Merriam-Webster's
Dictionary
of
Law

Merriam-Webster, Incorporated
Springfield, Massachusetts

A GENUINE MERRIAM-WEBSTER

The name *Webster* alone is no guarantee of excellence. It is used by a number of publishers and may serve mainly to mislead an unwary buyer.

Merriam-Webster™ is the name you should look for when you consider the purchase of dictionaries or other fine reference books. It carries the reputation of a company that has been publishing since 1831 and is your assurance of quality and authority.

Copyright © 1996 by Merriam-Webster, Incorporated

Library of Congress Cataloging in Publication Data
Main entry under title:

Merriam-Webster's Dictionary of Law
   p. cm.
 ISBN-13: 978-087779-604-6
 ISBN-10: 0-87779-604-1
  1. Law—United States—Dictionaries. 2. Law—Dictionaries.
I. Merriam-Webster, Inc.
KF156.M47 1996
340'.03—dc20   96-30463
              CIP

Made in the United States of America

1011121314TFP:RRD090807

Contents

Preface   iv

Explanatory Notes   vi

Abbreviations Used in This Book   xviii

Pronunciation Symbols   xix

List of Group Entries   xx

A Dictionary of Law   **1**

The Judicial System   543

Important Cases   565

Important Laws   580

Important Agencies   602

Constitution of the United States   619

Preface

The law touches the lives of all Americans. Even such commonplace activities as driving a car, depositing money in a bank, and entering a retail store have legal ramifications, although we are not ordinarily conscious of them. At other times—as when a relative dies or when we marry or divorce, file our income taxes, are injured in an accident, or sell or purchase a home—we may be acutely aware of the law's presence. At such times we feel the need to know the law and to understand the often unfamiliar terms that make up its language.

MERRIAM-WEBSTER'S DICTIONARY OF LAW is designed to meet these needs by offering convenient and comprehensive access to the language of law. It provides concise coverage of more than 10,000 legal words and phrases, based on a thorough examination of the legally relevant citations drawn from the nearly 15,000,000 citations in the Merriam-Webster offices and supplemented by a review of material available through various on-line legal databases. To make the dictionary easier to use, the information provided here is presented in a style that will be familiar to all users of standard desk dictionaries. Entries include definitions, pronunciations, variant spellings, grammatical information, etymologies for many words, and other conventional dictionary features. None of this information is intended to substitute for the expertise of a lawyer, but it will help to make encounters with law and lawyers less mysterious.

Because the language of law can often seem to be a foreign tongue, the definitions in this dictionary are written in a style that as far as possible expresses unfamiliar legal concepts in ordinary English, without introducing inaccuracies caused by oversimplification. If an unfamiliar legal term occurs in a definition, the user can find it entered and defined at its own place in the dictionary. Further, any word that occurs in Merriam-Webster's Dictionary of Law is entered either in this book or, if it is not a legal term, in a current edition of any of Merriam-Webster's hardback or paperback adult dictionaries.

As a further aid in clarifying obscure terminology, extensive use is made throughout the book of verbal illustrations—often direct quotations from legal sources—demonstrating how words are actually used. Many entries also include notes, sometimes quite extensive, providing supplementary information that is helpful in understanding a term or a point of law.

To make it easier for the user to compare closely related terms, such terms are grouped together when appropriate at the main entries through which they are related, so that, for example, various kinds of trusts are defined together under *trust*. For entries that are not grouped together, extensive cross-references lead the user to related or comparable terms. Status labels provide an indication of where or when a term is used; for example, many entries include the label *in the civil law of Louisiana*, which indicates that the labeled word or sense is limited in use to the only state in the United States whose law system is based on civil law rather than common law.

In this dictionary, those entries known to be trademarks or service marks are so labeled and are treated in accordance with a formula approved by the United States Trademark Association. No entry in this dictionary, however, should be regarded as affecting the validity of any trademark or service mark.

Merriam-Webster's Dictionary of Law is the product of a collective effort by members of the Merriam-Webster editorial staff. Initial editorial guidance was provided by Frederick C. Mish, Editor in Chief, John M. Morse, Executive Editor, and E. Ward Gilman, Director of Defining. The editor was assisted in preparing definitions by Thomas F. Pitoniak and Amy West. Peter D. Haraty provided assistance in handling financial terminology. Joanne M. Despres and James L. Rader researched and wrote the etymologies. Brian M. Sietsema provided the pronunciations. Jennifer N. Cislo verified the accuracy of quotations. The many cross-references were handled by Maria A. Sansalone, with the assistance of Donna L. Rickerby. The manuscript was copyedited by Stephen J. Perrault. Back-matter sections were researched and written by Michael Shally-Jensen, with contributions from Amy West. Proofreading was handled by Cynthia S. Ashby, Jill J. Cooney, Thomas F. Pitoniak, James L. Rader, and Maria A. Sansalone. The manuscript was deciphered and typed by Mary M. Dunn, Florence A. Fowler, Joan E. Matteson, and Deborah A. Merkman, all under the supervision of Veronica P. McLymont, and by Georgette B. Boucher. Indispensable clerical assistance was provided by Carol A. Fugiel, Ruth W. Gaines, and Patricia M. Jensen. Robert D. Copeland prepared the electronic text for release to the compositor, with the assistance of Jill J. Cooney; he also directed the book through its typesetting stages. Madeline L. Novak handled project coordination and scheduling.

Linda Picard Wood, J.D.
Editor

Explanatory Notes

Entries

MAIN ENTRIES

A boldface letter or a combination of such letters, including punctuation marks and diacritics where needed, that is set flush with the left-hand margin of each column of type is a main entry or entry word. The main entry may consist of letters and/or numbers set solid or separated by hyphens, periods, parentheses, diagonals, or spaces:

ex·clu·sive *adj*

attorney–at–law *n*

C.N. *abbr*

401(k) plan *n*

d/b/a *abbr*

wash sale *n*

The material in lightface type that follows each main entry on the same line and on succeeding indented lines explains and justifies its inclusion in the dictionary.

Variation in the styling of compound words in English is frequent and widespread. It is often completely acceptable to choose freely among open, hyphenated, and closed alternatives (as *quasicontract*, *quasi-contract*, or *quasi contract*). However, to show all the stylings that are found for English compounds would require space that can be better used for other information. So this dictionary limits itself to a single styling for a compound:

fact·find·er

straight–line

quasi easement

When a compound is widely used and one styling predominates, that styling is shown. When a compound is uncommon or when the evidence indicates that two or three stylings are approximately equal in frequency, the styling shown is based on the analogy of parallel compounds.

ORDER OF MAIN ENTRIES

The main entries follow one another in alphabetical order letter by letter without regard to intervening spaces or hyphens: *equal opportunity* follows *equality* and *lease-up* follows *leasehold mortgage*. Those containing an Arabic numeral are alphabetized as if the numeral were spelled out, according to their pronunciation: *401(k) plan*, in which *0* is pronounced like the letter *o*, comes between *four month rule* and *fourth degree*.

Solid compounds come first and are followed by hyphenated compounds and then open compounds. Lowercase entries come before entries that begin with a capital letter or are composed of capital letters. Full words come before parts of words made up of the same letters:

break–in . . . *n*

break in *vi*

co *abbr*

CO *abbr*

co- *prefix*

re . . . *prep*

re- *prefix*

GROUP ENTRIES

Some nouns that are part of legal terminology regularly appear in fixed open compounds with two or more different modifiers (for example, *contract* in compounds like *express contract*, *gratuitous contract*, and *implied contract*). A selected group of such nouns are entered with the open compounds in which they appear following immediately as subentries. Entries arranged in this way are called group entries. A list of the nouns receiving group entry treatment appears on page xx.

At a group entry, the main entry and any appropriate elements, such as functional labels, status labels, definitions, and cross-references, are followed by two or more subentries, entered in alphabetical order. A subentry is an open compound (e.g., *express contract*) whose major element is the noun (*contract*) at whose alphabetical place the subentry is entered. It is printed in boldface italics, with end-of-line division, pronunciation, and status label where appropriate. It is followed by a definition that may be divided into senses, and may include a called also note, usage note, directional cross-reference, or a supplemental information note. Subentries are always open compounds. A closed compound whose major element is the group entry noun will nevertheless be placed at its own alphabetical place in the vocabulary rather than as a subentry. Therefore, while *hostile witness* appears as a subentry at *witness*, *eyewitness* appears at its own alphabetical location in *E*.

A number of the group entries have subentries at more than one sense. Sense 2c of *declaration* is followed by the subentries *declaration against interest*, *dying declaration*, *self-serving declaration*, and *spontaneous declaration*. Sense 4 of *declaration* is followed by the subentries *declaration of condominium*, *declaration of homestead*, and *declaration of trust*.

If there is only one open compound that would fall under a sense at a group entry, it is entered at its own alphabetical location rather than following the group entry sense. For example, at the group entry *deposit*, where there are subentries at senses 2a and 3a, the open compound *security deposit* relates instead to sense 2b. Because it is the only compound that falls under that sense, *security deposit* is defined at its own

alphabetical place in *S* rather than at *deposit*. A *see also* cross-reference appears at the group entry indicating where such an open compound can be found.

Additionally, each subentry can be found at its own alphabetical place with a *see* cross-reference indicating the group entry at which the subentry can be found. See the Cross-Reference section of these Explanatory Notes for more information.

HOMOGRAPHS

When one main entry has exactly the same written form as another, the two are distinguished by superscript numerals preceding each word:

^{1}**bail** . . . *n* ^{1}**in•vest** . . . *vt*

^{2}**bail** *vt* ^{2}**invest** *vb*

Usually, as in the example *bail* above, the two homographs are different parts of speech and one has been derived from the other by functional shift. Sometimes, however, the two homographs will be words that are historically unrelated beyond the accident of spelling, or only indirectly related to each other, as are the two verb entries for *invest*.

GUIDE WORDS

To help in finding a particular word, the alphabetically first boldface entry on each left-hand page is printed at the top of that page. Likewise, the alphabetically last boldface entry is printed at the top of each right-hand page. These two guide words indicate the alphabetical range of entries on the two pages:

162   **enjoinable**
      equal opportunity   **163**

The entry used for a guide word need not be a main entry. Another boldface word —

a variant, an inflected form, or a defined or undefined run-on — may be selected as a guide word, although inflected forms that appear cut back and italic boldface subentries are disregarded.

When a page consists entirely of italic boldface subentries, as is the case on page 255, the group entry word (*interest* for this example) will be used as the guide word.

All guide words must themselves be in alphabetical order from page to page throughout the dictionary; thus, the alphabetically last boldface word on a page is not used if it follows alphabetically the first guide word on the next page:

74   chapter 7

child   75

On the pages where these guide words are found, *children*, a boldface inflected form at the entry *child*, is the last entry alphabetically, but it is not used as the guide word for the right page because it follows alphabetically the entry *child abuse*, which is the first guide word on the next page. To use *children* would violate the alphabetical order of guide words from page to page, and so the boldface entry word *child* is used instead.

END-OF-LINE DIVISION

The centered dots within entry words indicate division points at which a hyphen may be put at the end of a line of print or writing. Thus the noun *ar•bi•trar•i•ness* may be ended on one line with:

ar-

arbi-

arbitrar-

arbitrari-

and continued on the next with:

bitrariness

trariness

iness

ness

Centered dots are not shown after a single initial letter or before a single terminal letter because printers seldom cut off a single letter:

erase *vt*

¹guilty *adj*

idem . . . *pron*

Nor are they shown at second and succeeding homographs unless these differ among themselves:

¹es•crow . . . *n*   **¹re•cord** . . . *vt*

²escrow *vt*   **²rec•ord** . . . *n*

There are acceptable alternative end-of-line divisions just as there are acceptable variant spellings and pronunciations. No more than one division, however, is shown for an entry in this dictionary.

A double hyphen at the end of a line in this dictionary (as in the entry *generation-skipping transfer tax*) stands for a hyphen that belongs at that point in a hyphenated word and that is retained when the word is written as a unit on one line.

VARIANTS

When a main entry is followed by the word *or* and another spelling, the two spellings are equal variants. Both are standard, and either one may be used according to personal inclination:

bus•ing *or* **bus•sing**

If two variants joined by *or* are out of alphabetical order, they remain equal variants. The one printed first is, however, slightly more common than the second:

en•roll *or* **en•rol**

When another spelling is joined to the main entry by the word *also*, the spelling after *also* is a secondary variant and occurs less frequently than the first:

en banc *also* **in banc**

Secondary variants belong to standard usage and may be used according to personal inclination.

Variants whose spelling places them alphabetically more than one entry away from the main entry are entered at their own alphabetical places (and also appear at the main entry):

> **indorse, indorsee** . . . *var of* ENDORSE, EN-DORSEE

Variants having a usage label appear only at their own alphabetical places:

> **gaol, gaoler** *chiefly Brit var of* JAIL, JAILER

SUPPLEMENTAL INFORMATION NOTES

At some entries or subentries, a note consisting of one or more sentences may follow the definition and cross-references. These notes give additional information about the entry word. They are indicated by the symbol ◇:

> **labor union** *n* . . . ◇ Labor unions and employers are subject to the provisions of the National Labor Relations Act [which] authorized the establishment of the National Labor Relations Board . . .
>
> **idem** . . . *pron* . . . ◇ *Idem* is usu. used in the form of its abbreviation *id.*

RUN-ON ENTRIES

A main entry may be followed by one or more derivatives or by a homograph with a different functional label. These are run-on entries. Each is introduced by a lightface dash and each has a functional label. They are not defined, however, since their meanings are readily derivable from the meaning of the root word:

> ²**use** . . . *vt* . . . — **user** *n*
>
> **ju·di·cial** . . . *adj* . . . — **ju·di·cial·ly** *adv*
>
> **il·le·git·i·mate** . . . *adj* . . . — **illegitimate** *n*

A main entry may be followed by one or more phrases containing the entry word or an inflected form of it. These are also run-on entries. Each is introduced by a lightface dash but there is no functional label. They are, however, defined since their meanings are more than the sum of the meanings of their elements:

> **tri·al** *n* . . . — **at trial :** . . .
>
> **es·sence** . . . *n* . . . — **of the essence :** . . .
>
> **en·dorse** . . . *vt* . . . — **endorse in blank :** . . .

Defined phrases of this sort are run on at the entry constituting the first major element in the phrase, which is ordinarily a verb or a noun:

> ¹**is·sue** . . . *n* . . . — **at issue** *also* **in issue** . . .

A run-on entry is an independent entry with respect to function and status. Labels at the main entry do not apply unless they are repeated.

Pronunciation

The matter between a pair of reversed virgules \ \ following the entry word indicates the pronunciation. The symbols used are explained in the chart on page xix. An abbreviated list appears at the bottom of the second column of each right-hand page of the vocabulary. Pronunciation respellings are provided for every word that is not familiar in some meaning to most sixth-graders, according to *The Living Word Vocabulary: A National Vocabulary Inventory* by Edgar Dale and Joseph O'Rourke (Chicago: World Book-Childcraft International, Inc., 1981). The pronunciations for these familiar "core vocabulary" items may be found in *Merriam-Webster's Collegiate Dictionary, Tenth Edition.*

A hyphen is used in the pronunciation to show syllabic division. These hyphens sometimes coincide with the centered dots in the entry word that indicate end-of-line division:

> **ju·di·cial** \jü-'di-shəl\

Sometimes they do not:

> **fab·ri·cate** \'fa-brə-ˌkāt\

A high-set mark ' indicates major (primary) stress or accent; a low-set mark ˌ indicates minor (secondary) stress or accent:

jail•house \'jāl-ˌhaůs\

The stress mark stands at the beginning of the syllable that receives the stress. A syllable with neither a high-set mark nor a low-set mark is unstressed:

gov•ern \'gə-vərn\

The presence of variant pronunciations indicates that not all educated speakers pronounce words the same way. A second-place variant is not to be regarded as less acceptable than the pronunciation that is given first. It may, in fact, be used by as many educated speakers as the first variant, but the requirements of the printed page are such that one must precede the other:

ca•su•al•ty \'ka-zhəl-tē, 'ka-zhə-wəl-\
nu•ga•to•ry \'nü-gə-ˌtōr-ē, 'nyü-\

Entry words which are direct borrowings from French or Latin are often given two pronunciations, with the anglicized variants first and thereafter a rendering of the French or classical Latin pronunciation.

ha•be•as \'hā-bē-əs, 'hä-bā-äs\

When a main entry or a subentry is a compound word and has less than a full pronunciation, the missing part is to be supplied from a pronunciation in another entry elsewhere in this dictionary which gives the pronunciation for one or more elements of the compound word. For example, at the entry *idem sonans* a pronunciation is shown only for *sonans*. The pronunciation of *idem* is shown at the separate entry for that word.

In general, no pronunciation is indicated for open compounds consisting of two or more English words that either have own-place entry or are considered "core vocabulary" according to the criteria listed in the first paragraph of this section:

inheritance tax *n*

Only the first entry in a sequence of numbered homographs is given a pronunciation if their pronunciations are the same:

¹gross \'grōs\ *adj*

²gross *n*

Functional Labels

An italic label indicating a part of speech or some other functional classification follows the pronunciation or, if no pronunciation is given, the main entry.

sub•stan•tial . . . *adj*

du•ty *n*

eq•ui•ta•bly *adv*

²aliunde *prep*

steal . . . *vt*

If a verb is both transitive and intransitive, the labels *vt* and *vi* introduce the subdivisions:

take . . . *vb* . . . *vt* . . . ~ *vi*

A boldface swung dash ~ is used to stand for the main entry and separate the subdivisions of the verb. If there is no subdivision, *vt* or *vi* takes the place of *vb*:

bring . . . *vt*

ap•pear *vi*

Labeling a verb as transitive, however, does not preclude occasional intransitive use (as in absolute constructions).

Other italicized labels used to indicate functional classifications are:

id *abbr*

Breath•a•ly•zer . . . *trademark*

co- . . . *prefix*

oyez . . . *vb imper*

Re•al•tor . . . *collective mark*

Two functional labels are sometimes combined:

en banc . . . *adv or adj*

Inflected Forms

Most inflected forms are covered explicitly or by implication at the main entry for the base form. These are the plurals of nouns, the principal parts of verbs (the past tense, the past participle when it differs from the past tense, and the present participle), and the comparative and superlative forms of adjectives and adverbs. In general, it may be said that when these inflected forms are created in a manner considered regular in English (as by adding -s or -es to nouns, -ed and -ing to verbs, and -er and -est to adjectives and adverbs) and when it seems that there is nothing about the formation likely to give the dictionary user doubts, the inflected form is not shown:

²grant *n*

gar•nish . . . *vt*

ef•fec•tive *adj*

spe•cial *adj*

On the other hand, if the inflected form is created in an irregular way or if the dictionary user is likely to have doubts about it (even though it is formed regularly), the inflected form is shown in boldface, either in full or cut back to a convenient and easily recognizable point.

The inflected forms of nouns, verbs, adjectives, and adverbs are shown in this dictionary when suffixation brings about a change in final *y* to *i*, when the word ends in -*ey*, when there are variant inflected forms, when the plural of a noun is identical to its base form, and when the dictionary user might have doubts about the spelling of the inflected form:

¹guilty *adj* **guilt•i•er; -est**

at•tor•ney . . . *n, pl* **-neys**

bur•glary . . . *n, pl* **-glar•ies**

nex•us . . . *n, pl* **nex•us•es** *or* **nexus**

The inflected form is shown for any entry consisting of two or more words when the form is unusual or likely to raise doubts:

Judge Advocate General *n, pl* **Judge Advocates General**

attorney general *n, pl* **attorneys general** *or* **attorney generals**

Nouns that are plural in form and that regularly occur in plural construction are labeled *n pl*. Nouns that are plural in form but are not always construed as plural are appropriately labeled:

proceeds . . . *n pl*

ir•rec•on•cil•able dif•fer•enc•es . . . *n pl but sing or pl in constr*

The inflected forms of verbs, adjectives, and adverbs are also shown whenever suffixation brings about a doubling of a final consonant, elision of a final *e*, or a radical change in the base word itself:

en•trap . . . *vt* **en•trapped; en•trap•ping**

as•sume *vt* **as•sumed; as•sum•ing**

break . . . *vb* **broke** . . . **bro•ken** . . . **break•ing**

¹good *adj* **bet•ter; best**

jus . . . *n, pl* **ju•ra**

Capitalization

Most entries in this dictionary begin with a lowercase letter. A few of these have an italicized label *often cap*, which indicates that the word is as likely to be capitalized as not, that it is as acceptable with an uppercase initial as it is with one in lowercase. Some entries begin with an uppercase letter or are composed entirely of uppercase letters, which indicates that the word is usually capitalized as shown. The absence of an initial capital or of an *often cap* label indicates that the word is not ordinarily capitalized:

habeas cor•pus . . . *n*

board *n, often cap*

Breath•a•ly•zer . . . *trademark*

FAA *abbr*

The capitalization of entries that are open or hyphenated compounds is similarly indicated by the form of the entry or by an italicized label:

HUD–1 settlement statement . . . *n*

free ex•er•cise clause *n, often cap F&E&C*

United States marshal *n*

Jane Roe . . . *n*

A word that is capitalized in some senses and lowercase in others shows variations from the form of the main entry by the use of italicized labels at the appropriate senses:

bill of rights . . . *often cap B&R* . . . ; *esp, cap B&R* : . . .

Appropriate capitalization is also given for subentered open compounds:

bank . . . *n* . . . *Federal Re•serve bank* . . .

hear•ing *n* . . . *Mapp hearing* . . .

Attributive Nouns

The italicized label *often attrib* placed after the functional label *n* indicates that the noun is often used as an adjective equivalent in attributive position before another noun:

equal opportunity *n, often attrib*

land•mark *n, often attrib*

Examples of the attributive use of these nouns are *equal opportunity employment* and *landmark decision*.

Etymology

Etymologies in this dictionary are in boldface square brackets following the part-of-speech label and preceding the definition. The purpose of the etymologies is to provide a concise historical framework for the language most characteristic of law and the courtroom. In addition to basic legal terminology, phrases borrowed from foreign languages — most often Latin and Anglo-French — and words now uncommon in everyday English, whether exclusively legal in sense or not, have also been given etymologies.

Usually only one word of a set of related words — either the most basic word or the historically oldest — is given an etymology. For example, of the three words *defeasance, defeasible,* and *indefeasible,* only *defeasance* has an etymology. If a word or phrase that would otherwise deserve an etymology occurs within an open compound and is not given an etymology at that entry, the reader should take it as an indication that the word or phrase has its own entry and etymology. Hence, *vicinage* in the entry *jury of the vicinage* does not have an etymology at *jury of the vicinage* but rather at its own entry *vicinage*. Similarly, the phrase *inter vivos* at the subentry *gift inter vivos* under *gift* is not explained by an etymology in the subentry because *inter vivos* is an independent entry in the dictionary with its own etymology.

Words whose primary field of reference is not legal, as well as common words whose legal senses have developed from more general meanings, have not been given etymologies; the reader seeking the origin of such words can find them in *Merriam-Webster's Collegiate Dictionary, Tenth Edition.* Subentries have also not usually been given etymologies unless they contain a foreign phrase not found elsewhere in the dictionary.

In general, the kind of philological detail appropriate to an unabridged dictionary or a dictionary of etymology has been excluded in order to give the user information most pertinent to the origin of legal words. The form of a word in Middle English is not generally shown unless it is in some respect crucial to the word's history. The Germanic and Indo-European prehistory of words such as *right* and *witness* descended directly from Old English has also not been shown. In cases where English may have borrowed a Latin word through the mediation of French, in which the word also occurs as a learned borrowing, French is not shown as an intermediary language unless the word has undergone significant modification in form or sense. The Latin sources of French words inherited from the spoken Latin of Roman Gaul are normally shown, though the passage from one language to another may be bridged by the phrase "ultimately from," to indicate that intermediate linguistic forms unattested in writing have been omitted from the etymology.

Earlier historical periods of languages cited in the etymologies include the following:

Old English: from the earliest documents to about 1100
Middle English: from about 1100 to about 1500
(English words not otherwise qualified are to be understood as Modern English, i.e., the English in use after 1500)
Latin: from the earliest extant literature to about A.D.200
Late Latin: from about 200 to 600
Medieval Latin: from about 600 to 1500
New Latin: after about 1500
Old French: from the earliest documents to about 1300
Middle French: from about 1300 to 1600
French: after about 1600, i.e., Modern French

The term *Anglo-French* in this dictionary refers broadly to French as used in England after the Norman Conquest; it includes what is often called "law French," an ossified form of medieval French that those involved with the law in England used for reports and notes as late as the seventeenth century. (Prior to the seventeenth century most legal proceedings in the British Isles were recorded in either Anglo-French or Latin, not English.) Strictly speaking, Anglo-French — at least in its earlier stages, when it was still a living tongue — was simply one of several dialectal variants of medieval French; its sound system and grammar were strongly influenced by western and northern dialects, especially the speech of Normandy

(sometimes called "Old North French"). By convention, however, the etymologies treat Anglo-French words as if they were descended or borrowed from forms characteristic of the medieval French of the Paris region — the dialect on which Modern French is based.

Usage

USAGE LABELS

Status labels are used in this dictionary to signal that a word or a sense of a word has particular application in the law. The law of all of the states of the United States is based chiefly on the common law that originated in England and was further developed in this country. The law of Louisiana, however, is based on the civil law as set out in the Code Civil (or the Napoleonic Code). A word or sense limited in use to Louisiana civil law has a label indicating such use:

in•nom•i•nate . . . *adj, in the civil law of Louisiana*

Words current in all states have no label.

A word or sense limited in use to England has an appropriate label:

as•sur•ance *n* . . . 3 *chiefly Brit*

A subject label or guide phrase is sometimes used to indicate the specific application of a word or sense:

ef•fec•tive *adj* . . . 4 *of a rate of interest*

in•ven•to•ry . . . *n* . . . 2 . . . **a** *under the Bankruptcy Code*

In general, however, subject orientation is given in the definition:

dis•clo•sure . . . *n* . . . **a** : a lender's revelation of information to a consumer under the Truth in Lending Act that enables the consumer to make an intelligent decision about the loan

equitable distribution *n* : the distribution of marital assets by a court in a divorce action in accordance with statutory guidelines that are designed to produce a fair but not necessarily equal division of the property

ILLUSTRATIONS OF USAGE

Definitions are sometimes followed by verbal illustrations that show a typical use of the word in context. These illustrations are enclosed in angle brackets, and the word being illustrated is usually replaced by a lightface swung dash. The swung dash stands for the boldface entry word, and it may be followed by an italicized suffix:

board *n* . . . **2 a :** . . . ⟨a ~ of selectmen⟩

fed·er·al *adj* . . . **1** . . . ⟨a ~ government⟩

ad·min·is·ter . . . *vt* . . . **3 a** . . . ⟨~ an oath⟩

de·tain *vt* . . . **2** . . . ⟨~*ed* the driver and asked to see his license⟩

The swung dash is not used when the form of the boldface entry word is changed in suffixation, and it is not used for open compounds:

de·cer·ti·fy . . . *vt* . . . ⟨*decertified* the class action suit⟩

Illustrative quotations are also used to show words in typical contexts. Quotations used in this book are taken from statutes, cases, treatises and other legal publications, constitutions, and other reputable sources. Quotations from the Constitution of the United States indicate the article or amendment in which the quotation may be found:

es·tab·lish *vt* . . . **3** . . . ⟨Congress shall have power . . . to ~ post offices and post roads — *U.S. Constitution* art. I⟩

Note that omissions in quotations are indicated by suspension points.

Quotations from cases are followed by a case citation:

grieve . . . *vi* . . . ⟨as a union member, Jackson was obligated to ~ — not sue — *Jackson v. Liquid Carbonic Corp.*, 863 F.2d 111 (1988)⟩

A code, model code, or statutory compilation from which a quotation is taken is indicated by name:

eq·ui·ta·ble . . . *adj* **1** . . . ⟨shall allocate . . . appropriations in an ~ manner — *U.S. Code*⟩

break . . . *vt* . . . **2** . . . **b** . . . ⟨~*s* prison or escapes or flees from justice — *Colorado Revised Statutes*⟩

If a quotation is taken from a compilation of rules of procedure or evidence, the rule quoted is also indicated:

ap·pear *vi* **1 :** . . . ⟨to ~ before the officer who is to take the deposition — *Federal Rules of Civil Procedure* Rule 37(d)⟩

The names of individuals quoted follow the quotation:

ap·pli·ca·tion *n* . . . ⟨most ~*s* request bail . . . or an extension of time to file — W. J. Brennan, Jr.⟩

USAGE NOTES

Definitions are sometimes followed by brief usage notes that give supplementary information. A usage note is introduced by a lightface dash:

ar·rear . . . *n* **1 a** . . . — usu. used in pl.

hon·or·able *adj* . . . — used as a title for various government officials

²accord *n* . . . **3** . . . — usu. used in the phrase *accord and satisfaction*

Sometimes a usage note calls attention to one or more terms with the same denotation as a main entry or a subentered term:

check–kit·ing . . . *n* **:** the practice of drawing on uncollected funds . . . — called also *kiting*

The called also term is shown in italic type. If such a term is solid in form or is a closed compound word and falls alphabetically more than one entry away from a main entry, it is entered at its own place with the sole definition being a synonymous cross-reference to the entry where it appears in the usage note:

kit·ing . . . *n* **:** CHECK-KITING

Called also terms can also be found at subentries, with corresponding synonymous cross-references at their alphabetical locations, when appropriate:

forward contract . . . — called also *forward*

forward *n* : FORWARD CONTRACT at CONTRACT

See the section on Cross-Reference for information on the use of "at" and "in this entry" following synonymous cross-references.

Sometimes a usage note is used in place of a definition:

oyez . . . *vb imper* . . . — used by a court officer (as a bailiff) . . .

Sense Division

A boldface colon is used in this dictionary to introduce a definition:

²**interpleader** *n* : a person who is a party to an interpleader action

It is also used to separate two or more definitions of a single sense:

idem . . . *pron* . . . : something previously mentioned : the same authority

Boldface Arabic numerals separate the senses of a word that has more than one sense:

²**harbor** *vt* **1** : to receive secretly and conceal . . . **2** : to have (an animal) in one's keeping

Boldface lowercase letters separate the subsenses of a word:

give *vt* . . . **2 a** : to transfer from one's authority or custody . . . **b** : to execute and deliver . . . **c** : to communicate or impart to another

A lightface colon following a definition and immediately preceding two or more subsenses indicates that the subsenses are subsumed by the preceding definition:

li•a•bil•i•ty . . . *n* . . . **2** : something for which one is liable: as **a** : a financial obligation . . . **b** : accountability and responsibility to another enforceable by civil remedies or criminal sanctions

work•ing capital : the capital available for use in the course of business activity: **a**

: current assets . . . **b** : all capital of a business . . .

The word *as* may or may not follow the lightface colon. Its presence (as at *liability*) indicates that the following subsenses are typical or significant examples. Its absence (as at *working capital*) indicates that the subsenses which follow are exhaustive.

The system of separating the various senses of a word by numerals and letters is a lexical convenience. It reflects something of their semantic relationship, but it does not evaluate senses or set up a hierarchy of importance among them.

Sometimes a particular semantic relationship between senses is suggested by the use of one of four italic sense dividers: *esp, specif, also,* or *broadly.*

The sense divider *esp* (for *especially*) is used to introduce the most common meaning subsumed in the more general preceding definition:

iden•ti•ty *n* . . . **2** . . . **b** : distinguishing character of a person; *esp* : information that distinguishes a person

The sense divider *specif* (for *specifically*) is used to introduce a common but highly restricted meaning subsumed in the more general preceding definition:

jail . . . *n* : a place of confinement for persons held in lawful custody; *specif* : such a place under the jurisdiction of a local government . . . for . . . persons awaiting trial

The sense divider *also* is used to introduce a meaning that is closely related to but may be considered less important than the preceding sense:

join•der . . . *n* . . . ***permissive joinder*** : a joining in a suit as coplaintiffs . . . that share common issues . . . ; *also* : a joining in one suit of any legal . . . claims a party has against the opposing party

The sense divider *broadly* is used to introduce an extended or wider meaning of the preceding definition:

face *n* . . . **2** : the inscribed or printed side of something . . . ; *broadly* : the front side of something inscribed . . . on both sides

Information coming between the entry word and the first definition of a multisense word applies to all senses and subsenses. Information applicable only to some senses or subsenses is given between the appropriate boldface numeral, letter, or italic sense divider and the symbolic colon. A variety of kinds of information is offered in this way:

in•den•ture . . . *n* . . . **1** : a document . . . *specif, in bankruptcy law* : . . .

¹fi•nance *n* **1** *pl*

float•er *n* **1** [from the notion that the policy "floats" with the goods it insures . . .]

seize *vt* . . . **1** *or* **seise**

gain *n* . . . **2** *pl, in the civil law of Louisiana*

Cross-Reference

Various kinds of cross-references are used in this dictionary: directional, synonymous, cognate, and inflectional. In each instance the cross-reference is readily recognized by the lightface small capitals in which it is printed.

A cross-reference following a lightface dash and beginning with *see, see also,* or *compare* is a directional cross-reference. It directs the dictionary user to look elsewhere for further information. A *see also* or *compare* cross-reference is regularly appended to a definition:

dis•in•her•it . . . *vt* . . . — see also ELECTIVE SHARE

dis•crim•i•nate . . . *vi* . . . — see also . . . *Civil Rights Act of 1964* in the IMPORTANT LAWS section

good faith *n* . . . — . . . compare BAD FAITH

A subentry that shows a *compare* cross-reference to another subentry within the same group entry will have "in this entry" following the words in small capitals:

loan *n* . . . *loan for con•sump•tion* . . . — compare . . . LOAN FOR USE in this entry

A subentry or main entry that shows a *compare* or *see also* cross-reference to a subentry of a group entry will provide subentry and group entry information as follows:

life insurance *n* . . . *variable life insurance* . . . — compare *variable annuity* at AN-NUITY

²gross *n* . . . — see also *easement in gross* at EASEMENT

A *see* cross-reference stands alone, and indicates where a subentry may be found:

aleatory contract — see CONTRACT

A cross-reference immediately following a boldface colon is a synonymous cross-reference. It may stand alone as the only definitional matter for an entry or for a sense or subsense of an entry; it may follow an analytical definition; it may be one of two synonymous cross-references separated by a comma:

gender discrimination . . . . *n* : SEX DISCRIMINATION

¹lay *vt* . . . **2 a** : to put forward : ASSERT

leave *vt* . . . : BEQUEATH, DEVISE

A synonymous cross-reference indicates that a definition at the entry cross-referred to can be substituted as a definition for the entry or the sense or subsense in which the cross-reference appears. When a subentry is defined by a synonymous cross-reference to a subentry or sense of the same group entry, the reader will find "in this entry" following the synonymous cross reference, so that, for example, at sense 1 of the group entry for *interest* we find:

Article Nine security interest : SECURITY INTEREST 2 in this entry

which indicates that the definition for this subentry can be found at sense 2 of the subentry *security interest*.

At a subentry's alphabetical location, as noted above, a *see* cross reference directs the reader to the appropriate group entry:

Article Nine security interest — see INTEREST 1

The word that appears in small capitals may or may not show a sense number following it to indicate the appropriate sense.

A cross-reference following an italic *var of* is a cognate cross-reference and may carry a limiting label:

disseize *var of* DISSEISE

gaol, **gaoler** *chiefly Brit var of* JAIL, JAILER

A cross-reference following an italic label that identifies an entry as an inflected form of a noun, of an adjective or adverb, or of a verb is an inflectional cross-reference. Inflectional cross-references appear only when the inflected form falls at least one entry away from the entry cross-referred to:

dicta *pl of* DICTUM

borne *past part of* BEAR

When guidance seems needed as to which one of several homographs or which sense or subsense of a multisense word is being referred to, a superscript numeral may precede the cross-reference or a sense number may follow it or both:

legal opinion *n* : OPINION 2a

When a synonymous cross-reference is made to a subentry, the group entry at which the subentry can be found will be indicated following the word "at":

²**call** *n* . . . **2** : CALL OPTION at OPTION 3

compensatory damages *n* : ACTUAL DAMAGES at DAMAGE 2

Abbreviations Used in This Book

abbr	abbreviation	*Nat'l*	National
adj	adjective	*N.E.*	North Eastern Reporter
adv	adverb	*N.E.2d*	North Eastern Reporter, Second Series
amend.	amendment		
art.	article	*No.*	Number
A.2d	Atlantic Reporter, Second Series	*n pl*	noun plural
Ass'n	Association	*N.W.*	North Western Reporter
B.R.	Bankruptcy Reporter	*N.W.2d*	North Western Reporter, Second Series
Brit	British		
Cal.	California	*N.Y.S.*	New York Supplement Reporter
Cal. App.	California Appellate Reports	*N.Y.S.2d*	New York Supplement Reporter, Second Series
Cal. Rptr.	California Reporter		
cap	capital, capitalized	*occas.*	occasionally
Co.	Company	*Ohio App.*	Ohio Appellate Reports
Commn.	Commission	*orig.*	originally
constr	construction	*P.*	Pacific Reporter
Constr.	Construction	*Pac.*	Pacific
Corp.	Corporation	*part*	participle
Ctr.	Center	*Pharm.*	Pharmaceutical
Cty.	County	*pl*	plural
DA	District Attorney	*prep*	preposition
Dept.	Department	*pres.*	present
Dev.	Development	*prob.*	probably
Dist.	District, Distributors	*Prod(s).*	Product(s), Production(s)
e.g.	exempli gratia ("for example")	*P.2d*	Pacific Reporter, Second Series
esp	especially	*q.v.*	quod vide ("which see")
et seq.	et sequentes, et sequentia ("and the following")	*R.*	Railroad
		R.R.	Railroad
F.	Federal Reporter	*S.A.*	South America
Fed.	Federal	*Sav.*	Savings
Fin.	Finance, Financial, Financing	*Sch(s).*	School(s)
F.2d	Federal Reporter, Second Series	*2d*	Second
F. Supp.	Federal Supplement	*Serv(s).*	Services
F.3d	Federal Reporter, Third Series	*S.E.2d*	South Eastern Reporter, Second Series
Hosp.	Hospital		
i.e.	id est ("that is")	*sing*	singular
imper	imperative	*So. 2d*	Southern Reporter, Second Series
Inc.	Incorporated	*specif*	specifically
Indem.	Indemnity	*S.W.2d*	South Western Reporter, Second Series
Indus.	Industry, Industries, Industrial		
Ins.	Insurance	*Sys.*	System(s)
Int'l	International	*Tel.*	Telephone, Telegraph
Jr.	Junior	*U.S.*	United States, United States Reports
Labs.	Laboratories	*usu*	usually
Ltd.	Limited	*v.*	versus
Med.	Medical	*var*	variant
Mfg.	Manufacturing	*vb*	verb
Mortg.	Mortgage	*vi*	intransitive verb
Mut.	Mutual	*vt*	transitive verb
n	noun		

Pronunciation Symbols

ə . . . . abut, collect, suppose

ˈə, ˌə . . . . humdrum

ᵊ . . . . (in ᵊl, ᵊn) battle, cotton; (in lᵊ, mᵊ, rᵊ) French table, prisme, titre

ər . . . . . . operation, further

a . . . . map, patch

ā . . . . day, fate

ä . . . . bother, cot, father

à . . . . French patte

au̇ . . . . . . now, out

b . . . . baby, rib

ch . . . . . . chin, catch

d . . . . did, adder

e . . . . set, red

ē . . . . beat, easy

f . . . . fifty, cuff

g . . . . go, big

h . . . . hat, ahead

hw . . . . . whale

i . . . . tip, banish

ī . . . . site, buy

j . . . . job, edge

k . . . . kin, cook

k̲ . . . . . . German Buch, Scots loch

l . . . . lily, cool

m . . . . . . murmur, dim

n . . . . nine, own

ⁿ . . . . indicates that a preceding vowel is pronounced through both nose and mouth, as in French bon \bōⁿ\

ŋ . . . . sing, singer, finger, ink

ō . . . . bone, hollow

ȯ . . . . saw

œ . . . . . . French bœuf, German Hülle

œ̄ . . . . . . French feu, German Hühle

ȯi . . . . . . toy

p . . . . pepper, lip

r . . . . rarity

s . . . . source, less

sh . . . . . . shy, mission

t . . . . tie, attack

th . . . . . . thin, ether

t̲h̲ . . . . . . then, either

ü . . . . boot, few \ˈfyü\

u̇ . . . . put, pure \ˈpyu̇r\

ue . . . . . . German füllen

ūe . . . . . . French rue, German fühlen

v . . . . vivid, give

w . . . . . . we, away

y . . . . yard, cue \ˈkyü\

ʸ . . . . indicates that a preceding \l\, \n\, or \w\ is modified by having the tongue approximate the position for \y\, as in French digne \dēnʸ\

z . . . . zone, raise

zh . . . . . . vision, pleasure

\ . . . . slant line used in pairs to mark the beginning and end of a transcription: \ˈpen\

ˈ . . . . mark at the beginning of a syllable that has primary (strongest) stress: \ˈshə-fəl-ˌbōrd\

ˌ . . . . mark at the beginning of a syllable that has secondary (next-strongest) stress: \ˈshə-fəl-ˌbōrd\

- . . . . mark of a syllable division in pronunciations (the mark of end-of-line division in boldface entries is a centered dot •)

List of Group Entries

The following is a list of entries containing subentered terms. For more information on group entries, see the section Group Entries in the Explanatory Notes.

abstention	deduction	impossibility	performance
administrator	decree	injunction	plea
agency	deed	intent	pleading
agent	defense	interest	possession
alimony	delivery	intervention	power
annuity	demurrer	issue	power of appointment
arbitration	denial	joinder	power of attorney
arrest	deposit	judgment	prescription
assault	depreciation	jurisdiction	presumption
asset	devise	knowledge	principal
assignment	discharge	larceny	privilege
attack	dismissal	lease	proceeding
authority	dissolution	legacy	promise
bailment	dividend	letter	property
bank	divorce	letter of credit	question
basis	donation	liability	remainder
battery	draft	lien	reorganization
beneficiary	duty	life insurance	reserve
benefit	easement	listing	robbery
bequest	endorsement	loan	sale
bill	error	loss	search
bill of lading	estate	malice	security
bond	estoppel	manslaughter	segregation
breach	eviction	matter	sentence
capital	evidence	merger	servitude
case	exemption	mistake	stock
cause	expense	mortgage	strike
challenge	fact	motion	succession
chattel	failure of issue	murder	surplus
check	fee	negligence	tenancy
chose	fee simple	note	testimony
company	finding	notice	theft
condition	force	nuisance	title
consideration	fraud	nullity	trespass
conspiracy	fruit	obligation	trust
contempt	fund	obsolescence	use
contraband	gain	opinion	verdict
contract	gift	option	warrant
conversion	good	order	warranty
corporation	guardian	owner	waste
creditor	habeas corpus	ownership	will
custody	hearing	paper	witness
damage	heir	partner	writ
debt	homicide	partnership	
declaration	immunity	party	

ABA *abbr* American Bar Association

aban·don *vt* **1 :** to give up with the intent of never again asserting or claiming an interest in (a right or property) **2 :** to disassociate oneself from or forsake in spite of a duty or responsibility to ⟨~ one's child⟩ **3 :** to renounce one's obligations and rights under ⟨~ a contract⟩ **4 :** to fail purposely to bring to completion or fruition ⟨~ a crime⟩ ⟨~ a lawsuit⟩

abandoned property — see PROPERTY

aban·don·ment *n* **1 :** the act of abandoning property or a right: as **a :** relinquishment by an inventor of the right to enforce a patent — see also DEDICATION **b :** an author's relinquishment to the public domain of his or her copyrighted work **c :** relinquishment of a trademark established by a failure to use the trademark and an intention never to resume use **d :** the act of an insured in surrendering all rights to damaged or lost property to an insurer as a total loss — compare SALVAGE 2b **e :** relinquishment by a trustee in bankruptcy of interest in property in the bankruptcy estate often for a nominal sum **2 :** the act of abandoning a person: as **a :** failure to have contact with a spouse that is intended to create a permanent separation **b :** failure to communicate with or provide financial support for one's child over a period of time that shows a purpose to forgo parental duties and rights **3 :** the act of abandoning a contract **4 a :** the act of abandoning a course of action (as a crime) **b :** the affirmative defense (as recognized under the Model Penal Code) of voluntary withdrawal from the commission of a crime resulting from the actor's change of heart and not from intervening circumstances

abate \ə-ˈbāt\ *vb* **abat·ed; abat·ing** [Old French *abattre*, literally, to knock down,

from *a-*, prefix stressing result + *battre* to beat] *vt* **1 a :** to put an end to or do away with ⟨~ a nuisance⟩ **b :** make void **:** NULLIFY ⟨~ an action⟩ **2 :** to reduce in amount esp. proportionately ⟨~ a tax⟩ — *vi* **1 :** to become defeated or become null or void ⟨when a public officer is a party to an appeal . . . in an official capacity and during its pendency dies . . . the action does not ~ —*Federal Rules of Appellate Procedure* Rule 43⟩ **2 :** to decrease in amount or value ⟨the legacies *abated* proportionately⟩ ◊ A problem arises in estate law when the amount of the bequests and devises made in a will exceeds the assets available in the estate. In such a case, some or all of the bequests and devises may have to be abated to make up the deficit. Under the Uniform Probate Code, property in the estate that is not specifically given under the will abates first, residuary devises abate second, general devises abate third, and specific devises abate last.

abate·ment \ə-ˈbāt-mənt\ *n* **1 :** the act or process of abating or the state of being abated ⟨challenged the ~ of her bequest⟩ ⟨~ of a private nuisance by self-help —W. L. Prosser and W. P. Keeton⟩ **2 :** an amount abated **:** DEDUCTION; *esp* **:** a deduction from the full amount of a tax **— in abatement :** subject to termination because of a formal or procedural defect ⟨there shall be no reversal in the Supreme Court . . . for error in ruling upon matters *in abatement* —*U.S. Code*⟩

ab·duct \ab-ˈdəkt, əb-\ *vt* **:** to carry or lead (a person) away by threat or use of

\ə\abut \ᵊ\kitten \ər**further** \a\ash \ā\ace
\ä\cot, cart \au̇\out \ch\chin \e\bet \ē\easy
\g\go \i\hit \ī\ice \j\job \ŋ\sing \ō\go \ȯ\law
\ȯi\boy \th\thin \t͟h\the \ü\loot \u̇\foot \y\yet
\zh\vision *see also* Pronunciation Symbols page

force or often by fraud; *also* : to restrain or conceal (a person) for the purpose of preventing escape or rescue — see also KIDNAPPING — **ab·duc·tor** \-'dək-tər\ *n*
ab·duc·tion \ab-'dək-shən, əb-\ **1 a** : the action of abducting ⟨~ of a robbery victim⟩ **b** : the tort or felony of abducting a person **2** : the unlawful carrying away of a wife or female child or ward for the purpose of marriage or sexual intercourse ◊ Sense 2 has its roots in common law. As statutorily defined, mainly in the nineteenth century, abduction is generally stated to include taking away or detention of a woman under a certain age, usu. 16 or 18, with or without her consent or knowledge of her age.

abet \ə-'bet\ *vt* **abet·ted; abet·ting** : to assist, encourage, instigate, or support with criminal intent in attempting or carrying out a crime — often used in the phrase *aid and abet* *n* — **abet·tor** *also* **abet·ter** \ə-'be-tər\ *n*

abey·ance \ə-'bā-əns\ *n* [Middle French *abeance* expectation (of a title or claimant), from *abaer* to expect, from *a-*, prefix stressing result + *baer* to gape, aim at] **1** : a lapse in the succession of property during which there is no person in whom title to the property is vested — usu. used with *in* ⟨the estate was in ~⟩ **2** : temporary inactivity or suppression : cessation or suspension for a period of time — usu. used with *in* or *into* ⟨to hold the entry of summary judgment in ~ —J. H. Friedenthal *et al.*⟩

abide *vt* **abode** *or* **abid·ed; abid·ing** : to accept without objection — **abide by** : to act or behave in accordance with or in obedience to

ab in·con·ve·ni·en·ti \,ab-,in-kən-,vē-nē-'en-tē, -,tī; ,äb-,in-kòn-,wā-nē-'en-tē\ *adv* [New Latin] : from inconvenience or hardship — used to refer to a rule in law that an argument from inconvenience is a strong argument

ab ini·tio \,ab-ə-'ni-shē-,ō, ,äb-i-'nē-tē-,ō\ *adv* [Latin] : from the beginning ⟨a contract found to be void *ab initio*⟩

ab in·tes·ta·to \,ab-,in-tes-'tä-tō, ,äb-,in-tes-'tä-tō\ *adv* [Latin] *in the civil law of Louisiana* : from an intestate

ab·jure \ab-'jür, əb-\ *vt* **ab·jured; ab·jur·ing** [Latin *abjurare*, from *ab-* off + *jurare* to swear] : RENOUNCE; *specif* : to disclaim formally or renounce upon oath ⟨solemnly ~*s* his allegiance to his former country⟩ — **ab·ju·ra·tion** \,ab-jə-'rā-shən\ *n*

able *adj* **1** : possessed of needed powers or of needed resources to accomplish an objective ⟨~ to perform under the contract⟩ **2** : having freedom from restriction or obligation or from conditions preventing an action ⟨~ to vote⟩ **3** : legally qualified : possessed of legal competence ⟨~ to inherit property⟩

ab·nor·mal·ly dan·ger·ous ac·tiv·i·ty *n* : an activity esp. that is not common in or appropriate to an area, that creates a high degree of risk of harm to someone or something despite the exercise of due care, and whose value to the community in the area is outweighed by the risk of harm — compare ULTRAHAZARDOUS ACTIVITY ◊ Abnormally dangerous activities are subject to strict liability. *Abnormally dangerous activity* and *ultrahazardous activity* are sometimes used interchangeably.

abode *past and past part of* ABIDE
abol·ish *vt* : to end the observance or effect of : ANNUL
abort \ə-'bòrt\ *vt* : to induce the expulsion of (a human fetus)
abor·tion \ə-'bòr-shən\ *n* **1** : the termination of a pregnancy after, accompanied by, or closely followed by the death of the embryo or fetus; *esp* : the medical procedure of inducing expulsion of a human fetus to terminate a pregnancy **2** : the crime of procuring or performing an illegal abortion ⟨a conspiracy to commit ~ —W. R. LaFave and A. W. Scott, Jr.⟩ — see also *Roe v. Wade* and *Webster v. Reproductive Health Services* in the IMPORTANT CASES section
abor·tion·ist \ə-'bòr-shə-nist\ *n* : one who induces abortions
¹above *adv* **1** : higher on the same page or

on a preceding page ⟨the discussion ∼⟩ **2** : higher or superior in rank or authority ⟨the court ∼⟩ — **above the line** : in calculations that yield adjusted gross income or profit

²above *adj* : written or discussed higher on the same page or on a preceding page ⟨the ∼ argument⟩

abridge \ə-'brij\ *vt* **abridged; abridg·ing** : to diminish or reduce in scope ⟨no State shall make or enforce any law which shall ∼ the privileges and immunities of the citizens of the United States —*U.S. Constitution* amend. XIV⟩ — **abridg·ment** *or* **abridge·ment** *n*

ab·ro·gate \'a-brə-ˌgāt\ *vt* **-gat·ed; -gat·ing** [Latin *abrogare*, from *ab-* off + *rogare* ask, ask for approval of (a law)] : to abolish by authoritative, official, or formal action : ANNUL, REPEAL ⟨a recent addition to [section] 51B ∼*s* statutory and common-law privileges —J. S. J. Elder and A. G. Rodgers⟩ — **ab·ro·ga·tion** \ˌa-brə-'gā-shən\ *n*

ab·scond \ab-'skänd, əb-\ *vi* : to depart secretly : withdraw and hide oneself; *specif* : to evade the legal process of a court by hiding within or secretly leaving its jurisdiction ⟨∼*ed* with the funds⟩ ⟨∼ from New York⟩ ⟨∼ to Canada⟩ — **ab·scond·er** *n*

ab·sence with·out leave : the military offense of being absent without leave

ab·sen·tee \ˌab-sən-'tē\ *n* : one that is absent: as **a** : a proprietor who lives away from his or her business or estate **b** : a potential party to a legal action who is not present or does not have a representative present at a proceeding — **absentee** *adj*

absentee bal·lot *n* : a ballot submitted (as by mail) in advance of an election by a voter who is unable to be present at the polls

ab·sent with·out leave : absent from one's place of duty in the armed forces without authority

ab·so·lute *adj* **1 a** : free from qualification, condition, exception, or restriction ⟨ 't even seem ∼ have these qual-

ifications —*Long v. Rockwood*, 277 U.S. 142 (1927)⟩ — see also *absolute ownership* at OWNERSHIP; compare QUALIFIED **b** *in the civil law of Louisiana* : having or allowing no legal effect ⟨an ∼ impediment⟩ **2** : final and not liable to modification — sometimes used after the word it modifies ⟨divorce ∼⟩; compare NISI — **ab·so·lute·ly** *adv*

absolute assignment — see ASSIGNMENT

absolute defense — see DEFENSE 2a

absolute divorce — see DIVORCE

absolute estate — see ESTATE 1

absolute fee — see FEE 1

absolute immunity — see IMMUNITY

absolute liability — see LIABILITY 2b

absolutely privileged communication *n* : PRIVILEGED COMMUNICATION 2a

absolute nullity — see NULLITY

absolute ownership — see OWNERSHIP

absolute priority rule *n* : a rule that provides for the satisfaction in full of claims of senior creditors before any payments can be made to junior creditors under a chapter 11 bankruptcy plan

absolute privilege — see PRIVILEGE 1a

absolute right *n* : an unqualified right : a legally enforceable right to take some action or to refrain from acting at the sole discretion of the person having the right

absolute sale — see SALE

ab·solve \əb-'zälv, -'sälv\ *vt* **ab·solved; ab·solv·ing 1** : to set free or release from some obligation or responsibility ⟨a judgment terminating a parent's rights . . . ∼*s* that parent of all future support obligations —*In re Bruce R.*, 662 A.2d 107 (1995)⟩ **2** : to determine to be free of fault, guilt, or liability ⟨a jury *absolved* the defendant of any negligence —*Harbaugh v. Darr*, 438 P.2d 74 (1968)⟩

ab·sorb *vt* **1** : to make (a right guaranteed by the U.S. Constitution) applicable to the states **2 a** : to bear or assume the

\ə\abut	\ᵊ\kitten	\ər\further	\a\ash \ā\ace
\ä\cot, cart	\au̇\out	\ch\chin	\e\bet \ē\easy
\g\go	\i\hit \ī\ice	\j\job	\ŋ\sing \ō\go \ȯ\law
\ȯi\boy	\th\thin	\th\the	\ü\loot \u̇\foot \y\yet
\zh\vision	*see also* Pronunciation Symbols page		

burden of ⟨expenses were ~ed by the company⟩ **b : to lessen the tax liability for ⟨has other losses to ~ the income —D. Q. Posin⟩

ab·sorp·tion *n* **:** the application to the states of rights guaranteed by the U.S. Constitution ⟨while *Powell* [*v. Alabama*] was sometimes described as having absorbed the right to counsel, the Court there clearly limited any such ~ —W. R. LaFave and J. H. Israel⟩

ab·stain \əb-'stān, ab-\ *vi* **:** to refrain from exercising federal jurisdiction over a case **:** cause an abstention

ab·sten·tion \əb-'sten-chən\ *n* **:** the staying of the exercise of federal jurisdiction in a case that involves a question of state law or policy which the federal court prefers to have resolved by a state court or agency

Bur·ford abstention \'bər-fərd-\ **:** an abstention grounded on the involvement in the federal case of a challenge to the exercise of a usu. complex state administrative function

Col·o·ra·do Riv·er abstention \,kä-lə-'ra-dō-, -'rä-\ **:** an abstention grounded esp. on the involvement in the federal case of questions of state concern that are also at issue in a parallel case in state court

Pull·man abstention \'pùl-mən-\ **:** an abstention grounded on the involvement in the federal case of the interpretation of an ambiguously worded state law whose constitutionality would have to be determined by the federal court ◊ A party to a case subjected to a Pullman abstention may reserve the right to return to federal court once the state court has resolved the state law question. Pullman abstentions are the most common type of abstention.

Thi·bo·daux abstention \,tē-bə-'dō-\ **:** an abstention grounded on the involvement in the federal case of an issue that greatly affects and concerns a state

Youn·ger abstention \'yəŋ-gər-\ **:** an abstention grounded on the plaintiff's invocation of federal jurisdiction for the purpose of restraining an ongoing usu. criminal state proceeding that has been brought in good faith and not for harassment

ab·stract \'ab-,strakt\ *n* **1 :** a summary of a legal document **2 :** ABSTRACT OF TITLE — **ab·stract** \ab-'strakt, 'ab-,strakt\ *vt*

ab·stract·er *also* **ab·strac·tor** \ab-'strak-tər\ *n* **:** a person who searches out and summarizes information to be used as reference or proof; *specif* **:** a person who prepares abstracts of title

**abstract of title : **a summary statement of the successive conveyances and other facts on which a title to a piece of land rests

abstractor *var of* ABSTRACTER

¹abuse \ə-'byüz\ *vt* **abused; abus·ing 1 :** to put to a use other than the one intended: as **a :** to put to a bad or unfair use ⟨*abusing* the powers of office⟩ **b :** to put to improper or excessive use ⟨~ narcotics⟩ **2 a :** to inflict physical or emotional mistreatment or injury on (as one's child) purposely or through negligence or neglect and often on a regular basis **b :** to engage in sexual activity with (a child under an age specified by statute) **3 :** to attack harshly with words ⟨~ a police officer⟩ ⟨~ a debtor⟩ — **abus·er** *n*

²abuse \ə-'byüs\ *n* **1 :** improper, unfair, or excessive use ⟨~ of authority⟩ ⟨drug ~⟩ **2 a :** the infliction of physical or emotional injury; *also* **:** the crime of inflicting such injury — see also BATTERED CHILD SYNDROME, BATTERED WOMAN'S SYNDROME; compare CRUELTY, NEGLECT **b :** SEXUAL ABUSE **3 :** a verbal attack (as on a police officer in the performance of his or her duty); *also* **:** the crime of making such an attack

**abuse of discretion : **an error of judgment by a trial court in making a ruling that is clearly unreasonable, erroneous, or arbitrary and not justified by the facts or the law applicable in the case — compare CLEARLY ERRONEOUS

**abuse of process : **the tort of bringing and following through with a civil or criminal action for a purpose known to be different from the purpose for which the action was designed — compare MALICIOUS PROSECUTION

abu·sive \ə-'byü-siv, -ziv\ *adj* **1** : characterized by wrong or improper use or action ⟨~ tax shelters⟩ **2** : inflicting verbal or physical abuse ⟨~ parents⟩ — **abu·sive·ly** *adv*

abut \ə-'bət\ *vb* **abut·ted; abut·ting** *vi* : to touch along a border or with a projecting part — used with *on, upon,* or *against* ⟨the land ~s on the road⟩ ~ *vt* : to border on : reach or touch with an end ⟨two lots that ~ each other⟩

abut·ment \ə-'bət-mənt\ *n* : the place at which abutting occurs ⟨at the ~ of two properties⟩

abut·tal \ə-'bət-ᵊl\ *n* : a boundary of land with respect to other contiguous lands or roads by which it is bounded

abut·ter \ə-'bə-tər\ *n* : one that abuts; *specif* : the owner of an abutting property ⟨the ~s on a street⟩

abut·ting \ə-'bə-tiŋ\ *adj* : that abuts or serves as an abutment

ac·cede \ak-'sēd, ik-\ *vi* **ac·ced·ed; ac·ced·ing** **1 a** : to become a party (as to an agreement) by associating oneself with others ⟨they were invited to ~ to the covenant⟩ **b** : to express approval or give consent ⟨the banker asks for collateral. The debtor . . . ~s, and transfers some of his property —*In re Patterson,* 139 F. Supp. 830 (1956)⟩ **2** : to assume an office or position ⟨*acceded* to the governorship⟩ **3 a** : to become added by way of growth, increase, improvement, or labor ⟨the various improvements . . . had *acceded* to the realty and had become "fixtures" —*Graham v. Henderson,* 608 S.W.2d 150 (1980)⟩ **b** : to come into control or ownership of something ⟨a trustee in bankruptcy specifically ~s to all property of the debtor —*Directory Int'l Inc. v. Bates Mfg. Co.,* 91 B.R. 738 (1988)⟩

ac·cel·er·ate *vb* **-at·ed; -at·ing** *vt* : to bring about at an earlier time: as **a** : to advance (the maturity date of a security agreement) so that payment of the debt in full is due immediately — see also ACCELERA-

TION CLAUSE **b** : to cause (a future interest in property) to vest by removing the preceding interests (as by failure or premature termination) ~ *vi* : to enforce an acceleration clause ⟨held that the creditor's right to ~ was suspended —J. J. White and R. S. Summers⟩ — **ac·cel·er·a·tion** *n*

Accelerated Cost Recovery Sys·tem *n* : a method of calculating depreciation introduced in the Economic Recovery Tax Act of 1981 that results in faster recovery of costs for property put into service after 1980 by assigning it a shorter useful life than that previously allowed by the tax code

accelerated depreciation — see DEPRECIATION

acceleration clause *n* : a clause (as in a loan agreement) that accelerates the date of payment in full under specified circumstances (as default by the debtor)

ac·cept \ik-'sept, ak-\ *vt* **1 a** : to receive with consent ⟨~ a gift⟩ ⟨~ service⟩ **b** : to assent to the receipt of and treat in such a way as to indicate ownership of ⟨~*ed* the shipment despite discovering defects in the merchandise⟩ — compare REJECT ◊ Under section 2-606(1) of the Uniform Commercial Code, a buyer accepts goods if: 1) he or she indicates to the seller after a reasonable opportunity to inspect them that he or she will keep them; 2) he or she fails to effectively reject them; 3) he or she acts in a way that is inconsistent with seller's ownership of the goods. **2** : to make an affirmative or favorable response to; *specif* : to indicate by words or action one's assent to (an offer) and willingness to enter into a contract ◊ A contract is created when the offer is accepted. **3** : to assume orally, in writing, or by conduct an obligation to pay ⟨~*ing* a draft⟩ **4** *of a deliberative body* : to receive (a report) officially (as from a committee)

~ *vi* **1** : to receive favorably something offered — usu. used with *of* ⟨no person ... shall ... ~ of any present —*U.S. Constitution* art. I⟩ **2** : to receive and assume ownership of goods ⟨under section 2-606(1), buyer has ~*ed* if he has done any of the acts described therein —J. J. White and R. S. Summers⟩ — **ac•cep•tance** \ik-'sep-təns, ak-\ *n* — **ac•cept•er** *or* **ac•cep•tor** \-tər\ *n*

acceptance of responsibility : a convicted federal defendant's acknowledgment of and remorse for his or her crime such that the sentencing judge has the discretion under the federal sentencing guidelines to reduce the offense level and so impose a less severe sentence

ac•cess \'ak-ˌses\ *n, often attrib* **1** : permission, liberty, or ability to enter, approach, communicate with, or pass to and from a place, thing, or person ⟨public ~ to federal land⟩ ⟨~ to the courts⟩ **2** : opportunity for sexual intercourse **3** : a landowner's legal right to pass from his or her land to a highway and to return without being obstructed **4** : freedom or ability to obtain, make use of, or participate in something ⟨the right to equal treatment holds with respect to a limited set of interests — like voting — and demands that every person have the same ~ to these interests —L. H. Tribe⟩ **5 a** : a way by which a thing or place may be approached or reached **b** : passage to and from a place ⟨provide a means of ~ to the land⟩ **6** : opportunity to view or copy a copyrighted work

accessary *var of* ACCESSORY

ac•ces•sion \ik-'se-shən, ak-\ *n* **1** : increase by something added; *specif* : the mode of acquiring property by which the owner of property (as a building, land, or cattle) becomes the owner of an addition by growth, improvement, increase, or labor **2** : the act of assenting or agreeing

ac•ces•so•ri•al \ˌak-sə-'sōr-ē-əl\ *adj* **1** : of or relating to an accessory ⟨~ acts⟩ **2** : of lesser importance ⟨the principal has the principal or primary duty and the surety an ~ or a secondary duty —*Restatement of Security*⟩

ac•ces•so•ry *also* **ac•ces•sa•ry** \ik-'se-sə-rē, ak-\ *n, pl* **-ries** [Medieval Latin *accessorius* subordinate matter, accomplice to a crime, from Latin *accedere* to go to, agree, assent] **1** : a person who is not actually or constructively present but with criminal intent contributes as an assistant or instigator to the commission of a felony — called also *accessory before the fact;* compare *principal in the second degree* at PRINCIPAL ◊ The traditional distinction between accessories before the fact and principals, that accessories were not present and principals were present at the commission of the crime, is not recognized under most modern state statutes. Accessories before the fact are usu. considered principals. **2** : a person who knowing that a felony has been committed aids, assists, or shelters the offender with the intent to defeat justice — called also *accessory after the fact* ◊ Many state statutes now omit the term *accessory after the fact* and instead characterize the accessory as having committed a particular offense, such as obstructing justice. **3** : the crime of being an accessory — usu. used with *to* and specifying the crime ⟨convicted of murder and ~ to murder —H. B. Zobel⟩; compare SUBSTANTIVE CRIME — **ac•ces•so•ry•ship** *n*

accessory after the fact : ACCESSORY 2

accessory before the fact : ACCESSORY 1

accessory contract — see CONTRACT

ac•ci•dent *n* : an unexpected usu. sudden event that occurs without intent or volition although sometimes through carelessness, unawareness, ignorance, or a combination of causes and that produces an unfortunate result (as an injury) for which the affected party may be entitled to relief under the law or to compensation under an insurance policy — see also UNAVOIDABLE ACCIDENT ◊ The term *accident* has been held to include intentional acts (such as an assault and battery) under workers' compensation laws. — **ac•ci•den•tal** *adj* — **ac•ci•den•tal•ly** *also* **ac•ci•dent•ly** *adv*

accident insurance *n* : insurance against

loss to the insured through accidental bodily injury

ac·com·mo·date \ə-'kä-mə-ˌdāt\ *vt* **-dated; -dat·ing** **1 :** to make a change or provision for ⟨~ a disability⟩ — see also REASONABLE ACCOMMODATION **2 :** to accept without compensation responsibility for a debt of (another person) in the event of nonpayment as a way of reassuring a reluctant creditor — see also *accommodation paper* at PAPER, *accommodation party* at PARTY 1a ◊ To accommodate a debtor effectively, the party must sign the debt instrument, adding words describing limitations or conditions to the accommodation, if any. — **ac·com·mo·da·tion** \ə-ˌkä-mə-'dā-shən\ *n*

accommodated party — see PARTY 1a

accommodation paper — see PAPER

accommodation party — see PARTY 1a

ac·com·plice \ə-'käm-pləs, -'kəm-\ *n* [alteration (from incorrect division of *a complice*) of *complice*, from Middle French, associate, from Late Latin *complic-, complex* partner, confederate] **:** one who intentionally and voluntarily participates with another in a crime by encouraging or assisting in the commission of the crime or by failing to prevent it though under a duty to do so ⟨the ~ of the burglar⟩ ⟨an ~ in a robbery⟩

¹ac·cord \ə-'kȯrd\ *vt* **1 :** to bring into agreement **2 :** to grant or give esp. as appropriate, due, or earned ~ *vi* **:** to be consistent or in harmony ◊ *Accord* in this sense is often used to introduce a case or an authority that accords with the case or authority just cited, as for example in a sentence like ". . . a decision based on equitable principles. *Accord Smith v. Jones*, 1 F.2d 2 (1900)."

²accord *n* **1 :** agreement of opinion ⟨both cases in ~⟩ **2 :** a formal act of agreement **:** TREATY ⟨an economic ~⟩ **3 :** an accepted offer by which the parties agree that a specified future performance will discharge in full an obligation when performed even though the performance is of less value than the original obligation; *also* **:** the defense that an accord was agreed upon — usu. used in the phrase

accord and satisfaction; called also *executory accord;* compare COMPOSITION, COMPROMISE, NOVATION, SATISFACTION, *substituted contract* at CONTRACT, TRANSACTION 3

¹ac·count *n* **1 a :** a record of debit and credit entries to cover transactions involving a particular item (as cash or notes receivable) or a particular person or concern **b :** a statement of transactions during a fiscal period showing the resulting balance — sometimes used in the pl. ⟨trustees filed annual ~s as required by statute —W. M. McGovern, Jr. *et al.*⟩ **2 :** a periodically rendered reckoning (as one listing charged purchases and credits) **3 :** a sum of money or its equivalent deposited in the common cash of a bank and subject to withdrawal at the option of the depositor **4 :** a right under Article 9 of the Uniform Commercial Code to payment for goods or services which is not contained in an instrument or chattel paper and that may or may not have been earned by performance

²account *vi* **:** to give a financial account ⟨a duty to ~⟩

ac·count·able \ə-'kaün-tə-bəl\ *adj* **1 :** LIABLE ⟨~ for the burglary⟩ **2 :** obliged to accept responsibility ⟨the bank ~ for payment of the check⟩ — **ac·count·abil·i·ty** \ə-ˌkaün-tə-'bi-lə-tē\ *n*

ac·count·ing *n* **1 :** an often court-ordered presentment or examination of accounts ⟨a complete ~ would be necessary to determine the nature of the expenditures —*Case & Comment*⟩ **2 :** the settlement by judicial action of the assets of a partnership (as upon dissolution)

account pay·able \-'pā-ə-bəl\ *n, pl* **accounts payable :** the balance due to a creditor on a current account

account re·ceiv·able \-ri-'sē-və-bəl\ *n, pl* **accounts receivable :** a balance due from a debtor on a current account

account ren·dered \-'ren-dərd\ *n, pl*

accounts rendered : an account presented by a creditor to a debtor for examination and settlement

account stat·ed \-'stā-təd\ *n, pl* **accounts stated** : an account presented by a creditor to his or her debtor which by implied or express acceptance has been agreed upon by both parties as correct

ac·cred·it·ed investor \ə-'kre-də-təd-\ *n* : an investor that qualifies under the Securities Act of 1933 and related Securities and Exchange Commission regulations as one having at least a specified net worth and a certain level of knowledge and experience in financial matters

ac·crete \ə-'krēt\ *vb* **ac·cret·ed; ac·cret·ing** *vi* : to grow or become attached by accretion ~ *vt* : to cause to adhere or become attached

ac·cre·tion \ə-'krē-shən\ *n* **1** : the process or a result of growth or enlargement: as **a** : the increase or extension of the boundaries of land or the consequent acquisition of land accruing to the owner by the gradual or imperceptible action of natural forces (as by the washing up of sand or soil from the sea or a river or by a gradual recession of the water from the usual watermark); *also* : accession in which the boundaries of land are enlarged by this process — compare AVULSION, RELICTION **b** : increase in the amount or extent of any kind of property or in the value of any property ⟨~s to a trust fund resulting from the increase in value of . . . securities in which its corpus is invested —*In re Estate of Gartenlaub,* 244 P. 348 (1926)⟩ ◊ Accretion in value of the principal of a trust is generally not considered income. **c** : enlargement of a bargaining unit by the addition of new employees **2** *in the civil law of Louisiana* : the passing to an heir or conjoint legatee of the right to accept a portion of a succession resulting from the failure of a coheir or colegatee to take his or her own share

ac·cru·al \ə-'krü-əl\ *n* **1** : the action or process of accruing ⟨claim must be brought within two years of the date of

~⟩ **2 a** : something that accrues; *esp* : an amount of money that periodically accumulates for a specific purpose (as payment of taxes or interest) **b** : something that has accrued during a specified period

accrual basis — see BASIS 2

accrual bond — see BOND 2

accrual method *n* : ACCRUAL BASIS at BASIS

ac·crue \ə-'krü\ *vb* **ac·crued; ac·cru·ing** [Middle French *accreue* increase, addition to a property, from feminine of *accreu,* past participle of *acreistre* to increase] *vi* **1** : to come into existence as an enforceable claim : vest as a right ⟨action . . . does not ~ until the plaintiff knew or reasonably should have known that he may have suffered injury —*National Law Journal*⟩ ◊ Statutes of limitations begin to run when a cause of action accrues. **2** : to come by way of increase or addition : arise as a growth or result — usu. used with *to* or *from* ⟨advantages *accruing* to society from the freedom of the press⟩ ⟨interest ~s to the seller as a result of the delay⟩ **3** : to be periodically accumulated in the process of time whether as an increase or a decrease ⟨the *accruing* of taxes⟩ ⟨allowing the receivable interest to ~⟩ ~ *vt* **1** : to accumulate or have due after a period of time ⟨authorized by law to ~ leave . . . in the maximum amount of 120 days —*U.S. Code*⟩ **2** : to enter in the books as an accrual

ac·cu·mu·late *vb* **-lat·ed; -lat·ing** *vt* : to gather esp. little by little; *specif* : to add (income from a fund) back into the principal ~ *vi* : to increase gradually in amount or number

accumulated earnings tax *n* : a tax levied on the taxable income of a corporation that is accumulated by the corporation rather than distributed to shareholders and that is not retained for the reasonable needs of the business

ac·cu·mu·la·tion *n* : increase or growth by addition esp. when continuous or repeated; *specif* : an increase in the amount of a fund or property by the continuous addition to it of the income or interest it generates ⟨to treat a stock dividend as principal when local law classifies it as income may be deemed an ~ —W. M. McGovern, Jr. *et al.*⟩ — see also *accumulation trust* at TRUST ◊ Because they prevent the enjoyment and benefit of wealth, accumulations are deemed contrary to public policy. A provision in a will for an accumulation will be invalidated if found to be unreasonable by the court.

accumulation trust — see TRUST

ac•cu•sa•tion \ˌa-kyə-'zā-shən\ *n* **1 :** a formal charge of wrongdoing, delinquency, or fault ⟨the accused shall enjoy the right . . . to be informed of the nature and cause of the ~ —*U.S. Constitution* amend. VI⟩ — compare ALLEGATION, INDICTMENT, INFORMATION **2 :** the offense or fault of which one is accused ⟨the ~ was murder⟩

ac•cus•a•to•ri•al \ə-ˌkyü-zə-'tōr-ē-əl\ *adj* **:** of, relating to, or being a form of criminal prosecution in which a person is accused of a crime and is tried in public by a judge who is not also the prosecutor — compare ADVERSARY, INQUISITORIAL — **ac•cus•a•to•ri•al•ly** *adv*

ac•cus•a•to•ry \ə-'kyü-zə-ˌtōr-ē\ *adj* **1 :** containing or expressing an accusation ⟨the ~ pleading⟩ **2 :** ACCUSATORIAL

ac•cuse *vb* **ac•cused; ac•cus•ing** [Latin *accusare* to find fault with, charge with a crime, from *ad* to, at + *causa* legal case, trial] *vt* **:** to charge with an offense judicially or by a public process — compare INDICT ~ *vi* **:** to make or bring an accusation — **ac•cus•er** *n*

ac•cused \ə-'kyüzd\ *n, pl* **accused :** a person who has been arrested for or formally charged with a crime **:** the defendant in a criminal case ⟨the ~ shall enjoy the right to a speedy and public trial —*U.S. Constitution* amend. VI⟩ ◊ Certain rights guaranteed by the Constitution, such as the right to counsel, become effective once a person is characterized as an accused.

ac•knowl•edge *vt* **-edged; -edg•ing 1 :** to indicate recognition and acceptance of ⟨the power of taxation in the general and state governments is *acknowledged* to be concurrent —*McCulloch v. Maryland,* 17 U.S. 316 (1819)⟩ **2 a :** to show by word or act that one has knowledge of and accepts responsibility for (a duty, obligation, or indebtedness) **b :** to admit paternity of ⟨*will* ~ the child as his⟩ — compare FILIATE **3 :** to make known to a sender or giver the receipt of (what has been sent or given) or the fact of (one's having received what has been sent or given) ⟨~ receipt of a letter⟩ **4 :** to recognize as genuine so as to give validity **:** avow or admit in legal form ⟨the execution of any such power of attorney shall be *acknowledged* before one of the officers —*U.S. Code*⟩

ac•knowl•edg•ment *also* **ac•knowl•edge-ment** *n* **1 a :** the act of acknowledging **b :** the act of admitting paternity — compare FILIATION **2 :** a thing done or given in recognition of something received ⟨an ~ came in the mail⟩ **3 a :** a declaration or avowal of one's act or a fact to give it legal validity; *specif* **:** a declaration before a duly qualified public officer (as a notary public) by a person who has executed an instrument that the execution was the person's free act and deed **b :** the formal certificate made by an officer before whom one has acknowledged a deed including as an essential part the signature and often the seal of the officer

ACLU *abbr* American Civil Liberties Union

ac•quest /ə-'kwest, a-/ *n, in the civil law of Louisiana* **:** ACQUET

ac•quet /'a-kət, a-'kā, ə-'kwet/ *n* [French *acquêt* acquisition, from Old French *acquest*, ultimately from Latin *acquirere* to acquire] *in the civil law of Louisiana* **:** property acquired through means other than inheritance

\ə\abut \ᵊ\kitten \ər\further \a\ash \ā\ace
\ä\cot, cart \au̇\out \ch\chin \e\bet \ē\easy
\g\go \i\hit \ī\ice \j\job \ŋ\sing \ō\go \ȯ\law
\ȯi\boy \th\thin \t͟h\the \ü\loot \u̇\foot \y\yet
\zh\vision *see also* Pronunciation Symbols page

ac·qui·esce \ˌa-kwē-'es\ *vi* **-esced; -esc-ing** : to accept, comply, or submit tacitly or passively — often used with *in* and sometimes with *to* — **ac·qui·es·cence** \ˌa-kwē-'es-ᵊns\ *n*

ac·quire \ə-'kwīr\ *vt* **ac·quired; ac·quir-ing** : to come into possession, ownership, or control of : obtain as one's own ⟨the target's directors don't want the company to be *acquired* —R. C. Clark⟩ ⟨the court *acquired* jurisdiction⟩ — **ac·quir·er** *also* **ac·qui·ror** \ə-'kwīr-ər\ *n*

ac·qui·si·tion \ˌa-kwə-'zi-shən\ *n* **1** : the act or action of acquiring; *specif* : the obtaining of controlling interest in a company — compare MERGER, TAKEOVER **2** : a thing gained or acquired

acquisitive prescription — see PRESCRIPTION

ac·quis·i·tor \ə-'kwi-zə-tər\ *n* : one that acquires : ACQUIRER

ac·quit \ə-'kwit\ *vb* **ac·quit·ted; ac·quit-ting** [Old French *acquiter* to pay off, absolve, acquit, from *a-*, prefix marking causation + *quite* free (of an obligation)] *vt* : to discharge completely: as **a** : to release from liability for a debt or other obligation — usu. used in agreements ⟨forever release, ~, and discharge each other⟩ **b** : to absolve (a criminal defendant) of a charge by judicial process **c** : to clear of wrongdoing ⟨the fact . . . does not ~ them of misrepresentation —*In re Hiller*, 694 P.2d 540 (1985)⟩ ~ *vi* : to absolve a defendant of criminal liability ⟨must ~ if any reasonable doubt existed —*Commonwealth v. Gagliardi*, 638 N.E.2d 20 (1994)⟩ — compare CONVICT

ac·quit·tal \ə-'kwit-ᵊl\ *n* **1** : release or discharge from debt or other liability **2** : a setting free or deliverance from the charge of an offense by verdict of a jury, judgment of a court, or other legal process — see also IMPLIED ACQUITTAL, *judgment of acquittal* at JUDGMENT 1a; compare CONVICTION

ac·quit·tance \ə-'kwit-ᵊns\ *n* : ACQUITTAL 1

ac·quit·tee \ə-ˌkwi-'tē\ *n* : a person who is acquitted of a criminal charge

ACRS *abbr* Accelerated Cost Recovery System

¹act *n* **1 a** : something done by a person in accordance with his or her free will ⟨a tortious ~⟩ — see also ACTUS REUS **b** : the failure to do something that one has a legal duty to do — called also *negative act* **2 a** *often cap* : the formal product of a legislative body : the formally declared will of a legislature the final requirement of which is usu. the signature of the proper executive officer : STATUTE ⟨an ~ of Congress⟩ **b** : a decision or determination of a sovereign, a legislative council, or a court of justice — compare BILL 1 **3** *often cap* : a formal record of something done or transacted ⟨given as my free ~ and deed⟩ ⟨matters of procedure are provided for in that *Act* —*Federal Rules of Civil Procedure* Rule 81(a)(6)⟩

²act *vi* **1** : to carry into effect a determination of the will : take action **2** : to discharge the duties of a specified office or post : perform a specified function — used with a prepositional phrase ⟨declaring what officer shall then ~ as President —*U.S. Constitution* art. II⟩ **3** : to give a decision or award (as by vote of a deliberative body or by judicial decree) — often used with *on* ⟨adjourned with several important matters still not ~*ed* on⟩ — **ac·tor** \'ak-tər\ *n*

ac·tio de in rem ver·so \'ak-shē-ō-ˌdē-in-'rem-'vər-sō, 'äk-tē-ō-ˌdā-in-'rem-'ver-sō\ *n* [Latin, legal action over something converted to the benefit (of the principal in the law of agency)] *in the civil law of Louisiana* : a doctrine equivalent to the common-law doctrine of unjust enrichment

ac·tion *n* [Latin *actio* legal proceeding, from *agere* to do, carry out, initiate legal proceedings] **1 a** : a judicial proceeding for the enforcement or protection of a right, the redress or prevention of a wrong, or the punishment of a public offense — compare *special proceeding* at PROCEEDING **b** : the right to bring or maintain such a legal or judicial proceeding **2** : an act or decision by an executive or legislative body of a government (as an administrative agency) or of an organization (as a Board of Directors) ⟨the power of courts to invalidate statutes and executive ~*s* —R. H. Bork⟩ **3** : a voluntary act of will that manifests itself externally : a mode of conduct

ac·tion·able \'ak-shə-nə-bəl\ *adj* : subject to or providing grounds for an action or suit at law ⟨slander is ~⟩

action of debt : DEBT 2

action on the case : TRESPASS ON THE CASE at TRESPASS

ac·tive *adj* **1** : characterized or accomplished by action or effort ⟨~ concealment⟩ — compare PASSIVE **2** : engaged or participating in action or activity ⟨paying child support but not otherwise an ~ parent⟩

active trust — see TRUST

act of God *often cap* A : an extraordinary natural event (as a flood or earthquake) that cannot be reasonably foreseen or prevented — compare FORCE MAJEURE, INEVITABLE ACCIDENT, UNAVOIDABLE ACCIDENT ◊ It is a defense against liability for injury if the injury is directly and exclusively caused by an act of God.

act of state doctrine : a court-made doctrine barring U.S. courts from judging the validity of an official act of a foreign country committed within its own borders

ac·tu·al *adj* : existing in fact or reality — compare CONSTRUCTIVE — **ac·tu·al·ly** *adv*

actual agency — see AGENCY 2a

actual authority — see AUTHORITY

actual cash value *n* **1** : the cost of replacing or repairing damaged property less any applicable depreciation **2** : FAIR MARKET VALUE

actual cause — see CAUSE 1

actual controversy *n* : a real dispute between parties with true adverse legal interests based on facts existing at the time the suit is brought

actual damages — see DAMAGE 2

actual delivery — see DELIVERY

actual eviction — see EVICTION

actual express authority — see AUTHORITY

actual fraud — see FRAUD

actual implied authority — see AUTHORITY

actual knowledge — see KNOWLEDGE

actual loss — see LOSS

actual malice — see MALICE

actual notice — see NOTICE

actual possession — see POSSESSION

actual total loss — see LOSS

ac·tu·ar·i·al \ˌak-chə-'wer-ē-əl, ˌak-shə-\ *adj* **1** : of or relating to actuaries **2** : relating to statistical calculation esp. of life expectancy — **ac·tu·ar·i·al·ly** *adv*

ac·tu·ary \'ak-chə-ˌwer-ē, -shə-\ *n, pl* **-ar·ies** : a person who calculates insurance and annuity premiums, reserves, and dividends

ac·tus re·us \'ak-təs-'rē-əs, 'äk-tùs-'rä-ùs\ *n* [New Latin, guilty deed] : the wrongful act that makes up the physical action of a crime — see also CRIME; compare MENS REA

ACV *abbr* actual cash value

ADA *abbr* Americans with Disabilities Act — see also the IMPORTANT LAWS section

ADC *abbr* Aid to Dependent Children

ad dam·num \'ad-'dam-nəm, 'äd-'däm-nùm\ *n* [Latin, in accordance with the loss] : the claim for damages in a civil lawsuit ⟨defendant's motion seeking to reduce the *ad damnum* demanded in the complaint⟩

¹**ad·dict** \ə-'dikt\ *vt* : to cause (a person) to become physiologically dependent upon a drug

²**ad·dict** \'a-dikt\ *n* : one who is addicted to a drug

ad·dic·tion \ə-'dik-shən\ *n* : compulsive physiological need for a habit-forming drug (as heroin)

ad·dic·tive \ə-'dik-tiv\ *adj* : causing or characterized by addiction ⟨~ drugs⟩

\ə\abut \ᵊ\kitten \ər\further \a\ash \ā\ace
\ä\cot, cart \aù\out \ch\chin \e\bet \ē\easy
\g\go \i\hit \ī\ice \j\job \ŋ\sing \ō\go \ò\law
\òi\boy \th\thin \th̲\the \ü\loot \ù\foot \y\yet
\zh\vision *see also* Pronunciation Symbols page

ad·di·tur \\'a-di-tər, 'ä-di-ˌtür\ *n* [Latin, it is increased] : the increase by a court of the jury's award of damages which the court deems insufficient — compare REMITTITUR ◊ The Supreme Court held in *Dimick v. Schiedt*, 293 U.S. 474 (1935) that additur violates the Seventh Amendment and so is not permissible in federal courts. Many state courts allow additur, however, when the defendant agrees to the increased award on the condition that the court deny plaintiff's motion for a new trial.

add–on *adj* **1** : being or able to be added on 〈~ no-fault benefits〉 **2** : able to be added to 〈~ certificates of deposit〉

adeem \ə-'dēm\ *vt* [from *ademption*, after such pairs as *redemption* : *redeem*] : to revoke or satisfy (as a legacy) by ademption

ademp·tion \ə-'demp-shən\ *n* [Latin *ademptio*, from *adimere* to take away, from *ad* to + *emere* to buy, obtain] **1** : the revocation of a gift in a will inferred from the disposal (as by sale) of the property by the maker of the will before he or she dies **2** : the revocation of a gift in a will inferred from the maker's gift before his or her death of the same or similar property to the recipient named in the will — compare ADVANCEMENT ◊ Only gifts that are characterized as specific devises, bequests, or legacies are subject to ademption.

ad·e·quate *adj* : lawfully and reasonably sufficient 〈~ grounds for a lawsuit〉

adequate consideration — see CONSIDERATION

adequate protection *n* : such action as is judicially determined to protect a secured creditor's interest in property that is part of a bankrupt estate ◊ The U.S. Bankruptcy Code offers a list of examples of actions that are predetermined to provide adequate protection. When a court finds that a secured creditor is not adequately protected, the creditor may obtain relief from the automatic stay from creditors' collection attempts that is effected by the debtor's filing for bankruptcy.

adhesion contract — see CONTRACT

¹ad hoc \'ad-'häk, -'hōk; 'äd-'hōk\ *adv* [Latin, for this] : for the particular end or case at hand without consideration of wider application

²ad hoc *adj* **1** : concerned with a particular end or purpose 〈an *ad hoc* investigating committee〉 **2** : formed or used for specific or immediate problems or needs 〈*ad hoc* solutions〉

ad idem \'ad-'ī-dəm, 'äd-'ē-dem\ *adv* [Latin, to the same] : in agreement : at a meeting of the minds 〈the parties were *ad idem*〉

ad interim \'ad-'in-tə-rəm, 'äd-, -ˌrim\ *adj* [Latin, for the intervening time] : made or serving temporarily or for the time being 〈an *ad interim* committee〉

ad·jec·tive law \'a-jik-tiv-\ *n* : the portion of the law that deals with the rules of procedure governing evidence, pleading, and practice — compare SUBSTANTIVE LAW

ad·journ \ə-'jərn\ *vt* : to put off further proceedings of either indefinitely or until a later stated time : close formally 〈~*ing* the session〉 ~ *vi* : to suspend a session or meeting till another time or indefinitely : suspend formal business or procedure and disband 〈the congress will ~ next month〉 — **ad·journ·ment** *n*

ad·judge \ə-'jəj\ *vt* **ad·judged; ad·judg·ing** **1** : ADJUDICATE **2** : to award, grant, or impose judicially 〈~ costs to the plaintiff〉 — **ad·judg·ment** *n*

ad·ju·di·cate \ə-'jü-di-ˌkāt\ *vb* **-cat·ed; -cat·ing** [Latin *adjudicare* to award in judgment, from *ad* to, for + *judicare* to judge — see JUDGE] *vt* **1** : to settle either finally or temporarily (the rights and duties of the parties to a judicial or quasi-judicial proceeding) on the merits of the issues raised **2** : to pass judgment on as a judge : settle judicially **3** : to pronounce judicially to be 〈was *adjudicated* a bankrupt〉 〈was *adjudicated* the child's father〉 **4** : to convey by judicial sale ~ *vi* : to come to a judicial decision : act as judge 〈the court *adjudicated* upon the case〉 — **ad·ju·di·ca·tion** \ə-ˌjü-di-'kā-shən\ *n* — **ad·ju·di·ca·tive** \ə-'jü-di-ˌkā-tiv, -kə-\ *n* — **ad·ju·di·ca·tor** \-ˌkā-tər\ *n*

adjudicative fact — see FACT
ad·just *vt* **1 a** : to determine the amount to be paid under an insurance policy in settlement of (a loss) **b** : to make new arrangements with creditors for the payment of (the debts of a debtor in bankruptcy) **2** : to calculate in accordance with a system ⟨~*ing* the basis⟩
adjustable rate mortgage — see MORTGAGE
adjusted basis — see BASIS 3
adjusted gross income *n* : an individual's gross income decreased by the amount of deductions allowed esp. for business expenses
adjustment bond — see BOND 2
ad li·tem \'ad-'lī-təm, 'äd-'lē-tem\ *adj or adv* [Latin] : for the lawsuit or action ⟨trustee *ad litem*⟩
ad·min·is·ter \əd-'mi-nə-stər\ *vb* **-is·tered; -is·ter·ing** *vt* **1** : to manage the affairs of (as a government or agency) **2 a** : to direct or supervise the execution, use, or conduct of ⟨~ a trust fund⟩ **b** : to settle (an estate) under a court appointment as administrator or executor **3 a** : to give ritually ⟨~ an oath⟩ **b** : to give (as a narcotic) for the purpose of ingesting ~ *vi* **1** : to perform the office of an administrator or executor **2** : to manage or conduct affairs — **ad·min·is·tra·ble** \əd-'mi-nə-strə-bəl\ *adj*
ad·min·is·trate \əd-'mi-nə-ˌstrāt\ *vb* **-trat·ed; -trat·ing** : ADMINISTER
ad·min·is·tra·tion \əd-ˌmi-nə-'strā-shən\ *n* **1** : the act or process of administering ⟨the ~ of justice⟩ **2 a** : the management and disposal under court authority of the estate of a deceased person by an executor or an administrator **b** : the management of an estate (as of a minor) by a trustee or guardian appointed to take charge of it **c** : the management of assets held in a trust **3** : the execution of public affairs as distinguished from policy-making **4 a** : a body of persons (as of an organization) who administer **b** *often cap* : a group that makes up the executive branch of a presidential government **c** : a governmental agency or board **5** : the term

of office of an administrative officer or body
ad·min·i·stra·tive \əd-'mi-nə-ˌstrā-tiv\ *adj* **1** : of or relating to the performance of a function : MINISTERIAL ⟨~ communications include . . . instructions that encourage a jury to continue its deliberations —*National Law Journal*⟩ **2** : of or relating to the executive branch of a government — compare LEGISLATIVE, JUDICIAL **3** : of or relating to a government agency ⟨~ remedies⟩
administrative agency *n* : AGENCY 4
Administrative Court *n* : a court sitting in the District Court or Superior Court in Maine that handles matters involving real estate licenses
administrative crime *n* : violation of a regulation of a government agency that is punishable as a crime
administrative hearing — see HEARING
administrative inspection *n* : ADMINISTRATIVE SEARCH at SEARCH
administrative judge *n* : ADMINISTRATIVE LAW JUDGE
administrative law *n* : the branch of the law dealing with government agencies
administrative law judge *n* : an officer in a government agency with quasi-judicial functions including conducting hearings, making findings of fact, and making recommendations for resolution of disputes concerning the agency's actions — called also *administrative judge*
administrative search — see SEARCH
administrative warrant — see WARRANT
ad·min·i·stra·tor \əd-'mi-nə-ˌstrā-tər\ *n* **1** : a person appointed by a probate court to manage the distribution of the assets in the estate of a person who has died without leaving a valid will or leaving a will that does not name an executor able or willing to perform — see also ADMINISTRATRIX, *letters of administration* at

\ə\abut \ə\kitten \ər\further \a\ash \ā\ace
\ä\cot, cart \au̇\out \ch\chin \e\bet \ē\easy
\g\go \i\hit \ī\ice \j\job \ŋ\sing \ō\go \ȯ\law
\ȯi\boy \th\thin \t͟h\the \ü\loot \u̇\foot \y\yet
\zh\vision *see also* Pronunciation Symbols page

LETTER 2; compare EXECUTOR, PER-
SONAL REPRESENTATIVE
administrator ad litem : an administrator appointed to represent an estate that
is a necessary party to a lawsuit
administrator cum testamento annexo
: ADMINISTRATOR WITH THE WILL AN-
NEXED in this entry
administrator de bonis non \-dē-'bō-
nis-'nän, -dā-'bō-nis-'nōn\ : an administrator appointed to administer the
remaining assets in the estate when the
preceding administrator or executor
can or will no longer perform
administrator pen·den·te li·te \-pen-
'den-tē-'lī-tē, -pen-'den-tā-'lē-tā\ : SPE-
CIAL ADMINISTRATOR 2 in this entry
administrator with the will annexed
: an administrator appointed to administer an estate where the will names no
executor or where the named executor
is incapable of performing or unwilling
to perform — called also *administrator
cum testamento annexo*
ancillary administrator : a subordinate
administrator appointed to administer
the assets of an estate that are located
in a different jurisdiction from the one
where the deceased was domiciled and
where the primary administration of the
estate is taking place
foreign administrator : an administrator appointed in another state
general administrator : an administrator appointed to administer the entire estate of a deceased person in accordance
with the laws of intestacy or in accordance with the will if there is one — compare SPECIAL ADMINISTRATOR in this
entry
independent administrator : an administrator whose administration of the estate is entirely or mostly unsupervised
by the probate court
public administrator 1 : a public officer who administers the estates of deceased people when there is no one else
willing or entitled to perform 2 : an
administrator appointed in some states
for the sole purpose of being respon-

sible for the assets in an estate pending
settlement of a dispute or when there
is doubt as to who should be appointed
administrator
special administrator 1 : an administrator appointed to administer only a designated part of the deceased person's
estate 2 : an administrator appointed for
the sole purpose of being responsible for
the assets in an estate usu. in some emergency (as a will contest) — compare
GENERAL ADMINISTRATOR in this entry
2 : a person that administers; *esp, often
cap* : the head of a government agency
administrator ad litem — see ADMINI-
STRATOR
administrator cum testamento annexo
— see ADMINISTRATOR
administrator de bonis non — see AD-
MINISTRATOR
administrator pendente lite — see AD-
MINISTRATOR
administrator with the will annexed —
see ADMINISTRATOR
ad·min·i·stra·trix \əd-,mi-nə-'strā-triks\
n, pl **-tra·tri·ces** \-'strā-trə-,sēz\ : a woman administrator esp. of an estate
ad·mi·ral·ty \'ad-mə-rəl-tē\ *n* : the court
having jurisdiction over questions of
maritime law; *also* : MARITIME LAW
ad·mis·si·ble \əd-'mi-sə-bəl, ad-\ *adj* : capable of being allowed or permitted ⟨the
difficulty would be lessened if entries in
books of account were ~ as prima facie
evidence —B. N. Cardozo⟩ — **ad·mis-
si·bil·i·ty** \-,mi-sə-'bi-lə-tē\ *n*
ad·mis·sion *n* 1 : the act or process of admitting ⟨~ into evidence⟩ 2 a : a party's
acknowledgment that a fact or statement
is true ◊ In civil cases admissions are often agreed to and offered in writing to the
court before trial as a method of reducing the number of issues to be proven at
trial. b : a party's prior out-of-court statement or action that is inconsistent with
his or her position at trial and that tends
to establish guilt — compare CONFES-
SION, *declaration against interest* at DEC-
LARATION ◊ Under the Federal Rules of
Evidence an admission is not hearsay. Si-

lence can sometimes be construed as an admission where a person would reasonably be expected to speak up.

ad·mit *vb* **ad·mit·ted; ad·mit·ting** *vt* **1** : to concede as true or valid : make an admission of **2** : to allow to be entered or offered ⟨*admitted* the document into evidence⟩ ⟨~ a will to probate⟩ — *vi* : to make acknowledgment — used with *to* ⟨~*s* to the murder⟩

admitted asset — see ASSET 2

adopt \ə-'däpt\ *vt* **1** : to take voluntarily (a child of other parents) as one's own child esp. in compliance with formal legal procedures — see also EQUITABLE ADOPTION **2** : to take or accept as if one's own ⟨[the company] ~*ed* the signature on the financing statement —*Barber-Greene Co. v. Nat'l City Bank of Minneapolis*, 816 F.2d 1267 (1987)⟩ **3** : to accept formally and put into effect ⟨~ a constitutional amendment⟩ — **adopt·able** \ə-'däp-tə-bəl\ *adj* — **adopt·abil·i·ty** \ə-,däp-tə-'bi-lə-tē\ *adv* — **adop·tion** \ə-'däp-shən\ *n*

adopt·ee \ə-,däp-'tē\ *n* : a person who is adopted

adoption by estoppel : EQUITABLE ADOPTION

adop·tive \ə-'däp-tiv\ *adj* **1 a** : having adopted ⟨an ~ parent⟩ **b** : having been adopted ⟨an ~ child⟩ **2** : made or acquired by accepting as one's own the words or actions of another ⟨to constitute an ~ admission . . . defendant must actually understand what was said and have an opportunity to deny it —*United States v. White*, 766 F. Supp. 873 (1991)⟩

ADR *abbr* **1** administrative dispute resolution, alternative dispute resolution **2** asset depreciation range

ads *abbr* [Medieval Latin *ad sectam*] at the suit of

adult *n* : a person who has reached an age specified by law — compare CHILD, INFANT, MINOR

adul·ter·ate \ə-'dəl-tə-,rāt\ *vt* **-at·ed; -at·ing** : to corrupt, debase, or make impure by the addition of a foreign or inferior substance or element; *esp* : to prepare for sale by omitting a valuable ingre-

dient or by replacing more valuable ingredients with less valuable or inert and usu. harmful ingredients or with ingredients different from those claimed ◇ Under the federal Food, Drug, and Cosmetic Act, a device such as a piece of medical equipment that is defective in some way is considered adulterated. — **adul·ter·a·tion** \ə-,dəl-tə-'rā-shən\ *n* — **adul·ter·a·tor** \ə-'dəl-tə-,rā-tər\ *n*

adul·ter·ous \ə-'dəl-tə-rəs\ *adj* : relating to, characterized by, or given to adultery — **adul·ter·ous·ly** *adv*

adul·tery \ə-'dəl-tə-rē\ *n* : voluntary sexual activity (as sexual intercourse) between a married man and someone other than his wife or between a married woman and someone other than her husband; *also* : the crime of adultery — compare FORNICATION — **adul·ter·er** \ə-'dəl-tə-rər\ *n* — **adul·ter·ess** \-tə-rəs\ *n*

ad val \'ad-'val\ *abbr* ad valorem

ad va·lo·rem \'ad-və-'lōr-əm, 'äd-vä-'lō-rem\ *adj* [Latin, according to the value] : imposed at a rate based on a percent of value ⟨an *ad valorem* tax on real estate⟩

¹**ad·vance** *vt* **ad·vanced; ad·vanc·ing** : to supply or provide ahead of time: as **a** : to give (a gift) by way of or as an advancement **b** : to supply (as money) beforehand in expectation of repayment or other future adjustment

²**advance** *n* : a provision of something (as goods or money) before a return is received; *also* : the money or goods supplied

advance directive *n* : a document (as a living will or durable power of attorney) in which a person expresses his or her wishes regarding medical treatment in the event of incapacitation

ad·vance·ment *n* : something given in advance; *specif* : money or property given as a gift by a living person (as by a parent) to a child) with the intention that the

\ə\abut \ᵊ\kitten \ər\further \a\ash \ā\ace
\ä\cot, cart \aü\out \ch\chin \e\bet \ē\easy
\g\go \i\hit \ī\ice \j\job \ŋ\sing \ō\go \ò\law
\òi\boy \th\thin \th̲\the \ü\loot \ù\foot \y\yet
\zh\vision *see also* Pronunciation Symbols page

amount the recipient inherits under the law from the person's estate will be reduced proportionately — compare ADEMPTION ◊ Advancements apply only when the person making the gift dies without a will. The Uniform Probate Code requires written evidence that the gift was intended to be an advancement. A person who gives a gift that is not intended as an advancement cannot later change it to an advancement. A gift given as an advancement can, however, be changed into an outright gift.

advance sheet *n* : the published opinions of a court available in a temporary form (as in loose pages held in a binder) — compare REPORTER

ad·ver·sar·i·al \ˌad-vər-'ser-ē-əl\ *adj* : of, relating to, or characteristic of an adversary or adversary procedures : ADVERSARY

¹ad·ver·sary \'ad-vər-ˌser-ē\ *n* : one that contends with or opposes another; *esp* : any of the opposing parties in a legal action

²adversary *adj* : of, relating to, or involving opposing parties or interests; *specif* : of, relating to, or involving a system of justice in which opposing parties usu. represented by counsel present evidence to an impartial decision-maker (as a jury) by a process of questioning witnesses under the supervision of a judge — compare ACCUSATORIAL, INQUISITORIAL

ad·verse \ad-'vərs, 'ad-ˌvərs\ *adj* : opposed to one's interests : operating to one's detriment ⟨an ∼ verdict⟩

adverse party — see PARTY 1b

adverse possession — see POSSESSION

adverse witness — see WITNESS

ad·vice \əd-'vīs\ *n* **1** : recommendation regarding a decision or course of conduct ⟨he shall have power, by and with the ∼ and consent of the Senate, to make treaties — *U.S. Constitution* art. II⟩ ⟨∼ of counsel⟩ **2** : an official notice concerning a business transaction

ad·vise \əd-'vīz\ *vb* **ad·vised; ad·vis·ing** *vt* **1** : to give advice to : COUNSEL ⟨∼ them to draw up a will⟩ **2** : to give information

or notice to ⟨∼ them of their rights⟩ — *vi* **1** : to give advice ⟨∼ on legal matters⟩ **2** : to take counsel ⟨∼ with your lawyer⟩ —

ad·vis·er *also* **ad·vi·sor** \əd-'vī-zər\ *n*

ad·vise·ment \əd-'vīz-mənt\ *n* **1** : careful consideration : DELIBERATION ⟨take the matter under ∼⟩ **2** : the act or process of advising ⟨∼ of the debtor on matters relating to . . . his debts —J. H. Williamson⟩

ad·vi·so·ry \əd-'vī-zə-rē\ *adj* **1** : having or exercising power to advise ⟨an ∼ committee⟩ **2** : containing or giving advice ⟨an ∼ verdict⟩

advisory jury *n* : a jury impaneled at the discretion of a trial judge to assist the judge in deciding a case ◊ Advisory juries are allowed in cases in which there is no right to a jury or in which the right to a jury has been waived. The judge may follow or disregard the advisory jury's verdict.

advisory opinion — see OPINION

ad·vo·ca·cy \'ad-və-kə-sē\ *n* **1** : the profession or work of an advocate **2** : the action of advocating, pleading for, or supporting a cause or proposal ⟨a consequence of his moving ∼ —W. O. Douglas⟩

¹ad·vo·cate \'ad-və-kət, -ˌkāt\ *n* [Latin *advocatus* adviser to a party in a lawsuit, counselor, from past participle of *advocare* to summon, employ as counsel, from *ad* to + *vocare* to call] **1** : a person (as a lawyer) who works and argues in support of another's cause esp. in court **2** : a person or group that defends or maintains a cause or proposal ⟨a consumer ∼⟩

²ad·vo·cate \'ad-və-ˌkāt\ *vb* **-cat·ed; -cat·ing** *vt* : to argue in favor of ∼ *vi* : to act as an advocate ⟨shall ∼ for minority business —V. M. Rivera⟩

AFDC *abbr* Aid to Families with Dependent Children

aff'd *abbr* affirmed

af·fi·ant \ə-'fī-ənt\ *n* [Middle French, from present participle of *affier* to pledge faith, swear, from Medieval Latin *affidare*, ultimately from Latin *ad* to +

fidere to trust] : a person who swears to an affidavit — compare DEPONENT, WITNESS

af·fi·da·vit \ˌa-fə-'dā-vət\ *n* [Medieval Latin, he/she has pledged faith, third singular perfect of *affidare* — see AFFIANT] : a sworn statement in writing made esp. under oath or on affirmation before an authorized magistrate or officer — compare DEPOSITION, EXAMINATION

¹af·fil·i·ate \ə-'fi-lē-ˌāt\ *vb* **-at·ed; -at·ing** *vt* **1** : to bring or receive into close association as a member or division **2** : to join or associate as a member or division ~ *vi* : to connect or associate oneself — usu. used with *with* ⟨has just *affiliated* with the huge corporation⟩ — **af·fil·i·a·tion** \ə-ˌfi-lē-'ā-shən\ *n*

²af·fil·i·ate \ə-'fi-lē-ət\ *n* : an affiliated person or organization; *specif* : a business entity effectively controlling or controlled by another or associated with others under common ownership or control — compare PARENT 2, SUBSIDIARY

af·fine \a-'fīn, ə-\ *n* [Middle French *affin*, from Latin *affinis*, from *affinis* related, from *ad* to + *finis* end, border] : a relative by marriage — compare BLOOD RELATIVE — **af·fi·nal** \-'fī-nəl\ *adj*

af·fin·i·ty \ə-'fi-nə-tē\ *n, pl* **-ties** : relationship by marriage — compare CONSANGUINITY

af·firm \ə-'fərm\ *vt* **1** : to assert as true or factual **2** : to assert (as a judgment) as valid or confirmed ⟨*~ed* the lower court's ruling⟩ — compare REMAND, REVERSE ~ *vi* **1** : to make a solemn declaration under the penalties of perjury in place of swearing an oath to which one conscientiously objects **2** : to uphold the judgment or actions of a lower court ⟨the appeals court *~ed*⟩ — **af·fir·mance** \ə-'fər-məns\ *n* — **af·fir·ma·tion** \ˌa-fər-'mā-shən\ *n*

af·fir·ma·tive \ə-'fər-mə-tiv\ *adj* **1** : asserting the existence of certain facts esp. in support of a cause of action ⟨~ proof⟩ **2** : resulting from an intentional act ⟨~ concealment⟩ **3** : involving or requiring application of effort ⟨an ~ duty⟩ **4**

: favoring or supporting a proposition or motion ⟨an ~ vote⟩ — **af·firma·tive·ly** *adv*

affirmative action *n* : an active effort (as through legislation) to improve the employment or educational opportunities of members of minority groups or women

affirmative defense — see DEFENSE 2a

affirmative easement — see EASEMENT

affirmative injunction — see INJUNCTION

affirmative relief *n* : relief requested by the defendant to a lawsuit for injury which he or she claims to have suffered during the same factual situation the plaintiff claims to have been injured in and for which he or she could also bring a lawsuit

affirmative warranty — see WARRANTY 3

af·fix \ə-'fiks, a-\ *vt* **1** : to attach physically **2** : to attach or add in any way ⟨~ a signature to a document⟩ **3** : to make by or as if by pressure ⟨~ my seal⟩

af·fray \ə-'frā\ *n* [Middle French *affrai, effrai* fright, disturbance, from *affraier, effreer* to terrify] : a fight between two or more people in a public place that disturbs the peace

afft *abbr* affidavit

AFL–CIO *abbr* American Federation of Labor-Congress of Industrial Organization

afore·thought \ə-'fōr-ˌthȯt\ *adj* : previously in mind : PREMEDITATED

a for·ti·o·ri \ˌä-ˌfȯr-shē-'ōr-ˌī, ˌä-ˌfȯr-shē-'ōr-ē, -ˌfȯr-tē-\ *adv* [New Latin, from the stronger (argument)] : all the more certainly : with greater reason : with still more convincing force — used in drawing a conclusion that is thought to be even more certain than another ⟨the evident purpose of the latter statute — to provide a distinct and more severe sentencing scheme for violent habitual of-

\ə\abut \ᵊ\kitten \ər\further \a\ash \ā\ace
\ä\cot, cart \aú\out \ch\chin \e\bet \ē\easy
\g\go \i\hit \ī\ice \j\job \ŋ\sing \ō\go \ȯ\law
\ȯi\boy \th\thin \t͟h\the \ü\loot \ú\foot \y\yet
\zh\vision *see also* Pronunciation Symbols page

fenders — plainly suggests that the Legislature intended it to apply, *a fortiori*, to murderers as well as to criminals who commit other violent, but less serious, felonies —*People v. Jenkins*, 893 P.2d 1224 (1995)⟩

after–acquired *adj* : acquired after a certain event (as the perfection of a security interest)

after–acquired property — see PROPERTY

after–acquired title — see TITLE

after–born *adj* : born after a certain event (as a father's death or the execution of a will)

AG *abbr* attorney general

age *n* : the time of life at which some particular qualification, power, or capacity arises ⟨the voting ~ is 18⟩ — see also LEGAL AGE, MAJORITY

age discrimination *n* : unfair or unequal treatment of an employee by an employer because of the employee's age — see also *Age Discrimination in Employment Act* in the IMPORTANT LAWS section

agen•cy *n, pl* **-cies 1** : the person or thing through which power is exerted or an end is achieved ⟨death by criminal ~ —W. R. LaFave and A. W. Scott, Jr.⟩ **2 a** : a consensual fiduciary relationship in which one party acts on behalf of and under the control of another in dealing with third parties; *also* : the power of one in such a relationship to act on behalf of another ◊ A principal is bound by and liable for acts of his or her agent that are within the scope of the agency.

ac•tu•al agency : the agency that exists when an agent is in fact employed by a principal — see also EXPRESS AGENCY and IMPLIED AGENCY in this entry

agency by estoppel : an agency that is not created as an actual agency by a principal and an agent but that is imposed by law when a principal acts in such a way as to lead a third party to reasonably believe that another is the principal's agent and the third party is injured by relying on and acting in accordance with that belief ◊ A principal has a duty to correct a third party's mistaken belief in an agent's authority to act on the principal's behalf. If the principal could have corrected the misunderstanding but failed to do so, he or she is estopped from denying the existence of the agency and is bound by the agent's acts in dealing with the third party.

agency cou•pled with an interest : an agency in which the agent has an interest in the property regarding which he or she is acting on the principal's behalf

ap•par•ent agency : AGENCY BY ESTOPPEL in this entry

exclusive agency : an agency common in real estate sales in which the property owner agrees to employ no agents to sell the property other than the one hired for a specified period

express agency : an actual agency created by the written or spoken words of the principal authorizing the agent to act — compare IMPLIED AGENCY in this entry

general agency : an agency in which the agent is authorized to perform on behalf of the principal in all matters in furtherance of a particular business of the principal — compare SPECIAL AGENCY in this entry

implied agency : an actual agency created by acts of a principal that reasonably imply an intention to create an agency relationship — compare EXPRESS AGENCY in this entry

ostensible agency : AGENCY BY ESTOPPEL in this entry

special agency : an agency in which the agent is authorized to perform only specified acts or to act only in a specified transaction — compare GENERAL AGENCY in this entry

universal agency : GENERAL AGENCY in this entry

b : the office and function of an agent ⟨even when granted discretion in carrying out his ~ —R. C. Clark⟩ **c** : the law concerned with the relationship of a principal and an agent **3** : an establishment engaged in doing the business of another: as **a** : an establishment authorized by an insurance company to sell insurance policies and provide services offered by the insurer **b** : an establishment authorized by property owners to find a buyer for their property ◊ Many businesses that use the term *agency* are not truly agencies as defined in sense 2. **4** : a department or other unit of government created by legislation to administer the law in a particular area of public concern — called also *administrative agency;* see also EN-ABLING STATUTE, EXHAUSTION OF REME-DIES, *Administrative Procedure Act* in the IMPORTANT LAWS section ◊ When a legislature determines that government involvement is needed in a particular social activity or problem, it may write legislation creating an agency either directly or by authorizing the executive to set it up. Agencies exist at the federal, state, and local level. Most federal agencies are attached to the executive branch of government. Some agencies (such as the Environmental Protection Agency) are called an agency. An agency may, however, be called such other names as *board* (as the National Labor Relations Board), *commission* (as the Securities and Exchange Commission), *administration* (as the Social Security Administration), and *service* (as the Internal Revenue Service). Agencies at the federal level are governed by the provisions of the Administrative Procedure Act, which is found at title 5 of the U.S. Code.

independent agency : an agency that is not part of any of the three branches of government

regulatory agency : an agency that is authorized by the legislature to establish and enforce rules regulating its particular area of concern — often used interchangeably with *agency* or *administrative agency*

agency by estoppel — see AGENCY 2a

agency coupled with an interest — see AGENCY 2a

agency shop *n* : a shop in which the labor union serves as the bargaining agent for and receives dues from all employees in the bargaining unit regardless of union membership — compare OPEN SHOP, UNION SHOP

agent *n* **1** : someone or something that acts or exerts power : a moving force in achieving some result **2** : a person guided or instigated by another in some action ⟨where the heads of departments are the political . . . ~s of the executive, merely to execute the will of the president —*Marbury v. Madison,* 5 U.S. 137 (1803)⟩ — see also INNOCENT AGENT **3 a** : a person or entity (as an employee or independent contractor) authorized to act on behalf of and under the control of another in dealing with third parties — see also AGENCY 2, FIDUCIARY RE-LATIONSHIP, SUBAGENT; compare FIDUCI-ARY, PRINCIPAL, SERVANT

apparent agent : an agent acting under an agency by estoppel

bar·gain·ing agent : a labor union that represents the employees in a bargaining unit in negotiating with their employer through collective bargaining

business agent : an agent that handles business affairs for another person or organization; *esp* : a paid official of a union who carries on union business between the employees and the employer

collective bargaining agent : BAR-GAINING AGENT in this entry

del credere agent : an agent that guarantees to his or her principal that third parties involved in the transaction will pay or perform

exclusive agent : an agent acting under an exclusive agency

general agent : an agent acting under a general agency

legislative agent : an agent (as for an

\ə\abut \ᵊ\kitten \ər**further** \a\ash \ā\ace
\ä\cot, cart \aú\out \ch**chin** \e\bet \ē**easy**
\g\go \i\hit \ī\ice \j**job** \ŋ\sing \ō\go \ò\law
\òi**boy** \th\thin \t͟h\the \ü\loot \ú\foot \y\yet
\zh**vision** *see also* Pronunciation Symbols page

interest group) that lobbies a legislature esp. professionally

managing agent : an agent or employee of a corporation or other business entity who has a position that involves the use of judgment and discretion and who is considered under the law as capable of accepting service of process and answering questions under cross-examination on behalf of the business entity

ostensible agent : an agent acting under an agency by estoppel

special agent : an agent authorized to do one or more specific acts under particular instructions or within restrictions implied by the nature of the authorized acts : an agent acting under a special agency — compare GENERAL AGENT in this entry

transfer agent : an officer, bank, or trust company that acts on behalf of a publicly held corporation in handling the transfer of stock and other securities and keeping records of the owners

universal agent : an agent acting under a general agency **b** : a representative of a corporation designated to accept service of process on behalf of the corporation usu. as required by statute **c** : a person or organization that finds buyers or tenants for real estate owners usu. for a commission **d** : an independent sales or service representative of an insurance company — compare BROKER **4 a** : a representative, emissary, or official of a government ⟨a diplomatic ~⟩ **b** : an employee of a government agency usu. that is involved in law enforcement ⟨seized by DEA ~s⟩

age of consent : the age at which a person is deemed competent by law to give consent esp. to sexual intercourse or marriage — see also STATUTORY RAPE; compare EMANCIPATION, LEGAL AGE

age of majority : the age at which a person is granted by law the rights (as ability to sue) and responsibilities (as liability under contract) of an adult — compare EMANCIPATE ◊ At common law, the age

of majority was 21. Age of majority is now set by statute, in most states at 18. The age at which a person may perform various acts, as legally drink alcoholic beverages, make a binding contract, or make a valid will, does not necessarily correspond with the age of majority.

ag·gra·vate \'a-grə-ˌvāt\ *vt* **-vat·ed; -vat·ing** : to make more serious, more severe, or worse ⟨maliciousness *aggravated* the offense⟩ ⟨*aggravated* her preexisting condition⟩ ⟨*aggravating* factors⟩ — compare MITIGATE — **ag·gra·va·tion** \ˌa-grə-'vā-shən\ *n*

aggravated *adj* : characterized by aggravating elements (as the use of a deadly weapon) ⟨~ kidnapping⟩

aggravated assault — see ASSAULT

aggravated battery — see BATTERY

aggravated robbery — see ROBBERY

aggravating circumstance *n* : a circumstance relating to the commission of an act that increases the degree of liability or culpability ⟨punitive damages are recoverable in a conversion case when the evidence shows legal malice, willfulness, insult, or other *aggravating circumstances* —*Schwertfeger v. Moorehouse,* 569 So. 2d 322 (1990)⟩; *also* : a circumstance (as lack of remorse) relating to an offense or defendant that receives consideration by the court esp. in imposing a death sentence — compare MITIGATING CIRCUMSTANCE

ag·gra·va·tor \'a-grə-ˌvā-tər\ *n* : one that aggravates; *esp* : AGGRAVATING CIRCUMSTANCE ⟨weigh the ~s and the mitigators in fixing a sentence⟩

¹ag·gre·gate \'a-grə-gət\ *adj* : taken as a total ⟨~ liability⟩

²ag·gre·gate \'a-grə-ˌgāt\ *vb* **-gat·ed; -gat·ing** *vt* **1** : to combine or gather into a whole ⟨class members may ~ their individual claims⟩ — compare JOIN **2** : to amount to ⟨an award *aggregating* $100,000⟩ ~ *vi* : to form an aggregate ⟨they may not ~ if their claims are regarded as "separate and distinct" — J. M. Landers *et al.*⟩

³ag·gre·gate \'a-grə-gət\ *n* **1** : total amount

⟨may sue in federal court if the ~ of the claims exceeds $50,000⟩ **2 :** a whole made up of individual units ⟨the ~ of operative facts⟩

ag·gre·ga·tion \‚a-grə-'gā-shən\ *n* **1 :** the collecting of individual units (as damages) into a whole **2 :** a collection of separate parts that is unpatentable because no integrated mechanism or new and useful result is produced — compare COMBINATION, EQUIVALENT

ag·grieve \ə-'grēv\ *vt* **ag·grieved; ag·griev·ing :** to inflict injury on: as **a :** to adversely affect the interests of ⟨was not the party *aggrieved* by the exemption⟩ **b :** to infringe or deny the rights of ⟨a person *aggrieved* by an unlawful search and seizure —*Federal Rules of Criminal Procedure* Rule 41(e)⟩

aggrieved *adj* **:** having a grievance: as **a :** suffering from an infringement or denial of rights **b :** having interests adversely affected ⟨~ creditors⟩

aggrieved party — see PARTY 1b

aggrieved person *n* **:** AGGRIEVED PARTY at PARTY 1b

AGI *abbr* adjusted gross income

agree *vb* **agreed; agree·ing** *vt* **:** to share an opinion that ⟨*agreed* the terms were fair⟩ ~ *vi* **1 :** to share an opinion, understanding, or intent ⟨unable to ~ on a verdict —*New York Law Journal*⟩ **2 :** to indicate willingness or acceptance **:** give assent or approval ⟨*agreeing* to this proposal⟩

agree·ment *n* **1 a :** the act or fact of agreeing ⟨by mutual ~⟩ **b :** unity of opinion, understanding, or intent; *esp* **:** the mutual assent of contracting parties to the same terms ⟨if they reach ~⟩ ◇ Under common law, agreement is a necessary element of a valid contract. Under Uniform Commercial Code section 1-201(3), agreement is the bargain of the contracting parties as represented explicitly by their language or implicitly by other circumstances (as a course of dealings). **2 a :** an expression (as a settlement, covenant, or contract) of the intent or willingness of two or more parties to

bind at least one to terms usu. determined by negotiation ⟨an ~ must be sufficiently definite before a court can enforce it — J. D. Calamari and J. M. Perillo⟩ **b :** the language or instrument embodying such an expression ⟨signed the ~⟩

¹aid *vt* **:** to provide with what is useful in achieving an end ⟨conspiracy to counsel or ~ draft resisters —K. A. Cohen⟩ — often used in the phrase *aid and abet;* see also ABET ~ *vi* **:** to be of use ⟨*aided* in the commission of the crime⟩ — **aid·er** *n*

²aid *n* **1 :** an act of aiding ⟨render ~ to the principal⟩ **2 :** help given; *esp* **:** tangible means of assistance (as money or supplies) ⟨~ to the disabled⟩ ⟨giving ~ and comfort to the enemy⟩

aid·er by verdict \'ā-dər-\ [probably from *aid* + *-er* (as in *disclaimer, retainer*)] **:** the presumption after a verdict that all facts necessary to the verdict were proven **:** the correcting of a pleading defect (as failing to allege a fact) by the verdict in order to conform to the evidence

air·craft piracy *n* **1 :** the hijacking of an aircraft esp. in flight; *specif* **:** the act of seizing control of an aircraft by force, violence, threat, or intimidation with wrongful intent **2 :** the felony of hijacking or seizing control of an aircraft — called also *air piracy*

air right *n* **:** a property right to the space above a surface or object (as a building) that may be sold or leased for development purposes ⟨make use of the *air rights* above the Terminal —*Penn Central Transportation Co. v. City of New York*, 438 U.S. 104 (1978)⟩

AJ *abbr* Administrative Judge

aka *abbr* also known as

al·der·man \'ȯl-dər-mən\ *n* **:** a member of a city legislative body

al·der·wom·an \'ȯl-dər-‚wu̇-mən\ *n* **:** a female member of a city legislative body

ale·a·to·ry \'ā-lē-ə-ˌtōr-ē\ *adj* [Latin *aleatorius* of a gambler, from *aleator* gambler, dice player, from *alea*, a dice game] : depending on an uncertain event or contingency as to both profit and loss ⟨the ∼ nature of a lawyer's contingency fee arrangement⟩
aleatory contract — see CONTRACT
aleatory promise — see PROMISE
ALI *abbr* American Law Institute
¹**alias** \'ā-lē-əs, 'āl-yəs\ *adv* [Latin, otherwise, from *alius* other] : otherwise called : also known as ⟨John Thomas Nolan, ∼ Legs Diamond⟩
²**alias** *n* : an assumed or additional name
³**alias** *adj* : issued after the original instrument has not produced any action ⟨an ∼ tax warrant⟩ ⟨an ∼ summons⟩ — compare PLURIES
alias writ — see WRIT
al·i·bi *n* [Latin, elsewhere, from *alius* other] : a defense of having been somewhere other than at the scene of a crime at the time the crime was committed; *also* : the fact or state of having been elsewhere at the time a crime was committed ◊ Federal Rule of Criminal Procedure 12.1 requires the defendant to provide notice upon written demand of an intention to offer a defense of alibi. Likewise, the prosecution must provide to the defendant upon written demand the names of witnesses that will be used to rebut the defense.
alibi witness — see WITNESS
¹**alien** \'ā-lē-ən, 'āl-yən\ *adj* [Latin *alienus* not one's own, foreign] : relating, belonging, or owing allegiance to another country or government
²**alien** *n* : a foreign-born resident who has not been naturalized and is still a subject or citizen of a foreign country ⟨illegal ∼s⟩ ⟨an ∼ admitted to the United States for permanent residence — *U.S. Code*⟩
³**alien** *vt* : ALIENATE
alien·able \'āl-yə-nə-bəl, 'ā-lē-ə-\ *adj* : that may be changed over to another's ownership ⟨an ∼ interest in property⟩ —
alien·abil·i·ty \ˌāl-yə-nə-'bil-ə-tē, ˌā-lē-ə-\ *n*

alien·age \'āl-yə-nij, 'ā-lē-ə-\ *n* : the status of an alien
alien·ate \'ā-lē-ə-ˌnāt\ *vt* **-at·ed; -at·ing** [Latin *alienare*, from *alienus* not one's own] : to give away or sell (property or a property right) to another ⟨will not sell, transfer, assign, hypothecate or otherwise ∼ any of his voting shares —*Strickland v. Rahaim*, 549 So. 2d 58 (1989)⟩ — compare DEVISE — **alien·ation** \ˌā-lē-ə-'nā-shən, ˌāl-yə-\ *n*
alienation of affections : the diversion of a person's affection from someone (as a spouse) who has certain rights or claims to such affection usu. to a third person who is held to be the instigator or cause of the diversion — called also *alienation of affection;* compare CRIMINAL CONVERSATION ◊ In most jurisdictions alienation of affections is no longer recognized as a basis for a civil suit.
alien·ee \ˌā-lē-ə-'nē, ˌāl-yə-\ *n* : a person to whom property or a property right has been alienated
alien·ist \'ā-lē-ə-nist, 'āl-yə-\ *n* : a psychiatrist who specializes in the legal aspects of psychiatry (as determining sanity or capacity to stand trial)
alien·or \ˌā-lē-ə-'nȯr, ˌāl-yə-\ *n* : a person who alienates property or a property right to another
al·i·mo·ny \'a-lə-ˌmō-nē\ *n* [Latin *alimonia* sustenance, from *alere* to nourish] **1** : an allowance made to one spouse by the other for support pending or after legal separation or divorce — compare CHILD SUPPORT

   alimony in gross : LUMP SUM ALIMONY in this entry
   alimony pen·den·te li·te \-pen-'den-tē-'lī-ˌtē, -pen-'den-tā-'lē-tā\ : alimony granted pending a suit for divorce or separation that includes a reasonable allowance for the prosecution of the suit — called also *temporary alimony*
   lump sum alimony : alimony awarded after divorce that is a specific vested amount not subject to change — called also *alimony in gross*
   per·ma·nent alimony : alimony

awarded after divorce which consists of payments at regular intervals that may change in amount or terminate (as upon the payee's remarriage)

tem·po·rary alimony : ALIMONY PENDENTE LITE in this entry

2 : means of living, support, or maintenance ⟨fathers and mothers owe ~ to their illegitimate children —*Louisiana Civil Code*⟩

alimony in gross — see ALIMONY

alimony pendente lite — see ALIMONY

alimony trust — see TRUST

al·i·quot \'a-lə-ˌkwät, -kwət\ *adj* [Medieval Latin *aliquotus* contained an exact number of times in something else, from Latin *aliquot* some, several] : of, relating to, or being a fraction or percentage of a whole ⟨may deduct an ~ part of the cost —D. Q. Posin⟩

ALI test \ˌā-ˌel-'ī-\ *n* : SUBSTANTIAL CAPACITY TEST

¹al·i·un·de \ˌa-lē-'ən-dē, ˌä-lē-'ùn-dā\ *adv or adj* [Latin, from *alius* other + *unde* whence] : from another source ⟨must be proven ~⟩ ⟨proof ~⟩

²aliunde *prep* : from a source other than ⟨that he was shot . . . was proven ~ the admissions —*United States v. Strickland*, 493 F.2d 182 (1974)⟩

aliunde rule *n* : a rule of evidence that a verdict may not be challenged by a juror's testimony without evidence from another source — used primarily in Ohio

ALJ *abbr* administrative law judge

al·le·ga·ta \ˌa-lə-'gā-tə, ˌä-le-'gä-tä\ *n pl* [New Latin, plural of *allegatum*, from Medieval Latin *allegare* to allege, from Latin, to dispatch, adduce in support] : facts alleged or allegations made in a pleading — compare PROBATA

al·le·ga·tion \ˌa-lə-'gā-shən\ *n* **1** : the act of alleging **2 a** : a statement not yet proven ⟨~s in an affidavit⟩ **b** : a statement by a party to a lawsuit of what the party will attempt to prove : AVERMENT — compare ACCUSATION, INDICTMENT, INFORMATION, PROOF

al·lege \ə-'lej\ *vt* **al·leged; al·leg·ing** [Old French *alegier* to alleviate, free, confused with Old French *alleguer* to allege, from Medieval Latin *allegare* — see ALLEGATA] **1** : to state without proof or before proving **2** : to state (as a fact) in a pleading : AVER ⟨failed to ~ malice⟩

al·leged \ə-'lejd, -'le-jəd\ *adj* **1** : asserted to be true; *esp* : stated in an allegation ⟨~ crimes⟩ **2** : accused but not yet proven or convicted ⟨trial of ~ war criminals —R. G. Neumann⟩

al·leg·ed·ly \ə-'le-jəd-lē\ *adv* : by or according to an allegation ⟨defendant's response ~ showed malice⟩

Al·len charge \'a-lən-\ *n* [from the Supreme Court case *Allen v. United States*, 164 U.S. 492 (1896), which upheld the right of a trial judge to make such a charge] : a charge to a deadlocked jury to make a further effort to reach a verdict esp. by each juror considering the others' opinions with deference — called also *dynamite charge*

al·lied line \ə-'līd-, 'a-ˌlīd-\ *n* : insurance (as for earthquake or water damage) provided by policies separate from a fire policy

al·lo·ca·ble \'a-lə-kə-bəl\ *adj* : capable of being allocated or assigned

al·lo·ca·tur \ˌa-lō-'kā-tər, ˌä-lō-'kä-tùr\ *n* [Medieval Latin, it is allowed] : permission to appeal ⟨granted ~ in order to determine whether the lower courts were in error —*City of Pittsburgh v. Commonwealth*, 653 A.2d 1210 (1995)⟩ — used primarily in Pennsylvania

al·lo·cute \'a-lə-ˌkyüt\ *vi* **-cut·ed; -cut·ing** : to make an allocution

al·lo·cu·tion \ˌa-lə-'kyü-shən\ *n* [Latin *allocutio*, from *alloqui* to speak to, from *ad* to + *loqui* to speak] : a formal speech; *esp* : one made by a defendant at the time of sentencing

al·longe \ə-'länj, a-'lōⁿzh\ *n* [French, literally, something that lengthens, from Old French *alonge*, from *alongier* to make

\ə\abut	\ᵊ\kitten	\ər\further	\a\ash \ā\ace
\ä\cot, cart	\aù\out	\ch\chin	\e\bet \ē\easy
\g\go	\i\hit	\ī\ice	\j\job \ŋ\sing \ō\go \ò\law
\òi\boy	\th\thin	\th̲\the	\ü\loot \ù\foot \y\yet
\zh\vision		*see also* Pronunciation Symbols page	

long, ultimately from Latin *longus* long]
: a paper attached to an instrument to provide space for additional endorsements
: RIDER ◊ Under Uniform Commercial Code section 3-202(2), an allonge must be so firmly affixed to the instrument that it becomes part of it in order for the endorsements to be valid. Endorsements on an allonge are often considered invalid if there is still room on the instrument for endorsements.

al·low \ə-'laù\ *vt* : to give approval of or permission for: as **a** : to grant fulfillment of ⟨~*ed* her petition for relief⟩ **b** : to decide in favor of ⟨~ a deduction on a tax return⟩ **c** : to permit to be presented ⟨~*s* his claim⟩ ⟨more jurisdictions will ~ the cause of action⟩ — **al·low·abil·i·ty** \ə-ˌlaù-ə-'bi-lə-tē\ *adv* — **al·low·able** \ə-'laù-ə-bəl\ *adj*

al·low·ance \ə-'laù-əns\ *n* **1** : an allotted share: as **a** : a sum granted as a reimbursement or payment for expenses ⟨an ~ to support the deceased's family⟩ ⟨deduction for a moving ~⟩ **b** : a sum granted as a reduction or increase ⟨an ~ for depreciation⟩ **2** : an act of allowing ⟨~ of a deduction⟩

al·lu·vi·on \ə-'lü-vē-ən\ *n* : material (as clay, silt, sand, or gravel) deposited by running water; *esp* : the land added by the gradual or imperceptible accumulation of such material along a bank or shore ⟨~ formed in front of the property of several owners is divided equitably —*Louisiana Civil Code*⟩

al·ter ego \'òl-tər-'ē-gō\ *n* [Latin, literally, second I] : second self; *esp* : a person or entity vicariously liable for another (as an agent) ⟨had the officer been the *alter ego* of the corporation —J. J. White and R. S. Summers⟩ — compare INSTRUMENTAL-ITY ◊ The concept of a legal alter ego is used primarily to hold the controlling parties of a corporation personally liable instead of limiting liability to the corporate entity.

¹al·ter·nate \'òl-tər-nət, 'al-\ *adj* **1** : occurring or succeeding by turns **2** : being an alternative ⟨~ juror⟩

²alternate *n* **1** : ALTERNATIVE **2** : one that substitutes for another ⟨twelve jurors and three ~*s*⟩

alternate valuation *n* : the appraisal of a deceased person's gross estate at the fair market value six months after the person's death

¹al·ter·na·tive \òl-'tər-nə-tiv, al-\ *adj* **1** : ALTERNATE 1 **2** : offering or expressing a choice ⟨an ~ contract⟩ — see also *alternative pleading* at PLEADING 1b **3** : existing or functioning outside the established system; *also* : different from the usual or conventional ⟨~ sentencing⟩

²alternative *n* **1** : a proposition or situation offering a choice between two or more things only one of which may be chosen **2 a** : one of two or more things, courses, or propositions to be chosen **b** : something which can be chosen instead — **in the alternative 1** : for or as an alternative ⟨asked for specific performance, or, *in the alternative*, damages of $20,000⟩ ⟨a new trial may be asked for *in the alternative*⟩ **2** : in such a way that offers a choice ⟨relief *in the alternative* . . . may be demanded —*Federal Rules of Civil Procedure* Rule 8(a)⟩ ⟨plead *in the alternative*⟩

alternative dispute resolution *n* : a forum or means for resolving disputes (as arbitration or private judging) that exists outside the state or federal judicial system

alternative liability — see LIABILITY 2b

alternative minimum tax *n* : a federal tax that prevents a person or entity (as a corporation) with taxable income from avoiding tax liability and that imposes tax liability in the amount of the excess of the tentative minimum tax over regular tax liability — see also TAX PREFERENCE ITEM

alternative order — see ORDER 4b

alternative pleading — see PLEADING 1

alternative writ — see WRIT

am·bu·lance chas·er *n* : a lawyer or lawyer's agent who solicits accident victims to sue for damages

am·bu·la·to·ry \'am-byə-lə-ˌtōr-ē\ *adj* [Latin *ambulatorius*, literally, movable, transferable, from *ambulare* to walk, move, be transferred] : capable of being altered ⟨a will is ~ until the testator's death⟩

ameliorating waste — see WASTE

ame·lio·ra·tive waste \ə-'mēl-yə-,rā-tiv-\ *n* : AMELIORATING WASTE at WASTE

ame·na·ble \ə-'mē-nə-bəl, -'me-\ *adj* **1** : legally subject or answerable ⟨the corporation is not ~ to suit in New York⟩ **2 a** : suited by nature ⟨an adult is not ~ to a juvenile treatment program⟩ **b** : readily yielding, submitting, or cooperating ⟨defendant is ~ to rehabilitation —*National Law Journal*⟩ — **ame·na·bil·i·ty** \ə-,mē-nə-'bi-lə-tē, -,me-\ *n*

amend *vt* **1** : to change or modify for the better **2** : to alter esp. in the wording; *esp* : to alter formally by modification, deletion, or addition ⟨*~ed* the statute⟩ ⟨~ the complaint to cure the defect⟩ — **amend·able** *adj*

amen·da·to·ry \ə-'men-də-,tōr-ē\ *adj* : intended or serving to amend ⟨an ~ endorsement⟩

amended pleading — see PLEADING 1

amend·ment *n* **1** : an act of amending; *esp* : an alteration in wording ⟨*~s* to cure the defect in the pleading⟩ **2** : an alteration proposed or put into effect by legislative or constitutional procedure ⟨the Congress . . . shall propose *~s* to this Constitution —*U.S. Constitution* art. V⟩

amerce·ment \ə-'mərs-mənt\ *n* [Anglo-French *amercement*, from *amercier* to fine, from Old French *a merci* at one's mercy] : a fine or damages imposed at the discretion of the court

am·i·ca·ble action \'a-mi-kə-bəl-\ *n* : a case brought before a court by consent of the parties in order to get a ruling on a point of law — used esp. in Pennsylvania

amici *pl of* AMICUS

ami·cus \ə-'mē-kəs, -'mī-\ *n*, *pl* **ami·ci** \-'mē-,kē, -'mī-,sī\ : AMICUS CURIAE

amicus cu·ri·ae \-'kyur-ē-,ī, -'kur-, -ē-,ē\ *n*, *pl* **amici curiae** [New Latin, literally, friend of the court] : one (as an individual or organization) that is not a party to a particular lawsuit but is allowed to advise

the court regarding a point of law or fact directly concerning the lawsuit ⟨a brief of an *amicus curiae* may be filed —*Federal Rules of Appellate Procedure* Rule 29⟩ — called also *friend of the court*

am·nes·ty \'am-nəs-tē\ *n*, *pl* **-ties** : an act of clemency by an authority (as a government) by which pardon is granted esp. to a group of individuals ⟨illegal-alien farm workers seeking ~ —*National Law Journal*⟩

amor·tize \'a-mər-,tīz, ə-'mȯr-\ *vt* **-tized; -tiz·ing** : to reduce (an amount) gradually: as **a** : to pay off (as a loan) gradually usu. by periodic payments of principal and interest or payments to a sinking fund **b** : to gradually reduce the cost of (as an asset) esp. for tax purposes by making periodic charges to income over a time span ⟨~ the machinery over five years⟩ — see also DEPRECIATION; compare CAPITALIZE, DEDUCT — **amor·tiz·a·ble** *adj* — **amor·ti·za·tion** \,a-mər-tə-'zā-shən, ə-,mȯr-\ *n*

AMW *abbr* average monthly wage

an·ces·tor *n* **1 a** : a person from whom an individual is descended : ASCENDANT **b** : a person from whom an estate descends — compare HEIR **2** : one that precedes ⟨~ in title⟩

an·cient *adj* : existing from a long past date; *specif* : having had an uninterrupted existence of 20 to 30 or more years ◇ Things and esp. documents that are ancient benefit from a presumption that they are valid even though proof of their validity may be unavailable due to lapse of memory, absence of witnesses, or loss of documents.

an·cil·lary \'an-sə-,ler-ē, an-'si-lə-rē\ *adj* **1** : having a subordinate, subsidiary, or secondary nature ⟨~ functions⟩ ⟨an ~ agreement⟩ **2** : serving as a supplement or addition ⟨~ documents⟩ **3** : directly related ⟨~ claims⟩

\ə\abut \ᵊ\kitten \ər\further \a\ash \ā\ace
\ä\cot, cart \aů\out \ch\chin \e\bet \ē\easy
\g\go \i\hit \ī\ice \j\job \ŋ\sing \ō\go \ȯ\law
\ȯi\boy \th\thin \t̲h̲\the \ü\loot \ů\foot \y\yet
\zh\vision *see also* Pronunciation Symbols page

ancillary administrator — see ADMINI-STRATOR

ancillary jurisdiction — see JURISDIC-TION

an·i·mus \'a-nə-məs\ *n* [Latin, mind, soul] : INTENT ⟨discriminatory ∼⟩ — compare MENS REA

animus fu·ran·di \-fyú-'ran-,dī, -fü-'rän-dē\ *n* [New Latin] : the intent to steal

animus tes·tan·di \-tes-'tan-,dī, -tes-'tän-dē\ *n* [New Latin] : the intent to make a testament or will

an·nex \ə-'neks, 'a-,neks\ *vt* **1** : ATTACH **2** ⟨correspondence ∼*ed* to the petition⟩ ⟨a greenhouse ∼*ed* to the building⟩ **2** : to incorporate (as a territory) within a political domain ⟨the district ∼*es* only shards of 24 additional parishes —*Hays v. Louisiana*, 839 F. Supp. 1188 (1993)⟩ — **an·nex·ation** \,a-nek-'sā-shən\ *n*

Annot. *abbr* annotation

an·no·tate \'a-nə-,tāt\ *vb* **-tat·ed; -tat·ing** *vi* : to make or write an annotation ∼ *vt* : to make or write annotations for — **an·no·ta·tor** \-,tā-tər\ *n*

an·no·ta·tion \,a-nə-'tā-shən\ *n* **1** : a note added (as to a statute) by way of comment or explanation often furnishing summaries of relevant court decisions **2** *cap* : an informational and descriptive note or essay (as about a case or legal issue) esp. in *American Law Reports*

an·nu·al exclusion *n* : the maximum amount that a person can give each year as a gift without having to pay a gift tax ◊ The annual exclusion is currently $10,000 per donee.

annual meet·ing *n* : a meeting of shareholders that the law requires a corporation to hold each year for the election of directors and the transaction of other business — compare SPECIAL MEETING ◊ In order for a vote taken at an annual meeting to be valid, shareholders must have received notice of the time, place, and date of the meeting within a certain period, and there must be enough shareholders present to make a quorum.

annual re·port *n* : a written report distributed to shareholders each year by a corporation that sets forth financial information (as an auditor's report, the selling prices of the corporation's stock, and the yearly profit) as well as statements by the corporation's management

an·nu·i·tant \ə-'nü-ə-tənt, -'nyü-\ *n* : a person entitled to receive benefits or payments from an annuity

an·nu·ity \ə-'nü-ə-tē, -'nyü-\ *n, pl* **-ities** [Medieval Latin *annuitas*, from Latin *annuus* yearly] **1** : an amount payable at regular intervals (as yearly or quarterly) for a certain or uncertain period **2** : the grant of or the right to receive an annuity ⟨his will included *annuities* for several old friends⟩ **3** : a contract (as with an insurance company) under which one or more persons receive annuities in return for prior fixed payments made by themselves or another (as an employer)

annuity cer·tain pl **annuities certain** : an annuity payable over a specified period even if the annuitant dies

annuity due pl **annuities due** : an immediate annuity in which the payment of the benefits is made at the beginning of each payment interval rather than at the end

contingent annuity : an annuity whose starting or ending date depends on the occurrence of an event (as the death of the annuitant) whose date is uncertain

conventional annuity : an annuity under which the annuitant receives a specified minimum amount at each payment — compare VARIABLE ANNUITY in this entry

deferred annuity : an annuity in which payment of benefits is delayed until a particular time (as at retirement) — compare IMMEDIATE ANNUITY in this entry

group annuity : a pension plan paying annuity benefits at retirement for all eligible persons under a single master contract usu. issued to an employer for the benefit of its employees

im·me·di·ate annuity : an annuity purchased with a single premium in which payment of benefits begins within the first payment interval (as within a year) — compare DEFERRED ANNUITY in this entry

joint–and–survivor annuity : an annuity payable as long as any of the two or more annuitants remains alive — called also *joint-and-last-survivor annuity, joint and survivorship annuity, joint life and survivorship annuity;* compare JOINT LIFE ANNUITY in this entry

joint life annuity : an annuity payable only until the death of any of the annuitants — called also *joint annuity;* compare JOINT-AND-SURVIVOR ANNUITY in this entry

life annuity : an annuity payable during the annuitant's lifetime and terminating at death — called also *straight life annuity*

life income–pe•ri•od cer•tain annuity : an annuity that guarantees a minimum number of payments even if the annuitant dies before the minimum amount is paid or a minimum number of payments plus income for life if the annuitant is still alive after the minimum amount is paid

refund annuity : an annuity in which payments to the annuitant or to the annuitant's estate or to a beneficiary are guaranteed to equal at least the amount of the premium paid for the annuity

straight life annuity : LIFE ANNUITY in this entry

var•i•able annuity \'ver-ē-ə-bəl-\ : an annuity that is backed primarily by a fund of common stocks and whose payments go up or down depending on how well the stocks perform — compare CONVENTIONAL ANNUITY in this entry, *variable life insurance* at LIFE INSURANCE

annuity certain — see ANNUITY

annuity due — see ANNUITY

an•nul \ə-'nəl\ vt **an•nulled; an•nul•ling** **1** : to declare (a marriage) to have never validly existed — compare DIVORCE **2 a** : to make legally void **b** : to declare to no longer have legal effect

an•nul•ment \ə-'nəl-mənt\ n **1** : the act of annulling : the state of being annulled **2** : a declaration by a court that a marriage is invalid — compare DIVORCE

¹an•swer n **1** : the defendant's written response to the plaintiff's complaint in a civil suit in which he or she may deny any of plaintiff's allegations, offer any defenses, and make any counterclaims against the plaintiff, cross-claims against other defendants, or third-party claims against third parties otherwise not involved in the lawsuit **2** : a written response to a counterclaim, cross-claim, or third-party claim : REPLY — see also *responsive pleading* at PLEADING 1 ◊ In federal cases, answers are governed by Rule 12 of the Federal Rules of Civil Procedure. Under Rule 12, certain defenses (as lack of jurisdiction) may be made by motion rather than included in the answer.

²answer *vi* **1** : to serve or file an answer **2** : to make oneself responsible or accountable (as for the debt of another) — *vt* **1** : to reply to in an answer ⟨~ the complaint⟩ **2** : to make a defense against (as a charge or accusation) — **an•swer•able** *adj*

an•te•ce•dent \ˌan-tə-'sēd-ᵊnt\ *adj* : earlier in time or order

antecedent debt — see DEBT

an•te•nup•tial \ˌan-tə-'nəp-shəl, -chəl\ *adj* : made or occurring before marriage ⟨an ~ obligation⟩

antenuptial agreement *n* : an agreement made between a man and a woman before marrying in which they give up future rights to each other's property in the event of a divorce or death — called also *prenuptial agreement*

antenuptial will — see WILL

an•ti•chre•sis \ˌan-ti-'krē-sis, ˌan-ˌtī-, ˌan-tē-\ *n* [New Latin, from Greek, from *anti-* opposite + *chrēsis* use, from *chrēsthai* to use, need] *in the civil law of Louisiana* : a

\ə\abut \ᵊ\kitten \ər\further \a\ash \ā\ace \ä\cot, cart \au̇\out \ch\chin \e\bet \ē\easy \g\go \i\hit \ī\ice \j\job \ŋ\sing \ō\go \ȯ\law \ȯi\boy \th\thin \th̲\the \ü\loot \u̇\foot \y\yet \zh\vision *see also* Pronunciation Symbols page

written pledge and transfer from a debtor to a creditor of possession of immovable property giving the creditor the right to the fruits (as rents) of the property which are to be deducted from the interest or principal of the debt — compare PAWN

an·tic·i·pate \an-'ti-sə-ˌpāt\ *vt* **-pat·ed; -pat·ing 1 :** to bar or invalidate (a patent) by anticipation ⟨the patent on the compound had been *anticipated* by the Beilstein reference —*Misani v. Ortho Pharm. Corp.*, 210 A.2d 609 (1965)⟩ **2 :** to negate the novelty of (an invention) by its appearance in prior art ⟨appeared to have *anticipated* a variable light makeup mirror —*Wilson v. Bristol-Myers Co.*, 503 N.Y.S.2d 334 (1986)⟩

an·tic·i·pa·tion \an-ˌti-sə-'pā-shən\ *n* **:** the knowledge or use of an invention in the U.S. or the patenting or describing of the invention in a publication in the U.S. or a foreign country before the discovery by a patent applicant ◇ Case law has established that every claim or element of a claim has to be disclosed in the prior art in order for a patent application to be barred by anticipation. If an application is amended to consist of claims not disclosed in the prior art, invalidation by anticipation can be avoided.

an·tic·i·pa·tory \an-'ti-sə-pə-ˌtōr-ē\ *adj* **:** of or relating to a prior action that takes into account or forestalls a later action ⟨an ~ challenge brought for declaratory and injunctive relief —L. H. Tribe⟩ — **an·tic·i·pa·tor·i·ly** \-ˌti-sə-pə-'tōr-ə-lē\ *adv*

anticipatory breach — see BREACH 1b

anticipatory repudiation *n* **:** a refusal by one party to a contract to perform his or her future obligations under the contract that is expressed either by a clear statement of refusal or by a statement or action that clearly implies refusal

anticipatory search warrant — see WARRANT

anticipatory warrant *n* **:** ANTICIPATORY SEARCH WARRANT at WARRANT

an·ti–lapse statute \ˌan-ˌtī-'laps-, ˌan-tē-\ *n* **:** a statute providing that in the event a person who would have received a gift

under a will dies before the person who made the will dies then the gift is distributed to the heirs of the person who would have received the gift — compare LAPSE

an·ti·trust \ˌan-tē-'trəst, ˌan-ˌtī-\ *adj* **:** of, relating to, or being legislation against or opposition to business trusts or combinations; *specif* **:** consisting of laws to protect trade and commerce from unlawful restraints and monopolies or unfair business practices — see also *Clayton Antitrust Act* and *Sherman Antitrust Act* in the IMPORTANT LAWS section

App *abbr* appeals

ap·par·ent *adj* **1 :** capable of being easily seen, perceived, or discovered ⟨~ defects⟩ ⟨~ ambiguity⟩ **2 :** having a right to succeed to a title or estate that cannot be defeated **3 :** appearing to one's senses and esp. one's vision or to one's understanding as real or true on the basis of evidence that may or may not be correct or factual ⟨an ~ ability to cause injury⟩ ⟨the ~ scope of the agent's authority⟩ — **ap·par·ent·ly** *adv*

apparent agency — see AGENCY 2a

apparent agent — see AGENT

apparent authority — see AUTHORITY

apparent easement — see EASEMENT

apparent heir — see HEIR

apparent servitude — see SERVITUDE

¹ap·peal \ə-'pēl\ *n* [Old French *apel*, from *apeler* to call, accuse, appeal, from Latin *appellare*] **:** a proceeding in which a case is brought before a higher court for review of a lower court's judgment for the purpose of convincing the higher court that the lower court's judgment was incorrect; *also* **:** a proceeding for the review of an agency decision at a higher level within the agency or in a court — see also AFFIRM; compare CERTIORARI, NEW TRIAL, REHEARING ◇ The scope of an appeal is limited. The higher court will review only matters that were objected to or argued in the lower court during the trial. No new evidence can be presented on appeal. — **ap·peal·abil·i·ty** \ə-ˌpē-lə-'bi-lə-tē\ *n* — **ap·peal·able** \ə-'pē-lə-bəl\ *adj*

²**appeal** *vt* : to take (a lower court's decision) before a higher court for review : undertake an appeal of (a case) ~ *vi* : to take a lower court's decision to a higher court for review

appeal bond — see BOND 1a

ap·peals court *n* : a court that hears appeals; *esp* : an intermediate level appellate court

ap·pear *vi* **1** : to present oneself before a person or body having authority ⟨to ~ before the officer who is to take the deposition — *Federal Rules of Civil Procedure* Rule 37(d)⟩: as **a** : to present oneself in court as a party to a lawsuit often through the representation of an attorney; *also* : to participate as a party to a lawsuit in a way other than by physical presence (as by mail) **b** : to present oneself in court as the attorney for a party to a lawsuit ⟨~*ing* for the defendant⟩ **2** : to have an outward look ⟨conduct that ~*s* unethical⟩

ap·pear·ance *n* **1** : the presentation of oneself in court as a party to or as an attorney for a party to a lawsuit; *also* : a document filed in court by an attorney declaring his or her representation of a party to a lawsuit — see also GENERAL APPEARANCE, SPECIAL APPEARANCE **2** : outward look ⟨a lawyer should avoid the ~ of impropriety⟩

appearance bond — see BOND 1a

ap·pel·lant \ə-'pe-lənt\ *n* : a person or party who appeals a court's judgment — compare APPELLEE

ap·pel·late \ə-'pe-lət\ *adj* : of or relating to appeals or the power to hear appeals ⟨the ~ process⟩ ⟨an ~ court⟩

appellate jurisdiction — see JURISDICTION

ap·pel·lee \ˌa-pə-'lē\ *n* : the party to an appeal arguing that the lower court's judgment was correct and should stand — compare APPELLANT

ap·pli·ca·tion *n* : a request for action or relief ⟨most ~*s* request bail . . . or an extension of time to file — W. J. Brennan, Jr.⟩; *also* : a form used to make such a request ⟨an insurance ~⟩

ap·point \ə-'pȯint\ *vt* **1** : to name officially to a position ⟨~*ed* to the agency's top post⟩ ⟨~*ed* conservator of the estate⟩ **2** : to determine the distribution of (property) by exercising the authority granted by a power of appointment ⟨a general power to ~ the corpus of a trust — W. M. McGovern, Jr. *et al.*⟩ ~ *vi* : to exercise a power of appointment — see also POWER OF APPOINTMENT — **ap·point·ive** \ə-'pȯin-tiv\ *adj* — **ap·point·ment** *n*

ap·poin·tee \ə-ˌpȯin-'tē, ˌa-\ *n* **1** : a person who is appointed to a position **2** : a person to whom property is appointed under a power of appointment

appointive asset — see ASSET 2

ap·por·tion \ə-'pȯr-shən\ *vt* : to make a usu. proportionate division or distribution of (an amount due) according to a plan: as **a** : to divide (an amount due in tax or other liability) among the parties responsible for respective shares of the payment — compare CONTRIBUTION **b** : to assign (a portion of the consideration agreed to in a contract) as payment for the other party's partial performance **c** : to distribute (corporate dividends) based on some proportion **d** : to assign (legislative representatives and taxes) among the states as provided by law — **ap·por·tion·able** *adj* — **ap·por·tion·ment** *n*

ap·po·site \'a-pə-zət\ *adj* : highly pertinent or appropriate

ap·prais·al \ə-'prā-zəl\ *n* : a valuation of property by the estimate of an authorized person: as **a** : the determination of the fair value of a corporation's stock by a judicial proceeding that a dissenting shareholder is usu. entitled by statute to demand in a case of extraordinary corporate action (as a merger) — see also ¹DISSENT 1 **b** : the estimation of the value of real estate for the purpose of taxation, sale, or securing a mortgage **c** : the estimation of the value of damage done to property for the purpose of adjusting an insurance claim

appraisal clause *n* : a provision in an insurance policy for a procedure to be followed in determining the amount of a loss when the insured and the insurer cannot agree

ap·praise \ə-'prāz\ *vt* **ap·praised; ap·prais·ing** : to estimate the value of : make an appraisal of — **ap·prais·er** *n*

ap·pre·ci·ate \ə-'prē-shē-,āt, -'pri-, -sē-\ *vb* **-at·ed; -at·ing** *vt* **1** : to judge or understand the significance of ⟨incapable of *appreciating* the difference between right and wrong —B. N. Cardozo⟩ **2** : to raise the market value of — compare DEPRECIATE ~ *vi* : to rise in market value — **ap·pre·ci·a·tion** \ə-,prē-shē-'ā-shən, -,pri-, -sē-\ *n*

ap·pre·hend \,a-prə-'hend\ *vt* [Latin *apprehendere* to seize, arrest, from *ad* to + *prehendere* to seize] : ARREST

ap·pre·hen·sion \,a-pri-'hen-chən\ *n* : ARREST

ap·pro·pri·ate \ə-'prō-prē-,āt\ *vt* **-at·ed; -at·ing** [Late Latin *appropriare* to take possession of, from *ad* to, for + *proprius* one's own] **1** : to set apart for or assign to a particular recipient, purpose, or use ⟨the legislature *appropriating* funds for the program⟩ **2** : to take or make use of without authority or right — **ap·pro·pri·a·tion** \ə-,prō-prē-'ā-shən\ *n*

appropriations bill — see BILL 1

ap·prove *vt* **ap·proved; ap·prov·ing** : to give formal or official sanction to : RATIFY ⟨Congress *approved* the proposed budget⟩

ap·pur·te·nance \ə-'pərt-ᵊn-əns\ *n* [Anglo-French *apurtenance*, alteration of Old French *apartenance*, from *apartenant* appurtenant] : property (as an outbuilding or fixture) or a property right (as a right of way) that is incidental to a principal property and that passes with the principal property upon transfer

ap·pur·te·nant \ə-'pərt-ᵊn-ənt\ *adj* [Anglo-French *apurtenant*, alteration of

Old French *apartenant*, present participle of *apartenir* to belong, appertain] : annexed or belonging to a more important property

appurtenant easement — see EASEMENT

APR *abbr* annual percentage rate

ar·bi·ter \'är-bə-tər\ *n* [Latin, onlooker, arbitrator] : ARBITRATOR

ar·bi·trage \'är-bə-,träzh\ *n* [French, literally, arbitration, decision-making] **1** : the purchase of a security, commodity, or foreign currency in one market for the purpose of immediately selling it at a higher price in another market **2** : the purchase of the stock of a takeover target esp. for the purpose of selling it to the raider for a profit

ar·bi·tra·geur \,är-bə-,trä-'zhər\ *or* **ar·bi·trag·er** \'är-bə-,trä-zhər\ *n* : one that practices arbitrage

ar·bi·tral \'är-bə-trəl\ *adj* : of or relating to arbitrators or arbitration

ar·bit·ra·ment \är-'bi-trə-mənt\ *n* **1** : the settling of a dispute by an arbitrator **2** : ARBITRATOR'S AWARD

ar·bi·trary \'är-bə-,trer-ē\ *adj* **1** : depending on individual discretion (as of a judge) and not fixed by standards, rules, or law ⟨the manner of punishment is ~⟩ **2** **a** : not restrained or limited in the exercise of power ⟨an ~ government⟩ **b** : marked by or resulting from the unrestrained exercise of power ⟨protection from ~ arrest and detention⟩ **3** **a** : based on preference, bias, prejudice, or convenience rather than on reason or fact ⟨an ~ standard⟩ ⟨different provisions for the married and the unmarried were irrational and ~ —K. A. Cohen⟩ **b** : existing or coming about seemingly at random or by chance or as an unreasonable act of individual will without regard for facts or applicable law — often used in the phrase *arbitrary and capricious* ⟨an agency finding or conclusion of lack of evidence would be ~ and capricious if the record afforded no substantial basis for such a finding —*Irvin v. Hobby*, 131 F. Supp. 851 (1955)⟩ ◊ Under section 706 of the Administrative Procedure Act, a court

shall set aside an agency's action, findings, or conclusions determined upon review to be arbitrary. — **ar·bi·trar·i·ly** \ˌär-bə-'trer-ə-lē\ adv — **ar·bi·trar·i·ness** \'är-bə-ˌtrer-ē-nəs\ n
arbitrary mark n : a trademark, service mark, or trade name that is not indicative of the nature of the goods or services
ar·bi·trate \'är-bə-ˌtrāt\ vb **-trat·ed; -trat·ing** vt **1** : to act as arbitrator for **2** : to bring to arbitration for settlement ⟨agreed to ~ their dispute⟩ ~ vi : to act as arbitrator — **ar·bi·tra·tive** \-ˌtrā-tiv\ adj
ar·bi·tra·tion \ˌär-bə-'trā-shən\ n [Latin arbitratio, from arbitrari to judge, arbitrate, from arbiter onlooker, arbitrator] : the process of resolving a dispute (as between labor and management) or a grievance outside of the court system by presenting it to an impartial third party or panel for a decision that may or may not be binding — compare MEDIATION
final offer arbitration : interest arbitration in which the arbitrator must accept or reject the final offer of any party and may not decide to compromise
grievance arbitration : arbitration of a dispute over something in an existing collective bargaining agreement — called also *rights arbitration*; compare INTEREST ARBITRATION in this entry
interest arbitration : arbitration of a dispute over the provisions to be entered in a new contract — compare GRIEVANCE ARBITRATION in this entry
rights arbitration : GRIEVANCE ARBITRATION in this entry
— **ar·bi·tra·tion·al** \ˌär-bə-'trā-shə-nəl\ adj
ar·bi·tra·tor \'är-bə-ˌtrā-tər\ n : an impartial person or group that is given the power by disputing parties to resolve their dispute — compare MEDIATOR
arbitrator's award n : the decision an arbitrator makes concerning a dispute — called also *arbitrament*
A reorganization — see REORGANIZATION
ar·gue vb **ar·gued; ar·gu·ing** vi **1** : to give reasons for or against a matter in dispute ⟨*arguing* for an extension⟩ **2** : to present

a case in court ⟨will ~ for the defense⟩ ~ vt **1 a** : to give reasons for or against ⟨*argued* the issue before the judge⟩ **b** : to prove or try to prove by giving reasons or evidence ⟨will ~ invasion of privacy⟩ **2** : to present in court ⟨lawyers in court filing briefs and *arguing* appeals —Rorie Sherman⟩ — **ar·gu·able** adj
ar·gu·en·do \ˌär-gyü-'wen-dō\ adv [New Latin] : for the sake of argument ⟨assuming ~ that the allegations are true⟩
ar·gu·ment n **1** : a reason or the reasoning given for or against a matter under discussion — compare EVIDENCE, PROOF **2** : the act or process of arguing, reasoning, or discussing; esp : ORAL ARGUMENT
argumentative denial — see DENIAL
ARM abbr adjustable rate mortgage
armed \'ärmd\ adj **1** : having a weapon ⟨an ~ assailant⟩ **2** : involving the use of a weapon ⟨an ~ attack⟩
armed robbery — see ROBBERY
arm's length n : the condition of the parties to a business deal in which each has independent interests and one does not dominate the other — often used in the phrase *at arm's length* ⟨a contract made at *arm's length*⟩ — **arm's-length** adj
ar·raign \ə-'rān\ vt [Anglo-French *arrainer*, from Old French *araisnier* to address, call to account, from *a-*, prefix stressing goal of an action + *raisnier* to speak] : to bring (a defendant) before a judge or magistrate to hear the charges and to plead usu. either guilty or not guilty — compare INDICT ◊ For a person to be formally arraigned, he or she must be called by name before a judge or magistrate. The judge or magistrate makes sure that the defendant is the person named in the complaint, indictment, or information, which is then read to formally notify the defendant of the charges. The defendant may then enter a plea of guilty, not guilty, or another plea allowed by law

such as nolo contendere. In some cases, as when the defendant is not yet represented by a lawyer, the judge or magistrate may enter a plea of not guilty on the defendant's behalf. **— ar·raign·ment** *n*

arraignment on the warrant : INITIAL APPEARANCE

¹ar·ray \ə-'rā\ *vt* **:** to set (a jury) for trial; *specif* **:** to set (a jury) by calling out the names of the jurors one at a time — compare IMPANEL

²array *n* **:** the group of people summoned to serve as jurors from which the jury will be chosen; *also* **:** a list of the jurors' names — see also *challenge to the array* at CHALLENGE; compare VENIRE

ar·rear \ə-'rir\ *n* **1 a :** the condition of being behind in one's duties or esp. financial obligations — usu. used in pl. ⟨in ~*s* with the rent⟩ **b :** the condition of being due at the end of a term rather than the beginning — usu. used in pl. ⟨mortgage payments are made in ~*s*⟩ **2 :** an unpaid and overdue debt — usu. used in pl. ⟨paying off the ~*s* of the previous owners⟩

ar·rear·age \ə-'rir-ij\ *n* **1 :** the condition of being in arrears **2 :** something that is in arrears; *esp* **:** something unpaid and overdue **:** ARREAR — often used in pl. ⟨the Virginia court reduced the ~*s* to a final judgment —*National Law Journal*⟩

¹ar·rest \ə-'rest\ *n* [Middle French *arest*, from *arester* to stop, seize, arrest, ultimately from Latin *ad* to, at + *restare* to stay] **:** the restraining and seizure of a person whether or not by physical force by someone acting under authority (as a police officer) in connection with a crime in such a manner that it is reasonable under the circumstances for the person to believe that he or she is not free to leave — see also MIRANDA WARNINGS, *probable cause* at CAUSE 2, WARRANT; compare STOP

citizen's arrest : an arrest made not by a law officer but by any citizen who derives the authority to arrest from the fact of being a citizen ◊ Under common law, a citizen may make an arrest for any felony actually committed, or for a breach of the peace committed in his or her presence.

civil arrest : the arrest and detention of a defendant in a civil suit until he or she posts bail or pays the judgment — see also CAPIAS AD RESPONDENDUM ◊ Civil arrest is restricted or prohibited in most states.

custodial arrest : an arrest of a person accompanied by or followed by taking the person into custody

false arrest : an arrest made without legal authority — called also *unlawful arrest* ◊ If a person is taken into custody, no matter how briefly, a false arrest is also false imprisonment.

pre·text arrest \'prē-ˌtekst-\ **:** the arrest of a person for a minor crime (as a traffic violation) for the real purpose of getting an opportunity to investigate (as through a search) the person's possible involvement in a more serious crime for which there are no lawful grounds to make an arrest — called also *pretextual arrest*

unlawful arrest : FALSE ARREST in this entry

— under arrest : in the condition of being restrained under legal authority

²arrest *vt* **:** to place under arrest — **ar·rest·er** *also* **ar·res·tor** *n*

ar·res·tee \ə-ˌres-'tē\ *n* **:** a person who is or was under arrest

arrest of judgment [*arrest* stoppage] **:** a judge's stopping of a judgment because of a defect (as that the acts proven do not constitute a crime) for which the judgment could be reversed

arrest warrant — see WARRANT

ar·son \'ärs-ᵊn\ *n* [Anglo-French *arsoun*, alteration of Old French *arsin*, literally, conflagration, from *ars*, past participle of *ardre* to burn] **:** the act or crime of willfully, wrongfully, and unjustifiably setting property on fire often for the purpose of committing fraud (as on an insurance company) — **ar·son·ist** \-ist\ *n*

art *abbr* article

ar·ti·cle *n* **1 a :** a separate and usu. numbered or otherwise marked section (as of a statute, indictment, will, or other writing) **b :** a separate point, charge, count, or clause **c :** a condition or stipulation in a document (as a contract) **2 :** a document setting forth the terms of an agreement — usu. used in pl. ⟨~s of merger⟩ **3** *pl* : ARTICLES OF INCORPORATION

Article Nine security interest — see INTEREST 1

Article I court *n* : LEGISLATIVE COURT

articles of association 1 : the instrument under which an association is organized **2 :** ARTICLES OF INCORPORATION

articles of incorporation : a document by which a corporation is formed that sets forth basic information (as the corporation's name, purpose, directors, and stock) usu. as required by statute — see also CERTIFICATE OF INCORPORATION; compare BYLAWS, CHARTER ◊ In most states a corporation is created upon the filing of the articles of incorporation with the secretary of state.

Article III court *n* : a court created in accordance with Article III of the U. S. Constitution whose judges have positions for life and cannot have their salaries reduced — compare LEGISLATIVE COURT ◊ The purpose of the salary and position guarantees enjoyed by the judges of Article III courts is to ensure that their decisions are not influenced by fear of losing their positions or salaries.

ar·tic·u·la·ble \är-'ti-kyə-lə-bəl\ *adj* : capable of being expressed, explained, or justified ⟨police had observed drug sale and stopped defendant on ~ reasonable suspicion that he was dealing drugs —*National Law Journal*⟩

ar·ti·fice \'är-tə-fəs\ *n* : a clever strategy usu. intended to deceive or defraud

ar·ti·fi·cial *adj* **1 a :** made by humans ⟨~ accessions⟩ — compare NATURAL **b** : caused or produced by a human and esp. social or political agency ⟨an ~ price advantage⟩ **2 :** arising through operation of law — **ar·ti·fi·cial·ly** *adv*

artificial person *n* : LEGAL PERSON — compare NATURAL PERSON

as·cen·dant \ə-'sen-dənt\ *n* : ANCESTOR

as is clause *n* : a clause in an agreement providing that the buyer accepts the item for sale in its presently existing condition without modification or repair ◊ Under Uniform Commercial Code section 2-316, an as is clause releases the seller from responsibility for the quality of the item for sale.

as·por·ta·tion \ˌas-pər-'tā-shən\ *n* [Latin *asportatio*, from *asportare* to carry off, from *abs-* away + *portare* to carry] : a carrying away; *specif* : the carrying away of someone else's property that is an element of larceny

as·sail·ant \ə-'sā-lənt\ *n* : a person who commits criminal assault

¹as·sault \ə-'solt\ *n* [Old French *assaut*, literally, attack, ultimately from Latin *assultus*, from *assilire* to leap (on), attack] **1 :** the crime or tort of threatening or attempting to inflict immediate offensive physical contact or bodily harm that one has the present ability to inflict and that puts the victim in fear of such harm or contact — compare BATTERY **2 :** the crime of assault accompanied by battery; *specif* : SEXUAL ASSAULT in this entry — called also *assault and battery*

aggravated assault : a criminal assault accompanied by aggravating factors: as **a :** a criminal assault that is committed with an intent to cause or that causes serious bodily injury esp. through the use of a dangerous weapon **b :** a criminal assault accompanied by the intent to commit or the commission of a felony (as rape) — compare SIMPLE ASSAULT in this entry

assault with intent : a criminal assault committed with the intent to commit another specified crime ⟨*assault with intent* to rob⟩ ⟨charged with *assault with intent* to kill⟩

civil assault : an assault considered as

a tort rather than as a crime — compare CRIMINAL ASSAULT in this entry

criminal assault : an assault considered as a crime rather than as a tort — compare CIVIL ASSAULT in this entry ◊ An assault may be both a criminal assault and a civil assault.

felonious assault : a criminal assault that is classified as a felony and involves the infliction of serious bodily injury by the use of a dangerous weapon

indecent assault : intentional offensive sexual contact that does not amount to sexual intercourse or involve penetration and that is committed without consent of the victim and without the intent to commit rape

sexual assault : sexual contact usu. that is forced upon a person without consent or inflicted upon a person who is incapable of giving consent (as because of age or physical or mental incapacity) or who places the assailant (as a doctor) in a position of trust — see also RAPE ◊ Sexual assault in its most serious forms (often classified as first degree sexual assault) involves nonconsensual sexual penetration. In its less serious forms it may be the equivalent of statutory rape.

simple assault : a criminal assault that is not accompanied by any aggravating factors (as infliction of serious injury or use of a dangerous weapon) — compare AGGRAVATED ASSAULT in this entry ◊ Simple assault is usu. classified as a misdemeanor.

²**assault** *vt* : to make an assault on; *specif* : to subject to a sexual assault ~ *vi* : to make an assault — **as·sault·er** *n* — **as·saul·tive** \ə-'sȯl-tiv\ *adj* — **as·saul·tive·ly** *adv* — **as·saul·tive·ness** *n*

assault and battery *n* : ASSAULT 2

assault with intent — see ASSAULT

as·sem·ble *vb* **-bled; -bling** *vt* : to bring or summon together into a group esp. in a particular place for a particular purpose ~ *vi* : to come or meet together in a group often formally or for a common purpose ⟨the right of the people peaceably to ~ —*U.S. Constitution* amend. I⟩

as·sem·bly *n, pl* **-blies 1 a** : a company of persons collected together in one place usu. for some common purpose **b** *cap* : a legislative body esp. that makes up the lower house of a legislature — see also GENERAL ASSEMBLY, LEGISLATIVE ASSEMBLY **2** : the act of coming together : the condition of being assembled — see also UNLAWFUL ASSEMBLY

¹**as·sent** \ə-'sent\ *vi* : to agree to something esp. freely and with understanding : give one's assent

²**assent** *n* : agreement to a matter under consideration esp. based on freedom of choice and a reasonable knowledge of the matter ⟨their mutual ~ to the terms of the contract⟩

as·sert \ə-'sərt\ *vt* : to present and demand recognition of ⟨~ a claim⟩ — **as·ser·tion** \ə-'sər-shən\ *n*

as·sess \ə-'ses\ *vt* **1** : to determine the rate or amount of (as a tax) **2 a** : to impose (as a tax) according to an established rate **b** : to subject to a tax, charge, or levy ⟨each property owner was ~*ed* an additional five dollars⟩ **3** : to make an official valuation of (property) for the purposes of taxation — **as·sess·able** \ə-'se-sə-bəl\ *adj* — **as·sess·ment** *n*

assessment lien — see LIEN

as·ses·sor \ə-'se-sər\ *n* **1** : one appointed or elected to assist a judge or magistrate; *esp* : one with special knowledge of the subject to be decided — see also MASTER **2** : one that assesses; *specif* : one that is authorized to assess property for taxation

as·set \'a-ˌset, -sət\ *n* [back-formation from *assets*, singular, sufficient property to pay debts and legacies, from Anglo-French *asetz*, from Old French *asez* enough] **1** : the entire property of a person, business organization, or estate that is subject to the payment of debts — used in pl.; compare EQUITY **2** : an item of property owned

admitted asset : an asset allowed by law to be included in determining the financial condition of an insurance company — compare NONADMITTED ASSET in this entry *appointive asset* : an asset in an estate that is to be distributed under a power of appointment

capital asset : a tangible or intangible long-term asset esp. that is not regularly bought or sold as part of the owner's business; *specif*: any asset classified as a capital asset by law (as section 1221 of the Internal Revenue Code)

cur•rent asset : a short-term asset (as inventory, an account receivable, or a note) that can be quickly converted into cash

equitable asset : an asset esp. in an estate that is subject to the payment of debts only in a court of equity

fixed asset : a tangible asset (as a piece of equipment) that is of a permanent or long-term nature

intangible asset : an asset (as goodwill or a patent) that does not have physical form

marital asset : an asset acquired by either spouse or both spouses during a marriage ◊ Marital assets are generally subject to equitable distribution on divorce.

net assets **1** : the excess of assets over liabilities — called also *net worth* **2** : admitted assets considered as a whole

net quick assets : the excess of quick assets over current liabilities

non•ad•mit•ted asset : an asset not allowed by law to be included in determining the financial condition of an insurance company because it cannot be quickly converted into cash without incurring a loss — compare ADMITTED ASSET in this entry

quick assets : cash, accounts receivable, and other current assets except inventories

tangible asset : an asset that has physical form and is capable of being appraised at an actual or approximate value

wast•ing asset : property (as a copyright or oil well) that will eventually expire or be used up and lose its value

asset–backed security — see SECURITY

a̶̶ ̶̶̶̶̶reciation range *n* : a range of

useful lives assigned to types of property under the Internal Revenue Code for purposes of depreciation

¹**as•sign** \ə-'sīn\ *vt* **1** : to transfer (property or rights) to another ⟨the general practice by inventors of ~*ing* patent rights —J. K. Owens⟩ **2** : to appoint to a post or duty ⟨~*ed* to represent the defendant⟩ **3** : to fix or specify in relationship or correspondence ⟨no party may ~ as error the giving or the failure to give an instruction unless that party objects thereto —*Federal Rules of Civil Procedure* Rule 51⟩ — **as•sign•abil•i•ty** \ə-ˌsī-nə-'bi-lə-tē\ *n* — **as•sign•able** \ə-'sī-nə-bəl\ *adj* — **as•sign•or** \ə-'sī-nər\ *n*

²**assign** *n* : ASSIGNEE

assigned risk *n* : a poor risk (as an accident-prone driver) that insurance companies would normally reject but are forced to insure by state law

as•sign•ee \ˌa-sə-'nē, ˌa-ˌsī-, ə-ˌsī-\ *n* : a person to whom a right or property is transferred

as•sign•ment *n* **1** : the act of assigning **2 a** : a position, post, or office to which one is assigned **b** : a task assigned **3** : a present transfer of property or rights

absolute assignment : an assignment in which the transfer is complete and leaves the assignor with no interest in the property or right transferred

assignment for the benefit of creditors : assignment of property by a debtor to an assignee to be held in trust and used to pay off the debtor's debts

assignment of income : an assignment by one taxpayer to another of income for the purpose of avoiding taxes

assignment of lease : an assignment by a tenant of all of his or her remaining rights in a property under a lease — compare SUBLEASE

effective assignment : an assignment by which the assignor's interest in the prop-

\ə\abut \ᵊ\kitten \ər\further \a\ash \ā\ace
\ä\cot, cart \aù\out \ch\chin \e\bet \ē\easy
\g\go \i\hit \ī\ice \j\job \ŋ\sing \ō\go \ò\law
\òi\boy \th\thin \t̲h̲\the \ü\loot \ù\foot \y\yet
\zh\vision *see also* Pronunciation Symbols page

erty or right being assigned is terminated and transferred to the assignee

equitable assignment : an assignment (as of property in which one has a future interest) that is not valid at law but that would be upheld in a court of equity

general assignment : an assignment for the benefit of creditors of all of a debtor's property to be distributed fairly to the creditors — compare PREFERENCE

wage assignment : an assignment by an employee by which an amount of his or her wages are transferred to another party (as a creditor) before the wages are paid to the employee — compare GARNISHMENT

assignment for the benefit of creditors — see ASSIGNMENT

assignment of error : a declaration by a party to a legal action specifying the errors made by the court during the trial that the party seeks to have corrected (as by a new trial)

assignment of income — see ASSIGNMENT

assignment of lease — see ASSIGNMENT

as·sis·tance of counsel : the help of a lawyer which a defendant in a criminal prosecution is guaranteed by the Sixth Amendment to the U.S. Constitution — see also INEFFECTIVE ASSISTANCE OF COUNSEL, *Powell v. Alabama* in the IMPORTANT CASES section ◊ The Supreme Court held in *Powell v. Alabama* that the Sixth Amendment requires the state to provide a lawyer to a defendant too poor to hire one.

as·so·ci·ate \ə-'sō-shē-ət, -sē-ət, -shət\ *n* : a lawyer employed by a law firm — compare PARTNER

associate justice *n* : a justice of a court of last resort who is not the chief justice

as·so·ci·a·tion *n* 1 : a group of persons who share common interests or a common purpose and who are organized with varying degrees of formality — compare CORPORATION 2 : the act of having contact or communication with or keeping company with another ⟨freedom of ∼⟩ 3 : the sharing (as by a aider and abet-

tor) in the criminal intent of a person who commits a crime

as·sume *vt* **as·sumed; as·sum·ing 1** : to voluntarily take upon oneself ⟨∼ a risk⟩ **2** : to take over (the debts or obligations of another) as one's own ⟨∼ a mortgage⟩

as·sump·sit \ə-'səmp-sit\ *n* [Medieval Latin, he/she undertook] : an express or implied promise or contract or quasi contract the breach of which may be grounds for a suit; *also* : a common-law action that may be brought for such a breach — compare COVENANT, DEBT ◊ The action of assumpsit developed in early English law and is still available in the U.S. in some jurisdictions.

as·sump·tion of risk : a doctrine that a person may in advance relieve another person of the obligation to act towards him or her with due care and may accept the chance of being injured; *also* : an affirmative defense that the plaintiff cannot receive compensation for injuries from the defendant because the plaintiff freely and knowingly assumed the risk of injury and relieved the defendant of the obligation to act with reasonable care — compare *contributory negligence* at NEGLIGENCE, VOLENTI NON FIT INJURIA ◊ Assumption of risk may be express or may be implied from the plaintiff's words and actions. Assumption of risk has been abolished in certain types of cases, such as workers' compensation cases.

as·sur·ance *n* **1 a** : the act of assuring **b** : GUARANTEE 3 **2** : the act of conveying real property; *also* : the document by which it is conveyed **3** *chiefly Brit* : INSURANCE

as·sure *vt* **as·sured; as·sur·ing 1** *chiefly Brit* : INSURE **2 a** : to inform positively ⟨the seller *assured* the buyer of his honesty⟩ **b** : to provide a guarantee of

as·sured *n, pl* **assured** *or* **assureds** : INSURED

asy·lum \ə-'sī-ləm\ *n* : protection from arrest and extradition given esp. to political refugees by a nation or by an embassy or other agency that has diplomatic immunity

asylum state *n* : a state that is holding a fugitive from justice from another state pending extradition

ATF *abbr* Bureau of Alcohol, Tobacco, and Firearms — see also the IMPORTANT AGENCIES section

at–risk rule *n* : any of several rules enacted by the Tax Reform Act of 1976 that restrict the deduction from income a taxpayer may take for a loss to the amount for which the taxpayer is personally liable

atro·cious \ə-'trō-shəs\ *adj* : characterized by extreme cruelty or viciousness ⟨~ assault and battery⟩

att *abbr* attorney

at·tach *vb* [Anglo-French *attacher* to lodge (an action in court), seize (a person or property) by legal authority, from Old French *atachier* to fasten, fix, alteration of *estachier*, from *estache* stake] *vt* **1** : to obtain a court order against (property of another person) that directs an officer of the court (as a sheriff) to seize or take control of the property — compare GARNISH, LEVY ◊ A plaintiff may attach a defendant's property as a way of obtaining jurisdiction for the purpose of bringing a lawsuit or to prevent the defendant from getting rid of property that may be needed to pay a judgment to the plaintiff. **2** : to join or make a part of ⟨affidavits ~*ed* to the suit —Rosalind Resnick⟩ **3** : to create a security interest in (property) and so acquire the right to foreclose on or otherwise deal with property for payment of a debt and to exercise one's rights in the property against third parties — see also *security interest* at INTEREST 1; compare PERFECT ~ *vi* : to become effective: as **a** : to come into existence as a security interest ⟨from the date the interest ~*es*⟩ **b** : to become operative esp. as a right ⟨the right to counsel ~*es* only at or after the initiation of adversary judicial proceedings —*United States v. Gouveia*, 467 U.S. 180 (1984)⟩ — see also JEOPARDY — **at·tach·able** *adj* — **at·tach·ment** *n*

attachment bond — see BOND 1a

attachment lien — see LIEN

at·tack *n* : an attempt to prove something invalid or incorrect esp. through judicial procedures ⟨made an ~ on the will as not properly witnessed⟩; *specif* : an attempt to have the judgment of a court corrected or overruled

   collateral attack : an attack on a judgment made during or by a proceeding brought for a different purpose — see also *habeas corpus ad subjiciendum* at HABEAS CORPUS

   direct attack : an attack on a judgment made in a proceeding (as an appeal) brought for the specific purpose of having the judgment corrected or overturned

— **attack** *vb*

at·tain·der \ə-'tān-dər\ *n* [Anglo-French *atteinder*, from *ateindre* to convict, sentence, literally, to reach, attain, ultimately from Latin *attingere* to reach, from *ad* to + *tangere* to touch] : the termination of the civil rights of a person upon a sentence of death or outlawry for treason or a felony — see also *bill of attainder* at BILL 1, CORRUPTION OF BLOOD ◊ In English law up to the nineteenth century, attainder was the harsh consequence of conviction for treason or a felony. It resulted in the forfeiture of the convicted person's property. It also involved corruption of blood, which barred the person from inheriting, retaining, or passing title, rank, or property. A person outlawed lost the right to seek protection under the law. Article III, Section 3 of the U.S. Constitution prohibits corruption of blood or forfeiture upon a conviction for treason "except during the life of the person attainted," and Article I, Section 9 prohibits bills of attainder. Attainder was abolished in England in 1870.

at·taint \ə-'tānt\ *vt* [Anglo-French *ateint*, past participle of *ateindre* — see ATTAIN-

---

\ə\abut \ᵊ\kitten \ər\further \a\ash \ā\ace
\ä\cot, cart \aů\out \ch\chin \e\bet \ē\easy
\g\go \i\hit \ī\ice \j\job \ŋ\sing \ō\go \ò\law
\òi\boy \th\thin \t͟h\the \ü\loot \ů\foot \y\yet
\zh\vision *see also* Pronunciation Symbols page

DER] : to subject (a person) to the consequences of attainder

at·tempt *n* : the crime of having the intent to commit and taking action in an effort to commit a crime that fails or is prevented — called also *criminal attempt;* see also IMPOSSIBILITY ◊ There is no settled answer to how close to completing a crime a person must be to be guilty of attempt, but attempt must generally consist of more than preparation.

at·tempt·ed *adj* : characterized by an intent to commit and effort taken to commit a specified crime that fails or is prevented ⟨~ forgery⟩

at·ten·u·a·tion \ə-ˌten-yu̇-'wā-shən\ *n* : a lessening of the amount, force, or magnitude of something; *specif* : a weakening of the connection between an illegal police procedure and the evidence obtained by it such that the evidence is admissible at trial as an exception to the exclusionary rule

at·test \ə-'test\ *vb* [Latin *attestari*, from *ad* to + *testari* to call to witness, from *testis* witness] *vt* : to bear witness to : affirm to be true or genuine; *specif* : to authenticate (as a will) by signing as a witness ~ *vi* : to bear witness : TESTIFY — often used with *to* — **at·tes·ta·tion** \ˌa-ˌtes-'tā-shən\ *n*

attestation clause *n* : a clause at the end of a will in which the witnesses state that the will was signed and witnessed with all the formalities required by law and which often sets forth those requirements

at·torn \ə-'tərn\ *vi* [Anglo-French *aturner* to transfer (allegiance of a tenant to another lord), from Old French *atorner* to turn (to), arrange, from *a-* to + *torner* to turn] : to agree to be the tenant of a new landlord or owner of the same property — **at·torn·ment** *n*

at·tor·ney \ə-'tər-nē\ *n, pl* **-neys** [Anglo-French *atorné* legal representative, from past participle of *atorner* to designate, appoint, from Old French, to prepare, arrange — see ATTORN] : a person authorized to act on another's behalf; *esp* : LAW-YER — see also ATTORNEY-IN-FACT; compare COUNSEL

attorney–at–law *n, pl* **attorneys–at–law** : LAWYER — compare ATTORNEY-IN-FACT

attorney general *n, pl* **attorneys general** *or* **attorney generals** : the chief law officer of a nation or state who represents the government in litigation and serves as its principal legal advisor

attorney–in–fact *n, pl* **attorneys–in–fact** : an attorney who may or may not be a lawyer who is given written authority to act on another's behalf esp. by a power of attorney — compare ATTORNEY-AT-LAW

attractive nuisance — see NUISANCE

at·tri·bu·tion \ˌa-trə-'byü-shən\ *n* : a rule in tax law that in certain cases deems property owned by one person or business entity to be owned by another or others

atty *abbr* attorney

atty gen *abbr* attorney general

auc·tion *n* : a public sale of property to the highest bidder — see also RESERVE

au·dit \'ȯ-dət\ *n* **1** : a formal examination of an organization's or an individual's financial records often for the purpose of uncovering fraud or inaccurate tax returns; *also* : the final report of such an examination **2** : a methodical examination and review — **audit** *vb*

audit committee *n* : a corporate committee made up of usu. outside directors who review audits and evaluations of the corporation and its officers

au·di·tor \'ȯ-də-tər\ *n* **1** : a person qualified and authorized to examine and verify financial records **2** : a referee appointed by a court in a civil action; *esp* : one designated to prepare an account for the court — see also MASTER

augmented estate — see ESTATE 3a

au·then·tic act *n, in the civil law of Louisiana* : a writing executed in accordance with law which requires that each party to the writing sign it before a public officer (as a notary public) and two witnesses and that the public officer and witnesses also sign the writing

au·then·ti·cate *vt* **-cat·ed; -cat·ing 1** : to

prove or serve to prove that (something) is genuine; *esp* : to prove that (an item of evidence) is genuine for the purpose of establishing admissibility **2** : to make (a written instrument) valid and effective by marking esp. with one's signature ⟨~ a check⟩

au·thor·i·ty *n, pl* **-ties 1** : an official decision of a court used esp. as a precedent **2 a** : a power to act esp. over others that derives from status, position, or office ⟨the ~ of the president⟩; *also* : JURISDICTION **b** : the power to act that is officially or formally granted (as by statute, corporate bylaw, or court order) ⟨within the scope of the treasurer's ~⟩ ⟨police officers executing a warrant . . . are not required to "knock and announce" their ~ and purposes before entering —*National Law Journal*⟩ **c** : power and capacity to act granted by someone in a position of control; *specif* : the power to act granted by a principal to his or her agent

  actual authority : the authority that a principal in reality has granted to an agent

  actual express authority : the actual authority of an agent specifically stated or written by the principal

  actual implied authority : the actual authority of an agent that the principal has not specified but has purposely or through negligence allowed the agent to believe has been granted

  apparent authority : the authority that a principal purposely or through negligence allows a third party to believe that the principal's agent has although such authority has not in reality been granted — called also *authority by estoppel*, *ostensible authority* ◊ A principal is bound by the acts of an agent acting with apparent authority.

  express authority : authority that is explicitly granted to an agent by a principal — called also *expressed authority*, *stipulated authority*

  implied authority : the authority to perform acts that are customary, necessary, and understood by an agent as authorized in performing acts for which the principal has given express authority

  ostensible authority : APPARENT AUTHORITY in this entry

  stipulated authority : EXPRESS AUTHORITY in this entry

3 : a person in a position of power and esp. a public office — usu. used in pl. ⟨the local *authorities*⟩ **4 a** : a government agency or corporation that administers a revenue-producing public enterprise ⟨the transit ~⟩ **b** : a government agency or public office responsible for an area of regulation ⟨should apply for a permit to the permitting ~⟩

authority by estoppel : APPARENT AUTHORITY at AUTHORITY

au·tho·rize \'ȯ-thə-ˌrīz\ *vt* **-rized; -riz·ing 1** : to give permission to **2** : to give authority to act to — **au·tho·ri·za·tion** \ˌȯ-thə-rə-'zā-shən\ *n*

au·to·mat·ic *adj* : happening or existing through the operation of a preexisting arrangement that is triggered by some event; *specif* : happening or existing through the operation of law ⟨~ reversal⟩ ⟨an ~ appeal⟩ — **au·to·mat·i·cal·ly** *adv*

automatic stay *n* : a stay that comes into operation upon the filing of a bankruptcy petition in accordance with bankruptcy law that prevents creditors from attempting to collect from the debtor for debts incurred before the filing

au·to·mo·bile exception *n* : an exception to the prohibition on warrantless searches that allows a police officer to search an automobile without a search warrant in cases where the officer has probable cause to believe that the automobile contains evidence of a crime and that the evidence would be disposed of if the officer were to leave to obtain a warrant

\ə**abut**	\ᵊ**kitten**	\ər**further**	\a**ash**	\ā**ace**
\ä**cot, cart**	\aù**out**	\ch**chin**	\e**bet**	\ē**easy**
\g**go**	\i**hit**	\ī**ice**	\j**job**	\ŋ**sing**	\ō**go**	\ȯ**law**
\òi**boy**	\th**thin**	\t̲h̲**the**	\ü**loot**	\ù**foot**	\y**yet**
\zh**vision**	*see also* Pronunciation Symbols page			

automobile guest statute *n* : GUEST STAT-
UTE

au•ton•o•my \ȯ-'tä-nə-mē\ *n* : the quality or state of being self-governing; *esp*
: the right of self-government — **au•ton-
o•mous** \-məs\ *adj* — **au•ton•o•mous•ly**
adv

au•top•sy \'ȯ-ˌtäp-sē, -təp-\ *n, pl* **-sies** : an
examination of a body after death usu. involving dissection esp. to determine the
cause of death — called also *post mortem,
post mortem examination* — **autopsy** *vt*

au•tre•fois acquit \'ō-trə-ˌfwä-\ *n* [Anglo-
French, formerly acquitted] : a defendant's plea stating that he or she has already been tried for and acquitted of the
same offense

autrefois convict *n* [Anglo-French, formerly convicted] : a defendant's plea
stating that he or she has already been
tried for and convicted of the same offense

aver \ə-'vər\ *vt* **averred; aver•ring** : to assert or declare positively esp. in a pleading : ALLEGE ⟨not necessary to ~ the capacity of a party to sue —*Federal Rules
of Civil Procedure* Rule 9(a)⟩ ◊ Federal
Rule of Civil Procedure 8(e)(1) requires
that averments in a pleading be "simple,
concise, and direct," and states that "no
technical forms of pleading or motions
are required." — **aver•ment** *n*

avoid *vt* [modification of Old French
esvuider to destroy, literally, to empty,
from *es-* out + *vuider* to empty] **1** : to
make void or undo : ANNUL ⟨the trustee
may ~ any transfer of interest of the
debtor in property —*U.S. Code*⟩ **2** : to
respond to (an allegation or averment) by
declaring that facts alleged do not result
in liability ⟨averments in a pleading to

which no responsive pleading is required
or permitted shall be taken as denied or
~*ed* —*Federal Rules of Civil Procedure*
Rule 8(d)⟩ — see also CONFESSION AND
AVOIDANCE; compare DENY **3** : to prevent the occurrence of or responsibility
for esp. through lawful means ⟨~ a tax⟩
— compare EVADE — **avoid•abil•i•ty** *n*
— **avoid•able** *adj* — **avoid•ance** *n*

avoidable con•se•quenc•es *n* : MITIGA-
TION OF DAMAGES 1

avul•sion \ə-'vəl-shən\ *n* [Latin *avulsio*
act of tearing away, from *avellere* to tear
away, from *a-* off, away + *vellere* to pull,
pluck] : a sudden cutting off of land by
flood or change in the course of a body
of water; *esp* : one that separates a portion from one person's property and joins
it to the property of another — compare
ACCRETION

¹award *vt* [Anglo-French *awarder,
agarder* to look at, decide on, impose, alteration of Old French *esguarder* to look
at, from *es-*, intensive prefix + *guarder*
to guard] **1** : to give in accordance with
a judicial or administrative determination
or decision ⟨~ punitive damages⟩ **2** : to
grant as deserved ⟨~*ed* the contract to the
lowest bidder⟩

²award *n* **1** : a judgment or final decision: as **a** : ARBITRATOR'S AWARD **b** : a
formal decision regarding benefits in a
workers' compensation claim **2** : something granted esp. on the basis of merit
or entitlement: as **a** : a contract won by
a successful bidder **b** : relief usu. in the
form of money (as damages or alimony)
granted to a party in a legal proceeding

AWOL \'ā-ˌwȯl, 'ā-ˌdə-bəl-ˌyü-ˌō-'el\
abbr absent without leave

B

baby bond — see BOND 2
bach·e·lor of laws \'ba-chə-lər\ *often cap* ***B&L*** **1 :** the lowest degree conferred by a law school in Canada and formerly in the U.S. — see also JURIS DOCTOR **2 :** an undergraduate degree in law conferred by a school of law in England and Wales
back *adj* **1 :** being overdue or in arrears ⟨~ rent⟩ **2 :** being retroactive esp. as compensation ⟨reinstated with ~ pay⟩
bad *adj* **:** not valid **:** VOID ⟨~ notice⟩; *esp* **:** not covered by sufficient funds ⟨a ~ check⟩
bad debt — see DEBT
bad faith *n* **:** intentional deception, dishonesty, or failure to meet an obligation or duty ⟨no evidence of *bad faith*⟩ — compare GOOD FAITH — **in bad faith :** with or characterized by intentional deception or dishonesty ⟨possessor *in bad faith*⟩ ⟨an obligation to not act *in bad faith* —*Hillesland v. Federal Land Bank Ass'n*, 407 N.W.2d 206 (1987)⟩
¹bail \'bāl\ *n* [Anglo-French, act of handing over, delivery of a prisoner into someone's custody in exchange for security, from *bailler* to hand over, entrust, from Old French, from Latin *bajulare* to carry (a burden)] **1 :** the temporary release of a prisoner in exchange for security given for the prisoner's appearance at a later hearing ⟨while free on ~⟩ **2 :** the security given for a prisoner's release; *also* **:** the amount or terms of the security ⟨excessive ~ shall not be required —*U.S. Constitution* amend. VIII⟩ ⟨posted cash ~⟩ ⟨motion to reduce ~⟩ **3 :** one who provides bail and is liable for the released prisoner's appearance ⟨~ may arrest or authorize arrest of principal —*Code of Alabama*⟩ — **jump bail :** to flee the jurisdiction while released on bail — **make bail :** to be released on bail

²bail *vt* **1 :** to release on bail **2 :** to obtain the release of by giving bail — often used with *out* **3 :** to place (personal property) under a bailment ⟨identity of the article claimed to have been ~*ed* —*Peet v. Roth Hotel Co.*, 253 N.W. 546 (1934)⟩ ◊ Property is usually bailed by putting it temporarily in the custody of another for a specific purpose, as safekeeping or delivery to a third party.
bail·able \'bā-lə-bəl\ *adj* **1 :** eligible for bail ⟨a provision that all prisoners are ~ before conviction⟩ **2 :** appropriate for or allowing bail ⟨offenses that were not ~⟩
bail bond — see BOND 1a
bail·ee \bā-'lē\ *n* **:** an individual or entity (as a business organization) having possession of another's personal property under a bailment ◊ Carriers and warehouses are two examples of bailees. A bailee's liability for loss or damage to property is determined by the terms of the bailment or the law of the jurisdiction.
bai·liff \'bā-ləf\ *n* [Anglo-French, steward, king's official, from *bail* stewardship, custody, handing over — see BAIL] **:** an officer of some courts in the U.S. whose duties usu. include keeping order in the courtroom and guarding prisoners or jurors in deliberation
bail·ment \'bāl-mənt\ *n* [Anglo-French *bayllment*, from *bailler* to hand over — see BAIL] **:** the transfer of possession but not ownership of personal property (as goods) for a limited time or specified purpose (as transportation) such that the individual or business entity taking possession is liable to some extent for loss

\ə\abut \ᵊ\kitten \ər\further \a\ash \ā\ace
\ä\cot, cart \au̇\out \ch\chin \e\bet \ē\easy
\g\go \i\hit \ī\ice \j\job \ŋ\sing \ō\go \ȯ\law
\ȯi\boy \th\thin \t͟h\the \ü\loot \u̇\foot \y\yet
\zh\vision *see also* Pronunciation Symbols page

or damage to the property — compare DEPOSIT, *loan for consumption* and *loan for use* at LOAN ◊ The typical elements of a bailment are delivery of the personal property, acceptance of the delivery, and possession or control of the property. Any of these elements may be actual or constructive. Bailments may be created by contracts, either express or implied, which require agreement, and the agreement may also be express or implied. Contracts for the lease of a car, for sale of goods on consignment, and for the transport of goods are examples of bailments.

bailment for hire : a bailment that either benefits both parties or only the bailee; *esp* : one in which the bailee receives compensation — called also *bailment for mutual benefit, compensated bailment*

constructive bailment : a bailment imposed by law when the bailee comes into possession of the property by accident or mistake (as by finding it or receiving a mistaken delivery) — called also *involuntary bailment*

gratuitous bailment : a bailment in which there is no compensation or benefit to one party; *esp* : one that benefits only the bailor — compare COMMODATUM

involuntary bailment : CONSTRUCTIVE BAILMENT in this entry

bailment for hire — see BAILMENT

bailment for mutual benefit : BAILMENT FOR HIRE at BAILMENT

bail·or \bā-'lòr, 'bā-lər\ *n* : an individual or entity (as a business organization) placing personal property in the possession of another under a bailment

bait and switch *n* : a fraudulent or deceptive sales practice in which a purchaser is attracted by advertisement of a low-priced item but then is encouraged to purchase a higher-priced one — called also *bait advertising*

bal·ance sheet *n* : a statement of financial condition at a given date

bal·anc·ing test *n* : a test in which opposing rights, interests, or policies are assigned a degree or level of importance and the ruling of the court is determined by which is considered greater ◊ Balancing tests are often used for determining the constitutionality of laws and regulations touching on constitutional rights.

bal·lis·tics \bə-'lis-tiks\ *n pl but sing or pl in constr* **1 a** : the science of the motion of projectiles (as bullets) in flight **b** : the flight characteristics of a projectile (as a bullet) **2** : the study of the processes within a firearm as it is fired

bal·loon *adj* : being or having a final installment that is much larger than preceding ones in an installment or term loan ⟨a ~ payment⟩ ◊ In contrast to an amortized loan, a balloon loan is generally repaid in periodic payments of interest and a large, lump sum payment of principal at the end of the term.

balloon mortgage — see MORTGAGE

¹ban *vt* **banned; ban·ning** : to prohibit or forbid esp. by legal means (as by statute or order) ⟨~ solicitation⟩; *also* : to prohibit the use, performance, or distribution of ⟨legislation to ~ DDT⟩

²ban *n* : prohibition esp. by statute or order ⟨a ~ on automatic weapons⟩

bank \'baŋk\ *n* : an organization for the custody, loan, or exchange of money, for the extension of credit, and for facilitating the transmission of funds

branch bank : a banking facility that is a separate but dependent part of a chartered bank; *esp* : a facility that performs some banking functions and is separate from a main office

bridge bank : a national bank that is chartered for a limited time to operate an insolvent bank until it is sold

central bank : a national bank that establishes monetary and fiscal policy and controls the money supply and interest rate

collecting bank : a bank other than the payor bank that is handling for collection a negotiable instrument or a promise or order to pay money

commercial bank : a bank organized

chiefly to handle the everyday financial transactions of businesses (as through deposit accounts and commercial loans) *cooperative bank* : an association (as a credit union) owned by and offering banking services for its members; *specif* : SAVINGS AND LOAN ASSOCIATION *depositary bank* : the first bank to take a negotiable instrument or promise or order to pay money unless the instrument, promise, or order is presented for immediate payment over the counter *federal land bank* : a land bank that is under federal charter and regulated by the Farm Credit Administration *Federal Re·serve bank* : one of 12 central banks set up under the Federal Reserve Act to hold reserves for and extend credit to affiliated banks in their respective districts *intermediary bank* : a bank other than the depositary or payor bank to which a negotiable instrument or promise or order to pay is transferred in the course of collection *land bank* 1 : a bank that provides financing for land development and farm mortgages esp. by issuing stock — see also FEDERAL LAND BANK in this entry 2 : a trust that holds land for purposes of preservation or conservation *national bank* : a bank operating under federal charter and supervision *nonbank bank* : a financial organization (as a branch of an out-of-state bank) that either accepts demand deposits or makes commercial loans *payor bank* : a bank that is the drawee of a draft *presenting bank* : a bank other than a payor bank that presents a negotiable instrument or promise or order to pay money *sav·ings bank* : a bank organized to hold depositors' funds in interest-bearing accounts and to make long-term investments (as in home mortgage loans) *state bank* : a bank operating under state charter and law — **bank·er** \'baŋ-kər\ *n*

bank account trust — see TRUST
bank check — see CHECK
bank discount *n* : the interest that is discounted in adv·ce on a note and computed on the face value of the note
banker's acceptance *n* : a short-term credit instrument issued by an importer's bank that guarantees payment of an exporter's invoice
bank·ing \'baŋ-kiŋ\ *n* : the business of a bank or banker
bank note — see NOTE
¹bank·rupt \'baŋ-,krəpt\ *n* : a debtor (as an individual or organization) whose property is subject to administration under the bankruptcy laws for the benefit of the debtor's creditors ⟨was adjudicated a ~⟩ — see also DEBTOR
²bankrupt *adj* : ruined financially; *esp* : judicially declared a bankrupt ⟨the company is ~⟩ — compare INSOLVENT
³bankrupt *vt* : to reduce to bankruptcy ⟨was ~ed by attorney's fees⟩
bank·rupt·cy \'baŋ-,krəp-sē\ *n, pl* **-cies** 1 : the quality or state of a bankrupt ⟨filed for ~⟩ 2 : the administration of an insolvent debtor's property by the court for the benefit of the debtor's creditors ⟨the debt was discharged in ~⟩ ⟨~ proceedings⟩ — see also ADEQUATE PROTECTION, *Bankruptcy Code* in the IMPORTANT LAWS section; compare INSOLVENCY, RECEIVERSHIP ◊ Bankruptcy protects the debtor from debt collection by creditors. A debtor may file for bankruptcy, which is called "voluntary bankruptcy," or a creditor may petition the court to declare the debtor bankrupt, which is called "involuntary bankruptcy." Involuntary bankruptcy is allowed only under chapter 7 or chapter 11 of the U.S. Bankruptcy Code. There are four types of relief available to individuals or corporations under the Bankruptcy Code: liquidation (chapter 7), reorganization (chapter 11), debt ad-

\ə\abut \ᵊ\kitten \ər\further \a\ash \ā\ace \ä\cot, cart \au̇\out \ch\chin \e\bet \ē\easy \g\go \i\hit \ī\ice \j\job \ŋ\sing \ō\go \ȯ\law \ȯi\boy \th\thin \t͟h\the \ü\loot \u̇\foot \y\yet \zh\vision *see also* Pronunciation Symbols page

justment for a family farmer (chapter 12), and debt adjustment for an individual with a regular income (chapter 13). Municipalities may file for bankruptcy under chapter 9. Generally, not all debts are repaid in a bankruptcy. The court determines which debts are to be repaid according to their priority, and the debtor is typically granted a discharge from unpaid debts that are dischargeable under the Bankruptcy Code.

bankruptcy clause *n* : IPSO FACTO CLAUSE

bankruptcy court *n* : a court that is a unit of a federal District Court and has original jurisdiction over bankruptcy cases ◇ Bankruptcy courts were created by Congress as part of the 1898 Bankruptcy Act. Article I, Section 8 of the U.S. Constitution gives Congress the power to establish "uniform laws on the subject of bankruptcies throughout the United States."

bankruptcy estate — see ESTATE 2

bankruptcy trustee *n* : TRUSTEE IN BANKRUPTCY

¹bar \'bär\ *n, often attrib* **1 a** : the railing in a courtroom that encloses the area around the judge where prisoners are stationed in criminal cases or where the business of the court is transacted in civil cases — compare BENCH 1, DOCK, JURY BOX, STAND **b** : COURT, TRIBUNAL ⟨the younger judge brought a fresh viewpoint to the ~⟩ **2 a** : the whole body of lawyers; *esp* : those qualified to practice in the courts of a particular jurisdiction ⟨admitted to the Arizona ~⟩ ⟨the bankruptcy ~⟩ — compare BENCH 3b **b** : the profession or occupation of lawyer **c** : BAR EXAMINATION ⟨passed the ~⟩ **3** : something that prevents admission, progress, or action: as **a** : an intangible impediment, obstacle, or barrier ⟨the restrictive covenant raised a racial ~⟩ ⟨consent of the victim is a ~ to conviction⟩ **b** : the permanent preclusion of a claim or action esp. due to the loss of a previous suit based on the same cause of action and between the same parties ⟨its earlier successful suit against the

purchaser for the price was a ~ to the present suit — *Martino v. McDonald's System, Inc.*, 598 F.2d 1079 (1979)⟩ ⟨a statute of limitations ~ to the present action⟩ — compare *collateral estoppel* at ESTOPPEL 2a, MERGER 4, RES JUDICATA 2 — **at bar** : before the court ⟨in the case *at bar*⟩ — **at the bar** : in the legal profession ⟨pressures faced by women *at the bar* — R. E. Hauser⟩

²bar *vt* **barred; bar·ring 1** : to keep out : EXCLUDE ⟨cannot ~ the items from sale⟩ **2** : to prevent from doing or accomplishing (something) ⟨plaintiff's conduct may ~ her recovery⟩ ⟨the contract ~s his reinstatement⟩ **3** : PRECLUDE: as **a** : to act as a bar to (as a claim or action) ⟨liberative prescription ~s actions — *Louisiana Civil Code*⟩ ⟨final judgment *barred* the subsequent claim⟩ **b** : to prevent (a party) from bringing a claim or action ⟨plaintiffs are *barred* by the judgment . . . from relitigating their claims — *Roach v. Teamsters Local Union No. 688*, 595 F.2d 446 (1979)⟩ — see also ESTOP; compare MERGE 2 — **bar·ra·ble** *adj*

bar association *n* : a professional association made up of members of a particular bar (as of a state)

bare·boat charter \'bar-,bōt-\ *n* : DEMISE 3

bare license *n* **1** : authority to enter another's property that is granted to a person (as a salesperson) for that person's benefit **2** : a license to use copyrighted material that does not confer an exclusive right to use the material

bare licensee *n* : one who has a bare license — called also *naked licensee*

bar examination *n* : an examination that is usu. administered by a jurisdiction's bar association and which a lawyer must pass prior to admission to the bar of that jurisdiction

¹bar·gain *n, often attrib* [Old French *bargaigne* negotiation, haggling, from *bargaignier* to haggle] **1** : an agreement between parties that settles what each gives or receives (as a promise or performance) in a transaction between them — compare CONTRACT **2 a :** something acquired by or as if by bargaining **b :** something whose value considerably exceeds its cost ⟨a ∼ purchase⟩

²bargain *vi* **1 a :** to negotiate over the terms of an agreement (as a contract) **b :** to engage in collective bargaining ⟨the employer must ∼ with the union⟩ **2 :** to agree to certain terms or conditions **:** come to terms ⟨plaintiff ∼*ed* with the store for a lower price⟩ ∼ *vt* **:** to convey according to a bargain ⟨does hereby grant, ∼, sell, alien and confirm to the party of the second part, the following described property⟩ — often used with *sell* in deeds to indicate that the conveyor is receiving consideration in exchange for the property

bar·gain·able *adj* **:** subject to bargaining; *esp* **:** legitimately subject to collective bargaining ⟨a ∼ issue⟩

bargain and sale deed — see DEED

bargaining agent — see AGENT

bargaining unit *n* **:** the group of employees for whom a labor union negotiates a collective bargaining agreement — called also *collective bargaining unit*

bar·ra·try \'bar-ə-trē\ *n, pl* **-tries** [Middle French *baraterie* deception, from *barater* to deceive, cheat] **1 :** an unlawful act or fraudulent breach of duty by a ship's master or crew that injures the interests of the ship's or cargo's owners — often used in marine insurance policies ◊ Examples of barratry include embezzling cargo, stealing a ship's equipment, or willfully sinking a ship. **2 :** the persistent incitement of litigation

bar·ris·ter \'bar-ə-stər\ *n* [Middle English *barrester*, from *barre* bar + *-ster* (as in *legister* lawyer)] **1 :** a lawyer who argues cases before a British court; *esp* **:** one who is allowed to argue before a British high court — compare SOLICITOR ◊ Many countries in the Commonwealth (as England and Australia) and the Republic of Ireland divide the legal profession into barristers and solicitors. In Canada, every lawyer is both a barrister and a so-

licitor, although individual lawyers may describe themselves as one or the other. Scotland uses the term *advocate* to refer to lawyers allowed to argue cases in its courts. **2 :** LAWYER

bar·ris·ter–at–law \-'lȯ\ *n, pl* **barristers–at–law :** BARRISTER 1 — often used as a formal title

¹bar·ter \'bär-tər\ *vi* **:** to trade by exchanging one commodity or service for another ∼ *vt* **:** to trade or exchange by or as if by bartering — compare SELL

²barter *n* **:** the art or practice of carrying on trade or exchange by or as if by bartering **:** exchange of one commodity or service for another — compare SALE

ba·sis \'bā-səs\ *n, pl* **ba·ses** \-ˌsēz\ **1 :** something (as a principle or reason) on which something else is established ⟨the court could not imagine any conceivable ∼ for the statute⟩ — see also RATIONAL BASIS **2 :** a basic principle or method; *esp* **:** the principle or method by which taxable income is calculated ◊ The Internal Revenue Code has set some limits on which method a taxpayer may use for figuring taxable income. For example, a corporation with gross receipts under $5,000,000 may be a cash-basis taxpayer.

ac·cru·al basis : a method of accounting in which income and expenses are recorded in the period when they are earned or incurred regardless of when the payment is received or made — called also *accrual method*

cash basis : a method of accounting in which income and expenses are recorded in the period when payment is received or made — called also *cash method*

3 : the value (as cost or fair market value) of an asset used in calculating capital gains or losses for income tax purposes

adjusted basis : the basis of an asset increased or decreased to reflect changes

---

\ə\abut \ᵊ\kitten \ər\further \a\ash \ā\ace
\ä\cot, cart \au̇\out \ch\chin \e\bet \ē\easy
\g\go \i\hit \ī\ice \j\job \ŋ\sing \ō\go \ȯ\law
\ȯi\boy \th\thin \t̲h\the \ü\loot \u̇\foot \y\yet
\zh\vision *see also* Pronunciation Symbols page

in value (as through improvement or depreciation)

car•ry•over basis \'kar-ē-,ō-vər-\ : the basis of a donated or transferred asset that is equal to the basis of the asset when it was in the hands of the donor or transferor ◊ Carryover basis generally applied to gifts, transfers in trust, and property acquired from a decedent.

cost basis : the basis of an asset equal to the amount paid for the asset plus other acquisition costs (as a brokerage fee)

stepped–up basis \'stept-'əp-\ : a basis (as a carryover or cost basis) that is increased (as to fair market value) by other than an improvement or depreciation adjustment

sub•sti•tut•ed basis : the basis of property received in exchange for property of a like kind that is equal to the basis of the property given with adjustments for additional consideration received or gains and losses realized

bas•tard \'bas-tərd\ *n* : an illegitimate child ◊ The word *bastard* is no longer used in legal contexts. — **bas•tardy** \'bas-tər-dē\ *n*

Bat•son challenge \'bat-sən-\ *n* [from *Batson v. Kentucky*, 476 U.S. 79 (1986), the Supreme Court ruling that prohibited the striking of jurors on a racial basis] : an objection in which one party argues that the other has used the peremptory challenge to strike one or more prospective jurors from the panel for a discriminatory purpose in violation of the equal protection guarantee of the U.S. Constitution — called also *Batson objection;* compare THIRD-PARTY STANDING ◊ Batson challenges were originally applied to racial discrimination in jury selection but are now also applied when gender or sometimes ethnic background is an issue. The party making the objection usu. must establish by evidence a prima facie case of discrimination, at which point the other party has the burden of advancing a neutral reason for the strike.

bat•tered child syn•drome \-'sin-,drōm, -drəm\ *n* : the combination of grave physical injuries (as broken bones and bruises) that results from gross child abuse ◊ Evidence of battered child syndrome is often used to establish that a child's death was not accidental.

battered wo•man's syndrome *n* : the psychological symptoms suffered by a woman repeatedly abused by a mate (as a husband) ◊ Battered woman's syndrome is used as a defense to violent criminal charges (as homicide). Evidence of repeated abuse is used to show that the defendant acted in self-defense even though the threat or danger was not imminent. Battered woman's syndrome is also used as a mitigating factor in sentencing.

bat•tery \'ba-tə-rē, -trē\ *n* [Old French *batterie* beating, from *battre* to beat, from Latin *battuere*] : the crime or tort of intentionally or recklessly causing offensive physical contact or bodily harm (as by striking or by administering a poison or drug) that is not consented to by the victim — compare ASSAULT

aggravated battery : criminal battery that is accompanied by aggravating factors: as **a** : criminal battery that causes or is intended to cause serious bodily injury esp. through the use of a dangerous weapon **b** : criminal battery committed on a protected person (as a minor or a police officer) — compare SIMPLE BATTERY in this entry ◊ Aggravated battery is usu. classified as a felony.

sex•u•al battery : intentional and offensive sexual contact and esp. sexual intercourse with a person who has not given or (as in the case of a child) is incapable of giving consent; *broadly* : forced or coerced contact with the sexual parts of either the victim or the perpetrator — see also RAPE ◊ This is a broad definition of the offense. The specific elements of this crime vary from state to state, and some states use more narrow definitions.

simple battery : criminal battery that is not accompanied by aggravating factors (as a dangerous weapon) — compare AGGRAVATED BATTERY in this entry ◊ Simple battery is usu. classified as a misdemeanor.

bear \'bar\ *vb* **bore** \'bōr\; **borne** \'bōrn\ *also* **born** *vt* **1** : to physically carry (as an object or message) ⟨the right of the people to keep and ~ arms — *U.S. Constitution* amend. II⟩ **2** : YIELD ⟨the stock will ~ a dividend⟩ **3 a** : to admit of : ALLOW ⟨whatever price the market will ~⟩ **b** : ASSUME, ACCEPT ⟨you ~ legal responsibility for him⟩ — *vi* : to relate or have relevance ⟨will admit evidence ~*ing* on her defense⟩

¹bear·er \'bar-ər\ *n* : a person holding a check, draft, or other negotiable instrument for payment esp. marked payable to bearer or having a blank endorsement

²bearer *adj* : freely transferable by the holder with or without endorsement and with full title passing by delivery to the transferee: as **a** : not having a registered owner **b** : not designating a specific payee ⟨a ~ instrument⟩ ⟨~ checks⟩ — compare ORDER

bearer bond — see BOND 2
bearer paper — see PAPER
bearer security — see SECURITY
be·fore *prep* **1** : in the presence of ⟨then personally appeared ~ me⟩ **2** : to be judged or acted on by ⟨a case ~ the court⟩ ⟨a bill coming up ~ Congress⟩
be·lief *n* : a degree of conviction of the truth of something esp. based on a consideration or examination of the evidence — compare KNOWLEDGE, SUSPICION
be·lieve *vt* **be·lieved; be·liev·ing** : to consider to be true or honest
bel·lig·er·en·cy *n* \bə-'li-jə-rən-sē\ : the state of being at war or in conflict; *specif* : the status whereby a recognized military force is granted the protection of the international laws of war
¹bel·lig·er·ent \bə-'li-jə-rənt\ *adj* **1** : waging war : carrying on war; *specif* : belonging to or recognized as an organized military power protected by and subject to the laws of war **2** : inclined to or exhibiting hostility or a combative temperament

²belligerent *n* : a belligerent nation, state, or person
¹be·low *adv* **1** : in a lower court ⟨the presumption that the decisions ~ . . . are correct — W. J. Brennan, Jr.⟩ **2** : lower on the same page or on a following page ⟨the paragraph ~⟩
²below *prep* : lower in place, rank, or value than — **below the line** : in calculations that yield taxable income ⟨deductions taken *below the line*⟩
bench *n* **1** : the place where a judge sits in court ⟨asked counsel to approach the ~⟩ — compare BAR 1a, DOCK, JURY BOX, SIDEBAR, STAND **2** : the court or system of courts serving an area ⟨the state ~⟩ ⟨the federal ~⟩ **3 a** : the office of a judge ⟨appointed to the ~⟩ **b** : the body of persons who hold positions as judges ⟨members of the ~ and bar⟩ — compare BAR 2a **c** : a judge or panel of judges hearing a case ⟨unless the lawyer is responding to a question from the ~ —R. H. Bork⟩
bench ruling *n* : an oral ruling on a case given by the judge while still on the bench
bench trial *n* : a trial in which there is no jury and the judge decides the case — compare JURY TRIAL
bench warrant — see WARRANT
ben·e·fi·cial \,be-nə-'fi-shəl\ *adj* **1** : providing benefits or advantages **2** : receiving or entitling one to receive an advantage, benefit, or use ⟨a ~ shareholder⟩ ⟨a ~ estate⟩ — **ben·e·fi·cial·ly** \-shə-lē\ *adv*
beneficial interest — see INTEREST 1
beneficial owner — see OWNER
beneficial use — see USE 1b, 2
ben·e·fi·cia·ry \,be-nə-'fi-shē-,er-ē, -'fi-shə-rē\ *n, pl* **-ries** : a person or entity (as a charity or estate) that receives a benefit from something: as **a** : the person or entity named or otherwise entitled to receive the principal or income or

both from a trust — compare SETTLOR, TRUSTEE

contingent beneficiary : a beneficiary that may receive proceeds from a trust depending on the occurrence of a specified event (as the death of another beneficiary)

income beneficiary : a beneficiary that according to the provisions of a trust is to receive income but not the principal of the trust ◊ A trust may provide for income to be paid to someone (as a spouse) for his or her lifetime and then for payment of the principal to another person. A trustee is sometimes allowed to distribute some of the principal of the trust to an income beneficiary when necessary for the support of the beneficiary if support of the beneficiary was the purpose of the trust.

b : the person or entity named by the insured of a life insurance policy to receive the proceeds upon the insured's death

contingent beneficiary : a beneficiary named to receive the insurance proceeds if the primary beneficiary has died — called also *secondary beneficiary*

primary beneficiary \'prī-,mer-ē-, -mə-rē-\ : a beneficiary named to receive the insurance proceeds before any other

secondary beneficiary \'sek-ən-,der-ē-\ : CONTINGENT BENEFICIARY in this entry

c : a person or entity entitled under a letter of credit to demand payment from the issuer of the letter **d** : a person or entity that benefits from a promise, agreement, or contract; *esp* : THIRD-PARTY BENEFICIARY in this entry ⟨the contractual *beneficiaries* . . . are mortgagees and investors —*Key Pac. Mortg. Inc. v. Industrial Indem. Co.*, 845 P.2d 1087 (1993)⟩

creditor beneficiary : a direct beneficiary whom the party paying for the other party's performance intends to benefit as payment for a debt or obligation — compare DONEE BENEFICIARY in this entry

direct beneficiary : a third-party beneficiary to a contract whom the parties to

the contract intended to benefit — compare INCIDENTAL BENEFICIARY in this entry

donee beneficiary : a direct beneficiary whom the party paying for the other party's performance intends to benefit as a gift or donation

incidental beneficiary : a third-party beneficiary to a contract whom the parties to the contract did not intend to benefit — compare DIRECT BENEFICIARY in this entry

third–party beneficiary : a person or entity that is not a party to but has rights under a contract made by two other parties

beneficiary heir — see HEIR

ben•e•fit *n* **1** : something that provides an advantage or gain; *specif* : an enhancement of property value, enjoyment of facilities, or increase in general prosperity arising from a public improvement

general benefit : a benefit to the community at large resulting from a public improvement

special benefit : a benefit from a public improvement that directly enhances the value of particular property and is not shared by the community at large ◊ In proceedings for a partial taking for the purpose of a public improvement, the condemning authority may use a special benefit to the remaining land as a set-off against the landowner's damages for the taking.

2 *in the civil law of Louisiana* : a right esp. that serves to limit a person's liability

benefit of dis•cus•sion : the right of a surety being sued to compel the suing creditor to sue the principal first

benefit of di•vi•sion : the right of a surety being sued to compel the suing creditor to also sue the cosureties; *also* : the right of the surety to be liable only for his or her proportionate share of the debt

benefit of inventory : the right of an heir to be held liable for the debts of the estate only to the extent of the assets in the estate ◊ The heir obtains the benefit of inventory by having a qualified public

officer (as a notary public) make an inventory of the assets in the estate within the time period set by statute.
3 a : financial help in time of disability, sickness, old age, or unemployment **b :** payment or service provided for under an annuity, pension plan, or insurance policy — see also DEATH BENEFIT **c :** FRINGE BENEFIT — **benefit** *vb*

benefit of discussion — see BENEFIT 2

benefit of division — see BENEFIT 2

benefit of inventory — see BENEFIT 2

benefit of the bargain : the advantage that would be or have been gained under a contract if completed as agreed; *specif*: the difference between the actual value of property and the value of property as it is represented in case of misrepresentation — called also *benefit of one's bargain, loss of bargain;* compare OUT-OF-POCKET RULE

be·queath \bi-'kwēth, -'kwēth\ *vt* [Old English *becwethan* to speak to, address, leave by will, from *be-* to, about + *cwethan* to say] **:** to give by will — used esp. of personal property but sometimes of real property; see also LEGACY, LEGATEE; compare DEVISE

be·quest \bi-'kwest\ *n* **:** an act of bequeathing; *also* **:** something bequeathed **:** LEGACY

de·mon·stra·tive bequest \di-'män-strə-tiv-\ **:** a bequest of a particular amount of money or property to be distributed first from one source in the estate and then from other sources to the extent that the first is insufficient

general bequest **:** a bequest that is to be distributed from the general assets of the estate and that is not a particular thing

specific bequest \spə-'si-fik-\ **:** a bequest of a particular item or part of an estate or that is payable only from a specified source in the estate and not from the general assets

best evidence — see EVIDENCE

best evidence rule *n* **:** a rule of evidence: in order to prove what is said or pictured in a writing, recording, or photograph the original must be provided unless the original is lost, destroyed, or otherwise unobtainable — called also *original writing rule*

bes·ti·al·i·ty \ˌbes-chē-'a-lə-tē, ˌbēs-\ *n* **:** the crime of engaging in sexual relations with an animal — see also CRIME AGAINST NATURE

BFOQ *abbr* bona fide occupational qualification

BIA *abbr* Bureau of Indian Affairs — see also the IMPORTANT AGENCIES section

bi·as \'bī-əs\ *n* **:** a personal and often unreasoned judgment for or against one side in a dispute **:** PREJUDICE ⟨a judge disqualified because of ∼⟩

bi·cam·er·al \ˌbī-'ka-mə-rəl\ *adj* **:** having, consisting of, or based on two legislative chambers ⟨a ∼ legislature⟩ — **bi·cam·er·al·ism** \ˌbī-'ka-mə-rə-ˌli-zəm\ *n* — **bi·cam·er·al·i·ty** \ˌbī-ˌka-mə-'ra-lə-tē\ *n*

¹**bid** \'bid\ *vb* **bid; bid·ding** *vt* **:** to offer (a price) for payment or acceptance ∼ *vi* **:** to make a bid **:** state what one will pay or take in payment ⟨a contractor *bidding* for a job⟩ — **bid·der** *n*

²**bid** *n* **1 :** the act of one who bids **2 a :** a statement of what one will pay for something **b :** a statement of what one (as a contractor) will charge for something (as supplies or labor) **3 :** an opportunity to bid

bid bond — see BOND 1a

big·a·mous \'bi-gə-məs\ *adj* **1 :** guilty of bigamy ⟨a ∼ spouse⟩ **2 :** involving bigamy ⟨a ∼ marriage⟩

big·a·my \'bi-gə-mē\ *n* [Medieval Latin *bigamia,* ultimately from Latin *bi-* two + Greek *gamos* marriage] **:** the crime of marrying someone while still legally married to someone else — compare POLYGAMY — **big·a·mist** \-mist\ *n*

Big Pot *n* **:** MAIN POT

bi·lat·er·al \ˌbī-'la-tə-rəl\ *adj* **:** affecting, obligating, or shared by both parties ⟨a

\ə\abut	\ᵊ\kitten	\ər\further	\a\ash	\ā\ace
\ä\cot, cart	\au̇\out	\ch\chin	\e\bet	\ē\easy
\g\go	\i\hit	\ī\ice	\j\job	\ŋ\sing	\ō\go	\ȯ\law
\ȯi\boy	\th\thin	\th\the	\ü\loot	\u̇\foot	\y\yet
\zh\vision	*see also* Pronunciation Symbols page			

~ agreement⟩ — **bi·lat·er·al·ly** \-rə-lē\ *adv*

bilateral contract — see CONTRACT

bill *n* **1 :** a draft of a law presented to a legislature for enactment; *also* : the law itself ⟨the GI ~⟩

ap·pro·pri·a·tions bill \ə-ˌprō-prē-'ā-shənz-\: a bill providing money for government expenses and programs ◊ Appropriations bills originate in the House of Representatives.

bill of attainder 1 : a legislative act formerly permitted that attainted a person and imposed a sentence of death without benefit of a judicial trial — see also ATTAINDER; compare BILL OF PAINS AND PENALTIES in this entry **2 :** a legislative act that imposes any punishment on a named or implied individual or group without a trial ◊ Bills of attainder are prohibited by Article I of the U.S. Constitution.

bill of pains and penalties : a legislative act formerly permitted that imposed a punishment less severe than death without benefit of a judicial trial — compare BILL OF ATTAINDER in this entry ◊ The term *bill of attainder* is often used to include bills of pains and penalties. Bills of pains and penalties are included in the constitutional ban on bills of attainder.

clean bill : a bill in its form as amended and newly introduced to the legislature by a legislative committee

engrossed bill : a bill printed in the form in which it was passed by one chamber of Congress and certified by the appropriate legislative official

enrolled bill : a copy of a bill in the form in which it is passed in the legislature including all changes introduced before enactment that is kept as evidence of the law

House bill : a bill originating in the House of Representatives

money bill : REVENUE BILL in this entry

om·ni·bus bill \'äm-ni-ˌbəs-\: a bill that includes a number of miscellaneous provisions or appropriations

private bill **:** a bill affecting a particular person, organization, or locality as distinguished from all the people or the whole area of a political unit

public bill **:** a bill affecting the community (as a nation or state) at large

revenue bill **:** a bill (as for imposing a tax) for raising money for any public purpose — called also *money bill* ◊ The U.S. Constitution requires all bills for raising revenue to originate in the House of Representatives.

2 : the pleading used to begin a suit in equity that sets forth the basis for one's claim against another — called also *bill in equity* **3 a :** a form or device of procedure used in civil actions

bill in the na·ture of a bill of review **:** an equitable bill seeking to have a court decree set aside that is brought by someone who was not a party to the original suit usu. before the decree is entered in the record — compare BILL OF REVIEW in this entry ◊ Bills in the nature of a bill of review were abolished in federal practice by Federal Rule of Civil Procedure 60(b).

bill in the na·ture of interpleader **:** a bill of interpleader in which the plaintiff is allowed to claim an interest in the subject matter of the suit — compare BILL OF INTERPLEADER in this entry, INTERPLEADER ◊ In federal practice, bills in the nature of interpleader have been abandoned in favor of interpleader as described in Federal Rule of Civil Procedure 22.

bill of complaint **:** COMPLAINT — used esp. in equity actions

bill of costs **:** a bill setting forth the expenses in connection with a suit that a party seeks to have paid by an opposing party

bill of exceptions **:** a bill setting forth the exceptions and objections to rulings made at trial and the evidence relevant to them for the purpose of appeal or other review ◊ Bills of exceptions are no longer required in federal practice under the Federal Rules of Civil Procedure, but they are still used in some state courts.

bill of interpleader : a bill brought by a plaintiff who seeks a court determination of the conflicting claims of two or more defendants to the subject matter of the suit (as money owed by the plaintiff) and who has no interest in the subject matter and no preference as to which defendant prevails — called also *strict bill of interpleader;* compare BILL IN THE NATURE OF INTERPLEADER in this entry, INTERPLEADER ◊ Under most modern rules of procedure, the requirements for interpleader have been relaxed and the distinction between a bill of interpleader and a bill in the nature of interpleader no longer exists.

bill of par·tic·u·lars \-pər-'ti-kyə-lərz\ : a bill containing a detailed listing and explanation of the claims made by the plaintiff ◊ Under Federal Rule of Civil Procedure 12, bills of particulars have been abandoned in favor of the expanded rules for discovery and the motion for a more definite statement.

bill of peace : an equitable bill used to settle the rights of parties in one suit and avoid repeated litigation

bill of review : an equitable bill used to start a suit to have the final judgment of a previous suit set aside — compare BILL IN THE NATURE OF A BILL OF REVIEW in this entry ◊ Bills of review are used when another device for review, such as appeal, is not available, as when the period to bring it has expired. Bills of review are abolished in federal practice by Federal Rule of Civil Procedure 60(b).

creditor's bill : an equitable bill by which a creditor who has won a court judgment against a debtor can compel payment from the debtor out of the property that is not otherwise reachable by legal process

cross bill : an equitable bill by which a party to a suit can bring a claim against any other party ◊ Under Federal Rule of Civil Procedure 13, cross bills are replaced by counterclaims and cross-claims.

strict bill of interpleader : BILL OF INTERPLEADER in this entry

b : a device or instrument used in criminal procedure

bill of indictment : an instrument that contains the charges against a defendant and that is presented to a grand jury for determination after a preliminary hearing whether there is enough evidence to issue an indictment — called also *indictment;* compare NO BILL and TRUE BILL in this entry

bill of information : INFORMATION

bill of par·tic·u·lars \-pər-'ti-kyə-lərz\ : a bill that a defendant may request in which the prosecution sets out in detail the facts forming the basis for the criminal charges against the defendant

no bill : a bill returned by a grand jury that has determined the evidence in a bill of indictment to be insufficient to warrant prosecution; *also* : the finding of the grand jury that the evidence is insufficient — called also *ignoramus, no true bill*

true bill : a bill returned by a grand jury that has found the evidence in a bill of indictment sufficient to warrant prosecution : INDICTMENT

4 : an itemized account of goods sold, services performed, or work done **5** : a written instrument setting out the terms of a transaction involving goods: as **a** : BILL OF LADING **b** : BILL OF SALE **6** : a piece of paper money **7** : a written instrument providing proof of an obligation to pay money

bill of credit : an instrument written by a banker certifying to another that a person named in the instrument is entitled to draw on the banker's funds or credit up to a certain amount : LETTER OF CREDIT

\ə\abut \ᵊ\kitten \ər\further \a\ash \ā\ace
\ä\cot, cart \au̇\out \ch\chin \e\bet \ē\easy
\g\go \i\hit \ī\ice \j\job \ŋ\sing \ō\go \ȯ\law
\ȯi\boy \th\thin \t͟h\the \ü\loot \u̇\foot \y\yet
\zh\vision *see also* Pronunciation Symbols page

bill of exchange : an instrument by one party directing another party to pay a named third party or anyone bearing it a specific amount of money on a named future date or on demand; *also* : DRAFT

due bill : a bill given by a bank to the purchaser of a security in place of the security itself that entitles the purchaser to receive payment upon presentation

Treasury bill : a short-term obligation sold by the government at a discount that bears no interest but is payable at its face value at maturity — compare *Treasury bond* at BOND 2, *Treasury note* at NOTE

bill·able hour \'bi-lə-bəl-\ *n* : an hour that a lawyer spends engaged in work that can be charged to a client at the hourly rate

bill in equity : BILL 2

bill in the nature of a bill of review — see BILL 3a

bill in the nature of interpleader — see BILL 3a

bill of attainder — see BILL 1

bill of complaint — see BILL 3a

bill of costs — see BILL 3a

bill of credit — see BILL 7

bill of exceptions — see BILL 3a

bill of exchange — see BILL 7

bill of indictment — see BILL 3b

bill of information — see BILL 3b

bill of interpleader — see BILL 3a

bill of lad·ing \-'lā-diŋ\ : a document issued by a carrier that lists goods being shipped and specifies the terms of their transport ◊ A bill of lading serves as a receipt for the goods, a contract for the transport of the goods, and a document of title showing that the person in possession of the bill has title to the goods.

clean bill of lading : a bill of lading that does not have any notations written or otherwise marked on it that qualify or amend the bill

negotiable bill of lading : ORDER BILL OF LADING in this entry

nonnegotiable bill of lading : STRAIGHT BILL OF LADING in this entry

order bill of lading : a bill of lading under which the goods are to be delivered

to the person named in the bill or to the named person's order or to the bearer of the bill — called also *negotiable bill of lading;* compare STRAIGHT BILL OF LADING in this entry

straight bill of lading : a bill of lading that names the only person to whom the goods may be delivered — called also *nonnegotiable bill of lading;* compare ORDER BILL OF LADING in this entry

bill of pains and penalties — see BILL 1

bill of particulars — see BILL 3a, b

bill of peace — see BILL 3a

bill of review — see BILL 3a

bill of rights \-'rīts\ *often cap B&R* : a summary of fundamental rights and privileges guaranteed to a people against violation by the government; *esp, cap B&R* : the first 10 amendments to the U.S. Constitution — see also the CONSTITUTION in the back matter

bill of sale : a formal instrument for the conveyance or transfer of title to goods and chattels

bind \'bīnd\ *vt* **bound** \'baùnd\; **bind·ing 1 a** : to make responsible for an obligation (as under a contract) ⟨agents have the power to ~ the insurer —R. I. Mehr⟩ **b** : to burden with an obligation ⟨prevented married women from ~*ing* their property —J. H. Friedenthal *et al.*⟩ **2** : to exert control over : constrain by legal authority ⟨this court is *bound* by precedent⟩ **3** : to bring (an insurance policy) into effect by an oral communication or a binder

bind·er \'bīn-dər\ *n* **1** : a temporary insurance contract that provides coverage until the policy is issued **2** : a receipt for money paid to the owner of real estate or to the owner's agent to secure the right to purchase the real estate upon agreed terms; *also* : the money itself

binding *adj* **1** : imposing a legal obligation ⟨the agreement is ~ on the parties⟩ : requiring submission to a specified authority ⟨the suppression order was ~ on the Department of Transportation —*National Law Journal*⟩

bind over *vt* **1** : to put under a bond to do something (as appear in court) under court authority **2** : to transfer (a case or defendant) to another forum after a finding of probable cause at a preliminary hearing ◊ In states that require indictment by a grand jury in felony cases, a case will be bound over to the grand jury if the judge or magistrate finds at the preliminary hearing that there is probable cause to believe that the defendant committed the crime. In states that use an information, the case is bound over to the trial court upon a finding of probable cause. ⁓ *vi* : to bind a case over ⟨questioned the magistrate's decision to *bind over*⟩ — **bind•over** *n*

birth moth•er *n* : the woman who gave birth to a child esp. as distinguished from the child's adoptive mother

black•acre \'blak-,ā-kər\ *n* : a fictitious piece of real property — used in the study of property law

black–let•ter *adj* : having wide acceptance and great authority and often written down ⟨⁓ law⟩

black•mail \'blak-,māl\ *n* [originally, payment extorted from farmers in Scotland and northern England, from *black* + dialectal *mail* payment, rent] : extortion or coercion by often written threats esp. of public exposure, physical harm, or criminal prosecution — **blackmail** *vt* — **black•mail•er** \-,mā-lər\ *n*

blank endorsement — see ENDORSEMENT

blan•ket *adj* **1** : covering or affecting all members of a group or class ⟨⁓ health coverage⟩ **2** : covering or affecting all situations ⟨a ⁓ release of liability⟩

blanket bond — see BOND 1a

blanket insurance *n* **1** : insurance under which all of the members of a class or group are covered but are not named — see also GROUP INSURANCE **2** : insurance under which property of more than one type or at more than one location is covered

blanket mortgage — see MORTGAGE

blas•pheme \blas-'fēm, 'blas-,fēm\ *vb* **blas•phemed; blas•phem•ing** *vt* : to commit blasphemy against ⟨⁓ God⟩ ⁓ *vi* : to commit blasphemy

blas•phe•my \'blas-fə-mē\ *n, pl* **-mies** : the crime of insulting or showing contempt or lack of reverence for God or a religion and its doctrines and writings and esp. God as perceived by Christianity and Christian doctrines and writings — see also *Amendment 1* to the CONSTITUTION in the back matter ◊ In many states, blasphemy statutes have been repealed as contrary to the First Amendment.

block•age *n* : the condition of a large block of items of property (as shares of stock) that requires special valuation for purposes of estate and gift tax because the value of the items sold as a block differs from their value if sold individually

block•bust•ing *n* : profiteering by inducing property owners to sell hastily and often at a loss by appeals to fears of lowered values because of threatened minority encroachment and then reselling at inflated prices ◊ Many states have statutes prohibiting blockbusting by real estate agents.

block grant *n* : an unrestricted federal grant

blood rel•a•tive *n* : a relative by common descent — compare AFFINE

blot•ter *n* : POLICE REGISTER

blue chip *n* : a stock issue of high investment quality that usu. pertains to a substantial well-established company and enjoys public confidence in its worth and stability — **blue–chip** *adj*

blue flu *n* : an organized absence from work by police officers on the pretext of sickness that is staged for the purpose of protest

blue law *n* [*blue* puritanical] : a statute regulating work, commerce, and amusements on Sunday ◊ Existing blue laws derive from the numerous extremely rigorous laws designed to regulate morals and conduct that were enacted in colonial New England.

\ə\abut \ᵊ\kitten \ər\further \a\ash \ā\ace \ä\cot, cart \au̇\out \ch\chin \e\bet \ē\easy \g\go \i\hit \ī\ice \j\job \ŋ\sing \ō\go \ȯ\law \ȯi\boy \th\thin \t͟h\the \ü\loot \u̇\foot \y\yet \zh\vision *see also* Pronunciation Symbols page

blue pen•cil rule *n* : a rule in contracts: a court may strike parts of a covenant not to compete in order to make the covenant reasonable

blue–rib•bon *adj* : consisting of individuals selected for quality, reputation, or authority ⟨a ~ committee⟩

blue–rib•bon jury *n* : SPECIAL JURY

blue–sky *adj* **1** : having little or no value ⟨~ stock⟩ **2** : of or relating to blue-sky laws

blue–sky law *n* : a law providing for the regulation (as through registration) of the sale of securities (as stock) for the purpose of preventing fraud

board *n, often cap* **1 a** : a group of individuals having managerial, supervisory, investigatory, or advisory powers over a public or private business, trust, or other organization or institution ⟨*Board* of Regents⟩ ⟨*Board* of Bar Overseers⟩ **b** : BOARD OF DIRECTORS **2 a** : a group of citizens elected to administer the business of or an aspect of the business of a political unit (as a town or county) ⟨a ~ of selectmen⟩ **b** : a federal, state, or local government agency — see also *National Labor Relations Board* in the IMPORTANT AGENCIES section **3** : a securities or commodities exchange — see also BOARD OF TRADE

board of directors *often cap B&D* : a group of individuals elected by the shareholders of a corporation to manage the corporation's business and appoint its officers

board of trade : a commodities exchange

bodi•ly harm *n* : BODILY INJURY

bodily heir — see HEIR

bodily injury *n* : any damage to a person's physical condition including pain or illness — called also *bodily harm;* compare EMOTIONAL DISTRESS, SERIOUS BODILY INJURY

body corporate *n, pl* **bod•ies corporate** : CORPORATION

body pol•i•tic \-'pä-lə-tik\ *n, pl* **bod•ies politic** : a group of individuals organized under a single governmental authority

boil•er•plate \'boi-lər-,plāt\ *n* : standardized text in documents (as contracts)

boil•er room *n* : a room equipped with telephones used for making high-pressure usu. fraudulent sales pitches

bol•ster \'bōl-stər\ *vt* : to use evidence usu. improperly to give weight to (evidence already introduced)

bo•na fide \'bō-nə-,fīd, 'bä-nə-; ,bō-nə-'fī-dē, -'fī-də\ *adj* [Latin, in good faith] **1 a** : characterized by good faith and lack of fraud or deceit ⟨a *bona fide* offer⟩ **b** : valid under or in compliance with the law ⟨retirement incentives made part of a *bona fide* employee benefit plan⟩ **2** : made with or characterized by sincerity ⟨a *bona fide* belief⟩ **3** : being real or genuine ⟨*bona fide* residents⟩

bona fide holder *n* : a holder of a negotiable instrument who acquired title to the instrument in the ordinary course of business for value before it became due and without knowledge of any defect in title — compare HOLDER IN DUE COURSE

bona fide occupational qualification *n* : a requirement (as relating to sex, religion, national origin, or age) for a particular job that does not violate the constitutional bans on discrimination — see also *Civil Rights Act of 1964* and *Age Discrimination in Employment Act* in the IMPORTANT LAWS section, *Equal Employment Opportunity Commission* in the IMPORTANT AGENCIES section, *Amendment XIV* to the CONSTITUTION in the back matter; compare DISPARATE IMPACT, DISPARATE TREATMENT

bona fide purchaser *n* : a purchaser who purchases in good faith without notice of any defect in title and for a valuable consideration — called also *bona fide purchaser for value* ◊ There are particular requirements for a bona fide purchaser of a security set out in Uniform Commercial Code section 8-302. Under this section a bona fide purchaser is one who buys a security in good faith and without notice of any adverse claims and who takes delivery of a certificated security either as a bearer security or as a registered security issued to him or her or endorsed to him or her or by a blank endorsement or to whom the transfer of an uncertificated security is registered on the books of the issuer, or as otherwise provided in section 8-313.

bo•na fi•des \‚bō-nə-'fī-‚dēz, *commonly* 'bō-nə-‚fīdz\ *n* [Latin] : GOOD FAITH ⟨the fact that the plaintiff conducted an investigation demonstrated its *bona fides* —*Jeannette Glass Co. v. Indemnity Ins. Co. of North America*, 88 A.2d 407 (1952) (dissent)⟩

bo•na va•can•tia \'bō-nə-vā-'kan-shē-ə\ *n pl* [Latin, ownerless goods] : goods that are unclaimed and without an apparent owner ⟨it was trash, in the nature of *bona vacantia*, which the defendants had abandoned —*United States v. Calise*, 217 F. Supp. 705 (1962)⟩

¹bond *n* **1 a** : a usu. formal written agreement by which a person undertakes to perform a certain act (as appear in court or fulfill the obligations of a contract) or abstain from performing an act (as committing a crime) with the condition that failure to perform or abstain will obligate the person or often a surety to pay a sum of money or will result in the forfeiture of money put up by the person or surety; *also* : the money put up ◊ The purpose of a bond is to provide an incentive for the fulfillment of an obligation. It also provides reassurance that the obligation will be fulfilled and that compensation is available if it is not fulfilled. In most cases a surety is involved, and the bond makes the surety responsible for the consequences of the obligated person's behavior. Some bonds, such as fidelity bonds, function as insurance agreements, in which the surety promises to pay for financial loss caused by the bad behavior of an obligated person or by some contingency over which the person may have no control.

appeal bond : a cost bond required by a rule of procedure (as Federal Rule of Appellate Procedure 7) to be given by an appellant in order to cover the costs of an appeal

appearance bond : an often unsecured bond given by a defendant in a criminal trial to guarantee the defendant's appearance in court as scheduled

attachment bond **1** : a bond given by a plaintiff seeking to attach the defendant's property that ensures payment to the defendant of any damages suffered because of the attachment in the event the plaintiff loses the suit **2** : a bond given by a defendant in order to have an attachment released that ensures payment of a judgment awarded to the plaintiff

bail bond : a bond given by a criminal defendant or by his or her surety to ensure compliance with the terms of bail and esp. with the requirement that the defendant appear in court as scheduled

bid bond : a surety bond often required of contractors bidding on construction work to ensure that the successful bidder will accept the job and will also provide a performance bond

blanket bond : a fidelity bond covering all persons or all of a category of persons employed (as by a bank) or holding office (as of a trustee in bankruptcy)

com•ple•tion bond : PERFORMANCE BOND in this entry

contract bond : a bond given to protect a person or business entity against loss caused by a breach of a contract (as for building, construction, or supply)

cost bond : a bond given by a plaintiff to ensure payment of court costs

depository bond : a bond given by a bank often for deposits from state or municipal governments that covers the amount of the deposit in the event of the bank's insolvency

fidelity bond : a bond or other form of contract to cover an employer against financial loss due to the dishonesty of an employee

\ə\abut	\ᵊ\kitten	\ər\further	\a\ash	\ā\ace
\ä\cot, cart	\aú\out	\ch\chin	\e\bet	\ē\easy
\g\go	\i\hit	\ī\ice	\j\job	\ŋ\sing	\ō\go	\ò\law
\òi\boy	\th\thin	\t͟h\the	\ü\loot	\ù\foot	\y\yet
\zh\vision	*see also* Pronunciation Symbols page

injunction bond : a bond required to be given by the applicant for an injunction to cover costs and damages incurred by a party found to have been wrongfully enjoined

judicial bond : a bond (as an appeal bond or bail bond) required to be given in a court proceeding

license bond : a surety bond required by law or as a condition to the conduct of a specific business or profession — called also *permit bond*

pay•ment bond : a surety bond that covers payment to certain parties (as suppliers) in the event that a contractor breaches a construction contract

peace bond : a bond required to be given by a defendant to ensure good behavior and discourage breaches of the peace

penal bond : a bond that ensures payment of a stipulated sum in the event of a party's nonperformance and that is often required for government contracts

performance bond : a surety bond that ensures a property owner (as a developer or municipality) of the completion of a construction contract or payment of actual damages to the extent of the bond in the event that the contractor fails to complete it — called also *completion bond*

permit bond : LICENSE BOND in this entry

personal bond : a criminal defendant's unsecured promise to appear in court as scheduled after release from custody

replevin bond : a bond given by a plaintiff in a replevin action to cover losses to the defendant or court officer seizing the property in the defendant's possession and transferring it to the plaintiff in the event that the plaintiff loses the case

supersedeas bond : a bond given by an appellant in order to obtain a stay of the judgment awarded at trial and for the purpose of ensuring that if the appellant loses the appeal the appellee will be paid the judgment plus any damages incident to the delay caused by the appeal

surety bond : a bond in which a surety agrees to assume responsibility for the performance of an obligation of another in the event of a default

b : one who acts as a surety **2** : an interest-bearing document giving evidence of a debt issued by a government body or corporation that is sometimes secured by a lien on property and is often designed to take care of a particular financial need — see also COLLATERALIZED MORTGAGE OBLIGATION

accrual bond : a bond that is usu. the last tranche of a collateralized mortgage obligation and from which no payments of principal or interest are made until the earlier tranches are paid in full — called also *Z-bond*

adjustment bond : a bond that is issued in settlement of a prior obligation as part of a business reorganization and on which interest payments are usu. contingent upon earnings

ba•by bond : a bond having a face value of usu. $500 or less

bearer bond : a fully negotiable bond payable to its bearer — compare REGISTERED BOND in this entry

book–entry bond : a bond whose ownership is recorded by computer but for which no certificate is issued

convertible bond : a bond that may be exchanged for another type of security (as common stock) at prearranged terms

coupon bond : a bearer bond that has coupons that must be cut off and presented for payment of interest

debenture bond : a bond backed by the general credit of the issuer rather than by a specific lien on particular assets : DEBENTURE

discount bond : a bond with a market value lower than its face value

flower bond : a Treasury bond that may be redeemed at face value before maturity if used in settling federal estate taxes

guaranteed bond : a bond on which payment of interest or principal or both is guaranteed by a corporation other than the issuer

income bond : a bond that pays interest at a rate based on the issuer's earnings

junk bond : a high-risk bond that offers a high yield and is often issued to finance the takeover of a company

mortgage bond : a bond secured by a mortgage on property — compare DEBENTURE

municipal bond : a bond issued by a municipality to fund the expenses of running the government or of specific programs or projects

registered bond : a bond registered in the name of the holder on the books of the company and issued with the name of the holder written on the bond certificate — compare BEARER BOND in this entry

revenue bond : a bond issued by a public agency authorized to build, acquire, or improve a revenue-producing property (as a toll road) and payable solely out of the revenue derived from such property

sav•ings bond : a nontransferable registered bond issued by the U.S. government in denominations of $50 to $10,000

se•ri•al bond : one of a series of bonds maturing periodically rather than on a single maturity date

Treasury bond : a long-term government bond issued by or under the authority of the U.S. Treasury — compare *Treasury bill* at BILL, *Treasury note* at NOTE

ze•ro–coupon bond : a bond that is sold at a price significantly below face value, pays no annual interest, and is redeemable at full value at maturity — compare STRIP

²**bond** *vt* **1** : to convert into a debt secured by bonds **2** : to provide a bond for ⟨~ an employee⟩

bond•ed \'bän-dəd\ *adj* : in, operating under, or placed under a bond ⟨a ~ official⟩

bond for deed : CONTRACT FOR DEED at CONTRACT — used in Louisiana

bond•hold•er \'bänd-ˌhōl-dər\ *n* : a person or business entity that holds a government or corporation bond — compare STOCKHOLDER

bonds•man \'bändz-mən\ *n* : one who accepts responsibility as surety for the obligations of another and esp. for bail

¹**book** *n* **1** : a record of a business's financial transactions or financial condition — often used in pl. ⟨the ~s show a profit⟩ **2** : POLICE REGISTER **3** : the bets registered by a bookmaker; *also* : the business or activity of giving odds and taking bets

²**book** *vt* : to make (an arrested person) undergo booking

book–entry bond — see BOND 2

book•ie \'bu̇-kē\ *n* : BOOKMAKER

book•ing *n* : a procedure at a jail or police station following an arrest in which information about the arrest (as the time, the name of the arrested person, and the crime for which the arrest was made) is entered in the police register ◊ The arrested person is usu. photographed and fingerprinted at the time of the booking.

book•mak•er \'bu̇k-ˌmā-kər\ *n* : a person who determines odds and receives and pays off bets — called also *bookie*

book•mak•ing \-ˌmā-kiŋ\ *n* : the practices of a bookmaker

book value *n* : the value of something as shown on bookkeeping records as distinguished from market value: as **a** : the value of an asset equal to cost less depreciation **b** : the value of a corporation's capital stock expressed as its original cost less depreciation and liabilities

boot *n* [obsolete or dialect *boot* compensation, from Old English *bōt* advantage, compensation] : additional money or property received to make up the difference in an exchange of business or investment property that is of like kind but unequal in value ◊ Under Internal Revenue Code section 1031, no tax liability results from an exchange solely of like-kind property used in a business or trade or held for investment. If the exchange includes boot, however, under section 1245

\ə\abut \ᵊ\kitten \ər\further \a\ash \ā\ace
\ä\cot, cart \au̇\out \ch\chin \e\bet \ē\easy
\g\go \i\hit \ī\ice \j\job \ŋ\sing \ō\go \ȯ\law
\ȯi\boy \th\thin \t͟h\the \ü\loot \u̇\foot \y\yet
\zh\vision   *see also* Pronunciation Symbols page

the boot will be treated as ordinary income.

¹boot·leg *n* : something bootlegged — **bootleg** *adj*

²bootleg *vb* **boot·legged; boot·leg·ging** *vt* **1** : to produce, reproduce, or distribute without authorization or license **2** : SMUGGLE — compare PIRATE ~ *vi* : to engage in bootlegging — **boot·leg·ger** *n*

border search — see SEARCH

bore *past of* BEAR

borne *past part of* BEAR

bor·row *vt* : to take or receive temporarily; *specif* : to receive (money) with the intention of returning the same plus interest — **bor·row·er** *n*

bot·tom·ry \'bä-təm-rē\ *n* [alteration of earlier *bottomary*, modification of Dutch *bodemerij*, from *bodem* bottom, hull, ship] : a contract under which the owner of a ship pledges the ship as collateral for a loan to finance a journey ⟨money lent on ~ for . . . equipping the vessel —*Louisiana Civil Code*⟩ — compare RESPONDENTIA

¹bound *n* **1** : BOUNDARY — usu. used in pl. ⟨metes and ~*s*⟩ **2** : something that limits or restrains ⟨within the ~*s* of the law⟩

²bound *past and past part of* BIND

³bound *vt* : to form the boundary of or enclose ⟨property ~*ed* on the north by a stone wall⟩

⁴bound *adj* : placed under a legal or moral restraint or obligation

bound·ary *n, pl* **-ar·ies** : a theoretical line that marks the limit of an area of land

boun·ty \'baùn-tē\ *n, pl* **boun·ties** **1** : generosity in bestowing gifts esp. by will **2** : a reward, premium, or subsidy esp. offered by a government

boy·cott \'bòi-ˌkät\ *vt* : to engage in a concerted refusal to have dealings with (as a store, business, or organization) usu. to express disapproval or to force acceptance of certain conditions — see also PRIMARY BOYCOTT, SECONDARY BOYCOTT ◊ A boycott of a business by its competitors, suppliers, or buyers that has the effect of preventing the business's access to the market is a violation of the Sherman Antitrust Act. — **boycott** *n*

Bra·dy ma·te·ri·al \'brā-dē-\ *n* [from *Brady v. Maryland*, 373 U.S. 83 (1963), in which the Supreme Court ruled that suppression by the prosecution of evidence favorable to a defendant who has requested it violates due process] : evidence known to the prosecution that is favorable to a defendant's case and material to the issue of guilt or to punishment and that the prosecution is obligated to disclose to the defense : exculpatory evidence known to the prosecution that must be disclosed

brain death \'brān-ˌdeth\ *n* : the final stopping of activity in the central nervous system esp. as indicated by a flat electroencephalogram for a usu. statutorily predetermined period of time — **brain–dead** \'brān-ˌded\ *adj*

branch *n* : a part of a complex body: as **a** : one of the three main divisions of the U.S. or a state government — see also EXECUTIVE, JUDICIARY, LEGISLATURE **b** : a division of a business or organization ⟨an insurer's ~ office⟩ — see also *branch bank* at BANK

branch bank — see BANK

Bran·deis brief \'bran-ˌdīs-\ *n* [from Louis D. Brandeis (1856–1941), who introduced evidence of social and economic factors in his arguments before the Supreme Court in the case *Muller v. Oregon*] : a brief containing information and statistics relevant to social and economic problems in addition to arguments of law and fact

brand name *n* : TRADE NAME

breach \'brēch\ *n* **1** **a** : a violation in the performance of or a failure to perform an obligation created by a promise, duty, or law without excuse or justification *breach of duty* : a breach of a duty esp. by a fiduciary (as an agent or corporate officer) in carrying out the functions of his or her position *breach of trust* : a breach by a trustee of the terms of a trust (as by stealing from or carelessly mishandling the funds)

breach of war·ran·ty : a breach by a seller of the terms of a warranty (as by the failure of the goods to conform to the seller's description or by a defect in title) ◊ A seller may be liable for a breach of warranty even without any negligence or misconduct. **b** : failure without excuse or justification to fulfill one's obligations under a contract — called also *breach of contract*; compare REPUDIATION
an·tic·i·pa·to·ry breach : a breach of contract that occurs as a result of a party's anticipatory repudiation of the contract
ef·fi·cient breach : breach of contract in economic theory in which it is more profitable for the breaching party to breach the contract and pay damages than to perform under the contract
ma·te·ri·al breach : a breach of contract that is so substantial that it defeats the purpose of the parties in making the contract and gives the nonbreaching party the right to cancel the contract and sue for damages — compare *substantial performance* at PERFORMANCE ◊ Whether a breach is material is a question of fact. Under the Restatement (Second) of Contracts, a material breach gives rise to the right to suspend performance but not to cancel the contract until there is a total breach.
par·tial breach : a breach of contract in which the breaching party's nonperformance is minor and gives rise to the right to sue for damages but not to suspend performance or cancel the contract — compare *part performance* at PERFORMANCE
to·tal breach : a breach of contract under the Restatement (Second) of Contracts that is so substantial that it gives rise to the right to cancel the contract and sue for damages
2 a : a violation or disturbance of something (as a law or condition) ⟨find both the State and the minor guilty of gross *~es* of the rules of procedure —*In re D.L.B.,* 429 N.E.2d 615 (1981)⟩ ⟨a *~* of security⟩; *esp* : BREACH OF THE PEACE   **b**

: an act of breaking out ⟨*~* of prison⟩ **3** : the condition of having committed a breach of contract — used in the phrase *in breach* ⟨a terminating party who is not in *~* is entitled to expenses —*C&S/Sovran Corp. v. First Fed. Sav. Bank of Brunswick,* 463 S.E.2d 892 (1995)⟩ — **breach** *vb* — **breach·er** *n*
breach of contract : BREACH 1b
breach of duty — see BREACH 1a
breach of the peace   1 : a disturbance of public peace or order ⟨insulting language causing a *breach of the peace*⟩ — see also FIGHTING WORDS **2** : the offense of causing a breach of the peace — compare DISORDERLY CONDUCT
breach of trust — see BREACH 1a
breach of warranty — see BREACH 1a
break \'brāk\ *vb* **broke** \'brōk\; **bro·ken** \'brō-kən\; **break·ing** \'brā-kiŋ\ *vt* **1 a** : VIOLATE, TRANSGRESS ⟨*~* the law⟩ **b** : to invalidate (a will) by a court proceeding **2** **a** : to open (another's real property) by force or without privilege (as consent) for entry — often used in the phrase *break and enter* ⟨one who *~s* and enters a dwelling-house of another —W. R. LaFave and A. W. Scott, Jr.⟩ **b** : to escape by force from ⟨*~s* prison or escapes or flees from justice —*Colorado Revised Statutes*⟩ **3** : to cause (a strike) to fail and discontinue by means (as force) other than bargaining *~ vi* : to escape with forceful effort — often used with *out* ⟨prisoners wounded while attempting to *~* out⟩ — **break in·to** : to enter by force or without privilege ⟨an officer may *break into* a building —*Arizona Revised Statutes*⟩
break–in \'brāk-ˌin\ *n* : the act or action of breaking in
break in *vi* : to enter something (as a building or computer system) without privilege (as consent) or by force
break·ing and entering *n* : the act of

gaining passage into and entering another's property (as a building or vehicle) without privilege or by force; *also* : the crime of breaking and entering — see also BURGLARY

Breath·a·ly·zer \'bre-thə-ˌlī-zər\ *trademark* — used for a device that is used to determine the alcohol content of a breath sample

B reorganization — see REORGANIZATION

¹bribe *n* : a benefit (as money) given, promised, or offered in order to influence the judgment or conduct of a person in a position of trust (as an official or witness) — compare KICKBACK

²bribe *vt* **bribed; brib·ing** : to influence (a person) by giving a bribe

brib·ery *n, pl* **-er·ies** : the crime of giving or taking a bribe

bridge bank — see BANK

bridge loan — see LOAN

¹brief *n* [Old French *bref, brief* letter, writ indicating legal proceedings, from Late Latin *brevis, breve* short document, summary, from Latin *brevis*, adjective, short] **1** : a concise statement of a client's case written for the instruction of an attorney usu. by a law clerk — called also *memorandum* **2** : a formal written presentation of an argument that sets forth the main points with supporting precedents and evidence ◊ Briefs are filed either by a party or an amicus curiae with a court usu. regarding a specific motion (as for summary judgment) or point of law. The form of the brief is determined by the procedural rules of that court or jurisdiction.

²brief *vt* : to write a brief concerning (a motion or question of law)

bright line *n* : a clear distinction that resolves a question or matter in dispute — **bright–line** *adj*

bring \'briŋ\ *vt* **brought** \'brȯt\; **bringing** \'briŋ-iŋ\ : to begin or commence (a legal proceeding) through proper legal procedure: as **a** : to put (as a lawsuit) before a court ⟨this is an action *brought* to recover damages⟩ **b** : to formally assert

(as a charge or indictment) ⟨whether to ~ charges against him⟩

broke *past of* BREAK

broken *past part of* BREAK

bro·ker \'brō-kər\ *n* : an agent who negotiates contracts of sale (as of real estate or securities) or other agreements (as insurance contracts or mortgages) between the parties for a fee or commission — compare DEALER, FINDER ◊ An insurance broker differs from an insurance agent in that a broker is usu. considered an agent of the insured, even though he or she may receive a commission from an insurance company. A broker may sell the products of a number of insurers, and an insurer has no liability for a broker's wrongful actions (as misrepresentation or fraud). A securities broker often acts also as a dealer and so is often referred to as a broker-dealer.

bro·ker·age \'brō-kə-rij\ *n* **1** : the business or establishment of a broker **2** : a broker's fee or commission

brought *past and past part of* BRING

bug *vt* **bugged; bug·ging** : to plant a concealed microphone in ⟨~ an office⟩ — compare EAVESDROP, WIRETAP

building lease — see LEASE

¹bulk \'bəlk\ *n* : a large mass — **in bulk 1** : not divided into parts or packaged in separate units **2** : in large quantities

²bulk *adj* **1** : being in bulk ⟨~ shipment of wheat⟩ ⟨~ foods⟩ **2** : of or relating to materials in bulk ⟨~ buyer⟩

bulk sale — see SALE

bulk transfer *n* : BULK SALE at SALE

bur·den *n* **1** : something that is a duty, obligation, or responsibility ⟨the prosecution has the ~ of proving every element of the offense⟩ ⟨the statute imposes undue ~s⟩ ⟨~ of pleading the necessary elements⟩ **2** : BURDEN OF PROOF ⟨the husband had not carried his ~ on the insanity issue —*Case & Comment*⟩

burden of coming forward with the evidence : BURDEN OF PRODUCTION

burden of going forward with the evidence : BURDEN OF PRODUCTION

burden of per·sua·sion \-pər-'swā-zhən\

: the responsibility of persuading the trier of fact (as a judge or jury) that the existence of a fact or element (as of an offense or affirmative defense) is more probable than not — compare STANDARD OF PROOF ◊ If a party fails to meet its burden of persuasion, the trier of fact must find against that party regarding the fact or element.

burden of production : the responsibility of the party that is presenting an issue or fact to produce evidence sufficient to support a favorable finding on that issue or fact — called also *burden of coming forward with the evidence, burden of going forward with the evidence* ◊ The burden of production must be met in order to avoid a dismissal or directed verdict. Both parties to a suit usu. have burdens of production during the course of a suit, and often motions (as for summary judgment) impose a burden of production.

burden of proof : the responsibility of producing sufficient evidence in support of a fact or issue and favorably persuading the trier of fact (as a judge or jury) regarding that fact or issue ⟨the *burden of proof* is sometimes upon the defendant to show his incompetency —W. R. LaFave and A. W. Scott, Jr.⟩ — compare STANDARD OF PROOF ◊ The legal concept of the burden of proof encompasses both the burdens of production and persuasion. *Burden of proof* is often used to refer to one or the other. *Burden of proof* and *burden of persuasion* are also sometimes used to refer to the standard of proof.

Burford abstention — see ABSTENTION

bur·glar \'bər-glər\ *n* : a person who commits a burglary

bur·glar·ize \'bər-glə-ˌrīz\ *vt* **-ized; -iz·ing** : to commit a burglary at ⟨*burglarized* the apartment⟩

bur·glary \'bər-glə-rē\ *n, pl* **-glar·ies** [Anglo-French *burglarie*, modification of Medieval Latin *burgaria*, from *burgare* to break into (a house)] : the act of breaking and entering an inhabited structure (as a house) esp. at night

with intent to commit a felony (as murder or larceny); *also* : the act of entering or remaining unlawfully (as after closing to the public) in a building with intent to commit a crime (as a felony) ◊ The crime of burglary was originally defined under the common law to protect people, since there were other laws (as those defining larceny and trespass) that protected property. State laws have broadened the common-law crime. Entering at night is often no longer required and may be considered an aggravating factor. The building may be something other than a dwelling, such as a store or pharmacy. Some states (as Louisiana) have included vehicles under their burglary statute. There are degrees of burglary, and some of the usual aggravating factors are the presence of people and use of a deadly weapon. — **bur·glar·ious** \ˌbər-'glar-ē-əs\ *adj*

bur·gle \'bər-gəl\ *vt* **bur·gled; bur·gling** : BURGLARIZE

business agent — see AGENT

busi·ness compulsion *n* : ECONOMIC DURESS

business deduction — see DEDUCTION

business disparagement *n* : DISPARAGEMENT 1

business expense — see EXPENSE

business judgment — see JUDGMENT 2

business judgment rule *n* : a rule of law that provides corporate immunity to directors of corporations protecting them from liability for the consequences of informed decisions made in good faith

business records exception *n* : an exception to the hearsay rule that allows admission into evidence of records, reports, compilations of data, or memoranda of an event, act, condition, opinion, or diagnosis that are made at or near the time of the event by a person with knowledge or from information transmitted by

---

\ə\abut \ᵊ\kitten \ər\further \a\ash \ā\ace
\ä\cot, cart \aů\out \ch\chin \e\bet \ē\easy
\g\go \i\hit \ī\ice \j\job \ŋ\sing \ō\go \ȯ\law
\ȯi\boy \th\thin \t̲h̲\the \ü\loot \ů\foot \y\yet
\zh\vision *see also* Pronunciation Symbols page

a person with knowledge and that are made as a regular practice of the business

business trust — see TRUST

bus·ing *or* **bus·sing** \'bə-siŋ\ *n* : the act of transporting by bus; *esp* : the transporting of children to a school outside their neighborhood in order to establish a racial balance at that school

but–for *adj* : of or relating to the necessary cause (as a negligent act) without which a particular result (as damage) would not have occurred ⟨a *but-for* test of causation⟩ — compare SUBSTANTIAL FACTOR

but–for cause — see CAUSE 1

buy·back \'bī-,bak\ *n* : an act or instance of buying something back; *esp* : the repurchase by a corporation of shares of its own common stock on the open market

buy·er in ordinary course of business : a bona fide purchaser who in a normal or regular business procedure buys goods from a seller in the business of selling goods of that kind ◇ Under the Uniform Commercial Code a buyer in ordinary course of business takes the purchased goods free of the property interests of a third party. The consideration exchanged for the goods is restricted to cash, other property, or credit. The purchase also cannot be a transfer in bulk or serve as security for or satisfaction of a debt. Pawnbrokers are specifically excluded from qualifying as buyers in ordinary course of business.

buy·out \'bī-,aút\ *n* : an act or instance of buying out

buy out *vt* **1** : to purchase the share or interest of **2** : to purchase the entire tangible and intangible assets of (a business)

by·law \'bī-,ló\ *n* [Middle English *bilage, bilawe* local law, probably ultimately from Old Norse *bȳr* town + *lǫg* law] **1** : a rule adopted by an organization chiefly for the government of its members and the management of its affairs **2** : a local ordinance — often used in pl.

by·pass shelter trust *n* : BYPASS TRUST at TRUST

bypass trust — see TRUST

C

c *abbr* copyright

¹cal·en·dar *n* **1** : a list of cases ready to be heard on a procedural action ⟨the motion ~⟩; *specif* : a list of cases ready for trial — called also *list;* compare DOCKET ◊ Generally it is up to the party that wants to go to trial to have a case placed on the calendar. The party must file with the court a notice that the case is ready for trial and that a jury trial, if desired, is demanded. **2** : a list of bills or other items reported out of committee for consideration by a legislative assembly

²calendar *vt* : to place (a case) on a calendar ⟨the Appellate Division, Second Department, is now *~ing* civil appeals *—New York Law Journal*⟩ — compare DOCKET

calendar call *n* : a session of the court which is held to inquire into the status of cases and in which the cases are called by name and are scheduled for trial if the parties indicate readiness — called also *call of the list*

¹call *vt* **1** : to announce or recite loudly ⟨*~ed* the civil trial list⟩ **2** : to admit (a person) as a barrister ⟨was *~ed* to the bar⟩ **3** : to demand payment of esp. by formal notice ⟨~ a loan⟩ **4** : to demand presentation of (as a bond or option) for redemption ◊ A security issuer may call a security only if calling it is previously provided for, as, for example, in the indenture for a bond or in the stock agreement for preferred stock. The issuer usu. pays the holder a premium for a called security.

²call *n* **1** : a demand for payment of money: as **a** : a notice by the U.S. Treasury to depositories to transfer part of its deposit balance to the Federal Reserve bank **b** : a notice to a stockholder or subscriber to pay an assessment or an installment of subscription to capital **2** : CALL OPTION

at OPTION 3 **3 a** : a formal announcement or recitation ⟨the daily ~ of the motion calendar⟩ **b** : ROLL CALL ⟨the speaker ordered a ~ of the house⟩

call·able *adj* : capable of being called; *specif* : subject to a demand for presentation for payment ⟨a ~ bond⟩

call in *vt* : CALL 4

call of the list : CALENDAR CALL

call option — see OPTION 3

can·cel *vt* **-celed** *or* **-celled; -cel·ing** *or* **-cel·ling 1** : to destroy the force, validity, or effectiveness of: as **a** : to render (one's will or a provision in one's will) ineffective by purposely making marks through or otherwise marring the text of — compare REVOKE ◊ The text of the will or of the will's provision need not be rendered illegible in order for a court to find that there was an intent to cancel it. **b** : to make (a negotiable instrument) unenforceable esp. by purposely marking through or otherwise marring the words or signature ◊ As stated in section 3‑604 of the Uniform Commercial Code, a party that is entitled to enforce a negotiable instrument may cancel the instrument, whether or not for consideration, and discharge the obligation of the other party to pay. **c** : to mark (a check) to indicate that payment has been made by the bank ◊ A check is no longer negotiable once it has been cancelled. **d** : to withdraw an agreement to honor (a letter of credit) ⟨when an issuer wrongfully *~s* or otherwise repudiates a credit before presentment of a draft *—Uniform Commercial Code*⟩ **2** : to put an end to (a contract): as **a** : to end

\ə\abut \ᵊ\kitten \ər\further \a\ash \ā\ace
\ä\cot, cart \aú\out \ch\chin \e\bet \ē\easy
\g\go \i\hit \ī\ice \j\job \ŋ\sing \ō\go \ó\law
\ói\boy \th\thin \t̲h̲\the \ü\loot \ú\foot \y\yet
\zh\vision *see also* Pronunciation Symbols page

(a contract) by discharging the other party from obligations as yet unperformed **b** : to end (a contract) in accordance with the provisions of U.C.C. section 2-106 or a similar statute because the other party has breached — compare RESCIND, TERMINATE ◊ Section 2-106 provides that a party that cancels a contract because of the other party's breach is entitled to seek remedies for breach of all or part of the contract. **c** : to put an end to (a lease contract) because of the default of the other party ◊ Under U.C.C. section 2A-505, a party that cancels because of the other party's default may seek remedies for the default of all or any unperformed part of the lease contract. **3** : to terminate (an insurance policy) before the end of policy period usu. as allowed by policy provisions — **can·cel·able** *or* **can·cel·la·ble** *adj*

can·cel·la·tion *also* **can·cel·a·tion** *n* **1** : the act or an instance of cancelling **2** : a mark made to cancel something (as a check)

C & F *abbr* cost and freight

can·on \'ka-nən\ *n* [Greek *kanōn* rod, measuring line, rule] **1 a** : a regulation or doctrine decreed by a church council **b** : a provision of canon law **2 a** : an accepted principle or rule ⟨~*s* of descent⟩ **b** : a body of principles, rules, standards, or norms

canon law *n* : a body of religious law governing the conduct of members of a particular faith; *esp* : the codified church law of the Roman Catholic Church ◊ Common law has been influenced by canon law in the areas of marriage and inheritance. Roman Catholic canon law, like the civil law, has been modeled on ancient Roman law. The source for Roman Catholic canon law is the *Code of Canon Law. The Rudder* (Pedalion) is a source for Greek Orthodox canon law. Jewish canon law is contained in the Talmud.

can·vass *also* **can·vas** \'kan-vəs\ *vb* **-vassed** *also* **-vased; -vass·ing** *also* **-vas·ing** *vt* **1 a** : to examine in detail; *specif* : to examine (votes) officially for authenticity **b** : to make the subject of discussion or debate **2** : to go through (a district) or go to (persons) in order to solicit orders or political support or to determine opinions or sentiments ~ *vi* : to seek or solicit orders or votes

ca·pac·i·ty *n, pl* **-ties 1** : a qualification, power, or ability (as to give consent or make a testament) created by operation of law **2** : an individual's ability or aptitude; *esp* : mental ability as it relates to responsibility for the commission of a crime (as murder) — see also DIMINISHED CAPACITY; compare COMPETENCY, INCAPACITY, INSANITY

ca·pi·as ad re·spon·den·dum \'kā-pē-əs-ad-ˌrē-spän-'den-dəm, 'kä-pē-ˌäs-äd-ˌrä-spòn-'den-dùm\ *or* **capias** *n* [Medieval Latin, you may seize (the person) to (make him/her) answer the charge] : a writ or process commanding an officer to place a person under civil arrest in order to answer a charge

capias ad sat·is·fac·ien·dum \-ˌsa-tis-ˌfä-shē-'en-dəm, -ˌsä-tis-ˌfä-kē-'en-dùm\ *n* [Medieval Latin, you may seize (the person) to (make him/her) satisfy (the claim)] : a writ or process commanding an officer to place a person (as a debtor) under civil arrest until a claim is satisfied

¹cap·i·tal *adj* [Latin *capitalis*, from *caput* head, a person's life (as forfeit)] **1 a** : punishable by death ⟨~ murder⟩ **b** : involving execution ⟨a ~ case⟩ **2** [Medieval Latin *capitalis* chief, principal, from Latin *caput* head] : being the seat of government ⟨the ~ city⟩ **3** : of or relating to capital; *esp* : of or relating to capital assets ⟨a ~ account⟩ ⟨whether the gain is ~ or ordinary⟩

²capital *n* **1** : accumulated assets (as money) invested or available for investment: as **a** : goods (as equipment) used to produce other goods **b** : property (as stocks) used to create income — see also *capital stock* at STOCK

debt capital : capital that is raised by borrowing (as by issuing bonds or securing loans) *equity capital* : capital (as retained earnings) that is free of debt; *esp* : PAID-IN CAPITAL in this entry

fixed capital : capital that is invested on a long-term basis; *esp* : capital that is invested in fixed assets

legal capital : STATED CAPITAL in this entry

moneyed capital : capital that consists of or represents money that is used or invested (as by a bank or investment company) for the purpose of making a profit on it as money — see also *moneyed corporation* at CORPORATION

paid–in capital : equity capital that is received in exchange for an interest (as shares of stock) in the ownership of a business

risk capital : VENTURE CAPITAL in this entry

stat•ed capital : the total par value or stated value of no par issues of outstanding capital stock — called also *legal capital*

ven•ture capital : the initial usu. paid‑in capital of a new enterprise involving risk but offering potential above‑average profits — called also *risk capital*

work•ing capital : the capital available for use in the course of business activity: **a** : current assets less current liabilities **b** : all capital of a business except the fixed capital

2 : NET WORTH **3** : a city serving as a seat of government ⟨the state ~⟩

capital asset — see ASSET 2

capital contribution *n* : a contribution of funds or property to the capital of a business by a partner, owner, or shareholder ◊ Under the Internal Revenue Code, a capital contribution is generally excluded from a company's gross income, unless it is a loan from a shareholder that the company is released from repaying.

capital expenditure *n* : an amount paid out that creates a long-term benefit (as one lasting beyond the taxable year); *esp* : costs that are incurred in the acquisition or improvement of property (as capital assets) or that are otherwise chargeable to a capital account ◊ Capital expenditures are not deductible for income tax purposes. They are generally added to the property's basis.

capital expense — see EXPENSE

capital gain — see GAIN

cap•i•tal•i•za•tion \ˌka-pət-ᵊl-ə-'zā-shən, -ᵊl-ī-\ *n* **1** : the act or process of capitalizing ⟨~ of earnings⟩ **2** : a sum resulting from a process of capitalizing; *esp* : PAID‑IN CAPITAL at CAPITAL ⟨inadequate ~⟩ **3** : total capital liabilities of a business including both equity capital and debt capital ◊ Equity capital is considered a liability because the investors may recall some or all of it (as by redeeming stock). Inadequate capitalization of a business is considered by courts in cases dealing with equitable subordination of creditors or piercing the corporate veil. **4** : the total par value or the stated value of no-par issues of authorized capital stock

cap•i•tal•ize \'ka-pət-ᵊl-ˌīz\ *vt* **-ized**; **-iz•ing** **1 a** : to convert into capital ⟨~ the company's earnings⟩ **b** : to treat as a capital expenditure rather than an ordinary and necessary expense ⟨the cost of the merger must be *capitalized*⟩ **2 a** : to compute the present value of (an income extended over a period of time) — compare AMORTIZE **b** : to convert (a periodic payment) into an equivalent capital sum ⟨*capitalized* annuities⟩ **3** : to supply capital for ⟨had *capitalized* the business with her own savings⟩

capital loss — see LOSS

capital punishment *n* : DEATH PENALTY

capital stock — see STOCK

capital surplus — see SURPLUS

cap•i•ta•tion \ˌka-pə-'tā-shən\ *n* [Late Latin *capitatio*, from Latin *caput* head] **1** : a direct uniform tax imposed on each head or person : POLL TAX ⟨no ~, or other direct, tax shall be laid —*U.S. Con-*

stitution art. I⟩ **2** : a uniform per person payment or fee

ca·pri·cious \kə-'pri-shəs, -'prē-\ *adj* **1** : governed or characterized by impulse or whim: as **a** : lacking a rational basis **b** : likely to change suddenly **2** : not supported by the weight of evidence or established rules of law — often used in the phrase *arbitrary and capricious* — **ca·pri·cious·ly** *adv* — **ca·pri·cious·ness** *n*

cap·tion \'kap-shən\ *n* [Medieval Latin *captio* act of taking, from Latin *capere* to take] : the part of a legal document that states the court, the names of the parties, the docket number, the title of the document, and sometimes the name of the judge

care *n* **1** : watchful or protective attention, caution, concern, prudence, or regard usu. towards an action or situation; *esp* : DUE CARE ⟨a person has a duty to use ∼ in dealing with others, and failure to do so is negligence —R. I. Mehr⟩ — see also DUE CARE, NEGLIGENCE, STANDARD OF CARE ◊ Statute, case law, and custom often impose a duty of care. The degree or standard of care owed varies depending on the circumstances. For example, a landlord has to exercise greater care in relation to a tenant than to a trespasser. **2 a** : personal supervision or responsibility : CHARGE **b** : MAINTENANCE

ca·reer offender *n* : a habitual or repeat criminal; *esp* : an offender with two or more prior convictions for violent or drug-related crimes — called also *career criminal* ◊ Under federal sentencing guidelines career offenders are given maximum sentences.

care·less *adj* : not showing due care : NEGLIGENT ⟨∼ driving⟩ — compare RECKLESS

car·jack·ing \'kär-ˌja-kiŋ\ *n* : theft by force or intimidation of an auto that has a driver or passenger present

car·nal knowledge \'kär-nəl-\ *n* : an act of esp. illegal sexual intercourse ⟨whoever has *carnal knowledge* of a female forcibly and against her will —*District of Colum-*

bia Code Annotated⟩; *also* : the crime of committing such an act ⟨was charged with *carnal knowledge* of a juvenile⟩ — see also RAPE ◊ Carnal knowledge is sometimes an element of the statutory definition of rape in addition to being a separate offense.

car·ri·er *n* **1** : an individual or entity engaged in transporting passengers or goods for hire by land, water, or air; *specif* : COMMON CARRIER **2** : an insurer that assumes the risks of a policy that it issues to a policyholder

carrier's lien — see LIEN

car·ry·back \'kar-ē-ˌbak\ *n* : the portion of an income tax deduction (as for a net operating loss) or credit which cannot be taken entirely in a given period and which may be deducted from taxable income of a prior period — compare CARRYOVER

car·ry·for·ward \ˌkar-ē-'fōr-wərd\ *n* : CARRYOVER

car·ry·over \'kar-ē-ˌō-vər\ *n* : the portion of a deduction (as for a net operating loss) or credit which cannot be taken entirely in a given period and which may be deducted from taxable income of a later period — compare CARRYBACK

carryover basis — see BASIS 3

¹case *n* [Latin *casus* accident, event, set of circumstances, literally, act of falling] **1 a** : a civil or criminal suit or action ⟨the judicial power shall extend to all ∼s, in law and equity, arising under this Constitution —*U.S. Constitution* art. III⟩ — see also CONTROVERSY

case at bar : a case being considered by the court ⟨the facts of the *case at bar*⟩

case of first im·pres·sion : a case that presents an issue or question never before decided or considered by the court

com·pan·ion case : a case that is heard with another case because it involves similar or related questions of law

test case **1** : a representative case whose outcome will serve as precedent for future cases and esp. for pending cases involving similar or related issues or circumstances and often some of the same

parties ◊ A test case is selected from a number of cases in order to avoid a flood of litigation. All of the parties to the cases must agree to accept the outcome of the test case as binding. **2 :** a proceeding usu. in the form of a suit for injunction brought to obtain a decision as to the constitutionality of a statute **b :** the reported facts, procedural history, and esp. decision in an action
land•mark case **:** a case that marks a significant turning point on a particular issue
lead•ing case **:** a case so well reasoned and important in the rules of law determined and in the principles declared that it becomes well-known and is frequently cited by courts and lawyers as settling the points of law ruled upon and as useful in resolving new questions of law
c : the evidence and arguments presented by a party in court — see also CASE STATED
case in chief **:** the main part of a party's case including arguments for which the party bears the burden of proof but not including rebuttal
prima facie case **:** a case established by evidence that is sufficient to raise a presumption of fact or establish the fact in question unless rebutted
2 : TRESPASS ON THE CASE at TRESPASS
²case *vt* **cased; cas•ing :** to inspect or study with intent to rob ⟨*casing* a store⟩
case at bar — see CASE 1a
case in chief — see CASE 1c
case law *n* **:** law established by judicial decisions in cases as distinguished from law created by legislation — called also *decisional law;* see also COMMON LAW
case•load \'kās-ˌlōd\ *n* **:** the number of cases handled (as by a court or a lawyer) often in a particular period
case of first impression — see CASE 1a
case stat•ed *n* **:** a statement agreed upon by the parties to a lawsuit that sets forth the facts of the case and the parties' request for a judgment by the court based on those

cas for•tuit \'kä-fōr-'twē\ *n* [Anglo‑French] **:** FORTUITOUS EVENT
cash *n* **1 :** ready money **2 :** money or its equivalent (as a check) paid for goods or services at the time of purchase or delivery — **cash against documents :** a sight draft in exchange for a bill of lading ⟨agree that the buyer will pay *cash against documents*⟩
cash basis — see BASIS 2
cash collateral *n* **:** cash or cash equivalents (as negotiable instruments, securities, and documents of title) as specified in section 363 of chapter 11 of the Bankruptcy Code in which both the estate and another entity have an interest — see also *Bankruptcy Code* in the IMPORTANT LAWS section
cashier's check — see CHECK
cash merger — see MERGER
cash meth•od *n* **:** CASH BASIS at BASIS
cash out *vt* **1 :** to prematurely redeem the securities of (a holder) often as part of a merger ⟨the merging company will *cash out* the minority shareholders⟩ **2 a :** to accept payment for (a security) in full often unwillingly ⟨the shareholders were required to *cash out* their shares⟩ **b :** to dispose of (one's goods or assets) by sale ⟨*cashed out* his investment⟩ — **cash-out** *n*
cash sale — see SALE
cash surrender value *n* **:** the amount of money an insurer will pay the insured upon surrender of a life insurance policy usu. calculated as the reserve held by the insurer against the policy less a charge for surrender and any outstanding indebtedness
cash value *n* **:** MARKET VALUE
ca•su•al *adj* **1 a :** not expected or foreseen **b :** not done purposefully : ACCIDENTAL **2 a :** employed for irregular periods ⟨a ~ worker⟩ **b :** engaging in an activity on an occasional basis ⟨a ~ seller⟩

\ə\abut \ᵊ\kitten \ər\further \a\ash \ā\ace
\ä\cot, cart \aú\out \ch\chin \e\bet \ē\easy
\g\go \i\hit \ī\ice \j\job \ŋ\sing \ō\go \ò\law
\òi\boy \th\thin \t͟h\the \ü\loot \ú\foot \y\yet
\zh\vision *see also* Pronunciation Symbols page

ca·su·al·ty \'ka-zhəl-tē, 'ka-zhə-wəl-\ *n, pl* **-ties** **1** **:** an unfortunate occurrence; *esp* **:** a serious and often disastrous accident ⟨conversion of property . . . arising from fire, storm, shipwreck, or other ~ —*Internal Revenue Code*⟩ **2 :** something lost, stolen, damaged, or destroyed — see also *casualty gain* at GAIN, *casualty loss* at LOSS

casualty gain — see GAIN

casualty loss — see LOSS

Casualty Pot *n* **:** a step in calculating tax liability under Internal Revenue Code section 1231 in which qualified casualty gains and losses are added together to determine if the result is a net loss or net gain — compare MAIN POT ◊ Property that qualifies for inclusion in the Casualty Pot consists of casualties of depreciable and real property used in a trade or business for more than one year and capital assets held for more than one year in connection with a trade or business or transaction made for profit. If the net result of the calculation is a loss, then the ordinary rules for gains and losses apply to the casualties. If the net result is a gain, the entire amount passes into the Main Pot.

ca·sus omis·sus \'kä-səs-ə-'mi-səs, 'kä-süs-ō-'mi-sùs\ *n* [New Latin] **:** a situation omitted from or not provided for by statute or regulation and therefore governed by the common law

cau·cus \'kò-kəs\ *n* **:** a closed meeting of a group of persons belonging to the same political party or faction usu. to select candidates or to decide on policy —

caucus *vi*

cau·sa \'kò-zə, 'kaù-sä\ *n, pl* **cau·sae** \'kò-zī, -zē; 'kaù-,sī\ [Latin] **:** CAUSE — used in various Latin phrases

causae *pl of* CAUSA

caus·al \'kò-zəl\ *adj* **1 :** of, relating to, or constituting a cause ⟨~ negligence⟩ **2** **:** involving causation or a cause ⟨no ~ relationship between driving without insurance and the accident —*National Law Journal*⟩ ⟨a ~ link exists between the deceptive act and the injury —*National Law Journal*⟩ **3 :** arising from a cause

cau·sal·i·ty \kò-'za-lə-tē\ *n, pl* **-ties** **:** the relationship between cause and effect

causa mor·tis \-'mòr-tis\ *adj* [Latin *mortis causa* in contemplation of death] **:** made or done in contemplation of one's impending death ⟨rejected his claim that the gift was *causa mortis* —W. M. McGovern, Jr. *et al.*⟩ — usu. used following the term it modifies; see also *gift causa mortis* at GIFT; compare INTER VIVOS

cau·sa·tion \kò-'zā-shən\ *n* **1 a :** the act or process of causing ⟨proof of objective ~ of injury by the perpetrator —Alan Freeman⟩ **b :** the act or agency that produces an effect ⟨evidence was presented on doctor's malpractice . . . for . . . proof of ~ —*National Law Journal*⟩ ⟨if plaintiffs could establish . . . that the caps were manufactured by one of the defendants, the burden of proof as to ~ would shift to all the defendants —*Sindell v. Abbott Laboratories*, 607 P.2d 924 (1980)⟩ **2** **:** the relation between cause and effect esp. as an element to be proven in a tort or criminal case ⟨must be "legal" ~ between the acts and the results —W. R. LaFave and A. W. Scott, Jr.⟩ — see also CHAIN OF CAUSATION

caus·a·tive \'kò-zə-tiv\ *adj* **1 :** effective or operating as a cause ⟨the ~ negligent act⟩ **2 :** CAUSAL 2 ⟨the ~ link between stress and coronary artery disease —*National Law Journal*⟩

¹cause *n* **1 :** something that brings about an effect or result ⟨the negligent act which was the ~ of the plaintiff's injury⟩ ◊ The cause of an injury must be proven in both tort and criminal cases.

actual cause : CAUSE IN FACT in this entry

but–for cause : CAUSE IN FACT in this entry

cause in fact : a cause without which the result would not have occurred — called also *actual cause, but-for cause*

concurrent cause : a cause that joins simultaneously with another cause to produce a result — called also *concurring cause;* compare INTERVENING CAUSE

and SUPERSEDING CAUSE in this entry
direct cause : PROXIMATE CAUSE in this entry
ef·fi·cient intervening cause : SUPERSEDING CAUSE in this entry
intervening cause **1** : an independent cause that follows another cause in time in producing the result but does not interrupt the chain of causation if foreseeable — called also *supervening cause;* compare CONCURRENT CAUSE and SUPERSEDING CAUSE in this entry **2** : SUPERSEDING CAUSE in this entry
legal cause : PROXIMATE CAUSE in this entry
procuring cause : one (as a broker) that sets in motion a continuous series of events culminating esp. in the sale or leasing of real estate ⟨entitled to a commission as the *procuring cause* of the sale even though the listing had expired⟩
pro·duc·ing cause : an efficient, exciting, or contributing cause (as an act, practice, or event) that produces an injury which would not have occurred without it ⟨claimed that the workplace accident was a *producing cause* of his disability⟩ — used esp. in workers' compensation and consumer protection cases ◊ A producing cause lacks the element of foreseeability associated with a proximate cause, being more exclusively concerned with causation in fact.
proximate cause : a cause that sets in motion a sequence of events uninterrupted by any superseding causes and that results in a usu. foreseeable effect (as an injury) which would not otherwise have occurred — called also *direct cause, legal cause;* see also *Palsgraf v. Long Island Railroad Co.* in the IMPORTANT CASES section; compare REMOTE CAUSE in this entry
remote cause : a cause that is followed by a superseding cause interrupting the chain of causation; *also* : a cause that in ordinary experience does not lead to a particular effect — compare PROXIMATE CAUSE in this entry
superseding cause : an unforeseeable

intervening cause that interrupts the chain of causation and becomes the proximate cause of the effect — called also *efficient intervening cause, intervening cause;* compare CONCURRENT CAUSE and INTERVENING CAUSE 1 in this entry
supervening cause : INTERVENING CAUSE in this entry
2 : a reason or justification for an action or state (as belief): as **a** : GOOD CAUSE in this entry ⟨an appeal dismissed for ~⟩ **b** : JUST CAUSE in this entry ⟨behavior that constitutes ~ to terminate an employee⟩ ◊ The circumstances under which cause, good cause, just cause, probable cause, reasonable cause, or sufficient cause exists are determined on a case by case basis. These terms are often used interchangeably, and the distinctions between them are sometimes unclear.
good cause : a substantial reason put forth in good faith that is not unreasonable, arbitrary, or irrational and that is sufficient to create an excuse for an act under the law ⟨unable to show *good cause* for failure to pay child support⟩ ⟨neglect of duty is *good cause* for removal of a trustee⟩
just cause **1** : cause that a person of ordinary intelligence would consider a fair and reasonable justification for an act — used esp. in cases involving termination of employment and denial of unemployment benefits **2** : GOOD CAUSE in this entry
prob·a·ble cause \'prä-bə-bəl-\ **1** : a reasonable ground in fact and circumstance for a belief in the existence of certain circumstances (as that an offense has been or is being committed, that a person is guilty of an offense, that a particular search will uncover contraband, that an item to be seized is in a particular place, or that a specific fact or

\ə**abut** \ə**kitten** \ər**further** \a**ash** \ā**ace**
\ä**cot, cart** \aů**out** \ch**chin** \e**bet** \ē**easy**
\g**go** \i**hit** \ī**ice** \j**job** \ŋ**sing** \ō**go** \ô**law**
\ôi**boy** \th**thin** \t͟h**the** \ü**loot** \ů**foot** \y**yet**
\zh**vision** *see also* Pronunciation Symbols page

cause of action exists) ⟨when supported by *probable cause*, warrantless search of vehicle may extend to every part of vehicle where objects of search might be concealed — *State v. Nixon*, 593 N.E.2d 1210 (1992)⟩ — called also *reasonable cause, sufficient cause;* compare REASONABLE SUSPICION ◊ The Fourth Amendment to the U.S. Constitution stipulates that "no warrants shall issue, but upon probable cause." Probable cause is also required for a warrantless arrest. Probable cause is an objective standard rather than a function of subjective opinion or suspicion not grounded in fact or circumstance. However, the facts or circumstances need not be of the nature of certainty necessary to establish proof in court. **2** : justification for an administrative search based on a showing that it is to be conducted in accordance with standardized nonarbitrary regulatory procedures designed to further public interest in regulatory enforcement that outweighs the intrusiveness of the search

reasonable cause **1** : PROBABLE CAUSE in this entry; *also* : a fact or circumstance that justifies a reasonable suspicion — compare REASONABLE SUSPICION **2** : a reason that would motivate a person of ordinary intelligence under the circumstances ⟨*reasonable cause* to believe abuse had occurred⟩ **3** : something (as an event or the exercise of ordinary care or prudence) that excuses or justifies failure to file a tax return on time

sufficient cause : cause that is deemed enough to provide an excuse under the law: as **a** : GOOD CAUSE in this entry — often used in the phrase *good and sufficient cause* **b** : PROBABLE CAUSE in this entry

3 a : a ground of a legal action ⟨tortious conduct is not a ~ of divorce embraced within the statutory cause of cruel and inhuman treatment — *Case & Comment*⟩ **b** : CASE ⟨questions of law . . . determinative of the ~ then pending —

R. T. Gerwatowski⟩ **4** *in the civil law of Louisiana* : the reason for making a contract — compare FRUSTRATION 2 ◊ Under the Louisiana Civil Code, if a contract's cause is illicit or immoral, the contract is absolutely null. If the cause fails after the contract is made (as when a leased building cannot be occupied because of a fire), the contract may either be not enforced or only partially enforced.

²cause *vt* **caused**; **caus•ing 1** : to serve as the cause of ⟨the scales struck the plaintiff, *causing* injuries for which she sues — *Palsgraf v. Long Island R.R. Co.*, 162 N.E.99 (1928)⟩ **2** : to effect by command, authority, or force ⟨the administrator shall ~ an investigation to be made⟩

cause in fact — see CAUSE 1

cause of action 1 : the grounds (as violation of a right) that entitle a plaintiff to bring a suit ⟨an amended pleading reiterating a *cause of action* for lost profits — J. H. Friedenthal *et al.*⟩; *also* : the part of a suit brought on those grounds ⟨removed the *cause of action* to the district court⟩ **2** : RIGHT OF ACTION 1 ⟨the court, led by Justice Brennan, said Congress intended to provide a private *cause of action* — *National Law Journal*⟩

ca•ve•at \'ka-vē-ˌät, -ˌat; 'kä-vē-ˌät, 'kā-vē-ˌat\ *n* [Latin, may he/she beware] **1 a** : a warning enjoining one from certain acts or practices **b** : an explanation to prevent a misinterpretation **2** : a notice to a court or judicial officer to suspend a proceeding until the opposition can be heard ⟨a ~ entered in the probate court to stop the proving of the will⟩ — **caveat** *vb*

ca•ve•a•tee \ˌka-vē-ä-'tē, -a-'tē; ˌkä-vē-ä-'tē, ˌkä-vē-a-\ *n* : one against whose interest a caveat is entered or filed

caveat emp•tor \-'emp-tər, -ˌtòr\ *n* [New Latin, may the buyer beware] : a principle in commercial transactions: without a warranty the buyer takes the risk as to the condition of the property or goods — compare *products liability* at LIABILITY 2b, WARRANTY

ca•ve•a•tor \'ka-vē-ˌä-tər, -ˌa-, -ˌā-; 'kä-vē-

ˌä-tər, ˌka-vē-ä-ˈtȯr\ *n* : one who enters or files a caveat

CD *abbr* certificate of deposit

cease–and–desist order — see ORDER 3b

cede \ˈsēd\ *vt* **ced·ed; ced·ing 1** : to yield or grant usu. by treaty **2** : ASSIGN, TRANSFER **3** : to transfer (all or part of one's liability as an insurer under an insurance policy) by reinsurance to another insurer

¹cen·sor *vt* : to examine (as a publication or film) in order to suppress or delete any contents considered objectionable

²censor *n* : one that censors

cen·sor·ship *n* : the institution, system, or practice of censoring — compare FREEDOM OF SPEECH, PRIOR RESTRAINT

cen·sure \ˈsen-chər\ *n* : an expression of official disapproval ⟨a House resolution approving a ~ of the representative⟩ — **censure** *vt*

cen·sus *n* : a usu. complete count of a population (as of a state); *esp* : a periodic governmental count of a population that usu. includes social and economic information (as occupations, ages, and incomes) — see also *Article I* and *Amendment XVI* of the CONSTITUTION in the back matter

central bank — see BANK

CEO \ˌsē-ē-ˈō\ *n* [chief executive officer] : the executive with the chief decisionmaking authority in an organization or business

CERCLA \ˈsər-klə\ *abbr* Comprehensive Environmental Response, Compensation, and Liability Act of 1980 — see also the IMPORTANT LAWS section

cert *abbr* certiorari

¹cer·tif·i·cate \sər-ˈti-fi-kət\ *n* **1 a** : a document containing a certified statement as to the truth of something ⟨a birth ~⟩ **b** : a document certifying that a person has fulfilled the requirements of and may practice in a specified field ⟨a teaching ~⟩ **2** : CERTIFICATION ⟨the signature . . . constitutes a ~ that the attorney or party has read the document —*U.S. Code*⟩ **3** : a document that is proof of ownership or indebtedness ⟨stock ~s⟩ ⟨gold ~s⟩

²cer·tif·i·cate \sər-ˈti-fi-ˌkāt\ *vt* **-cat·ed; -cat·ing** : to testify or authorize by a certificate; *esp* : to recognize as having met special qualifications (as of a governmental agency or professional board) within a field — see also *certificated security* at SECURITY — **cer·tif·i·ca·to·ry** \-kə-ˌtȯrē\ *adj*

certificated security — see SECURITY

certificate of con·ve·nience and necessity : a certificate issued by an agency granting a company authority to operate a public service esp. as a utility or transportation company

certificate of deposit : a money-market bond of a preset face value (as $10,000) paying fixed interest and redeemable without penalty only on maturity (as after two years)

certificate of incorporation 1 : a certificate issued by a state's secretary of state that shows acceptance of a corporation's articles of incorporation **2** : ARTICLES OF INCORPORATION

certificate of occupancy : a certificate issued by a local authority indicating that a building meets building-code requirements

certificate of title 1 : a certificate of ownership stating that the title to the specified property is free and clear except for any encumbrance (as a mortgage) listed on it: as **a** : a certificate issued by a motor vehicle registry — called also *title* **b** : a certificate issued by a registry of deeds — see also TORRENS SYSTEM **2** : a document issued by a title abstracter (as an attorney) giving a legal opinion as to the status of a property's title based on a title search or abstract of title — compare DEED

cer·ti·fi·ca·tion \ˌsər-ti-fi-ˈkā-shən\ *n* **1 a** : the act of certifying **b** : the state of being certified — see also CERTIORARI ◊ Certification of an interlocutory decision by a trial court allows an appellate court to review the decision and to answer a con-

\ə\abut \ᵊ\kitten \ər\further \a\ash \ā\ace
\ä\cot, cart \au̇\out \ch\chin \e\bet \ē\easy
\g\go \i\hit \ī\ice \j\job \ŋ\sing \ō\go \ȯ\law
\ȯi\boy \th\thin \th\the \ü\loot \u̇\foot \y\yet
\zh\vision *see also* Pronunciation Symbols page

trolling question of law. Certification is often used in state courts as well as federal courts and, where available, allows a federal court to refer a question of state law to the state's highest court. Certification is also used to refer to a judge's order that allows a suit to be maintained as a class action. **2 :** a certified statement

certified check — see CHECK

certified question — see QUESTION 2

cer•ti•fy \'sər-tə-,fī\ *vt* **-fied; -fy•ing** [Medieval Latin *certificare*, from Late Latin, to assure, convince, from Latin *certus* certain + *-ficare* to make] **1 :** to state authoritatively: as **a :** to give assurance of the validity of ⟨~ corporate records⟩ **b :** to present in formal communication (as an order) esp. for review by an appellate court ⟨the court may ~ the question to the Supreme Judicial Court —R. T. Gerwatowski⟩ — see also CERTIFICATION **c :** to state as being true or as reported or as meeting a standard ⟨refused to ~ the suit as a class action and dismissed it — Marcia Coyle⟩ **2 :** to guarantee (a personal check) as to signature and amount by so indicating (as by stamping *certified*) on the face — see also *certified check* at CHECK **3 a :** CERTIFICATE, LICENSE **b :** to designate (a labor union) as an exclusive bargaining agent or representative

cer•tio•ra•ri \,sər-shē-ə-'rar-ē, ,sər-shə-, -'rär-\ *n* [Medieval Latin *certiorari* (*volumus*) (we wish) to be informed (words used in the Latin texts of such writs)] **:** an extraordinary writ issued by a superior court (as the Supreme Court) to call up the records of a particular case from an inferior judicial body (as a Court of Appeals) — see also the JUDICIAL SYSTEM in the back matter; compare APPEAL ◊ Certiorari is one of the two ways to have a case from a U.S. Court of Appeals reviewed by the U.S. Supreme Court. Certification is the other. The Supreme Court may also use certiorari to review a decision by a state's highest court when there is a question as to the validity of a federal treaty or statute, or of a state statute on constitutional grounds. Certi-

orari is also used within state court systems.

ces•sion \'se-shən\ *n* **1 :** an act of ceding **:** a yielding (as of property) to another: as **a** *in the civil law of Louisiana* **:** assignment or transfer of property rights by a debtor to a creditor **b :** transfer of liability by an insurer to a reinsurer **c :** transfer of control of or sovereignty over specific property or territory esp. by treaty ⟨such district . . . as may, by ~ of particular States . . . become the seat of the government of the United States —*U.S. Constitution* art. I⟩ **2 :** the monetary amount of liability ceded by an insurer to a reinsurer — compare CONCESSION

ces•tui \'se-tē, 'sā-; 'ses-,twē, ses-'twē\ *n* [Anglo-French, originally oblique form of *cest* this person, this] **:** BENEFICIARY

cestui que trust \-kē-'trəst, -ki-\ *n, pl* **cestuis que trust** *or* **cestuis que trus•tent** \-'trəs-tənt\ [Anglo-French, probably alteration of *cestui que use*] **:** the beneficiary of a trust — compare TRUSTEE

ces•tui que use \-'yüz\ *n* [Anglo-French, the person for whose use (a fief is granted)] **:** the beneficiary of a use

cf *abbr* [Latin *confer*] compare

CFR *abbr* Code of Federal Regulations — see also the IMPORTANT LAWS section

chain conspiracy — see CONSPIRACY

chain gang *n* **:** a group of convicts chained together esp. to work outside a prison

chain of causation : the causal connection between an original cause and its subsequent effects esp. as a basis for criminal or civil liability ⟨intervening acts of third parties will not break the *chain of causation* —*Brownell v. Figel*, 950 F.2d 1285 (1991)⟩ — see also NEXUS

chain of title : the succession of conveyances of the title to a particular item of real property (as a house) ◊ The chain of title is usually stated or shown in an abstract of title.

¹chal•lenge *vt* **chal•lenged; chal•leng•ing 1 :** to dispute esp. as being invalid or unjust ⟨counsel *challenged* this interpretation⟩ **2 :** to question formally (as by a suit or motion) the legality or legal qualifications of ⟨~ the regulations⟩; *esp* : to make a challenge to (a trier of fact) ⟨the grounds for *challenging* prospective jurors — W. R. LaFave and A. W. Scott, Jr.⟩ — compare RECUSE

²**challenge** *n* **1** : a calling into question; *esp* : a questioning of validity or legality : OBJECTION ⟨when the ~ to the statute is in effect a ~ of this basic assumption — *Kramer v. Union Free School Dist. No. 15*, 395 U.S. 621 (1969)⟩ — see also BATSON CHALLENGE **2** : a request to disqualify a trier of fact (as a jury member or judge) — compare RECUSAL, STRIKE

challenge for cause : a challenge esp. of a prospective juror based on a specific and stated cause or reason

challenge to the array : a challenge of an entire jury that raises objections to the selection process

peremptory challenge : a challenge esp. of a prospective juror that does not require a stated cause or reason

challenge for cause — see CHALLENGE

challenge to the array — see CHALLENGE

cham·ber *n* **1** : a judge's office; *specif* : the private office where a judge carries on business other than court sessions (as conferences or signing papers) — usu. used in pl. ⟨four other judges met in my *chambers* —R. H. Bork⟩ ⟨a hearing in *chambers*⟩ **2 a** : a hall for the meetings of a deliberative, legislative, or judicial body or assembly ⟨to run back into the House ~ —Tip O'Neill⟩ **b** : a legislative or judicial body : HOUSE ⟨approved by two-thirds of each ~ of Congress — *U.S. Code*⟩

cham·per·tous \'cham-pər-təs\ *adj* : of, relating to, or being a champerty ⟨a ~agreement⟩

cham·per·ty \'cham-pər-tē\ *n, pl* **-ties** [Anglo-French *champartie* bargaining for a share of disputed property, from *champart* share of crops paid as rent, share of property in dispute, from *champ* field + *part* portion] : an unenforceable agreement by which a person with otherwise no interest in a lawsuit agrees to aid in or carry on its litigation in considera-

tion of a share of the subject matter of the suit (as property or damages) — compare MAINTENANCE

chan·cel·lor \'chan-sə-lər\ *n* [Old French *chancelier* royal secretary, from Late Latin *cancellarius* doorkeeper, clerk, from Latin *cancellus* latticework barrier] **1** : the head of a chancery: as **a** : the Lord Chancellor of Great Britain **b** : a judge in a court of equity in various states **2 a** : a university president **b** : the chief executive officer in some state systems of higher education **3** : the chief minister of state in some European countries (as Germany)

chan·cery \'chan-sə-rē\ *n* [Middle English *chauncery*, alteration of *chancellerie* chancellor's office] **1** *cap* : the court having equity jurisdiction in England and Wales and presided over by the Lord Chancellor of Great Britain ◊ Formerly a separate court, the Chancery is now a division of the Supreme Court of Judicature in England. **2 a** : COURT OF EQUITY ⟨cases decided in ~⟩ **b** : the principles and practice of judicial equity ⟨court of ~⟩ — see also EQUITY; compare LAW ◊ There are chancery courts in Arkansas, Delaware, Mississippi, New Jersey, and Tennessee.

change of venue : a procedure available under title 28 section 1404 of the U.S. Code for the transfer of a case by a court in which the case is brought to another court where the case could have been properly brought and which would be more convenient for the parties and witnesses and better serve the interests of justice — compare FORUM NON CONVENIENS

chap·ter 11 *n* : chapter 11 of the U.S. Bankruptcy Code — see also *Bankruptcy Code* in the IMPORTANT LAWS section

chapter 9 *n* : chapter 9 of the U.S. Bankruptcy Code — see also *Bankruptcy Code* in the IMPORTANT LAWS section

\ə\abut \ᵊ\kitten \ər\further \a\ash \ā\ace
\ä\cot, cart \aù\out \ch\chin \e\bet \ē\easy
\g\go \i\hit \ī\ice \j\job \ŋ\sing \ō\go \ò\law
\òi\boy \th\thin \th̲\the \ü\loot \ù\foot \y\yet
\zh\vision *see also* Pronunciation Symbols page

chapter 7 *n* : chapter 7 of the U.S. Bankruptcy Code — see also *Bankruptcy Code* in the IMPORTANT LAWS section
chapter 13 *n* : chapter 13 of the U.S. Bankruptcy Code — see also *Bankruptcy Code* in the IMPORTANT LAWS section
chapter 12 *n* : chapter 12 of the U.S. Bankruptcy Code — see also *Bankruptcy Code* in the IMPORTANT LAWS section
character evidence — see EVIDENCE
character witness — see WITNESS
¹charge *n* **1 a** : something required : OBLIGATION **b** : personal management or supervision ⟨put the child in his ~⟩ **c** : a person or thing placed under the care of another **2** : an authoritative instruction or command; *esp* : instruction in points of law given by a judge to a jury ⟨conviction . . . reversed, because of trial court's ~ —W. R. LaFave and A. W. Scott, Jr.⟩ **3 a** : an incurred expense **b** : the price demanded for something (as admission or use) ⟨a finance ~⟩ **c** : a debit to an account; *esp* : a debit resulting from unexpected operating expenses ⟨a ~ against earnings⟩ **4** : a formal allegation of an offense or wrongdoing ⟨based on a ~ that was dismissed —*National Law Journal*⟩ — see also COMPLAINT, INDICTMENT, INFORMATION
²charge *vt* **charged; charg·ing 1 a** : to impose a task or responsibility on ⟨was *charged* with protecting civil rights⟩ **b** : to command or instruct with authority; *esp* : to give a charge to (a jury) ⟨the jury should have been *charged* on common= law negligence —*National Law Journal*⟩ **2 a** : to make an accusation against esp. in order to bring to trial ⟨*charging* her with attempted robbery⟩ — see also ACCUSE, INDICT **b** : to allege esp. as an accusation ⟨crimes *charged* in the indictment⟩ **3 a** : to impose a financial liability on ⟨~ the estate⟩ **b** : to impose or record as a financial burden or liability ⟨~ the debts to the estate⟩ ⟨*charging* the loss against earnings⟩ **4 a** : to fix or ask as a fee or payment ⟨~ $4 for parking⟩ **b** : to ask payment of (an individual or organization) ⟨~ a client for expenses⟩ — **charge·able** *adj*

charge off *vt* : to treat as a loss or expense; *specif* : to deduct as a bad debt ⟨part of the debt is *charged off* — Code of Federal Regulations⟩
charging lien — see LIEN
char·i·ta·ble *adj* : of or relating to charity ⟨~ contributions⟩
charitable deduction — see DEDUCTION
charitable immunity — see IMMUNITY
charitable lead trust — see TRUST
charitable remainder — see REMAINDER
charitable remainder annuity trust — see TRUST
charitable remainder trust — see TRUST
charitable remainder unitrust — see TRUST
charitable trust — see TRUST
char·i·ty *n, pl* **-ties** : a gift for humanitarian, philanthropic, or other purposes beneficial to the public (as maintaining a public building); *also* : an institution (as a hospital or school) or organization founded by such a gift — compare PRIVATE FOUNDATION ◊ Statutory definitions of what institutions and organizations qualify as charities vary. Organizations that are primarily involved in political campaigns or lobbying do not qualify as charities for tax purposes, but trusts for them may be considered charitable. In addition to tax-exempt status, charities have also generally been granted immunity from tort suits.
¹char·ter *n* [Old French *chartre* letter, formal document, from Late Latin *chartula*, from Latin, diminutive of *charta* sheet of papyrus] **1 a** : a grant or guarantee of rights, powers, or privileges from an authority or agency of a state or country ⟨a state bank ~⟩ — compare CONSTITUTION **b** : a written instrument that creates and defines the powers and privileges of a city, educational institution, or corporation — compare ARTICLES OF INCORPORATION **2** : a written instrument from the authorities of a society creating a lodge, branch, or chapter **3** : a lease of a ship esp. for the delivery of cargo — called also *charter party*
²charter *vt* **1** : to establish, enable, or con-

vey by charter ⟨∼ a bank⟩ **2** : to lease or hire for usu. exclusive and temporary use ⟨∼ a ship⟩

charter party *n* : CHARTER 3

chat·tel \'chat-ᵊl\ *n* [Old French *chatel* goods, property, from Medieval Latin *capitale*, from neuter of *capitalis* chief, principal — see CAPITAL] : an item of tangible or intangible personal property; *esp* : CHATTEL PERSONAL in this entry ◊ In some jurisdictions the term *chattel* is restricted to items of tangible and movable personal property. Other jurisdictions also classify intangible assets and property items as chattels.

  chattel personal pl chattels personal : an item of tangible movable personal property (as livestock or an automobile) that is not permanently connected with real estate

  chattel real pl chattels real : an interest (as a leasehold or profit a prendre) in an item of immovable property (as land or a building) that is less than a freehold estate — compare FIXTURE ◊ Interests that are considered chattels real have been treated by the common law as personal property despite being interests in real property.

chattel mortgage — see MORTGAGE

chattel paper — see PAPER

chattel personal — see CHATTEL

chattel real — see CHATTEL

check *n* **1** : something that limits or restrains — see also CHECKS AND BALANCES **2** : a written order signed by its maker directing a bank to pay a specified sum to a named person or to that person's order on demand — see also NEGOTIABLE INSTRUMENT; compare DRAFT

  bank check : a check drawn by a bank on its deposits in another bank

  ca·shier's check : a check drawn by a bank on its own funds and signed by the cashier or another bank official

  certified check : a check certified to be good by the bank upon which it is drawn by the signature of usu. the cashier or paying teller with the word *certified* or *accepted* across the face of the check

  NSF check [*N*ot *S*ufficient *F*unds] : a check drawn on an account with insufficient funds from which to make payment

check–kit·ing \'chek-ˌkī-tiŋ\ *n* : the practice of drawing on uncollected funds during the time needed to clear a check deposited in a bank esp. if the check is worthless — called also *kiting* ◊ Check-kiting typically works this way: a check drawn on insufficient funds in one bank is deposited in a second bank, and the funds represented by the check are immediately withdrawn from the second bank. The money is ultimately deposited in the first bank to cover the check before it clears, which usually takes several days.

check·off *n* **1** : the deduction of union dues from a worker's paycheck by the employer **2** : designation on an income tax return of a small amount of money to be applied to a special fund (as for campaign financing)

check off *vt* : to deduct (union dues) from a worker's paycheck

check·point *n* : a point at which an inspection or investigation is performed ⟨a ∼ to uncover drunk drivers⟩

checks and bal·anc·es \-'ba-lən-səz\ *n pl* : the powers (as judicial review, the presidential veto, and the congressional override) conferred on each of the three branches of government by which each restrains the others from exerting too much power

chief judge *n* : the principal, presiding, or most senior judge of esp. a lower level court or of a circuit

chief justice *n* : a chief judge of a usu. higher level court; *specif, often cap* : the chief justice of the U.S. Supreme Court — **chief jus·tice·ship** *n*

child *n, pl* **chil·dren 1** : a son or daughter of any age and usu. including one formally adopted — compare ISSUE ◊ The

\ə\abut \ᵊ\kitten \ər\further \a\ash \ā\ace
\ä\cot, cart \au̇\out \ch\chin \e\bet \ē\easy
\g\go \i\hit \ī\ice \j\job \ŋ\sing \ō\go \ȯ\law
\ȯi\boy \th\thin \t̲h̲\the \ü\loot \u̇\foot \y\yet
\zh\vision *see also* Pronunciation Symbols page

word *child* as used in a statute or will is often held to include a stepchild, an illegitimate child, a person for whom one stands in loco parentis, or sometimes a more remote descendant, such as a grandchild. In interpreting the word *child* as used in a will, the court will try to effectuate the intent of the person who made the will as it can be determined from the language of the will. **2** : a person below an age specified by law : INFANT, MINOR ⟨assault on a ~ under 16 years of age⟩ — compare ADULT ◊ A person who is below the statutory age but is married will usually be considered an adult.

child abuse *n* : ABUSE 2

child labor law *n* : a law regulating or prohibiting the employment of a person who is below a specified age

child support *n* : payment made for the support of the children of divorced or separated parents while the children are minors or until they reach an age set by the separation agreement or in a court order — compare ALIMONY ◊ Child support is usu. paid by the parent who is without custody. In the case of joint custody, both parents usu. pay child support.

chill *vt* : to discourage esp. through fear of penalty : have a chilling effect on ⟨statutes which may ~ the exercise of . . . free expression —M. H. Redish⟩

chilling effect *n* : a usu. undesirable discouraging effect or influence ⟨the *chilling effect* it will have on the assertion of legitimate claims —S. V. Bomse⟩ — used esp. of First Amendment violations

cho·ate \'kō-ət, -ˌāt\ *adj* [back-formation from *inchoate*] : being complete and superior to subsequent liens — see also *choate lien* at LIEN; compare INCHOATE — **cho·ate·ness** *n*

choate lien — see LIEN

choice of evils defense — see DEFENSE 2a

choice of law : an issue in conflicts of law as to what law (as among laws of different states or multiple federal laws) should be applied in a case — compare COMITY, FEDERALISM, FULL FAITH AND CREDIT

chop–shop \'chäp-ˌshäp\ *n* : a place where stolen automobiles are stripped of salable parts

chose \'shōz\ *n* [Anglo-French, literally, thing, from Old French, from Latin *causa* legal case, reason, cause] : a piece of personal property

   chose in action : a right to something (as payment of a debt or damages for injury) that can be recovered in a lawsuit; *also* : a document (as a check or stock certificate) embodying such a right

   chose in possession : something that is in one's actual possession or can be possessed

chose in action — see CHOSE

chose in possession — see CHOSE

churn \'chərn\ *vt* : to make (the account of a client) excessively active by frequent purchases and sales primarily in order to generate commissions ◊ Churning is a violation of federal securities laws.

CI *abbr* certificate of insurance; cost and insurance

CIA *abbr* Central Intelligence Agency — see also the IMPORTANT AGENCIES section

CID *abbr* civil investigative demand

C.I.F. *abbr* cost, insurance, and freight

cir·cuit *n* **1 a** : a route formerly taken by traveling judges **b** : a district established within a state or the federal judicial system — see also the JUDICIAL SYSTEM in the back matter **2** *cap* : the court of appeals for a circuit in the federal judicial system ⟨after the 9th *Circuit*'s ruling — V. M. Sher⟩

circuit court *n* : a court that sits in more than one place in a judicial district: as **a** : a state court usu. with original jurisdiction and sometimes with appellate jurisdiction **b** : any of the federal courts of appeals — not used technically; see also the JUDICIAL SYSTEM in the back matter ◊ Before 1948, the U.S. Courts of Appeals were known as Circuit Courts of Appeals.

circuit judge *n* : a judge who holds office in a circuit court

circuit justice *n* : a justice of the Supreme

Court of the United States who is also assigned to sit as a judge of a circuit court **cir·cum·stance** *n* **1 a :** a condition, fact, or event accompanying, conditioning, or determining another ⟨the ~*s* constituting fraud or mistake shall be stated —*Federal Rules of Civil Procedure* Rule 9(b)⟩ **b :** a piece of evidence that indicates the probability or improbability of an event ⟨a statement . . . offered to exculpate the accused is not admissible unless corroborating ~*s* clearly indicate the trustworthiness of the statement —*State v. Lopez*, 764 P.2d 1111 (1988)⟩ **2** *pl* **:** situation with regard to wealth ⟨the ~*s* of the parties before the divorce⟩

cir·cum·stan·tial \ˌsər-kəm-'stan-chəl\ *adj* **:** belonging to, consisting in, or dependent on circumstances — **cir·cum·stan·tial·ly** *adv*

circumstantial evidence — see EVIDENCE

ci·ta·tion \sī-'tā-shən\ *n* **1 :** a writ giving notice to a person to appear in court: as **a :** a process served upon an interested party in a probate proceeding **b :** a notice to a person that he or she is charged with a petty offense (as a traffic violation); *also* **:** the document embodying the notice ◊ Citations are issued in minor criminal cases as an alternative to arrest. Often a person may consent in writing to the penalty specified on the citation and forgo an appearance in court. **2 :** the citing of a previously decided case or recognized legal authority as support for an argument; *also* **:** the caption used for referring to such a case or authority esp. as published in a reporter — **ci·ta·tion·al** \-shə-nəl\ *adj*

ci·ta·tor \sī-'tā-tər, 'sī-ˌtā-\ *n* **:** a published list of cases, statutes, and other sources of law showing their subsequent history (as of being cited in other cases) and status (as in having been overruled by another case) — see also SHEPARDIZE

cite \'sīt\ *vt* **cit·ed; cit·ing** [Latin *citare* to rouse, call on, summon] **1 :** to demand the appearance of in court : serve with a citation ⟨had been *cited* for contempt⟩ ⟨you are hereby *cited* to show cause in the

Probate Court⟩ **2 :** to quote or refer to as a precedent or authority ⟨the plaintiff ~*s* several cases for the proposition⟩

cit·i·zen *n* [Anglo-French *citezein*, alteration of Old French *citeien*, from *cité* city] **1 :** a native or naturalized individual who owes allegiance to a government (as of a state or nation) and is entitled to the enjoyment of governmental protection and to the exercise of civil rights — see also *Scott v. Sandford* in the IMPORTANT CASES section, *Amendment XIV* to the CONSTITUTION in the back matter; compare RESIDENT ◊ Under the Fourteenth Amendment, "all persons born or naturalized in the United States, and subject to the jurisdiction thereof, are citizens of the United States and of the state wherein they reside." A person born outside of the U.S. to parents who were born or naturalized in the U.S. is also a citizen of the U.S. A corporation is not considered a citizen for purposes of the privileges and immunities clause of the Fourteenth Amendment. A corporation is, however, deemed a citizen of the state in which it is incorporated or has its principal place of business for purposes of diversity jurisdiction. **2 :** a resident of a town or state who is also a U.S. native or was naturalized in the U.S.

citizen in·for·mant \-in-'fȯr-mənt\ *n* **:** an informant who is motivated to assist law enforcement officers by good citizenship as distinguished from one seeking some gain (as payment or concessions from police) — called also *citizen informer* ◊ The information given by a citizen informant is presumed under the law to be reliable.

citizen's arrest — see ARREST

cit·i·zen·ship *n* **1 :** the status of being a citizen **2 :** the quality of an individual's behavior as a citizen **3 :** DOMICILE — used esp. in federal diversity cases;

\ə\abut	\ᵊ\kitten	\ər\further	\a\ash	\ā\ace
\ä\cot, cart	\au̇\out	\ch\chin	\e\bet	\ē\easy
\g\go	\i\hit	\ī\ice	\j\job	\ŋ\sing	\ō\go	\ȯ\law
\ȯi\boy	\th\thin	\t͟h\the	\ü\loot	\u̇\foot	\y\yet
\zh\vision	*see also* Pronunciation Symbols page

see also *diversity jurisdiction* at JURISDIC-TION

citizen suit *n* : a suit brought by citizens under a provision of an environmental law (as the Resource Conservation and Recovery Act) that gives citizens a private right of action against violators of the law and authorizes the court to award injunctive relief and sometimes to impose penalties

city attorney *n* : an attorney holding a public office whose function is to advise and represent the city in legal matters ◊ The office of the city attorney has many different titles. In some places the city attorney is called *city solicitor* or *city counselor*. At the town level, the title used is often *town counsel*. In Boston, the title *corporation counsel* is used. In Cleveland, it is *director of law*.

city clerk *n* : a public officer charged with recording the official proceedings and vital statistics of a city

city council *n* : the legislative body of a city

city court *n* : a court having jurisdiction over local civil matters and often petty criminal matters (as violations of city ordinances)

city solicitor *n* : CITY ATTORNEY

civ·ic \'si-vik\ *adj* : of or relating to a citizen, a city, citizenship, or civil affairs

civ·il \'si-vəl\ *adj* [Latin *civilis*, from *civis* citizen] 1 : concerning, befitting, or applying to individual citizens or to citizens as a whole ⟨a ~ duty⟩ — see also CIVIL RIGHT 2 : marked by public order : peaceable in behavior 3 : of or relating to a legal system based on Roman law as opposed to the English common law — see also the JUDICIAL SYSTEM in the back matter 4 : relating to private rights and to judicial proceedings in connection with them; *esp* : relating to legal matters other than those characterized as criminal ⟨a ~ action⟩ ⟨a ~ infraction⟩ 5 : defined by law : LEGAL ⟨a ~ disability⟩ 6 : of, relating to, or involving the general public, their activities, needs, ways, or civic affairs as distinguished from spe-

cial (as military or religious) affairs ⟨the ~ authorities⟩ ⟨the ~ service⟩ — **civ·il·ly** *adv*

civil arrest — see ARREST

civil assault — see ASSAULT

civil commitment *n* : court-ordered institutionalization of a person suffering from mental illness, alcoholism, or drug addiction usu. upon a finding that the person is dangerous to himself or herself or to others

civil conspiracy — see CONSPIRACY

civil contempt — see CONTEMPT

civil court *n* : a court having trial jurisdiction over usu. minor civil matters

civil damage act : DRAM SHOP ACT

civil death *n* : the status of a living person equivalent in its legal consequences to natural death; *specif* : deprivation of certain civil rights upon conviction for a serious crime

civil dis·obe·di·ence *n* : refusal to obey governmental demands or commands esp. as a nonviolent and usu. collective means of forcing concessions from the government

civil fruit — see FRUIT

1ci·vil·ian *n* : a specialist in Roman or modern civil law

2civilian *adj* : of or relating to civil law as distinguished from common law

civil law *n, often cap C&L* 1 : Roman law esp. as set forth in the Code of Justinian 2 : the body of law developed from Roman law and used in Louisiana, in continental Europe, and in many other countries outside of the English-speaking world including esp. those that were colonized by countries of continental Europe — see also the JUDICIAL SYSTEM in the back matter; compare COMMON LAW ◊ Although Louisiana is the only state in the U.S. whose law is based entirely on civil law, remnants of civil law remain in other states (as Texas and California) in which countries of continental Europe had a strong influence. 3 : the law established by a nation or state for its own jurisdiction 4 : the law that applies to private rights esp. as opposed to the law that applies to criminal matters — compare CRIMINAL LAW

civil liability — see LIABILITY 2b

civil liability act *n* : DRAM SHOP ACT

civil liberty *n* : freedom from arbitrary interference in one's pursuits (as in expressing thoughts, practicing a religion, or pursuing a living) by individuals or esp. by the government and esp. as constitutionally guaranteed — usu. used in pl.; see also CIVIL RIGHT

civil possession — see POSSESSION

civil procedure *n* : the steps taken and methods used in bringing and conducting a civil action; *also* : a course of study in the rules of procedure in civil actions

civil right *n* : CIVIL LIBERTY; *esp* : any of the civil liberties guaranteed by the 13th, 14th, and 15th Amendments to the Constitution and by the Civil Rights Acts — usu. used in pl.; see also *Civil Rights Act of 1964* in the IMPORTANT LAWS section

C.J. *abbr* **1** chief justice **2** chief judge

claim *n* [Old French, from *clamer* to call, claim, from Latin *clamare* to shout, proclaim] **1 a** : a demand for something (as money) due or believed to be due; *specif* : a demand for a benefit (as under the workers' compensation law) or contractual payment (as under an insurance policy) **b** : a paper embodying such a demand ⟨filing a ~ with the court⟩ **2** : a title to something (as a debt or privilege) in the possession of another ⟨assigned her ~ to the proceeds⟩ **3 a** : a right to seek a judicial remedy arising from a wrong or injury suffered ⟨a plaintiff who has been injured in an accident has ... one ~ for a broken arm, another for a ruptured spleen, and so forth —J. H. Friedenthal *et al.*⟩; *also* : the formal assertion of such a right ⟨bringing a ~ in the district court⟩ **b** : CAUSE OF ACTION 1 ⟨a plaintiff stated a ~ against a seller of applesauce when she alleged that her children ... ate the applesauce ... and were then so discomforted that they had to have their stomachs pumped —J. J. White and R. S. Summers⟩ — see also RES JUDICATA ◊ A cause of action may en-

compass more than one claim as the term is used in sense 3a. *Claim* is often used to mean *cause of action*, however, esp. in modern federal practice. **c** : a right to payment or to an equitable remedy as set forth in the Bankruptcy Code — see also PROOF OF CLAIM **4** : a formal assertion made by an applicant for a patent of the novelty and patentability of an invention with a description of the invention and its purpose — **claim** *vt*

claim and delivery *n* : a statutory action to obtain temporary possession of property held by another until title to the property is determined by final judgment of the court

claim·ant \'klā-mənt\ *n* : one that asserts a claim esp. formally

claim preclusion *n* : RES JUDICATA 2b

claims made policy *n* : an insurance policy providing coverage only for claims that are filed during the policy period — called also *discovery policy;* compare OCCURRENCE POLICY

class *n* : a group of persons or things having characteristics in common: as **a** : a group of persons who have some common relationship to a person making a will and are designated to receive a gift under the will but whose identities will not be determined until sometime in the future — see also *class gift* at GIFT **b** : a group of securities (as stocks or bonds) having similar distinguishing features (as voting rights or priority of redemption) **c** : a group whose members are represented in a class action **d** : PROTECTED CLASS **e** : a group of crimes forming a category distinguished by a common characteristic (as the use of violence or the requirement for a maximum penalty)⟨murder is a ~ A felony⟩

class action *n* : an action in which a representative plaintiff sues or a representative defendant is sued on behalf of a class of plaintiffs or defendants who have the same interests in the litigation as their representative and whose rights or liabilities can be more efficiently determined as a group than in a series of individual suits — called also *class action suit, class suit;* see also CERTIFICATION; compare CONSOLIDATE, JOINDER, *test case* at CASE ◇ Rule 23 of the Federal Rules of Civil Procedure sets out the prerequisites for having an action certified as a class action in federal court. Section (a) permits a class action if "(1) the class is so numerous that joinder of all members is impracticable, (2) there are questions of law or fact common to the class, (3) the claims or defenses of the representative parties are typical of the claims or defenses of the class, and (4) the representative parties will fairly and adequately protect the interests of the class." If the action satisfies these requirements, it must then fit into one of three categories: (1) where individual litigation would have varying results requiring the opposing party to act inconsistently toward the class members or would affect the interests of class members who are not parties to the individual action; (2) where the opposing party has acted or refused to act on grounds that are applicable to the class members as a whole and therefore injunctive or declaratory relief with respect to the class members as a whole is appropriate; or, (3) where the questions of law or fact common to the class members outweigh questions that apply to only particular individuals so that a class action is the best method to determine respective rights and liabilities. Using these guidelines, the judge will decide if an action should be certified as a class action.

class gift — see GIFT

clas·si·fi·ca·tion *n* : the act or method of distributing into a class or category according to characteristics; *also* : a class or category determined by characteristics — see also SUSPECT CLASSIFICATION

class suit *n* : CLASS ACTION

clause \'klòz\ *n* : a distinct section of a writing; *specif* : a distinct article, stipulation, or proviso in a formal document ⟨a no-strike ~ in the collective bargaining agreement⟩ — **claus·al** \'klò-zəl\ *adj*

Cl. Ct. *abbr* Claims Court

CLE *abbr* continuing legal education

clean *adj* : free of amendments or annotations

clean bill — see BILL 1

clean bill of lading — see BILL OF LADING

clean hands *n pl* : innocence of wrongdoing or deceit ⟨plaintiff must come into court with *clean hands*⟩ — see also CLEAN HANDS DOCTRINE

clean hands doctrine *n* : a doctrine that originated in equity and that bars a plaintiff from seeking judicial relief regarding a matter in which he or she is not free of guilt and does not have clean hands

clean–up doctrine *n* : a doctrine of jurisdiction that allows a court of chancery which has acquired jurisdiction in a case to decide both equitable and legal questions provided that the legal questions are incidental to the equitable ones

clear *adj* **1** : unencumbered by outstanding claims or interests ⟨a search showed the title was ~⟩ **2** : free from doubt or ambiguity

clear and con·vinc·ing *adj* : conforming to or being the standard of proof required for some civil cases or motions in which the party bearing the burden of proof must show that the truth of the allegations is highly probable ⟨*clear and convincing* proof⟩ — compare REASONABLE DOUBT, PREPONDERANCE OF THE EVIDENCE

clear and convincing evidence — see EVIDENCE

clear and pres·ent dan·ger *n* : a risk or threat to safety or other public interests that is serious and imminent; *esp* : one that justifies limitation of a right (as freedom of speech or press) by the legislative or executive branch of government ⟨a *clear and present danger* of harm to others or himself⟩ — see also FREEDOM OF SPEECH, *Schenck v. United States* in the IMPORTANT CASES section, *Amend-*

ment I to the CONSTITUTION in the back matter

clear error — see ERROR

clear·ing·house \'klir-iŋ-ˌhaůs\ *n* : an institution that arranges for payment of checks owed by one bank to another

clear·ly erroneous *adj* : being or containing a finding of fact that is not supported by substantial or competent evidence or by reasonable inferences ⟨findings of fact . . . shall not be set aside unless *clearly erroneous* —*Federal Rules of Civil Procedure* Rule 52(a)⟩ — see also *Amendment VII* to the CONSTITUTION in the back matter; compare ABUSE OF DISCRETION, DE NOVO ◊ The requirement that findings be clearly erroneous to be set aside is a standard of review used esp. by an appellate court when reviewing a trial judge's (as opposed to a jury's) findings of fact for error.

clear title — see TITLE

clem·en·cy \'kle-mən-sē\ *n, pl* **-cies** **1** : willingness or ability to moderate the severity of a punishment (as a sentence) **2** : an act or instance of mercy, compassion, or forgiveness — see also AMNESTY, COMMUTE, PARDON, REPRIEVE

¹clerk *n* **1** : an official responsible (as to a court) for correspondence, records, and accounts and having specified powers or authority (as to issue writs) ⟨a city ~⟩ ⟨~ of court⟩ **2 a** : a person employed to keep records or accounts or to perform general office work **b** : a person (as a law student or graduate) employed by an attorney or judge to assist with case-related tasks (as research) — compare PARALEGAL — **clerk·ship** *n*

²clerk *vi* : to act or work as a clerk ⟨*~ed* for a Supreme Court justice⟩

client security fund — see FUND 1

Clifford trust — see TRUST

¹close *vb* **closed; clos·ing** *vt* **1** : to bring to an end or to a state of completion ⟨*closed* the case⟩ ⟨~ an estate by liquidating its assets⟩ ⟨*closing* his account⟩ **2** : to conclude discussion or negotiation about; *also* : to bring to completion by performing something previously agreed

⟨*closing* a merger⟩ ⟨~ the property sale⟩ ~ *vi* **1** : to enter into or complete an agreement (as for the sale of real estate) ⟨they *closed* on the house⟩ **2** : to come to an end or to a state of completion ⟨after the class *closes*, the trust shall continue . . . until the death of the last surviving member of the class —*Louisiana Revised Statutes*⟩

²close *n* : an enclosed area ⟨break another's ~⟩

close corporation — see CORPORATION

closed *adj* **1** : confined to a few ⟨~ membership⟩ **2** : excluding outsiders or witnesses : conducted in secrecy ⟨~ hearings⟩

closed–end *adj* : having a fixed capitalization of shares that are traded on the market at prices determined by supply and demand ⟨a ~ investment company⟩ — compare OPEN-END

closed shop *n* : a business in which the employer by agreement hires and retains only union members — see also *Labor Management Relations Act* in the IMPORTANT LAWS section; compare OPEN SHOP, UNION SHOP ◊ Closed shops are illegal under the Labor Management Relations Act.

close·ly held \'klōs-lē-'held\ *adj* : having most stock shares and corporate voting rights in the hands of a few shareholders

closely held corporation *n* : CLOSE CORPORATION at CORPORATION

clos·ing \'klō-ziŋ\ *n* : the fulfillment or performance of a contract esp. for the sale of real estate; *also* : a meeting at which the closing of a contract takes place ⟨represented us at the ~⟩ ◊ At the closing for the completion of the sale of real property, the purchase price is paid and title is transferred to the purchaser or mortgagor.

closing argument *n* : the final address to the jury by the attorney for each side of

\ə\abut \ə\kitten \ər\further \a\ash \ā\ace \ä\cot, cart \aů\out \ch\chin \e\bet \ē\easy \g\go \i\hit \ī\ice \j\job \ŋ\sing \ō\go \ȯ\law \ȯi\boy \th\thin \t͟h\the \ü\loot \ů\foot \y\yet \zh\vision *see also* Pronunciation Symbols page

a case in which the attorney usu. summarizes the evidence and his or her client's position — called also *closing statement, final argument, summation, summing-up* ◊ Rule 29.1 of the Federal Rules of Criminal Procedure requires the prosecution to open the closing argument after the closing of the evidence. The defense replies, and the prosecution may offer a rebuttal.

clo•ture \'klō-chər\ *n* [French *clôture*, literally, closure] : the closing or limitation of debate in a legislative body esp. by calling for a vote — **cloture** *vt*

cloud on title : an interest (as a lien) in real property that if valid impairs the owner's title — compare QUIET

CMO \,sē-,em-'ō\ *n* : COLLATERALIZED MORTGAGE OBLIGATION

C.M.R. *abbr* Court of Military Review

C.N. *abbr* Code Napoleon — see also the IMPORTANT LAWS section

c\o *abbr* care of

co *abbr* 1 company 2 county

CO *abbr* 1 commanding officer 2 conscientious objector 3 corrections officer

co- *prefix* 1 : with : together : joint : jointly ⟨*co*defendant⟩ 2 a : associated in an action with another : fellow ⟨*co*-conspirator⟩ b : having a usu. lesser share in duty or responsibility : alternate : deputy ⟨*co*-counsel⟩

COBRA \'kō-brə\ *abbr* Consolidated Omnibus Budget Reconciliation Act of 1986 — see also *Employee Retirement Income Security Act* in the IMPORTANT LAWS section

co–con•spir•a•tor \,kō-kən-'spir-ə-tər\ *n* : a fellow conspirator ◊ Under Federal law, a statement made by a co-conspirator during and to further the conspiracy is admissible as evidence, but there must be other evidence establishing both the conspiracy and the defendant's participation.

co–coun•sel \,kō-'kaùn-səl\ *n* : an attorney who assists in or shares the responsibility of representing a client

COD *abbr* cash on delivery, collect on delivery

code *n* [Old French, from Medieval Latin

codex, from Latin *caudex, codex* tree trunk, set of wood writing tablets, book] 1 : a systematic compilation or revision of law or legal principles that is arranged esp. by subject: as **a** : one that contains the law of a specific jurisdiction or topic promulgated by legislative authority ⟨U.S. *Code*⟩ ⟨*Code* of Massachusetts Regulations⟩ ⟨building ~⟩ — see also IMPORTANT LAWS in the back matter; compare CASE LAW, DIGEST, STATUTE **b** : one that serves as a model for legislation but is not itself a law ⟨Model Penal *Code*⟩ 2 : a set of rules or regulations that is promulgated by a body (as a professional organization) and that regulates its industrial or professional practices ⟨ABA *Code* of Professional Responsibility⟩

co•debt•or \,kō-'de-tər\ *n* : one that shares liability for a debt : a fellow debtor

co•de•fen•dant \,kō-di-'fen-dənt, -,dant\ *n* : a joint defendant

code pleading — see PLEADING 2

cod•i•cil \'kä-də-səl, -,sil\ *n* [Latin *codicillus*, literally, writing tablet, diminutive of *codic-, codex* book — see CODE] : a formally executed document made after a will that adds to, subtracts from, or changes the will — see also REPUBLISH

cod•i•fy \'kä-də-,fī, 'kō-\ *vt* **-fied; -fy•ing** : to reduce (laws) to a code — **cod•i•fi•ca•tion** \,kä-də-fə-'kā-shən, ,kō-\ *n*

co•erce \kō-'ərs\ *vt* **co•erced; co•erc•ing** : to subject (a person) to coercion — compare IMPORTUNE, SOLICIT

co•er•cion \kō-'ər-zhən, -shən\ *n* : the use of express or implied threats of violence or reprisal (as discharge from employment) or other intimidating behavior that puts a person in immediate fear of the consequences in order to compel that person to act against his or her will ; *also* : the defense that one acted under coercion — see also DEFENSE, DURESS; compare UNDUE INFLUENCE

co•er•cive \kō-'ər-siv\ *adj* 1 : serving or intended to coerce 2 : resulting from coercion ⟨to protect women from ~ intimacy —Kimberle Crenshaw⟩

co–fel·on \ˌkō-'fe-lən\ *n* : one who commits a felony with another

cog·ni·za·ble \'käg-nə-zə-bəl, käg-'nī-\ *adj* **1** : capable of being known; *specif* : capable of being recognized as a group because of a common characteristic (as race or gender) ◊ Systematic exclusion of members of a cognizable group from a jury violates the Sixth Amendment to the Constitution, which requires that jurors be selected from jury pools that represent a fair cross section of the community. **2** : capable of being judicially heard and determined ⟨a ~ claim⟩

cog·ni·zance \'käg-nə-zəns\ *n* [Old French *connoissance* right to acknowledge and adjudicate issues, literally, knowledge, acquaintance, from *connoistre* to be acquainted with] : JURISDICTION

cog·no·vit clause \käg-'nō-vit-, kòg-'nō-wit-\ *n* [New Latin *cognovit (actionem)* he\she has acknowledged (the action)] : a clause in an agreement in which one party authorizes the entry of judgment against himself or herself in the event of his or her breach or default

cognovit judgment — see JUDGMENT 1a

cognovit note — see NOTE

co·hab·it \kō-'ha-bət\ *vi* : to live together as a married couple or in the manner of a married couple — **co·hab·i·ta·tion** \kō-ˌha-bə-'tā-shən\ *n*

co·heir \ˌkō-'er\ *n* : a joint heir

co·in·sur·ance \ˌkō-in-'shùr-əns, kō-'in-ˌshùr-\ *n* **1** : joint assumption of risk (as by two underwriters) with another **2** : insurance (as fire insurance) in which the insured is obligated to maintain coverage on a risk at a stipulated percentage of its total value or in the event of loss to suffer a penalty in proportion to the deficiency

co·in·sure \ˌkō-in-'shùr\ *vt* : to insure jointly — **co·in·sur·er** *n*

COLA \'kō-lə\ *abbr* **1** cost-of-living adjustment **2** cost-of-living allowance

cold blood \'kōld-'bləd\ *n* : a state of mind marked by premeditation and deliberateness — usu. used in the phrase *in cold blood* ⟨killed the victim in *cold blood*⟩; compare COOL STATE OF BLOOD, HEAT OF

PASSION — **cold–blood·ed** \'kōld-'blə-dəd\ *adj*

co·leg·a·tee \ˌkō-ˌle-gə-'tē\ *n* : a joint legatee

col·lab·o·rate \kə-'la-bə-ˌrāt\ *vi* **-rat·ed; -rat·ing** : to work jointly with others in some endeavor

col·late \kə-'lāt, kä-, kō-; 'kä-ˌlāt, 'kō-\ *vb* **-lat·ed; -lat·ing** [back-formation from *collation*, from Latin *collatio (bonorum)* bringing together (of property) for distribution to heirs] *vt, in the civil law of Louisiana* : to return to an estate for equal division ⟨children or grandchildren, coming to the succession of their fathers, mothers or other ascendants, must ~ what they have received —*Louisiana Civil Code*⟩ ~ *vi, in the civil law of Louisiana* : to return property or legacies to an estate for division ⟨shall then be obliged to ~ up to the sum necessary —*Louisiana Civil Code*⟩

¹col·lat·er·al \kə-'la-tə-rəl, -'la-trəl\ *adj* **1 a** : accompanying as a secondary fact, activity, or agency but subordinate to a main consideration **b** : not directly relevant or material ⟨a ~ evidentiary matter⟩ ⟨a ~ issue⟩ **2** : belonging to the same ancestral stock but not in a direct line of descent — compare LINEAL **3 a** : of, relating to, or being collateral used as a security (as for payment of a debt) **b** : secured by collateral ⟨a ~ loan⟩ — **col·lat·er·al·ly** *adj*

²collateral *n* **1** : a collateral relative **2** : property pledged by a borrower to protect the interests of the lender in the event of the borrower's default; *specif, under Article 9 of the Uniform Commercial Code* : property subject to a security interest

collateral agreement *n* : an agreement related to and consistent with but independent of a larger written agreement

collateral attack — see ATTACK

collateral estoppel — see ESTOPPEL 2a

\ə\abut \ᵊ\kitten \ər\further \a\ash \ā\ace
\ä\cot, cart \aù\out \ch\chin \e\bet \ē\easy
\g\go \i\hit \ī\ice \j\job \ŋ\sing \ō\go \ò\law
\òi\boy \th\thin \t͟h\the \ü\loot \ù\foot \y\yet
\zh\vision *see also* Pronunciation Symbols page

collateral fact — see FACT

collateral fraud — see FRAUD

col·lat·er·al·ize \kə-'la-tə-rə-,līz, -'la-trə-\ *vt* **-ized; -iz·ing 1 :** to make (a loan) secure with collateral **2 :** to use (as securities) for collateral

collateralized mortgage obligation *n* **:** a bond collateralized by a pool of mortgage obligations or pass-through securities and paid according to the maturity and amortization schedule of its class and not directly from the underlying obligations — called also *CMO;* see also REMIC; compare *pass-through security* at SECURITY, TRANCHE

collateral mortgage — see MORTGAGE

collateral negligence — see NEGLIGENCE

collateral note — see NOTE

collateral order doc·trine \-'däk-trən\ *n* **:** an exception to the final judgment rule that allows review of orders conclusively determining a disputed question when the question is independent and separable from the rest of the case for purposes of review and is too important to be denied review until the rest of the case is adjudicated

collateral power — see POWER 2b

collateral proceeding — see PROCEEDING

collateral promise — see PROMISE

collateral source rule *n* **:** a rule in torts: the amount of damages to be paid to a plaintiff by a defendant will not be reduced by payments received by the plaintiff from other sources (as medical insurance)

col·la·tion \kə-'lā-shən, kä-, kō-\ *n* [French, from Latin *collatio bonorum* (in Roman law) contribution made by emancipated heirs to an estate under an intestate succession, literally, bringing together of goods] *in the civil law of Louisiana* **:** the actual or supposed return of goods to the mass of the succession that is made by an heir who received property in advance for the purpose of having the property divided with the rest of the succession — compare HOTCHPOT ◊ Children and grandchildren of a decedent must return anything that they received in advance by donation inter vivos. Further, they cannot claim legacies made to them unless made expressly by the decedent as an advantage over their coheirs to be received besides their portion of the succession. Donations made to a grandchild by a grandparent during the life of the child's father are not subject to collation. A collation may be made in kind by the actual delivering up of the thing given, or by taking less from the succession in proportion to the value of the thing received in advance.

collecting bank — see BANK

col·lec·tion by affidavit : a procedure available for small estates in some states as an alternative to court administration in which a person named in a will may file an affidavit asserting his or her entitlement to payment after a waiting period — compare SUMMARY DISTRIBUTION

col·lec·tive \kə-'lek-tiv\ *adj* **:** involving all members of a group as distinct from individual members — **col·lec·tive·ly** *adv*

collective bargaining *n* **:** negotiation between an employer and a labor union usu. on wages, benefits, hours, and working conditions — see also *bargaining agent* at AGENT, BARGAINING UNIT, *Labor Management Relations Act* in the IMPORTANT LAWS section

collective bargaining agent — see AGENT

collective bargaining agreement *n* **:** an agreement between an employer and a labor union produced through collective bargaining **:** LABOR CONTRACT at CONTRACT

collective bargaining unit *n* **:** BARGAINING UNIT

collective mark *n* **:** a trademark or a service mark of a group (as a cooperative association)

col·lo·qui·um \kə-'lō-kwē-əm\ *n* [Latin, talk, discussion, from *colloqui* to converse] **:** the part of a complaint for defamation in which the plaintiff avers that the defamatory remarks related to him or her

col·lo·quy \'kä-lə-kwē\ *n* **:** a discussion during a hearing between the judge and the defendant usu. to ascertain the defendant's understanding of his or her rights and of the court proceedings

col·lude \kə-'lüd\ *vi* **col·lud·ed; col·lud·ing** : to agree or cooperate secretly for a fraudulent or otherwise illegal purpose

col·lu·sion \kə-'lü-zhən\ *n* : the act or an instance of colluding — **col·lu·sive** \-siv\ *adj*

collusive joinder — see JOINDER

Coll·yer Doc·trine \'käl-yər-'däk-trən\ *n* [from *Collyer Insulated Wire*, 192 N.L.R.B. 837 (1971), the ruling that resulted in it] : a doctrine in labor law under which the National Labor Relations Board will defer an issue brought before it to arbitration if the issue can be resolved under the collective bargaining agreement in arbitration — compare SPIELBERG DOCTRINE

col·or *n* : a legal claim to or appearance of a right or authority ⟨threats that gave ~ to an act of self-defense⟩ — usu. used in the phrase *under color of* ⟨a police officer held liable for violating the plaintiff's civil rights under ~ of state law⟩ ⟨a second "search" under ~ of warrant — W. R. LaFave and J. H. Israel⟩

col·or·able *adj* : having an appearance of truth, validity, or right ⟨if a ~ claim — or better — can be pleaded —D. F. Kolb and M. P. Carroll⟩ — **col·or·ably** *adv*

Colorado River abstention — see ABSTENTION

color of office : the pretense or appearance of official authority in one who is without the authority claimed

color of title 1 : an apparent but invalid title based upon a written instrument or record; *also* : the instrument itself **2** : an apparent ownership claimed by adverse possession

co–mak·er \'kō-,mā-kər\ *n* : one of two or more persons who sign an instrument to indicate a promise to pay a financial obligation ◊ Any co-maker may be sued for the entire amount of the indebtedness, although a co-maker who is forced to pay more than his or her share may seek contribution from the other co-makers.

com·bi·na·tion *n* **1 a** : an alliance of individuals, states, or esp. corporations united to achieve a common (as economic) end — see also COMBINATION IN RESTRAINT OF TRADE; compare JOINT VENTURE 1, MERGER **b** : CONSPIRACY 2 : a union of old or new elements or parts that is patentable because it produces a new and useful result — compare AGGREGATION 2, EQUIVALENT

combination in restraint of trade : any monopoly or attempt at monopoly or any contract, combination, or conspiracy intended to restrain trade or commerce that violates the anti-trust laws — see also *Sherman Antitrust Act* in the IMPORTANT LAWS section

come down *vi* **came down; coming down** : to be announced ⟨the decision *came down* from the Supreme Court⟩

come for·ward *vi* : to make a presentation of something to the court — usu. used with *with* ⟨must *come forward* with materials to show that there is a genuine issue of fact —J. H. Friedenthal *et al.*⟩ ⟨*coming forward* with the evidence⟩

come on *vi* : to be brought forward (as a case in court) ⟨the first prize case of the war . . . *came on* for trial —W. G. Young⟩

co·mi·ty \'kä-mə-tē, 'kō-\ *n* **1** : COMITY OF NATIONS **2** : the informal and voluntary recognition by courts of one jurisdiction of the laws and judicial decisions of another — called also *judicial comity;* compare CHOICE OF LAW, FEDERALISM, FULL FAITH AND CREDIT

comity of na·tions \-'nā-shənz\ **1** : the courtesy and friendship of nations marked esp. by mutual recognition of executive, legislative, and judicial acts **2** : the group of nations practicing international comity

com·ment *n* **1** *often cap* **a** : an essay analyzing, criticizing, or explaining a subject ⟨a ~ published in the Yale Law Review⟩ **b** : an explanatory remark appended to

\ə\abut \ə\kitten \ər\further \a\ash \ā\ace \ä\cot, cart \aú\out \ch\chin \e\bet \ē\easy \g\go \i\hit \ī\ice \j\job \ŋ\sing \ō\go \ò\law \òi\boy \th\thin \th\the \ü\loot \ù\foot \y\yet \zh\vision *see also* Pronunciation Symbols page

a section of text (as of enacted code) **2** : an expression of an opinion or attitude about something: as **a** : a remark to a jury by a judge or prosecutor about evidence ◊ A prosecutor may not remark to the jury that a defendant's failure to testify implies guilt, and a judge may not remark to the jury his or her opinion about what the evidence does or does not prove. **b** : a written expression of opinion or information solicited by an agency about a subject of its rulemaking — see also INFORMAL RULEMAKING

com·merce *n* **1** : the exchange or buying and selling of goods, commodities, property, or services esp. on a large scale and involving transportation from place to place : TRADE **2** — see also COMMERCE CLAUSE, *Fair Labor Standards Act* in the IMPORTANT LAWS section **2** : the act of engaging in sexual intercourse

commerce clause *n, often cap both Cs* : a clause in Article I, Section 8 of the U.S. Constitution that empowers Congress to regulate interstate commerce and commerce with foreign countries and that forms the constitutional basis for much federal regulation — see also *Article I* of the CONSTITUTION in the back matter

commerce power — see POWER 2a

com·mer·cial *adj* : of or relating to commerce ⟨~ regulations⟩ — **com·mer·cial·ly** *adv*

commercial bank — see BANK

commercial disparagement *n* : DISPARAGEMENT 1

commercial frustration *n* : FRUSTRATION

commercial impracticability *n* : IMPRACTICABILITY 2

commercial law *n* : the legal rules and principles bearing on commercial transactions and business organizations — see also *Uniform Commercial Code* in the IMPORTANT LAWS section

commercial letter of credit — see LETTER OF CREDIT

commercially reasonable *adj* : fair, done in good faith, and corresponding to commonly accepted commercial practices ⟨a secured party after default may sell . . .

the collateral in its then condition or following any *commercially reasonable* preparation — *Uniform Commercial Code*⟩

commercial paper — see PAPER

commercial partnership — see PARTNERSHIP

commercial speech *n* : speech (as advertising) that proposes a commercial transaction — compare PURE SPEECH, SYMBOLIC SPEECH ◊ Commercial speech is entitled to a lesser level of protection under the First Amendment than speech which is an expression of one's thoughts.

commercial unit *n* : an item or group of items defined under section 2-105 of the Uniform Commercial Code as being viewed in commerce as a single whole that would be diminished in value if divided ◊ Under U.C.C. section 2-606, when a part of a commercial unit is accepted by a buyer, the entire commercial unit is deemed to be accepted.

com·min·gle \kə-'miŋ-gəl, kä-\ *vb* **-gled; -gling** *vt* : to combine (funds or properties) into a common fund or stock ~ *vi* : to become commingled

com·mis·sion *n* **1** : a formal written authorization to perform various acts and duties ⟨a notary's ~⟩ **2 a** : authority to act for, in behalf of, or in place of another **b** : a task or matter entrusted to one as the agent for another **3 a** : a group of persons directed to perform a duty **b** *usu cap* : a government agency ⟨Federal Trade *Commission*⟩ — see also AGENCY **c** : a city council having legislative and executive functions **4** : an act of committing something ⟨~ of the crime⟩ **5** : a fee paid to an agent or employee for transacting a piece of business or performing a service; *esp* : a percentage of the money received paid to the agent responsible for the business — **commission** *vt*

com·mis·sion·er *n* : a person with a commission: as **a** : a member of a commission **b** *often cap* : the officer in charge of a government agency ⟨a police ~⟩

com·mit *vb* **com·mit·ted; com·mit·ting** *vt* **1 a** : to put into another's charge or trust

: ENTRUST, CONSIGN ⟨*committed* her children to her sister's care⟩ **b** : to place in a prison or mental hospital esp. by judicial order ⟨was found to be gravely disabled and was involuntarily *committed* to the Central Louisiana State Hospital — *In the Matter of K.G.*, 531 So. 2d 575 (1988)⟩ — compare INSTITUTIONALIZE, INTERDICT **c** : to send (as a legislative bill) to a committee for consideration and report ⟨~ the crime bill to the joint committee⟩ **2** : to carry into action deliberately : PERPETRATE ⟨to define and punish piracies and felonies *committed* on the high seas — *U.S. Constitution* art. I⟩ **3** : OBLIGATE, BIND ~ *vi* : to obligate or bind oneself ⟨would not ~ to the irrevocable order⟩

commitment *n* **1** : an act of committing: as **a** : placement in or assignment to a prison or mental hospital ⟨petition for ~⟩ — compare INCOMPETENT, INTERDICTION ◊ Commitment to a mental health facility is called *civil commitment* when it is not part of a criminal proceeding. Civil commitment proceedings are initiated by the patient, in the case of voluntary commitment, or by someone (as a family member or government agent) authorized by statute to petition for the patient's involuntary commitment. Some form of a hearing and periodic review is required in involuntary commitment proceedings. A criminal defendant may be committed to a mental hospital as a result of being found incompetent to stand trial, not guilty by reason of insanity, or incompetent to be sentenced. **b** : an act of referring a matter to a legislative committee **c** : a warrant committing someone to a prison **2** : an agreement or promise to do something in the future; *esp* : a promise to assume a financial obligation at a future date ⟨cannot meet their loan ~*s*⟩

com·mit·tee *n* **1** : a person to whom a charge (as an incompetent) is committed — compare CONSERVATOR, CURATOR, GUARDIAN, TUTOR **2 a** : a body of persons delegated or assigned to consider, investigate, act on, or report on

some matter; *esp* : a group of fellow legislators chosen by a legislative body to consider legislative matters (as drafting bills or conducting hearings) ⟨the Senate judiciary ~⟩ — see also CONFERENCE COMMITTEE, JOINT COMMITTEE **b** : a private organization for the promotion of a common object ⟨political action ~*s*⟩ — compare COUNCIL

committee of the whole : the whole membership of a legislative house (as the House of Representatives) sitting as a committee and operating under informal parliamentary rules — called also *Committee of the Whole House on the State of the Union*

com·mo·da·tum \ˌkä-mə-ˈdā-təm, ˌkō-mō-ˈdä-tùm\ *n* [Latin, loan, from neuter of *commodatus*, past participle of *commodare* to lend, bestow] : a gratuitous loan of movable property to be used and returned by the borrower : LOAN FOR USE at LOAN — compare DEPOSIT, *gratuitous bailment* at BAILMENT, *loan for consumption* at LOAN

com·mod·i·ty \kə-ˈmä-də-tē\ *n, pl* **-ties** : a class of economic goods; *esp* : an item of merchandise (as soybeans) whose price is the basis of futures trading

¹com·mon *adj* **1 a** : of or relating to a community at large : PUBLIC ⟨~ defense⟩ **b** : known to the community ⟨a ~ thief⟩ **2** : belonging to or shared by two or more persons or things or by all members of a group ⟨when the insured and the beneficiary perish in a ~ disaster⟩ ⟨~ areas of the building⟩ **3** : of or relating to common stock ⟨~ shares⟩

²common *n* **1** *pl, cap* : HOUSE OF COMMONS **2** : the legal right of taking a profit in another's land in common with the owner or others ⟨the ~ of estovers⟩ ⟨the ~ of pasture⟩ **3** : a piece of land subject to common use: as **a** : land jointly owned and used esp. for pasture **b** : a public

\ə\abut \ᵊ\kitten \ər\further \a\ash \ā\ace
\ä\cot, cart \aù\out \ch\chin \e\bet \ē\easy
\g\go \i\hit \ī\ice \j\job \ŋ\sing \ō\go \ò\law
\ói\boy \th\thin \th̲\the \ü\loot \ù\foot \y\yet
\zh\vision *see also* Pronunciation Symbols page

open area in a municipality **4** : a condition of shared ownership : a condition in which a right is shared with an interest held by another person ⟨held the estate in ~⟩ — see also *tenancy in common* at TENANCY; compare SEVERALTY 1 **5** : COMMON STOCK at STOCK

common carrier *n* : a business or agency that is available to the public for transportation of persons, goods, or messages — compare CONTRACT CARRIER

common easement — see EASEMENT

common law *n* : a body of law that is based on custom and general principles and embodied in case law and that serves as precedent or is applied to situations not covered by statute ⟨the *common law* of torts⟩: as **a** : the body of law that was first developed in the English courts of law as distinguished from equity and that allows for particular remedies (as damages or replevin) ⟨in suits at *common law* . . . the right of trial by jury shall be preserved —*U.S. Constitution* amend. VII⟩ — compare EQUITY 2 **b** : the body of law developed in England that is the basis of U.S. federal law and of state law in all states except Louisiana — see also the JUDICIAL SYSTEM in the back matter; compare CIVIL LAW 2, STATUTORY LAW

common–law *adj* **1** : of, relating to, or based on the common law ⟨*common-law* immunity⟩ **2** : relating to or based on a common-law marriage ⟨her *common-law* husband⟩

common–law copyright *n* : a copyright in common law protecting unpublished works ◊ Works created after January 1, 1978, are protected by statutory rather than common-law copyright while unpublished.

common–law lien — see LIEN

common–law marriage *n* : a marriage that is without a ceremony and is based on the parties' agreement to consider themselves married and usu. also on their cohabitation for a period and their public recognition of the marriage — compare CONCUBINAGE ◊ Most jurisdictions no longer allow this type of marriage to be formed, although they may recognize such marriages formed prior to a certain date or formed in a jurisdiction that does permit common-law marriages.

common–law trust — see TRUST

common nuisance — see NUISANCE

Common Pleas *n* : COURT OF COMMON PLEAS

common property — see PROPERTY

common stock — see STOCK

common trust fund — see FUND 1

com·mon·wealth \'kä-mən-,welth\ *n* **1** : a nation, state, or other political unit: as **a** : one founded on law and united by compact or tacit agreement by the people for the common good **b** : one in which supreme authority is vested in the people **c** : REPUBLIC **2** : a state of the U.S. — used officially of Kentucky, Massachusetts, Pennsylvania, and Virginia **3** *often cap* : an association of self-governing autonomous states more or less loosely associated in a common allegiance (as to the British crown) **4** *often cap* : a political unit having local autonomy but voluntarily united with the U.S. — used officially of Puerto Rico and the Northern Mariana Islands

Commonwealth Court *n* : a court in Pennsylvania that hears cases involving administrative agencies or other governmental bodies

com·mu·ni·ca·tion \kə-,myü-nə-'kā-shən\ *n* : the expression to another of information or thoughts through speech, writing, or gestures — see also CONFIDENTIAL COMMUNICATION, PRIVILEGED COMMUNICATION

com·mu·ni·ca·tive \kə-'myü-nə-,kā-tiv, -kə-tiv\ *adj* **1** : tending or serving to communicate ⟨a ~ gesture⟩ **2** : of or relating to communication

communicative evidence — see EVIDENCE

com·mu·ni·ty *n, pl* **-ties 1** : the people who live in a particular place or region and usu. are linked by some common interests **2 a** : the mass of community property owned by a husband and wife ⟨a spouse may not . . . lease to a third person his undivided interest in the ~ or in particular things of the ~ —*Louisiana Civil Code*⟩ **b :** the entity created upon the marriage of a husband and wife for the purposes of ownership of property in community property states ⟨an agreement terminating the ~⟩ — see also *community property* at PROPERTY, REGIME

community property — see PROPERTY

commutative contract — see CONTRACT

com·mute \kə-'myüt\ *vt* **com·mut·ed; com·mut·ing 1 :** to convert (as a payment) into another form **2 :** to change (a penalty) to one less severe esp. out of clemency — compare PARDON — **com·mu·ta·tion** \ˌkä-myə-'tā-shən\ *n* — **com·mu·ta·tive** \kə-'myü-tə-tiv, 'kä-myə-ˌtā-tiv\ *adj*

companion case — see CASE 1a

com·pa·ny *n, pl* **-nies :** an association of persons for carrying on a commercial or industrial enterprise — compare CORPORATION, PARTNERSHIP

finance company **:** a company that makes usu. small short-term loans to individuals

growth company **:** a company that grows at a greater rate than the economy as a whole and that usu. directs a relatively high proportion of income back into the business

holding company **:** a company whose sole function is to own and control other companies

investment company **:** a company that earns income solely or primarily by holding and investing in securities issued by other companies or by government agencies

joint-stock company **:** a business organization whose capital is represented by shares owned by stockholders each of whom is personally liable for the company's debts

limited liability company **:** an unincorporated company formed under applicable state statute whose members cannot be held liable for the acts, debts, or obligations of the company and that may elect to be taxed as a partnership

mutual company **:** an insurance company whose capital is owned by its policyholders

surety company **:** a company that provides surety bonds for a fee

trust company **:** a company and often a commercial bank acting as trustee for individuals and businesses and providing related financial or estate planning services

company union *n* **:** an unaffiliated labor union of the employees of a single company ◊ Historically, the company union was one formed or dominated by the company. Such unions have been long held to be illegal.

com·pa·ra·ble worth \'käm-pə-rə-bəl-'wərth, 'käm-prə-\ *n* **:** the concept that women and men should receive equal pay for jobs calling for comparable skill and responsibility

com·par·a·tive \kəm-'par-ə-tiv\ *adj* **:** characterized by systematic comparison ⟨~ contribution, which apportions according to . . . respective fault —W. L. Prosser and W. P. Keeton⟩ — **com·par·a·tive·ly** *adv*

comparative fault *n* **:** a doctrine in torts in which the fault attributable to each party is compared and any award to the plaintiff is reduced in proportion to the plaintiff's share of the fault **:** COMPARATIVE NEGLIGENCE b at NEGLIGENCE — compare *contributory negligence* at NEGLIGENCE, *strict liability* at LIABILITY 2b

comparative law *n* **:** the study of the differences, similarities, and interrelationships of different systems of law

comparative negligence — see NEGLIGENCE

com·pel \kəm-'pel\ *vt* **com·pelled; com·pel·ling :** to cause to do or occur by overwhelming pressure and esp. by authority or law ⟨cannot ~ the defendant to testify⟩ ⟨the result . . . is *compelled* by, the

\ə\abut \ᵊ\kitten \ər\further \a\ash \ā\ace \ä\cot, cart \aú\out \ch\chin \e\bet \ē\easy \g\go \i\hit \ī\ice \j\job \ŋ\sing \ō\go \ȯ\law \ȯi\boy \th\thin \th\the \ü\loot \ù\foot \y\yet \zh\vision *see also* Pronunciation Symbols page

original understanding of the fourteenth amendment's equal protection clause — R. H. Bork⟩

compelling *adj* : that compels : tending to demand action or to convince ⟨a ~ need for disclosure⟩ ⟨a ~ argument⟩

compelling state interest — see INTEREST 3a

com·pen·sa·ble \kəm-'pen-sə-bəl\ *adj* : entitling an individual to compensation ⟨a ~ job-related injury⟩

com·pen·sate \'käm-pən-ˌsāt, -ˌpen-\ *vt* **-sat·ed; -sat·ing** : to make an appropriate and usu. counterbalancing payment to ⟨~the victims for their injuries⟩ ⟨adequately *compensated* for her work⟩ — **com·pensa·to·ry** \kəm-'pen-sə-ˌtōr-ē\ *adj*

compensated bailment *n* : BAILMENT FOR HIRE at BAILMENT

com·pen·sa·tion \ˌkäm-pən-'sā-shən\ *n* **1** : the act of compensating **2** *in the civil law of Louisiana* : the ending of mutual obligations between two people for money or quantities of fungible things usu. by operation of law but sometimes by an agreement **3** : something that makes up for a loss ⟨received ~ for the breach of contract⟩; *specif* : payment to unemployed or injured workers or their dependents — see also UNEMPLOYMENT COMPENSATION, WORKERS' COMPENSATION **4** : payment for a thing of value tendered or a service rendered ⟨the Senators and Representatives shall receive ~ for their services — *U.S. Constitution* art. I⟩

compensatory damages *n* : ACTUAL DAMAGES at DAMAGE 2

com·pe·tence \'käm-pə-təns\ *n* : the quality or state of being competent: as **a** : possession of sufficient knowledge or skill **b** : legal authority, ability, or admissibility ⟨a court of general ~⟩ ⟨the ~ of witnesses⟩ ⟨challenge the ~ of the evidence⟩

com·pe·ten·cy \'käm-pə-tən-sē\ *n* **1** : the quality or state of being mentally competent — compare CAPACITY, INCOMPETENCE, INSANITY **2** : the quality or state

of being legally qualified or adequate ⟨the ~, quantum and legal effect of evidence — *State v. Scoggin*, 72 S.E.2d 54 (1952)⟩

com·pe·tent \'käm-pə-tənt\ *adj* **1** : having or showing requisite or adequate ability or qualities ⟨a ~ lawyer⟩ ⟨~ representation by counsel⟩ **2 a** : free from addiction or mental defect that renders one incapable of taking care of oneself or one's property **b** : capable of understanding one's position as a criminal defendant and the nature of the criminal proceedings and able to participate in one's defense — compare CAPACITY, INCOMPETENT, INSANITY **3** : legally qualified or adequate: as **a** : having the necessary power or authority ⟨a judge of ~ jurisdiction — *U.S. Code*⟩ **b** : qualified for presentation in court : admissible as evidence or capable of giving admissible evidence ⟨a ~ witness⟩ **c** : INTELLIGENT ⟨a ~ waiver⟩

competent evidence — see EVIDENCE

com·pi·la·tion \ˌkäm-pə-'lā-shən\ *n* : a collection of preexisting materials and data so arranged to form a new original work under the law of copyright

com·plain *vi* : to make a complaint

com·plain·ant \kəm-'plā-nənt\ *n* : the party (as a plaintiff or petitioner) who makes the complaint in a legal action or proceeding

com·plaint *n* **1** : the initial pleading that starts a lawsuit and that sets forth the allegations made by the plaintiff against the defendant and the plaintiff's demand for relief — see also PRAYER, PROCESS, WELL-PLEADED COMPLAINT RULE; compare ANSWER **2** : a document sworn to by a victim or police officer that sets forth a criminal violation and that serves as the charging instrument by which charges are filed and judicial proceedings commenced against a defendant in a magistrate's court — compare DECLARATION, INDICTMENT, INFORMATION **3** : PETITION

complete defense : DEFENSE 2a

completed gift — see GIFT

com·plete diversity *n* : diversity of citizenship in which the citizenship of all the plaintiffs to an action differs from that of all the defendants — see also DIVERSITY OF CITIZENSHIP, *diversity jurisdiction* at JURISDICTION; compare MINIMAL DIVERSITY

complete interdiction *n* : INTERDICTION 1

completion bond — see BOND 1a

complex trust — see TRUST

com•pli•ance \kəm-'plī-əns\ *n* **1** : an act or process of complying with a demand or recommendation **2** : observance of official requirements

com•po•nent part \kəm-'pō-nənt-, 'käm-ˌpō-nənt-\ *n* : something (as a building or part of a building) that cannot be removed without substantial damage to itself or to the immovable property to which it is attached

com•po•si•tion *n* : an agreement between an insolvent debtor and several creditors whereby partial payment of the debts discharges in full the original obligations — compare ACCORD, COMPROMISE

com•pos men•tis \'käm-pəs-'men-təs, 'kȯm-pȯs-'men-tis\ *adj* [Latin, literally, having possession of one's mind] : COMPETENT

com•pound \kəm-'paȯnd\ *vt* **1** : to agree for a consideration not to prosecute (an offense) ◇ Compounding a felony is a common-law crime. **2** : to pay (interest) on both the accrued interest and the principal

compound interest — see INTEREST 5

com•pre•hen•sive \ˌkäm-pri-'hen-siv\ *adj* : covering completely or broadly ⟨a ~insurance policy⟩

comprehensive general liability insurance *n* : liability insurance for a business that usu. covers losses from products liability, premises liability, and some liabilities that the insured assumes under a contract (as a lease)

¹com•pro•mise *n* : an agreement resolving differences by mutual concessions esp. to prevent or end a lawsuit

²compromise *vb* **-mised; -mis•ing** *vt* : to resolve or dispose of by a compromise ⟨cases in which a dispute is *compromised*

—E. A. Farnsworth and W. F. Young⟩ ~ *vi* : to enter into a compromise

compromise verdict — see VERDICT

comp•trol•ler \kən-'trō-lər, 'kämp-ˌtrō-\ *n* : the head accounting officer of a company or government

comptroller general *n* : the accounting officer of the U.S. who investigates financial claims against or on behalf of the government

Comptroller of the Cur•ren•cy \-'kər-ən-sē\ : the appointed U.S. official who oversees the financial soundness of federally chartered banks

com•pul•sion \kəm-'pəl-shən\ *n* **1** : an act of compelling (as by threat or intimidation); *specif* : COERCION ⟨a payment exacted by lawless ~ —E. A. Farnsworth and W. F. Young⟩ **2** : the state of being compelled; *specif* : DURESS ◇ Compulsion can make a contract voidable or be a ground for damages or restitution. Compulsion may also be a defense to a criminal act.

com•pul•so•ry \kəm-'pəl-sə-rē\ *adj* **1** : required or compelled by law : MANDATORY, OBLIGATORY ⟨~ arbitration⟩ ⟨~insurance⟩; *specif* : required to be brought or asserted in a pleading because of having arisen from the transaction or occurrence that is the subject of litigation ⟨a ~ counterclaim⟩ ⟨~ reconvention⟩ — compare ELECTIVE, PERMISSIVE **2** : using compulsion : COMPELLING ⟨~ measures⟩ — **com•pul•so•ri•ly** \-sə-rə-lē\ *adv*

compulsory joinder — see JOINDER

compulsory process *n* : process served on witnesses to compel their testimony for the defense at trial ◇ A criminal defendant has a constitutional right to compulsory process.

con•ceal *vt* **1** : to prevent disclosure of or fail to disclose (as a provision in a contract) esp. in violation of a duty to disclose **2 a** : to place out of sight ◇ A

\ə\abut \ᵊ\kitten \ər\further \a\ash \ā\ace
\ä\cot, cart \aȯ\out \ch\chin \e\bet \ē\easy
\g\go \i\hit \ī\ice \j\job \ŋ\sing \ō\go \ȯ\law
\ȯi\boy \th\thin \t̲h̲\the \ü\loot \u̇\foot \y\yet
\zh\vision *see also* Pronunciation Symbols page

weapon need only be placed out of ordinary observation in order to be considered a concealed weapon. **b** : to prevent or hinder recognition, discovery, or recovery of ⟨*~ing* stolen property⟩ — **conceal·ment** *n*

con·cert·ed \kən-'sər-təd\ *adj* **1** : mutually contrived or agreed upon ⟨the ~ pursuit of lawful . . . ends —L. H. Tribe⟩ **2** : acting together toward a common end ⟨~ wrongdoers⟩

concerted ac·tiv·i·ty \-ak-'ti-və-tē\ *n, pl* **-ties** : an employee action (as canvassing other employees) that concerns wages or working conditions of others in addition to the employee and that contemplates group activity ◊ Concerted activities are protected by the National Labor Relations Act and cannot be used as a reason to discharge or discipline an employee.

con·cert of action \'kän-sərt-\ **1** : a theory in torts that imposes liability on all defendants who have committed tortious acts that contributed to the plaintiff's injury even though only one actually caused the injury — compare *alternative liability* at LIABILITY 2b **2** : a rule in criminal law that holds an aider and abettor liable for commission of a criminal act by the principal ◊ Concert of action does not apply where the crime requires more than one person for its commission.

con·ces·sion *n* **1** : an act or instance of conceding or yielding **2** : something conceded: as **a** : ACKNOWLEDGMENT, ADMISSION **b** : something granted esp. as an inducement (as to enter into an agreement) **c** : a grant of real property esp. by a government in return for services or for a particular use (as settlement) **d** : a right to undertake a specified activity for profit on another's real property ⟨a logging ~⟩ **e** : a lease that grants a right to engage in a profitable activity on another's real property; *also* : the property or portion of the property subject to such a lease

con·cil·i·a·tion \kən-ˌsi-lē-'ā-shən\ *n* : the settlement of a dispute by mutual and friendly agreement with a view to avoiding litigation — **con·cil·i·a·tor** \kən-'si-lē-ˌā-tər\ *n*

con·clu·sion \kən-'klü-zhən\ *n* **1** : a judgment or opinion inferred from relevant facts ⟨our ~ upon the present evidence — *Missouri v. Illinois*, 200 U.S. 496 (1905)⟩ **2 a** : a final summarizing (as of a closing argument) **b** : the last or closing part of something **3** : an opinion or judgment offered without supporting evidence; *specif* : an allegation made in a pleading that is not based on facts set forth in the pleading

con·clu·sion·ary \kən-'klü-zhə-ˌner-ē\ *adj* : CONCLUSORY

conclusion of fact : a fact inferred to exist from other facts actually proved by evidence

conclusion of law : the court's statement of the law applicable to a case in view of facts found to be true : the judgment required by law when applied to the facts — called also *finding of law*

con·clu·sive *adj* **1** : of, relating to, or being a conclusion **2** : putting an end to debate or question esp. by reason of inability to be refuted — **con·clu·sive·ly** *adv* — **con·clu·sive·ness** *n*

conclusive presumption — see PRESUMPTION

con·clu·so·ry \kən-'klü-sə-rē\ *adj* : consisting of or relating to a conclusion or assertion for which no supporting evidence is offered ⟨~ allegations⟩

con·cu·bi·nage \kän-'kyü-bə-nij\ *n* : the relationship between persons who are cohabiting without the benefit of marriage — used esp. in the civil law of Louisiana; compare COMMON-LAW MARRIAGE ◊ Under Louisiana law, concubinage does not give rise to any rights in the parties to each other's property.

con·cur \kən-'kər\ *vi* **con·curred; con·cur·ring 1** : to happen at the same time **2** : to express agreement ⟨he shall have power . . . to make treaties, provided two-thirds of the Senators present ~ —*U.S. Constitution* art. II⟩; *specif* : to join in an appellate decision — compare DISSENT ◊ A judge or justice may concur with the decision of the court but not agree with the reasons set forth in the opinion. Often a separate opinion is written in such a case.

con·cur·rence \kən-'kər-əns\ *n* **1** : the simultaneous occurrence of events or circumstances **2** : an agreement in judgment; *specif* : a judge's or justice's separate opinion that differs in reasoning but agrees in the decision of the court

con·cur·rent \kən-'kər-ənt\ *adj* **1** : occurring, arising, or operating at the same time often in relationship, conjunction, association, or cooperation ⟨the power of taxation in the general and state governments is acknowledged to be ∼ —*McCulloch v. Maryland*, 17 U.S. 316 (1819)⟩ ⟨a ∼ tortious act⟩ — see also *concurrent cause* at CAUSE, *concurrent sentence* at SENTENCE **2** : insuring the same property to the same extent under identical terms ⟨∼ fire policies⟩ **3** : exercised over the same matter or area by two different authorities — see also *concurrent jurisdiction* at JURISDICTION, *concurrent power* at POWER 2a — **con·cur·rent·ly** *adv*

concurrent cause — see CAUSE 1

concurrent condition — see CONDITION

concurrent jurisdiction — see JURISDICTION

concurrent power — see POWER 2a

concurrent resolution *n* : a resolution passed by both houses of a legislative body that lacks the force of law — compare JOINT RESOLUTION

concurrent sentence — see SENTENCE

concurring cause *n* : CONCURRENT CAUSE at CAUSE 1

concurring opinion — see OPINION

con·demn \kən-'dem\ *vt* **1** : to impose a penalty on; *esp* : to sentence to death **2** : to adjudge unfit for use or consumption **3** : to declare convertible to public use under the right of eminent domain : TAKE — **con·dem·nable** \kən-'dem-nə-bəl, -'de-mə-\ *adj* — **con·dem·na·tion** \ˌkän-ˌdem-'nā-shən\ *n* — **con·demn·er** *or* **con·dem·nor** \kən-'de-mər, -'dem-ˌnȯr\ *n*

con·dem·nee \ˌkän-dem-'nē\ *n* : the owner of property that is condemned

¹con·di·tion *n* **1** : an uncertain future act or event whose occurrence or nonoccurrence determines the rights or obligations of a party under a legal instrument and esp. a contract; *also* : a clause in the instrument describing the act or event and its effect

concurrent condition : a condition that is to be fulfilled by one party at the same time that a mutual condition is to be fulfilled by another party

condition implied in law : CONSTRUCTIVE CONDITION in this entry

condition pre·ce·dent \-pri-'sēd-ᵊnt, -'pre-sə-dənt\ : a condition that must be fulfilled before performance under a contract can become due, an estate can vest, or a right can become effective

condition subsequent : a condition whose fulfillment defeats or modifies an estate or right already in effect or vested or discharges an already existing duty under a contract

constructive condition : a condition created by operation of law — called also *condition implied in law;* compare EXPRESS CONDITION in this entry

express condition : a condition created and explicitly stated by the parties to a contract — compare CONSTRUCTIVE CONDITION in this entry

po·tes·ta·tive condition \'pō-tes-ˌtā-tiv\ *in the civil law of Louisiana* : a condition whose fulfillment was completely within the power of the obligated party ◊ Article 1770 of the Louisiana Civil Code eliminates the term *potestative condition*, stating that suspensive conditions which depend on the whim of the obligated party make the obligation null, and that resolutory conditions which depend on the will of the obligated party must be fulfilled in good faith.

\ə\abut \ᵊ\kitten \ər\further \a\ash \ā\ace
\ä\cot, cart \aù\out \ch\chin \e\bet \ē\easy
\g\go \i\hit \ī\ice \j\job \ŋ\sing \ō\go \ȯ\law
\ȯi\boy \th\thin \t͟h\the \ü\loot \ù\foot \y\yet
\zh\vision *see also* Pronunciation Symbols page

re•so•lu•to•ry condition \,re-zə-'lü-tə-rē-, ri-'zäl-yü-,tōr-ē-\ *in the civil law of Louisiana* : a condition that upon fulfillment terminates an already enforceable obligation and entitles the parties to be restored to their original positions — see also POTESTATIVE CONDITION in this entry

suspensive condition in the civil law of Louisiana : a condition which must be fulfilled before an obligation is enforceable — see also POTESTATIVE CONDITION in this entry **2** : a state of being ⟨a latent defective ∼⟩ **3** : one of the rights or obligations of the policyholder or the insurer set forth in an insurance policy — **con•di•tion•al** *adj* — **con•di•tion•al•ly** *adv*

²**condition** *vt* **con•di•tioned; con•di•tion•ing** : to make subject to conditions ⟨the sale . . . was orally *conditioned* upon approval of the patent —J. D. Calamari and J. M. Perillo⟩

conditional delivery — see DELIVERY

conditional fee — see FEE 1

conditionally privileged communication *n* : PRIVILEGED COMMUNICATION 2b

conditional obligation — see OBLIGATION

conditional privilege *n* : QUALIFIED PRIVILEGE at PRIVILEGE 1a

conditional sale — see SALE

conditional use — see USE 2

conditional will — see WILL

condition implied in law *n* — see CONDITION

condition precedent — see CONDITION

condition subsequent — see CONDITION

con•do•min•i•um \,kän-də-'mi-nē-əm\ *n, pl* **-ums** [New Latin, joint dominion, from Latin *com-* with, together + *dominium* rule, ownership] **1** : ownership of real property that is characterized by separate ownership of portions of the property (as units in an apartment building) and undivided or joint ownership of the remainder (as the common areas of an apartment building) ⟨the conversion of real property to the ∼ form of ownership —*Troy Ltd. v. Renna*, 727 F.2d 287

(1984)⟩ — compare COOPERATIVE **2** : real property (as an apartment or building) having condominium ownership ⟨a two-bedroom ∼⟩

con•do•na•tion \,kän-də-'nā-shən\ *n* [Medieval Latin *condonatio* remission, pardon, from Latin *condonare* to give away, absolve] : voluntary overlooking or pardon of an offense; *specif* : express or implied and usu. conditional forgiveness of a spouse's marital wrong (as adultery or cruelty)

con•done \kən-'dōn\ *vt* **con•doned; con•don•ing** [Latin *condonare* to give away, absolve] : to pardon or overlook voluntarily

con•duct \'kän-,dəkt\ *n* **1 a** : the act, manner, or process of carrying on or managing ⟨his ∼ of the case was negligent⟩ **b** : an act or omission to act ⟨a crime is that ∼ which is defined as criminal —*Louisiana Revised Statutes*⟩ **2** : mode or standard of personal behavior

con•fer•ence \'kän-frəns, -fə-rəns\ *n* **1** : a meeting for consultation, deliberation, discussion, or interchange of opinions ⟨a ∼ on environmental law⟩ — see also JUDICIAL CONFERENCE, PRETRIAL CONFERENCE **2** : a meeting of members of the two branches of a legislature esp. to adjust differences in the provisions of a bill passed in different forms by the two branches; *also* : CONFERENCE COMMITTEE **3** : CAUCUS

conference committee *n* : a joint committee that is appointed to hold a conference on differing versions of a bill

con•fess \kən-'fes\ *vt* : to admit (as a charge or allegation) as true, proven, or valid ⟨unless you answer, the petition shall be taken as *confessed*⟩ ∼ *vi* : to make a confession — **con•fes•sor** \kən-'fe-sər\ *n*

con•fes•sion *n* **1** : an act of confessing **2** : an acknowledgment of a fact or allegation as true or proven; *esp* : a written or oral statement by an accused party acknowledging the party's guilt (as by admitting commission of a crime) — compare ADMISSION, *declaration*

against interest at DECLARATION, SELF=
INCRIMINATION ◊ Courts differ on how a
confession establishes the accused's
guilt; for example, in some jurisdictions
the confession has to establish all the necessary elements of the crime. In order
to be admissible as evidence, a confession must be voluntary. A guilty plea is
considered a judicial confession.

confession and avoidance *n* : a common=
law plea in which a party confesses an
allegation but alleges additional facts to
avoid the intended legal effect of the original allegation — compare DEMURRER

confession of judgment *n* : acknowledgment by a debtor of a claim and consent
that a judgment may be entered usu. without notice or hearing for the amount of
the claim when it is due and unpaid —
compare *cognovit note* at NOTE

con•fi•den•tial \ˌkän-fi-'den-chəl\ *adj* **1**
: known or conveyed only to a limited
number of people ⟨a ~ disclosure⟩ **2**
: marked by or indicative of intimacy,
mutual trust, or willingness to confide
esp. between parties one of whom is in
a position of superiority ⟨the ~ relationship of doctor and patient⟩ **3** : containing
information whose unauthorized disclosure could be prejudicial to the national
interest — **con•fi•den•ti•al•i•ty** \ˌkän-fi-
ˌden-chē-'a-lə-tē\ *n* — **con•fi•den•tial•ly**
adv

con•fi•den•tial communication \ˌkän-fə-
'den-chəl-\ *n* : a communication between
parties to a confidential relation (as husband and wife, attorney and client, or
doctor and patient) such that the recipient of the communication has a privilege
exempting him or her from disclosing
it as a witness — called also *privileged
communication*

confidential relationship *n* : FIDUCIARY
RELATIONSHIP

con•fine *vt* **con•fined; con•fin•ing** : to hold
within a location; *specif* : IMPRISON

con•fine•ment *n* **1** : the act of confining **2**
: the state of being confined

con•firm *vt* **1 a** : to make valid by necessary formal approval ⟨the debtor's chap-

ter 13 plan ~*ed* by the court⟩ **b** : to vote
approval of ⟨~ a nomination⟩ **2** : to give
formal acknowledgment of receipt of **3**
: to remove doubt about by authoritative
act or indisputable fact ⟨a consent decree
~*ing* Capt. Brown's right to his cargo —
W. G. Young⟩

con•fir•ma•tion \ˌkän-fər-'mä-shən\ *n* **1**
: the act or process of confirming, assuring, or upholding ⟨seeking ~ of the
agreement⟩; *specif* : the ratification of an
executive act by a legislative body ⟨sen-
ate ~ of the Supreme Court nominee⟩ **2**
: something that confirms: as **a** : an express or implied contract by which a person makes a voidable agreement binding;
specif : a definite expression or written
memorandum that verifies or substanti-
ates an agreement previously made orally
or informally **b** *in the civil law of Louisiana* : a declaration whereby a person
corrects the parts of an obligation that are
null to make them enforceable **c** : a conveyance by which valid title to an estate is
transferred to a person already in possession or by which an estate is increased

confirmation hearing — see HEARING

con•fis•cate \'kän-fə-ˌskāt\ *vt* **-cat•ed;
-cat•ing** : to seize without compensation
as forfeited to the public treasury — compare CRIMINAL FORFEITURE ◊ Illegal
items such as narcotics or firearms, or
profits from the sale of illegal items, may
be confiscated by law enforcement officers. Additionally, government action
that reduces the value of property to a person or entity as to make it nearly worthless has been held to constitute confisca-
tion. Examples of such government action include the passage of zoning laws
that prevent the use of land for its designated purpose and the setting of utility rates so low that the utility company
cannot realize a reasonable return on its
investment. — **con•fis•ca•tion** \ˌkän-fə-

\ə\abut \ᵊ\kitten \ər\further \a\ash \ā\ace
\ä\cot, cart \aů\out \ch\chin \e\bet \ē\easy
\g\go \i\hit \ī\ice \j\job \ŋ\sing \ō\go \ȯ\law
\ȯi\boy \th\thin \ṯh\the \ü\loot \ů\foot \y\yet
\zh\vision *see also* Pronunciation Symbols page

'skā-shən\ *n* — **con•fis•ca•tor** \'kän-fə-ˌskā-tər\ *n* — **con•fis•ca•to•ry** \kən-'fis-kə-ˌtōr-ē\ *adj*

con•flict of interest \'kän-ˌflikt-\ **1** : a conflict between the private interests and the official or professional responsibilities of a person in a position of trust **2** : a conflict between competing duties (as in an attorney's representation of clients with adverse interests) — see also *ABA Model Rules of Professional Conduct* in the IMPORTANT LAWS section

conflict of laws : opposition or conflict between the applicable laws of different states or jurisdictions regarding the rights of the parties in a case; *also* : a branch of law that deals with the resolution of such conflict and the determination of the law applicable to cases in which the laws of different jurisdictions are asserted

con•form \kən-'form\ *vi* : to be in accordance : correspond in character; *specif* : to be in accordance with the provisions of a contract — **con•for•mance** \kən-'for-məns\ *n* — **con•for•mi•ty** \kən-'for-mə-tē\ *n*

con•front \kən-'frənt\ *vt* : to face or bring face-to-face for the purpose of challenging esp. through cross-examination ⟨the accused shall enjoy the right . . . to be ~ed with the witnesses against him — *U.S. Constitution* amend. VI⟩ — **con•fron•ta•tion** \ˌkän-frən-'tā-shən\ *n*

confrontation clause *n, often cap both Cs* : the clause in the Sixth Amendment to the U.S. Constitution guaranteeing to defendants in criminal prosecutions the right to be confronted with the witnesses against them esp. for the purpose of conducting cross-examination — see also CONFRONT

con•fu•sion *n* **1** *in the civil law of Louisiana* : a uniting of two interests or rights in property into one — compare MERGER 1 **2** *in the civil law of Louisiana* : the termination of an obligation by a person acquiring the right from which the obligation arose **3** : the mixing or blending together of goods or commodities so that the individual owners cannot identify

their own property — called also *confusion of goods*

cong *abbr* **1** congress **2** congressional

con•glom•er•ate \kən-'glä-mə-rət\ *n* : a widely diversified company; *esp* : a corporation that acquires other companies whose activities are unrelated to the corporation's primary activity

con•gress *n* [Latin *congressus* meeting, encounter, from *congredi* to approach, meet] **1** : a formal meeting of delegates **2 a** : the supreme legislative body of a nation and esp. a republic **b** *cap* : the legislative branch of the United States government; *specif* : the U.S. House of Representatives **3** *cap* **a** : the U.S. legislature as it is composed for an enumerated two-year period ⟨the 101st *Congress*⟩ **b** : a single session of the U.S. legislature — see also HOUSE OF REPRESENTATIVES, SENATE, *Article I* of the CONSTITUTION in the back matter — **con•gres•sion•al** *adj* — **con•gres•sion•al•ly** *adv*

congressional district *n* : a territorial division of a state from which a member of the U.S. House of Representatives is elected

Congressional Record *n* : the published record of the daily proceedings in the U.S. Senate and House of Representatives

con•gress•man *n, pl* **con•gress•men** : a member of Congress; *esp* : a member of the U.S. House of Representatives

con•gress•peo•ple *n pl* : members of Congress : congressmen and congresswomen

con•gress•per•son *n* : a congressman or congresswoman

con•gress•wom•an *n, pl* **con•gress•wom•en** : a female member of Congress; *esp* : a female member of the U.S. House of Representatives

con•joint *adj, in the civil law of Louisiana* : JOINT — **con•joint•ly** *adv*

conjoint legacy — see LEGACY

con•ju•gal \'kän-jə-gəl\ *adj* : of or relating to marriage or to married persons and their relationships

conjugal rights *n pl* : the rights and privileges (as to love, affection, sexual relations, companionship, comfort, and services) implied by and involved in the marriage relationship

con·ni·vance \kə-'nī-vəns\ *n* : the act of conniving esp. with regard to a spouse's marital misconduct (as adultery); *also* : a defense to a charge of marital misconduct in a divorce proceeding — compare CONDONATION

con·nive \kə-'nīv\ *vt* **con·nived; con·niving** [Latin *con(n)ivere* to close one's eyes, knowingly overlook something] : to assent knowingly and wrongfully without opposition to another's wrongdoing; *specif* : to knowingly consent to a spouse's marital misconduct and esp. to adultery

con·san·guine \kän-'saŋ-gwən\ *adj* : CONSANGUINEOUS

con·san·guin·e·ous \ˌkän-ˌsan-'gwi-nē-əs, -ˌsaŋ-\ *adj* : of the same blood or origin; *specif* : descended from the same ancestor — **con·san·guin·e·ous·ly** *adv*

con·san·guin·i·ty \ˌkän-ˌsan-'gwi-nə-tē, -ˌsaŋ-\ *n* : the quality or state of being consanguineous

con·science *adj* : exempting persons whose religious beliefs forbid compliance ⟨~ laws, which allow physicians . . . to refuse to participate in abortions — W. J. Curran⟩

con·scien·tious objection \ˌkän-chē-'en-chəs-\ *n* : objection on moral or religious grounds (as to military service or bearing arms) — **conscientious objector** *n*

con·scio·na·ble \'kän-chə-nə-bəl\ *adj* : guided by conscience : characterized by fairness and justice — compare UNCONSCIONABLE — **con·scio·na·bil·i·ty** \ˌkän-chə-nə-'bi-lə-tē\ *n*

con·sec·u·tive *adj* : following one after the other in order — **con·sec·u·tive·ly** *adv*

consecutive sentence — see SENTENCE

con·sen·su·al \kən-'sen-chə-wəl\ *adj* **1** : existing or made by mutual consent without any further act (as a writing) **2** : involving or based on mutual consent ⟨~ sexual intercourse⟩

con·sen·sus ad idem \kən-'sen-səs-'ad-'ī-dəm, -'äd-'ē-dem\ *n* [Latin, agreement with respect to the same thing] : MEETING OF THE MINDS

con·sent *n* **1 a** : compliance in or approval of what is done or proposed by another; *specif* : the voluntary agreement or acquiescence by a person of age or with requisite mental capacity who is not under duress or coercion and usu. who has knowledge or understanding — see also AGE OF CONSENT, INFORMED CONSENT, RAPE, STATUTORY RAPE **b** : a defense claiming that the victim consented to an alleged crime (as rape) **2** : agreement as to action or opinion ⟨shall have power, by and with the advice and ~ of the Senate, to make treaties —*U.S. Constitution* art. II⟩ ⟨a contract is formed by the ~ of the parties established through offer and acceptance —*Louisiana Civil Code*⟩; *specif* : voluntary agreement by a people to organize a civil society and give authority to a government — **consent** *vi* — **con·sent·er** *n*

consent decree — see DECREE

consent judgment — see JUDGMENT 1a

consent order — see ORDER 3b

consent search — see SEARCH

con·se·quen·tial \ˌkän-si-'kwen-chəl\ *adj* : of the nature of an indirect or secondary result

consequential damages — see DAMAGE 2

consequential loss — see LOSS

con·ser·va·tor \kən-'sər-və-tər, 'kän-sər-ˌvā-\ *n* **1** : a person, official, or institution appointed by a court to take over and manage the estate of an incompetent — compare COMMITTEE, CURATOR, GUARDIAN, RECEIVER, TUTOR **2** : a public official charged with the protection of something affecting public welfare and interests; *specif* : an official placed in charge of a bank because its affairs are not in a satisfactory condition — **con·ser·va·tor·ship** *n*

con·sid·er·a·tion *n* : something (as an act

or forbearance or the promise thereof) done or given by one party for the act or promise of another — see also CONTRACT; compare MOTIVE ◊ Except in Louisiana, consideration is a necessary element to the creation of a contract. The consideration must result from bargaining by the parties, and must be the thing that induces the mutual promises.

adequate consideration : a consideration that is reasonably equivalent in value to the thing for which it is given

fair consideration : a consideration that is reasonable and given in good faith; *specif* : something with a reasonably equivalent value that under the laws of fraudulent conveyances is given in good faith in exchange for the transfer of property

good consideration **1** : a consideration based on a family relationship or natural love and affection **2** : VALUABLE CONSIDERATION in this entry ◊ When used as defined in sense 1, *good consideration* is the opposite of *valuable consideration*. However, *good consideration* is also sometimes used to mean *valuable consideration*. Good consideration of the kind denoted by sense 1 cannot create an enforceable contract.

new consideration : something according to section 6-106 of the Uniform Commercial Code that becomes payable in exchange for the transfer of bulk goods

nominal consideration : consideration consisting of a nominal amount

past consideration : something that has already been given or some act that has already been performed that cannot therefore be induced by the other party's thing, act, or promise in exchange and is not truly a consideration

valuable consideration : a consideration that confers some benefit having pecuniary value on one party to a contract or imposes a detriment having pecuniary value on the other

con·sign \kən-'sīn\ *vt* : to entrust (one's goods) to the possession of a dealer to be sold for profit or returned if unsold

— compare BAIL, ENTRUST — **con·sign·ment** *n* — **con·sign·or** \kən-'sī-nər, ˌkän-ˌsī-'nȯr\ *n*

con·sign·ee \kən-ˌsī-'nē; ˌkän-ˌsī-'nē, kən-, -sə-\ *n* : a person to whom goods are consigned

con·sol·i·date \kən-'sä-lə-ˌdāt\ *vt* **-dat·ed; -dat·ing** : to join together into one whole: as **a** : to combine (two or more lawsuits or matters that involve a common question of law or fact) into one — compare CLASS ACTION ◊ Consolidation of matters in the federal courts is governed by Rule 42 of the Federal Rules of Civil Procedure. Consolidated cases may become one single action with a single judgment, or may retain their individual identities although tried together. The court may also try one representative case and render a judgment binding on the other cases. **b** : to combine (two or more corporations) to form one new corporation — compare MERGER — **con·sol·i·da·tion** \kən-ˌsä-lə-'dā-shən\ *n*

con·sor·tium \kən-'sȯr-shəm; -shē-əm\ *n*, *pl* **-sor·tia** \-shə, -shē-ə\ *also* **-sortiums** [Latin, sharing, partnership, from *consort-, consors* sharer, partner] **1** : an agreement, combination, or group (as of companies) formed to undertake an enterprise beyond the resources of any one member **2** [Medieval Latin, marital partnership, from Latin] : the right of one spouse to the company, affection, and assistance of and to sexual relations with the other; *also* : the right of a parent or child to the company, affection, and assistance of the other ⟨suing for loss of ~⟩ — compare SOCIETY

con·spir·a·cy \kən-'spir-ə-sē\ *n*, *pl* **-cies** [Latin *conspiratio*, from *conspirare* to conspire — see CONSPIRE] **1** : an agreement between two or more people to commit an act prohibited by law or to commit a lawful act by means prohibited by law; *also* : the crime or tort of participating in a conspiracy — compare SUBSTANTIVE CRIME ◊ Some states require an overt act in addition to the agreement to constitute conspiracy.

chain conspiracy : a conspiracy in

which the conspirators act separately and successively (as in distributing narcotics)

civil conspiracy : a conspiracy that is not prosecuted as a crime but that forms the grounds for a lawsuit

criminal conspiracy : a conspiracy prosecuted as a crime **2** : a group of conspirators

con·spir·a·tor \kən-'spir-ə-tər\ *n* : one who conspires

con·spir·a·tor·i·al \kən-'spir-ə-'tōr-ē-əl\ *adj* : of, relating to, or suggestive of a conspiracy — **con·spir·a·tor·i·al·ly** *adv*

con·spire \kən-'spīr\ *vi* **con·spired; con·spir·ing** [Latin *conspirare* to be in harmony, to join in an unlawful agreement, from *com*- together + *spirare* to breathe] : to join in a conspiracy — compare SOLICIT

con·sta·ble \'kän-stə-bəl, 'kən-\ *n* [Old French *conestable* military commander, chief of the royal household, from Late Latin *comes stabuli*, literally, officer of the stable] : a public officer usu. of a town or township responsible for keeping the peace and for minor judicial duties

con·stit·u·en·cy \kən-'sti-chə-wən-sē\ *n*, *pl* **-cies 1** : a body of citizens entitled to elect a representative (as to a legislative or executive office) **2** : the residents in an electoral district **3** : an electoral district

¹con·stit·u·ent \kən-'sti-chə-wənt\ *n* **1** : one who authorizes another to act as agent : PRINCIPAL **2** : a member of a constituency

²constituent *adj* : having the power to create a government or to frame or amend a constitution ⟨a ~ assembly⟩

con·sti·tute \'kän-stə-ˌtüt, -ˌtyüt\ *vt* **1** : to appoint to an office or function ⟨those who are *constituted* heirs or named legatees —*Louisiana Civil Code*⟩ ⟨legal authority ~s all magistrates⟩ **2** : ESTABLISH, FOUND ⟨to ~ tribunals inferior to the supreme Court —*U.S. Constitution* art. I⟩ **3 a** : to put (as an agreement) into required form **b** : to qualify as ⟨a letter vill —W. M. McGovern, Jr. *et* re to act may ~ negligence⟩ **c**

: to form the substance or whole of ⟨the bonds *constituted* the entire estate⟩

con·sti·tu·tion *n* [Latin *constitutio* system, fundamental principles (of an institution), from *constituere* to set up, establish] **1** : the basic principles and laws of a nation, state, or social group that determine the powers and duties of the government and guarantee certain rights to the people in it **2** : a written instrument containing the fundamental rules of a political or social organization; *esp, cap* : the U.S. Constitution — see also the JUDICIAL SYSTEM and the CONSTITUTION in the back matter; compare CHARTER, DECLARATION ◊ A constitution was originally simply a law, ordinance, or decree usu. made by a king, emperor, or other superior authority. A constitution now usu. contains the fundamental law and principles with which all other laws must conform. Unlike the U.S. Constitution, the British Constitution is not set down in a comprehensive document, but is found in a variety of statutes (as the Magna Carta) and in common law. Canada inherited many of the rules and practices that are considered part of the British Constitution, but the Constitution of Canada is also set down in comprehensive documents, such as the Constitution Act, 1982 and the Constitution Act, 1867 (formerly called the British North America Act, 1867).

con·sti·tu·tion·al *adj* **1** : consistent with or authorized by the constitution of a state or society ⟨~ rights⟩ **2** : regulated by, dependent on, or ruling according to a constitution ⟨a ~ monarchy⟩ **3** : of, relating to, or dealing with a constitution or its interpretation, formulation, or amendment ⟨a ~ convention⟩ ⟨~ lawyers⟩ — **con·sti·tu·tion·al·ly** *adv*

constitutional court *n* : a court established by a constitution; *esp* : the federal courts established by Article III of the U.S. Constitution — compare LEGISLATIVE COURT

\ə\abut \ᵊ\kitten \ər\further \a\ash \ā\ace
\ä\cot, cart \au̇\out \ch\chin \e\bet \ē\easy
\g\go \i\hit \ī\ice \j\job \ŋ\sing \ō\go \ȯ\law
\ȯi\boy \th\thin \t͟h\the \ü\loot \u̇\foot \y\yet
\zh\vision *see also* Pronunciation Symbols page

constitutional fact — see FACT
constitutional immunity — see IMMU-
NITY
con·sti·tu·tion·al·i·ty \ˌkän-stə-ˌtü-shə-
'na-lə-tē, -ˌtyü-\ *n* : the quality or state
of being constitutional; *esp* : conformity with the provisions of a constitution ⟨questioned the ~ of the income
tax⟩
constitutional law *n* : a body of statutory
and case law that is based on, concerns,
or interprets a constitution
con·struc·tion \kən-'strək-shən\ *n* : the
act or result of construing, interpreting,
or explaining meaning or effect (as of a
statute or contract) ⟨the ~ placed upon
an agreement —J. D. Calamari and J. M.
Perillo⟩
construction mortgage — see MORTGAGE
con·struc·tive \kən-'strək-tiv\ *adj* : created by a legal fiction: as **a** : inferred by
a judicial construction or interpretation
b : not actual but implied by operation
of the law ⟨made a ~ entry when he refused to take the opportunity for a voluntary departure —*Harvard Law Review*⟩
— compare ACTUAL — **con·struc·tive·ly**
adv
constructive bailment — see BAILMENT
constructive condition — see CONDITION
constructive contempt — see CONTEMPT
constructive contract — see CONTRACT
constructive custody — see CUSTODY c
constructive delivery — see DELIVERY
constructive desertion *n* : the act of one
spouse forcing the other (as by violence)
to abandon the home or relationship
◊ Constructive desertion, like desertion,
is a ground for divorce.
constructive discharge — see DISCHARGE
constructive dividend — see DIVIDEND
constructive eviction — see EVICTION
constructive force — see FORCE 3
constructive fraud — see FRAUD
constructive intent — see INTENT
constructive knowledge — see KNOWL-
EDGE
constructive notice — see NOTICE
constructive possession — see POSSES-
SION

constructive receipt *n* : the receipt of taxable income (as interest on a savings account) that is implied by the income's
ready availability to the taxpayer although it has not actually been collected
constructive service *n* : SUBSTITUTED
SERVICE
constructive total loss — see LOSS
constructive trust — see TRUST
con·sul \'kän-səl\ *n* : an official appointed
by a government to reside in a foreign
country in order to represent the commercial interests of citizens of the appointing
country — **con·su·lar** \-sə-lər\ *adj* —
con·sul·ship *n*
con·sul·ate \'kän-sə-lət\ *n* **1** : the office,
term of office, or jurisdiction of a consul
2 : the residence or official premises of a
consul
con·sum·er *n* : one that utilizes economic
goods; *specif* : an individual who purchases goods for personal use as distinguished from commercial use
consumer credit *n* : credit extended by
merchants or banks to finance the purchase of consumer goods (as home appliances) or services (as travel or hotel
accommodations) — compare *consumer
debt* at DEBT
consumer debt — see DEBT
consumer goods — see GOOD 2
consumer lease — see LEASE
consumer price index *n* : an index measuring the change in the cost of typical
wage-earner purchases of goods and services in some base period — called also
cost-of-living index
con·tem·ner *also* **con·tem·nor** \kən-'tem-
nər\ *n* : one who commits contempt
con·tempt \kən-'tempt\ *n* **1** : willful disobedience or open disrespect of the orders, authority, or dignity of a court or
judge acting in a judicial capacity by dis-
ruptive language or conduct or by failure
to obey the court's orders; *also* : the offense of contempt — called also *contempt
of court*
   civil contempt : contempt that consists
of disobedience to a court order in favor
of the opposing party ◊ The sanctions

for civil contempt end upon compliance with the order.

constructive contempt : INDIRECT CONTEMPT in this entry

criminal contempt : contempt consisting of conduct that disrupts or opposes the proceedings or power of the court ◇ The sanctions for criminal contempt are designed to punish as well as to coerce compliance.

direct contempt : contempt committed in the presence of the court or in a location close enough to disrupt the court's proceedings

in•di•rect contempt : contempt (as disobedience of a court order) that occurs outside of the presence of the court 2 : willful disobedience to a lawful order of or willful obstruction of a legislative body in the course of exercising its powers ⟨~ of Congress⟩ — **in contempt** : in the state of having been found guilty of contempt ⟨refused to testify and were held *in contempt* —A. M. Dershowitz⟩

contempt of court : CONTEMPT 1

¹con•test \kən-'test\ *vt* : to dispute or challenge through legal procedures ⟨~ a will⟩

²con•test \'kän-ˌtest\ *n* : a challenge brought through formal or legal procedures ⟨boundary controversies or other ~s between states —Felix Frankfurter⟩; *specif* : WILL CONTEST — see also NO CONTEST CLAUSE

con•tes•tant *n* : one that initiates or participates in a contest

con•tin•gen•cy \kən-'tin-jən-sē\ *n, pl* **-cies** 1 : the quality or state of being contingent 2 : a contingent event or condition: as **a** : an event that may but is not certain to occur ⟨a ~ that made performance under the contract impossible⟩ **b** : something likely to come about as an adjunct to or result of something else; *specif* : CONTINGENCY FEE at FEE 2 ⟨whether a case is on a ~ or billed at an hourly rate —D. R. Frederico⟩

contingency fee — see FEE 2

con•tin•gent \kən-'tin-jənt\ *adj* 1 : likely but not certain to happen — compare EXECUTORY 2 : intended for use in circumstances not completely foreseen ⟨a

~ fund⟩ 3 : dependent on or conditioned by something else ⟨a ~ claim⟩ ⟨a legacy ~ on the marriage⟩ — compare VESTED

contingent annuity — see ANNUITY

contingent beneficiary — see BENEFICIARY a, b

contingent estate — see ESTATE 1

contingent fee *n* : CONTINGENCY FEE at FEE 2

contingent interest — see INTEREST 1

contingent liability — see LIABILITY 2a

contingent remainder — see REMAINDER

con•tin•u•ance \kən-'ti-nyə-wəns\ *n* : the postponement of the court proceedings in a case to a future day

con•tin•ue *vt* **-tin•ued; -tinu•ing** : to postpone (a legal proceeding) to a future day

con•tin•u•ing *adj* 1 : marked by uninterrupted extension in time or sequence ⟨a ~ criminal enterprise⟩ 2 : needing no renewal ⟨~ shareholders⟩

continuing trespass — see TRESPASS

¹con•tra \'kän-trə\ *prep* [Latin] : in opposition or contrast to

²contra *adj* : placed or set in opposition ⟨~ parties⟩

con•tra•band \'kän-trə-ˌband\ *n* [Italian *contrabbando* act of smuggling, from *contra*- against + *bando* edict, law] : property that is unlawfully produced, possessed, or transported

contraband per se : property that is in and of itself unlawful to possess, produce, or transport

derivative contraband : property that is unlawful because it is used in committing an unlawful act

contraband per se — see CONTRABAND

contra bonos mores *adj* [Late Latin] : against good morals : harmful to the moral welfare of society ⟨an act *contra bonos mores*⟩

¹con•tract \'kän-ˌtrakt\ *n* [Latin *contractus* from *contrahere* to draw together, enter into (a relationship or agreement), from

\ə\abut \ᵊ\kitten \ər\further \a\ash \ā\ace
\ä\cot, cart \au̇\out \ch\chin \e\bet \ē\easy
\g\go \i\hit \ī\ice \j\job \ŋ\sing \ō\go \ȯ\law
\ȯi\boy \th\thin \t͟h\the \ü\loot \u̇\foot \y\yet
\zh\vision *see also* Pronunciation Symbols page

com- with, together + *trahere* to draw] **1** : an agreement between two or more parties that creates in each party a duty to do or not do something and a right to performance of the other's duty or a remedy for the breach of the other's duty ; *also* : a document embodying such an agreement — see also ACCEPT, ²BARGAIN, BREACH, CAUSE 4, CONSENT, CONSIDERATION, DUTY, MEETING OF THE MINDS, OBLIGATION, OFFER, PERFORMANCE, PROMISE, RESCIND, SOCIAL CONTRACT, SUBCONTRACT, *Uniform Commercial Code* in the IMPORTANT LAWS section ◊ Contracts must be made by parties with the necessary capacity (as age or mental soundness) and must have a lawful, not criminal, object. Except in Louisiana, a valid contract also requires consideration, mutuality of obligations, and a meeting of the minds. In Louisiana, a valid contract requires the consent of the parties and a cause for the contract in addition to capacity and a lawful object.

accessory contract : a contract (as a security agreement) made to secure the performance of another obligation — compare PRINCIPAL CONTRACT in this entry

ad•he•sion contract \ad-'hē-zhən-\ : CONTRACT OF ADHESION in this entry

aleatory contract : a contract in which either party's performance is dependent on an uncertain event

bilateral contract : a contract in which both parties have promised to perform — compare UNILATERAL CONTRACT in this entry

commutative contract in the civil law of Louisiana : a contract in which the obligations of the parties to perform are equal to each other in value

constructive contract : QUASI CONTRACT in this entry

contract for deed : LAND INSTALLMENT CONTRACT in this entry

contract implied in fact : IMPLIED CONTRACT 1 in this entry

contract implied in law : QUASI CONTRACT in this entry

contract of adhesion : a contract that is not negotiated by the parties and that is usu. embodied in a standardized form prepared by the dominant party

contract under seal : a contract that does not require consideration in order to be binding but that must be sealed, delivered, and show a clear intention of the parties to create a contract under seal ◊ Contracts under seal were in use long prior to the development of the requirement of consideration. They originally usu. were impressed with an actual seal, but today the word *seal*, the abbreviation *L.S.*, or words such as "signed and sealed" or "witness my seal" may take the place of the seal. Without a clear indication of the parties' intention, however, the presence of a seal, such as a corporate seal, is insufficient to create a contract under seal. Contracts under seal have a substantially longer statute of limitations than contracts based on consideration.

des•ti•na•tion contract : a contract for goods stipulating that the seller assumes the risk of loss from damage to the goods until they arrive at the destination specified in the contract — compare SHIPMENT CONTRACT in this entry

du•al contract : one of two contracts made by the same parties with regard to the same transaction; *specif* : one of two contracts made with regard to the sale of real estate of which one states an inaccurately high price for the purpose of defrauding a lender into providing a larger loan

executory contract : a contract that sets forth promises that are not yet performed

express contract : a contract created by the explicit language of the parties — compare IMPLIED CONTRACT in this entry

formal contract : a contract made binding by the observance of required formalities regardless of the giving of consideration; *specif* : a contract that is a contract under seal, a recognizance, a letter of credit, or a negotiable instrument — called also *special contract, specialty*

forward contract : a privately negotiated investment contract in which a buyer commits to purchase something (as a quantity of a commodity, security, or currency) at a predetermined price on a set future date — called also *forward*

futures contract : a contract purchased or sold on an exchange in which a party agrees to buy or sell a quantity of a commodity on a specified future date at a set price : FUTURE — called also *future contract*

gratuitous contract *in the civil law of Louisiana* : a contract in which one party promises to do something without receiving anything in return — compare ONEROUS CONTRACT in this entry

guaranteed investment contract : an investment contract under which an institutional investor deposits a lump sum of money (as a pension fund) with an insurance company that guarantees the return of principal and a specific amount of interest at the end of the contract term; *also* : such a contract considered as an investment ⟨purchased a *guaranteed investment contract*⟩ — called also *GIC*

il·lu·so·ry contract \i-'lü-sə-rē-, -zə-\ : a contract in which at least one party makes an illusory promise

implied contract 1 : a contract that a court infers to exist from the words and conduct of the parties — called also *contract implied in fact, implied in fact contract;* compare EXPRESS CONTRACT in this entry **2** : QUASI CONTRACT in this entry

implied in law contract : QUASI CONTRACT 1 in this entry

informal contract : any contract that is not a formal contract — called also *simple contract*

innominate contract *in the civil law of Louisiana* : a contract that is given no special designation as to its purpose —

compare NOMINATE CONTRACT in this entry

installment contract : a contract in which performance is tendered in installments (as by separate periodic delivery of goods)

investment contract : an agreement or transaction in which a party invests money in a common enterprise the profits from which are derived from the efforts of others

labor contract : a contract between an employer and a labor union reached through and containing the results of collective bargaining : COLLECTIVE BARGAINING AGREEMENT

land installment contract : a contract for the purchase of real property in which the seller retains the deed to the property or otherwise continues to have an interest in it until the buyer makes payments in installments equal to the full purchase price or as much of the purchase price as agreed upon — called also *contract for deed, land contract*

maritime contract : a contract directly relating to the navigation, business, or commerce of the high seas or other navigable waters and falling within the jurisdiction of the admiralty court

nominate contract *in the civil law of Louisiana* : a contract given a special designation (as sale, insurance, or lease) — compare INNOMINATE CONTRACT in this entry

onerous contract *in the civil law of Louisiana* : a contract in which each party obligates himself or herself in exchange for the promise of the other — compare GRATUITOUS CONTRACT in this entry

option contract : a contract in which a time period is specified within which an offer must be accepted

out·put contract : a contract in which

\ə\abut \ᵊ\kitten \ər\further \a\ash \ā\ace \ä\cot, cart \aú\out \ch\chin \e\bet \ē\easy \g\go \i\hit \ī\ice \j\job \ŋ\sing \ō\go \ò\law \òi\boy \th\thin \ṯh\the \ü\loot \ù\foot \y\yet \zh\vision *see also* Pronunciation Symbols page

the buyer agrees to buy and the seller agrees to sell all of a kind of goods that the seller produces

principal contract : a contract from which a secured obligation arises — compare ACCESSORY CONTRACT in this entry

quasi contract 1 : an obligation that is not created by a contract but that is imposed by law to prevent the unjust enrichment of one party from the acts of another party — called also *contract implied in law, implied in law contract* **2** *in the civil law of Louisiana* : a lawful and voluntary act that benefits another for which the law imposes an obligation on the beneficiary or a third party to compensate the actor — compare OFFENSE 2

re•quire•ments contract : a contract in which the seller agrees to sell and the buyer agrees to buy all of a kind of goods that the buyer requires

ship•ment contract : a contract in which the seller bears the risk of loss from damage to the goods only until they are brought to the place of shipment — compare DESTINATION CONTRACT in this entry

simple contract : INFORMAL CONTRACT in this entry

special contract 1 : a contract containing provisions and stipulations not ordinarily found in contracts of its kind **2** : FORMAL CONTRACT in this entry

substituted contract : a contract between parties to a prior contract that takes the place of and discharges the obligations under the prior contract — compare ACCORD 3, NOVATION

synallagmatic contract *in the civil law of Louisiana* : BILATERAL CONTRACT in this entry

unilateral contract : a contract in which only one party is obligated to perform — compare BILATERAL CONTRACT in this entry

yellow–dog contract : an illegal employment contract in which a worker disavows membership in and agrees not to join a labor union in order to get a job **2** : an insurance policy **3** : the study of the law regarding contracts — usu. used in pl.

²contract *vt* **1** : to undertake or establish by a contract **2** : to purchase (as goods or services) on a contract basis — often used with *out* ∼ *vi* : to make a contract

contract bond — see BOND 1a

contract carrier *n* : a transport line that carries persons or property under contract to one or a limited number of shippers — compare COMMON CARRIER

contract clause *n, often cap both Cs* : the clause in Article I, Section 10 of the U.S. Constitution that prohibits states from passing any laws that render contracts invalid or impair the obligations under them

contract implied in fact — see CONTRACT

contract implied in law — see CONTRACT

contract of adhesion — see CONTRACT

con•trac•tor \'kän-ˌtrak-tər, kən-'trak-\ *n* : one that contracts: as **a** : one that contracts to perform work or provide supplies **b** : one that contracts to erect buildings

con•trac•tu•al \kən-'trak-chə-wəl\ *adj* : of, relating to, or constituting a contract ⟨a ∼ agreement⟩ — **con•trac•tu•al•ly** *adv*

contract under seal — see CONTRACT

con•trib•ute *vb* **-ut•ed; -ut•ing** *vt* : to make a contribution of ∼ *vi* : to make a contribution

con•tri•bu•tion *n* **1** : payment of a share of an amount for which one is liable: as **a** : shared payment of a judgment by joint tortfeasors esp. according to proportional fault — compare APPORTION a **b** : pro rata apportionment of loss among all the insurance policies covering the same person or property — compare INDEMNITY **2** : the money paid by one responsible for a share **3** : payment to a common fund (as by an employer or employee to an insurance plan or retirement fund)

con•trib•u•to•ry \kən-'tri-byə-ˌtōr-ē\ *adj* **1** : characterized by or making contributions to a common fund or enterprise; *specif* : of, relating to, or being an em-

ployee benefit plan to which both employers and employees make contributions 2 : helping to bring about an end or result ⟨~ infringement⟩
contributory fault *n* : responsibility for aiding in the accomplishment of a bad result (as an injury); *specif* : responsibility of a promisor for causing his or her promise to be impossible to perform ◊ A promisor who is guilty of contributory fault cannot invoke the defense of impossibility.
contributory negligence — see NEGLIGENCE
con·trol *vt* **con·trolled; con·trol·ling** **1** : to exercise restraining or directing influence over esp. by law **2** : to have power or authority over ⟨precedent ~*s* the outcome in this case⟩ **3** : to have controlling interest in — **control** *n*
controlled sub·stance *n* : a substance (as a drug) whose use and possession is regulated by law (as title 21, chapter 13 of the U.S. Code)
con·trol·ler \kən-'trō-lər, 'kän-ˌtrō-\ *n* : COMPTROLLER
controlling *adj* **1 a** : exercising domination or influence ⟨the ~ principles of law⟩ **b** : DISPOSITIVE ⟨judgment debtor's stipulation to pay a specified amount is not ~ —J. H. Friedenthal *et al.*⟩ **2** : having controlling interest ⟨~ shareholders⟩
controlling interest — see INTEREST 1
con·tro·ver·sy \'kän-trə-ˌvər-sē, *Brit also* kən-'trä-vər-sē\ *n, pl* **-sies** **1** : a state of dispute or disagreement ⟨suits at common law, where the value in ~ shall exceed twenty dollars —*U.S. Constitution* amend. VII⟩ **2** : a civil action involving a real and immediate dispute between parties with adverse interests ◊ Article III of the U.S. Constitution gives the judiciary the power to decide cases and controversies. Article III's limitation of the judicial power to cases or controversies requires that an action brought in the federal court involve parties with standing to sue and questions that are ripe and not moot. — **con·tro·ver·sial** \ˌkän-trə-'vər-shəl, -'vər-sē-əl\ *adj*

con·tu·ma·cy \kən-'tü-mə-sē, -'tyü-; 'kän-tə-mə-sē, -tyə-\ *n* [Latin *contumacia*, literally, defiance, obstinacy] : willful disobedience of a court order — **con·tu·ma·cious** \ˌkän-tü-'mā-shəs, -tyü-\ *adj*
con·ven·tion *n* **1** : an agreement between nations for regulation of matters affecting all of them **2** : an agreement enforceable in law : CONTRACT **3** : an assembly of persons met for a common purpose; *esp* : a meeting of the delegates of a political party for the purpose of formulating a platform and selecting candidates for office
con·ven·tion·al /kən-'ven-chə-nəl/ *adj* **1** : based on, settled by, or formed by agreement : CONTRACTUAL — compare JUDICIAL 2, LEGAL 2c **2** : of, like, or relating to a convention or public meeting
conventional annuity — see ANNUITY
conventional loan — see LOAN
conventional mortgage — see MORTGAGE
conventional obligation — see OBLIGATION
con·ver·sion \kən-'vər-zhən\ *n* **1 a** : the act of changing from one form or use to another **b** : the act of exchanging one kind of property for another; *esp* : the act of exchanging preferred stocks or bonds for shares of common stock of the same company usu. at a preset ratio or price and at a preset time
equitable conversion : the constructive conversion of real property into personal property esp. as a result of a contract for sale of land or testamentary instructions to sell real estate and divide the proceeds ◊ Equitable conversion is a legal fiction under which the seller of a real property becomes, upon the execution of a contract for the sale of the property, the owner of personal property in the form of legal title to the property that secures payment of the purchase

price. The purchaser is deemed to be the holder of equitable title in and owner of the real property, having the rights and being subject to the liabilities that attend that status. In the case of a will in which a property owner authorizes the sale of real property and distribution of the proceeds, the property transforms into personalty by equitable conversion upon the owner's death.

involuntary conversion : the conversion of property into other property as compensation for the theft, destruction, seizure, requisition, or condemnation of the original property ◊ For income tax purposes, involuntary conversions are generally taxable, and the gain or loss is computed by offsetting the basis of the property against the compensation received (as from insurance).
2 : the crime or tort of interfering with the ownership of another's movable or personal property without authorization or justification (as a lien) and esp. of depriving the owner of use and possession — see also FRAUDULENT CONVERSION

con•vert \kən-'vərt\ *vt* **1 a** : to change from one form or use to another **b** : to exchange (property) for another esp. of a different kind 〈if property . . . is compulsorily or involuntarily *~ed* —*Internal Revenue Code*〉; *esp* : to exercise the right of conversion by exchanging (preferred shares or bonds) for common stock **2** : to appropriate (another's property) by conversion 〈the bailee *~ed* the goods to his own use〉 — see also EMBEZZLE — **con•vert•er** *n* — **con•ver•ti•ble** \kən-'vər-tə-bəl\ *adj*
convertible bond — see BOND 2
convertible security — see SECURITY
con•vey \kən-'vā\ *vt* **con•veyed; con•vey•ing** : to transfer or transmit (property or property rights) to another esp. by a writing (as a deed or will) 〈agreed to *~* to the estate his Manhattan town house —R. H. Jensen〉 — compare ALIENATE, DEVISE, DONATE, GIVE, GRANT, SELL — **con•vey•ee** \kən-ˌvā-'ē\ *n* — **con•vey•or** \kən-'vā-ər\ *n*

con•vey•ance \kən-'vā-əns\ *n* **1** : an act of conveying 〈a *~* of land〉 **2** : an instrument (as a deed) that conveys property rights (as title) 〈lack of delivery of a *~* —J. D. Calamari and J. M. Perillo〉
con•vey•an•cing *n* : the act or business of drawing up conveyances (as deeds or leases) — **con•vey•an•cer** *n*
¹**con•vict** \kən-'vikt\ *vt* [Latin *convictus* past participle of *convincere* to find guilty, prove, from *com-* with, together + *vincer* to conquer] : to find guilty of a criminal offense 〈was *~ed* of fraud〉 — compare ACQUIT
²**con•vict** \'kän-ˌvikt\ *n* : a person convicted of and serving a sentence for a crime
con•vic•tion *n* **1** : the act or process of convicting; *also* : the final judgment entered after a finding of guilt 〈a prior *~* of murder〉 〈would not overturn the *~*〉 — compare ACQUITTAL ◊ Jurisdictions differ as to what constitutes conviction for various statutes (as habitual offender statutes). *Conviction* is rarely applied to civil cases. **2** : GUILT 〈the judge will enter a judgment of *~* —W. R. LaFave and J. H. Israel〉
cool *vi* : to lose passion : become calm — sometimes used with *off* or *down* 〈the time elapsing . . . is such that a reasonable man thus provoked would have *~ed* — W. R. LaFave and A. W. Scott, Jr.〉
cool•ing–off pe•ri•od *n* : a period of time (as after a sale or a call to strike) to allow further consideration or negotiation — see also *Labor Management Relations Act* in the IMPORTANT LAWS section
cooling time *n* : time in which to become calm following provocation — compare HEAT OF PASSION ◊ If a court finds that the cooling time was sufficient or reasonable, a defendant may not use provocation to reduce a murder charge to involuntary manslaughter.
cool state of blood : an emotional condition in which a person's anger or passion is not great enough to overcome his or her faculties or ability to reason — often used in statutory definitions of murder; compare COLD BLOOD, HEAT OF PASSION

¹cooperative *adj* : of, relating to, or organized as a cooperative

²co·op·er·a·tive *n* : an enterprise or organization (as for banking and credit services or the ownership of residential property) that is owned by and operated for the benefit of those using its services — called also *co-op;* compare CONDOMINIUM 1

cooperative bank — see BANK

co·or·di·na·tion of benefits \kō-ˌȯrd-ᵊn-ˈā-shən-\ : the distribution of compensation or coverage from more than one insurance policy

co–own·er \ˈkō-ˌō-nər\ *n* : one of two or more individuals or entities owning property together (as by joint tenancy, tenancy in common, or tenancy by the entirety)

co·par·ce·nary \ˌkō-ˈpärs-ᵊn-ˌer-ē\ *n, pl* **-nar·ies 1** : joint heirship **2** : joint ownership

co·par·ce·ner \ˌkō-ˈpärs-ᵊn-ər\ *n* : a joint heir

co·par·ty \ˌkō-ˈpär-tē, ˈkō-ˌ\ *n* : a party (as a coplaintiff or codefendant) on the same side of an action

co·plain·tiff \ˌkō-ˈplān-təf\ *n* : a joint plaintiff

¹copy·right \ˈkä-pē-ˌrīt\ *n* : a person's exclusive right to reproduce, publish, or sell his or her original work of authorship (as a literary, musical, dramatic, artistic, or architectural work) — see also COMMON⸱ LAW COPYRIGHT, *fair use* at USE 2, INFRINGE, *intellectual property* at PROPERTY, INTERNATIONAL COPYRIGHT, ORIGINAL, PUBLIC DOMAIN; compare PATENT, TRADEMARK ◊ Copyrights are governed by the Copyright Act of 1976 contained in title 17 of the U.S. Code. The Act protects published or unpublished works that are fixed in a tangible medium of expression from which they can be perceived. The Act does not protect matters such as an idea, process, system, or discovery. Protection under the Act extends for the life of the creator of the work plus fifty years after his or her death. For works created before January 1, 1978, but not copyrighted or in the public domain, the copyright starts on January 1, 1978, and extends for the same period as for other works, but in any case will not expire before December 31, 2002. Prior to the enactment of the Act, copyright protection was available for unpublished works only under common law. The Act abolishes the common-law rights, as well as any rights available under state statute, in favor of the rights available under the provisions of the Act. The Act provides for certain exceptions, however, including rights to protection for works not fixed in a tangible medium of expression, and rights regarding any cause of action arising from events occurring before January 1, 1978. — **copyright** *adj*

²copyright *vt* : to secure a copyright on — **copy·right·abil·i·ty** \ˌkä-pē-ˌrī-tə-ˈbi-lə-tē\ *n* — **copy·right·able** \ˈkä-pē-ˌrī-tə-bəl\ *adj*

cor·am no·bis \ˈkȯr-əm-ˈnō-bəs, ˈkō-räm-ˈnō-bēs\ *n* [Latin, in our presence] : WRIT OF ERROR CORAM NOBIS at WRIT

core proceeding — see PROCEEDING

co·re·spon·dent \ˌkō-ri-ˈspän-dənt\ *n* **1** : a joint respondent **2** : a person named as guilty of adultery with the defendant in a divorce suit

cor·o·ner \ˈkȯr-ə-nər\ *n* [Anglo-French, recorder of crown pleas, from *corone* crown] : a public officer whose principal duty is to inquire by an inquest into the cause of death when there is reason to think the death may not be due to natural causes

corpora *pl of* CORPUS

cor·po·ral punishment \ˈkȯr-pə-rəl-\ *n* : punishment inflicted on a person's body — see also CRUEL AND UNUSUAL PUNISHMENT ◊ The prohibition on cruel and unusual punishment in the Eighth Amendment to the U.S. Constitution imposes limits on the use of corporal pun-

\ə\abut \ᵊ\kitten \ər\further \a\ash \ā\ace
\ä\cot, cart \aú\out \ch\chin \e\bet \ē\easy
\g\go \i\hit \ī\ice \j\job \ŋ\sing \ō\go \ȯ\law
\ȯi\boy \th\thin \t̲h\the \ü\loot \ú\foot \y\yet
\zh\vision *see also* Pronunciation Symbols page

ishment on convicted offenders and prisoners. The U.S. Supreme Court has found the Eighth Amendment to be inapplicable to the use of corporal punishment on schoolchildren.

¹cor•po•rate \'kȯr-pə-rət\ *adj* : of or relating to a business corporation

²corporate *n* : a bond issued by a business corporation

corporate immunity — see IMMUNITY

corporate liability — see LIABILITY 2b

corporate op•por•tu•ni•ty doctrine *n* : a doctrine of corporate law stating that fiduciaries of the corporation (as directors or officers) may not take for themselves a business opportunity offered to the corporation

cor•po•ra•tion \ˌkȯr-pə-'rā-shən\ *n* [Late Latin *corporatio*, from Latin *corporare* to form into a body, from *corpor-*, *corpus* body] : an invisible, intangible, artificial creation of the law existing as a voluntary chartered association of individuals that has most of the rights and duties of natural persons but with perpetual existence and limited liability — see also PIERCE; compare ASSOCIATION, PARTNERSHIP, SOLE PROPRIETORSHIP

close corporation \'klōs-\ : a corporation whose shares are held by a small number of individuals (as management) and not publicly traded; *specif* : SMALL BUSINESS CORPORATION in this entry — called also *closely held corporation;* compare PUBLIC CORPORATION 2 in this entry

foreign corporation : a corporation organized under the laws of a state or government other than that in which it is doing business

government corporation : PUBLIC CORPORATION 1 in this entry

moneyed corporation : a corporation (as a bank) authorized to engage in the investment, exchange, or lending of moneyed capital

municipal corporation : a political unit created or otherwise given corporate status (as by a charter) by a superior governing authority (as a state) and endowed with powers of local self-government (as eminent domain); *broadly* : a public corporation (as a utility) created to act as an agency of administration and local self-government ◊ As a result of its incorporation, a municipal corporation has the capacity to sue and be sued. Citizens as well as officials are usu. considered part of a municipal corporation.

professional corporation : a corporation organized by one or more licensed individuals (as a doctor or lawyer) to provide professional services and obtain tax advantages

public corporation **1** : a government-owned corporation (as a utility or railroad) engaged in a profit-making enterprise that may require the exercise of powers unique to government (as eminent domain) — called also *government corporation, publicly held corporation* **2** : a business corporation whose stocks are publicly traded — called also *publicly held corporation;* compare CLOSE CORPORATION in this entry

S corporation : a small business corporation that is treated for federal tax purposes as a partnership — called also *subchapter S corporation*

shell corporation **1** : a corporation that exists as a legal entity without independent assets or operations as an instrument by which another company or corporation can carry out dealings usu. unrelated to its primary business **2** : a corporation formed for purposes of tax evasion or acquisition or merger rather than for a legitimate business purpose

small business corporation : a corporation described in section 1361 of the Internal Revenue Code that has 35 shareholders or less and only one class of stock and that may if eligible elect to be an S corporation and taxed accordingly

subchapter S corporation : S CORPORATION in this entry

corporation counsel *n* : the city attorney in some cities (as Boston)

cor·po·re·al \kȯr-'pōr-ē-əl\ *adj* : having, consisting of, or relating to a physical material body — compare INCORPOREAL — **cor·po·re·al·ly** *adv*

cor·pus \'kȯr-pəs, -ˌpu̇s\ *n, pl* **cor·po·ra** \-pə-rə\ : the main body of a thing; *specif* : the principal of a fund, trust, or estate as distinct from income or interest : RES

corpus de·lic·ti \-di-'lik-ˌtī, -dā-, -tē\ *n* [New Latin, literally, the body of the offense] : the substance of a crime that the prosecutor must prove and that consists of an injury or loss (as death of a victim or disappearance of property) and the criminal act that resulted in it

corpus jur·is \-'ju̇r-is, -'yu̇r-ēs\ *n* [Medieval Latin, literally, a body of law] : a comprehensive collection of the law of a judicial system or of a country or jurisdiction

cor·re·al \'kȯr-ē-əl, kə-'rē-əl\ *adj* [Latin *correus* person accused along with another, from *com-* with, together + *reus* accused person] *in the civil law of Louisiana* : SOLIDARY — **cor·real·i·ty** \ˌkȯr-ē-'a-lə-tē\ *n*

cor·rec·tion *n* **1** : a decline in market price or business activity following and counteracting a rise **2** : the treatment and rehabilitation of offenders through a program involving penal custody, parole, and probation — often used in pl. — **cor·rec·tion·al** *adj*

cor·rob·o·rate \kə-'rä-bə-ˌrāt\ *vt* **-rat·ed; -rat·ing** [Latin *corroboratus*, past participle of *corroborare* to strengthen, from *com-*, prefix marking completion + *robur* strength, literally, oak tree] : to support with evidence or authority : strengthen or make more certain — **cor·rob·o·ra·tion** \kə-ˌrä-bə-'rā-shən\ *n* — **cor·rob·o·ra·tive** \kə-'rä-bə-ˌrā-tiv, -rə-tiv\ *adj*

corroborating evidence — see EVIDENCE

corroborative evidence *n* : CORROBORATING EVIDENCE at EVIDENCE

¹cor·rupt \kə-'rəpt\ *adj* : having an unlawful or evil motive; *esp* : characterized by improper and usu. unlawful conduct intended to secure a benefit for oneself or another (as by taking or giving bribes) — **cor·rupt·ly** *adj* — **cor·rupt·ness** *n*

²corrupt *vt* **1** : to change from good to bad in principles or moral values ⟨~*ing* a minor⟩ **2** : to subject (a person) to corruption of blood — **cor·rup·ti·bil·i·ty** \kə-ˌrəp-tə-'bi-lə-tē\ *n* — **cor·rup·ti·ble** \kə-'rəp-tə-bəl\ *adj* — **cor·rup·ti·bly** *adv* — **cor·rup·tion** \kə-'rəp-shən\ *n*

corruption of blood : the effect of an attainder which bars a person from inheriting, retaining, or transmitting any estate, rank, or title ⟨no attainder of treason shall work *corruption of blood* —*U.S. Constitution* art. III⟩

corrupt practices act *n* : a law regulating the amount and source of political campaign contributions and requiring detailed reports of expenditures

co·sig·na·to·ry \kō-'sig-nə-ˌtōr-ē\ *n* : a joint signer

co·sign·er \'kō-ˌsī-nər\ *n* : COSIGNATORY; *esp* : a joint signer of a promissory note

cost *n* **1** : the amount or equivalent paid or charged for something **2** *pl* : expenses incurred in litigation; *esp* : those given by the law or the court to the prevailing party against the losing party

cost and freight *adj* : including the cost of goods being shipped and the freight charges

cost basis — see BASIS 3

cost bond — see BOND 1a

cost, insurance, and freight *adj* : including the cost of goods being shipped and the freight and insurance charges

cost of liv·ing : the cost of purchasing those goods and services which are included in an accepted standard level of consumption

cost of living clause *n* : a clause in an agreement (as a collective bargaining agreement) that provides for increase of payments (as wages) made under the

\ə\abut \ᵊ\kitten \ər\further \a\ash \ā\ace
\ä\cot, cart \au̇\out \ch\chin \e\bet \ē\easy
\g\go \i\hit \ī\ice \j\job \ŋ\sing \ō\go \ȯ\law
\ȯi\boy \th\thin \t͟h\the \ü\loot \u̇\foot \y\yet
\zh\vision *see also* Pronunciation Symbols page

agreement in some proportion to the increase in the cost of living

cost–of–living index *n* : CONSUMER PRICE INDEX

cost recovery *n* : DEPRECIATION

co·sure·ty \ˌkō-'shùr-ə-tē\ *n, pl* **-ties** : any of two or more sureties liable on the same obligation — **co·sure·ty·ship** *n*

co·ten·an·cy \ˌkō-'te-nən-sē\ *n, pl* **-cies** : JOINT TENANCY at TENANCY

co·ten·ant \ˌkō-'te-nənt\ *n* : JOINT TENANT

co·trust·ee \ˌkō-ˌtrəs-'tē\ *n* : a joint trustee

coun·cil \'kaùn-səl\ *n* : a governmental body: as **a** : a group elected as a legislative body ⟨city ~⟩ **b** : an administrative body ⟨~ on aging⟩ **c** : an executive body whose members are equal in power and authority — compare COMMITTEE 2b

coun·cil·lor *or* **coun·ci·lor** \'kaùn-sə-lər\ *n* : a member of a council — **coun·cil·lor·ship** *n*

coun·cil·man *n, pl* **-men** : a member of a council : COUNCILLOR

coun·cil·wom·an *n, pl* **-wom·en** : a woman who is a member of a council

¹coun·sel \'kaùn-səl\ *n, pl* **counsel** [Old French *conseil* advice, from Latin *consilium* discussion, advice, council, from *consulere* to consult] : LAWYER: as **a** : a lawyer participating in the management or trial of a case in court ⟨ . . . to have the assistance of ~ for his defense — *U.S. Constitution* amend. VI⟩ ⟨a right to ~⟩ **b** : a lawyer appointed or engaged to advise or represent a client in legal matters (as negotiations or the drafting of documents) — compare ATTORNEY ◊ A judge who has acted as counsel in a matter (as by advising an investigator) is disqualified from hearing the case. — **of counsel 1** : assisting another lawyer in a case ⟨was attorney *of counsel*⟩ **2** : employed on a part-time basis ⟨a tax attorney will move also and become *of counsel* — *National Law Journal*⟩

²counsel *vt* **-seled** *or* **-selled**; **-sel·ing** *or* **-sel·ling** : ADVISE

coun·se·lor \'kaùn-sə-lər\ *n* : COUNSEL

counselor–at–law *n, pl* **counselors–at–**law : COUNSEL — compare ATTORNEY⁰ AT-LAW

count *n* : CHARGE; *specif* : a charge (as in a complaint or indictment) that separately states a cause of action or esp. offense ⟨guilty on all ~s⟩

coun·ter- \'kaùn-tər\ *prefix* **1 a** : contrary : opposite ⟨*counter*letter⟩ **b** : opposing : retaliatory ⟨*counter*action⟩ **2** : complementary : corresponding ⟨*counter*sign⟩ **3** : duplicate : substitute ⟨*counter*part⟩

coun·ter·claim \'kaùn-tər-ˌklām\ *n* : a claim for relief that is asserted against an opposing party after an original claim has been made — compare *affirmative defense* at DEFENSE, CROSS-ACTION, CROSS-APPEAL, CROSS-CLAIM, INTERPLEADER, THIRD-PARTY CLAIM — **counterclaim** *vb*

¹coun·ter·feit \'kaùn-tər-ˌfit\ *adj* [Middle French *contrefait*, past participle of *contrefaire* to imitate, draw, paint, from *contre-* counter- + *faire* to make] : made in imitation of a genuine article (as a document) without authorization and esp. with intent to deceive or defraud

²counterfeit *vt* : to make an imitation of without authorization and esp. with intent to deceive or defraud ⟨whoever falsely makes, alters, forges, or ~s any deed — *U.S. Code*⟩ — **coun·ter·feit·er** *n*

³counterfeit *n* : something counterfeit ⟨all ~s of any coins or obligations — *U.S. Code*⟩ — compare FORGERY

counterletter *n, in the civil law of Louisiana* : a secret agreement that expresses the true intent of the parties to a simulation; *esp* : a writing embodying the agreement ⟨~ can have no effects against third persons in good faith — *Louisiana Civil Code*⟩ ◊ An agreement stating that the conveyor of some land is still the owner, even though the other party has been given a bill of sale, is an example of a counterletter.

coun·ter·of·fer \'kaùn-tər-ˌȯ-fər\ *n* : an offer that is made in response to another and that has additional or differing terms ◊ Under common law, a counteroffer does not constitute an acceptance of an offer and is often considered a rejection of the offer. — **counteroffer** *vi*

coun·ter·part \'kaún-tər-ˌpärt\ *n* : one of two corresponding or duplicate copies of a legal instrument

coun·ter·sign \'kaún-tər-ˌsīn\ *n* : a signature attesting the authenticity of a document already signed by another

counter will — see WILL

coun·ty attorney \'kaún-tē-\ *n* : a district attorney for a county

county commission *n* **1** : a commission for a county **2** : a court in West Virginia having jurisdiction over certain probate matters including civil commitments

county court *n, often cap both Cs* : a court in some states that has a designated jurisdiction usu. both civil and criminal within the limits of a county

county court at law *n, often cap C&C&L* : a court in some of the more populated counties of Texas that takes on some of the responsibilities of the constitutional county court

county recorder's court *n, often cap C&R&C* : a court of limited jurisdiction in several counties in Georgia

cou·pon \'kü-ˌpän, 'kyü-\ *n* [French, from Old French, piece, from *couper* to cut] : a statement of due interest to be cut from a debt instrument and esp. a bearer bond when payable and presented for payment; *also* : the interest rate of a coupon

coupon bond — see BOND 2

course of dealing : the conduct of parties to a business deal during past business deals that may be used as a basis for understanding each other's expressions and conduct during the current deal — compare COURSE OF PERFORMANCE, USAGE OF TRADE

course of performance : the conduct of parties during a business deal requiring repeated performances that creates an understanding between the parties as to performance and that may be used to help interpret their agreement in instances of dispute — compare COURSE OF DEALING, PRACTICAL CONSTRUCTION, USAGE OF TRADE

court \'kōrt\ *n* [Old French, enclosed space, royal entourage, court of justice, from Latin *cohort-, cohors* farmyard,

armed force, retinue] **1 a** : an official assembly for the administration of justice : a unit of the judicial branch of government 〈the judicial power of the United States shall be vested in one supreme Court, and in such inferior ~*s* as the Congress may from time to time ordain and establish — *U.S. Constitution* art. III〉 — see also the JUDICIAL SYSTEM in the back matter **b** : a session of such a court **c** *usu cap* : the Supreme Court of the United States **2** : a place (as a building, hall, or room) for the administration of justice 〈order in the ~〉 **3** : a judge or judges acting in official capacity 〈an issue to be decided by the ~〉 〈the ~ may neither preside at nor attend the meeting of creditors —J. H. Williamson〉 **4** *usu cap* : a legislative body 〈the General *Court* of Massachusetts〉 **5** : a body (as the International Court of Justice) exercising judicial powers over its members or the members of a body represented by it 〈an ecclesiastical ~〉 — **out of court** : without a court hearing : by private arrangement 〈settled *out of court*〉

Court Christian *n* : ECCLESIASTICAL COURT

court·house *n* : a building in which court is regularly held

¹court–mar·tial \'kōrt-ˌmär-shəl\ *n, pl* **courts–martial** *also* **court–martials** **1** : a court consisting of commissioned officers and in some instances enlisted personnel for the trial of members of the armed forces or others within its jurisdiction **2** : a trial by a court-martial

²court–martial *vt* **-mar·tialed** *also* **-martialled; -mar·tial·ing** *also* **-mar·tial·ling** : to subject to trial by court-martial

court of admiralty : ADMIRALTY

court of appeals *often cap C&A* : a court hearing appeals from the decisions of lower courts: as **a** : an intermediate court of the U.S. federal judicial system **b** : a state appellate court — called also *court*

\ə\abut \ᵊ\kitten \ər\further \a\ash \ā\ace
\ä\cot, cart \aú\out \ch\chin \e\bet \ē\easy
\g\go \i\hit \ī\ice \j\job \ŋ\sing \ō\go \ȯ\law
\ȯi\boy \th\thin \t̲h̲\the \ü\loot \ú\foot \y\yet
\zh\vision   *see also* Pronunciation Symbols page

of appeal; see also the JUDICIAL SYS-TEM in the back matter ◊ Not all of the states have intermediate-level courts but of those that do, many are called the Court of Appeals or, in California and Louisiana, the Court of Appeal. In Hawaii, such a court is called the Intermediate Court of Appeals. In some states, appeals are divided between a court of criminal appeals and a court of civil appeals. In the District of Columbia, Maryland, and New York the court of last resort is called the Court of Appeals, and the intermediate court in Maryland is called the Court of Special Appeals. In West Virginia the court of last resort is called the Supreme Court of Appeals. In England the Court of Appeal is a division of the Supreme Court of Judicature.

court of chancery *often cap both Cs* : COURT OF EQUITY

Court of Civil Appeals : the intermediate court in Alabama for appeals of civil matters

court of claims 1 *often cap both Cs* : a court (as in Illinois, Michigan, New York, and West Virginia) that has jurisdiction primarily over cases involving claims against the state **2** *cap* : a former court succeeded by the United States Claims Court — see also UNITED STATES COURT OF FEDERAL CLAIMS

court of common pleas *often cap C&C&P* : an intermediate-level court in some states (as Arkansas, Connecticut, and Ohio) having limited jurisdiction over various civil and criminal matters

court of criminal appeals 1 *often cap C&C&A* : a court of appeals in some states (as Alabama, Oklahoma, Tennessee, and Texas) that hears criminal appeals **2** *cap* : the intermediate appellate military court made up of military personnel and having the power to review questions of fact as well as law ◊ This court was called the Court of Military Review until 1994.

court of domestic re•la•tions *often cap C&D&R* : FAMILY COURT

court of equity *often cap C&E* : a court

having jurisdiction over suits in equity and administering justice and providing remedies according to the rules and principles of equity — compare COURT OF LAW ◊ Rule 1 of the Federal Rules of Civil Procedure abolishes the distinction between law and equity, and therefore there are no longer courts of equity in the federal system.

court of inquiry : a military court that inquires into and reports on some military matter (as an officer's questionable conduct)

court of last re•sort : a court of final appeal in a jurisdiction — see also COURT OF APPEALS, SUPREME COURT, SUPREME COURT OF APPEALS, SUPREME JUDICIAL COURT

court of law : COURT 1; *specif* : a court that hears cases and decides them on the basis of statutes and common law — compare COURT OF EQUITY

Court of Military Review : COURT OF CRIMINAL APPEALS 2

court of record : a court whose acts and proceedings are kept on permanent record

Court of Spe•cial Appeals : the intermediate appellate court in Maryland

Court of the Exchequer : EXCHEQUER 2

court reporter *n* : a stenographer who records and transcribes a verbatim report of all proceedings in a court of law

court•room *n* : a room where court is held

cov•e•nant \'kə-və-nənt\ *n* **1** : an official agreement or compact ⟨an international ~ on human rights⟩ **2 a** : a contract in its entirety or a promise within a contract for the performance or nonperformance of a particular act ⟨a ~ not to sue⟩; *specif* : a promise relating to the transfer, possession, or ownership of real property — see also COVENANT NOT TO COMPETE, RESTRICTIVE COVENANT **b** : a warranty in a deed assuring the grantee esp. against defects in title ⟨a ~ for quiet enjoyment⟩ — see also RUN **3** : a common-law action to recover damages for breach of a contract under seal — compare ASSUMPSIT, DEBT — **covenant** *vb*

cov·e·nan·tee \ˌkə-və-ˌnan-ˈtē, -nən-\ *n* : a person to whom or an entity to which a promise in the form of a covenant is made

covenant not to com·pete *n* : a covenant in an agreement (as for the sale of a business) by which one party agrees not to engage in the same business or a similar business in a particular area for a period of time

covenant of warranty : WARRANTY 1

cov·e·nan·tor \ˈkə-və-ˌnan-tər, -nən-; ˌkə-və-ˌnan-ˈtȯr\ *n* : the party to a covenant who is bound to perform the obligation expressed in it

¹cov·er *vt* **1** : INSURE ⟨this policy ~s other family drivers⟩ **2** : to give protection against or compensation or indemnification for ⟨doesn't ~ flood damage⟩ — *vi* : to obtain cover ⟨where the seller anticipatorily repudiates a contract and the buyer does not ~ —*Cosden Oil & Chemical Co. v. Karl O. Helm AG*, 736 F.2d 1064 (1984)⟩

²cover *n* : purchase of goods in substitution for those originally contracted for when the seller fails to fulfill the contract ⟨the buyer is always free to choose between ~ and damages for nondelivery —*Uniform Commercial Code*⟩; *also* : the substituted goods ◊ Under the Uniform Commercial Code, when a seller does not perform on a contract, the buyer has the option of covering, with the seller paying the difference between the cost of the cover and the original contract price, or seeking damages for nonperformance. Reselling is the seller's comparable remedy when a buyer does not perform under a contract.

cov·er·age \ˈkə-və-rij\ *n* **1** : protection or indemnification by an insurance policy ⟨the policy provides extensive ~ against burglary⟩ **2** : a risk assumed by the terms of an insurance contract ⟨the policy lists four ~s: liability, medical payments, uninsured motorists, and physical damage⟩

covered option — see OPTION 3

cov·er·ture \ˈkə-vər-ˌchu̇r, -chər\ *n* [Anglo-French, literally, shelter, cover-

ing, from Old French, from *covert*, past participle of *covrir* to cover] : the inclusion of a woman in the legal person of her husband upon marriage under common law ◊ Because of coverture, married women formerly did not have the legal capacity to hold their own property or contract on their own behalf. These disabilities have been removed for the most part by statute.

CP *abbr* court of common pleas

CPSC *abbr* Consumer Product Safety Commission — see also the IMPORTANT AGENCIES section

craft union *n* : a labor union with membership limited to workers in the same craft (as carpentry or plumbing) — compare INDUSTRIAL UNION

¹cred·it *n* **1** : RECOGNITION — see also FULL FAITH AND CREDIT **2 a** : the balance in an account which may be drawn upon and repaid later — compare LOAN **b** : the use of resources (as money) in the present obtained by the debtor's promise to repay the creditor in the future usu. with interest as compensation to the creditor and often secured by a pledge of property or the right to attach the debtor's income in case of a failure to repay — see also CONSUMER CREDIT; compare DEBT **c** : financial reputation ⟨to borrow money on the ~ of the United States —*U.S. Constitution* art. I⟩ **d** : LETTER OF CREDIT **3 a** : a deduction from an expense or asset account **b** : a reduction of an amount otherwise due; *esp* : TAX CREDIT ⟨a ~ for child-care expenses⟩ — compare DEDUCTION, EXCLUSION, EXEMPTION

²credit *vt* **1** : to supply goods on credit to **2** : to trust in the truth of **3 a** : to enter upon the credit side of an account **b** : to place an amount to the credit of ⟨~ his account with ten dollars⟩

credit bu·reau *n* : a private business that compiles information on consumers'

\ə\abut \ᵊ\kitten \ər\further \a\ash \ā\ace \ä\cot, cart \au̇\out \ch\chin \e\bet \ē\easy \g\go \i\hit \ī\ice \j\job \ŋ\sing \ō\go \ȯ\law \ȯi\boy \th\thin \t͟h\the \ü\loot \u̇\foot \y\yet \zh\vision *see also* Pronunciation Symbols page

creditworthiness and provides this information to lenders

credit insurance *n* : insurance paid for by a debtor to assure payment of any outstanding credit balance in the event of death or disability

cred·i·tor \'kre-də-tər, -ˌtȯr\ *n* : a person to whom a debt is owed; *esp* : a person to whom money or goods are due — compare DEBTOR, OBLIGOR

  general creditor : a creditor who is not secured by a lien or other security interest — called also *unsecured creditor*

  judgment creditor : a creditor who has a money judgment entered against the debtor and may enforce the judgment (as by attachment or writ of execution)

  known creditor : a creditor whose potential claim is known or should be known by a debtor and who is entitled to notice of a corporate dissolution or of a date at which claims will be barred (as in bankruptcy)

  lien creditor : a creditor who is secured by a lien (as by attachment)

  secured creditor : a creditor who has a security interest (as a mortgage)

  unsecured creditor : GENERAL CREDITOR in this entry

creditor beneficiary — see BENEFICIARY b

creditor's bill — see BILL 3a

credit shelter trust — see TRUST

credit union *n* : a cooperative association that makes small loans to its members at low interest rates and offers other banking services (as savings and checking accounts)

cred·it·wor·thy \'kre-dit-ˌwər-thē\ *adj* : likely to be able to repay loans or consumer credit — **cred·it·wor·thi·ness** *n*

C reorganization — see REORGANIZATION

crime \'krīm\ *n* [Middle French, from Latin *crimen* fault, accusation, crime] **1** : conduct that is prohibited and has a specific punishment (as incarceration or fine) prescribed by public law — compare DELICT, TORT **2** : an offense against public law usu. excluding a petty viola-

tion — see also FELONY, MISDEMEANOR ◊ Crimes in the common-law tradition were originally defined primarily by judicial decision. For the most part, common-law crimes are now codified. There is a general principle "nullum crimen sine lege," that there can be no crime without a law. A crime generally consists of both conduct, known as the actus reus, and a concurrent state of mind, known as the mens rea. **3** : criminal activity

crime against hu·man·i·ty : an inhumane act (as enslavement) committed against civilians before or during a war for which criminal liability is imposed by a domestic or international tribunal — see also WAR CRIME

crime against nature : a sexual act (as of bestiality) that is regarded by the law as abnormal; *also* : the crime of committing such an act

cri·men fal·si \'krī-mən-'fȯl-ˌsī, 'krē-men-'fäl-sē\ *n* [Latin, literally, crime of falsehood] : a crime (as perjury or fraud) involving deceit or falsification

crime of violence : a crime that by its nature poses a substantial risk that force will be used against a person or property ◊ A record of crimes of violence is used esp. to determine career offender status under federal sentencing guidelines.

¹crim·i·nal \'kri-mə-nəl\ *adj* **1** : relating to, involving, or being a crime ⟨~ neglect⟩⟨~ conduct⟩ **2** : relating to crime or its prosecution ⟨brought a ~ action⟩ ⟨~ code⟩ — compare CIVIL 4, PENAL

²criminal *n* **1** : one who has committed a crime **2** : a person who has been convicted of a crime

criminal assault — see ASSAULT

criminal attempt *n* : ATTEMPT

criminal conspiracy — see CONSPIRACY

criminal contempt — see CONTEMPT

criminal con·ver·sa·tion *n* : the tort of committing adultery with another's spouse — compare ALIENATION OF AFFECTIONS ◊ This tort is no longer recognized in most jurisdictions.

criminal court *n* : a court that has jurisdiction to try criminal defendants

criminal forfeiture *n* : the forfeiture of property used in committing a crime — see also SEIZE; compare CONFISCATE

criminal homicide — see HOMICIDE

criminal intent — see INTENT

crim·i·nal·ist \'kri-mə-nə-list\ *n* : one who practices criminalistics as a profession

crim·i·nal·is·tics \ˌkri-mə-nə-'lis-tiks\ *n pl but sing in constr* : application of scientific techniques in collecting and analyzing physical evidence in criminal cases

crim·i·nal·i·ty \ˌkri-mə-'na-lə-tē\ *n* **1** : the quality or state of being criminal ⟨can't understand the ∼ of his act⟩ **2** : CRIME 3 ⟨violent ∼⟩

crim·i·nal·ize \'kri-mə-nə-ˌlīz\ *vt* **-ized; -iz·ing** : to make criminal : OUTLAW ⟨the statute *criminalizing* the use of contraceptives —R. H. Bork⟩ — compare ILLEGALIZE — **crim·i·nal·i·za·tion** \ˌkri-mə-nə-lə-'zā-shən, -ˌlī-\ *n*

criminal law *n* : public law that deals with crimes and their prosecution — compare CIVIL LAW ◊ Substantive criminal law defines crimes, and procedural criminal law sets down criminal procedure. Substantive criminal law was originally common law for the most part. It was later codified and is now found in federal and state statutory law.

criminal lawyer *n* : a lawyer who specializes in criminal law

criminal liability — see LIABILITY 2b

crim·i·nal·ly *adv* **1** : according to criminal law ⟨∼ liable⟩ ⟨∼ insane⟩ **2** : in a manner that constitutes a crime ⟨∼ negligent⟩

criminal negligence — see NEGLIGENCE

criminal procedure *n* : the steps taken and methods used in bringing and conducting a criminal action; *also* : a course of study in the rules of procedure in criminal actions

criminal syndicalism *n* : advocacy of unlawful means (as acts of violence) to bring about a change in industry or government — compare SABOTAGE, SEDITION

criminal trespass — see TRESPASS

crim·i·no·gen·ic \ˌkri-mə-nō-'je-nik\ *adj* : producing or leading to crime ⟨to narrow the demoralizing and ∼ abyss between affluent and poor —Elliott Currie⟩

crim·i·nol·o·gy \ˌkri-mə-'nä-lə-jē\ *n* : the scientific study of crime as a social phenomenon, of criminals, and of penal treatment — **crim·i·no·log·i·cal** \ˌkri-mə-nə-'lä-jə-kəl\ *adj* — **crim·i·no·log·i·cal·ly** *adv* — **crim·i·nol·o·gist** \ˌkri-mə-'nä-lə-jist\ *n*

crit·i·cal stage *n* : a stage in a criminal proceeding at which the accused's rights or defenses may be affected and which triggers the Sixth Amendment right to counsel — see also *Amendment VI* to the CONSTITUTION in the back matter

cross–ac·tion *n* : an action brought by a defendant in an existing action against a plaintiff or codefendant — compare COUNTERCLAIM, CROSS-APPEAL, CROSS-CLAIM, THIRD-PARTY CLAIM

cross–ap·peal *n* : an appeal taken by an appellee against the appellant — compare COUNTERCLAIM, CROSS-ACTION, CROSS-CLAIM — **cross–appeal** *vb*

cross–appellant *n* : a party that cross-appeals

cross bill — see BILL 3a

cross–claim *n* : a claim against a party on the same side of an action (as a coplaintiff or codefendant) — compare COUNTER-CLAIM, CROSS-ACTION, CROSS-APPEAL, THIRD-PARTY CLAIM ◊ Under Rule 13(g) of the Federal Rules of Civil Procedure, a cross-claim must be related to the original action in that it arises from the same transaction or occurrence as the original action or a counterclaim, or involves property that is the subject matter of the original action. — **cross–claim** *vi*

cross–claimant *n* : a party that cross-claims

cross–collateral *n* : collateral given to secure preexisting unsecured debt in return for new loans

cross–collateralize *vt* **-ized; -iz·ing** : to

\ə\abut \ᵊ\kitten \ər\further \a\ash \ā\ace
\ä\cot, cart \au̇\out \ch\chin \e\bet \ē\easy
\g\go \i\hit \ī\ice \j\job \ŋ\sing \ō\go \ȯ\law
\ȯi\boy \th\thin \t͟h\the \ü\loot \u̇\foot \y\yet
\zh\vision *see also* Pronunciation Symbols page

secure (a preexisting debt) with cross‐ collateral — **cross–collateralization** *n*

cross–complaint *n* **1** : a claim brought by a defendant against another party to the lawsuit **2** : a claim brought by a defendant against a person not a party to the original lawsuit for a related cause of action

cross–examination *n* : the examination of a witness who has already testified in order to check or discredit the witness's testimony, knowledge, or credibility — see also CONFRONTATION CLAUSE; compare DIRECT EXAMINATION, RECROSS‐ EXAMINATION, REDIRECT EXAMINATION ◊ In accordance with Rule 611 of the Federal Rules of Evidence, cross‐ examination should only refer to matters that were covered during direct examination or that are relevant to the witness's credibility. Anything exceeding these limits is permissible at the court's discretion. Rule 611 also states that "ordinarily leading questions should be permitted on cross-examination." — **cross– examine** *vb* — **cross–examiner** *n*

cross–license *vt* **-censed; -cens•ing** : to license (a patent or invention) to another to use in return for a similar license ⟨*cross– licensed* its patents with a Japanese company⟩

cross–mo•tion \'krȯs-ˌmō-shən\ *n* : a motion that attempts to counter a similar motion filed by an opposing party ⟨after the plaintiffs moved to recuse his counsel, the defendant filed a ~ to disqualify theirs⟩

cross remainder — see REMAINDER

cru•el and in•hu•man treatment *n* : CRU-ELTY 2

cruel and un•usu•al punishment *n* : punishment that is offensive to the contemporary morality or jurisprudence (as by being degrading, inflicting unnecessary and intentional pain, or being disproportionate to the offense) ⟨nor *cruel and un-usual punishments* inflicted — *U.S. Constitution* amend. VIII⟩ — see also *Gregg v. Georgia* in the IMPORTANT CASES section; compare CORPORAL PUNISHMENT,

DEATH PENALTY ◊ A cruel and unusual punishment is essentially one that the courts consider to violate the Eighth Amendment based on a variety of criteria. The interpretation of what constitutes cruel and unusual punishment has changed over time and has varied from jurisdiction to jurisdiction. Most forms of corporal punishment formerly used at common•law have been found to be cruel and unusual punishments. The U.S. Supreme Court has held that the death penalty in itself does not constitute cruel and unusual punishment, although mandatory death sentences do.

cru•el•ty *n, pl* **-ties 1 a** : an intentional or criminally negligent act that causes pain and suffering ⟨~ to animals⟩ ⟨~ to children⟩ **b** : mistreatment or neglect that causes pain and suffering — compare ABUSE ◊ Cruelty is an aggravating circumstance to a crime (as murder). **2** : a spouse's conduct that endangers life or health or causes mental suffering or fear — called also *cruel and inhuman treatment* ◊ Cruelty is a ground for divorce.

Ct *abbr* court

cta *abbr* cum testamento annexo

cul•pa•ble \'kəl-pə-bəl\ *adj* : deserving condemnation or blame as wrong or harmful — **cul•pa•bil•i•ty** \ˌkəl-pə-'bi-lə-tē\ *n* — **cul•pa•ble•ness** *n* — **cul•pa•bly** *adv*

culpable negligence *n* : CRIMINAL NEGLI-GENCE at NEGLIGENCE

cum tes•ta•men•to an•nexo \'kəm-ˌtes-tə-'men-tō-ə-'nek-sō\ *adj* [New Latin, literally, with a will attached] : attended by a will — see also *administrator cum testamento annexo* at ADMINISTRATOR

cu•mu•la•tive \'kyü-myə-lə-tiv, -ˌlā-\ *adj* **1** : increasing by successive additions **2** : tending to prove the same point ⟨~ testimony⟩ **3** : following in time

cumulative dividend — see DIVIDEND

cumulative evidence — see EVIDENCE

cumulative preferred stock — see STOCK

cumulative sentence — see SENTENCE

cumulative voting *n* : a system of voting for corporate directors in which each shareholder is entitled to as many votes as he or she has shares times the number of directors to be elected — compare STRAIGHT VOTING

cu·ra·tive \'kyùr-ə-tiv\ *adj* : serving or intended to cure defects ⟨~ instructions to the jury⟩

cu·ra·tor \'kyùr-ˌā-tər, kyù-'rā-tər\ *n* [Latin, guardian, from *curare* to take care of] *in the civil law of Louisiana* : a person appointed by a court to care for the property of an absent person or to care for the person or property of someone mentally incapable of doing so — compare COMMITTEE, CONSERVATOR, GUARDIAN, INTERDICT, TUTOR — **cu·ra·tor·ship** *n*

cure *vb* **cured; cur·ing** *vt* : to deal with in a way that eliminates or corrects: as **a** : to use judicial procedures to undo (damage to a litigant's case caused by procedural errors made during a trial) ⟨subsequent proceedings *cured* harm caused by trial court's error in impermissibly allowing ... statements of government witness — *National Law Journal*⟩; *also* : to judicially correct or negate (procedural errors) ⟨~ a defect in the pleadings⟩ **b** : to correct or make acceptable (a defective performance or delivery under a contract) ⟨the nonconformity would be seasonably *cured* —J. J. White and R. S. Summers⟩ **c** : to negate (a default by a debtor in bankruptcy) by restoring the debtor and creditor to their positions before the default ~ *vi* : to eliminate or correct a defect; *esp* : to correct or make acceptable a defective performance or delivery under a contract ⟨the seller may seasonably notify the buyer of his intention to ~ and may then within the contract time make a conforming delivery —*Uniform Commercial Code*⟩ — **cur·able** *adj* — **cur·abil·i·ty** *n* — **cure** *n*

current asset — see ASSET 2

cur·te·sy \'kər-tə-sē\ *n, pl* **-sies** [Anglo⸗ French *curteisie*, literally, favor, courtesy, originally in the phrase *par la corteysie de Engleterre* (tenancy) by courtesy of (the law of) England (as op-

posed to natural right)] : a husband's interest at common law in a life estate upon the death of his wife in the real property that she either solely owned or inherited provided that they bore a child capable of inheriting the property — compare DOWER, ELECTIVE SHARE

cur·ti·lage \'kərt-ᵊl-ij\ *n* [Anglo-French *curtillage* enclosed land belonging to a house, kitchen garden, from Old French *cortillage* kitchen garden, from *cortil* garden, ultimately from Latin *cohort-, cohors* farmyard] : the area surrounding and associated with a home ◊ The curtilage of a house is included in the Fourth Amendment prohibition on unreasonable searches and seizures.

cus·to·di·al \kə-'stō-dē-əl\ *adj* **1** : occurring during or in connection with custody ⟨a ~ interrogation⟩ **2** : having sole custody or custody a greater portion of the time ⟨a ~ parent⟩

custodial arrest — see ARREST

cus·to·di·an *n* : an individual entrusted with guarding and keeping property or having custody of a person: as **a** : the warden of a prison **b** : a person given custody of a child by court order **c** : a person named to manage a child's property under the Uniform Transfers to Minors Act **d** : a person or entity appointed by a bankruptcy court to take charge of the debtor's property for purposes of administration — **cus·to·di·an·ship** *n*

cus·to·dy *n* [Latin *custodia*, from *custod-, custos* guardian] : care or control exercised by a person or authority over something or someone: as **a** : supervision and control over property that usu. includes liability for damage that may occur **b** : care and maintenance of a child that includes the right to direct the child's activities and make decisions regarding the child's upbringing — compare VISITATION

\ə\abut	\ᵊ\kitten	\ər\further	\a\ash	\ā\ace
\ä\cot, cart	\aú\out	\ch\chin	\e\bet	\ē\easy
\g\go	\i\hit	\ī\ice	\j\job	\ŋ\sing	\ō\go	\ò\law
\òi\boy	\th\thin	\th̲\the	\ü\loot	\ù\foot	\y\yet
\zh\vision	*see also* Pronunciation Symbols page

joint custody : custody of a child shared by divorced or separated parents who alternate physical custody of and share in decisions regarding the child — called also *shared custody*

phys·i·cal custody : custody that includes sharing a residence with a child

shared custody : JOINT CUSTODY in this entry

sole custody : custody of a child awarded to only one person and usu. to a parent

tem·po·rary custody : custody awarded until a final judgment in a matter (as a divorce) is made

c : official restraint on freedom (as by arrest or imprisonment or by release on bail, personal recognizance, probation, or parole) — compare ARREST

con·struc·tive custody : custody of a person (as a parolee) who is not under immediate physical control but whose freedom is controlled or restrained by legal authority

pe·nal custody : custody of a person (as in a correctional institution) as a form of punishment

phys·i·cal custody : custody of a person (as an arrestee) whose freedom is under the actual and immediate control of an official ◊ A person need not be in physical custody to be entitled to habeas corpus protection.

pre·ven·tive custody : custody of a person (as a criminal defendant awaiting trial) for the purpose of preventing further possible dangerous or criminal behavior

pro·tec·tive custody : physical custody of a person for his or her own safety

cus·tom *n* **1** : a practice common to many or to a particular place or institution; *esp* : a long-established practice that is generally recognized as having the force of law — see also SECTION 1983; compare USAGE **2** *pl* **a** : duties, tolls, or imposts imposed by the law of a country on imports or exports **b** *usu sing in constr* : the agency, establishment, or procedure for collecting such customs

cus·to·mer *n* **1** : a person or business that purchases a commodity or service **2 a** : a person or entity having an account with a bank or on whose behalf the bank has agreed to collect items **b** : a person or entity for whom an issuer issues a letter of credit

cy·ber·law \'sī-bər-ˌlȯ\ *n* : the area of law dealing with regulation of use of the Internet

¹cy pres \ˌsē-'prā\ *n* [Anglo-French, as near (as possible)] : a rule in the law of trusts and estates that provides for the interpretation of instruments as nearly as possible in conformity with the intention of the testator when literal construction is illegal, impracticable, or impossible

²cy pres *adv* : in accordance with the rule of cy pres

D

D *abbr* **1** district **2** defendant
DA *abbr* **1** deposit account **2** district attorney
¹dam·age *n* [Old French, from *dam* injury, harm, from Latin *damnum* financial loss, fine] **1** : loss or harm resulting from injury to person, property, or reputation **2** *pl* : the money awarded to a party in a civil suit as reparation for the loss or injury for which another is liable — see also ADDITUR, COVER, MITIGATE, REMITTITUR; compare *declaratory judgment* at JUDGMENT 1a, INJUNCTION, *specific performance* at PERFORMANCE ◊ The trier of fact determines the amount of damages to be awarded to the prevailing party. More than one type of damages may be awarded for a single injury.
actual damages : damages deemed to compensate the injured party for losses sustained as a direct result of the injury suffered — called also *compensatory damages*
consequential damages : SPECIAL DAMAGES in this entry
direct damages : damages for a loss that is an immediate, natural, and foreseeable result of the wrongful act — compare SPECIAL DAMAGES in this entry
ex·em·pla·ry damages \ig-'zem-plə-rē-\ : PUNITIVE DAMAGES in this entry
ex·pec·ta·tion damages : damages recoverable for breach of contract and designed to put the injured party in the position he or she would have been in had the contract been completed — called also *expectancy damages*
general damages **1** : damages for a loss that is the natural, foreseeable, and logical result of a wrongful act — compare SPECIAL DAMAGES in this entry **2** : damages for losses (as pain and suffering, inconvenience, or loss of lifestyle) whose monetary values are difficult to assign
he·don·ic damages \hi-'dä-nik-\ : damages deemed to compensate for the loss of enjoyment of life resulting from a wrongful act ◊ Hedonic damages are not recognized in all jurisdictions.
incidental damages : damages recoverable under section 2-715 of the Uniform Commercial Code in breach of contract cases for losses that include expenses incurred in handling and caring for goods which were the subject of the contract, reasonable expenses incurred in obtaining cover, and any other reasonable expenses resulting from the breach that do not fall into any other category
liquidated damages : damages whose amount is agreed upon by the parties to a contract as adequately compensating for loss in the event of a breach — called also *stipulated damages* ◊ Liquidated damages in an amount exceeding that needed to reasonably compensate the injured party constitute a penalty and are therefore void.
mor·a·to·ry damages *in the civil law of Louisiana* : damages recoverable for loss resulting from an obligor's delay in performing ◊ Compensatory damages are recoverable in a case of failure to perform.
nominal damages : damages awarded in a small amount (as one dollar) in cases in which a party has been injured but no loss resulted from the injury or in which the injured party failed to prove that loss resulted from the injury
presumed damages : damages that are

\ə\abut   \ᵊ\kitten   \ər\further   \a\ash   \ā\ace
\ä\cot, cart   \au̇\out   \ch\chin   \e\bet   \ē\easy
\g\go   \i\hit   \ī\ice   \j\job   \ŋ\sing   \ō\go   \ȯ\law
\ȯi\boy   \th\thin   \t̲h̲\the   \ü\loot   \u̇\foot   \y\yet
\zh\vision   *see also* Pronunciation Symbols page

presumed under the law to result naturally and necessarily from a tortious act and that therefore do not require proof

punitive damages : damages awarded in cases of serious or malicious wrongdoing to punish or deter the wrongdoer or deter others from behaving similarly — called also *exemplary damages, smart money*

special damages : damages awarded in an amount deemed to compensate for losses that arise not as a natural result of the injury but because of some particular circumstance of the injured party; *specif* : damages relating to a business, profession, or property that are easily calculable in monetary terms — called also *consequential damages;* compare DIRECT DAMAGES in this entry, GENERAL DAMAGES in this entry ◊ Because special damages do not arise in every case, they must be specifically requested in the pleadings. This is an issue of particular importance in cases of harm to reputation, such as slander, libel, and malicious prosecution.

stipulated damages in *the civil law of Louisiana* : LIQUIDATED DAMAGES in this entry

tre·ble damages \'tre-bəl-\ : damages awarded in an amount that is three times the amount for which the trier of fact finds the wrongdoer liable ◊ Treble damages are recoverable where authorized by statute and are usu. imposed as a punishment.

3 *pl* : losses for which damages are recoverable ⟨did not incur ~s, because he was unlikely to win the foreclosure case —Rosalind Resnick⟩

²damage *adj* : of or relating to damages ⟨a ~ action⟩ ⟨a ~ remedy⟩

dam·num abs·que in·ju·ria \'dam-nəm-'ab-skwē-in-'jur-ē-ə, 'däm-nùm-'äb-skwä-in-'yü-rē-ä\ [Late Latin, loss without unlawful conduct] : a loss for which the law provides no means of recovery — compare INJURIA ABSQUE DAMNO

dan·ger·ous *adj* **1** : creating a risk of bodily injury ⟨a ~ condition of a public building⟩ **2** : able or likely to inflict esp. serious bodily injury ⟨a ~ criminal with no regard for human life⟩ ⟨a ~ animal⟩; *also* : DEADLY **3** : likely to engage in repeated criminal activity ⟨a ~ offender⟩ ◊ The activity that an offender is likely to engage in need not involve violence in order for the offender to be deemed dangerous.

dangerous instrument *n* : an object capable of causing bodily injury either because of an inherent quality or because of the manner in which it is used — called also *dangerous instrumentality* ◊ An object is more likely to be deemed a dangerous instrument on the basis of how it is used in criminal cases than in tort cases. For example, a sidewalk has been held to be a dangerous instrument in a criminal case in which the defendant struck the victim's head against it. In tort cases, esp. where strict liability is to be imposed, the object usu. has to have some inherently dangerous quality.

dangerous weap·on *n* : an object that when used as an instrument of offense is capable of causing serious bodily injury — compare DEADLY WEAPON

date of record : RECORD DATE

da·tion en paie·ment \'dā-shən-en-'pā-mənt, dà-'syóⁿ-äⁿ-pā-'mäⁿ\ [French, literally, act of giving in payment] in *the civil law of Louisiana* : a mode of discharging a debt by the debtor's giving to the creditor with the creditor's consent something that satisfies the debt but differs from the form of payment originally called for by the debt — called also *giving in payment*

da·tive \'dā-tiv\ *adj* [Medieval Latin *dativus* subject to appointment, from Latin, assigned (of a guardian), from *datus*, past participle of *dare* to give] in *the civil law of Louisiana* **1** : appointed by a judge **2** : established by judicial appointment ⟨~ tutorship⟩

day in court : a day or opportunity to appear in a legal proceeding to be heard or to assert one's rights

days of grace : GRACE PERIOD

d/b/a *abbr* doing business as

DB&C *abbr* dwelling, buildings, and contents

d.b.n. *abbr* de bonis non

D.C. *abbr* district court

DEA *abbr* Drug Enforcement Administration — see also the IMPORTANT AGENCIES section

dead hand *n* : MORTMAIN

dead·lock \'ded-ˌläk\ *n* : a state of inaction resulting from the opposition of equally powerful uncompromising persons or factions: as **a** : the state of a jury unable to agree on a verdict — see also ALLEN CHARGE **b** : IMPASSE **c** : a state in which corporate directors are unable to perform their functions because of shareholder voting — **deadlock** *vb*

dead·ly *adj* **dead·li·er; -est** : likely to cause or capable of causing death; *also* : DANGEROUS 2 ◊ *Deadly* and *dangerous* are sometimes used interchangeably, esp. in connection with weapons or instruments.

deadly force — see FORCE 3

deadly weap·on *n* : an object whose purpose is to cause death or that when used as an instrument of offense is capable of causing death or sometimes serious bodily harm — compare DANGEROUS WEAPON ◊ An unloaded firearm has been generally held to be a deadly weapon. Although usu. distinct, the terms *deadly weapon* and *dangerous weapon* are sometimes used interchangeably.

dead man's statute *n* : a law barring the testimony of a person with an interest in an estate regarding any conversation with or any event taking place in the presence of the decedent — called also *dead man act, dead man's act*

¹deal *vb* **dealt; deal·ing** *vt* : to carry on the business of buying or esp. selling (something) ⟨~*ing* drugs⟩ ~ *vi* **1** : to engage in bargaining **2** : to sell or distribute something as a business or for money ⟨~*ing* in real estate⟩ ⟨~ in stolen property⟩

²deal *n* **1** : an act of dealing : a business transaction **2** : an arrangement for mutual advantage (as for a defendant to testify in exchange for immunity from prosecution)

deal·er *n* : one that deals; *specif* : a person or entity that buys and sells securities for his or her or its own account and not for others — compare BROKER

death *n* : a permanent cessation of all vital bodily functions : the end of life — see also BRAIN DEATH, CIVIL DEATH ◊ Death is usu. defined by statute and for purposes of criminal homicide has been held to include brain death.

death benefit *n* : money payable to the beneficiary of a deceased as a benefit (as under a policy of life or accident insurance or a pension plan) ◊ The right to death benefits is generally terminated in cases of fraud, as when an insured commits suicide after purchasing a policy or when the beneficiary murders the insured.

death certificate *n* : a document setting forth information (as age, occupation, and place of birth) relating to a dead person and including a doctor's certification of the cause of death ◊ Death certificates are issued by a particular public official, as a city or town clerk. A death certificate is required to document a person's death for certain purposes, as to file an estate tax return or to probate an estate.

death knell exception \-'nel-\ *n* : a rule of procedure allowing immediate review of an interlocutory order when denial of review would result in irreparable injury

death penalty *n* : death as punishment for a crime — called also *capital punishment;* see also CRUEL AND UNUSUAL PUNISHMENT, *Gregg v. Georgia* in the IMPORTANT CASES section ◊ The U.S. Supreme Court has held that the death penalty is not inherently violative of the Eighth Amendment's prohibition on

\ə\abut \ᵊ\kitten \ər\further \a\ash \ā\ace
\ä\cot, cart \au̇\out \ch\chin \e\bet \ē\easy
\g\go \i\hit \ī\ice \j\job \ŋ\sing \ō\go \ȯ\law
\ȯi\boy \th\thin \t͟h\the \ü\loot \u̇\foot \y\yet
\zh\vision *see also* Pronunciation Symbols page

cruel and unusual punishment, provided that the method is not deemed cruel and that the punishment is not excessive in relation to the crime. A statute mandating the death penalty is unconstitutional, however. A sentencing judge is required to consider any mitigating circumstances before imposing the death penalty for a crime.

death qual·i·fi·ca·tion *n* : the process of excluding a juror from the jury of a case in which the death penalty may be imposed on the grounds that the juror's objection to the death penalty would prevent him or her from making an impartial decision as to the defendant's guilt

death row *n* : a prison area housing inmates sentenced to death — **death row** *adj*

death sentence — see SENTENCE

death tax *n* : a tax assessed on the transfer of property (as an estate, inheritance, legacy, or succession) after the transferor's death — compare ESTATE TAX, GENERATION-SKIPPING TRANSFER TAX, GIFT TAX

death warrant — see WARRANT

de·bar \dē-'bär\ *vt* **de·barred; de·bar·ring** : to bar from having or doing something; *specif* : to exclude from contracting with the federal government or a federal contractor 〈was *debarred* from bidding〉 — compare DISBAR — **de·bar·ment** *n*

de be·ne es·se \dē-'bē-nē-'e-sē, di-; dā-'be-ne-'e-se\ *adj* [Medieval Latin, literally, of well-being (i.e., morally acceptable, but subject to legal validation)] : subject to future exception : CONDITIONAL, PROVISIONAL 〈depositions *de bene esse*〉

de·ben·ture \di-'ben-chər\ *n* [Anglo-French *debentour* and Medieval Latin *debentura*, perhaps from Latin *debentur* they are owed] : an unsecured bond that is backed by the issuer's general credit rather than a specific lien — called also *debenture bond;* see also INDENTURE; compare *mortgage bond* at BOND ◊ Debentures are often convertible to stocks.

debenture bond — see BOND 2

de bo·nis non \dē-'bō-nis-'nän, dā-'bō-nēs-'nȯn\ *adj* [short for *de bonis non administratis,* from Medieval Latin, of the goods not administered (by the executor)] : concerning the goods of a decedent that are not yet administered — see also *administrator de bonis non* at ADMINISTRATOR

debt *n* [Old French *dette,* ultimately from Latin *debita,* plural of *debitum* debt, from neuter of *debitus,* past participle of *debere* to owe] **1** : something owed: as **a** : a specific sum of money or a performance due another esp. by agreement (as a loan agreement) 〈to pay the ~*s* . . . of the United States —*U.S. Constitution* art. I〉 〈a ~ for alimony〉 **b** : an obligation to pay or perform on another's claim 〈discharged the ~〉 — compare ASSET, EQUITY 4 ◊ It is often up to the courts to decide what is or is not a debt under various laws. Courts disagree whether criminal restitution is a debt under the Bankruptcy Code. The historical practice of imprisoning debtors for nonpayment is no longer used.

antecedent debt : debt that is incurred prior to a property transfer paying or securing the debt — compare PREFERENCE

bad debt : a debt that cannot be collected ◊ An income tax deduction is allowed for bad debts.

consumer debt : debt that is incurred by an individual primarily for the purchase of consumer goods or services — compare CONSUMER CREDIT

judgment debt : a debt established by a judgment and enforceable by a legal process (as an execution of judgment or attachment)

c : a state of owing 〈in ~〉 **d** : the aggregate of money owed 〈the national ~〉 **2** : the common-law action for the recovery of a specified sum of money or a sum that can be simply and certainly determined — called also *action of debt, writ of debt;* compare ASSUMPSIT, COVENANT

debt adjustment *n* : the arrangements made for the repayment or satisfaction of debts in an amount or manner that differs from the original arrangements esp. in accordance with a bankruptcy plan under chapter 13 of the Bankruptcy Code

debt capital — see CAPITAL

debt·or *n* : a person who owes a debt — see also BANKRUPT; compare CREDITOR, OBLIGEE, OBLIGOR ◊ The Bankruptcy Act of 1978 calls the person concerned in a bankruptcy case the "debtor" as opposed to the "bankrupt."

debtor in possession : a debtor who remains in possession of an estate during chapter 11 or 12 bankruptcy and has the same duties as a trustee in bankruptcy

debtor's estate *n* : BANKRUPTCY ESTATE at ESTATE 2

debt security — see SECURITY

debt service *n* : the amount of interest and principal payments due annually on long-term debt

de·ce·dent \di-'sēd-ᵊnt\ *n* [Latin *decedent-, decedens*, present participle of *decedere* to depart, die] : a deceased person ⟨the estate of the ~⟩

de·ceit *n* : deliberate and misleading concealment, false declaration, or artifice : DECEPTION ⟨theft by ~⟩; *also* : the tort of committing or carrying out deceit ⟨an action for ~⟩ — see also FRAUD, MISREPRESENTATION

de·ceive *vb* **de·ceived; de·ceiv·ing** *vt* : to cause to accept as true or valid what is false or invalid ~ *vi* : to practice deceit — compare DEFRAUD, MISLEAD

de·cep·tion \di-'sep-shən\ *n* **1** : an act of deceiving **2** : something that deceives : DECEIT

de·cep·tive \di-'sep-tiv\ *adj* : tending or having capacity to deceive ⟨~ trade practices⟩ — compare FRAUDULENT, MISLEADING

de·cer·ti·fy \dē-'sər-tə-ˌfī\ *vt* **-fied; -fy·ing** : to withdraw or revoke the certification of ⟨*decertified* the class action suit⟩; *esp* : to withdraw the certification of (a labor union) as a collective bargaining agent ⟨petitions to ~ the union⟩ ◊ The National Labor Relations Board will decertify a union after an election in which the majority of members do not support the union or after participation in an illegal

strike. — **de·cer·ti·fi·ca·tion** \dē-ˌsər-tə-fə-'kā-shən\ *n*

de·cide *vb* **de·cid·ed; de·cid·ing** *vt* : to determine (as a case or issue) by making a decision (as a final judgment) : ADJUDICATE 1, 2 — compare FIND, HOLD ~ *vi* : to make a decision

de·ci·sion \di-'si-zhən\ *n* : an authoritative determination (as a decree or judgment) made after consideration of facts or law; *also* : a report or document containing such a determination — see also MEMORANDUM DECISION; compare DISPOSITION, FINDING, HOLDING, JUDGMENT, OPINION, RULING, VERDICT ◊ A decision, while being an authoritative determination of a disputed issue, does not have to be a final determination closing the case. Some interlocutory decisions may be appealed. — **de·ci·sion·al** \-zhə-nəl\ *adj*

decisional law *n* : CASE LAW

de·clar·ant \di-'klar-ənt\ *n* : a person who makes a statement or declaration

dec·la·ra·tion *n* **1** : the act of declaring ⟨~ of dividends⟩ ⟨~ of war⟩ **2 a** : the first pleading in a common-law action — compare COMPLAINT, INDICTMENT **b** : a statement usu. not under oath made by a party to a legal transaction ⟨the attorney must later sign an affidavit or ~ stating that he has informed the debtor —J. H. Williamson⟩ **c** : a statement not under oath being offered as evidence

declaration against interest : a statement made by someone unavailable as a witness that is against that person's own interests (as pecuniary or property interests) or may subject that person to liability — compare ADMISSION, CONFESSION, SELF-INCRIMINATION ◊ A declaration against interest is an exception to the hearsay rule. A statement that is offered to clear the accused is not admissible without corroborating circum-

---

\ə\abut \ᵊ\kitten \ər\further \a\ash \ā\ace
\ä\cot, cart \aù\out \ch\chin \e\bet \ē\easy
\g\go \i\hit \ī\ice \j\job \ŋ\sing \ō\go \ò\law
\òi\boy \th\thin \th̲\the \ü\loot \ù\foot \y\yet
\zh\vision *see also* Pronunciation Symbols page

stances under the Federal Rules of Evidence.

dy•ing declaration : a statement that is made by a person who firmly believes that he or she is about to die and has no hope of recovery and that concerns the circumstances or cause of the presumed death — compare EXCITED UTTERANCE, RES GESTAE ◊ Dying declarations are an exception to the hearsay rule and can be admitted as evidence only if the declarant is unavailable as a witness.

self–serving declaration : a statement made out of court that is in the declarant's own interest

spon•ta•ne•ous declaration \spän-'tā-nē-əs-\ : an excited utterance that is made without time for fabrication — called also *spontaneous exclamation, spontaneous utterance;* compare RES GESTAE ◊ Spontaneous declarations are exceptions to the hearsay rule under the excited utterance exception.

3 : something that is declared: as **a** : a statement proclaiming the principles, aims, or policies of a group or government ⟨~ of rights⟩ — compare CONSTITUTION, PROCLAMATION **b** : a statement of the value of property that is subject to a tax (as a duty); *also* : a statement of the amount of tax estimated to be due (as on property or income) — see also ESTIMATED TAX; compare RETURN **c** : a statement of information (as year, make, and model) regarding the subject (as a car) and coverage of an insurance policy **4** : a statement creating or giving notice of the creation of a legal entity, relationship, or status; *also* : the instrument embodying such a statement

declaration of condominium : a declaration of the creation of a condominium that includes a description of the common and individual interests and obligations — compare *master deed* at DEED

declaration of homestead : a declaration by a qualified property owner by which the protection of a homestead exemption is effectuated

declaration of trust : a declaration by one holding or taking title to property in which he or she acknowledges that the property is held in trust for another

5 : DECLARATORY JUDGMENT at JUDGMENT 1a

declaration against interest — see DECLARATION 2c

declaration of condominium — see DECLARATION 4

declaration of homestead — see DECLARATION 4

declaration of trust — see DECLARATION 4

de•clar•a•to•ry \di-'klar-ə-,tōr-ē\ *adj* : serving to declare, set forth, or explain: as **a** : declaring what is the existing law **b** : declaring a legal right or interpretation ⟨~ relief⟩ — see also *declaratory judgment* at JUDGMENT 1a

declaratory judgment — see JUDGMENT 1a

de•clare *vt* **de•clared; de•clar•ing 1** : to make known formally, officially, or explicitly ⟨*declaring* who shall then act as President —*U.S. Constitution* amend. XX⟩ **2 a** : to make a full statement of (one's taxable property) ⟨didn't ~ some of his income⟩ **b** : to state the value of (one's taxable or dutiable property) ⟨*declared* the diamond earrings⟩ **3** : to make payable ⟨~ dividends⟩ — **de•clar•er** *n*

de•cree \di-'krē\ *n* [Old French *decré*, from Latin *decretum*, from neuter of *decretus*, past participle of *decernere* to decide] **1** : an order having the force of law ⟨by judicial ~⟩ **2** : a judicial decision esp. in an equity or probate court; *broadly* : JUDGMENT ⟨divorce ~⟩ ⟨interlocutory ~⟩

consent decree : a decree entered by a court that is determined by the parties' agreement : a settlement between the parties that is subject to judicial approval and supervision; *specif* : such a decree by which the accused agrees to cease alleged illegal activities without admitting guilt

decree nisi pl decrees nisi : a provisional decree that will become final unless cause is shown why it should not

◊ Some states grant divorces using decrees nisi. The decree nisi creates a time period (as of 3 months) allowing for possible reconciliation or for completion of various arrangements (as custody).

decree pro confesso : a decree entered by a court based on a defendant's default and the presumption that the allegations are confessed — compare *default judgment* at JUDGMENT 1a

final decree : a decree that disposes of an action by determining all matters in dispute including esp. the parties' rights — compare *final judgment* at JUDGMENT 1a

interlocutory decree : a decree that is made during the course of an action and that does not settle all matters in dispute — decree *vb*

decree nisi — see DECREE

decree pro confesso — see DECREE

de•crim•i•nal•ize \dē-'kri-mən-ᵊl-ˌīz\ *vt* **-ized; -iz•ing** : to remove or reduce the criminal classification or status of — **de•crim•i•nal•iza•tion** \dē-ˌkri-mən-ᵊl-ə-'zā-shən\ *n*

ded•i•ca•tion \ˌde-di-'kā-shən\ *n* : a giving up of property to public use that precludes the owner from asserting any further interest in it: as **a** : an intentional donation of land for public use that is accepted by the proper public authorities **b** : intentional or negligent surrender to the public of intellectual property that could have been protected by copyright or patent

de•duct *vt* : to take away (an amount) from a total; *specif* : to take as a deduction ⟨must be capitalized . . . rather than immediately ~*ed* —D. Q. Posin⟩ — compare AMORTIZE

¹de•duc•ti•ble \di-'dək-tə-bəl\ *adj* : allowable as a deduction — **de•duc•ti•bil•i•ty** \-ˌdək-tə-'bi-lə-tē\ *n*

²deductible *n* : a clause in an insurance policy that relieves the insurer of responsibility for an initial specified loss of the kind insured against; *also* : the amount specified in such a clause — compare FRANCHISE 4a

de•duc•tion *n* **1** : an amount allowed by tax laws to be subtracted from income in order to decrease the amount of income tax due — see also *Internal Revenue Code* in the IMPORTANT LAWS section; compare CREDIT, EXCLUSION, EXEMPTION

busi•ness deduction : a deduction usu. taken from gross income that is allowed for losses or expenses attributable to business activities or to activities engaged in for profit

charitable deduction : a deduction allowed for a contribution to a charity usu. that is qualified under the tax law (as sections 170 and 2055 of the Internal Revenue Code)

de•pen•den•cy deduction : a deduction allowed to be taken in a set amount for a qualified dependent (as under sections 151 and 152 of the Internal Revenue Code)

itemized deduction : a deduction for a specifically recorded item that is allowed to be taken from adjusted gross income if the total of such deductions exceeds the standard deduction

marital deduction **1** : a deduction allowed under the Internal Revenue Code to be taken from the gross estate that amounts to the value of any property interest which is included in the estate and which was given by a decedent to the surviving spouse provided that the interest is not terminable during the life of the survivor **2** : a deduction allowed under the IRC of the value of any gift inter vivos subject to gift tax by one spouse to the other

personal deduction : a deduction allowed to be taken for losses or expenses that are not necessarily attributable to a business activity or an activity engaged in for profit

personal exemption deduction : a deduction for an amount set by tax law

\ə\abut \ᵊ\kitten \ər\further \a\ash \ā\ace
\ä\cot, cart \au̇\out \ch\chin \e\bet \ē\easy
\g\go \i\hit \ī\ice \j\job \ŋ\sing \ō\go \ȯ\law
\ȯi\boy \th\thin \th̲\the \ü\loot \u̇\foot \y\yet
\zh\vision *see also* Pronunciation Symbols page

that under section 151 of the Internal Revenue Code includes the dependency deduction

stan·dard deduction : a deduction of an amount set by tax law that is allowed to be taken from adjusted gross income unless the taxpayer elects to itemize deductions **2** *in the civil law of Louisiana* : an item of property or an amount that an heir has a right to take from the mass of the succession before any of it is partitioned (as for a debt owed by the deceased to the heir)

¹deed *n* **1** : something done : ACT 1 ⟨my free act and ~⟩ **2** : a written instrument by which a person transfers ownership of real property to another — see also DELIVER, GRANTEE, GRANTOR, RECORDING ACT, REGISTRY, TITLE; compare CERTIFICATE OF TITLE ◊ A deed must be properly executed and delivered in order to be effective. Additionally, the grantor must have freely intended to make the transfer at the time of the conveyance. Deeds are recorded at the local registry of deeds to give notice of ownership.

bargain and sale deed 1 : a contract resulting from a bargain between a buyer and a seller of real property that creates a use in the buyer and therefore transfers title to the buyer by operation of law **2** : a deed in which the grantor makes no warranties of title to the grantee

deed of trust : an instrument securing a debt in which a debtor conveys the legal ownership of real property to a trustee to be held in trust for the benefit of the creditor or to be sold upon the debtor's default to pay the debt : a mortgage with a power of sale — called also *trust deed*

master deed : a deed that submits the land described therein to the provisions of a state's law regarding condominiums and sets out various information (as about the units, common areas, bylaws, and rights of the owners) as required under state law — compare *declaration of condominium* at DECLARATION 4

quitclaim deed 1 : a deed that grants

only whatever title or interest the grantor had to the property without any warranty as to the title **2** : SPECIAL WARRANTY DEED in this entry — compare WARRANTY DEED in this entry

sheriff's deed : a deed given to a buyer of property purchased at a sheriff's sale

special warranty deed : a deed in which the property transferred is warranted to be free of all liens or encumbrances made by, through, or under the grantor

tax deed : a deed evidencing the transfer of title acquired by the grantee as purchaser of property at a tax sale — compare TAX CERTIFICATE

trust deed : DEED OF TRUST in this entry

unit deed : a deed conveying a condominium unit

warranty deed : a deed warranting that the grantor has a good title free and clear of all encumbrances and will defend the grantee against all claims — compare QUITCLAIM DEED in this entry

²deed *vt* : to convey by deed

deed of trust — see DEED

deep pock·et *n* **1** : a person or organization having substantial financial resources esp. for the purpose of paying damages **2** *pl* : substantial financial resources

Deep Rock doctrine *n* [from *Deep Rock*, a debtor corporation found to have been used for fraudulent transfers to its parent corporation in the Supreme Court case *Taylor v. Standard Gas and Electric Co.* (*Deep Rock*), 306 U.S. 307(1939)] : a doctrine holding that the claim of a stockholder and esp. a stockholder with controlling interest who makes a loan to his or her own corporation will be subordinated to the claims of outside creditors if the corporation is deemed undercapitalized

def. *abbr* defendant

de·face \di-'fās\ *vt* **de·faced; de·fac·ing** : to deface or mar the face or surface of — **de·face·ment** *n* — **de·fac·er** *n*

¹de fac·to \di-'fak-tō, dā-, dē-\ *adv* [Medieval Latin, literally, from the fact] : in reality : ACTUALLY ⟨these two constraints have been lifted, one *de facto* and one de jure —Susan Lee⟩

²de facto *adj* **1 :** ACTUAL; *esp* **:** being such in effect though not formally recognized — see also *de facto segregation* at SEGREGATION **2 :** exercising power as if legally constituted or authorized ⟨a *de facto* government⟩ ⟨a *de facto* judge⟩ — compare DE JURE

de facto merger — see MERGER

de facto segregation — see SEGREGATION

de•fal•cate \di-'fal-ˌkāt, -'fȯl-, dē-; 'de-fəl-ˌkāt\ *vi* **-cat•ed; -cat•ing :** to commit defalcation — compare EMBEZZLE — **de•fal•ca•tor** \-ˌkā-tər\ *n*

de•fal•ca•tion \ˌdē-ˌfal-'kā-shən, -ˌfȯl-, di-; ˌde-fəl-'kā-shən\ *n* [earlier, deduction, lessening, shortcoming, from Medieval Latin *defalcatio* discounting of debt, from *defalcare* to cut down, deduct, from Latin *de-* away from + *falc-, falx* sickle] **1 :** failure to account for or pay over money that has been entrusted to one's care; *also* **:** an instance of such failure — compare EMBEZZLE, MISAPPROPRIATE ◊ Defalcation does not necessarily involve culpability or misconduct. **2 :** a failure to meet a promise or expectation ⟨the school committee's ~s did not end with its refusal to submit a desegregation plan —S. L. Lynch⟩

de•fa•ma•tion \ˌde-fə-'mā-shən\ *n* **1 :** communication to third parties of false statements about a person that injure the reputation of or deter others from associating with that person — see also LIBEL, SLANDER, *New York Times Co. v. Sullivan* in the IMPORTANT CASES section; compare DISPARAGEMENT, FALSE LIGHT, SLANDER OF TITLE **2 :** a defamatory communication ⟨every repetition of the ~ is a publication —W. L. Prosser and W. P. Keeton⟩

defamation of title : SLANDER OF TITLE

de•fam•a•to•ry \di-'fa-mə-ˌtȯr-ē\ *adj* **:** tending to disgrace or lower public opinion of a person or to harm a person's reputation

de•fame \di-'fām\ *vt* **de•famed; de•fam•ing** [Medieval Latin *defamare*, alteration

of Latin *diffamare* to spread news of, defame, from *dis-*, prefix marking dispersal or removal + *fama* reputation] **:** to make the subject of defamation — **de•fam•er** *n*

de•fault \di-'fȯlt, 'dē-ˌfȯlt\ *n* [Anglo-French *defalte, defaute* lack, fault, failure to answer a summons, from *defaillir* to be lacking, fail, from *de-*, intensive prefix + *faillir* to fail] **1 :** failure to do something required by duty (as under a contract or by law): as **a :** failure to comply with the terms of a loan agreement or security agreement esp. with regard to payment of the debt **b** *in the civil law of Louisiana* **:** a delay in performing under a contract that is recognized by the other party ◊ A party whose performance under a contract is delayed is not automatically in default. Rather, the law of Louisiana requires that the other party "put him or her in default" by a written or witnessed oral request for performance, by filing suit, or by invoking a specific provision in the contract. Moratory damages may be recoverable for loss caused by the delay. **2 :** failure to defend against a claim in court (as by failing to file pleadings or to appear in court) — see also *default judgment* at JUDGMENT 1a — **default** *vb* — **de•fault•er** *n* — **in default :** in the condition of having defaulted

default judgment — see JUDGMENT 1a

de•fea•sance \di-'fē-zəns\ *n* [Anglo-French *defesance*, literally, undoing, destruction, from Old French *deffesant*, present participle of *deffaire* to destroy, undo — see DEFEAT] **1 a :** a condition (as in a deed or will) that upon fulfillment terminates a property interest **b :** an instrument setting forth such a condition **2 :** a rendering null or void

de•fea•si•ble \di-'fē-zə-bəl\ *adj* **:** subject to or capable of being annulled or made void ⟨a ~ interest⟩ ⟨his rights are not ~ by

\ə\abut \ᵊ\kitten \ər\further \a\ash \ā\ace \ä\cot, cart \au̇\out \ch\chin \e\bet \ē\easy \g\go \i\hit \ī\ice \j\job \ŋ\sing \ō\go \ȯ\law \ȯi\boy \th\thin \t͟h\the \ü\loot \u̇\foot \y\yet \zh\vision *see also* Pronunciation Symbols page

agreement —J. D. Calamari and J. M. Perillo⟩

defeasible fee — see FEE 1

de·feat *vt* [Anglo-French *defait*, past participle of *defaire* to undo, defeat, from Old French *deffaire, desfaire*, from *de-*, prefix marking reversal of action + *faire* to do] **1 a :** to render null ⟨third parties will ~ an attached but "unperfected" security interest —J. J. White and R. S. Summers⟩ **b :** to prevent or undo the effectiveness or establishment of ⟨~ jurisdiction⟩ ⟨defendant took stand and ~*ed* intoxication defense —*National Law Journal*⟩ **2 a :** to prevail over **b :** to thwart the claim of ⟨~ creditors⟩ ⟨an intent to ~ the surviving spouse of his ... elective share —*Tennessee Code Annotated*⟩ — **defeat** *n*

de·fect \'dē-ˌfekt, di-'fekt\ *n* : something or a lack of something that results in incompleteness, inadequacy, or imperfection: as **a :** a flaw in something (as a product) esp. that creates an unreasonable risk of harm in its normal use — see also LATENT DEFECT **b :** an error or omission in a court document (as an indictment or pleading) **c :** some imperfection in the chain of title to property that makes the title unmarketable — **de·fec·tive** \di-'fek-tiv\ *adj* — **de·fec·tive·ly** *adv* — **de·fec·tive·ness** *n*

de·fend *vt* **1 :** to drive danger or attack away from ⟨using a weapon to ~ oneself⟩ **2 :** to act as attorney for (a defendant) ⟨appointed to ~ the accused⟩ **3 :** to deny or oppose the rights of a plaintiff in regard to (a suit or claim) ⟨intend to ~ the case⟩ ~ *vi* **1 :** to take action against attack or challenge ⟨not justified in striking first, but may ~⟩ **2 :** to present a defense ⟨may not thereafter ~ on grounds of insanity —W. R. LaFave and A. W. Scott, Jr.⟩

de·fen·dant \di-'fen-dənt, -ˌdant\ *n* : the party against whom a criminal or civil action is brought — see also ANSWER, CODEFENDANT; compare ACCUSED, PLAINTIFF

de·fend·er *n* : a lawyer who represents defendants; *esp* : PUBLIC DEFENDER

de·fense \di-'fens, 'dē-ˌfens\ *n* **1 :** the act or action of defending — see also SELF-DEFENSE **2 a :** the theory or ground that forms the basis for a defendant's opposition to an allegation in a complaint or to a charge in a charging instrument (as an indictment); *also* : the evidence and arguments presented supporting the defendant's opposition — see also ACCORD, ALIBI, ASSUMPTION OF RISK, COERCION, CONSENT, *contributory negligence* at NEGLIGENCE, DENIAL, DIMINISHED CAPACITY, DURESS, ENTRAPMENT, ESTOPPEL, FRAUD, INFANCY, INSANITY, INTOXICATION, LACHES, MISTAKE, NECESSITY, RES JUDICATA, STATUTE OF LIMITATIONS

absolute defense : COMPLETE DEFENSE in this entry

affirmative defense : a defense that does not deny the truth of the allegations against the defendant but gives some other reason (as insanity, assumption of risk, or expiration of the statute of limitations) why the defendant cannot be held liable ◊ The defendant bears the burden of proof as to affirmative defenses.

choice of evils defense : a defense to a criminal charge based on the assertion that the criminal act was committed to avoid the commission of an even greater evil — called also *lesser evils defense* ◊ In jurisdictions that recognize the choice of evils defense, it encompasses both of the older defenses of duress and necessity.

complete defense : a defense that shields the defendant from any liability and bars any recovery by the plaintiff — compare PARTIAL DEFENSE in this entry

lesser evils defense : CHOICE OF EVILS DEFENSE in this entry

meritorious defense : a defense that is based on evidence sufficient to warrant setting aside a default judgment against the defendant in civil litigation

partial defense : a defense by which the defendant reduces the amount of damages of which he or she is liable — compare COMPLETE DEFENSE in this entry b : a basis upon which an obligor of a negotiable instrument may avoid liability under the instrument

personal defense : a defense of an obligor under a negotiable instrument that can be asserted against anyone but a holder in due course

real defense : a defense of an obligor of a negotiable instrument that may be asserted even against a holder in due course ◊ Section 3-305(a)(1) of the Uniform Commercial Code sets out the real defenses as infancy, duress, lack of legal capacity, illegality of the transaction, fraud in the factum, and discharge of the obligor by a bankruptcy court. By exclusion, all other defenses are personal defenses.

3 : the defending side in a legal proceeding ⟨the ~ rests⟩ — compare PROSECUTION

defense bar *n* : the segment of the bar in a given area that consists of lawyers who primarily represent defendants ⟨the New York criminal *defense bar*⟩

de·fen·sive *adj* **1** : serving to defend or as part of a defense ⟨a ~ pleading⟩ **2** : devoted to resisting or preventing aggressive actions ⟨a ~ recapitalization . . . to escape a takeover attempt —Barbara Franklin⟩ — **de·fen·sive·ly** *adv*

de·ferred \di-'fərd\ *adj* : withheld or delayed for or until a stated time ⟨a ~ payment⟩ ⟨~ prosecution⟩

deferred annuity — see ANNUITY

deferred compensation *n* : current compensation (as wages or salary) deferred until a later time usu. for the purpose of investment (as in a retirement plan)

deferred income *n* : current income forgone to produce a later higher income (as at retirement)

de·fi·cien·cy \di-'fi-shən-sē\ *n, pl* **-cies** : an amount that is lacking or inadequate: as **a** : the difference between the amount of tax owed and the amount of tax paid **b** : the difference between the amount owed under a security agreement and the amount the creditor is able to recover upon default of the debtor by selling the collateral

deficiency judgment — see JUDGMENT 1a

de·file \di-'fīl\ *vt* **de·filed; de·fil·ing** : to dishonor by physical acts (as trampling, dirtying, or mutilating) ⟨*defiling* the flag⟩ — **de·file·ment** *n* — **de·fil·er** *n*

de·fined benefit plan *n* : a pension plan in which the amount of benefits paid to an employee after retirement is fixed in advance in accordance with a formula given in the plan

defined contribution plan *n* : a pension plan in which the amount of the contributions made by the employer is fixed in advance and earnings are distributed proportionately

definite failure of issue — see FAILURE OF ISSUE

de·fraud \di-'fròd\ *vt* : to deprive of something by fraud — **de·fraud·er** *n*

de·gree *n* **1** : a step in a direct line of descent or in the line of ascent to a common ancestor **2 a** : a measure of the seriousness of a crime — see also FIFTH DEGREE, FIRST DEGREE, FOURTH DEGREE, SECOND DEGREE, THIRD DEGREE ◊ Crimes are rated by degrees for the purpose of imposing more severe punishments for more serious crimes. **b** : a measure of care; *also* : a measure of negligence esp. in connection with bailments — see also CARE, NEGLIGENCE

de·hors \dē-'hòrz, də-'hòr\ *prep* [Anglo-French, outside of] : out of (as an agreement, record, or will) : foreign to

de–im·mo·bi·lize \ˌdē-i-'mō-bə-ˌlīz\ *vt* **-ized; -iz·ing** : to free from immobilization; *specif* : to return (a component part of immovable property) to the status of movable property (as by detachment or removal) — **de–im·mo·bi·li·za·tion** \-ˌmō-bə-lə-'zā-shən, -lī-\ *n*

de ju·re \dē-'jùr-ē, dā-'yùr-ā\ *adv or adj* [Medieval Latin, literally, from the law] **1** : by right : of right ⟨a de jure officer⟩ **2** : in accordance with law — see

\ə\abut \ˌ\kitten \ər\further \a\ash \ā\ace \ä\cot, cart \aù\out \ch\chin \e\bet \ē\easy \g\go \i\hit \ī\ice \j\job \ŋ\sing \ō\go \ò\law \òi\boy \th\thin \th\the \ü\loot \ù\foot \y\yet \zh\vision *see also* Pronunciation Symbols page

also *de jure segregation* at SEGREGATION; compare DE FACTO

de jure segregation — see SEGREGATION

del cre•de•re \del-'krā-də-ˌrā\ *adj* [Italian, of belief, of trust] : relating to or guaranteeing performance or payment by third persons to a principal in connection with transactions entered into by an agent for the principal usu. in return for higher commissions

del credere agent — see AGENT

de•lec•tus per•son•ae \di-'lek-təs-pər-'sō-nē, dā-'lek-tu̇s-per-'sō-nī\ *n* [Latin, choice of person] : the selection of a person satisfactory to oneself for a position (as of partner) involving trust and confidence in the other's character, capacities, or responsibility

del•e•ga•ble \'de-lə-gə-bəl\ *adj* : capable of being delegated — **del•e•ga•bil•i•ty** \ˌde-lə-gə-'bi-lə-tē\ *n*

del•e•gant \'de-lə-gənt\ *n* : one that delegates

¹del•e•gate \'de-li-gət\ *n* [Medieval Latin *delegatus*, from Latin, past participle of *delegare* to appoint, put in charge] : a person empowered to act on behalf of another: as **a** : a person who is authorized to perform another's duties under a contract **b** : a representative to a convention (as of a political party) or conference **c** : a representative of a U.S. territory in the House of Representatives **d** : a member of the lower house of the legislature of Maryland, Virginia, or West Virginia

²del•e•gate \'de-li-ˌgāt\ *vb* **-gat•ed; -gat-ing** *vt* **1** : to entrust or transfer (as power, authority, or responsibility) to another: as **a** : to transfer (one's contractual duties) to another **b** : to empower a body (as an administrative agency) to perform (a governmental function) — see also NONDELEGATION DOCTRINE **2** : to appoint as one's representative ∼ *vi* : to transfer responsibility or authority

del•e•ga•tee \ˌde-li-gə-'tē\ *n* : DELEGATE

del•e•ga•tion \ˌde-li-'gā-shən\ *n* **1** : the act of delegating **2** : a group of persons chosen to represent others

¹de•lib•er•ate \di-'li-bə-ˌrāt\ *vb* **-at•ed; -at-**

ing *vi* : to think about and weigh or discuss issues and decisions carefully ⟨the jury retired to ∼⟩ ∼ *vt* : to think about or evaluate

²de•lib•er•ate \di-'li-bə-rət\ *adj* **1** : characterized by or resulting from careful consideration; *esp* : characterized by or resulting from evaluation done in a cool state of blood and with a fixed purpose ⟨∼ murder⟩ — compare PREMEDITATED **2** : characterized by an understanding of the nature of a thing or act and its consequences ⟨∼ falsehoods⟩ — **de•lib•er-ate•ly** *adv* — **de•lib•er•ate•ness** *n*

deliberate homicide — see HOMICIDE

de•lib•er•a•tion \di-ˌli-bə-'rā-shən\ *n* **1 a** : the act of deliberating — compare PREMEDITATION **b** : a discussion and consideration by a group of persons (as a jury or legislature) of the reasons for or against a measure **2** : the quality or state of being deliberate ⟨killing with ∼⟩ — **de•lib•er-a•tive** \dē-'li-bə-ˌrā-tiv, -brə-tiv\ *adj*

deliberative process privilege — see PRIVILEGE 1b

de•lict \di-'likt\ *n* [Latin *delictum* misdeed, offense, from neuter past participle of *delinquere* to commit (an offense), err] **1** *in the civil law of Louisiana* : OFFENSE 2; *esp* : an offense other than breach of contract that creates an obligation for damages ◊ *Delict* is the civil law equivalent of the common-law *tort.* **2** : a criminal offense — **de•lic•tu•al** \di-'lik-chə-wəl\ *adj*

de•lin•quen•cy \di-'liŋ-kwən-sē\ *n, pl* **-cies 1 a** : the quality or state of being delinquent **b** : JUVENILE DELINQUENCY ⟨contributing to the ∼ of a minor⟩ **2** : a debt on which payment is overdue ⟨consumer loan *delinquencies*⟩

¹de•lin•quent \di-'liŋ-kwənt\ *n* : a delinquent person; *esp* : JUVENILE DELINQUENT

²delinquent *adj* [Latin *delinquent-, delinquens*, present participle of *delinquere* to commit (an offense), err] **1 a** : offending by neglect or violation of duty or law ⟨∼ acts⟩ **b** : characterized by juvenile delinquency ⟨∼ youth⟩ **2** : being overdue in

payment ⟨~ taxes⟩ ⟨was ~ in his child support payments⟩
de·list \dē-'list\ *vt* : to remove from a list; *esp* : to remove (a security) from the list of securities that may be traded on a particular exchange
de·liv·er *vt* **-ered; -er·ing** : to transfer possession of (property) to another : put into the possession or exclusive control of another ⟨a deed must be ~*ed* to be effective —W. M. McGovern, Jr. *et al.*⟩ — see also GIFT; compare BAIL, CONVEY, DONATE, GIVE, SELL — **de·liv·er·able** *adj*
de·liv·ery *n, pl* **-er·ies** : an act that shows a transferor's intent to make a transfer of property (as a gift); *esp* : the transfer of possession or exclusive control of property to another
actual delivery : a delivery (as by hand or shipment) of actual physical property (as jewelry or stock certificates)
conditional delivery : a delivery after which ownership will be transferred upon fulfillment of a condition — compare *gift causa mortis* at GIFT ◊ A conditional delivery is usu. made in order to make a transfer revocable.
constructive delivery : a delivery of a representation of property (as a written instrument) or means of possession (as a key) that is construed by a court as sufficient to show the transferor's intent or to put the property under the transferee's control — called also *symbolic delivery*
¹de·mand *n* **1** : a formal request or call for something (as payment for a debt) esp. based on a right or made with force ⟨a shareholder must first make a ~ on the corporation's board of directors to act — R. C. Clark⟩ ⟨a written ~ for payment⟩ **2** : something demanded ⟨any ~*s* against the estate⟩ — see also CLAIM — **on demand** : upon presentation and request for payment
²demand *vt* : to ask or call for with force, authority, or by legal right : claim as due ⟨any party may ~ a trial by jury of any issue triable of right by a jury —*Federal Rules of Civil Procedure* Rule 38(b)⟩ — **·able** *adj*

demand deposit — see DEPOSIT 2a
demand loan — see LOAN
demand note — see NOTE
de·mea·nor \di-'mē-nər\ *n* : outward manner : way of conducting oneself ◊ A jury may consider a witness's demeanor on the stand in determining the witness's credibility.
de min·i·mis \dē-'mi-nə-məs, dā-'mē-ni-mis\ *adj* [New Latin, concerning trifles] : lacking significance or importance : so minor as to be disregarded — compare SUBSTANTIAL ◊ An action may be dismissed if the claim or cause is considered de minimis.
de minimis non cu·rat lex \-'nän-'kyür-ət-'leks, -'nȯn-'kü-rät-\ *n* [New Latin, the law does not concern itself with trifles] : the principle that the law is not concerned with insignificant or minor matters
¹de·mise \di-'mīz\ *vt* **de·mised; de·mis·ing** : to convey (possession of property) by will or lease ⟨the *demised* premises⟩
²demise *n* [Anglo-French, from feminine past participle of *demettre* to convey by lease, from Old French, to put down, give up, renounce, from Latin *demittere* to let fall and *dimittere* to release] **1** : the conveyance of property by will or lease : LEASE **2** : the transmission of property by testate or intestate succession **3** : charter of a boat in which the owner surrenders completely the possession, command, and navigation of the boat — called also *bareboat charter*
de·moc·ra·cy \di-'mä-krə-sē\ *n, pl* **-cies 1 a** : government by the people; *esp* : rule of the majority **b** : a government in which the supreme power is vested in the people and exercised by them directly or indirectly through a system of representation usu. involving periodically held free elections **2** : a political unit that has a democratic government — **dem·o·crat·ic** \¸de-

mə-'kra-tik\ *adj* — **dem•o•crat•i•cal•ly** *adv*

demonstrative bequest — see BEQUEST

demonstrative evidence — see EVIDENCE

demonstrative legacy — see LEGACY

de•mur \di-'mər\ *vi* **de•murred; de•mur•ring** : to interpose a demurrer ⟨~ to the declaration⟩ — **de•mur•ra•ble** *adj*

de•mur•rer \di-'mər-ər\ *n* [Anglo-French, from *demurrer* to file a demurrer, literally, to stay, dwell, delay, from Old French *demorer*, from Latin *demorari* to delay] : a plea in response to an allegation (as in a complaint or indictment) that admits its truth but also asserts that it is not sufficient as a cause of action — compare CONFESSION AND AVOIDANCE ◊ Demurrers are no longer used in federal civil or criminal procedure but are still used in some states. General demurrers are replaced in the Federal Rules of Civil Procedure by motions to dismiss for failure to state a claim on which relief may be granted. Special demurrers are replaced by motions for more definite statement. In the Federal Rules of Criminal Procedure, a motion to dismiss or to grant appropriate relief takes the place of a demurrer. Demurrers are sometimes used to question a court's jurisdiction.

demurrer to the evidence : a demurrer that asserts that the evidence is not sufficient to create a question of fact for the jury to decide

general demurrer : a demurrer that challenges the sufficiency of the substance of allegation

special demurrer : a demurrer that challenges the structure or form of an allegation as uncertain or ambiguous ◊ A special demurrer must specify the defect in the allegation.

demurrer to the evidence — see DEMURRER

den *abbr* denied

de•ni•al \di-'nī-əl\ *n* 1 : refusal to grant or allow something ⟨~ of due process⟩ ⟨~ of a motion⟩ 2 a : an assertion that an allegation is false b : a defense asserting that an opposing party's allegations are false — compare *affirmative defense* at DEFENSE 2a, TRAVERSE ◊ Under the Federal Rules of Civil Procedure, allegations that are not denied are taken as admitted, and a statement that a party has insufficient knowledge or information to form a belief as to the truth of an allegation is taken as a denial. A denial must sufficiently state which allegations or parts of allegations are being denied.

ar•gu•men•ta•tive denial \,är-gyə-'men-tə-tiv-\ : a denial that asserts facts inconsistent with an allegation made by an adverse party

general denial 1 : a denial of all the allegations in a complaint 2 : a denial of all the allegations of a particular paragraph or group of paragraphs in a complaint

specific denial 1 : GENERAL DENIAL 2 in this entry 2 : a denial of parts of an allegation in a complaint

de no•vo \dē-'nō-vō, dā-\ *adv or adj* [Medieval Latin, literally, from (the) new] : over again : as if for the first time: **a** : allowing independent appellate determination of issues (as of fact or law) ⟨a *de novo* review⟩ **b** : allowing complete retrial upon new evidence — compare ABUSE OF DISCRETION, CLEARLY ERRONEOUS ◊ A de novo review is an in-depth review. Decisions of federal administrative agencies are generally subject to de novo review in the U.S. District Courts, and some lower state court decisions are subject to de novo review at the next level.

de•ny *vt* **de•nied; de•ny•ing** 1 : to declare untrue ⟨a party . . . shall admit or ~ the averments —*Federal Rules of Civil Procedure* Rule 8(b)⟩ — compare AVOID 2 : to refuse to grant ⟨*denied* the motion for a new trial⟩

de•pe•cage \,dā-pə-'säzh\ *n* [French *dépeçage* dismemberment, from *dépecer* to carve up, analyze minutely] : a rule in conflicts of law: the laws of different states may be applied to different issues in the same dispute

dependency deduction — see DEDUCTION

dependency exemption — see EXEMPTION

¹**de•pen•dent** *adj* **1 :** determined or conditioned by another **:** CONTINGENT **2 a :** relying on another for esp. financial support **b :** lacking the necessary means of support or protection and in need of aid from others (as a public agency) ⟨have the child declared ~ and taken away from his or her parents —L. H. Tribe⟩ **3 :** subject to another's jurisdiction ⟨the United States and its ~ territories⟩

²**dependent** *n* **:** a person who is dependent; *esp* **:** a close relative or member of a taxpayer's household who receives over half of his or her support from the taxpayer and is a U.S. citizen, national, or resident, or a resident of a bordering country (as Mexico) — see also *dependency exemption* at EXEMPTION

dependent relative revocation *n* **:** a doctrine holding that if the destruction, cancellation, or revocation of a will is dependent on the making of a new will which is not made or is found to be invalid then the original will is still in effect

de•ple•tion \di-'plē-shən\ *n* **:** the reduction of the value of the assets of a company engaged in removing natural resources (as by mining) because of the decrease over time of the natural resources (as coal) available in or on the land being worked

de•po•nent \di-'pō-nənt\ *n* **:** a person who gives a deposition — compare AFFIANT, WITNESS

de•port \di-'pōrt\ *vt* **:** to send (an alien) out of a country by order of deportation — compare EXCLUDE — **de•port•able** *adj*

de•por•ta•tion \ˌdē-ˌpōr-'tā-shən\ *n* **:** an act or instance of deporting; *specif* **:** the removal from a country of an alien whose presence is illegal or detrimental to the public welfare — compare EXCLUSION

de•por•tee \ˌdē-ˌpōr-'tē\ *n* **:** a person who has been deported or is under an order of deportation

de•pose \di-'pōz\ *vb* **de•posed; de•pos•ing** *vt* **1 :** to testify to under oath or by sworn affidavit **2 :** to take testimony from esp. by deposition ⟨plaintiffs . . . were entitled to ~ experts retained by the defendants — *National Law Journal*⟩ — compare EXAMINE ~ *vi* **:** TESTIFY ⟨the plaintiff *deposed* in person to many specific facts — *Mintz v. Atlantic Coast Line R. Co.*, 72 S.E.2d 38 (1952)⟩

¹**de•pos•it** \di-'pä-zət\ *vt* **1 :** to place for safekeeping or as security ⟨may ~ the property with the court⟩; *esp* **:** to put in a bank account **2** *in the civil law of Louisiana* **:** to place (movable property) under a deposit ⟨the depository can not make use of the thing ~*ed* — *Louisiana Civil Code*⟩ — **de•pos•i•tor** \di-'pä-zə-tər\ *n*

²**deposit** *n* **1 :** the state of being deposited (as in an account) ⟨holding the property on ~⟩ — compare ESCROW, TRUST **2 :** something placed for safekeeping: as **a :** money deposited in a bank esp. to one's credit

demand deposit **:** a bank deposit that can be withdrawn without prior notice

general deposit **:** a deposit of money in a bank that is to the credit of the depositor thereby giving the depositor the right to money and creating a debtor-creditor relationship

special deposit **:** a deposit that is made for a specific purpose, that is to be returned to the depositor, and that creates a bailment or trust

time deposit **:** a bank deposit that can be withdrawn only after a set period of time or with prior notice

b : something given as security — see also SECURITY DEPOSIT ◊ A deposit may be applied to a purchase price or may be considered partial payment. **3** *in the civil law of Louisiana* **a :** the gratuitous transfer of possession of movable property to another for a limited time or specified purpose such that the depositary is liable to some extent for loss or damage

\ə\abut \ᵊ\kitten \ər\further \a\ash \ā\ace
\ä\cot, cart \aú\out \ch\chin \e\bet \ē\easy
\g\go \i\hit \ī\ice \j\job \ŋ\sing \ō\go \ò\law
\ói\boy \th\thin \th̲\the \ü\loot \ú\foot \y\yet
\zh\vision *see also* Pronunciation Symbols page

to the property — see also SEQUESTRA-TION; compare BAILMENT, HIRING, *loan for consumption* and *loan for use* at LOAN ◊ Like the common-law bailment, the civil law deposit requires either actual or constructive delivery.

necessary deposit : a deposit compelled by a sudden emergency ◊ The Louisiana Civil Code deems the deposit of travelers' belongings with an innkeeper a necessary deposit.

voluntary deposit : a deposit that is made by the mutual consent of the depositor and depositary ◊ The consent required may be express or implied, and because of the requirements of consent, only persons with the capacity to contract can make a voluntary deposit.

b : the movable property that is the object of a deposit ⟨the depositary is bound to use the same diligence in preserving the ~ that he uses in preserving his own property —*Louisiana Civil Code*⟩ **4** : an act of depositing ⟨upon the ~ of the money in the escrow account⟩ **5** : DEPOSITORY ⟨night ~⟩

de·pos·i·tary \di-'pä-zə-ˌter-ē\ *n*, *pl* **-taries** : an individual or entity (as a business organization) that holds a deposit ⟨the ~ ought to restore the precise object which he received —*Louisiana Civil Code*⟩; *also* : DEPOSITORY

depositary bank — see BANK

de·po·si·tion \ˌde-pə-'zi-shən\ *n* [Late Latin *depositio* testimony, from Latin, act of depositing, from *deponere* to put down, deposit] **1 a** : a statement that is made under oath by a party or witness (as an expert) in response to oral examination or written questions and that is recorded by an authorized officer (as a court reporter); *broadly* : AFFIDAVIT **b** : the certified document recording such a statement — compare INTERROGATORY **2** : the hearing at which a deposition is made ⟨order that the testimony at a ~ be recorded by other than stenographic means —*Federal Rules of Civil Procedure* Rule 38(b)⟩ ◊ A deposition can be used as a method of discovery, to preserve the testimony of a witness who is likely to become unavailable for trial, or for impeachment of testimony at trial. Depositions are distinguished from affidavits by the requirement that notice and an opportunity to cross-examine the deponent must be given to the other party.

de·pos·i·to·ry \di-'pä-zə-ˌtōr-ē\ *n*, *pl* **-ries** **1** : a place where something is deposited esp. for safekeeping ⟨night ~⟩; *specif* : a bank chosen for the depositing of government funds **2** : DEPOSITARY

depository bond — see BOND 1a

de·praved \di-'prāvd\ *adj* : marked by moral corruption or perversion as shown by a capacity for extreme and wanton physical cruelty ⟨the ~ state of mind of the murderer⟩ ⟨the ~ nature of the crime⟩

depraved–heart murder — see MURDER

de·prav·i·ty \di-'pra-və-tē\ *n*, *pl* **-ties** **1** : the quality or state of being depraved **2** : a corrupt act or practice

de·pre·cia·ble \di-'prē-shə-bəl\ *adj* : capable of being depreciated ⟨~ property⟩

de·pre·ci·ate \di-'prē-shē-ˌāt\ *vb* **-at·ed; -at·ing** *vt* : to subject to depreciation : lower the value of ~ *vi* : to fall in value — compare APPRECIATE

de·pre·ci·a·tion \di-ˌprē-shē-'ā-shən\ *n* **1** : any decrease in the value of property (as machinery) for the purpose of taxation that cannot be offset by current repairs and is carried on company books as a yearly charge amortizing the original cost over the useful life of the property

accelerated depreciation : the depreciation of property that was put into use prior to 1980 which is allowed at a faster rate than normal under the depreciation rules in force before the adoption of the Accelerated Cost Recovery System

straight–line depreciation : depreciation of an asset by a fixed percentage of its original cost based on its estimated life **2** : a loss in the value of property due to physical deterioration and wear or to obsolescence and lack of adaptability

de·prive *vt* **de·prived; de·priv·ing** : to

take away or withhold something from ⟨no person shall . . . be *deprived* of life, liberty, or property, without due process of law —*U.S. Constitution* amend. V⟩ — **dep·ri·va·tion** \‚de-prə-'vā-shən, ‚dē-‚prī-\ *n*

deprived *adj* : marked by deprivation esp. of the necessities of life or care in a healthful environment ⟨a ~ child⟩

dep·u·tize \'de-pyə-‚tīz\ *vb* -**tized; -tiz·ing** *vt* : to appoint as deputy — *vi* : to act as deputy

dep·u·ty \'de-pyə-tē\ *n, pl* -**ties** [Middle French *député* person appointed to exercise authority, from past participle of *deputer* to appoint, depute] **1** : a person appointed as a substitute with power to act **2** : a second in command or assistant who usu. takes charge when his or her superior is absent; *specif* : DEPUTY SHERIFF

deputy sheriff *n* : an assistant appointed to take on some of the duties of a sheriff

der·e·lic·tion \‚der-ə-'lik-shən\ *n* **1 a** : an intentional abandonment **b** : a state of being abandoned **2** : a recession of water leaving permanently dry land **3** : an intentional or conscious neglect ⟨~ of duty⟩

¹de·riv·a·tive \də-'ri-və-tiv\ *n* : a contract or security that derives its value from that of an underlying asset (as another security) or from the value of a rate (as of interest or currency exchange) or index of asset value (as a stock index) ◊ Derivatives often take the form of customized contracts transacted outside of security exchanges, while other contracts, such as standard index options and futures, are openly traded on such exchanges. Derivatives often involve a forward contract.

²derivative *adj* **1** : arising out of or dependent on the existence of something else — compare DIRECT **2** : of, relating to, or being a derivative ⟨a ~ transaction⟩ — **de·riv·a·tive·ly** *adv*

derivative action *n* : a suit brought by a shareholder on behalf of a corporation or by a member on behalf of an association to assert a cause of action usu.

against an officer which the corporation or association has itself failed to assert for its injuries — called also *derivative suit, shareholder's derivative suit;* compare DIRECT ACTION 2 ◊ A shareholder or member bringing a derivative action must describe in the complaint attempts to obtain action from the corporate directors or association authorities, or from other shareholders or members, and the reasons these attempts failed. The plaintiff must fairly and adequately represent the other similarly situated shareholders or members, and the action may not be collusive. Federal Rule of Civil Procedure 23.1 governs derivative actions brought in federal court.

derivative contraband — see CONTRABAND

derivative evidence — see EVIDENCE

derivative suit *n* : DERIVATIVE ACTION

derivative work *n* : a piece of intellectual property that substantially derives from an underlying work ◊ Use of a derivative work that is derived from an underlying copyrighted work is infringement if the permission of the copyright owner is not obtained.

der·o·ga·tion \‚der-ə-'gā-shən\ *n* [Latin *derogatio* partial abrogation of a law, from *derogare* to detract from the force of (a law)] : a taking away or detraction from something (as the force of a law) ⟨the executive was without power to act in ~ of international law —Jules Lobel⟩

de·scend \di-'send\ *vi* : to pass by inheritance — **de·scen·di·bil·i·ty** \-‚sen-də-'bil-ə-tē\ *n* — **de·scend·ible** \-'sen-də-bəl\ *adj*

de·scen·dant *also* **de·scen·dent** \di-'sen-dənt\ *n* : a blood relative of a later generation

de·scent *n* : transmission or devolution of the estate of a person who has died with-

\ə\abut \ə\kitten \ər\further \a\ash \ā\ace
\ä\cot, cart \au̇\out \ch\chin \e\bet \ē\easy
\g\go \i\hit \ī\ice \j\job \ŋ\sing \ō\go \ȯ\law
\ȯi\boy \th\thin \th\the \ü\loot \u̇\foot \y\yet
\zh\vision *see also* Pronunciation Symbols page

out a valid will — compare DISTRIBU-
TION

de·scrip·tion *n* : a representation in words of the nature and characteristics of a thing: as **a** : a specification of the boundaries of a piece of land (as for a deed) **b** : an explanation of an invention in a patent application or printed publication

de·scrip·tive mark *n* : a trademark or service mark that conveys the idea of the qualities, characteristics, or effects of a product or service and that is protectable when it creates an association in the mind of the public between the mark and the producer or product or service

de·seg·re·gate \dē-'se-grə-ˌgāt\ *vt* **-gat-ed; -gat·ing** : to eliminate segregation in; *specif* : to free from any law, provision, or practice requiring isolation of the members of a particular race in separate units ~ *vi* : to become desegregated

de·seg·re·ga·tion \dē-ˌse-grə-'gā-shən\ *n* **1** : the action or an instance of desegregating **2** : the state of being desegregated

de·ser·tion *n* : the forsaking of a person, post, or relationship: as **a** : permanent withdrawal from living with one's spouse without the spouse's consent and without cause or justification ◊ Desertion is a ground for divorce in many states. **b** : intentional permanent termination of custody over one's child; *also* : ABANDONMENT **c** : abandonment of military duty without leave and without the intent to return

de·sign·er drug *n* : a synthetic version of a controlled substance (as heroin) that is produced with a slightly altered molecular structure to avoid having it classified as an illegal drug

de·sign patent *n* : a patent that protects the appearance of a product against infringement

de·sire *vt* **de·sired; de·sir·ing** : to wish for earnestly — see also PRECATORY ◊ Courts have variously interpreted *desire* in wills to indicate either a direction of the testator that must be followed or

merely an expression of what the testator hoped would happen.

destination contract — see CONTRACT

de·struc·ti·bil·i·ty of contingent remainders : a now largely abolished rule in the law of estates that a contingent remainder that fails to vest upon the termination of the preceding estate is destroyed — see also *executory interest* at INTEREST

de·sue·tude \'de-swi-ˌtüd, -ˌtyüd; di-'sü-ə-ˌtüd\ *n* [Latin *desuetudo* disuse, from *desuescere* to lose the habit of] : a doctrine holding that a statute may be abrogated because of its long disuse

de·tain *vt* **1** : to hold or keep in custody or possession ⟨property wrongfully ~*ed*⟩ ⟨a juvenile ~*ed* in a care facility⟩ **2** : to restrain from proceeding ⟨~*ed* the driver and asked to see his license⟩

de·tain·ee \di-ˌtā-'nē\ *n* : a person who is detained; *esp* : a person held in custody prior to trial or hearing

de·tain·er \di-'tā-nər\ *n* [Anglo-French *detenoure*, from *detenir* to restrain, detain, from Old French, from Latin *detinere*] **1** : the act of keeping something in one's possession; *specif* : UNLAWFUL DETAINER **2** : detention in custody **3** : a notification sent by a prosecutor, judge, or other official advising a prison official that a prisoner is wanted to answer criminal charges and requesting continued detention of the prisoner or notification of the prisoner's impending release — compare EXTRADITION

de·tec·tive *n* : a person engaged or employed in detecting lawbreakers or in getting information that is not readily or publicly accessible ⟨a police ~⟩ ⟨hired a private ~⟩

de·ten·tion *n* **1** : the act or fact of detaining or holding back; *esp* : a holding in custody **2** : the state of being detained; *esp* : a period of temporary custody prior to a trial or hearing — see also PREVENTIVE DETENTION

de·ter·min·able *adj* **1** : capable of being determined, ascertained, or decided upon **2** : liable to be terminated upon the occurrence of a contingency

determinable easement — see EASEMENT
determinable fee — see FEE 1
determinate sentence — see SENTENCE
de·ter·mi·na·tion *n* : a decision of a court or administrative agency regarding an issue, case, or claim
determination letter — see LETTER 1
de·ter·mi·na·tive \di-'tər-mə-,nā-tiv, -nə-tiv\ *adj* : having the power or tendency to determine ⟨a fact ∼ of the issue⟩
de·ter·mine *vt* -mined; -min·ing : to make a determination regarding
de·ter·rence \di-'tər-əns, -'ter-\ *n* : the inhibition of criminal behavior by fear esp. of punishment
det·i·net \'de-ti-,net\ *n* [Medieval Latin, he/she withholds] : a common-law action alleging that the defendant is withholding money or items owed (as under a contract) — compare DETINUIT
det·i·nue \'det-ᵊn-,ü, -,yü\ *n* [Anglo-French *detenue*, from feminine past participle of *detenir* to detain — see DETAINER] : a common-law action for the recovery of personal property belonging to the plaintiff that is wrongfully detained by the defendant — compare TROVER
de·tin·u·it \de-'ti-nü-it, -nyü-\ *n* [Medieval Latin, he/she withheld] : an action for replevin where the plaintiff already has the goods that are the subject of the suit — compare DETINET
det·ri·ment \'de-trə-mənt\ *n* 1 : INJURY, LOSS; *also* : the cause of an injury or loss 2 : a giving up of a thing or mode of conduct to which one is entitled that constitutes consideration for a contract — called also *legal detriment* — **det·ri·men·tal** \,de-trə-'men-təl\ *adj* — **det·ri·men·tal·ly** *adv*
dev·a·sta·vit \,de-və-'stā-vit\ *n* [Medieval Latin, he/she has spoiled (someone's property)] 1 : mismanagement or waste of the assets in the estate of a deceased person by the fiduciary in charge of the estate (as the executor) 2 : a common-law writ seeking a remedy for devastavit
de·vest \di-'vest\ *vt* : DIVEST
dev·i·sa·vit vel non \,de-və-'zā-vit-,vel-'nän, ,dā-vē-'sä-vit-,vel-'nōn\ *n* [New

Latin, (whether) he/she bequeaths or not] : a document that sets forth the questions of fact pertinent to the validity of an alleged will and is sent from a court of probate or chancery to a court of law for a jury trial for judgment as to the validity of the will — called also *devisat vel non*
¹de·vise \di-'vīz\ *vt* **de·vised; de·vis·ing** [Anglo-French *deviser* to divide, share, bequeath, ultimately from Latin *dividere* to divide] : to give (property) by will; *specif* : to give (real property) by will — compare ALIENATE, BEQUEATH, CONVEY — **de·vis·able** *adj* — **de·vi·sor** \,de-və-'zòr; di-'vī-,zòr, -zər\ *n*
²devise *n* 1 : a gift of property made in a will; *specif* : a gift of real property made in a will — see also ABATE, ADEMPTION; compare DISTRIBUTION ◊ Formerly *devise* was used to refer only to gifts of real property, and *legacy* and *bequest* were used only to refer to gifts of personal property. These distinctions are no longer closely followed. The Uniform Probate Code uses *devise* to refer to any gifts made in a will.
executory devise : a devise of an interest in land that will vest in the future upon the occurrence of a contingency and that can follow a fee simple estate ◊ Executory devises were invented as a way of getting around the rule in Shelley's case, which is now largely abolished.
general devise : a devise that is to be distributed from the general assets of an estate and that is not of a particular thing
re·sid·u·ary devise \ri-'zi-jə-,wer-ē-\ : a devise of whatever is left in an estate after all other debts and devises have been paid or distributed
specific devise : a devise of a particular item or part of an estate that is payable only from a specified source in the estate and not from the general assets

\ə\abut \ᵊ\kitten \ər\further \a\ash \ā\ace
\ä\cot, cart \aù\out \ch\chin \e\bet \ē\easy
\g\go \i\hit \ī\ice \j\job \ŋ\sing \ō\go \ò\law
\òi\boy \th\thin \th\the \ü\loot \ù\foot \y\yet
\zh\vision *see also* Pronunciation Symbols page

2 : a clause in a will disposing of property and esp. real property **3** : property disposed of by a will

de•vi•see \ˌde-və-'zē, di-ˌvī-'zē\ *n* : one to whom a devise of property is made — compare HEIR, LEGATEE, NEXT OF KIN

de•vo•lu•tion \ˌde-və-'lü-shən, ˌdē-\ *n* : the transfer (as of rights, powers, property, or responsibility) to another

de•volve \di-'völv, -'välv\ *vi* **de•volved; de•volv•ing** [Medieval Latin *devolvi*, passive of *devolvere* to roll down, from Latin, from *de* down, away + *volvere* to roll] **1** : to pass by transfer or succession ⟨the estate *devolved* to a distant cousin⟩ **2** : to fall or be passed usu. as an obligation or responsibility ⟨in case of the removal of the President from office, or of his . . . inability to discharge the powers and duties of the said office, the same shall ~ on the Vice President — *U.S. Constitution* art. II⟩

DFA *abbr* delayed funds availability

dick•er \'di-kər\ *vi* **dick•ered; dick•er•ing** : to seek to arrive at a workable and agreeable arrangement by negotiating and haggling

dicta *pl of* DICTUM

dic•tum \'dik-təm\ *n, pl* **dic•ta** \-tə\ [Latin, utterance, from neuter of *dictus*, past participle of *dicere* to say] : a view expressed by a judge in an opinion on a point not necessarily arising from or involved in a case or necessary for determining the rights of the parties involved — called also *obiter dictum;* compare HOLDING, JUDGMENT, PRECEDENT, STARE DECISIS ◊ Dicta have persuasive value in making an argument, but they are not binding as precedent.

di•es non \'dī-ēz-'nän, 'dē-es-'nȯn\ *also* **dies non ju•rid•i•cus** \-jù-'ri-di-kəs, -yù-'rē-di-kùs\ *n* [New Latin *dies non juridicus* nonjuridical day] : a day when courts do not sit or carry on business

di•gest \'dī-ˌjest\ *n* [Latin *digesta*, from neuter plural of *digestus*, past participle of *digerere* to disperse, arrange] : a compilation of legal rules, statutes, or decisions systematically arranged

dilatory plea — see PLEA

dil•i•gence \'di-lə-jəns\ *n* : earnest and persistent application of effort esp. as required by law; *also* : CARE 1 — see also DUE DILIGENCE

di•lute \dī-'lüt, də-\ *vt* **di•lut•ed; di•lut•ing** : to cause dilution of

di•lu•tion \dī-'lü-shən, də-\ *n* **1** : a lessening of real value (as of equity) by a decrease in relative worth; *specif* : a decrease of the value per share of common stock caused by an increase in the total number of shares **2** : a lessening of the value of a trademark that is caused by use of the mark by another and that creates potential confusion on the part of the consumer **3** : a weakening of the voting rights of a group of citizens (as a minority) because the representatives they elect have no greater legislative power than the representatives elected by smaller voting groups

di•min•ished capacity \də-'mi-nisht-\ *n* **1** : an abnormal mental condition that renders a person unable to form the specific intent necessary for the commission of a crime (as first-degree murder) but that does not amount to insanity — called also *diminished responsibility, partial insanity;* compare INSANITY, IRRESISTIBLE IMPULSE TEST, M'NAGHTEN TEST, SUBSTANTIAL CAPACITY TEST **2 a** : a defense based on a claim of diminished capacity **b** : the doctrine that diminished capacity may negate an element of a crime ◊ If diminished capacity is shown, negating an element of the crime with which a defendant is charged, the defendant can only be convicted of a lesser offense that does not include the element.

dim•i•nu•tion \ˌdi-mə-'nü-shən, -'nyü-\ *n* : the act, process, or an instance of making less ⟨prohibiting the ~ of a judge's compensation — *U.S. Code*⟩

diminution in value : a theory of property damages in which the measure of damages for the breach of a contract or lease is equal to the difference between the value of the property in the condition promised and the value as it exists

diplomatic immunity — see IMMUNITY
¹di·rect *vt* **1** : to order with authority ⟨the testator ~*ed* that the car go to his niece⟩ **2** : to order entry of (a verdict) without jury consideration ⟨the court ~*ed* a verdict in favor of the defendant⟩ **3** : to act as director of ~ *vi* : to act as director
²direct *adj* **1 a** : stemming immediately from a source ⟨~ costs⟩ ⟨a ~ claim⟩ — compare DERIVATIVE **b** : being or passing in a straight line from parent to offspring : LINEAL ⟨a ~ ancestor⟩ — compare COLLATERAL **2** : marked by absence of any intervening agency, instrumentality, or influence ⟨~ consequences⟩ **3** : effected by the action of the people or the electorate and not by representatives ⟨~ democracy⟩ **4** : characterized by close logical, causal, or consequential relationship ⟨a ~ interest in the outcome of the litigation⟩ — **di·rect·ly** *adv*
³direct *n* : DIRECT EXAMINATION ⟨testimony given on ~⟩
direct action *n* **1** : an action in which the plaintiff sues a person's insurer without first obtaining a judgment against the insured or joining the insured **2** : a suit by a shareholder for an injury to himself or herself independent from any injury to the corporation — called also *individual action;* compare DERIVATIVE ACTION
direct appeal *n* **1** : an appeal from an order of a three-judge court granting or denying an interlocutory or permanent injunction that may be taken directly to the U.S. Supreme Court under title 28 section 1253 of the U.S. Code **2** : DIRECT REVIEW
direct attack — see ATTACK
direct beneficiary — see BENEFICIARY d
direct cause — see CAUSE 1
direct contempt — see CONTEMPT
direct damages — see DAMAGE 2
directed verdict — see VERDICT
directed verdict of acquittal — see VERDICT
direct estoppel — see ESTOPPEL 2a
direct evidence — see EVIDENCE
direct examination *n* : the first examination of a witness by the party calling the witness — compare CROSS-EXAMINATION, REDIRECT EXAMINATION ◇ Leading questions are not allowed on direct examination unless the witness is shown to be hostile.
direct insurance *n* : an insurance contract in which the insurer agrees to pay the insured for a designated loss — compare REINSURANCE
direct loss — see LOSS
di·rec·tor *n* **1** : the head of an organized group or administrative unit or agency **2** : any of a group of persons usu. elected by shareholders and entrusted with the overall control of a corporation ◇ Directors owe a fiduciary duty to the shareholders in the exercise of their powers. Directors have the power to appoint and dismiss officers, declare and pay dividends on stock, initiate major corporate actions such as mergers or dissolution, and determine other matters affecting the corporation. — **di·rec·tor·ship** *n*
di·rec·tor·ate \də-'rek-tə-rət, dī-\ *n* **1** : a board of directors (as of a corporation) **2** : membership on a board of directors
director of law : CITY ATTORNEY
direct review *n* : judicial review of a case obtained through ordinary appellate procedure rather than through a collateral attack
direct skip *n* : a generation-skipping transfer of an interest in property to a skip person : a transfer that is to a person two or more generations below the person making the transfer or to a trust in which all interest is held by such persons and that is subject to generation-skipping transfer taxes — compare TAXABLE DISTRIBUTION, TAXABLE TERMINATION
direct tax *n* : a tax imposed on a taxpayer himself or herself or on his or her property — compare EXCISE

\ə\abut \ᵊ\kitten \ər\further \a\ash \ā\ace
\ä\cot, cart \au̇\out \ch\chin \e\bet \ē\easy
\g\go \i\hit \ī\ice \j\job \ŋ\sing \ō\go \ȯ\law
\ȯi\boy \th\thin \t̲h̲\the \ü\loot \u̇\foot \y\yet
\zh\vision *see also* Pronunciation Symbols page

dis•abil•i•ty *n, pl* **-ties 1** : inability to pursue an occupation because of a physical or mental impairment; *specif* : inability to engage in any substantial gainful activity because of a medically determinable physical or mental impairment that can be expected to result in death or to be of long continued or indefinite duration in accordance with the Social Security Act — see also BENEFIT, *Americans with Disabilities Act* in the IMPORTANT LAWS section; compare INCAPACITY, OCCUPATIONAL DISEASE **2** : lack of legal qualification to do something ⟨a minor's ~⟩

dis•able *vt* **dis•abled; dis•abl•ing 1** : to deprive of legal right, qualification, or capacity **2** : to make incapable or ineffective; *specif* : to cause to have a disability — **dis•able•ment** *n*

disabled *adj* : having a disability

dis•af•firm \,di-sə-'fərm\ *vt* : CANCEL, RESCIND — used esp. of a contract made by a minor — **dis•af•fir•mance** \,di-sə-'fər-məns\ *n* — **dis•af•fir•ma•tion** \,dis-,a-fər-'mā-shən\ *n*

dis•al•low \,di-sə-'laů\ *vt* **1** : to deny the truth, force, or validity of ⟨*~ed* the deduction⟩ ⟨~ a bankruptcy claim⟩ **2** : to refuse to allow ⟨~ payment of benefits⟩ — **dis•al•low•ance** *n*

dis•bar \dis-'bär\ *vt* : to expel from the bar or the legal profession : deprive (an attorney) of a license to practice law usu. for engaging in unethical or illegal practices — compare DEBAR — **dis•bar•ment** *n*

¹dis•charge \dis-'chärj, 'dis-,chärj\ *vt* **1** : to release from an obligation: as **a** : to relieve of a duty under an instrument (as a contract or a negotiable instrument); *also* : to render (an instrument) no longer enforceable ⟨a formal instrument . . . may be *discharged* by either cancellation or surrender —J. D. Calamari and J. M. Perillo⟩ **b** : to release (a debtor in bankruptcy) from liability for his or her debts **2** : to release from confinement, custody, or care ⟨~ a prisoner⟩ **3 a** : to dismiss from employment : terminate the employment of **b** : to release from service or duty ⟨~ a jury⟩ ⟨~ a witness⟩ **4 a** : to get rid of (as a debt or obligation) by performing an appropriate action **b** : to fulfill a requirement for ⟨evidence which is required to ~ the burden of going forward —W. R. LaFave and A. W. Scott, Jr.⟩ **5** : to order (a legislative committee) to end consideration of a bill in order to bring it before the house for action — **discharge•abil•i•ty** \dis-,chär-jə-'bi-lə-tē\ *n* — **dis•charge•able** \dis-'chär-jə-bəl\ *adj*

²dis•charge \'dis-,chärj\ *n* **1 a** : the act of relieving of something that burdens or oppresses : RELEASE **b** : something that discharges or releases; *esp* : a certification of or a document proving release or payment **2** : the state of being discharged or released ⟨a party seeking a total ~⟩ **3** : release from confinement ⟨ordering a conditional ~ of the alien on habeas corpus —*Harvard Law Review*⟩ **4** : the act of removing an obligation or liability (as by payment of a debt or performance of a duty) **5 a** : a dismissal from employment or office

  constructive discharge : discharge of an employee effected by making the employee's working conditions so intolerable that he or she reasonably feels compelled to resign

  retaliatory discharge : a wrongful discharge that is done in retaliation for an employee's conduct (as reporting an employer's criminal activity) and that clearly violates public policy

  wrongful discharge : discharge of an employee for illegal reasons or for reasons that are contrary to public policy (as in retaliation for the employee's refusal to engage in unlawful activity) **b** : a release from service or duty

discharge hearing — see HEARING

dis•ci•pli•nary rule \'di-sə-plə-,ner-ē-\ *n* : a rule that is set out in the ABA Model Code of Professional Responsibility and whose violation may result in disciplinary action against the violating lawyer — compare ETHICAL CONSIDERATION

dis•claim \dis-'klām\ *vi* : to make a disclaimer ~ *vt* **1** : to reject or relinquish a claim to (as an interest in an estate) **2 a :** to deny or reject the right, validity, or authority of **b :** to negate or limit the rights under (a warranty) — **dis•claim•ant** \-'klā-mənt\ *n*

dis•claim•er \dis-'klā-mər\ *n* [Anglo-French *desclamer*, from *desclamer* to disavow, deny, from Old French *des-*, prefix marking reversal + *clamer* to claim — see CLAIM] **1 :** a refusal or disavowal of something that one has a right to claim; *specif* : a relinquishment or formal refusal to accept an interest or estate — see also QUALIFIED DISCLAIMER **2 :** a denial of responsibility for a thing or act: as **a :** a negation or limitation of the rights under a warranty given by a seller to a buyer **b :** a denial of coverage by an insurance company **3 :** a writing that embodies a disclaimer

dis•close \dis-'klōz\ *vt* : to make known or reveal to another or to the public

dis•clo•sure \dis-'klō-zhər\ *n* : an act or instance of disclosing: as **a :** a lender's revelation of information to a consumer under the Truth in Lending Act that enables the consumer to make an intelligent decision about the loan **b :** the revelation to investors of financial information about a corporation or municipality and about the security it is offering for sale — see also PROSPECTUS, REGISTRATION STATEMENT ◊ Disclosure is required for a public offering. **c :** revelation by a corporate insider (as an officer) for approval of a business transaction that involves self-dealing **d :** a debtor in bankruptcy's revelation to creditors of a bankruptcy plan

dis•con•tin•u•ance \ˌdis-kən-'ti-nyə-wəns\ *n* **1 :** the usu. voluntary termination of an action by a plaintiff by motion or by failure to pursue the claim **2 :** the abandonment of a property or of a particular use of the property under the zoning laws

¹dis•count \'dis-ˌkaunt\ *n* : a reduction made from the gross amount or value of something: as **a :** a reduction made from a regular or list price or a proportionate deduction from a debt account usu. made for prompt payment or for payment in cash **b :** a reduction made for interest in advancing money upon or purchasing a note not yet due **c :** a reduction in the price of a bond — see also *discount bond* at BOND 2 **d :** the sale of securities that are issued below and redeemed at face value — compare PREMIUM 1

²dis•count \'dis-ˌkaunt, dis-'kaunt\ *vt* **1 a :** to make a deduction from usu. for cash or prompt payment **b :** to sell or offer at a lowered price **2 :** to lend money on after deducting a discount ⟨banks ~ negotiable instruments⟩ **3 :** to take into account (a future event or prospect) in making present calculations ~ *vi* : to give or make discounts

³dis•count \'dis-ˌkaunt\ *adj* **1 a :** selling goods or services at a discount ⟨a ~ broker⟩ **b :** offered or sold at a discount ⟨~ securities⟩ **2 :** reflecting a discount ⟨the ~ price⟩

dis•count•able \dis-'kaun-tə-bəl\ *adj* **1 :** set apart for discounting ⟨within the ~ period⟩ **2 :** subject to being discounted ⟨a ~ note⟩

discount bond — see BOND 2

discount rate *n* **1 :** the interest on an annual basis deducted in advance on a loan **2 :** the interest levied by the Federal Reserve for advances and rediscounts

discount share *n* : a share of corporate stock issued at less than par value

dis•cov•er *vt* **1 :** to find out about, recognize, or realize for the first time ⟨when the victim ~s the fraud⟩ — see also DISCOVERY RULE **2 a :** to make the subject of discovery **b :** to learn of or obtain (information) through discovery — **dis•cov•er•able** *adj*

dis•cov•ered peril *n* : LAST CLEAR CHANCE

dis•cov•ery *n, pl* **-er•ies 1 :** the act or process of discovering **2 :** something discovered ⟨applied for a patent for the

\ə\abut \ə\kitten \ər\further \a\ash \ā\ace \ä\cot, cart \au\out \ch\chin \e\bet \ē\easy \g\go \i\hit \ī\ice \j\job \ŋ\sing \ō\go \o\law \oi\boy \th\thin \t͟h\the \ü\loot \u̇\foot \y\yet \zh\vision *see also* Pronunciation Symbols page

~⟩ **3 a :** the methods used by parties to a civil or criminal action to obtain information held by the other party that is relevant to the action — see also DEPOSITION, INTERROGATORY, REQUEST FOR PRODUCTION **b :** the disclosure of information held by the opposing party in an action ⟨a party may obtain ~ of the existence and contents of any insurance agreement — *Federal Rules of Civil Procedure* Rule 26(b)(2)⟩ — see also PRIVILEGE, WORK PRODUCT DOCTRINE ◊ Discovery allowed under Federal Rule of Civil Procedure 26 is far-reaching. With some exceptions, a party may obtain discovery of any relevant information as long as it is not privileged, including information that itself would not be admissible at trial but that is likely to lead to the discovery of admissible evidence. Criminal discovery, however, has been more controversial. Under Federal Rule of Criminal Procedure 16, a defendant may obtain discovery of his or her own written or recorded statements or confessions, results of examinations and tests, his or her recorded testimony before a grand jury, and testimony to be given by the prosecution's expert witnesses. A defendant may also inspect the prosecution's books, documents, photographs, objects, and other items of evidence. Under Federal Rule of Criminal Procedure 12.1, the prosecution must also disclose the names of witnesses that will be called to rebut the defendant's alibi defense. The defendant must also permit the prosecution to inspect books, documents, photographs, and objects and must disclose reports of examinations or tests and testimony of expert witnesses.

discovery immunity — see IMMUNITY

discovery policy *n* : CLAIMS MADE POLICY

discovery rule *n* : a rule in tort law: the statute of limitations for a cause of action does not begin to run until the time that the injured party discovers or reasonably should have discovered the injury

dis·cre·tion \dis-'kre-shən\ *n* : power of free decision or latitude of choice within certain bounds imposed by law ⟨reached the age of ~⟩ ⟨struck down death penalty provisions administered through unbridled jury ~ —L. H. Tribe⟩: as **a :** the power of a judge to use his or her own judgment in making decisions guided by what is fair and equitable and by principles of law — see also ABUSE OF DISCRETION **b :** the power of a public official or employee to act and make decisions based on his or her own judgment or conscience within the bounds of reason and the law

dis·cre·tion·ary \dis-'kre-shə-,ner-ē\ *adj* : left to discretion : exercised at one's own discretion; *specif* : relating to the policy-making function of a public official — see also *Federal Tort Claims Act* in the IMPORTANT LAWS section; compare MINISTERIAL ◊ A public official generally has qualified immunity from lawsuits that arise from his or her discretionary acts.

discretionary immunity — see IMMUNITY

discretionary trust — see TRUST

dis·crim·i·nate \dis-'kri-mə-,nāt\ *vi* **-nat·ed; -nat·ing :** to make a difference in treatment or favor on a basis other than individual merit; *esp* : to make a difference in treatment on a basis prohibited by law (as national origin, race, sex, religion, age, or disability) — see also BONA FIDE OCCUPATIONAL QUALIFICATION, EQUAL PROTECTION, REVERSE DISCRIMINATION, SUSPECT CLASS, *Civil Rights Act of 1964* in the IMPORTANT LAWS section, *Amendment XIV* to the CONSTITUTION in the back matter — **dis·crim·i·na·tion** \dis-,kri-mə-'nā-shən\ *n*

dis·crim·i·na·to·ry \dis-'kri-mə-nə-,tōr-ē\ *adj* **1 :** applying discrimination in treatment **2 :** having unlawful discrimination as an effect

dis·en·fran·chise \,dis-ᵊn-'fran-,chīz\ *vt* **-chised; -chis·ing :** DISFRANCHISE — **dis·en·fran·chise·ment** *n*

dis·en·tit·le \dis-ᵊn-'tīt-ᵊl\ *vt* : to deprive of title, claim, or right

dis•fran•chise \dis-'fran-,chīz\ *vt* **-chised; -chis•ing** : to deprive of a franchise, of a legal right, or of some privilege or immunity; *esp* : to deprive of the right to vote

dis•gorge \dis-'gorj\ *vt* **dis•gorged; disgorg•ing** : to give up (as illegally gained profits) on request, under pressure, or by court order esp. to prevent unjust enrichment ⟨ordered a . . . salesman to ~ about $468,000 he had earned by defrauding Iowa banks —*National Law Journal*⟩ — **dis•gorge•ment** *n*

disguised donation — see DONATION

dis•her•i•son \dis-'her-ə-zən\ *n* [Anglo= French *dishereison, desheriteson,* from Old French *deseriteison,* from *desheriter* to disinherit, from *des-,* prefix marking reversal + *heriter* to inherit, from Late Latin *hereditare*] : the act of disinheriting

¹dis•hon•or *n* : refusal on the part of the issuer (as a bank) to pay or accept commercial paper (as a check) when it is presented — see also WRONGFUL DISHONOR

²dishonor *vt* : to refuse to pay or accept ⟨a bank ~*ing* the checks for insufficient funds⟩

dis•in•her•i•son \,dis-in-'her-ə-zən\ *n* [alteration (influenced by *inherit*) of *disherison*] *in the civil law of Louisiana* : DISHERISON — see also *forced heir* at HEIR ◊ The Louisiana Civil Code sets out the situations in which disinherison is allowed.

dis•in•her•it \,dis-ᵊn-'her-ət\ *vt* : to prevent deliberately from inheriting something (as by making a will) — see also ELECTIVE SHARE — **dis•in•her•i•tance** \-'her-ə-təns\ *n*

dis•in•ter•est•ed \dis-'in-tə-rəs-təd, -'in-trəs-, -'in-tə-,res-\ *adj* : free of any interest esp. of a pecuniary nature : IMPARTIAL ⟨a ~ person to witness the will⟩

dis•in•ter•me•di•a•tion \dis-,in-tər-,mē-dē-'ā-shən\ *n* [from the investor's bypassing of the intermediate institution] : the diversion of savings from accounts with low fixed interest rates to direct investment in high-yielding instruments

dis•in•vest \,dis-ᵊn-'vest\ *vi* **1** : to reduce

or eliminate capital investment (as in an industry or area) **2** : to give up an investment ⟨insiders force the noncontrolling shareholders to . . . ~ —R. C. Clark⟩ ~ *vt* : to cause to give up an investment ⟨no one is being . . . ~*ed* or cashed out — R. C. Clark⟩

dis•junc•tive allegation \dis-'jəŋk-tiv-\ *n* : an allegation that is unclear in meaning because it includes the word *or* in charging the defendant with two or more wrongful acts ◊ Disjunctive allegations are inadmissible.

dis•miss *vt* **1** : to remove from position or service ⟨~*ed* the employee⟩ **2** : to bring about or order the dismissal of (an action) ⟨the suit was ~*ed*⟩ ~ *vi* : to bring about or order a dismissal ⟨the plaintiff moved to ~⟩

dis•mis•sal *n* **1** : removal from a position or service **2 a** : the termination of an action or claim usu. before the presentation of evidence by the defendant

involuntary dismissal **1** : the dismissal of an action by the court because of the plaintiff's failure to pursue his or her case **2** : the dismissal of an action by the court upon motion of the defendant after presentation of plaintiff's case made on the grounds that the plaintiff has shown no right to relief ◊ An involuntary dismissal under Federal Rule of Civil Procedure 41(b) prevents the plaintiff from bringing suit again based on the same claim.

voluntary dismissal : the dismissal of an action by the plaintiff ◊ Under Federal Rule of Civil Procedure 41(a), a plaintiff may dismiss an action without a court order anytime before the defendant serves an answer or moves for summary judgment, or by stipulation of the parties. Otherwise, a court order is required. A court-ordered dismissal will not prevent the plaintiff from bring-

\ə\abut \ᵊ\kitten \ər\further \a\ash \ā\ace
\ä\cot, cart \au̇\out \ch\chin \e\bet \ē\easy
\g\go \i\hit \ī\ice \j\job \ŋ\sing \ō\go \ȯ\law
\ȯi\boy \th\thin \t͟h\the \ü\loot \u̇\foot \y\yet
\zh\vision *see also* Pronunciation Symbols page

ing the action again unless the order so states. A dismissal without a court order will not bar the plaintiff from bringing the action again unless the plaintiff has brought the same action already.
b : the cancellation of an indictment, information, complaint, or charge ◊ Under Federal Rule of Criminal Procedure 48, the attorney for the government may dismiss the indictment, information, or complaint with the court's approval. The court may also dismiss it if there is unnecessary delay in the government's prosecution of the case. **c :** a document setting forth the request for a dismissal ⟨plaintiff filed a ~⟩

dis·or·der·ly con·duct *n* : conduct that is likely to lead to a disturbance of the public peace or that offends public decency; *also* : the petty offense of engaging in disorderly conduct — compare BREACH OF THE PEACE ◊ The term *disorderly conduct* is used in statutes to identify various acts against the public peace. It has been held to include the use of obscene language in public, the blocking of public ways, and the making of threats. A statute must identify acts that constitute disorderly conduct with sufficient clarity in order to avoid being held unconstitutional because of vagueness.

dis·par·age·ment \di-'spar-ij-mənt\ *n* **1** : the publication of false and injurious statements that are derogatory of another's property, business, or product — called also *business disparagement, commercial disparagement, disparagement of property, slander of goods, trade libel* **2** : SLANDER OF TITLE

disparagement of property 1 : DISPARAGEMENT 1 **2 :** SLANDER OF TITLE

disparagement of title : SLANDER OF TITLE

dis·par·ate impact \'dis-pə-rət-, dis-'par-ət-\ *n* : an unnecessary discriminatory effect on a protected class caused by a practice or policy that appears to be nondiscriminatory — compare BONA FIDE OCCUPATIONAL QUALIFICATION, DISPARATE TREATMENT

disparate treatment *n* : treatment of an individual (as an employee or prospective juror) that is less favorable than treatment of others for discriminatory reasons (as race, religion, national origin, sex, or disability) — compare BONA FIDE OCCUPATIONAL QUALIFICATION, DISPARATE IMPACT

dis·pos·able income *n* : income available for disposal: as **a :** the income remaining to an individual after deduction of taxes **b :** the income of a debtor in bankruptcy that is not necessary to support the debtor or the debtor's dependents

disposable portion *n, in the civil law of Louisiana* : the portion of a testate succession that may be donated to legatees other than the forced heir — compare MARITAL PORTION

dis·pose of *vt* **dis·posed of; dis·pos·ing of** **1 :** to transfer to the control or ownership of another ⟨*disposed of* the property by will⟩ **2 :** to deal with conclusively : determine finally ⟨received petitions for injunctions . . . The common theme in *disposing of* these —W. J. Brennan, Jr.⟩

dis·po·si·tion *n* **1 a :** the final determination of a matter (as a case or motion) by a court or quasi-judicial tribunal ⟨the beneficiary of such a ~ of charges against him —*United States v. Smith*, 354 A.2d 510 (1976)⟩ — compare DECISION, HOLDING, JUDGMENT, OPINION, RULING, VERDICT **b :** the sentence given to a convicted criminal defendant ⟨probation is often a desirable ~ —W. R. LaFave and J. H. Israel⟩; *also* : the sentence given to or treatment prescribed for a juvenile offender **2 :** transfer to the care, possession, or ownership of another ⟨to either a surviving spouse or a charity, those ~s are totally exonerated from the payment of taxes —*Matter of McKinney*, 477 N.Y.S.2d 367 (1984)⟩; *also* : the power of such transferral **3 :** the state or condition of being predisposed : PREDISPOSITION

dis·pos·i·tive \dis-'pä-zə-tiv\ *adj* **1 :** directed toward or effecting a disposition (as of a case) ⟨an endless variety of ~ . . .

pretrial motions —Robert Shaw⁼ Meadow⟩ **2 :** relating to a disposition of property ⟨~ words in a will⟩ **3 :** providing a final resolution (as of an issue) **:** having control over an outcome ⟨~ of the question⟩

dis•pos•sess \ˌdis-pə-'zes\ *vt* **:** to put out of possession or occupancy — compare EVICT — **dis•pos•ses•sion** \-'ze-shən\ *n* — **dis•pos•ses•sor** \-'ze-sər\ *n*

dispossessory warrant — see WARRANT

¹dis•pute \di-'spyüt\ *vb* **dis•put•ed; dis•put•ing** *vi* **:** to engage in a dispute ⟨*disputing* with management over contract terms⟩ ~ *vt* **:** to engage in a dispute over ⟨*disputing* the correct application of the contract provision⟩; *esp* **:** to oppose by argument or assertion ⟨*disputed* changes to the grievance procedure⟩ — **dis•put•able** \di-'spyü-tə-bəl, 'dis-pyə-tə-bəl\ *adj*

²dispute *n* **:** an assertion of opposing views or claims **:** a disagreement as to rights; *esp* **:** one that is the subject of proceedings for resolution (as arbitration)

dis•qual•i•fi•ca•tion \dis-ˌkwä-lə-fə-'kā-shən\ *n* **1 :** something that disqualifies or incapacitates **2 :** the act of disqualifying **:** state of being disqualified ⟨~ of a juror for bias⟩

dis•qual•i•fy \dis-'kwä-lə-ˌfī\ *vt* **-fied; -fy•ing 1 :** to deprive of the required qualities, properties, or conditions ⟨a financial interest in the case that *disqualified* the judge⟩ **2 :** to deprive of a right or privilege esp. after a hearing ⟨misconduct that *disqualified* the employee from receiving unemployment benefits⟩

dis•seise *or* **dis•seize** \dis-'sēz\ *vt* **disseised** *or* **dis•seized; dis•seis•ing** *or* **dis•seiz•ing** [Anglo-French *disseisir* to dispossess, from Old French *dessaisir*, from *des-*, prefix marking reversal + *saisir* to put in possession of] **:** to deprive of seisin wrongfully **:** unjustly dispossess —

dis•sei•sor \-'sē-zər\ *n*

dis•sei•see \dis-ˌsē-'zē\ *n* **:** one who is disseised

dis•sei•sin *or* **dis•sei•zin** \di-'sēz-ᵊn\ *n* [Anglo-French *disseisine*, from Old French *dessaisine*, from *dessaisir* to dis-

possess — see DISSEISE] **:** the act of disseising **:** the state of being disseised

disseize *var of* DISSEISE

disseizin *var of* DISSEISIN

¹dis•sent \di-'sent\ *vi* **1 :** to withhold assent or approval ⟨unfair squeezeout transactions—the kind to which public shareholders seem most likely to ~ —R. C. Clark⟩ — see also APPRAISAL ◊ A shareholder who dissents from a proposed transaction may demand that the corporation buy his or her shares after an appraisal. **2 :** to differ in opinion; *esp* **:** to disagree with a majority opinion ⟨three of the justices ~*ed*⟩ — compare CONCUR — **dis•sent•er** *n*

²dissent *n* **1 :** difference of opinion; *esp* **:** a judge's disagreement with the decision of the majority **2 :** DISSENTING OPINION at OPINION **3 :** the judge or group of judges that dissent — compare MAJORITY

dissenting opinion — see OPINION

dis•si•pate \'di-sə-ˌpāt\ *vt* **-pat•ed; -pat•ing :** to use (marital assets) for one's own benefit and to the exclusion of one's spouse for a purpose unrelated to the marriage at a time when the marriage is undergoing an irretrievable breakdown — **dis•si•pa•tion** \ˌdi-sə-'pā-shən\ *n*

dis•so•lu•tion \ˌdi-sə-'lü-shən\ *n* **:** the act or process of ending: as **a :** the termination of an organized body (as a court) **b :** the ending of a partnership relationship caused by the withdrawal of one of the partners from the relationship **c :** the termination of a corporation

involuntary dissolution : dissolution of a corporation by a court in response to a shareholder petition based on statutorily prescribed grounds

voluntary dissolution : dissolution of a corporation upon the initiative of the directors and with approval of a certain percentage of the shareholders

d : the termination of an injunction or stay

\ə\abut \ᵊ\kitten \ər\further \a\ash \ā\ace
\ä\cot, cart \au̇\out \ch\chin \e\bet \ē\easy
\g\go \i\hit \ī\ice \j\job \ŋ\sing \ō\go \ȯ\law
\ȯi\boy \th\thin \t͟h\the \ü\loot \u̇\foot \y\yet
\zh\vision *see also* Pronunciation Symbols page

by court order e : the termination of a marriage by divorce

dis•solve *vt* **dis•solved; dis•solv•ing :** to bring about the dissolution of — **dissolv•able** *adj*

Dist. Ct. *abbr* District Court

dis•tin•guish *vt* **:** to identify or explain differences in or from ⟨~*ed* the cases on factual grounds⟩

dis•train \di-'strān\ *vb* [Anglo-French *destreindre*, literally, to constrict, force, from Old French, from Late Latin *distringere* to hinder, punish, from Latin, to pull in different directions, distract, from *dis-* apart + *stringere* to draw tight] *vt* **1 :** to force or compel to satisfy an obligation by means of a distress **2 :** to seize by distress — compare ENTER ~ *vi* **:** to levy a distress — **dis•train•able** *adj* — **dis•train•er** \-'strā-nər\ *or* **dis•train•or** \di-'strā-nər, ˌdis-trā-'nōr\ *n*

dis•traint \di-'strānt\ *n* **:** the act or action of distraining

dis•tress *n* [Anglo-French *destrece*, literally, tightness, anguish, deprivation, from Old French, ultimately from Late Latin *districtus* severe, from past participle of *distringere* to hinder, punish — see DISTRAIN] **1 :** seizure and detention of the goods of another as pledge or to obtain satisfaction of a claim by the sale of the goods seized; *specif* **:** seizure by a landlord of a tenant's property to obtain satisfaction of arrearages in rent ◊ Distress is regulated by statute where available. It has been held unconstitutional by some courts. **2 :** pain or suffering affecting the body, a bodily part, or the mind — see also EMOTIONAL DISTRESS

distress warrant — see WARRANT

dis•trib•ute \di-'stri-byüt\ *vt* **-ut•ed; -uting 1 :** to divide among several or many **:** APPORTION **2 :** to give out or deliver esp. to members of a group — see also DIVIDEND

dis•trib•u•tee \di-ˌstri-byü-'tē\ *n* **:** one to whom something is or will be distributed; *esp* **:** one sharing in or entitled to share in an estate

dis•tri•bu•tion \ˌdis-trə-'byü-shən\ *n* **1**

: the act or process of distributing: as **a :** the apportionment by a court of the property and esp. personal property of an intestate among those entitled to it according to statute — compare DESCENT, DEVISE ◊ The laws dealing with intestate succession are often called laws of descent and distribution. **b :** the payment or transfer to a beneficiary of interest to which he or she is entitled under a trust **c :** the transfer by a corporation or mutual fund of money or property to a shareholder in his or her capacity as a shareholder **d :** the initial offering to the public of a security by a corporation **e :** the delivery of a controlled substance **2 :** something distributed — **dis•tri•bu•tive** \di-'stri-byü-tiv\ *adj*

dis•trict *n* **:** a territorial division (as of a nation, state, county, or city) for administrative, judicial, electoral, or other purposes: as **a :** an administrative unit esp. of a town or city established for the performance of a special governmental function ⟨the water ~⟩ ⟨park ~⟩ **b :** CONGRESSIONAL DISTRICT **c :** one of the divisions of the United States or of the individual states served by a particular federal or state court — see also the JUDICIAL SYSTEM in the back matter

district attorney *n* **:** the prosecuting officer of a judicial district — see also STATE'S ATTORNEY

district court *n, often cap D&C* **:** a trial court having general or limited jurisdiction in a judicial district: as **a :** one of the federal trial courts sitting in a federal district **b :** a trial court within a state court system — see also the JUDICIAL SYSTEM in the back matter

District Court of Appeal : any of the appellate courts in Florida

district judge *n* **:** the judge of a district court

District Justice Court *n* **:** a court in Pennsylvania having limited jurisdiction over minor civil and criminal cases

dis•turb *vt* **1 :** to destroy the tranquillity or composure of **2 :** to throw into disorder

~ *vi* : to cause disturbance — **disturb the peace** : to cause a disturbance
dis·tur·bance *n* : an interruption of peace or order; *specif* : an interruption of the quiet enjoyment of one's property
di·verse *adj* : differing from one another; *specif* : differing in citizenship from another party to an action ⟨a ~ defendant⟩ — see also *diversity jurisdiction* at JURISDICTION; compare NONDIVERSE
di·ver·sion \də-'vər-zhən, dī-\ *n* : the act or an instance of diverting: as **a** : an unauthorized rerouting or appropriation ⟨~ of funds⟩ **b** : suspension of the prosecution of a charge for a period of time during which the defendant participates in a rehabilitation program or makes restitution and after which the charges are dismissed if the rehabilitation or restitution is completed — compare PROBATION — **di·ver·sion·ary** \-'vər-zhə-ˌner-ē, -shə-\ *adj*
di·ver·si·ty \də-'vər-sə-tē, dī-\ *n* : DIVERSITY OF CITIZENSHIP
diversity jurisdiction — see JURISDICTION
diversity of citizenship : a condition in which the parties to an action are of diverse state or national citizenship — see also COMPLETE DIVERSITY, *diversity jurisdiction* at JURISDICTION, MINIMAL DIVERSITY, *Article III* of the CONSTITUTION in the back matter
di·vert \də-'vərt, dī-\ *vt* **1** : to turn from one course or use to another ⟨funds illegally ~ed⟩ **2** : to place (a defendant) under a diversion — **di·vert·er** *n*
di·vest \dī-'vest, də-\ *vt* [Anglo-French *devestir*, literally, to undress, from Old French *desvestir*, from *de(s)*-, prefix marking reversal + *vestir* to dress, from Latin *vestire*] : to deprive or dispossess (oneself) of property through divestiture — **di·vest·ment** *n*
di·ves·ti·ture \dī-'ves-ti-ˌchùr, də-, -chər\ *n* **1** : the sale or transfer of title to a property (as an operating division) under court order (as in bankruptcy) **2** : the sale of an asset (as a business division) that is unprofitable, does not enhance a corpo-

rate restructuring, or is felt to be morally reprehensible
di·vid·ed *adj* **1 a** : separated into parts, classes, or portions ⟨~ coverage⟩ ⟨~ custody⟩ **b** *in the civil law of Louisiana* : separately owned, possessed, or held : no longer held in indivision ⟨owner of a ~ part or of the entire estate following partition —*Louisiana Civil Code*⟩ ⟨granted in ~ portions⟩ **2** : not united : failing to agree ⟨a ~ Court⟩
div·i·dend \'di-və-ˌdend\ *n* **1** : the part of corporate net earnings distributed usu. periodically (as quarterly) to stockholders in the form of cash, additional shares, or property either as a set amount per share or a percentage of par value
constructive dividend : a benefit (as unreasonable compensation or use of corporate property) or transfer of funds from a corporation to a shareholder that is interpreted by a taxing authority as a dividend
cumulative dividend : a dividend distributed to preferred stockholders that is added to and paid with the next payment or future payments if not paid when due
extraordinary dividend : a dividend declared in addition to a regular dividend because of unanticipated profits or a nonrecurring increase of revenue
2 : a share of the surplus earnings of a mutual insurance company paid to policyholders either in the form of cash disbursements or through reduction of premiums **3** : a payment disbursed to investors from the income of a mutual fund
dividend option — see OPTION 4
di·vis·i·ble \də-'vi-zə-bəl\ *adj* : capable of being divided esp. into independent parts (as promises or interests) ⟨a ~ contract⟩ — compare ENTIRE — **di·vis·i·bil·i·ty** \də-ˌvi-zə-'bi-lə-tē\ *n*
¹di·vorce *n* [Middle French, from Latin *divortium*, from *divortere, divertere* to

\ə\abut \ᵊ\kitten \ər\further \a\ash \ā\ace
\ä\cot, cart \au̇\out \ch\chin \e\bet \ē\easy
\g\go \i\hit \ī\ice \j\job \ŋ\sing \ō\go \ȯ\law
\ȯi\boy \th\thin \th̲\the \ü\loot \u̇\foot \y\yet
\zh\vision *see also* Pronunciation Symbols page

leave one's marriage partner, from *di-* away, apart + *vertere* to turn] : the dissolution of a valid marriage granted esp. on specified statutory grounds (as adultery) arising after the marriage — compare ANNULMENT ◊ The most common grounds for divorce are absence from the marital home, drug or alcohol addiction, adultery, cruelty, conviction of a crime, desertion, insanity, and nonsupport.

absolute divorce : a divorce that completely and permanently dissolves the marital relationship and terminates marital rights (as property rights) and obligations (as fidelity)

divorce a men·sa et tho·ro \-,ā-'men-sə-,et-'thȯr-ō, -,ä-'men-sä-,et-'thō-rō\ : a separation governed by a court order : LEGAL SEPARATION

divorce a vin·cu·lo mat·ri·mo·nii \-,ā-'viŋ-kyù-,lō-,ma-trə-'mō-nē-,ī, -,ä-'viŋ-kü-,lō-,mä-trē-'mō-nē-,ē\ : ABSOLUTE DIVORCE in this entry

limited divorce : an intentional cessation of cohabitation between spouses : SEPARATION

no–fault divorce : an absolute divorce that is not based on either spouse's fault and that is granted usu. on the grounds of an irretrievable breakdown or when husband and wife have lived apart for a statutorily specified period of time

²divorce *vb* **di·vorced; di·vorc·ing** *vt* **1** : to dissolve the marriage of (a husband and wife) by judgment or decree of divorce **2** : to sever the marital relationship with (a spouse) by a judgment or decree of divorce ~ *vi* : to obtain a divorce

divorce a mensa et thoro — see DIVORCE

divorce a vinculo matrimonii — see DIVORCE

DNA fingerprinting \,dē-,en-'ā-\ *n* : a method of identification esp. for evidentiary purposes by analyzing and comparing the DNA from tissue samples

DNR *abbr* do not resuscitate

do *vb* **did; done; do·ing; does** *vt* **1** : PERFORM, EXECUTE **2** : COMMIT ⟨*did* this act of cruelty⟩ *verbal auxiliary* — used with

the infinitive without *to* to form present and past tenses in legal and parliamentary language ⟨~ hereby bequeath⟩ — **do business** : to be engaged in business activities (as soliciting sales); *specif* : to engage in activities sufficient to subject a foreign company to the personal jurisdiction of a state ⟨was sufficient to constitute *doing business* in the state —*International Shoe Co. v. Washington*, 326 U.S. 310 (1945)⟩ — see also DOING BUSINESS STATUTE

DOA *abbr* dead on arrival

dock *n* [Dutch dialect *docke, dok* pen, cage] : the place in a criminal court where a prisoner stands or sits during trial — compare BAR, BENCH, JURY BOX, SIDE-BAR, STAND

¹dock·et \'dä-kət\ *n* [earlier *doggette, docquet* summary, abstract, of unknown origin] **1 a** : a formal abridged record of the proceedings (as motions, orders, and judgments) in a legal action ⟨the clerk shall keep a ~ in each case —*U.S. Code*⟩ **b** : a register of such records **2 a** : a list of legal actions to be heard by a court ⟨the nearly 500 such cases on court ~*s* — Rorie Sherman⟩ — compare CALENDAR **b** : the caseload of a court ⟨a great part of our ~ consisted of regulatory agency cases —R. H. Bork⟩

²docket *vt* : to enter in a docket (as of a case or a court) ⟨closure motions must be ~*ed* sufficiently in advance —W. R. LaFave and J. H. Israel⟩ — compare CALENDAR

docket num·ber *n* : the number assigned to a particular case on a court's docket

doc·tor of juridical sci·ence *often cap D&J&S* : DOCTOR OF THE SCIENCE OF LAW

doctor of jurisprudence *often cap D&J* **1** : JURIS DOCTOR **2** : DOCTOR OF THE SCIENCE OF LAW

doctor of law *often cap D&L* : JURIS DOCTOR

doctor of laws *often cap D&L* : an honorary law degree — compare DOCTOR OF THE SCIENCE OF LAW, JURIS DOCTOR, MASTER OF LAWS

doctor of the sci·ence of law *often cap*

D&S&L : a degree conferred for advanced study, research, and completion and approval of a dissertation in law — compare DOCTOR OF LAWS, JURIS DOCTOR, MASTER OF LAWS

doc·trine \'däk-trən\ *n* : a principle established through judicial decisions — compare LAW, PRECEDENT — **doc·tri·nal** \-trə-nəl\ *adj*

¹**doc·u·ment** \'dä-kyə-mənt\ *n* **1** : a writing (as a deed or lease) conveying information — see also INSTRUMENT **2 a** : something (as a writing, photograph, or recording) that may be used as evidence **b** : an official paper (as a license) relied on as the basis, proof, or support of something (as a right or privilege)

²**doc·u·ment** \'dä-kyə-,ment\ *vt* **1 a** : to furnish documentary evidence of **b** : to provide with exact references to authoritative supporting information **2** : to furnish (as a ship) with documents (as ship's papers)

doc·u·men·ta·ry \,dä-kyə-'men-tə-rē\ *adj* : being, consisting of, or contained in documents ⟨~ evidence⟩

documentary draft — see DRAFT

document of title : a document (as a warehouse receipt) which is issued by or addressed to a bailee and which in the ordinary course of business is considered to show that the person in possession of it is entitled to receive, hold, and dispose of the bailed goods covered by it

DOD *abbr* Department of Defense — see also the IMPORTANT AGENCIES section

DOE *abbr* Department of Energy — see also the IMPORTANT AGENCIES section

D'Oench doctrine \'dench-\ *n* [from *D'Oench, Duhme & Co., Inc. v. Federal Deposit Insurance Company*, 315 U.S. 447 (1942), the Supreme Court case establishing the doctrine] : a doctrine in banking law: a party (as a borrower or guarantor) cannot assert an unrecorded agreement with a failed bank against attempts by the federal insurer (as the Federal Deposit Insurance Corporation) or its assigns to collect on a promissory note (as a loan) — called also *D'Oench Duhme doctrine*

DOI *abbr* Department of the Interior — see also the IMPORTANT AGENCIES section

doing business statute *n* : a state long-arm statute that creates personal jurisdiction over companies establishing minimum contacts by doing business in that state

dol \'dōl, 'dȯl\ *n, in the civil law of Louisiana* : fraud committed to induce another to make a contract — compare FRAUDE

DOL *abbr* Department of Labor — see also the IMPORTANT AGENCIES section

do·mes·tic \də-'mes-tik\ *adj* **1** : of or relating to the household or family ⟨a ~ servant⟩ ⟨~ relations⟩ — see also FAMILY COURT **2** : of, relating to, or originating within a country or state and esp. one's own country or state ⟨the state has personal jurisdiction over ~ corporations⟩ — compare FOREIGN, MUNICIPAL

domestic vi·o·lence *n* : violence committed by one family or household member against another — see also *restraining order* at ORDER

¹**do·mi·cile** \'dä-mə-,sīl, 'dō-\ *n* [Latin *domicilium* dwelling place, home] **1** : the place where an individual has a fixed and permanent home for legal purposes — called also *legal residence* **2** : the place where an organization (as a corporation) is chartered or that is the organization's principal place of business — compare CITIZENSHIP, RESIDENCE ◊ The domicile of an individual or organization determines the proper jurisdiction and venue for legal process. The courts of a person's domicile have personal jurisdiction. For persons lacking capacity (as minors), domicile is often statutorily determined as the domicile of the guardian.

²**domicile** *vt* **-ciled; -cil·ing** : to establish in or provide with a domicile ⟨an alien

\ə\abut \ə\kitten \ər\further \a\ash \ā\ace
\ä\cot, cart \au̇\out \ch\chin \e\bet \ē\easy
\g\go \i\hit \ī\ice \j\job \ŋ\sing \ō\go \ȯ\law
\ȯi\boy \th\thin \t̲h̲\the \ü\loot \u̇\foot \y\yet
\zh\vision *see also* Pronunciation Symbols page

admitted to the United States for permanent residence shall be deemed a citizen of the State in which such alien is *domiciled* — *U.S. Code*⟩ ⟨any state in which a corporation is *domiciled* —L. H. Tribe⟩

¹dom·i·cil·i·ary \ˌdä-mə-'si-lē-ˌer-ē, ˌdō-\ *adj* : of, relating to, or constituting a domicile ⟨~ jurisdiction⟩

²domiciliary *n, pl* **-ar·ies** : a person who is domiciled in a particular jurisdiction (as a country) ⟨a French ~⟩ — compare RESIDENT

dominant estate — see ESTATE 4

do·min·ion \də-'min-yən\ *n* **1 a** : supreme authority : SOVEREIGNTY **b** : a territory over which such authority is exercised **c** *often cap* : a self-governing nation (as Canada) of the Commonwealth other than the United Kingdom that acknowledges the British monarch as the head of state **2** : the power (as authority) or right (as ownership) to use or dispose of property; *specif* : absolute or exclusive use, control, ownership, or possession of property ⟨the transferred property is placed beyond the donor's ~ and control —W. M. McGovern, Jr. *et al.*⟩ ⟨the bailee exercised ~ over the vehicle⟩

do·nate *vb* **do·nat·ed; do·nat·ing** *vt* : to transfer by a gift or donation ⁓ *vi* : to make a donation — compare GIVE, SELL

do·na·tio inter vivos \dō-'nä-shē-ō-, dō-'nä-tē-ō-\ *n* [Latin, literally, gift between living people] : DONATION INTER VIVOS at DONATION

donatio mortis causa *n* [Latin, literally, gift in contemplation of death] : DONATION MORTIS CAUSA at DONATION

do·na·tion *n* **1** : the making of an esp. charitable gift **2** *in the civil law of Louisiana* : a voluntary transfer of ownership of property from one person to another — compare SALE

  dis·guised donation : a transfer of property (as a sale) that does not have a sufficient reciprocal consideration (as a proportional price) so that it is considered a gratuitous donation and must meet the statutory requirements for a donation (as a notarial act) to be valid —

called also *donation in disguise;* compare SIMULATION

  donation in·ter vi·vos \-ˌin-tər-'vī-ˌvōs, -ˌin-ter-'vē-ˌvōs\ : a donation that transfers property owned by the donor and that takes effect upon the donee's acceptance — compare *gift inter vivos* at GIFT

  donation mor·tis cau·sa \-'mȯr-tis-'kȯ-zə, -'mȯr-tēs-'kau̇-sä\ : a donation that is to take effect on the donor's death and that is revocable — compare *gift causa mortis* at GIFT

3 : something that is transferred by a donation

donation in disguise : DISGUISED DONATION at DONATION

donation inter vivos — see DONATION

donation mortis causa — see DONATION

do·na·tive \'dō-nə-tiv\ *adj* **1** : having the character of a donation ⟨a ~ transfer⟩ **2** : of or relating to donation ⟨~ intent⟩ ⟨~ capacity⟩

do·nee \ˌdō-'nē\ *n* : one that receives or is granted something (as a gift or power)

donee beneficiary — see BENEFICIARY d

do·nor \'dō-nər, -ˌnȯr\ *n* : one that gives, donates, grants, or confers something; *specif* : SETTLOR

dormant partner — see PARTNER

DOT *abbr* Department of Transportation — see also the IMPORTANT AGENCIES section

do·tal \'dōt-ᵊl\ *adj* [Latin *dotalis*, from *dot-, dos* dowry] : of, relating to, or being separate property brought to a marriage by the wife

dou·ble dip·per *n* : an individual who engages in double dipping

double dip·ping *n* : the usu. illicit practice of accepting income from two mutually exclusive sources (as from a government pension and a government salary or from two insurers for the same loss)

double indemnity *n* : a provision in a life insurance or accident policy whereby the company agrees to pay twice the face of the contract in case of accidental death

double jeopardy *n* : the prosecution of a person for an offense for which he or she has already been prosecuted — see also JEOPARDY, *Amendment V* to the CONSTITUTION in the back matter; compare MERGER 3 ◊ The Fifth Amendment to the Constitution states that no person shall "be subject for the same offense to be twice put in jeopardy of life or limb." The double jeopardy clause bars second prosecutions after either acquittal or conviction, and prohibits multiple punishments for the same offense.

double taxation *n* : taxation by the same authority of the same property for the same period and the same purpose

dow·er \'daù-ər\ *n* [Anglo-French, from Old French *douaire*, modification of Medieval Latin *dotarium*, from Latin *dot-*, *dos* gift, dowry] : the life estate in a man's real property to which his wife is entitled upon his death under common law and some state statutes — compare CURTESY, ELECTIVE SHARE

DR *abbr* disciplinary rule

¹**draft** *n* **1** : a preliminary version of something (as a law) **2 a** : a system for or act of selecting individuals from a group (as for military service) **b** : the act or process of selecting an individual (as for political candidacy) without his or her expressed consent **3** : an order for the payment of money drawn by one person or bank on another — see also DRAWEE, DRAWER; compare CHECK

documentary draft : a draft that will be honored only upon the presentation of certain documents (as an invoice or certificate of title)

sight draft : a draft payable on presentation

time draft : a draft payable a specified number of days after the date of the draft or of its presentation

²**draft** *vt* **1** : to select for some purpose; *specif* : to conscript for military service **2** : to compose or prepare esp. the preliminary version of ⟨*~ing* legislation⟩ — *vi* : to practice draftsmanship — **draft·er** *n*

drafts·man \'drafts-mən\ *n* : a person who prepares or composes legal or legislative documents — **drafts·man·ship** *n*

dram shop act \'dram-\ *n* : a law imposing civil liability on the owner of an establishment that sells alcoholic beverages to an intoxicated person who causes injury to another as a result of the intoxication — called also *civil damage act*, *civil liability act*

draw *vb* **drew; drawn; draw·ing** *vt* **1** : to compose by random selection ⟨*~* a jury⟩ **2** : to take (money) from a place of deposit **3** : to write and sign (a draft) in due form for use in making a demand ⟨*~* a check⟩ **4** : to write out in due form ⟨hired an attorney to *~* our wills⟩ — *vi* : to make a written demand for payment of money on deposit

draw·ee \drȯ-'ē\ *n* : the party (as a bank) on which a draft is drawn — compare DRAWER, PAYEE

draw·er \'drȯ-ər\ *n* : the party that draws a draft — compare DRAWEE, PAYEE

D reorganization — see REORGANIZATION

driv·ing under the influence : the offense of operating a motor vehicle while intoxicated by drugs or esp. alcohol — called also *driving while intoxicated*, *drunk driving*, *drunken driving* ◊ Most states specify by statute a level of alcohol in the blood that creates a presumption that the person is under the influence of alcohol. The blood alcohol content is required to be .10 percent in most states.

drug–free zone *n* : a statutorily designated area or place (as a public park or beach or a school bus) within which the distribution of or possession with intent to distribute a controlled substance is an aggravated felony; *esp* : such an area including and extending outward usu. 1000 feet from the real property of a public or private school ⟨it is irrelevant whether a person is aware that he or she is carrying on the prohibited drug activity in a *drug-*

\ə\abut \ᵊ\kitten \ər\further \a\ash \ā\ace
\ä\cot, cart \aủ\out \ch\chin \e\bet \ē\easy
\g\go \i\hit \ī\ice \j\job \ŋ\sing \ō\go \ȯ\law
\ȯi\boy \th\thin \t͟h\the \ü\loot \ủ\foot \y\yet
\zh\vision *see also* Pronunciation Symbols page

free zone —*State v. Silva-Baltazar,* 886 P.2d 138 (1994)⟩

dry trust — see TRUST

du·al capacity doctrine *n* : a doctrine that provides an exception to the exclusive remedy of workers' compensation by allowing an employee to sue his or her employer when the injury caused by the employer to the employee is unrelated to the employee's capacity as an employee

dual contract — see CONTRACT

dual sovereignty doctrine *n* : a doctrine holding that more than one sovereign (as a state government and the federal government) may prosecute an individual without violating the prohibition against double jeopardy if the individual's act breaks the laws of each sovereignty

du·bi·tan·te \ˌdü-bi-'tan-tē, ˌdyü-, -'tän-\ *adj* [Latin, ablative singular masculine of *dubitans*, present participle of *dubitare* to doubt] : having doubts — used of a judge who expresses doubt about but does not dissent from a decision reached by a court

due *adj* [Old French *deu*, past participle of *devoir* to owe, from Latin *debere*] **1 a** : satisfying or capable of satisfying an obligation, duty, or requirement under the law ⟨the buyer's ~ performance under the contract⟩ ⟨~ proof of loss⟩ **b** : proper under the law ⟨obstructing ~ administration of justice⟩ **2** : capable of being attributed — used with *to* ⟨any loss ~ to neglect⟩ **3 a** : having reached the date at which payment is required : PAYABLE **b** : owed though not yet required to be paid **4** : REASONABLE 1a, b

due bill — see BILL 7

due care *n* : the care that an ordinarily reasonable and prudent person would use under the same or similar circumstances — called also *ordinary care, reasonable care;* see also DUE DILIGENCE; compare FAULT, NEGLIGENCE

due diligence *n* **1** : such diligence as a reasonable person under the same circumstances would use : use of reasonable but not necessarily exhaustive efforts — called also *reasonable diligence* ◊ *Due*

diligence is used most often in connection with the performance of a professional or fiduciary duty, or with regard to proceeding with a court action. *Due care* is used more often in connection with general tort actions. **2 a** : the care that a prudent person might be expected to exercise in the examination and evaluation of risks affecting a business transaction **b** : the process of investigation carried on usu. by a disinterested third party (as an accounting or law firm) on behalf of a party contemplating a business transaction (as a corporate acquisition or merger, loan of finances, or esp. purchase of securities) for the purpose of providing information with which to evaluate the advantages and risks involved ⟨the greatest exposure . . . for failure to conduct adequate *due diligence* arises in the context of public offerings of securities —G. M. Lawrence⟩ **c** : the defense (as to a lawsuit) that due diligence was conducted

due process *n* **1** : a course of formal proceedings (as judicial proceedings) carried out regularly, fairly, and in accordance with established rules and principles — called also *procedural due process* **2** : a requirement that laws and regulations must be related to a legitimate government interest (as crime prevention) and may not contain provisions that result in the unfair or arbitrary treatment of an individual — called also *substantive due process* ◊ The guarantee of due process is found in the Fifth Amendment to the Constitution, which states "no person shall . . . be deprived of life, liberty, or property, without due process of law," and in the Fourteenth Amendment, which states "nor shall any state deprive any person of life, liberty, or property without due process of law." The boundaries of due process are not fixed and are the subject of endless judicial interpretation and decision-making. Fundamental to procedural due process is adequate notice prior to the government's deprivation of one's life, liberty, or property, and an opportunity to be heard and defend one's rights

to life, liberty, or property. Substantive due process is a limit on the government's power to enact laws or regulations that affect one's life, liberty, or property rights. It is a safeguard from governmental action that is not related to any legitimate government interest or that is unfair, irrational, or arbitrary in its furtherance of a government interest. The requirement of due process applies to agency actions. **3** : the right to due process ⟨acts that violated *due process*⟩
due process clause *n* : a clause in a constitution prohibiting the government from depriving a person of life, liberty, or property without due process of law; *specif, often cap D&P&C* : such a clause found in the Fifth and Fourteenth Amendments to the U.S. Constitution
due process of law : DUE PROCESS
DUI *abbr* driving under the influence
du·ly \'dü-lē, 'dyü-\ *adv* : in a due manner or time ⟨failed to ~ deliver⟩
dump *vt* : to sell in quantity at a very low price; *specif* : to sell abroad at less than the market price at home
¹du·pli·cate \'dü-pli-ˌkāt, 'dyü-\ *vt* **-cat·ed; -cat·ing** : to make a duplicate of — **du·pli·ca·tive** \-ˌkā-tiv\ *adj*
²du·pli·cate \'dü-pli-kət, 'dyü-\ *n* : either of two things exactly alike and often produced at the same time; *specif* : a counterpart identified in the Federal Rules of Evidence Rule 1001 as produced by the same impression as the original or from the same matrix or by means of photography, mechanical, or electronic rerecording, chemical reproduction, or another technique which accurately reproduces the original — compare ORIGINAL
du·pli·ca·tion \ˌdü-pli-'kā-shən, ˌdyü-\ *n* : the act, process, or result of duplicating
du·plic·i·tous \dü-'pli-sə-təs, dyü-\ *adj* : marked by duplicity ⟨a ~ indictment⟩
du·plic·i·ty \dü-'pli-sə-tē, dyü-\ *n, pl* **-ties** [Late Latin *duplicitat-, duplicitas* duality, double-dealing, from Latin *duplex* twofold] **1** : the use of deceptive words or actions **2** : the use of more than one claim, allegation, or defense in a single

paragraph of a pleading; *esp* : the improper charging of more than one offense in one count in a charging instrument (as an indictment) — compare MISJOINDER, MULTIPLICITY
durable goods — see GOOD 2
durable power of attorney — see POWER OF ATTORNEY
du·ra·bles \'dùr-ə-bəlz, 'dyùr-\ *n pl* : consumer goods (as vehicles or appliances) that are typically used repeatedly over a period of years — called also *durable goods*
du·ran·te ab·sen·tia \dù-'ran-tē-əb-'sen-chē-ə, dyù-, -chə; dü-'rän-tā-äb-'sen-tē-ä\ *adv* [New Latin] : during absence
du·ress \dù-'res, dyù-\ *n* [Anglo-French *duresce*, literally, hardness, harshness, from Old French, from Latin *duritia*, from *durus* hard] : wrongful and usu. unlawful compulsion (as threats of physical violence) that induces a person to act against his or her will : COERCION; *also* : the affirmative defense of having acted under duress — see also ECONOMIC DURESS; compare NECESSITY, UNDUE INFLUENCE ◊ A person may be able to avoid the consequences of his or her acts under the law if they were performed while under duress. For example, a contract made under duress is voidable by the coerced party. Similarly, a will signed under duress is invalid. Duress may also be used to justify a criminal act. A threat to bring a lawsuit is not duress.
duress of goods : a wrongful threat to detain or the actual detaining of another party's property that leaves the party no alternative but to agree to a transaction
Dur·ham rule \'dùr-əm-, 'dər-\ *n* [from *Durham v. United States*, 214 F.2d 862 (1954), a case heard by the District of Columbia Court of Appeals that established the rule] : a rule of criminal law used in some states that holds that in order to find

\ə\abut \ᵊ\kitten \ər\further \a\ash \ā\ace
\ä\cot, cart \aù\out \ch\chin \e\bet \ē\easy
\g\go \i\hit \ī\ice \j\job \ŋ\sing \ō\go \ò\law
\òi\boy \th\thin \th\the \ü\loot \ù\foot \y\yet
\zh\vision *see also* Pronunciation Symbols page

a defendant not guilty by reason of insanity the defendant's criminal act must be the product of a mental disease or defect — compare IRRESISTIBLE IMPULSE TEST, M'NAGHTEN TEST, SUBSTANTIAL CAPACITY TEST

du·ti·able \'dü-tē-ə-bəl, 'dyü-\ *n* : subject to a duty ⟨purchased ~ items while overseas⟩

du·ty *n*, *pl* **du·ties** [Anglo-French *deuté* indebtedness, obligation, from *deu* owing, due, from Old French — see DUE] **1** : tasks, service, or functions that arise from one's position ⟨performing a police officer's *duties*⟩; *also* : a period of being on duty — see also JURY DUTY **2** : an obligation assumed (as by contract) or imposed by law to conduct oneself in conformance with a certain standard or to act in a particular way ⟨~ of good faith⟩ ⟨a ~ to warn of danger⟩ — see also PUBLIC DUTY DOCTRINE, SPECIAL DUTY DOCTRINE

duty of can·dor \-'kan-dər\ : a duty obligating directors of a corporation to disclose all material facts known to them about a transaction when they are seeking shareholder approval

duty of care : a duty to use due care toward others in order to protect them from unnecessary risk of harm

duty of fair representation : a duty obligating a labor union to represent the employees in its collective bargaining unit fairly and in good faith

duty of loy·al·ty : a duty obligating directors of a corporation to refrain from using their positions to further their own interests rather than the interests of the shareholders (as by self-dealing or fraud)

fiduciary duty : a duty obligating a fiduciary (as an agent or trustee) to act with loyalty and honesty and in a manner consistent with the best interests of the beneficiary of the fiduciary relationship (as a principal or trust beneficiary) **3** : TAX; *esp* : a tax on imports — **off duty** : not engaged in a duty ⟨a police officer who is *off duty*⟩ — **on duty** : engaged in a duty

duty of candor — see DUTY
duty of care — see DUTY
duty of fair representation — see DUTY
duty of loyalty — see DUTY

dwell·ing *n* : a structure where a person lives and esp. sleeps — called also *dwelling house;* see also BURGLARY ◊ Courts disagree as to how permanent or consistent the habitation of a structure must be in order for it to be considered a dwelling, but most courts agree that a dwelling includes its curtilage.

DWI *abbr* driving while intoxicated

dying declaration — see DECLARATION 2c

dy·na·mite charge *n* [probably from the notion of exploding the metaphorical blockage impeding a decision by a deadlocked jury] : ALLEN CHARGE

E

ear·mark·ing doctrine *n* [probably so called because the loan has been earmarked, i.e., specifically designated, by the debtor to pay a specific creditor] **:** a doctrine in bankruptcy law: a loan made by a third person to a debtor to enable the debtor to pay off a specified creditor cannot be avoided by the trustee as a preference since the debtor never actually had control of the funds and the transfer does not diminish the debtor's estate

earned income *n* **:** income (as wages, salary, professional fees, or commissions) that results from the personal labor or services of an individual — compare UNEARNED INCOME

earned premium *n* **:** the difference between the amount of premium paid by the insured and the amount returned to the insured by the insurer upon cancellation of a policy before its term expires

earned surplus — see SURPLUS

ear·nest \'ər-nəst\ *n* [Anglo-French *ernes(t)*, *erles*, alteration of Old French *erres*, plural of *erre* pledge, earnest, alteration of Latin *arra*, short for *arrabo*, from Greek *arrhabōn*, of Semitic origin] **:** something of value given by a buyer to a seller to bind a bargain

earnest money *n* **:** money used as earnest

earn·ings *n pl* **1 :** something (as wages or dividends) earned as compensation for labor or the use of capital **2 :** the balance of revenue for a specified period that remains after deducting related costs and expenses incurred — compare PROFIT

ease·ment \'ēz-mənt\ *n* [Anglo-French *esement*, literally, benefit, convenience, from Old French *aisement*, from *aisier* to ease, assist] **:** an interest in land owned by another that entitles its holder to a specific limited use or enjoyment (as the right to cross the land or have a view continue

unobstructed over it) — see also *dominant estate* and *servient estate* at ESTATE 4; compare LICENSE, PROFIT 2, RIGHT OF WAY, SERVITUDE

affirmative easement **:** an easement entitling a person to do something affecting the land of another that would constitute trespass or a nuisance if not for the easement — compare NEGATIVE EASEMENT in this entry

apparent easement **:** an easement whose existence is detectable by its outward appearance (as by the presence of a water pipe)

ap·pur·te·nant easement \ə-'pərt-ᵊn-ənt-\ **:** EASEMENT APPURTENANT in this entry

common easement **:** an easement in which the owner of the land burdened by the easement retains the privilege of sharing the benefits of the easement — called also *nonexclusive easement;* compare EXCLUSIVE EASEMENT in this entry

determinable easement **:** an easement that will terminate upon the happening of a specific event or contingency

easement appurtenant pl easements appurtenant **:** an easement attached to and benefiting a dominant estate and burdening a servient estate — compare EASEMENT IN GROSS in this entry ◊ Easements appurtenant run with the land and are therefore passed when the property is transferred.

easement by estoppel **:** an easement that is created when the conduct of the owner of land leads another to reasonably be-

\ə\abut \ᵊ\kitten \ər\further \a\ash \ā\ace
\ä\cot, cart \aú\out \ch\chin \e\bet \ē\easy
\g\go \i\hit \ī\ice \j\job \ŋ\sing \ō\go \ò\law
\ói\boy \th\thin \th\the \ü\loot \ú\foot \y\yet
\zh\vision *see also* Pronunciation Symbols page

lieve that he or she has an interest in the land so that he or she acts or does not act in reliance on that belief

easement by implication : an easement that is created by operation of law when an owner severs property into two parcels in such a way that an already existing, obvious, and continuous use of one parcel (as for access) is necessary for the reasonable enjoyment of the other parcel — called also *easement by necessity, implied easement, way of necessity*

easement by prescription : an easement created by the open, notorious, uninterrupted, hostile, and adverse use of another's land for 20 years or for a period set by statute — called also *prescriptive easement*

easement in gross : an easement that is a personal right of its holder to a use of another's land and that is not dependent on ownership of a dominant estate — called also *personal easement;* compare EASEMENT APPURTENANT in this entry ◊ Utility companies often own easements in gross.

exclusive easement : an easement that the holder has the right to enjoy to the exclusion of all others — compare COMMON EASEMENT in this entry

implied easement : EASEMENT BY IMPLICATION in this entry

negative easement : an easement that entitles the holder to prevent the owner of land from using the land for a purpose or in a way that would otherwise be permitted

nonexclusive easement : COMMON EASEMENT in this entry

personal easement : EASEMENT IN GROSS in this entry

prescriptive easement : EASEMENT BY PRESCRIPTION in this entry

quasi easement : the use by the owner of two adjoining parcels of land of one of the parcels to benefit the other ◊ A quasi easement may become an easement upon the transfer of one or both of the parcels.

reciprocal negative easement : an easement created by operation of law and held by the owner of a lot in a residential development that entitles the holder to enforce restrictions that were part of the general development scheme against the developer and subsequent buyers who purchase free of the restrictions

easement appurtenant — see EASEMENT

easement by estoppel — see EASEMENT

easement by implication — see EASEMENT

easement by necessity : EASEMENT BY IMPLICATION at EASEMENT

easement by prescription — see EASEMENT

easement in gross — see EASEMENT

eaves•drop *vi* **eaves•dropped; eaves•drop•ping** : to listen secretly to what is being said in private without the consent of the speaker — compare BUG, WIRETAP — **eaves•drop•per** *n*

EC *abbr* ethical consideration

ec•cle•si•as•ti•cal court \i-ˌklē-zē-'as-ti-kəl-\ *n* : a court having jurisdiction in ecclesiastical affairs : a tribunal in an ecclesiastical body — called also *Court Christian*

ecclesiastical law *n* : CANON LAW

eco•nom•ic duress *n* : wrongful or unlawful conduct that creates fear of economic hardship which prevents the exercise of free will in engaging in a business transaction; *also* : the defense of economic duress — called also *business compulsion*

economic obsolescence — see OBSOLESCENCE

economic re•al•i•ties test *n* : a judicial method of determining the nature of a business transaction or situation; *esp* : a test used by courts for the purpose of determining if a person is an employee by considering such things as the extent of the alleged employer's ability to control, hire, fire, and discipline the person, the nature of the person's duties, and the payment of wages

economic strike — see STRIKE

EEO *abbr* equal employment opportunity

EEOC *abbr* Equal Employment Opportunity Commission — see also the IMPORTANT AGENCIES section
¹ef·fect *n* **1** : something that is produced by an agent or cause **2** *pl* : PERSONAL PROPERTY 1 at PROPERTY : GOODS ⟨the right of the people to be secure in their persons, houses, papers, and ~s, against unreasonable searches and seizures —*U.S. Constitution* amend. IV⟩ **3** : the quality or state of being operative ⟨when the new law goes into ~⟩
²effect *vt* **1** : to cause to come into being **2** : to bring about often by surmounting obstacles ⟨~ a settlement of the dispute⟩ **3** : to put into operation ⟨the duty of the legislature to ~ the will of the citizens⟩
ef·fec·tive *adj* **1** : producing a desired effect ⟨an ~ revocation of the contract⟩ **2** : capable of bringing about an effect ⟨~ assistance of counsel⟩ — see also INEFFECTIVE ASSISTANCE OF COUNSEL **3** : being in effect **4** *of a rate of interest* : equal to the rate of simple interest that yields the same amount when the rate is paid once at the end of the interest period as a quoted rate of interest does when calculated at compound interest over the same period — compare NOMINAL — **ef·fec·tive·ness** *n*
effective assignment — see ASSIGNMENT
efficient breach — see BREACH 1b
efficient intervening cause — see CAUSE 1
ef·fi·cient market *n* : a securities and commodities market whose prices always reflect the most accurate and up-to-date information — compare FRAUD ON THE MARKET THEORY
egre·gious \i-ˈgrē-jəs\ *adj* : extremely and conspicuously bad
¹egress \ˈē-ˌgres\ *n* [Medieval Latin *egressus*, literally, act of going out, departure, from Latin, from *egredi* to go out, from *e-* out + *gradi* to make one's way] **1** : the action or right of going or coming out **2** : a place or means of going out or exiting — compare INGRESS
²egress \i-ˈgres\ *vi* : to go or come out
eight–hour law *n* : a law fixing the working day for specified types of employment at eight hours and frequently providing for time-and-a-half compensation for hours worked after eight hours
eject \i-ˈjekt\ *vt* : DISPOSSESS
eject·ment \i-ˈjekt-mənt\ *n* : an action at common law that is to determine the right to possession of property and for the recovery of damages and that is brought by a plaintiff who claims to hold superior title
ejus·dem gen·er·is \ē-ˈjəs-dəm-ˈje-nə-ris, ā-ˈyüs-dem-ˈge-ne-rēs\ *adj* [Latin] : of the same kind or class ⟨was *ejusdem generis* with the other items listed⟩
ejusdem generis rule *n* : a rule of construction: general words (as in a statute) that follow specific words in a list must be construed as referring only to the types of things identified by the specific words
elect *vt* **1** : to select by vote for an office, position, or membership **2** : to make a selection of ⟨~ed her statutory share over the gift under the will⟩ ~ *vi* : to choose an elective share ⟨the right of a spouse to ~ against the will⟩
elec·tion *n* **1 a** : the act or process of electing **b** : an instance of the electorate voting for candidates for an elective office **c** : the fact of being elected **2** : the right, power, or privilege of making a choice: as **a** : the right of a spouse to choose a statutorily prescribed amount of a deceased spouse's estate or whatever was devised to him or her under the will **b** : the right of a person who has an interest in property that a deceased has disposed of by will either to claim his or her right to the property or to accept what he or she was devised under the will instead **c** : the right of a party to a contract that has been breached by the other party to choose to continue or terminate the contract — see also ELECTION OF REMEDIES, EQUITABLE ELECTION

\ə\abut \ᵊ\kitten \ər\further \a\ash \ā\ace
\ä\cot, cart \aù\out \ch\chin \e\bet \ē\easy
\g\go \i\hit \ī\ice \j\job \ŋ\sing \ō\go \ò\law
\òi\boy \th\thin \th̲\the \ü\loot \ù\foot \y\yet
\zh\vision *see also* Pronunciation Symbols page

election of remedies 1 : the act of electing a remedy from those available for an injury **2 :** the doctrine that a plaintiff who elects a remedy for his or her injury is barred from pursuing another remedy that is inconsistent with the one elected

elec·tive *adj* **1 a :** chosen by popular election ⟨an ~ official⟩ **b :** of or relating to election **c :** based on the right or principle of election ⟨the presidency is an ~ office⟩ **2 a :** permitting a choice — compare COMPULSORY **b :** available as a choice ⟨~ insurance coverage⟩ **c :** beneficial to the patient but not essential for survival ⟨~ surgery⟩

elective share *n* **:** the share (as one third) of an estate set by statute that a widow or widower or sometimes a child is entitled to claim in lieu of any provisions made in a will or in the event of being disinherited unjustifiably — called also *forced share;* compare CURTESY, DOWER

elec·tor *n* **1 :** a person who is qualified to vote **2 :** a member of the electoral college in the U.S.

elec·tor·al college *n, often cap E&C* **:** a body of electors; *specif* **:** the body of electors chosen from each state to elect the president and vice president of the U.S. ◊ Under Article II, Section 1 of the U.S. Constitution, each state chooses electors in the same number that the state has senators and representatives. The electors have the discretion to choose the candidate they vote for, but in practice the electors vote for the candidate that wins the most votes in their respective states. In all the states except Maine, the candidate that wins a plurality of the popular votes wins all of the state's electoral votes.

elec·tor·ate *n* **:** a body of people entitled to vote

elec·tric chair *n* **1 :** a chair used in performing a legal electrocution **2 :** the penalty of death by electrocution

elec·tro·cute *vt* **-cut·ed; -cut·ing** [*electro-,* combining form meaning "electric" + exe*cute*] **:** to execute (a convicted criminal) by electricity — **elec·tro·cu·tion** *n*

elee·mo·sy·nary \ˌe-li-ˈmäs-ᵊn-ˌer-ē,

-ˈmōs-ᵊn-, -ˈmäz-ᵊn-\ *adj* **:** of, relating to, or supported by charity

el·e·ment *n* **:** one of the constituent parts (as a particular act, a mental state, or an attendant circumstance) of a crime as defined by statute that the prosecution must prove to win a conviction

eli·sor \i-ˈlī-zər\ *n* [Anglo-French *ellisour, eslisour,* literally, one who selects (jurors in the sheriff's stead), elector, from *eslire* to select, from Old French, ultimately from Latin *eligere* to choose, elect] **:** a judicial officer appointed to act in the stead of a sheriff when the sheriff and any other authorized official (as a coroner) are unable or unqualified to act

eman·ci·pate \i-ˈman-sə-ˌpāt\ *vt* **-pat·ed; -pat·ing 1 :** to free from restraint, control, or the power of another; *esp* **:** to free from bondage ⟨*emancipated* the slaves⟩ — compare ENFRANCHISE **2 :** to release from the care, responsibility, and control of one's parents — compare AGE OF MAJORITY, LEGAL AGE ◊ The circumstances under which a minor may become emancipated vary from state to state. In many states, however, the marriage of a minor results in his or her emancipation.

eman·ci·pa·tion \i-ˌman-sə-ˈpā-shən\ *n* **:** the act or process of emancipating

emas·cu·late \i-ˈmas-kyə-ˌlāt\ *vt* **-lat·ed; -lat·ing :** to deprive (as a law or judicial opinion) of force or effectiveness

¹em·bar·go \im-ˈbär-gō, em-\ *n, pl* **-goes** [Spanish, from *embargar* to bar] **1 :** an order of a government prohibiting the departure of commercial ships from its ports **2 :** a legal prohibition on commerce ⟨an ~ on arms shipments⟩ **3 :** an order by a common carrier or public regulatory agency prohibiting or restricting freight transportation

²embargo *vt* **-goed; -go·ing :** to place an embargo on

em·bez·zle \im-ˈbe-zəl\ *vt* **em·bez·zled; em·bez·zling** [Anglo-French *embeseiller* to make away with, from *en-,* prefix stressing completion + *beseller* to snatch, misappropriate, from Old French, to destroy] : to convert (property entrusted to one's care) fraudulently to one's own use — compare DEFALCATE — **em·bez·zle-ment** *n* — **em·bez·zler** *n*

em·ble·ments \'em-blǝ-mǝns\ *n pl* [Anglo-French, from Middle French *emblaement* act of sowing grain, from *emblaer* to sow with grain, from *en-*, causative prefix + Old French *blet, ble* grain] : crops from annual cultivation legally belonging to the tenant

em·brace·or \im-'brā-sǝr\ *n* [Anglo⸗ French, from Old French *embraserre* one who inflames, from *embraser* to set on fire, from *en-*, causative prefix + *brase, brese* live coals] : a person who has committed embracery

em·brac·ery \im-'brā-sǝ-rē\ *n, pl* **-er·ies** : an attempt to influence a jury in a corrupt manner

emer·gen·cy *n, pl* **-cies** 1 : an unforeseen combination of circumstances or the resulting state that calls for immediate action 2 : an urgent need for assistance or relief ⟨a state of ~⟩

emergency doctrine *n* 1 : SUDDEN EMERGENCY DOCTRINE 2 : EMERGENCY EXCEPTION

emergency exception *n* : an exception to the requirement for a search warrant in a situation in which a police officer has reason to believe that immediate action including a search is necessary to protect life or prevent serious injury

em·i·nent do·main /'e-mǝ-nǝnt-/ *n* : the right of the government to take property from a private owner for public use by virtue of the superior dominion of its sovereignty over all lands within its jurisdiction — see also CONDEMN, EXPROPRIATE, TAKE 1b ◇ The Fifth Amendment to the U.S. Constitution requires the government to compensate the owner of property taken by eminent domain, stating "nor shall private property be taken for public use, without just compensation." State constitutions contain similar provisions requiring that the property owner receive just compensation for the property taken.

em·is·sary \'e-mǝ-,ser-ē\ *n, pl* **-sar·ies** : a representative usu. empowered to act more or less independently (as in collecting or conveying information or in negotiating)

emol·u·ment \i-'mäl-yǝ-mǝnt\ *n* : a return arising from office or employment usu. in the form of compensation or perquisites ⟨the President shall, at stated times, receive for his services, a compensation . . . and he shall not receive within that period any other ~ —*U.S. Constitution* art. II⟩

emo·tion·al distress *n* : a highly unpleasant emotional reaction (as anguish, humiliation, or fury) which results from another's conduct and for which damages may be sought — called also *emotional harm, mental anguish, mental distress, mental disturbance, mental suffering;* see also OUTRAGE, ZONE OF DANGER ◇ Damages may be recoverable for emotional distress that is caused intentionally or negligently. Recovery for negligent infliction of emotional distress often requires that the plaintiff suffer a physical injury as well.

empanel *var of* IMPANEL

em·ploy·ee *or* **em·ploye** *n* : a person usu. below the executive level who is hired by another to perform a service esp. for wages or salary and is under the other's control — see also RESPONDEAT SUPERIOR; compare INDEPENDENT CONTRACTOR ◇ In determining whether an individual is an employee, courts look at several factors, including the nature of the compensation paid, provision for employee benefits, whether the hired party is in business, tax treatment of the hired party, source of the equipment used, and location of the work. Statutes, such as workers' compensation acts and labor laws, usu. include a definition of *employee* as it is used in the statute.

\ǝ\abut \ˈǝ\kitten \ǝr\further \a\ash \ā\ace
\ä\cot, cart \aù\out \ch\chin \e\bet \ē\easy
\g\go \i\hit \ī\ice \j\job \ŋ\sing \ō\go \ò\law
\òi\boy \th\thin \t͟h\the \ü\loot \ù\foot \y\yet
\zh\vision *see also* Pronunciation Symbols page

employee stock ownership plan *n* : ESOP

em·ploy·er *n* : one that hires others to perform a service or engage in an activity in exchange for compensation — see also RESPONDEAT SUPERIOR

em·ploy·ment *n* **1** : an activity or service performed for another esp. for compensation or as an occupation **2** : the act of employing : the state of being employed

employment tax *n* : a tax imposed on the basis of an employee-employer relationship

em·pow·er \im-'pau̇-ər\ *vt* : to give official authority or legal power to ⟨no branch of government should be ~*ed* unilaterally to impose a serious penalty —L. H. Tribe⟩

en·abl·ing *adj* : giving legal power, capacity, or sanction ⟨~ legislation⟩

enabling statute *n* : a statute that confers (as to an administrative agency) the power or authority to engage in conduct not previously allowed

en·act \i-'nakt\ *vt* : to establish by legal and authoritative act : make into law ⟨~ a bill⟩

en·act·ing clause *n* : the clause of an act that formally expresses legislative authorization and usu. begins with "Be it enacted"

en·act·ment *n* **1** : the act of enacting : the state of being enacted **2** : something (as a law) that has been enacted

en banc *also* **in banc** *also* **in bank** \in-'baŋk, äⁿ-'bäⁿk\ *adv or adj* [Anglo-French *en banke*, literally, on the bench] : with all judges or a quorum of judges present : in full court ⟨an *en banc* rehearing⟩ ⟨heard very few matters *en banc* — H. B. Zobel⟩

en·croach \in-'krōch\ *vi* [Anglo-French *encrocher*, probably alteration of *acrocher* to catch hold of, seize, usurp, from Old French, from *a-*, prefix stressing goal + *croc* hook] : to enter esp. gradually or stealthily into the possessions or rights of another ⟨~*es* on an adjoining property⟩

en·croach·ment *n* **1** : an act or instance of encroaching **2** : something (as a structure) that encroaches on another's land ⟨possession of the one-foot ~⟩

en·cum·ber *also* **in·cum·ber** \in-'kəm-bər\ *vt* **-bered; -ber·ing** : to burden with a claim (as a mortgage or lien) ⟨~*ed* the land with a mineral lease⟩

en·cum·brance *also* **in·cum·brance** \in-'kəm-brəns\ *n* : a claim (as a lien) against property; *specif* : an interest or right (as an easement or a lease) in real property that may diminish the value of the estate but does not prevent the conveyance of the estate ⟨that these premises are free from all ~*s*⟩

en·cum·branc·er \in-'kəm-brən-sər\ *n* : a person who holds an encumbrance

en·dan·ger *vt* : to bring into danger or peril **~** *vi* : to create a dangerous situation ⟨charged with driving to ~⟩

en·dan·ger·ment *n* : the crime or tort of exposing others to possible harm or danger

en·dorse *also* **in·dorse** \in-'dȯrs\ *vt* **en·dorsed** *also* **in·dorsed; en·dors·ing** *also* **in·dors·ing** [Anglo-French *endosser*, *endorser* and Medieval Latin *indorsare*, both ultimately from Latin *in* on + *dorsum* back] **1** : to write on the back of; *esp* : to sign one's name as payee on the back of (an instrument) in order to receive the cash or credit represented on the face ⟨~ a check⟩ **2** : to inscribe (as one's signature or a notation accompanied by one's signature) on an instrument (as a note or bill) esp. to transfer or guarantee it **3** : to transfer (an instrument) to another by inscribing one's signature ⟨assume that payee ~*s* a note to creditor as security for a debt — *Uniform Commercial Code*⟩ **4** : to inscribe (as an official document) with a notation (as of date or title) — **endorse in blank** : to inscribe (an instrument) with a blank endorsement

en·dors·ee *also* **in·dors·ee** \in-ˌdȯr-'sē, ˌen-\ *n* : one to whom something is endorsed

en·dorse·ment *also* **in·dorse·ment** *n* **1** : the act or process of endorsing **2** : an inscription (as a signature or notation) on a document or instrument; *esp* : an inscription usu. on the back of a negotiable instrument that transfers or guarantees the instrument *blank endorsement* : an endorsement (as a signature) of a negotiable instrument that does not name a transferee and that makes the instrument payable to bearer — called also *endorsement in blank*

qualified endorsement : an endorsement of a negotiable instrument with words (as "without recourse") that limit or qualify the endorser's liability

restrictive endorsement : an endorsement of a negotiable instrument with words (as "for deposit only") that limit the further negotiation of the instrument ◇ A restrictive endorsement does not prevent further negotiation of the instrument under the Uniform Commercial Code.

spe•cial endorsement : an endorsement of a negotiable instrument with words (as "Pay to Jane Doe") that make the instrument payable to a specified person **3** : a provision added to an insurance policy that alters its coverage ⟨a theft ∼⟩ **endorsement in blank** : BLANK ENDORSEMENT at ENDORSEMENT

en•dors•er *also* **in•dors•er** *n* : one who endorses something

en•dow \in-'daù\ *vt* [Anglo-French *endower*, from Old French *en-*, prefix stressing completion + *douer* to endow, from Latin *dotare*, from *dot-*, *dos* gift, dowry] : to furnish with income; *esp* : to make a grant of money providing for the continuing support or maintenance of ⟨a scholarship ∼*ed* by the testator⟩

en•dow•ment *n* **1** : the act or process of endowing **2** : a result or product of endowing: as **a** : the income of an institution derived from donations ⟨the university's ability to attract ∼⟩ **b** : the property (as a fund) donated to an institution or organization that is invested and producing income ⟨an ∼ to maintain the gallery⟩ **3** : an endowed organization or institution : FOUNDATION ⟨chairwoman of the state's arts ∼⟩ **4** : ENDOWMENT INSURANCE

endowment insurance *n* : life insurance in which the benefit is paid to the policyowner if he or she is still living at the end of the policy's term (as 20 years)

en•feoff \en-'fef, -'fēf\ *vt* [Anglo-French *enfeoffer*, from Old French *en-*, causative prefix + *fief* fief] : to invest (a person) with a freehold estate by feoffment

en•feoff•ment *n* **1** : the act of enfeoffing **2** : the instrument by which one is enfeoffed

en•force *vt* **en•forced; en•forc•ing** : to cause to take effect or to be fulfilled ⟨*enforcing* the divorce decree⟩ ⟨Congress shall have power to ∼ this article by appropriate legislation —*U.S. Constitution* amend. XIX⟩

en•force•able *adj* : capable of being enforced esp. as legal or valid ⟨creditors with ∼ contract rights —L. H. Tribe⟩

en•force•ment *n* : the act or process of enforcing ⟨∼ of the debt⟩

en•fran•chise \in-'fran-ˌchīz\ *vt* **-chised; -chis•ing** : to grant franchise to; *esp* : to admit to the privileges of a citizen and esp. to voting rights ⟨the Twenty-sixth Amendment *enfranchised* all citizens over 18 years of age⟩ — compare EMANCIPATE

en•fran•chise•ment *n* **1** : the act of enfranchising **2** : the state of being enfranchised

en•gross \in-'grōs\ *vt* [Anglo-French *engrosser* to put (a legal document) in final form, from Medieval Latin *ingrossare*, from *in grossam* (put) into final form, literally, (written) in large (letter)] : to prepare the usu. final handwritten or printed text of (as a bill or resolution) esp. for final passage or approval ⟨the amendment was ordered to be ∼*ed* —*Congressional Record*⟩ — see also *engrossed bill* at BILL 1; compare ENROLL ◇ A bill or resolution is engrossed in the Congress and some state legislatures before its third reading and final passage by one of the legislative houses. — **en•gross•ment** *n*

engrossed bill — see BILL 1

en•join \in-'jóin\ *vt* [Anglo-French

\ə\abut \ə\kitten \ər\further \a\ash \ā\ace \ä\cot, cart \aù\out \ch\chin \e\bet \ē\easy \g\go \i\hit \ī\ice \j\job \ŋ\sing \ō\go \ò\law \ói\boy \th\thin \t͟h\the \ü\loot \ù\foot \y\yet \zh\vision *see also* Pronunciation Symbols page

enjoindre to impose, constrain, from Old French, from Latin *injungere* to attach, impose, from *in-* on + *jungere* to join] : to prohibit by judicial order : issue an injunction against ⟨a three-judge district court had ~*ed* the plans —W. J. Brennan, Jr.⟩ — **en•join•able** *adj*

en•joy•ment *n* : personal benefit, use, or possession (as of rights or property) ⟨widows and widowers were relegated to lifetime ~ of the marital estates —W. M. McGovern, Jr. *et al.*⟩; *specif* : the receipt of the fruits or profits of property — see also RIGHT OF USE, USUFRUCT

en•roll *or* **en•rol** *vt* **en•rolled; en•roll•ing 1** : to insert, register, or enter in a list, catalog, or roll ⟨*enrolled* the deed⟩ **2** : to prepare a final copy of (a bill passed by a legislature) in written or printed form — see also *enrolled bill* at BILL 1; compare ENGROSS — **en•roll•ment** *n*

enrolled bill — see BILL 1

¹**en•tail** \in-ˈtāl\ *vt* [Middle English *entaillen*, from *en-*, causative prefix + *taille* restriction on inheritance; see TAIL] : to make (an estate in real property) a fee tail : limit the descent of (real property) by restricting inheritance to specific descendants who cannot convey or transfer the property ⟨estates are ~*ed* entire on the eldest male heir —Benjamin Franklin⟩ — **en•tail•ment** *n*

²**entail** *n* **1** : an act or instance of entailing real property; *also* : the practice of entailing property ⟨the repeal of the laws of ~ would prevent the accumulation and perpetuation of wealth in select families —Thomas Jefferson⟩ — see also *De Donis Conditionalibus* in the IMPORTANT LAWS section **2** : an entailed estate in real property ⟨if ~*s* had not become barrable —Eileen Spring⟩ **3** : the fixed line of descent of an entailed estate

en•ter *vi* : to go or come in; *specif* : to go upon real property by right of entry esp. to take possession ⟨lessor shall have the right to ~ and take possession⟩ — often used in deeds and leases ~ *vt* **1** : to come or go into ⟨he breaks into and ~*s* a vehicle —*Code of Alabama*⟩ — see also BREAK,

BREAKING AND ENTERING **2** : RECORD, REGISTER **3** : to put in correct form before a court or on a record ⟨~*ed* judgment against the defendant⟩ ⟨~*ing* a plea⟩ — compare RENDER **4** : to go upon (real property) by right of entry esp. to take possession ⟨if the lessee defaults, the lessor may ~ the premises⟩ — compare DISTRAIN — **en•ter•able** *adj* — **enter into** : to make oneself a party to or in ⟨no State shall *enter into* any treaty, alliance or confederation —*U.S. Constitution* art. I⟩ ⟨*entered into* a lease⟩

en•ter•prise \ˈen-tər-ˌprīz\ *n* : an economic organization or activity; *esp* : a business organization

enterprise liability — see LIABILITY 2b

en•tire *adj* : not capable of being divided into independent parts (as promises) : constituting an undivided unit ⟨an ~ contract⟩ — compare DIVISIBLE, SEVERABLE

en•tire•ty *n, pl* **-ties 1** : the state of being entire or complete ⟨in its ~⟩ **2** : an undivided whole; *specif* : an interest in real property that cannot be divided — compare MOIETY — **by the entirety** *also* **by the entireties** : by a husband and wife with undivided interests in the whole estate and a right of survivorship ⟨an estate held *by the entireties*⟩ — see also *tenancy by the entirety* at TENANCY

en•ti•tle *vt* **-tled; -tling** : to give an enforceable right to claim something ⟨her will ~*s* her daughters to half of her estate⟩

en•ti•tle•ment *n* **1** : the state or condition of being entitled : CLAIM ⟨evidence of victim's ~ to money seized —*National Law Journal*⟩ **2** : a right to benefits that is granted esp. by law or contract (as an insurance policy) ◊ Some courts have held that entitlements are a property interest and therefore subject to procedural due process under the Fifth and Fourteenth Amendments to the U.S. Constitution when denied by federal or state governments. **3** : a government program that provides benefits to members of a group that has a statutory entitlement;

also : the benefits distributed by such a program

en·ti·ty \'en-ti-tē\ *n, pl* **-ties** : an organization (as a business or governmental unit) that has a legal identity which is separate from those of its members — see also AL-TER EGO, INSTRUMENTALITY, JURIDICAL PERSON, LEGAL PERSON, PIERCE

en·trap \in-'trap\ *vt* **en·trapped; en·trap·ping** : to cause (a person) to commit a crime by means of undue persuasion, encouragement, or fraud in order to later prosecute ⟨police ~ him into violating the literal terms of a criminal statute —W. R. LaFave and A. W. Scott, Jr.⟩

en·trap·ment *n* **1** : the action or process of entrapping ⟨~ is un-American and has no place in law enforcement —Tip O'Neill⟩ **2** : the state or condition of being entrapped; *also* : the affirmative defense of having been entrapped by a government agent (as an officer or informant) — see also PREDISPOSE ◊ Entrapment is available as a defense only when an agent of the state or federal government has provided the encouragement or inducement. This defense is sometimes allowed in administrative proceedings (as for the revocation of a license to practice medicine) as well as criminal proceedings. In order to establish entrapment, the defendant has the burden of proving either that he or she would not have committed the crime but for the undue persuasion or fraud of the government agent, or that the encouragement was such that it created a risk that persons not inclined to commit the crime would commit it, depending on the jurisdiction. When entrapment is pleaded, evidence (as character evidence) regarding the defendant that might otherwise have been excluded is allowed to be admitted.

en·trust *also* **in·trust** *vt* **1** : to deliver something to (a person) under a charge or duty **2** : to give (something) over to the care of another; *specif* : to deliver to a merchant who may transfer ownership to a buyer in the ordinary course of — used esp. in the *Uniform*

Commercial Code; see also NEGLIGENT ENTRUSTMENT; compare BAIL, CONSIGN — **en·trust·ment** *n*

en·try *n, pl* **en·tries** **1** : the privilege of entering real property — see also RIGHT OF ENTRY **2** : the act of entering real property ⟨a warrantless ~ by the officer⟩ — see also TRESPASS **3** : the act of making or entering a record (as a plea or judgment) ⟨an ~ of default⟩; *also* : a record entered ⟨a docket ~⟩

enumerated powers — see POWER 2a

en·vi·ron·men·tal crime *n* : an act that is destructive to the environment and that has been criminalized by statute

environmental im·pact statement *n* : a technical report that details the effect proposed legislation or action will have on the natural and human environment and that is sometimes required to be furnished esp. by a governmental body (as an administrative agency or a municipality) for official and public review in the regulatory and decision-making process — called also *environmental impact report*

EOE *abbr* equal opportunity employer

EPA *abbr* Environmental Protection Agency — see also the IMPORTANT AGENCIES section

¹equal *adj* [Latin *aequalis*, from *aequus* level, equal] **1** : like in quality, nature, or status **2** : like for each member of a group, class, or society **3** : regarding or affecting all objects in the same way : IMPARTIAL

²equal *n* : one that is equal

equal·i·ty *n* : the quality or state of being equal: as **a** : sameness or equivalence in number, quantity, or measure **b** : likeness or sameness in quality, power, status, or degree

equal op·por·tu·ni·ty *n, often attrib* : freedom from discrimination (as in employment) on the basis of race, color, religion, national origin, sex, disability,

\ə\abut \ə\kitten \ər\further \a\ash \ā\ace
\ä\cot, cart \aù\out \ch\chin \e\bet \ē\easy
\g\go \i\hit \ī\ice \j\job \ŋ\sing \ō\go \ò\law
\òi\boy \th\thin \th\the \ü\loot \ù\foot \y\yet
\zh\vision   *see also* Pronunciation Symbols page

age, or sometimes sexual orientation — see also *Equal Employment Opportunity Commission* in the IMPORTANT AGENCIES section

equal opportunity employer *n* : an employer who agrees not to discriminate against any employee or job applicant because of race, color, religion, national origin, sex, physical or mental disability, or age

equal protection *n* : a guarantee under the Fourteenth Amendment to the U.S. Constitution that a state must treat an individual or class of individuals the same as it treats other individuals or classes in like circumstances — called also *equal protection of the law;* see also RATIONAL BASIS TEST, STRICT SCRUTINY, SUSPECT CLASSIFICATION, *Amendment XIV* to the CONSTITUTION in the back matter ◊ The equal protection requirement of the Constitution protects against legislation that affects individuals differently without a rational basis for doing so. In reviewing claims of denial of equal protection, a court will uphold legislation that has a rational basis unless the legislation affects a fundamental right or involves a suspect classification, such as race. In such a case, the court will use a strict scrutiny standard of review and will strike down legislation that does not show a compelling need for discriminating.

equal protection clause *n, often cap E&P&C* : the clause in the Fourteenth Amendment to the U.S. Constitution that prohibits any state from denying to any person within its jurisdiction the equal protection of the laws

equal protection of the law : EQUAL PROTECTION

equip·ment *n* : the implements used in an operation or activity; *specif, in the Uniform Commercial Code* : goods that are bought for or used in a business enterprise or by a debtor which is a nonprofit organization or a government agency and that are not inventory, farm products, or consumer goods

eq·ui·ta·ble \'e-kwi-tə-bəl\ *adj* **1** : hav-

ing or exhibiting equity : dealing fairly and equally ⟨shall allocate . . . appropriations in an ~ manner —*U.S. Code*⟩ **2** : existing or valid in equity or as a matter of equity as distinguished from law ⟨an ~ defense⟩ — compare LEGAL 4 — **eq·ui·ta·bil·i·ty** \ˌe-kwi-tə-'bi-lə-tē\ *n* — **eq·ui·ta·ble·ness** *n* — **eq·ui·ta·bly** *adv*

equitable adoption *n* : an adoption recognized by the law in order to allow claims (as to assets in an estate or to insurance or government benefits) in cases in which there is an express or implied contract to adopt and clear evidence of an intention to adopt but no performance of the procedures required by statute for an adoption — called also *adoption by estoppel*

equitable asset — see ASSET 2

equitable assignment — see ASSIGNMENT

equitable conversion — see CONVERSION

equitable distribution *n* : the distribution of marital assets by a court in a divorce action in accordance with statutory guidelines that are designed to produce a fair but not necessarily equal division of the property

equitable election *n* : the choice that a beneficiary of an instrument (as a will) must make to forgo a challenge to the instrument and accept the benefit or vice versa

equitable estate — see ESTATE 1

equitable estoppel — see ESTOPPEL 1

equitable fraud — see FRAUD

equitable interest — see INTEREST 1

equitable lien — see LIEN

equitable mortgage — see MORTGAGE

equitable owner — see OWNER

equitable recoupment *n* : a doctrine that allows the government to collect a tax or a taxpayer to collect a refund of tax after the running of the statute of limitations for such collection in cases where the statute of limitations creates an inequitable result

equitable relief *n* : relief (as an injunction) available under a court's equitable powers

equitable subordination *n* : the subordination of a creditor's claim in a bankruptcy proceeding imposed by the court when the creditor has an unfair advantage over other creditors because of improper conduct or an advantageous position (as of a corporate insider)

equitable subrogation *n* : SUBROGATION 1

equitable title — see TITLE

equitable tolling *n* : a doctrine or principle of tort law: a statute of limitations will not bar a claim if despite use of due diligence the plaintiff did not or could not discover the injury until after the expiration of the limitations period

eq·ui·ty \\'e-kwə-tē\\ *n, pl* **-ties** [Latin *aequitat-, aequitas* fairness, justice, from *aequus* equal, fair] **1 a** : justice according to fairness esp. as distinguished from mechanical application of rules ⟨prompted by considerations of ~⟩ ⟨comity between nations, and ~ require it to be paid for —F. A. Magruder⟩ **b** : something that is equitable : an instance of equity ⟨the inequities produced by the system are outnumbered by the *equities*⟩ **2 a** : a system of law originating in the English chancery and comprising a settled and formal body of substantive and procedural rules and doctrines that supplement, aid, or override common and statutory law ⟨the judicial power shall extend to all cases, in law and ~, arising under this Constitution —*U.S. Constitution* art. III⟩ — see also CHANCERY; compare COMMON LAW, LAW ◊ The courts of equity arose in England from a need to provide relief for claims that did not conform to the writ system existing in the courts of law. Originally, the courts of equity exercised great discretion in fashioning remedies. Over time, they established precedents, rules, and doctrines of their own that were distinct from those used in the courts of law. Although for a time the courts of equity rivaled the law courts in power, the law courts maintained an advantage partly as a result of forcing the equity courts to hear only those cases for which there was no adequate remedy at law. The courts of law and equity were

united in England in 1873. Courts of equity also developed in the United States, but in most states and in the federal system courts of law and courts of equity have been joined. The courts apply both legal and equitable principles and offer both legal and equitable relief, although generally equitable relief is still granted when there is no adequate remedy at law. **b** : the principles that developed in the courts of equity : justice in accordance with equity ⟨~ treats a devisee who procures a will by fraud as a constructive trustee —W. M. McGovern, Jr. *et al.*⟩; *also* : justice in accordance with natural law **c** : a court of equity ⟨sat alone for some time in ~ —O. W. Holmes, Jr.⟩ **3** : a body of doctrines and rules developed to enlarge, supplement, or override any narrow or rigid system of law **4 a** : a right, claim, or interest existing or valid in equity **b** : the money value of a property or of an interest in property in excess of any claims or liens (as mortgage indebtedness) against it **c** : a risk interest or ownership right in property; *specif* : the ownership interests of shareholders in a company **d** : the common stock of a corporation — compare ASSET, DEBT

equity capital — see CAPITAL

equity court *n* : a court with equity jurisdiction : COURT OF EQUITY

equity loan *n* : HOME EQUITY LOAN at LOAN

equity of redemption 1 : the right of a defaulting mortgagor to redeem the mortgaged property before an absolute foreclosure **2** : the interest or estate remaining to a mortgagor in mortgaged property; *also* : the value of such interest

equity security — see SECURITY

eq·uiv·a·lent *n* : something that performs substantially the same function as another thing in substantially the same way — compare AGGREGATION, COMBINATION,

\ə\abut \ə\kitten \ər\further \a\ash \ā\ace
\ä\cot, cart \aú\out \ch\chin \e\bet \ē\easy
\g\go \i\hit \ī\ice \j\job \ŋ\sing \ō\go \ò\law
\òi\boy \th\thin \t̲h̲\the \ü\loot \ú\foot \y\yet
\zh\vision *see also* Pronunciation Symbols page

INVENTION ◊ Under patent law, a patentee may bring a claim for infringement against the inventor of an equivalent.

erase *vt* **erased; eras•ing** : to seal and protect (criminal records) from disclosure

erect *vt* : to give legal existence to by a formal act of authority ⟨no new State shall be formed or ~*ed* within the jurisdiction of any other State — *U.S. Constitution* art. IV⟩ — **erec•tion** *n*

E reorganization — see REORGANIZATION

Erie doctrine \'ir-ē-\ *n* [from the Supreme Court case *Erie Railroad Co. v. Tompkins*, which resulted in definition of the doctrine] : a doctrine that a federal court exercising diversity jurisdiction over a case for which no federal law is relevant must apply the law of the state in which it is sitting — called also *Erie Rule;* see also *Erie Railroad Co. v. Tompkins* in the IMPORTANT CASES section

ERISA \e-'ri-sə\ *abbr* Employee Retirement Income Security Act of 1974 — see also the IMPORTANT LAWS section

err \'er, 'ər\ *vi* : to make an error ⟨the court ~*ed* in denying the motion⟩

er•ro•ne•ous \i-'rō-nē-əs, e-\ *adj* : containing or characterized by error — see also CLEARLY ERRONEOUS — **er•ro•ne•ous•ly** *adv* — **er•ro•ne•ous•ness** *n*

er•ror *n* : an act that through ignorance, deficiency, or accident departs from or fails to achieve what should be done ⟨procedural ~*s*⟩; *esp* : a mistake made by a lower court in conducting judicial proceedings or making findings in a case ⟨to compel to conclusion that a manifest ~ has been done — *Moses v. Burgin*, 445 F.2d 369 (1971)⟩ — often used without an article ⟨had been ~ to give the jury special interrogatories — K. A. Cohen⟩; see also ASSIGNMENT OF ERROR, CLEARLY ERRONEOUS ◊ Generally a party must object to an error at trial in order to raise it as an issue on appeal.

  clear error : an error made by a judge in his or her findings of fact which is such that it leaves the reviewing court with the firm and definite conviction that a mistake has been made ◊ A clear error may or may not warrant reversal.

  fundamental error : PLAIN ERROR in this entry — used esp. in criminal cases

  harmless error : an error that does not affect a substantial right or change the outcome of a trial and does not warrant reversal or other modification of the lower court's decision on appeal

  invited error : an error resulting from a party's own request for or encouragement of an action by the court ◊ A party may not seek relief based on invited error that he or she has induced.

  manifest error : an error that is obvious and indisputable and that warrants reversal on appeal

  plain error : an obvious and prejudicial error that affects the substantial rights of the parties and that results or probably results in a miscarriage of justice ◊ Plain error warrants reversal on appeal even in the absence of objection to the error at trial.

  prejudicial error : an error that affects or presumptively affects the outcome of a trial

  reversible error : a substantial and prejudicial error warranting reversal on appeal

ERTA *abbr* Economic Recovery Tax Act of 1981 — see also the IMPORTANT LAWS section

es•ca•la•tor clause \'es-kə-ˌlā-tər-\ *n* **1** : a clause in a contract that provides for an increase in the amount of the payments made under the contract to reflect an increase in costs or the raising of a government-imposed cap on costs **2** : a clause in an employment contract that provides for an increase in wages to reflect a rise in the cost of living but prohibits a decrease to reflect a drop in the cost of living

¹es•cape *vi* **es•caped; es•cap•ing** : to depart from lawful custody with the intent of avoiding confinement or the administration of justice

²**escape** *n* **1** : an act or instance of escaping **2** : the criminal offense of escaping

escape clause *n* : a clause in a contract that allows a party to avoid liability under the contract for specified reasons; *esp* : a provision in an insurance policy that denies coverage when other insurance covers the risk

es·ca·pee \is-ˌkā-'pē, ˌes-kā-\ *n* : a person who escapes

¹**es·cheat** \is-'chēt\ *n* [Anglo-French *eschete* reversion of property, from Old French *escheoite* accession, inheritance, from feminine past participle of *escheoir* to fall (to), befall, ultimately from Latin *ex-* out + *cadere* to fall] **1** : escheated property **2** : the reversion of property to the state upon the death of the owner when there are no heirs

²**escheat** *vt* : to cause to revert by escheat ∼ *vi* : to revert by escheat — **es·cheat·able** *adj*

¹**es·crow** \'es-ˌkrō\ *n* [Anglo-French *escroue* deed delivered on condition, literally, scroll, strip of parchment, from Old French *escroe*] **1** : an instrument and esp. a deed or money or property held by a third party to be turned over to the grantee and become effective only upon the fulfillment of some condition **2** : a fund or deposit designed to serve as an escrow — **in escrow** : held as an escrow : in trust as an escrow ⟨had $1000 *in escrow* to pay taxes⟩ — compare TRUST

²**escrow** *vt* : to cause to be held as an escrow : place in escrow

es·crow·ee \ˌes-krō-'ē, es-'krō-ē\ *n* : the one holding an escrow

ESOP \'ē-ˌes-ˌō-'pē\ *n* [employee *s*tock *o*wnership *p*lan] : a program by which a corporation's employees may acquire its capital stock

es·pi·o·nage \'es-pē-ə-ˌnäzh, -ˌnäj, -nij\ *n* : the practice of gathering, transmitting, or losing through gross negligence information relating to the defense of the U.S. with the intent that or with reason to believe that the information will be used to the injury of the U.S. or the advantage of a foreign nation

esq. *abbr* esquire

es·quire \'es-ˌkwīr\ *n* [Middle French *escuier* squire, from Late Latin *scutarius* shield bearer, from Latin *scutum* shield] — used as a title of courtesy for lawyers usu. placed in its abbreviated form after the name and capitalized ⟨John R. Smith, *Esq.*⟩ ⟨Jane L. Smith, *Esq.*⟩

es·sence \'es-ᵊns\ *n* **1** : the real or ultimate nature of a thing : the properties that make a thing what it is ⟨his award is legitimate only so long as it draws its ∼ from the collective bargaining agreement — *United Steel Workers v. Enterprise Wheel and Car Corp.*, 363 U.S. 593 (1960)⟩ — see also ESSENCE TEST **2** : the predominant purpose of a thing ⟨the ∼ of the contract⟩ — **of the essence** : of the utmost importance; *specif* : so material in nature that failure to satisfy its requirements constitutes a breach of contract ⟨time is *of the essence*⟩

essence test *n* : a rule in labor law: a reviewing court may set aside an arbitrator's award only if it is unreasonable and does not derive from the collective bargaining agreement

es·sen·tial element *n* : an element of a tort or esp. a crime that must be alleged in the complaint or charging instrument (as the indictment) in order to make out a prima facie case

es·tab·lish *vt* **1** : to institute (as a law) permanently by enactment or agreement ⟨we the people of the United States . . . do ordain and ∼ this Constitution — *U.S. Constitution* preamble⟩ **2** : to make firm or stable **3** : to bring into existence : FOUND ⟨Congress shall have power . . . to ∼ post offices and post roads — *U.S. Constitution* art. I⟩; *specif* : to found (a national bank) pursuant to a charter **4** : to make (a church) a national or state institution — see also ESTABLISHMENT, ESTABLISHMENT CLAUSE **5** : to put beyond doubt

\ə\abut	\ᵊ\kitten	\ər\further	\a\ash	\ā\ace
\ä\cot, cart	\au̇\out	\ch\chin	\e\bet	\ē\easy
\g\go	\i\hit	\ī\ice	\j\job	\ŋ\sing	\ō\go	\ȯ\law
\ȯi\boy	\th\thin	\t͟h\the	\ü\loot	\u̇\foot	\y\yet
\zh\vision	*see also* Pronunciation Symbols page		

: PROVE **6** : to place in a position of being accepted or followed ⟨a rule ~*ed* by case law⟩

es·tab·lish·ment *n* **1** : something established: as **a** : a church recognized by law as the official church of a nation or state and supported by civil authority **b** : a permanent civil or military organization **c** : a place of residence or esp. business with its furnishings and staff **2 a** : an act of establishing **b** : the state of being established

establishment clause *n, often cap E&C* : a clause in the U.S. Constitution forbidding Congress from establishing a state religion — see also *Amendment I* to the CONSTITUTION in the back matter; compare FREE EXERCISE CLAUSE

es·tate \i-'stāt\ *n* [Anglo-French *estat*, literally, state, condition, from Old French, from Latin *status*, from *stare* to stand] **1** : the interest of a particular degree, nature, quality, or extent that one has in land or other property — compare FEE, *future interest* at INTEREST, REMAINDER, REVERSION, TENANCY

absolute estate : an estate that confers an absolute right to property and that is subject to no limitations, restrictions, or conditions : FEE SIMPLE ABSOLUTE at FEE SIMPLE

contingent estate : an estate whose vesting is conditioned upon the happening or failure of some uncertain event

equitable estate : the estate of one that has a beneficial right to property which is legally owned by a trustee or a person regarded at equity as a trustee (as in the case of a use or power) — compare LEGAL ESTATE in this entry

estate at sufferance : the estate in property held by one who remains in possession of or on the property after his or her lawful right to do so has ended

estate at will : an estate in property subject to termination at the will of another person

estate by the entirety : an estate held by a husband and wife together in which the whole property belongs to each of them

and passes as a whole to the survivor upon the death of either of them to the exclusion of the deceased spouse's heirs — called also *estate by the entireties;* compare *joint tenancy, tenancy by the entirety,* and *tenancy in common* at TENANCY

estate for years : an estate that terminates after a set period

estate in expectancy : an estate the enjoyment of which will take place at a future time : FUTURE INTEREST at INTEREST

estate of inheritance : an estate that can be inherited (as a fee simple as opposed to a life estate)

estate on condition : an estate subject to a contingency whose happening permits the grantor of the estate to terminate it if he or she so chooses — compare *fee simple determinable* at FEE SIMPLE

estate pur autre vie : a life estate measured by the life of a third person rather than that of the person enjoying the property

estate tail pl estates tail : an estate granted to a person and his or her direct descendants subject to a reverter or remainder upon the inheritance of the property by a grantee without direct descendants : FEE TAIL at FEE

legal estate : an estate to which one person (as a trustee) has legal title but of which another person has the right to the beneficial use — compare EQUITABLE ESTATE in this entry

life estate : an estate in property held only during or measured in duration by the lifetime of a specified individual and esp. the individual enjoying the property — see also LIFE TENANT ◊ Life estates are not estates of inheritance.

vested estate : an estate in which one has a right to enjoyment currently or sometime in the future

2 : all or designated items of a person's or entity's property considered as a whole

bankruptcy estate : the estate of a debtor in bankruptcy that includes all the debtor's legal and equitable interests in property as set out in the bankruptcy laws — called also *debtor's estate;* see also BANKRUPTCY, TRUSTEE IN BANKRUPTCY

personal estate : all of a person's property except real property; *broadly* : all of the property belonging to a person

separate estate : an estate whose ownership and control is enjoyed by a person free from any rights or control of another (as a spouse)

3 a : the assets and liabilities left by a person at death — see also BEQUEST, DEVISE, FREEHOLD, HEIR, INHERITANCE, INTESTATE, LEASEHOLD, LEGACY, PROBATE, TESTATE, WILL

aug•ment•ed estate \ȯg-'men-təd-\ : a deceased person's probate estate increased in accordance with statutory provisions and esp. by the addition of any property transferred by the deceased within two years of death, any joint tenancies, and any transfers in which the deceased retained either the right to revoke or the income for life ◊ In some states, the surviving spouse's elective share is distributed from the augmented estate.

gross estate : the estate of a person upon death defined by federal estate laws to include all of the deceased's real and personal property at death that may be passed by will or by intestate succession as well as specified property transferred by the deceased before death

probate estate : all of a deceased person's estate that is administered under the jurisdiction of the probate court ◊ Some assets, such as certain insurance proceeds, generally do not become part of the probate estate and are said to "pass outside of probate."

residuary estate : all of what is left of an estate once the deceased person's debts and administration costs have been paid and all specific and general bequests and devises have been distributed — called also *residual estate*

taxable estate : the estate of a deceased person that is subject to estate tax ◊ Under federal estate tax law, the taxable estate is the gross estate less allowed deductions.

b : the aggregate of a deceased person's property considered as a legal entity **4** : a tract of land esp. affected by an easement

dominant estate : a tract of land that is benefited by an easement burdening a servient estate

servient estate : a tract of land that is burdened by an easement benefiting a dominant estate

estate at sufferance — see ESTATE 1
estate at will — see ESTATE 1
estate by the entirety — see ESTATE 1
estate for years — see ESTATE 1
estate in expectancy — see ESTATE 1
estate of inheritance — see ESTATE 1
estate on condition — see ESTATE 1
estate plan•ner *n* : a professional or business that provides advice regarding estate planning and sometimes prepares necessary legal documents
estate plan•ning *n* : the arranging for the disposition and management of one's estate at death through the use of wills, trusts, insurance policies, and other devices
estate pur autre vie — see ESTATE 1
estate tail — see ESTATE 1
estate tax *n* : an excise in the form of a percentage of the taxable estate that is imposed on a property owner's right to transfer the property to others after his or her death — called also *succession tax;* see also UNIFIED TRANSFER TAX; compare GIFT TAX, INHERITANCE TAX
es•ti•mat•ed tax *n* : a tax paid usu. quarterly by certain entities (as corporations or trusts) or individuals on income that is not subject to withholding ◊ A declaration of estimated tax is not required for federal income taxes for tax years af-

\ə\abut　\ᵊ\kitten　\ər\further　\a\ash　\ā\ace
\ä\cot, cart　\aú\out　\ch\chin　\e\bet　\ē\easy
\g\go　\i\hit　\ī\ice　\j\job　\ŋ\sing　\ō\go　\ȯ\law
\ȯi\boy　\th\thin　\t͟h\the　\ü\loot　\ú\foot　\y\yet
\zh\vision　*see also* Pronunciation Symbols page

ter 1984. Some states, however, require declarations to be filed.

es·top \es-'täp\ *vt* **es·topped; es·top·ping** [Anglo-French *estop(p)er*, literally, to stop up, from Middle French *estouper*, ultimately from Latin *stuppa* hemp fiber (used for plugging holes)] **:** to impede or bar by estoppel

es·top·pel \e-'stä-pəl\ *n* [probably from Middle French *estoupail* plug, stopper, from *estouper* to stop up — see ESTOP] **1 :** a bar to the use of contradictory words or acts in asserting a claim or right against another; *esp* **:** EQUITABLE ESTOPPEL in this entry — compare WAIVER

equitable estoppel **:** an estoppel that prevents a person from adopting a new position that contradicts a previous position maintained by words, silence, or actions when allowing the new position to be adopted would unfairly harm another person who has relied on the previous position to his or her loss — called also *estoppel in pais* ◊ Traditionally equitable estoppel required that the original position was a misrepresentation which was being denied in the new position. Some jurisdictions retain the requirement of misrepresentation.

estoppel by deed **:** an estoppel precluding a person from denying the truth of any matter that he or she asserted in a deed esp. regarding his or her title to the property — compare *after-acquired title* at TITLE

estoppel by silence **:** an estoppel preventing a person from making an assertion to another's disadvantage when the person previously had the opportunity and duty to speak but failed to do so

estoppel in pais **:** EQUITABLE ESTOPPEL in this entry

file wrapper estoppel **:** an estoppel in patent law barring an applicant who has acquiesced in the rejection of a broad claim in the application for a patent from later asserting that a claim deliberately more restricted is equivalent to the origi-

nal claim — called also *prosecution history estoppel*

promissory estoppel **:** an estoppel that prevents a promisor from denying the existence of a promise when the promisee reasonably and foreseeably relies on the promise and to his or her loss acts or fails to act and suffers an injustice that can only be avoided by enforcement of the promise

prosecution his·to·ry estoppel **:** FILE WRAPPER ESTOPPEL in this entry

quasi estoppel **:** an equitable estoppel that does not require misrepresentation by one party nor reliance or ignorance by the other party

2 a : a bar to the relitigation of issues

collateral estoppel **:** estoppel by judgment barring the relitigation of issues litigated by the same parties on a different cause of action; *broadly* **:** estoppel by judgment barring the relitigation of issues litigated by the same parties on a different or the same cause of action

direct estoppel **:** estoppel by judgment barring the relitigation of issues litigated by the same parties on the same cause of action

estoppel by judgment **:** a bar to the relitigation in a second action of issues already determined in a previous action; *esp* **:** COLLATERAL ESTOPPEL in this entry — called also *estoppel by verdict, issue preclusion;* see also FORMER ADJUDICATION; compare MERGER 4, RES JUDICATA

b : the affirmative defense of estoppel — **by estoppel :** arising from the operation of estoppel ⟨an entrapment *by estoppel*⟩

estoppel by deed — see ESTOPPEL 1
estoppel by judgment — see ESTOPPEL 2a
estoppel by silence — see ESTOPPEL 1
estoppel by verdict : ESTOPPEL BY JUDGMENT at ESTOPPEL 2a
estoppel in pais — see ESTOPPEL 1

es·to·vers \es-'tō-vərz\ *n pl* [Anglo-French, plural of *estover* necessity, allowance, from *estoveir* to be necessary, from Old French, ultimately from Latin *est opus* it is necessary] : necessary supplies; *esp* : wood that a tenant is allowed to take from the landlord's premises (as for necessary repairs or fuel)

et al. *abbr* [Latin *et alia*] and others

eth·i·cal \'e-thi-kəl\ *adj* **1** : of or relating to ethics **2** : conforming to accepted professional standards of conduct — **eth·i·cal·ly** *adv*

ethical consideration *n* : a recommendation made in the ABA Model Code of Professional Responsibility of what would or would not be ethical behavior by a lawyer under specified circumstances — compare DISCIPLINARY RULE

eth·ics \'e-thiks\ *n pl but sing or pl in constr* : the principles of conduct governing an individual or a profession — see also *ABA Model Rules of Professional Conduct* in the IMPORTANT LAWS section

et ux \,et-'əks, -'ək-sər; -'üks, -'ük-ˌsȯr\ [Latin *et uxor*] : and wife

et vir \,et-'vir\ [Latin] : and husband

Eu·clid·e·an zoning \yü-'kli-dē-ən-\ *n* [from *Village of Euclid, Ohio et al. v. Ambler Realty Co.*, 272 U.S. 365 (1926), case in which the Supreme Court upheld the right of a locality to enforce such a system] : a system of zoning whereby a town or community is divided into areas in which specific uses of land are permitted

Eu·ro·cur·ren·cy \,yür-ō-'kər-ən-sē\ *n, pl* **-cies** : currency (as from the U.S. and Japan) held outside its country of origin and used in the money markets of Europe

Eu·ro·dol·lar \,yür-ō-'dä-lər\ *n* : a U.S. dollar held as Eurocurrency

eu·tha·na·sia \,yü-thə-'nā-zhə\ *n* : the act or practice of killing or permitting the death of hopelessly sick or injured persons in a relatively painless way for reasons of mercy — called also *mercy killing* — **eu·tha·na·sic** \-'nā-zik, -sik\ *adj*

evade \i-'vād\ *vt* **evad·ed; evad·ing 1** : to unlawfully fail to pay (taxes) through fraudulent or deceptive means — com-

pare AVOID **2** : to avoid answering directly ⟨trying to ~ the question⟩

eva·sion \i-'vā-zhən\ *n* **1** : a means of evading **2** : the act or an instance of evading — see also TAX EVASION

eva·sive \i-'vā-siv, -ziv\ *adj* : tending or intending to evade ◊ Under Federal Rule of Civil Procedure 37(a)(3), an evasive or incomplete answer to an interrogatory or to a question at a deposition is treated as a failure to answer and may be subject to an opponent's motion to compel an answer. — **eva·sive·ly** *adv* — **eva·sive·ness** *n*

event *n* **1** : something that happens : OCCURRENCE **2** : the issue or outcome of a legal action or proceeding as finally determined

evict \i-'vikt\ *vt* [Medieval Latin *evictus*, past participle of *evincere* to recover (property) by legal process, from Latin, to vanquish, regain possession of] : to put (a tenant) out of property by force, by virtue of a paramount title, or esp. by legal process

evic·tion \i-'vik-shən\ *n* : the dispossession of a tenant of leased property by force or esp. by legal process
actual eviction : eviction that involves the physical expulsion of a tenant
constructive eviction : eviction effected by substantially interfering with a tenant's enjoyment of the property (as by allowing the property to become uninhabitable) so that the tenant is regarded as evicted under law
retaliatory eviction : wrongful eviction of a tenant in reaction to the tenant's exercising of a right (as of reporting health code violations) contrary to the landlord's interest

¹ev·i·dence \'e-və-dəns, -ˌdens\ *n* [Medieval Latin *evidentia*, from Latin, that which is obvious, from *evident-, evidens* clear, obvious, from *e-* out of, from +

\ə\abut \ᵊ\kitten \ər\further \a\ash \ā\ace
\ä\cot, cart \au̇\out \ch\chin \e\bet \ē\easy
\g\go \i\hit \ī\ice \j\job \ŋ\sing \ō\go \ȯ\law
\ȯi\boy \th\thin \t̲h̲\the \ü\loot \u̇\foot \y\yet
\zh\vision *see also* Pronunciation Symbols page

videns, present participle of *videre* to see]
: something that furnishes or tends to furnish proof; *esp* : something (as testimony, writings, or objects) presented at a judicial or administrative proceeding for the purpose of establishing the truth or falsity of an alleged matter of fact — see also ADMISSIBLE, BEST EVIDENCE RULE, EXCLUSIONARY RULE, EXHIBIT, FOUNDATION, OBJECTION, PREPONDERANCE OF THE EVIDENCE, RELEVANT, SCINTILLA, STATE'S EVIDENCE, SUPPRESS, TESTIMONY, WITNESS, *Federal Rules of Evidence* in the IMPORTANT LAWS section; compare ALLEGATION, ARGUMENT, PROOF

best evidence : evidence that is the most reliable and most direct in relationship to what it is offered to prove — see also BEST EVIDENCE RULE

char·ac·ter evidence : evidence of a particular human trait (as honesty or peacefulness) of a party or witness — see also *character witness* at WITNESS ◊ Under the Federal Rules of Evidence, character evidence generally may not be used to prove that a person acted in accordance with that character. It is admissible for that purpose, however, if a criminal defendant offers it about himself or herself or about the victim, or if the prosecution offers evidence to rebut the defendant's evidence in either of those circumstances. The prosecution may also rebut a claim of self-defense by presenting evidence of the peaceful character of the victim. Additionally, the character of a witness with regard to truthfulness may be attacked or supported by opinion or by evidence of reputation.

circumstantial evidence : evidence that tends to prove a factual matter by proving other events or circumstances from which the occurrence of the matter at issue can be reasonably inferred — compare DIRECT EVIDENCE in this entry

clear and convincing evidence : evidence showing a high probability of truth of the factual matter at issue — compare PREPONDERANCE OF THE EVIDENCE, REASONABLE DOUBT

com·mu·ni·ca·tive evidence \kə-'myü-nə-kə-tiv-, -ˌkā-tiv-\ : TESTIMONIAL EVIDENCE in this entry

competent evidence : evidence that is admissible, relevant, and material to the factual matter at issue

corroborating evidence : evidence that is independent of and different from but that supplements and strengthens evidence already presented as proof of a factual matter — called also *corroborative evidence;* compare CUMULATIVE EVIDENCE in this entry

cumulative evidence : evidence that is of the same kind as evidence already offered as proof of the same factual matter — compare CORROBORATING EVIDENCE in this entry

de·mon·stra·tive evidence : evidence in the form of objects (as maps, diagrams, or models) that has in itself no probative value but is used to illustrate and clarify the factual matter at issue; *broadly* : PHYSICAL EVIDENCE in this entry — called also *illustrative evidence*

derivative evidence : evidence obtained as a result of the unlawful gathering of primary evidence — called also *indirect evidence, secondary evidence;* see also FRUIT OF THE POISONOUS TREE

direct evidence : evidence that if believed immediately establishes the factual matter to be proved by it without the need for inferences; *esp* : evidence of a factual matter offered by a witness whose knowledge of the matter was obtained through the use of his or her senses (as sight or hearing) — compare CIRCUMSTANTIAL EVIDENCE in this entry

evidence in chief : evidence that is to be used by a party in making its case in chief

exculpatory evidence : evidence that tends to clear a defendant from fault or guilt — see also BRADY MATERIAL ◊ The prosecution in a criminal case is obligated to disclose to the defense any exculpatory evidence in its possession.

extrinsic evidence 1 : evidence regarding an agreement that is not included in the written version of the agreement ◊ A court may use extrinsic evidence to make sense of an ambiguity in a writing subject to some limitations. 2 : evidence about a witness's character obtained from the testimony of other witnesses rather than from cross-examination of the witness himself or herself ◊ A witness may not be impeached by the use of extrinsic evidence.

hearsay evidence : a statement made out of court and not under oath and offered in evidence as proof that what is stated is true : HEARSAY

il·lus·tra·tive evidence : DEMONSTRATIVE EVIDENCE in this entry

impeachment evidence : evidence that may be used to impeach a witness because it tends to harm the witness's credibility

indirect evidence : DERIVATIVE EVIDENCE in this entry

intrinsic evidence : evidence that exists within a writing ⟨the will contains ample *intrinsic evidence* of the testator's intent —*Stoner v. Custer*, 251 N.E.2d 668 (1968)⟩ — compare EXTRINSIC EVIDENCE in this entry

material evidence : evidence that is likely to affect the determination of a matter or issue; *specif* : evidence that warrants reopening of a claim or reversal of a conviction because but for the circumstance that the evidence was unavailable the outcome of the first proceeding would have been different

no evidence : evidence presented that is insufficient to prove a matter of esp. vital fact : a point of error that insufficient evidence has been presented to support a finding

parol evidence : evidence of matters spoken (as an oral agreement) that are related to but not included in a writing — see also PAROL EVIDENCE RULE

physical evidence : tangible evidence (as a weapon, document, or visible injury) that is in some way related to the incident that gave rise to the case — called also *real evidence;* compare DEMONSTRATIVE EVIDENCE and TESTIMONIAL EVIDENCE in this entry

presumptive evidence : PRIMA FACIE EVIDENCE in this entry

prima facie evidence : evidence that is sufficient to prove a factual matter at issue and justify a favorable judgment on that issue unless rebutted

primary evidence 1 : BEST EVIDENCE in this entry 2 : evidence obtained as a direct result of an unlawful search

real evidence : PHYSICAL EVIDENCE in this entry

rebuttal evidence : evidence that tends to refute or discredit an opponent's evidence

relevant evidence : evidence that tends to prove or disprove any issue of fact that is of consequence to the case

secondary evidence : DERIVATIVE EVIDENCE in this entry

substantial evidence : evidence greater than a scintilla of evidence that a reasonable person would find sufficient to support a conclusion

substantive evidence : evidence offered to prove a factual issue rather than merely for impeachment

testimonial evidence : evidence given in writing or speech or in another way that expresses the person's thoughts — compare PHYSICAL EVIDENCE in this entry ◊ Only testimonial evidence is protected by the Fifth Amendment's privilege against self-incrimination.

— in evidence : as evidence ⟨introduced a letter *in evidence*⟩

²**evidence** *vt* **-denced; -denc·ing** : to provide evidence of

evidence in chief — see EVIDENCE

ev·i·den·tial \ˌe-və-'den-chəl\ *adj* : EVIDENTIARY 1 — **ev·i·den·tial·ly** *adv*

ev·i·den·tia·ry \ˌe-və-'den-chə-rē, -chē-

\ə\abut \ə\kitten \ər\further \a\ash \ā\ace
\ä\cot, cart \au̇\out \ch\chin \e\bet \ē\easy
\g\go \i\hit \ī\ice \j\job \ŋ\sing \ō\go \ȯ\law
\ȯi\boy \th\thin \th\the \ü\loot \u̇\foot \y\yet
\zh\vision *see also* Pronunciation Symbols page

‚er-ē\ *adj* **1** : being, relating to, or affording evidence ⟨photographs of ∼ value⟩ **2** : conducted so that evidence may be presented ⟨an ∼ hearing⟩ — **ev·i·den·tia·ri·ly** *adv*

evidentiary fact — see FACT

evidentiary harpoon *n* [from the comparison of such evidence to a harpoon, which can be retracted after it has injured its target] : evidence consisting esp. of a police officer's statement that is improper and is knowingly offered by the prosecution to prejudice the defendant in the eyes of the jury

ex- *prefix* [Latin *ex* from, out of] : free from : without

Ex. *abbr* Exchequer

ex ae·quo et bo·no \‚eks-'ē-kwō-et-'bō-nō, -'ī-kwō-\ [Latin] : according to what is equitable and good : on the merits of the case — often used in international law when a matter is to be decided according to principles of equity rather than by points of law

ex·am·i·na·tion *n* : the act or process of examining; *esp* : a formal questioning esp. in a court proceeding — see also CROSS-EXAMINATION, DIRECT EXAMINATION, RECROSS-EXAMINATION, REDIRECT EXAMINATION; compare AFFIDAVIT, DEPOSITION

ex·am·ine *vt* **ex·am·ined; ex·am·in·ing 1** : to investigate or inspect closely ⟨∼ the title⟩ — compare AUDIT **2** : to question closely esp. in a court proceeding — compare DEPOSE

ex·am·in·er *n* : a person who examines: as **a** : a court officer empowered to administer an oath and take testimony **b** : a person whose work is to inspect usu. a specified thing or situation ⟨a bank ∼⟩

ex·cept \ik-'sept\ *vt* : to take or leave out (as from insurance coverage or a deed) : EXCLUDE ⟨specifically ∼*ed* the air carriers and unions from the provisions — M. A. Kelly⟩ ∼ *vi* : OBJECT; *esp* : to file a bill of exceptions or make a formal exception ⟨∼*ed* to the judge's order⟩

ex·cep·tion *n* **1** : something that is ex-

cepted or excluded; *esp* : a situation to which a rule does not apply ⟨the supreme Court shall have appellate jurisdiction, both as to law and fact, with such ∼*s*, and under such regulations as the Congress shall make —*U.S. Constitution* art. III⟩ **2** : an act of excepting; *esp* : exclusion of a section of real property from a conveyance — compare RESERVATION **3** : a usu. written objection esp. to a judge's ruling ⟨demurrers, pleas, and ∼*s* for insufficiency of a pleading shall not be used —*Federal Rules of Civil Procedure* Rule 7(c)⟩ — used esp. in equity proceedings

ex·cess *adj* : more than a usual or specified amount; *specif* : additional to an amount specified under another insurance policy ⟨∼ coverage⟩ ⟨∼ insurance⟩

ex·ces·sive *adj* : exceeding what is proper, necessary, or normal; *specif* : being out of proportion to the offense ⟨∼ bail⟩

excessive verdict — see VERDICT

ex·change *n* **1 a** : a giving of something of value (as real property) in return for something of equal value (as money or property of a like kind) **b** *in the civil law of Louisiana* : a giving of something of value in return for something of equal value except money — compare SALE **2** : an organized market or center for trading in securities or commodities

ex·che·quer \'eks-‚che-kər, iks-'che-\ *n* [Anglo-French *eschecker, eschequ(i)er*, from Old French *eschequier* royal treasury, reckoning board or cloth marked with squares, literally, chessboard, from *eschec* chess] **1** *cap* : a royal office in medieval England at first responsible for the collection and management of the royal revenue and later for the adjudication of revenue cases **2** *cap* : a former superior court having law and equity jurisdiction in England and Wales over primarily revenue cases and now merged with the Queen's Bench Division of the High Court of Justice — called also *Court of the Exchequer* ◊ The Exchequer was created in England by the Norman kings. In addition to being divided into a court of common law and a court of equity, at one point the Exchequer also had jurisdiction over all actions, except those involving real property, between two subjects of the Crown. In 1841, the Exchequer's equity jurisdiction, except over revenue cases, was transferred to the Court of Chancery, and in 1881 the Exchequer was merged into the Queen's Bench Division of the High Court of Justice. **3** *often cap* : the office in Great Britain and Northern Ireland responsible for the collection and care of the national revenue

ex•cise \'ek-ˌsīz, -ˌsīs\ *n* **1** : a tax levied on the manufacture, sale, or consumption of a commodity — compare INCOME TAX, PROPERTY TAX **2** : any of various taxes on privileges often assessed in the form of a license or other fee — see also *Article I* of the CONSTITUTION in the back matter; compare DIRECT TAX — **excise** *vt*

excise tax *n* : EXCISE

ex•cit•ed ut•ter•ance *n* : a statement that concerns a startling event (as a physical assault) and that is made by a person while under stress caused by the event — see also RES GESTAE, *spontaneous declaration* at DECLARATION; compare *dying declaration* at DECLARATION ◊ Excited utterances are an exception to the hearsay rule. They may be admitted as evidence even if the declarant is available as a witness.

ex•clud•able \ik-'sklü-də-bəl\ *adj* : subject to being excluded ⟨because the witness was available, the hearsay testimony was ~ —*National Law Journal*⟩ — **ex•clud•abil•i•ty** \ik-ˌsklü-də-'bi-lə-tē\ *n*

ex•clude \ik-'sklüd\ *vt* **ex•clud•ed; ex•clud•ing 1** : to prevent or restrict the entry or admission of ⟨~ hearsay evidence⟩ **2** : to remove from participation, consideration, or inclusion (as in insurance coverage) ⟨the *excluded* perils include acts of war⟩

ex•clu•sion \ik-'sklü-zhən\ *n* **1** : the act of excluding or state of being excluded; *specif* : refusal of entry into the U.S. by immigration officials ⟨review of deportation and ~ orders⟩ — compare DEPORTATION **2** : something that excludes

or is excluded: as **a** : a part of an insurance contract that excludes specified risks from coverage — compare CONDITION, DECLARATION **b** : an amount that is excluded from tax liability ⟨a $10,000 annual per donee ~ for gifts —W. M. McGovern, Jr. *et al.*⟩ — compare CREDIT, DEDUCTION, EXEMPTION — **ex•clu•sion•ary** \-zhə-ˌner-ē\ *adj*

exclusionary rule *n* : any of various rules that exclude or suppress evidence; *specif* : a rule of evidence that excludes or suppresses evidence obtained in violation of a defendant's constitutional rights — see also FRUIT OF THE POISONOUS TREE, GOOD FAITH EXCEPTION, *Mapp v. Ohio* and *Wong Sun v. United States* in the IMPORTANT CASES section ◊ The U.S. Supreme Court established the rule that evidence gathered by a governmental agent in violation of esp. the Fourth and Fifth Amendments to the U.S. Constitution cannot be admitted against a defendant. The rule is available primarily in criminal trials or quasi-criminal proceedings (as punitive administrative hearings) and must also be observed by state courts. There are various statutory exclusionary rules in addition to the rule established by the Supreme Court.

ex•clu•sive *adj* **1 a** : excluding or having power to exclude others ⟨~ right to their respective writings and discoveries —*U.S. Constitution* art. I⟩ **b** : being independent from or not shared by others : SOLE ⟨~ control⟩ ⟨~ use⟩ **2** : limiting or limited to possession, ownership, or use by a single individual or group ⟨an ~ contract⟩ ⟨an ~ lease⟩

exclusive agency — see AGENCY 2a

exclusive agency listing — see LISTING

exclusive agent — see AGENT

exclusive easement — see EASEMENT

exclusive jurisdiction — see JURISDICTION

\ə\abut	\ᵊ\kitten	\ər\further	\a\ash	\ā\ace
\ä\cot, cart	\au̇\out	\ch\chin	\e\bet	\ē\easy
\g\go	\i\hit	\ī\ice	\j\job	\ŋ\sing	\ō\go	\ȯ\law
\ȯi\boy	\th\thin	\t͟h\the	\ü\loot	\u̇\foot	\y\yet
\zh\vision	*see also* Pronunciation Symbols page

exclusive right to sell listing — see LISTING

ex·con·trac·tu \'eks-kən-'trak-tü, -tyü; -kȯn-'träk-tü\ *adj* [Latin] : arising from or based on a contract ⟨damages *ex contractu*⟩ — compare EX DELICTO

ex·cul·pate \'ek-skəl-ˌpāt, ek-'skəl-\ *vt* -pat·ed; -pat·ing [Medieval Latin *exculpare*, from Latin *ex*- out of + *culpa* blame] : to clear from alleged fault or guilt ⟨a statement . . . offered to ~ the accused is not admissible unless corroborating circumstances clearly indicate the trustworthiness of the statement —*Federal Rules of Evidence* Rule 804(b)(3)⟩ — compare ACQUIT, EXONERATE — **ex·cul·pa·tion** \ˌek-skəl-'pā-shən\ *n*

ex·cul·pa·to·ry \ek-'skəl-pə-ˌtōr-ē\ *adj* : tending or serving to exculpate ⟨an ~ clause in a contract⟩ — compare INCULPATORY

exculpatory evidence — see EVIDENCE

exculpatory no doctrine *n* : a doctrine in federal criminal law: an individual cannot be charged with making a false statement if the statement is a false denial of guilt made in response to a federal investigator's question ◊ This doctrine is based on the Fifth Amendment protection against self-incrimination, and is often used as a defense to a charge of knowingly making a false statement. The doctrine is recognized in most federal Courts of Appeals.

ex·cus·able *adj* : having a basis for being excused or justified

excusable homicide — see HOMICIDE

excusable neglect *n* : the failure of a party to follow a required procedure in a timely fashion that results from a circumstance (as an accident) which is considered by the court to be sufficient reason to excuse that party — compare UNAVOIDABLE CASUALTY ◊ Excusable neglect allows a party to seek relief from a default judgment, to file late, or to be granted a deadline extension.

ex·cus·al \ik-'skyü-zəl\ *n* : the act or an instance of excusing ⟨~ of a juror⟩ — compare CHALLENGE

¹ex·cuse \ik-'skyüz\ *vb* **ex·cused; ex·cus-**ing *vt* **1** : to grant exemption or release to ⟨*excused* the prospective juror⟩ ⟨*excused* the witness after an hour of testimony⟩ **2** : JUSTIFY ~ *vi* : to serve as an excuse or justification ⟨exigent circumstances may ~ —J. J. White and R. S. Summers⟩

²ex·cuse \ik-'skyüs\ *n* **1** : EXCUSAL **2 a** : a circumstance that allows for release under the law from an obligation, duty, or contractual liability — compare ACT OF GOD, FORCE MAJEURE, FORTUITOUS EVENT, IMPOSSIBILITY OF PERFORMANCE **b** : a circumstance (as a physical threat) that grants immunity for otherwise tortious or criminal conduct — compare JUSTIFICATION, PRIVILEGE

ex·de·lic·to \'eks-di-'lik-tō, -dā-'lēk-tō\ *adj* [Latin, of or by reason of a wrong] : arising from or based on a tort or delict (as a breach of duty) ⟨the action is *ex delicto*⟩ — compare EX CONTRACTU

ex–dis·tri·bu·tion \ˌeks-ˌdis-trə-'byü-shən\ *adv or adj* : without the right to a pending distribution (as of capital gains from a mutual fund) ⟨shares traded ~⟩

ex–dividend \'eks-\ *adv or adj* : without a dividend ◊ A stock is said to be sold "ex-dividend" when the sale occurs just before the next dividend on the stock is due to be paid, so that the payment date comes after the order to buy is executed but before the stock changes hands. In such cases, the dividend is paid to the seller, and the price of the stock is reduced by an appropriate amount.

ex·e·cute \'ek-si-ˌkyüt\ *vt* **-cut·ed; -cut·ing 1** : PERFORM: as **a** : to carry out fully ⟨includes not only *executed* violence, but also threatened violence —*Louisiana Civil Code*⟩ **b** : to do what is provided or required by ⟨~ a contract⟩ ⟨~ a search warrant⟩ **c** : to deem (a use in property) to confer full seisin in a cestui que use by operation of the Statute of Uses **2** : to perform what is required to give validity to; *esp* : to complete (as by signing and delivering) in proper form ⟨~ a note⟩ ⟨~ a deed⟩ **3** : to put to death in compliance with a judicial death sentence

executed trust — see TRUST

ex·e·cu·tion \ˌek-si-'kyü-shən\ *n* **1** : the act or process of executing ⟨witnessed the ~ of the will⟩ **2** : a putting to death as fulfillment of a judicial death sentence **3** : the process of enforcing a judgment (as against a debtor); *also* : a judicial writ (as fieri facias) by which an officer is empowered to carry a judgment into effect — see also LEVY

ex·e·cu·tion·er \ˌek-si-'kyü-shə-nər\ *n* : one who puts another to death in fulfillment of a judicial death sentence

execution sale — see SALE

¹ex·ec·u·tive *adj* **1** : of or relating to the execution or carrying out of laws ⟨serving a warrant is an ~ function⟩; *esp* : belonging to the branch of government that is charged with such powers as diplomatic representation, overseeing the execution of laws, and appointment of officials — see also ADMINISTRATIVE, *Article II* of the CONSTITUTION in the back matter; compare JUDICIAL, LEGISLATIVE **2 a** : of or relating to execution **b** : having administrative or managerial responsibility ⟨an ~ director⟩ **3** : of, relating to, or issued by an executive ⟨an ~ pardon⟩

²executive *n* **1 a** : the executive branch of a government — compare JUDICIARY, LEGISLATURE **b** : the person or persons making up that branch — see also GOVERNOR, MAYOR, PRESIDENT **2** : a person who exercises administrative or managerial control

executive agreement *n* : an agreement (as an armistice) between the U.S. and a foreign government that is made by the president and usu. deals with a subject within the president's powers — compare TREATY ◊ An executive agreement does not carry the same weight as a treaty unless it is supported by a joint resolution. Unlike a treaty, an executive agreement can supersede a conflicting state law but not a federal law.

executive immunity — see IMMUNITY

executive order *n* : an order issued by a government's executive on the basis of authority specifically granted to the executive branch (as by the U.S. Constitu-

tion or a congressional act) ⟨the National Security Agency was created by an *executive order*⟩ — compare PROCLAMATION, STATUTE ◊ An executive order from the president does not have the force of law until it is printed in the Federal Register.

executive power — see POWER 2a

executive privilege — see PRIVILEGE 1b

executive session *n* : a closed session (as of the U.S. Senate) in which executive business (as consideration of appointments or ratification of treaties) is taken care of — compare LEGISLATIVE SESSION

ex·ec·u·tor \ig-'ze-kyə-tər\ *n* : a person named by a testator to execute or carry out the instructions in a will — compare ADMINISTRATOR

executor fund — see FUND 1

ex·ec·u·to·ry \ig-'ze-kyə-ˌtōr-ē\ *adj* : designed or of such a nature as to be performed in the future or to take effect on a future contingency ⟨cancellation of the ~ portion of the contract —J. J. White and R. S. Summers⟩ — compare CONTINGENT

executory accord *n* : ACCORD 3

executory contract — see CONTRACT

executory devise — see DEVISE

executory interest — see INTEREST 1

executory limitation *n* : a limitation that creates an executory interest ⟨a fee simple subject to an *executory limitation*⟩ — see also *executory interest* at INTEREST

executory remainder — see REMAINDER

executory trust — see TRUST

ex·ec·u·trix \ig-'ze-kyə-ˌtriks\ *n, pl* **ex·ec·u·tri·ces** \ˌze-kyə-'trī-ˌsēz\ *or* **ex·ec·u·trix·es** \-'ze-kyə-ˌtrik-səz\ : a woman who is an executor

exemplary damages — see DAMAGE 2

¹ex·empt \ig-'zempt\ *adj* : free or released from some obligation or duty to which others are subject : not subject or liable ⟨certain properties are declared to be ~

\ə\abut	\ᵊ\kitten	\ər\further	\a\ash	\ā\ace
\ä\cot, cart	\aů\out	\ch\chin	\e\bet	\ē\easy
\g\go	\i\hit	\ī\ice	\j\job	\ŋ\sing	\ō\go	\ô\law
\ôi\boy	\th\thin	\th\the	\ü\loot	\ů\foot	\y\yet
\zh\vision	*see also* Pronunciation Symbols page			

and cannot be taken by a person's creditors —J. H. Williamson⟩

²**exempt** *vt* : to release or exclude from some liability (as in taxation), obligation, or duty to which others are subject ⟨~*s* the income of a spendthrift trust —W. M. McGovern, Jr. *et al.*⟩

exempted security — see SECURITY

ex·emp·tion \ig-'zemp-shən\ *n* **1** : the act of exempting or state of being exempt **2** : one that exempts or is exempted: as **a** : an amount of income exempted from taxation that may be deducted from adjusted gross income under the tax laws — see also *Internal Revenue Code* in the IMPORTANT LAWS section; compare DEDUCTION, EXCLUSION, TAX CREDIT

de·pen·den·cy exemption \də-'pen-dən-sē-\ : an exemption that is allowed for each dependent who qualifies under the tax laws (as sections 151 and 152 of the Internal Revenue Code) ◊ Under the federal income tax laws, the dependency exemption is allowed for each dependent whose gross income is less than the exemption or who is a child of the taxpayer and is under 19 or a student under 24.

personal exemption : an exemption that is allowed for the taxpayer or for the taxpayer and spouse if filing a joint return

b : the right created by federal and state laws to exempt specified types of property from a bankruptcy estate ⟨precludes the debtor from using the ~*s* in the Bankruptcy Code⟩; *also* : a type of property that may be claimed as exempt — see also *Bankruptcy Code* in the IMPORTANT LAWS section **c** : HOMESTEAD EXEMPTION

¹**ex·er·cise** \'ek-sər-ˌsīz\ *n* **1** : the discharge of an official function or professional occupation **2** : the act or an instance of carrying out the terms of an agreement (as an option)

²**exercise** *vt* **-cised; -cis·ing 1** : to make effective in action ⟨*exercising* power⟩ **2** : to bring to bear ⟨~ influence⟩ **3** : to implement the terms of (as an option) — **ex·er-**

cis·able \ˌek-sər-'sī-zə-bəl, 'ek-sər-ˌsī-\ *adj*

ex facie \ˌeks-'fā-shē-ˌē, -'fä-kē-e\ *adv* [New Latin, literally, from the appearance] : on its face ⟨valid *ex facie*⟩ — compare PRIMA FACIE

ex·haust *vt* : to use up or consume entirely: as **a** : to try all of (available remedies) ⟨the applicant has ~*ed* the remedies available in the court of the State —*U.S. Code*⟩ **b** : to bring (a claim) through all available prior levels of review ⟨each of his claims would now be ~*ed* —W. R. LaFave and J. H. Israel⟩

ex·haus·tion *n* : the act or process of exhausting ⟨even after the ~ of direct appellate review —W. R. LaFave and J. H. Israel⟩; *specif* : EXHAUSTION OF REMEDIES

exhaustion of remedies : a doctrine of civil and criminal procedure: a remedy cannot be sought in another forum (as a federal district court) until the remedies or claims have been exhausted in the forum having original jurisdiction (as a state court, tribal court, or administrative agency) — compare *primary jurisdiction* at JURISDICTION ◊ The doctrine of exhaustion of remedies was first developed by judges in case law based on comity. It is used primarily in administrative law cases and federal habeas corpus cases, and it is now incorporated in the federal habeas corpus statute (section 2254 of title 28 of the U.S. Code). It may also be applied when an administrative agency has original jurisdiction over a claim. It is used in proceedings in tribal courts.

¹**ex·hib·it** *vt* **1** : to submit (as a document) to a court or officer in the course of proceedings; *also* : to present or offer officially or in legal form **2** : to present to view or display outwardly — **ex·hib·i·tor** *n*

²**exhibit** *n* **1 a** : a document or object produced and identified in court as evidence **b** : a document labeled with an identifying mark (as a number or letter) and appended to a writing (as a brief) to which

it is relevant **2** : something exhibited **3** : an act or instance of exhibiting

ex·i·gen·cy \'ek-sə-jən-sē, ik-'si-jən-sē\ *n, pl* **-cies 1** : that which is required in a particular situation — usu. used in pl. **2 a** : the quality or state of being exigent **b** : a state of affairs that makes urgent demands

ex·i·gent \'ek-sə-jənt\ *adj* : requiring immediate aid or action — see also EXIGENT CIRCUMSTANCES

exigent circumstances *n pl* : circumstances that are of such urgency as to justify a warrantless entry, search, or seizure by police when a warrant would ordinarily be required — compare KNOCK AND ANNOUNCE RULE, *no-knock search warrant* at WARRANT

ex mal·e·fic·io \'eks-,ma-lə-'fi-shē-ō, -,mä-le-'fē-kē-ō\ *adj* [Late Latin, in the phrase *obligatio ex maleficio* obligation arising from a misdeed] : arising from wrongdoing : created by law in response to a wrongdoing ⟨a trustee *ex maleficio*⟩

ex of·fic·io \'eks-ə-'fi-shē-ō, -sē-ō\ *adv or adj* [Late Latin] : by virtue or because of an office ⟨the Vice President serves *ex officio* as president of the Senate⟩ ⟨an *ex officio* member of the board⟩

ex·on·er·ate \ig-'zä-nə-,rāt, eg-\ *vt* **-at·ed; -at·ing** [Latin *exonerare* to relieve, free, discharge, from *ex-* out + *onerare* to burden, from *oner-, onus* load] **1** : to relieve esp. of a charge, obligation, or hardship **2** : to clear from accusation or blame — compare ACQUIT, EXCULPATE

ex·on·er·a·tion \ig-,zä-nə-'rā-shən, eg-\ *n* **1** : the act of disburdening or discharging (as from a charge, liability, obligation, duty, or responsibility); *also* : the state of being so freed **2 a** : the right of a person who has paid a debt for which he or she is only secondarily liable to be reimbursed by the person primarily liable **b** : the right of a surety to require a person or estate that is subject to a liability for which the surety is secondarily liable to discharge the liability thus relieving the surety; *also* : the equitable remedy by which the surety compels discharge of the liability

Ex. Ord. *abbr* executive order

exp. *abbr* expense, export, express

ex par·te \'eks-'pär-tē, -tā\ *adv or adj* [Medieval Latin, on behalf (of)] : on behalf of or involving only one party to a legal matter and in the absence of and usu. without notice to the other party ⟨an *ex parte* motion⟩ ⟨relief granted *ex parte*⟩ — used in citations to indicate the party seeking judicial relief in a case ⟨*Ex Parte* Jones, 7 U.S. 2 (1866)⟩ — compare IN RE, INTER PARTES

ex·pa·tri·ate \ek-'spā-trē-,āt\ *vb* **-at·ed; -at·ing** *vt* : to voluntarily withdraw (oneself) from allegiance to one's native country ~ *vi* : to renounce allegiance to one's country and abandon one's nationality voluntarily — **ex·pa·tri·ate** \-trē-ət\ *n* — **ex·pa·tri·a·tion** \ek-,spā-trē-'ā-shən\ *n*

ex·pec·tan·cy *n, pl* **-cies** : something expected: as **a** : an interest held by a person who may receive something (as a bequest) in the future but has no enforceable right to it **b** : the benefit that will be received from a contract if performed

expectancy damages *n pl* : EXPECTATION DAMAGES at DAMAGE 2

expectancy interest *n* : EXPECTATION INTEREST at INTEREST 1

expectation damages — see DAMAGE 2

expectation interest — see INTEREST 1

ex·pec·ta·tion of privacy : a belief in the existence of freedom from unwanted esp. governmental intrusion in some thing or place — compare ZONE OF PRIVACY ◊ In order to successfully challenge a search or seizure as a violation of the Fourth Amendment to the U.S. Constitution, a plaintiff must show that he or she had manifested a subjective expectation of privacy in the area of the search or the object seized and that the expectation is one that society is willing to recognize as reasonable or legitimate.

ex·pen·di·ture \ik-'spen-di-chər, -,chür\ *n*
1 : the act or process of paying out **2**
: something paid out — see also CAPITAL
EXPENDITURE

¹**ex·pense** *n* **:** financial burden or outlay;
specif **:** an item of business outlay chargeable against revenue for a specific period
   busi·ness expense **:** an expense made
   in furtherance of one's business esp. as
   part of the cost of operating a business in
   the taxable year in which the expense is
   incurred — compare CAPITAL EXPENSE
   and PERSONAL EXPENSE in this entry
   ◊ Business expenses are generally tax
   deductible in the year the expense is
   incurred.
   capital expense **:** an expense made in a
   business that will provide a long-term
   benefit **:** CAPITAL EXPENDITURE ◊ Capital expenses are not tax deductible as
   business expenses but may be used for
   depreciation or amortization.
   mov·ing expense **:** an expense incurred
   in changing one's residence that is tax
   deductible if incurred for business reasons (as when one's job requires relocation)
   ordinary and necessary expense **:** an
   expense that is normal or customary and
   helpful and appropriate for the operation of a particular business or trade and
   that is made during the taxable year —
   called also *ordinary and necessary business expense* ◊ Ordinary and necessary
   expenses are tax deductible.
   per·son·al expense **:** an expense incurred in the course of one's personal affairs as distinguished from the course of
   one's employment or the operation of a
   business — compare BUSINESS EXPENSE
   in this entry ◊ Personal expenses are
   usu. not tax deductible.
²**expense** *vt* **ex·pensed; ex·pens·ing 1 :** to
charge with expenses **2 :** to write off as
an expense
ex·pert *n* **:** a person with special or superior skill or knowledge in a particular
area — see also *expert witness* at WIT
NESS

expert witness — see WITNESS
ex·port \ek-'spōrt, 'ek-,spōrt\ *vt* **:** to carry
or send (as a commodity) to some other
place (as another country) ~ *vi* **:** to send
something abroad — **ex·port** \'ek-,spōrt\
n — **ex·por·ta·bil·i·ty** \ek-,spōr-tə-'bi-lə-
tē\ *n* — **ex·por·ta·ble** \ek-'spōr-tə-bəl\
adj
ex·pose *vt* **ex·posed; ex·pos·ing 1 :** to
subject to risk from a harmful action or
condition: as **a :** to make (one) open to
liability or financial loss **b :** to leave
(a child) uncared-for and lacking shelter from the elements **2 :** to cause to be
visible or open to view: as **a :** to offer
publicly for sale ⟨all of which I shall ~
for sale at public auction —*Detroit Law
Journal*⟩ **b :** to purposely uncover (one's
private body parts) or leave open to view
in a place or situation in which such conduct is likely to be deemed offensive or
indecent esp. as set forth by statute — see
also INDECENT EXPOSURE
¹**ex post facto** \'eks-,pōst-'fak-tō\ *adv* [Late
Latin, literally, from a thing done afterward] **:** after the fact **:** RETROACTIVELY
⟨cannot judge *ex post facto*⟩
²**ex post facto** *adj* **1 :** done, made, or formulated after the fact **:** RETROACTIVE **2**
: of or relating to an ex post facto law ⟨the
chief concerns of the *ex post facto* ban —
L. H. Tribe⟩
ex post facto clause *n, often cap
E&P&F&C* **:** the clause in Article I, Section 9 of the U.S. Constitution forbidding
Congress from passing any ex post facto
laws
ex post facto law *n* **:** a civil or criminal law
with retroactive effect; *esp* **:** a law that
retroactively alters a defendant's rights
esp. by criminalizing and imposing punishment for an act that was not criminal or
punishable at the time it was committed,
by increasing the severity of a crime from
its level at the time the crime was committed, by increasing the punishment for
a crime from the punishment imposed at
the time the crime was committed, or by
taking away from the protections (as evidentiary protection) afforded the defen-

dant by the law as it existed when the act was committed ◊ Ex post facto laws are prohibited by Article I, Section 9 of the U.S. Constitution.

ex·po·sure *n* **1** : the fact or condition of being exposed; *also* : the possibility of loss caused by an outside source — used in insurance **2** : the act or an instance of exposing **3** : something that exposes someone or something; *esp* : something (as a condition, situation, or action) that creates a risk of financial loss esp. for which one may be insured ⟨two forms of insurance are needed to cover the ~ fully —R. I. Mehr⟩; *also* : the extent to which one is at risk

¹ex·press *adj* : directly and distinctly stated or expressed rather than implied or left to inference — compare IMPLIED

²express *vt* : to make known (one's thoughts, ideas, or opinions) by words, conduct, or symbols — see also EXPRESSION

express agency — see AGENCY 2a

express authority — see AUTHORITY

express condition — see CONDITION

express contract — see CONTRACT

expressed authority *n* : EXPRESS AUTHORITY at AUTHORITY

ex·pres·sion *n* **1** : an act, process, or instance of representing or conveying in words or some other medium : SPEECH ⟨protected ~ under the First Amendment⟩ **2** : a mode or means of expressing an idea, opinion, or thought ◊ An expression is protectible under copyright law, but an idea is not.

ex·pres·sio uni·us est ex·clu·sio al·ter·i·us \ik-'spre-shē-ō-yü-'nī-əs-,est-ik-'sklü-zē-ō-ól-'tir-ē-əs, ek-'spre-sē-ō-ü-'nē-ùs-,est-ek-'sklü-sē-ō-äl-te-'rē-ùs\ [New Latin, the explicit mention of one (thing) is the exclusion of another] : a principle in statutory construction: when one or more things of a class are expressly mentioned others of the same class are excluded

ex·pres·sive *adj* **1** : of or relating to expression **2** : serving to express or represent ⟨~ conduct protected by the First

Amendment⟩ — **ex·pres·sive·ly** *adv* — **ex·pres·sive·ness** *n*

ex·press·ly *adv* : in an express manner : in definite and distinct terms ⟨acceptance is ~ conditional⟩

express malice *n* : ACTUAL MALICE 1 at MALICE

express notice — see NOTICE

express trust — see TRUST

express warranty — see WARRANTY 2a

ex·pro·pri·ate \ek-'sprō-prē-,āt\ *vt* **-at·ed; -at·ing** : to take (property) of an individual in the exercise of state sovereignty (as by eminent domain) — **ex·pro·pri·a·tion** \ek-,sprō-prē-'ā-shən\ *n*

ex·punc·tion \ik-'spəŋk-shən\ *n* : the act of expunging : the state of being expunged

ex·punge \ik-'spənj\ *vt* **ex·punged; ex·pung·ing** : to cancel out or destroy completely ⟨~ the court records of an acquitted defendant⟩ — **ex·punge·ment** *n*

ex rel. *abbr* ex relatione

ex re·la·tio·ne \'eks-ri-,lä-shē-'ō-nē, -re-,lä-tē-'ō-nä\ *prep* [Medieval Latin] : by or on the relation or information of ◊ The abbreviation for *ex relatione, ex rel.,* is used in the title of informations and special proceedings to designate the interested individual, called the relator, at whose instance the state or public officer is acting.

ex–rights \,eks-'rīts\ *adv or adj* : without rights ◊ The purchaser of stock traded ex-rights does not acquire the right to purchase new securities at a discount prior to their public issuance because such right was retained by the seller.

exrx *abbr* executrix

ex·ten·sion *n* : an increase in length of time; *specif* : an increase in the time allowed under an agreement

ex·tin·guish *vt* **1** : to cause the nonexistence of : do away with **2** : to cause (as a claim or right) to be void : NULLIFY

\ə\abut　\ᵊ\kitten　\ər\further　\a\ash　\ā\ace
\ä\cot, cart　\au̇\out　\ch\chin　\e\bet　\ē\easy
\g\go　\i\hit　\ī\ice　\j\job　\ŋ\sing　\ō\go　\ȯ\law
\ȯi\boy　\th\thin　\t͟h\the　\ü\loot　\u̇\foot　\y\yet
\zh\vision　*see also* Pronunciation Symbols page

3 : to get rid of (a debt or other liability) by payment or other compensatory adjustment — **ex·tin·guish·able** *adj* — **ex·tin·guish·ment** *n*

ex·tort \ik-'stort\ *vt* [Latin *extortus*, past participle of *extorquere* to remove by twisting, obtain by force, from *ex-* out + *torquere* to twist] **:** to obtain (as money) from a person by force, intimidation, or undue or unlawful use of authority or power — **ex·tort·er** *n* — **ex·tor·tive** \-'stor-tiv\ *adj*

ex·tor·tion \ik-'stor-shən\ *n* **1 :** the act or practice of extorting esp. money or other property; *specif* **:** the act or practice of extorting by a public official acting under color of office **2 :** the crime of extorting — **ex·tor·tion·ate** \-shə-nət\ *adj* — **ex·tor·tion·er** *n* — **ex·tor·tion·ist** \-shə-nist\ *n*

ex·tract \'ek-ˌstrakt\ *n* **:** a certified copy of a document that forms part of or is preserved in a public record

ex·tra·dite \'ek-strə-ˌdīt\ *vt* **-dit·ed; -dit·ing 1 :** to deliver up to extradition **2 :** to obtain the extradition of — **ex·tra·dit·abil·i·ty** \ˌek-strə-ˌdī-tə-'bi-lə-tē\ *n* — **ex·tra·dit·able** \'ek-strə-ˌdī-tə-bəl\ *adj*

ex·tra·di·tion \ˌek-strə-'di-shən\ *n* [French, from Latin *ex-* out + *traditio* act of handing over, from *tradere* to hand over] **:** the surrender of an accused usu. under the provisions of a treaty or statute by one sovereign (as a state or nation) to another that has jurisdiction to try the accused and that has demanded his or her return — see also ASYLUM STATE; compare DETAINER, RENDITION ◊ Article IV of the U.S. Constitution states: "A person charged in any State with treason, felony, or other crime, who shall flee from justice, and be found in another State, shall on demand of the executive authority of the State from which he fled, be delivered up, to be removed to the State having jurisdiction of the crime."

extradition warrant — see WARRANT

ex·tra·ju·di·cial \ˌek-strə-jü-'di-shəl\ *adj* **1 :** not involving, occurring in, or forming part of a legal proceeding ⟨a creditor's ∼ repossession of property⟩ ⟨an ∼ investigation⟩; *esp* **:** OUT-OF-COURT ⟨an ∼ identification⟩ **2 :** stemming from something outside of a court proceeding ⟨a judge disqualified for bias that is ∼ and not derived from the evidence presented⟩ **3 :** occurring or arising outside of the course of judicial duties ⟨a judge's ∼ conduct⟩ — **ex·tra·ju·di·cial·ly** *adv*

ex·tra·lat·er·al right \ˌek-strə-'la-tə-rəl-\ *n* **:** the right of the holder of a mining claim on public land to mine veins whose tops are present on the surface of the claim even though the veins extend under the surface outside of the claim

ex·tra·le·gal \ˌek-strə-'lē-gəl\ *adj* **:** not regulated or sanctioned by law — **ex·tra·le·gal·ly** *adv*

ex·tra·or·di·nary \ek-'stor-də-ˌner-ē, ˌek-strə-'or-\ *adj* **1 a :** going beyond what is usual, regular, or customary; *specif* **:** of, relating to, or having the nature of a proceeding or action not normally required by law or not prescribed for the regular administration of law ⟨an ∼ session of the legislature⟩ ⟨granted ∼ relief⟩ — compare ORDINARY **b :** of or relating to a financial transaction that is not expected to be repeated ⟨an ∼ charge against earnings⟩ ⟨an ∼ gain⟩ **2 :** employed for or sent on a special function or service ⟨an ambassador ∼⟩

extraordinary dividend — see DIVIDEND

extraordinary remedy *n* **:** a procedure for obtaining judicial relief allowed when no other method is available, appropriate, or useful — see also HABEAS CORPUS, MANDAMUS, QUO WARRANTO

extraordinary writ — see WRIT

ex·tra·ter·ri·to·ri·al \ˌek-strə-ˌter-ə-'tōr-ē-əl\ *adj* **:** existing or taking place outside the territorial limits of a jurisdiction

ex·tra·ter·ri·to·ri·al·i·ty \ˌek-strə-ˌter-ə-ˌtōr-ē-'a-lə-tē\ *n* **:** exemption from the application or jurisdiction of local law or tribunals

ex·treme cruelty *n* **:** behavior toward a spouse that involves physical violence or threats thereof, acts calculated to destroy the peace of mind or health of the

spouse, or acts destructive of the purpose of the marriage; *also* **:** a ground for divorce based on a spouse's extreme cruelty
ex·trin·sic \ek-'strin-zik, -sik\ *adj* **:** not contained in or occurring in something (as a contract) ⟨an ~ representation⟩
extrinsic evidence — see EVIDENCE
extrinsic fraud — see FRAUD
ex–warrants \ˌeks-'wȯr-ənts\ *adv or adj*

: without warrants ◊ The purchaser of stock traded ex-warrants does not receive any warrants that were formerly traded with the stock.
eye·wit·ness *n* **:** one who sees an occurrence or object or sometimes experiences it through other senses (as hearing) and usu. reports or testifies about it

---

\ə\abut   \ᵊ\kitten   \ər\further   \a\ash   \ā\ace
\ä\cot, cart   \au̇\out   \ch\chin   \e\bet   \ē\easy
\g\go   \i\hit   \ī\ice   \j\job   \ŋ\sing   \ō\go   \ȯ\law
\ȯi\boy   \th\thin   \th̲\the   \ü\loot   \u̇\foot   \y\yet
\zh\vision   *see also* Pronunciation Symbols page

F

FAA *abbr* Federal Aviation Administration — see also the IMPORTANT AGENCIES section

fab·ri·cate \'fa-brə-ˌkāt\ *vb* **-cat·ed; -cat·ing** *vt* : to make up (as testimony) with an intent to deceive ~ *vi* : to make something up with an intent to deceive ⟨there was a motive to ~ —Gary Taylor⟩

face *n* **1 a** : outward appearance **b** : the surface or superficial reading or meaning of something (as a document or statute) that does not take into account outside information ⟨the ~ of [the] deed reveals that she had two purposes in mind — *State v. Rand*, 366 A.2d 183 (1976)⟩ — often used in the phrases *on its face* and *on the face of* ⟨is. . .neutral *on its face* but has a discriminatory effect on women —Marcia Coyle⟩ ⟨did not see *on the face of* the amendment that it was precisely directed at public as distinguished from private destruction —*O'Brien v. United States*, 376 F.2d 538 (1967)⟩ **2** : the inscribed or printed side of something (as a document); *broadly* : the front side of something inscribed or printed on both sides ⟨the ~ of a stock certificate⟩ **3** : FACE VALUE

face amount *n* : the amount of money payable under an insurance policy at the time of a loss

face value *n* : the value indicated on the face of something (as a stock certificate)

fa·cial *adj* : involving or apparent from the face of something (as a statute) ⟨~ discrimination⟩ ⟨a ~ challenge to the law⟩ — **fa·cial·ly** *adv*

fa·cil·i·tate \fə-'si-lə-ˌtāt\ *vt* **-tat·ed; -tat·ing** : to make easier : help bring about ⟨a vehicle used to ~ commission of the offense⟩ — **fa·cil·i·ta·tion** \fə-ˌsi-lə-'tā-shən\ *n*

fa·cil·i·ty of pay·ment clause \fə-'si-lə-tē-\ : a clause in an insurance policy permitting the insurer to pay the death benefit to a relative of the insured or to any other person esp. by reason of the person's incurring expenses (as funeral expenses) on the insured's behalf

fact *n* [Latin *factum* deed, real happening, something done, from neuter of *factus*, past participle of *facere* to do, make] **1** : something that has actual existence : a matter of objective reality **2** : any of the circumstances of a case that exist or are alleged to exist in reality : a thing whose actual occurrence or existence is to be determined by the evidence presented at trial — see also *finding of fact* at FINDING, JUDICIAL NOTICE, *question of fact* at QUESTION, TRIER OF FACT; compare LAW, OPINION

adjudicative fact : a fact particularly related to the parties to an esp. administrative proceeding — compare LEGISLATIVE FACT in this entry

collateral fact : a fact that has no direct relation to or immediate bearing on the case or matter in question — compare MATERIAL FACT in this entry

constitutional fact : a fact that relates to the determination of a constitutional issue (as violation of a constitutional right) — used esp. of administrative findings of fact

evidentiary fact : a fact that is part of the situation from which a case arises and that is established by testimony or other evidence — called also *mediate fact, predicate fact*; compare ULTIMATE FACT in this entry

legislative fact : a fact of general social, economic, or scientific relevance that does not change from case to case — compare ADJUDICATIVE FACT in this entry

material fact : a fact that affects decision making: as **a** : a fact upon which the outcome of all or part of a lawsuit depends **b** : a fact that would influence a reasonable person under the circumstances in making an investment decision (as in purchasing a security or voting for a corporate officer or action)
mediate fact : EVIDENTIARY FACT in this entry
predicate fact : EVIDENTIARY FACT in this entry
ul·ti·mate fact \'əl-ti-mət-\ : a conclusion of law or esp. mixed fact and law that is necessary to the determination of issues in a case and that is established by evidentiary facts — compare EVIDENTIARY FACT in this entry
—**in fact** : as a factual matter : established by fact rather than as a matter of law
fact·find·er \'fakt-ˌfīn-dər\ *n* : one that tries to determine the facts of a case, situation, or relationship: as **a** : an impartial examiner designated by a government agency to appraise the facts underlying a particular matter (as a labor dispute) **b** : TRIER OF FACT
fact·find·ing *n* : the act or process of determining the facts and often the issues involved in a case, situation, or relationship; *specif* : a method of labor dispute resolution in which an impartial factfinder holds hearings and from the evidence gathered makes determinations as to the facts and issues of the dispute and sometimes makes recommendations for resolution ◊ At the trial level, factfinding is done by the jury, or by the judge in a non-jury trial. At agency proceedings, factfinding is done by an officer or by a commission, council, or other body.
fac·tor *n* [Medieval Latin, doer, maker, agent, from Latin, maker, from *facere* to do, make] **1** : one who acts or transacts business for another: as **a** : a commercial agent who buys or sells goods for others on commission **b** : one that lends money to producers and dealers (as on the security of accounts receivable) **2** : a

person or thing that actively contributes to the production of a result (a difference in salary based on a ~ other than sex)
fac·tor·ing *n* : the purchasing of accounts receivable from a business by a factor who assumes the risk of loss in return for some agreed discount
factor's lien — see LIEN
fact pleading — see PLEADING 2
fac·tu·al \'fak-chə-wəl\ *adj* **1** : of or relating to facts (~ issues) **2** : restricted to or based on fact — **fac·tu·al·i·ty** \ˌfak-chə-'wa-lə-tē\ *n* — **fac·tu·al·ly** *adv* — **fac·tu·al·ness** *n*
factual impossibility — see IMPOSSIBILITY
fac·tum \'fak-təm\ *n* [New Latin, from Latin, act, deed; see FACT] **1** : a person's act and deed; *specif* : the due execution of a will **2** : FACT
fa·cul·ta·tive reinsurance \'fa-kəl-ˌtā-tiv-\ *n* [alluding to the *faculty* (i.e., power or prerogative) of the reinsurer to accept or reject the agreement] : a separate reinsurance agreement drawn up for a single risk — compare TREATY REINSURANCE
fail *vi* **1** : to be or become inadequate or unsuccessful esp. in fulfilling certain formal requirements (even though one or more terms are left open a contract for sale does not ~ for indefiniteness —*Uniform Commercial Code*) **2** : to become bankrupt or insolvent ~ *vt* : to leave undone or neglect to do (~ to appear in court) (~ to read a contract)
fail·ure *n* **1** : omission of occurrence or performance; *specif* : a failing to perform a duty or expected action (a ~ to mitigate damages) (~ to prosecute) **2** : a lack of success or adequacy (~ of a suit) **3** : a failing in business
failure of consideration : the neglect, refusal, or failure of a party to a contract to perform as promised or furnish the consideration promised; *also* : the extin-

\ə\abut \ᵊ\kitten \ər\further \a\ash \ā\ace
\ä\cot, cart \au̇\out \ch\chin \e\bet \ē\easy
\g\go \i\hit \ī\ice \j\job \ŋ\sing \ō\go \ȯ\law
\ȯi\boy \th\thin \th̲\the \ü\loot \u̇\foot \y\yet
\zh\vision   *see also* Pronunciation Symbols page

guishment of the consideration or of the worth of the consideration promised

failure of issue : lack of living issue (as of a person named to take under a will) at death

definite failure of issue : a failure of issue determined at a specific time set in a will (as at the death of a named taker)

indefinite failure of issue : a failure of issue for which no time period is fixed in a will

fair *adj* **1** : characterized by honesty and justice : free from self-interest, deception, injustice, or favoritism ⟨a ~ and impartial tribunal⟩ **2** : reasonable as a basis for exchange ⟨a ~ wage⟩ ⟨a ~ valuation⟩ **3** : consistent with merit or importance ⟨~ and just compensation for the injuries⟩ **4** : conforming with established laws or standards : being in accordance with a person's rights under the law ⟨~ judicial process⟩ — **fair·ly** *adv* — **fairness** *n*

fair comment *n* : a common-law privilege to criticize and comment on matters of public interest without being liable for defamation provided that the comment is an honest expression of opinion and free of malice

fair consideration — see CONSIDERATION

fair dealing *n* : the transacting of business in a manner characterized by candor and full disclosure and free of self-dealing; *specif* : such transacting undertaken by a corporate officer on his or her own behalf

fair hearing — see HEARING

fair market value *n* : a price at which buyers and sellers both having reasonable knowledge of the property and being under no compulsion are willing to do business

fairness doctrine *n* : a doctrine requiring broadcasters to provide an opportunity for response to personal attacks aired by the broadcaster and esp. for the airing of conflicting viewpoints on controversial issues

fair play and substantial justice *n* : a requirement or standard of fairness which a court's assertion of personal jurisdiction over a nonresident defendant must meet in order to avoid a violation of the defendant's right to due process — see also MINIMUM CONTACTS, *International Shoe Co. v. Washington* in the IMPORTANT CASES section ◊ In *International Shoe Co. v. Washington*, the Supreme Court held that in order for a state court to exercise jurisdiction over a defendant whose residence is elsewhere, the court must establish that the defendant has such minimum contacts with the state that the exercise of jurisdiction over the defendant does not offend traditional notions of fair play and substantial justice. Among the factors used to make this determination are the difficulty for the defendant of appearing in the court, the state's interest in deciding the case, and the plaintiff's interest in the convenience of the court and the effectiveness of the relief to be obtained there.

fair representation *n* : a union's representation in good faith of all employees within the bargaining unit without unfairly discriminating against any

fair–trade *vt* : to market (a commodity) in compliance with the provisions of a fair-trade agreement — **fair trade** *n* — **fair trader** *n*

fair–trade agreement *n* : an agreement between a producer and a seller that commodities bearing a trademark, label, or trade name belonging to the producer be sold at or above a specified price ◊ Most fair-trade agreements are illegal.

fair trial *n* : a trial that is conducted fairly, justly, and with procedural regularity by an impartial judge and in which the defendant is afforded his or her rights under the U.S. Constitution or the appropriate state constitution or other law ◊ Among the factors used to determine whether a defendant received a fair trial are these: the effectiveness of the assistance of counsel, the opportunity to present evidence and witnesses, the opportunity to rebut the opposition's evidence and cross-examine the opposition's witnesses, the presence of an impartial jury, and the judge's freedom from bias.

fair use — see USE 2
fair value *n* **1 :** a reasonable value (as one set by courts and regulatory commissions) for property **2 :** FAIR MARKET VALUE
fair warning *n* **:** sufficient notification in a statute that particular conduct constitutes a crime — see also VOID-FOR-VAGUENESS DOCTRINE
faith *n* **1 a :** allegiance or loyalty to a duty or a person **b :** sincerity or honesty of intentions — see also BAD FAITH, GOOD FAITH **2 :** fidelity to one's promises and obligations
Fal·cid·i·an por·tion \fòl-'si-dē-ən-, fal-\ *n* [from *Falcidius*, Roman tribune who proposed the law passed in 40 B.C. that established the portion] **:** the one-fourth portion of a succession that may be retained by the instituted heir in civil law if more than three-fourths of the succession was bequeathed to other legatees — compare LEGITIME, MARITAL PORTION ◊ The Falcidian portion is expressly abolished in the Louisiana Civil Code.
false *adj* **1 :** not genuine, authentic, or legitimate — compare COUNTERFEIT **2 a :** not true or correct; *esp* **:** intentionally or knowingly untrue or incorrect ⟨injured by ~ accusations⟩ **b :** intended to mislead or deceive **:** DECEPTIVE, MISLEADING — compare FRAUDULENT — **false·ly** *adv* — **false·ness** *n*
false ad·ver·tis·ing *n* **:** the crime or tort of publishing, broadcasting, or otherwise publicly distributing an advertisement that contains an untrue, misleading, or deceptive representation or statement which was made knowingly or recklessly and with the intent to promote the sale of property, goods, or services to the public
false arrest — see ARREST
false imprisonment *n* **:** the tort of intentionally restraining another by physical force or the threat of physical force without privilege or authority — see also *false arrest* at ARREST
false light *n* **:** an untrue or misleading portrayal ⟨unreasonably placed their fam-

ily in a *false light* before the public — *Cantrell v. Forest City Publishing Co.*, 419 U.S. 245 (1974)⟩; *also* **:** an invasion of privacy tort that is based on injury to the victim's reputation by such a portrayal (as in a publication) — compare DEFAMATION, LIBEL, SLANDER ◊ The false light cause of action is not recognized in all jurisdictions. Where it is recognized, the misrepresentation creating the false light does not need to be defamatory, but it must be offensive or objectionable to a reasonable person and made with knowledge of its inaccuracy.
false pre·tens·es \-'pre-ˌten-səz, -pri-'ten-\ *n pl* **:** false representations concerning past or present facts that are made with the intent to defraud another; *also* **:** the crime of obtaining title to another's property by false pretenses — compare *larceny by trick* at LARCENY, THEFT
false promise — see PROMISE
false representation *n* **:** an untrue or incorrect representation regarding a material fact that is made with knowledge or belief of its inaccuracy — see also MISREPRESENTATION
false statement *n* **:** a statement that is known or believed by its maker to be incorrect or untrue and is made esp. with intent to deceive or mislead ⟨submitted a *false statement* to obtain the loan⟩; *also* **:** the federal crime of concealing a material fact, making a false statement, or using documents known to be falsified — see also EXCULPATORY NO DOCTRINE; compare PERJURY
false swearing *n* **:** the making of false statements under oath or affirmation in a setting other than a judicial proceeding; *also* **:** the crime of false swearing — compare PERJURY
fal·si·fi·ca·tion \ˌfòl-si-fə-'kā-shən\ *n* **:** an act or instance of falsifying
fal·si·fy \'fòl-si-ˌfī\ *vt* **-fied; -fy·ing :** to

\ə\abut \ᵊ\kitten \ər\further \a\ash \ā\ace
\ä\cot, cart \aú\out \ch\chin \e\bet \ē\easy
\g\go \i\hit \ī\ice \j\job \ŋ\sing \ō\go \ò\law
\òi\boy \th\thin \th\the \ü\loot \ú\foot \y\yet
\zh\vision *see also* Pronunciation Symbols page

make false: as **a :** to make (as a document) false by mutilation, alteration, or addition ⟨the motel clerk had *falsified* the records —M. A. Kelly⟩ **b :** to report (as information) falsely ⟨the informant *falsified* his testimony⟩

fal·si·ty \'fȯl-sə-tē\ *n, pl* **-ties 1 :** something false **2 :** the quality or state of being false ⟨did not establish the ~ of the statement⟩

fam·i·ly \'fam-lē, 'fa-mə-\ *n, pl* **-lies 1 :** a group of individuals related by blood, marriage, or adoption **2 :** a group of usu. related individuals who live together under common household authority and esp. who have reciprocal duties to each other ◊ The interpretation of the word *family* in a law context depends upon the area of the law concerned (as contract or zoning law), the purpose of the document (as a statute or contract) in which it is used, and the facts of the case. Often for zoning purposes, the occupants of a group home are considered a family if the organization is like that of a family or if the home is going to be a permanent rather than a transitional residence for the occupants. — **fa·mil·ial** \fə-'mil-yəl\ *adj*

family car doctrine *n :* FAMILY PURPOSE DOCTRINE

family court *n :* a court that has jurisdiction and often advisory powers over domestic disputes involving the rights and duties of husband, wife, parent, or child esp. in matters affecting the support, custody, and welfare of children — compare JUVENILE COURT

Family Division *n :* a division of the High Court of Justice having jurisdiction over matters of family law and uncontested probate matters

family farm·er *n :* an individual or business entity whose debts and income arise primarily from a family owned and operated farming operation as set out in the Bankruptcy Code — see also *Bankruptcy Code* in the IMPORTANT LAWS section ◊ Only a person who qualifies as a family farmer with a regular annual income under the Bankruptcy Code may file for

bankruptcy under chapter 12, although a family farmer may also have the option of filing under chapter 7 or chapter 13.

family law *n :* an area of law dealing with family relations including divorce, adoption, paternity, custody, and support

family meeting *n, in the civil law of Louisiana :* a formal extrajudicial meeting of relatives or next friends of a minor or interdict held esp. to advise a court, curator, or tutor

family partnership — see PARTNERSHIP

family purpose doctrine *n :* a doctrine in tort law: the owner of a car is vicariously liable for damages incurred by a family member while using the car with the owner's permission — called also *family car doctrine* ◊ This doctrine is recognized only in some jurisdictions and has been rejected in most.

FAS *abbr* free alongside (ship)

fa·tal *adj* **1 :** causing failure of a legal claim or cause of action ⟨a ~ defect in the proceedings —W. R. LaFave and J. H. Israel⟩ **2 :** making something (as a contract) invalid or unenforceable ⟨there is a ~ indefiniteness with the result that the agreement is void —J. D. Calamari and J. M. Perillo⟩ — **fa·tal·ly** *adv*

fatico hearing — see HEARING

fault *n* [Anglo-French *faute* lack, failing, ultimately from Latin *fallere* to deceive, disappoint] **1 :** a usu. intentional act forbidden by law; *also :* a usu. intentional omission to do something (as to exercise due care) required by law — see also NEGLIGENCE; compare NO-FAULT, *strict liability* at LIABILITY ◊ Sometimes when *fault* is used in legal contexts it includes negligence, sometimes it is considered synonymous with *negligence,* and sometimes it is distinguished from *negligence.* Fault and negligence are the usual bases for liability in the law of torts. **2 :** responsibility for an act or omission that causes damage or injury to another ⟨relative degrees of ~⟩ — see also COMPARATIVE FAULT — **at fault :** liable or responsible based on fault ⟨was not *at fault*⟩

fa·vor *n* **1 :** BIAS **2 :** BENEFIT — **in favor**

of : to the benefit of ⟨a judgment *in favor of* the defendant⟩ — **in one's favor** : to one's benefit ⟨a donation inter vivos made *in his favor*⟩

FBI *abbr* Federal Bureau of Investigation — see also the IMPORTANT AGENCIES section

FCIC *abbr* Federal Crop Insurance Corporation

FDA *abbr* Food and Drug Administration — see also the IMPORTANT AGENCIES section

fdba *abbr* formerly doing business as

FDIC *abbr* Federal Deposit Insurance Corporation — see also the IMPORTANT AGENCIES section

feath·er·bed·ding \'fe-t͟hər-ˌbe-diŋ\ *n* [from the notion of making oneself comfortable through the receipt of excessive or unjustified compensation for little or no work] : the unfair labor practice of causing an employer to pay for services which are not performed (as by requiring more workers than necessary) — see also *Labor Management Relations Act* in the IMPORTANT LAWS section

Fed \'fed\ *n* : the Board of Governors of the Federal Reserve System — see also *Federal Reserve System* in the IMPORTANT AGENCIES section

fed·er·al *adj* [Latin *foeder-, foedus* compact, league] **1** : of or constituting a form of government in which power is distributed between a central authority and a number of constituent territorial units (as states) ⟨a ∼ government⟩ **2** : of or relating to the central government of a federation as distinguished from the governments of the constituent territorial units (as states); *esp* : of or relating to the laws made and enforced by the federal government ⟨a ∼ crime⟩ — **fed·er·al·ly** *adv*

Federal Circuit *n* : a circuit that has nationwide jurisdiction over appeals or reviews of certain customs, trademark and patent cases (as actions for patent applications or patent interference), and claims against the U.S. from district courts or federal agencies and that has appellate ju-risdiction over cases in the United States Court of Federal Claims, the United States Court of International Trade, and the United States Court of Veterans Appeals

federal common law *n* : case law developed in the federal courts — see also *Erie Railroad Co. v. Tompkins* in the IMPORTANT CASES section ◊ Federal common law is applied primarily in admiralty and maritime cases, disputes between states, matters of international relations, and in cases regarding the proprietary interests of the U.S. Federal common law is used when federal statutory law does not completely address an issue or problem.

federal court *n* : a court established by the federal government and having jurisdiction over questions of federal law — see also JUDICIAL SYSTEM and *Article I* and *Article III* of the CONSTITUTION in the back matter

fed·er·al·ism \'fe-drə-ˌli-zəm, 'fe-də-rə-\ *n, often cap* : distribution of power in a federation between the central authority and the constituent units (as states) involving esp. the allocation of significant lawmaking powers to those constituent units — compare COMITY, FULL FAITH AND CREDIT, STATES' RIGHTS

federal labor union *n* : a union that is chartered by the AFL-CIO

federal preemption *n* : a doctrine in law that allows a federal law to take precedence over or to displace a state law in certain matters of national importance (as interstate commerce)

federal question — see QUESTION 2

federal question jurisdiction — see JURISDICTION

Federal Register *n* : the daily bulletin of administrative and executive rules, regulations, orders, and notices that is published by the federal government — see also *Code of Federal Regulations* in

\ə\abut \ᵊ\kitten \ər\further \a\ash \ā\ace
\ä\cot, cart \au̇\out \ch\chin \e\bet \ē\easy
\g\go \i\hit \ī\ice \j\job \ŋ\sing \ō\go \ȯ\law
\ȯi\boy \th\thin \t͟h\the \ü\loot \u̇\foot \y\yet
\zh\vision *see also* Pronunciation Symbols page

the IMPORTANT LAWS section ◊ The Federal Register in effect updates the Code of Federal Regulations daily.

Federal Reserve bank — see BANK

Fed. R. App. P. *abbr* Federal Rules of Appellate Procedure

Fed. R. Civ. P. *abbr* Federal Rules of Civil Procedure — see also the IMPORTANT LAWS section

Fed. R. Crim. P. *abbr* Federal Rules of Criminal Procedure — see also the IMPORTANT LAWS section

Fed. Reg. *abbr* Federal Register

Fed. R. Evid. *abbr* Federal Rules of Evidence — see also the IMPORTANT LAWS section

fee *n* [Middle English, fief, from Old French *fé, fief*, ultimately from a Germanic word akin to Old High German *fehu* cattle] **1** : an inheritable freehold estate in real property; *esp* : FEE SIMPLE — compare LEASEHOLD, *life estate* at ESTATE

absolute fee : a fee granted with no restrictions or limitations on alienability : FEE SIMPLE ABSOLUTE at FEE SIMPLE

conditional fee : a fee that is subject to a condition: as **a** : FEE SIMPLE CONDITIONAL at FEE SIMPLE **b** : FEE SIMPLE ON CONDITION SUBSEQUENT at FEE SIMPLE

defeasible fee : a fee that is subject to terminating or being terminated

determinable fee : a defeasible fee that terminates automatically upon the occurrence of a specified event : FEE SIMPLE DETERMINABLE at FEE SIMPLE

fee patent : a fee simple absolute that is granted by a patent from the U.S. government; *also* : a patent that grants a fee simple absolute ⟨the land shall have the same status as though such *fee patent* had never been issued — *U.S. Code*⟩ ◊ Allotments of parcels of land in reservations are held in private ownership by fee patents.

fee tail : a fee which is granted to an individual and to that individual's descendants, which is subject to a reversion or a remainder if a tenant in tail dies with no lineal descendants, and which is not freely alienable — see also ¹ENTAIL, *De Donis Conditionalibus* in the IMPORTANT LAWS section; compare *fee simple conditional* at FEE SIMPLE ◊ The fee tail developed out of the fee simple conditional as a means to ensure that property would remain intact and in the family. Instead of giving the grantee a fee simple absolute once he or she has a child, which the grantee could then alienate (as by selling), the fee tail creates a future interest in the descendants which prevents the grantee and the descendants from alienating the property. A fee tail is created by a conveyance to the grantee and to the heirs of the grantee's body. In most jurisdictions, the fee tail is not recognized.

2 : a fixed amount or percentage charged; *esp* : a sum paid or charged for a service ⟨attorney ~*s*⟩

contingency fee : a fee for the services of a lawyer paid upon successful completion of the services and usu. calculated as a percentage of the gain obtained for the client — called also *contingency, contingent fee;* compare CHAMPERTY, MAINTENANCE

filing fee : a fee charged for the filing of a document ◊ Filing fees are ordinarily charged in civil matters with the filing of the complaint.

jury fee : a fee that is assessed in some courts as part of the cost of a civil jury trial

origination fee : a fee charged by a lender for the preparation and processing of a loan

— in fee : under title that creates a fee

fee patent — see FEE 1

fee simple *n, pl* **fees simple** [*simple* without limitation (as to heirs) and unrestricted (as to transfer of ownership)] : a fee that is alienable (as by deed, will, or intestacy) and of potentially indefinite duration; *esp* : FEE SIMPLE ABSOLUTE in this entry

fee simple absolute : a fee that is freely inheritable and alienable without any limitations or restrictions on transfers and that is of indefinite duration ◊ A fee simple absolute is conveyed by language granting the estate "to the grantee and his or her heirs," "to the grantee, his heirs and assigns," or "to the grantee." The term *heirs* is considered in this context a word of limitation, and so this does not create a future interest in the estate in the heirs but simply makes the estate freely alienable.

fee simple conditional : a fee granted to an individual and to that individual's descendants which is subject to a reversion or remainder if the grantee has no lineal descendants but which becomes a fee simple absolute and freely alienable upon the birth of a direct descendant — see also *De Donis Conditionalibus* in the IMPORTANT LAWS section; compare *fee tail* at FEE ◊ The fee simple conditional is not recognized in England or the United States except in South Carolina.

fee simple determinable : a defeasible fee that automatically terminates upon the occurrence of a specified event or condition and which reverts to the grantor — compare *estate on condition* at ESTATE ◊ A fee simple determinable is conveyed by language which states that the estate automatically terminates and reverts to the grantor, and which expresses duration ("so long as," "until," "during the time that").

fee simple on condition sub·se·quent \-'səb-si-kwənt\ : a defeasible fee that may be terminated by the grantor or assigns upon the occurrence of an event — called also *fee simple subject to condition subsequent* ◊ A fee simple on condition subsequent is conveyed by language that creates a right of entry or power of termination in the grantor and that expresses condition ("on condition that," "provided that").

— **in fee simple** : under title that creates a fee simple (as a fee simple absolute) ⟨entitled him to ownership of the disputed property *in fee simple* —*National Law Journal*⟩

fee simple absolute — see FEE SIMPLE
fee simple conditional — see FEE SIMPLE
fee simple determinable — see FEE SIMPLE
fee simple on condition subsequent — see FEE SIMPLE
fee simple subject to condition subsequent : FEE SIMPLE ON CONDITION SUBSEQUENT at FEE SIMPLE
fee tail — see FEE 1
fel·low–ser·vant rule *n* : a common-law rule or doctrine in tort law: an employer is not liable for injuries inflicted on one employee by the fault of another employee during the course of his or her employment ◊ This rule is no longer used in most jurisdictions as a result of federal and state workers' compensation statutes.
fel·on \'fe-lən\ *n* [Anglo-French *felon, fel*, literally, evildoer, from Old French, probably of Germanic origin] : one who has committed a felony
fe·lo·ni·ous \fə-'lō-nē-əs\ *adj* : of, relating to, or constituting a felony ⟨~ sale of cocaine⟩ — **fe·lo·ni·ous·ly** *adv*
felonious assault — see ASSAULT
felonious homicide — see HOMICIDE
fel·o·ny \'fe-lə-nē\ *n, pl* **-nies** : a crime that has a greater punishment imposed by statute than that imposed on a misdemeanor; *specif* : a federal crime for which the punishment may be death or imprisonment for more than a year — see also ATTAINDER, TREASON ◊ Originally in English law a felony was a crime for which the perpetrator would suffer forfeiture of all real and personal property as well as whatever sentence was imposed. Under U.S. law, there is no forfeiture of all of the felon's property (real or personal) and such forfeiture is not part of the definition of a felony. For certain crimes, however (as for a conviction under the Racketeer Influenced

\ə\abut \ə\kitten \ər\further \a\ash \ā\ace
\ä\cot, cart \au\out \ch\chin \e\bet \ē\easy
\g\go \i\hit \ī\ice \j\job \ŋ\sing \ō\go \o\law
\oi\boy \th\thin \th\the \ü\loot \u\foot \y\yet
\zh\vision *see also* Pronunciation Symbols page

and Corrupt Organizations Act or a narcotics law), specific property, such as that used in or gained by the crime, is subject to forfeiture. Every state has its own statutory definition of a felony. Most are in line with the federal definition of a felony as a crime which carries a sentence of imprisonment for more than one year or the death penalty (where applicable). Other states, like Louisiana, define a felony as a crime which carries a sentence of death or imprisonment at hard labor.

felony murder — see MURDER

¹fence *n* **1** : a barrier intended to prevent escape or intrusion or to mark a boundary **2 a** : a receiver of stolen goods **b** : a place where stolen goods are bought

²fence *vt* **fenced; fenc•ing 1 a** : to enclose with a fence **b** : to keep in or out with a fence **2** : to sell (stolen property) to a fence

feoff \'fef, 'fēf\ *vt* [Anglo-French *feoffer*, from *fie, fief* fief] : ENFEOFF

feoff•ee \fe-'fē, fē-'fē\ *n* : a person to whom a feoffment is made

feoff•ment \'fef-mənt, 'fēf-\ *n* : the historical method of granting a freehold estate in land by actual delivery of possession orig. by livery of seisin

feof•for \'fe-fər, 'fē-\ *n* : one who makes a feoffment

fe•rae na•tu•rae \'fir-ē-nə-'chŭr-ē, -'tŭr-, -'tyŭr-; 'fer-ˌī-nä-'tü-ˌrī\ *adj* [New Latin, literally, of a wild nature] : wild by nature : not usu. tamed ◊ Animals like wild ducks or bees are considered ferae naturae. At common law they cannot be claimed as one's property except under certain circumstances, as when captured.

Fer•es doctrine \'fer-is-\ *n* [from *Feres v. United States*, 340 U.S. 135 (1950), the case which established the doctrine] : a doctrine in tort law: a member of the military is barred from recovering damages from the government under the Federal Tort Claims Act for injuries sustained in the course of activity incident to his or her military service — called also *Feres rule*

fer•tile oc•to•ge•nar•i•an rule \-ˌäk-tə-jə-

'ner-ē-ən-\ *n* : a presumption at common law that a woman of any age is capable of having children for purposes of determining the applicability of the rule against perpetuities

fe•ti•cide \'fē-tə-ˌsīd\ *n* : the act of causing the death of a fetus

FHA *abbr* Federal Housing Administration — see also the IMPORTANT AGENCIES section

fi•at \'fē-ˌät, -ˌat, -ət; 'fī-ˌat\ *n* **1** : DECREE **2** : an authoritative but arbitrary order ⟨a brazen act of judicial ∼ —L. H. Tribe⟩

FICA \'fī-kə\ *abbr* Federal Insurance Contributions Act

fic•tion *n* : LEGAL FICTION — **fic•tion•al** *adj*

fic•ti•tious *adj* **1** : of, relating to, or characteristic of a legal fiction **2** : FALSE — **fic•ti•tious•ly** *adv* — **fic•ti•tious•ness** *n*

fictitious name *n* : a name (as *John Doe*) used in a complaint when the party's name is unknown at the time of filing or when the party's identity is being kept private

fictitious payee *n* : a person named as payee in an instrument who does not in fact exist or who does exist but to whom the maker of the instrument does not intend to convey any interest in the instrument

fictitious person *n* : a supposed but in fact nonexistent person referred to in some legal documents or proceedings; *also* : FICTITIOUS PAYEE

fidei commissa *pl of* FIDEI COMMISSUM

fi•dei com•mis•sum \'fī-dē-ˌā-kə-'mi-səm, 'fē-dā-ˌē-kò-'mē-sùm\ *n, pl* **fidei com•mis•sa** \-sə, -sä\ [Latin *fidei commissum*, from neuter past participle of *fideicommittere* to bequeath (a thing) with the request that it be delivered to a third person, from *fidei*, dative of *fides* trust + *committere* to place in the hands of, entrust] *in the civil law of Louisiana* : a gift (as by will) of property in which a person is invested with title and which the person is directed to convey to another person or to make a particular disposition of — compare SUBSTITUTION

◇ Fidei commissa are prohibited by the Louisiana Civil Code.

fi·del·i·ty \fə-'de-lə-tē, fī-\ *n* : the quality or state of being faithful or loyal; *esp* : loyalty to one's spouse in refraining from adultery and sometimes in submitting to a spouse's reasonable sexual desires

fidelity bond — see BOND 1a

fidelity insurance *n* : insurance against loss caused by the dishonesty or nonperformance of an employee of the insured

¹fi·du·cia·ry \fə-'dü-shə-rē, -'dyü-, -shē-ˌer-ē\ *n, pl* **-ries** : one often in a position of authority who obligates himself or herself to act on behalf of another (as in managing money or property) and assumes a duty to act in good faith and with care, candor, and loyalty in fulfilling the obligation : one (as an agent) having a fiduciary duty to another — see also *fiduciary duty* at DUTY, FIDUCIARY RELATIONSHIP; compare PRINCIPAL

²fiduciary *adj* [Latin *fiduciarius*, from *fiducia* trust, transfer of a property on trust] **1** : of, relating to, or involving a confidence or trust ⟨a guardian acting in his ~ capacity⟩ **2** : of or relating to a fiduciary or the position of a fiduciary ⟨a ~ bond⟩

fiduciary duty — see DUTY

fiduciary re·la·tion·ship *n* : a relationship in which one party places special trust, confidence, and reliance in and is influenced by another who has a fiduciary duty to act for the benefit of the party — called also *confidential relationship, fiduciary relation;* see also *fiduciary duty* at DUTY ◇ A fiduciary relationship may be created by express agreement of the parties, or it may be imposed by law where established by the conduct of the parties. Typical fiduciary relationships exist between agents and principals, attorneys and clients, executors or administrators and legatees or heirs, trustees and beneficiaries, corporate directors or officers and stockholders, receivers or trustees in

bankruptcy and creditors, guardians and wards, and confidential advisors and those advised.

fiduciary shield doctrine *n* : a doctrine barring a state from exercising personal jurisdiction over a nonresident defendant as an individual if the acts for which the defendant is being sued were performed in his or her capacity as a corporate agent or employee

fi·e·ri fa·ci·as \'fī-ə-rē-'fā-shē-əs, -sē-; 'fē-e-rē-'fä-kē-ˌäs\ *n* [Medieval Latin, literally, may you cause it to be done, from words used in the writ, typically *de terris et cattalis fieri facias* may you raise from the lands and chattels (of the defendant) (a given sum)] : a writ authorizing a sheriff to seize and sell certain items of the property of a debtor in order to satisfy a creditor's judgment against the debtor — see also EXECUTION

fi. fa. *abbr* fieri facias

FIFO \'fī-ˌfō\ *abbr* first in, first out

fifth degree *n* : the grade sometimes given to the least serious form of a crime ⟨theft in the *fifth degree*⟩

fight·ing words *n pl* : words which by their very utterance are likely to inflict harm on or provoke a breach of the peace by the average person to whom they are directed ◇ Fighting words are not protected speech under the First Amendment to the U.S. Constitution.

¹file *vb* **filed; fil·ing** *vt* **1 a** : to submit (a legal document) to the proper office (as the office of a clerk of court) for keeping on file among the records esp. as a procedural step in a legal transaction or proceeding ⟨*filed* a tax return⟩ ⟨a financing statement *filed* with the Secretary of State⟩ ⟨*filing* a notice of appeal⟩; *also* : RECORD ⟨*filed* a mortgage in the Registry of Deeds⟩ ◇ In nearly all cases, a document is deemed to be filed when it is actually received by the office to which

\ə\abut \ᵊ\kitten \ər\further \a\ash \ā\ace
\ä\cot, cart \aù\out \ch\chin \e\bet \ē\easy
\g\go \i\hit \ī\ice \j\job \ŋ\sing \ō\go \ò\law
\òi\boy \th\thin \t͟h\the \ü\loot \ù\foot \y\yet
\zh\vision *see also* Pronunciation Symbols page

it is directed. A few cases, however, have held that a document is filed upon the mailing of it. **b :** to place (as a document) on file among the records of an office esp. by formally receiving and endorsing ⟨a complaint *filed* by the clerk despite the absence of the filing fee⟩ **2 :** to return (the documentation in a case) to the records of a clerk of court without any determination of the case; *broadly* : to conclude (a case) without a determination on its merits **3 :** to initiate (a judicial or administrative proceeding) by submitting the proper documents or following proper procedure : BRING ⟨threatened to ~ charges⟩ ⟨two separate actions were *filed* by representatives of the estates — J. H. Friedenthal *et al.*⟩ ~ *vi* **1 :** to register as a candidate esp. in a primary election **2 :** to place items in a file
²file *n* **:** a collection of papers or publications usu. arranged or classified; *specif* : the papers that make up the record of a case — **on file :** in or as if in a file for ready reference
file wrap·per *n* **:** a written record in a patent office of the application and negotiations for a patent preceding the issuance of the patent — see also *file wrapper estoppel* at ESTOPPEL 1
file wrapper estoppel — see ESTOPPEL 1
fil·i·ate \'fi-lē-ˌāt\ *vt* **-at·ed; -at·ing :** to declare (a child) the descendant of a particular parent and esp. a father ⟨has not been *filiated* by the initiative of the parent —*Louisiana Civil Code*⟩ — compare ACKNOWLEDGE 2b, LEGITIMATE ◊ A child may be illegitimate but filiated. Both legitimation and acknowledgment filiate an illegitimate child. Adopted children are filiated by the adoption proceeding.
fil·i·a·tion \ˌfi-lē-'ā-shən\ *n* [Late Latin *filiatio* relationship of a son and father, from Latin *filius* son] **1 :** a legal relationship of a parent and esp. a father and child that creates rights and obligations ⟨used to help prove ~ in a paternity suit —*LeBlanc v. LeBlanc*, 427 So. 2d 1361 (1986)⟩ — see also LEGITIMATE

FILIATION; compare ACKNOWLEDGMENT, PATERNITY ◊ The Louisiana Supreme Court has held that children not entitled to legitimate filiation to the alleged parent, or not legitimated or formally acknowledged by the alleged parent, may establish filiation in a filiation proceeding. This has led to some instances where the legitimate children of one father have been allowed to prove filiation to another father. Such an action does not make the children illegitimate but does create a status of dual paternity. **2 :** adjudication of paternity or filiation ⟨the court has made an order of ~ —*Idaho Code*⟩
¹fil·i·bus·ter \'fi-lə-ˌbəs-tər\ *n* **:** the use of extreme dilatory tactics in an attempt to delay or prevent action esp. in a legislative assembly; *also* : an instance of this practice
²filibuster *vb* **-tered; -ter·ing** *vi* **:** to engage in a filibuster ~ *vt* **:** to subject to a filibuster
filing *n* **1 :** an act or instance of filing something **2 :** a document filed
filing fee — see FEE 2
fi·li·us nul·li·us \'fi-lē-əs-'nə-lē-əs, -nə-'lī-əs; 'fē-lē-ùs-'nù-lē-ùs\ *n* [Medieval Latin, literally, no one's son] **:** an illegitimate child **:** BASTARD — called also *filius populi*
fi·nal *adj* **1 :** ending a court action or proceeding leaving nothing further to be determined by the court or to be done except execution of the judgment but not precluding appeal — used of an order, decision, judgment, decree, determination, or sentence; see also FINALITY, FINAL JUDGMENT RULE; compare INTERLOCUTORY **2 :** being a decision that precludes the right to appeal or to continue a case in any other court upon the merits: as **a :** being a decision for which availability of appeal has been exhausted and concerning which a writ of certiorari has been denied or the time to petition for certiorari has expired **b :** being a decision of the Supreme Court of the U.S. that terminates the litigation between parties on the merits and leaves nothing for the lower

court to do in case of an affirmance except to execute the judgment **3 :** being the last in a series, process, or progress ⟨a ~ payment⟩

final account *n* **:** a statement usu. submitted at the close of a matter (as the administration of an estate or a bankruptcy proceeding) showing transactions not previously reported by the fiduciary handling the matter

final argument *n* **:** an argument made to the jury or to the judge in a bench trial by both sides of a case after all the evidence has been presented

final decree — see DECREE

final injunction — see INJUNCTION

fi·nal·i·ty \fī-'na-lə-tē, fə-\ *n* **1 :** the state or condition of being final **2 :** the principle that appeals may only be taken from final orders or judgments

final judgment — see JUDGMENT 1a

final judgment rule *n* **:** a rule of procedure: an appeal may be taken only after final determination of all issues involved in a case

final offer arbitration — see ARBITRATION

final order — see ORDER 3b

final rule *n* **:** a rule promulgated by an administrative agency after the public has had an opportunity to comment on the proposed rule

¹**fi·nance** *n* **1** *pl* **:** money or other liquid resources of a government, business, group, or individual **2 :** the system that includes the circulation of money, the granting of credit, the making of investments, and the provision of banking facilities **3 :** the science or study of the management of funds **4 :** the obtaining of funds or capital **:** FINANCING

²**finance** *vt* **fi·nanced; fi·nanc·ing 1 a :** to raise or provide funds or capital for ⟨~ a takeover⟩ **b :** to furnish with necessary funds **2 :** to sell something to on credit

finance company — see COMPANY

finance lease — see LEASE

fi·nan·cial *adj* **:** relating to finance or financiers — **fi·nan·cial·ly** *adv*

f̶   ̶esponsibility law *n* **:** a law that

requires a driver involved in an accident to provide proof of the ability to pay a judgment obtained against him or her

financial statement *n* **:** a statement of one's status with regard to money or wealth — compare FINANCING STATEMENT

fi·nan·cier *n* **1 :** one who specializes in raising and expending public moneys **2 :** one who deals with finance and investment on a large scale

fi·nanc·ing *n* **:** the act or process or an instance of raising or providing funds; *also* **:** the funds thus raised or provided

financing statement *n* **:** a statement that contains information about a security interest in collateral used to secure a debt and that is filed to provide notice to other creditors of the security interest — see also PERFECT b, *Uniform Commercial Code* in the IMPORTANT LAWS section; compare FINANCIAL STATEMENT ◊ Under Article 9 of the Uniform Commercial Code, a financing statement must 1) give the names of the debtor and the secured party, 2) be signed by the debtor, 3) give the address of the secured party, 4) give the address of the debtor, and 5) indicate the items of collateral.

find *vb* **found; find·ing** *vt* **1 :** to come upon accidentally or through effort ⟨*found* a valuable antique in the old desk⟩ ⟨*found* a buyer for the property⟩ **2 :** to make a judicial determination regarding ⟨*found* the testimony not credible⟩ ⟨*found* the defendant guilty⟩ — compare DECIDE, HOLD ~ *vi* **:** to make a judicial determination ⟨the jury *found* in favor of the plaintiff⟩

find·er *n* **1 :** one that finds ⟨the ~ of lost property has a right to it as against the world, except against the true owner — *McDonald v. Railway Express Agency*, 81 S.E.2d 525 (1954)⟩ **2 :** one that for a fee discovers a financial opportunity, passes

\ə\abut \ə\kitten \ər\further \a\ash \ā\ace
\ä\cot, cart \au̇\out \ch\chin \e\bet \ē\easy
\g\go \i\hit \ī\ice \j\job \ŋ\sing \ō\go \ȯ\law
\ȯi\boy \th\thin \t̶h̶\the \ü\loot \u̇\foot \y\yet
\zh\vision   *see also* Pronunciation Symbols page

passes it on to another, and may act as a go-between for but does not participate in subsequent negotiations between the involved parties — compare BROKER

finder of fact : TRIER OF FACT

find·ing *n* **:** a determination resulting from judicial or administrative examination or inquiry (as at trial) esp. into matters of fact as embodied in the verdict of a jury or decision of a court, referee, or administrative body or officer; *also, usu pl* **:** a written statement of such determinations — see also FACTFINDING; compare DECISION, HOLDING, OPINION, RULING

finding of fact **:** a determination made by the trier of fact as to a factual issue based on the evidence presented in a case ◊ Conclusions of law are based on findings of fact.

finding of law **:** a court's determination of the law as applied to a case **:** CONCLUSION OF LAW

gen·er·al finding **:** a finding that the facts in general support a judgment in favor of one of the parties

spe·cial finding **:** a finding setting out the ultimate facts upon which the court's judgment is based

finding of fact — see FINDING

finding of law — see FINDING

¹fine *n* [Anglo-French *fin, fine* & Medieval Latin *finis* end, boundary, agreement, payment for release or privilege, monetary penalty, from Latin *finis* end, boundary] **1 :** a sum imposed as punishment for an offense — compare RESTITUTION **2** **:** a forfeiture or penalty paid to an injured party in a civil action

²fine *vt* **fined; fin·ing :** to impose a fine on **:** punish by fine

fine print *n* **:** a part of an agreement or document spelling out restrictions or limitations often in small type or obscure language

fin·ger *vt* **fin·gered; fin·ger·ing :** to accuse or identify as guilty ⟨was *fingered* simply because he fit the stereotype of a young, black street criminal —Jack Ewing⟩

fin·ger·print *n* **:** the impression of a fingertip on any surface; *also* **:** an ink impression of the lines upon the fingertip taken for the purpose of identification (as during the booking procedure following an arrest) — see also DNA FINGERPRINTING — **fingerprint** *vt* — **fin·ger·print·ing** *n*

fire·man's rule *n* **:** a doctrine holding that a property owner or occupant is not liable for unintentional injuries suffered by firefighters or police officers in responding to a problem on the property

firm *n* [German *Firma*, from Italian, signature, ultimately from Latin *firmare* to make firm, confirm] **1 :** the name or title under which a company transacts business **2 :** a partnership of two or more persons that is not recognized as a legal person distinct from the members composing it **3 :** a business unit or enterprise

firm offer *n* **:** a binding written offer to buy or sell that cannot be revoked for a stipulated period of time or for a reasonable time that in no event exceeds three months

first blush *n* **:** initial view, appearance, or consideration — used esp. in the phrase *at first blush* ⟨an award can be set aside as excessive if at *first blush* it indicates prejudice on the part of the jury⟩

first degree *n* **:** the grade given to the most serious forms of crimes ⟨burglary in the *first degree*⟩ — **first–degree** *adj*

first–degree murder — see MURDER

first im·pres·sion *n* **:** first consideration or judgment — see also *case of first impression* at CASE

first in, first out *adj* **:** being or relating to a method of valuing inventories by which items in the lot first received are assumed to be issued or sold first and requisitions are priced at the cost per item of the oldest lot on hand — compare LAST IN, FIRST OUT

first lien — see LIEN

first mortgage — see MORTGAGE

first offender *n* **:** one convicted of an offense for the first time

fis•cal \'fis-kəl\ *adj* [Latin *fiscalis*, from *fiscus* basket, treasury] **1** : of or relating to taxation, public revenues, or public debt ⟨~ policy⟩ **2** : of or relating to financial matters — **fis•cal•ly** *adv*

fiscal year *n* : an accounting period of 12 months

fish•ing ex•pe•di•tion \-ₗek-spə-'di-shən\ *n* **1** : an inquiry (as by the use of discovery) that is unnecessarily extensive or unrelated to the lawsuit **2** : an investigation that does not stick to a stated objective but hopes to uncover incriminating or newsworthy evidence

fix *vt* **1 a** : to make firm, stable, or stationary **b** : to attach physically **2** : to influence the actions, outcome, or effect of by improper or illegal methods ⟨conspiracy to defraud the government by ~*ing* income tax cases —W. R. LaFave and A. W. Scott, Jr.⟩ — **fix** *n* — **fix•er** *n*

fixed amount option *n* : INSTALLMENTS= FOR-A-FIXED-AMOUNT OPTION at OPTION 4

fixed asset — see ASSET 2

fixed capital — see CAPITAL

fixed charge *n* : a regularly recurring expense (as rent, taxes, or interest) that must be met when due

fixed–income security — see SECURITY

fixed liability — see LIABILITY 2a

fixed period option *n* : INSTALLMENTS= FOR-A-FIXED-PERIOD OPTION at OPTION 4

fixed rate *n* : a rate (as of interest) that stays the same ⟨a mortgage with a *fixed rate*⟩

fixed rate mortgage — see MORTGAGE

fix•ture *n* : an item of movable property so incorporated into a real property that it may be regarded as legally a part of it

fla•gran•te de•lic•to \flə-'grän-tē-də-'lik-tō, -'gran-; flä-'grän-tä-dä-'lēk-tō\ *adv or adj* [Medieval Latin, literally, while the crime is blazing] : in the very act of committing a misdeed ⟨was caught *flagrante delicto*⟩; *also* : in the midst of sexual activity

¹flat *adj* : not varying ⟨a ~ rate⟩; *specif, of a tax* : having a rate that remains constant for any taxable base

²flat *adv* : without interest charge; *esp* : without allowance or charge for accrued interest ⟨bonds sold ~⟩

flat rule *n* : PER SE RULE

¹float *n* **1** : an amount of money represented by checks outstanding and in process of collection **2** : the time between a transaction (as the writing of a check or a purchase on credit) and the actual withdrawal of funds to cover it

²float *vi, of a currency* : to find a level in the international exchange market in response to the law of supply and demand and without any restrictive effect of artificial support or control ~ *vt* **1** : to place (an issue of securities) on the market **2** : to obtain money for the establishment or development of (an enterprise) by issuing and selling securities **3** : NEGOTIATE 1 ⟨~ a loan⟩

float•er *n* **1** [from the notion that the policy "floats" with the goods it insures, wherever they might be located] : a policy or supplemental attachment to a policy insuring specific items of personal property (as jewelry or art); *specif* : a policy of insurance to protect against loss or damage of goods in transit or goods (as jewels) naturally subject to use in various places — called also *floating policy* **2** : a debt security that yields an indexed variable rate of interest; *esp* : FLOATING RATE NOTE at NOTE

float•ing *adj* **1** : not presently committed or invested ⟨~ capital⟩ **2** : short-term and usu. not funded ⟨~ debt⟩ **3** : having no fixed value or rate ⟨~ currencies⟩ ⟨~ interest rates⟩

floating lien — see LIEN

floating policy *n* : FLOATER

floating rate note — see NOTE

floating zone *n* : a zone that is to be used for a designated purpose and that is approved as to particular characteristics (as size and type of buildings) but whose

location is to be determined in the future
flood·gate *n* : something serving to restrain an outburst (as of litigation) — usu. used in pl. ⟨a decision that will open the *floodgates* for other claims⟩
floor *n* **1 a :** a main level space (as in a stock exchange or legislative chamber) distinguished from a platform or gallery **b :** members of an assembly ⟨took questions from the ~⟩ **c :** the right to address an assembly ⟨the senator from Utah has the ~⟩ **2 :** a lower limit ⟨a five percent ~ on deductions for medical expenses⟩
floor plan·ning *n* : a method of financing a retail sales business in which the retailer gives a security interest in all of the inventory to the lender or seller
flo·tage \'flō-tij\ *n* : FLOTSAM
flot·sam \'flät-səm\ *n* : floating wreckage of a ship or its cargo — compare JETSAM
flower bond — see BOND 2
FLRA *abbr* Federal Labor Relations Authority — see also the IMPORTANT AGENCIES section
fly·ing squad *n* : a usu. small standby group of people ready to move or act quickly; *esp* : a police unit formed to respond quickly in an emergency — called also *flying squadron*
F.O.B. *abbr* free on board
FOIA *abbr* Freedom of Information Act — see also the IMPORTANT LAWS section
fo·lio \'fō-lē-ˌō\ *n* : a certain number of words taken as a unit or division in a document for purposes of measurement or reference ◊ A folio by statutory provision generally consists of 100 words.
fol·low *vt* : to be in accordance with (a prior decision) : accept as authoritative — see also PRECEDENT; compare OVERRULE
for *prep* **1 :** because of ⟨a statute void ~ vagueness⟩ **2 :** on behalf of : as the representative of ⟨attorney general's office ~ petitioner⟩
for·bear·ance *also* **fore·bear·ance** \fȯr-

'bar-əns\ *n* : a refraining from the enforcement of something (as a debt, right, or obligation) that is due
¹force *n* **1 :** a cause of motion, activity, or change
   intervening force : a force that acts after another's negligent act or omission has occurred and that causes injury to another : INTERVENING CAUSE at CAUSE
   irresistible force : an unforeseeable event esp. that prevents performance of an obligation under a contract : FORCE MAJEURE
2 : a body of persons available for a particular end ⟨the labor ~⟩; *specif* : POLICE FORCE — usu. used with *the* **3 :** violence, compulsion, or constraint exerted upon or against a person or thing
   constructive force : the use of threats or intimidation for the purpose of gaining control over or preventing resistance from another
   deadly force : force that is intended to cause or that carries a substantial risk of causing death or serious bodily injury — compare NONDEADLY FORCE in this entry ◊ As a general rule, deadly force may be used without incurring criminal or tort liability when one reasonably believes that one's life or safety is in danger. In some cases, a person's unreasonable belief in the need for deadly force has been used to justify reducing a charge of murder to voluntary manslaughter. Additionally, a police officer is generally justified in using deadly force to prevent the escape of a suspect who threatens the officer or who the officer has probable cause to believe has committed a violent crime.
   lawful force : force that is considered justified under the law and does not create criminal or tort liability — compare UNLAWFUL FORCE in this entry
   mod·er·ate force \'mä-də-rət-\ : NONDEADLY FORCE in this entry
   non·dead·ly force : force that is intended to cause minor bodily injury; *also* : a threat (as by the brandishing of a gun) to use deadly force — called

also *moderate force;* compare DEADLY FORCE in this entry

reasonable force : Lawful force that is reasonably necessary to accomplish a particular end (as preventing theft of one's property)

unlawful force : force that is not justified under the law and therefore is considered a tort or crime or both — compare LAWFUL FORCE in this entry

— **in force** : valid and operative ⟨a life insurance policy *in force*⟩

²force *vt* **forced; forc·ing 1 a** : to compel by physical means often against resistance ⟨*forced* him into the car⟩ **b** : to break open or through ⟨*forced* the door⟩ — see also FORCIBLE ENTRY **2** : to impose or require by law — see also ELECTIVE SHARE, *forced heir* at HEIR, *forced sale* at SALE

force and effect *n* : legal efficacy ⟨have the *force and effect* of a formal acceptance — *Louisiana Civil Code*⟩

forced heir — see HEIR

forced portion *n* : LEGITIME

forced sale — see SALE

forced share *n* : ELECTIVE SHARE

force ma·jeure \'fȯrs-ma-'zhər, -mà-'zhœr\ *n* [French, superior force] **1** : superior or insuperable force **2** : an event (as war, labor strike, or extreme weather) or effect that cannot be reasonably anticipated or controlled : FORTUITOUS EVENT — compare ACT OF GOD, INEVITABLE ACCIDENT

force majeure clause *n* : a clause in an agreement that excuses performance in the event that a force majeure makes the performance impracticable or impossible

for·ci·ble \'fȯr-sə-bəl\ *adj* : effected by force or threat of force used against opposition or resistance ⟨a ~ felony⟩ — **for·ci·bly** *adv*

forcible entry *n* **1** : the unlawful taking of possession of real property by force or threats of force against the lawful possessor — see also FORCIBLE ENTRY AND DETAINER **2** : unlawful entry into or onto another's property esp. when accompanied by force ⟨*forcible entry* of an automobile⟩

forcible entry and detainer *n* **1** : the forcible entry upon and keeping of real property without authority of law **2** : the statutory proceeding to regain possession of real property taken through a forcible entry and detainer

forebearance *var of* FORBEARANCE

fore·close \fȯr-'klōz\ *vb* [Anglo-French *forclos*, past participle of *foreclore* to preclude, prevent, from *fors* outside + *clore* to close] *vt* : to subject to foreclosure proceedings ~ *vi* : to foreclose a mortgage or other security interest — compare REPOSSESS, SEIZE 2

fore·clos·ure \fȯr-'klō-zhər\ *n* **1** : a legal proceeding that bars or extinguishes a mortgagor's equity of redemption in mortgaged real property — see also *deficiency judgment* at JUDGMENT, REDEEM, RIGHT OF REDEMPTION, STATUTORY FORECLOSURE, STRICT FORECLOSURE 1 **2** : the extinguishment (as under the provisions of Article 9 of the Uniform Commercial Code) of the rights of a debtor in personal property subject to a security interest by judicial proceedings and esp. by judicial sale — see also STRICT FORECLOSURE 2

foreclosure sale — see SALE

for·eign *adj* : not being within the jurisdiction of a political unit (as a state); *esp* : being from or in a state other than the one in which a matter is being considered ⟨a ~ company doing business in South Carolina⟩ ⟨a ~ executor submitting to the jurisdiction of this court⟩ ⟨a ~ judgment⟩ — compare DOMESTIC

foreign administrator — see ADMINISTRATOR

foreign corporation — see CORPORATION

fore·man *n, pl* **fore·men** : a male or female member of a jury who acts as the leader and speaks for the jury

fo·ren·sic \fə-'ren-sik, -zik\ *adj* [Latin *forensis* public, forensic, from *forum* fo-

\ə\abut \ᵊ\kitten \ər\further \a\ash \ā\ace
\ä\cot, cart \au̇\out \ch\chin \e\bet \ē\easy
\g\go \i\hit \ī\ice \j\job \ŋ\sing \ō\go \ȯ\law
\ȯi\boy \th\thin \t̲h̲\the \ü\loot \u̇\foot \y\yet
\zh\vision *see also* Pronunciation Symbols page

rum] **1 :** belonging to, used in, or suitable to the courts or to public discussion and debate **2 :** relating to or dealing with the application of scientific knowledge (as of medicine or linguistics) to legal problems ⟨~ pathology⟩ ⟨~ experts⟩ — **fo·ren·si·cal·ly** *adj*

fore·per·son *n* : FOREMAN

fore·see *vt* **fore·saw; fore·seen; fore·see·ing** : to be aware of the reasonable possibility of (as an occurrence or development) beforehand

fore·see·abil·i·ty \fōr-ˌsē-ə-'bi-lə-tē\ *n* **1** : the quality or state of being foreseeable ⟨reasonable ~ of probable consequences —*Gerwin v. Southeastern Cal. Ass'n of Seventh Day Adventists*, 14 Cal. App. 3d 209 (1971)⟩ **2 :** the doctrine esp. of tort and contract law that liability is limited to losses that are foreseeable — see also *Palsgraf v. Long Island Railroad Co.* in the IMPORTANT CASES section

fore·see·able \fōr-'sē-ə-bəl\ *adj* : such as reasonably can or should be anticipated : such that a person of ordinary prudence would expect to occur or exist under the circumstances ⟨a ~ risk⟩ ⟨the ~ expenses⟩ ⟨a ~ plaintiff⟩ — **fore·see·ably** *adv*

¹for·feit \'fȯr-fət\ *n* [Anglo-French, from Middle French *forfait*, past participle of *forfaire* to commit a crime, from *fors* outside + *faire* to do] : something forfeited or subject to being forfeited

²forfeit *vt* **1 :** to lose or lose the right to by some default, failure, or neglect of obligation or duty or by some offense ⟨shall ~ to the United States . . . any proceeds which the person obtained, directly or indirectly, from racketeering activity — *U.S. Code*⟩ **2 :** to subject to forfeiture ⟨it shall be placed in the custody of the Collector, who . . . shall cause a notice of the seizure and intention to ~ and sell the same —*Morgan v. United States*, 107 F. Supp. 501 (1952)⟩ — **for·feit·abil·i·ty** \ˌfȯr-fə-tə-'bi-lə-tē\ *n* — **for·feit·able** *adj*

³forfeit *adj* : forfeited or subject to forfeiture

for·fei·ture \'fȯr-fə-ˌchu̇r\ *n* **1 :** the loss of a right, money, or esp. property because of one's criminal act, default, or failure or neglect to perform a duty — compare WAIVER **2 :** something (as money or property) that is forfeited as a penalty

forge *vb* **forged; forg·ing** *vt* : to make, alter, or imitate (as a writing) falsely with intent to defraud : COUNTERFEIT ~ *vi* : to commit forgery — **forg·er** *n*

forg·ery *n, pl* **-er·ies 1 :** the act of falsely making, altering, or imitating (as a document or signature) with intent to defraud; *also* : the crime of committing such an act **2 :** something that is forged

form *n* **1 :** the structure of something (as a document) as distinguished from its matter ⟨a defect in ~, not substance⟩ **2** : established procedure according to rule or practice — see also FORM OF ACTION **3 :** a printed or typed document with blank spaces for insertion of required or requested information ⟨tax ~s⟩

for·mal *adj* **1 :** relating to or involving outward form, structure, or arrangement rather than content ⟨a ~ defect in the pleadings⟩ **2 :** requiring special or established solemnities or formalities esp. in order to be effective or valid under the law ⟨received ~ notice⟩ ⟨a ~ criminal charge⟩ **3 :** being such only as a matter of form : NOMINAL ⟨a ~ party to a lawsuit⟩

formal contract — see CONTRACT

formal rulemaking *n* : rulemaking by a government agency that is on the record after an opportunity for an agency hearing in accordance with the formal procedures set forth in sections 556 and 557 of the Administrative Procedure Act — compare INFORMAL RULEMAKING ◊ Formal rulemaking is usu. only done where specifically required by the legislation mandating the agency action.

for·mer adjudication *n* : a procedural doctrine that bars relitigation by the same parties of the same issues or claims upon which a judgment has already been rendered ◊ Estoppel by judgment and res judicata are the two branches of former adjudication, although *res judicata* is often used broadly to mean *former adjudication.*

former jeopardy *n* **1** : a common-law plea in bar of autrefois acquit or autrefois convict **2** : DOUBLE JEOPARDY

former testimony — see TESTIMONY

form of action : any of the personal actions (as assumpsit, detinue, or replevin) formerly brought at common law — see also WRIT ◊ Rule 2 of the Federal Rules of Civil Procedure states "there shall be one form of action to be known as 'civil action.'"

Form 10–K *n* : a financial disclosure form required by the Securities and Exchange Commission to be filed annually by companies issuing securities or having a threshold amount of gross assets

for·ni·ca·tion \ˌfȯr-nə-'kā-shən\ *n* [Late Latin *fornicatio*, from *fornicare* to have intercourse with prostitutes, from Latin *fornic-, fornix* arch, vault, brothel] : consensual sexual intercourse between a man and esp. single woman who are not married to each other; *also* : the crime of engaging in fornication — compare ADULTERY ◊ Where still considered a crime, fornication is classified as a misdemeanor.

for·swear \fȯr-'swar\ *vb* **-swore** \-'swȯr\; **-sworn** \-'swȯrn\; **-swear·ing** *vt* **1** : to reject, renounce, or deny under oath **2** : to renounce earnestly ～ *vi* : to swear falsely : commit false swearing

for·tu·i·tous event \fȯr-'tü-ə-təs-, -'tyü-\ *n* : an event of natural or human origin that could not have been reasonably foreseen or expected and is out of the control of the persons concerned (as parties to a contract) : FORCE MAJEURE — called also *cas fortuit*; see also FRUSTRATION; compare INEVITABLE ACCIDENT

fo·rum \'fō-rəm\ *n* **1** : PUBLIC FORUM **2 a** : a judicial body or assembly : COURT ⟨allowed the defendant in a state court action to choose the federal ～ by removing the case —M. H. Redish⟩ **b** : the territorial jurisdiction of a court ⟨due process requires defendant to have minimum level of contacts with ～ before personal juris-

diction may be exercised —*National Law Journal*⟩

forum non con·ve·ni·ens \ˌnän-kən-'vē-nē-ˌenz, -ˌnȯn-kȯn-'vā-nē-ˌens\ *n* [New Latin, literally, unsuitable tribunal] : a doctrine allowing a court with jurisdiction over a case to dismiss it because the convenience of the parties and the interest of justice would be better served if the case were brought in a court having proper jurisdiction in another venue — compare CHANGE OF VENUE

forum se·lec·tion clause *n* : a clause in an agreement in which the parties stipulate the forum in which any disputes arising between them will be resolved

forum shop *vi* : to engage in forum shopping

forum shop·ping *n* : the practice of choosing the court in which to bring an action from among those courts that could properly exercise jurisdiction based on a determination of which court is likely to provide the most favorable outcome

for·ward *n* : FORWARD CONTRACT at CONTRACT

forward contract — see CONTRACT

¹fos·ter *adj* : affording, receiving, or sharing nurture or parental care though not related by blood or legal relationships ⟨a ～ child⟩ ⟨a ～ parent⟩

²foster *vt* **fos·tered; fos·ter·ing** : to give parental care to

foster home *n* : a household in which care is provided to a child who has been orphaned or removed from the home of his or her natural parents (as for reasons of abuse, neglect, or delinquency)

¹found *past and past part of* FIND

²found *vt* : to establish (as an institution) often with provision for future maintenance

foun·da·tion *n* **1** : a basis upon which something stands or is supported; *specif* : a witness's preliminary testimony given

\ə\abut	\ᵊ\kitten	\ər\further	\a\ash \ā\ace
\ä\cot, cart	\au̇\out	\ch\chin	\e\bet \ē\easy
\g\go	\i\hit	\ī\ice	\j\job \ŋ\sing \ō\go \ȯ\law
\ȯi\boy	\th\thin	\t͟h\the	\ü\loot \u̇\foot \y\yet
\zh\vision	*see also* Pronunciation Symbols page		

to identify or explain evidence being offered at trial and establish its connection to the issue for which it is offered ⟨the lack of any ~ for the orthopedic surgeon's familiarity with the . . . standard of care rendered the surgeon's opinion testimony inadmissible —*National Law Journal*⟩ ◊ Before evidence can be admitted at trial, the foundation for it must be laid by the party offering it. A foundation must also be laid for the qualification of a witness as an expert, or for the assertion of a privilege. **2 a :** funds given for the permanent support of an institution : ENDOWMENT **b :** an organization or institution established by endowment with provision for future maintenance — **foun·da·tion·al** *adj*

found·er *n* : one that founds or establishes: as **a :** one that establishes a foundation **b** : FOUNDING FATHER

found·ing fa·ther *n, often cap both Fs* : a leading figure in the founding of the U.S.; *specif* : a member of the Constitutional Convention of 1787

four cor·ners *n pl* : the contents of a document as interpreted without reference to or consideration of outside information : the face of a document ⟨any evidence offered . . . must appear within the *four corners* of the will —*Crump's Estate v. Freeman*, 614 P.2d 1096 (1980)⟩

four corners rule *n* : a rule holding that if a document (as a contract, deed, or will) appears on its face to be complete no outside evidence may be used to challenge it ◊ The number of states that accept the four corners rule is in decline.

four–month rule *n* : a rule requiring that an action be taken within four months: as **a :** a rule in some states requiring that a defendant be tried within four months of the arrest, charge, or arraignment **b :** a rule set out in section 9-103(1)(d) of the Uniform Commercial Code that provides a secured creditor four months to perfect a security interest again in the state to which the collateral perfected previously in another state has been moved

401(k) plan \'fȯr-ˌō-ˌwən-'kā-\ *n* [after the section of the Internal Revenue Code that established it] : a retirement savings plan under which an employee may elect to have pretax contributions from his or her wages or salary deferred to a trust for investment

fourth degree *n* : a grade given to less serious forms of crimes ⟨manslaughter in the *fourth degree*⟩

frame *vt* **framed; fram·ing 1 :** to formulate the contents of and draw up (as a document) ⟨in the two hundred years since our Constitution was *framed* —W. J. Brennan, Jr.⟩ **2 :** to contrive the evidence against (as an innocent person) so that a verdict of guilty is assured

fram·er *n* : a drafter of legislation; *specif, cap* : one of the drafters of the U.S. Constitution and esp. of the articles and the Bill of Rights

frame–up \'frām-ˌəp\ *n* : an act or series of acts in which someone is framed

fran·chise \'fran-ˌchīz\ *n* [Anglo-French, literally, freedom, liberty, from Middle French, from *franchir* to free, from Old French *franc* free] **1 :** a special right or privilege granted by the government to an individual, group, or business entity: as **a :** a right to conduct a business and esp. to be and to exercise the powers of a corporation **b :** a right granted to a public utility company to provide services and to use public land for that purpose **2 :** a constitutional or statutory right; *esp* : the right to vote — used with *the* ⟨restricting them in employment, education, the ~, legal personality, and public accommodation —W. H. Burns⟩ **3 :** a right or license that is granted to an individual or group to market a company's goods or services in a particular territory under the company's trademark, trade name, or service mark and that often involves the use of rules and procedures designed by the company and services (as advertising) and facilities provided by the company in return for fees, royalties, or other compensation; *also* : a business granted such a right or license ⟨ran a fast-food ~⟩ **4 a :** an amount of liability (as a percentage or sum) specified in an insurance contract below which an insurer disclaims liability and above which the insurer assumes total liability — compare DEDUCTIBLE **b :** group insurance covering fewer than the minimum number of participants required by law for such coverage

fran·chi·see \‚fran-‚chī-'zē\ *n* : one granted a franchise

franchiser *var of* FRANCHISOR

franchise tax *n* : a business tax imposed upon various corporations granted a franchise

fran·chi·sor \‚fran-‚chī-'zȯr, 'fran-‚chī-zər\ *also* **fran·chis·er** \'fran-‚chī-zər\ *n* : one granting a franchise; *also* : FRANCHISEE

Franks hearing — see HEARING

frat·ri·cide \'fra-trə-‚sīd\ *n* [Middle French, from Latin *fratricida*, from *fratr-*, *frater* brother + *-cida* killing] **1 :** one that murders or kills his or her own brother or sister or an individual (as a countryman) having a relationship like that of a brother or sister **2 :** the act of a fratricide — **frat·ri·cid·al** \‚fra-trə-'sīd-ᵊl\ *adj*

fraud *n* [Latin *fraud-*, *fraus*] **1 a :** any act, expression, omission, or concealment calculated to deceive another to his or her disadvantage; *specif* : a misrepresentation or concealment with reference to some fact material to a transaction that is made with knowledge of its falsity or in reckless disregard of its truth or falsity and with the intent to deceive another and that is reasonably relied on by the other who is injured thereby **b :** the affirmative defense of having acted in response to a fraud **2 :** the crime or tort of committing fraud ⟨convicted of securities ∼⟩ — see also MISREPRESENTATION ◊ A tort action based on fraud is also referred to as an action of deceit.

actual fraud : fraud committed with the actual intent to deceive and thereby injure another — called also *fraud in fact;* compare CONSTRUCTIVE FRAUD in this entry

collateral fraud : EXTRINSIC FRAUD in this entry

constructive fraud : conduct that is considered fraud under the law despite the absence of an intent to deceive because it has the same consequences as an actual fraud would have and it is against public interests (as because of the violation of a public or private trust or confidence, the breach of a fiduciary duty, or the use of undue influence) — called also *legal fraud;* compare ACTUAL FRAUD in this entry

equitable fraud : CONSTRUCTIVE FRAUD in this entry — used esp. in New Jersey

extrinsic fraud : fraud (as that involved in making a false offer of compromise) that induces one not to present a case in court or deprives one of the opportunity to be heard; *also* : fraud that is not involved in the actual issues presented to a court and that prevents a full and fair hearing — called also *collateral fraud;* compare INTRINSIC FRAUD in this entry

fraud in fact : ACTUAL FRAUD in this entry

fraud in law : fraud that is presumed to have occurred in light of the circumstances irrespective of intent to deceive

fraud in the factum : fraud in which the deception causes the other party to misunderstand the nature of the transaction in which he or she is engaging esp. with regard to the contents of an instrument (as a contract or promissory note) — called also *fraud in the execution;* compare FRAUD IN THE INDUCEMENT in this entry

fraud in the inducement : fraud in which the deception leads the other party to engage in a transaction the nature of which he or she understands — compare FRAUD IN THE FACTUM in this entry

\ə\abut \ᵊ\kitten \ər\further \a\ash \ā\ace
\ä\cot, cart \au̇\out \ch\chin \e\bet \ē\easy
\g\go \i\hit \ī\ice \j\job \ŋ\sing \ō\go \ȯ\law
\ȯi\boy \th\thin \t͟h\the \ü\loot \u̇\foot \y\yet
\zh\vision *see also* Pronunciation Symbols page

fraud on the court : fraud involving conduct that undermines the integrity of the judicial process (as by improperly influencing a judge, jury, or other court personnel); *also* : EXTRINSIC FRAUD in this entry

intrinsic fraud : fraud (as by the use of false or forged documents, false claims, or perjured testimony) that deceives the trier of fact and results in a judgment in favor of the party perpetrating the fraud — compare EXTRINSIC FRAUD in this entry

legal fraud **1** : CONSTRUCTIVE FRAUD in this entry **2** : ACTUAL FRAUD in this entry — used esp. in New Jersey

mail fraud : fraud committed by use of the postal service esp. as described in title 18 section 1341 of the U.S. Code

wire fraud : fraud committed by using a means of electronic communication (as a telephone) — see also *Wire Fraud Act* in the IMPORTANT LAWS section

fraude \'fröd\ *n* [French, fraud] *in the civil law of Louisiana* : fraud committed in the performance of a contract — compare DOL

fraud in fact — see FRAUD
fraud in law — see FRAUD
fraud in the execution : FRAUD IN THE FACTUM at FRAUD
fraud in the factum — see FRAUD
fraud in the inducement — see FRAUD
fraud on the court — see FRAUD
fraud on the market the·o·ry *n* : a theory of liability in securities fraud cases: a defendant's material misrepresentation regarding a security traded in the open market that affects the price of the security is presumed to have been relied on by a plaintiff who purchased the security and suffered a loss — compare EFFICIENT MARKET

fraud·u·lent *adj* : characterized by, based on, or done by fraud — compare DECEPTIVE, FALSE, MISLEADING — **fraud·u·lent·ly** *adv*

fraudulent concealment *n* : the intentional failure to disclose a material fact and esp. the existence of a cause of action by one under a duty to make such a disclosure to another who acts or fails to act in reliance and suffers a loss

fraudulent conversion *n* : conversion committed with the intent of defrauding someone

fraudulent conveyance *n* : a conveyance of property made for the purpose of rendering the property unavailable for satisfaction of a debt or otherwise hindering or defeating the rights of creditors; *specif* : a conveyance of property that is made in return for inadequate consideration by one who is insolvent or who is rendered insolvent, undercapitalized, or unable to pay his or her debts as a result of the conveyance or that is made with the intent of hindering, delaying, or defrauding his or her creditors — called also *fraudulent transfer;* compare PREFERENCE ◊ A fraudulent conveyance is generally voidable by a court or, in a bankruptcy case, by the trustee in bankruptcy.

F.R.Civ.P. *abbr* Federal Rules of Civil Procedure — see also the IMPORTANT LAWS section

[1]free *adj* **1 a** : having the legal and political rights of a citizen ⟨representatives . . . shall be determined by adding to the whole number of ~ persons —*U.S. Constitution* art. I⟩ **b** : enjoying civil and political liberty ⟨a ~ people⟩ **c** : enjoying political independence or freedom from outside domination ⟨these united colonies are, and of right ought to be ~ and independent States —*Declaration of Independence*⟩ **d** : not subject to the control or domination of another **2** : made or done as a matter of choice and right : not compelled or restricted ⟨no law respecting an establishment of religion, or prohibiting the ~ exercise thereof —*U.S. Constitution* amend. I⟩ ⟨a ~ and voluntary confession⟩ **3** : relieved from or lacking a burden (as a lien or other encumbrance on title) ⟨a buyer in ordinary course of business . . . takes ~ of a security interest created by his seller —*Uniform Commercial Code*⟩ **4** : not bound, confined, or detained by force ⟨~ on bail⟩ **5 a :** having no trade restrictions **b :** not subject to government regulation **c** *of foreign exchange* **:** not subject to restriction or official control **6 :** not costing or charging anything — **free•ly** *adv* — **for free :** without charge

²**free** *vt* **freed; free•ing 1 :** to cause to be free **2 :** to relieve or rid of what constrains, confines, restricts, or burdens

free along•side ship *adv or adj* **:** with delivery at the side of the ship free of charges and the buyer's liability then beginning

free•dom *n* **1 :** the quality or state of being free: as **a :** the absence of necessity, coercion, or constraint in choice or action **b :** liberation from slavery or restraint or from the power of another **c :** the quality or state of being exempt or released from something onerous **2 a :** a political or civil right **b :** FRANCHISE 2

freedom of association : the right guaranteed esp. by the First Amendment to the U.S. Constitution to join with others either in personal relationships or as part of a group usu. having a common viewpoint or purpose and often exercising the right to assemble and to free speech

freedom of contract : a power or right to contract and freely determine the provisions of contracts without arbitrary or unreasonable legal restrictions esp. as guaranteed under the contract clause of Article I, Section 10 of the U.S. Constitution — called also *freedom to contract, liberty of contract*

freedom of expression : FREEDOM OF SPEECH

freedom of re•li•gion : the right esp. as guaranteed under the free exercise clause of the First Amendment to the U.S. Constitution to practice one's religion or exercise one's beliefs without intervention by the government and to be free of the exercise of authority by a church through the government — see also FREE EXERCISE CLAUSE ◊ The freedom of religion as guaranteed by the First Amendment can

be overcome by a showing by the government of a compelling state interest. On this basis, practices used in some religions, such as drug use and bigamy, are prohibited despite the First Amendment guarantee.

freedom of speech : the right to express information, ideas, and opinions free of government restrictions based on content and subject only to reasonable limitations (as the power of the government to avoid a clear and present danger) esp. as guaranteed by the First and Fourteenth Amendments to the U.S. Constitution — see also FREE SPEECH; compare CENSORSHIP, PRIOR RESTRAINT

freedom of the press : the right to publish and disseminate information, thoughts, and opinions without restraint or censorship as guaranteed under the First Amendment to the U.S. Constitution ◊ The First Amendment's guarantees of freedom of speech and freedom of the press are closely intertwined, and many cases relating to freedom of the press are couched in terms of the freedom of speech.

freedom of the seas : the right of a merchant ship to travel any waters except territorial waters either in peace or war

freedom to contract : FREEDOM OF CONTRACT

free exercise clause *n, often cap F&E&C* **:** the clause in the First Amendment to the U.S. Constitution prohibiting Congress from making any law prohibiting the free exercise of religion — see also FREEDOM OF RELIGION; compare ESTABLISHMENT CLAUSE

free expression *n* **:** FREE SPEECH

free•hold \'frē-ˌhōld\ *n* [translation of Anglo-French *frank tenement* freehold estate] **:** a tenure of real property the duration of which cannot be determined and by which an estate in fee simple or fee tail

\ə\abut \ə\kitten \ər\further \a\ash \ā\ace
\ä\cot, cart \au̇\out \ch\chin \e\bet \ē\easy
\g\go \i\hit \ī\ice \j\job \ŋ\sing \ō\go \ȯ\law
\ȯi\boy \th\thin \t̲h̲\the \ü\loot \u̇\foot \y\yet
\zh\vision *see also* Pronunciation Symbols page

or for life is held; *also* : an estate held by such tenure — compare LEASEHOLD — **freehold** *adj or adv*

free·hold·er *n* : the owner of a freehold estate

free on board *adv or adj* : without charge for delivery to and placing on board a carrier at a specified point

free speech *n* **1** : speech that is protected by the First Amendment to the U.S. Constitution ⟨setting off an alarm bell is not *free speech* —A. M. Dershowitz⟩ **2** : FREEDOM OF SPEECH ⟨an unconstitutional restraint on *free speech* —*National Law Journal*⟩

freeze *vt* **froze; fro·zen; freez·ing 1** : to cause to become fixed, immovable, unavailable, or unalterable ⟨∼ interest rates⟩ **2** : to immobilize (as by government regulation or the action of a financial institution) the expenditure, withdrawal, or exchange of ⟨∼ foreign assets⟩ **3** : to restructure (the capital of a close corporation) so that the value is reflected mostly in preferred stock rather than common stock ◊ Once capital is frozen, the common shares can be transferred to the heirs of the owner without taxation while the owner continues to enjoy the income from preferred stock dividends during his or her lifetime. — **freeze** *n*

freez·ee \ˌfrē-'zē\ *n* : one subject to a freezeout

freeze·out \'frēz-ˌaút\ *n* : a corporate action (as a merger) taken by those in control of the corporation (as controlling shareholders or the board of directors) for the purpose of causing the minority shareholders to lose their equity in the corporation (as by the sale of their shares) — compare SQUEEZEOUT

freeze out *vt* : to subject to a freezeout

F reorganization — see REORGANIZATION

fresh *adj* **1 a** : free of the detrimental effects of delay (as the fading of memories) **b** : characterized by promptness **2** : experienced, made, or received newly or anew ⟨a resumed interrogation requiring ∼ Miranda warnings⟩

fresh complaint *n* : a report of a sexual offense by the victim to someone in a position of trust (as a police officer, parent, or friend) made with reasonable promptness

fresh complaint rule *n* : a rule of evidence: the testimony of a witness to whom a victim of a sexual offense made a fresh complaint is admissible to corroborate the victim's testimony — called also *fresh complaint doctrine*

fresh pur·suit *n* **1** : the immediate and continuous pursuit by police officers of a suspect who is fleeing to avoid arrest that under common law and some state codes gives the officers the right to cross jurisdictional lines in order to make an arrest **2** : HOT PURSUIT

friend·ly *adj* : agreeable to those affected : not hostile ⟨a ∼ takeover⟩

friend of the court : AMICUS CURIAE

fringe benefit *n* : an employment benefit (as a pension, a paid holiday, or health insurance) granted by an employer that has a monetary value but that does not affect basic wage rates

frisk *vt* : to run the hand rapidly over the outer clothing of (a suspect) for the purpose of finding concealed weapons — compare SEARCH ◊ The purpose of frisking a suspect is to insure the safety of an officer making an investigation against concealed weapons, not to uncover evidence. The officer must be justified in his or her encounter of the suspect and must have a reasonable suspicion that the suspect is armed. The scope of the frisk must be limited to the discovery of weapons. — **frisk** *n*

friv·o·lous \'fri-və-ləs\ *adj* : lacking in any arguable basis or merit in either law or fact ◊ In an attempt to discourage frivolous lawsuits, Rule 11 of the Federal Rules of Civil Procedure requires the signature of an attorney or party on any pleading, motion, or other paper to certify that to the signer's knowledge it is grounded in fact and warranted by law or otherwise brought in good faith and not for an improper purpose. A court is authorized to impose sanctions for violation of the rule.

front *n* : something or someone (as a person or group) used to mask the identity or true character or activity of the actual person or organization in control — **front** *vb*

front·age \'frən-tij\ *n* **1** : a piece of land that lies adjacent (as to a street or the ocean) **2** : the land between the front of a building and the street **3** : the length of a frontage

froze *past of* FREEZE

frozen *past part of* FREEZE

fruit *n* **1 a** : something (as evidence) that is obtained or gathered during an action or operation (as a search) ⟨moved to suppress evidence seized from the room on the grounds that it was obtained as the ~ of an illegal arrest —*National Law Journal*⟩ **b** *pl* : FRUIT OF THE POISONOUS TREE ⟨the Court was asked to extend the . . . *fruits* doctrine —*Oregon v. Elstad*, 470 U.S. 298 (1985)⟩ **2 a** *in the civil Law of Louisiana* : property (as income or goods) produced by or derived from other movable or immovable property without diminution of its substance ⟨co-owners share the ~s and products of the thing held —*Louisiana Civil Code*⟩ — compare PRODUCT 3

civil fruit : the revenue derived from property esp. by virtue of an obligation (as a lease)

natural fruit : an animal or plant product (as a crop)

b : income that is produced or earned by other property or services

fruit of the poisonous tree 1 : a doctrine of evidence: evidence that is derived from or gathered during an illegal action (as an unlawful search) cannot be admitted into court **2** : evidence that is inadmissible under an evidentiary exclusionary rule because it was derived from or gathered during an illegal action — see also *Wong Sun v. U.S.* in the IMPORTANT CASES section; compare INDEPENDENT SOURCE, INEVITABLE DISCOVERY, PLAIN VIEW

frus·trate \'frəs-ˌtrāt\ *vt* **frus·trat·ed;**

frus·trat·ing : to make invalid or ineffectual : DEFEAT ⟨the remedial purposes of the Workers' Compensation Act should not be *frustrated* by rigid technical standards —*Palmer v. Bath Iron Works Corp.*, 559 A.2d 340 (1989)⟩

frus·tra·tion \ˌfrəs-'trā-shən\ *n* **1 a** : the act of frustrating **b** : the state or an instance of being frustrated **c** : something that frustrates **2** : a common-law doctrine of contract law: parties to a contract may be excused from performance even though performance is still possible if the reason for making the contract is partially or completely frustrated by a fortuitous event or by circumstances which are not the fault of either party — called also *frustration of purpose*, *frustration of the venture;* compare CAUSE 4, FORCE MAJEURE CLAUSE, IMPOSSIBILITY, IMPRACTICABILITY ◊ In order for frustration to be used as a successful defense to a breach of contract claim, the reason for making the contract must have been contemplated or recognized by both the contracting parties even though it was not expressed in the contract.

Frye test \'frī-\ *n* [from *United States v. Frye*, 293 F. 1013 (1923), the case that established the rule] : a common-law rule of evidence: the results of scientific tests or procedures are admissible as evidence only when the tests or procedures have gained general acceptance in the particular field to which they belong — called also *Frye rule* ◊ In *Daubert v. Merrell Dow Pharmaceuticals*, 509 U.S. 579 (1993), the Supreme Court held that the Federal Rules of Evidence supersede the Frye test, and as a result scientific evidence (as expert testimony) needs to meet only the requirements of the Federal Rules of Evidence in order to be admissible.

FTC *abbr* Federal Trade Commission —

\ə\abut \ᵊ\kitten \ər\further \a\ash \ā\ace
\ä\cot, cart \au̇\out \ch\chin \e\bet \ē\easy
\g\go \i\hit \ī\ice \j\job \ŋ\sing \ō\go \ȯ\law
\ȯi\boy \th\thin \t͟h\the \ü\loot \u̇\foot \y\yet
\zh\vision *see also* Pronunciation Symbols page

see also the IMPORTANT AGENCIES section

FTCA *abbr* Federal Tort Claims Act — see also the IMPORTANT LAWS section

fu·gi·tive \'fyü-jə-tiv\ *n* : a person who flees; *esp* : a person who flees one jurisdiction (as a state) for another in order to elude law enforcement personnel

fugitive from justice warrant *n* : FUGITIVE WARRANT at WARRANT

fugitive warrant — see WARRANT

full age *n* : AGE OF MAJORITY

full bench *n* : FULL COURT

full court *n* : a court with all or the required number of the judges present — called also *full bench;* compare EN BANC, PANEL

full faith and credit *n* : the recognition and enforcement of the public acts, records, and judicial proceedings of one state by another — see also *Article IV* of the CONSTITUTION in the back matter; compare CHOICE OF LAW, COMITY, FEDERALISM ◊ Unlike comity, full faith and credit is a requirement created by the U.S. Constitution and the U.S. Code. A public law or a judicial decision may not, however, be entitled to full faith and credit for specific reasons (as for having been decided by a court not having jurisdiction). Full faith and credit is given only in civil cases; states recognize each other's criminal laws through the mechanism of extradition.

full faith and credit clause *n*, *often cap both Fs & both Cs* : the clause in Article IV of the U.S. Constitution that requires states to give full faith and credit to the public acts, records, and judicial proceedings of the other states

full interdiction *n* : INTERDICTION 1

full re·port·ing clause *n* : a clause in an insurance policy which provides that the indemnity will not exceed that proportion of loss which the last reported value of the property bears to the actual value

fully funded *adj* : having financial resources adequate to meet current retirement plan payments even in the event of bankruptcy

functional obsolescence — see OBSOLESCENCE

func·tus of·fi·cio \'fəŋk-təs-ə-'fi-shē-ō, 'fuŋk-tüs-ō-'fē-kē-ō\ *adj* [Latin, having performed his duty, having served its purpose] : of no further official authority or legal effect ⟨the warrant . . . had been returned and was *functus officio* —*Cady v. Dombrowski,* 413 U.S. 433 (1973)⟩ ⟨once an arbitrator makes an award she is *functus officio*⟩ — used esp. of an officer who is no longer in office or of an instrument that has fulfilled its purpose

¹fund *n* **1** : a sum of money or other resources whose principal or interest is set aside for a specific objective

cli·ent security fund : a fund established by each state to compensate clients for losses suffered due to their attorneys' misappropriation of funds

common trust fund : an in-house trust fund established by a bank trust department to pool the assets of many small trusts for greater diversification in investing

executor fund : a fund established in estate planning to provide for the payment of final expenses by an executor

joint wel·fare fund : a fund that is established by collective bargaining to provide health and welfare benefits to employees and that is jointly administered by representatives of labor and management

paid–in fund : a reserve cash fund in lieu of a capital stock account set up by mutual insurance companies to cover unforeseen losses

sink·ing fund : a fund set up and accumulated by regular deposits for paying off the principal on a debt or for other specified purposes (as self-insurance)

strike fund : a fund accumulated by a union through special assessments or from general funds and used to pay striking workers or for other strike-related activities

Taft–Hart·ley fund \'taft-'härt-lē-\ [after the Taft-Hartley Act of 1947, which established it] : JOINT WELFARE FUND in this entry

trust fund : property (as money or securities) settled or held in a trust **2** : an organization administering a special fund

growth fund : a mutual fund that invests in the stock of growth companies

hedge fund : an investing group usu. in the form of a limited partnership that employs speculative techniques in the hope of obtaining large capital gains

index fund : a mutual fund that invests to reflect the composition of the market as a whole by matching its investments to a stock index

mutual fund : an investment company that invests its shareholders' money in a usu. diversified group of securities of other companies

vul·ture fund : an investment company that buys up bankrupt or insolvent companies with the goal of reorganizing them so they can be profitably resold as going concerns

²fund *vt* **1 a** : to make provision of resources for discharging the principal or interest of **b** : to provide financial resources for **2** : to place in a fund **3** : to convert into a debt that is payable either at a distant date or at no definite date and that bears a fixed interest

fundamental error — see ERROR

fun·da·men·tal fairness *n* **1** : the balance or impartiality (of a court proceeding) that is essential to due process **2** : a subjective standard by which a court pro-

ceeding is deemed to have followed due process

fundamental right *n* : a right that is considered by a court (as the U.S. Supreme Court) to be explicitly or implicitly expressed in a constitution (as the U.S. Constitution) ◇ A court must review a law that infringes on a fundamental right under a standard of strict scrutiny. A fundamental right can be limited by a law only if there is a compelling state interest.

¹fun·gi·ble \ˈfən-jə-bəl\ *adj* [New Latin *fungibilis*, from Latin *fungi* to perform] : being something (as money or a commodity) one part or quantity of which can be substituted for another of equal value in paying a debt or settling an account ⟨oil, wheat, and lumber are ~ commodities⟩

²fungible *n* : something that is fungible

fungible goods — see GOOD 2

fu·ture *n* : a contract traded on an exchange in which a party agrees to buy or sell a quantity of a bulk commodity (as soybeans) at a specified future date and at a set price — usu. used in pl. ◇ If the price of the commodity has gone up when the future date arrives, the buyer in the contract profits. If the price has gone down, the seller profits.

future contract *n* : FUTURES CONTRACT at CONTRACT

future goods — see GOOD 2

future interest — see INTEREST 1

futures contract — see CONTRACT

futures option — see OPTION 3

G

GAAP *abbr* generally accepted accounting principles

gag order — see ORDER 3b

gag rule *n* : a law, order, or ruling that prohibits free debate or expression of ideas, information, or opinions ⟨a long-standing Florida *gag rule* barring people from discussing complaints they made against police officers —*National Law Journal*⟩; *specif* : a rule limiting or prohibiting debate on an issue in a legislative assembly (as the U.S. House of Representatives)

gain *n* **1** : an increase in value, capital, or amount — compare LOSS

   capital gain : a gain realized on the sale or exchange of a capital asset (as a stock or real estate)

   casualty gain : a gain realized by an insured because property insurance benefits paid for a loss from a casualty or theft are greater than the adjusted value of the insured asset

   long–term capital gain : a capital gain realized on the sale or exchange of an asset held for more than a specified period (as a year)

   ordinary gain : a gain from the exchange or sale of an asset that is not capital

   short–term capital gain : a capital gain realized on the sale or exchange of an asset held for less than a specified period (as a year) that is treated as ordinary income under federal income tax laws

2 *pl, in the civil law of Louisiana* : a class of community property that reflects the increase in property value contributed by the common skill or labor of the spouses — **gain** *vb*

gain·shar·ing \'gān-₁shar-iŋ\ *n* : incentive-based compensation that ties wage increases or bonuses to increased productivity rather than profit increases

GAL *abbr* guardian ad litem

gam·ble \'gam-bəl\ *vb* **gam·bled; gam·bling** *vi* : to risk something of value for the chance of winning a prize — *vt* : to risk (something) for the chance of winning a prize — **gam·bler** \-blər\ *n*

game *vi* **gamed; gam·ing** : to play for a stake : GAMBLE

gang *n* : a group of persons associating for antisocial and often criminal purposes and activities

gang·land \'gaŋ-₁land\ *n, often attrib* : the world of organized crime

gang·ster *n* : a member of a gang of criminals

GAO *abbr* General Accounting Office — see also the IMPORTANT AGENCIES section

gaol, gaol·er *chiefly Brit var of* JAIL, JAILER

gap–fill·er \'gap-₁fi-lər\ *n* : a term supplied by a law or a court when the parties to an agreement fail to make provisions for a particular matter (as a price or a remedy for breach)

gar·nish \'gär-nish\ *vt* [Anglo-French *garniss-*, stem of *garnir* to garnish, give legal summons, warn, from Old French, of Germanic origin; akin to Old High German *warnōn* to take heed] **1** : to subject (property or money) to garnishment **2** : to seek satisfaction of (a debt) through garnishment — compare ATTACH, LEVY

¹gar·nish·ee \₁gär-nə-'shē\ *n* : a third party holding garnished property or money of a debtor

²garnishee *vt* **-eed; -ee·ing** : GARNISH

gar·nish·ment \'gär-nish-mənt\ *n* : a remedial device used by a creditor to have property of the debtor or money owed to the debtor that is in the possession of a third party attached to pay the debt to the creditor; *specif* : attachment of the debtor's wages to satisfy a judgment — compare *wage assignment* at ASSIGNMENT

gar·nish·or \'gär-ni-shər, -ˌshȯr\ *n* : a creditor who brings a garnishment proceeding against a garnishee

GATT \'gat\ *abbr* General Agreement on Tariffs and Trade — see also the IMPORTANT LAWS section

gave *past of* GIVE

GBMI *abbr* guilty but mentally ill

gen·der discrimination \'jen-dər-\ *n* : SEX DISCRIMINATION

gen·er·al \'jen-rəl, 'je-nə-\ *adj* **1** : involving, applicable to, or affecting the whole **2** : involving, relating to, or applicable to every member of a class, kind, or group **3** : not confined by specialization or limitation **4** : relating to, determined by, or concerned with main elements rather than limiting details ⟨a ~ resemblance⟩ **5** : holding superior rank or taking precedence over others similarly titled ⟨the ~ manager⟩

general act *n* : GENERAL LAW

general administrator — see ADMINISTRATOR

general agency — see AGENCY 2a

general agent — see AGENT

general appearance *n* : a court appearance by which a party submits to the jurisdiction of the court esp. by asking for any relief other than a ruling that the court has no jurisdiction over the appearing party — compare SPECIAL APPEARANCE ◊ General and special appearances are not used in the federal courts or in state courts that follow the Federal Rules of Civil Procedure.

general assembly *n* **1** : a legislative assembly; *esp* : a U.S. state legislature **2** *cap G&A* : the supreme deliberative body of the United Nations

general assignment — see ASSIGNMENT

general benefit — see BENEFIT 1

general bequest — see BEQUEST

general contractor *n* : a person or business entity that contracts to be in charge of a building project usu. involving the use of subcontractors — called also *orig-*

inal contractor, prime, prime contractor

general counsel *n* : a lawyer at the head of a legal department (as of a corporation or government agency)

General Court *n* : a legislative assembly; *specif* : the state legislature in Massachusetts and New Hampshire

general court–martial *n* : a court-martial consisting of a military judge and usu. at least five members and having authority to impose a sentence of dishonorable discharge or death — compare SPECIAL COURT-MARTIAL, SUMMARY COURT-MARTIAL

general creditor — see CREDITOR

general damages — see DAMAGE 2

general demurrer — see DEMURRER

general denial — see DENIAL

general deposit — see DEPOSIT 2a

general devise — see DEVISE

general election *n* : an election usu. held at regular intervals in which candidates are elected in all or most constituencies of a nation or state

general finding — see FINDING

general intangible *n* : any personal property that is not an account, chattel paper, document, instrument, goods, or money esp. as identified by section 9-106 of the Uniform Commercial Code

general intent — see INTENT

general jurisdiction — see JURISDICTION

general law *n* : a law that is unrestricted as to time, is applicable throughout the entire territory subject to the power of the legislature that enacted it, and applies to all persons in the same class — called also *general act, general statute;* compare LOCAL LAW 1a, PUBLIC LAW, SPECIAL LAW

general legacy — see LEGACY

general lien — see LIEN

general mortgage — see MORTGAGE

general partner — see PARTNER

\ə\abut \ᵊ\kitten \ər\further \a\ash \ā\ace
\ä\cot, cart \au̇\out \ch\chin \e\bet \ē\easy
\g\go \i\hit \ī\ice \j\job \ŋ\sing \ō\go \ȯ\law
\ȯi\boy \th\thin \th̠\the \ü\loot \u̇\foot \y\yet
\zh\vision *see also* Pronunciation Symbols page

general partnership — see PARTNERSHIP

general power — see POWER 2b

general power of appointment — see POWER OF APPOINTMENT

general power of attorney — see POWER OF ATTORNEY

general publication *n* : communication or dissemination of a copyrightable work that implies a dedication of the work to the public or an abandonment of the copyright — compare LIMITED PUBLICATION

general sentence — see SENTENCE

General Ses·sions Court \-'se-shənz-\ *n* : a court sitting in each county seat in Tennessee and having limited jurisdiction over civil matters and some minor criminal matters

general statute *n* : GENERAL LAW

general strike — see STRIKE

general verdict — see VERDICT

general verdict rule *n* : a rule providing that if a jury returns a general verdict in favor of one party it is presumed to have found in favor of that party on every issue

general warrant — see WARRANT

general wel·fare clause \-'wel-,far-\ *n, often cap G&W&C* : a clause in Article I, Section 8 of the U.S. Constitution empowering Congress to provide for the general welfare of the United States (as through the collection of taxes)

gen·er·a·tion–skip·ping tax *n* : GENERATION-SKIPPING TRANSFER TAX

generation–skipping transfer *n* : a transfer of property or of an interest in property that is to a person of a generation more than one generation below that of the transferor and that can be characterized as a taxable termination, a taxable distribution, or a direct skip — see also DIRECT SKIP, *generation-skipping trust* at TRUST, SKIP PERSON, TAXABLE DISTRIBUTION, TAXABLE TERMINATION ◊ A transfer from a grandparent to a grandchild qualifies as a generation-skipping transfer, as does a transfer of a life estate to a child with a remainder in the grandchild. Such transfers are subject to a generation‑skipping transfer tax.

generation–skipping transfer tax *n* : a transfer tax on a generation-skipping transfer — called also *generation‑skipping tax*

generation–skipping trust — see TRUST

ge·ner·ic \jə-'ner-ik\ *adj* **1** : common or descriptive and not entitled to trademark protection : NONPROPRIETARY ⟨the ~ name of a drug⟩ **2** : having a nonproprietary name ⟨~ drugs⟩

geno·cide \'je-nə-,sīd\ *n* : acts committed with intent to partially or wholly destroy a national, ethnic, racial, or religious group; *also* : the crime of committing such acts

gen·u·ine *adj* : actually having the reputed or apparent qualities or character; *specif* : free of forgery or counterfeiting — see also *genuine issue* at ISSUE — **gen·u·ine·ly** *adv* — **gen·u·ine·ness** *n*

genuine issue — see ISSUE

geo·graph·ic market *n* : the geographic area in which there is effective competition in the sale of products or services — used in antitrust matters

¹ger·ry·man·der \'jer-ē-,man-dər *also and originally* 'ger-ē-\ *n* [Elbridge *Gerry* (1744–1814) + sala*mander;* from the shape of an election district formed during Gerry's governorship of Massachusetts] **1** : the act or method of gerrymandering **2** : a district or pattern of districts varying greatly in size or population as a result of gerrymandering

²gerrymander *vt* **-dered; -der·ing 1** : to divide (a territorial unit) into election districts to give one political party an electoral majority in a large number of districts while concentrating the voting strength of the opposition in as few districts as possible **2** : to divide (an area) into political units to give special advantages to one group ⟨~ a school district⟩

GIC \,jē-,ī-'sē\ *n* : GUARANTEED INVESTMENT CONTRACT at CONTRACT

gift *n* **1** : an intentional and gratuitous transfer of real or personal property by a donor with legal capacity who actually or constructively delivers the property to the donee with the intent of giving up dominion over the property and investing it in the donee who accepts it; *broadly* : a voluntary transfer of property without compensation — see also DELIVERY; compare DONATION, SALE

class gift : a usu. testamentary gift of a sum to a group of unspecified persons whose number and identity and share of the gift will be determined sometime in the future (as at the death of the donor)

com·plet·ed gift : a gift in which the dominion and control of the property is placed beyond the donor's reach

gift cau·sa mor·tis \-'kò-zə-'mòr-tis, -'kaù-sä-'mòr-tēs\ *pl* **gifts causa mortis** : a gift of esp. personal property made in contemplation of impending death that is delivered with the intent that the gift take effect only in the event of the donor's death and that it be revoked in the event of survival — compare *donation inter vivos* and *donation mortis causa* at DONATION, GIFT INTER VIVOS and TESTAMENTARY GIFT in this entry

gift in·ter vi·vos \-'in-tər-'vī-vōs; -'in-ter-'vē-vōs, -'wē-wōs\ *pl* **gifts inter vivos** : a gift made during the lifetime of the donor and delivered with the intent of surrendering immediately and irrevocably dominion and control over the property — compare *donation inter vivos* at DONATION, GIFT CAUSA MORTIS and TESTAMENTARY GIFT in this entry

gift over pl gifts over : a gift esp. by will of property that takes effect upon the termination or failure of a preceding estate (as a life estate) in the property

manual gift : a gift esp. under the civil law of Louisiana made of a movable corporeal object by actual delivery and involving no formalities

split gift : a gift made by a spouse to a third person that for purposes of gift tax may be considered as given one= half by each spouse to take advantage of tax avoidance devices (as the annual exclusion)

sub·sti·tu·tion·al gift \,səb-stə-'tü-shə-nəl-, -'tyü-\ : a gift to a legatee or devisee in substitution for another devisee

or legatee who cannot take under the will (as because of death) — called also *substitute gift*

testamentary gift : a gift that does not become effective until the death of the donor; *specif* : a gift made in a will — compare GIFT CAUSA MORTIS and GIFT INTER VIVOS in this entry **2** : something voluntarily transferred without compensation **3** : a transfer of property for less than adequate consideration other than in the ordinary course of business — used in the law of gift tax ◊ The amount by which the value of property so transferred exceeds the consideration paid is included in the total amount of taxable gifts made during a calendar year.

gift causa mortis — see GIFT
gift inter vivos — see GIFT
gift over — see GIFT
gift tax *n* : an excise tax imposed on a donor for gifts of property made during the donor's lifetime — see also ANNUAL EXCLUSION, GIFT 3 *split gift* at GIFT, UNIFIED TRANSFER TAX; compare DEATH TAX, ESTATE TAX, GENERATION-SKIPPING TRANSFER TAX

gist \'jist\ *n* [Anglo-French, in the phrase *laccion gist* the action lies or is based (on), from *gisir* to lie (of process), from Old French *gesir* to lie, ultimately from Latin *jacere*] : the ground or foundation of a legal action without which it would not be sustainable

give *vt* **gave; giv·en; giv·ing 1 a** : to make a gift of ⟨I ~ the remainder of my estate to my wife⟩ — compare CONVEY, SELL **b** : to grant or bestow by formal action ⟨the law ~s citizens the right to vote⟩ **2 a** : to transfer from one's authority or custody ⟨the sheriff *gave* the prisoner to the warden⟩ **b** : to execute and deliver ⟨all officers must ~ bond⟩ **c** : to communicate or impart to another ⟨failed to ~ adequate

\ə\abut \ᵊ\kitten \ər\further \a\ash \ā\ace
\ä\cot, cart \aù\out \ch\chin \e\bet \ē\easy
\g\go \i\hit \ī\ice \j\job \ŋ\sing \ō\go \ò\law
\òi\boy \th\thin \th\the \ü\loot \ù\foot \y\yet
\zh\vision   *see also* Pronunciation Symbols page

notice⟩ **d** : to offer or submit for the consideration of another ⟨~ testimony in court⟩ **3** : to yield possession of by way of exchange ⟨will ~ top dollar for your used car⟩ **4 a** : to impose as punishment **b** : to award by formal verdict ⟨judgment was *given* against the plaintiff⟩ — **giv•er** *n*

give•back \'giv-,bak\ *n* : a previous gain (as an increase in wages or benefits) given back to management by workers (as in a labor contract)

giving in payment : DATION EN PAIEMENT

GNP *abbr* gross national product

go forward *vi* **went forward; gone forward; going forward** : to proceed with a lawsuit or a matter (as the presentation of evidence) in a lawsuit

go•ing and com•ing rule *n* : a rule that an employee cannot receive workers' compensation benefits for injuries suffered while coming to or going from work — see also SPECIAL HAZARD RULE, SPECIAL MISSION EXCEPTION

going con•cern *n* : a business that is in operation

going concern value *n* : the value of the assets of an enterprise or of the enterprise itself considered as an operating business and therefore based on earning power and prospects rather than on the value of the same assets or the same business in the event of liquidation

going private *n* : the process of transforming a public corporation into a close corporation by terminating the registration of the corporation's stock, the listing of the stock on an exchange, or the active trading of the stock on the market

going private transaction *n* : a corporate action (as a recapitalization, share repurchase, or tender offer) taken as part of going private

gold•en para•chute *n* : an agreement providing for generous compensation to an executive upon dismissal (as because of a merger)

¹good *adj* **bet•ter; best** **1** : commercially sound or reliable ⟨a ~ risk⟩ **2 a** : valid or effectual under the law **b** : free of defects **3 a** : characterized by honesty and

fairness **b** : conforming to a standard of virtue ⟨shall hold their offices during ~ behavior —*U.S. Constitution* art. III⟩; *also* : characterized by or relating to good behavior

²good *n* **1** : advancement of prosperity and well-being ⟨for the ~ of the community⟩ **2** : an item of tangible movable personal property having value but usu. excluding money, securities, and negotiable instruments — usu. used in pl.: as **a** *pl* : all things under section 2-105 of the Uniform Commercial Code that are movable at the time of identification to the contract for sale other than the money that is to be paid, investment securities, and choses in action **b** *pl* : all things under section 9-104 of the Uniform Commercial Code that are movable at the time that a security interest in them attaches or that are fixtures but excluding money, documents, instruments, accounts, chattel paper, general intangibles, and minerals or the like before extraction

consumer goods : goods purchased primarily for personal, family, or household uses

du•ra•ble goods : consumer goods that last and are used for a number of years : DURABLES

fungible goods : goods of which any unit is by nature or by usage of trade the equivalent of any other unit esp. as defined by section 1-201 of the Uniform Commercial Code

future goods : goods that are the subject of a contract but are not yet existing or specified

hard goods : DURABLE GOODS in this entry

house•hold goods : goods used in connection with the home; *specif* : furniture, furnishings, and personal effects used in a dwelling as defined by section 7-209 of the Uniform Commercial Code

mo•bile goods : goods as defined in section 9-103 of the Uniform Commercial Code that are mobile, are of a type (as vehicles) usu. used in more than one jurisdiction, are not covered by a certificate of title, and are either the equipment of a debtor or inventory leased by a debtor

ordinary goods : goods as defined by section 9-103 of the Uniform Commercial Code that are anything other than those covered by a certificate of title, mobile goods, or minerals

pro•duc•er goods : goods (as tools and raw materials) used to produce other goods and satisfy human wants only indirectly

soft goods : consumer goods that are not durable goods

good cause — see CAUSE 2

good consideration — see CONSIDERATION

good faith *n* [translation of Latin *bona fides*] : honesty, fairness, and lawfulness of purpose : absence of any intent to defraud, act maliciously, or take unfair advantage ⟨filed the suit in *good faith*⟩ ⟨negotiating in *good faith*⟩ — see also GOOD FAITH EXCEPTION, GOOD FAITH PURCHASER; compare BAD FAITH ◊ The meaning of *good faith*, though always based on honesty, may vary depending on the specific context in which it is used. A person is said to buy in good faith when he or she holds an honest belief in his or her right or title to the property and has no knowledge or reason to know of any defect in the title. In section 1-201 of the Uniform Commercial Code, *good faith* is defined generally as "honesty in fact in the conduct or transaction concerned." Article 2 of the U.C.C. says "good faith in the case of a merchant means honesty in fact and the observance of reasonable commercial standards of fair dealing in the trade." Similarly, Article 3 on negotiable instruments defines *good faith* as "honesty in fact and the observance of reasonable commercial standards of fair dealing," a definition which also applies to the provisions of Article 4 on bank deposits and collections and Article 4A on funds transfers. The U.C.C. imposes an obligation of good faith on the performance of every contract or duty under its purview. The law also generally requires good faith of fiduciaries and agents acting on behalf of their principals. There is also a requirement under the National Labor Relations Act that employers and unions bargain in good faith.

good faith exception *n* : an exception to the exclusionary rule: evidence obtained by the use of a warrant later found to be unsupported by probable cause is admissible if the investigating officers acted in reasonable reliance that the warrant was valid — see also *Mapp v. Ohio* in the IMPORTANT CASES section

good faith purchaser *n* : a purchaser who gives value for an asset in good faith and without knowledge of adverse claims — called also *good faith purchaser for value*

good sa•mar•i•tan \-sə-'mar-ə-tən\ *n* [from the *good Samaritan* in the New Testament parable (Luke 10:30–37)] : one who voluntarily renders aid to another in distress although under no duty to do so

Good Samaritan law *n* : a law providing immunity from liability to a good samaritan (as an off-duty physician) whose negligent administration of aid causes injury

goods and chattels *n pl* : personal property of any kind but sometimes limited to tangible property

good time *n* : a deduction for good behavior made from a convict's term of imprisonment

good title — see TITLE

good•will \'gùd-,wil\ *n* **1** : an intangible asset that is made up of the favor or prestige which a business has acquired beyond the mere value of what it sells due to the personality or experience of those conducting it, their reputation for skill or dependability, the business's location, or

\ə\abut \ᵊ\kitten \ər\further \a\ash \ā\ace
\ä\cot, cart \au̇\out \ch\chin \e\bet \ē\easy
\g\go \i\hit \ī\ice \j\job \ŋ\sing \ō\go \ȯ\law
\ȯi\boy \th\thin \t̲h̲\the \ü\loot \u̇\foot \y\yet
\zh\vision *see also* Pronunciation Symbols page

any other circumstance incidental to the business that tends to draw and retain customers **2 a :** the value of projected increases in the earnings of a business esp. as part of its purchase price **b :** the excess of the purchase price of a business above the value assigned for tax purposes to its other net assets ◊ The Internal Revenue Code requires the purchaser of a business to allocate the purchase price among the various types of assets. Frequently the purchase price is greater than the sum of the values of the individual assets. The excess is labeled *goodwill*. Because of its indefinite life, goodwill is not amortizable as an asset. The purchaser will therefore usu. try to keep the allocation to goodwill as small as possible.

gov·ern \'gə-vərn\ *vt* **1 :** to exercise continuous sovereign authority over; *esp* : to control and direct the administration of policy in **2 :** to exert a determining or guiding influence in or over ⟨the testator's assets are ~*ed* by will substitutes — W. M. McGovern, Jr. *et al.*⟩ **3 :** to serve as a precedent or deciding principle for ⟨the law ~*ing* bills of lading⟩ ⟨*United States v. Leon* ~*s* the case at bar⟩ — **gov·er·na·ble** \'gə-vər-nə-bəl\ *adj*

gov·ern·ment \'gə-vər-mənt, -vərn-\ *n* **1 :** the act or process of governing; *specif* : authoritative direction or control **2 :** the office, authority, or function of governing **3 :** the continuous exercise of authority over and the performance of functions for a political unit : RULE **4 a :** the organization, machinery, or agency through which a political unit exercises authority and performs functions and which is usu. classified according to the distribution of power within it **b :** the complex of political institutions, laws, and customs through which the function of governing is carried out **5 :** the body of persons that constitutes the governing authority of a political unit or organization: as **a :** the officials comprising the governing body of a political unit and constituting the organization as an active agency **b** *cap* **:** the executive branch of the U.S. fed-

eral government **c :** the prosecution in a criminal case in its capacity as agents of the political unit ⟨the ~ failed to prove guilt beyond a reasonable doubt⟩ — **gov·ern·men·tal** *adj* — **gov·ern·men·tal·ly** *adv*

governmental immunity — see IMMUNITY

government corporation — see CORPORATION

government security — see SECURITY

gov·er·nor \'gə-vər-nər\ *n* : one that governs: as **a :** one that exercises authority esp. over an area or group **b :** an official elected or appointed to act as ruler, chief executive, or nominal head of a political unit; *specif* : the chief executive of a U.S. state **c :** the managing director and usu. the principal officer of an institution or organization **d :** a member of a group that controls or directs an institution ⟨the Federal Reserve System's Board of *Governors*⟩ — **gov·er·nor·ship** *n*

gr *abbr* granted

grace *n* **1 :** a special favor : PRIVILEGE ⟨considered by many authorities to be a matter of ~ and not of right —*The Mentally Disabled and the Law*⟩ **2 a :** a temporary exemption **b :** the prerogative of mercy exercised (as by a chief executive) or granted in the form of equitable relief

grace pe·ri·od *n* : a period of time beyond a scheduled date during which a required action (as payment of an obligation) may be taken without incurring the ordinarily resulting adverse consequences (as penalty or cancellation): as **a :** a period of 30 days or one month during which premiums on insurance policies may be paid without penalty **b :** a period of ten days during which certain security interests (as those in fixtures or purchase money security interests) must be perfected in order to have priority over conflicting security interests under Article 9 of the Uniform Commercial Code — called also *days of grace*

grad·u·at·ed \'gra-jə-,wā-təd\ *adj, of a tax* : increasing in rate with increase in taxable base : PROGRESSIVE

grand *adj* : of, relating to, or being a crime involving the theft of money or property valued at over a set amount ⟨convicted of ~ embezzlement⟩ — see also *grand larceny* at LARCENY, *grand theft* at THEFT; compare PETTY

grand·fa·ther *vt* : to permit to continue under a grandfather clause ⟨current residents will be ~*ed* under the regulation⟩ — often used with *in*

grandfather clause *n* : a clause creating an exemption (as from a law or regulation) based on circumstances previously existing; *specif* : a provision inserted in the constitutions of some southern states after the Civil War requiring high standards of literacy and substantial property qualifications of voters except for descendants of men voting before 1867

grand juror *n* : a member of a grand jury

grand jury *n* : a jury that examines accusations against persons charged with crime and if the evidence warrants makes formal charges on which the accused persons are later tried — see also *no bill* and *true bill* at BILL 3b, INDICTMENT; compare PETIT JURY, SPECIAL GRAND JURY

grand larceny — see LARCENY

grand theft — see THEFT

¹grant *vt* **1** : to permit as a right or privilege ⟨~ a new trial⟩ ⟨the Supreme Court ~*ed* certiorari⟩ **2** : to bestow or transfer formally; *specif* : to transfer the possession or title of by a deed : CONVEY

²grant *n* **1** : the act of granting **2** : something granted; *esp* : a gift (as of land or money) for a particular purpose **3 a** : a transfer of property by deed or writing **b** : the instrument by which such a transfer is made; *also* : the property so transferred

grant·ee \gran-'tē\ *n* : one to whom a grant is made; *specif* : one to whom a grant by deed is made

grant·or \'gran-tər, -ˌtȯr; gran-'tȯr\ *n* : one that makes a grant: as **a** : one that conveys property or a right in property by deed **b** : SETTLOR **c** : one (as an organization) that provides aid in the form of grants (as for education)

grantor trust — see TRUST

gra·tu·i·tous \grə-'tü-ə-təs, -'tyü-\ *adj* : not involving a return benefit, compensation, or consideration — compare ONEROUS — **gra·tu·i·tous·ly** *adv*

gratuitous bailment — see BAILMENT

gratuitous contract — see CONTRACT

gratuitous promise — see PROMISE

gra·va·men \grə-'vā-mən\ *n* [Medieval Latin, from Late Latin, burden, from Latin *gravare* to burden, from *gravis* heavy, grave] : GIST

gray market *n* : a market employing irregular but not illegal methods; *esp* : a market that legally circumvents authorized channels of distribution to sell goods at prices lower than those intended by the manufacturer

great bodily injury *n* : physical injury suffered by the victim of a violent crime that causes a substantial risk of death, extended loss or impairment of a body part or function, or permanent disfigurement : physical injury that is more serious than that ordinarily suffered in a battery

Great Writ *n* : HABEAS CORPUS AD SUBJICIENDUM at HABEAS CORPUS — used with *the*

green card *n* [from the fact that it was formerly colored green] : an identity card attesting the permanent resident status of an alien in the U.S.

green·mail \'grēn-ˌmāl\ *n* [*green* (money) + *-mail* (as in *blackmail*)] : the practice of buying enough of a company's stock to threaten a hostile takeover and reselling it to the company at a price above market value; *also* : the money paid for such stock — **greenmail** *vt* — **green·mail·er** *n*

G reorganization — see REORGANIZATION

griev·ance \'grē-vəns\ *n* **1** : a cause of distress (as an unsatisfactory working condi-

\ə\abut \ᵊ\kitten \ər\further \a\ash \ā\ace
\ä\cot, cart \au̇\out \ch\chin \e\bet \ē\easy
\g\go \i\hit \ī\ice \j\job \ŋ\sing \ō\go \ȯ\law
\ȯi\boy \th\thin \th\the \ü\loot \u̇\foot \y\yet
\zh\vision *see also* Pronunciation Symbols page

tion or unfair labor practice) felt to afford a reason for complaint or dispute; *esp* : a violation of a collective bargaining agreement usu. by the employer **2** : the formal expression of a grievance brought esp. by an employee as the initial step toward resolution through a grievance procedure — see also ARBITRATION, *grievance arbitration* at ARBITRATION, MEDIATION

grievance arbitration — see ARBITRATION

grievance committee *n* : a committee formed by a labor union or by employer and employees jointly to discuss and where possible eliminate grievances

grievance procedure *n* : the several stages or steps established for the resolution of grievances ◊ A grievance procedure typically calls for initial complaints to a supervisor and leads ultimately to arbitration as a final step.

griev•ant \'grē-vənt\ *n* : one who submits a grievance for resolution through a grievance procedure and esp. for arbitration

grieve *vb* **grieved; griev•ing** *vt* : to submit (a grievance) to a grievance procedure ⟨wage claims . . . had been contractually *grieved* —M. A. Kelly⟩ ~ *vi* : to bring a grievance under a grievance procedure ⟨as a union member, Jackson was obligated to ~ — not sue —*Jackson v. Liquid Carbonic Corp.*, 863 F.2d 111 (1988)⟩

¹gross \'grōs\ *adj* [Middle English, immediately obvious, from Middle French *gros* thick, coarse, from Latin *grossus*] **1** : flagrant or extreme esp. in badness or offensiveness : of very blameworthy character ⟨a ~ violation of the rules of ethics⟩ ⟨a ~ abuse of trust⟩ **2** : consisting of an overall total exclusive of deductions ⟨~ annual earnings⟩ — compare NET — **gross•ly** *adv* — **gross•ness** *n*

²gross *n* : overall total exclusive of deductions — **in gross 1** : as a lump sum — see also *lump sum alimony* at ALIMONY **2** : independently existing, belonging to a person, and not attached to

land — see also *easement in gross* at EASEMENT

³gross *vt* : to earn or bring in (an overall total) exclusive of deductions (as for taxes or expenses)

gross estate — see ESTATE 3a

gross income *n* : all income derived from any source except for items specifically excluded by law ◊ Section 61 of the Internal Revenue Code lists fifteen nonexclusive items that should be included in gross income. They are (1) compensation for services, including fringe benefits and commissions; (2) gross income derived from business; (3) gains derived from dealings in property; (4) interest; (5) rents; (6) royalties; (7) dividends; (8) alimony and separate maintenance payments; (9) annuities; (10) income from life insurance and contracts for endowment insurance; (11) pensions; (12) income from discharge of a debt; (13) distributive share of partnership gross income; (14) income received (as by an estate or heir) by reason of a person's death; and (15) income from an interest in an estate or trust.

gross national product *n* : the total value of the goods and services produced by the residents of a nation during a specified period (as a year)

gross negligence — see NEGLIGENCE

gross receipts *n pl* : the total amount of value in money or other consideration received by a taxpayer in a given period for goods sold or services performed

¹ground *n* **1** : the foundation or basis on which knowledge, belief, or conviction rests : a premise, reason, or collection of data upon which something (as a legal action or argument) relies for validity ⟨sued the city on the ~ that the city . . . had wrongfully released . . . records —*City of Lawton v. Moore*, 868 P.2d 690 (1993)⟩ ⟨listed adultery and alcoholism as the ~*s* for divorce⟩ **2** : a piece or parcel of land ⟨the design being to create high ~ for use during overflow periods —*Bright v. Perkins*, 239 S.W.2d 281 (1951)⟩ ⟨a sudden disruption of a piece of ~ from one

man's land —*Porter v. Arkansas Western Gas Co.*, 482 S.W.2d 598 (1972)⟩ — **ground·less** *adj* — **ground·less·ly** *adv* — **ground·less·ness** *n*
²ground *vt* : to furnish a ground for : set on a basis ⟨that court ~*ed* the disclosure requirement in negligence law — *Scott v. Bradford*, 606 P.2d 554 (1979)⟩ ⟨an argument ~*ed* on erroneous assumptions⟩
ground lease — see LEASE
ground rent *n* **1** : the rent paid by a lessee for the use of land esp. for building **2** : a rent charge reserved to himself or herself or his or her heirs by the grantor of land in fee simple, on perpetual lease, or on lease for a renewable term of years ◊ *Ground rent* in this sense is found chiefly in Pennsylvania and Maryland.
group annuity — see ANNUITY
group boycott *n* : an agreed-upon refusal by competitors to deal with another business unless it refrains from dealing with a potential competitor trying to enter the market
group insurance *n* : insurance issued upon a group of persons under a single or blanket insurance policy
growth company — see COMPANY
growth fund — see FUND 2
growth stock — see STOCK
gua·ran·tee \ˌgar-ən-'tē, ˌgär-\ *n* [probably alteration of *guaranty*] **1** : GUARANTOR **2** : GUARANTY 1 **3** : an assurance that a condition will be fulfilled: as **a** : an agreement by which one person undertakes to secure another in the possession or enjoyment of something **b** : an assurance of the quality or of the length of use to be expected from a product offered for sale often with a promise of reimbursement **4** : GUARANTY 4, 5 ⟨constitutional ~*s*⟩ — **guarantee** *vt*
guaranteed bond — see BOND 2
guaranteed investment contract — see CONTRACT
guar·an·tor \ˌgar-ən-'tòr, ˌgär-; 'gar-ən-tər, 'gär-\ *n* : one that makes or gives a guaranty

guar·an·ty \'gar-ən-tē, 'gär-\ *n, pl* **-ties** [Old French *garantie*, from *garantir* to guarantee, from *garant* warrant] **1** : a pledge to pay another's debt or to perform another's duty in case of the other's default or inadequate performance — compare LETTER OF CREDIT **2** : GUARANTEE 3 **3** : GUARANTOR **4** : something given as security : PLEDGE **5** : the protection of a right afforded by legal provision (as in a constitution)
guard·ian \'gär-dē-ən\ *n* : one who has or is entitled or legally appointed to the care and management of the person or property of another — compare COMMITTEE, CONSERVATOR, CURATOR, RECEIVER, TUTOR
guardian ad li·tem \-ad-'lī-təm, -äd-'lē-tem\ : a guardian appointed by a court to represent in a particular lawsuit the interests of a minor, a person not yet born, or a person judged incompetent
guardian by nature : NATURAL GUARDIAN in this entry
natural guardian : a guardian by natural relationship having custody of the person but not the property of a minor ◊ Under common law the father is considered the natural guardian of a child until his death or incapacitation, whereupon the mother becomes the natural guardian. Many states have passed statutes giving both parents equal rights as guardians.
statutory guardian : a guardian appointed by statutory authority
testamentary guardian : a person named in a will to serve as a guardian
— **guard·ian·ship** *n*
guardian ad litem — see GUARDIAN
guardian by nature — see GUARDIAN
guest statute *n* : a statute that prevents non-paying passengers from suing the driver or owner of a car for accidental injuries except in cases of gross negligence

\ə\abut	\ᵊ\kitten	\ər\further	\a\ash	\ā\ace
\ä\cot, cart	\au̇\out	\ch\chin	\e\bet	\ē\easy
\g\go	\i\hit	\ī\ice	\j\job	\ŋ\sing	\ō\go	\ȯ\law
\ȯi\boy	\th\thin	\t͟h\the	\ü\loot	\u̇\foot	\y\yet
\zh\vision	*see also* Pronunciation Symbols page

or willful or wanton misconduct — called also *automobile guest statute*

guilt *n* [Old English *gylt* delinquency] : the fact of having committed an offense esp. against the law ⟨not enough evidence to establish ~⟩ — compare INNOCENCE

¹**guilty** *adj* **guilt·i·er; -est 1 :** having committed a crime : justly charged with a specified crime ⟨~ of larceny⟩ **2 :** involving guilt or culpability⟨~ knowledge⟩

²**guilty** *n* **1 :** a plea of a criminal defendant who does not intend to contest the charges **2 :** a verdict of a jury that be-

lieves the defendant committed the crime charged — compare NOLO CONTENDERE, NOT GUILTY, NOT GUILTY BY REASON OF INSANITY

guilty but mentally ill *n* : a verdict available in some jurisdictions in cases involving an insanity defense in which the defendant is considered as if having been found guilty but is committed to a mental hospital rather than imprisoned if an examination shows a need for psychiatric treatment — compare NOT GUILTY BY REASON OF INSANITY

H

ha•be•as \'hā-bē-əs, 'hä-bā-äs\ *n*, *often attrib* : HABEAS CORPUS AD SUBJICI-ENDUM at HABEAS CORPUS
habeas cor•pus \-'kȯr-pəs, -ˌpu̇s\ *n* [Medieval Latin, literally, you should have the body (the opening words of the writ)] : any of several writs originating at common law that are issued to bring a party before the court; *esp* : HABEAS CORPUS AD SUBJICIENDUM in this entry ⟨the privilege of the writ of *habeas corpus* shall not be suspended, unless when in cases of rebellion or invasion the public safety may require it — *U.S. Constitution* art. I⟩
habeas corpus ad fa•ci•en•dum et re•ci•pi•en•dum \-ˌad-ˌfa-sē-'en-dəm-et-ri-ˌsi-pē-'en-dəm, -ˌfa-shē-'en-; -ˌäd-ˌfä-kē-'en-du̇m-et-rā-ˌkē-pē-'en-du̇m\ [New Latin, literally, you should have the body for doing and receiving] : HABEAS CORPUS CUM CAUSA in this entry
habeas corpus ad pro•se•quen•dum \-ˌad-ˌprä-si-'kwen-dəm, -ˌäd-ˌprō-sā-'kwen-du̇m\ [New Latin, literally, you should have the body for prosecuting] : a writ for removing a prisoner for trial in the jurisdiction of the issuing court where the prisoner committed a crime
habeas corpus ad sub•ji•ci•en•dum \-ˌad-səb-ˌji-sē-'en-dəm, -ˌji-shē-; -ˌäd-su̇b-ˌyi-kē-'en-du̇m\ [New Latin, literally, you should have the body for submitting] : an extraordinary writ issued upon a petition challenging the lawfulness of restraining a person who is imprisoned or otherwise in another's custody — called also *the Great Writ* ◇ Habeas corpus ad subjiciendum is an extraordinary remedy, and is by far the most frequently used writ of habeas corpus. It is an independent civil action and a form of collateral attack to determine not the guilt or innocence of the person held in custody, but whether the custody is unlawful under the U.S. Constitution. Common grounds for relief under the writ include a conviction based on illegally obtained evidence, a denial of effective assistance of counsel, or a conviction by a jury that was improperly selected and impaneled. The degree of restraint on a person's liberty that is necessary to constitute custody entitling a person to habeas corpus relief is not viewed uniformly by the courts. Use of the writ is not limited to criminal matters. It is also available in civil matters, as, for example, to challenge a person's custody of a child or the institutionalization of a person declared incompetent.
habeas corpus ad tes•ti•fi•can•dum \-ˌad-ˌtes-ti-fi-'kan-dəm, -ˌäd-ˌtes-tē-fē-'kän-du̇m\ [New Latin, literally, you should have the body for testifying] : a writ for bringing a person into a court as a witness
habeas corpus cum cau•sa \-kəm-'kȯ-zə, -ˌku̇m-'kau̇-sä\ [New Latin, literally, you should have the body with the cause] : a writ issued from a superior court to an inferior court requiring that a defendant be produced along with the cause for which the defendant has been taken and held — called also *habeas corpus ad faciendum et recipiendum*
habeas corpus ad faciendum et recipiendum — see HABEAS CORPUS
habeas corpus ad prosequendum — see HABEAS CORPUS

\ə\abut \ᵊ\kitten \ər\further \a\ash \ā\ace \ä\cot, cart \au̇\out \ch\chin \e\bet \ē\easy \g\go \i\hit \ī\ice \j\job \ŋ\sing \ō\go \ȯ\law \ȯi\boy \th\thin \t̲h̲\the \ü\loot \u̇\foot \y\yet \zh\vision *see also* Pronunciation Symbols page

habeas corpus ad subjiciendum — see HABEAS CORPUS

habeas corpus ad testificandum — see HABEAS CORPUS

habeas corpus cum causa — see HABEAS CORPUS

ha·ben·dum \hə-'ben-dəm\ *n* [New Latin, from Latin, to be had, neuter of *habendus*, future passive participle of *habēre* to have, to hold (the first word of this part of the deed)] : the part of a deed that limits and defines an estate of ownership granted and sometimes the type of tenancy by which the estate is to be held ◊ The habendum is now often just a formality.

hab·it·able \'ha-bi-tə-bəl\ *adj* : suitable and fit for a person to live in : free of defects that endanger the health and safety of occupants — see also *warranty of habitability* at WARRANTY — **hab·it·abil·i·ty** \ˌha-bi-tə-'bi-lə-tē\ *n* — **hab·it·able·ness** *n* — **hab·it·ably** *adv*

hab·i·ta·tion \ˌha-bə-'tā-shən\ *n* **1 a** : the act of occupying or inhabiting **b** *in the civil law of Louisiana* : the right of a person to dwell in the house of another **2** : a dwelling place

ha·bit·u·al \hə-'bi-chə-wəl\ *adj* **1** : practicing or acting in some manner by force of custom, habit, or addiction ⟨a ~ drunkard⟩ **2** : being such a specified number of times or with designated regularity ⟨~ offenders⟩ **3** : involved in the practice of a person's usual behavior ⟨her ~ residence⟩

habitual criminal *n* : one convicted of a crime who has a certain number of prior convictions for offenses of a specified kind (as felonies) and is thereby under some statutes subject to an increased penalty (as life imprisonment)

habitual criminal law *n* : a law that imposes greater penalties if a convicted defendant has previously been convicted of one or more crimes ◊ Some such laws have been challenged on the ground of violating the prohibition on cruel and unusual punishment in the Eighth Amendment to the U.S. Constitution or on the ground of being an ex post facto law.

half blood *n* : the relation between persons having only one parent in common; *also* : a person so related to another

half·way house *n* : a residence for formerly institutionalized individuals (as mental patients, drug addicts, or convicts) that is designed to facilitate their readjustment to private life

hand down *vt* **1** : to deliver (the decision or opinion of an appellate court) to the proper office of an inferior court **2** : to make an official formulation of and announce (the decision of a court)

han·di·cap *n* : a physical disability (as a bodily impairment or a devastating disease)

han·di·capped *adj* : having a disability that substantially limits a major life activity (as caring for oneself, working, or having sensory functions)

hand note — see NOTE

hand up *vt* : to deliver (an indictment) to a judge or higher judicial authority

hang *vb* **hung** *also* **hanged; hang·ing** *vt* : to suspend by the neck until dead esp. as a form of execution — often *hanged* in the past tense ~ *vi* **1** : to die by hanging — often *hanged* in the past tense ⟨he ~*ed* for his crimes⟩ **2** : to be unable to reach a decision or verdict ⟨the jury *hung* on 19 counts against [him] —Randall Samborn⟩

ha·rass \hə-'ras, 'har-əs\ *vt* [Middle French *harasser* to exhaust, fatigue, from *harer* to set a dog on, from Old French *hare*, interjection used to incite dogs] : to subject persistently and wrongfully to annoying, offensive, or troubling behavior ⟨a collection agency ~*ing* a debtor⟩ — see also SEXUAL HARASSMENT — **ha·rass·er** *n* — **ha·rass·ment** *n*

¹har·bor *n* : a place of security and comfort — see also SAFE HARBOR

²harbor *vt* **1** : to receive secretly and conceal (a fugitive from justice) **2** : to have (an animal) in one's keeping ⟨may not ~a dog without a permit⟩ — **har·bor·er** *n*

hard goods — see GOOD 2

hard labor *n* : compulsory labor imposed upon prisoners as part of a sentence or as prison discipline

harm *n* : loss of or damage to a person's right, property, or physical or mental well-being : INJURY — **harm** *vt*

harm•ful *adj* : of a kind likely to cause harm — **harm•ful•ly** *adv* — **harm•ful•ness** *n*

harm•less *adj* **1** : free from harm, liability, or loss — often used in the phrase *to hold harmless* — see also HOLD HARMLESS **2** : lacking capacity or intent to injure — **harm•less•ly** *adv* — **harm•less•ness** *n*

harmless error — see ERROR

hate crime *n* : a crime that violates the victim's civil rights and that is motivated by hostility to the victim's race, religion, creed, national origin, sexual orientation, or gender

haz•ard \'ha-zərd\ *n* : a condition that tends to create or increase the possibility of loss — used esp. in insurance law

haz•ard•ous *adj* : creating a hazard : involving or exposing one to risk (as of loss or harm) ⟨a ~ occupation⟩ ⟨a ~ substance⟩ — **haz•ard•ous•ly** *adv* — **haz•ard•ous•ness** *n*

H.B. *abbr* House bill

head *n* : any of a number of individuals — **by heads** : with an equal share to each individual : PER CAPITA — used in the rules of intestate succession in Louisiana

head•note \'hed-₁nōt\ *n* : a summary prefixed to the report of a decided legal case stating the principles or rulings of the decision and usu. the main facts of the case

head of house•hold : an unmarried individual who is not a surviving spouse and who maintains a household which for more than one-half of the taxable year is the principal abode of a person who qualifies as a dependent under section 2(b) of the Internal Revenue Code

head stew•ard \-'stü-ərd, -'styü-\ *n* : the chief union representative in a plant

head tax *n* : a tax that imposes the same amount of tax on every individual in a class or group

health insurance *n* : insurance against loss through illness or injury of the insured; *esp* : insurance providing compensation for medical expenses and often income for disability

hear *vt* **heard; hear•ing 1 a** : to give a hearing to ⟨the court *heard* the claims⟩ ⟨the judge agreed to ~ argument on the objection⟩ **b** : to conduct a hearing about ⟨the magistrate's authority to ~ a matter properly before him⟩ **2 a** : to take testimony from ⟨the committee will ~ 30 witnesses⟩ **b** : to take (as testimony) at a hearing ⟨the judge *heard* statements from the victim's family⟩

hear•ing *n* **1** : a proceeding of relative formality at which evidence and arguments may be presented on the matter at issue to be decided by a person or body having decision-making authority — compare TRIAL ◊ The purpose of a hearing is to provide the opportunity for each side of a dispute, and esp. a person who may be deprived of his or her rights, to present its position. A hearing, along with notice, is a fundamental part of procedural due process. Hearings are also held, as for example by a legislature or an administrative agency, for the purpose of gathering information and hearing the testimony of witnesses.

administrative hearing : a hearing conducted by an official (as an administrative law judge) or a body (as a review board) of an administrative agency regarding an agency action and esp. an action under dispute

confirmation hearing **1** : a hearing conducted by the U.S. Senate to examine a nominee for the U.S. Supreme Court ◊ Article II of the U.S. Constitution provides for presidential appointment of Supreme Court justices "by and with the advice and consent of the Senate." **2** : a hearing held in a bankruptcy

\ə\abut \ᵊ\kitten \ər\further \a\ash \ā\ace
\ä\cot, cart \au̇\out \ch\chin \e\bet \ē\easy
\g\go \i\hit \ī\ice \j\job \ŋ\sing \ō\go \ȯ\law
\ȯi\boy \th\thin \t͟h\the \ü\loot \u̇\foot \y\yet
\zh\vision *see also* Pronunciation Symbols page

case prior to the confirmation of a proposed bankruptcy plan

discharge hearing : a hearing in a bankruptcy case in which a debtor is informed that his or her discharge has been granted or is told the reasons why it has not been granted

fair hearing : a hearing that is conducted impartially and in accordance with due process and for which the defendant has reasonable opportunity to prepare, the assistance of counsel, the right to present evidence, the opportunity to cross-examine adverse witnesses, and often the right to a jury

fat·i·co hearing \'fa-ti-kō-\ : a hearing sometimes held prior to the sentencing of a convicted criminal at which the parties may offer evidence as to appropriate sentencing

Franks hearing \'fraŋks-\ : a hearing to determine whether statements made by police officers in an affidavit that was used to obtain a search warrant by which evidence incriminating the defendant was found are false and constitute perjury or reckless disregard for the truth

Hunt·ley hearing \'hənt-lē-\ : a Jackson-Denno hearing in the form of procedure used in New York

Jack·son–Den·no hearing \'jak-sən-'de-nō-\ : a hearing to determine if a confession or statements made by a defendant were given involuntarily and so should be suppressed as evidence

Mapp hearing \'map-\ : a hearing to determine whether evidence should be suppressed on the ground that it was obtained as the result of an illegal search and seizure

preliminary hearing : a hearing held after a criminal defendant's first appearance in court esp. for the purpose of determining whether there is probable cause to believe that the defendant committed the felony with which he or she is charged — called also *preliminary examination, probable cause hearing*

pre·ter·mi·na·tion hearing \prē-,tər-mə-'nā-shən-\ : a hearing held prior to the termination of a property interest (as employment or a benefit)

probable cause hearing : PRELIMINARY HEARING in this entry

reaffirmation hearing : a hearing in a bankruptcy case at which a debtor may reaffirm dischargeable debts ◊ The reaffirmation hearing and discharge hearing are usu. held simultaneously.

suppression hearing : a hearing held in a criminal case to determine the admissibility of evidence that the defendant seeks to suppress — see also *motion to suppress* at MOTION

taint hearing : a hearing held in a criminal case to determine if the prosecution's evidence is inadmissible because of some taint (as because it was obtained through procedures that violated the defendant's constitutional rights)

valuation hearing : a hearing held in a bankruptcy case to determine the value of the debtor's property in which a creditor claims a lien or security interest

Wade hearing \'wād-\ : a hearing in a criminal case to determine whether a witness's identification of the defendant (as in court or in a lineup) is tainted (as because of unfairly suggestive procedures) and therefore inadmissible as evidence

2 : a trial in equity practice

hear·say \'hir-,sā\ *n* : a statement made out of court and not under oath which is offered as proof that what is stated is true — called also *hearsay evidence*

hearsay evidence — see EVIDENCE

hearsay rule *n* : a rule barring the admission of hearsay as evidence ◊ The hearsay rule is stated in Rule 802 of the Federal Rules of Evidence. Hearsay is inadmissible as evidence because of the unavailability of cross-examination to test the accuracy of the statement. There are numerous exceptions to the rule, however, mainly for statements made under circumstances that assure reliability. Statements made spontaneously, for example, or as part of a business or medical record are inherently trustworthy and thus excepted from the rule. A statement need not be made orally for purposes of the hearsay rule. Written statements, gestures, and even motion pictures are included.

heat of passion : an agitated state of mind (as anger or terror) prompted by provocation sufficient to overcome the ability of a reasonable person to reflect on and control his or her actions — called also *heat of blood, heat of passion on sudden provocation, hot blood, sudden heat, sudden heat of passion, sudden passion;* see also MANSLAUGHTER; compare COLD BLOOD, COOL STATE OF BLOOD

hedge \'hej\ *vi* **hedged; hedg·ing** : to reduce possible losses in speculative transactions by engaging in offsetting transactions (as futures trading)

hedge fund — see FUND 2

hedg·ing *n* : the practice of engaging in offsetting financial transactions to reduce losses

hedonic damages — see DAMAGE 2

hei·nous \'hā-nəs\ *adj* : enormously and shockingly evil ⟨a ~ crime⟩ — **hei·nous·ly** *adv* — **hei·nous·ness** *n*

heir \'ar\ *n* : one who inherits or is entitled to succeed to the possession of property after the death of its owner: as **a** : one who by operation of law inherits the property and esp. the real property of a person who dies without leaving a valid will — used in jurisdictions whose law is based on English common law; called also *heir at law, heir general, legal heir;* compare ISSUE **b** *in the civil law of Louisiana* : one who succeeds to the estate of a person by will or esp. by operation of law — see also INTESTACY, UNWORTHY; compare ANCESTOR, DEVISEE, LEGATEE, NEXT OF KIN, SUCCESSOR

apparent heir : HEIR APPARENT in this entry

beneficiary heir in the civil law of Louisiana : an heir who exercises the benefit of inventory which limits the amount of his or her liability for the decedent's debts

bodi·ly heir : HEIR OF THE BODY in this entry

forced heir : an heir who cannot be disinherited except for causes recognized by law; *esp, in the civil law of Louisiana* : an heir who because of youth or mental or physical infirmity cannot care for himself or herself and who cannot be deprived of his or her lawful portion of the decedent's estate by disinherison without just cause — see also LEGITIME

heir ab in·tes·ta·to \-,ab-,in-tes-'tā-tō, -,äb-,in-tes-'tä-tō\ *pl* **heirs ab intestato** *in the civil law of Louisiana* : an heir that takes only by operation of the laws governing intestate succession

heir apparent pl heirs apparent : an heir whose right to an inheritance cannot be voided or undone except by exclusion under a valid will if he or she survives the ancestor — called also *apparent heir;* compare HEIR PRESUMPTIVE in this entry

heir at law : HEIR a

heir general pl heirs general : HEIR a

heir in tail : an heir to a fee-tail estate — called also *heir of entail*

heir of the body : an heir who is a lineal descendant esp. as contrasted with a collateral descendant — called also *bodily heir*

heir presumptive pl heirs presumptive : an heir whose right to inherit may be defeated by the birth of a nearer relative or by exclusion under a valid will — called also *presumptive heir;* compare HEIR APPARENT in this entry

instituted heir in the civil law of Louisiana : an heir who is named in the will but whose legacy will fall to a substitute legatee under a vulgar substitution in the event that he or she refuses the legacy or dies before the testator — called also *instituted legatee irregular heir in the civil law of Louisiana* : an heir who inherits a right of action to the estate as distinguished from seisin ◊ This class of heirs was eliminated as of January 1, 1982. Formerly, a decedent's illegitimate children and spouse were considered irregular heirs.

legal heir : HEIR a; *specif, in the civil law of Louisiana* : an heir who receives seisin immediately after the death of the intestate by operation of law — compare IRREGULAR HEIR in this entry ◊ Prior to 1982 the Louisiana Civil Code distinguished between legal and irregular heirs who were required to go through an additional procedure in order to receive possession of the property. This division of heirs was eliminated in the 1981 revision of the Civil Code.

natural heir : an heir (as a child) whose status as an heir arises from esp. close blood relationship as distinguished from one (as the state) whose status arises by operation of statute

presumptive heir : HEIR PRESUMPTIVE in this entry

pretermitted heir : a descendant of a testator who would be an heir under the laws of intestacy but who is not named to take under the will ◊ Most states have statutes requiring a share of the estate to go to a pretermitted heir on the assumption that the omission was unintentional.

right heir **1** : an heir by blood **2** : the particular heir granted or devised an estate tail as distinguished from the heirs in general

testamentary heir in the civil law of Louisiana : an heir who inherits under a will

— **heir·less** *adj* — **heir·ship** *n*
heir ab intestato — see HEIR
heir apparent — see HEIR
heir at law — see HEIR
heir general — see HEIR
heir in tail — see HEIR
heir of the body — see HEIR
heir presumptive — see HEIR
held *past and past part of* HOLD

her·e·dit·a·ment \ˌher-ə-'di-tə-mənt\ *n* [Medieval Latin *hereditamentum*, from Late Latin *hereditare* to inherit, from Latin *hered-*, *heres* heir] : inheritable property
he·red·i·tary \hə-'re-də-ˌter-ē\ *adj* [Latin *hereditarius*, from *hereditas* inheritance, from *hered-*, *heres* heir] **1** : received or passing by inheritance or required to pass by inheritance ⟨~ shares⟩ **2** : having ownership or possession through inheritance ⟨a ~ chief⟩
her·i·ta·ble \'her-ə-tə-bəl\ *adj* : INHERITABLE
heritable obligation — see OBLIGATION
HGN test \ˌāch-ˌjē-'en-\ *n* : HORIZONTAL GAZE NYSTAGMUS TEST
HHS *abbr* Department of Health and Human Services — see also the IMPORTANT AGENCIES section
high court *n* **1** : a court of last resort in the U.S.; *esp* : SUPREME COURT **2** *cap* : HIGH COURT OF JUSTICE
High Court of Justice : a part of the Supreme Court of Judicature of England and Wales that includes the Chancery, Family, and King's Bench or Queen's Bench divisions — called also *High Court*
high crime *n* : a crime of infamous nature contrary to public morality but not technically constituting a felony; *specif* : an offense that the U.S. Senate deems to constitute an adequate ground for removal of the president, vice president, or any civil officer as a person unfit to hold public office and deserving of impeachment
high–low agreement *n* : a settlement that is contingent on a jury's award of damages and that sets a minimum amount that the defendant will pay the plaintiff if the award is below that amount and a maximum amount that the defendant will pay if the award is above that amount
hi·jack \'hī-ˌjak\ *vt* : to seize possession or control of (a vehicle) from another person by force or threat of force; *specif* : to seize possession or control of (an aircraft) esp. by forcing the pilot to divert the aircraft to another destination — **hijack** *n* — **hi·jack·er** *n*

hi·jack·ing *n* : the felony of hijacking a vehicle

¹hire *n* **1** : payment for the temporary use of something or for labor or services **2 a** : the act or an instance of hiring ⟨from the date of ~ until now⟩ **b** : the state of being hired : EMPLOYMENT ⟨while he was in the ~ of the defendant⟩ **3** : one who is hired ⟨all new ~s will enjoy the same medical benefits⟩ — **for hire** : available for use or service in return for payment

²hire *vb* **hired; hir·ing** *vt* **1** : to engage the personal services of or the temporary use of for a fixed sum **2** : to grant the personal services of or the temporary use of ~ *vi* : to take employment — **hir·er** *n*

hiring hall *n* : a union-operated placement office where registered applicants are referred to jobs usu. in the order of their registration

hit–and–run *adj* **1** : having left the scene of a motor vehicle accident without stopping to fulfill the duties imposed by law (as rendering aid or giving identification) ⟨a ~ driver⟩ **2** : involving or concerning a hit-and-run driver ⟨a ~ accident⟩ ⟨~ statutes⟩

hit–skip *adj* : HIT-AND-RUN

Hodge Podge \'häj-ˌpäj\ *n* : MAIN POT

hold *vt* **held; hold·ing 1 a** : to have lawful possession or ownership of ⟨*held* the property as tenants in common⟩ ⟨the band ~s the title to the car⟩ **b** : to have as a privilege or position of responsibility ⟨~*ing* a retail liquor license⟩ ⟨the judges ... shall ~ their offices during good behavior — *U.S. Constitution* art. III⟩ **2** : to restrain the liberty of; *specif* : to keep in custody ⟨the defendant will be *held* without bail⟩ **3** : to cause to be conducted ⟨will ~ a hearing on the matter⟩ **4** : to rule as the holding of a case ⟨the court *held* that such conduct violated the statute⟩ — compare DECIDE, FIND

hold·er *n* **1** : a person that holds: as **a** : OWNER ⟨the ~ of a patent⟩ — often used in combination ⟨a stock*holder*⟩ **b** : one that holds or occupies the property of another by agreement and esp. under a : a person who under the Uni-

form Commercial Code is in possession of a negotiable instrument that names and is made payable to the possessor or that is payable to bearer **b** : a person under the U.C.C. in possession of goods named in a document of title if the goods are deliverable to bearer or to the order of the possessor **3** *in the civil law of Louisiana* : an individual (as a trustee or debtor) or legal or commercial entity that under the Civil Code's provisions for disposition of unclaimed property is in possession of property belonging to another

holder for value : a holder to whom an instrument is issued or transferred in exchange for something of value (as a promise of performance, a security interest or lien in the instrument not obtained by judicial process, payment of or use of the instrument as security for a claim against another person, a negotiable instrument, or the incurring of an irrevocable obligation to a third party)

holder in due course : the holder of a negotiable instrument that is complete and regular on its face and that is taken in good faith and for value without notice that it is overdue or has been dishonored or that there is any defense against it or claim to it by any party — compare BONA FIDE HOLDER ◊ A holder in due course takes the negotiable instrument free of any claims to it and of most defenses of a party to it. Federal Trade Commission rules have abolished the status of holder in due course in consumer transactions.

hold harmless *adj* : of, relating to, or being an agreement between parties in which one assumes the potential liability for injury that may arise from a situation and thus relieves the other of liability ⟨a *hold harmless* agreement⟩ ⟨a *hold harmless* clause⟩ — compare RELEASE

¹hold·ing *n* **1** : a ruling of a court upon an

\ə\abut \ə\kitten \ər\further \a\ash \ā\ace \ä\cot, cart \au\out \ch\chin \e\bet \ē\easy \g\go \i\hit \ī\ice \j\job \ŋ\sing \ō\go \ȯ\law \ȯi\boy \th\thin \th\the \ü\loot \u̇\foot \y\yet \zh\vision *see also* Pronunciation Symbols page

issue of law raised in a case : the pronouncement of law supported by the reasoning in a court's opinion — compare DECISION, DICTUM, DISPOSITION, FINDING, JUDGMENT, OPINION, RULING, VERDICT **2** : any property that is owned or possessed — usu. used in pl. ⟨an increase in the company's ~*s*⟩

²**holding** *adj* : intended for temporary custody or detention ⟨a ~ facility⟩ ⟨a ~ cell⟩

holding company — see COMPANY

holding pe·ri·od *n* : the length of time a taxpayer holds property for purposes of determining if any gain realized or loss incurred from it is long-term or short‑term

hold over *vi* : to remain in a position or condition ⟨one who *holds over* in possession of a building after the expiration of a term of years —B. N. Cardozo⟩ — **hold·over** *n*

holdover tenancy — see TENANCY

hold·up *n* : an attempted or completed robbery carried out with the use of force and esp. at gunpoint

hold up *vt* : to make the victim of a holdup : rob at gunpoint

ho·lo·graph \'hō-lə-ˌgraf, 'hä-\ *n* [Late Latin *holographus*, from Late Greek *holographos*, from Greek *holos* whole, complete + *graphein* to write] : a document (as a will or a deed) entirely in the handwriting of the person whose act it purports to be — **ho·lo·graph·ic** \ˌhō-lə-ˈgra-fik, ˌhä-\ *adj*

holographic will — see WILL

home equity conversion mortgage — see MORTGAGE

home equity line *n* : HOME EQUITY LOAN at LOAN

home equity line of credit : HOME EQUITY LOAN at LOAN

home equity loan — see LOAN

home invasion *n* : the crime of entering a dwelling and committing or with intent to commit a crime (as assault) while armed and while another is lawfully present

home·own·er's insurance \'hōm-ˌō-nərz\ *n* : insurance that covers primarily a person's residence and that also covers the owner for liability resulting from his or her personal acts

home rule *n* : self-government or limited autonomy in internal affairs by a dependent political unit (as a territory or municipality); *also* : the political theory or principle of self-government

home·stead \'hōm-ˌsted, -stid\ *n* **1 a** : the home and adjoining land with any buildings that is occupied usu. by a family as its principal residence **b** : an estate created by law in a homestead esp. for the purpose of taking advantage of a homestead exemption **2** : a tract of land acquired from U.S. public lands by filing a record and living on and cultivating the tract

homestead exemption *n* : an exemption from liability that prevents creditors from obtaining satisfaction from a debtor's homestead — see also *declaration of homestead* at DECLARATION 4 ◊ The laws governing the homestead exemption vary greatly from state to state. Most states have limits on the amount for which a debtor is exempted, but a few have no limits at all. Others have limits that are dependent on the size or type of property or the age of the property owner.

ho·mi·ci·dal \ˌhä-mə-ˈsīd-ᵊl, ˌhō-\ *adj* : of, relating to, or tending toward homicide

ho·mi·cide \'hä-mə-ˌsīd, 'hō-\ *n* [Latin *homicidium*, from *homo* human being + *caedere* to cut, kill] **1** : a person who kills another **2** : the killing of one human being by another — compare MANSLAUGHTER, MURDER

criminal homicide : homicide committed by a person with a criminal state of mind (as intentionally, with premeditation, knowingly, recklessly, or with criminal negligence)

deliberate homicide : homicide caused purposely and knowingly — used in Montana

excusable homicide : homicide that is committed by accident or misfortune by a person doing a lawful act by lawful means with usual and ordinary caution and without any unlawful intent and that is excused under the law with no criminal punishment imposed; *also* : JUSTIFIABLE HOMICIDE in this entry

felonious homicide : homicide committed without justification

homicide by misadventure : homicide that occurs as the result of an accident caused by a person doing a lawful act with no unlawful intent

justifiable homicide : homicide that is committed in self-defense, in defense of another and esp. a member of one's family or sometimes in defense of a residence, in preventing a felony esp. involving great bodily harm, or in performing a legal duty and that is justified under the law with no criminal punishment imposed; *also* : EXCUSABLE HOMICIDE in this entry

negligent homicide : homicide caused by a person's criminally negligent act

reckless homicide : homicide caused by a person's reckless acts ◊ In Illinois, involuntary manslaughter committed by use of a motor vehicle is called reckless homicide.

ve·hic·u·lar homicide \vē-'hi-kyə-lər-\ : homicide committed by the use of a vehicle (as an automobile or boat)

homicide by misadventure — see HOMICIDE

ho·mol·o·gate \hō-'mä-lə-ˌgāt\ *vt* **-gat·ed; -gat·ing** [Medieval Latin *homologatus*, past participle of *homologare* to agree, from Greek *homologein*, from *homologos* agreeing] : to approve or confirm officially — **ho·mol·o·ga·tion** \hō-ˌmä-lə-'gā-shən\ *n*

hon *abbr* honorable

hon·es·ty clause *n* : FULL REPORTING CLAUSE

hon·or *vt* **hon·ored; hon·or·ing 1** : to accept and pay ⟨the bank ~*ed* the check⟩ **2** : to purchase or discount (a draft) in compliance with a letter of credit

hon·or·able *adj* : entitled to honor — used as a title for various government officials

honorary trust — see TRUST

hor·i·zon·tal \ˌhȯr-ə-'zän-təl, ˌhär-\ *adj* : relating to, directed toward, or consist-

ing of individuals or entities of similar status or on the same level — **hor·i·zon·tal·ly** *adv*

horizontal agreement *n* : an agreement among economic competitors on the same level of production or distribution — compare VERTICAL AGREEMENT ◊ Horizontal agreements are generally considered illegal as violating antitrust laws.

horizontal gaze ny·stag·mus test \-ni-'stag-məs-\ *n* : a test for intoxication (as of a driver) based on observation of involuntary jerking movements of the eyes as they follow horizontal motion

horizontal price–fix·ing *n* : a generally illegal arrangement among competitors to charge the same price for an item — compare VERTICAL PRICE-FIXING

horizontal privity *n* **1** : the relationship between the parties to a covenant that is based on a mutual or successive interest in the land burdened or benefited by the covenant **2** : the relationship between the original supplier of a product and an ultimate user or a bystander affected by it — used esp. in connection with breaches of warranty

horizontal restraint *n* : a restraint of trade involving an agreement among competitors at the same distribution level for the purpose of minimizing competition

horizontal unionism *n* : a form of labor organization in which unions are made up of workers with the same or similar skills or crafts or having the same status

hos·tile *adj* **1** : having an intimidating, antagonistic, or offensive nature ⟨a ~ work environment⟩ **2 a** : of or relating to an opposing party in a legal action ⟨a ~ claim⟩ **b** : adverse to the interests of a party to a legal action ⟨if the interests of the party joined involuntarily render him ~ to the original plaintiff, he must remain a de-

\ə\abut \ᵊ\kitten \ər\further \a\ash \ā\ace
\ä\cot, cart \aù\out \ch\chin \e\bet \ē\easy
\g\go \i\hit \ī\ice \j\job \ŋ\sing \ō\go \ȯ\law
\ȯi\boy \th\thin \th\the \ü\loot \ù\foot \y\yet
\zh\vision *see also* Pronunciation Symbols page

fendant —J. H. Friedenthal *et al.*⟩ **3 a**
: adverse to or incompatible with the interests of a property owner ⟨a ~ use⟩ —
see also *adverse possession* at POSSES-
SION, *easement by prescription* at EASE-
MENT, PRESCRIPTION 1 **b** : unwelcome
by or contrary to the interests of corporate stockholders or management ⟨a
~ takeover bid⟩
hostile en·vi·ron·ment harassment *n*
: employment discrimination consisting
of unwelcome verbal or physical conduct
(as comments, jokes, or acts) relating to
the victim's constitutionally or statutorily
protected classification (as race, religion,
ethnic origin, or age) that has the effect of
substantially interfering with a person's
work performance or of creating a hostile
work environment; *esp* : HOSTILE ENVI-
RONMENT SEXUAL HARASSMENT
hostile environment sexual harassment
n : sexual harassment that has the effect
of unreasonably interfering with a victim's work performance or creating an intimidating, hostile, or offensive working
environment that affects the victim's psychological well-being — called also *hostile environment harassment;* compare
QUID PRO QUO SEXUAL HARASSMENT
hostile possession — see POSSESSION
hostile witness — see WITNESS
hot blood *n* : HEAT OF PASSION
¹hot car·go *n* : products made by nonunion employees or by employees considered to be treated unfairly by their
employer
²hot cargo *adj* : of, relating to, or being
an agreement between labor and an employer barring the employer from using
or otherwise dealing with the products
of another employer whose employees
are nonunion ◊ Hot cargo agreements,
clauses, and provisions were outlawed
by the Labor Management Reporting and
Disclosure Act.
hotch·pot \'häch-ˌpät\ *n* [Anglo-French
hochepot, from Old French, thick soup or
stew, from *hochier* to shake + *pot* pot] **1**
: the combining of properties into a common lot to ensure equality of division

among those entitled to a share of an estate which requires that advancements (as
to a child) be made up to the estate by contribution or by an accounting — compare
COLLATION **2** : MAIN POT
hot pur·suit *n* : the immediate and continuous pursuit by police officers of a fleeing
suspect whose possible escape justifies
the failure of the officers to obtain a warrant before making an entry, search, seizure, or arrest
house *n* **1 a** : a building (as a single or
multiple family house, apartment, or hotel room) serving as living quarters and
usu. including the curtilage **b** : a building (as one's residence or a locked place
of business) in which one is entitled to
protection (as from warrantless searches
and seizures) under the Fourth Amendment to the U.S. Constitution **2 a** : a legislative assembly esp. that constitutes a
division of a bicameral body ⟨the votes of
both *houses* shall be determined by yeas
and nays —*U.S. Constitution* art. I⟩ **b**
: the building or chamber where such an
assembly meets **c** : a quorum of such an
assembly
House bill — see BILL 1
house·break·ing \'haùs-ˌbrā-kiŋ\ *n* : the
act of breaking into and entering the
dwelling house of another for the purpose
of committing a felony — **house·break-
er** *n*
house counsel *n* : a lawyer employed by
a business to work in-house on its legal
matters
house·hold·er \'haùs-ˌhōl-dər\ *n* : a person
who occupies a house alone or as head
of a household; *specif* : one who makes a
declaration of homestead
household goods — see GOOD 2
House of Commons : the lower house of
the British and Canadian parliaments —
called also *Commons*
house of correction : an institution where
persons who have committed minor offenses and who are considered capable
of reformation are confined — compare
HOUSE·OF DETENTION, JAIL, LOCKUP,
PENITENTIARY, PRISON

house of delegates : HOUSE 2a; *esp* : the lower house of the state legislature in Maryland, Virginia, and West Virginia

house of detention : a place where prisoners and occasionally witnesses are detained pending a trial — compare HOUSE OF CORRECTION, JAIL, LOCKUP, PENITENTIARY, PRISON

House of Lords : the upper house of the British parliament composed of the lords temporal and spiritual — called also *Lords*

house of representatives : the lower house of a legislative body; *esp, cap H&R* : the lower house of the U.S. Congress or a state legislature

hous·ing court *n* : a court having limited jurisdiction over certain property and housing cases (as landlord and tenant disputes)

HR *abbr* House of Representatives

H Res *abbr* House resolution

HR–10 plan \ͺāch-ͺär-'ten-\ *n* [from *H.R. 10*, the 1965 U.S. House of Representatives bill that established the plan] : KEOGH PLAN

HUD \'həd\ *abbr* Department of Housing and Urban Development — see also the IMPORTANT AGENCIES section

HUD–1 settlement statement \'həd-'wən-\ *n* [Department of *H*ousing and *U*rban *D*evelopment (which publishes the form) + *1* (indicating its place in a sequence of such forms)] : a form signed at closing that sets out expenses, disburse-ments, and adjustments relating to the purchase of real property

hung *past and past part of* HANG

hung jury *n* : a jury whose members are unable to agree on a verdict

Huntley hearing — see HEARING

hy·brid \'hī-brid\ *adj* : consisting of diverse components: as **a** : of, relating to, or being a lawsuit brought by an employee under the Labor Management Relations Act against both the employer for breach of contract and the union for breach of the duty of fair representation **b** : of, relating to, or being representation of a criminal defendant in which the defendant represents himself or herself with the assistance of a lawyer

hybrid security — see SECURITY

hy·poth·e·cary \hi-'pä-thə-ͺker-ē, hī-\ *adj, in the civil law of Louisiana* : of or relating to an obligation, right, or security in property of a debtor given to a creditor by contract or by operation of law without transfer of possession or title to the creditor

hy·poth·e·cate \hi-'pä-thə-ͺkāt, hī-\ *vt* **-cat·ed; -cat·ing** [Medieval Latin *hypothecare* to pledge, from Late Latin *hypotheca* pledge, from Greek *hypothēkē*, from *hypotithenai* to put under, deposit as pledge] : to pledge as security without delivery of title or possession — compare PAWN — **hy·poth·e·ca·tion** \-ͺpä-thə-'kā-shən\ *n*

hypothetical question — see QUESTION 1

I

ICC *abbr* **1** International Chamber of Commerce **2** Interstate Commerce Commission — see also the IMPORTANT AGENCIES section

id. *abbr* idem

idem \'ī-dəm, 'ē-dem\ *pron* [Latin, same] **:** something previously mentioned **:** the same authority — used in citations to cases and other works to refer to an immediately preceding reference; compare INFRA, SUPRA ◊ *Idem* is usu. used in the form of its abbreviation *id.* ⟨In *Bally*, the plaintiff also claimed . . . 403 Mass. at 720-21. The [court] denied the claim . . . *Id.* at 721 —R. T. Gerwatowski⟩

idem so·nans \-'sō-ˌnanz, -ˌnänz\ *adj* [Latin, sounding the same] **:** relating to or being two names having the same or similar pronunciation or sound ⟨the two names are not *idem sonans* —*Johnson v. Estelle*, 704 F.2d 232 (1983)⟩ ⟨the *idem sonans* test⟩ — compare MISNOMER ◊ An idem sonans name allows a pleading or other document (as a warrant) to be considered valid despite the minor misspelling of a name or other misidentification of a party (as in identifying a corporation as a partnership). The fact that two trademarks are idem sonans may be used to establish the likelihood of confusion on the part of consumers in a trademark infringement case.

iden·ti·fy *vt* **-fied; -fy·ing** **1 :** to consider as united or associated (as in interests or principles) ⟨can ask leading questions of a witness who is *identified* with an adverse party⟩ **2 :** to establish the identity of ⟨*~ing* the suspect⟩ **3 :** to specify or designate (goods) as the object of a contract — used in the phrase *identify to the contract* ⟨the disputed beans were goods *identified* to the contract⟩ ◊ Under the Uniform Commercial Code, once goods are identified to a contract, the buyer has a special property interest and an insurable interest in the goods. This gives the buyer the right to seek damages and other relief. This identification can be done at any time and in any manner agreed to by the parties or as otherwise specified in the U.C.C. — **iden·ti·fi·able** *adj* — **iden·ti·fi·ca·tion** *n*

iden·ti·ty *n, pl* **-ties 1 :** sameness of essential character or aspect ⟨collateral estoppel requires ~ of the issues and the parties⟩ **2 a :** separate or distinct existence ⟨when movables lose their ~ or become an integral part of the immovable —*Louisiana Civil Code*⟩ **b :** distinguishing character of a person; *esp* **:** information (as a name or address) that distinguishes a person ⟨is required to reveal the ~ of an informer⟩ ⟨but for a mistake concerning the ~ of the proper party —*Federal Rules of Civil Procedure* Rule 15(c)⟩ **3 :** the condition of being the same as a thing or person described, claimed, or accused ⟨character evidence of a suspect's past crimes may be admitted to prove the ~ of a crime's perpetrator⟩

identity theft — see THEFT

id·i·ot \'i-dē-ət\ *n* **:** a person with esp. profound mental retardation ◊ While the terms *idiot, imbecile,* and *moron* survive in many state codes and statutes, they are generally no longer used in both medical and legal contexts. The modern terminology distinguishes between mild, moderate, severe, and profound levels of retardation. Historically persons with mental retardation have suffered legal disabilities (as in not being allowed to marry or vote). Generally today, an adult with mental retardation who is his or her own guardian does not suffer these disabilities.

ig·no·ra·mus \ˌig-nə-'rā-məs\ n : NO BILL at BILL 3b

il·le·gal \il-'lē-gəl\ adj : contrary to or in violation of a law : ILLICIT, UNLAWFUL ⟨an ~ contract⟩ — il·le·gal·ly adv

il·le·gal·i·ty \ˌi-li-'ga-lə-tē\ n, pl -ties 1 : the quality or state of being illegal 2 : an illegal action

il·le·ga·lize \il-'lē-gə-ˌlīz\ vt : to make or declare illegal — compare CRIMINALIZE

il·le·git·i·ma·cy \ˌi-li-'ji-tə-mə-sē\ n : the quality or state of being illegitimate

il·le·git·i·mate \ˌi-li-'ji-tə-mət\ adj 1 : not recognized by the law as offspring; specif : born out of marriage ◊ An illegitimate child is usu. legitimated by his or her parents' later marriage. Illegitimate children generally have the same inheritance rights under intestate successions as legitimate children; statutes limiting their inheritance rights have been found to violate the equal protection clause. 2 : not valid according to law — illegitimate n

il·lic·it \il-'li-sət\ adj : not permitted : UNLAWFUL ⟨an ~ motive to defeat or evade the taxes —In re Haas, 48 F.3d 1153 (1995)⟩

Illinois land trust — see TRUST

il·lu·so·ry \i-'lü-sə-rē, -zə-rē\ adj : likely to mislead or deceive : FALSE, DECEPTIVE ⟨an ~ plea bargain leading to a longer sentence than expected⟩

illusory contract — see CONTRACT

illusory promise — see PROMISE

illustrative evidence — see EVIDENCE

im·be·cile \'im-bə-sil, -ˌsīl\ n : a mentally retarded or deficient person; esp : a severely mentally retarded person — used esp. formerly; see also IDIOT

im·ma·te·ri·al \ˌi-mə-'tir-ē-əl\ adj : not essential, pertinent, or of consequence ⟨the jury could have discounted the medical history evidence, or while accepting its accuracy, found it ~ —Willett v. State, 911 S.W.2d 937 (1995)⟩ — compare IRRELEVANT — im·ma·te·ri·al·i·ty \ˌi-mə-ˌtir-ē-'a-lə-tē\ n

immediate annuity — see ANNUITY

im·mo·bi·lize \i-'mō-bə-ˌlīz\ vt -lized; -liz·ing : to make immobile; specif : to turn (movable property) into immovable property (as by incorporating it into a building) — im·mo·bi·li·za·tion \i-ˌmō-bə-lə-'zā-shən\ n

¹im·mov·able \im-'mü-və-bəl\ adj : incapable of being moved — see also immovable property at PROPERTY

²immovable n : an item of immovable property (as land, standing timber, or a building) ⟨a manufactured home placed upon a lot or tract of land shall be an ~ —Louisiana Revised Statutes⟩; also : an interest or right (as a servitude) in an item of immovable property ⟨a predial servitude is an incorporeal ~ —Louisiana Civil Code⟩ — often used in pl.; compare MOVABLE

immovable property — see PROPERTY

im·mune \i-'myün\ adj : having immunity : EXEMPT

im·mu·ni·ty \i-'myü-nə-tē\ n, pl -ties [Latin immunitas, from immunis exempt from public service, exempt, from in- non- + -munis (from munia services)] 1 : exemption from a duty or liability that is granted by law to a person or class of persons ⟨a defendant may not take the stand in his own behalf and then claim ~ from cross-examination —W. R. LaFave and A. W. Scott, Jr.⟩; also : the affirmative defense of having such an exemption

absolute immunity : immunity from all personal civil liability without limits or conditions (as a requirement of good faith) — compare QUALIFIED IMMUNITY in this entry

charitable immunity : immunity from civil liability esp. for negligent torts that is granted to a charitable or nonprofit organization (as a hospital)

constitutional immunity : immunity (as from a tax) that is granted or created by a constitution (as the U.S. Constitution)

corporate immunity : immunity from

\ə\abut \ə\kitten \ər\further \a\ash \ā\ace \ä\cot, cart \au̇\out \ch\chin \e\bet \ē\easy \g\go \i\hit \ī\ice \j\job \ŋ\sing \ō\go \ȯ\law \ȯi\boy \th\thin \th\the \ü\loot \u̇\foot \y\yet \zh\vision   see also Pronunciation Symbols page

personal liability for tortious acts that is granted to an officer of a corporation who acted in good faith and within the course of his or her duties — see also BUSINESS JUDGMENT RULE; compare PIERCE

dip·lo·mat·ic immunity : immunity (as from taxes or prosecution) granted to a diplomat

discovery immunity : IMMUNITY 2

discretionary immunity : qualified immunity from civil liability for tortious acts or omissions that arise from a government employee's discretionary acts performed as part of the employee's duties — see also the *Federal Tort Claims Act* in the IMPORTANT LAWS section ◇ The Federal Tort Claims Act includes an additional requirement of acting in good faith for the discretionary immunity granted to the federal government.

executive immunity : immunity granted to officers of the executive branch of government from personal liability for tortious acts or omissions done in the course of carrying out their duties ◇ While the president's executive immunity is absolute, the immunity of other federal executive officials is qualified.

governmental immunity : discretionary immunity granted to a governmental unit (as an agency) or its employees; *broadly* : SOVEREIGN IMMUNITY in this entry

judicial immunity : absolute immunity from civil liability that is granted to judges and other court officers (as prosecutors and grand juries) and quasi‌judicial officials for tortious acts or omissions done within the scope of their jurisdiction or authority

legislative immunity : absolute immunity from civil liability that is granted to legislators for tortious acts or omissions done in the course of legislative activities — see also SPEECH OR DEBATE CLAUSE

official immunity : discretionary immunity from personal liability that is granted to public officers for tortious acts and omissions — compare GOVERNMENTAL IMMUNITY in this entry

qualified immunity : immunity from civil liability that is conditioned or limited (as by a requirement of good faith or due care); *specif* : official immunity from damages for acts that violate another's civil rights that is granted if it can be shown that the acts do not violate clearly established statutory or constitutional rights of which a reasonable person would be aware — see also *Civil Rights Act* in the IMPORTANT LAWS section

sovereign immunity : the absolute immunity of a sovereign government (as a state) from being sued — see also *Federal Tort Claims Act* in the IMPORTANT LAWS section, *Amendment XI* to the CONSTITUTION in the back matter ◇ For an action to be brought against a state or the federal government, sovereign immunity must be waived by the government.

trans·ac·tion·al immunity \tran-'zak-shə-nəl-, -'sak-\ : immunity from criminal prosecution granted to a witness for an offense related to his or her compelled testimony — see also USE IMMUNITY in this entry

use immunity : immunity granted to a witness in a criminal case that prevents the use of the witness's compelled testimony against that witness in a criminal prosecution ◇ Transactional and use immunity are granted to preserve the constitutional protection against self‌incrimination. The states grant either form of this immunity, while the federal government grants only use immunity. A witness with use immunity may still be prosecuted, but only based on evidence not gathered from the protected testimony.

2 : a usu. statutory prohibition that excludes specific documents or information from discovery — called also *discovery immunity*

im·mu·nize \'i-myə-ˌnīz\ *vt* **-nized; -niz-**

ing : to grant immunity to ⟨the ultimately ill-fated effort to ~ state judges from the burdens of the federal income tax —J. K. Owens⟩ — im•mu•ni•za•tion \ˌi-myə-nə-ˈzā-shən\ *n*
im•pair \im-ˈper\ *vt* **1** : to damage or make worse by or as if by diminishing ⟨~ed health⟩ **2** : to diminish the value of (property or property rights); *specif* : to diminish the value of (legal contractual obligations) to the point that a party loses the benefit of the contract or the contract otherwise becomes invalid ⟨a law ~ing a state's own obligations was entitled to less deference —Gerald Gunther⟩ — see also CONTRACT CLAUSE — im•pair•ment *n*
im•pan•el \im-ˈpan-ᵊl\ *or* em•pan•el \im-, em-\ *vt* -eled *or* -elled; -el•ing *or* -el•ling : to form (a jury) esp. by summoning and selecting the members; *specif* : to enroll (a list of selected jurors) in a court — compare ARRAY — im•pan•el•ment *n*
im•par•tial \im-ˈpär-shəl\ *adj* : not partial or biased : treating or affecting all equally — im•par•ti•al•i•ty \im-ˌpär-shē-ˈa-lə-tē\ *n* — im•par•tial•ly *adv*
impartial chair•man *n* : ARBITRATOR, MEDIATOR; *specif* : an arbitrator who serves on a committee or board — compare UMPIRE
im•passe \ˈim-ˌpas, im-ˈpas\ *n* : a point in esp. labor negotiations at which reaching an agreement is impossible because neither party is willing to compromise or change position
im•peach \im-ˈpēch\ *vt* [Anglo-French *empecher*, from Old French *empeechier* to hinder, from Late Latin *impedicare* to fetter, from Latin *in-* + *pedica* fetter, from *ped-, pes* foot] **1** : to charge with a crime or misconduct; *specif* : to charge (a public official) before a competent tribunal (as the U.S. Senate) with misconduct in office — see also *Article I* and *Article II* of the CONSTITUTION in the back matter ◊ Impeachment is the first step in removing an officer from office. The president, vice president, and other federal officers (as judges) may be impeached by the House of Representatives. (Members of Congress themselves are not removed by being impeached and tried, but rather are expelled by a two-thirds majority vote in the member's house.) The House draws up articles of impeachment that itemize the charges and their factual bases. The articles of impeachment, once approved by a simple majority of the House members, are then submitted to the Senate, thereby impeaching the officer. The Senate then holds a trial, at the conclusion of which each member votes for or against conviction on each article of impeachment. Two-thirds of the Senate members present must vote in favor of conviction. Once convicted, the officer can be removed from office. Although the Constitution specifies that an officer is to be impeached for high crimes and misdemeanors, impeachment can also occur for misconduct that is not necessarily criminal (as violation of the Constitution). Because impeachment is the first step taken to remove an officer from office, *impeach* is often used in general contexts to refer to the removal itself, but that is not its specific legal meaning. An officer generally cannot be impeached for acts done prior to taking office. **2** : to cast doubt on: as **a** : to attack the validity of (a judgment or verdict) because of judicial or juror misconduct **b** : to challenge the credibility of (a witness) or the validity of (a witness's testimony) ⟨a witness, including a criminal defendant who testifies in his own behalf, may be ~ed on the ground of former conviction —W. R. LaFave and A. W. Scott, Jr.⟩ — see also *impeachment evidence* at EVIDENCE; compare REHABILITATE ◊ A witness may be impeached by character evidence or circumstantial evidence relating to the credibility of the witness, and esp. on the grounds of prior convictions,

\ə\abut \ᵊ\kitten \ər\further \a\ash \ā\ace
\ä\cot, cart \au̇\out \ch\chin \e\bet \ē\easy
\g\go \i\hit \ī\ice \j\job \ŋ\sing \ō\go \ȯ\law
\ȯi\boy \th\thin \th̲\the \ü\loot \u̇\foot \y\yet
\zh\vision *see also* Pronunciation Symbols page

prior inconsistent statements, contradiction by other evidence, and the witness's reputation for truth, prior acts of misconduct, and partiality. — **im·peach·able** *adj* — **im·peach·ment** *n*

impeachment evidence — see EVIDENCE

im·ped·i·ment \im-'pe-də-mənt\ *n* : something that prevents or interferes with a process, power, or right ⟨should have known of the legal ~s to the execution of any judgment against the police jury —*Penalber v. Blount*, 550 So. 2d 577 (1989)⟩; *specif* : a bar to the formation of a valid contract or marriage — compare NULLITY

im·per·fect *adj* : not perfect or complete: as **a** : not enforceable : enforceable only under certain conditions ⟨an ~ obligation⟩ **b** : lacking an element otherwise required by law — compare PERFECT

imperfect self–defense *n* : a defense based on self-defense that does not shield the defendant from all liability but reduces the liability esp. because the defendant actually but unreasonably believed that he or she was in imminent danger of death or great bodily injury ◊ Imperfect self-defense is not recognized in all jurisdictions. When it is successfully used in criminal cases it eliminates the element of malice, reducing the level of the offense from murder to manslaughter.

im·per·mis·si·ble \ˌim-pər-'mi-sə-bəl\ *adj* : not permissible — **im·per·mis·si·bly** *adv*

im·per·son·ate \im-'pər-sə-ˌnāt\ *vt* **-at·ed; -at·ing** : to assume (another's or a fictitious identity) without authority and with fraudulent intent ⟨~ a police officer⟩ ⟨*impersonated* a public servant by saying he was from the water department⟩ — **im·per·son·a·tor** \-ˌnā-tər\ *n*

im·per·so·na·tion \im-ˌpər-sə-'nā-shən\ *n* : the act or an instance of impersonating another; *also* : the crime of impersonation

im·plead \im-'plēd\ *vt* [Anglo-French *empleder*, from Old French *emplaidier*, from *en*- thoroughly + *plaidier* to plead] : to bring into a lawsuit; *specif* : to bring

(a third party who is or may be liable to the plaintiff or defendant) into a suit — compare INTERPLEAD, INTERVENE, JOIN

im·plead·er \im-'plē-dər\ *n* : the act or procedural device of impleading a third party; *specif* : a petition or complaint brought in a lawsuit by a plaintiff or defendant against a third party who may be liable to that plaintiff or defendant — called also *third-party practice;* compare COUNTERCLAIM, CROSS-CLAIM, INTERPLEADER, INTERVENTION, JOINDER

im·pli·cate \'im-plə-ˌkāt\ *vt* **-cat·ed; -cat·ing** : to involve as a consequence, corollary, or natural inference ⟨firing the federal employee because of her protest ~s the First Amendment⟩

im·pli·ca·tion \ˌim-plə-'kā-shən\ *n* **1** : the act of implicating : the state of being implicated **2** : the act of implying : the state of being implied **3** : something implied

im·plic·it \im-'pli-sət\ *adj* : capable of being recognized though unexpressed : IMPLIED — **im·plic·it·ly** *adv*

im·plied \im-'plīd\ *adj* : not directly or specifically made known (as in the terms of a contract); *specif* : recognized (as by a court) as existing by reason of an inference and esp. on legal or equitable grounds ⟨for breach of ~ covenants in oil and gas leases —*National Law Journal*⟩ — compare EXPRESS — **im·pli·ed·ly** \im-'plī-əd-lē\ *adv*

implied acquittal *n* : an acquittal of a more serious offense (as first-degree murder) that is considered to result from a verdict which convicts the defendant of a lesser included offense while remaining silent on the greater one ◊ A greater offense and a lesser included offense are the same offense under a double jeopardy analysis. Therefore, a conviction of a lesser included offense and implied acquittal of the greater offense bars retrial on the greater offense.

implied agency — see AGENCY 2a

implied authority — see AUTHORITY

implied contract — see CONTRACT

implied easement — see EASEMENT

implied in fact *adj* : recognized by infer-

ence based on the facts (as the parties' conduct or statements)
implied in fact contract : IMPLIED CONTRACT at CONTRACT
implied in law *adj* : created and imposed by law (as statutory or case law) ⟨it contradicted an *implied in law* term of the writing —J. D. Calamari and J. M. Perillo⟩
implied in law contract — see CONTRACT
implied malice — see MALICE
implied notice — see NOTICE
implied power — see POWER 2a, b
implied promise — see PROMISE
implied trust — see TRUST
implied warranty — see WARRANTY 2a
im•ply \im-'plī\ *vt* **im•plied; im•ply•ing** **1** : to recognize as existing by inference or necessary consequence esp. on legal or equitable grounds ⟨in ordinary circumstances . . . the law would ∼ that it was the duty of the hospital to use due care —*Haase v. Starnes*, 915 S.W.2d 675 (1996)⟩ **2** : to make known indirectly
im•por•tune \ˌim-pȯr-'tün, -'tyün; im-'pȯr-ˌtyün, -chən\ *vb* **-tuned; -tun•ing** *vt* : to press or urge with troublesome persistence ⟨who solicits, requests, commands, ∼s or intentionally aids another person to engage in conduct which constitutes an offense —*General Statutes of Connecticut*⟩ ∼ *vi* : to beg, urge, or press another persistently or troublesomely — compare COERCE, SOLICIT
im•pos•si•bil•i•ty *n, pl* **-ties** **1** : the quality or state of being impossible; *also* : the affirmative defense that something (as performance) is impossible **2** : something impossible **3** : IMPOSSIBILITY OF PERFORMANCE in this entry
factual impossibility : impossibility based on factual circumstances; *specif* : a partial defense to criminal liability based on the incompletion of an intended criminal act ◊ Factual impossibility is not a complete defense and does allow prosecution for attempt or for another inchoate offense. For example, if the defendant constructed a bomb that failed to explode, factual impossi-

bility would be a defense against murder charges, but not attempted murder.
impossibility of performance **1** : a doctrine in contract law that a party may be released from liability for breach of contract for failing to perform an obligation that is rendered impossible by uncontrollable circumstances (as death or failure of the means of delivery) **2** : a defense to breach of contract or a basis for release from contractual obligations because of impossibility of performance — compare FRUSTRATION, IMPRACTICABILITY
legal impossibility : impossibility based on or with reference to a law; *specif* : a complete defense to criminal liability based on the commitment of acts that are not criminal or illegal ◊ Legal impossibility is founded on the principle that an act is not a crime unless there is a law prohibiting it.
impossibility of performance — see IMPOSSIBILITY
im•pos•si•ble *adj* : not possible : incapable of being done, attained, or fulfilled ⟨a party's performance is ∼ in part⟩
im•pos•tor *or* **im•pos•ter** \im-'päs-tər\ *n* : one that assumes a false identity or title for the purpose of deception : IMPERSONATOR
im•pound \im-'paùnd\ *vt* : to take control of in the custody of the law or by legal authority ⟨∼ a vehicle⟩ ⟨the police ∼*ed* the dwelling until the search warrant was obtained⟩ — **im•pound•ment** *n*
im•prac•ti•ca•bil•i•ty \im-ˌprak-ti-kə-'bi-lə-tē\ *n* **1** : the state of being impracticable **2** : a doctrine in contract law: relief from obligations under a contract may be granted when performance has been rendered excessively difficult, expensive, or harmful by an unforeseen contingency; *also* : a defense to breach of contract on the ground that it has been rendered

\ə\abut \ᵊ\kitten \ər\further \a\ash \ā\ace
\ä\cot, cart \aù\out \ch\chin \e\bet \ē\easy
\g\go \i\hit \ī\ice \j\job \ŋ\sing \ō\go \ò\law
\òi\boy \th\thin \t̲h̲\the \ü\loot \ù\foot \y\yet
\zh\vision *see also* Pronunciation Symbols page

impracticable — called also *commercial impracticability, impracticability of performance;* compare FRUSTRATION, *impossibility of performance* at IMPOSSIBILITY ◊ Under section 2-615 of the Uniform Commercial Code, the impracticability must arise "by the occurrence of contingency the non-occurrence of which was a basic assumption on which the contract was made" or by compliance with the law. **3** : excessive difficulty in carrying out a procedure (as joinder)

im·prac·ti·ca·ble \im-'prak-ti-kə-bəl\ *adj* : excessively difficult to perform esp. by reason of an unforeseen contingency ⟨a contract made ~ by the new regulation⟩

im·pre·scrip·ti·ble \,im-prē-'skrip-tə-bəl\ *adj* : not subject to prescription : INALIENABLE

im·pris·on *vt* : to confine in prison esp. as punishment for a crime — compare FALSE IMPRISONMENT — **im·pris·on·ment** *n*

im·prop·er *adj* : not proper: as **a** : not in accord with correct procedure ⟨an ~ venue⟩ **b** : WRONGFUL; *specif* : in violation of a constitution ⟨the denial of trial by jury was held ~⟩ — **im·prop·er·ly** *adv*

im·prove·ment *n* : a usu. permanent addition to or modification of real property that enhances its capital value and is distinguished from an ordinary repair in being designed to make the property more useful or valuable

im·pute \im-'pyüt\ *vt* **im·put·ed; im·put·ing** **1** : to consider or calculate as a value or cost (as for taxation); *broadly* : to reckon as an actual thing ⟨~ a benefit from the use of the car⟩ **2** *in the civil law of Louisiana* : to direct (payment) to principal or interest **3** : to attribute to a party esp. because of responsibility for another ⟨~ knowledge to his corporate superior⟩ — **im·pu·ta·tion** \,im-pyə-'tā-shən\ *n*

imputed income *n* : income calculated from the supposed value of intangible or non-cash sources

in *prep* : under the law of : based on ⟨brought an action ~ negligence —*National Law Journal*⟩

in ab·sen·tia \,in-ab-'sen-chə\ *adv* [Latin] : in absence ⟨sentenced *in absentia*⟩

in·ad·mis·si·ble \,in-əd-'mi-sə-bəl\ *adj* : not admissible ⟨~ evidence⟩ ⟨~ testimony⟩ — **in·ad·mis·si·bil·i·ty** \-,mi-sə-'bi-lə-tē\ *n* — **in·ad·mis·si·bly** *adv*

in·ad·ver·tence \,in-əd-'vərt-ᵊns\ *n* : an accidental oversight (as failing to sign a form)

in·ad·ver·tent discovery \,in-əd-'vərt-ᵊnt-\ *n* : unexpected finding of incriminating evidence in plain view by the police — compare INEVITABLE DISCOVERY ◊ In *Coolidge v. New Hampshire*, 403 U.S. 443 (1971), the U.S. Supreme Court held that evidence found by inadvertent discovery may be seized under the plain view exception to the warrant requirement for searches and seizures. In *Horton v. California*, 496 U.S. 128 (1990), however, the Court, while not overturning *Coolidge*, decided that inadvertent discovery is not a necessary condition for application of the plain view exception to seizures.

in·alien·able \in-'āl-yə-nə-bəl, -'ā-lē-ə-\ *adj* : incapable of being alienated, surrendered, or transferred ⟨~ rights⟩ — **in·alien·abil·i·ty** \-,āl-yə-nə-'bi-lə-tē, -,ā-lē-ə-\ *n* — **in·alien·ably** *adv*

in banc *var of* EN BANC

in cam·e·ra \,in-'kam-rə, -'ka-mə-\ *adv or adj* [New Latin, literally, in a chamber] : in private; *esp* : in a judge's chambers ⟨the judge reviewed the sensitive material *in camera*⟩ ⟨an *in camera* proceeding⟩ — compare OPEN COURT

in·ca·pa·ble *adj* : lacking legal qualification or power (as by reason of mental incompetence) — see also INCAPACITY

in·ca·pac·i·tate \,in-kə-'pa-sə-,tāt\ *vt* **-tat·ed; -tat·ing** **1** : to make legally incapable or ineligible ⟨mental illness alone will not ~ a person from making a valid contract —*Landmark Med. Ctr. v. Gauthier*, 635 A.2d 1145 (1994)⟩ **2** : to deprive of capacity or natural power ⟨an injury that ~s the employee⟩ — **in·ca·pac·i·ta·tion** \-,pa-sə-'tā-shən\ *n*

in·ca·pac·i·ty \,in-kə-'pa-sə-tē\ *n, pl* **-ties**

1 : the quality or state of being incapable; *esp* : lack of legal qualifications due to age or mental condition — compare CA- PACITY 2 : the inability of an injured worker to perform the duties required in a job for which he or she is qualified — compare DISABILITY 1

in·car·cer·ate \in-'kär-sǝ-ˌrāt\ *vt* -at·ed; -at·ing [Latin *incarceratus*, past participle of *incarcerare*, from *in-* in + *carcer* prison] : IMPRISON — **in·car·ce·ra·tion** \in-ˌkär-sǝ-'rā-shǝn\ *n*

incentive stock option — see OPTION 3

in·cest \'in-ˌsest\ *n* [Latin *incestus* sexual impurity, from *incestus* impure, from *in-* not + *castus* pure] : sexual intercourse between persons so closely related that they are forbidden by law to marry; *also* : the crime of engaging in such sexual intercourse

Inch·ma·ree clause \'inch-mǝ-rē-\ *n* [after *Inchmaree*, a British steamer whose 1884 sinking in Liverpool harbor resulted in its formulation] : a clause in a marine insurance policy that covers damage or loss caused by the negligence of a vessel's own captain or crew or by any defect in the ship's hull or machinery

in·cho·ate \in-'kō-ǝt, 'iŋ-kō-ˌāt\ *adj* 1 a : not yet made complete, certain, or specific : not perfected — see also *inchoate lien* at LIEN b : not yet transformed into actual use or possession ⟨until an employee has earned his retirement pay . . . [it] is but an ~ right —*Peterson v. Fire & Police Pension Ass'n*, 759 P.2d 720 (1988)⟩ 2 : of or relating to a crime (as attempt, solicitation, or conspiracy) which consists of acts that are preliminary to another crime and that are in themselves criminal — compare CHOATE

inchoate lien — see LIEN

¹in·ci·dent \'in-sǝ-dǝnt, -ˌdǝnt\ *n* 1 : a distinct occurrence or event ⟨an ~ of sexual harassment⟩ 2 : a subordinate, dependent, or consequential element ⟨the search was a legitimate ~ to the arrest⟩ ⟨child support and other ~s of divorce⟩

²incident *adj* : having a subordinate or dependent relation to something specified ⟨a search ~ to arrest⟩

in·ci·den·tal \ˌin-sǝ-'dent-ᵊl\ *adj* 1 : subordinate or secondary in importance or position ⟨~ benefits⟩ 2 : INCIDENT 3 : occurring by chance or in isolation ⟨~ use of a person's image⟩ — **in·ci·den·tal·ly** *adv*

incidental beneficiary — see BENEFICI-ARY d

incidental damages — see DAMAGE 2

incident of ownership : any of several rights (as the right to change beneficiaries) that may be exercised over a life insurance policy which are used as criteria for the inclusion of the value of a policy in a decedent's gross estate for purposes of estate tax

in·cite \in-'sīt\ *vt* **in·cit·ed; in·cit·ing** : to urge on ⟨~ a riot⟩ — **in·cite·ment** *n*

in·clud·ed offense *n* : LESSER INCLUDED OFFENSE ⟨permitted . . . to plead guilty to a logical *included offense* —W. R. LaFave and J. H. Israel⟩

in·come *n* : a gain or recurrent benefit usu. measured in money that derives from capital or labor; *also* : the amount of such gain received in a period of time ⟨an ~ of $20,000 a year⟩

income beneficiary — see BENEFICIARY a

income bond — see BOND 2

income tax *n* : a tax on the net income of an individual or a business — compare EXCISE, PROPERTY TAX

in com·men·dam \ˌin-kǝ-'men-dǝm\ *adj* [New Latin, translation of French (*societé*) *en commandité* (company) in limited partnership] *in the civil law of Louisiana* : characterized by partnership liability that is limited to the amount of capital contribution — see also *partner in commendam* at PARTNER, *partnership in commendam* at PARTNERSHIP

in·com·pe·tence \in-'käm-pǝ-tǝns\ *n* : the state or fact of being incompetent — compare COMPETENCY

in·com·pe·ten·cy \in-'käm-pǝ-tǝn-sē\ *n* : INCOMPETENCE

\ǝ\abut \ᵊ\kitten \ǝr\further \a\ash \ā\ace
\ä\cot, cart \aů\out \ch\chin \e\bet \ē\easy
\g\go \i\hit \ī\ice \j\job \ŋ\sing \ō\go \ȯ\law
\ȯi\boy \th\thin \t͟h\the \ü\loot \ů\foot \y\yet
\zh\vision *see also* Pronunciation Symbols page

¹in•com•pe•tent \in-'käm-pə-tənt\ *adj* **1**
: not legally qualified: as **a** : lacking legal capacity (as because of age or mental
deficiency) **b** : incapable due to mental
or physical condition — compare COM-
PETENT **c** : lacking authority, power, or
qualifications required by law ⟨an ~
court⟩ ⟨~ evidence⟩ **2** : unable or failing
to perform adequately ⟨fired for being ~⟩
⟨an ~ attorney⟩ — compare INEFFECTIVE
ASSISTANCE OF COUNSEL
²incompetent *n* : a person who is incompetent — compare INTERDICT
in•con•tes•ta•bil•i•ty clause \,in-kən-,tes-
tə-'bi-lə-tē-\ *n* : a clause in an insurance
policy that forbids the insurer from disputing the policy (as on the ground that
the insured made false statements) after a
set period of time
in•con•ve•nient forum \,in-kən-'vē-
nyənt-\ *n* : an inappropriate or oppressive
forum (as one in a distant jurisdiction)
for a legal action; *esp* : one to which
the doctrine of forum non conveniens is
applicable
in•cor•po•rate \in-'kȯr-pə-,rāt\ *vb* -rat•ed;
-rat•ing *vt* **1** : to unite with something
else to form a whole ⟨~ the agreement
into the divorce⟩ **2** : to form (as a business) into a legal corporation **3** : to include (rights guaranteed by the Bill of
Rights) within the guarantees of the Fourteenth Amendment — see also SELEC-
TIVE INCORPORATION, TOTAL INCORPO-
RATION ~ *vi* : to form a legal corporation — in•cor•po•ra•tion \in-,kȯr-pə-
'rā-shən\ *n* — **incorporate by reference**
: to make (the terms of a contemporaneous or earlier document) part of another document (as a codicil) by specific
reference in that document — see also
REPUBLISH
in•cor•po•ra•tor \in-'kȯr-pə-,rā-tər\ *n*
: any of the persons who join as original
members in incorporating a company
in•cor•po•re•al \,in-kȯr-'pōr-ē-əl\ *adj* : not
tangible : having no material body or
form ⟨~ hereditaments⟩ ⟨an ~ right⟩ —
compare CORPOREAL
in•crim•i•nate \in-'kri-mə-,nāt\ *vt* -nat-

ed; -nat•ing **1** : to charge with involvement in a crime ⟨he was *incriminated* in
the conspiracy⟩ **2** : to suggest or show involvement of in a crime ⟨among the evidence that *incriminated* him was a box
of trigger devices⟩ — see also SELF-
INCRIMINATION — in•crim•i•na•tion \in-
,kri-mə-'nā-shən\ *n* — in•crim•i•na•to-
ry \in-'kri-mə-nə-,tōr-ē\ *adj*
incriminating *adj* : showing or suggesting
involvement in a crime ⟨~ testimony⟩
in•cul•pa•to•ry \in-'kəl-pə-,tōr-ē\ *adj* : IN-
CRIMINATING ⟨made ~ statements to the
police⟩ — compare EXCULPATORY
incumber *var of* ENCUMBER
incumbrance *var of* ENCUMBRANCE
in•cur \in-'kər\ *vt* in•curred; in•cur•ring
: to become liable or subject to : bring
down upon oneself ⟨~ obligations⟩ ⟨~
expenses⟩
indecent assault — see ASSAULT
in•de•cent exposure *n* : the exposing of
one's private body parts (as the genitals)
either recklessly or intentionally and under circumstances likely to cause offense
or affront ◊ Indecent exposure is generally classified as a misdemeanor.
in•de•fea•si•ble \,in-di-'fē-zə-bəl\ *adj* : not
capable of being annulled or voided ⟨an
~ right⟩ — in•de•fea•si•bly *adv*
indefinite failure of issue — see FAILURE
OF ISSUE
in•dem•ni•fi•ca•tion \in-,dem-ni-fə-'kā-
shən\ *n* **1 a** : the action of indemnifying
b : the condition of being indemnified **2**
: INDEMNITY 2b
in•dem•ni•fy \in-'dem-nə-,fī\ *vt* -fied;
-fy•ing [Latin *indemnis* unharmed, from
in- not + *damnum* damage] **1** : to secure
against hurt, loss, or damage **2** : to compensate or reimburse for incurred hurt,
loss, or damage — in•dem•ni•fi•er *n*
in•dem•ni•tee \in-,dem-nə-'tē\ *n* : one that
is indemnified
in•dem•ni•tor \in-'dem-nə-tər, -,tȯr\ *n*
: one that indemnifies
in•dem•ni•ty \in-'dem-nə-tē\ *n, pl* -ties **1**
a : security against hurt, loss, or damage **b** : exemption from incurred penalties or liabilities **2 a** : INDEMNIFICA-

TION 1 **b** : something (as a payment) that indemnifies — compare CONTRIBU-TION

in·den·ture \in-'den-chər\ *n* [Old French *endenture* an indented document, from *endenter* to indent (divide a document into sections with irregular edges that can be matched for authentication), from *en-* thoroughly + *dent* tooth] **1** : a document stating the terms under which a security (as a debenture or other bond) is issued; *specif, in bankruptcy law* : a document (as a mortgage or deed of trust) under which there is outstanding security constituting a claim against a debtor, a claim secured by a lien on any of the debtor's property, or an equity security of the debtor **2** : a deed or other document to which two or more parties (as both grantor and grantee) are bound

in·de·pen·dent *adj* **1** : not dependent on others (as parents) for livelihood; *esp* : not a dependent ⟨declared she was ~ on her financial aid form⟩ **2 a** : not affiliated with another usu. larger unit ⟨an ~ adjuster⟩ **b** : not contingent on something else ⟨an ~ promise⟩ — **in·de·pen·dence** *n* — **in·de·pen·dent·ly** *adv*

independent administrator — see AD-MINISTRATOR

independent agency — see AGENCY 4

independent contractor *n* : one that contracts to do work or perform a service for another and that retains total and free control over the means or methods used in doing the work or performing the service — compare EMPLOYEE

independent counsel *n* : an official appointed by the court at the request of the U.S. Attorney General to investigate and prosecute criminal violations by high government officials, members of Congress, or directors of a presidential reelection campaign after a preliminary investigation by the Attorney General finds specific and credible evidence that a crime may have been committed ◊ The use of an independent counsel was codified in the Ethics in Government Act of 1978 and is designed to ensure an impartial inves-

tigation (as when the Attorney General would face a conflict of interest). The independent counsel was formally called a special prosecutor until 1983.

independent source *n* **1** : a source of evidence that is not connected with unlawful conduct which uncovers the same evidence **2** : a doctrine that permits use of evidence obtained independently of unlawful conduct which uncovers the same evidence or use of evidence that would have been inevitably discovered without the unlawful procedure that led to its discovery — compare FRUIT OF THE POISON-OUS TREE, INEVITABLE DISCOVERY

indeterminate sentence — see SENTENCE

¹in·dex *n* : a numerical measure or indicator (as of inflation or economic performance) — see also CONSUMER PRICE INDEX

²index *vt* : to link (as wages, rates, or investments) to an index ⟨under the contract wages were ~*ed* to inflation⟩

index fund — see FUND 2

index option — see OPTION 3

Indian title — see TITLE

in·di·cia \in-'di-shē-ə\ *n pl* [Latin, plural of *indicium* sign, from *indicare* to point out] : distinctive indications ⟨~ of reliability⟩

in·dict \in-'dīt\ *vt* [alteration of earlier *indite*, from Anglo-French *enditer*, from Old French, to write down, ultimately from Latin *indicere* to proclaim, from *in-* toward + *dicere* to say] : to charge with a crime by the finding or presentment of a grand jury in due form of law — compare ACCUSE, ARRAIGN, CHARGE

in·dict·able \in-'dī-tə-bəl\ *adj* : making one liable to indictment ⟨an ~ offense⟩

in·dict·ment \in-'dīt-mənt\ *n* **1** : the action or the legal process of indicting **2 a** : a formal written statement framed by a prosecuting authority and found by a grand jury that charges a person or persons with an offense — compare COM-

\ə\abut \ᵊ\kitten \ər\further \a\ash \ā\ace \ä\cot, cart \aú\out \ch\chin \e\bet \ē\easy \g\go \i\hit \ī\ice \j\job \ŋ\sing \ō\go \ó\law \ói\boy \th\thin \t̲h̲\the \ü\loot \ú\foot \y\yet \zh\vision *see also* Pronunciation Symbols page

PLAINT, INFORMATION **b** : BILL OF IN-DICTMENT at BILL 3b

in•di•gence \'in-də-jəns\ *n* : impoverished hardship and deprivation

in•di•gent \'in-də-jənt\ *adj* : suffering from indigence ⟨the ~ defendant was provided with counsel⟩ — **indigent** *n*

in•dig•ni•ty \in-'dig-nə-tē\ *n, pl* **-ties** : persistent and intolerable behavior toward a spouse esp. as a manifestation of settled estrangement

indirect contempt — see CONTEMPT

indirect evidence — see EVIDENCE

indirect loss — see LOSS

in•di•rect tax \ˌin-də-'rekt-, -dī-\ *n* : EXCISE

in•dis•pen•sa•ble \ˌin-di-'spen-sə-bəl\ *adj* : having rights so connected to the claims of the parties to an action that the action cannot be adjudicated without affecting those rights — see also *indispensable party* at PARTY

indispensable party — see PARTY 1b

in•di•vid•u•al action *n* : DIRECT ACTION 2

individual policy pension trust — see TRUST

individual re•tire•ment account *n, often cap I&R&A* : IRA

in•di•vis•i•ble \ˌin-də-'vi-zə-bəl\ *adj* : consisting of one whole whose parts cannot be divided or treated individually ⟨an ~ obligation⟩ — **in•di•vis•i•bil•i•ty** \-ˌvi-zə-'bi-lə-tē\ *n* — **in•di•vis•i•bly** *adv*

in•di•vi•sion \ˌin-də-'vi-zhən\ *n, in the civil law of Louisiana* : a state of undivided wholeness : state of being owned by two or more co-owners each having an undivided interest in the property as a whole ⟨an estate held in ~⟩ ⟨they receive this usufruct in ~ —*Louisiana Civil Code*⟩ — see also *ownership in indivision* at OWNERSHIP

indorse, indorsee, indorsement, indorser *var of* ENDORSE, ENDORSEE, ENDORSEMENT, ENDORSER — used primarily in the context of the Uniform Commercial Code

in•duce•ment \in-'düs-mənt, -'dyüs-\ *n* **1** : factual matter presented by way of introduction or background to explain the principal allegations of a legal cause (as of slander or libel) — compare INNUENDO **2** : a significant offer or act that promises or encourages ⟨the ~*s* amounted to entrapment⟩

in•dus•tri•al union *n* : a labor union that admits to membership workers in an industry regardless of their occupation or craft — compare CRAFT UNION

in•ef•fec•tive assistance of counsel : representation of a criminal defendant that is so flawed as to deprive the defendant of a fair trial ⟨claimed *ineffective assistance of counsel* following his conviction⟩ — called also *ineffective assistance* ◊ Ineffective assistance of counsel is a violation of the guarantee of the assistance of counsel that is provided in the Sixth Amendment to the U.S. Constitution. A claim of ineffective assistance of counsel may be brought as a result of government interference with the attorney-client relationship that precludes effective representation, as when an informant is present during conversations between the attorney and the defendant. The existence of a conflict of interest on the part of the attorney may also be the basis for a claim. Most claims are, however, based on the attorney's failure to provide competent representation. Competent representation does not require the best representation, only a performance that is reasonable under prevailing professional norms.

in•eq•ui•ta•ble \in-'e-kwi-tə-bəl\ *adj* : contrary to the principles of equity : not fair or just ⟨~ conduct⟩ — **in•eq•ui•ta•bly** *adv*

in•eq•ui•ty \in-'e-kwə-tē\ *n, pl* **-ties** : INJUSTICE; *also* : an instance of injustice

in esse \in-'e-sē, -sā\ *adv or adj* [Medieval Latin] : in actual existence — compare IN POSSE

in•ev•i•ta•ble accident \in-'e-vi-tə-bəl-\ *n* : an accident not caused by human negligence — compare ACT OF GOD, FORCE MAJEURE, FORTUITOUS EVENT

inevitable discovery *n* : a doctrine in criminal law: evidence obtained by methods that are unconstitutional may be admissible if it would have been inevitably discovered without the unlawful methods — compare FRUIT OF THE POISONOUS TREE, INADVERTENT DISCOVERY, INDEPENDENT SOURCE, PLAIN VIEW

in fa·cie cu·ri·ae \in-'fā-shē-'kyủr-ē, -'fā-shē-,ē-'kyủr-ē-,ē; in-'fä-kē-e-'kü-rē-,ī\ *adv or adj* [New Latin] : before or in the presence of the court ⟨contempt *in facie curiae*⟩

in·fa·mous \'in-fə-məs\ *adj* : of, relating to, or being a crime punishable by imprisonment (as a year or more in a penitentiary) that can lead to loss of rights and privileges upon conviction; *also* : convicted of such a crime

in·fan·cy \'in-fən-sē\ *n, pl* **-cies** **1** : the legal status of an infant : MINORITY **2** : the affirmative defense of lacking legal capacity (as to make a contract or commit a crime) because of being too young and esp. because one's age is below an age set by statute

in·fant \'in-fənt\ *n* : a person who is not of the age of majority : MINOR — compare ADULT

in·fan·ti·cide \in-'fan-tə-,sīd\ *n* : the killing of a newly or recently born child

in fa·vor·em li·ber·ta·tis \,in-fə-'vōr-əm-,li-bər-'tā-təs, ,in-fä-'vō-rem-,lē-ber-'tä-tis\ [Late Latin] : in favor of freedom or liberty ⟨any doubt as to the free use of immovable property must be resolved *in favorem libertatis* —*Louisiana Civil Code*⟩

in·fer \in-'fər\ *vb* **in·ferred; in·fer·ring** *vt* : to derive as a conclusion from facts or premises ⟨could ∼ acceptance of the offer from the offeree's response⟩ ∼ *vi* : to draw inferences — **in·fer·able** *also* **in·fer·ri·ble** \in-'fər-ə-bəl\ *adj*

in·fer·ence \'in-fə-rəns\ *n* **1** : the act or process of inferring; *specif* : the act of passing from one proposition, statement, or judgment considered as true to another whose truth is believed to follow logically from that of the former **2** : something inferred; *esp* : a proposition arrived at by inference — see also *permissive presump-*

tion at PRESUMPTION **3** : the premises and conclusions of a process of inferring

in·fer·en·tial \,in-fə-'ren-chəl\ *adj* **1** : relating to, involving, or resembling inference **2** : deduced or deducible by inference

in·fer·en·tial·ly *adv* : by way of inference : through inference

in·fe·ri·or *adj* : of lower status, rank, or priority

inferior court *n* : a court that is subordinate to and whose decisions are subject to review by the highest court in a judicial system (as of a state or country); *specif* : a court having limited and specified jurisdiction rather than general jurisdiction

in·feu·da·tion \,in-fyü-'dā-shən\ *n* [Medieval Latin *infeudatio*, from *infeudare* to enfeoff, from *in-* in + *feudum* feoff] : ENFEOFFMENT

in fi·e·ri \,in-'fē-ə-rē\ *adj* [Medieval Latin] **1** : being in the process of accomplishment : PENDING **2** : beginning to have existence : not yet completely formed

in flagrante delicto *adv* : FLAGRANTE DELICTO

in·flam·ma·to·ry \in-'fla-mə-,tōr-ē\ *n* : tending to cause anger, animosity, or indignation ⟨the use of an alias by a defendant is ... almost always ∼ —F. D. Doucette⟩ ◊ Evidence, and esp. photographic evidence, may be deemed inadmissible if its inflammatory nature seriously outweighs its probative value or relevance. The mere fact that evidence is graphic or gruesome, however, is not enough to render it inadmissible.

in·flic·tion of emotional distress : the tort of intentionally or negligently causing emotional distress — called also *infliction of mental distress;* see also EMOTIONAL DISTRESS

in·flu·ence *n* **1 a** : the act or power of

\ə\abut   \ᵊ\kitten   \ər\further   \a\ash   \ā\ace
\ä\cot, cart   \aủ\out   \ch\chin   \e\bet   \ē\easy
\g\go   \i\hit   \ī\ice   \j\job   \ŋ\sing   \ō\go   \ȯ\law
\ȯi\boy   \th\thin   \t̲h̲\the   \ü\loot   \ủ\foot   \y\yet
\zh\vision   *see also* Pronunciation Symbols page

producing an effect without any apparent exertion of force or direct exercise of command **b :** corrupt interference with authority for personal gain **2 :** the power or capacity of causing an effect in indirect or intangible ways **3 :** one that exerts influence — **in•flu•enc•er** *n* — **under the influence :** affected by alcohol or another intoxicant ⟨was arrested for driving *under the influence*⟩

in•for•mal *adj* : marked by the absence of required forms or procedures or by the relaxation of prescribed rules ⟨an ~ hearing⟩

informal agency action *n* : an action (as investigation, publicity, or supervision) of an administrative agency that is not adjudication or rulemaking

informal contract — see CONTRACT

informal proof of claim : a writing by a creditor that contains a demand for payment of a debt and an intention to hold the debtor's bankruptcy estate liable but that is not in the form prescribed in the Bankruptcy Code for proofs of claim ◊ If an informal proof of claim is filed with the bankruptcy court within the time allowed for filing proofs of claim, the court may allow the creditor to file a proof of claim in its correct form and consider it as having been filed on the date that the informal proof of claim was filed.

informal rulemaking *n* : rulemaking by a government agency in accordance with the provisions of section 553 of the Administrative Procedure Act — called also *notice-and-comment rulemaking;* compare FORMAL RULEMAKING ◊ Section 553 requires that prior to the promulgation of a proposed rule notice of the rule or of the issues involved must be published in the Federal Register, followed by a period during which interested persons may submit data, views, comments, or arguments.

in•for•mant \in-ˈfȯr-mənt\ *n* : one who informs against another; *specif* : one who makes a practice esp. for money of informing police of others' criminal activities

informant's privilege — see PRIVILEGE 1b

in for•ma pau•pe•ris \ˌin-ˈfȯr-mə-ˈpȯ-pə-rəs, -ˈfȯr-mä-ˈpau̇-pe-rēs\ *adj or adv* [Medieval Latin, in the form of a pauper] : as a poor person : relieved of the fees and costs of a legal action because of inability to pay ⟨allowed to file an appeal *in forma pauperis*⟩ ⟨*in forma pauperis* status⟩

in•for•ma•tion *n* : an instrument containing a formal accusation of a crime that is issued by a prosecuting officer and that serves the same function as an indictment presented by a grand jury — compare COMPLAINT 2, INDICTMENT ◊ About half the states in the United States allow prosecutors to issue informations. The rest require indictment.

in•for•ma•tion•al picketing *n* : picketing by a labor union for the purpose of informing the public about a matter of concern to the union

information letter — see LETTER 1

in•formed *adj* : based on or made with essential information ⟨an ~ judgment⟩

informed consent *n* : consent to medical treatment by a patient or to participation in a medical experiment by a subject after achieving an understanding of what is involved and esp. of the risks

in•form•er *n* : INFORMANT

informer's privilege *n* : INFORMANT'S PRIVILEGE at PRIVILEGE 1b

in•fra \ˈin-frə, -ˌfrä\ *adv* : in the following text : BELOW ⟨see textual discussion accompanying note 22 ~ —D. Q. Posin⟩ — used in books, articles, and cases to refer the reader to later pages, sections, or footnotes of the text — compare IDEM, SUPRA

in•frac•tion \in-ˈfrak-shən\ *n* : the act of infringing : VIOLATION — **in•fract** \-ˈfrakt\ *vt*

in frau•dem le•gis \in-ˈfrȯ-dəm-ˈlē-jis, -ˈfrau̇-dem-ˈlä-gēs\ *adv* [Latin] : in circumvention of the rules of law

in•fringe \in-ˈfrinj\ *vb* **in•fringed; in•fring•ing** [Medieval Latin *infringere*, from Latin, to break, crush, from *in-* in + *frangere* to break] *vt* : to encroach upon

in a way that violates law or the rights of another ⟨the right of the people to keep and bear arms, shall not be *infringed* — *U.S. Constitution* amend. II⟩; *esp* : to violate a holder's rights under (a copyright, patent, trademark, or trade name) ∼ *vi* : ENCROACH — **in·fring·er** *n*
in·fringe·ment *n* : the act or an instance of infringing; *esp* : the unauthorized use of copyrighted or patented material or of a trademark, trade name, or trade dress — see also EQUIVALENT, FAIR USE ◊ Infringement of a trademark, trade name, or trade dress involves use of one by the infringer that is the same as that of the owner or so similar that it is likely to deceive or to cause confusion or mistake on the part of the average purchaser. Infringement of a copyright involves the copying of a material and substantial portion of the protected work. If the alleged infringer denies copying, the copyright holder may be able to prove infringement with circumstantial evidence of the infringer's access to the protected work and of similarities between the two works.
in fu·tu·ro \ˌin-fyü-'chùr-ō, -fü-'tü-rō\ *adv* [Medieval Latin] : in the future
in glo·bo \in-'glō-bō\ *adv* [Latin, in a mass] : as a unit rather than separately ⟨child support *in globo* for two or more children —*Louisiana Civil Code*⟩
in·grat·i·tude *n* : forgetfulness of or lack of appreciation for kindness or esp. a gift received ◊ Under the civil law of Louisiana, a gift may be revoked on the ground of ingratitude if the recipient of the gift tries to kill the person who gave the gift, is guilty of cruelly mistreating or injuring the giver, or refuses the giver food when it is needed.
in·gress \'in-ˌgres\ *n* 1 : the act of entering 2 : the power or liberty of access — compare EGRESS
in·her·ent defect \in-'hir-ənt-, -'her-\ *n* : LATENT DEFECT
in·her·ent·ly dangerous *adj* 1 : of, relating to, or being an activity or occupation whose nature presents a risk of grave in-

jury without the use of and sometimes despite the use of special skill and care 2 : of, relating to, or being an instrumentality or product that poses a risk of danger stemming from its nature and not from a defect
in·her·it \in-'her-it\ *vb* [Middle French *enheriter* to make one an heir, from Late Latin *inhereditare*, from Latin *in-* in + *hereditas* inheritance] *vt* 1 : to receive (property) from an estate by operation of the laws of intestacy; *broadly* : to receive (property) either by will or through intestate succession 2 : SUCCEED ∼ *vi* : to take or hold a possession or rights by inheritance — **in·her·i·tor** \in-'her-i-tər\ *n*
in·her·it·able \in-'her-i-tə-bəl\ *adj* 1 : capable of being inherited 2 : capable of taking by inheritance — **in·her·i·ta·bil·i·ty** \in-ˌher-i-tə-'bi-lə-tē\ *n* — **in·her·it·able·ness** *n*
in·her·i·tance \in-'her-ə-təns\ *n* 1 : the act of inheriting: as **a** : the acquisition of real or personal property under the laws of intestacy or sometimes by will **b** : the succession upon the death of an owner either by will or by operation of law to all the estate, rights, and liabilities of the decedent 2 **a** : something that is or may be inherited **b** : something to which one is entitled as heir ⟨increasing the son's potential ∼ under [the] will —*Lesnick v. Lesnick*, 577 So. 2d 856 (1991)⟩
inheritance tax *n* : an excise tax that is levied upon the privilege of receiving property as heir or next of kin under the law of intestacy and that is measured by the value of the property received — compare ESTATE TAX
ini·tial appearance \i-'ni-shəl-\ *n* : the first appearance of a criminal defendant before a judge or usu. a magistrate — called also *arraignment on the warrant*, *initial presentment*
ini·tia·tive \i-'ni-shə-tiv, -shē-ə-tiv\ *n* 1

\ə\abut	\ᵊ\kitten	\ər\further	\a\ash	\ā\ace
\ä\cot, cart	\aù\out	\ch\chin	\e\bet	\ē\easy
\g\go	\i\hit	\ī\ice	\j\job	\ŋ\sing	\ō\go	\ò\law
\òi\boy	\th\thin	\th̲\the	\ü\loot	\ù\foot	\y\yet
\zh\vision	*see also* Pronunciation Symbols page

: the esp. introductory series of steps taken to cause a desired result ⟨the deposing party would ordinarily be required to take the ~ in arranging a deposition —*Andrews v. Bradshaw*, 895 P.2d 973 (1995)⟩ **2 a** : the right to initiate legislative action **b** : a procedure enabling a specified number of voters by petition to propose a law and secure its submission to the electorate or to the legislature for approval — see also REFERENDUM — **on one's own initiative** : at one's own discretion : independently of outside influence, suggestion, or control ⟨the court may reduce a sentence *on its own initiative* —*Ghrist v. People*, 897 P.2d 809 (1995)⟩

in·junc·tion \in-'jəŋk-shən\ *n* [Middle French *injonction*, from Late Latin *injunction-*, *injunctio*, from Latin *injungere* to enjoin, from *in-* in + *jungere* to join] : an equitable remedy in the form of a court order compelling a party to do or refrain from doing a specified act — compare *cease-and-desist order* at ORDER 3b, DAMAGE, *declaratory judgment* at JUDGMENT 1a, MANDAMUS, *specific performance* at PERFORMANCE, STAY ◊ An injunction is available as a remedy for harm for which there is no adequate remedy at law. Thus it is used to prevent a future harmful action rather than to compensate for an injury that has already occurred, or to provide relief from harm for which an award of money damages is not a satisfactory solution or for which a monetary value is impossible to calculate. A defendant who violates an injunction is subject to penalty for contempt.

affirmative injunction : an injunction requiring a positive act on the part of the defendant : MANDATORY INJUNCTION in this entry

final injunction : PERMANENT INJUNCTION in this entry

interlocutory injunction : an injunction that orders the maintenance of the status quo between the parties prior to a final determination of the matter; *specif* : PRELIMINARY INJUNCTION in this entry

mandatory injunction : an injunction that compels the defendant to do some positive act rather than simply to maintain the situation as it was when the action was brought — compare PROHIBITORY INJUNCTION in this entry

per·ma·nent injunction : an injunction imposed after a hearing and remaining in force at least until the defendant has complied with its provisions — called also *final injunction, perpetual injunction*

preliminary injunction : an interlocutory injunction issued before a trial for purposes of preventing the defendant from acting in a way that will irreparably harm the plaintiff's ability to enforce his or her rights at the trial — called also *temporary injunction;* compare *temporary restraining order* at ORDER ◊ Before a preliminary injunction can be issued, there must be a hearing with prior notice to the defendant. Under Federal Rule of Civil Procedure 65, the hearing and the trial may be consolidated.

prohibitory injunction : an injunction that prohibits the defendant from taking a particular action and maintains the positions of the parties until there is a hearing to determine the matter in dispute

tem·po·rary injunction : PRELIMINARY INJUNCTION in this entry

injunction bond — see BOND 1a

in·junc·tive \in-'jəŋk-tiv\ *adj* : of or relating to an injunction ⟨granted ~ relief⟩

in·jure *vt* **in·jured; in·jur·ing 1** : to interfere with or violate the legally protected interests of: as **a** : to harm the physical, emotional, or mental well-being of **b** : to cause (another) to suffer from damage to, deprivation of, or interference with property or a property interest **c** : to violate the constitutionally or otherwise legally protected rights of **2** : to mar or impair the soundness or appearance of (as a building) : DEFACE

in ju·re \in-'jùr-ē, -'yü-rā\ *adv* [Latin] : in right, law, or justice

in·ju·ria \in-'jùr-ē-ə\ *n, pl* **injurias** [Latin,

unlawful conduct, unjust treatment] : invasion of another's rights for which one may bring an action

injuria abs•que dam•no \-'ab-skwē-'dam-nō, -'äb-skwā-'däm-nō\ *n* [Latin, injury without damage] : a wrong that causes no damage sustaining an action for relief ⟨the lack of a warning label on the electric broom ... is at best *injuria absque damno* —*Lee v. Regina Corp.*, 253 F. Supp. 825 (1966)⟩ — called also *injuria absque damnum;* compare DAMNUM ABSQUE INJURIA

in•ju•ri•ous \in-'jùr-ē-əs\ *adj* : inflicting or tending to inflict injury — **in•ju•ri•ous•ly** *adv*

injurious false•hood *n* : DISPARAGEMENT

in•ju•ry *n, pl* **-ries** [Latin *injuria*, from *injurus* injurious, from *in-* not + *jur-, jus* right] **1** : an act that wrongs or harms another; *specif* : a violation of a legally protected interest (as the physical or mental well-being, property, reputation, or rights of another) for which the law allows an action for legal or equitable relief **2** : hurt, damage, or loss sustained

in•jus•tice *n* **1** : absence of justice : violation of what is considered right and just or of the rights of another **2** : an unjust act

in–kind *adj* **1 a** : made in a form other than money ⟨an ~ contribution to a political campaign⟩ **b** : made without conversion (as of assets) into money ⟨an ~ distribution of assets⟩ **2** : made in a form or amount equivalent to another ⟨an ~ payment to substitute for meals⟩

in•land marine insurance *n* : insurance against loss of or damage to property transported in domestic commerce, instrumentalities of transport and communication, and personal property — compare MARINE INSURANCE, OCEAN MARINE INSURANCE

¹in lim•i•ne \in-'li-mə-nē, -'lē-mi-nā\ *adv* [Latin, on the threshold] : at the beginning : as a preliminary matter; *specif* : before a particular procedure or proceeding takes place

²in limine *adj* : of, relating to, or being a motion, petition, or order regarding the admissibility of evidence whose exclusion is sought esp. on the ground that it is prejudicial

in lo•co pa•ren•tis \in-'lō-kō-pə-'ren-tis\ *adv* [Latin] : in the place of a parent ⟨either parent of a minor, guardian, or a person standing *in loco parentis* to the minor —*Code of Alabama*⟩ ◊ In order for a person to be considered in loco parentis, he or she must have intentionally assumed the rights and duties of a parent.

in•mate \'in-,māt\ *n* : a person confined in an institution (as a prison or hospital)

in•no•cence \'i-nə-səns\ *n* : freedom from fault or guilt under the law: as **a** : the state of not being guilty of a particular crime or offense — compare GUILT **b** : the state of not being guilty of an act that constitutes a ground for divorce **c** : ignorance on the part of a party to a transaction of facts that would lead a person of ordinary prudence to make inquiries

in•no•cent \'i-nə-sənt\ *adj* : characterized by innocence

innocent agent *n* : one who unknowingly, unintentionally, or under force or coercion commits a criminal act on behalf of another

innocent misrepresentation *n* : a representation that is made in good faith and believed to be true by the one making it but that is in fact false

innocent party — see PARTY 1b

innocent purchaser *n* : one who purchases property for consideration in good faith and without knowledge of facts that would lead to the suspicion that the seller does not have good title

innocent spouse \-'spaùs\ *n* : a spouse who may be relieved of liability for taxes on an amount of income that the other spouse failed to include on a joint return filed with the Internal Revenue Service ◊ In order to be relieved of tax liability, the innocent spouse must prove that the other

\ə\abut	\ə\kitten	\ər\further	\a\ash	\ā\ace
\ä\cot, cart	\aù\out	\ch\chin	\e\bet	\ē\easy
\g\go	\i\hit	\ī\ice	\j\job	\ŋ\sing	\ō\go	\ò\law
\ò\boy	\th\thin	\th\the	\ü\loot	\ù\foot	\y\yet
\zh\vision	*see also* Pronunciation Symbols page

spouse omitted the amount of income, that he or she did not know and had no reason to know that the income had been omitted, and that it is unfair under the circumstances to hold the innocent spouse liable.

in·nom·i·nate \in-'nä-mə-nət\ adj, in the civil law of Louisiana : having no special name or designation — compare NOMINATE

innominate contract — see CONTRACT

Inns of Court 1 : the four sets of buildings in London belonging to four societies of students and practitioners of the law 2 : the four societies that alone admit to practice at the English bar

in·nu·en·do \,i-nyü-'wen-dō\ n : a parenthetical explanation of the text of a legal document; esp : an explanation in a complaint for defamation of the defamatory meaning of a statement by the defendant which is not defamatory on its face — compare INDUCEMENT

in·of·fi·cious \,i-nə-'fi-shəs\ adj [Latin inofficiosus (of a will) ignoring the testator's duty to his relatives, from in- not + officiosus kind, dutiful, from officium service, kindness, duty] : of or relating to a disposition of property that has the effect of depriving descendants of the shares of a succession to which they are entitled by law

in·op·er·a·tive \i-'nä-pə-rə-tiv\ adj : having no force or effect ⟨an ~ will⟩

in pais \in-'pā\ adv [Anglo-French en pais in the country, outside court] 1 : out of court : without judicial proceedings 2 a : not in writing b : not of record

in pa·ri cau·sa \in-'pä-rē-'kȯ-zə, -'kau̇-sä\ adv [Late Latin, in a like case] : in a case where all parties stand equal in right according to law

¹in pari de·lic·to \-di-'lik-tō, -dä-\ adv [New Latin, in like offense] : in equal fault or wrong — used of parties to a lawsuit

²in pari delicto n : a doctrine that bars a plaintiff who has participated in wrongdoing from recovering damages for loss resulting from the wrongdoing

in pari ma·te·ria \-mə-'tir-ē-ə, -mä-\ adv [Late Latin, in a like matter] : on the same subject or matter : in a similar case ◊ It is a doctrine in statutory construction that statutes that are in pari materia must be construed together.

in per·so·nam \,in-pər-'sō-nəm\ adv or adj [Latin, against a person] : against a person for the purpose of imposing a liability or obligation to do or not do something ⟨an action in personam⟩ ⟨an in personam suit⟩ — see also in personam jurisdiction at JURISDICTION; compare IN REM, QUASI IN REM

in personam judgment — see JUDGMENT 1a

in personam jurisdiction — see JURISDICTION

in pos·se \in-'pä-sē\ adv or adj [Medieval Latin, in possibility] : not in actuality : having a potential to exist — compare IN ESSE

in prae·sen·ti \,in-prē-'zen-,tī, -prī-'sen-tē\ adv [Latin] : in the present

in pro·pria per·so·na \in-'prō-prē-ə-pər-'sō-nə, -per-'sō-nä\ adv [Latin] : in one's own person : without the assistance of an attorney : PRO SE ⟨the defendant appeared in propria persona⟩

in·quest \'in-,kwest\ n [Anglo-French enqueste, from Old French, ultimately from Latin inquirere to ask about, from in- within, into + quaerere to seek] 1 : a judicial or official inquiry or examination often before a jury ⟨a coroner's ~⟩ — compare TRIAL 2 : a body of people (as a jury) assembled to hold a judicial or official inquiry; also : the finding of such an inquiry or the document recording it

in·qui·ry \'in-,kwīr-ē, in-'kwīr-ē; 'in-kwə-rē, 'iŋ-\ n, pl -ries 1 : a request for information ⟨such doubt as would cause a reasonable person to make an ~⟩ 2 : a systematic official investigation often of a matter of public interest esp. by a body (as a legislative committee) with power to compel testimony — on inquiry : having notice that inquiry should be made

inquiry notice n : IMPLIED NOTICE at NOTICE

in·qui·si·tion \ˌin-kwə-'zi-shən, ˌiŋ-\ *n* **1** : the act of inquiring or examining **2** : a judicial or official inquiry or examination usu. before a jury; *also* : the finding that results from such an inquiry
in·qui·si·to·ri·al \in-ˌkwi-zə-'tōr-ē-əl\ *adj* **1** : constituting or relating to a system of justice in which the judge conducts an inquiry developing the facts of the litigant's case — compare ACCUSATORIAL, ADVERSARY **2** : having the authority to conduct official investigations
in re \in-'rē, -'rā\ *prep* [Latin] : in the matter of — used in the title or name of a case where the proceeding is in rem or quasi in rem and not in personam (as in a matter involving a probate or bankruptcy estate, a guardianship, or an application for laying out a public highway) and occasionally in the title of an ex parte proceeding (as in an application for a writ of habeas corpus)
in rem \in-'rem\ *adv or adj* [Latin] : against or with respect to a thing (as a right, status, or interest in property) without reference to the persons involved ⟨when the Government is proceeding against property *in rem* —Austin v. United States, 509 U.S. 602 (1993)⟩ ⟨an *in rem* action⟩ — see also *in rem jurisdiction* at JURISDICTION; compare IN PERSONAM, QUASI IN REM
in rem judgment — see JUDGMENT 1a
in rem jurisdiction — see JURISDICTION
INS *abbr* Immigration and Naturalization Service — see also the IMPORTANT AGENCIES section
in·sane *adj* : affected with insanity
insane de·lu·sion *n* : a false belief in a nonexistent state of facts in which no rational person would believe that deprives a person of the capacity to make a will and renders any will made invalid
in·san·i·ty *n* **1** : unsoundness of mind or lack of the ability to understand that prevents one from having the mental capacity required by law to enter into a particular relationship, status, or transaction or that releases one from criminal or civil responsibility: as **a** : a disease, defect, or condition of the mind that renders one un-

able to understand the nature of a criminal act or the fact that it is wrong or to conform one's conduct to the requirements of the law being violated **b** : inability to understand and participate in legal proceedings brought against one : INCOMPETENCE **c** : inability to understand the nature and purpose of a punishment (as the death penalty) to which one has been sentenced **d** : inability to understand the nature and consequences of one's acts (as making a will) or of events, matters, or proceedings in which one is involved — see also COMMITMENT, DURHAM RULE, IRRESISTIBLE IMPULSE TEST, M'NAGHTEN TEST, NOT GUILTY BY REASON OF INSANITY, SUBSTANTIAL CAPACITY TEST; compare CAPACITY, COMPETENCY, COMPETENT, DIMINISHED CAPACITY, SANITY **2** : the affirmative defense of having acted while insane
in·scribe *vt* **in·scribed; in·scrib·ing** : to set down in writing (as the terms of a mortgage) to create a lasting public record — **in·scrip·tion** *n*
in·se·cure *adj* : having a good faith belief that the prospect of receiving payment or performance from a party with whom one has contracted is impaired — **in·se·cu·ri·ty** *n*
insecurity clause *n* : a clause in an agreement (as a security agreement) allowing a party who deems himself or herself insecure to require immediate payment or performance or the giving of collateral
in·side information *n* : information not known to the public that one has obtained by virtue of being an insider — called also *insider information*
in·sid·er *n* : a person who is in a position of power or has access to confidential information: as **a** : one (as an officer, director, employee, relative, or owner of more than 10% of the corporation's stock) who is in a position to have special knowl-

\ə\abut \ᵊ\kitten \ər\further \a\ash \ā\ace \ä\cot, cart \au̇\out \ch\chin \e\bet \ē\easy \g\go \i\hit \ī\ice \j\job \ŋ\sing \ō\go \ȯ\law \ȯi\boy \th\thin \t̲h̲\the \ü\loot \u̇\foot \y\yet \zh\vision *see also* Pronunciation Symbols page

edge of the affairs of or to influence the decisions of a company **b** : an individual (as a relative or an influential party) or entity (as a corporate affiliate) having a close relationship with a debtor such that transactions are not made at arm's length and are subject to closer scrutiny than the transactions of those dealing at arm's length

insider preference *n* : a transfer of property by a debtor in bankruptcy to an insider made more than ninety days prior to but within one year of the bankruptcy petition

insider trader *n* : one that engages in insider trading

insider trading *n* : the illegal use of esp. material inside information for profit in financial trading — see also TIPPEE

in so·li·do \in-'sä-lə-dō, -'sō-lē-ˌdō\ *adv or adj* [New Latin] *in the civil law of Louisiana* : for the whole : involving all ⟨an *in solido* obligation⟩ ⟨if several persons have jointly borrowed the same object, they are bound for it *in solido* to the lender — *Louisiana Civil Code*⟩ — compare JOINT AND SEVERAL

in·sol·ven·cy \in-'säl-vən-sē\ *n, pl* **-cies** **1** : the fact or state of being insolvent — compare BANKRUPTCY **2** : insufficiency (as of an estate) to discharge all enforceable debts ◊ Insolvency matters are covered under the Bankruptcy Code.

in·sol·vent \in-'säl-vənt\ *adj* **1** : having ceased paying or unable to pay debts as they fall due in the usual course of business — compare BANKRUPT **2** : having liabilities in excess of a reasonable market value of assets held **3** : insufficient to pay all debts ⟨an ~ estate⟩ — **insolvent** *n*

in·spect *vt* **1** : to view closely and critically **2** : to examine officially ⟨~ the facility for code violations⟩ — *vi* : to make an inspection

in·spec·tion *n* : a careful and critical examination: as **a** : a buyer's examination of goods prior to payment or acceptance esp. in accordance with section 2-513 of the Uniform Commercial Code **b** : an

examination of articles of commerce to determine their fitness for transportation or sale **c** : an investigation of an applicant for insurance **d** : an examination or survey of a community, of premises, of a facility, or of a vehicle by an authorized person (as to determine compliance with regulations or susceptibility to fire or other hazards); *specif* : ADMINISTRATIVE SEARCH at SEARCH **e** : examination of documents, things, or property for purposes of making discovery for trial

in·spec·tor *n* **1** : a person employed or authorized to inspect something **2** : a police officer in charge of a number of precincts and ranking below a superintendent or deputy superintendent

in·stall·ment *n* : one of the parts into which a debt is divided when payment is made at intervals — **installment** *adj*

installment contract — see CONTRACT

installments–for–a–fixed–amount option — see OPTION 4

installments–for–a–fixed–period option — see OPTION 4

in·stance \'in-stəns\ *n* [French, from Late Latin *instantia*, from Latin, the fact of being present or impending, vehemence in speech, urgency, from *instant-*, *instans* insistent, pressing, from present participle of *instare* to be pressing, stand upon] : the institution or prosecution of a lawsuit ⟨a court of first ~⟩

in·stant *adj* : being under present consideration ⟨the questions presented in the ~ case⟩

¹in·sti·tute *vt* **-tut·ed; -tut·ing** **1** : to establish in a particular position or office; *specif, in the civil law of Louisiana* : to appoint as heir — see also *instituted heir* at HEIR **2** : to get started : BRING ⟨~ a lawsuit⟩

²institute *n* **1** : an elementary principle recognized as authoritative **2** *pl* : a collection of principles; *esp* : a legal compendium

instituted heir — see HEIR

instituted legatee *n* : INSTITUTED HEIR at HEIR

in·sti·tu·tion *n* **1** : the act of instituting **2** : a significant practice, relationship, or organization in a society or culture ⟨the ~ of marriage⟩ **3** : an established organization or corporation esp. of a public character; *specif* : a facility for the treatment or training of persons with mental deficiencies

in·sti·tu·tion·al·ize \ˌin-stə-'tü-shə-nə-ˌlīz, -'tyü-\ *vt* **-ized; -iz·ing** : to put in the care of an institution — compare COMMIT

in·struct *vt* : to provide (a jury) with explanation and directions regarding the law applicable to a case ⟨the judge ~ed the jury that the plaintiff bears the burden of proof⟩ ⟨the jury was ~ed to ignore the attorney's comments⟩ ~ *vi* : to give instructions to a jury ⟨the trial judge refused to ~ on manslaughter —W. R. LaFave and A. W. Scott, Jr.⟩

instructed verdict — see VERDICT

in·struc·tion *n* : an explanation of an applicable principle of law given by a judge to a jury before the jury retires to consider its verdict — called also *jury charge, jury instruction* ◊ Under both the Federal Rules of Civil Procedure and the Federal Rules of Criminal Procedure, at the close of evidence, or before the close if the court reasonably so directs, any party may file written requests for the instructions to be given to the jury by the court. The court must advise the parties of its decision regarding the instructions prior to closing argument so that the parties may address the instructions during argument. Any objections to the instructions must be made before the jury retires for deliberation.

in·stru·ment *n* **1** : a means or implement by which something is achieved, performed, or furthered ⟨an ~ of crime⟩ **2** : a document (as a deed, will, bond, note, certificate of deposit, insurance policy, warrant, or writ) evidencing rights or duties esp. of one party to another under the law ⟨no person is liable on an ~ unless his signature appears thereon — *Uniform Commercial Code*⟩ ⟨an indictment

is a form of charging ~⟩; *specif* : NEGOTIABLE INSTRUMENT

in·stru·men·tal·i·ty \ˌin-strə-mən-'ta-lə-tē, -ˌmen-\ *n, pl* **-ties** **1** : something through which an end is achieved or occurs ⟨damages incurred in a single incident through an ~ owned by the employer⟩ **2** : something that serves as an intermediary or agent through which one or more functions of a larger controlling entity are carried out : a part or branch esp. of a governing body — compare ALTER EGO

in·sur·able \in-'shùr-ə-bəl\ *adj* : capable of or appropriate for being insured against loss, damage, or death : affording a sufficient ground for insurance — **in·sur·abil·i·ty** \in-ˌshùr-ə-'bi-lə-tē\ *n*

insurable interest — see INTEREST 1

in·sur·ance \in-'shùr-əns, 'in-ˌshùr-\ *n* **1** : the action, process, or means of insuring or the state of being insured usu. against loss or damage by a contingent event (as death, fire, accident, or sickness) **2 a** : the business of insuring persons or property **b** : coverage by contract whereby for an agreed payment one party agrees to indemnify or guarantee another against loss by a specified contingency or peril **c** : the principles and practice of the business of insuring **3** : the sum for which something is insured

insurance adjuster *n* : a person employed by insurer or insured to determine the loss under an insurance policy

insurance certificate *n* **1** : a certificate issued by an insurer to a shipper as evidence that a shipment of merchandise is covered under a marine insurance policy **2** : a certificate issued in place of an insurance policy by an insurer to one insured as evidence of membership in an insurance or pension plan

insurance policy *n* : a writing whereby a contract of insurance is made in which

\ə\abut	\ᵊ\kitten	\ər\further	\a\ash	\ā\ace
\ä\cot, cart	\au̇\out	\ch\chin	\e\bet	\ē\easy
\g\go	\i\hit	\ī\ice	\j\job	\ŋ\sing	\ō\go	\ȯ\law
\ȯi\boy	\th\thin	\t͟h\the	\ü\loot	\u̇\foot	\y\yet
\zh\vision	*see also* Pronunciation Symbols page			

the rights and duties of the insurer and the insured are set out

insurance trust — see TRUST

in•sure \in-'shùr\ *vb* **in•sured; in•sur•ing** *vt* : to assure against a loss by a contingent event on certain stipulated conditions or at a given rate of premium : give, take, or procure insurance on or for ~ *vi* : to contract to give insurance : UNDERWRITE; *also* : to procure or effect insurance

in•sured *n* : a person whose life, physical well-being, or property is the subject of insurance

insured plan *n* : a pension or retirement plan managed by an insurance company under which contributions are used to purchase life insurance or annuities as a means of funding the benefits promised

in•sur•er \in-'shùr-ər\ *n* : one that contracts to indemnify another by way of insurance : an insurance company or underwriter

in•sur•gence \in-'sər-jəns\ *n* : insurgent rebellion

in•sur•gen•cy \in-'sər-jən-sē\ *n, pl* **-cies** : the quality or state of being insurgent; *specif* : a condition of revolt against a recognized government that does not reach the proportions of an organized revolutionary government and is not recognized as belligerency

¹in•sur•gent \in-'sər-jənt\ *n* **1** : a person who rises in revolt against civil authority or an established government; *esp* : one not recognized as a belligerent **2** : one that acts contrary to the established leadership (as of a political party, union, or corporation) or its decisions and policies

²insurgent *adj* : rising in opposition to civil or political authority or against an established government

insuring agreement *n* : the part of an insurance policy setting out in basic terms what the policy covers

insuring clause *n* : a clause in an insurance policy that sets out the risk assumed by the insurer or defines the scope of the coverage afforded

in•sur•rec•tion \,in-sə-'rek-shən\ *n* : the act or an instance of revolting esp. vio-

lently against civil or political authority or against an established government; *also* : the crime of inciting or engaging in such revolt ⟨whoever incites, sets on foot, assists, or engages in any rebellion or ~ against the authority of the United States ... shall be fined not more than $10,000 or imprisoned not more than ten years — *U.S. Code*⟩

¹in•sur•rec•tion•ary \,in-sə-'rek-shə-,ner-ē\ *adj* : of, relating to, or constituting insurrection; *also* : given to or tending to induce insurrection

²insurrectionary *n* : a participant in insurrection : INSURGENT

¹in•tan•gi•ble \in-'tan-jə-bəl\ *adj* : incapable of being touched : having no physical existence : not tangible or corporeal

²intangible *n* : something intangible; *specif* : an asset (as goodwill or a patent right) that is not corporeal

intangible asset — see ASSET 2

intangible property — see PROPERTY

intangible tax *n* : a tax imposed on the privilege of owning, transferring, devising, profiting by, or otherwise dealing with or benefiting from intangibles

in•te•grate *vb* **-grat•ed; -grat•ing** *vt* **1** : to form, coordinate, or blend into a functioning or unified whole **2** : to end the segregation of and bring into equal membership in society or an organization ~ *vi* : to become integrated

integrated *adj* **1** : composed to form a complete or coordinated entity; *specif* : being a final and complete expression of an agreement that cannot be contradicted or modified by extrinsic evidence ⟨an ~ writing⟩ **2** : marked by the unified control of all aspects of industrial production from raw materials through distribution of finished products ⟨~ companies⟩ ⟨~ production⟩ **3** : characterized by integration and esp. racial integration ⟨~ schools⟩ ⟨an ~ society⟩

integrated bar *n* : a bar having compulsory membership of all lawyers practicing in a specific area (as a state) — called also *unified bar;* compare VOLUNTARY BAR

in·te·gra·tion *n* : the act or process or an instance of integrating: as **a** : a writing that embodies a complete and final agreement between parties **b** : incorporation as equals into society or an organization of individuals of different groups (as races)

integration clause *n* : a clause in a contract stating that the contract is a complete and final statement of the agreement between the parties

intellectual property — see PROPERTY

in·tel·li·gent *adj* : having or indicating a high or satisfactory degree of intelligence and mental capacity; *esp* : having or indicating an understanding of the nature and consequences of an act or decision ⟨a knowing and ~ waiver of counsel⟩ — compare KNOWING ◊ Under *Miranda v. Arizona*, 384 U.S. 436 (1966), a waiver of rights must be knowing and intelligent. — in·tel·li·gent·ly *adv*

in·tend \in-'tend\ *vt* : to have in one's mind as a purpose or goal ⟨did not ~ to kill her⟩

in·tend·ed *adj* : specifically planned or contemplated ⟨an ~ injury⟩⟨~ uses⟩⟨the ~ beneficiary⟩

in·tend·ment \in-'tend-mənt\ *n* : the true meaning or intention esp. of a law

in·tent \in-'tent\ *n* **1** : the act or fact of intending: as **a** : the design or purpose to commit a wrongful or criminal act — called also *criminal intent;* compare KNOWLEDGE, MENS REA, MOTIVE, NEGLIGENCE **b** : the purpose to commit a tortious act having consequences that the actor desires and believes or knows will occur

constructive intent : intent that is inferred to exist (as from willfulness or recklessness) in relation to an act

criminal intent : INTENT 1a

general intent : intent to perform an illegal act without the desire for further consequences or a precise result ⟨there was a *general intent* to assault but not to kill⟩

specific intent : intent to perform an illegal act with the knowledge or purpose

that particular results will or may ensue ⟨assaulted him with *specific intent* to kill⟩

transferred intent **1** : intent attributed to a person who intends to cause another harm when the harm is accidentally inflicted on an unintended victim **2** : a doctrine in tort and criminal law: a wrongdoer who causes harm to a person other than the one intended may nevertheless be held to have intended the harmful result

2 a : INTENDMENT — see also LEGISLATIVE INTENT **b** : the purpose of a document (as a contract or will) **c** : the aim or goal of a person in creating a document or taking an action ⟨the court's attempt to fulfill the donor's ~⟩ ⟨the ~ of the contracting parties implied by their language⟩ — see also ORIGINAL INTENT — **with intent** : with the intent to commit another sometimes specified crime ⟨entered the apartment *with intent* to commit theft therein⟩ ⟨a drug dealer charged with possession *with intent*⟩

in·ten·tion \in-'ten-chən\ *n* : something intended : INTENT ⟨the ~ of the testator⟩ ◊ *Intent* is more commonly used than *intention* when speaking technically esp. about the criminal and tort concepts of intent (senses 1a and 1b).

in·ten·tion·al \in-'ten-chə-nəl\ *adj* : done with intent ⟨an ~ tort⟩⟨~ discrimination⟩ — in·ten·tion·al·ly *adv*

in·ter alia \'in-tər-'ā-lē-ə, -'ä-\ *adv* [Latin] : among other things ⟨contends, *inter alia,* that the claim is moot⟩

in·ter·cept *vt* : to receive (a communication or signal directed elsewhere) usu. secretly ⟨shall not be unlawful ... for a person acting under color of law to ~ a wire, oral, or electronic communication where such person is a party to the communication —*U.S. Code*⟩ — in·ter·cep·tion *n*

\ə\abut \ᵊ\kitten \ər\further \a\ash \ā\ace
\ä\cot, cart \aú\out \ch\chin \e\bet \ē\easy
\g\go \i\hit \ī\ice \j\job \ŋ\sing \ō\go \ò\law
\òi\boy \th\thin \t̲h̲\the \ü\loot \ù\foot \y\yet
\zh\vision *see also* Pronunciation Symbols page

¹in·ter·dict \'in-tər-ˌdikt\ *n* **1** : something that prohibits **2** : one that has been interdicted — compare WARD
²in·ter·dict \ˌin-tər-'dikt\ *vt* **1** *in the civil law of Louisiana* : to deprive (a person) of the right to care for one's own person or affairs because of mental incapacity — compare COMMIT, CURATOR, TUTOR **2** : to authoritatively prohibit or bar (an act or conduct) **3** : to intercept or cut off (as a drug shipment) by force
in·ter·dic·tion \ˌin-tər-'dik-shən\ *n* **1** *in the civil law of Louisiana* : removal of the right to care for one's own person and affairs — called also *complete interdiction, full interdiction;* compare LIMITED INTERDICTION **2** : the act or an instance of interdicting ⟨∼ of drugs⟩
in·ter·est \'in-trəst; 'in-tə-rəst, -ˌrest\ *n* [probably alteration of earlier *interesse*, from Anglo-French, from Medieval Latin, from Latin, to be between, make a difference, concern, from *inter-* between, among + *esse* to be] **1** : a right, title, claim, or share in property
Article Nine security interest : SECURITY INTEREST 2 in this entry
beneficial interest : the right to the use and benefit of property ⟨a *beneficial interest* in the trust⟩
contingent interest : a future interest whose vesting is dependent upon the occurrence or nonoccurrence of a future event — compare VESTED INTEREST in this entry
controlling interest : sufficient stock ownership in a corporation to exert control over policy
equitable interest : an interest (as a beneficial interest) that is held by virtue of equitable title or that may be claimed on the ground of equitable relief ⟨claimed an *equitable interest* in the debtor's assets⟩
executory interest : a future interest other than a remainder or reversion that may take effect upon the divesting of a prior interest or one created simultaneously ◊ Unlike a remainder, an executory interest does not require the expira-

tion of a prior interest. It was designed to guard against the destructibility of contingent remainders set forth in the rule in Shelley's case.
expectation interest : the interest of a party to a breached contract in receiving the benefit of the bargain by being put in a position as good as that which would have resulted had the contract been performed — called also *expectancy interest;* compare RELIANCE INTEREST in this entry
future interest : an interest in property limited or created so that its owner will come into the use, possession, or enjoyment of it at some future time — see also CONTINGENT INTEREST and EXECUTORY INTEREST in this entry; compare REMAINDER, REVERSION
insurable interest : an interest or stake in property or in a person that arises from the potential for esp. financial loss upon the destruction of the property or the death of the person and that is a requirement for enforcing an insurance contract ◊ The purpose of requiring an insurable interest is to prevent the use of insurance as a form of gambling or as a method of profiting from destruction.
legal interest : an interest that is recognized in law (as by legal title) — compare EQUITABLE INTEREST in this entry, *legal title* at TITLE
life interest : an interest lasting for the duration of a person's life that forecloses the ability to affect the property beyond that term — compare *life estate* at ESTATE 1
possessory interest : an interest (as a right) involving or arising out of the possession of property ◊ A possessory interest is based on control rather than use. Thus a lessee who occupies and controls the use of property has a possessory interest, while a party who has an easement does not.
purchase money security interest **1** : the security interest held by the seller of collateral to secure payment of all or part of the price **2** : the security interest

of a person that gives value to a debtor so that the debtor may acquire rights in or the use of collateral

reliance interest : the interest of a party to a breached contract in being compensated for detriments suffered (as expenses incurred) in reliance on the agreement — compare EXPECTATION INTEREST in this entry

reversionary interest : an interest in property (as a possibility of reverter or a power of termination) remaining in the transferor of the property or in his or her successor in interest

security interest **1** : an interest in property that exists by contract as security for payment or performance of an obligation ⟨the *security interest* of a mortgagee in the mortgaged property⟩; *also* : LIEN ◊ While a lien may be created by statutory or judicial means without any agreement providing for security (as in the case of a tax lien or judgment lien), a security interest and lien may inhere in the same claim, as when a mortgage comprises both a lien on and security interest in the mortgaged property. **2** : an interest in personal property or fixtures created by a security agreement that secures payment or performance of an obligation ⟨the creditor had a *security interest* in the inventory and accounts receivable of the business⟩ — called also *Article Nine security interest;* see also ATTACH 3, ²PERFECT b, PURCHASE MONEY SECURITY INTEREST in this entry ◊ Security interests in personal property are governed by Article 9 of the Uniform Commercial Code. The security interest set out in Article 9 largely replaces the traditional devices for security, such as the pledge and chattel mortgage. A security interest in property that has attached enables a creditor to obtain satisfaction of a debt out of the property without the need to obtain a judgment in court and levy on the property. Further, it provides the creditor with priority over competing claims against the property.

terminable interest : an interest (as in a life estate) that will terminate upon the occurrence of an event or the passing of time

vested interest : a present and certain right to the present or future enjoyment of property — compare CONTINGENT INTEREST in this entry

working interest : the interest of a party that holds the right to oil, gas, or minerals on a property and that bears production costs — see also OVERRIDING ROYALTY

2 : a specific concern or level of involvement (as financial involvement) esp. that warrants recognition or causes bias ⟨had a right to intervene because of an ~ in the litigation⟩ ⟨recused himself due to an ~ in the matter⟩ — see also CONFLICT OF INTEREST **3** : something that causes or warrants particular attention: as **a** : a principle, purpose, or object of concern

compelling state interest : a governmental interest (as in educating children or protecting the public) which is so important that it outweighs individual rights

public interest **1 a** : the general welfare and rights of the public that are to be recognized, protected, and advanced ⟨the attorney general has standing as a representative of the *public interest*⟩ **b** : a specific public benefit or stake in something ⟨the *public interest* in controlling crime⟩ **2** : the concern or attention of the public ⟨a matter of widespread *public interest*⟩ **b** : a right esp. that arises from a constitution (as the U.S. Constitution); *esp* : such a right considered as an issue or claim created in or involving a particular situation or thing ⟨no person will be deprived of his ~s in the absence of a proceeding in which he may present his case — *Marshall v. Jerrico, Inc.,* 446 U.S. 238 (1980)⟩

\ə\abut \ᵊ\kitten \ər\further \a\ash \ā\ace
\ä\cot, cart \au̇\out \ch\chin \e\bet \ē\easy
\g\go \i\hit \ī\ice \j\job \ŋ\sing \ō\go \ȯ\law
\ȯi\boy \th\thin \t̲h̲\the \ü\loot \u̇\foot \y\yet
\zh\vision *see also* Pronunciation Symbols page

liberty interest : an interest in freedom from governmental deprivation of liberty esp. without due process ⟨the *liberty interest* implicated by the needless discouragement of the exercise of the right to counsel —*State v. Albert*, 899 P.2d 103 (1995) (dissent)⟩

privacy interest : an interest in freedom from governmental intrusion into matters in which one has a reasonable expectation of privacy ⟨we have no *privacy interest* protected by the federal Constitution in limiting public or government access to knowledge of our financial transactions —L. H. Tribe⟩

property interest : an interest in freedom from governmental deprivation of property and sources of financial gain (as employment or a government benefit) without due process; *broadly* : something (as a job or benefit) to which one has a legitimate claim of entitlement and that cannot be taken away without due process as distinguished from the unprotected object of a need, desire, or expectation

4 : the well-being of a person — often used in pl. ⟨does not serve the child's best ~*s*⟩ **5** : a charge for the use of another's money that is usu. a percentage of the money being used ⟨an account yielding 7% ~⟩ ⟨paid back the loan with ~⟩

compound interest : interest computed on the sum of the original principal and accrued interest

legal interest : a lawful interest rate and esp. the highest rate allowed ⟨proposals to increase the *legal interest* on department store credit cards to 15% —*American Banker*⟩; *also* : interest computed at such a rate ⟨awarded the defendant *legal interest*⟩ — compare USURY

qualified residence interest : interest that is deductible from adjusted gross income under federal tax law when it is paid on debt that is secured by one's residence and that was incurred for the acquisition, construction, improvement, or refinancing of the residence or through a home equity loan

simple interest : interest computed on the principal of a loan or account

interest arbitration — see ARBITRATION

in·ter·est·ed *adj* : having a recognizable interest in a matter — compare INTEREST 2

interest–only option — see OPTION 4

in·ter·fere *vi* -fered; -fer·ing **1** : to act in a way that impedes or obstructs others **2** : to enter into the concerns of others

in·ter·fer·ence *n* **1 a** : the act or an instance of interfering ⟨~ with contract⟩ **b** : something that interferes **2** : a hearing to determine the priority of invention at issue in a patent dispute

¹**in·ter·im** \'in-tə-rəm\ *n* : an intervening time — see also AD INTERIM

²**interim** *adj* : done, made, appointed, or occurring for an interim ⟨an ~ disposition⟩

in·ter·in·sur·ance \ˌin-tər-in-'shūr-əns, -'in-ˌshūr-\ *n* : RECIPROCAL INSURANCE

interinsurance exchange *n* : RECIPROCAL EXCHANGE

in·ter·in·sur·er \ˌin-tər-in-'shūr-ər\ *n* : an underwriter of reciprocal insurance

in·ter·lock \ˌin-tər-'läk\ *vi* : to be or become mutually connected; *also* : to be consistent in regard to major elements ⟨confessions that ~⟩

interlocking confession *n* : a confession of a defendant in a joint trial that agrees in important respects with that of a codefendant ◊ The use of interlocking confessions at trial can pose difficult problems when a defendant's confession incriminates a codefendant. If the first defendant does not testify, the other may be deprived of the right to confront an accuser.

interlocking director *n* : one that serves as a director of two or more corporations at one time

interlocking directorate *n* : a directorate linked with that of another corporation by interlocking directors

in·ter·loc·u·to·ry \ˌin-tər-'lä-kyə-ˌtōr-ē\ *adj* [Medieval Latin *interlocutorius*, from Late Latin *interloqui* to pronounce an interlocutory sentence, from Latin, to speak between] : not final or definitive

⟨an ~ order⟩; *broadly* : made or done during the progress of an action esp. when delay would cause irreversible injury ⟨an ~ appeal⟩
interlocutory decree — see DECREE
interlocutory injunction — see INJUNCTION
in·ter·me·di·ary \ˌin-tər-'mē-dē-ˌer-ē\ *n, pl* **-ar·ies** : one that acts as a means or go-between in a matter involving other parties ⟨a reinsurance ~⟩ — see also LEARNED INTERMEDIARY — **intermediary** *adj*
intermediary bank — see BANK
in·ter·me·di·ate \ˌin-tər-'mē-dē-ət\ *adj* **1** : being or occurring at the middle place, stage, or degree or between extremes ⟨an ~ order⟩ **2** : of, relating to, or being a level of judicial scrutiny to ensure equal protection of the laws that is applied to a statute involving classification of persons and that is more intensive than the rational basis test and not as severe as strict scrutiny ⟨~ review⟩ ⟨~ scrutiny⟩ — **in·ter·me·di·ate·ly** *adv*
intermediate court *n* : a court (as an appeals court) beneath the court of last resort in a jurisdiction
Intermediate Court of Appeals : the court of appeals in Hawaii
in·ter·nal law *n* : the law of a state regulating its internal affairs — compare INTERNATIONAL LAW, WHOLE LAW
in·ter·na·tion·al copyright \ˌin-tər-'nash-ə-nəl-\ *n* : a copyright secured by international treaties
International Court of Justice : the principal judicial instrumentality of the United Nations which has jurisdiction to settle disputes between nations that have consented to such jurisdiction and to provide other branches of the U.N. (as the General Assembly) with advisory opinions — called also *World Court*
international law *n* : a body of laws, rules, or legal principles that are based on custom, treaties, or legislation and that control or affect the rights and duties of nations in relation to each other — compare INTERNAL LAW
international will — see WILL

in·ter par·tes \'in-tər-'pär-tēz, 'in-ter-'pär-tās\ *adv or adj* [Latin] : between parties ⟨a consent decree is not simply a contract *inter partes*, unlike a settlement⟩; *specif* : having or involving adverse parties ⟨an issue of an invalid application may also arise in *inter partes* proceedings where an adversary raises the issue —*In re Compagnie Generale Maritime*, 993 F.2d 841 (1993) (dissent)⟩ — compare EX PARTE
in·ter·plead \ˌin-tər-'plēd\ *vb* [Anglo-French *enterpleder*, from *enter-* between, among + *pleder* to plead, from Old French *plaidier*] *vt* : to bring (adverse claimants) into court by interpleader ⟨the defendants can ~ injured stock purchasers if they fear the latter may have a superior claim . . . to the agents' illicit profits —R. C. Clark⟩ — compare IMPLEAD, INTERVENE ~ *vi* : to go to trial with each other in order to settle adverse claims to property held by or an obligation owed by a third party (as an insurance company) ⟨may be joined as defendants and required to ~ when their claims are such that the plaintiff is or may be exposed to double or multiple liability — *Official Code of Georgia Annotated*⟩
¹in·ter·plead·er \ˌin-tər-'plē-dər\ *n* [Anglo-French *enterpleder*, from *enter-pleder*, verb] : a proceeding by which a person compels parties making the same claim against him or her to litigate the matter between themselves — see also *bill in the nature of interpleader* and *bill of interpleader* at BILL 3a; compare COUNTERCLAIM, CROSS-CLAIM, IMPLEADER, INTERVENTION, JOINDER ◊ When an interpleader is initiated, the person holding the property or owing the obligation that is the subject of the adverse claims usu. must deposit the property or post a bond with the court.
²interpleader *n* : a person who is a party to an interpleader action

in·ter·pret \in-'tər-prət\ *vt* : to explain or tell the meaning of (as a document) esp. in order to determine intent ⟨they must ~ the provisions of the Constitution —L. H. Tribe⟩
in·ter·pre·ta·tion \in-ˌtər-prə-'tā-shən\ *n* : the act or result of interpreting — compare CONSTRUCTION — **in·ter·pre·ta·tive** \in-'tər-prə-ˌtā-tiv, -tə-tiv\ *adj* — **in·ter·pre·tive** \in-'tər-prə-tiv\ *adj*
interpretive rule *n* : a rule issued by an administrative agency that only clarifies or explains existing laws or regulations — called also *interpretative rule;* compare LEGISLATIVE RULE ◊ An interpretive rule does not have to meet the requirements set out in the Administrative Procedure Act for notice to the public and opportunity for comment that apply to legislative rules. An interpretive rule does not have the force of law.
in·ter·ro·gate \in-'ter-ə-ˌgāt\ *vt* **-gat·ed; -gat·ing** : to question formally and systematically; *esp* : to gather information from (a suspect) by means that are reasonably likely to elicit incriminating responses — see also MIRANDA RIGHTS ◊ Under *Rhode Island v. Innis,* 446 U.S. 291 (1980), interrogating includes not just express questioning, but also any words or actions that the police should know are reasonably likely to elicit an incriminating response. Asking questions that are normally asked in the course of arrest or booking (such as questions about name or age) is not considered interrogation. — **in·ter·ro·ga·tion** \in-ˌter-ə-'gā-shən\ *n* — **in·ter·ro·ga·tor** \in-'ter-ə-ˌgā-tər\ *n*
in·ter·rog·a·to·ry \ˌin-tə-'rä-gə-ˌtōr-ē\ *n, pl* **-ries** : a written question required by law to be answered under the direction of a court; *esp* : a written question directed by one party to another regarding information that is within the scope of discovery — see also *general verdict* and *special verdict* at VERDICT, SPECIAL INTERROGATORY ◊ Interrogatories are widely used as a discovery device in civil procedure and also have limited use in

criminal proceedings. An interrogatory may be objected to and does not have to be answered if the court determines that it is excessive or burdensome. An interrogatory may also be submitted by a judge to a jury when the court asks for a general verdict and wants to know the basis of the decision, or when the court requires the jury to return a special verdict.
in ter·ror·em \ˌin-te-'rōr-əm, -em\ *adv or adj* [Latin, so as to produce terror] : by way of threat or intimidation : serving or intended to threaten or intimidate ⟨overbroad covenants not to compete which have *in terrorem* effect on employees —J. D. Calamari and J. M. Perillo⟩ ◊ *In terrorem* is most commonly used to describe a condition in a will that threatens an heir with forfeiture if he or she challenges the validity of the will.
in·ter se \ˌin-tər-'sē, -'sā\ *adv or adj* [Latin] : among or between themselves ⟨the individual rights or obligations of the parties *inter se* —Goozh v. Capitol Souvenir Co.,* 462 A.2d 1140 (1983)⟩
in·ter·spou·sal \ˌin-tər-'spaů-zəl, -səl\ *adj* : being between spouses ⟨~ gifts⟩
in·ter·state commerce \'in-tər-ˌstāt-\ *n* : commerce, traffic, transportation, and exchange between states of the U.S. — see also COMMERCE CLAUSE ◊ While interstate commerce has been narrowly interpreted in judicial decisions in the past, more recent decisions have interpreted it more broadly and have allowed Congress to regulate internal or local activities that affect interstate commerce. For example, cattle crossing a state line while grazing and the movement of pollutants across state lines have been considered interstate commerce by federal courts in order to uphold Congress's regulatory jurisdiction.
in·ter·vene \ˌin-tər-'vēn\ *vi* **-ven·ed; -ven·ing 1** : to occur, fall, or come between points of time or events ⟨may be held liable even though other independent agencies ~ between his negligence

and the ultimate result —*Hooks Superx, Inc. v. McLaughlin,* 642 N.E.2d 514 (1994)⟩ **2 a :** to come in or between by way of hindrance or modification ⟨~ to stop a fight⟩ **b :** to become a party to a legal proceeding begun by others in order to protect an alleged interest in the subject matter of the proceeding ⟨the Commissioner of Internal Revenue was granted leave to ~ —P. A. Freund⟩ — compare IMPLEAD, INTERPLEAD, JOIN — **in•ter•ve•nor** \-'vē-nər, -ˌnȯr\ *n*
intervening cause — see CAUSE 1
intervening force — see FORCE 1
in•ter•ven•tion \ˌin-tər-'ven-chən\ *n* : the act or an instance of intervening; *specif* : the act or procedure by which a third party becomes a party to a pending proceeding between other parties in order to protect his or her own interest in the subject matter of the suit — compare IMPLEADER, INTERPLEADER, JOINDER ◊ Intervention developed as a procedure in equity courts. There is some overlap between joinder and intervention because of the merger of law and equity in federal practice.
intervention of right : intervention allowed in federal civil procedure when a statute grants an absolute right to intervene or when the applicant claims an interest in the subject of the proceeding that the applicant may be impeded from protecting by the disposition of the proceeding ◊ Intervention of right will not be granted if the court considers that the applicant's interest is already adequately represented.
permissive intervention : intervention allowed in federal civil procedure when a statute grants a conditional right to intervene or when the applicant's claim has a question of law or fact in common with the proceeding
intervention of right — see INTERVENTION
in•ter vi•vos \'in-tər-'vī-vōs, -'vē-\ *adv or adj* [Late Latin] : between living persons ⟨an *inter vivos* transfer⟩ — see also *do- 'er vivos* at DONATION, *gift inter*

vivos at GIFT, *inter vivos trust* at TRUST; compare CAUSA MORTIS
inter vivos trust — see TRUST
in•tes•ta•cy \in-'tes-tə-sē\n, *pl* **-cies 1 :** the state of dying intestate : an intestate state or condition ⟨the invalidation of the will resulted in her ~⟩ **2 :** INTESTATE SUCCESSION at SUCCESSION ⟨wills should be construed to avoid ~ whenever possible — *Smith v. Estate of Peters,* 741 P.2d 1172 (1987)⟩ ⟨the remaining property passed by ~ to the heirs⟩
¹in•tes•tate \in-'tes-ˌtāt\ *adj* [Latin *intestatus,* from *in-* not + *testatus* testate] **1 :** having not made a valid will ⟨died ~⟩ **2 :** not disposed of by a valid will ⟨~ property⟩ ⟨an ~ estate⟩; *specif* : transmitted according to statutory rules governing intestate succession **3 :** of or relating to intestate succession ⟨~ laws⟩
²intestate *n* : a person who dies intestate
intestate succession — see SUCCESSION
in•tim•i•date \in-'ti-mə-ˌdāt\ *vt* **-dat•ed; -dat•ing 1 :** to make timid or fearful; *esp* : to compel or deter by or as if by threats — see also COERCION **2 :** to engage in the crime of intimidating (as a witness, juror, public officer in the performance of his or her duty, or victim of a robbery or other crime) — **in•tim•i•dat•ing•ly** *adv* — **in•tim•i•da•tion** \in-ˌti-mə-'dā-shən\n — **in•tim•i•da•tor** \in-'ti-mə-ˌdā-tər\ *n*
in to•to \in-'tō-tō\ *adv* [Latin, on the whole] : as a whole : in total ⟨admitted the disputed testimony *in toto*⟩ ⟨refused to allow the will *in toto*⟩
in•tox•i•cate \in-'täk-sə-ˌkāt\ *vt* **-cat•ed; -cat•ing :** to excite or stupefy by alcohol or a drug esp. to the point where physical and mental control is markedly diminished — see also DRIVING UNDER THE INFLUENCE
in•tox•i•ca•tion \in-ˌtäk-sə-'kā-shən\ *n* **1 :** the state or condition of being intoxicated **2 :** a defense based on inability to

\ə\abut \ᵊ\kitten \ər\further \a\ash \ā\ace
\ä\cot, cart \au̇\out \ch\chin \e\bet \ē\easy
\g\go \i\hit \ī\ice \j\job \ŋ\sing \ō\go \ȯ\law
\ȯi\boy \th\thin \t̲h̲\the \ü\loot \u̇\foot \y\yet
\zh\vision *see also* Pronunciation Symbols page

form the requisite specific intent to commit a crime due to intoxication

intra- *prefix* **1 :** within 〈*intra*state〉 **2 :** during 〈*intra*day〉

in·tra·day \ˌin-trə-'dā\ *adj* : occurring in the course of a single day 〈the ~ financing practices of Government securities dealers —*Federal Register*〉

in·tra·state \ˌin-trə-'stāt, 'in-trə-ˌstāt\ *adj* : existing within a state 〈interstate and ~ commerce〉

in·tra vi·res \'in-trə-'vī-rēz, -'vē-rās\ *adv* [New Latin] : within the powers 〈a corporate director acting *intra vires*〉 — compare ULTRA VIRES

in·trin·sic \in-'trin-zik, -sik\ *adj* : belonging to the essential nature or constitution of a thing

intrinsic evidence — see EVIDENCE

intrinsic fraud — see FRAUD

in·tro·duce *vt* -duced; -duc·ing : to present and offer (evidence) at trial

in·trude \in-'trüd\ *vb* **in·trud·ed; in·trud·ing** *vi* **1 :** to enter by intrusion **2 :** ENCROACH 〈a search that ~*s* on a person's privacy〉 ~ *vt* : to encroach on or upon without permission or right — **in·trud·er** *n*

in·tru·sion \in-'trü-zhən\ *n* **1 a :** the entry at common law of a stranger after a particular estate of freehold is determined before the person who holds it in remainder or reversion has taken possession **b :** the act of wrongfully entering upon, seizing, or taking possession of the property of another **2 :** a trespassing on or encroachment upon something (as a right) 〈the Fourth Amendment demands that the showing of justification match the degree of ~ —*Berger v. New York*, 388 U.S. 41 (1968)〉

in·tru·sive \in-'trü-siv\ *adj* : characterized by intrusion — **in·tru·sive·ly** *adv* — **in·tru·sive·ness** *n*

intrust *var of* ENTRUST

in·ure \i-'nùr, -'nyùr\ *vi* **in·ured; in·ur·ing** : to become of advantage — usu. used in the phrase *inure to the benefit of*

in utero \in-'yü-tə-rō\ *adv or adj* [Latin] : in the uterus : before birth 〈an injury

suffered *in utero*〉 〈that her condition could possibly be linked to *in utero* exposure —*Burgess v. Eli Lilly & Co.*, 995 F.2d 646 (1993)〉

in·vade *vt* **in·vad·ed; in·vad·ing 1 :** to encroach upon : INFRINGE 〈*invading* a constitutional right〉 **2 :** to make payments out of (a fund from which payments are not ordinarily made) 〈authorized the trustee to ~ the principal for educational expenses〉

in·val·id \in-'va-ləd\ *adj* : being without force or effect under the law 〈declared the will ~〉 — **in·val·id·ly** *adv*

in·val·i·date \in-'va-lə-ˌdāt\ *vt* : to make or declare invalid 〈the high court *invalidating* the statute〉 — **in·val·i·da·tion** \in-ˌva-lə-'dā-shən\ *n*

in·va·lid·i·ty \ˌin-və-'li-də-tē\ *n* : lack of validity : state of being invalid

in·va·sion \in-'vā-zhən\ *n* : the act of or an instance of invading

invasion of privacy : the tort of unjustifiably intruding upon another's right to privacy by appropriating his or her name or likeness, by unreasonably interfering with his or her seclusion, by publicizing information about his or her private affairs that a reasonable person would find objectionable and in which there is no legitimate public interest, or by publicizing information that unreasonably places him or her in a false light — see also PRIVACY; compare RIGHT OF PRIVACY, ZONE OF PRIVACY

in·vei·gle \in-'vā-gəl, -'vē-\ *vt* **in·vei·gled; in·vei·gling :** to lure by false representations or other deceit 〈whoever unlawfully . . . ~*s*, decoys, kidnaps, abducts, or carries away and holds for ransom or reward or otherwise any person . . . shall be punished by imprisonment — *U.S. Code*〉

in·vent *vt* : to create or produce for the first time — **in·ven·tor** *n*

in·ven·tion *n* : a device, process, or discovery under U.S. patent law that is new and useful, that reflects extraordinary creative ability or skill, and that makes a distinct and recognized contribution to and advancement of science; *also* : the act or process of creating such an invention — compare AGGREGATION, COMBINATION, EQUIVALENT

in•ven•to•ry \'in-vən-ˌtōr-ē\ *n, pl* **-ries 1** : an itemized list of current assets: as **a** : a written list or catalog of the property of an individual, organization, or estate or succession that is made by a fiduciary under oath and that usu. describes and assigns a value to the items or classes of property **b** : aggregate value assigned to an inventory **2** : goods or materials held on hand: as **a** *under the Bankruptcy Code* : materials including personal property leased or furnished, held for sale or lease, or to be furnished under a contract for service, raw materials, work in process, or materials used or consumed in a business or held for sale or lease **b** *under section 9-109 of the Uniform Commercial Code* : goods that are held by a person who holds them for sale or lease or to be furnished under contracts of service or if he or she has so furnished them or that are raw materials, works in process, or materials used or consumed in a business

inventory search — see SEARCH

in ven•tre sa mere \in-'ven-trē-sä-'mer, -'ven-trə-\ [Anglo-French, *en ventre sa mere* in his/her mother's womb] : in the womb : IN UTERO

in•verse condemnation \'in-ˌvərs-\ *n* : an action brought against the government by a landowner to obtain just compensation for a taking of property effected without a formal exercise of eminent domain; *also* : the taking alleged in such an action

¹in•vest \in-'vest\ *vt* [Medieval Latin *investire*, from Latin, to clothe, from *in-* in + *vestis* garment] **1** : to install in an office or position **2 a** : to furnish with or formally grant power or authority **b** : to grant someone control or authority over : VEST

²invest *vb* [Italian *investire* to clothe, invest money, from Latin, to clothe] *vt* **1** : to commit (money) in order to earn a financial return **2** : to make use of for

future benefits or advantages — *vi* : to commit funds or purchase something of intrinsic value for future gain : make an investment — often used with *in* ⟨~*ing* in precious metals⟩ — **in•ves•tor** *n*

in•ves•ti•gate \in-'ves-tə-ˌgāt\ *vb* **-gat•ed; -gat•ing** *vt* : to observe or study by close examination and systematic inquiry; *specif* : to make (a criminal suspect) the subject of inquiry and study for the purpose of establishing probable cause — *vi* : to make a systematic examination; *esp* : to conduct an official inquiry — **in•ves•ti•ga•tion** \in-ˌves-tə-'gā-shən\ *n* — **in•ves•ti•ga•tion•al** \-shə-nəl\ *adj* — **in•ves•ti•ga•tive** \in-'ves-tə-ˌgā-tiv\ *adj* — **in•ves•ti•ga•tor** \-ˌgā-tər\ *n* — **in•ves•ti•ga•to•ry** \in-'ves-tə-gə-ˌtōr-ē\ *adj*

investigative stop *n* : TERRY STOP

in•ves•ti•ture \in-'ves-tə-ˌchùr, -chər, -ˌtyùr\ *n* **1** : the act of establishing in office or ratifying **2** : LIVERY OF SEISIN

¹in•vest•ment *n* : INVESTITURE 1

²investment *n* **1** : the outlay of money usu. for income or profit : capital outlay; *also* : the sum invested or the property purchased **2** : the commitment of funds with a view to minimizing risk and safeguarding capital while earning a return — compare SPECULATION

investment company — see COMPANY

investment contract — see CONTRACT

investment income *n* : income (as interest, dividends, annuities, or royalties) that is not derived in the ordinary course of a trade or business

investment trust — see TRUST

in•vid•i•ous \in-'vi-dē-əs\ *adj* : of, relating to, or being discrimination that arises from the creation of a classification that is arbitrary, irrational, or capricious and not related to a legitimate purpose — **in•vid•i•ous•ly** *adv* — **in•vid•i•ous•ness** *n*

invited error — see ERROR

in·vi·tee \ˌin-ˌvī-'tē, -və-\ *n* : an invited person; *specif* : a person (as a customer) who is present in a place by the express or implied invitation of the occupier in control of the place under circumstances that impose a duty on the occupier to use reasonable care to protect the safety of the invited person — compare LICENSEE, TRESPASSER

in·vo·ca·tion \ˌin-və-'kā-shən\ *n* **1** : a calling upon for authority or justification **2** : an act of legal implementation ⟨an ~ of the contract clause⟩

in·voice \'in-ˌvȯis\ *n* **1** : an itemized statement furnished to a purchaser by a seller and usu. specifying the price of goods or services and the terms of sale : BILL **2** : a consignment of merchandise

in·voke \in-'vōk\ *vt* **in·voked; in·vok·ing** **1** : to appeal to as furnishing authority or motive **2** : to put into legal effect or call for the observance of : ENFORCE ⟨*invoking* his Fifth Amendment privilege⟩ **3** : to introduce or put into operation ⟨*invoking* economic sanctions⟩ **4** : to be the cause of ⟨the . . . decision *invoked* the final hardship — *U.S. Code*⟩

in·vol·un·tary \in-'vä-lən-ˌter-ē\ *adj* : done, made, or initiated contrary to or without one's choice ⟨an ~ confession⟩ ⟨an ~ lien⟩ ⟨an ~ plaintiff joined in the action⟩ — **in·vol·un·tar·i·ly** *adv*

involuntary bailment — see BAILMENT

involuntary bankruptcy *n* : bankruptcy declared upon petition of creditors — see also BANKRUPTCY

involuntary conversion — see CONVERSION

involuntary dismissal — see DISMISSAL

involuntary dissolution — see DISSOLUTION

involuntary lien — see LIEN

involuntary manslaughter — see MANSLAUGHTER

involuntary trust — see TRUST

IOLTA *abbr* Interest on Lawyers' Trust Accounts

ip·so fac·to \'ip-sō-'fak-tō\ *adv* [New Latin, literally, by the fact itself] : by that very fact or act : as an inevitable result ⟨drove the getaway car and was *ipso facto* an accessory⟩

ipso facto clause *n* : a clause in an agreement stipulating the consequences (as termination of a lease or acceleration of a payment) of the insolvency of one of the parties — called also *bankruptcy clause*, *ipso facto bankruptcy clause* ◊ An ipso facto clause is invalid under the Bankruptcy Code because a trustee is not bound by any provision or applicable law that is conditioned on the debtor's insolvency.

ip·so ju·re \'ip-sō-'jùr-ē, -'yü-rä\ *adv* [Latin] : by the law itself : by the operation of law ⟨the securities sale was *ipso jure* unlawful⟩

IRA \ˌī-ˌär-'ā, 'ī-rə\ *n* [*i*ndividual *r*etirement *a*ccount] : an account in which a person may deposit up to a stipulated amount each year and that is not taxable until retirement or early withdrawal ◊ Deposits to an IRA may not be completely or partially deductible from adjusted gross income if one's income exceeds a set level.

I.R.C. *abbr* Internal Revenue Code — see also the IMPORTANT LAWS section

ir·ra·tio·nal \ir-'ra-shə-nəl\ *adj* : not rational: as **a** : not governed by reason, mental clarity, or understanding **b** : not governed by a fair consideration of facts or evidence; *broadly* : ARBITRARY ⟨an ~ decision to deny the permit⟩ — **ir·ra·tio·nal·i·ty** \ir-ˌra-shə-'na-lə-tē\ *n* — **ir·ra·tio·nal·ly** *adv*

ir·re·but·ta·ble presumption \ˌir-i-'bə-tə-bəl-\ *n* : CONCLUSIVE PRESUMPTION at PRESUMPTION

ir·rec·on·cil·able dif·fer·enc·es \ir-ˌre-kən-'sī-lə-bəl-\ *n pl but sing or pl in constr* : substantial incompatibility between marriage partners that is a broad ground for esp. no-fault divorce — compare IRRETRIEVABLE BREAKDOWN OF THE MARRIAGE

ir·reg·u·lar \ir-'re-gyə-lər\ *adj* : not in accord with laws, rules, procedures, or established custom — **ir·reg·u·lar·ly** *adv*

irregular heir — see HEIR

ir·reg·u·lar·i·ty \ir-ˌre-gyə-'lar-ə-tē\ *n, pl* **-ties** : something that is irregular ⟨an ~ in the proceeding⟩

ir·rel·e·vance \ir-'re-lə-vəns\ *n* **1** : the quality or state of being irrelevant **2** : something that is irrelevant

ir·rel·e·van·cy \ir-'re-lə-vən-sē\ *n, pl* **-cies** : IRRELEVANCE

ir·rel·e·vant \ir-'re-lə-vənt\ *adj* : not relevant : not applicable or pertinent ⟨~ allegations⟩ ⟨~ evidence⟩ — compare IMMATERIAL — **ir·rel·e·vant·ly** *adv*

ir·re·me·di·a·ble \ˌir-rə-'mē-dē-ə-bəl\ *adj* : impossible to remedy, correct, or redress ⟨~ harm⟩ ⟨~ conduct⟩ — **ir·re·me·di·a·bly** *adv*

irremediable break·down of the marriage : IRRETRIEVABLE BREAKDOWN OF THE MARRIAGE

ir·rep·a·ra·ble \i-'re-pə-rə-bəl, -prə-bəl\ *adj* : impossible to repair, remedy, or undo — **ir·rep·a·ra·bly** *adv*

irreparable injury *n* : serious injury to a party that justifies relief esp. by preliminary injunction — called also *irreparable damage*, *irreparable harm* ◊ Typical irreparable injury is not remediable by monetary compensation.

irresistible force — see FORCE 1

ir·re·sis·ti·ble im·pulse \ˌir-rə-'zis-tə-bəl-\ *n* : an overpowering impulse produced by mental disease or defect that leads to the commission of a criminal act (as murder)

irresistible impulse test *n* : a test used in some jurisdictions when considering an insanity defense that involves a determination of whether an impulse to commit a criminal act was irresistible due to mental disease or defect regardless of whether the defendant knew right from wrong — compare DIMINISHED CAPACITY, DURHAM RULE, M'NAGHTEN TEST, SUBSTANTIAL CAPACITY TEST

ir·re·triev·able break·down of the marriage \ˌir-rə-'trē-və-bəl-\ : a broad ground for divorce that is predicated on the development of incompatibility between marriage partners and that is used in many states as the sole ground of no-

fault divorce — called also *irremediable breakdown of the marriage, irretrievable breakdown;* compare IRRECONCILABLE DIFFERENCES

ir·re·ver·si·ble \ˌir-rə-'vər-sə-bəl\ *adj* : not reversible ⟨an ~ decision⟩

ir·rev·o·ca·ble \ir-'re-və-kə-bəl\ *adj* : not capable of being revoked ⟨the offer was ~ for ten days⟩ — **ir·rev·o·ca·bil·i·ty** *n* — **ir·rev·o·ca·bly** *adv*

irrevocable letter of credit — see LETTER OF CREDIT

irrevocable power of attorney — see POWER OF ATTORNEY

irrevocable trust — see TRUST

IRS *abbr* Internal Revenue Service — see also the IMPORTANT AGENCIES section

is·su·able \'i-shü-ə-bəl\ *adj* **1** : open to contest, debate, or litigation ⟨an ~ fact⟩; *also* : made on the merits and subject to dispute ⟨an ~ plea⟩ ⟨an ~ defense⟩ **2** : authorized for issue ⟨bonds ~ under the merger terms⟩

is·su·ance \'i-shü-əns\ *n* : the act or an instance of issuing ⟨the ~ of the injunction was upheld⟩

¹is·sue \'i-ˌshü, -ˌsyü\ *n* **1** *pl* : proceeds from a source of revenue (as an estate) ⟨rents, ~s, and profits⟩ **2** : one or more lineal descendants ⟨died without ~⟩ — compare CHILD, HEIR **3 a** : a vital question or problem ⟨cited a national security ~⟩ ⟨raised an ~ of public safety⟩ **b** : a matter of dispute between two or more parties; *specif* : a single material point of fact or law in litigation that is affirmed by one side and denied by the other and that is a subject of the final determination (as by jury) of the proceedings
genuine issue : an issue of fact that requires adjudication by trial rather than summary judgment because sufficient evidence exists to support a verdict for the party opposing the motion for summary judgment ◊ The burden is on the

party moving for summary judgment to show that no genuine issue is in dispute. *issue of fact* : a dispute about a material fact that is raised by pleadings and that must be resolved by a decision under the law in order to become res judicata *issue of law* : a question specifically regarding the application of law to a case ⟨instructed the jury on various *issues of law* —*United States v. Levine*, 41 F.3d 607 (1994)⟩ **c** : the point at which a legal matter is ready for determination (as by trial) ⟨filed pleadings and brought the case to ∼⟩ **4 a** : the offering or selling of a group of securities by a corporation or government ⟨a new bond ∼⟩ **b** : the securities offered or sold in such a group ⟨sold the entire ∼⟩ — **at issue** *also* **in issue** : under discussion or in dispute

²**is·sue** \'i-shü\ *vb* **is·sued; is·su·ing** *vi* **1** : ACCRUE ⟨profits *issuing* from the sale of the stock⟩ **2** : to become available or be put forth by authority ⟨waited for the search warrant to ∼⟩ ∼ *vt* : to put forth or distribute usu. officially ⟨∼ a subpoena⟩⟨∼ bonds⟩⟨∼ credit⟩ — **is·su·er** *n*
issue of fact — see ISSUE
issue of law — see ISSUE
issue preclusion *n* : ESTOPPEL BY JUDGMENT at ESTOPPEL 2a
item \'ī-təm\ *n* **1** : a distinct part in an enumeration, account, or series **2** : a financial instrument (as a check or draft)
item·i·za·tion \ˌī-tə-mə-'zā-shən\ *n* : the act of itemizing; *also* : an itemized list
item·ize \'ī-tə-ˌmīz\ *vt* **-ized; -iz·ing** : to list in detail or by particulars ⟨∼ deductions⟩
itemized deduction — see DEDUCTION

J

J. *abbr* **1** judge **2** justice **3** judgment

JA *abbr* judge advocate

jack·et *n* **:** a standard insurance policy to which other coverage or exclusions may be attached

Jackson–Denno hearing — see HEARING

JAG *abbr* judge advocate general

jail \'jāl\ *n* **:** a place of confinement for persons held in lawful custody; *specif* **:** such a place under the jurisdiction of a local government (as a county) for the confinement of persons awaiting trial or those convicted of minor crimes — compare HOUSE OF CORRECTION, HOUSE OF DETENTION, LOCKUP, PENITENTIARY, PRISON — **jail** *vt*

jail·er *n* **:** a keeper of a jail

jail·house \'jāl-,haùs\ *n* **:** JAIL

jailhouse lawyer *n* **:** a prison inmate self-taught in the law who tries to gain release through legal maneuvers or who advises fellow inmates on their legal problems

Jane Roe \'jān-'rō\ *n* **:** a female party to a legal proceeding whose true identity is unknown or whose true name is being withheld — compare JOHN DOE, RICHARD ROE

jay·walk \'jā-,wòk\ *vi* **:** to cross a street carelessly or in an illegal manner so as to be endangered by traffic

JD *abbr* **1** justice department **2** juvenile delinquent

J.D. *abbr* juris doctor

jeop·ar·dy \'je-pər-dē\ *n* **1** **:** exposure to or imminence of death, loss, or injury **2** **:** the danger of conviction that an accused person is subjected to when on trial for a criminal offense — see also DOUBLE JEOPARDY ◊ Jeopardy attaches, or comes into effect for double jeopardy purposes, when a jury is sworn in or, in a non-jury trial, when the judge begins to hear evidence. The Fifth Amendment

to the U.S. Constitution forbids double jeopardy for the same offense, and this applies whether the first trial ends in acquittal, conviction, or a mistrial. If a mistrial occurs due to a manifest necessity or if a defendant appeals a conviction, however, the rule against double jeopardy does not apply. The issue of manifest necessity is determined by the trial judge and, if necessary, by an appeals court.

jeopardy assessment *n* **:** a special immediate assessment of an alleged tax deficiency levied under federal law when a taxing officer believes that delay may jeopardize collection of the claim

jet·sam \'jet-səm\ *n* **:** the part of a ship, its equipment, or its cargo that is cast overboard to lighten the load in time of distress and that sinks or is washed ashore — compare FLOTSAM

JJ. *abbr* **1** judges **2** justices

JNOV *abbr* judgment notwithstanding the verdict

¹job *vb* **jobbed; job·bing** *vi* **1** **:** to do odd or occasional pieces of work for hire **2** **:** to carry on the business of a middleman or wholesaler ~ *vt* **1** **:** to buy and sell (as stock) for profit **2** **:** to hire or let by the job or for a period of service **3** **:** to do or cause to be done by separate portions or lots **:** SUBCONTRACT

²job *n* **1 a** **:** a piece of work; *esp* **:** a small miscellaneous piece of work undertaken on order at a stated rate **b** **:** the object or material on which work is being done **2 a** **:** a specific duty, role, or function ⟨a ~ description⟩ **b** **:** a regular remunerative position — **on the job** **:** at work

\ə\abut \ᵊ\kitten \ər\further \a\ash \ā\ace
\ä\cot, cart \aù\out \ch\chin \e\bet \ē\easy
\g\go \i\hit \ī\ice \j\job \ŋ\sing \ō\go \ò\law
\òi\boy \th\thin \th\the \ü\loot \ù\foot \y\yet
\zh\vision *see also* Pronunciation Symbols page

job action *n* : a temporary action (as a slowing of work) by workers on the job that is meant as a protest to force compliance with demands — compare STRIKE

job•ber *n* **1** : a wholesaler who operates on a small scale or who sells only to retailers and institutions **2** : a person who works by the job

john \'jän\ *n* : a prostitute's client

John Doe \'jän-'dō\ *n* : a party to legal proceedings (as a suspect) whose true name is unknown or withheld — compare JANE ROE, RICHARD ROE

John Doe summons *n* : a summons made out to an unidentified defendant who is referred to in the summons as John Doe

join *vt* **1** : to unite so as to form one unit ⟨~ the claims in one action⟩ **2 a** : to align oneself with esp. in a legal matter ⟨she ~*ed* her husband as plaintiff⟩ **b** : to cause or order (a person) to become a party to a lawsuit ⟨if the person has not been so ~*ed*, the court shall order that the person be made a party *—Federal Rules of Civil Procedure* Rule 19(a)⟩ — compare CONSOLIDATE, IMPLEAD, INTERPLEAD, INTERVENE **c** : to enter into or participate in ⟨~ the suit⟩ ~ *vi* **1** : to come together so as to form a unit ⟨the other victims of the scheme ~*ed* in the suit⟩ **2** : to commence involvement or participation ⟨if the person should ~ as a plaintiff but refuses to do so, the person may be made a defendant, or . . . an involuntary plaintiff *—Federal Rules of Civil Procedure* Rule 19(a)⟩ — **join•able** *adj* — **join issue** *or* **join the issue 1** : to accept, fix on, or clearly define an issue as the subject of a legal dispute ⟨refused to *join issue* by filing an answer with the court⟩ **2** : to take an opposed position on some question ⟨*join issue* with the conclusion⟩

join•der \'jȯin-dər\ *n* [Anglo-French, from *joinder* to join, from Old French *joindre*, from Latin *jungere*] : the act or an instance of joining: as **a** : a joining of parties as coplaintiffs or codefendants in a suit; *also* : a joining of claims by one or more plaintiffs in a suit — see also MISJOINDER; compare COUNTERCLAIM,

CROSS-CLAIM, IMPLEADER, INTERPLEADER, INTERVENTION, SEVER 3c

collusive joinder : an addition of a party to a suit made for the purpose of manufacturing federal jurisdiction ◊ Under the Federal Rules of Civil Procedure a federal district court will not have jurisdiction when collusive joinder is made.

compulsory joinder : joinder of a party to a suit required by the court when the party is indispensable to complete relief for parties already involved or when the party claims an interest that may substantially affect the other parties or may be put at risk by the action

joinder of remedies : a joining of two claims in one action even though one cannot be recognized until the other is resolved; *specif* : the combination of legal and equitable claims in one action when a fraudulent conveyance must first be set aside legally before equitable relief can be granted to a creditor

permissive joinder : a joining in a suit as coplaintiffs or codefendants of any parties that share common issues of law or fact in regard to the same occurrences or transactions; *also* : a joining in one suit of any legal, equitable, or maritime claims a party has against the opposing party **b** : a joining of offenses or defendants in an indictment, information, or prosecution **c** : a formal answer (as denial of fact) to an issue tendered ⟨moved for summary judgment after ~ of issue⟩ **d** : a joining into a common transaction ⟨requires the ~ of both spouses *—W. M. McGovern, Jr. et al.*⟩

joinder of remedies — see JOINDER

joint *adj* **1** : common to two or more: as **a** : involving the combined activity or negligence of two or more ⟨a ~ tort⟩ — see also JOINT TORTFEASOR; compare SEVERAL **b** : shared by or affecting two or more as a unit ⟨a ~ account⟩ **2** : united, joined, or sharing with another (as in a right or status) ⟨~ heirs⟩

joint ad•ven•ture *n* : JOINT VENTURE

joint–and–last–survivor annuity *n*

: JOINT-AND-SURVIVOR ANNUITY at AN-NUITY

joint–and–last–survivorship option — see OPTION 4

joint and mutual will — see WILL

joint and reciprocal will *n* : JOINT AND MUTUAL WILL at WILL

joint and several *adj* : relating or belonging to two or more parties together and separately ⟨*joint and several* duties of the partners⟩ — see also *joint and several liability* at LIABILITY 2b; compare IN SOLIDO, JOINT 1b, JOINTLY — **jointly and severally** *adv*

joint and several liability — see LIABILITY 2b

joint–and–survivor annuity — see ANNUITY

joint and survivorship annuity *n* : JOINT-AND-SURVIVOR ANNUITY at ANNUITY

joint annuity *n* : JOINT LIFE ANNUITY at ANNUITY

joint committee *n* : a committee made up of members of both houses of a legislature (as for purposes of investigation or oversight) — compare CONFERENCE COMMITTEE

joint custody — see CUSTODY b

joint enterprise *n* **1** : JOINT VENTURE **2** : an undertaking of two or more parties for a common purpose in which each shares a common interest and an equal right of control (as of a vehicle) ◊ In regard to a tort involving such an enterprise, a third party may impute negligence of one party (as a driver) to another in the enterprise.

joint liability — see LIABILITY 2b

joint life and survivorship annuity *n* : JOINT-AND-SURVIVOR ANNUITY at ANNUITY

joint life annuity — see ANNUITY

joint·ly *adv* : in a joint manner; *esp* : so as to be or become subject to joint liability

joint obligation — see OBLIGATION

joint rate *n* : a single rate charged by two or more carriers to transport a shipment of goods over a route

joint resolution *n* : a resolution passed by both houses of a legislative body that has

the force of law when signed by or passed over the veto of the executive — compare CONCURRENT RESOLUTION

joint–stock company — see COMPANY

joint tenancy — see TENANCY

joint tenant *n* : one who holds an estate by or in joint tenancy

joint tortfeasor *n* : any of two or more parties held jointly or severally liable for the same tort — see also CONTRIBUTION, *joint liability* at LIABILITY 2b

joint ven·ture \-'ven-chər\ *n* **1** : a cooperative business agreement or partnership between two or more parties that is usu. limited to a single enterprise and that involves the sharing of resources, control, profits, and losses — compare COMBINATION **2** : a criminal undertaking by two or more persons in which each intentionally takes part — used in the law of Massachusetts

joint welfare fund — see FUND 1

joint will — see WILL

journalist's privilege — see PRIVILEGE 1b

joy·rid·ing *n* : the unauthorized and esp. reckless taking and driving of another's vehicle for a period of time — **joy·ride** *n*

J.P. *abbr* justice of the peace

J.S.D. *abbr* [New Latin *juris scientiae doctor*] doctor of juridical science; doctor of the science of law

¹judge \'jəj\ *vb* **judged; judg·ing** [Old French *jugier*, from Latin *judicare*, from *judic-*, *judex* judge, from *jus* right, law + *dicere* to decide, say] *vt* **1** : to hear and decide (as a litigated question) in a court of justice ⟨~ a case⟩ **2** : to pronounce after inquiry and deliberation ⟨he was *judged* incompetent⟩ ~ *vi* : to make a determination : DECIDE ⟨~ between two accounts⟩

²judge *n* : a public official vested with the authority to hear, determine, and preside over legal matters brought in court; *also*

\ə\abut \ᵊ\kitten \ər\further \a\ash \ā\ace
\ä\cot, cart \au̇\out \ch\chin \e\bet \ē\easy
\g\go \i\hit \ī\ice \j\job \ŋ\sing \ō\go \ȯ\law
\ȯi\boy \th\thin \t͟h\the \ü\loot \u̇\foot \y\yet
\zh\vision *see also* Pronunciation Symbols page

: one (as a justice of the peace) who performs one or more functions of such an official

judge advocate *n, pl* **judge advocates 1** : an officer serving under the Judge Advocate General **2** : an officer charged with administering military justice (as by acting as legal counsel or conducting an appellate review)

Judge Advocate General *n, pl* **Judge Advocates General** : the senior legal officer and chief legal adviser in the army, navy, or air force

judge–made *adj* : created by judges or judicial decision — used esp. of law established by due judicial interpretation of statutes

judg·ment *also* **judge·ment** \'jəj-mənt\ *n* **1 a** : a formal decision or determination on a matter or case by a court; *esp* : FINAL JUDGMENT in this entry — compare DICTUM, DISPOSITION, FINDING, HOLDING, OPINION, RULING, VERDICT ◊ Under Rule 54 of the Federal Rules of Civil Procedure, *judgment* encompasses a decree and any order from which an appeal lies.

cog·no·vit judgment \käg-'nō-vit-\ : an acknowledgment by a debtor of the existence of a debt with agreement that an adverse judgment may be entered without notice or a hearing : CONFESSION OF JUDGMENT

consent judgment : a judgment approved and entered by a court by consent of the parties upon agreement or stipulation : CONSENT DECREE at DECREE

declaratory judgment : a judgment declaring a right or establishing the legal status or interpretation of a law or instrument ⟨seeking a *declaratory judgment* that the regulation is unconstitutional⟩ — compare DAMAGE 2, INJUNCTION, *specific performance* at PERFORMANCE

default judgment : a judgment entered by a court after an entry of default against a party for failure to appear, to file a pleading, or to take other required procedural steps — called also *judgment*

by default; compare *decree pro confesso* at DECREE

deficiency judgment : a judgment in favor of a creditor for the balance of a debt that is not satisfied in full by the security; *esp* : such a judgment following the foreclosure of a mortgage

final judgment : a judgment that leaves nothing further to be done on a matter except execution

in personam judgment : PERSONAL JUDGMENT in this entry

in rem judgment : JUDGMENT IN REM in this entry

judgment by default : DEFAULT JUDGMENT in this entry

judgment in per·so·nam \-ˌin-pər-'sō-nəm, -per-'sō-näm\ *pl* *judgments in personam* : PERSONAL JUDGMENT in this entry

judgment in rem \-in-'rem\ *pl* *judgments in rem* : a judgment affecting the status of a particular thing (as an item of property) or subject matter : a judgment rendered by a court exercising in rem jurisdiction — compare PERSONAL JUDGMENT in this entry

judgment ni·si \-'nī-ˌsī, -'nē-sē\ *pl* *judgments nisi* : a judgment that is not final or absolute ⟨after default and *judgment nisi* requiring them to show cause why it should not be made final — *Code of Alabama*⟩

judgment non ob·stan·te ve·re·dic·to \-'nän-əb-'stan-tē-ˌver-ə-'dik-tō, -'nòn-òb-'stän-tā-ˌvā-rā-'dēk-tō\ *pl* *judgments non obstante veredicto* [*non obstante veredicto*, from Medieval Latin, notwithstanding the verdict] : JUDGMENT NOTWITHSTANDING THE VERDICT in this entry

judgment not·with·stand·ing the verdict : a judgment that may be granted upon a motion by a defendant whose motion for a directed verdict was denied and that sets aside the jury's verdict in favor of a judgment in accordance with the motion for directed verdict — called also *judgment non obstante veredicto*

judgment of acquittal : a judgment that

is rendered upon motion of the defendant or the court's own motion at the close of the evidence and that acquits the defendant of one or more of the offenses charged when the evidence is insufficient to sustain a conviction — called also *directed verdict, directed verdict of acquittal*
judgment on the merits : a judgment made after consideration of the substantive as distinguished from procedural issues in a case
judgment on the pleadings : SUMMARY JUDGMENT in this entry
money judgment : a judgment directing the payment of a sum of money
ni•hil–di•cit judgment \'nī-həl-'di-sit-, -'dī-; 'nē-hil-'dē-kit-\ : a judgment entered against a defendant who has failed to make an effective answer (as because the answer is withdrawn or does not respond to the merits of the plaintiff's case) — called also *nil dicit judgment*
personal judgment : a judgment determining the rights and liabilities of a particular person : a judgment rendered by a court exercising personal jurisdiction over a person — compare JUDGMENT IN REM in this entry
summary judgment : judgment that may be granted upon a party's motion when the pleadings, discovery, and any affidavits show that there is no genuine issue of material fact and that the party is entitled to judgment in its favor as a matter of law ◊ According to Rule 56 of the Federal Rules of Civil Procedure, a motion for summary judgment may be made at any time after 20 days following the commencement of the action. Summary judgment may be granted on all or on just part of a case.
b : an obligation (as a debt) created by a decree of a court ⟨collection of . . . automobile ~s from uninsured motorists — *Harvard Law Review*⟩; *also* : an official document embodying such a decision or decree **c** : a declaration by a court of the conviction of a criminal defendant

and the punishment to be imposed; *specif* : SENTENCE **2** : the action of judging : the mental or intellectual process of forming an opinion or making a decision; *also* : an opinion or decision so formed
business judgment : a decision by a person or body (as a board of directors) having authority to act on behalf of a business and usu. marked by reasonableness and the exercise of due care; *also* : the faculty of making such decisions
substituted judgment : a decision regarding medical treatment made by a person (as a family member) on behalf of a person who is incompetent and unable to decide for himself or herself
judgment by default — see JUDGMENT 1a
judgment creditor — see CREDITOR
judgment debt — see DEBT
judgment debtor *n* : one who is obligated to pay a debt or damages in accordance with a judgment entered by a court
judgment in personam — see JUDGMENT 1a
judgment in rem — see JUDGMENT 1a
judgment lien — see LIEN
judgment nisi — see JUDGMENT 1a
judgment non obstante veredicto — see JUDGMENT 1a
judgment notwithstanding the verdict — see JUDGMENT 1a
judgment n.o.v. *abbr* [Medieval Latin *n*on *o*bstante *v*eredicto] judgment notwithstanding the verdict
judgment of acquittal — see JUDGMENT 1a
judgment on the merits — see JUDGMENT 1a
judgment on the pleadings — see JUDGMENT 1a
judgment–proof *adj* : of or being one (as a judgment debtor) from whom nothing

\ə\abut \ᵊ\kitten \ər\further \a\ash \ā\ace
\ä\cot, cart \aú\out \ch\chin \e\bet \ē\easy
\g\go \i\hit \ī\ice \j\job \ŋ\sing \ō\go \ó\law
\ói\boy \th\thin \t͟h\the \ü\loot \ú\foot \y\yet
\zh\vision *see also* Pronunciation Symbols page

can be recovered because he or she has no property, his or her property is not within the jurisdiction where the judgment was obtained, or he or she is protected from execution of the judgment by statute
ju·di·ca·to·ry \'jü-di-kə-ˌtōr-ē\ *n, pl* **-ries** [Medieval Latin *judicatorium* court of law, from *judicare* to judge] **1 :** a court of justice or legal tribunal **2 :** a governing body of a religious organization — **judicatory** *adj*
ju·di·cial \jü-'di-shəl\ *adj* [Latin *judicialis*, from *judicium* judgment, from *judic-, judex* judge, from *jus* right, law + *dicere* to determine, say] **1 a :** of or relating to a judgment, the function of judging, the administration of justice, or the judiciary **b :** of, relating to, or being the branch of government that is charged with trying all cases that involve the government and with the administration of justice within its jurisdiction — compare ADMINISTRATIVE 2, EXECUTIVE 1, LEGISLATIVE **2 :** created, ordered, or enforced by a court ⟨a ~ foreclosure⟩ — compare CONVENTIONAL 1, LEGAL 2c — **ju·di·cial·ly** *adv*
judicial act *n* **:** an act deriving from the normal exercise of judicial power within the proper jurisdiction — used as a criterion for absolute judicial immunity
judicial ac·ti·vism \-'ak-tə-ˌvi-zəm\ *n* **:** the practice in the judiciary of protecting or expanding individual rights through decisions that depart from established precedent or are independent of or in opposition to supposed constitutional or legislative intent — compare JUDICIAL RESTRAINT
judicial bond — see BOND 1a
judicial comity *n* **:** COMITY 2
judicial conference *n* **:** a conference of judges and sometimes other concerned individuals (as members of the bar) at which important judicial affairs are reviewed and conducted for the purpose of improving the administration of justice
judicial confession *n* **:** a confession made in a legal proceeding (as in a trial) ⟨a

guilty plea supported by a *judicial confession*⟩
judicial discretion *n* **:** DISCRETION a
judicial immunity — see IMMUNITY
judicial lien — see LIEN
judicial mortgage — see MORTGAGE
judicial notice *n* **:** recognition by the court of a fact that is not reasonably disputable and without the introduction of supporting evidence ⟨took *judicial notice* that January 1 is a legal holiday⟩ ⟨a motion for *judicial notice* of a fact⟩
judicial power — see POWER 2a
judicial restraint *n* **:** a refraining in the judiciary from departure from precedent and the formulation of broad doctrine — compare JUDICIAL ACTIVISM
judicial review *n* **1 :** REVIEW **2 :** a constitutional doctrine that gives to a court system the power to annul legislative or executive acts which the judges declare to be unconstitutional; *also* **:** the process of using this power — see also CHECKS AND BALANCES, *Marbury v. Madison* in the IMPORTANT CASES section
judicial sale — see SALE
judicial separation *n* **:** LEGAL SEPARATION
judicial writ — see WRIT
ju·di·cia·ry \jü-'di-shē-ˌer-ē, -'di-shə-rē\ *n, pl* **-ries 1 a :** a system of courts of law **b :** the judges of these courts **2 :** a branch of government in which judicial power is vested — compare EXECUTIVE, LEGISLATURE — **judiciary** *adj*
ju·nior \'jü-nyər\ *adj* **:** of lower standing or rank **:** SUBORDINATE ⟨a ~ lienholder⟩
junior lien — see LIEN
junk bond — see BOND 2
jura *pl of* JUS
ju·ral \'jùr-əl\ *adj* [Latin *jur-, jus* law] **1 :** of or relating to law **2 :** of or relating to rights or obligations
ju·rat \'jùr-ət, -ˌat\ *n* [short for Latin *juratum* (*est*) it has been sworn] **:** a certification added to an affidavit stating when, before whom, and where the affidavit was made
ju·rid·i·cal \jù-'ri-di-kəl\ *adj* [Latin *juridicus*, from *jur-, jus* law + *dicere* to

say] **1** : of or relating to the administration of justice or the office of a judge ⟨raises a ~ question regarding trial⟩ **2** : of or relating to law or jurisprudence : LEGAL ⟨nowhere in . . . ~ opinions can we discover any overriding rule —*Brown v. Superior Court of Sacramento Cty.*, 655 P.2d 1260 (1982)⟩

juridical act *n, in the civil law of Louisiana* : an expression of will that is intended to have legal consequences ⟨the concurrence of a spouse is a *juridical act — Louisiana Civil Code*⟩

juridical person *n, in the civil law of Louisiana* : an entity (as a partnership or corporation) that is given rights and responsibilities — compare NATURAL PERSON ◊ The rights and responsibilities of a juridical person are distinct from those of the natural persons constituting it.

ju·ris·con·sult \ˌjūr-əs-'kän-ˌsəlt, -kən-'səlt\ *n* [Latin *jurisconsultus,* from *juris,* genitive of *jus* law, right + *consultus,* past participle of *consulere* to consult] : JURIST; *esp* : one learned in international and public law

ju·ris·dic·tion \ˌjūr-əs-'dik-shən\ *n* [Latin *jurisdictio,* from *juris,* genitive of *jus* law + *dictio* act of saying, from *dicere* to say] **1** : the power, right, or authority to interpret, apply, and declare the law (as by rendering a decision) ⟨to be removed to the State having ~ of the crime —*U.S. Constitution* art. IV⟩ ⟨a court of competent ~ ⟩ — see also SITUS, *International Shoe Co. v. Washington* in the IMPORTANT CASES section; compare VENUE ◊ Jurisdiction determines which court system should properly adjudicate a case. Questions of jurisdiction also arise regarding quasi⁼ judicial bodies (as administrative agencies) in their decision-making capacities.

ancillary jurisdiction : jurisdiction giving a court the power to adjudicate claims (as counterclaims and cross⁼ claims) because they arise from a cause of action over which the court has original jurisdiction; *specif* : supplemental jurisdiction acquired by a federal court allowing it to adjudicate claims that are

based on state law but that form part of a case brought to the court under its diversity jurisdiction — compare PENDENT JURISDICTION in this entry ◊ Ancillary jurisdiction allows a single court to decide an entire case instead of dividing the claims among several courts and proceedings, and allows a federal court to decide a claim that would otherwise be properly brought to a state court.

appellate jurisdiction : the jurisdiction granted to particular courts to hear appeals of the decisions of lower tribunals and to reverse, affirm, or modify those decisions — compare ORIGINAL JURISDICTION in this entry

concurrent jurisdiction : jurisdiction that is shared by different courts and that may allow for removal ⟨two states may have *concurrent jurisdiction* over crimes committed on boundary rivers —W. R. LaFave and A. W. Scott, Jr.⟩

diversity jurisdiction : the jurisdiction granted to federal courts over civil disputes involving parties having diverse citizenship (as in being from different states) where the matter in controversy exceeds a statutory amount (as $50,000) — see also *Article III* of the CONSTITUTION in the back matter ◊ The diversity jurisdiction of the district courts requires that there be complete diversity of the parties, which means that no party on one side has the same citizenship as a party on the other side. Interpleader in federal district courts, however, requires only minimal diversity, which means that at least one party has citizenship that differs from the others. The federal courts have traditionally refused to exercise their diversity jurisdiction over cases involving domestic relations and probate.

exclusive jurisdiction : jurisdiction

\ə\abut \ᵊ\kitten \ər\further \a\ash \ā\ace
\ä\cot, cart \au̇\out \ch\chin \e\bet \ē\easy
\g\go \i\hit \ī\ice \j\job \ŋ\sing \ō\go \ȯ\law
\ȯi\boy \th\thin \t̲h̲\the \ü\loot \u̇\foot \y\yet
\zh\vision *see also* Pronunciation Symbols page

granted only to a particular court to the exclusion of others ⟨federal courts have *exclusive jurisdiction* over bankruptcy cases⟩

federal question jurisdiction : the jurisdiction granted to federal courts over civil actions arising under the Constitution, federal laws, or treaties of the U.S. : federal jurisdiction over cases involving a federal question — see also WELLPLEADED COMPLAINT RULE ◊ The federal courts have usually interpreted the statutory phrase "arising under" rather strictly. U.S. Supreme Court decisions have held that the plaintiff's pleading must establish that the cause of action raises an issue of federal law (as by depending on construction or application of a federal law).

general jurisdiction : jurisdiction that is not limited (as to a particular class of cases); *specif* : the personal jurisdiction granted a court over a party allowing the court to adjudicate a cause of action that does not arise out of or is not related to the party's contacts within the territory of that court

in per·so·nam jurisdiction \,in-pər-'sō-nəm-, -per-'sō-näm-\ : the jurisdiction granted a court over persons before it that allows the court to issue a binding judgment : PERSONAL JURISDICTION in this entry

in rem jurisdiction \in-'rem-\ : the jurisdiction granted a court over property that allows the court to issue binding judgments (as an order for partition) affecting a person's interests in the property — compare PERSONAL JURISDICTION in this entry

jurisdiction in personam : IN PERSONAM JURISDICTION in this entry

jurisdiction in rem : IN REM JURISDICTION in this entry

limited jurisdiction : jurisdiction that is restricted (as to a type of case)

original jurisdiction : the jurisdiction granted a court to try a case in the first instance, make findings of fact, and render a usu. appealable decision ⟨the district courts shall have *original jurisdiction* of all civil actions arising under the Constitution, laws, or treaties of the United States — *U.S. Code*⟩

pendent jurisdiction : supplemental jurisdiction that allows a federal court to adjudicate state law claims which form part of a case that was brought to it under its federal question jurisdiction; *also* : PENDENT PARTY JURISDICTION in this entry — compare ANCILLARY JURISDICTION in this entry

pendent party jurisdiction : supplemental jurisdiction that allows a federal court to adjudicate a state law claim asserted against a third party which is part of a case brought to it under its original jurisdiction

personal jurisdiction : the jurisdiction granted a court over the parties before it that allows it to issue a binding judgment — see also DOING BUSINESS STATUTE, FAIR PLAY AND SUBSTANTIAL JUSTICE, LONG-ARM STATUTE, MINIMUM CONTACTS; compare SUBJECT MATTER JURISDICTION in this entry ◊ The U.S. Supreme Court has held in a series of decisions that the exercise of personal jurisdiction must meet the requirements of due process and must not violate notions of fair play and substantial justice. The constitutional standard to determine whether a party is subject to the personal jurisdiction of a court is whether that party has had minimum contacts within the territory (as a state) of that court.

primary jurisdiction : the jurisdiction granted by a judicially created doctrine to an administrative agency to decide certain controversies initially before relief is sought in the courts — compare EXHAUSTION OF REMEDIES

quasi in rem jurisdiction : the jurisdiction of a court over a person which is based on the person's interests in property under the court's jurisdiction and which allows the court to issue a binding judgment against the person — see also SEQUESTRATION; compare PERSONAL JURISDICTION in this entry

specific jurisdiction : personal jurisdiction granted a court over a party that allows it to adjudicate only a cause of action that arises out of or is related to the party's contacts within the territory of that court — compare GENERAL JURISDICTION in this entry
subject matter jurisdiction : the jurisdiction of a court over the subject, type, or cause of action of a case that allows the court to issue a binding judgment ⟨housing court lacks *subject matter jurisdiction* to adjudicate fraudulent conveyance actions —*National Law Journal*⟩ — compare PERSONAL JURISDICTION in this entry ◊ Diversity jurisdiction, federal question jurisdiction, and jurisdiction over admiralty and bankruptcy cases are examples of the federal courts' subject matter jurisdiction. Subject matter jurisdiction is generally established by statute.
supplemental jurisdiction : jurisdiction granted federal courts over claims that could not be heard in a federal court on their own but that are so closely related to claims over which the court has original jurisdiction that they form part of the same case — see also ANCILLARY JURISDICTION and PENDENT JURISDICTION in this entry ◊ Supplemental jurisdiction was created by a federal statute that codified the judicially created doctrines of ancillary and pendent jurisdiction.
2 : the authority (as of a state) to govern or legislate ⟨the trade bill was within the Ways and Means committee's ~⟩ ⟨whether a foreign state shall be subject to the ~ of another⟩; *broadly* : the power or right to exercise authority ⟨the department of consumer affairs has ~ over such complaints⟩ **3** : the limits or territory within which authority may be exercised ⟨no new State shall be formed or erected within the ~ of any other State —*U.S. Constitution* art. IV⟩ — called also *territorial jurisdiction* — **ju·ris·dic·tion·al** \-shə-nəl\ *n* — **ju·ris·dic·tion·al·ly** *adv*
jurisdictional amount *n* : the amount or value that a matter in controversy must exceed in order for the federal courts to have diversity jurisdiction ◊ The jurisdictional amount is set by statute and is currently $50,000.
jurisdictional strike — see STRIKE
jurisdiction in personam — see JURISDICTION
jurisdiction in rem — see JURISDICTION
ju·ris doc·tor \'jùr-əs-,däk-tər\ *n, often cap J&D* [New Latin, doctor of law] : the lowest degree conferred by a law school usu. after three years of full-time study or its equivalent — compare MASTER OF LAWS, DOCTOR OF LAWS, DOCTOR OF THE SCIENCE OF LAW ◊ The juris doctor replaced the bachelor of laws as the first degree conferred by a law school in 1969. Not all states mention the J.D. or LL.B. specifically as a requirement for admission to the bar, but all states do require graduation from a law school.
ju·ris·prude \'jùr-əs-,prüd\ *n* [back-formation (influenced by *prude*) from *jurisprudence*] : an individual who makes ostentatious show of learning in jurisprudence and the philosophy of law or who regards legal doctrine with undue solemnity or veneration ⟨philosophers and ~*s* might long and profoundly debate the question of which was the greater right and which was the lesser —*Howell v. State*, 425 A.2d 1361 (1981)⟩
ju·ris·pru·dence \,jùr-əs-'prüd-ᵊns\ *n* [Late Latin *jurisprudentia* knowledge of or skill in law, from Latin *juris*, genitive of *jus* right, law + *prudentia* wisdom, proficiency] **1 a** : a system or body of law ⟨in the federal ~⟩; *esp* : a body of law dealing with a specific issue or area ⟨labor ~⟩ **b** : the course of court decisions as distinguished from legislation and doctrine ⟨the ~ decided under the source provisions —*Louisiana Civil Code*⟩ **2** : the science or philosophy of law ⟨they have

\ə\abut \ᵊ\kitten \ər\further \a\ash \ā\ace
\ä\cot, cart \aù\out \ch\chin \e\bet \ē\easy
\g\go \i\hit \ī\ice \j\job \ŋ\sing \ō\go \ò\law
\òi\boy \th\thin \th̲\the \ü\loot \ù\foot \y\yet
\zh\vision *see also* Pronunciation Symbols page

no theories of ~ but . . . decide each case on its facts —R. H. Bork⟩ — **ju•ris•pru•den•tial** \ˌjùr-əs-prü-'den-chəl\ *adj*
jurisprudence con•stante \-kòn-'stänt\ *n* [French, uniform jurisprudence] : a doctrine in the civil law of Louisiana: a long series of previous decisions applying a particular rule of law carries great weight and may be determinative in subsequent cases; *also* : the rule of law applied in the jurisprudence constante — compare STARE DECISIS
ju•ris•pru•dent \ˌjùr-əs-'prüd-ᵊnt\ *n* [Late Latin *jurisprudent-, jurisprudens*, from Latin *juris*, genitive of *jus* right, law + *prudent-, prudens* foreseeing, skilled, prudent] : JURIST
ju•rist \'jùr-ist\ *n* [Middle French *juriste*, from Medieval Latin *jurista*, from Latin *jur-, jus* law] : an individual having a thorough knowledge of law; *esp* : JUDGE ⟨the state's top ~ violated the U.S. Constitution when he banned the filming — *National Law Journal*⟩
ju•ris•tic \jù-'ris-tik\ *adj* **1** : of or relating to a jurist or jurisprudence ⟨~ scholarship⟩ ⟨~ thought⟩ **2** : of, relating to, or recognized in law ⟨all of these considerations are of little or no ~ significance — *Wilson v. Lund*, 491 P.2d 1287 (1971)⟩
juristic person *n* : JURIDICAL PERSON
ju•ror \'jùr-ər, -ˌòr\ *n* : a member of a jury ⟨an alternate ~⟩; *broadly* : an individual who is summoned but not yet selected to serve on a jury
ju•ry \'jùr-ē\ *n, pl* **ju•ries** [Anglo-French *juree*, from feminine past participle of Old French *jurer* to swear, from Latin *jurare*, from *jur-, jus* law] : a body of individuals sworn to give a decision on some matter submitted to them; *esp* : a body of individuals selected and sworn to inquire into a question of fact and to give their verdict according to the evidence — occasionally used with a pl. verb ⟨the ~ are always to decide whether the inference shall be drawn —Oliver Wendell Holmes, Jr.⟩ — see also ADVISORY JURY, ARRAY, GRAND JURY, INQUEST, JURY NULLIFICATION, PETIT JURY,

SPECIAL JURY, TRIAL JURY, VENIRE, *Amendment VI* to the CONSTITUTION in the back matter ◊ The jury of American and English law most likely originated in early Anglo-Norman property proceedings, where a body of 12 knights or freemen who were from the area, and usu. familiar with the parties, would take an oath and answer questions put to them by a judge in order to determine property rights. Jury verdicts began to be used in felony cases in the early 1200s as the use of the trial by ordeal declined. The questions put to those early juries were usu. questions of fact or mixed questions of fact and law. Modern juries may deal with questions of law in addition to questions of fact when rendering general verdicts, or in specific cases under state law. Federal juries are usu. limited to dealing with questions of fact. The modern jury can vary in size depending on the proceeding but is usu. made up of 6 or 12 members. According to federal law, federal grand and petit juries must be "selected at random from a fair cross-section of the community in the district or division wherein the court convenes." State jury selection varies and occasionally differs from federal, but the states still must meet constitutional requirements for due process. The U.S. Supreme Court has stated in a series of decisions that a jury is to be composed of "peers and equals," and that systematic exclusion of a particular class (as on the basis of gender, race, or ancestry) from a jury violates the equal protection clause and the defendant's right to a jury trial. A defendant is not, however, entitled to a jury of any particular composition.
jury box *n* **1** : the usu. enclosed place where the jury sits in a courtroom — compare BAR, BENCH, DOCK, SIDEBAR, STAND **2** : a box from which the names of prospective jurors are drawn by chance : JURY WHEEL
jury charge *n* : INSTRUCTION
jury commission *n* : a body of appointed public officers who maintain a jury list

and select the names of prospective jurors usu. at random by use of a jury wheel ◊ Jury commissions may be used in some federal district courts and state courts instead of or in addition to computerized jury selection. Jury commissions are usu. organized on the county level and are used in almost 20 states.

jury commissioner *n* : an individual who is a member of a jury commission; *specif* : the head of a jury commission

jury duty *n* : the obligation to serve on a jury; *also* : service on a jury — called also *jury service*

jury fee — see FEE 2

jury instruction *n* : INSTRUCTION

jury list *n* : a list of individuals qualified to be selected for jury duty ◊ The jury list is compiled in various ways in different jurisdictions, but it is usu. based on a list of registered voters or licensed drivers.

ju•ry•man \'juṙ-ē-mən, -ˌman\ *n, pl* **ju•ry•men** \-ˌmen\ : JUROR

jury nullification *n* : the acquitting of a defendant by a jury in disregard of the judge's instructions and contrary to the jury's findings of fact ◊ Jury nullification is most likely to occur when a jury is sympathetic toward a defendant or regards the law under which the defendant is charged with disfavor. Except for a statutory requirement to the contrary, a jury does not have to be instructed on the possibility of jury nullification.

jury of the vic•i•nage \-'vi-si-nij\ : a jury drawn from the neighborhood or political subdivision (as a county) in which the court is held

jury pool *n* : the body of prospective jurors summoned for jury duty

jury room *n* : the room where a jury deliberates

jury service *n* : JURY DUTY

jury trial *n* : a trial in which a jury serves as the trier of fact — called also *trial by jury;* see also *Article III, Article VI* and *VII, Amendments VI* and *VII* to the CONSTITUTION in the back matter; compare BENCH TRIAL ◊ The right to a jury trial is established in the U.S. Constitution,

but it is not an absolute right. The Supreme Court has stated that petty crimes (as those carrying a sentence of up to 6 months) do not require trial by jury. The right to a jury trial in a criminal case may be waived by the "express and intelligent consent" of the defendant, usu. in writing, as well as, in federal cases, the approval of the court and consent of the prosecutor. There is no right to a jury trial in equity cases. When a civil case involves both legal and equitable issues or procedure, either party may demand a jury trial (and failure to do so is taken as a waiver), but the judge may find that there is no right to jury trial because of equitable issues or claims.

jury–waived \'juṙ-ē-'wāvd\ *adj* : of, relating to, or being a trial in which the right to a jury trial has been waived

jury wheel *n* : a revolving container into which the names of prospective jurors from a jury list are placed and then drawn by chance

ju•ry•wom•an \'juṙ-ē-ˌwu̇-mən\ *n, pl* **-wom•en** \-ˌwi-mən\ : a female juror

jus \'jəs, 'yu̇s\ *n, pl* **ju•ra** \'jər-ə, 'yü-rä\ [Latin] **1** : LAW **2** : a legal principle or right

jus ac•cres•cen•di \-ˌa-krə-'sen-ˌdī, -ˌä-krä-'sken-dē\ *n* [Latin, literally, right of increasing] : a right of accrual; *specif* : RIGHT OF SURVIVORSHIP — compare ACCRETION

jus ad rem \-ad-'rem, -äd-\ *n* [Medieval Latin, right to a thing] : a personal right to possession of property that usu. arises from a contractual obligation (as a lease) — compare JUS IN RE

jus co•gens \-'kä-gənz, -'kō-gens\ *n* [New Latin, literally, constraining law] : a principle of international law that is based on values taken to be fundamental to the international community and that cannot be set aside (as by treaty) ⟨it is doubtful that any state has ever violated *jus cogens* norms on a scale rivaling that of the Third Reich —*Princz v. Federal Republic of Germany*, 26 F.3d 1166 (1994)⟩ ⟨genocide and slave trade are violations of *jus cogens*⟩

jus dis•po•nen•di \-,dis-pō-'nen-,dī, -dē\ *n* [Latin, right of disposing] : a right of disposal of property ⟨the stockholder's *jus disponendi* was destroyed⟩

jus gen•ti•um \-'jen-shē-əm, -chəm\ *n* [Latin, literally, law of nations] : a body of law recognized by nations that is binding and governs their relations with each other : INTERNATIONAL LAW — called also *law of nations* ◊ In Roman law, *jus gentium* referred to the rules and laws that were common to the various nations or peoples under the Roman empire and were used in cases between non-Roman citizens or between a Roman and a non-Roman citizen.

jus in re \-in-'rē, -'rā\ *n* [Medieval Latin, right in a thing] : a right of property ownership that is enforced by an action in rem — compare JUS AD REM

jus pri•va•tum \-prə-'vā-təm, -prī-; -prē-'vä-təm\ *n* [New Latin, from Latin, private law or right] : a right of private ownership — compare JUS PUBLICUM

jus pub•li•cum \-'pə-bli-kəm, -'pü-blē-,kùm\ *n* [New Latin, from Latin, public law or right] : a right of public ownership; *specif* : the right of ownership of real property that is held in trust by a government for the public ⟨tidal flats are subject to the *jus publicum* —*United States v. Hensel*, 509 F. Supp. 1376 (1981)⟩

jus san•gui•nis \-'saŋ-gwi-nis, -'säŋ-gwē-,nēs\ *n* [Latin, right of blood] : a rule of law that a child's citizenship is determined by that of his or her parents

jus so•li \-'sō-,lī, -lē\ *n* [Latin, right of the soil] : a rule of law that a child's citizenship is determined by his or her place of birth — see also *Amendment XIV* to the CONSTITUTION in the back matter

just *adj* [Latin *justus* lawful, merited, from *jus* right, law] : conforming to law or

to the underlying principles of law: as **a** : conforming to reason or a standard of correctness ⟨~ sanctions cannot be excessive in relation to the offense⟩ **b** : conforming with what is deemed fair or good ⟨the award of attorney's fees was ~⟩ ⟨the application of this rule retroactively is not ~⟩ — **just•ly** *adv* — **just-ness** *n*

just cause — see CAUSE 2

just compensation *n* : compensation for property taken under eminent domain that places a property owner in the same position as before the property is taken — see also EMINENT DOMAIN ◊ Just compensation is usu. the fair market value of the property taken. Attorney's fees or expenses are usu. excluded.

jus ter•tii \-'tər-shē-,ī, -'ter-, -shē-,ē\ *n* [Latin] : a right of a third party (as to property in another's possession); *also* : the right to assert the rights of another in a lawsuit ◊ In property actions the claims of a third party on the property cannot usu. be asserted as a defense by a litigant. A litigant may, however, have third-party standing to assert another's constitutional rights (as when an organization asserts the rights of its members) if there is a substantial relationship between the litigant and the third party, if it is impossible for the third party to assert its own rights, and if there is the risk that the third party's rights will be diluted without the litigant's assertion.

jus•tice \'jəs-təs\ *n* [Old French, from Latin *justitia*, from *justus* just] **1 a** : the quality of being just, impartial, or fair ⟨it is not the province of the court to decide upon the ~ or injustice . . . of these laws —*Scott v. Sanford*, 60 U.S. 393 (1857)⟩ **b** : the principle or ideal of just dealing; *also* : conformity to the principle or ideal of just dealing **2 a** : the administration of law ⟨a fugitive from ~⟩; *esp* : the establishment or determination of rights according to law or equity ⟨system of ~⟩ **b** : fair, just, or impartial legal process ⟨courts or tribunals . . . for the administration of international ~

—G. R. Winters⟩ **3** : JUDGE; *esp* : a judge of an appellate court or court of last resort (as a supreme court) ⟨insults to particular ~*s* and threats of civil disobedience were bandied freely —R. H. Bork⟩

justice court *n* : JUSTICE OF THE PEACE COURT

justice of the peace : a local judicial official who is empowered chiefly to administer oaths, perform marriage ceremonies, certify documents, and in some states may have additional judicial powers (as to issue summonses)

justice of the peace court : a local court of limited jurisdiction usu. over minor civil and criminal actions, small claims, and some felony preliminaries which is presided over by a justice of the peace and which usu. follows summary procedure ◊ Justice of the peace courts were formerly common but now are used or remain active to some extent in only a few states.

jus·ti·cia·ble \jǝ-'sti-shǝ-bǝl, -shē-ǝ-\ *adj* : capable of being decided according to legal principles by a court ⟨whether the tax laws unfairly burden the poor is not a ~ issue⟩; *esp* : triable in a court ⟨the claim is not ~ because the plaintiff has no present right to the property but may in the future⟩ — see also *political question* at QUESTION 2; compare MOOT — **jus·ti·cia·bil·i·ty** \jǝ-ˌsti-shǝ-'bi-lǝ-tē, -shē-ǝ-\ *n*

jus·ti·fi·able \ˌjǝs-tǝ-'fī-ǝ-bǝl\ *adj* : capable of being justified ⟨~ reliance⟩

justifiable homicide — see HOMICIDE

jus·ti·fi·ca·tion \ˌjǝs-tǝ-fǝ-'kā-shǝn\ *n* **1** : the act or an instance of justifying **2** : something that justifies; *specif* : a le-

gally sufficient reason or cause (as self-defense) for an act that would otherwise be criminal or tortious **3** : the affirmative defense of having a legally sufficient justification — compare EXCUSE

jus·ti·fy \'jǝs-tǝ-ˌfī\ *vb* **-fied; -fy·ing** *vt* **1** : to prove or show to be just, right, or reasonable ⟨does not ~ a denial of bail⟩ **2** : to show to have had a legally sufficient reason or cause ⟨a defendant may not set up his own standard of conduct to ~ or excuse himself —*State v. Doss,* 568 P.2d 1054 (1977)⟩ ~ *vi* **1** : to show a legally sufficient reason for an act **2** : to swear an oath as to the ownership of sufficient property ⟨they shall ~ in an amount no less than $200 —*Oregon Revised Statutes*⟩; *also* : to qualify as a surety by swearing such an oath ⟨the defendants sought to ~ as bail —*State v. Blaisdell,* 253 A.2d 341 (1969)⟩

just title — see TITLE

ju·ve·nile \'jü-vǝ-ˌnīl, -nǝl\ *n* : an individual who is under an age fixed by law (as 18 years) at which he or she would be charged as an adult for a criminal act — compare MINOR

juvenile court *n* : a court that has jurisdiction over juvenile delinquency proceedings or other civil proceedings involving minors or juveniles — compare FAMILY COURT

juvenile delinquency *n* : a violation of the law committed by a juvenile that would have been a crime if committed by an adult; *also* : antisocial behavior by juveniles that is subject to legal action

juvenile delinquent *n* : a juvenile who commits an act of juvenile delinquency — compare STATUS OFFENDER, YOUTHFUL OFFENDER

K

k/a *abbr* known as

K.B. *abbr* King's Bench

keep·er *n* : one that takes care of and often is legally responsible for something ⟨a dog's ~⟩ ⟨a ~ of the property⟩

Ke·ogh plan \'kē-ō-\ *n* [after Eugene J. *Keogh* (1907–89), U.S. Congressman whose 1965 bill established the plan] : an individual retirement account for the self-employed

key *adj* : of vital importance (as in a business organization) esp. so as to be specially insured to the benefit of an employer ⟨~ man⟩ ⟨~ employee insurance⟩

kick·back \'kik-,bak\ *n* : a payment (as of money or property) made to one in a position to open up or control a source of income for the payor ⟨convicted of receiving ~*s* for referrals⟩ — compare BRIBE, PAYOFF ◊ A kickback is specifically a payment for income received or to be received. The word is usu. not restricted to a return of funds.

kid·nap \'kid-,nap\ *vt* **kid·napped** *or* **kid-naped** \-,napt\; **kid·nap·ping** *or* **kid-nap·ing** \-,na-piŋ\ [probably back-formation from *kidnapper*, from *kid* child + obsolete *napper* thief] : to seize and confine or carry away by force or fraud and often with a demand for ransom — **kid·nap·per** *or* **kid·nap·er** \-,na-pər\ *n*

kid·nap·ping *or* **kid·nap·ing** *n* : an act or instance or the crime of seizing, confining, inveigling, abducting, or carrying away a person by force or fraud often with a demand for ransom or in furtherance of another crime

kin *n* : one's relatives — **kin·ship** \-,ship\ *n*

kind *n* **1** : a particular type, category, or class ⟨properties of like ~⟩ — see also LIKE-KIND EXCHANGE **2 a** : an unconverted form ⟨a partition of property in ~⟩;

broadly : a form other than money ⟨forbid a bribe in cash or in ~⟩ — see also IN-KIND **b** : the equivalent in value ⟨repay a loan in ~⟩

King's Bench *n* : a division of the High Court of Justice of England and Wales that hears civil cases (as commercial cases) and appeals of criminal cases — used during the reign of a king; compare QUEEN'S BENCH

kit·ing \'kī-tiŋ\ *n* : CHECK-KITING

knock and an·nounce rule *n* : a rule of criminal procedure requiring that police announce their authority and purpose before entering a premises in execution of a search or arrest warrant unless special circumstances (as risk of harm to the police) warrant unannounced or forcible entry — compare EXIGENT CIRCUMSTANCES, *no-knock search warrant* at WARRANT

know·ing *adj* **1** : having or reflecting knowledge ⟨a ~ and intelligent waiver of counsel⟩ — see also INTELLIGENT **2** : DELIBERATE 2 ⟨~ possession⟩ ⟨~ endangerment⟩ — compare MENS REA — **know·ing·ly** *adv*

know·ledge *n* **1 a** : awareness or understanding esp. of an act, a fact, or the truth : ACTUAL KNOWLEDGE 1 in this entry **b** : awareness that a fact or circumstance probably exists; *broadly* : CONSTRUCTIVE KNOWLEDGE in this entry — see also SCIENTER, WILLFUL BLINDNESS ◊ Knowledge fundamentally differs from intent in being grounded in awareness rather than purpose.

actual knowledge **1** : direct and clear awareness (as of a fact or condition) ⟨the bank had *actual knowledge* that the name and account number referred to different persons⟩ **2** : awareness of such information as would cause a reasonable person to inquire further; *specif* : such awareness considered as a timely and sufficient substitute for actual notice (as of a work-related injury or of a bankruptcy proceeding) ⟨ruled that the employer did not have actual notice or *actual knowledge* within 90 days⟩

constructive knowledge : knowledge (as of a condition or fact) that one using ordinary care or diligence would possess ⟨had *constructive knowledge* of the presence of narcotics on his property⟩

personal knowledge : direct knowledge of a matter or of the truth or falsity of an allegation ⟨a witness may not testify to a matter unless evidence is introduced sufficient to support a finding that the witness has *personal knowledge* of the matter — *Federal Rules of Evidence* Rule 602⟩

superior knowledge : knowledge greater than that possessed by another; *esp* : awareness of a condition or fact that affects another who was not aware of it ⟨denied having had *superior knowledge* of the hazard⟩ ⟨*superior knowledge* of a factor in the performance of a contract⟩ **2** : the range of one's information, understanding, or expertise ⟨answered to the best of his ∼⟩

known creditor — see CREDITOR

280

L

labor contract — see CONTRACT

labor organization *n* : an organization, agency, committee, group, or plan in which employees take part that deals with employers about such matters as wages and grievances; *esp* : LABOR UNION ◇ Designation by the court as a labor organization subject to applicable statutes can confer a variety of liabilities and protections, esp. in regard to antitrust issues, unfair labor and management practices, and right-to-work laws.

labor union *n* : a labor organization usu. consisting of workers of the same trade that is formed for the purpose of advancing its members' interests (as through collective bargaining) in respect to wages, benefits, and working conditions — see also CRAFT UNION, BARGAINING UNIT ◇ Labor unions and employers are subject to the provisions of the National Labor Relations Act (NLRA or Wagner Act), as amended by the Labor Management Relations (Taft-Hartley) Act and the Labor Management Reporting and Disclosure (Landrum-Griffin) Act. The NLRA authorized the establishment of the National Labor Relations Board, the federal agency which administers the provisions of the Act.

la·ches \'la-chəz, 'lā-, -shəz\ *n, pl* **laches** [Anglo-French *lachesce, laschesce* negligence, from Old French *lasche* lax, ultimately from Latin *laxare* to loosen, from *laxus* slack] **1** : undue delay in asserting a right or privilege — compare STATUTE OF LIMITATIONS **2 a** : a doctrine permitting dismissal of a suit because a plaintiff's unreasonable delay in asserting a right or privilege has been detrimental to the defendant's ability to make a defense (as by resulting in the unavailability of witnesses or evidence) ⟨a suit barred

by ~⟩ **b** : an affirmative defense based on this doctrine

laid *past and past part of* LAY

lain *past part of* LIE

land *n* **1** : an area of the earth usu. inclusive of improvements, bodies of water, and natural or man-made objects and extending indefinitely upward and downward — compare AIR RIGHT **2** : an estate, interest, or right in land ⟨~ means both surface and mineral rights — *California Public Resources Code*⟩

land bank — see BANK

land contract *n* : LAND INSTALLMENT CONTRACT at CONTRACT

land court *n* : a court having jurisdiction over registration of title to land and matters incidental thereto — see also TORRENS SYSTEM ◇ In the United States only Massachusetts and Hawaii have land courts.

land installment contract — see CONTRACT

land·lord *n* : the owner of property (as houses, apartments, or land) that is leased or rented to another

landlord's lien — see LIEN

land·mark *n, often attrib* **1** : an object (as a stone or tree) that marks a boundary of land **2** : an event or development that marks a turning point or stage ⟨a ~ decision⟩ **3** : a structure (as a building) of unusual historical or aesthetic interest; *esp* : one that is officially designated and set aside for preservation

landmark case — see CASE 1b

land trust — see TRUST

lap·ping \'la-piŋ\ *n* [gerund of *lap* to overlap] : the practice of misappropriating entrusted funds and then covering up the act by using other entrusted funds or funds subsequently received in a continuous process of concealment

¹lapse \'laps\ *n* : a termination or failure due to events, neglect, or time: as **a** : the failure of a bequest (as because the intended recipient dies before the testator) — compare ANTI-LAPSE STATUTE **b** : the termination of an insurance policy because of nonpayment of premiums or nonrenewal

²lapse *vb* **lapsed; laps·ing** *vi* : to terminate, become ineffective, or fail ⟨the bequest *lapsed* when the son died before the father⟩ ⟨allowed the insurance policy to ~⟩ ~ *vt* : to cause (as a policy) to lapse ⟨the company *lapsed* the policy⟩

lar·ce·nous \'lär-sə-nəs\ *adj* **1** : of, relating to, or having the nature of larceny ⟨~ intent⟩ ⟨a ~ scheme⟩ **2** : committing larceny

lar·ce·ny \'lär-sə-nē\ *n, pl* **-nies** [modification of Anglo-French *larcine* theft, from Old French *larrecin*, from Latin *latrocinium* robbery, from *latron-*, *latro* mercenary soldier, brigand] : the unlawful taking and carrying away of personal property with the intent to deprive the rightful owner of it permanently; *also* : any of several types of theft (as embezzlement or obtaining another's property by false pretenses) that have been traditionally distinguished from larceny ◊ Under the Model Penal Code and in states that follow it, larceny is a type of theft. In states where larceny is currently defined as a separate crime, it may include the crimes that were distinct from it under common law.

    grand larceny : felonious larceny of property having a value greater than an amount fixed by law; *also* : larceny accompanied by aggravating circumstances (as the use of threats)

    larceny by trick : larceny of property obtained by the use of misrepresentation esp. in getting an owner to hand over something in the belief that it is for temporary purposes — compare FALSE PRETENSES

    larceny from the person : larceny of property held by or within the immediate control of its owner

pet·it larceny \'pe-tē-\ : larceny of property having a market value below an amount fixed by law — called also *petty larceny* ◊ Petit larceny is a misdemeanor.

larceny by trick — see LARCENY

larceny from the person — see LARCENY

las·civ·i·ous \lə-'si-vē-əs\ *adj* : reflecting or producing sexual desire or behavior esp. that is considered indecent or obscene ⟨lewd and ~ behavior⟩

last antecedent rule *n* : a doctrine in the interpretation of statutes: qualifying words or phrases refer only to the last antecedent word or phrase unless the context or entire act clearly requires otherwise — called also *last antecedent doctrine*

last clear chance *n* : a doctrine in the law of negligence: the contributory negligence of a plaintiff in putting himself or herself in peril will not bar recovery from a defendant who could have avoided injuring or killing the plaintiff by the use of ordinary care — called also *discovered peril*

last in, first out *adj* : being or relating to a method of valuing inventories by which items from the last lot received are assumed to be sold first and all requisitions are priced at the cost per item of the lot last stocked — compare FIRST IN, FIRST OUT

last injurious exposure rule *n* : a rule placing liability for workers' compensation on the last employer of a worker disabled as a result of injuries or conditions suffered under two or more successive employers

la·tent \'lāt-ᵊnt\ *adj* : existing in hidden or dormant form but usu. capable of being brought to light — compare PATENT

latent am·bi·gu·i·ty \-ˌam-bə-'gyü-ə-tē\ *n* : an uncertainty which does not appear on the face of a legal instrument (as a contract or will) but which arises from a consideration of extrinsic facts or evidence — compare PATENT AMBIGUITY

latent defect *n* : a defect (as in a product or property) that is not discoverable by reasonable or customary inspection ⟨a *latent defect* excluded from the homeowner's insurance⟩

laun·der *vt* : to transfer (money or instruments deriving from illegal activity) so as to conceal the true nature and source ⟨~ money through an offshore account⟩

law \'lȯ\ *n* [Old English *lagu*, of Scandinavian origin] **1** : a rule of conduct or action prescribed or formally recognized as binding or enforced by a controlling authority: as **a** : a command or provision enacted by a legislature — see also STATUTE 1 **b** : something (as a judicial decision) authoritatively accorded binding or controlling effect in the administration of justice ⟨that case is no longer the ~ of this circuit⟩ **2 a** : a body of laws ⟨the ~ of a state⟩; *broadly* : laws and justice considered as a general and established entity ⟨the ~ looks with disfavor on restraints on alienation⟩ **b** : COMMON LAW — compare EQUITY 2 **3 a** : the control or authority of the law ⟨maintain ~ and order⟩ **b** : one or more agents or agencies involved in enforcing laws **c** : the application of a law or laws as distinct from considerations of fact ⟨an error of ~⟩ — see also *issue of law* at ISSUE, *matter of law* at MATTER, *question of law* at QUESTION 2 **4** : the whole body of laws and doctrines relating to one subject ⟨contract ~⟩ ⟨the ~ of attractive nuisance⟩ **5 a** : the legal profession ⟨practice ~⟩ **b** : the nature, use, and effects of laws and legal systems as an area of knowledge or society ⟨the politics of ~⟩ — compare JURISPRUDENCE — **at law** : under or within the provisions of the law esp. as opposed to equity ⟨a remedy *at law*⟩

law–abid·ing \'lȯ-ə-ˈbī-diŋ\ *adj* : abiding by or obedient to the law — **law–abid·ing·ness** *n*

law clerk *n* : one (as a law school graduate) who provides a judge, magistrate, or lawyer with assistance in such matters as research and analysis

law·ful *adj* **1 a** : being in harmony with the law ⟨a ~ judgment⟩ ⟨a ~ purpose⟩ **b** : constituted, authorized, or established by law ⟨a ~ duty⟩ **2** : LAW-ABIDING ⟨~ citizens⟩ — **law·ful·ly** *adv* — **law·ful·ness** *n*

lawful age *n* : LEGAL AGE

lawful force — see FORCE 3

law·less *adj* **1** : not restrained or controlled by law **2** : ILLEGAL ⟨a ~ act⟩ — **law·less·ly** *adv* — **law·less·ness** *n*

law·mak·er *n* : one that makes laws; *esp* : LEGISLATOR — **law·mak·ing** *n*

law merchant *n* : the commercial rules developed under English common law that influenced modern commercial law and that are referred to as supplementing rules set down in the Uniform Commercial Code and in state codes

law of na·tions : JUS GENTIUM

law of the case : a doctrine in legal procedure: an issue esp. of law that has been decided (as by an appeals court) will not be reconsidered in the same case unless compelling circumstances warrant such reconsideration; *also* : a matter of law considered as settled in a case ⟨the jury instructions were not objected to and thus became the *law of the case*⟩

law of the land 1 : the established law of a nation or region **2** : DUE PROCESS

law of the sea *often cap L&S* : a body of international law promulgated by United Nations convention and covering a range of ocean matters including territorial zones, access to and transit on the sea, environmental preservation, and the resolution of international disputes

law review *n*, *often cap L&R* : a periodical (as one published by a law school or bar association) containing notes and articles analyzing and evaluating subject areas and developments in the law

law·suit *n* : an action brought in a court for the purpose of seeking relief from or remedy for an alleged wrong : SUIT

law·yer \'lȯ-yər\ *n* : one whose profession is to advise clients as to legal rights and obligations and to represent clients in legal proceedings

law·yer·ing *n* : the profession or work of a lawyer

¹lay *vt* **laid; lay·ing 1** : to impose as a duty, burden, or punishment ⟨~ a tax⟩ **2 a** : to put forward : ASSERT ⟨~ a claim⟩ **b** : to submit for examination and determination ⟨*laid* a case before the commission⟩

²lay *past of* LIE

lay witness — see WITNESS

LBO *abbr* leveraged buyout

L/C *abbr* letter of credit

¹lead *vt* **led; lead·ing** : to suggest the desired answer to (a witness) by asking leading questions

²lead *n* : something serving as a tip, indication, or clue ⟨the police have only one ~ in the murder investigation⟩

leading case — see CASE 1b

leading object rule *n* : MAIN PURPOSE RULE

leading question — see QUESTION 1

¹leaf·let *n* : a usu. folded printed sheet intended for free distribution

²leaflet *vi* **-let·ed** *or* **-let·ted; -let·ing** *or* **-let·ting** : to hand out leaflets ⟨invalidated an ordinance banning all *leafleting* — David Kairys⟩

learn·ed intermediary \'lər-nəd-\ *n* : a person and esp. a physician who is properly warned of the dangers of a product by the manufacturer in accordance with the learned intermediary doctrine

learned intermediary doctrine *n* : a doctrine of products liability law: the manufacturer of a prescription drug fulfills its duty to warn of potentially harmful effects of the drug by informing the prescribing physician and is not also obligated to warn the user

¹lease \'lēs\ *n* [Anglo-French *les*, from *lesser* to grant by lease, from Old French *laisser* to let go, from Latin *laxare* to loosen, from *laxus* slack] **1 a** : a contract by which an owner of property conveys exclusive possession, control, use, or enjoyment of it for a specified rent and a specified term after which the property reverts to the owner; *also* : the act of

such conveyance or the term for which it is made — see also SUBLEASE; compare EASEMENT, LICENSE, *security interest* at INTEREST 1, TENANCY ◊ Article 2A of the Uniform Commercial Code, which governs leases where adopted, defines *lease* as "a transfer of the right to possession and use of goods for a term in return for consideration."

build·ing lease : GROUND LEASE in this entry

consumer lease : a lease made by a lessor regularly engaged in the selling or leasing of a product to a lessee who is leasing the product primarily for his or her personal or household use

finance lease : a lease in which the lessor acquires goods from a supplier in accordance with the specifications of the lessee ◊ Under section 2A-103 of the Uniform Commercial Code, before the lessor signs the lease or the lease becomes effective, the lessee must receive or approve of a copy of the contract by which the goods were acquired or must receive a statement of terms (as warranties, disclaimers, and liquidated damages) relating to the contract or notification of where such information can be obtained.

ground lease : a lease of land usu. for a long term in consideration of the payment of rent and with the agreement that the lessee build or improve a structure on the land — called also *building lease*

mineral lease : a lease granting the right to work a mine and extract the minerals or other valuable deposits from it under prescribed conditions (as of time, price, or royalties) — called also *mining lease*

net lease : a lease requiring the lessee to assume all operation expenses (as for maintenance, insurance, and taxes) in addition to the payment of rent

operating lease : a lease of property

\ə\abut \ᵊ\kitten \ər\further \a\ash \ā\ace
\ä\cot, cart \au̇\out \ch\chin \e\bet \ē\easy
\g\go \i\hit \ī\ice \j\job \ŋ\sing \ō\go \ȯ\law
\ȯi\boy \th\thin \t͟h\the \ü\loot \u̇\foot \y\yet
\zh\vision *see also* Pronunciation Symbols page

and esp. equipment for a term which is shorter than the property's useful life and in which the lessor is responsible for certain expenses (as taxes) **per·pet·u·al lease** \pər-'pe-chù-wəl-\ : a lease renewable forever at the lessee's option
proprietary lease : a lease used to convey to a member of a cooperative the exclusive possession of a residential unit
true lease : a lease that resembles a security agreement but retains the attributes of a lease
b : property and esp. real property that is leased **2** *in the civil law of Louisiana* : a contract by which a person provides labor or services for a price
²lease *vb* **leased; leas·ing** *vt* **1** : to grant by lease to another ⟨~s mopeds to tourists⟩ **2** : to hold under a lease ⟨a company *leasing* a fleet of cars for its executives⟩ ~ *vi* **1** : to be under a lease or subject to a lease ⟨the vacation house ~s for $500 a week⟩ **2** : to grant property by a lease ⟨have *leased* to students in the past⟩
lease·back \'lēs-ˌbak\ *n* : the sale of property with the understanding that the seller can lease it back from the new owner — often used in the phrase *sale and leaseback*
lease·hold \'lēs-ˌhōld\ *n* : a tenure of real property held by a lessee under a lease : a lessee's estate in the property; *also* : the property so held — compare FEE, FREEHOLD
lease·hold·er *n* : one having a leasehold
leasehold insurance *n* : insurance against loss to a lessee (as of profits derived from a sublease) because of cancellation of a lease as a result of fire or other specified peril
leasehold mortgage — see MORTGAGE
lease–up *n* : the act or practice of finding or acquiring tenants
leash law *n* : a law and esp. an ordinance requiring that a dog be restrained when not confined to its owner's property
leave *vt* **left; leav·ing** : BEQUEATH, DEVISE
led *past and past part of* LEAD
leg *abbr* **1** legal **2** legislative, legislature

leg·a·cy \'le-gə-sē\ *n, pl* **-cies** [Medieval Latin *legatio*, from Latin *legare* to bequeath] : a gift of property by will; *specif* : a gift of personal property by will : BEQUEST — see also ADEMPTION; compare DEVISE
conjoint legacy *in the civil law of Louisiana* : a legacy by a single disposition to more than one legatee or of indivisible property to more than one legatee
de·mon·stra·tive legacy \di-'män-strə-tiv-\ : a legacy payable from a designated fund or asset or from the general assets of the estate to the extent the specified fund or asset fails to satisfy legacy
general legacy : a legacy payable out of the general assets of the estate
legacy under a universal title *in the civil law of Louisiana* : a legacy that consists of a specified proportion (as one-half), a specified type (as movables), or a specified proportion of a specified type of the testator's property
particular legacy *in the civil law of Louisiana* : any legacy that is not a universal legacy or a legacy under a universal title — called also *legacy under particular title*
residuary legacy : a legacy that consists of all of the testator's estate which has not been distributed through other legacies or charges upon the estate
specific legacy : a legacy payable only from a specific fund or asset in the estate
universal legacy *in the civil law of Louisiana* : a legacy by which a testator gives to one or more legatees all of his or her property at the time of death
legacy under a universal title — see LEGACY
legacy under particular title : PARTICULAR LEGACY at LEGACY
le·gal \'lē-gəl\ *adj* [Latin *legalis*, from *leg-, lex* law] **1** : of or relating to law or the processes of law ⟨a ~ question⟩ ⟨take ~ action⟩ **2 a** : deriving authority from or founded on law ⟨a ~ tariff rate⟩ ⟨a ~

government⟩ **b** : fulfilling the requirements of law ⟨a ~ voter⟩ **c** : having a status derived from law : recognized as such by law ⟨a ~ certainty⟩ **d** : created by operation of esp. statutory law ⟨~ incompetence⟩ ⟨a ~ presumption⟩ — compare CONVENTIONAL 1, JUDICIAL 2 **e** : established by law ⟨the ~ test for mental capacity⟩ **3** : conforming to or permitted by law : LAWFUL ⟨a referendum to make gambling ~⟩ **4** : recognized or made effective under principles of law as distinguished from principles of equity : deriving from or existing or valid in law as distinguished from equity — see also EQUITY; compare EQUITABLE **5 a** : of, relating to, or having the characteristics of the profession of law or one of its members ⟨a corporate ~ department⟩ ⟨the ~ community⟩ **b** : of or relating to the study of law ⟨continuing ~ education⟩ — **le·gal·ly** *adv*

legal age *n* : an age at which a person becomes entitled under the law to engage in a particular activity or becomes responsible for particular acts ⟨the *legal age* for drinking in this state⟩; *broadly* : AGE OF MAJORITY — compare AGE OF CONSENT, EMANCIPATE

legal aid *n* : aid provided by an organization established to serve the legal needs of the poor

legal aid society *n* : an organization providing government-funded legal aid to the poor

legal capital — see CAPITAL

legal cause — see CAUSE 1

legal cer·tain·ty test *n* : a rule in federal civil procedure: a defendant's challenge to diversity jurisdiction made on the basis that the amount of money involved in the controversy falls short of the jurisdictional amount will be defeated if the plaintiff provides proof that the amount is certain to be met — called also *legal certainty rule*, *legal certainty standard*

legal detriment *n* : DETRIMENT 2

legal entity *n* : an entity (as a corporation or labor union) having under the law rights and responsibilities and esp. the capacity to sue and be sued

le·gal·ese \ˌlē-gə-ˈlēz, -ˈlēs\ *n* : the specialized language of the legal profession

legal estate — see ESTATE 1

legal fiction *n* : something asssumed in law to be fact irrespective of the truth or accuracy of that assumption ⟨the *legal fiction* that a day has no fractions —*Fields v. Fairbanks North Star Borough*, 818 P.2d 658 (1991)⟩

legal fraud — see FRAUD

legal heir — see HEIR

legal impossibility — see IMPOSSIBILITY

legal interest — see INTEREST 1, 5

le·gal·i·ty \li-ˈga-lə-tē\ *n, pl* **-ties** **1** : attachment to or observance of law **2** : the quality or state of being legal : LAWFULNESS **3** *pl* : obligations imposed by law

le·gal·ize \ˈlē-gə-ˌlīz\ *vt* **-ized; -iz·ing** : to make legal; *esp* : to give legal validity or sanction to — **le·gal·i·za·tion** *n* — **le·gal·iz·er** *n*

legal list *n* : a statutory list of types of investments that fiduciaries are permitted to make on behalf of others — compare PRUDENT MAN RULE

legal malice *n* : IMPLIED MALICE at MALICE

legal mortgage — see MORTGAGE

legal name *n* **1** : a person's name that is usu. the name given at birth and recorded on the birth certificate but that may be a different name that is used by a person consistently and independently or that has been declared the person's name by a court ◊ If a person seeks to change a name by judicial process, the court may not deny the change absent any indication of a fraudulent purpose. In some states, a woman's legal name is presumed to include her husband's last name. **2** : the designation chosen by a business entity (as a corporation) and reported to

\ə\abut   \ᵊ\kitten   \ər\further   \a\ash   \ā\ace
\ä\cot, cart   \au̇\out   \ch\chin   \e\bet   \ē\easy
\g\go   \i\hit   \ī\ice   \j\job   \ŋ\sing   \ō\go   \ȯ\law
\ȯi\boy   \th\thin   \t͟h\the   \ü\loot   \u̇\foot   \y\yet
\zh\vision   *see also* Pronunciation Symbols page

the state (as in the articles of incorporation)

legal opinion *n* : OPINION 2a

legal owner — see OWNER

legal person *n* : a body of persons or an entity (as a corporation) considered as having many of the rights and responsibilities of a natural person and esp. the capacity to sue and be sued

legal personality *n* : the quality or state of being a legal person

legal representative *n* : one who represents or stands in the place of another under authority recognized by law esp. with respect to the other's property or interests: as **a** : PERSONAL REPRESENTATIVE **b** : an agent having legal status; *esp* : one acting under a power of attorney

legal reserve — see RESERVE

legal residence *n* : DOMICILE 1

legal separation *n* : a separation of spouses which does not involve a dissolution of the marriage but in which certain arrangements (as for maintenance and custody) are ordered by the court — called also *divorce a mensa et thoro, judicial separation, separation from bed and board*

legal servitude — see SERVITUDE

legal tender *n* : money that is legally valid for the payment of debts and that must be accepted for that purpose when offered

legal title — see TITLE

le·ga·tee \ˌle-gə-'tē\ *n* : one to whom a legacy is bequeathed — compare DEVISEE, HEIR, NEXT OF KIN, SUCCESSOR

leg·is·late \'le-jəs-ˌlāt\ *vb* **-lat·ed; -lat·ing** *vi* : to perform the function of legislation; *specif* : to make or enact laws ∼ *vt* : to cause, create, provide, or bring about by legislation

leg·is·la·tion \ˌle-jəs-'lā-shən\ *n* **1** : the making or giving of laws; *specif* : the exercise of the power and function of making rules that have the force of authority by virtue of their promulgation by an official organ of the state **2** : the enactments of a legislator or legislative body **3** : a matter of business for or under consideration by a legislative body ⟨recently proposed ∼⟩

leg·is·la·tive \'le-jəs-ˌlā-tiv\ *adj* **1 a** : having the power or performing the function of legislating **b** : belonging to the branch of government that is charged with such powers as making laws, levying and collecting taxes, and making financial appropriations — compare ADMINISTRATIVE 2, EXECUTIVE, JUDICIAL **2 a** : of or relating to a legislature ⟨∼ committees⟩ **b** : composed of members of a legislature ⟨∼ caucus⟩ **c** : created or effectuated by a legislature esp. as distinguished from an executive or judicial body **d** : designed to assist a legislature or its members ⟨a ∼ research agency⟩ **3** : of, concerned with, or created by legislation — **leg·is·la·tive·ly** *adv*

legislative agent — see AGENT

legislative assembly *n, often cap L&A* **1** : a bicameral legislature **2** : the lower house of a bicameral legislature

legislative council *n, often cap L&C* : a permanent committee chosen from both houses that meets between sessions of a state legislature to study problems and plan a legislative program

legislative counsel *n* : a lawyer or group of lawyers employed to assist legislators in the procedures (as holding hearings and drafting bills) for enacting legislation

legislative court *n* : a court (as the United States Tax Court and the territorial courts) created by Congress under Article I of the U.S. Constitution whose judges are subject to removal from office and salary reduction — called also *Article I court;* compare ARTICLE III COURT

legislative day *n* : a period of time during which a legislature is in session that commences with the opening of a daily session and ends with adjournment and that may last more than one calendar day

legislative fact — see FACT

legislative history *n* : a published record (as of drafts and commentary by the drafters) relating to the passing of particular legislation

legislative immunity — see IMMUNITY

legislative intent *n* : the ends sought to be achieved by a legislature in an enactment ◊ Courts often look to legislative intent for guidance in interpreting and applying a law. The legislative history, the language of the law, and the wrong to be corrected may provide indications of the legislative intent.

legislative power — see POWER 2a

legislative rule *n* : a rule adopted by a government agency in accordance with the notice and comment requirements of the Administrative Procedure Act that has the force of law and imposes new duties on the regulated parties — called also *substantive rule;* compare INTERPRETIVE RULE

legislative session *n* : a session of the U.S. Senate that is not an executive session

legislative veto *n* : a resolution passed by one or both houses of a legislature that is intended to nullify an administrative regulation or action

leg·is·la·tor \'le-jəs-ˌlā-tər, -ˌtòr\ *n* [Latin *legis lator,* literally, proposer of a law, from *legis* (genitive of *lex* law) + *lator* proposer, from *ferre* (past participle *latus*) to carry, propose] : a person who makes laws esp. for a political unit; *esp* : a member of a legislative body — **leg·is·la·to·ri·al** \ˌle-jəs-lə-'tōr-ē-əl\ *adj* — **leg·is·la·tor·ship** *n*

leg·is·la·ture \'le-jəs-ˌlā-chər, -ˌchùr\ *n* : a body of persons having the power to legislate; *specif* : an organized body having the authority to make laws for a political unit (as a nation or state) — compare EXECUTIVE, JUDICIARY

le·git·i·ma·cy \li-'ji-tə-mə-sē\ *n* : the quality or state of being legitimate

¹le·git·i·mate \lə-'ji-tə-mət\ *adj* [Medieval Latin *legitimatus,* past participle of *legitimare* to give legal status to, from Latin *legitimus* legally sanctioned, from *leg-, lex* law] **1** : conceived of or born of parents lawfully married to each other or having been made through legal procedure equal in status to one so conceived or born; *also* : having rights and obligations under the law as the child of such

birth **2** : being neither spurious nor false ⟨a ~ grievance⟩ **3** : being in accordance with law or with established legal forms and requirements ⟨a ~ government⟩ **4** : conforming to recognized principles or accepted rules and standards ⟨a ~ claim of entitlement⟩ ⟨a ~ business reason⟩ — **le·git·i·mate·ly** *adv*

²le·git·i·mate \lə-'ji-tə-ˌmāt\ *vt* **-mat·ed; -mat·ing** : to make legitimate: as **a** : to give legal status or authorization to **b** : to show or affirm to be justified or have merit **c** : to put (an illegitimate child) in the state of a child born of married parents before the law by legal means — compare FILIATE — **le·git·i·ma·tion** \lə-ˌji-tə-'mā-shən\ *n*

legitimate filiation *n, in the civil law of Louisiana* : filiation created by a child being born during a marriage or adopted

legitimate por·tion *n* : LEGITIME

le·git·i·me \lə-'ji-tə-mē\ *n* [French, from Latin *legitima (pars)* the lawful (share)] *in the civil law of Louisiana* : the portion (as one-fourth) of a testate succession that is reserved for a forced heir — called also *forced portion;* compare DISPOSABLE PORTION, FALCIDIAN PORTION, MARITAL PORTION ◊ The fraction used to calculate the legitime will vary depending on the number of forced heirs.

le·git·i·mize \lə-'ji-tə-ˌmīz\ *vt* **-mized; -miz·ing** : LEGALIZE, LEGITIMATE

lem·on law *n* : a statute that grants the purchaser of a car specific remedies (as a refund) if the car has a defect that impairs or significantly affects its use, value, or safety and that cannot be repaired within a specified period

lend *vb* lent; lend·ing *vt* **1** : to give for temporary use on condition that the same or its equivalent be returned **2** : to let out (money) for temporary use on condition of repayment with interest ~ *vi* : to make a loan — **lend·able** *adj* — **lend·er** *n*

\ə\abut \ᵊ\kitten \ər\further \a\ash \ā\ace
\ä\cot, cart \aù\out \ch\chin \e\bet \ē\easy
\g\go \i\hit \ī\ice \j\job \ŋ\sing \ō\go \ò\law
\òi\boy \th\thin \t̲h̲\the \ü\loot \ù\foot \y\yet
\zh\vision *see also* Pronunciation Symbols page

le·sion \'lē-zhən\ *n* [Anglo-French, damage, injury, from Latin *laesio,* from *laedere* to injure] *in the civil law of Louisiana* : loss from failure to receive a threshold amount or value (as one-half market value) for immovable property conveyed or transferred by a commutative contract (as a sale or exchange) ⟨a new partition may be demanded for the least ~ —*Louisiana Civil Code*⟩ — called also *lesion beyond moiety;* compare UNJUST ENRICHMENT

les·see \le-'sē\ *n* : a person who has possession of real or personal property under a lease; *specif* : a tenant of real property under a lease

less·er \'le-sər\ *adj* : of less size, quality, degree, or significance; *specif* : of lower criminal liability ⟨duress has been held a good defense to such ~ crimes as robbery, burglary and malicious mischief — W. R. LaFave and A. W. Scott, Jr.⟩

lesser evils defense — see DEFENSE 2a

lesser included offense *n* : a crime (as unlawful entry) that is by definition included in the commission of another crime (as burglary) which has additional elements and greater criminal liability — called also *included offense* ◊ A criminal defendant may be convicted of a lesser included offense if not charged specifically with that crime.

les·sor \'le-ˌsȯr, le-'sȯr\ *n* : a person who conveys the possession of real or personal property under a lease

let *vb* **let; let·ting** *vt* **1** : to offer or grant for rent, lease, or hire : LEASE ⟨may not be alienated, ~, or encumbered⟩ ⟨corporeal things may be ~ out⟩ **2** : to assign esp. after bids ⟨were attempting to ~ a contract without going through the bidding process —*Union Springs Tel. Co. v. Rowell,* 623 So. 2d 732 (1993)⟩ ~ *vi* **1** : to become rented, leased, or hired **2** : to become awarded to a contractor

let·ter *n* **1** : a direct written statement addressed to an individual or organization; *broadly* : an official communication — see also COUNTERLETTER

determination letter : a letter from an administrative agency (as the Internal Revenue Service) usu. in response to a request in which a determination, decision, or ruling (as whether an organization qualifies as charitable) is made

information letter : a letter from an administrative agency usu. in response to a request that provides information and esp. that simply calls attention to an interpretation or principle of law

letter of intent : a letter in which the intention to enter into a formal agreement (as a contract) or to take some specified action is stated

letter ro·ga·to·ry \-'rō-gə-ˌtȯr-ē\ [probably partial translation of Medieval Latin *littera rogatoria* letter of request] : a formal written request by a court to a court in a foreign jurisdiction to summon and examine a witness in accordance with that jurisdiction's procedures (as oral interrogatories) — usu. used in pl.

90–day letter : a letter from the Internal Revenue Service notifying a taxpayer of a determination of a deficiency ◊ A taxpayer has 90 days from the date of the mailing of the 90-day letter to petition for a redetermination of the deficiency in the U.S. Tax Court.

no–action letter : a letter from an attorney for the Securities and Exchange Commission recommending that the Commission take no prosecutorial action with regard to a suspected and investigated violation of SEC rules or regulations

opinion letter : a letter in which an opinion (as of a court or attorney) is given

ruling letter : DETERMINATION LETTER in this entry

30–day letter : a letter from the Internal Revenue Service to a taxpayer who has been audited and disputes the auditor's determination that sets out the taxpayer's right to appeal ◊ A taxpayer has 30 days from the time of the mailing of the 30-day letter to respond.

2 : a written communication usu. from a court containing a grant (as of a right) or an appointment — usu. used in pl. ⟨~*s* of guardianship⟩

letter of attorney : POWER OF ATTORNEY

letter of marque \-'märk\ [Anglo-French *mark, marque* right of retaliation, from Middle French *marque*, from Old Provençal *marca*, from *marcar* to mark, seize as pledge] : a letter from a government formerly used to grant a private person the power to seize the subjects of a foreign state; *specif* : authority granted to a private person to fit out an armed ship to plunder the enemy — usu. used in pl.; often used in the phrase *letters of marque and reprisal* ⟨the Congress shall have power . . . to declare war, grant *letters of marque* and reprisal, and make rules concerning captures on land and water — *U.S. Constitution* art. I⟩

letters of administration : a letter from a probate court that appoints the addressee administrator of an estate

letters patent : a letter (as from a government) that grants a designated person a right (as to property) and that is in a form open for public inspection : PATENT

letters testamentary : a letter from a probate court that appoints or confirms the addressee as executor of an estate

3 : LETTER OF CREDIT

letter of attorney — see LETTER 2

letter of credit : a document issued to a beneficiary at the request of the issuer's customer in which the issuer (as a bank) promises to honor a demand for payment by the beneficiary in order to satisfy or secure the customer's debt — compare GUARANTY ◊ A letter of credit is usu. requested by a buyer of merchandise (the issuer's customer) to be issued to the seller (the beneficiary) in order to secure the payment for the merchandise. In effect the letter of credit is considered to extend a line of credit or substitute the issuer's credit for the customer's.

commercial letter of credit : a letter of credit which is used to satisfy payment for merchandise and which usu. requires

the beneficiary to present a draft and some documentary proof (as of shipment or receipt of the merchandise) when making a demand for payment

irrevocable letter of credit : a letter of credit which the issuer cannot revoke or modify without the consent of the issuer's customer or the beneficiary

stand-by letter of credit : a letter of credit which is used to secure payment in case of default by the issuer's customer and which requires the beneficiary to present some documentary proof of such default when making a demand for payment

letter of intent — see LETTER 1

letter of marque — see LETTER 2

letter rogatory — see LETTER 1

letter ruling *n* : a ruling (as of a court or administrative agency) that is made in a letter (as an opinion or determination letter); *also* : DETERMINATION LETTER at LETTER 1

letters of administration — see LETTER 2

letters patent — see LETTER 2

letters testamentary — see LETTER 2

le·vari fa·ci·as \lə-'var-,ī-'fā-shē-əs, le-'vä-rē-'fä-kē-,äs\ *n* [New Latin, you should cause to be levied] : a common-law writ of execution for the satisfaction of a judgment debt from the goods and lands of the judgment debtor — used chiefly in Delaware; compare FIERI FACIAS

¹le·ver·age \'le-vrij, -və-rij\ *n* : the use of credit to enhance one's speculative capacity

²leverage *vt* **-aged; -ag·ing** : to provide (as a corporation) or supplement (as money) with leverage

leveraged buy·out \-'bī-,aůt\ *n* : the acquisition of a company usu. by members of its own management using debt to finance the purchase of equity with debt to be paid by future profits or sale of company assets

\ə\abut   \ᵊ\kitten   \ər\further   \a\ash   \ā\ace
\ä\cot, cart   \aů\out   \ch\chin   \e\bet   \ē\easy
\g\go   \i\hit   \ī\ice   \j\job   \ŋ\sing   \ō\go   \ô\law
\ôi\boy   \th\thin   \t̲h\the   \ü\loot   \ů\foot   \y\yet
\zh\vision   *see also* Pronunciation Symbols page

levi·able \'le-vē-ə-bəl\ *adj* **1 :** that may be levied ⟨a ~ tax⟩ **2 :** that may be levied upon ⟨~ assets⟩

¹levy \'le-vē\ *n, pl* **lev·ies 1 :** an act of levying: as **a :** the imposition or collection of a tax **b :** the seizure according to a writ of execution of real or personal property in a judgment debtor's possession to satisfy a judgment debt **2 :** an amount levied **:** TAX ⟨providing for a ~ of 3% on income up to $10,000 —D. Q. Posin⟩

²levy *vb* **lev·ied; levy·ing** *vt* **1 :** to impose or collect (as a tax or fine) with authority ⟨allow it to ~ stiffer penalties for some safety violations —*National Law Journal*⟩ **2 :** to enforce or carry into effect (a writ of execution) — compare ATTACH, GARNISH ~ *vi* **:** to enforce a writ of execution or attachment; *specif* **:** to make a seizure of real or personal property in a judgment debtor's possession ⟨they might as a last resort ~ on his merchandise —J. J. White and R. S. Summers⟩

lewd \'lüd\ *adj* **:** involving or being sexual conduct that is considered indecent or offensive **:** LICENTIOUS ⟨convicted of ~ and lascivious assault upon a child — *National Law Journal*⟩ — **lewd·ly** *adv* — **lewd·ness** *n*

lex fori \'leks-'fȯr-ˌ ī, -'fȯr-ē\ *n* [New Latin, law of the court] **:** the law of the court in which a proceeding is brought

lex lo·ci con·trac·tus \-'lō-ˌsī-kən-'trak-təs, -'lō-kē-kȯn-'träk-tu̇s\ *n* [New Latin, law of the place of the contract] **:** the law of the place where a contract was made or to be performed

lex loci de·lic·tii \-di-'lik-tē-ˌī, -dā-'lik-tē-ˌē\ *n* [New Latin, law of the place of the wrong] **:** the law of the place where an offense or tort occurred

li·a·bil·i·ty \ˌlī-ə-'bi-lə-tē\ *n, pl* **-ties 1 :** the quality or state of being liable **2 :** something for which one is liable: as **a :** a financial obligation **:** DEBT ⟨tax ~⟩ ⟨the bonds are *liabilities*⟩ — compare ASSET

contingent liability **:** an amount that may or may not be owed depending on the outcome of a contingency (as a cosigner's default on a loan)

fixed liability **:** a liability (as a bond or mortgage) that does not mature for at least one year from the date incurred or from a given date

b : accountability and responsibility to another enforceable by civil remedies or criminal sanctions ⟨~ for injuries caused by their product⟩

absolute liability **:** STRICT LIABILITY in this entry

alternative liability **:** joint liability imposed on multiple tortfeasors when there are simultaneous tortious acts (as defective manufacture of parts of a wheel by different manufacturers) and uncertainty as to which act was the proximate cause of an injury — compare CONCERT OF ACTION 1

civil liability **:** liability imposed under civil laws and civil process as distinguished from criminal laws; *also* **:** the state of being subject to civil sanctions (as restitution or damages) ⟨the acquittal does not relieve the corporation of *civil liability* for its fraud⟩ — see also TORT ◊ Civil liability is created by a legal theory or principle that places a duty or obligation (as to use due care) on the defendant.

corporate liability **:** liability of a corporation that is enforced by sanctions imposed against the corporation itself — see also PIERCE

criminal liability **:** liability imposed under criminal laws and by means of criminal prosecution; *also* **:** the state of being subject to criminal sanctions ⟨the *criminal liability* of an accomplice⟩

enterprise liability **:** liability imposed on a business enterprise esp. for on-the⸗job injuries to employees; *specif* **:** liability imposed on defendants who are all members of an industry that has produced a defective product when the specific manufacturer cannot be identified

joint and several liability **:** joint liability imposed on joint tortfeasors that allows enforcement of the entire judgment against any one of the tortfeasors ◊ In some jurisdictions, joint and several liability remains despite adoption of comparative fault, and in others it has been eliminated by comparative fault.

joint liability : liability that is shared (as by co-owners); *specif* : liability for a tort that is imposed on joint tortfeasors when they have acted in concert, owe the same duty to the plaintiff, have a legal relationship, or otherwise together have caused an injury to the plaintiff and that allows contribution or indemnity between the joint tortfeasors

liability in solido : SOLIDARY LIABILITY in this entry

liability without fault : STRICT LIABILITY in this entry

personal liability : liability imposed against an individual esp. for injuries that occur on the individual's property or as a result of the individual's activities

premises liability : liability arising from injuries or losses occurring on one's premises

primary liability : liability imposed directly on a person because of his or her own negligence, default, or legal undertaking

prod·ucts liability : liability imposed on a manufacturer or seller for a defective and unreasonably dangerous product; *specif* : strict liability for a defective product that does not require the plaintiff to have privity of contract with the seller or manufacturer — called also *product liability* ◊ A plaintiff usu. must show that a defective product was the proximate cause of injuries, was defective at the time of purchase, and was used for its intended purpose in order to establish a products liability claim.

secondary liability 1 : VICARIOUS LIABILITY in this entry **2** : liability (as of a guarantor) that arises from a legal obligation owed to an injured party to pay damages for another's failure to perform or negligent act

liability : liability assumed or

imposed on an individual separate from others

solidary liability *in the civil law of Louisiana* : liability that is shared by obligors and that makes any one obligor liable for the entire obligation to the obligee but also apportions the liability among the obligors so that contribution is allowed; *specif* : such liability for a tort that is imposed on joint tortfeasors — see also *solidary obligation* at OBLIGATION

strict liability : liability that is imposed without a finding of fault (as negligence or intent)

vicarious liability : liability that is imposed for another's acts because of imputed or constructive fault (as negligence) — see also RESPONDEAT SUPERIOR

3 : LIABILITY INSURANCE

liability in solido — see LIABILITY 2b

liability insurance *n* : insurance against loss resulting from civil liability for injury or damage to the persons or property of others — see also COMPREHENSIVE GENERAL LIABILITY INSURANCE

liability without fault — see LIABILITY 2b

li·a·ble \'lī-ə-bəl\ *adj* [ultimately from Old French *lier* to bind, from Latin *ligare*] **1** : answerable according to law : bound or obligated according to law or equity ⟨one is ~ as an accomplice to the crime of another —W. R. LaFave and A. W. Scott, Jr.⟩ ⟨the estate is ~ for succession taxes —*Commissioner of Revenue Services v. Estate of Culpepper*, 493 A.2d 297 (1985)⟩ **2 a** : being in a position to incur — used with *to* ⟨~ to a fire⟩ ⟨property ~ to duties⟩ **b** : subject or amenable according to law

¹li·bel \'lī-bəl\ *n* [Anglo-French, from Latin *libellus*, diminutive of *liber* book] **1** : COMPLAINT 1 — used esp. in admiralty and divorce cases **2 a** : a defamatory

\ə\abut \ᵊ\kitten \ər\further \a\ash \ā\ace
\ä\cot, cart \aù\out \ch\chin \e\bet \ē\easy
\g\go \i\hit \ī\ice \j\job \ŋ\sing \ō\go \ò\law
\òi\boy \th\thin \t̲h̲\the \ü\loot \ù\foot \y\yet
\zh\vision *see also* Pronunciation Symbols page

statement or representation esp. in the form of written or printed words; *specif* : a false published statement that injures an individual's reputation (as in business) or otherwise exposes him or her to public contempt **b** : the publication of such a libel **c** : the crime or tort of publishing a libel — see also SINGLE PUBLICATION RULE, *New York Times Co. v. Sullivan* in the IMPORTANT CASES section; compare DEFAMATION, SLANDER ◊ Although libel is defined under state case law or statute, the U.S. Supreme Court has enumerated some First Amendment protections that apply to matters of public concern. In *New York Times Co. v. Sullivan,* the Court held that in order to recover damages a public person (as a celebrity or politician) who alleges libel (as by a newspaper) has to prove that "the statement was made with 'actual malice' — that is, with knowledge that it was false or with reckless disregard of whether it was false or not" in order to recover damages. The Court has also held that the states cannot allow a private person to recover damages for libel against a media defendant without a showing of fault (as negligence) on the defendant's part. These protections do not apply to matters that are not of public concern (as an individual's credit report) and that are not published by a member of the mass media. A libel plaintiff must generally establish that the alleged libel refers to him or her specifically, that it was published to others, and that some injury (as to reputation) occurred that gives him or her a right to recover damages (as actual, general, presumed, or special damages). The defendant may plead and establish the truth of the statements as a defense. Criminal libel may have additional elements, as in tending to provoke a breach of peace or in blackening the memory of someone who is dead, and may not have to be published to someone other than the person libeled.

²libel *vt* **-beled** *also* **-belled; -bel·ing** *also* **-bel·ling 1** : to make or publish a libel against : to hurt the reputation of by libel

⟨respondent's complaint alleged that he had been *libeled* by statements in a full-page advertisement —*New York Times Co. v. Sullivan,* 376 U.S. 254 (1964)⟩ **2** : to proceed against in law by filing a libel (as against a ship or goods) ⟨several French ships were *libeled* in Boston — J. K. Owens⟩

libelant *var of* LIBELLANT

libelee *var of* LIBELLEE

li·bel·er \'lī-bə-lər\ *n* : a person who makes or publishes a libel

li·bel·lant *also* **li·bel·ant** \'lī-bə-lənt\ *n* **1** : a party who institutes a suit (as in admiralty) by a libel; *esp* : the petitioner or plaintiff in a divorce proceeding ⟨the ~ agreed to pay alimony⟩ **2** : LIBELER

li·bel·lee *also* **li·bel·ee** \ˌlī-bə-'lē\ *n* **1** : a party against whom a suit has been instituted by a libel; *esp* : the respondent or defendant in a divorce proceeding **2** : a person who has been libeled

li·bel·ous *also* **li·bel·lous** \'lī-bə-ləs\ *adj* : constituting or including libel ⟨a ~ magazine article⟩

libel per quod \-pər-'kwäd, -per-'kwōd\ *n* : libel that is actionable only when the plaintiff introduces additional facts to show defamation or claims special damages

libel per se \-pər-'sē, -per-'sā\ *n* : libel that is actionable without the plaintiff introducing additional facts to show defamation or claiming special damages

li·ber \'lī-bər, 'lē-ber\ *n* [Latin, book] : a book of records (as of deeds or wills) ⟨recorded in said Bureau in *Liber* 2564, at page 256⟩

lib·er·a·tive \'li-bə-ˌrā-tiv, -rə-tiv\ *adj* : serving to free or release (as from ownership or obligation) ⟨the ~ effects of tender and deposit⟩

liberative prescription — see PRESCRIPTION

lib·er·ty *n, pl* **-ties 1 a** : freedom from external (as governmental) restraint, compulsion, or interference in engaging in the pursuits or conduct of one's choice to the extent that they are lawful and not harmful to others **b** : enjoyment of the rights enjoyed by others in a society free of arbitrary or unreasonable limitation or interference **2 :** freedom from physical restraint **3 :** freedom from subjection to the will of another claiming ownership or services **4 :** RIGHT ⟨the right to a fair trial is a fundamental ~ secured by the Fourteenth Amendment —W. R. LaFave and J. H. Israel⟩

liberty clause *n, often cap L&C* **:** the due process clause found in the Fourteenth Amendment to the U.S. Constitution

liberty interest — see INTEREST 3b

liberty of contract : FREEDOM OF CONTRACT

¹li·cense \'līs-ᵊns\ *n* [Anglo-French, literally, permission, from Old French, from Latin *licentia*, from *licent-, licens*, present participle of *licēre* to be permitted, be for sale] **1 a :** a right or permission granted by a competent authority (as of a government or a business) to engage in some business or occupation, do some act, or engage in some transaction which would be unlawful without such right or permission; *also* **:** a document, plate, or tag evidencing a license granted **b :** revocable authority or permission given solely to one having no possessory rights in a tract of land to do something on that land which would otherwise be unlawful or a trespass — compare EASEMENT, LEASE **c :** a grant by the holder of a copyright or patent to another of any of the rights embodied in the copyright or patent short of an assignment of all rights **2 :** a defense (as to trespass) that one's act was in accordance with a license granted **3 a :** freedom that allows or is used with irresponsibility **b :** disregard for standards of personal conduct **:** LICENTIOUSNESS

²license *vt* **li·censed; li·cens·ing 1 :** to issue a license to **2 :** to permit or authorize by a license

license bond — see BOND 1a

li·cens·ee \ˌlīs-ᵊn-'sē\ *n* **:** one to whom a license is given ⟨a patent ~⟩; *specif* **:** one (as a firefighter in the course of his or her duty) who is on the property of another by authority of law or by the consent or invitation of the possessor — see also BARE LICENSEE, SOCIAL GUEST; compare INVITEE, TRESPASSER

licensee by in·vi·ta·tion : a social guest who is expressly or impliedly invited onto another's premises

li·cen·sor \'līs-ᵊn-sər, ˌlīs-ᵊn-'sȯr\ *n* **:** one that issues a license

li·cen·sure \'līs-ᵊn-shər, -ˌshu̇r\ *n* **:** the granting of licenses esp. to practice a profession; *also* **:** the state of being licensed

li·cen·tious \lī-'sen-chəs\ *adj* **:** disregarding legal restraints esp. with regard to sexual relations ⟨arrested as a prostitute for ~ sexual intercourse⟩ — **li·cen·tious·ly** *adv* — **li·cen·tious·ness** *n*

lic·it \'li-sət\ *adj* **:** conforming to the requirements of the law **:** not forbidden by law — **lic·it·ly** *adv*

lic·i·ta·tion \ˌli-sə-'tā-shən\ *n* [Latin *licitatio*, from *licitari* to bid a price, from *licere* to be for sale] **:** the act of offering for sale or bidding at an auction; *specif*, *in the civil law of Louisiana* **:** a mode of partitioning property held in common by sale at auction

lie \'lī\ *vi* **lay** \'lā\; **lain** \'lān\; **ly·ing :** to be sustainable or capable of being maintained **:** have grounds under the law ⟨holding that an action of battery would ~ —*Scott v. Bradford*, 606 P.2d 554 (1979)⟩ ⟨remedies for misrepresentation . . . will not ~ for misstatements of opinion —W. L. Prosser and W. P. Keeton⟩ ⟨appeals from the Tax Court ~ to the . . . Circuit Court —D. Q. Posin⟩ — **lie in grant :** to be transferable legally only by grant

lie de·tec·tor *n* **:** an instrument for detecting physiological evidence of the tension that accompanies lying — compare POLYGRAPH

\ə\abut \ᵊ\kitten \ər\further \a\ash \ā\ace
\ä\cot, cart \au̇\out \ch\chin \e\bet \ē\easy
\g\go \i\hit \ī\ice \j\job \ŋ\sing \ō\go \ȯ\law
\ȯi\boy \th\thin \t̲h\the \ü\loot \u̇\foot \y\yet
\zh\vision *see also* Pronunciation Symbols page

lien \\'lēn\\ *n* [Anglo-French, bond, obligation, literally, tie, band, from Old French, from Latin *ligamen*, from *ligare* to bind] : a charge or encumbrance upon property for the satisfaction of a debt or other duty that is created by agreement of the parties or esp. by operation of law; *specif* : a security interest created esp. by a mortgage

assessment lien : a lien that is on property benefiting from an improvement made by a municipality and that secures payment of the taxes assessed to pay for the improvement

attachment lien : a lien acquired on property by a creditor upon levy of an attachment

car•ri•er's lien : a lien against freight conferring on the carrier the right to retain the property until the amount due is paid

charging lien : a lien attaching to a judgment or recovery awarded to a plaintiff and securing payment of the plaintiff's attorney's fees and expenses — called also *special lien*

choate lien : a lien that requires no further action to be made enforceable and that identifies the lienor, the property subject to the lien, and the amount of the lien

common–law lien : a lien under common law giving a creditor (as a bailee) in possession of property the right to retain possession until payment of the amount due

equitable lien : a lien against property that does not require possession of the property and that is available in equity to prevent unjust enrichment

factor's lien : a lien against property held on consignment by a factor conferring the right to retain possession of the property until payment of the amount due ◊ Under Article 9 of the Uniform Commercial Code, a factor's lien is simply a security interest and, unlike a common-law lien, is enforceable even after the factor is no longer in possession of the property.

first lien : a lien taking precedence over all other claims, charges, or encumbrances of the same general category but not necessarily over those (as taxes) imposed by government sanction

floating lien : a lien created in a security agreement against property owned by the debtor at the time of the agreement's creation as well as property acquired after the agreement's creation

general lien **1** : a lien that is for the satisfaction of a balance due from an owner of property and that is not confined to the amount due in respect to the property itself **2** : RETAINING LIEN in this entry

inchoate lien : a lien for which some procedure remains unfinished or some term remains undetermined

involuntary lien : a lien that arises other than by the debtor's consent (as by operation of law)

judgment lien : a lien acquired against the property of a debtor by a creditor upon obtaining a favorable judgment

judicial lien : a lien obtained by a legal or equitable process (as judgment, levy, attachment, or execution)

junior lien : a lien that is lower in priority relative to other liens

landlord's lien : a lien against the goods and valuables of a tenant to secure payment of rent or sometimes repayment of money otherwise owed to a landlord

maritime lien : a lien arising under maritime law against a ship or its cargo (as for services or supplies tendered or for damages caused by a collision) which may be enforced by a court-ordered seizure of the property in order to satisfy the obligation

ma•te•ri•al•man's lien \\mə-'tir-ē-əl-mənz-\\ : a lien on property for materials supplied

me•chan•ic's lien : a lien against a building and its site to assure priority of payment for labor or services (as construction and sometimes design) or material

retaining lien : a lien that attaches to

the papers or property of a client which have come into his or her attorney's possession in the course of employment and that secures payment of the attorney's fees — called also *general lien*
senior lien : a lien that is higher in priority relative to other liens
special lien 1 : an equitable lien enforceable to compel performance of an obligation (as under a divorce settlement) **2** : CHARGING LIEN in this entry
specific lien : a lien upon specific property as security for the payment of a debt or the satisfaction of some other obligation arising out of a transaction or agreement involving that property — compare GENERAL LIEN in this entry
statutory lien : a lien imposed by statute
tax lien : a statutory lien on property for taxes due giving the taxing authority a security interest in the property — compare *tax sale* at SALE
vendor's lien : a lien on esp. real property securing payment in full of the purchase price by the buyer
voluntary lien : a lien created (as by contract) with the consent of the debtor
lien•able \'lē-nə-bəl\ *adj* : capable of being subjected to or made the subject of a lien
lien creditor — see CREDITOR
lien•ee \ˌlē-'nē\ *n* : one whose property is subject to a lien
lien•hold•er \'lēn-ˌhōl-dər\ *n* : LIENOR
lien•or \'lē-nər, ˌlē-'nȯr\ *n* : one holding a lien against the property of another
life annuity — see ANNUITY
life estate — see ESTATE 1
life expectancy *n* : the average life span of an individual
life in be•ing : the life of a particular person (as a lineal descendant) in existence at the time of the creation of a deed or will or at the time of the testator's death ⟨the interest must vest by the end of *lives in being* plus 21 years⟩ — see also RULE AGAINST PERPETUITIES
life income option — see OPTION 4

life income–period certain annuity — see ANNUITY
life insurance *n* : insurance providing for the payment of money to a designated beneficiary upon the death of the insured — see also ENDOWMENT INSURANCE
ordinary life insurance : WHOLE LIFE INSURANCE in this entry
straight life insurance : WHOLE LIFE INSURANCE in this entry
term life insurance : life insurance that provides coverage for a set term and does not accumulate cash surrender value
universal life insurance : life insurance characterized by flexible premiums, benefits, and payment schedules, by the indexing of cash value to money market interest rates, and by the periodic reporting of current value and company costs charged to the account
universal variable life insurance : VARIABLE UNIVERSAL LIFE INSURANCE in this entry
variable life insurance : life insurance in which all or part of the cash value of the policy is located in a tax-deferred investment portfolio with risk assumed by the insured for investment losses — compare *variable annuity* at ANNUITY
variable universal life insurance : universal life insurance that includes the investment component of variable life insurance — called also *universal variable life insurance*
whole life insurance : life insurance that provides coverage over the life of the insured and that can be sold for surrender value or used as the basis of low-interest loans — called also *ordinary life insurance, straight life insurance*
life interest — see INTEREST 1
life sentence — see SENTENCE
life tenancy — see TENANCY
life tenant *n* : a tenant having possession

\ə\abut \ᵊ\kitten \ər\further \a\ash \ā\ace \ä\cot, cart \au̇\out \ch\chin \e\bet \ē\easy \g\go \i\hit \ī\ice \j\job \ŋ\sing \ō\go \ȯ\law \ȯi\boy \th\thin \t̲h̲\the \ü\loot \u̇\foot \y\yet \zh\vision *see also* Pronunciation Symbols page

of property for the duration of his or her life : one having a life estate in property

LIFO *abbr* last in, first out

lift *vt* : to put an end to : make no longer effective ⟨~ the stay⟩

like–kind exchange *n* : an exchange of business or investment property of the same kind, class, or character and excluding securities that is made pursuant to section 1031 of the Internal Revenue Code and is thus exempt from taxation

lim·i·ta·tion *n* **1 a** : RESTRICTION ⟨a ~ on the rights of ownership⟩ **b** : a statement or stipulation in a deed or will placing limits on the disposition of an estate or interest esp. in regard to duration or heirs — see also WORD OF LIMITATION **2** : a certain period limited by statute after which actions or prosecutions cannot be brought in the courts — see also STATUTE OF LIMITATIONS

limited divorce — see DIVORCE

lim·it·ed forum *n* : LIMITED PUBLIC FORUM

limited interdict *n, in the civil law of Louisiana* : a person subject to limited interdiction

limited interdiction *n, in the civil law of Louisiana* : partial removal of one's rights ⟨under *limited interdiction* he could care for his person but not his estate⟩ — compare INTERDICTION

limited jurisdiction — see JURISDICTION

limited liability company — see COMPANY

limited liability partnership — see PARTNERSHIP

limited open forum *n* : LIMITED PUBLIC FORUM

limited partner — see PARTNER

limited partnership — see PARTNERSHIP

limited partnership roll·up transaction \-'rōl-,əp-\ *n* : the combining or reorganizing of one or more limited partnerships into an entity (as a master limited partnership or real estate investment trust) that can be publicly traded; *specif* : such a transaction in which some or all of the investors suffer adverse changes including the receipt of new securities without

an option to receive or retain securities having the same terms as those originally purchased — called also *partnership rollup, rollup*

limited power of appointment — see POWER OF APPOINTMENT

limited publication *n* : the communication of a work (as a text) to a selected group with the express or implied exclusion of the public and with common-law copyright thus preserved — compare GENERAL PUBLICATION

limited public figure *n* : LIMITED PURPOSE PUBLIC FIGURE

limited public forum *n* : a public forum created by the government voluntarily for expressive activity that may be restricted as to subject matter or class of speaker — called also *limited forum, limited open forum;* compare OPEN FORUM, PUBLIC FORUM ◇ The restriction of a limited public forum must be able to withstand strict judicial scrutiny of its effect on First Amendment rights.

limited purpose public figure *n* : a person who voluntarily and prominently participates in a public controversy for the purpose of influencing its outcome and who is thus required as a public figure to prove actual malice in a defamation suit — called also *limited public figure;* compare PUBLIC FIGURE

lin·eal \'li-nē-əl\ *adj* : consisting of or being in a direct male or female line of ancestry ⟨a ~ descendant⟩ — compare COLLATERAL 2

line–item veto *n* : an executive veto of a specific item in an appropriations bill

line of credit : an agreement specifying the maximum amount of credit allowed a borrower

line·up *n* : a line of persons assembled by police esp. for possible identification of a suspect by a witness to a crime — compare SHOWUP

liq·uid *adj* **1 a** : consisting of cash or capable of ready conversion into cash ⟨~ assets⟩ **b** : capable of covering current liabilities out of current assets esp. in a rapid manner ⟨a ~ insurer⟩ **2** : of

or relating to a security or commodity with enough shares or units outstanding to hinder significant price variation from large transactions
liq·ui·date \'li-kwə-ˌdāt\ *vb* **-dat·ed; -dat·ing** *vt* **1 :** to determine by agreement or litigation the precise amount of; *also* **:** to settle (a debt) by payment or other adjustment **2 a :** to determine the liabilities and apportion the assets of esp. in bankruptcy or dissolution ⟨~ a corporation⟩ — compare BANKRUPTCY **b :** to convert (as assets) into cash ⟨~ an estate⟩ ~ *vi* **:** to liquidate something (as a corporation) — **liq·ui·da·tion** \ˌli-kwə-'dā-shən\ *n*
liq·ui·dat·ed *adj* **1 :** settled or determined by liquidating — see also *liquidated damages* at DAMAGE 2 **2 :** capable of being readily fixed, calculated, or ascertained as a sum esp. without dispute or reliance on opinion or discretion
liquidated damages — see DAMAGE 2
liq·ui·dat·ing *adj* **:** produced or occurring as a result of liquidation ⟨a ~ dividend⟩ ⟨a ~ distribution⟩
liq·ui·da·tor \'li-kwə-ˌdā-tər\ *n* **:** one that liquidates; *esp* **:** an individual appointed by law to liquidate assets — compare RECEIVER
liq·uid·i·ty \li-'kwi-də-tē\ *n* **:** the quality or state of being liquid
lis pen·dens \'lis-'pen-ˌdenz\ *n* [Latin] **1 :** a pending suit **2 :** a written notice of a pending suit involving property usu. filed in the appropriate office (as a registry of deeds) — called also *notice of pendency* **3 a :** the jurisdiction and control of the court over property involved in a pending suit **b :** a doctrine under which one purchasing an interest in property involved in a pending suit does so subject to the adjudication of the rights of the parties to the suit
list *n* **:** CALENDAR
list·ing *n* **1 :** an arrangement, agreement, or contract for the marketing of real property through one or more real estate agents usu. for a specific period — called also *listing agreement*
  exclusive agency listing **:** a listing under which only one agent may sell the prop-

erty but without the right to a commission if the owner sells it directly ◊ An agent is usu. still entitled to a commission if the owner sells directly to a buyer who was introduced into the process by the agent, even if the sale occurs after the agreement expires.
  exclusive right to sell listing **:** a listing under which only one agent may sell the property and is entitled to a commission if the owner sells it directly to any party
  multiple listing **:** an agreement or arrangement under which real property is marketed through a service or association composed of several agents with a commission from the sale of a property shared between the selling agent and the agent that initiates the listing of it
  net listing **:** a listing under which the agent that sells a property retains as compensation the amount of the selling price that exceeds a specified sum
  open listing **:** a listing that does not preclude the use of multiple agents or a direct sale by the owner with no commission paid to an agent — called also *nonexclusive listing*
2 a : a record of a property or properties available through a real estate agent **b :** property listed in such a record
listing agreement *n* **:** LISTING 1
lit·i·gant \'li-ti-gənt\ *n* **:** an active party to litigation — **litigant** *adj*
lit·i·gate \'li-tə-ˌgāt\ *vb* **-gat·ed; -gat·ing** [Latin *litigatus*, past participle of *litigare*, from *lit-, lis* lawsuit + *agere* to drive] *vi* **:** to seek resolution of a legal contest by judicial process ⟨chose to ~ rather than settle⟩ ~ *vt* **:** to make the subject of a suit ⟨~ a claim⟩; *broadly* **:** to contest or resolve in court ⟨~ an insanity defense⟩ — **lit·i·ga·ble** \'li-tə-gə-bəl\ *adj* — **lit·i·ga·tion** \ˌli-tə-'gā-shən\ *n* — **lit·i·ga·tion·al** \-shənəl\ *adj* — **lit·i·ga·to·ry** \'li-tə-gə-ˌtōr-ē\ *adj*

\ə\abut \ᵊ\kitten \ər\further \a\ash \ā\ace \ä\cot, cart \au\out \ch\chin \e\bet \ē\easy \g\go \i\hit \ī\ice \j\job \ŋ\sing \ō\go \o\law \oi\boy \th\thin \th\the \ü\loot \u̇\foot \y\yet \zh\vision *see also* Pronunciation Symbols page

lit·i·ga·tor \'li-tə-,gā-tər\ *n* : one that litigates; *esp* : a lawyer skilled at litigation

li·ti·gious \li-'ti-jəs\ *adj* **1** : prone to engage in lawsuits or legal maneuvers esp. to an excessive degree ⟨a stubbornly ~ defendant⟩ **2** : subject to litigation ⟨acquired only a possible ~ claim —*Wells v. Joseph*, 95 So. 2d 843 (1957)⟩ **3** : of, relating to, or marked by litigation — **li·ti·gious·ly** *adv* — **li·ti·gious·ness** *n*

litigious right *n*, *in the civil law of Louisiana* : a right that can only be exercised after being litigated

lit·to·ral \'li-tə-rəl; ,li-tə-'ral, -'räl\ *adj* : of, relating to, or being property abutting an ocean, sea, lake, or pond — compare RIPARIAN

littoral right *n* : the right of one owning littoral land to have access to and use of the shore and water

liv·ery of seisin \'li-və-rē-\ [*livery* delivery, handing over, from Anglo-French *liveree*, from Old French *livré*, from *livrer* to hand over, from Latin *liberare* to free] : an ancient ceremony for conveyance of land by the symbolic transfer of a relevant item (as a key, twig, or turf) or by symbolic entry of the grantee — called also *investiture;* see also FEOFFMENT

living trust — see TRUST

liv·ing will *n* : a document in which the signer indicates preferences or directions for the administration and esp. the withdrawal or withholding of life-sustaining medical treatment in the event of terminal illness or permanent unconsciousness — see also ADVANCE DIRECTIVE; compare *durable power of attorney* at POWER OF ATTORNEY

LL.B. *abbr* bachelor of laws

LL.M. *abbr* [New Latin *legum magister*] master of laws

L.L.P. *abbr* limited liability partnership

load *n* : an amount added (as to the price of a security or the net premium in insurance) to represent selling expense and profit to the distributor — compare NO-LOAD

loan *n* **1 a** : money lent at interest **b** : something lent usu. for the borrower's temporary use **2** : a transfer or delivery of money from one party to another with the express or implied agreement that the sum will be repaid regardless of contingency and usu. with interest; *broadly* : the furnishing of something to another party for temporary use with the agreement that it or its equivalent will be returned ⟨the leasing of the vehicle was termed a ~ subject to usury statutes⟩

bridge loan : a short-term loan used as a means of financing a purchase or enterprise prior to obtaining other funds ⟨used a *bridge loan* to purchase a new home prior to the sale of their previous one⟩

con·ven·tion·al loan \kən-'ven-chə-nəl-\ : a loan for the purchase of real property that is secured by a first mortgage on the property rather than by any federal agency

demand loan : a loan that is subject to repayment upon demand of the lender

home equity loan : a loan or line of credit secured by the equity in one's home — called also *equity loan, home equity line, home equity line of credit;* see also *qualified residence interest* at INTEREST 5

loan for con·sump·tion \-kən-'sümp-shən\ : a loan in which the borrower is obligated to return property of the same kind as that borrowed and consumed — used chiefly in the civil law of Louisiana; compare BAILMENT, DEPOSIT, LOAN FOR USE in this entry

loan for use : a loan in which one party lends personal property to another with the understanding that the borrower will return the same property at a future time without compensation for its use : COMMODATUM — used chiefly in the civil law of Louisiana; compare BAILMENT, DEPOSIT, LOAN FOR CONSUMPTION in this entry

participation loan : a single loan in which two or more lenders participate

term loan : a loan extended to a business with provisions for repayment according to a schedule of amortization and usu. for a period of one to five years and sometimes fifteen years

loaned servant *n* **1** : an employee of one employer who is temporarily under the control of another — called also *loaned employee* **2** : a doctrine under which a loaned servant is considered an employee of the borrowing employer who is thus liable for negligence or workers' compensation

loan for consumption — see LOAN

loan for use — see LOAN

¹lob·by *n, pl* **lobbies** : a group of persons engaged in lobbying esp. as representatives of a particular interest group

²lobby *vb* **lob·bied; lob·by·ing** *vi* : to conduct activities aimed at influencing public officials and esp. members of a legislative body on legislation ~ *vt* : to attempt to influence or sway (as a public official) toward a desired action — **lob·by·er** *n* — **lob·by·ist** *n*

lo·cal *n* : LOCAL UNION

local act *n* : LOCAL LAW 1a

local action *n* : an action (as for trespassing) that must be brought in the venue that has jurisdiction over the situs or is otherwise designated by law — compare TRANSITORY ACTION

local law *n* **1 a** : a law limited in application to a particular district within a territory — called also *local act;* compare GENERAL LAW, PUBLIC LAW **b** : SPECIAL LAW 2 **2** : the laws and legal principles and rules of a state other than those concerned with conflicts of law

local union *n* : a local branch of a union (as a national or international union) made up of many branches — called also *local*

lock·down \'läk-ˌdaùn\ *n* : the confinement of prisoners to their cells for a temporary period as a security measure

lock·out \'läk-ˌaùt\ *n* : the withholding of employment by an employer in order to gain concessions from or resist demands of employees

lock·up *n* **1** : a cell or group of cells (as in a courthouse) or jail where persons are held prior to a court hearing — compare HOUSE OF CORRECTION, HOUSE OF DE-

TENTION, JAIL, PENITENTIARY, PRISON **2** : the tactic of arranging with a friendly party an option to buy a valuable portion of one's corporate assets in order to discourage a takeover by another party

lo·cus \'lō-kəs\ *n* : the place connected with a particular event having legal significance

locus poe·ni·ten·ti·ae \-ˌpe-nə-'ten-shē-ˌē, -ˌī\ *n* [Late Latin, literally, place of repentance] : an opportunity to withdraw from a contract or obligation before it is completed or to decide not to commit an intended crime

lode·star \'lōd-ˌstär\ *n* [perhaps from the notion of the lodestar as a guiding light or principle] : the amount obtained by multiplying the reasonable amount of hours spent by an attorney working on a case by the reasonable hourly billing rate for purposes of calculating an award of attorney's fees

lodg·er \'lä-jər\ *n* : a person who occupies a rented room in another's house; *specif* : a person who by agreement with the owner of a house acquires no property, interest, or possession therein but only the right to occupy a designated room or area that remains in the owner's legal possession

log *n* : REGISTER 1

log·roll·ing \'lòg-ˌrō-liŋ, 'läg-\ *n* [from the former American custom of neighbors assisting one another in rolling logs into a pile for burning] : the practice of including in a legislative bill unrelated provisions to attract a wider base of support and insure passage of the bill as a whole

loi·ter \'lòi-tər\ *vi* : to remain in or hang around an area for no obvious purpose; *specif* : to linger aimlessly for the purpose of committing a crime ⟨a statute forbidding any person from ~*ing* on school grounds⟩

\ə\abut \ᵊ\kitten \ər\further \a\ash \ā\ace \ä\cot, cart \aù\out \ch\chin \e\bet \ē\easy \g\go \i\hit \ī\ice \j\job \ŋ\sing \ō\go \ò\law \òi\boy \th\thin \th\the \ü\loot \ù\foot \y\yet \zh\vision *see also* Pronunciation Symbols page

long *adj* : owning or accumulating securities, goods, or commodities esp. in anticipation of a rise in prices ⟨a buyer ~ on wheat⟩ — compare SHORT

long–arm *adj* : of, relating to, or arising from a long-arm statute ⟨~ jurisdiction⟩ ⟨a ~ provision⟩

long–arm statute *n* : a state statute allowing for the assertion of personal jurisdiction over a nonresident defendant who has some connection (as ownership or use of property, transaction of business, or commission of a tort) with the state — called also *single-act statute;* see also DOING BUSINESS STATUTE, MINIMUM CONTACTS

long–term capital gain — see GAIN

loot *vt* **1** : to rob esp. during or following a catastrophe (as war, riot, or natural disaster) **2** : to rob esp. on a large scale and usu. by violence or corruption ~ *vi* : to engage in robbing esp. after a catastrophe — **loot•er** *n*

Lord Camp•bell's Act \'lòrd-'kam-bəlz-, -'ka-məlz-\ *n* [after Baron John Campbell (1779–1861), Scottish-born British jurist who played an instrumental role in the passage of the 1846 Fatal Accidents Act, which formed the basis for such laws] : a statute setting out the remedy available for wrongful death

Lord Chancellor *n* : an official in the British judicial system whose duties include heading the Chancery Division and presiding over the Supreme Court of Judicature and the House of Lords in its judicial capacity

Lords *n pl* : HOUSE OF LORDS

loss *n* **1** : physical, emotional, or esp. economic harm or damage sustained: as **a** : decrease in value, capital, or amount — compare GAIN **b** : an amount by which the cost of something (as goods or services) exceeds the selling price — compare PROFIT **c** : something unintentionally destroyed or placed beyond recovery **d** : the amount of an insured's financial detriment due to the occurrence of a stipulated event (as death, injury, destruction, or damage) in such a manner as to create liability in the insurer under the terms of the policy ◇ As a general rule, economic losses are deductible from adjusted gross income under section 165 of the Internal Revenue Code. There are, however, numerous exceptions and limitations.

  actual loss : the identifiable and calculable monetary detriment that is suffered or will be suffered as a result of an act or event

  actual total loss : a loss in marine insurance in which the property (as a vessel or cargo) cannot be repaired or recovered — compare CONSTRUCTIVE TOTAL LOSS in this entry

  capital loss : the amount by which the book value of a capital asset exceeds the amount realized from the sale or exchange of the asset

  casualty loss : loss of property as a result of a fire, storm, shipwreck, or other catastrophic event

  consequential loss : a loss that arises as an indirect result of an act or event — called also *indirect loss;* compare DIRECT LOSS in this entry

  constructive total loss : a loss in marine insurance in which the cost of repairing or recovering a ship or its cargo would be more than the ship or cargo is worth — compare ACTUAL TOTAL LOSS in this entry

  direct loss : a loss arising directly from an act or event — compare CONSEQUENTIAL LOSS in this entry

  in•di•rect loss : CONSEQUENTIAL LOSS in this entry

  net operating loss : the amount by which the expenses of operating a business exceed the income derived from it — see also CARRYBACK, CARRYOVER

  ordinary loss : a loss from the sale or exchange of any asset that is not a capital asset

  partial loss : a loss arising from damage to property that does not render it a total loss

  total loss : a loss arising from damage to property that is so substantial as to make the property valueless to an insured

2 : the act or fact of suffering physical, emotional, or esp. economic harm or detriment

loss lead·er *n* : something (as merchandise) sold at a loss in order to draw customers — **loss–leader** *adj*

loss of bargain : BENEFIT OF THE BARGAIN

loss ra·tio \-'rā-ˌshō, -'rā-shē-ˌō\ *n* : the ratio between insurance losses incurred and premiums earned during a given period

loss reserve — see RESERVE

lost *adj* **1** : not made use of, won, or claimed ⟨~ opportunity costs⟩ **2** : unintentionally gone out of or missing from one's possession or control **3** : ruined or destroyed physically; *also* : in an unknown physical condition or location ⟨a ~ ship⟩

lost property — see PROPERTY

lost vol·ume seller *n* : a seller who sells to a buyer after a previous buyer has breached a contract for sale but who would have been able to make a sale to the second buyer even if the first buyer had not breached — called also *lost volume dealer*

lot *n* **1** : a portion of land; *specif* : a measured parcel of contiguous land having fixed boundaries and recorded (as on a plat) with the appropriate authority or office (as a registry of deeds) **2** : a single article, a number of units of an article, or a parcel of articles offered as one item (as in an auction sale); *specif* : a parcel or single article under the Uniform Commercial Code which is the subject matter of a separate sale, lease, or delivery whether or not it is sufficient to perform the contract — see also ODD LOT, ROUND LOT

low·er court *n* : a court whose decisions are subject to review or to appeal to a higher court

L. Rev. *abbr* Law Review ⟨Harv. *L. Rev.*⟩

L.S. *abbr* [Latin *locus sigilli*] place of the seal — used on sealed documents

LSAT \ˌel-ˌes-ˌā-'tē, 'el-ˌsat\ *abbr* Law School Admission Test

lu·cra·tive \'lü-krə-tiv\ *adj* **1** : producing wealth or profit **2** : acquired, received, or had without burdensome conditions or giving of consideration — **lu·cra·tive·ly** *adv* — **lu·cra·tive·ness** *n*

lucrative title — see TITLE

lu·cri cau·sa \'lü-ˌkrī-'kȯ-zə, 'lü-krē-'kaủ-sä\ *n* [New Latin, literally, for the sake of gain] : intent to obtain a gain ⟨because *lucri causa* is required for larceny — W. R. LaFave and A. W. Scott, Jr.⟩

lump sum alimony — see ALIMONY

lu·na·cy \'lü-nə-sē\ *n* : INSANITY

lu·na·tic \'lü-nə-tik\ *n* : an insane person — used esp. formerly — **lunatic** *adj*

lux·u·ry tax *n* : an excise levied on the purchase of items that are not essential for support or maintenance

lying *pres part of* LIE

ly·ing in wait *adj* : holding oneself in a concealed position to watch and wait for a victim for the purpose of making an unexpected attack and murdering or inflicting bodily injury on the victim

lynch \'linch\ *vt* : to put to death (as by hanging) by mob action without legal sanction — **lynch·er** *n*

lynch·ing *n* **1** : the crime of lynching a person **2** : LYNCH LAW

lynch law *n* [after William Lynch (1742–1820), American vigilante] : the punishment of presumed crimes usu. by death without due process of law

\ə\abut \ᵊ\kitten \ər\further \a\ash \ā\ace
\ä\cot, cart \aủ\out \ch\chin \e\bet \ē\easy
\g\go \i\hit \ī\ice \j\job \ŋ\sing \ō\go \ȯ\law
\ȯi\boy \th\thin \t͟h\the \ü\loot \ủ\foot \y\yet
\zh\vision *see also* Pronunciation Symbols page

M

mag·is·trate \'ma-jə-ˌstrāt, -strət\ *n* [Latin *magistratus* magistracy, magistrate, from *magistr-, magister* master, political superior] **1 :** a civil or judicial official vested with limited judicial powers ⟨a family support ∼⟩ ⟨a traffic ∼⟩ **2 a :** a municipal, state, or federal judicial officer commonly authorized to issue warrants, hear minor cases, and conduct preliminary or pretrial hearings — called also *magistrate judge* **b :** an official (as a judge) authorized to perform the role or function of a magistrate ⟨∼ means an officer having power to issue a warrant for the arrest of a person charged with a public offense —*Arizona Revised Statutes*⟩

magistrate court *n* **:** a court presided over by a magistrate that has minor civil and criminal jurisdiction — called also *magistrate's court*

magistrate judge *n* **:** MAGISTRATE 2a

Mag·na Car·ta *or* **Mag·na Char·ta** \'mag-nə-'kär-tə\ *n* [Medieval Latin, literally, great charter] **:** a charter of liberties signed under duress by King John of England in 1215 that influenced the development of several modern legal and constitutional principles (as due process)

mail·box rule *n* **:** a rule treating the sending of something as constituting a filing or as a basis for assuming receipt; *specif* **:** a rule in contract law: a notice of acceptance of an offer sent to the offeror by reasonable means or as agreed by the parties is effective and is not affected by any notice of revocation of the offer subsequently received

mail fraud — see FRAUD

maim \'mām\ *vt* **:** to mutilate, disfigure, or wound seriously — compare MAYHEM

Main Pot *n* **:** a step in calculating tax liability under Internal Revenue Code section 1231 in which all qualified transactions are netted to determine if the result is a loss or gain — called also *Big Pot, Hodge Podge, hotchpot;* compare CASUALTY POT ◊ The transactions netted in the Main Pot are as follows: casualties in the Casualty Pot if they have netted a gain; sales, exchanges, or condemnations of depreciable or real property used in a business for more than one year; and condemnations of capital assets held for more than one year in connection with a trade or business or transaction entered into for profit. If the net result is a gain, then the transactions are treated as long-term capital gains and losses.

main pur·pose rule *n* **:** a doctrine in contract law: a promise to pay the debt of another need not be in writing to be enforceable if the promisor was motivated by a desire for advantage or benefit — called also *leading object rule;* compare STATUTE OF FRAUDS 1

main·te·nance *n* **1 a :** the act of providing basic and necessary support **b :** the state of having such support **2 :** a financial means of providing necessary assistance: as **a :** ALIMONY **b :** SUPPORT **3 :** the necessities of life provided for by payment of maintenance **4 :** the upkeep of property or equipment **5 :** unsought and unnecessary meddling in a lawsuit by assisting either party with means to carry it on — compare CHAMPERTY

ma·jor *n* **:** a person who has attained majority — compare MINOR

major dispute *n* **:** a labor dispute that pursuant to the Railway Labor Act concerns the making or modification rather than the interpretation of a collective bargaining agreement — called also *new contract dispute;* compare MINOR DISPUTE ◊ Under the Railway Labor Act, which is also referred to in airline cases, a major dispute must go to mediation or arbitration if necessary.

major federal action *n* : a proposed federal undertaking that pursuant to the National Environmental Policy Act must be the subject of an environmental impact statement if it would significantly affect the environment

ma·jor·i·tar·i·an \mə-ˌjȯr-i-'tar-ē-ən, -ˌjär-\ *adj* : characterized by the rule or decisions of a majority ⟨~ politics⟩

ma·jor·i·ty \mə-'jȯr-ə-tē\ *n, pl* **-ties** **1 a** : LEGAL AGE **b** : the status of one who has reached legal age **2 a** : a number or quantity greater than half of a total — compare PLURALITY **b** : the excess of a majority over the remainder of the total **3 a** : the group or political party whose votes predominate **b** : the judges voting in a particular case who together determine the prevailing decision — see also *majority opinion* at OPINION; compare DISSENT 3 — **majority** *adj*

majority lead·er *n* : a leader of the majority party in a legislative body

majority opinion — see OPINION

majority shareholder *n* : a shareholder who alone or in combination with others controls a majority of the outstanding shares in a corporation

mak·er *n* : one (as an issuer) that undertakes to pay a negotiable instrument and esp. a note ⟨sign a note as ~ rather than indorser⟩

mala in se *pl of* MALUM IN SE

mal·fea·sance \ˌmal-'fēz-ᵊns\ *n* [*mal-* bad + obsolete English *feasance* doing, execution, from Old French *faisance*, from *fais-*, stem of *faire* to make, do, from Latin *facere*] : the commission (as by a public official) of a wrongful or unlawful act involving or affecting the performance of one's duties — compare MISFEASANCE, NONFEASANCE

mal·ice \'ma-ləs\ *n* **1 a** : the intention or desire to cause harm (as death, bodily injury, or property damage) to another through an unlawful or wrongful act without justification or excuse **b** : wanton disregard for the rights of others or for

the value of human life **c** : an improper or evil motive or purpose ⟨if ~ cannot be proved or a benign purpose can be imagined —David Kairys⟩ **d** : ACTUAL MALICE 2 in this entry

actual malice **1** : malice proved by evidence to exist or have existed in one that inflicts unjustified harm on another: as **a** : an intent to injure or kill **b** : MALICE 2 — called also *express malice, malice in fact* **2 a** : the knowledge that defamatory statements esp. regarding a public figure are false **b** : RECKLESS DISREGARD OF THE TRUTH — see also PUBLIC FIGURE, *New York Times Co. v. Sullivan* in the IMPORTANT CASES section

implied malice : malice inferred from the nature or consequences of a harmful act done without justification or excuse; *also* : malice inferred from subjective awareness of duty or of the likely results of one's act — called also *legal malice, malice in law*

malice aforethought : actual or implied malice existing in or attributed to the intention of one that injures or esp. kills without justification or excuse and usu. requiring some degree of deliberation or premeditation or wanton disregard for life ⟨murder is the unlawful killing of a human being, or a fetus, with *malice aforethought —California Penal Code*⟩

malice in fact : ACTUAL MALICE 1 in this entry

malice in law : IMPLIED MALICE in this entry

2 : feelings of ill will, spite, or revenge ◊ Such feelings are usu. not an important component of malice in legal consideration unless punitive damages or actual malice is an issue.

malice aforethought — see MALICE

malice in fact — see MALICE

malice in law — see MALICE

ma·li·cious \mə-'li-shəs\ *adj* : given to,

\ə\abut	\ᵊ\kitten	\ər\further	\a\ash	\ā\ace
\ä\cot, cart	\aů\out	\ch\chin	\e\bet	\ē\easy
\g\go	\i\hit	\ī\ice	\j\job	\ŋ\sing	\ō\go	\ȯ\law
\ȯi\boy	\th\thin	\t̲h̲\the	\ü\loot	\ů\foot	\y\yet
\zh\vision	*see also* Pronunciation Symbols page

marked by, or arising from malice ⟨~ destruction of property⟩ — **ma·li·cious·ly** *adv* — **ma·li·cious·ness** *n*

malicious mis·chief *n* : the act or offense of intentionally damaging or destroying another's property (as from feelings of ill will) — compare VANDALISM

malicious prosecution *n* : the tort of initiating a criminal prosecution or civil suit against another party with malice and without probable cause; *also* : an action for damages based on this tort brought after termination of the proceedings in favor of the party seeking damages — called also *malicious use of process;* compare ABUSE OF PROCESS

mal·prac·tice \ˌmal-ˈprak-təs\ *n* : negligence, misconduct, lack of ordinary skill, or a breach of duty in the performance of a professional service (as in medicine) resulting in injury or loss

mal·um in se \ˈma-ləm-in-ˈsē, ˈmä-lùm-in-ˈsä\ *n, pl* **mala in se** \ˈma-lə-, ˈmä-\ [New Latin, offense in itself] : an offense that is evil or wrong from its own nature irrespective of statute — often used with a preceding noun (as *crime* or *act*) ⟨held that burglary was a crime *malum in se* — *State v. Stiffler*, 788 P.2d 2205 (1990)⟩; compare MALUM PROHIBITUM

malum pro·hib·i·tum \-prō-ˈhi-bə-təm\ *n, pl* **mala pro·hib·i·ta** \-ˈhi-bə-tə\ [New Latin, prohibited offense] : an offense prohibited by statute but not inherently evil or wrong ⟨is *malum prohibitum* and, therefore, does not demand mens rea — *Commonwealth v. Guthrie*, 616 A.2d 1019 (1992)⟩ — often used with a preceding noun (as *crime* or *act*) ⟨acts *malum prohibitum*⟩ — compare MALUM IN SE

managing agent — see AGENT

man·da·mus \man-ˈdā-məs\ *n* [Latin, we enjoin, from *mandare* to enjoin] : an extraordinary writ issued by a court of competent jurisdiction to an inferior tribunal, a public official, an administrative agency, a corporation, or any person compelling the performance of an act usu. only when there is a duty under the law to perform the act, the plaintiff has a clear right to such performance, and there is no other adequate remedy available; *also* : an action in the nature of a writ of mandamus in jurisdictions where the writ is abolished — compare *cease-and-desist order* at ORDER, INJUNCTION, STAY ◇ Mandamus is an extraordinary remedy and is issued usu. only to command the performance of a ministerial act. It cannot be used to substitute the court's judgment for the defendant's in the performance of a discretionary act. — **mandamus** *vb*

man·da·tary \ˈman-də-ˌter-ē\ *n, pl* **-tar·ies** : a person to whom the power to transact business for another under a mandate is given

¹man·date \ˈman-ˌdāt\ *n* [Latin *mandatum*, from neuter of *mandatus*, past participle of *mandare* to entrust, enjoin, probably irregularly from *manus* hand + *-dere* to put] **1 a** : a formal communication from a reviewing court notifying the court below of its judgment and directing the lower court to act accordingly **b** : MANDAMUS **2** *in the civil law of Louisiana* : an act by which a person gives another person the power to transact for him or her one or several affairs **3 a** : an authoritative command : a clear authorization or direction ⟨the ~ of the full faith and credit clause —*National Law Journal*⟩ **b** : the authorization to act given by a constituency to its elected representative

²mandate *vt* **man·dat·ed; man·dat·ing** : to make mandatory or required ⟨the Pennsylvania Constitution ~*s* a criminal defendant's right to confrontation —*National Law Journal*⟩

mandated reporter *n* : an individual who holds a professional position (as of social worker, physician, teacher, or counselor) that requires him or her to report to the appropriate state agency cases of child abuse that he or she has reasonable cause to suspect

man·da·to·ry \ˈman-də-ˌtȯr-ē\ *adj* : containing or constituting a command : being obligatory — **man·da·to·ri·ly** \-ˌtȯr-i-lē\ *adv*

mandatory injunction — see INJUNCTION

mandatory instruction *n* : an instruction that sets out a factual situation which if found by the jury to be supported by the evidence requires a certain verdict

mandatory presumption — see PRESUMPTION

mandatory sentence — see SENTENCE

¹man·i·fest \'ma-nə-ˌfest\ *adj* **1** : capable of being readily perceived by the senses and esp. by sight ⟨a ~ injury⟩ **2** : capable of being easily understood or recognized : clearly evident, obvious, and indisputable ⟨vacating an arbitrator's award because of the arbitrator's ~ disregard of the law⟩ — **man·i·fest·ly** *adv*

²manifest *vt* : to make evident or certain by showing or displaying ⟨~ing the intent to make a gift⟩ — **man·i·fes·ta·tion** \ˌma-nə-fə-'stā-shən, -ˌfe-'stā-\ *n*

³manifest *n* : a list of passengers or an invoice of cargo for a vehicle (as a ship or plane)

manifest error — see ERROR

manifest injustice *n* : an outcome in a case that is plainly and obviously unjust ⟨acceptance of an involuntary guilty plea constitutes *manifest injustice*⟩

manifest necessity *n* : a circumstance (as an incurable pleading defect, the unavailability of an essential witness, juror misconduct, or illness of counsel) which is of such an overwhelming and unforeseeable nature that the conduct of trial or reaching of a fair result is impossible and which necessitates the declaration of a mistrial ◊ If there is a manifest necessity for the declaration of a mistrial, the defendant may be retried without violation of the prohibition on double jeopardy.

manifest weight of the evidence : a deferential standard of review under which reversal of a decision or verdict requires showing that it is obviously erroneous and unsupported by the evidence and that an opposite conclusion is clearly evident

ma·nip·u·late \mə-'ni-pyə-ˌlāt\ *vt* **-lat·ed;** **-lat·ing** : to change by artful or unfair means so as to serve one's purpose; *specif* : to affect (the price of securities) artifi-

cially in order to deceive or mislead investors — **ma·nip·u·la·ble** \mə-'ni-pyə-lə-bəl\ *adj* — **ma·nip·u·la·tion** \mə-ˌni-pyə-'lā-shən\ *n* — **ma·nip·u·la·tive** \mə-'ni-pyə-ˌlā-tiv, -lə-tiv\ *adj* — **ma·nip·u·la·tive·ly** *adv* — **ma·nip·u·la·tive·ness** *n* — **ma·nip·u·la·tor** \mə-'ni-pyə-ˌlā-tər\ *n* — **ma·nip·u·la·to·ry** \mə-'ni-pyə-lə-ˌtȯr-ē\ *adj*

Mans·field rule \'manz-ˌfēld-\ *n, often cap R* [after William Murray, first Earl of Mansfield (1705–1793), British jurist who set forth the rule] : a rule that a juror's affidavit or testimony as to juror misconduct during deliberations may not be used to impeach the verdict

man·sion house *n* : a dwelling house of any size and any buildings (as barns or stables) within the curtilage

man·slaugh·ter \'man-ˌslȯ-tər\ *n* : the unlawful killing of a human being without malice — compare HOMICIDE, MURDER

involuntary manslaughter : manslaughter resulting from the failure to perform a legal duty expressly required to safeguard human life, from the commission of an unlawful act not amounting to a felony, or from the commission of a lawful act involving a risk of injury or death that is done in an unlawful, reckless, or grossly negligent manner — see also *reckless homicide* at HOMICIDE ◊ The exact formulation of the elements of involuntary manslaughter vary from state to state esp. with regard to the level of negligence required. In states that grade manslaughter by degrees, involuntary manslaughter is usu. graded as a second- or third-degree offense.

misdemeanor–manslaughter : involuntary manslaughter occurring during the commission of a misdemeanor — compare *felony murder* at MURDER

voluntary manslaughter : manslaugh-

\ə\abut \ᵊ\kitten \ər\further \a\ash \ā\ace
\ä\cot, cart \au̇\out \ch\chin \e\bet \ē\easy
\g\go \i\hit \ī\ice \j\job \ŋ\sing \ō\go \ȯ\law
\ȯi\boy \th\thin \t͟h\the \ü\loot \u̇\foot \y\yet
\zh\vision *see also* Pronunciation Symbols page

ter resulting from an intentional act done without malice or premeditation and while in the heat of passion or on sudden provocation ◊ In states that grade manslaughter by degrees, voluntary manslaughter is usu. a first-degree offense.

man·u·al \'man-yə-wəl\ *adj* : involving or as if involving use of the hands; *specif* : of, relating to, or being a gift of a corporeal movable object that is actually delivered ⟨a ~ donation⟩ — **man·u·al·ly** *adv*

manual gift — see GIFT

Mapp hearing — see HEARING

mar·gin \'mär-jən\ *n* **1** : the difference between net sales and the cost of the merchandise sold from which expenses are usu. met or profits derived **2** : the amount by which the market value of collateral is greater than the face value of a loan **3 a** : cash or collateral deposited in a regulated amount by a client with a broker who is financing the purchase of securities — see also REGULATION T **b** : a deposit made with a broker by a client who is trading in futures

margin account *n* : a client's account with a brokerage firm through which the client may buy securities on the firm's credit

margin stock — see STOCK

ma·rine insurance \mə-'rēn-\ *n* : insurance against loss by damage to or destruction of cargo or the means or instruments of its transportation whether on land, sea, or air — see also INLAND MARINE INSURANCE, OCEAN MARINE INSURANCE

mar·i·tal \'mar-ət-ᵊl\ *adj* : of or relating to marriage or the married state

marital asset — see ASSET 2

marital deduction — see DEDUCTION

marital deduction trust — see TRUST

marital portion *n, in the civil law of Louisiana* : a one-fourth portion that a surviving spouse is entitled to claim from the estate of a spouse who has died rich in comparison to the surviving spouse — compare DISPOSABLE PORTION, FALCIDIAN PORTION, LEGITIME

marital property — see PROPERTY

marital trust — see TRUST

mar·i·time \'mar-ə-ˌtīm\ *adj* : of or relating to navigation or commerce on navigable waters

maritime contract — see CONTRACT

maritime law *n* : law that relates to commerce and navigation on the high seas and other navigable waters and that is administered by the admiralty courts ◊ Article III of the U.S. Constitution confers the power to hear cases of maritime law on the federal courts.

maritime lien — see LIEN

¹mark *n* **1** : a character usu. in the form of a cross or X that is made as a substitute for a signature by a person who cannot or is unwilling to write **2** : a character, device, label, brand, seal, or other sign put on an article or used in connection with a service esp. to show the maker or owner, to certify quality, or for identification: **a** : TRADEMARK **b** : SERVICE MARK

²mark *vt* **1** : to fix or trace out the bounds or limits of ⟨a landowner ~*ing* his boundary⟩ **2** : to affix a significant identifying mark (as a trademark) to — **mark to the market 1** : to adjust (cash deposited with a lender of securities) to the prevailing market price **2** : to value (an option or futures contract) in accordance with the market value prevailing on the last business day of the year for tax purposes

mar·ket *n* **1** : the rate or price at which a security or commodity is currently selling : MARKET PRICE **2 a** : a geographical area of demand for commodities or services ⟨seeking new foreign ~*s*⟩ **b** : a formal organized system enabling the transaction of business between buyers and sellers of commodities ⟨a futures ~⟩ — see also STOCK MARKET **c** : a specified category of potential buyers ⟨the youth ~⟩ **3 a** : the course of commercial activity by which the exchange of commodities is accomplished ⟨the ~ is quiet⟩ **b** : an opportunity for selling ⟨developing new ~*s*⟩ **c** : the available supply of or potential demand for specified goods or services ⟨the labor ~⟩ ⟨the ~ for durable goods⟩ **d** : the area of economic activity in which buyers and sellers come together and the

Mary Carter agreement 307

forces of supply and demand affect prices ⟨studying ∼ forces and behavior⟩
mar·ket·able \'mär-kə-tə-bəl\ *adj* **1** : fit to be offered for sale : being such as may be justly or lawfully sold or bought ⟨∼ goods⟩ **2** : wanted by buyers ⟨∼ securities⟩ — **mar·ket·abil·i·ty** \ˌmär-kə-tə-'bi-lə-tē\ *n*
marketable title — see TITLE
market price *n* **1** : the price at which a security is currently selling on the market **2** : MARKET VALUE 1
market share *n* : the percentage of the market for a product or service that a company supplies
market value *n* **1** : the price at which a buyer is ready and willing to buy and a seller is ready and willing to sell **2** : MARKET PRICE 1
market value clause *n* : an insurance clause providing for payment of a loss of goods at market value rather than manufacturing cost
mar·riage \'mar-ij\ *n* **1** : the state of being united to a person of the opposite sex as husband or wife in a legal, consensual, and contractual relationship recognized and sanctioned by and dissolvable only by law — see also DIVORCE **2** : the ceremony containing certain legal formalities by which a marriage relationship is created
marriage certificate *n* : a document which certifies that a marriage has taken place, which contains information (as time and place) about the ceremony, and which is signed by the parties, witnesses, and officiant
marriage license *n* : a written authorization for the marriage of a named man and woman that is granted by a legally qualified government official
marriage settlement *n* **1** : ANTENUPTIAL AGREEMENT **2** : a written agreement regarding matters of support, custody, property division, and visitation upon a couple's divorce — called also *marriage settlement agreement*
¹mar·shal \'mär-shəl\ *n* **1** : a ministerial officer appointed for each judicial district

of the U.S. to execute the process of the courts and perform various duties similar to those of a sheriff **2** : a law officer in some cities (as New York) of the U.S. who is entrusted with particular duties (as serving the process of justice of the peace courts) **3** : the administrative head of the police or esp. fire department in some cities of the U.S.
²marshal *also* **marshall** *vt* **-shaled** *also* **-shalled; -shal·ing** *also* **-shal·ling** : to fix the order of (assets) with respect to liability or availability for payment of obligations; *also* : to fix the order of (as liens or remedies) with respect to priority against a debtor's assets — see also MARSHALING
marshaling *also* **marshalling** *n* : an equitable doctrine requiring that if one creditor can obtain satisfaction of a claim from only one fund and a second creditor can obtain satisfaction from more than one fund the second creditor must claim against the fund that the other creditor cannot reach
mar·tial law \'mär-shəl-\ *n* **1** : the law applied in occupied territory by the military authority of the occupying power **2** : the law administered by military forces that is invoked by a government in an emergency when civilian law enforcement agencies are unable to maintain public order and safety — compare MILITARY LAW
Mary Car·ter agreement \'mer-ē-'kär-tər-\ *n* [from *Booth v. Mary Carter Paint Co.*, 202 So. 2d 8 (1967), Florida appeals court case that popularized the agreement] : a secret agreement between a plaintiff and one or more but not all codefendants which limits the liability of the defendants by giving them an interest in the recovery awarded to the plaintiff ◇ In a Mary Carter agreement, the participating defendants agree to remain as parties to the lawsuit and guarantee pay-

\ə\abut \ᵊ\kitten \ər\further \a\ash \ā\ace
\ä\cot, cart \au̇\out \ch\chin \e\bet \ē\easy
\g\go \i\hit \ī\ice \j\job \ŋ\sing \ō\go \ȯ\law
\ȯi\boy \th\thin \t̲h̲\the \ü\loot \u̇\foot \y\yet
\zh\vision *see also* Pronunciation Symbols page

ment to the plaintiff of a settled amount if no recovery is awarded against the other defendants. The plaintiff agrees to offset their liability by, or sometimes even to pay them from, a recovery awarded from the other defendants. Some states allow the admission of Mary Carter agreements into evidence. In other states they are illegal.

¹mass *n* : an aggregation of usu. similar things (as assets in a succession) considered as a whole

²mass *adj* : participated in by or affecting a large number of individuals ⟨~ insurance underwriting⟩ ⟨~ tort litigation⟩

Massachusetts trust — see TRUST

¹mas·ter *n* **1** : an individual or entity (as a corporation) having control or authority over another: as **a** : the owner of a slave **b** : EMPLOYER — compare SERVANT **c** : PRINCIPAL 1a **2** : an officer of the court appointed (as under Federal Rule of Civil Procedure 53) to assist a judge in a particular case by hearing and reporting on the case, sometimes by making findings of fact and conclusions of law, and by performing various related functions ◊ Under the Federal Rules of Civil Procedure, a master may be a magistrate or else may be a person with some special expertise in the matter. The word *master* as used in the Federal Rules encompasses a referee, an auditor, an examiner, and an assessor. If the master makes findings of fact, they are reviewable by the court except when the case is not to be tried to the jury and the findings are clearly erroneous, or when the parties have stipulated that the master's findings are to be final.

²master *adj* : being the principal or controlling one : governing a number of subordinate like things ⟨a ~ insurance policy⟩

master deed — see DEED

master in chancery : a master in a court of equity ◊ Since courts of law and equity have been merged in the federal and most state systems, the master in chancery has been replaced by the master.

master limited partnership — see PARTNERSHIP

master of laws : a degree conferred for advanced study of law following the obtaining of a juris doctor — compare DOCTOR OF LAWS, DOCTOR OF THE SCIENCE OF LAW

¹ma·te·ri·al \mə-ˈtir-ē-əl\ *adj* **1** : of, relating to, or consisting of physical matter **2** : being of real importance or consequence **3** : being an essential component ⟨the ~ terms of the contract⟩ **4** : being relevant to a subject under consideration; *specif* : being such as would affect or be taken into consideration by a reasonable person in acting or making a decision — see also INSIDER TRADING — **ma·te·ri·al·i·ty** \mə-ˌtir-ē-ˈa-lə-tē\ *n* — **ma·te·ri·al·ly** *adv*

²material *n* : something used for or made the object of consideration or study; *specif* : EVIDENCE — see also BRADY MATERIAL

material alteration *n* : an alteration made to an instrument that adds or deletes any provision or changes the rights and obligations of any party under it

material breach — see BREACH 1b

material evidence — see EVIDENCE

material fact — see FACT

materialman's lien — see LIEN

material witness — see WITNESS

mat·ri·cide \ˈma-trə-ˌsīd\ *n* [Latin *matricidium*, from *matr-*, *mater* mother + *-cidium* killing] **1** : the murder of a mother by her son or daughter **2** [Latin *matricida*, from *matr-* + *-cida* killer] : a person who murders his or her mother

mat·ter *n* **1** : a subject of consideration, disagreement, or litigation: as **a** : a legal case, dispute, or issue ⟨a ~ within the court's jurisdiction⟩ — often used in titles of legal proceedings ⟨~ of Doe⟩ — see also IN RE **b** : one or more facts, claims, or rights examined, disputed, asserted, proven, or determined by legal process

matter in controversy 1 : MATTER 1 — called also *matter in dispute* **2** : the monetary amount involved in a case

matter in issue : a matter that is in dispute as part or all of a legal issue

matter of fact : a matter primarily involving proof or evidence rather than a question of law

matter of form : a matter concerning form or details often of a relatively inessential nature rather than substance ⟨a petition invalid because of a *matter of form*⟩

matter of law : a matter involving or consisting of the application of law ⟨entitled to judgment as a *matter of law* — *National Law Journal*⟩

matter of record : a matter (as a fact) entered on the record of a court or other official body ⟨the security interest was a *matter of record*⟩

matter of substance : a matter concerning the merits of a case rather than form or relatively inessential details

2 : written, printed, or postal material ⟨obscene ~⟩

matter in controversy — see MATTER
matter in dispute : MATTER IN CONTROVERSY at MATTER
matter in issue — see MATTER
matter of fact — see MATTER
matter of form — see MATTER
matter of law — see MATTER
matter of record — see MATTER
matter of substance — see MATTER

ma·ture \mə-'tür, -'chür\ *vb* **ma·tured; ma·tur·ing** *vt* : to bring to maturity ⟨a policy *matured* by the death of the insured⟩ ~ *vi* : to become due, payable, or enforceable; *specif* : to entitle one to immediate enjoyment of benefits ⟨her pension right *matured* upon retirement⟩ — compare VEST — **mature** *adj*

ma·tu·ri·ty \mə-'tür-ə-tē, -'chür-\ *n* : termination of the period that a note or other obligation has to run : state or condition of having become due

may·hem \'mā-,hem, -əm\ *n* [Anglo-French *mahaim, mahain,* literally, mutilation, from Old French *mahain,* from *mahaignier* to injure, mutilate] : willful and permanent crippling, mutilation, or disfigurement of any part of another's body; *also* : the crime of engaging in mayhem ◊ Under the Model Penal Code and the codes of the states that follow it,

mayhem is encompassed by assault and aggravated assault.

may·or \'mā-ər, 'mer\ *n* : an official elected or appointed to act as chief executive or nominal head of a city, town, or borough

mayor's court *n* : a court in some cities that is usu. presided over by the mayor and that has jurisdiction over violations of city ordinances and other minor criminal and civil matters

MBS *abbr* mortgage-backed security

Mc·Nabb–Mal·lo·ry rule \mək-'nab-'ma-lə-rē-\ *n* [after *McNabb v. United States,* 318 U.S. 332 (1943) and *Mallory v. United States,* 354 U.S. 449 (1957), U.S. Supreme Court cases that established the rule] : a doctrine in criminal procedure: an arrestee must be brought before a magistrate without unnecessary delay in order for a confession made during detention to be admissible ◊ In practice, the rule is not absolute. Under the U.S. Code, a delay of more than six hours in bringing an arrestee before a magistrate will not render a confession inadmissible if the delay was reasonable in light of distance and transportation.

me·an·der line \mē-'an-dər-\ *n* : a usu. irregular surveyed line following the outline of a body of water that is used to measure abutting property and is not a boundary line

means *n pl but sing or pl in constr* **1 a** : something enabling one to achieve a desired end ⟨a ~ of self-defense⟩ **b** : CAUSE 1 **2** : resources (as income and assets) at one's disposal

mea·sure of damages : the method under applicable principles of law for determining the damages sustained by a party

mechanic's lien — see LIEN
mediate fact — see FACT
me·di·a·tion \,mē-dē-'ā-shən\ *n* : nonbinding intervention between parties esp.

\ə\abut \ᵊ\kitten \ər\further \a\ash \ā\ace
\ä\cot, cart \au̇\out \ch\chin \e\bet \ē\easy
\g\go \i\hit \ī\ice \j\job \ŋ\sing \ō\go \ȯ\law
\ȯi\boy \th\thin \t̲h̲\the \ü\loot \u̇\foot \y\yet
\zh\vision   *see also* Pronunciation Symbols page

in a labor dispute to promote resolution of a grievance, reconciliation, settlement, or compromise — compare ARBITRATION

me•di•a•tor \'mē-dē-ˌā-tər\ *n* : one that works to effect reconciliation, settlement, or compromise between parties at variance — compare ARBITRATOR

med•ic•aid \'me-di-ˌkād\ *n, often cap* : a program of medical aid designed for those unable to afford regular medical care and financed by the state and federal governments

med•i•cal examiner *n* : a public officer who determines the necessity of and conducts autopsies to find the cause of death

medi•care \'me-di-ˌkar\ *n, often cap* : a government program of medical care esp. for the aged

meet•ing of creditors : a hearing held pursuant to section 341 of the Bankruptcy Code at which a bankrupt debtor is required to submit to examination under oath by creditors who may also elect a trustee if one has not already been appointed

meeting of the minds : assent to the mutually agreed upon and understood terms of an agreement by the parties to a contract that may be manifest by objective signs of intent (as conduct) ⟨the parties had not reached a *meeting of the minds*, and they did not have a specifically enforceable agreement —*Franklin v. Stern*, 858 P.2d 142 (1993) (dissent)⟩

mem•o•ran•dum \ˌme-mə-'ran-dəm\ *n, pl* **-dums** *or* **-da** \-də\ **1** : a usu. informal written communication **2** : a record (as a note) which is used by a party seeking to enforce an otherwise oral agreement in accordance with the Statute of Frauds to prove that the other party agreed to a contract and which need not contain all the terms of the contract itself **3** : BRIEF **4** : MEMORANDUM DECISION

memorandum clause *n* : a clause in a marine insurance policy setting forth exclusions or special terms for loss or damage to particular cargo

memorandum decision *n* : a document produced by the court stating a present or intended decision usu. previously announced from the bench without an accompanying opinion

memorandum opinion — see OPINION

¹men•ace \'me-nəs\ *n* **1** : a show of an intention to inflict esp. physical harm ⟨accomplished against a person's will by means of force, . . . ~, or fear of immediate and unlawful bodily injury —*California Penal Code*⟩ **2** : one who represents a threat

²menace *vb* **men•aced; men•ac•ing** *vt* **1** : to make a show of intention to harm **2** : to represent or pose a threat to ~ *vi* : to act in a threatening manner — **men•ac•ing•ly** *adv*

mens rea \'menz-'rē-ə, -'rā-\ *n, pl* **mentes re•ae** \'men-ˌtēz-'rē-ˌē, 'men-ˌtās-'rā-ˌī\ [New Latin, literally, guilty mind] : a culpable mental state; *esp* : one involving intent or knowledge and forming an element of a criminal offense ⟨murder contains a *mens rea* element⟩ — compare ACTUS REUS

men•tal an•guish *n* : a high degree of emotional pain, distress, torment, or suffering that may aggravate a crime or be a subject of an action for damages or wrongful death : EMOTIONAL DISTRESS

mental cruelty *n* : conduct by one spouse that renders the other's life miserable and unendurable and that is a ground for divorce

mental defect *n* : an abnormal mental condition (as mental retardation) that may be of a more fixed nature than a mental disease

mental deficiency *n* : failure in intellectual development that is marked by low intelligence or mental retardation and that may result in an inability to function competently in society

mental dis•ease *n* : an abnormal mental condition that interferes with mental or emotional processes and internal behavioral control and that is not manifest only in repeated criminal or antisocial conduct; *broadly* : MENTAL ILLNESS ◊ *Mental disease* and *mental illness* are in general use synonymous, but *mental* *disease* has developed a settled meaning in criminal law while *mental illness* is often explained or defined by reference to the medical community's understanding of the term.

mental disorder *n* : MENTAL ILLNESS 2

mental distress *n* : EMOTIONAL DISTRESS

mental disturbance *n* : EMOTIONAL DISTRESS

mental ill•ness *n* **1** : MENTAL DISEASE **2** : a mental condition marked primarily by sufficient disorganization of personality, mind, and emotions to seriously impair the normal psychological and often social functioning of the individual — called also *mental disorder*

mental suf•fer•ing *n* : EMOTIONAL DISTRESS

mentes reae *pl of* MENS REA

mer•chant \'mər-chənt\ *n* : a person who trades in goods esp. of a certain kind and possesses expertise in the area of the goods and the practices of trading in them or who employs others with such expertise ⟨a warranty that the goods shall be merchantable is implied in a contract for their sale if the seller is a ~ with respect to goods of that kind — *Uniform Commercial Code*⟩

mer•chant•able \'mər-chən-tə-bəl\ *adj* : of commercially acceptable quality : characterized by fitness for normal use, good quality, and accord with any statements or promises made on the packaging or label ⟨~ goods⟩ — see also *implied warranty* and *warranty of merchantability* at WARRANTY 2a — **mer•chant•abil•i•ty** \,mər-chən-tə-'bi-lə-tē\ *n*

merchantable title *n* : MARKETABLE TITLE at TITLE

mer•cy kill•ing *n* : EUTHANASIA

merge \'mərj\ *vb* **merged; merg•ing** *vt* **1** : to cause to unite, combine, or coalesce ⟨~ one corporation with another⟩ **2** : to cause to be incorporated and superseded ⟨one effect of a judgment is to ~ therein the cause of action on which the action is brought — *American Jurisprudence* 2d⟩ — compare BAR 3b ~ *vi* : to become combined : undergo merger

merg•er \'mər-jər\ *n* **1** : the absorption of a lesser estate or interest into a greater one held by the same person — compare CONFUSION **2** : the incorporation and superseding of one contract by another **3 a** : the treatment (as by statute) of two offenses deriving from the same conduct such that a defendant cannot be or is not punished for both esp. when one offense is incidental to or necessarily included in the other ⟨a ~ of offenses in a statute⟩ ⟨a ~ of convictions⟩ **b** : the doctrine according to which such offenses must be merged — compare DOUBLE JEOPARDY ◊ Merger commonly involves the interpretation of statutes and legislative intent in deciding whether two or more offenses deriving from the same conduct remain distinct. **4** : a doctrine in civil litigation: a judgment in favor of a plaintiff incorporates and supersedes the cause of action and any claims based on it and requires that further litigation in the case by the defendant be concerned with the judgment itself — compare BAR 3b, *estoppel by judgment* at ESTOPPEL 2a, RES JUDICATA **5** : the superseding of a prior agreement in a divorce case by the divorce decree **6 a** : the act or process of merging **b** : absorption by one corporation of another; *also* : any of various methods of combining two or more organizations (as business concerns) — compare CONSOLIDATE

cash merger : a merger in which shareholders in the company to be absorbed receive cash for their shares rather than shares in the absorbing company ⟨a tender offer to be followed by a *cash merger*⟩ — see also CASH OUT

de facto merger : a merger that is characterized by the issuance of stock to the corporation to be absorbed rather than an outright purchase of assets for cash, by continued participation of the shareholders, directors, and employees

\ə\abut　\ᵊ\kitten　\ər\further　\a\ash　\ā\ace
\ä\cot, cart　\aů\out　\ch\chin　\e\bet　\ē\easy
\g\go　\i\hit　\ī\ice　\j\job　\ŋ\sing　\ō\go　\ȯ\law
\ȯi\boy　\th\thin　\t͟h\the　\ü\loot　\ů\foot　\y\yet
\zh\vision　*see also* Pronunciation Symbols page

of the absorbed corporation, and by an assumption of liabilities by the absorbing corporation ◇ Shareholders in a de facto merger are considered to have the same right to an appraisal of the fair value of their shares as shareholders in a statutory merger.

short–form merger : an accelerated statutory merger between a subsidiary and a parent corporation that controls a large specified majority of shares in the subsidiary

statutory merger : a merger performed in accordance with relevant statutes that require specific procedures for the notification and approval of shareholders

merger clause *n* : a clause in a contract stating that the contract is a complete statement of the agreement and supersedes any prior terms, representations, or agreements whether made orally or in writing ⟨*merger clauses* do not apply to subsequent modifications —J. J. White and R. S. Summers⟩

mer·it \'mer-ət\ *n* **1** *pl* : the substance of a case apart from matters of jurisdiction, procedure, or form ⟨a ruling on the ~*s* of the case⟩ — see also *judgment on the merits* at JUDGMENT 1a **2** : legal significance, standing, or worth ⟨an argument without ~⟩

mer·i·to·ri·ous \ˌmer-ə-'tōr-ē-əs\ *adj* **1** : deserving of honor or esteem **2** : having merit ⟨a ~ claim⟩

meritorious defense — see DEFENSE 2a

merit shop *n* : OPEN SHOP

mesne process \'mēn-\ *n* [*mesne* intermediate, intervening, from Anglo-French, alteration of Old French *meien* middle, from Latin *medianus*, from *medius* middle] : process (as a writ) issued in the course of a proceeding

mesne profits *n pl* : profits (as from crops) earned by one in wrongful possession of property ⟨the rightful owner sued for *mesne profits*⟩

mes·suage \'mes-wij\ *n* [Anglo-French, probably alteration of Old French *mesnage* dwelling house, ultimately from Latin *mansion-*, *mansio* habitation,

dwelling, from *manēre* to remain, sojourn, dwell] : a dwelling house with the adjacent buildings and curtilage and other adjoining lands used in connection with the household

metes and bounds \'mēts-ənd-'baundz\ *n pl* [translation of Anglo-French *metes et boundes*] : the boundaries or limits of a tract of land esp. as described by reference to lines and distances between points on the land

met·ro·pol·i·tan court \ˌme-trə-'pä-lət-ᵊn-\ *n* : a court of limited jurisdiction found primarily in New Mexico

mil·i·tary commission *n* : a military court organized in time of war or suspension of the civil power to try offenses by persons (as civilians) not subject to trial by a court-martial

military government *n* : the government established by a military commander in conquered territory to administer the military law declared under military authority applicable to all persons in the conquered territory and superseding any incompatible local law

military law *n* : law enforced by military rather than civil authority; *specif* : law prescribed by statute for the government of the armed forces and accompanying civilian employees — compare MARTIAL LAW

mineral lease — see LEASE

min·er·al right *n* : the right or title to all or specified minerals in a given tract : the right to explore for and extract such minerals or to receive a royalty for them

min·i·mal diversity \'mi-nə-məl-\ *n* : diversity of citizenship of the parties to a lawsuit in which at least one plaintiff is a resident from a state different from at least one defendant — compare COMPLETE DIVERSITY ◇ Diversity jurisdiction requires complete diversity. Statutory interpleader requires only minimal diversity between the claimants, however.

min·i·mum contacts \'mi-nə-məm-\ *n pl* : the level of a nonresident defendant's connection with or activity in a state that is sufficient under due process to support the assertion of personal jurisdiction under a long-arm statute — see also DOING BUSINESS STATUTE, FAIR PLAY AND SUBSTANTIAL JUSTICE, *International Shoe Co. v. Washington* in the IMPORTANT CASES section ◊ In most cases, minimum contacts are shown by continuous and purposeful contact with the state usu. for business purposes. Once the minimum contacts requirement is met, the court must determine that the contacts are sufficient so that the assertion of jurisdiction will not offend the traditional notions of fair play and substantial justice.

minimum wage *n* : a wage fixed by contract or esp. by law as the least that may be paid either to employees generally or to a particular category of employees — compare SCALE

min·ing lease *n* : MINERAL LEASE at LEASE

mining partnership — see PARTNERSHIP

min·is·te·ri·al \ˌmi-nə-ˈstir-ē-əl\ *adj* **1** : being or having the characteristics of an act or duty prescribed by law as part of the duties of an administrative office **2** : relating to or being an act done after ascertaining the existence of a specified state of facts in obedience to legal and esp. statutory mandate without exercise of personal judgment or discretion — see also MANDAMUS; compare DISCRETIONARY

mini·trial \ˈmi-nē-ˌtrī-əl\ *n* : an informal trial-like proceeding used as a form of alternative dispute resolution

¹mi·nor *n* : a person who has not yet reached the age of majority — compare ADULT, JUVENILE, MAJOR

²minor *adj* **1 a** : being less important or serious ⟨a ~ official⟩ ⟨a ~ offense⟩ **b** : involving, relating to, or dealing with less important matters **2** : having the status of a minor ⟨~ children⟩

minor dispute *n* : a dispute between an employer and a union that under the Railway Labor Act can be resolved through interpretation of the existing collective bargaining agreement — compare MAJOR DISPUTE

mi·nor·i·ty *n*, *pl* **-ties 1 a** : the period before attainment of majority **b** : the state of being a minor **2** : the smaller of two groups constituting a whole: as **a** : a group (as in a legislative body) having less than the number of votes necessary for control **b** : a group of judges among those hearing an appeal who disagree with the majority's judgment : DISSENT **3** **c** : a group of jurisdictions taking a less widespread approach to or view of a legal question, issue, or problem **3 a** : a part of a population differing esp. from the dominant group in some characteristics (as race, sex, or national origin) and often subject to differential treatment **b** : a member of a minority ⟨an effort to hire more *minorities*⟩

minority shareholder *n* : a shareholder whose proportion of shares is too small to confer any power to exert control or influence over corporate action

min·ute \ˈmi-nət\ *n* **1** : a brief note (as of summary or recommendation) **2** : MEMORANDUM 1 **3** *pl* : the official record of the proceedings of a meeting or court

minute book *n* **1** : a book in which written minutes or other records are entered **2** : the official written record of the transactions of the stockholders and directors of a corporation

Mi·ran·da \mə-ˈran-də\ *adj* : of, relating to, or being one's Miranda rights ⟨a ~ waiver⟩

Miranda card *n* : a card on which Miranda rights are written for police officers to read to a person being arrested

Miranda rights *n pl* [from *Miranda v. Arizona*, the 1966 U.S. Supreme Court ruling establishing such rights] : the rights (as the right to remain silent, to have an attorney present, and to have an attorney appointed if indigent) of which an arrest-

\ə\abut \ᵊ\kitten \ər\further \a\ash \ā\ace
\ä\cot, cart \au̇\out \ch\chin \e\bet \ē\easy
\g\go \i\hit \ī\ice \j\job \ŋ\sing \ō\go \ȯ\law
\ȯi\boy \th\thin \th\the \ü\loot \u̇\foot \y\yet
\zh\vision   *see also* Pronunciation Symbols page

ing officer must advise the person being arrested — see also *Miranda v. Arizona* in the IMPORTANT CASES section ◊ A reading of the Miranda rights usu. includes a warning that anything said could be used as evidence. No statements made by an arrested person or evidence obtained therefrom may be introduced at trial unless the person was advised of or validly waived these rights. A fresh reading of the Miranda rights may be required by the passage of time after the initial reading, as for example if a previously silent person begins to speak or police interrogate a person more than once.

Miranda warnings *n pl* : the warnings given by police in advising an arrested person of his or her Miranda rights

mi·ran·dize \mə-'ran-ˌdīz\ *vt* **-dized; -diz·ing** : to recite the Miranda warnings to (a person under arrest)

mis·ad·ven·ture \ˌmi-səd-'ven-chər\ *n* : an accident that causes serious injury or death to a person and that does not involve negligence, wrongful purpose, or unlawful conduct

mis·ap·ply \ˌmi-sə-'plī\ *vt* **-plied; -ply·ing** : to misuse or spend (as public money) without proper authority; *specif* : to willfully and unlawfully convert (bank funds) for the use, benefit, or gain of oneself or a third party esp. through one's position as a bank employee or officer — **mis·ap·pli·ca·tion** \ˌmi-ˌsa-plə-'kā-shən\ *n*

mis·ap·pro·pri·ate \ˌmi-sə-'prō-prē-ˌāt\ *vt* : to appropriate wrongfully or unlawfully (as by theft or embezzlement) — **mis·ap·pro·pri·a·tion** \-ˌprō-prē-'ā-shən\ *n*

mis·brand \mis-'brand\ *vt* : to brand (as a food item or drug) falsely or in a misleading way; *specif* : to label in violation of statutory requirements

mis·car·riage of justice \ˌmis-'kar-ij-, 'mis-ˌkar-\ : an error at trial that probably led to a less favorable outcome for the appealing party

mis·con·duct \mis-'kän-dəkt\ *n* : intentional or wanton wrongful but usu. not criminal behavior: as **a** : deliberate or

wanton violation of standards of conduct by a government official **b** : wrongful behavior (as adultery) by a spouse that leads to the dissolution of the marriage **c** : an attorney's violation of the standards set for professional conduct; *also* : an attorney's and esp. a prosecutor's use of deceptive or reprehensible methods in presenting a case to a jury **d** : impermissible behavior by a juror (as communicating about the case with outsiders, witnesses, or others, reading or hearing news reports about the case, or independently introducing evidence to other jurors) **e** : an employee's deliberate or wanton disregard of an employer's interests or disregard or violation of the employer's standards or rules that is sufficient to justify a denial of unemployment compensation

mis·de·mean·ant \ˌmis-di-'mē-nənt\ *n* : one who commits a misdemeanor

mis·de·mean·or \ˌmis-di-'mē-nər\ *n* : a crime that carries a less severe punishment than a felony; *specif* : a crime punishable by a fine and by a term of imprisonment not to be served in a penitentiary and not to exceed one year — compare FELONY

misdemeanor–manslaughter — see MANSLAUGHTER

mis·fea·sance \mis-'fēz-ᵊns\ *n* [Anglo-French *misfesance*, from Middle French *mesfaire* to do wrong, from *mes-* wrongly + *faire* to make, do, from Latin *facere*] : the performance of a lawful action in an illegal or improper manner; *specif* : the performance of an official duty in an improper or unlawful manner or with an improper or corrupt motive — compare MALFEASANCE, NONFEASANCE

mis·join·der \mis-'join-dər\ *n* : an incorrect joinder of claims or parties in a legal action; *also* : an impermissible joinder of criminal charges or defendants — compare DUPLICITY, MULTIFARIOUS, MULTIPLICITY

mis·lead \mis-'lēd\ *vb* **-led** \-'led\; **-lead·ing** *vt* : to lead into a mistaken action or belief : to cause to have a false impression ~ *vi* : to create a false impression — compare DECEIVE

misleading *adj* : possessing the capacity or tendency to create a mistaken understanding or impression — compare DECEPTIVE, FRAUDULENT

mis·no·mer \ˌmis-'nō-mər\ *n* [Anglo‑French *mesnomer*, from *mesnomer* to misname, from Middle French *meswrongly* + *nommer* to name, from Latin *nominare*, from *nomin-*, *nomen* name] : the misnaming of a person in a legal document or proceeding (as in a complaint or indictment); *specif* : the institution of proceedings against and service of process on the correct party using the incorrect name — compare IDEM SONANS ◊ Amendment of the pleadings is generally allowed in cases of misnomer.

mis·pri·sion \mis-'pri-zhən\ *n* [Anglo‑French, error, wrongdoing, from Old French, from *mesprendre* to make a mistake, from *mes-* wrongly + *prendre* to take, from Latin *prehendere* to seize] **1** : neglectful or wrongful performance of an official duty **2** : a clerical error in a legal proceeding that can be corrected in a summary proceeding **3** : the concealment of a treason or felony and failure to report it to the prosecuting authorities by a person who has not committed it ⟨~ of felony⟩ ⟨~ of treason⟩

mis·rep·re·sent \mis-ˌre-pri-'zent\ *vt* : to make a misrepresentation about ~ *vi* : to make a misrepresentation — **mis·rep·re·sen·ta·tive** \-ˌre-pri-'zen-tə-tiv\ *adj* — **mis·rep·re·sen·ter** *n*

mis·rep·re·sen·ta·tion \mis-ˌre-pri-ˌzen-'tā-shən, -zən-\ *n* : an intentionally or sometimes negligently false representation made verbally, by conduct, or sometimes by nondisclosure or concealment and often for the purpose of deceiving, defrauding, or causing another to rely on it detrimentally; *also* : an act or instance of making such a representation

mis·take *n* **1** : an unintentional error esp. in legal procedure or form that does not indicate bad faith and that commonly warrants excuse or relief by the court ⟨the court's power to revise a judgment because of fraud, ~, or irregularity⟩ ⟨a clerical ~⟩ **2** : an erroneous belief: as **a** : a state of mind that is not in accordance with the facts existing at the time a contract is made and that may be a ground for the rescission or reformation of the contract **b** : a misconception at the time of an offense alleged by a defendant

mistake of fact **1** : a mistake regarding a fact or facts esp. that significantly affects the performance of a contract **2** : a criminal defense that attempts to eliminate culpability on the ground that the defendant operated from an unintentional misunderstanding of fact rather than from a criminal purpose

mistake of law : a mistake involving the misunderstanding or incorrect application of law in regard to an act, contract, transaction, determination, or state of affairs; *also* : a criminal defense alleging such a mistake ◊ In both contract and criminal law a mistake of law is a weaker ground for relief or acquittal than a mistake of fact.

mutual mistake : a mistake common to both parties to a contract who were in agreement about the purpose or terms of the contract ⟨reformed the contract because of a *mutual mistake*⟩

unilateral mistake : a mistake on the part of one party to a contract that is usu. not a ground for rescission or reformation unless one party stands to profit or benefit improperly from the mistake

mistake of fact — see MISTAKE

mistake of law — see MISTAKE

mis·tri·al \'mis-ˌtrī-əl\ *n* : a trial that terminates without a verdict because of error, necessity, prejudicial misconduct, or a hung jury — see also MANIFEST NECESSITY; compare DISMISSAL 2, TRIAL DE NOVO

mit·i·gate \'mi-tə-ˌgāt\ *vb* **-gat·ed; -gat-**

\ə\abut \ᵊ\kitten \ər\further \a\ash \ā\ace
\ä\cot, cart \au̇\out \ch\chin \e\bet \ē\easy
\g\go \i\hit \ī\ice \j\job \ŋ\sing \ō\go \ȯ\law
\ȯi\boy \th\thin \t͟h\the \ü\loot \u̇\foot \y\yet
\zh\vision *see also* Pronunciation Symbols page

ing *vt* **:** to lessen or minimize the severity of ⟨what actions the State took to ∼ the hazardous conditions —*Estate of Arrowwood v. State,* 894 P.2d 642 (1995)⟩ ⟨factors that ∼ the crime⟩ — see also MITIGATION OF DAMAGES 1; compare AGGRAVATE **∼** *vi* **:** to lessen or minimize the severity of one's losses or damage ⟨a failure to ∼⟩ — **mit·i·ga·tion** \ˌmi-tə-'gā-shən\ *n* — **mit·i·ga·tive** \'mi-tə-ˌgā-tiv\ *adj*

mitigating circumstance *n* **:** a circumstance in the commission of an act that lessens the degree of criminal culpability ⟨was convicted of manslaughter rather than murder because of *mitigating circumstances*⟩; *also* **:** a circumstance or factor relating to an offense or defendant that does not bear on the question of culpability but that receives consideration by the court esp. in lessening the severity of a sentence ⟨the *mitigating circumstance* of the defendant's terminal illness⟩ — compare AGGRAVATING CIRCUMSTANCE

mitigation of damages 1 : a doctrine in tort and contract law: a person injured by another is required to mitigate his or her losses resulting from the injury ⟨whether the patient shares any fault and whether the patient has satisfied the requirements of *mitigation of damages* —*D'Aries v. Schell,* 644 A.2d 134 (1994)⟩; *also* **:** an affirmative defense based on this doctrine — called also *avoidable consequences* **2 :** a reduction in the amount of damages awarded a party

mit·i·ga·tor \'mi-tə-ˌgā-tər\ *n* **:** one that mitigates; *specif* **:** MITIGATING CIRCUMSTANCE ⟨a statutory ∼⟩ — **mit·i·ga·to·ry** \'mi-ti-gə-ˌtòr-ē\ *adj*

mit·ti·mus \'mi-tə-məs\ *n* [Latin, we send] **:** a warrant issued to a sheriff commanding the delivery to prison of a person named in the warrant

M'Naght·en test \mək-'nät-ᵊn-\ *n* [after Daniel *M'Naghten,* defendant in 1843 murder case heard before the British House of Lords who was acquitted due to his insanity] **:** a standard under which a criminal defendant is considered to have been insane at the time of an act (as a killing) if he or she did not know right from wrong or did not understand the moral nature of the act because of a mental disease or defect — called also *M'Naghten rule;* compare DIMINISHED CAPACITY, DURHAM RULE, IRRESISTIBLE IMPULSE TEST, SUBSTANTIAL CAPACITY TEST ◊ Many jurisdictions have followed the Model Penal Code in basing criminal insanity on either of two factors: an inability to appreciate the wrongfulness of an act, which reflects the influence of the M'Naghten test, and an inability to conform one's behavior to the dictates of the law, which reflects the concept of the irresistible impulse. Both factors must be rooted in a mental disease or defect, which is also what the Durham rule requires of insanity.

MO *abbr* modus operandi

mobile goods — see GOOD 2

Mod·el Penal Code test *n* **:** SUBSTANTIAL CAPACITY TEST

moderate force — see FORCE 3

mo·dus ope·ran·di \ˌmō-dəs-ˌä-pə-'ran-dē, -ˌdī\ *n* [New Latin, manner of operating] **:** a distinct pattern or method of operation esp. that indicates or suggests the work of a single criminal in more than one crime

moi·e·ty \'mòi-ə-tē\ *n, pl* **-ties :** half of something (as an estate) ⟨an interest exceeding a ∼⟩ — compare ENTIRETY 2

mo·lest \mə-'lest\ *vt* **1 :** to annoy, disturb, or persecute esp. with hostile intent or injurious effect **2 :** to make annoying sexual advances to; *specif* **:** to force physical and usu. sexual contact on (as a child) — **mo·les·ta·tion** \ˌmō-ˌles-'tā-shən, ˌmä-, -ləs-\ *n* — **mo·lest·er** *n*

mon·ey \'mə-nē\ *n, pl* **moneys** *or* **mon·ies** \'mə-nēz\ **1 :** an accepted or authorized medium of exchange; *esp* **:** coinage or negotiable paper issued as legal tender by a government **2 a :** assets or compensation in the form of or readily convertible into cash **b :** capital dealt in as a commodity to be lent, traded, or invested ⟨mortgage ∼ available from a lender⟩ ⟨the ∼ supply⟩ **c** *pl* : sums of money ⟨collect tax *moneys*⟩

money bill — see BILL 1

mon•eyed \'mə-nēd\ *adj* : consisting in or derived from money ⟨a ~ obligation⟩

moneyed capital — see CAPITAL

moneyed corporation — see CORPORATION

money judgment — see JUDGMENT 1a

money market *n* : the trade in short-term negotiable instruments (as certificates of deposit or U.S. Treasury securities)

money order *n* : an order issued by a post office, bank, or telegraph office for payment of a specified sum of money usu. at any branch of the issuing organization

monies *pl of* MONEY

mo•nop•o•lize \mə-'nä-pə-ˌlīz\ *vt* **-lized; -liz•ing** : to get a monopoly of ⟨~ an industry⟩ — **mo•nop•o•li•za•tion** \-ˌnä-pə-lə-'zā-shən\ *n*

mo•nop•o•ly \mə-'nä-pə-lē\ *n, pl* **-lies 1** : exclusive control of a particular market that is marked by the power to control prices and exclude competition and that esp. is developed willfully rather than as the result of superior products or skill — see also ANTITRUST, *Sherman Antitrust Act* in the IMPORTANT LAWS section **2** : one that has a monopoly

¹moot \'müt\ *vt* : to make moot ⟨statute of limitations would ~ the effort —S. R. Sontag⟩

²moot *adj* [(of a trial or hearing) hypothetical, staged for practice, from *moot* hypothetical case for law students, argument, deliberative assembly, from Old English *mōt* assembly, meeting] : deprived of practical significance : made abstract or purely academic ⟨the case became ~ when the defendant paid the sum at issue⟩ — see also MOOTNESS DOCTRINE; compare JUSTICIABLE, RIPE — **moot•ness** \'müt-nəs\ *n*

moot court *n* : a mock court in which law students argue hypothetical cases for practice

mootness doctrine *n* : a doctrine in judicial procedure: a court will not hear or decide a moot case unless it includes an issue that is not considered moot because it involves the public interest or constitutional questions and is likely to be repeated and otherwise evade review or resolution

mor•al cer•tain•ty *n* : a state of subjective certainty leaving no real doubt about a matter (as a defendant's guilt) : certainty beyond a reasonable doubt

moral hazard *n* : the possibility of loss to an insurance company (as by arson) arising from the character or circumstances of the insured ⟨deductibles decrease *moral hazard*⟩

moral tur•pi•tude \-'tər-pə-ˌtüd, -ˌtyüd\ *n* **1** : an act or behavior that gravely violates the sentiment or accepted standard of the community **2** : a quality of dishonesty or other immorality that is determined by a court to be present in the commission of a criminal offense ⟨a crime involving *moral turpitude*⟩ — compare MALUM IN SE ◊ Whether a criminal offense involves moral turpitude is an important determination in deportation, disbarment, and other disciplinary hearings. Past crimes involving moral turpitude usu. may also be introduced as evidence to impeach testimony. Theft, perjury, vice crimes, bigamy, and rape have generally been found to involve moral turpitude, while liquor law violations and disorderly conduct generally have not.

moratoria *pl of* MORATORIUM

mor•a•to•ri•um \ˌmȯr-ə-'tȯr-ē-əm\ *n, pl* **-riums** *or* **-ria** [New Latin, from Late Latin, neuter of *moratorius* dilatory, from *morari* to delay, from *mora* delay] **1 a** : an authorized period of delay in the performance of an obligation (as the paying of a debt) **b** : a waiting period set by an authority **2** : a suspension of activity

mor•a•to•ry \'mȯr-ə-ˌtȯr-ē\ *adj* [French *moratoire*, from Late Latin *moratorius*]

\ə\abut \ᵊ\kitten \ər\further \a\ash \ā\ace
\ä\cot, cart \au̇\out \ch\chin \e\bet \ē\easy
\g\go \i\hit \ī\ice \j\job \ŋ\sing \ō\go \ȯ\law
\ȯi\boy \th\thin \t͟h\the \ü\loot \u̇\foot \y\yet
\zh\vision *see also* Pronunciation Symbols page

: of, relating to, or resulting from delay in the payment or performance of an obligation ⟨~ interest⟩

moratory damages — see DAMAGE 2

morgue \\'mȯrg\ *n* : a place where the bodies of persons found dead are kept until identified and claimed by relatives or released for burial or autopsy

mo•ron \\'mȯr-ˌän\ *n* : a moderately or mildly retarded person — used esp. formerly; see also IDIOT

¹mort•gage \\'mȯr-gij\ *n* [Anglo-French, from Old French, from *mort* dead (from Latin *mortuus*) + *gage* security] **1 a :** a conveyance of title to property that is given to secure an obligation (as a debt) and that is defeated upon payment or performance according to stipulated terms ⟨shows that a deed was intended only as a ~ —W. M. McGovern, Jr. *et al.*⟩ **b :** a lien against property that is granted to secure an obligation (as a debt) and that is extinguished upon payment or performance according to stipulated terms ⟨creditors with valid ~s against the debtor's property —J. H. Williamson⟩ **c :** a loan secured by a mortgage ⟨applied for a ~⟩

adjustable rate mortgage : a mortgage having an interest rate which is usu. initially lower than that of a mortgage with a fixed rate but which is adjusted periodically according to an index (as the cost of funds to the lender)

balloon mortgage : a mortgage having the interest paid periodically and the principal paid in one lump sum at the end of the term of the loan

blanket mortgage : a mortgage of or against all of the property of the mortgagor

chattel mortgage : a mortgage of or against personal or movable property (as an airplane) — compare PLEDGE, *security interest* 2 at INTEREST 1

collateral mortgage in the civil law of Louisiana : a mortgage against movable or immovable property that is given to secure a written obligation (as a note) which is pledged as collateral security

for a principal obligation — see also *collateral note* at NOTE

construction mortgage : a mortgage that secures a loan which finances construction

conventional mortgage **1** *in the civil law of Louisiana* : a mortgage that is created by a written contract **2 :** a mortgage that is not guaranteed by government agency

equitable mortgage : a constructive or implied mortgage : a transaction (as a conveyance) that does not have the form of a mortgage but is given the effect of a mortgage by a court of equity because the parties intended it to be a mortgage

first mortgage : a mortgage that has priority over all other security interests except those imposed by law

fixed rate mortgage : a mortgage having an interest rate that stays the same

general mortgage in the civil law of Louisiana : a blanket mortgage that burdens all present and future property

home equity conversion mortgage : REVERSE MORTGAGE in this entry

judicial mortgage in the civil law of Louisiana : a mortgage lien that secures a judgment debt and is created by filing a judgment with the recorder of mortgages

junior mortgage : SECOND MORTGAGE in this entry

leasehold mortgage : a mortgage under which a leasehold interest in property secures a loan or obligation

legal mortgage in the civil law of Louisiana : a mortgage that secures an obligation which is created by a law and which does not have to be stipulated to by the parties

open–end mortgage : a mortgage that secures a loan agreement which allows the mortgagor to borrow additional sums usu. up to a specified limit

purchase money mortgage : a mortgage that is given (as to a lender) to secure a loan for all or some of the purchase price of property; *also* : a mortgage given to a seller of property to secure the unpaid balance of the purchase price *reverse mortgage* : a mortgage that allows elderly homeowners to convert existing equity into available funds provided through a line of credit, a cash advance (as for the purchase of an annuity), or periodic disbursements to be repaid with interest when the home is sold or ceases to be the primary residence, when the borrower dies or some other specified event occurs, or at a fixed maturity date

second mortgage : a mortgage lien that is subordinate in priority to a first mortgage — called also *junior mortgage*

senior mortgage : FIRST MORTGAGE in this entry

special mortgage : a mortgage on specified property

wrap–around mortgage \'rap-ə-ˌraȯnd-\ : a second or later mortgage that incorporates the debt of a previous mortgage with additional debt for another loan **2 a** : an instrument embodying and containing the provisions of a mortgage ⟨executing and recording ~*s*⟩ **b** : the interest of a mortgagee in mortgaged property ⟨the bank holds the ~⟩

²mortgage *vt* **mort·gaged; mort·gag·ing**
1 : to grant or convey by a mortgage ⟨*mortgaged* the property to the bank⟩ **2** : to encumber with a mortgage

mort·gage·able \'mȯr-gi-jə-bəl\ *adj* : susceptible or capable of being mortgaged ⟨mineral rights are not ~ in this jurisdiction⟩ — **mort·gage·abil·i·ty** \ˌmȯr-gi-jə-'bi-lə-tē\ *n*

mortgage–backed security — see SECURITY

mortgage bond — see BOND 2

mortgage clause *n* : a clause in an insurance contract (as for fire insurance) that entitles a named mortgagee to be paid for damage or loss to the property — see also OPEN MORTGAGE CLAUSE, STANDARD MORTGAGE CLAUSE

mort·gag·ee \ˌmȯr-gi-'jē\ *n* : a party (as a business or individual) to whom or in whose favor property is mortgaged

mort·gag·or \ˌmȯr-gi-'jȯr\ *n* : a person who mortgages property

mor·tis cau·sa \'mȯr-tis-'kȯ-zə, -'kaȯ-sä\ *adj* : CAUSA MORTIS

mort·main \'mȯrt-ˌmān\ *n* [Anglo‑French, from Old French *mortemain*, from *morte* (feminine of *mort* dead, from Latin *mortuus*) + *main* hand, from Latin *manus*] **1** : the possession of real property in perpetuity by a corporate body (as a church); *also* : the condition of property in such possession **2** : the controlling influence of the past — not used technically

mortmain statute *n* : a statute that prohibits corporate bodies (as charities) from holding real property in perpetuity or that otherwise limits or regulates testamentary dispositions to usu. charitable corporations — called also *statute of mortmain*

most–fa·vored–na·tion clause *n* : a clause in a treaty granting to a nation in certain stipulated matters the same terms as are then or may thereafter be granted to any other nation

¹mo·tion *n* [Anglo-French, from Latin *motion- motio* movement, from *movēre* to move] **1** : a proposal for action; *esp* : a formal proposal made in a legislative assembly ⟨made a ~ to refer the bill to committee⟩ **2 a** : an application made to a court or judge to obtain an order, ruling, or direction ⟨a ~ to arrest judgment⟩; *also* : a document containing such an application **b** : the initiative of a court to issue an order, ruling, or direction ⟨the court is given discretion to order a pretrial conference either on its own ~ or at the request of a party —J. H. Friedenthal *et al.*⟩

motion for judgment on the pleadings : a motion made after pleadings have been entered that requests the court to issue a judgment at that point — compare *summary judgment* at JUDGMENT 1a ◊ Under the Federal Rules of Civil Procedure, if matters outside of the pleadings are presented to the court when a motion for judgment on the

\ə\abut \ᵊ\kitten \ər\further \a\ash \ā\ace
\ä\cot, cart \aȯ\out \ch\chin \e\bet \ē\easy
\g\go \i\hit \ī\ice \j\job \ŋ\sing \ō\go \ȯ\law
\ȯi\boy \th\thin \th̲\the \ü\loot \u̇\foot \y\yet
\zh\vision *see also* Pronunciation Symbols page

pleadings is made, the motion will be treated as a motion for summary judgment.

motion for more definite statement : a motion that is filed before an answer and that requests the court to order the plaintiff to clarify allegations in the complaint because the claims are so vague or ambiguous that an answer cannot reasonably be framed

motion in bar : a motion that bars an action (as trial or prosecution) — used esp. in Georgia and Illinois

motion in lim·i·ne \-in-'li-mə-nē\ : a usu. pretrial motion that requests the court to issue an interlocutory order which prevents an opposing party from introducing or referring to potentially irrelevant, prejudicial, or otherwise inadmissible evidence until the court has finally ruled on its admissibility

motion to suppress : a pretrial motion requesting the court to exclude evidence that was obtained illegally and esp. in violation of Fourth, Fifth, and Sixth Amendment protections

om·ni·bus motion \'äm-ni-bəs-\ : a motion that makes multiple requests ⟨filing an *omnibus motion* to dismiss and for a more definite statement —*Department of Ins. of Florida v. Coopers & Lybrand*, 570 So. 2d 369 (1990)⟩

²motion *vb* : MOVE ⟨~ed for a summary judgment⟩

motion for judgment on the pleadings — see MOTION

motion for more definite statement — see MOTION

motion in bar — see MOTION

motion in limine — see MOTION

motion to suppress — see MOTION

mo·tive *n* [Anglo-French *motif*, from Middle French *motif* adjective, moving, from Medieval Latin *motivus*, from Latin *motus*, past participle of *movēre* to move] : something (as a need or desire) that causes a person to act ◇ In criminal law, motive is distinguished from intent or mens rea. Although motive is not an element of a crime, evidence regarding

motives can be introduced to help establish intent. In contract law, motive is usu. distinguished from cause or consideration.

¹mov·able *or* **move·able** \'mü-və-bəl\ *adj* : capable of being moved

²movable *or* **moveable** *n* : an item of movable property; *also* : a right or interest (as a chattel mortgage) in an item of movable property ⟨bonds and annuities are incorporeal ~s⟩ — often used in pl.; compare IMMOVABLE

movable property — see PROPERTY

mov·ant *or* **mov·ent** \'mü-vənt\ *n* : the party who makes a motion

move *vb* **moved; mov·ing** *vi* : to make a motion ⟨*moved* to seize the property⟩ ~ *vt* : to request (a court) by means of a motion ⟨*moved* the court to vacate the order⟩

moveable *var of* MOVABLE

movent *var of* MOVANT

moving expense — see EXPENSE

moving papers *n pl* : the documents (as affidavits) containing and supporting a motion

moving violation *n* : a violation (as speeding or drunk driving) of motor vehicle or traffic laws that is made while the vehicle is moving

mug *vt* **mugged; mug·ging** : to assault (an individual) usu. with intent to rob

mug shot *n* : a police photograph of a suspect's face or profile that is taken when the suspect is booked

mulct \'məlkt\ *n* [Latin *multa, mulcta*] : FINE, PENALTY — **mulct** *vt*

mul·ti·far·i·ous \,məl-ti-'far-ē-əs\ *adj* : having or occurring in great variety : DIVERSE; *also* : uniting usu. in an improper way distinct and independent matters, subjects, or causes ⟨point one is ~, and we must break it down for analysis: a) the alleged reformation of the decree; and b) the order that appellant pay —*Spradley v. Hutchison*, 787 S.W.2d 214 (1990)⟩ — compare MISJOINDER — **mul·ti·far·i·ous·ness** *n*

mul·ti·ple–line insurance \'məl-ti-pəl-'līn-\ *n* : an insurance contract that provides coverage against multiple perils (as liability and loss of property)

multiple listing — see LISTING

mul·ti·plic·i·tous \ˌməl-tə-ˈpli-sə-təs\ *adj* : giving rise to or resulting from multiplicity ⟨a ~ indictment⟩ ⟨they are not ~ charges⟩

mul·ti·plic·i·ty \ˌməl-tə-ˈpli-sə-tē\ *n, pl* **-ties 1 a** : the quality or state of being multiple or various **b** : the charging of a single criminal act or offense as multiple separate charges or counts of an indictment or information ⟨~ does not require dismissal of the indictment — W. R. LaFave and J. H. Israel⟩ — compare DUPLICITY 2, MISJOINDER ◊ Multiplicity raises the risk of violating the double jeopardy protection against receiving multiple sentences for a single offense. Multiplicity is a defect that can be corrected without dismissal of the case. **2** : a great number ⟨joinder is allowed to avoid a ~ of actions⟩

1mu·nic·i·pal \myü-ˈni-sə-pəl\ *adj* **1** : of or relating to the internal affairs of a major political unit (as a nation) ⟨was sentenced by a court of ~, not international, jurisdiction⟩ — compare DOMESTIC **2 a** : of, relating to, or characteristic of a municipality ⟨the ~ counsel⟩ **b** : having local self-government ⟨a ~ district⟩ **3** : restricted to one locality

2municipal *n* : a security issued by a state or local government or by an authority set up by such a government — usu. used in pl.; see also *municipal bond* at BOND 2

municipal bond — see BOND 2

municipal corporation — see CORPORATION

municipal court *n* : a court that sits in some cities and larger towns and that usu. has limited civil and criminal jurisdiction over cases arising within the municipality; *also* : POLICE COURT

mu·nic·i·pal·i·ty \myü-ˌni-sə-ˈpa-lə-tē\ *n, pl* **-ties** : a primarily urban municipal corporation; *also* : the governing body of a municipality

mu·ni·ment \ˈmyü-nə-mənt\ *n* [Anglo-French, from Middle French, defense, from Latin *munimentum*, from *munire* to fortify] : a record (as a deed, statutory grant, or judgment) that passes title to real property and enables a person to defend the title or otherwise maintain a claim to real rights or privileges ⟨~ of title⟩ — often used in pl. ⟨the ~s of which the chain of record title is formed —*Connecticut General Statutes*⟩

1mur·der \ˈmər-dər\ *n* [partly from Old English *morthor;* partly from Old French *murdre,* of Germanic origin] : the crime of unlawfully and unjustifiably killing another under circumstances defined by statute (as with premeditation); *esp* : such a crime committed purposely, knowingly, and recklessly with extreme indifference to human life or during the course of a serious felony (as robbery or rape) — compare COLD BLOOD, COOLING TIME, HOMICIDE, MANSLAUGHTER ◊ Self-defense, necessity, and lack of capacity for criminal responsibility (as because of insanity) are defenses to a charge of murder. Most state statutes and the U.S. Code divide murder into two degrees. Florida, Minnesota, and Pennsylvania currently have three degrees of murder. Some states do not assign degrees of murder.

de·praved–heart murder \di-ˈprävd-ˈhärt-\ : a murder that is the result of an act which is dangerous to others and shows that the perpetrator has a depraved mind and no regard for human life ◊ Depraved-heart murder is usu. considered second- or third-degree murder.

felony murder : a murder that occurs in the commission of a serious felony (as burglary or sexual battery) — compare *misdemeanor-manslaughter* at MANSLAUGHTER ◊ Felony murder is usu. considered first-degree murder. Felony murder does not require specific intent

to kill, and an accessory to the felony may also be charged with the murder.
first–degree murder : a murder that is committed with premeditation or during the course of a serious felony (as kidnapping) or that otherwise (as because of extreme cruelty) requires the most serious punishment under the law
second–degree murder : a murder that is committed without premeditation but with some intent (as general or transferred intent) or other circumstances not covered by the first-degree murder statute
third–degree murder : a murder that is not first- or second-degree murder: as **a** : a murder committed in the perpetration of a felony not listed in the first-degree murder statute **b** : DEPRAVED-HEART MURDER in this entry
²murder *vt* : to kill (a human being) unlawfully and under circumstances constituting murder ~ *vi* : to commit murder
mur•der•er \'mər-dər-ər\ *n* : a person who commits murder
mu•tu•al \'myü-chə-wəl\ *adj* **1** : directed by each toward the other : RECIPROCAL ⟨~ orders of protection in domestic violence cases —L. H. Schafran and Norman Wikler⟩ **2** : shared in common : JOINT ⟨spouses' ~ obligation to sup-

port children of their marriage —*Louisiana Civil Code*⟩ **3** : of or relating to a plan whereby the members of an organization share in the profits and expenses; *specif* : of, relating to, or taking the form of an insurance method in which the policyholders constitute the members of the insuring company — **mu•tu•al•ly** *adv*
mutual company — see COMPANY
mutual fund — see FUND 2
mu•tu•al•i•ty \ˌmyü-chə-'wa-lə-tē\ *n* : the quality or state of being mutual: as **a** : the quality of a contract under which both parties are bound by obligations **b** : the state of debts for purposes of set-off under bankruptcy law in which the debts are owed between the same parties standing in the same capacity
mutual mistake — see MISTAKE
mutual will — see WILL
mu•tu•um \'myü-chù-wəm\ *n* [Latin, from neuter of *mutuus* borrowed, lent] : LOAN FOR CONSUMPTION at LOAN
mys•te•ri•ous dis•ap•pear•ance *n* : the loss of property under unknown or puzzling circumstances which are difficult to explain or understand
mys•tic testament \'mis-tik-\ *n* : MYSTIC WILL at WILL
mystic will — see WILL

N

na·ked *adj* **1 :** characterized by the lack of an interest or of exclusive control, use, or possession **2 :** not backed by the option writer's ownership of the commodity, the contract for the commodity, or the security
naked land trust — see TRUST
naked licensee *n* : BARE LICENSEE
naked option — see OPTION 3
naked owner — see OWNER
naked power — see POWER 2b
naked promise — see PROMISE
naked trust — see TRUST
national bank — see BANK
nat·u·ral *adj* **1 :** based on an inherent sense of right and wrong ⟨~ justice⟩ — see also NATURAL LAW, NATURAL RIGHT **2 a :** existing as part of or determined by nature ⟨the ~ condition of the land⟩ **b** : being in accordance with or arising from nature esp. as distinguished from operation of law — see also NATURAL PERSON; compare ARTIFICIAL **c** : arising from the usual course of events ⟨a ~ result of the accident⟩ **3 a :** begotten as distinguished from adopted **b** : being a relation by consanguinity as distinguished from adoption ⟨~ parents⟩ **4 :** ILLEGITIMATE ⟨a ~ child⟩ — **nat·u·ral·ly** *adv*
natural and prob·a·ble con·se·quence *n* : a consequence that one could reasonably expect to result from an act ⟨the injury was determined to be a *natural and probable consequence* of the defendant's negligence⟩
natural fruit — see FRUIT
natural guardian — see GUARDIAN
natural heir — see HEIR
nat·u·ral·ize \'na-chə-rə-ˌlīz\ *vt* **-ized; -iz·ing :** to admit (a person) to citizenship — **nat·u·ral·iza·tion** \ˌna-chə-rə-lə-'zā-shən\ *n*
r ⸱⸱⸱ **w** *n* : a body of law or a spe-

cific principle of law that is held to be derived from nature and binding upon human society in the absence of or in addition to positive law ◊ While natural law, based on a notion of timeless order, does not receive as much credence as it did formerly, it was an important influence on the enumeration of natural rights by Thomas Jefferson and others.
natural object *n* : a person likely to be the recipient of some thing or action; *esp* : a person who is close to or related to a person dying whether testate or intestate, who would reasonably be expected to receive a share of the estate, and who may be so recognized in the absence of a will or in a will contest — usu. used in the phrase *natural object of one's bounty* ⟨widows and children, who, as the *natural objects* of a testator's bounty, were . . . residuary legatees —*Lomon v. Citizens Nat'l. Bank & Trust of Muskogee*, 689 P.2d 306 (1984)⟩
natural obligation — see OBLIGATION
natural person *n* : a human being as distinguished from a person (as a corporation) created by operation of law — compare JURIDICAL PERSON, LEGAL PERSON
natural right *n* : a right considered to be conferred by natural law ⟨James Madison . . . distinguished *natural rights*, such as life and liberty, from rights that are part of the compact between citizen and government —L. H. Tribe⟩
natural servitude — see SERVITUDE
nav·i·ga·ble wa·ters \'na-vi-gə-bəl-\ *n pl* : waters that are capable of being navi-

\ə\abut \ᵊ\kitten \ər\further \a\ash \ā\ace
\ä\cot, cart \au̇\out \ch\chin \e\bet \ē\easy
\g\go \i\hit \ī\ice \j\job \ŋ\sing \ō\go \ȯ\law
\ȯi\boy \th\thin \t͟h\the \ü\loot \u̇\foot \y\yet
\zh\vision *see also* Pronunciation Symbols page

gated (as for commerce) and to which federal admiralty jurisdiction and specific environmental regulations apply ⟨it is the national goal that the discharge of pollutants into the *navigable waters* be eliminated by 1985 — *U.S. Code*⟩

nec·es·sar·ies \'ne-sə-ˌser-ēz\ *n pl* **1** : goods, services, or expenses that are considered necessary: as **a** : such goods, services, or expenses as are essential to the maintenance and support of a present or former spouse or of the child of divorced parents and for which one spouse or parent may seek reimbursement or contribution from the other **b** : essential goods or services furnished to a vessel whose supplier may be entitled to a maritime lien **2** : goods or services delivered to a minor that are considered by reference to his or her circumstances to warrant holding the minor to a contract for them despite an attempt to disaffirm it

nec·es·sary and proper clause *n, often cap N&P&C* [from the words of the clause] : the clause in Article I, Section 8 of the U.S. Constitution that empowers the Congress to make all laws necessary for executing its other powers and those of the federal government as a whole

necessary deposit — see DEPOSIT 3a

necessary party — see PARTY 1b

ne·ces·si·ty *n, pl* **-ties** **1 a** : the presence or pressure of circumstances that justify or compel a certain course of action; *esp* : a need to respond or react to a dangerous situation by committing a criminal act **b** : an affirmative defense originating in common law that the defendant had to commit a criminal act because of the pressure of a situation that threatened a harm greater than that resulting from the act — see also *choice of evils defense* at DEFENSE 2a; compare DURESS, UNDUE INFLUENCE **2** : something that is necessary esp. to subsistence ⟨obligated to provide the *necessities* of food, clothing, and shelter⟩

neg·a·tive act *n* : ACT 1b

negative averment *n* : a negative statement or allegation (as in a pleading) that constitutes a statement of fact and that must be proved by the party making it ⟨a *negative averment* alleging that the plaintiff did not have the capacity to sue⟩

negative easement — see EASEMENT

negative testimony — see TESTIMONY

ne·glect *n* : a disregard of duty resulting from carelessness, indifference, or willfulness; *esp* : a failure to provide a child under one's care with proper food, clothing, shelter, supervision, medical care, or emotional stability — compare ABUSE 2, NEGLIGENCE — **neglect** *vt* — **ne·glect·ful** *adj*

neg·li·gence \'ne-gli-jəns\ *n* : failure to exercise the degree of care expected of a person of ordinary prudence in like circumstances in protecting others from a foreseeable and unreasonable risk of harm in a particular situation; *also* : conduct that reflects this failure — called also *ordinary negligence, simple negligence;* compare ABUSE 2, DUE CARE, INTENT ◊ Negligence may render one civilly and sometimes criminally liable for resulting injuries.

collateral negligence : negligence on the part of an independent contractor that is not connected with a manner of working or risk ordinarily associated with particular work and for which the employer of the contractor is not liable

com·par·a·tive negligence \kəm-'par-ə-tiv-\ **1 a** : negligence of one among multiple parties involved in an injury that is measured (as in percentages) according to the degree of its contribution to the injury ⟨the *comparative negligence* of the plaintiff⟩ **b** : a doctrine, rule, or method of apportioning liability and damages in tort law: negligence and damages are determined by reference to the proportionate fault of the plaintiff and defendant with the negligence of the plaintiff not constituting an absolute bar to recovery from the defendant — compare CONTRIBUTORY NEGLIGENCE in this entry

◊ The great majority of states have replaced the doctrine of contributory negligence with that of comparative negligence. **2** : an affirmative defense alleging comparative negligence by the plaintiff

contributory negligence **1** : negligence on the part of a plaintiff that contributed to the injury at issue **2** : a now largely abolished doctrine in tort law: negligence on the part of a plaintiff that contributed to the injury at issue will bar recovery from the defendant; *also* : an affirmative defense based on this doctrine

criminal negligence : a gross deviation from the standard of care expected of a reasonable person that is manifest in a failure to protect others from a risk (as of death) deriving from one's conduct and that renders one criminally liable — called also *culpable negligence;* compare GROSS NEGLIGENCE in this entry

gross negligence : negligence that is marked by conduct that presents an unreasonably high degree of risk to others and by a failure to exercise even the slightest care in protecting them from it and that is sometimes associated with conscious and willful indifference to their rights — see also RECKLESSNESS; compare CRIMINAL NEGLIGENCE in this entry

negligence per se \-ˌpər-'sā, -'sē\ : negligence that consists of a violation of a statute esp. designed to protect the public safety ◊ Recovery may be had on a theory of negligence per se when the harm resulting from the violation is the type that the statute is designed to prevent, the plaintiff is a member of the class of persons sought to be protected by the statute, and the violation is the proximate cause of the plaintiff's injury.

ordinary negligence : NEGLIGENCE
passive negligence : failure to do something (as to discover a dangerous condition on one's property) that is not a breach of an affirmative duty and that

in combination with another's act is a cause of injury
simple negligence : NEGLIGENCE
slight negligence : failure to exercise the great degree of care typical of an extraordinarily prudent person ◊ The category of slight negligence is used much less frequently than ordinary negligence and gross negligence, the other members of a three-level classification that was formerly prevalent.

negligence per se — see NEGLIGENCE
neg·li·gent \'ne-gli-jənt\ *adj* : marked by, given to, or produced by negligence ⟨a ~ act⟩⟨the defendant was ~⟩ — **neg·li·gent·ly** *adv*

negligent en·trust·ment \-in-'trəst-mənt\ *n* : the entrusting of a dangerous article (as a motor vehicle) to one who is reckless or too inexperienced or incompetent to use it safely; *also* : a theory or doctrine making one liable for injury caused by a party to whom one negligently entrusted something

negligent homicide — see HOMICIDE
ne·go·tia·ble \ni-'gō-shə-bəl\ *adj* : capable of being negotiated; *esp* : transferable from one party to another by delivery with or without endorsement so that title passes to the transferee ⟨~ securities⟩ ⟨a ~ certificate of deposit⟩ — see also NEGOTIABLE INSTRUMENT — **ne·go·tia·bil·i·ty** \ni-ˌgō-shə-'bi-lə-tē\ *n*

negotiable bill of lading — see BILL OF LADING

negotiable instrument *n* : a transferable instrument (as a note, check, or draft) containing an unconditional promise or order to pay to a holder or to the order of a holder upon issue, possession, demand, or at a specified time ⟨was determined to be a holder in due course of a *negotiable instrument*⟩ — see also BEARER, HOLDER IN DUE COURSE

ne·go·ti·ate \ni-'gō-shē-ˌāt\ *vb* -at·ed;

\ə\abut	\ᵊ\kitten	\ər\further	\a\ash \ā\ace
\ä\cot, cart	\au̇\out	\ch\chin	\e\bet \ē\easy
\g\go	\i\hit \ī\ice	\j\job	\ŋ\sing \ō\go \ȯ\law
\ȯi\boy	\th\thin	\t͟h\the	\ü\loot \u̇\foot \y\yet
\zh\vision		*see also* Pronunciation Symbols page	

-at•ing *vi* : to confer with another so as to settle some matter — *vt* **1** : to bring about through conference, discussion, and agreement or compromise ⟨~ a contract⟩ **2 a** : to transfer (as an instrument) to another by delivery or endorsement **b** : to convert into cash or the equivalent value ⟨~ a check⟩ — **ne•go•ti•a•tion** \ni-ˌgō-shē-'ā-shən\ *n* — **ne•go•ti•a•tor** \ni-'gō-shē-ˌā-tər\ *n*

ne•go•ti•or•um ges•tio \ni-ˌgō-shē-'òr-əm-'jes-chē-ō\ *n* [Late Latin, from Latin, management of business] *in the civil law of Louisiana* : the management of or interference with the business or affairs of another without authority

negotiorum ges•tor \-'jes-tər, -ˌtòr\ *n* [Late Latin, from Latin, manager of business] *in the civil law of Louisiana* : an agent undertaking negotiorum gestio

net *adj* [Anglo-French, clean, pure, from Latin *nitidus* bright, neat, from *nitēre* to shine] : remaining after deduction of all charges, outlay, or loss ⟨the ~ proceeds⟩ — compare GROSS

net assets — see ASSET 2

net asset value *n* : the portion represented by one share of stock of the excess of the market value of a corporation's assets over its liabilities

net income *n* : the balance of gross income remaining after all allowable deductions and exemptions are taken

net lease — see LEASE

net listing — see LISTING

net operating loss — see LOSS

net premium *n* : an insurance premium consisting of the amount required to pay the insurance liability on its becoming due without paying any expenses or contingent charges

net quick assets — see ASSET 2

net valuation premium *n* : a premium for a life insurance policy set after a determination of the amount needed to cover liabilities and maintain policy reserves

net worth *n* : the excess of the value of assets over liabilities : NET ASSETS at ASSET 2

net worth meth•od *n* : a method used by the Internal Revenue Service to detect and calculate tax evasion in which the change in a taxpayer's net worth is compared to reported taxable income taking into account living expenses, allowable deductions and exemptions, and nontaxable income

¹neu•tral *n* : one that is neutral; *specif* : an impartial person used in alternative dispute resolution to help resolve or to determine the matters in dispute

²neutral *adj* : not engaged on either side; *specif* : not aligned with a political or ideological grouping — **neu•tral•ly** *adj* — **neu•tral•ness** *n*

ne var•i•e•tur \'nē-'var-ē-ˌē-tər, 'nā-'vä-rē-ˌā-tùr\ [Latin] : it must not be changed — used as an inscription on notarized documents esp. that are evidence of an encumbrance (as a mortgage)

new consideration — see CONSIDERATION

new contract dispute *n* : MAJOR DISPUTE

new trial *n* : a repeat inquiry by the same court into all or some of the issues in an action for the purpose of correcting a problem (as the improper admission of evidence) in the prior trial, determining the merits of a challenge (as that the verdict is contrary to law) to the prior outcome, or considering newly discovered evidence — compare APPEAL

new value *n* : something of value (as money, goods, services, credit, or release of previously transferred property) that is newly given ◊ A transfer by a debtor to a creditor that is intended as a contemporaneous exchange for new value and not as satisfaction for a preexisting debt may not be avoided by a trustee in bankruptcy as a voidable preference.

next friend *n* : a person appearing in or appointed by a court to act on behalf of a person (as a child) lacking legal capacity

next of kin 1 : one or more living persons in the nearest degree of relationship to a particular individual **2** : those persons entitled by statute to receive the property in an intestate's estate — compare HEIR

nex·us \'nek-səs\ *n, pl* **nex·us·es** *or* **nexus** \-səs, -ˌsüs\ [Latin, bond, tie, from *nectere* to bind] : a connection or link between things, persons, or events esp. that is or is part of a chain of causation

night·time *n* **1** : the time from dusk to dawn **2** : a statutorily set period usu. beginning shortly after dusk and ending shortly after dawn

night·walk·er \'nīt-ˌwȯ-kər\ *n* : a person who roams about at night soliciting others for illicit sexual acts — often preceded by *common*

ni·hil di·cit \'nī-əl-'dē-sit, 'nī-hil-, 'nē-hil-, -'dī-\ *n* [Latin, he says nothing] **1** : refusal or neglect by a defendant to plead or answer **2** : a judgment rendered against a defendant who refuses or neglects to plead or answer

nihil–dicit judgment — see JUDGMENT 1a

90–day letter — see LETTER 1

ni·si \'nī-ˌsī, 'nē-sē\ *adj* [Latin, unless] : taking effect at a later specified time unless previously modified or avoided by cause shown, further proceedings, or a condition fulfilled ⟨an order ∼⟩ — compare ABSOLUTE

nisi pri·us \-'prī-əs, -'prē-ùs\ *n* [Medieval Latin, unless before, the words introducing a clause in an English writ commanding a sheriff to provide a jury at the Court of Westminster on a certain day unless the judges of assize previously come to the county from which the jury is to be returned] : a court of record that tries an issue of fact before a jury and a single judge : TRIAL COURT; *also* : the proceedings in such a court : the conducting of jury trials ⟨long-distance travel eliminated the *nisi prius* practice of the justices —W. J. Brennan, Jr.⟩

NLRA *abbr* National Labor Relations Act — see also the IMPORTANT LAWS section

NLRB *abbr* National Labor Relations Board — see also the IMPORTANT AGENCIES section

NMI *abbr* no middle initial

no–ac·tion clause *n* : a clause in an insurance contract providing that the insurer does not have to pay unless and until a judgment against the insured is obtained

no–action letter — see LETTER 1

no bill — see BILL 3b

no contest *n* : NOLO CONTENDERE

no contest clause *n* : a clause inserted in a will that causes a legacy to be forfeited if the legatee challenges the will by bringing a will contest

no–du·ty doctrine *n* : a doctrine in tort law: a defendant cannot be held liable for an injury if no duty is owed to the plaintiff; *specif* : a doctrine holding that a person in possession of property is under no duty to protect an invitee from a known or obvious hazard and cannot be held liable for injury — called also *no-duty rule*

Noerr–Pen·ning·ton doctrine \'nȯr-'pe-niŋ-tən-\ *n* [after *Eastern Railroad Presidents Conference v. Noerr Motor Freight, Inc.*, 365 U.S. 127 (1961), and *United Mine Workers v. Pennington*, 381 U.S. 657 (1965), U.S. Supreme Court cases that established the doctrine] : a doctrine based on the First Amendment right of petition that exempts from antitrust liability the joint efforts of businesses to petition or influence government bodies provided that such activities are not sham

no evidence — see EVIDENCE

no–eye·wit·ness rule *n* : a rule in tort law: in the absence of testimony by eyewitnesses a jury may assume that a person has exercised reasonable care to preserve his or her own safety — used esp. in Iowa

no–fault *adj* **1** : of, relating to, or being a motor vehicle insurance plan under which someone injured in an accident is compensated usu. up to a stipulated limit for esp. actual losses (as for property

\ə\abut	\ᵊ\kitten	\ər\further \a\ash \ā\ace
\ä\cot, cart	\au̇\out	\ch\chin \e\bet \ē\easy
\g\go	\i\hit	\ī\ice \j\job \ŋ\sing \ō\go \ȯ\law
\ȯi\boy	\th\thin	\t͟h\the \ü\loot \u̇\foot \y\yet
\zh\vision	*see also*	Pronunciation Symbols page

damage, medical bills, and lost wages) by that person's own insurer regardless of who is responsible for the accident and is prohibited from or limited in his or her right to sue the responsible party **2 :** of or relating to no-fault divorce ⟨a ~ ground for dissolution⟩ — see also *no-fault divorce* at DIVORCE

no–fault divorce — see DIVORCE

no–knock *adj* **:** of, relating to, or being entry by police (as to make an arrest) into private premises without knocking and without identifying themselves ⟨a ~ raid⟩ — **no–knock** *n*

no–knock search warrant — see WARRANT

NOL *abbr* net operating loss

nolle \'nä-lē, 'nə-\ *n* **:** NOLLE PROSEQUI — **nolle** *vt*

nolle pros \-'präs\ *vt* **nolle prossed; nolle pros•sing :** NOL-PROS

nolle pros•e•qui \-'prä-sə-ˌkwī, -ˌkwē\ *n* [Latin, to be unwilling to pursue] **:** an entry in a criminal action denoting that the prosecutor will not prosecute the case further in whole or as to one or more of several counts or one or more of several defendants — compare NON PROSEQUITUR

no•lo \'nō-lō\ *n* **:** NOLO CONTENDERE

no–load \'nō-'lōd\ *adj* **:** charging no sales commission ⟨a ~ mutual fund⟩ — compare LOAD — **no–load** *n*

nolo con•ten•de•re \-kən-'ten-də-rē, -rā\ *n* [Latin, I do not wish to contend] **:** a plea by a defendant in a criminal prosecution that without admitting guilt subjects the defendant to conviction as in the case of a guilty plea but that does not bar denial of the truth of the charges in another proceeding (as a civil action based on the same acts) — called also *no contest, non vult contendere;* compare GUILTY, NOT GUILTY 1

nol–pros \'näl-'präs, 'nəl-\ *vb* **nol–prossed; nol–pros•sing** *vt* **:** to discontinue by entering a nolle prosequi ~ *vi* **:** to enter a nolle prosequi

nom•i•nal \'nä-mən-ᵊl\ *adj* **1 :** existing or being something in name or form but usu. not in reality ⟨defenses . . . raised by the corporation as ~ defendant in a derivative suit —R. C. Clark⟩ **2 :** being so small or trivial as to be a mere token ⟨charging a ~ fee⟩ **3** *of a rate of interest* **a :** equal to the annual rate of simple interest that would obtain if interest were not compounded when in fact it is compounded and paid for periods of less than a year **b :** equal to the percentage by which a repaid loan exceeds the principal borrowed with no adjustment made for inflation — compare EFFECTIVE 4 — **nom•i•nal•ly** *adv*

nominal consideration — see CONSIDERATION

nominal damages — see DAMAGE 2

nominal party — see PARTY 1b

¹nom•i•nate \'nä-mə-nət, -ˌnāt\ *adj* [Latin *nominatus*, past participle of *nominare* to call by name, from *nomin-, nomen* name] *in the civil law of Louisiana* **:** having a special or certain name — compare INNOMINATE

²nom•i•nate \'nä-mə-ˌnāt\ *vt* **-nat•ed; -nat•ing 1 :** to appoint or propose for appointment to an office, position, or place ⟨if the testator has *nominated* an executor of the will⟩ ⟨the President . . . shall ~ and by and with the advice and consent of the Senate, shall appoint ambassadors —*U.S. Constitution* art. II⟩ **2 :** to propose as a candidate for election to office — **nom•i•na•tion** \ˌnä-mə-'nā-shən\ *n*

nominate contract — see CONTRACT

nom•i•nee \ˌnä-mə-'nē\ *n* **1 :** a person named as the recipient of a grant, conveyance, or annuity **2 :** a person named or proposed for an office, duty, or position: as **a :** a person named to act as another's agent or representative **b :** a candidate selected to represent a party in an election **3 :** a person in whose name a stock or registered bond certificate is registered but who is not the actual owner

nominee trust — see TRUST

non- *prefix* **:** not **:** other than **:** reverse of **:** absence of

non·abil·i·ty \ˌnän-ə-'bi-lə-tē\ *n, pl* **-ties** : lack of legal capacity; *also* : a plea or exception raising lack of legal capacity

non·ac·qui·es·cence \ˌnän-ˌa-kwē-'es-ᵊns\ *n* : an administrative agency's disagreement with and refusal to follow judicial precedent in cases before the agency to which the precedent applies

nonadmitted asset — see ASSET 2

non·ap·pear·ance \ˌnän-ə-'pir-əns\ *n* : failure to appear in court to prosecute or defend

non·ar·bi·trary \ˌnän-'är-bə-ˌtrer-ē\ *adj* : not arbitrary

non·as·sign·able \ˌnän-ə-'sī-nə-bəl\ *adj* : not assignable

non·bank \ˌnän-'baŋk\ *adj* : being, done by, or involving some entity other than a bank ⟨~ lenders⟩ ⟨a ~ depositor⟩ — **non·bank·ing** *adj*

nonbank bank — see BANK

non·bind·ing \ˌnän-'bīn-diŋ\ *adj* : not binding ⟨a ~ referendum⟩

non·breach·ing \ˌnän-'brē-chiŋ\ *adj* : not breaching ⟨a ~ party⟩

non·cap·i·tal \ˌnän-'ka-pət-ᵊl\ *adj* : not involving the death penalty ⟨a ~ case⟩

non·cash \ˌnän-'kash\ *adj* : being other than cash ⟨~ income⟩

non·cit·i·zen \ˌnän-'si-tə-zən\ *n* : one who is not a citizen

non·claim statute \ˌnän-'klām-\ *n* : a statute prohibiting the initiation of a suit beyond a particular time period : STATUTE OF LIMITATIONS

non–com·mer·cial partnership *n* : NON-TRADING PARTNERSHIP at PARTNERSHIP

non com·pos men·tis \'nän-'käm-pəs-'men-təs\ *adj* [Latin, literally, not having mastery of one's mind] : not of sound mind : lacking mental ability to understand the nature, consequences, and effect of a situation or transaction

non·con·form·ing \ˌnän-kən-'for-miŋ\ *adj* : failing to conform or comply (as with contract requirements or specifications or a law)

nonconforming use — see USE 2

non·con·for·mi·ty \ˌnän-kən-'for-mə-tē\ *n, pl* **-ties** **1** : failure to conform to or comply with something (as contract requirements) ⟨acceptance of goods occurs when the buyer . . . will take or retain them in spite of their ~ — *Uniform Commercial Code*⟩ **2** : a particular aspect in which something is nonconforming ⟨cannot revoke an acceptance he made with knowledge of a ~ —J. J. White and R. S. Summers⟩

non·con·sen·su·al \ˌnän-kən-'sen-chə-wəl\ *adj* : not involving consent : not consented to

non·con·sum·able \ˌnän-kən-'sü-mə-bəl\ *n* : a thing (as land, furniture, or shares of stock) that may be enjoyed without altering its substance except for natural deterioration over time

non·con·trib·u·to·ry \ˌnän-kən-'tri-byə-ˌtōr-ē\ *adj* : making or involving no contribution; *specif* : involving, relating to, or being an employee benefit plan (as a pension plan) in which the employer pays the entire cost

non·con·trol·ling \ˌnän-kən-'trō-liŋ\ *adj* : not controlling

non–core \ˌnän-'kōr\ *adj* : of, relating to, or being a non-core proceeding

non–core proceeding — see PROCEEDING

non·crim·i·nal \ˌnän-'kri-mən-ᵊl\ *adj* : not criminal ⟨~ conduct⟩ ⟨~ proceedings⟩

non·cus·to·di·al \ˌnän-kə-'stō-dē-əl\ *adj* **1** : not taking place while in custody ⟨a ~ interrogation of a suspect⟩ **2** : of or being a parent who does not have sole custody of a child or who has custody a smaller portion of the time

nondeadly force — see FORCE 3

non·de·duc·ti·ble terminable interest rule \ˌnän-di-'dək-tə-bəl-\ *n* : a rule in estate tax law: the value of a property interest that passes to a surviving spouse may not be deducted if it passes from the surviving spouse to another person for less than adequate consideration upon the happening of some event (as the passing of a period of time)

non•del•e•ga•ble \,nän-'de-li-gə-bəl\ *adj* : not capable of being or permitted to be delegated — **non•del•e•ga•bil•i•ty** \-,de-li-gə-'bi-lə-tē\ *n*

non•del•e•ga•tion doctrine \,nän-,de-li-'gā-shən-\ *n* : a doctrine that Congress may not delegate its duties under the Constitution to other branches of government without violating the principle of separation of powers

non•dis•clo•sure \,nän-dis-'klō-zhər\ *n* : failure to disclose

non•di•verse \,nän-dī-'vərs, -də-\ *adj* : having the same citizenship as another party in a lawsuit ⟨a ~ defendant⟩ — compare DIVERSE

non est fac•tum \'nän-,est-'fak-təm, 'nōn-,est-'fäk-tùm\ *n* [New Latin, (it) is not (his or her) deed] : a defense by way of denial of a deed (as the execution of a contract)

non est in•ven•tus \-in-'ven-təs, -tùs\ *n* [Latin, he or she has not been found] : the return of a sheriff on a writ or process when the defendant or person to be served or arrested is not found in the jurisdiction

nonexclusive easement — see EASEMENT

non•ex•clu•sive listing *n* : OPEN LISTING at LISTING

non•fea•sance \,nän-'fēz-ᵊns\ *n* [*non-* + obsolete English *feasance* doing, execution, from Anglo-French *fesance*, from Old French *faisance* act, from *fais-*, stem of *faire* to do, from Latin *facere*] : the failure or omission to do something that should be done or esp. something that one is under a duty or obligation to do — compare MALFEASANCE, MISFEASANCE

nonforfeiture option — see OPTION 4

nonintervention will — see WILL

non•join•der \,nän-'join-dər\ *n* : the failure to join a party to a lawsuit

non•ju•di•cial \,nän-jù-'di-shəl\ *adj* : not judicial

non•ju•rid•i•cal \,nän-jə-'ri-di-kəl\ *adj* : not juridical

non–jury \,nän-'jùr-ē\ *adj* : of or relating to a case that is heard and decided by a judge or other qualified judicial officer (as a magistrate) without a jury

non•jus•ti•cia•ble \,nän-jə-'sti-shə-bəl, -'sti-shē-ə-\ *adj* : not appropriate or proper for judicial consideration or resolution — **non•jus•ti•cia•bil•i•ty** \-,sti-shə-'bi-lə-tē\ *n*

non•ne•go•tia•ble \,nän-ni-'gō-shə-bəl\ *adj* : not negotiable — **non•ne•go•tia•bil•i•ty** \-nə-,gō-shə-'bi-lə-tē\ *n*

nonnegotiable bill of lading — see BILL OF LADING

non•par \'nän-,pär, ,nän-'pär\ *adj* : NON-PARTICIPATING

non•par•tic•i•pat•ing \,nän-pär-'ti-sə-,pā-tiŋ\ *adj* : not participating; *specif* : not participating or not giving the right to participate in surplus or profit

non•per•fec•tion \,nän-pər-'fek-shən\ *n* : the failure to perfect

non•per•for•mance \,nän-pər-'for-məns\ *n* : neglect or failure to perform

non•pro•bate \,nän-'prō-,bāt\ *adj* : not involving or involved in a probate proceeding ⟨a ~ asset⟩

non•pro•pri•e•tary \,nän-prə-'prī-ə-,ter-ē\ *adj* : not proprietary

non•pros \,nän-'präs\ *vt* **non•prossed;** **non•pros•sing** : to enter a non prosequitur against

non pro•seq•ui•tur \'nän-prə-'se-kwə-tər, 'nōn-prō-'sā-kwi-,tùr\ *n* [Late Latin, he or she does not prosecute] : a judgment entered against a plaintiff for failure to appear to prosecute a suit — compare NOLLE PROSEQUI

non–pub•lic forum \,nän-'pə-blik-\ *n* : public property that has not by tradition or designation been opened as a public forum

non–pur•chase money \,nän-'pər-chəs-\ *adj* : not involving or being a debt secured by the property purchased with the money borrowed

non–re•course \,nän-'rē-,kòrs, -ri-'kòrs\ *adj* : of, relating to, or being a debt whose satisfaction may be obtained on default only out of the particular collateral given and not out of the debtor's other assets ⟨a

~ mortgage⟩ ⟨a ~ creditor⟩ — compare RECOURSE

non–recourse note — see NOTE

non·re·new·al \‚nän-ri-'nü-əl, -'nyü-\ *n* : failure to renew

non–skip person *n* : a person who is not a skip person

non·suit \‚nän-'süt\ *n* : a judgment entered against a plaintiff for failure to prosecute a case or inability to establish a prima facie case : DISMISSAL — **nonsuit** *vt*

non·sup·port \‚nän-sə-'pȯrt\ *n* : failure (as of a parent) to honor a statutory or contractual obligation to provide support; *also* : the crime of such failure to support

nontrading partnership — see PARTNERSHIP

non·union \‚nän-'yü-nyən\ *adj* **1** : not belonging to or connected with a labor union ⟨~ carpenters⟩ **2** : not recognizing or favoring labor unions or their members **3** : not produced or worked on by members of a labor union ⟨~ lettuce⟩

non·use \‚nän-'yüs\ *n* **1** : failure to use ⟨~ of land⟩ **2** : the fact or condition of not being used

non vult con·ten·dere \'nän-'vəlt-kən-'ten-də-rē, 'nōn-'vu̇lt-kȯn-'ten-de-‚rä\ *n* [Latin] : he or she does not wish to contend] : NOLO CONTENDERE — called also *non vult*

no par \'nō-'pär\ *adj* : having no par value ⟨a *no par* share⟩

no–par stock \'nō-'pär-\ *n* : NO-PAR VALUE STOCK at STOCK

no–par value stock — see STOCK

no·sci·tur a so·ci·is \'nō-si-tər-‚ä-'sō-sē-yəs, 'nō-skē-‚tu̇r-‚ä-'sō-kē-‚ēs\ *n* [Latin, it is known by its associates] : a doctrine or rule of construction: the meaning of an unclear or ambiguous word (as in a statute or contract) should be determined by considering the words with which it is associated in the context

no–strike *adj* : of, relating to, or being a provision in a collective bargaining agreement prohibiting employees from striking

no·tar·i·al \nō-'tar-ē-əl\ *adj* : of, relating to, or characteristic of a notary public; *also* : done, executed, framed, or taken by a notary public ⟨~ documents⟩ — **no·tar·i·al·ly** *adv*

no·ta·rize \'nō-tə-‚rīz\ *vt* **-rized; -riz·ing** : to acknowledge or attest as notary public ⟨~ a document⟩

no·ta·ry public \'nō-tə-rē-\ *n, pl* **no·ta·ries public** *or* **notary publics** [Latin *notarius* stenographer, from *nota* note, shorthand character] : a public officer who certifies and attests to the authenticity of writings (as deeds) and takes affidavits, depositions, and protests of negotiable instruments — called also *notary*

¹note *n* **1 a** : a written promise to pay a debt; *specif* : PROMISSORY NOTE in this entry

bank note : a promissory note issued by a bank payable to bearer on demand but without interest and circulating as money

cog·no·vit note \käg-'nō-vit-, kōg-\ : a note in which the maker acknowledges the debt and authorizes the entry of judgment against him or her without notice or a hearing : a note containing a confession of judgment

collateral note : a note secured esp. by a collateral mortgage and pledged to secure an obligation of which a hand note usu. serves as evidence

demand note : a note payable on demand — compare TIME NOTE in this entry

floating rate note : a negotiable note that yields an indexed and periodically adjusted variable rate of interest — called also *floater*

hand note : a note for an obligation secured by a collateral note

non–recourse note : a note whose satisfaction upon default may be obtained only out of the collateral securing it

promissory note : a note containing an unconditional promise to pay on demand or at a fixed or determined future time a particular sum of money to or to the order of a specified person or to the bearer

recourse note : a note whose satisfaction upon default may be obtained from the debtor's assets other than and in addition to the collateral securing it

re•new•al note : a note that continues an obligation due under a previous note

tax an•tic•i•pa•tion note : a note issued by a state or municipality on pending tax revenue to fund immediate governmental expenditures

time note : a note payable at a specified time in the future — compare DEMAND NOTE in this entry

Treasury note : a negotiable note issued by the U.S. government with a maturity date of one to ten years from the date of issue — called also *T-note;* compare *Treasury bill* at BILL 7, *Treasury bond* at BOND 2 **b** : a piece of paper money **2** : an exposition on a law-related topic esp. found in a law review

²note *vt* **noted; not•ing 1** : to recognize the existence or presence of ⟨*noted* probable jurisdiction⟩ **2** : to make a notarial memorandum of nonpayment of (a negotiable instrument) on presentation

not guilty *n* **1** : a plea by a criminal defendant who intends to contest the charges — compare GUILTY, NOLO CONTENDERE ◊ Under the Federal Rules of Criminal Procedure, if a defendant refuses to plead or if the defendant is a corporation that fails to appear the court must enter a plea of not guilty on the defendant's behalf. **2** : a verdict rendered by a jury acquitting a criminal defendant upon finding that the prosecution has not proven the defendant's guilt beyond a reasonable doubt

not guilty by reason of insanity 1 : a plea by a criminal defendant who intends to raise an insanity defense — used in jurisdictions that require such a plea in order for an insanity defense to be presented

2 : a verdict rendered by a jury in a criminal case that finds that the defendant was insane at the time of committing the crime as determined by application of the test for insanity used in the jurisdiction — compare GUILTY BUT MENTALLY ILL ◊ A verdict of not guilty by reason of insanity usu. results in the commitment of the defendant to a mental institution. Such a verdict, however, may allow the defendant to be released, sometimes into the custody or care of another (as a family member).

¹no•tice *n* **1 a** : a notification or communication of a fact, claim, demand, or proceeding — see also PROCESS, SERVICE ◊ The requirements of when, how, and what notice must be given to a person are often prescribed by a statute, rule, or contract. **b** : awareness of such a fact, claim, demand, or proceeding

actual notice **1** : actual awareness or direct notification of a specific fact, demand, claim, or proceeding ⟨had *actual notice* of the meeting⟩ — called also *express notice* **2** : IMPLIED NOTICE in this entry

constructive notice : notice that one exercising ordinary care and diligence as a matter of duty would possess and esp. that is imputed by law rather than from fact ⟨held to have *constructive notice* of the prior recorded deed⟩ — compare RECORDING ACT

express notice : ACTUAL NOTICE 1 in this entry

implied notice : notice that is imputed to a party having knowledge of a fact or circumstance that would cause a reasonable party to inquire further or having possession of a means of knowing a particular fact and that is considered a form of actual notice — called also *inquiry notice*

notice by publication : notice published in a public medium (as a newspaper) that is used, allowed, or required esp. in matters of public concern, land, or estates or after due diligence in attempting personal service of process

2 : ACTUAL NOTICE in this entry **3** : CONSTRUCTIVE NOTICE in this entry **4** : something (as information) that would cause a reasonable party to inquire further — see also IMPLIED NOTICE in this entry **5** : a written document containing notice ⟨filed a ~ of appeal⟩ **6** : recognition or attention esp. by a court — see also JUDICIAL NOTICE

²notice *vt* **no·ticed; no·tic·ing 1** : to make known through notice ⟨appeals *noticed* for the coming session⟩ ⟨a *noticed* shareholder meeting⟩ **2** : to recognize formally ⟨in a civil action or proceeding, the court shall instruct the jury to accept as conclusive any fact judicially *noticed* — *Federal Rules of Evidence* Rule 201(g)⟩ **3** : to serve a notice to; *also* : to bring about by means of notice ⟨allowed to ~ a deposition from the other party⟩

³notice *adj* : of, relating to, or being a recording act in which a party having an interest in property has priority over any earlier unrecorded claims of which the party had no notice — compare PURE RACE, RACE-NOTICE

no·tice–and–com·ment rulemaking *n* : INFORMAL RULEMAKING

notice by publication — see NOTICE

notice of pen·den·cy \-'pənd-ᵊn-sē\ : LIS PENDENS 2

notice pleading — see PLEADING 2

no·to·ri·ous \nō-'tōr-ē-əs\ *adj* : generally known and talked of ⟨adverse possession created by open, continuous, ~, and adverse use⟩

notorious possession — see POSSESSION

no true bill *n* : NO BILL at BILL 3b

no·va·tion \nō-'vā-shən\ *n* [Late Latin *novatio* renewal, legal novation, from Latin *novare* to make new, from *novus* new] : the substitution by mutual agreement of one obligation for another with or without a change of parties and with the intent to extinguish the old obligation ⟨no evidence that the contract was assigned, or that there was a ~ —*Boccardi v. Horn Constr. Corp.*, 612 N.Y.S.2d 180 (1994)⟩ — compare ACCORD 3, *substituted contract* at CONTRACT

nov·el·ty \'nä-vəl-tē\ *n, pl* **-ties** : the quality or state of being new : quality of being different from anything in prior existence ⟨satisfied the requirement of ~ for a patent on the design⟩

NSF check — see CHECK

nu·dum pac·tum \'nü-dəm-'pak-təm, 'nyü-, -'päk-\ *n* [Medieval Latin, naked pact] : an agreement or promise that is made without consideration and hence unenforceable ⟨a mere *nudum pactum*⟩ — compare *gratuitous promise* at PROMISE

nu·ga·to·ry \'nü-gə-ˌtōr-ē, 'nyü-\ *adj* [Latin *nugatorius*, from *nugari* to trifle, from *nugae* trifles] : being without operative legal effect ⟨held that such an interpretation would render the statute ~⟩

nui·sance \'nüs-ᵊns, 'nyüs-\ *n* [Anglo-French *nusaunce*, from Old French *nuire* to harm, from Latin *nocēre*] : something (as an act, object, or practice) that invades or interferes with another's rights or interests (as the use or enjoyment of property) by being offensive, annoying, dangerous, obstructive, or unhealthful

at·trac·tive nuisance 1 : a thing or condition on one's property that poses a risk to children who may be attracted to it without realizing the risk by virtue of their youth **2** : a doctrine or theory employed in most jurisdictions: a possessor of property may be liable for injury caused to a trespassing or invited child by a condition on the property if he or she failed to use ordinary care in preventing such injury (as by fencing in a pool) and had reason to foresee entry by the child and if the utility of the condition was minor compared to the likelihood of injury ⟨declined to extend the doctrine of *attractive nuisance* . . . to moving trains — *Honeycutt v. City of Wichita*, 796 P.2d 549 (1990)⟩ ◊ The doctrine of attrac-

tive nuisance originated in an 1873 U.S. Supreme Court case, *Sioux City & Pacific Railroad Co. v. Stout*, 84 U.S. 657 (1873), involving a trespassing child injured by a railroad turntable; an early premise was that the attractive nuisance caused the trespass, and so by extension the owner was responsible for the trespass as well. Subsequent modification of the doctrine has focused on the possessor's duty to use care in preventing injury, whether a child is a trespasser or invitee.
common nuisance : PUBLIC NUISANCE in this entry
nuisance at law : NUISANCE PER SE in this entry
nuisance in fact : an act, occupation, or structure that is considered a nuisance in relation to its circumstances or surroundings ⟨a lawful business may be a *nuisance in fact* in a particular location⟩ — called also *nuisance per accidens;* compare NUISANCE PER SE in this entry
nuisance per se : an act, occupation, or structure that is considered a nuisance regardless of its circumstances or surroundings ⟨a house of prostitution is a *nuisance per se*⟩ — called also *nuisance at law;* compare NUISANCE IN FACT in this entry
private nuisance : something (as an activity) that constitutes an unreasonable interference in the right to the use and enjoyment of one's property and that may be a cause of action in civil litigation
public nuisance : something that unreasonably interferes with the health, safety, comfort, morals, or convenience of the community and that is treated as a criminal violation ⟨declared that the landfill was a present and prospective *public nuisance* and ordered . . . operations to cease —*SCA Servs. v. Transportation Ins. Co.*, 646 N.E.2d 394 (1995)⟩ — called also *common nuisance*
nuisance at law — see NUISANCE
nuisance in fact — see NUISANCE

nuisance per accidens *n* : NUISANCE IN FACT at NUISANCE
nuisance per se — see NUISANCE
null \'nəl\ *adj* [Anglo-French *nul*, literally, not any, from Latin *nullus*, from *ne-* not + *ullus* any] : having no legal or binding force : VOID ⟨a ~ contract⟩
nul·li·fi·ca·tion \ˌnə-lə-fə-'kā-shən\ *n* : the act of nullifying : the state of being nullified — see also JURY NULLIFICATION
nul·li·fy \'nə-lə-ˌfī\ *vt* **-fied; -fy·ing** : to make null ⟨~ a contract⟩
nul·li·ty \'nə-lə-tē\ *n, pl* **-ties** **1** : the quality or state of being null **2** : an act, proceeding, or contract void of legal effect — compare IMPEDIMENT
absolute nullity *in the civil law of Louisiana* : a contract or act considered void by virtue of a transgression of the public order, interest, law, or morals ⟨a bigamous marriage is an *absolute nullity* — *Louisiana Civil Code*⟩; *also* : the quality or state of such a nullity ◊ A marriage that is an absolute nullity does not have to be annulled to terminate its legal effects (as property rights).
relative nullity *in the civil law of Louisiana* : a nullity that can be cured by confirmation because the object involved is considered valid; *also* : the quality or state of such a nullity ◊ A contract that is a relative nullity may be annulled and the parties restored to their original positions. A marriage that is a relative nullity must be annulled to terminate the legal effects (as property rights) of the marriage.
nu·mer·os·i·ty \ˌnü-mə-'rä-sə-tē, ˌnyü-\ *n* : the requirement that members of a proposed class formed for a class action be so numerous as to make joinder of the members impracticable
nunc pro tunc \'nəŋk-ˌprō-'təŋk, 'nu̇ŋk-ˌprō-'tu̇ŋk\ [New Latin] : now for then — used in reference to a judicial or procedural act that corrects an omission in the record, has effect as of an earlier date, or takes place after a deadline has expired ⟨a *nunc pro tunc* order⟩ ⟨permitted to file the petition *nunc pro tunc*⟩

nun·cu·pa·tive \\'nəŋ-kyə-ˌpā-tiv, nən-'kyü-pə-tiv\ *adj* [Medieval Latin *nuncupativus*, from Late Latin, so-called, from Latin *nuncupatus*, past participle of *nuncupare* to name, probably ultimately from *nomen* name + *capere* to take] : stated by spoken word

nuncupative will — see WILL

\ə\abut \ᵊ\kitten \ər\further \a\ash \ā\ace
\ä\cot, cart \aů\out \ch\chin \e\bet \ē\easy
\g\go \i\hit \ī\ice \j\job \ŋ\sing \ō\go \ȯ\law
\ȯi\boy \th\thin \th\the \ü\loot \ů\foot \y\yet
\zh\vision *see also* Pronunciation Symbols page

O

oath *n* **1 :** a solemn attestation of the truth of one's words or the sincerity of one's intentions; *specif* **:** one accompanied by calling upon a deity as a witness **2 :** a promise (as to perform official duties faithfully) corroborated by an oath — compare PERJURY — **under oath :** under a solemn and esp. legal obligation to tell the truth (as when testifying)

obi·ter dic·tum \'ō-bi-tər-'dik-təm, 'ä-bi-\ *n, pl* **obiter dic·ta** \-tə\ [Late Latin, literally, something said in passing] **:** an incidental and collateral remark that is uttered or written by a judge but is not binding **:** DICTUM

¹ob·ject \'äb-jikt\ *n* **1 :** something toward which thought, feeling, or action is directed — see also NATURAL OBJECT **2 :** the purpose or goal of something; *esp, in the civil law of Louisiana* **:** the purpose for which a contract or obligation is formed

²ob·ject \əb-'jekt\ *vt* **:** to state in opposition or as an objection ⟨~*ed* that the evidence was inadmissible⟩ ~ *vi* **:** to state opposition esp. to something in a judicial proceeding ⟨~*ed* to the testimony on the ground that it was hearsay⟩

ob·jec·tion *n* **1 :** an act or instance of objecting; *specif* **:** a statement of opposition to an aspect of a judicial or other legal proceeding ⟨file an ~ to a proposed bankruptcy plan⟩ **2 :** a reason or argument forming the ground of an objection ◊ Objections at trial are generally made for the purpose of opposing the admission of improper evidence. Such an objection must be made in a timely manner. Objections prevent the jury from seeing or hearing the evidence and preserve the issue for appeal. Objections may also be made on the ground of the opposing counsel's improper methods (as leading a witness) or for other technical reasons.

ob·li·gate \'ä-blə-ˌgāt\ *vt* **-gat·ed; -gat·ing** **1 :** to bind legally or morally ⟨was *obligated* to pay child support⟩ **2 :** to commit (as funds or property) to meet or provide security for an obligation — **oblig·a·to·ry** \ə-'bli-gə-ˌtōr-ē\ *adj*

ob·li·ga·tion \ˌä-blə-'gā-shən\ *n* **1 :** a promise, acknowledgment, or agreement (as a contract) that binds one to a specific performance (as payment); *also* **:** the binding power of such an agreement or indication ⟨held that the amendment did not unconstitutionally impair the ~*s* of contracts —*Davis v. American Family Mut. Ins. Co.*, 521 N.W.2d 366 (1994)⟩ **2 :** a debt security (as a corporate or government bond) — see also COLLATERALIZED MORTGAGE OBLIGATION **3 :** what one is obligated to do, satisfy, or fulfill: as **a :** a commitment to pay a particular amount of money ⟨does not create a debt, liability, or other ~, legal or moral —*State v. Florida Dev. Fin. Corp.*, 650 So. 2d 14 (1995)⟩; *also* **:** an amount owed in such a commitment **b :** a duty arising from law, contract, or morality ⟨had a legal ~ as an employer⟩ ⟨a contractual ~⟩ **4** *in the civil law of Louisiana* **:** a relationship that binds one party to a performance (as a payment or transfer) or nonperformance for another party — see also CONTRACT, OFFENSE, QUASI-OFFENSE ◊ An obligation under civil law may arise by operation of law, naturally, or by contract or other declaration of will. The elements of an obligation are: the parties, an object, the relationship by virtue of which one party is bound to perform for the other's benefit, and, in the case of conventional obligations, a cause.

conditional obligation : an obligation that is dependent on an uncertain event

conventional obligation : an obligation taking the form of a contract

heritable obligation : an obligation that may be enforced by the successor of the obligee or against the successor of the obligor

joint obligation **1** : an obligation binding different obligors to a performance for one obligee **2** : an obligation binding one obligor to a performance for different obligees ◊ In civil law, one of two or more obligors in a joint obligation is only liable for his or her portion of the performance.

natural obligation : an obligation arising from moral duty that is implied but not enforceable by the law

several obligation **1** : any of the obligations binding different obligors to separate performances for one obligee **2** : any of the obligations binding an obligor to separate performances for different obligees

solidary obligation : an obligation under which any of two or more obligors can be held liable for the entire performance (as payment of a debt) ◊ Solidary obligation is similar to joint and several liability in common law.

ob·li·gee \ˌä-blə-ˈjē\ *n* : one (as a creditor) to whom another is legally obligated ⟨an ~ protected by a surety bond⟩ — compare DEBTOR, OBLIGOR

ob·li·gor \ˌä-blə-ˈgȯr, -ˈjȯr\ *n* : one who is bound by an obligation to another ⟨an obligation extinguished by performance of the ~⟩ — compare CREDITOR, DEBTOR, OBLIGEE, PROMISOR, SURETY

ob·scene \äb-ˈsēn\ *adj* [Middle French, from Latin *obscenus, obscaenus* indecent, lewd] : extremely or deeply offensive according to contemporary community standards of morality or decency — see also *Roth v. United States* in the IMPORTANT CASES section ◊ The U.S. Supreme Court has ruled that *obscene* applies to materials that appeal predominantly to a prurient interest in sexual con-

duct, depict or describe sexual conduct in a patently offensive way, and lack serious literary, artistic, political, or scientific value. Material or expression deemed obscene by the court is not protected by the free speech guarantee of the First Amendment to the U.S. Constitution.

ob·scen·i·ty \äb-ˈse-nə-tē\ *n, pl* **-ties 1** : the quality or state of being obscene **2** : something (as an utterance or act) that is obscene; *also* : obscene material

ob·so·les·cence \ˌäb-sə-ˈles-ᵊns\ *n* : a loss in the utility or value of property that results over time from intrinsic limitations (as outmoded facilities) or external circumstances ◊ Obsolescence is usu. distinguished from depreciation and physical deterioration.

economic obsolescence : obsolescence that results from external factors (as location) that render a property obsolete, no longer competitive, unattractive to purchasers or investors, or of decreasing usefulness ⟨claimed that the appraisal failed to account for *economic obsolescence* resulting from an adjacent waste facility⟩

func·tion·al obsolescence \ˈfəŋk-shə-nəl-\ : obsolescence deriving from a lack of adequate or appropriate equipment, space, or design

ob·struc·tion of justice \əb-ˈstrək-shən-\ : the crime or act of willfully interfering with the process of justice and law esp. by influencing, threatening, harming, or impeding a witness, potential witness, juror, or judicial or legal officer or by furnishing false information in or otherwise impeding an investigation or legal process ⟨the defendant's *obstruction of justice* led to a more severe sentence⟩

ob·vi·ous *adj* : easily seen, discovered, or understood; *specif* : readily apparent to a person of ordinary skill in a particular art considering the scope and content of the

\ə\abut \ᵊ\kitten \ər\further \a\ash \ā\ace
\ä\cot, cart \au̇\out \ch\chin \e\bet \ē\easy
\g\go \i\hit \ī\ice \j\job \ŋ\sing \ō\go \ȯ\law
\ȯi\boy \th\thin \t͟h\the \ü\loot \u̇\foot \y\yet
\zh\vision *see also* Pronunciation Symbols page

prior art — see also PATENT ◊ An invention that is found to be obvious cannot be patented. — **ob•vi•ous•ness** *n*

oc•cu•pan•cy \'ä-kyə-pən-sē\ *n, pl* **-cies** 1 : the fact or condition of holding, possessing, or residing in or on something ⟨~ of the premises⟩ 2 : the act or fact of taking or having possession (as of abandoned property) to acquire ownership 3 : the fact or condition of being occupied ⟨~ by more than 400 persons is unlawful⟩ 4 : the use to which a property is put ⟨designed for industrial ~⟩

oc•cu•pant \'ä-kyə-pənt\ *n* 1 : one who occupies a particular place ⟨an ~ of the car⟩⟨the ~ of the apartment⟩ 2 : one who acquires title by occupancy

oc•cu•pa•tion•al disease \,ä-kyə-'pā-shə-nəl-\ *n* : an ailment that results from the characteristic conditions or functions of one's employment rather than from the ordinary risks to which the general public is exposed and that renders one eligible for workers' compensation — compare DISABILITY 1

oc•cu•pa•tion tax \,ä-kyə-'pā-shən-\ *n* : an excise imposed on persons for the privilege of carrying on a trade, business, or occupation

oc•cur•rence *n* : something that takes place; *esp* : an accident, event, or continuing condition that causes personal or property damage that is unintended or unexpected from the standpoint of an insured party making a claim

occurrence policy *n* : an insurance policy that provides coverage for an event occurring within the policy period even if the discovery or claim is made later — compare CLAIMS MADE POLICY

ocean ma•rine insurance *n* : insurance against risks incident to transportation by sea — compare INLAND MARINE INSURANCE, MARINE INSURANCE

odd–lot *adj* : of, relating to, or being the type of worker considered under the odd-lot doctrine ⟨an ~ worker without stable employment⟩

odd lot *n* : a quantity of stock that is less than the usual rounded amount (as 100 shares) — compare ROUND LOT

odd–lot doctrine *n* : a doctrine in workers' compensation law: a disabled worker who is not totally incapacitated for all work may nonetheless be considered totally disabled if there is no reasonably dependable market for his or her services

offence *var of* OFFENSE

of•fend•er \ə-'fen-dər\ *n* : one that commits an offense ⟨a repeat ~⟩

of•fense *or* **of•fence** \ə-'fens\ *n* 1 : a violation of the law; *esp* : a criminal act ⟨nor shall any person be subject for the same ~ to be twice put in jeopardy — *U.S. Constitution* amend. V⟩ — see also LESSER INCLUDED OFFENSE 2 *in the civil law of Louisiana* : an intentional unlawful act that causes damage to another and for which the law imposes an obligation for damages — compare *quasi contract* at CONTRACT, QUASI-OFFENSE ◊ Breach of contract, offenses, quasi-offenses, and quasi contracts are the bases for civil liability under the civil law. Offenses and quasi-offenses are comparable to common-law torts.

of•fen•sive \ə-'fen-siv\ *adj* 1 : of, relating to, or designed for attack ⟨~ weapons⟩ 2 : causing displeasure or resentment; *esp* : contrary to a particular or prevailing sense of what is decent, proper, or moral ⟨depicted sexual acts in a patently ~ way⟩ — see also OBSCENE — **of•fen•sive•ly** *adv* — **of•fen•sive•ness** *n*

of•fer \'ȯ-fər\ *n* 1 : a proposal, promise, or other manifestation of willingness to make and fulfill a contract or to bargain under proposed terms with another party that has the power to accept it upon receiving it ⟨denied accepting the ~⟩ — see also REVOKE, TENDER OFFER 2 : a price named by one proposing to buy (as in a bid, bargain, or settlement) : the amount of an offer to pay money ⟨decided the ~ was too low⟩ — **offer** *vb*

of•fer•ee \,ȯ-fə-'rē\ *n* : one to whom an offer is made ⟨a unilateral contract consists of a promise on the part of the offeror and performance of the requisite terms by the ~ —*Kloss v. Honeywell, Inc.*, 890 P.2d 480 (1995)⟩

of·fer·ing *n* : an issuance of securities for sale ⟨raise capital through a public ~ of stock⟩

of·fer·or \'ȯ-fə-rər, -ˌrȯr\ *n* : one that makes an offer to another ⟨acceptance of the offer terminates the power of revocation that the ~ ordinarily has —J. D. Calamari and J. M. Perillo⟩

of·fice *n* **1** : a special duty, charge, or position conferred by governmental authority and for a public purpose ⟨qualified to hold public ~⟩; *broadly* : a special duty or position of authority ⟨hold an ~ of trust⟩ **2** : a place where business or administration is conducted or services are performed **3** : a special administrative department or unit ⟨~ of the district attorney⟩

of·fic·er *n* **1** : one charged with administering or enforcing the law ⟨a police ~⟩ **2** : one who holds an office of trust, authority, or command ⟨the directors, ~s, employees, and shareholders of a corporation⟩ **3** : one who holds a position of authority or command in the armed forces ⟨insubordinate to his commanding ~⟩

¹of·fi·cial *n* : one who holds or is invested with an office esp. in government ⟨a municipal ~⟩

²official *adj* **1** : of, relating to, or holding an office, position, or trust ⟨~ duties⟩ **2** : fully authorized ⟨an ~ policy of the bank⟩ — **of·fi·cial·ly** *adv*

official immunity — see IMMUNITY

of·fi·ci·ant \ə-'fi-shē-ənt\ *n* : one (as a priest) who officiates at a religious rite

of·fi·cious in·ter·med·dler \ə-'fi-shəs-ˌin-tər-'med-ᵊl-ər\ *n* : one who unnecessarily meddles in the affairs of another and then seeks restitution or compensation for the beneficial results but who is barred from receiving it

¹off·set \'ȯf-ˌset\ *n* : a claim or amount that reduces or balances another claim or amount : SET-OFF ⟨the creditor's own debt was an ~⟩; *also* : the reduction or balance achieved by such a claim

²off·set \ˌȯf-'set\ *vt* : to balance, reduce, or calculate by reference to another amount ⟨~ the debt against a credit⟩

ol·i·gop·o·ly \ˌä-li-'gä-pə-lē, ˌō-\ *n*, *pl* **-lies** : a condition in which a few sellers dominate a particular market to the detriment of competition by others

olo·graph \'ō-lə-ˌgraf, 'ä-\ *n* : HOLOGRAPH — **olo·graph·ic** \ˌō-lə-'gra-fik, ˌä-\ *adj*

omis·sion \ō-'mi-shən\ *n* **1** : something neglected, left out, or left undone **2** : the act, fact, or state of leaving something out or failing to do something esp. that is required by duty, procedure, or law ⟨liable for a criminal act or ~⟩

omnibus bill — see BILL 1

om·ni·bus clause \'äm-ni-ˌbəs-\ *n* **1** : a clause in a will, decree, or security agreement that stipulates the disposition or status of property not specifically named **2** : a clause in a vehicle insurance policy that provides coverage for those who use the vehicle with the express or implied permission of the insured — see also STATUTORY OMNIBUS CLAUSE

omnibus motion — see MOTION

oner·ous \'ä-nə-rəs, 'ō-\ *adj* **1** : excessively burdensome or costly **2** : involving a return benefit, compensation, or consideration ⟨an ~ donation⟩ — used chiefly in the civil law of Louisiana; see also *onerous contract* at CONTRACT; compare GRATUITOUS

onerous contract — see CONTRACT

onerous title — see TITLE

op. *abbr* opinion

¹open *adj* **1** : exposed to general view or knowledge : free from concealment ⟨an ~, notorious, continuous, and adverse use of the property⟩ ⟨an ~ and obvious danger⟩ ◊ When a defect, hazard, or condition is open such that a reasonable person under the circumstances should have recognized the danger posed by it, a defendant is usu. relieved of liability for failure to warn. **2** : not restricted to a particular group or category of participants; *specif* : enterable by a registered voter regardless of political affiliation ⟨an

\ə\abut \ᵊ\kitten \ər\further \a\ash \ā\ace
\ä\cot, cart \au̇\out \ch\chin \e\bet \ē\easy
\g\go \i\hit \ī\ice \j\job \ŋ\sing \ō\go \ȯ\law
\ȯi\boy \th\thin \t͟h\the \ü\loot \u̇\foot \y\yet
\zh\vision *see also* Pronunciation Symbols page

~ primary⟩ **3 a** : being in effect or operation ⟨an ~ mine⟩ ⟨a bench warrant still ~⟩ **b** : available for use ⟨an ~ toll road⟩ **c** : not finally determined, decided, or settled : subject to further consideration ⟨an ~ question⟩ **d** : remaining effective or available for use until canceled ⟨an ~ insurance contract⟩ **4** : not repressed or regulated by legal controls ⟨a state with ~ gambling⟩

²open *vb* **opened; open·ing** *vt* **1** : to begin the process of ⟨~ the succession⟩ **2 a** : to make the statement by which the trial of (a case) is begun and put before the court **b** : to be the first to speak in summing up or arguing (a case) **3** : to restore or recall (as an order, rule, or judgment) from a finally determined state to a state in which the parties are free to prosecute or oppose by further proceedings ~ *vi* **1** : to begin action : commence on some course or activity ⟨the stock ~*ed* at par⟩ **2** : to begin the trial of a case ⟨defendant . . . has the option of presenting an opening statement immediately after plaintiff ~*s* — J. H. Friedenthal *et al.*⟩

open court *n* **1** : a recorded judicial proceeding that is presided over by a judge and attended by the parties and their attorneys and that is convened for the purpose of conducting official business — compare IN CAMERA **2** : a session of a court that is open to the public

open–end *adj* : organized to allow for contingencies: as **a** : permitting additional debt to be incurred under the original debt instrument subject to specified conditions — see also *open-end mortgage* at MORTGAGE **b** : having fluctuating capitalization of shares that are issued or redeemed at the current net asset value or at a figure in fixed ratio to this ⟨an ~ investment company⟩ — compare CLOSED-END **c** : calling for the filling by a particular contractor of all government needs for a specific product during a specified period ⟨an ~ contract⟩

open–end mortgage — see MORTGAGE

open fields doctrine *n* : a doctrine in criminal procedure: law enforcement officers may make a warrantless search of the area outside of the curtilage of a person's home without violating the Fourth Amendment to the U.S. Constitution — called also *open fields rule*

open forum *n* : a government property that is opened to the public for expressive activities of any kind — compare LIMITED PUBLIC FORUM

opening statement *n* : a statement to the jury by trial counsel before the presentation of evidence that usu. explains the nature of the case, the factual matters to be proven, and the evidence to be presented and that summarizes the arguments to be made; *also* : a similar statement made to the presiding authority (as an arbitrator) at a nonjudicial or quasi-judicial hearing (as an arbitration hearing)

open listing — see LISTING

open market *n* : a freely competitive market in which any buyer or seller may trade and in which prices are determined by competition

open mortgage clause *n* : a mortgage clause which provides that payments go first to the mortgagee to the extent of its interest and which makes the mortgagee's right to receive payment dependent on the mortgagor's right to recover under the policy — called also *simple mortgage clause*

open order — see ORDER 4b

open perils *adj* : of, relating to, or being an insurance contract that covers all perils unless specifically excluded

open shop *n* : an establishment in which eligibility for employment and retention on the payroll are not determined by membership or nonmembership in a labor union though there may be an agreement by which a union is recognized as sole bargaining agent — called also *merit shop;* compare AGENCY SHOP, CLOSED SHOP, UNION SHOP

op·er·at·ing \'ä-pə-ˌrā-tiŋ\ *adj* **1** : engaged in active business **2** : arising out of or relating to the current daily operations of a concern (as in transportation or manufacturing) as distinct from its finan-

cial transactions and permanent improvements ⟨~ expenses⟩ ⟨~ personnel⟩
operating lease — see LEASE
operating under the influence : DRIVING UNDER THE INFLUENCE
op·er·a·tion·al \ˌä-pə-'rā-shə-nəl\ *adj* : MINISTERIAL
op·er·a·tion of law \ˌä-pə-'rā-shən-\ : the application of law to a situation that gives rise to a result ⟨statutory liens and other forms of security that arise by *operation of law* —J. J. White and R. S. Summers⟩
opin·ion \ə-'pin-yən\ *n* **1 a** : a belief stronger than impression and less strong than positive knowledge **b** : a formal expression of a judgment or appraisal by an expert — see also *opinion testimony* at TESTIMONY; compare FACT **2 a** : advice or evaluation regarding the legal issues involved in a situation given by an attorney to a client ⟨an ~ of title⟩ — called also *legal opinion; see* also *opinion letter* at LETTER 1 **b** : an advisory opinion issued by an authorized public official (as an attorney general) or a recognized body (as the American Bar Association) **3 a** : the formal written expression by a court or judge of the reasons and principles of law upon which the decision in a case is based — compare HOLDING, JUDGMENT, RULING

advisory opinion : a nonbinding opinion or evaluation of a court or other judicial or quasi-judicial authority or body regarding the effect of the law on a situation that does not present an actual controversy between parties ⟨to answer questions which were not brought before this Court would be to issue an *advisory opinion* —JBC of Wyoming Corp. v. City of Cheyenne, 843 P.2d 1190 (1992)⟩ ◊ Advisory opinions are issued esp. by administrative agencies and by some state courts. Federal courts are constrained by the U.S. Constitution to deciding only cases or controversies and cannot issue advisory opinions.

concurring opinion : an opinion by a judge who agrees with the result in a case but not necessarily with the reasoning used to reach it

dissenting opinion : an opinion by a judge who disagrees with the result in a case

majority opinion : an opinion in a case that is written by one judge and in which a majority of the judges on the court join

memorandum opinion **1** : a brief opinion of a court that announces the result of a case without extensive discussion and that is usu. unpublished and cannot be cited as precedent **2** : an opinion of the U.S. Tax Court that is ordered not to be published but that is authoritative as precedent **3 a** : an opinion of a court that sets forth the court's views or intended decision in a case but does not constitute the judgment **b** : an opinion of a court or judge setting forth the conclusions and findings and containing or constituting the actual order, judgment, or decree in the case

per curiam opinion : a usu. very brief unanimous opinion attributed to the court as a whole and not to any particular judge

plurality opinion : an opinion with which a majority of the judges on the court concur in result but not in reasoning

separate opinion : an opinion written separately by a judge who dissents or who concurs only in the result of the majority opinion

slip opinion : an opinion published in temporary form soon after the decision is rendered **b** : a written explanation for a decision reached by an official (as an arbitrator) presiding over the nonjudicial resolution of a dispute
opinion letter — see LETTER 1
opinion testimony — see TESTIMONY
op·por·tu·ni·ty cost *n* : the cost of making

\ə\abut \ᵊ\kitten \ər\further \a\ash \ā\ace
\ä\cot, cart \aù\out \ch\chin \e\bet \ē\easy
\g\go \i\hit \ī\ice \j\job \ŋ\sing \ō\go \ò\law
\òi\boy \th\thin \t͟h\the \ü\loot \ù\foot \y\yet
\zh\vision *see also* Pronunciation Symbols page

an investment that is the difference between the return on one investment and the return on an alternative

opportunity for comment : the chance to express one's views on or provide information about a proposed action and esp. informal rulemaking by a government agency — called also *opportunity to comment*

opportunity to be heard : the chance to present one's views or objections before being deprived of a right by government authority — see also DUE PROCESS

opportunity to comment : OPPORTUNITY FOR COMMENT

op·pres·sion \ə-'pre-shən\ *n* : an unjust or excessive exercise of power: as **a** : unlawful, wrongful, or corrupt exercise of authority by a public official acting under color of authority that causes a person harm **b** : dishonest, unfair, wrongful, or burdensome conduct by corporate directors or majority shareholders that entitles minority shareholders to compel involuntary dissolution of the corporation **c** : inequality of bargaining power resulting in one party's lack of ability to negotiate or exercise meaningful choice — see also UNCONSCIONABILITY — **op·pres·sive** \ə-'pre-siv\ *adj*

¹op·tion \'äp-shən\ *n* **1** : the power or right to choose; *also* : a choice made or available **2** : a privilege of demanding fulfillment of a contract on any day within a specified time **3** : a contract conveying in exchange for the payment of a premium a right to buy or sell designated securities, commodities, or interests in property at a specified price during a stipulated period; *also* : the right conveyed by such a contract ⟨decided to exercise his ~⟩

call option : an option to buy at a fixed price at or within a certain time — compare PUT OPTION in this entry

covered option : an option in which the optionor owns the security or commodity to be conveyed under the option — compare NAKED OPTION in this entry

futures option : an option on futures

in·cen·tive stock option \in-'sen-tiv-\ : a stock option granted by a corporation to its officers and employees as supplementary compensation that is subject to special tax treatment under the Internal Revenue Code

index option : an option on a stock index

naked option : an option in which the optionor does not own the security or commodity and will have to purchase it at market price if the optionee decides to exercise the option — compare COVERED OPTION in this entry

put option : an option to sell for a fixed price at or within a specified time

stock option : an option giving the optionee the right to purchase a specified number of shares of stock from a corporation at a specified price at or within a specified time — see also INCENTIVE STOCK OPTION in this entry

4 : a right of an insured to choose the form in which various payments due him or her on a policy shall be made or applied

dividend option : an option allowing the owner of a participating insurance policy and esp. a life insurance policy to determine how dividends are to be paid (as in cash or by being applied as payment for additional insurance)

installments–for–a–fixed–amount option : a settlement option in which the insurer retains the policy proceeds and makes periodic payments of a fixed amount until the proceeds are exhausted — called also *fixed amount option*

installments–for–a–fixed–pe·ri·od option : a settlement option in which the policy proceeds are retained by the insurer and paid in installments over a fixed period of time — called also *fixed period option*

interest–only option : a settlement option in which the insurer retains the policy proceeds and makes interest payments at a guaranteed minimum rate

joint–and–last–survivorship option : an option in which the insurer makes periodic payments to two or more persons (as a husband and wife) of the proceeds or usu. cash value of a policy until the death of the last survivor

life income option : a settlement option in which the insurer retains the policy proceeds and makes periodic payments for the beneficiary's life or for a specified number of years even after the beneficiary's death with payments to a different recipient

non·for·fei·ture option \ˌnän-'fȯr-fə-ˌchu̇r-\ **:** an option (as to surrender the policy for its cash value or convert the policy to one with a smaller face amount or to a term policy with a shorter period) available to a policyholder who has ceased paying premiums

settlement option : an option to receive payments of the proceeds of a life insurance policy other than by lump sum

²**option** *vt* **:** to grant or take an option on ⟨started buying or ~*ing* riverfront land —Rita Koselka⟩

option contract — see CONTRACT

op·tion·ee \ˌäp-shə-'nē\ *n* **:** one who is granted or buys an option

op·tion·or \'äp-shə-nər, -ˌnȯr\ *n* **:** one who grants or sells an option

oral argument \'ȯr-əl-\ *n* **:** oral presentation of a party's position and the reasoning behind it before an esp. appellate court

oral trust — see TRUST

¹**or·der** *n* **1 :** a state of peace, freedom from unruly behavior, and respect for law and proper authority ⟨maintain law and ~⟩ **2 :** an established mode or state of procedure ⟨a call to ~⟩ **3 a :** a mandate from a superior authority — see also EXECUTIVE ORDER **b :** a ruling or command made by a competent administrative authority; *specif* **:** one resulting from administrative adjudication and subject to judicial review and enforcement ⟨an administrative ~ may not be inconsistent with the Constitution —*Wells v. State*, 654 So. 2d 145 (1995)⟩ **c :** an authoritative command issued by the court ⟨violated a court ~ and was jailed for contempt⟩

cease–and–de·sist order \ˌsēs-ənd-di-'zist-, -'sist-\ **:** an order from a court or quasi-judicial tribunal to stop engaging in a particular activity or practice (as an unfair labor practice) — compare INJUNCTION, MANDAMUS, STAY

consent order : an agreement of litigating parties that by consent takes the form of a court order

final order : an order of a court or quasi-judicial tribunal which leaves nothing further to be determined or accomplished in that forum except execution of the judgment and from which an appeal will lie

gag order : an order barring public disclosure or discussion (as by the involved parties or the press) of information relating to a case

order to show cause : an order requiring the prospective object of a legal action to show cause why that action should not take place — called also *show cause order*

pretrial order : a court order setting out the rulings, stipulations, and other actions taken at a pretrial conference

protection order : RESTRAINING ORDER 2 in this entry

protective order : an order issued for the protection of a particular party: as **a :** an order that limits, denies, or defers discovery by a party in order to prevent undue embarrassment, expense, oppression, or disclosure of trade secrets **b :** RESTRAINING ORDER 2 in this entry

qualified domestic relations order : an order, decree, or judgment that satisfies the criteria set out in section 414 of the Internal Revenue Code for the payment of all or part of individual pension, profit sharing, or retirement benefits usu. to a divorcing spouse (as for alimony or child support) ◊ The alienation or assignment of funds under a qualified domestic relations order does not affect the tax status of the plan from which such funds are paid.

re·strain·ing order \ri-'strā-niŋ-\ **1** : TEMPORARY RESTRAINING ORDER 1 in this entry **2** : an order of a specified duration issued after a hearing attended by all parties that is intended to protect one individual from violence, abuse, harassment, or stalking by another esp. by prohibiting or restricting access or proximity to the protected party ⟨excluded from the home by a *restraining order* issued because of domestic violence⟩ — called also *protection order, protective order;* compare TEMPORARY RESTRAINING ORDER 2 in this entry

show cause order : ORDER TO SHOW CAUSE in this entry

tem·po·rary restraining order 1 : an order of brief duration that is issued ex parte to protect the plaintiff's rights from immediate and irreparable injury by preserving a situation or preventing an act until a hearing for a preliminary injunction can be held **2** : a protective order issued ex parte for a brief period prior to a hearing on a restraining order attended by both parties and intended to provide immediate protection from violence or threatened violence

turn·over order \'tər-ˌnō-vər-\ : an order commanding one party to turn over property to another; *esp* : an order commanding a judgment debtor to turn over assets to a judgment creditor ⟨*turnover order* in aid of execution — *California Code of Civil Procedure*⟩ **c** : a command issued by a military superior **4 a** : a direction regarding the party to whom a negotiable instrument shall be paid ⟨pay to the ∼ of John Doe⟩ — see also MONEY ORDER, NEGOTIABLE INSTRUMENT **b** : an instruction or authorization esp. to buy or sell goods or securities or to perform work ⟨a purchase ∼⟩ ⟨a work ∼⟩

alternative order : an order to a broker in which alternative methods of carrying out the order (as by buying or selling) are set forth

open order 1 : an order to buy securities or commodity futures that remains effective until filled or canceled **2** : an order for merchandise expressed in very general terms so that the seller has considerable latitude in selecting the articles actually provided

stop order : an order to a broker to buy or sell a security when the price advances or declines to a designated level **c** : goods or items bought or sold ⟨the ∼ was received in good condition⟩ — **to order** : according to the specifications of an order esp. of a bearer or endorsee ⟨payable to bearer or *to order*⟩

²order *adj* : payable to a named person or to an individual that person names by an endorsement ⟨∼ instrument⟩ — compare BEARER

order bill of lading — see BILL OF LADING

or·dered liberty *n* : freedom limited by the need for order in society ◊ The concept of ordered liberty was the initial standard for determining what provisions of the Bill of Rights were to be upheld by the states through the due process clause of the Fourteenth Amendment. Today the Fourteenth Amendment is generally seen as encompassing all of the guarantees bearing on fundamental fairness that are included in or that arose from the Bill of Rights rather than a small class of provisions essential to ordered liberty.

order paper — see PAPER

order to show cause — see ORDER 3b

or·di·nance \'ȯrd-ᵊn-əns\ *n* : an authoritative decree or law; *esp* : a municipal regulation ⟨a zoning ∼⟩

or·di·nary *adj* : of a kind to be expected from the average person or in the normal course of events; *broadly* : of a common kind or degree ⟨an ∼ proceeding⟩ — compare EXTRAORDINARY

ordinary and necessary business expense *n* : ORDINARY AND NECESSARY EXPENSE at EXPENSE

ordinary and necessary expense — see EXPENSE

ordinary care *n* **1** : DUE CARE **2** : conformity to the reasonable business standards that prevail in a particular area for a particular business

ordinary course of business : the usual manner and range of a business esp. considered in relation to the amount, circumstances, and validity of a particular transfer ⟨the bankruptcy trustee voided a transfer that was not in the *ordinary course of business*⟩ — see also BUYER IN ORDINARY COURSE OF BUSINESS

ordinary gain — see GAIN

ordinary goods — see GOOD 2

ordinary income *n* : income that does not derive from the exchange or sale of capital assets or property used in one's trade or business and that for individuals includes compensation, interest, dividends, and short-term capital gains

ordinary life insurance — see LIFE INSURANCE

ordinary loss — see LOSS

ordinary negligence — see NEGLIGENCE

ore te·nus \'ōr-ē-'tē-nəs, 'ȯr-ā-'te-nu̇s\ *adv or adj* [Latin, by mouth] : made or presented orally ⟨*ore tenus* testimony⟩ ⟨evidence presented *ore tenus*⟩

or·gan·ic law *n* : the body of laws (as in a constitution or charter) that form the original foundation of a government; *also* : one of the laws that make up such a body

or·ga·ni·za·tion *n* : a body (as a corporation or union) that has a membership acting or united for a common purpose — **or·ga·ni·za·tion·al** *adj*

organizational pick·et·ing *n* : picketing by a labor union for recognition as the organization representing employees

organizational strike — see STRIKE

or·ga·nize *vb* **-nized; -niz·ing** *vt* **1 a** : to set up an administrative structure for **b** : to persuade to associate in an organization (as a union) **2** : to arrange by systematic planning and united effort ⟨∼ a strike⟩ ∼ *vi* : to form an organization; *esp* : to form or persuade workers to join a union

organized crime *n* : criminal activity on the part of an organized and extensive group of people — compare RACKETEERING

orig·i·nal *n* **1** : that from which a copy or reproduction is made ⟨both parties signed the ∼⟩ — compare DUPLICATE **2** : a work composed firsthand as the product of an author's creativity ◊ A work must be an original in order to obtain a copyright. — **original** *adj*

original contractor *n* : GENERAL CONTRACTOR

original intent *n* **1** : the actual aim or purpose esp. of the framers of the U.S. Constitution **2** : a conservative theory in constitutional law: only those guarantees intended by the framers and set forth in the text of the Constitution are valid — compare JUDICIAL RESTRAINT

orig·i·nal·i·ty *n* : the quality or fact of being the product of individual creation that warrants copyright protection for a particular work regardless of novelty

original jurisdiction — see JURISDICTION

original promise — see PROMISE

original writ — see WRIT

original writ·ing rule *n* : BEST EVIDENCE RULE

orig·i·nate \ə-'ri-jə-,nāt\ *vb* **-nat·ed; -nat·ing** *vt* : to give rise to; *specif* : to issue (a mortgage loan) usu. for subsequent sale in a pool of mortgage loans to a secondary market — compare SERVICE ∼ *vi* : to take or have origin — **orig·i·na·tion** \ə-,ri-jə-'nā-shən\ *n* — **orig·i·na·tor** \ə-'ri-jə-,nā-tər\ *n*

origination fee — see FEE 2

or·phan *n* : a child deprived by death of one or usu. both parents; *broadly* : a child without a parent or guardian

orphans' court *n* : a probate court with limited jurisdiction

OSHA \'ō-shə\ *abbr* Occupational Safety and Health Administration — see also the IMPORTANT AGENCIES section

ostensible agency — see AGENCY 2a

ostensible agent — see AGENT

ostensible authority — see AUTHORITY

\ə\abut \ᵊ\kitten \ər\further \a\ash \ā\ace
\ä\cot, cart \au̇\out \ch\chin \e\bet \ē\easy
\g\go \i\hit \ī\ice \j\job \ŋ\sing \ō\go \ȯ\law
\ȯi\boy \th\thin \th\the \ü\loot \u̇\foot \y\yet
\zh\vision *see also* Pronunciation Symbols page

ostensible ownership — see OWNERSHIP

Our Federalism *n* [from the language of a U.S. Supreme Court ruling in *Younger v. Harris*, 401 U.S. 37 (1971), which proclaimed that "Our Federalism" represents "a system in which there is sensitivity to the legitimate interests of both State and National Government. . . ."] : a doctrine in federal jurisprudence that limits federal interference in state civil and esp. criminal proceedings out of respect for the interests and policies of the states

oust·er \'aùs-tər\ *n* **1** : wrongful dispossession esp. of a cotenant **2** : a judgment removing a public officer or depriving a corporation of a public franchise

¹out·law \'aùt-,lò\ *n* [Old English *ūtlaga*, from Old Norse *ūtlagi*, from *ūt* out + *lag*, *lǫg* law] **1** : a person excluded from the benefit or protection of the law ⟨a trespasser is not an ~⟩ **2** : a lawless person or a fugitive from the law **3** : a person or organization (as a nation) under a ban or restriction or considered to be in defiance of norms or laws ⟨considered an ~ for its support of terrorism⟩

²outlaw *vt* : to make illegal — **out·law·ry** \'aùt-,lòr-ē\ *n*

out–of–court *adj* **1** : not made under oath or affirmation as part of a judicial proceeding (as a trial or deposition) ⟨an ~ statement⟩ **2** : not made or done as part of a judicial proceeding ⟨an ~ settlement⟩

out–of–pocket *adj* : requiring an outlay of cash ⟨~ expenses⟩

out–of–pocket rule *n* : a measure of damages from fraud used in some jurisdictions that is based on the difference between the amount paid by the plaintiff and the market value of the thing paid for rather than the value attributed by the defendant — compare BENEFIT OF THE BARGAIN

output contract — see CONTRACT

out·rage \'aùt-,rāj\ *n* **1** : a deeply offensive or violent act **2** : the tort of intentionally inflicting emotional distress

out·ra·geous \aùt-'rā-jəs\ *adj* : going beyond standards of decency : utterly intolerable in a civilized society ⟨~ conduct⟩ — **out·ra·geous·ly** *adv* — **out·ra·geous·ness** *n*

out·side director *n* : a corporate director who is neither an employee nor an officer

out·stand·ing *adj* **1** : not paid ⟨had several ~ debts⟩ **2** : publicly issued and sold ⟨a million shares ~⟩

over *adj* : based on the termination or failure of a prior estate ⟨a limitation ~⟩ — see also *gift over* at GIFT

over·age \'ō-və-rij\ *n* : an amount exceeding a certain sum or quantity: as **a** : a percentage of the amount of sales grossed by a retail store that is paid under the terms of a lease in addition to a fixed rent **b** : an amount by which a payment or cost exceeds an expected or budgeted amount **c** : SURPLUS

over·breadth \,ō-vər-'bredth, -'bretth; 'ō-vər-,\ *n* **1** : the quality or state of being overbroad ⟨a statute void for ~⟩ **2** : a doctrine in constitutional law: a law that prohibits protected conduct (as free speech) as part of its reach may be struck down as unconstitutional if the threat to protected activity is a substantial effect and if it cannot be clearly removed; *also* : a doctrine allowing a defendant accused of unprotected conduct to challenge a law for overbreadth esp. in the area of free speech

over·broad \,ō-vər-'bròd\ *adj* : not sufficiently restricted to a specific subject or purpose ⟨an ~ search⟩; *esp* : characterized by a prohibition or chilling effect on constitutionally protected conduct ⟨an ~ statute⟩ — compare VAGUE

over·draft \'ō-vər-,draft\ *n* **1** : the act or result of drawing on a bank account for more than the balance; *also* : the amount exceeding the balance in an overdraft **2** : a loan or credit extended on a current account esp. to established or institutional customers

over·draw \,ō-vər-'dró\ *vb* **-drew** \-'drü\; **-drawn** \-'dròn\; **-draw·ing** *vt* : to draw checks on (a bank account) for more than the balance ~ *vi* : to make an overdraft

over·head \'ō-vər-,hed\ *n* : business expenses (as rent or insurance) not chargeable to a particular part of the work or product

over·in·clu·sive \ˌō-vər-in-ˈklü-siv\ *adj* : including more than is necessary or advisable; *specif* : relating to or being legislation that burdens more people than necessary to accomplish the legislation's goal — compare UNDERINCLUSIVE

over·in·sur·ance \ˌō-vər-in-ˈshūr-əns\ *n* : insurance (as from two or more policies) that exceeds the value of the thing covered ⟨~ may lead to fraud by the insured⟩; *broadly* : excessive insurance (as from needlessly duplicative coverage)

over·pay·ment \ˈō-vər-ˌpā-mənt\ *n* : payment in excess of what is due

over·plus \ˈō-vər-ˌpləs\ *n* : SURPLUS

over·reach \ˌō-vər-ˈrēch\ *vt* : to make (someone or something) the subject of overreaching ⟨this uncounseled defendant was . . . ~*ed* by the prosecution's submission of misinformation to the court —*Townsend v. Burke*, 334 U.S. 736 (1948)⟩ ⟨must determine whether it ~*ed* privilege —*National Law Journal*⟩

over·reach·ing *n* **1** : conduct that exceeds established limits (as of authority or due process) ⟨claimed that ~ by the prosecution barred a retrial because of double jeopardy⟩ **2** : the gaining of an unconscionable advantage over another esp. by unfair or deceptive means ⟨if the contract was void for traditional reasons such as fraud or ~ —*Lugassy v. Independent Fire Ins. Co.*, 636 So. 2d 1332 (1994)⟩

¹over·ride \ˌō-vər-ˈrīd\ *vt* **-rode** \-ˈrōd\; **-rid·den** \-ˈrid-ᵊn\; **-rid·ing 1** : to prevail or take precedence over ⟨if, as is often the case, federal constitutional principles ~ state statutory or common law —H. P. Wilkins⟩ **2** : to set aside by virtue of superior authority ⟨*overrode* the jury's sentencing recommendation⟩; *esp* : ANNUL 2 ⟨~ a veto with the required majority⟩

²over·ride \ˈō-vər-ˌrīd\ *n* **1** : a commission paid to managerial personnel on sales made by subordinates — called also *override commission* **2** : ROYALTY **3** : an act or instance of overriding ⟨a legislative ~⟩

overriding royalty *n* : an interest in and royalty on the oil, gas, or minerals extracted from another's land that is carved out of the producer's working interest and is not tied to production costs — compare ROYALTY

over·rule \ˌō-vər-ˈrül\ *vt* **1** : to rule against ⟨the objection was *overruled*⟩ — compare SUSTAIN **2 a** : to rule against upon review by virtue of a higher authority : SET ASIDE, REVERSE ⟨the appeals court *overruled* the trial court's decision⟩ **b** : to set aside as a precedent or guide ⟨did not intend to *overrule* prior jurisprudence in that area⟩ ⟨refused to *overrule* the landmark case⟩ — compare FOLLOW

overt act \ō-ˈvərt-, ˈō-ˌvərt-\ *n* **1** : an act directed toward another person that indicates an intent to kill or harm and that justifies self-defense **2** : an outward act that is done in furtherance of a conspiracy, of treason, or of the crime of attempt and that is usu. a required element of such crimes for conviction even if it is legal in itself

over–the–count·er *adj* **1** : not traded or effected on an organized securities exchange ⟨~ transactions⟩ ⟨~ securities⟩ **2** : sold lawfully without a prescription ⟨~ drugs⟩

over·turn *vt* : OVERRULE

ow·el·ty \ˈō-əl-tē\ *n, pl* **-ties** [Anglo‑French *oelté* equality, from Latin *aequalitat-, aequalitas*] : a lien created or a pecuniary sum paid by order of the court to effect an equitable partition of property (as in divorce) when such a partition in kind would be impossible, impracticable, or prejudicial to one of the parties ⟨an ~ award⟩

own *vt* : to have or hold as property; *esp* : to have title to ⟨~ property⟩

own·er *n* : one with an interest in and often dominion over property: as **a** : LEGAL OWNER in this entry **b** : one with

\ə\abut \ᵊ\kitten \ər\further \a\ash \ā\ace
\ä\cot, cart \au̇\out \ch\chin \e\bet \ē\easy
\g\go \i\hit \ī\ice \j\job \ŋ\sing \ō\go \ȯ\law
\ȯi\boy \th\thin \th\the \ü\loot \u̇\foot \y\yet
\zh\vision *see also* Pronunciation Symbols page

the right to exclusive use, control, or possession of property **c** : a purchaser under a contract for the sale of real property — see also EQUITABLE OWNER in this entry

beneficial owner **1** : one holding a beneficial interest in a trust — compare *beneficial interest* at INTEREST 1 **2** : one enjoying the benefit of property of which another is the legal owner ⟨was the *beneficial owner* of property held by the parent corporation⟩ **3** : one who has or shares the power to control the voting or investment of stock ⟨was considered the *beneficial owner* of stock held by her minor children⟩

equitable owner : one (as a beneficiary of a trust) who is considered to have rights or obligations of an owner regardless of legal title on the ground of equity ⟨do not have legal title but, upon execution of the contract, they became *equitable owners* and have power to sue to protect their land —*Dessen v. Jones*, 551 N.E.2d 782 (1990)⟩

legal owner : one who has legal title to property; *broadly* : one determined by law to own property ⟨a dispute over who is *legal owner* of the money⟩

naked owner *in the civil law of Louisiana* : an owner of property burdened by a usufruct ⟨a usufructuary possesses the usufruct for himself and the thing for the *naked owner* —*Louisiana Civil Code*⟩

record owner : one who is the owner of property (as land or stock) according to current appropriate records ⟨received a tax bill as *record owner* of the land⟩ — called also *owner of record*

own·er·ship *n* : the state, relation, or fact of being an owner; *also* : the rights or interests of an owner ⟨reduced their ~ by one third⟩

absolute ownership : ownership esp. by a single person that is free of any encumbrances or limitations other than statutory law — compare *fee simple absolute* at FEE SIMPLE

os·ten·si·ble ownership \ä-'sten-sə-bəl\ : ownership that is apparent rather than actual and that sometimes is recognized in cases of purchase of the property by an innocent third party ⟨a dispute arising from the dealer's *ostensible ownership* and sale of the collateral⟩ ◊ A purchaser from a person with ostensible ownership of property may be able to defeat the claim to the property of the actual owner who created the ostensible ownership.

ownership in indivision *in the civil law of Louisiana* : ownership by two or more persons each having undivided shares in the property as a whole — compare *community property* at PROPERTY ◊ Ownership in indivision is ended by a partition of the property.

qualified ownership : ownership that is limited by time, the interest of another party, or restrictions on the use of the property ⟨had only *qualified ownership* of the fish and game on his property due to state restrictions⟩

ownership in indivision — see OWNERSHIP

oyez \ō-'yez, -'yā, -'yes; 'ō-ˌ\ *vb imper* [Anglo-French *oyez!* hear ye!, from Old French *oiez, oyez*, imperative plural of *oir* to hear, from Latin *audire*] — used by a court officer (as a bailiff) to gain the attention of people present at the commencement of a judicial proceeding

P

pack *vt* : to influence the composition of (as a political agency) so as to bring about a desired result ⟨~ a jury⟩

pac·ta sunt ser·van·da \'pak-tə-'sənt-sər-'van-də, 'päk-tä-'sůnt-ser-'vän-dä\ [Latin] : agreements must be kept

paid–in capital — see CAPITAL

paid–in fund — see FUND 1

paid–in surplus — see SURPLUS

paid–up *adj* : requiring no further payments ⟨a ~ insurance policy⟩

pain *n* **1** : PUNISHMENT **2 a** : physical discomfort associated with bodily disorder (as disease or injury) **b** : acute mental or emotional suffering — **pain·less** *adj* — **pain·less·ly** *adv* — **on pain of** *or* **un·der pain of** : subject to penalty or punishment of ⟨ordered not to leave the country *on pain of* death⟩

pain and suf·fer·ing *n* : mental or esp. physical distress for which one may seek damages in a tort action

pair–or–set clause *n* : a provision in an insurance policy giving the insurer the option in the case of loss of fewer than all items in a set to restore the set to its value before the loss or pay the difference between the value before and after the loss

PAL *abbr* passive activity loss

pal·i·mo·ny \'pa-lə-ˌmō-nē\ *n* [blend of *pal* and *alimony*] : a court-ordered allowance paid by one member of a couple formerly living together out of wedlock to the other — not used technically

palm off *vt* : to sell or attempt to sell (a product) by inducing buyers to believe that one's product is actually the product of another; *specif* : to attempt to sell (a product) under another's trademark or trade name

¹pan·der \'pan-dər\ *vt* : to sell or distribute by pandering ⟨had no protected right

to ~ prurient materials —*Dunigan Enterprises v. DA for the Northern District*, 415 N.E.2d 251 (1981)⟩ ~ *vi* : to engage in pandering ⟨counts included . . . conspiracy to ~ and receive the earnings of a prostitute —*State v. Tocco*, 750 P.2d 874 (1988)⟩

²pander *n* [Middle English *Pandare*, character who procured for Troilus the love of Cressida in *Troilus and Creseyde*, poem by Geoffrey Chaucer (ca. 1342–1400)] : one who engages in pandering : PANDERER

pan·der·er *n* : one who engages in pandering — compare PIMP, PROSTITUTE

pan·der·ing *n* **1** : the act or crime of recruiting prostitutes or of arranging a situation for another to practice prostitution — compare ²PIMP **2** : the act or crime of selling or distributing visual or print media (as magazines) designed to appeal to the recipient's sexual interest

pan·el *n* **1** : a group of community members summoned for jury service **2** : a group of usu. three judges among the judges sitting on an appellate court who hear a particular appeal — compare FULL COURT

PAP *abbr* personal automobile policy

pa·per *n* **1** : a piece of paper containing a written statement: as **a** : a formal written composition or document often intended for publication ⟨the Federalist ~s⟩ **b** : a document containing a statement of legal status, identity, authority, or ownership — often used in pl. whether applying to one or more items ⟨naturalization ~s⟩ ⟨this policy, including the endorsements

\ə\abut \ə\kitten \ər\further \a\ash \ā\ace \ä\cot, cart \aů\out \ch\chin \e\bet \ē\easy \g\go \i\hit \ī\ice \j\job \ŋ\sing \ō\go \ȯ\law \ȯi\boy \th\thin \th\the \ü\loot \ů\foot \y\yet \zh\vision *see also* Pronunciation Symbols page

and the attached ~*s* —*Mutual of Omaha*⟩ **c** **:** a document (as an answer, motion, or brief) prepared in furtherance of a legal action ⟨all ~*s* after the complaint required to be served upon a party shall be filed with the court —*Federal Rules of Civil Procedure* Rule 5(d)⟩ **2** **:** a document providing evidence of a financial obligation; *esp* **:** COMMERCIAL PAPER in this entry

accommodation paper **:** commercial paper used by one party to accommodate another party

bearer paper **:** commercial paper that is freely negotiable by the holder and is made payable to bearer — compare ORDER PAPER in this entry

chattel paper **:** paper that sets out both a buyer's obligation to repay and a lender's or a seller's security interest in the goods bought or that contains the provisions of a lease of the goods

commercial paper **:** a usu. negotiable instrument (as a note, draft, or certificate of deposit) arising out of a commercial transaction; *specif* **:** any of the instruments constituting the obligations of a business organization that are sold as investments

order paper **:** commercial paper that is payable to order — compare BEARER PAPER in this entry

— **on paper** **:** figured at face value

paper title — see TITLE

¹**par** \'pär\ *n* [Latin, one that is equal, from *par* equal] **:** the face amount of an instrument of value (as a check or note): as **a :** the monetary value assigned to each share of stock in the charter of a corporation **b :** the principal of a bond

²**par** *adj* **:** PARTICIPATING

para·graph *n* **:** a distinct often numbered or otherwise designated section of a document or writing (as a statute or pleading)

para·le·gal \ˌpar-ə-'lē-gəl\ *adj* **:** of, relating to, or being a paraprofessional who assists a lawyer — compare CLERK 2b —

paralegal *n*

paramount title — see TITLE

¹**par·aph** \'par-əf, pə-'raf\ *n, in the civil*

law of Louisiana **:** the signature of a notary public on a document accompanied by a date, identification of parties, seal, or other required elements

²**paraph** *vt, in the civil law of Louisiana* **:** to affix a paraph to ⟨~*ed* the mortgage⟩; *also* **:** to include (as particular words) in a paraph

par·cel \'pär-səl\ *n* **:** a tract or plot of land

par·ce·nary \'pärs-ᵊn-ˌer-ē\ *n, pl* -**nar·ies** [Anglo-French *parcenarie*, from Old French *parçonerie*, from *parçon* portion, from Latin *partition-, partitio* partition] **:** COPARCENARY

par·ce·ner \'pärs-ᵊn-ər\ *n* [Anglo-French, from Old French *parçonier*, from *parçon*] **:** COPARCENER

par·don *n* **1 :** a release from the legal penalties of an offense **2 :** an official warrant of remission of penalty as an act of clemency — compare COMMUTE **3 :** excuse or forgiveness for a fault or offense — **pardon** *vt*

par·ens pat·ri·ae \'par-ənz-'pa-trē-ˌē, -'pā-, -trē-ˌī; 'pär-ens-'pä-trē-ˌī\ *n* [Latin, parent of the country] **:** the state in its capacity as the legal guardian of persons not sui juris and without natural guardians, as the heir to persons without natural heirs, and as the protector of all citizens unable to protect themselves ⟨because the State is supposed to proceed in respect of the child as *parens patriae* and not as adversary —*Kent v. United States*, 383 U.S. 541 (1966)⟩

par·ent *n* **1 a :** a person who begets or brings forth offspring; *esp* **:** the natural parents of a child born of their marriage ◊ The biological father of an illegitimate child is usu. not considered the child's parent absent a judicial determination of paternity. There have been exceptions, based mainly on the father's attitude toward, support of, or involvement with the child. **b :** a person who legally adopts a child **c :** a person or entity that owes to a child a legally imposed duty of support **d :** a stepparent where designated by statute **2 :** an entity or group that gives rise to or acquires another usu. subsidiary entity or group ⟨a ~ company⟩; *specif* : a corporation that owns a required minimum percentage of the stock of another corporation — compare AFFILIATE — **par·ent** *adj* — **pa·ren·tal** \pə-'ren-təl\ *adj* — **pa·ren·tal·ly** *adv* — **par·ent·less** *adj* **par·en·te·la** \‚par-ən-'tē-lə\ *n* [Late Latin, from Latin *parent-*, *parens* parent + *-ela* (as in *clientela* clientele)] : the line of blood relatives : the kin of a person by descent — **par·en·te·lic** \-lik\ *adj* **par·ish** \'par-ish\ *n* : a civil division of the state of Louisiana corresponding to a county in other states **parish court** *n* : a court established for each Louisiana parish and having limited jurisdiction over civil and less serious criminal matters **par·lia·ment** \'pär-lə-mənt, 'pärl-yə-\ *n* [Anglo-French *parlement* conference, council, parliament, from *parler* to speak] **1 a** : an assemblage of the nobility, clergy, and commons called together by the British sovereign as the supreme legislative body in the United Kingdom **b** : a similar assemblage in another nation or state **2** : the supreme legislative body of a usu. major political unit that is a continuing institution comprising a series of individual assemblages **par·lia·men·tar·i·an** \‚pär-lə-‚men-'tar-ē-ən, ‚pärl-yə-, -mən-\ *n* **1** : an expert in the rules and usages of a parliament or other deliberative assembly; *specif, often cap* : an officer of a legislative body acting as adviser to the presiding officer on matters of procedure ◊ The parliamentarian of the U.S. House of Representatives is appointed by the Speaker of the House. The Secretary of the Senate appoints the Senate's parliamentarian with approval of the majority leader. **2** : a member of a parliament **par·lia·men·ta·ry** \‚pär-lə-'men-tə-rē, ‚pärl-yə-\ *adj* **1 a** : of or relating to a parliament **b** : enacted, done, or ratified by a parliament **2** : of, based on, or having the characteristics of parliamentary government **3** : of or relating to the mem-

bers of a parliament **4** : of or according to parliamentary law ⟨~ procedure⟩ **parliamentary government** *n* : a system of government having the real executive power vested in a cabinet composed of members of the legislature who are individually and collectively responsible to the legislature **parliamentary law** *n* : the rules and precedents governing the proceedings of deliberative assemblies and other organizations **pa·ro·chi·al** \pə-'rō-kē-əl\ *adj* : of or relating to a parish **¹par·ol** \'par-əl\ *n* [Anglo-French, speech, talk, from Old French *parole*] : an oral declaration or statement ⟨where the evidence of the gift rests in ~ *—Matter of Cohn*, 176 N.Y.S. 225 (1919) (dissent)⟩ **²parol** *adj* **1** : executed or made by word of mouth or by a writing not under seal ⟨a ~ agreement⟩ **2 a** : given or expressed by word of mouth : oral as distinguished from written **b** : relating to matters outside of a writing **pa·rol·able** \pə-'rō-lə-bəl\ *adj* : qualified for parole **pa·role** \pə-'rōl\ *n* [Old French, speech, word, prisoner's word of honor to fulfill stated conditions, from Late Latin *parabola* speech, parable, from Greek *parabolē* comparison] : a conditional release of a prisoner who has served part of a sentence and who remains under the control of and in the legal custody of a parole authority — compare PROBATION **pa·rol·ee** \pə-‚rō-'lē, -'rō-‚lē\ *n* : a prisoner released on parole **parol evidence** — see EVIDENCE **parol evidence rule** *n* : a rule of document interpretation: parol evidence offered to contradict or modify a writing (as a contract or will) is not admissible when the writing is unambiguous or was intended

\ə\abut \ə\kitten \ər\further \a\ash \ā\ace \ä\cot, cart \au̇\out \ch\chin \e\bet \ē\easy \g\go \i\hit \ī\ice \j\job \ŋ\sing \ō\go \ȯ\law \ȯi\boy \th\thin \t͟h\the \ü\loot \u̇\foot \y\yet \zh\vision *see also* Pronunciation Symbols page

to be a final expression of the author's wishes

par·ri·cide \'par-ə-ˌsīd\ *n* [Latin *parricida* killer of a close relative] **1 :** a person who murders his or her mother or father or sometimes a close relative **2 :** the act of a parricide

partial breach — see BREACH 1b

partial defense — see DEFENSE 2a

par·tial insanity *n* **:** DIMINISHED CAPACITY

partial responsibility *n* **:** DIMINISHED RESPONSIBILITY

partial verdict — see VERDICT

par·ti·ceps crim·i·nis \'par-ti-ˌseps-'kri-mə-nis, 'pär-\ *n* [Latin] **:** one who takes part in a crime **:** ACCOMPLICE

par·tic·i·pat·ing *adj* **1 :** involving participation by more than one person or agency **2 :** sharing in distributions: **a :** entitling the holder to a share in any distribution of surplus by the issuing insurance company **b :** entitled to a share in distributions that are in addition to regular fixed income ⟨~ shares⟩

par·tic·i·pa·tion *n* **1 :** the action or state of taking part in something: as **a :** association with others in a relationship (as a partnership) or an enterprise usu. on a formal basis with specified rights and obligations ⟨a loan made directly or in ~ with a bank⟩ **b :** PROFIT SHARING **2 a :** something in which shares are taken by more than one party **b :** something that results in a share (as of a distribution)

participation loan — see LOAN

par·tic·u·lar *adj, in the civil law of Louisiana* **:** of or relating to a designated property or to the inheritance of it — compare UNIVERSAL

particular legacy — see LEGACY

particular successor *n, in the civil law of Louisiana* **:** a successor (as a donee or buyer) who succeeds by particular title to the rights and obligations pertaining only to the property conveyed by the ancestor in title, who takes title and possession in his or her own right, and who is not liable for any debts of the succession — compare UNIVERSAL SUCCESSOR

particular title — see TITLE

par·ti·tion \pär-'ti-shən\ *n* **:** the severance voluntarily or by legal proceedings of common or undivided interests in property and esp. real property **:** division into severalty of property held jointly or in common or the sale of such property by a court with division of the proceeds — **partition** *vt*

part·ner *n* **:** one of two or more persons associated as joint principals in carrying on a business for the purpose of enjoying a joint profit **:** a member of a partnership; *specif* **:** a partner in a law firm

   dormant partner **:** SILENT PARTNER in this entry

   general partner **:** a partner whose liability for partnership debts and obligations is unlimited — compare LIMITED PARTNER in this entry

   limited partner **:** a partner in a venture who has no management authority and whose liability is limited to the amount of his or her investment — compare GENERAL PARTNER in this entry

   partner in com·men·dam \-in-kə-'men-dəm, -kō-'men-ˌdäm\ *in the civil law of Louisiana* **:** LIMITED PARTNER in this entry

   silent partner **:** a partner who takes no active part in conducting the partnership business but who receives a share of its profits and whose existence is often not made public — called also *dormant partner*

partner in commendam — see PARTNER

part·ner·ship *n* **:** an association of two or more persons or entities that conduct a business for profit as co-owners — see also *Uniform Partnership Act* in the IMPORTANT LAWS section; compare CORPORATION, JOINT VENTURE, SOLE PROPRIETORSHIP ◊ Except in civil law as practiced in Louisiana, where a partnership, like a corporation, is considered a legal person, a partnership is traditionally viewed as an association of individuals rather than as an entity with a separate and independent existence. A partnership cannot exist beyond the lives of the part-

ners. The partners are taxed as individuals and are personally liable for torts and contractual obligations. Each partner is viewed as the other's agent and, traditionally, is jointly and severally liable for the tortious acts of any one of the partners.
commercial partnership : TRADING PARTNERSHIP in this entry
family partnership : a partnership in which the partners are members of a family
general partnership : a partnership in which each partner is liable for all partnership debts and obligations in full regardless of the amount of the individual partner's capital contribution — compare LIMITED PARTNERSHIP in this entry
limited liability partnership : a partnership formed under applicable state statute in which the partnership is liable as an entity for debts and obligations and the partners are not liable personally
limited partnership : a partnership in which the business is managed by one or more general partners and is provided with capital by limited partners who do not participate in management but who share in profits and whose individual liability is limited to the amount of their respective capital contributions — compare GENERAL PARTNERSHIP in this entry
master limited partnership : a limited partnership that offers interests for sale on the market; *also* : the interests themselves sold as securities
mining partnership : a partnership in which two or more persons jointly own a mining claim and actually engage in extracting minerals with the purpose of sharing profits and losses
non·trad·ing partnership : a partnership that is not engaged in the buying and selling of goods — called also *noncommercial partnership;* compare TRADING PARTNERSHIP in this entry
partnership at will : a partnership whose duration is not fixed by contract and that is terminable at will by any partner
partnership by estoppel : a partnership

created by operation of law when a defendant by words or conduct represents himself or herself to the plaintiff or to the public as a partner and the plaintiff relies on the representation to his or her detriment
partnership in commendam in the civil law of Louisiana : LIMITED PARTNERSHIP in this entry
trading partnership : a partnership whose business involves the buying and selling of goods — called also *commercial partnership;* compare NONTRADING PARTNERSHIP in this entry
partnership at will — see PARTNERSHIP
partnership by estoppel — see PARTNERSHIP
partnership in commendam — see PARTNERSHIP
partnership rollup *n* : LIMITED PARTNERSHIP ROLLUP TRANSACTION
part performance — see PERFORMANCE
par·ty *n, pl* **parties** **1 a** : one (as a person, group, or entity) constituting alone or with others one of the sides of a proceeding, transaction, or agreement ⟨the *parties* to a contract⟩ ⟨a person who signed the instrument as a ~ to the instrument — *Uniform Commercial Code*⟩
accommodated party : a party to an instrument for whose benefit an accommodation party signs and incurs liability on the instrument : a party for whose benefit an accommodation is made
accommodation party : a party who signs and thereby incurs liability on an instrument that is issued for value and given for the benefit of an accommodated party
secured party : a party holding a security interest in another's property
third party : a person other than the principals ⟨insurance against injury to a *third party*⟩
b : one (as an individual, firm, or cor-

\ə\abut \ᵊ\kitten \ər\further \a\ash \ā\ace
\ä\cot, cart \aů\out \ch\chin \e\bet \ē\easy
\g\go \i\hit \ī\ice \j\job \ŋ\sing \ō\go \ȯ\law
\ȯi\boy \th\thin \t̲h̲\the \ü\loot \ů\foot \y\yet
\zh\vision   *see also* Pronunciation Symbols page

poration) that constitutes the plaintiff or defendant in an action; *also* : one so involved in the prosecution or defense of a judicial or quasi-judicial proceeding as to be bound or substantially affected by the decision or judgment therein

adverse party : a party to an action who is on the opposing side; *specif* : a party to a finally decided action whose interests would be served by having the judgment upheld on appeal and who is entitled to notice of an appeal

aggrieved party : a party with a legally recognized interest that is injuriously affected esp. by an act of a judicial or quasi-judicial body and that confers standing to appeal — called also *aggrieved person, party aggrieved*

indispensable party : a party whose rights are so connected with the claims being litigated in an action that no judgment can be rendered without affecting or impairing those rights, no complete disposition of the action can be made without the party's joinder, and whose nonjoinder will result in the dismissal of an action — compare NECESSARY PARTY in this entry ◊ Federal Rule of Civil Procedure 19 provides the courts with discretion in determining whether the absence of a party requires dismissal of an action, replacing an older and more rigid basis for determination. The rule states that "the court shall determine whether in equity and good conscience the action should proceed among the parties before it, or should be dismissed, the absent person being thus regarded as indispensable."

innocent party : a party having no fault in or responsibility for the situation for which judicial relief is sought : a party who comes into court with clean hands

necessary party : a party whose interests are so connected with an action that he or she should be joined in order to fully determine the controversy but whose nonjoinder because of a valid excuse will not result in dismissal — compare INDISPENSABLE PARTY in this entry

nominal party : a party who has no actual stake in the outcome of litigation and whose inclusion as a party is solely for the purpose of conforming with procedural rules

party aggrieved : AGGRIEVED PARTY in this entry

party in interest 1 : a person whose rights are or will be affected by an action taken esp. by a government or judicial body; *esp* : a person whose pecuniary interests are affected by a bankruptcy proceeding 2 : REAL PARTY IN INTEREST in this entry

proper party : a party whose interests are likely to be affected by litigation and whose inclusion in the litigation is preferable but not essential

real party in interest : a party who according to the applicable law is entitled to enforce the right that forms the basis of the claim regardless of who will actually benefit by the outcome ◊ Federal Rule of Civil Procedure 17(a) requires that "every action shall be prosecuted in the name of the real party in interest."

third party 1 : a person who is not a party to an action but who is or may be liable to the defendant in the action for all or part of the plaintiff's claim and against whom the defendant may bring a third-party complaint 2 : a person who is not a party to an action but who is or may be liable to the plaintiff in the action for all or part of a counterclaim and against whom the plaintiff may bring a third-party complaint — see also THIRD-PARTY COMPLAINT 2 : a group of persons usu. sharing a set of political ideals who are organized for the purpose of directing the policies of a government

party aggrieved — see PARTY 1b

party in interest — see PARTY 1b

par value *n* : PAR a

pass *vi* **1 a** : to issue a decision, verdict, or opinion ⟨the Supreme Court ~*ed* on a statute⟩ **b** : to be legally issued ⟨judgment ~*ed* by default⟩ **2** : to go from the control, ownership, or possession of one person or group to that of another ⟨title ~*es* to the buyer⟩ — *vt* **1** : to omit a regularly scheduled declaration and payment of (a dividend) **2 a** : to get the approval of ⟨the bill ~*ed* the House⟩ **b** : to give approval or legal sanction to ⟨the House ~*ed* the bill⟩ **3** : to transfer the right to or interest in ⟨the sale ~*es* the title to the goods⟩ **4** : to put in circulation ⟨~ bad checks⟩ — compare UTTER **5** : to pronounce (as a sentence or judgment) judicially ⟨the court ~*ed* a severe sentence⟩

pas·sim \'pa-səm, -ˌsim, 'pä-ˌsēm\ *adv* [Latin, here and there] : in one place and another — used in citations of cases, articles, or books to indicate that something (as a word, phrase, or idea) is found at many places in the work cited ⟨see *Arango*, 621 F.2d 1371, *passim*⟩

pas·sion \'pa-shən\ *n* : intense, driving, or overpowering feeling or emotion; *esp* : any violent or intense emotion that prevents reflection — see also HEAT OF PASSION

pas·sive \'pa-siv\ *adj* : not involving, deriving from, or requiring effort or active participation ⟨imposed a ~ duty not to interfere⟩; *specif* : of, relating to, or being business activity in which the investor does not have immediate control over the income-producing activity ⟨~ income⟩ ⟨~ losses⟩ ◊ Any rental activity is designated a passive activity under the Internal Revenue Code. Investment income is not considered income from a passive activity. — **pas·sive·ly** *adv* — **pas·sive·ness** *n*

passive negligence — see NEGLIGENCE

passive trust — see TRUST

pass off *vt* **1** : to make public or offer for sale (goods or services) with intent to deceive : PALM OFF ⟨*passing* his product *off* as that of the plaintiff's —W. L. Prosser and W. P. Keeton⟩ — see also UNFAIR COMPETITION **2** : to give a false identity or character to ⟨they created the documents on the day of the trial and *passed* them *off* as being made earlier⟩

pass–through security — see SECURITY

past consideration — see CONSIDERA-

past rec·ol·lec·tion re·cord·ed \-ˌre-kə-'lek-shən-\ *n* : a witness's written account of a past event prepared at a time when his or her memory of it was fresh; *also* : an exception to the hearsay rule allowing admission of such an account into evidence if the witness has insufficient present memory of the event or has no memory of having recorded it but is confident that the account is accurate — compare PRESENT RECOLLECTION REFRESHED ◊ A document containing a past recollection recorded may only be admitted as an exhibit if offered by an adverse party. Otherwise, it may only be read into evidence.

¹pat·ent \'pat-ᵊnt, *3 also* 'pāt-\ *adj* [Anglo-French, from Latin *patent-, patens*, from present participle of *patēre* to be open] **1 a** : open to public inspection — see also *letters patent* at LETTER **2 b** : secured or protected by a patent ⟨a nonexclusive ~ license to produce and sell the product⟩ ⟨sought to enforce her ~ rights against infringement⟩ **2** : of, relating to, or concerned with the granting of patents esp. for inventions ⟨a ~ lawyer⟩ ⟨involved in ~ litigation⟩ **3** : readily seen, discovered, or understood ⟨a ~ defect⟩ ⟨if no bad faith or abuse is ~⟩ — compare LATENT — **pat·ent·ly** *adv*

²pat·ent \'pat-ᵊnt\ *n* **1** : an official document conferring a right or privilege : LETTERS PATENT at LETTER **2 2 a** : the right to exclude others from making, using, or selling an invention or products made by an invented process that is granted to an inventor and his or her heirs or assigns for a term of years — see also *intellectual property* at PROPERTY; compare COPYRIGHT, TRADEMARK ◊ A patent may be granted for a process, act, or method that is new, useful, and not obvious, for a new use of a known process, machine, or composition of matter or material, as well as for an asexually repro-

\ə\abut \ᵊ\kitten \ər\further \a\ash \ā\ace \ä\cot, cart \au̇\out \ch\chin \e\bet \ē\easy \g\go \i\hit \ī\ice \j\job \ŋ\sing \ō\go \ȯ\law \ȯi\boy \th\thin \t̠h̠\the \ü\loot \u̇\foot \y\yet \zh\vision *see also* Pronunciation Symbols page

duced distinct and new variety of plant (excluding one propagated from a tuber), and for any new, original, and ornamental design for an article of manufacture. Design patents are issued for a term of 14 years. Patents issuing on applications made after June 8, 1995, for basic or plant patents (excluding design patents) are for a term of 20 years from the date of application. An inventor can file a provisional patent application, which requires less documentation and lower fees than a regular application, before reducing the invention to practice. This allows the inventor to claim "patent pending" status for the invention and to establish an earlier filing date and priority of the invention. A regular patent application must be made within a year of the provisional application or it will expire. Patents are considered personal property and may be sold, assigned, or otherwise transferred. Under common law, if a patented invention or discovery is made while the inventor is working for a company, and is made on company time with company facilities and materials, the employer receives an irrevocable, nonassignable, nonexclusive, royalty-free license to use it. Often an employee is required contractually to assign his or her patent to the employer. **b** : the writing securing such a right ⟨received his ~ in the mail⟩ **c** : a patented invention ⟨all substantial rights to a ~ — *Internal Revenue Code*⟩ **3** : an instrument making a conveyance of public lands ⟨to issue a ~ to each of said Indians for the village or town lot occupied by him — *U.S. Code*⟩ — see also *fee patent* at FEE 1

³pat·ent *vt* : to obtain or grant a right to (something) by a patent ⟨the land was ~*ed* to the railroad⟩; *specif* : to protect the rights to (an invention) by a patent ⟨printed matter cannot be ~*ed*⟩

pat·ent·able \'pat-ᵊn-tə-bəl\ *adj* : capable or susceptible of being patented ⟨an idea alone is not ~⟩ — **pat·en·ta·bil·i·ty** \ˌpat-ᵊn-tə-'bi-lə-tē\ *n*

patent am·bi·gu·i·ty \-ˌam-bə-'gyü-ə-tē\ *n* : an ambiguity in a legal document (as a

contract or will) that is apparent on the face of the document and arises from inconsistent or uncertain language — compare LATENT AMBIGUITY

pat·en·tee \ˌpat-ᵊn-'tē\ *n* : a person to whom a grant is made or privilege secured by patent ⟨the ~ assigned the patent to his employer⟩

patent medicine *n* : a packaged nonprescription drug which is protected by a trademark and whose contents are incompletely disclosed; *also* : any drug that is a proprietary

pa·ter·ni·ty \pə-'tər-nə-tē\ *n* **1** : the quality or state of being a father **2** : origin or descent from a father

pat·ri·cide \'pa-trə-ˌsīd\ *n* [Latin *patricida*, from *patr-*, *pater* father + *-cida* killer] **1** : an individual who murders his or her father **2** : the murder of an individual's own father

pat·ri·mo·ni·al \ˌpa-trə-'mō-nē-əl\ *adj* : of, relating to, or constituting a patrimony ⟨a ~ asset⟩

pat·ri·mo·ny \'pa-trə-ˌmō-nē\ *n*, *pl* **-nies** [Middle French *patrimonie*, from Latin *patrimonium*, from *patr-*, *pater* father] **1** : an estate inherited from one's father or ancestor ⟨to deprive her and her coheirs of their ~ —*Wells Fargo Bank v. Kincaid*, 260 Cal. App. 2d 120 (1968)⟩ **2** : an estate or endowment belonging to a church ⟨the property of a dissolved parish shall pass to the ~ of the diocese⟩ **3** *in the civil law of Louisiana* : the net assets of a person : the sum of a person's assets and liabilities ⟨reimbursement shall be made from the ~ of the spouse who owes reimbursement —*Louisiana Civil Code*⟩

pat·tern \'pa-tərn\ *n* **1** : a form or model proposed for imitation **2** : a recognizably consistent series of related acts ⟨found a ~ of discrimination in that company⟩ ⟨a ~ of racketeering activity⟩

pau·per \'pȯ-pər\ *n* : a person who is destitute and relying on charity; *specif* : a person who is relieved of the costs and expenses of a court proceeding because of poverty

¹pawn \'pȯn\ *n* **1 a** : a pledge and trans-

fer of possession of movable or personal property to a creditor which gives the creditor the privilege of satisfying the debt from the property (as by selling it) if the debt is not repaid within a specified time; *also* : the property pledged ⟨shall not take as a ~ any workman's tools⟩ — compare ANTICHRESIS **b** : the state of being so pledged or burdened by such a pledge ⟨goods held in ~⟩ **2** : the act of pawning
²**pawn** *vt* : to put (personal or movable property) in pawn ⟨when it is redeemed by the person who ~*ed* it⟩ — compare HYPOTHECATE — **pawn·er** \'pȯ-nər\ *or* **paw·nor** *same or* pȯ-'nȯr\ *n*
pawn·bro·ker \'pȯn-ˌbrō-kər\ *n* : a person who lends money on the security of personal or movable property pledged in his or her keeping or who buys personal property and gives the seller an opportunity to buy back the property
pawn·shop *n* : a pawnbroker's shop
pay·able *adj* : that may, can, or must be paid
pay·ee \ˌpā-'ē\ *n* : a person to whom money is to be or has been paid; *specif* : the person named in a bill of exchange, note, or check as the one to whom the amount is directed to be paid — compare DRAWEE, DRAWER
payer *var of* PAYOR
payment bond — see BOND 1a
pay·off \'pā-ˌȯf\ *n* **1** : the act or an instance of paying someone off : BRIBE — compare KICKBACK **2** : the act of paying a debt or creditor in full ⟨would release the lien upon the ~ of the balance⟩
pay off *vt* **1** : to pay (a debt or credit) in full ⟨the loan was *paid off*⟩ **2** : BRIBE
pay·o·la \pā-'ō-lə\ *n* : a secret or indirect payment (as to a disc jockey) for a commercial favor (as for promoting a particular record)
pay·or \'pā-ər, -ˌȯr; pā-'ȯr\ *also* **pay·er** \'pā-ər\ *n* : a person who pays; *specif* : the person by whom a note or bill has been or should be paid
payor bank — see BANK
pay·roll tax *n* : a tax that is levied as a per-

centage of an employee's pay and is usu. paid by the employer
PBGC *abbr* Pension Benefit Guaranty Corporation — see also *Pension and Welfare Benefits Administration* in the IMPORTANT AGENCIES section
P.C. *abbr* professional corporation
peace *n* : a state of tranquillity or quiet: as **a** : a state of security or order within a community provided for by law or custom ⟨keeping the ~⟩ **b** : freedom from civil disturbance
peace·able \'pē-sə-bəl\ *adj* : marked by freedom from dispute, strife, violence, or disorder ⟨the right to ~ assembly⟩ ⟨~ possession⟩ — **peace·ably** \-blē\ *adv*
peace bond — see BOND 1a
peace officer *n* : a civil officer (as a police officer) whose duty it is to preserve the public peace
pec·u·la·tion \ˌpe-kyə-'lā-shən\ *n* [Late Latin *peculation-, peculatio*, from Latin *peculari* to embezzle, from *peculium* private property, from *pecu* cattle] : misappropriation esp. of public funds
pe·cu·liar risk doctrine *n* : a doctrine that renders an employer (as a general contractor) liable for injury caused by an independent contractor if the employer failed to take reasonable precautions against a risk particular to the employee's work that the employer should have recognized
pe·cu·ni·ary \pi-'kyü-nē-ˌer-ē\ *adj* : consisting of, measured in, or relating to money ⟨~ damages⟩
pe·nal \'pēn-ᵊl\ *adj* **1** : of, relating to, or being punishment ⟨~ sanctions⟩ **2** : making one (as an offender) punishable ⟨a ~ offense⟩; *also* : CRIMINAL 2 **3** : used as a place of confinement and punishment ⟨a ~ institution⟩
penal action *n* : an action by the state or a private party that is for the purpose of imposing a statutorily prescribed penalty

\ə\abut \ᵊ\kitten \ər\further \a\ash \ā\ace \ä\cot, cart \aů\out \ch\chin \e\bet \ē\easy \g\go \i\hit \ī\ice \j\job \ŋ\sing \ō\go \ȯ\law \ȯi\boy \th\thin \t̲h̲\the \ü\loot \ů\foot \y\yet \zh\vision *see also* Pronunciation Symbols page

on one who violates a law and that is punitive rather than remedial in nature; *also* : a criminal prosecution

penal bond — see BOND 1a

penal code *n* : a code of laws concerning crimes and their punishments

penal custody — see CUSTODY c

penal law *n* **1** : a law prescribing a penalty (as a fine or imprisonment) for one who violates it **2** : PENAL CODE

penal statute *n* : PENAL LAW 1; *esp* : a law that calls for a penalty as opposed to one providing for a remedy for a wronged party

penal sum *n* : a sum to be paid as a penalty esp. under the terms of a bond

pen·al·ty \'pen-ᵊl-tē\ *n, pl* **-ties 1** : a punishment that is imposed on a wrongdoer by statute or judicial decision **2** : a pecuniary sum that by agreement is to be paid by a party who fails to fulfill an obligation to another and that is punitive rather than compensatory ⟨the court declined to enforce the contractual ~ and determined actual damages instead⟩

penalty clause *n* **1** : a clause (as in a contract) that calls for a penalty to be paid or suffered by a party under specified terms (as in the event of a breach) and that is usu. unenforceable ◊ A penalty clause differs from a liquidated damages clause by not being tied to an estimate of possible actual damages. **2** : a clause in a statute or judgment that sets forth a penalty for a specific act or omission (as failure to make a support payment on time)

pend \'pend\ *vi* : to be pending ⟨the action ~s as to the third party⟩

pen·den·cy \'pen-dən-sē\ *n* : the quality, state, or period of being pendent ⟨the ~ of the contract renewal⟩

pen·dent \'pen-dənt\ *adj* [Middle French *pendant* suspended, present participle of *pendre* to hang, ultimately from Latin *pendēre*] **1** : remaining undetermined : PENDING 1 ⟨a ~ suit⟩ **2** : of, relating to, or being the basis of pendent jurisdiction or pendent party jurisdiction ⟨the Supreme Court drew a sharp distinction between ~ claims and ~ parties —*Na-*

tional Law Journal⟩ **3** : DEPENDENT 1 ⟨is ~ upon another claim⟩

pen·den·te li·te \pen-'den-tē-'lī-tē, pen-'den-tā-'lē-tā\ *adv or adj* [New Latin] : during the suit : while litigation continues ⟨awarded joint legal custody of the child *pendente lite*⟩ ⟨*pendente lite* child support⟩

pendent jurisdiction — see JURISDICTION

pendent party jurisdiction — see JURISDICTION

¹pend·ing \'pen-diŋ\ *prep* **1** : during the time of **2** : while awaiting : in the time preceding ⟨held in escrow ~ the outcome of the suit⟩ ⟨free ~ trial⟩

²pending *adj* **1** : not yet decided ⟨a ~ suit⟩ **2** : to occur or be realized soon

pen·i·ten·tia·ry \ˌpe-nə-'ten-chə-rē\ *n, pl* **-ries** : a state or federal prison for the punishment and reformation of convicted felons — compare HOUSE OF CORRECTION, HOUSE OF DETENTION, JAIL, LOCKUP

penny stock — see STOCK

pe·nol·o·gy \pi-'nä-lə-jē\ *n* : a branch of criminology dealing with prison management and the treatment of offenders — **pe·no·log·i·cal** \ˌpē-nə-'läj-ə-kəl\ *adj* — **pe·nol·o·gist** \pi-'nä-lə-jist\ *n*

pen register *n* [perhaps from the original use of a pen to mark the dots or dashes used in counting the numbers dialed] : a device that registers the numbers dialed from a telephone — compare WIRETAP ◊ A court order is always required for the use of a pen register in a criminal investigation, but such use has not been considered a search or interception of communication by the U.S. Supreme Court. Some states have disagreed and discern a privacy interest in such information.

pen·sion *n* : money paid under given conditions to a person following retirement or to surviving dependents — see also DEFINED BENEFIT PLAN, DEFINED CONTRIBUTION PLAN

pe·num·bra \pi-'nəm-brə\ *n, pl* **-bras 1** : an area within which distinction or resolution is difficult or uncertain ⟨the public-private ~⟩ **2** : an extension of protection, reach, application, or consideration; *esp* : a body of rights held to be guaranteed by implication from other rights explicitly enumerated in the U.S. Constitution ⟨the First Amendment has a ~ where privacy is protected from governmental intrusion —*Griswold v. Connecticut*, 381 U.S. 479 (1965)⟩ — see also *Griswold v. Connecticut* in the IMPORTANT CASES section —

pe·num·bral \-brəl\ *adj*

pe·on·age \'pē-ə-nij\ *n* : labor in a condition of servitude to extinguish a debt ⟨the holding of any person to service or labor under the system known as ~ is abolished and forever prohibited —*U.S. Code*⟩

per \'pər\ *prep* : as stated by — used to indicate the author of an opinion with which the majority of judges concur

per an·num \pər-'a-nəm\ *adv* [Medieval Latin] : in or for each year ⟨interest of six percent *per annum*⟩

per cap·i·ta \pər-'ka-pə-tə\ *adv or adj* [Medieval Latin, by heads] **1** : equally to each individual ⟨all property to pass to the descendants *per capita*⟩ — used of a method of distributing an esp. intestate estate; compare PER STIRPES ◇ Per capita distribution of an estate provides each descendant with an equal share of the estate's assets regardless of the degree of his or her kinship. Children, grandchildren, great-grandchildren, etc., all receive equal shares. **2** : per unit of population : by or for each individual ⟨a high *per capita* tax burden⟩

per cu·ri·am \pər-'kyur-ē-,äm, -'kur-, -əm\ *adv or adj* [Latin, by the court] : by the court as a whole rather than by a single justice and usu. without extended discussion ⟨a *per curiam* affirmance⟩

per curiam opinion — see OPINION

¹per di·em \pər-'dē-əm, -'dī-\ *adv* [Latin] : by the day : for each day ⟨paid *per diem*⟩

²per diem *adj* **1** : based on use or service by the day ⟨*per diem* compensation⟩ **2** : paid or calculated by the day ⟨*per diem* interest⟩

³per diem *n* **1** : a daily allowance ⟨received a *per diem* for expenses⟩ **2** : a daily fee

⟨paid a *per diem* for maintenance of the equipment⟩

pe·remp·tion \pə-'remp-shən\ *n* [Late Latin *peremption-, peremptio*, the act of quashing, from Latin *perimere* to take away entirely, destroy, kill] *in the civil law of Louisiana* : the absolute extinguishment of a right that prevents the bringing of an action ⟨a claim barred by ~⟩; *also* : the period of time after which such an extinguishment automatically occurs — compare PRESCRIPTION

pe·remp·tive \pə-'remp-tiv\ *adj* : of, relating to, or creating peremption ⟨the ~ period⟩ ⟨a ~ statute⟩

¹pe·remp·to·ry \pə-'remp-tə-rē\ *adj* [Late Latin *peremptorius*, from Latin, destructive, from *perimere* to take entirely, destroy] **1** : permitting no dispute, alternative, or delay; *specif* : not providing an opportunity to show cause why one should not comply ⟨when the right to require the performance of the act is clear and it is apparent that no valid excuse can be given for not performing it, a ~ mandamus may be allowed —*Revised Statutes of Nebraska*⟩ **2** : not requiring cause — see also *peremptory challenge* at CHALLENGE — **pe·remp·to·ri·ly** \pə-'remp-tə-rə-lē, -,remp-'tōr-ə-lē\ *adv* — **pe·remp·to·ri·ness** \-'remp-tə-rē-nəs\ *n*

²peremptory *n, pl* **-ries** : PEREMPTORY CHALLENGE at CHALLENGE

peremptory challenge — see CHALLENGE

peremptory exception *n, in the civil law of Louisiana* : an exception pleaded by a defendant esp. on the basis that the law provides no remedy for the injury the plaintiff alleges, that the claim is barred by res judicata or prescription, or that an indispensable party has not been joined

peremptory instruction *n* : an instruction charging a jury that if they agree to the truth of certain stated facts then they must find for a particular party

peremptory writ — see WRIT

¹per·fect \'pər-fikt\ *adj* : entirely without fault or defect: as **a** : satisfying all requirements ⟨failed to make ~ tender⟩ **b** : free from any valid legal objection : valid and effective at law ⟨having ~ title to the property⟩ — compare IMPERFECT

²per·fect \pər-'fekt\ *vt* : to complete or put in final conformity with the law: as **a** : to make (an appeal) ready for transfer to an appeals court by satisfying procedural requirements **b** : to put (one's security interest) in a position or status having priority over subsequently perfected security interests or unperfected security interests by taking statutorily prescribed steps to give notice esp. by filing a financing statement or taking possession of the collateral ⟨was the first creditor to ~ its security interest in the debtor's collateral, and, thus, was the first in priority for the collateral —*Commercial Bank v. Pride Furniture, Inc.,* 877 P.2d 1222 (1994)⟩ — compare ATTACH 3 ~ *vi* : to make something (as a security interest) complete, in conformity with the law, or valid against third-party claims — **per·fec·tion** \pər-'fek-shən\ *n*

per·fect·ed \pər-'fek-təd\ *adj* : completed in accordance with statutory procedure for giving notice and thereby having a status of priority over security interests that are the subject of such procedure at a later date or that are not the subject of such procedure ⟨settling a priority contest between the two ~ security interests⟩

perfect tender rule *n* : a rule that permits a buyer to reject goods if they or the tender of delivery fail to conform to contract in any respect ⟨the *perfect tender rule* is preserved to the extent of permitting a buyer to reject goods for any defects —*Ramirez v. Autosport,* 440 A.2d 1345 (1982)⟩ ◊ The Uniform Commercial Code contains provisions for a seller's right to cure a nonconforming shipment that counteract the strictness of the perfect tender rule.

per·form *vt* **1** : to adhere to and fulfill the terms of ⟨~ an obligation⟩ **2** : to carry out

or bring about ⟨~ the work according to design⟩ **3** : to do according to prescribed ritual or law ⟨~ a marriage ceremony⟩ **4** : to give a public rendition or presentation of ⟨~ a copyrighted play⟩ ~ *vi* **1** : to adhere to and fulfill the terms of a contract, promise, or obligation ⟨failed to ~ under the agreement⟩ **2** : to carry out or present something

per·for·mance *n* **1** : work done in employment ⟨unsatisfactory ~⟩ **2 a** : what is required to be performed in fulfillment of a contract, promise, or obligation ⟨substituted a new ~ in novation of the contract⟩ **b** : the fulfillment of a contract, promise, or obligation

part performance **1** : partial performance of a contract, promise, or obligation **2** : a doctrine which provides an exception to the Statute of Frauds requirement that a contract be in writing by treating partial performance and the acceptance of it by the other party as evidence of an enforceable contract — compare *partial breach* at BREACH

specific performance **1** : the complete or exact fulfillment of the terms of a contract, promise, or obligation **2** : an equitable remedy that requires a party to fulfill the exact terms of a contract, promise, obligation, or decree mandating a remedy and that is used when legal remedies (as damages) are inadequate ⟨the common law prohibition against *specific performance* as a remedy for alleged breach of employment contract — *Chady v. Solomon Schechter Day Schs.,* 645 N.E.2d 983 (1995)⟩ — compare INJUNCTION

substantial performance **1** : performance of the essential terms of a contract, promise, or obligation ⟨a contractor is not entitled to a lien in the absence of *substantial performance* —*Casa Linda Tile & Marble Installers, Inc. v. Highlands Place 1981 Ltd.,* 642 So. 2d 766 (1994)⟩ **2** : a doctrine which permits a party (as a builder) that acted in good faith to recover from the other party to a contract for a performance that departs in minor respects from what was promised — compare *material breach* at BREACH

3 : a public rendition or presentation of an artistic work

performance bond — see BOND 1a

per·il \'per-əl\ *n* **1 :** exposure to the risk of death, destruction, or loss **2 :** the cause of a loss (as of property) ⟨insured their home against fire, floods, and other ~*s*⟩ — compare RISK

perils of the sea : perils that are peculiar to the sea but are of such an extraordinary nature and power that one cannot guard against them using ordinary skill and prudence ⟨the insurance company denied that such waves in that region were *perils of the sea*⟩

periodic tenancy — see TENANCY

per·jure \'pər-jər\ *vt* **per·jured; per·jur·ing :** to make a perjurer of (oneself)

perjured *adj* **1 :** guilty of perjury ⟨a ~ witness⟩ **2 :** marked by perjury ⟨~ testimony⟩

per·jur·er \'pər-jər-ər\ *n* **:** a person guilty of perjury

per·ju·ri·ous \pər-'jur-ē-əs, -'jər-\ *adj* **:** PERJURED ⟨~ statements⟩ ⟨a ~ witness⟩ — **per·ju·ri·ous·ly** *adv*

per·ju·ry \'pər-jə-rē\ *n, pl* **-ries** [Anglo⸗ French *perjurie, parjurie,* from Latin *perjurium,* from *perjurus* deliberately giving false testimony, from *per-* detrimental to + *jur-, jus* law] **:** the act or crime of knowingly making a false statement (as about a material matter) while under oath or bound by an affirmation or other officially prescribed declaration that what one says, writes, or claims is true — compare FALSE SWEARING

permanent alimony — see ALIMONY

permanent injunction — see INJUNCTION

per·mis·sive *adj* **1 :** based on or having permission ⟨~ occupancy⟩ ⟨a ~ user of the vehicle⟩ **2 :** granting permission or discretion (as to the court) ⟨a ~ statute⟩ **3 :** not compulsory: as **a :** allowed or made under a standard, rule, or provision that permits discretion or an option — see also *permissive intervention* at IN-

TERVENTION, *permissive presumption* at PRESUMPTION; compare COMPULSORY **b :** allowed under modern rules of civil procedure although not arising from the same transaction or occurrence as the one at issue in the original claim ⟨a ~ counterclaim⟩ — see also *permissive joinder* at JOINDER — **per·mis·sive·ly** *adv* — **per·mis·sive·ness** *n*

permissive inference *n* **:** PERMISSIVE PRESUMPTION at PRESUMPTION

permissive intervention — see INTERVENTION

permissive joinder — see JOINDER

permissive presumption — see PRESUMPTION

permissive waste — see WASTE

per·mit \'pər-ˌmit, pər-'mit\ *n* **:** a written warrant or license granted by one having authority ⟨a building ~⟩

permit bond — see BOND 1a

per·pe·trate \'pər-pə-ˌtrāt\ *vt* **-trat·ed; -trat·ing :** to carry out or bring about (as a crime) — **per·pe·tra·tion** \ˌpər-pə-'trā-shən\ *n* — **per·pe·tra·tor** \'pər-pə-ˌtrā-tər\ *n*

perpetual injunction *n* **:** PERMANENT INJUNCTION at INJUNCTION

perpetual lease — see LEASE

per·pet·u·ate \pər-'pe-chə-ˌwāt\ *vt* **-at·ed; -at·ing :** to preserve or make available (testimony) for later use at a trial by means of deposition esp. when the evidence so gathered would be otherwise unavailable or lost ◊ Courts will not allow the perpetuation of testimony at a pretrial proceeding if it appears to be an attempt to fish for useful material. — **per·pet·u·a·tion** \pər-ˌpe-chə-'wā-shən\ *n*

per·pe·tu·i·ty \ˌpər-pə-'tü-ə-tē, -'tyü-\ *n, pl* **-ties 1 :** the quality, state, or duration of being perpetual ⟨devised to them in ~⟩ **2 a :** the condition of a future estate limited in such a way as not to vest within the period fixed by law for the vesting of an estate; *also* : a limitation that gives rise to such a situation **b** : an estate that will not vest within the period fixed by law — see also RULE AGAINST PERPETUITIES, STATUTORY RULE AGAINST PERPETUITIES **3** : an annuity payable forever

per quod \pər-ˈkwäd, ˌper-ˈkwōd\ *adv or adj* [Latin, whereby] : on the basis of or with reference to extrinsic circumstances ⟨statements are considered defamatory *per quod* if the defamatory character of the statement is not apparent on its face —*Kolegas v. Heftel Broadcasting Corp.*, 607 N.E.2d 201 (1992)⟩ ⟨a *per quod* claim for loss of consortium⟩ — compare PER SE

¹per se \pər-ˈsā, ˌper-; pər-ˈsē\ *adv* [Latin, by, of, or in itself] **1** : inherently, strictly, or by operation of statute, constitutional provision or doctrine, or case law ⟨the transaction was illegal *per se*⟩ — see also *negligence per se* at NEGLIGENCE, *nuisance per se* at NUISANCE **2** : without proof of special damages or reference to extrinsic circumstances ⟨defamatory statements that were actionable *per se*⟩ — compare PER QUOD

²per se *adj* : being such inherently, clearly, or by operation of statute, constitutional provision or doctrine, or case law ⟨it is clear that licensing of adult entertainment establishments is not a *per se* violation of the First Amendment —*Club Southern Burlesque, Inc. v. City of Carrollton*, 457 S.E.2d 816 (1995)⟩ ⟨a *per se* conflict of interest⟩

per·se·cu·tion *n* : punishment or harassment usu. of a severe nature on the basis of race, religion, or political opinion in one's country of origin ⟨claimed ~ and sought asylum⟩

per se rule *n* **1** : a generalized rule applied without consideration for specific circumstances ⟨would go even further and apply a *per se rule* of invalidity to affirmative action programs —Alan Freeman⟩ — called also *flat rule* **2** : a rule that considers a particular restraint of trade to be manifestly contrary to competition and so does not require an inquiry into pre-cise harm or purpose for an instance of it to be declared illegal ⟨applied the *per se* rule to price-fixing by public utilities⟩ — compare RULE OF REASON

per·son *n* **1** : NATURAL PERSON **2** : the body of a human being; *also* : the body and clothing of a human being ⟨had drugs on his ~⟩ **3** : one (as a human being or corporation) that is recognized by law as the subject of rights and duties — see also JURIDICAL PERSON, LEGAL PERSON, PERSONALITY — **per·son·hood** *n*

per·son·al *adj* **1** : of, relating to, or affecting a person: as **a** : of, relating to, or based on the existence or presence of a person — see also PERSONAL INJURY, *personal jurisdiction* at JURISDICTION **b** : of, relating to, or restricted to a natural person and his or her rights, obligations, affairs, assets, or lifetime ⟨refused to disclose ~ information⟩ ⟨released on ~ recognizance⟩ **2** : of, relating to, or constituting personal property ⟨~ effects⟩ — see also *personal property* at PROPERTY; compare REAL — **per·son·al·ly** *adv*

personal bond — see BOND 1a

personal deduction — see DEDUCTION

personal defense — see DEFENSE 2b

personal easement — see EASEMENT

personal estate — see ESTATE 2

personal exemption — see EXEMPTION

personal exemption deduction — see DEDUCTION

personal expense — see EXPENSE

personal injury *n* : an injury to one's body, mind, or emotions; *broadly* : an injury that is not to one's property

per·son·al·i·ty *n, pl* **-ties 1** : the quality, state, or fact of being a person ⟨the corporation has legal ~⟩ **2** : the totality of an individual's behavioral and emotional characteristics ⟨a ~ disorder⟩

personal judgment — see JUDGMENT 1a

personal jurisdiction — see JURISDICTION

personal knowledge — see KNOWLEDGE

personal liability — see LIABILITY 2b

personal property — see PROPERTY

personal representative *n* : one recognized as the representative of another party or his or her interests; *specif* : an executor or administrator who may bring or be subject to an action or proceeding for or against a deceased person and his or her estate ⟨when a person who has brought an action for personal injury dies pending the action, such action may be revived in the name of his *personal representative* —*Code of Virginia*⟩

personal right *n* : a right that is based on one's status as an individual and does not derive from property

personal service *n* **1** : a service based on the intellectual or manual efforts of an individual (as for salary or wages) rather than a salable product of his or her skills **2** : physical delivery of process to a person to whom it is directed or to someone authorized to receive it on that person's behalf

personal servitude — see SERVITUDE

per·son·al·ty \'pərs-ᵊn-əl-tē\ *n* [Anglo‑French *personalté*, from Late Latin *personalit-*, *personalitas* personality] : PERSONAL PROPERTY at PROPERTY

per·son·ate \'pərs-ᵊn-ˌāt\ *vt* **-at·ed; -at·ing** : IMPERSONATE

per stir·pes \pər-'stər-pēz, per-'stir-pās\ *adv or adj* [Latin, by familial stocks] : by right of representation ⟨the estate was divided *per stirpes*⟩ — used of a method of distributing an esp. intestate estate; compare PER CAPITA ◊ Per stirpes distribution provides for division of an estate equally among the members of the group of descendants having a particular degree of kinship (as children), with the issue (that is, the offspring) of a deceased member of that group representing the deceased member, taking the deceased member's share, and dividing it equally among themselves. For example, if a decedent had three children, one of whom had already died leaving issue, the estate would be divided into thirds, with each living child receiving a one-third share, and the issue of the deceased child dividing a one-third share equally amongst themselves.

pet·it \'pe-tē\ *adj* [Anglo-French, minor, small] : PETTY

¹pe·ti·tion *n* **1** : a formal written request made to an official person or body (as a court or board) ⟨a ∼ for equitable relief⟩ ⟨the creditor filed a ∼ for involuntary bankruptcy⟩ **2** : a document embodying a formal written request

²petition *vt* : to direct a petition to ⟨∼ the court⟩ ∼ *vi* : to make a petition ⟨∼ for relief⟩ — **pe·ti·tion·er** *n*

petit juror *n* : a member of a petit jury

petit jury *n* : a jury of twelve persons that is impaneled to try and to decide the facts at issue in a trial — compare GRAND JURY

petit larceny — see LARCENY

pet·i·to·ry \'pe-tə-ˌtōr-ē\ *adj* [Latin *petitorius* of a claim to ownership, from *petere* to go to or toward, seek, request] : made under admiralty or civil law to establish a right to ownership rather than to possession of property ⟨a ∼ action⟩

petit theft *n* : PETTY THEFT at THEFT

pet·ty \'pe-tē\ *adj* : relatively minor in degree ⟨a ∼ offense punishable by not more than six months in prison⟩ — compare GRAND

petty larceny *n* : PETIT LARCENY at LARCENY

petty theft — see THEFT

phan·tom stock plan *n* : a form of executive compensation in which an employee is granted units representing shares of stock which are redeemable at a specified future date for the market value of an equivalent number of corporate shares but which in the interval are nontransferable, have no cash value, and confer none of the noneconomic rights (as voting) conferred by ordinary stock

physical custody — see CUSTODY b, c

physical evidence — see EVIDENCE

phys·i·cal taking *n* : a physical invasion or occupation of private property rights by a governmental action (as building a road)

\ə\abut \ᵊ\kitten \ər\further \a\ash \ā\ace
\ä\cot, cart \au̇\out \ch\chin \e\bet \ē\easy
\g\go \i\hit \ī\ice \j\job \ŋ\sing \ō\go \ȯ\law
\ȯi\boy \th\thin \th\the \ü\loot \u̇\foot \y\yet
\zh\vision   *see also* Pronunciation Symbols page

that exercises the right of eminent domain and for which just compensation must be given ⟨argued that requiring the easement constituted a *physical taking*⟩ — compare REGULATORY TAKING

¹pick·et *n* : a person posted by a labor organization at a place of employment affected by a labor dispute; *broadly* : a person posted for a demonstration or protest

²picket *vt* : to post pickets in front of : walk or stand in front of as a picket ⟨their tactics have included ~*ing* clinics —L. H. Tribe⟩ ~ *vi* : to demonstrate by use of pickets ⟨a currently certified union may ~ for recognition⟩; *also* : to serve as a picket — see also INFORMATIONAL PICKETING, ORGANIZATIONAL PICKETING, SECONDARY PICKETING; compare STRIKE ◊ While the right to peacefully picket for a lawful purpose is protected by the First Amendment to the U.S. Constitution, case law has recognized some limitations and the Labor Management Relations Act has placed some restrictions on organizational and secondary picketing. — **pick·et·er** *n*

picket line *n* : a line of people picketing a business, institution, or organization

pick·pock·et *n* : a thief who surreptitiously steals money or valuables from the pockets or person of an individual

piece·work \'pēs-ˌwərk\ *n* : work done by the piece and paid for at a set rate per unit

pierce *vt* **pierced; pierc·ing** : to see through the usu. misleading or false appearance of ⟨the object of summary judgment is to ~ the pleadings and allow a judgment on the merits —J. H. Friedenthal *et al.*⟩ ⟨the Internal Revenue Service may attempt to ~ the plain meaning of the agreement —W. M. McGovern, Jr. *et al.*⟩ — **pierce the corporate veil** : to disregard the corporate entity and reach the personal assets of the corporation's controlling parties : hold the controlling parties (as officers or shareholders) of a corporation personally liable for wrongful acts or debts of the corporation ⟨a . . . creditor in New York cannot *pierce the corporate veil* solely on

grounds of inadequate capitalization — R. C. Clark⟩ — compare *corporate immunity* at IMMUNITY ◊ An action to pierce the corporate veil is usu. grounded on the corporation's being an instrumentality or alter ego of the officers or shareholders and on some misuse (as fraud) of the officers' or shareholders' control over the corporation.

pil·fer \'pil-fər\ *vi* : to steal esp. in small amounts and often again and again ⟨accused of ~*ing* from passenger luggage⟩ ~ *vt* : to steal or steal from esp. in small quantities ⟨found ~*ing* goods from a store he was guarding⟩ — **pil·fer·age** \'pil-fə-rij\ *n*

pil·lage \'pi-lij\ *vb* **pil·laged; pil·lag·ing** *vt* : to loot or plunder esp. in war ~ *vi* : to take booty — **pillage** *n*

¹pimp \'pimp\ *n* : one who derives income from the earnings of a prostitute usu. by soliciting business — compare PANDERER

²pimp *vi* : to work as a pimp — compare PANDERING

pi·ra·cy \'pī-rə-sē\ *n, pl* **-cies 1** : an act of robbery esp. on the high seas; *specif* : an illegal act of violence, detention, or plunder committed for private ends by crew or passengers of a private ship or aircraft against another ship or aircraft on the high seas or in a place outside the jurisdiction of any state — see also AIRCRAFT PIRACY, *Article I* of the CONSTITUTION in the back matter **2 a** : the unauthorized copying, distribution, or use of another's production (as a film) esp. in infringement of a copyright ⟨software ~⟩ **b** : the unauthorized use, interception, or receipt of encoded communications (as satellite cable programming) esp. to avoid paying fees for use ⟨the statute's purpose is to proscribe the ~ of programming signals — *United States v. Harrell*, 983 F.2d 36 (1993)⟩ **3** : the crime of committing piracy

¹pi·rate \'pī-rət\ *n* : a person who commits piracy

²pirate *vb* **pi·rat·ed; pi·rat·ing** *vt* : to take or appropriate by piracy; *esp* : to copy, distribute, or use without authorization esp. in infringement of copyright ⟨the *pirated* software⟩ ⟨*pirating* cable signals⟩ ∼ *vi* : to commit piracy — compare BOOTLEG

Pl *abbr* pleas

PL *abbr* **1** plaintiff **2** public law

pla·gia·rize \'plā-jə-ˌrīz\ *vb* **-rized; -rizing** [from *plagiary* plagiarist, from Latin *plagiarius*, literally, kidnapper, from *plagium* netting of game, kidnapping, from *plaga* net] *vt* : to copy and pass off (the expression of ideas or words of another) as one's own : use (another's work) without crediting the source ⟨the book contained *plagiarized* material — *Smith v. Little, Brown & Co.*, 265 F. Supp. 451 (1965)⟩ ∼ *vi* : to present as new and original an idea or work derived from an existing source — **pla·gia·rism** \-ˌrizəm\ *n* — **pla·gia·rist** \-rist\ *n*

plain·clothes \'plān-'klōz, -'klō<u>th</u>z\ *adj* : dressed in civilian clothes while on duty — used esp. of a police officer

plain error — see ERROR

plain mean·ing rule *n* : a rule in statute or contract interpretation: when the language is unambiguous and clear on its face the meaning of the statute or contract must be determined from the language of the statute or contract and not from extrinsic evidence

plain·tiff \'plān-təf\ *n* [Middle French *plaintif*, from *plaintif*, adj., grieving, from *plaint* lamentation, from Latin *planctus*, from *plangere* to strike, beat one's breast, lament] : the party who institutes a legal action or claim (as a counterclaim) — see also COMPLAINANT, COMPLAINT, LIBELLANT; compare DEFENDANT, PROSECUTION

plaintiff in error : a party who proceeds by writ of error : APPELLANT

plain view *n* **1** : a location or field of perception in which something is plainly apparent **2** : a doctrine that permits the search, seizure, and use of evidence obtained without a search warrant when such evidence was plainly perceptible in the course of lawful procedure and the

police had probable cause to believe it was incriminating — see also INADVERTENT DISCOVERY; compare FRUIT OF THE POISONOUS TREE

plan *n* **1** : a diagram of an area of land (as a subdivision) filed in the registry of deeds — see also PLOT PLAN **2** : a detailed program; *esp* : one made under chapter 13 of the Bankruptcy Code that places future earnings under the control of a trustee, provides for the payment of creditors, and is subject to approval by the creditors

plat \'plat\ *n* [probably alteration of *plot*] : a plan, map, or chart of a piece of land with present or proposed features (as lots); *also* : the land represented

plea \'plē\ *n* [Anglo-French *plei, plai* legal action, trial, from Old French *plait, plaid*, from Medieval Latin *placitum*, from Latin, decision, decree, from neuter of *placitus*, past participle of *placēre* to please, be decided] **1 a** : an allegation of fact in civil litigation made in response to a claim — compare DEMURRER **b** : a defendant's answer to a plaintiff's claim in civil litigation ◊ Under the Federal Rules of Civil Procedure, and in states where they have been adopted, civil pleas are abolished, and answers and motions are used instead. Such pleas were used at common law.

dil·a·to·ry plea \'di-lə-ˌtōr-ē-\ : a common-law plea which is intended to defeat the pending action or proceeding without involving any decision on the merits of the case

plea in abatement : a plea entered by a party seeking postponement or dismissal of an action by setting forth some matter or defect regarding procedure, jurisdiction, or timing — called also *plea of abatement*

plea in bar : a plea that alleges the existence of an absolute bar (as a statute of limitations) to an action

\ə\abut \ᵊ\kitten \ər\further \a\ash \ā\ace \ä\cot, cart \au̇\out \ch\chin \e\bet \ē\easy \g\go \i\hit \ī\ice \j\job \ŋ\sing \ō\go \ȯ\law \ȯi\boy \th\thin \t̲h̲\the \ü\loot \u̇\foot \y\yet \zh\vision *see also* Pronunciation Symbols page

plea of abatement : PLEA IN ABATE-
MENT in this entry
2 a : an accused party's answer to a criminal charge or indictment **b** : a plea of
guilty **3** : an earnest entreaty
plea agreement *n* : an agreement reached
at the conclusion of plea bargaining
: PLEA BARGAIN
plea bargaining *n* : the negotiation of
an agreement between the prosecution
and the defense whereby the defendant
pleads guilty to a lesser offense or to
one or some of multiple offenses usu.
in exchange for more lenient sentencing
recommendations, a specific sentence, or
dismissal of other charges — **plea–
bargain** *vi* — **plea bargain** *n*
plead \'plēd\ [Anglo-French *plaider* to argue in a court of law, from Old French
plaid legal action, trial — more at PLEA]
vb **plead•ed** *or* **pled** *also* **plead** \'pled\;
plead•ing *vi* **1** : to make an allegation in
an action or other legal proceeding; *esp*
: to answer the pleading or charge of the
other party by denying facts therein stated
or by alleging new facts ⟨the defendant
shall be given a copy of the indictment
or information before the defendant is
called upon to ~ —*Kansas Statutes Annotated*⟩ — see also ALTERNATIVE **2** : to
make a specific plea ⟨~ not guilty⟩; *also*
: to make a plea of guilty ⟨agreed to ~ to
the lesser charge⟩ ~ *vt* **1** : to allege
in or by way of a pleading : state in a
pleading ⟨unless plaintiff ~*s* and proves
facts showing actual malice, he cannot
recover punitive damages —*Kumaran v.
Brotman*, 617 N.E.2d 191 (1993)⟩ ⟨~ a
case of fraudulent conveyance⟩ **2** : to offer as an excuse ⟨cannot ~ ignorance of
the law⟩ — **plead•able** *adj* — **plead-
er** *n*
plead•ing *n* **1 a** : one of the formal declarations (as a complaint or answer) exchanged by the parties in a legal proceeding (as a suit) setting forth claims, averments, allegations, denials, or defenses;
also : a written document embodying
such a declaration — see also RELATION
BACK **b** : any of the allegations, aver-

ments, claims, denials, or defenses set
forth in a pleading
alternative pleading : a pleading that
sets out an alternative theory in support of a plaintiff's claim for relief or a
defendant's defense
amended pleading : a pleading that is
filed to replace an original pleading and
that contains matters omitted from or
not known at the time of the original
pleading
re•spon•sive pleading \ri-'spän-siv-\ : a
pleading that directly responds to another pleading (as by denying in an answer allegations in a complaint)
sham pleading : a pleading that is factu-
ally false, is not made in good faith, and
that may be struck
supplemental pleading : a pleading that
supplements an earlier pleading with
matters that have occurred or come into
existence since the date of the original
pleading
2 : a process or system through which the
parties in a legal proceeding present their
allegations
code pleading : pleading (as fact pleading) done in accordance with the rules
set down in a code ◊ Code pleading began in 1848 in New York State and was
a departure from the complex system of
common-law pleading, which included
a lengthy set of stages by which a single
issue was produced, and which was determined by the type of writ under which
the plaintiff proceeded.
fact pleading : pleading that requires a
plaintiff to set out in the complaint facts
sufficient to establish a cause of action
— compare NOTICE PLEADING in this
entry
notice pleading : pleading that is characterized esp. by a simplified description sufficient to give notice of a claim
or defense rather than by a technical account of any facts pertinent to the claim
or defense — compare FACT PLEADING
in this entry ◊ Notice pleading is
allowed under the Federal Rules of Civil
Procedure and in a majority of states,

although complex cases often require substantial detail in the pleading.

plea in abatement — see PLEA

plea in bar — see PLEA

plea of abatement — see PLEA

pled *past and past part of* PLEAD

¹pledge \'plej\ *n* **1** : a delivery of esp. personal property as security for a debt or other obligation; *broadly* : the perfection of a security interest in collateral through possession of the collateral by a creditor or other promisee **2 a** : property and esp. personal property that is used as security esp. upon delivery; *broadly* : a security interest in collateral — compare *chattel mortgage* at MORTGAGE **b** : a contract under which the delivery of property (as personal property) as security takes place **3 a** : the state of being held as security or guaranty ⟨property held in ~⟩ **b** : something given as security for the performance of an act **4** : a binding promise to do or forbear

²pledge *vt* **pledged; pledg·ing 1** : to deliver or otherwise put forward as security for a debt or other obligation ⟨*pledged* his car as collateral for the loan⟩ **2** : to bind by a pledge ⟨we mutually ~ to each other our lives, our fortunes and our sacred honor —*Declaration of Independence*⟩ **3** : to assure or promise the performance or payment of — **pled·gor** \'ple-jər, ple-'jòr\ *or* **pledg·er** \'ple-jər\ *n*

pledg·ee \ple-'jē\ *n* : one to whom property is pledged

ple·na·ry \'plē-nə-rē, 'ple-\ *adj* : full and complete in every respect: as **a** : ABSOLUTE 1 ⟨~ power⟩ **b** : fully attended or constituted ⟨a ~ session of the legislature⟩ **c** : including all steps in due order ⟨a ~ proceeding⟩ — compare SUMMARY

plot plan *n* : a plan indicating the present or proposed use of a plot of land; *esp* : one for a residential lot that indicates the location of structures and other important elements (as a septic system)

pltf *abbr* plaintiff

plu·ral·i·ty \plů-'ra-lə-tē\ *n, pl* **-ties** : an amount or group (as of votes) that is greater than any other amount or group

within a total but that is not more than half; *esp* : a group of justices on an appeals court who do not form a majority but with whose opinion enough other justices concur to render it the decision of the court — see also *plurality opinion* at OPINION; compare MAJORITY

plurality opinion — see OPINION

plu·ri·es \'plůr-ē-,ēz\ *adj* : of, relating to, or being a writ issued after the first and alias writs have proven ineffectual

PMI *abbr* private mortgage insurance

pock·et veto *n* : a veto of legislation that occurs indirectly when an executive refrains from signing the legislation and the adjournment of the legislature prevents its automatic enactment (as upon expiration of ten days)

P.O.D. account \pē-,ō-'dē-\ *n* [*Payable On Death*] : an account payable on request to an original party or upon the party's death to one or more designated beneficiaries ◊ A P.O.D. account is one of the few vehicles for the transfer of a decedent's property outside of probate.

point *n* **1** : a particular detail, proposition, or issue of law; *specif* : POINT OF ERROR **2** : any of various incremental units used in measuring, fixing, or calculating something: as **a** : a unit used in calculating a sentence by various factors (as aggravating or mitigating circumstances) **b** : a unit used in the pricing of securities and valuation of markets **c** : a charge to a borrower (as a mortgagor) that is equal to one percent of the principal and that is made at closing — **in point** *or* **on point** : relevant to the legal issues at hand

point of error : a challenge by a party to a finding, ruling, or judgment of a trial court on the basis that it is contrary to the evidence or to the law

poi·son pill *n* : a financial tactic or provision used by a company to make an unwanted takeover prohibitively expensive or less desirable

¹po·lice *vt* **po·liced; po·lic·ing** : to control, regulate, or keep in order esp. as an official duty ⟨~ the area⟩

²police *n, pl* **police 1** : the control and regulation of affairs affecting the order and welfare of a political unit and its citizens **2 a** : the department of a government or other institution that maintains order and safety and enforces laws **b** : POLICE FORCE **c** *pl* : the members of a police force

police court *n* : a court of record in some states that has jurisdiction over various minor offenses and the power to bind over those accused of more serious offenses

police force *n* : a body of trained officers entrusted by a government with maintenance of public peace and order, enforcement of laws, and prevention and detection of crime

police jury *n* : the governing body of a Louisiana parish corresponding to a board of supervisors in the counties of other states

police power — see POWER 2a

police register *n* : a register kept by police of daily business (as arrests)

¹pol·i·cy \'pä-lə-sē\ *n, pl* **-cies** : an overall plan, principle, or guideline; *esp* : one formulated outside of the judiciary ⟨obligated to consider legislative ~ on the matter in their decision⟩

²policy *n, pl* **-cies** : a contract of insurance; *also* : the written instrument of such a contract

pol·i·cy·hold·er \'pä-lə-sē-ˌhōl-dər\ *n* : the owner of an insurance policy — called also *policyowner;* compare SUBJECT

pol·i·cy·own·er \'pä-lə-sē-ˌō-nər\ *n* : POLICYHOLDER

policy reserve — see RESERVE

political question — see QUESTION 2

po·lit·i·cal question doctrine *n* : a doctrine under which a court will refrain from adjudicating a question that is more properly resolved by the other branches of government because of its inherently political nature and not because of a lack of jurisdiction

poll tax \'pōl-\ *n* : a tax of a fixed amount per person levied on adults

po·lyg·a·my \pə-'li-gə-mē\ *n* : the offense of having several and specif. more than two spouses at one time — compare BIGAMY — **po·lyg·a·mous** \-məs\ *adj*

poly·graph \'pä-lē-ˌgraf\ *n* : an instrument that records physiological pulsations; *esp* : LIE DETECTOR — **poly·graph·ic** \ˌpä-lē-'gra-fik\ *adj*

Pon·zi scheme \'pän-zē-ˌskēm\ *n* [Charles A. *Ponzi* (ca. 1882–1949), Italian-born American swindler] : an investment swindle in which early investors are paid with sums obtained from later ones in order to create the illusion of profitability

¹pool *n* **1** : an aggregation of the interests, obligations, or undertakings of several parties working together ⟨an insurance ~⟩ **2** : a group of people available for some purpose — see also JURY POOL

²pool *vt* : to combine (as assets or votes) in a common form or effort; *esp* : to combine (interests) so as not to have a merger of companies considered a purchase for accounting purposes

pop·u·lar *adj* **1** : of or relating to the general public **2 a** : of, relating to, or by the people (as of a nation or state) as a whole as distinguished from a specific class or group **b** : based on or alleged to be based on the will of the people

por·nog·ra·phy \pȯr-'nä-grə-fē\ *n* : material that depicts erotic behavior and is intended to cause sexual excitement ◊ Pornographic material is protected expression unless it is determined to be obscene. However, child pornography is illegal under federal and state laws prohibiting the depiction of minors in sexual acts. — **por·nog·ra·pher** \pȯr-'nä-grə-fər\ *n* — **por·no·graph·ic** \ˌpȯr-nə-'gra-fik\ *adj* — **por·no·graph·i·cal·ly** *adv*

port·fo·lio \pȯrt-'fō-lē-ō\ *n* : the securities held by an investor : the commercial paper held by a financial institution (as a bank)

pos·i·tive law *n* : law established or recognized by governmental authority — compare NATURAL LAW

positive testimony — see TESTIMONY

pos·sess \pə-'zes\ *vt* : to have possession of
pos·ses·sion \pə-'ze-shən\ *n* **1** : the act,
fact, or condition of having control of
something: as **a** : ACTUAL POSSESSION
in this entry **b** : CONSTRUCTIVE POSSES-
SION in this entry **c** : knowing dominion
and control over a controlled substance
or other contraband **d** *in the civil law of
Louisiana* : the detention or enjoyment of
a corporeal thing **e** : control or occupancy
of property
actual possession **1** : direct occupancy,
use, or control of real property ⟨had *actual possession* of the land despite a lack
of legal title⟩ **2** : direct physical custody,
care, or control of property or contraband (as illegal drugs) ⟨*actual possession* is not necessary to sustain a conviction — *State v. Garrison*, 896 S.W.2d
689 (1995)⟩
adverse possession : actual possession
of another's real property that is open,
hostile, exclusive, continuous, adverse
to the claim of the owner, often under a
claim of right or color of title, and that
may give rise to title in the possessor if
carried out for a specified statutory period (as ten years); *also* : the method of
acquiring title by such possession — see
also HOSTILE POSSESSION and NOTORI-
OUS POSSESSION in this entry; compare
PRESCRIPTION
civil possession in the civil law of Louisiana : possession that exists by virtue
of an intent to be the owner of a property
even though one no longer occupies or
has physical control of it
constructive possession **1** : possession
that exists by virtue of a right (as by title)
rather than direct occupancy or control
2 : the knowing ability and sometimes
intent to exercise dominion and control
over something (as illegal drugs) either
directly or through others
hostile possession : possession (as in
adverse possession) that is antagonistic
to the claims of all others (as a record
owner) and that is carried out with the
intention to possess the property exclusively
notorious possession : possession (as in

adverse possession) that is so conspicu-
ous that it is generally known by people in the vicinity of the property and
so gives rise to a presumption that the
owner has notice of it
precarious possession in the civil law of
Louisiana : possession of property that
is exercised by another (as a lessee) with
the permission of or on behalf of the
owner — see also *acquisitive prescription* at PRESCRIPTION
2 : something controlled, occupied, or
owned ⟨personal ~*s*⟩
pos·ses·sor \pə-'ze-sər\ *n* : one that has
possession
pos·ses·so·ry \pə-'ze-sə-rē\ *adj* **1** : of,
arising from, involving, or having the nature of possession ⟨~ rights⟩ ⟨a ~ action⟩
2 : having possession ⟨a ~ owner⟩
possessory interest — see INTEREST 1
pos·si·bil·i·ty of reverter : a future interest in property that is retained by the
grantor of a conditional fee or determinable fee and by which property reverts to
the grantor upon the occurrence of a particular event or fulfillment of a particular
condition — compare REVERSION
post *vt* : to put up (as bond) ⟨~ bail⟩
post–con·vic·tion \ˌpōst-kən-'vik-shən\
adj : relating to or occurring in the period
following conviction ⟨~ review⟩
pos·ter·i·ty \pä-'ster-ə-tē\ *n* **1** : all of the
lineal descendants of a person **2** : all
future generations
post·ing *n* **1** : the transfer of an entry or
item from a book or file of original entry to the proper account in a ledger; *also*
: the record produced by such a transfer **2**
: the actual crediting or debiting of an account (as in payment of a draft) ⟨charged
interest from the ~ date of the credit card
transaction⟩
¹post mor·tem \ˌpōst-'mȯr-təm\ *adj* : done,
occurring, or collected after death
²post mortem *n* : AUTOPSY
post mortem examination *n* : AUTOPSY

\ə\abut	\ᵊ\kitten	\ər\further	\a\ash	\ā\ace
\ä\cot, cart	\aů\out	\ch\chin	\e\bet	\ē\easy
\g\go	\i\hit	\ī\ice	\j\job	\ŋ\sing	\ō\go	\ȯ\law
\ȯi\boy	\th\thin	\t̲h̲\the	\ü\loot	\ů\foot	\y\yet
\zh\vision	*see also* Pronunciation Symbols page			

post·nup·tial agreement \ˌpōst-'nəp-shəl-, -chəl-\ *n* : an agreement that is made between spouses regarding the division of marital property and that is usu. formulated in contemplation of separation or divorce

post·pone *vt* **post·poned; post·pon·ing 1** : to put off to a later time **2** : to place later in precedence, preference, or importance; *specif* : to subordinate (a lien) to a later lien — **post·pon·able** *adj* — **post·pone·ment** *n*

potestative condition — see CONDITION

¹pour–over \'pōr-ˌō-vər\ *adj* : providing for or creating the transfer of property in a decedent's estate or a trust to a pour-over trust ⟨a ~ provision⟩⟨a ~ bequest⟩ — see also *pour-over trust* at TRUST, *pour-over will* at WILL

²pour–over *n* : an act or instance of pouring over; *also* : a provision esp. in a will that calls for estate assets to be transferred to a pour-over trust

pour over *vi* : to be conveyed from an estate or trust to another trust; *broadly* : to be transferred as a residue or surplus ⟨the remainder of the estate will *pour over* to a charitable trust⟩ ~ *vt* : to cause to be conveyed esp. to a pour-over trust

pour–over trust — see TRUST

pour–over will — see WILL

pow·er *n* **1** : capability of acting or of producing an effect ⟨parties of unequal bargaining ~⟩ **2 a** : authority or capacity to act that is delegated by law or constitution — often used in pl.
commerce power often cap C&P : the power delegated to Congress under Article I, Section 8 of the U.S. Constitution to regulate commerce esp. among the states — see also COMMERCE CLAUSE
concurrent power : a power that is held simultaneously by more than one entity; *specif* : a power delegated to the federal government by the U.S. Constitution that is also held by the states
enu·mer·at·ed powers \i-'nü-mə-ˌrā-təd-, -'nyü-\ : the powers specifically named and delegated to the federal government or prohibited to be exercised by the states under the U.S. Constitution — compare RESERVED POWERS in this entry
executive power : the power delegated to the executive of a government; *specif* : any or all of the powers delegated to the president under Article II of the U.S. Constitution
implied power : a power that is reasonably necessary and appropriate to carry out the purposes of a power expressly granted; *esp* : a power that is not specifically delegated to the federal government by the U.S. Constitution but that is implied by the necessary and proper clause to be delegated for the purpose of carrying out the enumerated powers — see also *McCulloch v. Maryland* in the IMPORTANT CASES section
judicial power : the power granted to the judicial branch of a government; *specif* : the power delegated to the judiciary under Article III of the U.S. Constitution
legislative power : the power delegated to a legislative branch of a government; *specif* : any or all of the powers delegated to the Congress under Article I of the U.S. Constitution
police power : the power of a government to exercise reasonable control over persons and property within its jurisdiction in the interest of the general security, health, safety, morals, and welfare except where legally prohibited (as by constitutional provision)
reserved powers : the political powers reserved by a constitution to the exclusive jurisdiction of a specified political authority; *specif* : powers that are not expressly delegated to the federal government nor expressly prohibited to the states and are therefore left to the states under the Tenth Amendment to the U.S. Constitution — compare ENUMERATED POWERS in this entry
spend·ing power : the power granted to a government body to make expenditures; *specif* : the power delegated to Congress under Article I, Section 8 of the U.S. Constitution to pay the debts

and provide for the common defense and general welfare of the U.S.

tax·ing power : the power granted to a government body to lay and collect taxes; *specif* : such power delegated to Congress under Article I, Section 8 of the U.S. Constitution

war powers : the powers delegated to the executive and legislative branches of the federal government relating to the waging of war: as **a** : the power delegated to Congress under Article I, Section 8 of the U.S. Constitution to declare war **b** : the power delegated to the president under Article II, Section 2 of the U.S. Constitution to serve as commander in chief of the armed forces

b : an ability, authority, or right usu. conferred by one person upon another to do something that effects a change in a legal relationship; *specif* : such authority or right to affect another's interest in property (as by conveyance) — see also POWER OF APPOINTMENT, POWER OF ATTORNEY

collateral power : NAKED POWER in this entry

general power : a power that may be exercised in favor of anyone including the donee

implied power : the power of one acting under an implied agency

naked power : a power (as a power of sale) granted to one who has no interest in the property to which the power relates (as an executor who is not a legatee or devisee) — called also *collateral power;* compare POWER COUPLED WITH AN INTEREST in this entry

power ap·pen·dant \-ə-'pen-dənt\ : a power coupled with an interest (as a grant of a lease) that the donee can exercise only out of an estate (as a life estate) that he or she holds — called also *power appurtenant*

power cou·pled with an interest : a power accompanying an interest of the donee in the property to which the power relates

power in gross : a naked power exercis-

able by the donee only in the creation of estates that will not attach to the estate the donee holds or be satisfied out of the donee's own interest

power of acceptance : the power of an offeree to bind an offeror to a contract by accepting the offer

power of mod·i·fi·ca·tion \ˌmä-də-fə-'kā-shən\ : a power reserved in an instrument (as one creating a trust) to make changes by a specified method

power of revocation : a power usu. reserved by a person in an instrument (as one creating a trust) to revoke the legal relationship that the person has created or made a possibility

power of sale : a power granted (as in a will, trust, or mortgage) to sell the property to which the power relates often under specified circumstances (as upon the default of a mortgage)

power of termination : a power of a grantor or the grantor's successors in interest to enter upon an estate that was granted upon a condition after the breach of the condition in order to terminate the granted estate and revest it in the grantor or successors in interest — called also *right of entry*, *right of reentry*

special power : a power in which the person or class of persons to whom the disposition of property under the power is to be made is expressly designated and excludes the donee or where the power is to transfer, charge, or encumber any estate less than a fee simple

stock power : an irrevocable power of attorney used in making a transfer of a certificate of stock

3 a : possession of control, authority, or influence over others **b** : one having such power; *specif* : a sovereign state **c** : political control or influence

power appendant — see POWER 2b

\ə\abut \ᵊ\kitten \ər\further \a\ash \ā\ace
\ä\cot, cart \au̇\out \ch\chin \e\bet \ē\easy
\g\go \i\hit \ī\ice \j\job \ŋ\sing \ō\go \ȯ\law
\ȯi\boy \th\thin \t͟h\the \ü\loot \u̇\foot \y\yet
\zh\vision *see also* Pronunciation Symbols page

power appurtenant *n* : POWER APPEN-DANT at POWER 2b

power coupled with an interest — see POWER 2b

power in gross — see POWER 2b

power of acceptance — see POWER 2b

power of appointment : a power granted under a deed or will authorizing the donee to dispose of an estate in a specified manner for the benefit of the donee or of others

general power of appointment : a power of appointment which the donee may exercise in favor of anyone including himself or herself; *specif* : a power of appointment defined by the Internal Revenue Code as one exercisable in favor of the individual possessing the power, his or her estate, his or her creditors, or the creditors of his or her estate with certain specified qualifications

limited power of appointment : SPECIAL POWER OF APPOINTMENT in this entry; *also* : a power of appointment which the donee may exercise in favor of anyone but himself or herself

special power of appointment : a power of appointment which the donee may exercise in favor of only a designated person or class of persons not including himself or herself or his or her estate

testamentary power of appointment : a power of appointment that the donee may exercise only in his or her will

power of appointment trust — see TRUST

power of attorney : an instrument containing an authorization for one to act as the agent of the principal that terminates esp. upon revocation by the principal or death of the principal or agent — called also *letter of attorney*

du·ra·ble power of attorney \'dür-ə-bəl-, 'dyür-\ : a power of attorney that becomes effective upon the principal's becoming incompetent or unable to manage his or her affairs and that is often used as a form of advance directive — compare LIVING WILL

general power of attorney : a power of attorney authorizing the agent to carry on business or an enterprise for the principal — compare SPECIAL POWER OF ATTORNEY in this entry

irrevocable power of attorney : a power of attorney that cannot be revoked by the principal

special power of attorney : a power of attorney authorizing the agent to carry out a particular business transaction for the principal

power of modification — see POWER 2b

power of revocation — see POWER 2b

power of sale — see POWER 2b

power of termination — see POWER 2b

prac·ti·cal construction *n* **1** : the interpretation of the terms of a contract as shown by the performance of the parties that may be used by the court to help determine the intent of the parties; *also* : the doctrine that permits such a method of discerning intent — compare COURSE OF PERFORMANCE **2** : interpretation of a statute or document in a manner that does not defeat its purpose esp. when a strict interpretation would produce clearly unintended or absurd results

prac·tice *n* **1** : the form and manner of conducting judicial and quasi-judicial proceedings **2 a** : the continuous exercise of a profession; *also* : the performance of services that are considered to require an appropriate license ⟨engaged in the unauthorized ~ of law⟩ **b** : a professional business

prae·ci·pe *also* **pre·ci·pe** \'pre-sə-,pē, 'prē-\ *n* [Medieval Latin *precipe*, legal writ commanding a person to do something or show cause why he or she should not, from Latin *praecipe*, imperative of *praecipere* to give rules or precepts, admonish, enjoin] : a written request for an action (as the issuing of a writ of execution) from a party to a clerk of a court or sometimes to a judge ⟨filed a ~ for the writ of scire facias⟩ ⟨shall issue upon ~ of the plaintiff⟩ ◊ When addressed to a clerk, a praecipe is usu. a request for some action that does not require immediate judicial review, such as the issuing of a subpoena or the preparing of a record for appellate review. When addressed to a judge, as for jury instructions in some jurisdictions, a praecipe is similar to a motion. A praecipe originally was a writ issued by the king to a sheriff, telling the sheriff to command someone to do something (as to release land being withheld from another).

pray *vt* : to ask for ⟨plaintiff ~*s* judgment against the defendants for actual damages⟩ — used esp. in pleadings ⁓ *vi* : to make a request of a court esp. in a complaint or petition ⟨complainant ~*s* for declaratory relief⟩ ⟨~*ing* that the judgment be vacated⟩

prayer \'prer\ *n* : the part of a pleading (as a complaint) that specifies the relief sought; *also* : a request for relief or some other action by the court

pre- *prefix* **1 a** : earlier than : prior to : before ⟨*pre*marital⟩ ⟨*pre*judgment⟩ **b** : preparatory or prerequisite to ⟨*pre*hearing⟩ **2** : in advance : beforehand ⟨*pre*pay⟩

pre·am·ble \'prē-ˌam-bəl, prē-'am-\ *n* [Middle French *preambule*, from Medieval Latin *preambulum*, from Late Latin, neuter of *preambulus* walking in front of, from Latin *prae-* + *ambulare* to walk] : an introductory statement (as to a contract); *esp* : the introductory part of a constitution or statute that usu. states the reasons for and intent of the law ◊ While preambles do not state law and therefore are not judicially enforceable, they are used to determine legislative intent when interpreting statutes.

pre·car·i·ous \pri-'kar-ē-əs\ *adj* : depending on the will or pleasure of another ⟨a temporary and ~ office⟩ — see also *precarious possession* at POSSESSION

precarious possession — see POSSESSION

prec·a·to·ry \'pre-kə-ˌtōr-ē\ *adj* : expressing a wish or desire but not creating a legal obligation or affirmative duty ⟨a ~ remark⟩ ⟨the ~ words⟩ ◊ When interpreting wills, courts will look to whether a direction is precatory or mandatory in carrying out the testator's intent. Thus, courts generally will not construe language to create a trust if the language is only precatory and there is no evidence that the language was intended to create a trust. Words such as *with the hope that* or *it is my wish that* are often considered precatory.

¹pre·ce·dent \pri-'sēd-ᵊnt, 'pre-səd-\ *adj* [Middle French, from Latin *praecedent-*, *praecedens*, present participle of *praecedere* to go ahead of, come before] : prior in time, order, arrangement, or significance — see also *condition precedent* at CONDITION; compare SUBSEQUENT

²prec·e·dent \'pre-səd-ᵊnt\ *n* : a judicial decision that should be followed by a judge when deciding a later similar case — see also STARE DECISIS; compare DICTUM ◊ To serve as precedent for a pending case, a prior decision must have a similar question of law and factual situation. If the precedent is from the same or a superior jurisdiction (as the state's supreme court), it is binding upon the court and must be followed; if the precedent is from another jurisdiction (as another state's supreme court), it is considered only persuasive. Precedents may be overruled esp. by the same court that originally rendered the decision.

prec·e·den·tial \ˌpre-sə-'den-chəl\ *adj* : relating to, having the character of, or constituting precedent ⟨is of no ~ value⟩ ⟨has no ~ effect in this jurisdiction⟩

precipe *var of* PRAECIPE

pre·clude \pri-'klüd\ *vt* **pre·clud·ed; pre·clud·ing** : to prevent or exclude by necessary consequence ⟨the requirement of a marriage ceremony ~*s* the creation of common-law marriages in this jurisdiction⟩: as **a** : to prevent (a party) from litigating an action or claim esp. by collateral estoppel or res judicata ⟨they are *precluded* only because they failed to assert . . . the grounds for recovery they now assert —*Roach v. Teamsters Local Union No. 688*, 595 F.2d 446 (1979)⟩ **b**

\ə\abut \ᵊ\kitten \ər\further \a\ash \ā\ace
\ä\cot, cart \au̇\out \ch\chin \e\bet \ē\easy
\g\go \i\hit \ī\ice \j\job \ŋ\sing \ō\go \ȯ\law
\ȯi\boy \th\thin \t͟h\the \ü\loot \u̇\foot \y\yet
\zh\vision *see also* Pronunciation Symbols page

: to prevent (a claim or action) from being litigated esp. by collateral estoppel or res judicata ⟨the Civil Service Reform Act provides the exclusive address for adverse federal employment actions and thus ~*s* claims brought under the Tort Claims Act —*National Law Journal*⟩ — **pre·clu·sion** \-'klü-zhən\ *n* — **pre·clu·sive** \-'klü-siv\ *adj*

pred·a·to·ry \'pre-də-ˌtōr-ē\ *adj* : inclined or intended to injure competitors by unfair means ⟨subject to antitrust liability for ~ conduct —*National Law Journal*⟩ ⟨~ bidding⟩

predatory pric·ing *n* : the practice of pricing goods below cost and incurring a loss in order to reduce or eliminate competition ◊ Predatory pricing constitutes an antitrust violation.

pre·de·cease \ˌprē-di-'sēs\ *vt* -ceased; -ceas·ing : to die before (another person) ⟨when the child ~*s* the parent⟩

pre·de·ces·sor in interest \'pre-də-ˌse-sər, 'prē-\ : a person who previously held the rights or interests currently held by another : a party with whom another is in privity; *specif* : a party in a previously related civil case who was in a similar position and dealt with similar issues and facts as a party in the current case and so had the same motive as the current party in developing testimony at trial — see also *former testimony* at TESTIMONY

pre·di·al \'prē-dē-əl\ *adj* [Medieval Latin *praedialis*, from Latin *praedium* landed property, from *praed-*, *praes* bondsman, from *prae-* before + *vad-*, *vas* surety] *in the civil law of Louisiana* : of, consisting of, or relating to land ⟨a ~ lease⟩ ⟨leasing a ~ estate to a farmer⟩

predial servitude — see SERVITUDE

¹pred·i·cate \'pre-də-ˌkāt\ *vt* -cat·ed; -cat·ing : to set or ground on something : find a basis for — usu. used with *on* ⟨if Mary's claim is *predicated* simply on John's duty of support —W. M. McGovern, Jr. *et al.*⟩

²pred·i·cate \'pre-di-kət\ *adj* : relating to or being any of a series of criminal acts upon which prosecution for racketeering may be predicated ⟨a ~ act⟩ ⟨a ~ crime⟩

predicate fact — see FACT

pre·dis·pose \ˌprē-di-'spōz\ *vt* -posed; -pos·ing : to dispose or incline in advance; *specif* : to make ready and willing to commit a crime ⟨have been *predisposed* to engage in criminal behavior —W. R. LaFave and J. H. Israel⟩ ◊ Predisposition on the part of a defendant vitiates the defense of entrapment. — **pre·dis·po·si·tion** \ˌprē-ˌdis-pə-'zi-shən\ *n*

pre·empt \prē-'empt\ *vt* **1 a** : to acquire (land) by preemption **b** : to seize upon to the exclusion of others : take for oneself ⟨a senior user of a trademark could not ~ use of the mark in remote geographical markets —*Mesa Springs Enterprises v. Cutco Indus.*, 736 P.2d 1251 (1986)⟩ **2 a** : to replace or supersede (a law) by preemption ⟨such state laws are not ~*ed* by the federal Energy Reorganization Act of 1974 —*National Law Journal*⟩ **b** : to preclude or bar (an action) by preemption ⟨federal airline deregulation does not ~ claims under state contract law —*National Law Journal*⟩

pre·emp·tion \prē-'emp-shən\ *n* [Medieval Latin *praeemption-*, *praeemptio* previous purchase, from *praeemere* to buy before] **1 a** : the right of purchasing before others : PREEMPTIVE RIGHT **b** : a right to purchase a tract of public land before others that was given by the government to the actual occupant of the land ◊ This sense of *preemption* is primarily of historical importance. **2** : a doctrine in conflicts of law: when a superior government (as of a state) has undertaken to regulate a subject its laws supersede those of an inferior government (as of a municipality) ◊ According to the doctrine of preemption, federal law supersedes state law when federal law is in conflict with a state law on a subject or when there is congressional intent to regulate a subject to the exclusion of the states. Federal preemption is based on the supremacy clause of the U.S. Constitution and is closely related to the powers granted Congress in the commerce clause. **3** : an act or instance of preempting

pre·emp·tive \prē-'emp-tiv\ *adj* : of or relating to preemption

preemptive right *n* 1 : RIGHT OF FIRST REFUSAL 2 : the right of a shareholder to buy shares of newly issued stock in proportion to existing holdings before a public offering is made in order to prevent dilution of ownership interest or seizure of majority control by management

pre·exist·ing duty rule *n* : a common law rule of contracts: a party's offer of a performance already required under an existing contract is insufficient consideration for modification of the contract ◊ This rule is not applicable to sales contracts in jurisdictions that have enacted the Uniform Commercial Code. It is also not applicable where there has been a rescission of the contract followed by a new contract.

pre·fer \pri-'fər\ *vt* **pre·ferred; pre·fer·ring** 1 : to give (a creditor or debt) priority or preference ⟨any *preferred* charges such as child support or alimony —*In re Smiley,* 427 P.2d 179 (1967)⟩ 2 : to bring forward for determination; *esp* : to bring (a charge) against someone ⟨the various means by which a grand jury might ~ charges —*State v. Byrd,* 399 S.E.2d 267 (1990)⟩

pref·er·ence \'pre-frəns, -fə-rəns\ *n* 1 : the right to prior payment of a debt ⟨with ~ over the creditors of the heirs or legatees —*Louisiana Civil Code*⟩ 2 : the transfer of an insolvent debtor's interest in property to a creditor for an earlier debt that gives the creditor more than the creditor would otherwise receive (as under a bankruptcy settlement) — called also *voidable preference;* compare *antecedent debt* at DEBT, FRAUDULENT CONVEYANCE, *general assignment* at ASSIGNMENT ◊ Preferences can be voided by a bankruptcy trustee because they diminish the bankruptcy estate out of which other creditors will be paid. Preferences must be made during a period (as 90 days before the date of filing a bankruptcy petition) established by bankruptcy law in order to be voidable. Perfection or grant

of a security interest during this period is also a preference. The bankruptcy law states exceptions under which payments to creditors are not voidable preferences. 3 : PRIORITY

pref·e·ren·tial \,pre-fə-'ren-chəl\ *adj* 1 : of or constituting a preference ⟨a ~ transfer⟩ 2 : giving preference to union members esp. in hiring ⟨a ~ shop⟩ 3 : showing preference ⟨these creditors may obtain ~ treatment⟩

pre·fer·ment \pri-'fər-mənt\ *n* 1 : advancement or promotion in office or station 2 : the act of preferring (as charges) ⟨without ~ of allegations⟩

preferred risk *n* : an insured that an insurer deems has a lower than average chance of loss and that usu. may pay a lower premium ⟨because of the past accidents, he was not a *preferred risk*⟩

preferred share *n* : a share of preferred stock

preferred stock — see STOCK

pre·hear·ing \'prē-,hir-iŋ\ *adj* : preparatory to a hearing ⟨a ~ brief⟩ ⟨a ~ stipulation⟩

pre·judg·ment \,prē-'jəj-mənt\ *adj* : occurring before the rendering of judgment ⟨a ~ attachment⟩

¹prej·u·dice \'pre-jə-dəs\ *n* [Old French, from Latin *praejudicium* previous judgment, damage, from *prae-* before + *judicium* judgment] 1 : injury or detriment to one's legal rights or claims (as from the action of another): as **a** : substantial impairment of a defendant's ability to defend ⟨the court found no ~ to the defendant by the lengthy delay in bringing charges⟩ **b** : tendency for a decision on an improper basis (as past conduct) by a trier of fact ⟨whether an ex parte communication to a deliberating jury resulted in any reasonable possibility of ~ to the defendant —*National Law Journal*⟩ **c** : implied waiver of rights and privileges

\ə\abut	\ᵊ\kitten	\ər\further	\a\ash \ā\ace
\ä\cot, cart	\aù\out	\ch\chin	\e\bet \ē\easy
\g\go	\i\hit \ī\ice	\j\job	\ŋ\sing \ō\go \ò\law
\òi\boy	\th\thin	\th̲\the	\ü\loot \ù\foot \y\yet
\zh\vision	*see also* Pronunciation Symbols page		

not explicitly retained ⟨District Court erred in attaching ∼ to prisoner's complaint for injunctive relief —*National Law Journal*⟩ **2 :** a final and binding decision (as an adjudication on the merits) that bars further prosecution of the same cause of action or motion ⟨dismisses this case with ∼⟩ ⟨the dismissal was without ∼⟩ **3 a :** an irrational attitude of hostility directed against an individual, a group, a race, or their supposed characteristics ⟨the Constitution does not prohibit laws based on ∼ per se —R. H. Bork⟩ **b :** an attitude or disposition (as of a judge) that prevents impartiality ⟨that the judge before whom the matter is pending has a personal bias or ∼ . . . against him —*U.S. Code*⟩

²prejudice *vt* **-diced; -dic·ing 1 :** to injure or damage the rights of by some legal action or prejudice ⟨if it appears that a defendant or the government is *prejudiced* by a joinder of offenses —*Federal Rules of Criminal Procedure* Rule 14⟩ **2 :** to injure or damage (rights) by some legal action or prejudice ⟨that the denial *prejudiced* his right to a fair trial⟩ ⟨this clause does not ∼ other rights⟩

prej·u·diced \'pre-jə-dəst\ *adj* **:** resulting from or having a prejudice or bias for or esp. against ⟨alleged that the trial judge was ∼⟩

prej·u·di·cial \ˌpre-jə-'di-shəl\ *adj* **:** having the effect of prejudice: as **a :** tending to injure or impair rights ⟨such a transfer would be ∼ to other creditors⟩ **b :** leading to a decision or judgment on an improper basis ⟨the evidence was excluded because it was more ∼ than probative⟩

prejudicial error — see ERROR

pre·lim·i·nary \pri-'li-mə-ˌner-ē\ *adj* **:** coming before and usu. serving as a temporary or intermediate step to something ⟨∼ negotiations⟩ ⟨a ∼ payment plan⟩ — **preliminary** *n*

preliminary examination *n* **:** PRELIMINARY HEARING at HEARING

preliminary hearing — see HEARING

preliminary injunction — see INJUNCTION

pre·mar·i·tal \ˌprē-'mar-ət-ᵊl\ *adj* **:** ANTENUPTIAL

pre·med·i·tate \pri-'me-də-ˌtāt\ *vb* **-tat·ed; -tat·ing** *vt* **:** to think about or consider beforehand ⟨must ∼ the killing and deliberate about it —W. R. LaFave and A. W. Scott, Jr.⟩ ∼ *vi* **:** to think or consider beforehand

pre·med·i·tat·ed *adj* **:** having been thought about at some point before being committed ⟨any ∼ killing⟩; *also* **:** having been formed prior to commission of the act ⟨with ∼ malice⟩ — compare DELIBERATE

pre·med·i·ta·tion \pri-ˌme-də-'tā-shən\ *n* **:** an act or instance of premeditating; *specif* **:** consideration or planning of an act beforehand ⟨designed so that it requires ∼ to tamper with it⟩ ⟨murder in the first degree is the killing of a human being committed . . . intentionally and with ∼ —*Kansas Statutes Annotated*⟩ — see also COLD BLOOD, MURDER; compare INTENT ◊ The terms *premeditation, malice aforethought, deliberate,* and *willful* are often used in statutes either along with or instead of *intent* to describe the necessary mental state for a crime. In some jurisdictions the premeditation has to occur only moments before the act, while in others it must precede the act by an appreciable amount of time.

prem·is·es \'pre-mə-səz\ *n pl* **1 :** matters previously stated: as **a :** the preliminary part of a deed that includes a description of the real estate and that precedes the habendum **b :** the preliminary part of a bill in equity that states the facts, names the wrongs, and identifies the defendants **2 :** a tract of land with its component parts (as buildings); *also* **:** a building or part of a building usu. with its appurtenances (as grounds or easements)

premises liability — see LIABILITY 2b

pre·mi·um \'prē-mē-əm\ *n* **1 :** the difference between the face value or par value of a security and its market price when the latter is greater — compare DISCOUNT **2**

: the price paid for an insurance contract equal to the cost per unit times the number of units

pre·nup·tial agreement \prē-'nəp-shəl-, -chəl-\ *n* : ANTENUPTIAL AGREEMENT

pre–pack·aged bankruptcy \prē-'pa-kijd-\ *n* : a bankruptcy plan that has been negotiated between the debtor and creditors prior to the debtor's filing for bankruptcy

pre·pay \prē-'pā\ *vt* **pre·paid; pre·pay·ing** : to pay or pay the charge on in advance (as of date due or maturity date) ⟨no penalty for ~*ing* your student loan⟩ — **pre·pay·ment** *n*

pre·pon·der·ance of the evidence \pri-'pän-də-rəns-\ : the standard of proof in most civil cases in which the party bearing the burden of proof must present evidence which is more credible and convincing than that presented by the other party or which shows that the fact to be proven is more probable than not; *also* : the evidence meeting this standard ⟨plaintiffs must show by a *preponderance of the evidence* that defendant's negligence proximately caused the injuries⟩ — compare CLEAR AND CONVINCING, REASONABLE DOUBT

pre·pon·der·ate \pri-'pän-də-,rāt\ *vi* **-at·ed; -at·ing** : to have greater credibility or convincing weight : have an outweighing effect ⟨the evidence either was evenly balanced or *preponderated* in favor of the state —*Weston v. State*, 682 P.2d 1119 (1984)⟩ ⟨such evidence ~*s* against the board's decision⟩

prerogative writ — see WRIT

pre·scribe \pri-'skrīb\ *vb* **pre·scribed; pre·scrib·ing** *vi* **1** : to claim title or a right to something (as an easement) by prescription ⟨a precarious possessor cannot ~ against the owner⟩ **2** *in the civil law of Louisiana* : to become unenforceable or invalid by prescription ⟨any party having an interest in a money judgment may have it revived before it ~*s* —*Louisiana Civil Code*⟩ ~ *vt* **1** : to lay down as a rule or guide : specify with authority ⟨the times, places and manner of holding elections for Senators and Representatives, shall be *prescribed* in each State by the legislature thereof —*U.S. Constitution* art. I⟩ **2** *in the civil law of Louisiana* : to invalidate or bar the enforcement of by prescription ⟨this claim for damages shall not be *prescribed* so long as the minor's right of action exists against his tutor —*Louisiana Civil Code*⟩

pre·scrip·tion \pri-'skrip-shən\ *n* [partly from Middle French *prescription* establishment of a claim, from Late Latin *praescription-, praescriptio*, from Latin, act of writing at the beginning, order, from *praescribere* to write at the beginning, dictate, order; partly from Latin *praescription-, praescriptio* order] **1** : acquisition of an interest (as an easement) in real property that is usu. less than a fee by long-term, continuous, open, and hostile use and possession as determined by the law of a jurisdiction ⟨gained title by ~⟩ — see also *easement by prescription* at EASEMENT; compare *adverse possession* at POSSESSION **2** *in the civil law of Louisiana* **a** : the running of a period of time set by law after which a right is unenforceable in Louisiana courts but may be enforced in another state forum ⟨an interruption of ~⟩ ⟨by the ~ of ten years⟩; *also* : the bar to an action that results from prescription — see also PEREMPTORY EXCEPTION; compare PEREMPTION **b** : the creation of a right by the running of a period of time set by law; *esp* : ACQUISITIVE PRESCRIPTION in this entry ⟨predial servitudes on property of the state may not be acquired by ~ —*Louisiana Civil Code*⟩

ac·quis·i·tive prescription \ə-'kwi-zə-tiv-\ : acquisition of ownership or other real rights in movables or immovables by continuous, uninterrupted, peaceable, public, and unequivocal possession for a period of time (as 10 years) set

\ə\abut \ᵊ\kitten \ər\further \a\ash \ā\ace
\ä\cot, cart \aú\out \ch\chin \e\bet \ē\easy
\g\go \i\hit \ī\ice \j\job \ŋ\sing \ō\go \ó\law
\ói\boy \th\thin \t̲h̲\the \ü\loot \ú\foot \y\yet
\zh\vision *see also* Pronunciation Symbols page

by law; *also* : such possession that creates real rights ⟨*acquisitive prescription* is interrupted when the possessor acknowledges the right of the owner — *Louisiana Civil Code*⟩ ◊ The Louisiana Civil Code has set various periods of time for acquisitive prescription of movables and immovables. With the shorter periods (as 10 years for immovables or 3 years for movables) the Code also requires that the possessor possess in good faith and under just title. Acquisitive prescription does not run in favor of a person having precarious possession, because he or she possess the property on behalf of or with permission of the owner, until the possessor begins to possess the property on his or her own behalf (as after a lease terminates). *liberative prescription* : a period of time set by law (as one year) after which legal action is barred if no steps have been taken to enforce or litigate the right ⟨delictual actions are subject to a *liberative prescription* of one year — *Louisiana Civil Code*⟩ ◊ Liberative prescription is similar to the common: law statute of limitations. *prescription of nonuse* : the extinguishment or termination of a real right other than ownership as a result of the failure to exercise the right for a period of time (as 10 years) set by law; *also* : the period of time

3 : something prescribed as a rule ⟨created a legal ~ against such acts⟩

prescription of nonuse — see PRESCRIPTION

pre·scrip·tive \pri-'skrip-tiv\ *adj* **1** : serving to prescribe ⟨~ rules⟩ **2** : acquired by, founded on, or constituting prescription ⟨a ~ right⟩ ⟨a longer ~ period⟩

prescriptive easement — see EASEMENT

¹pre·sent \pri-'zent\ *vt* **1** : to lay before a court as an object of consideration ⟨~ a complaint⟩ ⟨~*ed* a defense of insanity⟩ **2** : to make a presentment of (an instrument) — **pre·sen·ta·tion** \ˌprē-ˌzen-'tā-shən, ˌpre-, -zən-\ *n* — **pre·sent·er** *n*

²pres·ent \'pre-zənt\ *adj* **1** : now existing

⟨a ~ undivided interest in the property⟩ ⟨a ~ ability to pay⟩ **2** : constituting the one actually involved or being considered ⟨the ~ case⟩ **3** : being in attendance : being in one place and not elsewhere ⟨no person shall be convicted without the concurrence of two thirds of the members ~ — *U.S. Constitution* art. I⟩

pre·sen·tence investigation \ˌprē-'sent-ᵊns-\ *n* : an investigation made by a probation officer in preparing a presentence report

presentence report *n* : a report prepared by a probation officer upon conviction of a defendant that assists the sentencing court in imposing an appropriate sentence ◊ The information contained in a presentence report includes the defendant's prior criminal history (if any) and relevant (as financial) circumstances, the appropriate classification of the defendant and of the offense under the established classification system, the kinds and range of sentences and programs available, and the impact of the offense on the victim.

presenting bank — see BANK

pre·sent·ment \pri-'zent-mənt\ *n* **1** : the act of presenting to an authority a formal statement of a matter to be dealt with; *specif* : the notice or accusation of an offense by a grand jury on the initiative of the jury members or on the basis of their own knowledge without a bill of indictment laid before them **2** : the act of producing or offering at the proper place and time a document (as a negotiable instrument) that calls for acceptance and payment by another : a demand for payment of an instrument upon a party liable for payment on behalf of the holder

present rec·ol·lec·tion re·freshed \-ˌre-kə-'lek-shən-\ *n* : a rule of evidence allowing the use of a writing to jog the memory of a witness and enable the witness to testify about things newly remembered — called also *present recollection revived;* compare PAST RECOLLECTION RECORDED

pres·ents \'pre-zənts\ *n pl* : the words, statements, or document (as a deed) under consideration ⟨know all persons by these ~⟩

present sense im·pres·sion *n* : an out-of-court statement that describes or explains an event or condition and that was made during or immediately after the time the event or condition was perceived; *also* : an exception to the hearsay rule allowing such a statement to be entered as evidence that what was asserted in the statement is true ◊ Present sense impressions are excepted from the hearsay rule because the immediacy of the response is considered to render the statement trustworthy. "Look out, he's got a gun," might be considered admissible as a present sense impression.

pre·serve \pri-'zərv\ *vt* **pre·served; pre·serv·ing 1** : to keep safe from injury, harm, or destruction ⟨expenses necessary to ~ the property⟩ **2 a** : to keep valid, intact, or in existence (as pending a proceeding) ⟨the right of a trial by jury shall be *preserved* — U.S. Constitution amend. VII⟩ ⟨the dismissal of a chapter 7 case . . . reinstates certain transfers voided or *preserved* in the case — J. H. Williamson⟩ **b** : to maintain for use or consideration at a later time esp. by keeping a record of ⟨deposed the witness to ~ her testimony⟩ ⟨a party has the option of *preserving* the objection raised — J. H. Friedenthal *et al.*⟩ — **pres·er·va·tion** \ˌpre-zər-'vā-shən\ *n*

pre·side \pri-'zīd\ *vi* **pre·sid·ed; pre·sid·ing 1** : to exercise guidance, direction, or control **2** : to occupy the place of authority : direct or regulate proceedings as chief officer

pres·i·den·cy \'pre-zə-dən-sē, -ˌden-\ *n, pl* **-cies 1 a** : the office of president **b** : the office of president of the U.S.; *also* : the American governmental institution comprising the office of president and various associated administrative and policy-making agencies **2** : the term during which a president holds office **3** : the action or function of one that presides

pres·i·dent \'pre-zə-dənt, -ˌdent\ *n* **1** : an official chosen to preside over a meeting or assembly **2** : an appointed governor of a subordinate political unit **3** : the chief officer of an organization (as a corporation or institution) usu. entrusted with the direction and administration of its policies **4** : the presiding officer of a governmental body ⟨the Vice President of the United States shall be *President* of the Senate — U.S. Constitution art. I⟩ **5 a** : an elected official serving as both chief of state and chief political executive in a republic having a presidential government **b** : an elected official having the position of chief of state but usu. only minimal political powers in a republic having a parliamentary government — **pres·i·den·tial** \ˌpre-zə-'den-chəl\ *adj* — **pres·i·den·tial·ly** *adv* — **pres·i·dent·ship** *n*

presidential government *n* : a system of government in which the president is constitutionally independent of the legislature

pre·sume \pri-'züm\ *vt* **pre·sumed; pre·sum·ing** : to suppose to be true without proof or before inquiry : accept as a presumption ⟨must ~ the defendant is innocent⟩

presumed damages — see DAMAGE 2

pre·sump·tion \pri-'zəmp-shən\ *n* : an inference as to the existence of a fact not certainly known that the law requires to be drawn from the known or proven existence of some other fact

conclusive presumption : a presumption that the law does not allow to be rebutted — called also *irrebuttable presumption;* compare REBUTTABLE PRESUMPTION in this entry

mandatory presumption : a presumption that a jury is required by law to make upon proof of a given fact — compare PERMISSIVE PRESUMPTION in this entry

permissive presumption : an inference

\ə\abut \ᵊ\kitten \ər\further \a\ash \ā\ace \ä\cot, cart \au̇\out \ch\chin \e\bet \ē\easy \g\go \i\hit \ī\ice \j\job \ŋ\sing \ō\go \ȯ\law \ȯi\boy \th\thin \th\the \ü\loot \u̇\foot \y\yet \zh\vision *see also* Pronunciation Symbols page

or presumption that a jury is allowed but not required to make from a given set of facts — called also *permissive inference;* compare MANDATORY PRESUMPTION in this entry

presumption of fact : a presumption founded on a previous experience or on general knowledge of a connection between a known fact and one inferred from it

presumption of innocence : a rebuttable presumption in the favor of the defendant in a criminal action imposing on the prosecution the burden of proving guilt beyond a reasonable doubt

presumption of intent : a permissive presumption that if a criminal defendant committed an act it was his or her intent to commit it

presumption of law : a presumption (as of the innocence of a criminal defendant) founded on a rule or policy of law regardless of fact

presumption of survivorship : the presumption in the absence of direct evidence that of two or more persons dying in a common disaster (as a fire) one was the last to die because of youth, strength, or other reasons rendering survivorship likely

rebuttable presumption : a presumption that may be rebutted by evidence to the contrary — compare CONCLUSIVE PRESUMPTION in this entry
presumption of fact — see PRESUMPTION
presumption of innocence — see PRESUMPTION
presumption of intent — see PRESUMPTION
presumption of law — see PRESUMPTION
presumption of survivorship — see PRESUMPTION
pre·sump·tive \pri-'zəmp-tiv\ *adj* **1** : based on presumption : presumed to have occurred ⟨a ~ violation of law⟩ **2** : giving grounds for reasonable opinion or belief — **pre·sump·tive·ly** *adv*
presumptive evidence — see EVIDENCE
presumptive heir — see HEIR
presumptive sentence — see SENTENCE

pre·tax \ˌprē-'taks\ *adj* : existing or occurring before the assessment or deduction of taxes ⟨~ income⟩ ⟨~ contributions⟩
pretermination hearing — see HEARING
pre·ter·mis·sion \ˌprē-tər-'mi-shən\ *n* : the act or an instance of pretermitting
pre·ter·mit \ˌprē-tər-'mit\ *vt* **-mit·ted; -mit·ting** [Latin *praetermittere,* from *praeter* by, past + *mittere* to let go, send] : to let pass without mention or notice — see also *pretermitted heir* at HEIR
pretext arrest — see ARREST
pre·tex·tu·al arrest \ˌprē-'teks-chə-wəl-\ *n* : PRETEXT ARREST at ARREST
pre·tri·al \ˌprē-'trī-əl\ *adj* : existing or occurring before trial ⟨a ~ motion⟩ ⟨a ~ detainee⟩
pretrial conference *n* : a proceeding attended by the parties to an action and a judge or magistrate and held at a party's request or on the judge's initiative for the purpose of focusing the issues, making discovery, entering into stipulations, obtaining rulings, and dealing with any matters that may facilitate fair and efficient disposition of the case including settlement
pretrial order — see ORDER 3b
pre·vail \pri-'vāl\ *vi* **1** : to obtain substantially the relief or action sought in a lawsuit **2** : to be frequent or predominant ⟨the ~*ing* rate⟩
pre·ven·tive detention \pri-'ven-tiv-\ *n* : detention of a defendant awaiting trial for the purpose of preventing further misconduct or protecting an individual or the public
price–fix·ing \'prīs-ˌfik-siŋ\ *n* : the usu. illegal setting of prices artificially (as by producers) contrary to free market operations — see also HORIZONTAL PRICE-FIXING, VERTICAL PRICE-FIXING
¹pri·ma fa·cie \'prī-mə-'fā-shə, -sē, -shē\ *adv* [Latin] : at first view : on first appearance absent other information or evidence ⟨guidelines which would *prima facie* accredit new entrance examinations as nondiscriminatory —S. L. Lynch⟩ — compare EX FACIE
²prima facie *adj* : sufficient to establish a

fact or case unless disproved ⟨*prima facie* proof⟩ ⟨a *prima facie* showing⟩
prima facie case — see CASE 1c
prima facie evidence — see EVIDENCE
¹pri•ma•ry \'prī-ˌmer-ē, -mə-rē\ *adj* **1** : of first rank, value, or importance **2** : belonging to the first group or order in successive divisions, combinations, or ramifications — **pri•mar•i•ly** \prī-'mer-ə-lē\ *adv*
²primary *n, pl* **-ries 1** : CAUCUS **2** : an election in which qualified voters nominate or express a preference for a particular candidate or group of candidates for political office, choose party officials, or select delegates for a party convention
primary beneficiary — see BENEFICIARY b
primary boycott *n* : an organized effort of a labor union and its members to discourage consumers from buying the products of a particular employer — compare SECONDARY BOYCOTT
primary evidence — see EVIDENCE
primary insurance coverage *n* : coverage under an insurance policy in which the insurer is immediately liable upon the happening of a covered event
primary jurisdiction — see JURISDICTION
primary liability — see LIABILITY 2b
primary market *n* : the market in which newly issued securities are sold — compare SECONDARY MARKET
primary strike — see STRIKE
¹prime *n* **1** : PRIME RATE **2** : GENERAL CONTRACTOR
²prime *vt* **primed; prim•ing** : to have priority over ⟨a perfected security interest ~s an unperfected one⟩
prime contractor *n* : GENERAL CONTRACTOR
prime interest rate *n* : PRIME RATE
prime min•is•ter \-'mi-nə-stər\ *n* **1** : the chief minister of a ruler or state **2** : the official head of a cabinet or ministry; *esp* : the chief executive of a parliamentary government — **prime min•is•te•ri•al** \-ˌmi-nə-'stir-ē-əl\ *adj* — **prime min•is•ter•ship** *n* — **prime min•is•try** \-'mi-nə-strē\ *n*

prime rate *n* : an interest rate formally announced by a bank to be the lowest available at a particular time to its most creditworthy customers — called also *prime, prime interest rate*
pri•mo•gen•i•ture \ˌprī-mō-'je-nə-ˌchu̇r\ *n* **1** : the state of being the firstborn of the children of the same parents **2** : exclusive right of inheritance; *specif* : a right to take all the real property of an estate belonging under English law to the eldest son or eldest male in the next degree of consanguinity if there is no son of an ancestor to the exclusion of all female and younger male descendants
¹prin•ci•pal \'prin-sə-pəl\ *adj* **1** : being the main or most important, consequential, or influential ⟨their ~ place of business⟩ ⟨the ~ obligor⟩ **2** : of, relating to, or constituting principal or a principal ⟨the ~ amount of the loan⟩
²principal *n* **1** : a participant in an action or transaction esp. having control or authority ⟨the ~s of a business⟩: as **a** : one who engages another to act for him or her subject to his or her general control or instruction : one from whom an agent derives authority to act — compare FIDUCIARY **b** : one who commits a crime or instigates, encourages, or assists another to commit it esp. when constructively or actually present — see also ACCESSORY 1
   principal in the first degree : a principal under common law who intentionally commits and is actually or constructively present at the commission of a crime
   principal in the second degree : a principal under common law who aids, encourages, or commands another to commit a crime and is actually or constructively present when it is committed
   c : the person primarily liable on a legal obligation or one who will ultimately bear the burden because of a duty to indemnify

\ə\abut \ᵊ\kitten \ər\further \a\ash \ā\ace
\ä\cot, cart \au̇\out \ch\chin \e\bet \ē\easy
\g\go \i\hit \ī\ice \j\job \ŋ\sing \ō\go \ȯ\law
\ȯi\boy \th\thin \t͟h\the \ü\loot \u̇\foot \y\yet
\zh\vision *see also* Pronunciation Symbols page

another as distinguished from one (as an endorser, surety, or guarantor) who is secondarily liable **2** : a capital sum earning interest, due as a debt, or used as a fund ⟨shall receive the income from the trust until age 18, and thereafter the ~⟩ ⟨payments shall be applied first to interest and then to ~⟩; *also* : the main body of an estate, devise, or bequest

principal contract — see CONTRACT

principal in the first degree — see PRINCIPAL

principal in the second degree — see PRINCIPAL

pri•or \'prī-ər\ *adj* **1** : earlier in time or order **2** : taking precedence (as in importance) ⟨a ~ lien⟩

prior art *n* : the processes, devices, and modes of achieving the end of an alleged invention that were known or knowable by due diligence before and at the date of the invention; *also* : the knowledge or description of such processes, devices, or modes — used chiefly in patent law

prior con•sis•tent statement \-kən-'sis-tənt-\ *n* : a witness's statement made out of court prior to testifying that is consistent with the witness's testimony — compare PRIOR INCONSISTENT STATEMENT ◊ A prior consistent statement may be offered as evidence to rebut a charge that a witness's testimony is fabricated, provided that the witness is available to be cross-examined. Under Federal Rule of Evidence 801(d)(1), a prior consistent statement of a witness testifying at trial and subject to cross-examination is not hearsay.

prior in•con•sis•tent statement \-,in-kən-sis-tənt-\ *n* : a witness's statement made out of court prior to testifying that is inconsistent with the witness's testimony and that may be offered to impeach the witness's credibility — compare PRIOR CONSISTENT STATEMENT ◊ If a prior inconsistent statement was made under oath subject to the penalties of perjury at a previous proceeding (as a deposition or grand jury hearing), the statement is not hearsay under Federal Rule of Evidence

801(d)(1) and may be offered to prove that what was asserted in the statement is true.

¹pri•or•i•ty \prī-'òr-ə-tē\ *n, pl* **-ties** : precedence in exercise of rights in the same subject matter ⟨secured interests have ~ over unsecured ones⟩

²priority *adj* **1** : having precedence over another in the exercise of rights in the same subject matter ⟨a ~ creditor⟩ ⟨a ~ claim⟩ **2** : of or relating to priority ⟨a ~ contest⟩

prior restraint *n* : governmental prohibition on expression (esp. by publication) before the expression actually takes place — see also *Near v. Minnesota* and *New York Times Co. v. United States* in the IMPORTANT CASES section; compare CENSORSHIP, FREEDOM OF SPEECH ◊ In *New York Times Co. v. United States*, the U.S. Supreme Court restated its position that "any system of prior restraints" bears "a heavy presumption against constitutional validity" and that the government "carries a heavy burden of showing justification for the imposition of such a restraint."

pris•on *n* : an institution usu. under state control for confinement of persons serving sentences for serious crimes — compare HOUSE OF CORRECTION, HOUSE OF DETENTION, JAIL, LOCKUP, PENITENTIARY

prison camp *n* : a camp for the confinement of reasonably trustworthy prisoners usu. employed on government projects

pris•on•er *n* : a person deprived of liberty and kept under involuntary restraint, confinement, or custody; *esp* : one under arrest, awaiting trial, on trial, or serving a prison sentence

pri•va•cy *n* : freedom from unauthorized intrusion : state of being let alone and able to keep certain esp. personal matters to oneself — see also EXPECTATION OF PRIVACY, INVASION OF PRIVACY, *privacy interest* at INTEREST 3b, RIGHT OF PRIVACY, *Griswold v. Connecticut* and *Roe v. Wade* in the IMPORTANT CASES section

privacy interest — see INTEREST 3b

pri·vate *adj* **1 a :** intended for or restricted to the use of a particular person or group or class of persons **:** not available to the public ⟨a ~ park⟩ **b :** not related to, controlled by, or deriving from the state ⟨a ~ school⟩ **2 a :** owned by or concerning an individual person or entity ⟨~ land⟩ **b :** not having shares that can be freely traded on the open market ⟨a ~ company⟩ **3 :** affecting the interests of a particular person, class or group of persons, or locality ⟨~ legislation⟩ ⟨~ rights⟩ **4 a :** not invested with or engaged in public office or employment ⟨a ~ citizen⟩ **b :** not related to or dependent on an official position ⟨~ correspondence⟩ **5 :** not known publicly or carried on in public; *esp* **:** intended only for the persons involved **6 :** made under private signature ⟨a ~ instrument⟩

private attorney general doctrine *n* **:** an equitable doctrine allowing the recovery of attorney's fees to a party whose suit has benefited a large number of people, requires private enforcement, and is of societal importance

private bill — see BILL 1

private detective *n* **:** PRIVATE INVESTIGATOR

private eye *n* **:** PRIVATE INVESTIGATOR

private foundation *n* **:** a tax-exempt foundation operated exclusively for humanitarian (as religious, charitable, educational, or scientific) purposes whose earnings do not benefit any private individual and which does not participate in or carry on any political propaganda or campaign — compare CHARITY

private investigator *n* **:** a person not a member of a police force who is licensed to do detective work (as investigation of suspected wrongdoing or searching for missing persons)

private law *n* **:** a branch of law concerned with private persons, property, and relationships — compare PUBLIC LAW

private letter ruling *n* **:** a letter from the Internal Revenue Service to an individual taxpayer setting out the agency's interpretation of the tax rules relating to a specific situation or transaction proposed by the taxpayer

private mortgage insurance *n* **:** insurance that a lender may require a borrower to purchase to cover losses in the event of default of a residential loan esp. when the borrower is giving the lender a mortgage on property in which the borrower has less than 20 percent equity

private nuisance — see NUISANCE

private offering *n* **:** the sale of an issue of securities directly by the issuer to one or a few large investors without any public offering — called also *private placement;* compare PUBLIC OFFERING ◊ A private offering is exempt from the requirements of filing a registration statement with the Securities and Exchange Commission and distributing prospectuses to potential buyers before the sale.

private person *n* **1 :** an individual who is not a public figure or in the military services **2** *in the civil law of Louisiana* **:** a juridical person governed by private law

private sale — see SALE

private signature *n, in the civil law of Louisiana* **:** a signature made on a writing (as an instrument or will) that is not witnessed or notarized — **under private signature :** executed outside of the presence of a notary public or witnesses

private treaty *n* **:** a sale of property on terms determined between the buyer and the seller ⟨got better prices by *private treaty* than his neighbors did at auction⟩

pri·va·tize \'prī-və-ˌtīz\ *vt* **-tized; -tiz·ing :** to make private; *esp* **:** to change (as a business or industry) from public to private control or ownership — **pri·va·ti·za·tion** \ˌprī-və-tə-'zā-shən, -ˌtī-\ *n*

priv·i·lege *n* [Latin *privilegium* law affecting a specific person, special right, from *privus* private + *leg-, lex* law] **1 :** a right, license, or exemption from duty or liability granted as a special benefit, advantage, or favor: as **a** : an exemption from liability where an action is deemed to be justifiable (as in the case of self-defense) or because of the requirements of a position or office; *also* : the affirmative defense that an action is privileged — compare EXCUSE

absolute privilege : a privilege that exempts a person from liability esp. for defamation regardless of intent or motive; *specif* : a privilege that exempts high public officials (as legislators) from liability for statements made while acting in their official capacity without regard to intent or malice

qualified privilege : a privilege esp. in the law of defamation that may be defeated esp. by a showing of actual malice — called also *conditional privilege*

b : an exemption from a requirement to disclose information (as for trial) that is granted because of a relationship or position that demands confidentiality ⟨the attorney-client ~⟩ ⟨the doctor-patient ~⟩ ⟨the marital ~⟩ ⟨the priest-penitent ~⟩ — see also CONFIDENTIAL COMMUNICATION

deliberative process privilege : a privilege exempting the government from disclosure (as in discovery) of government agency materials containing opinions, recommendations, and other communications that are part of the decision-making process within the agency

executive privilege : a privilege exempting the executive branch of government from disclosing communications if such disclosure would adversely affect the functions and decision-making process of that branch — see also *United States v. Nixon* in the IMPORTANT CASES section ◊ Executive privilege is based on the separation of powers doctrine. In *United States v. Nixon*, the Supreme Court held that this privilege is not absolute and that without a claim of a need to protect military, diplomatic, or national security secrets, the need for evidence in a criminal trial

will outweigh a general assertion of executive privilege.

informant's privilege : the privilege of the government to withhold the identity of an informant who has provided evidence for a criminal trial — called also *informer's privilege*

jour·nal·ist's privilege : REPORTER'S PRIVILEGE in this entry

privilege against self–incrimination : a privilege under the Fifth Amendment to the U.S. Constitution protecting a person from compulsion to make self-incriminating statements

reporter's privilege : a privilege protecting a reporter from compulsion to reveal information acquired in the course of gathering news — called also *journalist's privilege*

c : something specially permitted or granted as a matter of discretion that may be limited or taken away ⟨right to . . . mooring permit is not necessarily created because discretionary state ~ was generously granted in [the] past —*National Law Journal*⟩ — compare RIGHT **d** *in the civil law of Louisiana* : a right of a creditor conferred by the nature of a debt to have priority over the debtor's other creditors **2** : any of various fundamental or specially sacred rights considered as particularly guaranteed to all persons by a constitution and esp. by the privileges and immunities clause of the U.S. Constitution

privilege against self–incrimination — see PRIVILEGE 1b

priv·i·leged *adj* : not subject to the usual rules or penalties because of some special circumstance; *esp* : not subject to disclosure esp. in an adjudicative proceeding

privileged communication *n* **1** : CONFIDENTIAL COMMUNICATION **2 a** : a defamatory communication that does not expose the party making it to the liability that would follow from it if not privileged — called also *absolutely privileged communication* **b** : a defamatory statement made by one person to another who is in a confidential relation (as that of a prospective employer) or who has an interest therein that may upon proof of bad faith or actual malice be deprived of its privileged character — called also *conditionally privileged communication*

privileges and immunities clause *n, often cap P&I&C* **1** : a clause in Article IV of the U.S. Constitution stating that the citizens of each state of the U.S. shall be entitled to all the privileges and immunities of citizens of the other states **2** : a clause in Amendment XIV to the U.S. Constitution stating that no state shall make or enforce any law that abridges the privileges or immunities of the citizens of the U.S. — called also *privileges or immunities clause*

priv·i·ty \\'pri-və-tē\\ *n, pl* **-ties** [Old French *privité* privacy, secret, from Medieval Latin *privitat-, privitas*, from Latin *privus* private] **1** : the direct connection or relationship between parties to a contract or transaction (as a purchase) ⟨~ of contract⟩ — see also HORIZONTAL PRIVITY 2, VERTICAL PRIVITY 2 ◊ Formerly a suit for breach of warranty or negligence arising from a product could only be brought by a party to the original contract or transaction, and only against the party (as a retailer) directly dealt with. Only these parties had privity. Under modern laws and doctrines of strict liability and implied warranty, however, the right to sue has been extended to those, such as third-party beneficiaries and members of a purchaser's household, whose use of a product is foreseeable. **2 a** : a mutual or successive interest esp. in the same rights of property (as by inheritance or purchase); *also* : the condition of having such an interest — see also HORIZONTAL PRIVITY 1, VERTICAL PRIVITY 1 **b** : an interest in a transaction, contract, or esp. action that does not derive from direct participation but from a relationship to one of the parties or from having an interest identical to one in the original subject matter; *also* : the condition or relationship of having such an interest ⟨a party in ~⟩ — see also PREDECESSOR IN

INTEREST ◊ A claim may be barred by res judicata or collateral estoppel if the plaintiff's interests are identical, by relationship or subject matter, to those of a party to a previous action in which the plaintiff did not participate but which is deemed to have resulted in an adjudication of the plaintiff's rights. **3** : private or joint knowledge of a private matter; *esp* : awareness (as of wrongdoing) implying concurrence

privy \\'pri-vē\\ *n, pl* **priv·ies** [Anglo-French *privé*, from Old French, intimate, confidant, from *privé* intimate, familiar, from Latin *privatus* private] : one having privity; *esp* : one who acquires an interest in the subject matter (as property) of prior or pending litigation and is bound by the judgment as if he or she were a party to the action

prize *n* **1** : property (as a ship) lawfully captured in time of war **2** : the wartime capture of a ship and its cargo at sea

probable cause — see CAUSE 2

probable cause hearing — see HEARING

pro·ba·ta \\prō-'bā-tə, -'bä-\\ *n pl* : things conclusively established or proved — compare ALLEGATA

¹pro·bate \\'prō-ˌbāt\\ *n* [Latin *probatum*, neuter of *probatus*, past participle of *probare* to test, approve, prove] **1 a** : the process of proving in a court of competent jurisdiction (as a probate court) that an instrument is the valid last will and testament of a deceased person; *broadly* : the process of administering an estate **b** : the judicial determination that a will is valid **2** : the officially authenticated copy of a probated will **3 a** : PROBATE COURT **b** : matters that fall under the jurisdiction of a probate court

²probate *vt* **pro·bat·ed; pro·bat·ing** **1** : to establish (a will) as valid through probate **2 a** : to put (a convicted offender) on probation **b :** to replace (a sentence) with probation

probate court *n* **:** a court that has jurisdiction over the probate of wills and administration of estates and sometimes over the affairs of minors and persons adjudged incompetent — compare ORPHANS' COURT

probate estate — see ESTATE 3a

pro·ba·tion \prō-'bā-shən\ *n* [Middle French, critical examination and evaluation, from Latin *probation-, probatio,* from *probare* to test, approve, prove] **1 a :** subjection to a period of evaluation and possible termination at the commencement of employment in a position for which one's fitness is to be determined **b :** subjection to a period of review in the course of employment or education as a result of a violation of standards and with the possibility of dismissal if standards are not met **2 a :** the suspension of all or part of a sentence and its replacement by freedom subject to specific conditions and the supervision of a probation officer ⟨it is the intent of the legislature that the granting of ~ shall be a matter of grace conferring no vested right to its continuance — *Michigan Statutes Annotated*⟩ — compare DIVERSION, PAROLE **b :** probation as a sentence in itself **c :** the period or state of being subject to probation ⟨arrested while on ~⟩ — **pro·ba·tional** \-shə-nəl\ *adj* — **pro·ba·tion·al·ly** *adv* — **pro·ba·tion·ary** \-shə-ˌner-ē\ *adj*

pro·ba·tion·able \prō-'bā-shə-nə-bəl\ *adj* **:** not precluding probation **:** punishable by probation ⟨a ~ offense⟩

pro·ba·tion·er \prō-'bā-shə-nər\ *n* **:** one (as an offender or employee) who is on probation

probation officer *n* **:** an officer appointed to investigate, report on, and supervise the conduct of convicted offenders on probation

pro·ba·tive \'prō-bə-tiv\ *adj* **1 :** serving or tending to prove ⟨evidence of the use of an alias by a defendant is often ~ of nothing — *Case & Comment*⟩ — compare

PREJUDICIAL **2 :** of or relating to proof ⟨evidence with ~ value⟩

pro bono \ˌprō-'bō-nō\ *adv or adj* [Latin *pro bono publico* for the public good] **:** being, involving, or doing legal work donated esp. for the public good ⟨*pro bono* counsel⟩

pro·ce·den·do \ˌprō-sə-'den-dō\ *n* [Latin, ablative of *procedendum,* gerund of *procedere* to proceed] **:** an extraordinary writ ordering a lower court to proceed to or execute a judgment

pro·ce·dur·al \prə-'sē-jə-rəl\ *adj* **:** of or relating to procedure ⟨sentence reversed as result of ~ error in sentencing — *National Law Journal*⟩ — compare SUBSTANTIVE — **pro·ce·dur·al·ly** *adv*

procedural default *n* **:** a failure to follow state appellate procedure (as in the exhaustion of state remedies) that bars federal esp. habeas corpus review of a case in the absence of a showing of cause for and prejudice from the failure or sometimes in the absence of proof that the bar would result in a miscarriage of justice

procedural due process *n* **:** DUE PROCESS 1

procedural law *n* **:** law that prescribes the procedures and methods for enforcing rights and duties and for obtaining redress (as in a suit) and that is distinguished from law that creates, defines, or regulates rights ⟨the federal courts in diversity actions must apply state substantive law and federal *procedural law* — *Miller v. American Dredging Corp.,* 595 So. 2d 615 (1992)⟩; *also* **:** a particular law of this nature — compare SUBSTANTIVE LAW

procedural unconscionability *n* **:** unconscionability that derives from the process of making a contract rather than from inherent unfairness or unreasonableness in the terms of the contract — compare SUBSTANTIVE UNCONSCIONABILITY ◊ Procedural unconscionability is based on factors, such as consumer ignorance or a great deal of unexplained fine print, that serve to deprive a party of a meaningful choice.

pro·ce·dure \prə-'sē-jər\ *n* **1** : one or more methods or steps for the enforcement or administration of rights, duties, justice, or laws ⟨civil ∼⟩ ⟨police ∼⟩ — compare PROCEDURAL LAW, SUBSTANTIVE LAW **2** : a particular and esp. established way of doing something ⟨a medical ∼⟩ ⟨security ∼s⟩

pro·ceed·ing *n* **1** : a particular step or series of steps in the enforcement, adjudication, or administration of rights, remedies, laws, or regulations: as **a** : an action, hearing, trial, or application before the court

collateral proceeding : a proceeding that concerns an order, motion, petition, or writ deriving from or sought in relation to another proceeding (as a trial) ⟨a *collateral proceeding* on a motion to have the judge in a pending trial disqualified⟩; *esp* : one in which a collateral attack on a judgment is made ⟨sought to avoid the effect of the judgment in a *collateral proceeding* after denial of a direct appeal⟩

core proceeding : a proceeding (as one instituted by a debtor against a creditor) that is integral to the administration of a bankruptcy estate and so falls under the jurisdiction of the bankruptcy court

non–core proceeding : a proceeding involving a matter that relates to a bankruptcy case but that does not arise under bankruptcy laws, that could be adjudicated in a state court, and over which a bankruptcy court has limited authority

special proceeding : a proceeding (as for condemnation or disbarment) that may be commenced independently of a pending action by petition or motion and from which a final order affecting a substantial right may be immediately appealed ⟨*special proceedings* created exclusively by statute where a special procedure is appropriate and warranted —*Sosebee v. County Line Sch. Dist.*, 897 S.W.2d 556 (1995)⟩

y *proceeding* : a civil or criminal proceeding in the nature of a trial that is conducted without formalities (as indictment, pleadings, and usu. a jury) for the speedy and peremptory disposition of a matter

supplementary proceeding : a proceeding to discover the assets of a judgment debtor; *also* : a proceeding that in some way supplements another

b : a hearing conducted by an administrative body **c** : a criminal prosecution or investigation **2** *pl* : an official record of things done or said

pro·ceeds \'prō-ˌsēdz\ *n pl* **1** : money or other property received as the result of a sale or other transaction esp. involving collateral ⟨retain a security interest in the ∼ of collateral⟩ **2** : money received from an insurance policy

pro·cess \'prä-ˌses, 'prō-\ *n* **1** : a continuous operation, art, or method esp. in manufacture ⟨whoever invents or discovers any new and useful ∼ . . . may obtain a patent therefor —*U.S. Code*⟩ **2 a** : PROCEDURE 1 — see also ABUSE OF PROCESS, DUE PROCESS **b** : a means (as a summons) used to compel a defendant to appear in court; *broadly* : a means by which a court acquires or exercises jurisdiction over a person or property — see also MESNE PROCESS; compare NOTICE, SERVICE ◊ In civil procedure, service of a summons on a defendant is considered constitutionally sufficient process, although usu. a copy of the complaint must also be provided according to the local rule of procedure.

pro·cès ver·bal \prō-ˌsā-vər-'bäl, -ˌver-\ *n*, *pl* **procès ver·bals** \-'bälz\ [French, literally, verbal trial] *in the civil law of Louisiana* : an official written record of a proceeding (as a judicial sale of property)

pro·claim \prō-'klām\ *vt* : to declare or declare to be solemnly, officially, or for-

mally ⟨~*ed* the island a U.S. territory⟩
proc·la·ma·tion \,prä-klə-'mā-shən\ *n* **1** : the act of proclaiming **2** : something proclaimed; *specif* : an official formal public announcement (as a public notice, edict, or decree) — compare DECLARATION, EXECUTIVE ORDER
pro con·fes·so \,prō-kən-'fe-sō\ *adv* [Latin] : as though confessed ⟨the plaintiff's pleadings were taken *pro confesso* since the defendant did not appear⟩ — see also *decree pro confesso* at DECREE
proc·u·ra·tion \,prä-kyə-'rā-shən\ *n* **1** *in the civil law of Louisiana* : POWER OF ATTORNEY **2** : PROCUREMENT 1
pro·cure \prə-'kyùr\ *vt* **pro·cured; pro·cur·ing** : to obtain, induce, or cause to take place — **pro·cur·able** *adj* — **pro·cur·er** *n*
pro·cure·ment *n* **1** : the act of procuring **2** : the purchasing, leasing, renting, or selling of materials, services, equipment, or construction
procuring cause — see CAUSE 1
producer goods — see GOOD 2
producing cause — see CAUSE 1
prod·uct \'prä-,dəkt\ *n* **1** : the result of work or thought **2 a** : the output of an industry or firm **b** : a thing created by manufacturing **3** *in the civil law of Louisiana* : something (as timber or a mineral) that is derived from something else and that diminishes the substance of the thing from which it is derived — compare FRUIT 2a
products liability — see LIABILITY 2b
professional corporation — see CORPORATION
pro·fes·sion·al service *n* : a service requiring specialized knowledge and skill usu. of a mental or intellectual nature and usu. requiring a license, certification, or registration
pro·fil·ing *n* : the practice of singling out persons for law enforcement procedures on the basis of predetermined characteristics; *specif*: the discriminatory practice of profiling based on race or ethnicity ⟨racial ~⟩
prof·it *n* **1** : gain in excess of expenditures: as **a** : the excess of the selling price of goods over their cost **b** : net income from a business, investment, or capital appreciation — compare EARNINGS, LOSS **2** : a benefit or advantage from the use of property — see also MESNE PROFITS, PROFIT A PRENDRE; compare EASEMENT, RIGHT OF WAY, SERVITUDE
prof·it·able \'prä-fə-tə-bəl\ *adj* : affording profits : yielding advantageous returns or results — **prof·it·abil·i·ty** \,prä-fə-tə-'bi-lə-tē\ *n* — **pro·fit·able·ness** *n* — **prof·it·ably** *adv*
profit a pren·dre *or* **profit à prendre** \'prä-fət-ä-'prän-dər\ *n, pl* **profits à prendre** *or* **profits à prendre** [Anglo-French, literally, profit to be taken] : a right, privilege, or interest that allows one to use the soil or products (as fish and game) of another's property
prof·i·teer \,prä-fə-'tir\ *n* : one who makes what is considered an unreasonable profit esp. on the sale of essential goods during times of emergency (as during wartime) — **profiteer** *vi*
profit shar·ing *n* : a plan under which employees receive a part of the profits of an enterprise
pro for·ma \prō-'fòr-mə\ *adj* [Latin, for the sake of form] **1** : made or carried out in a perfunctory manner or as a formality **2** : provided or made in advance to describe items or projections ⟨a *pro forma* invoice⟩
pro·gres·sive *adj* : increasing in rate as the base increases ⟨a ~ tax⟩
pro hac vi·ce \'prō-'hak-'vī-sē, -'häk-'vē-kä\ *adv* [Latin] : for this occasion ⟨a motion to admit the attorney *pro hac vice* as counsel of record —*Huff v. State*, 622 So. 2d 982 (1993)⟩ — used esp. when an out-of-state attorney is allowed to practice in a case without the appropriate state bar license
pro·hi·bi·tion \,prō-ə-'bi-shən\ *n* **1 a** : an extraordinary writ issued by a higher court commanding an inferior court to keep within its proper jurisdiction (as by ceasing a prosecution) **b** : an order to refrain or stop **2 a** : something (as a law)

that prohibits a certain act or procedure **b** *cap* **:** the period from 1920 to 1933 in the U.S. when the manufacture, transportation, and sale of alcoholic liquors was prohibited by the Eighteenth Amendment to the U.S. Constitution — **pro·hib·i·tive** \prō-'hi-bə-tiv\ *adj* — **pro·hib·i·tive·ly** *adv* — **pro·hib·i·to·ry** \-'hi-bə-ˌtōr-ē\ *adj* **prohibitory injunction** — see INJUNCTION

pro·jet \prō-'zhā, -'zhet\ *n* [French, literally, plan] *in the civil law of Louisiana* **:** a draft of a proposed code or constitution

prom·ise *n* **:** a declaration or manifestation esp. in a contract of an intention to act or refrain from acting in a specified way that gives the party to whom it is made a right to expect its fulfillment

aleatory promise **:** a promise (as to compensate an insured individual for future loss) whose fulfillment is dependent on a fortuitous or uncertain event

collateral promise **:** a promise usu. to pay the debt of another that is ancillary to an original promise, is not made for the benefit of the party making it, and must be in writing to be enforceable

false promise **:** a promise that is made with no intention of carrying it out and esp. with intent to deceive or defraud

gratuitous promise **:** a promise that is made without consideration and is usu. unenforceable — called also *naked promise*; compare NUDUM PACTUM ◊ A gratuitous promise may be enforceable under promissory estoppel.

illusory promise **:** a purported promise that does not actually bind the party making it to a particular performance ⟨an *illusory promise* depending solely on the will of the supposed promisor⟩

implied promise **:** a promise that is considered to exist despite the lack of an agreement or express terms to that effect and the breach of which may be recognized as a cause of action ⟨claimed a breach of an *implied promise* that he

would not be terminated at will⟩ — see also PROMISE IMPLIED IN FACT and PROMISE IMPLIED IN LAW in this entry

naked promise **:** GRATUITOUS PROMISE in this entry

original promise **:** a promise (as in a suretyship) usu. to pay the debt of another that is made primarily for the benefit of the party making it and need not be in writing to be enforceable — compare COLLATERAL PROMISE in this entry, MAIN PURPOSE RULE

promise implied in fact **:** an implied promise that exists by inference from specific facts, circumstances, or acts of the parties

promise implied in law **:** an implied promise that exists on the basis of a legally enforceable duty and not on the basis of words or conduct which are promissory in form or support an inference of a promise ⟨a *promise implied in law* that one will be compensated for services rendered and accepted⟩

prom·is·ee \ˌprä-mə-'sē\ *n* **:** one to whom a promise is made

promise implied in fact — see PROMISE

promise implied in law — see PROMISE

prom·i·sor \ˌprä-mə-'sōr\ *also* **prom·is·er** \'prä-mə-sər\ *n* **:** one that makes a promise — compare OBLIGOR, OFFEROR

prom·is·so·ry \'prä-mə-ˌsōr-ē\ *adj* **:** containing or conveying a promise or assurance ⟨~ terms⟩

promissory estoppel — see ESTOPPEL 1

promissory note — see NOTE

promissory warranty — see WARRANTY 3

pro·mot·er *n* **:** one who alone or with others actively participates in the formation of a business or venture ⟨~*s* owe a fiduciary duty to the corporation they are promoting —R. C. Clark⟩

\ə**abut** \ᵊ**kitten** \ər**further** \a**ash** \ā**ace** \ä**cot, cart** \aú**out** \ch**chin** \e**bet** \ē**easy** \g**go** \i**hit** \ī**ice** \j**job** \ŋ**sing** \ō**go** \ò**law** \òi**boy** \th**thin** \th̲**the** \ü**loot** \ú**foot** \y**yet** \zh**vision** *see also* Pronunciation Symbols page

prom·ul·gate \'prä-məl-ˌgāt, prō-'məl-\ *vt* **-gat·ed; -gat·ing 1 :** to make known or public **2 :** to put (as a regulation) into effect — **prom·ul·ga·tion** \ˌprä-məl-'gä-shən, ˌprō-ˌməl-\ *n* — **prom·ul·ga·tor** \'prä-məl-ˌgā-tər, prō-'məl-\ *n*

proof *n* [alteration of Middle English *preove*, from Old French *preuve*, from Late Latin *proba*, from Latin *probare* to prove] **1 :** the effect of evidence sufficient to persuade a reasonable person that a particular fact exists — see also EVIDENCE **2 :** the establishment or persuasion by evidence that a particular fact exists — see also BURDEN OF PROOF **3 :** something (as evidence) that proves or tends to prove the existence of a particular fact — see also CLEAR AND CONVINCING, PREPONDERANCE OF THE EVIDENCE, REASONABLE DOUBT, STANDARD OF PROOF; compare ALLEGATION, ARGUMENT **4 :** PROBATE 1a

proof of claim : a written statement that sets forth a claim against a bankrupt debtor or the probate estate of a deceased debtor

proof of loss : a statement submitted to an insurer setting forth a loss that the insured expects to be covered; *also :* proof that such a loss has occurred

proof of service : a statement submitted (as by a sheriff) to the court as evidence of successful service of process to a party

proof of will : PROBATE 1a

prop·er *adj* **:** marked by fitness or correctness; *esp :* being in accordance with established procedure, law, jurisdiction, or standards of care, fairness, and justice ⟨argued that the shareholder was acting in bad faith and lacked a ~ purpose for examining its records⟩ — **prop·er·ly** *adv*

proper look·out *n* **:** the due degree of vigilance expected of the operator of a vehicle or train in avoiding collisions with vehicles or pedestrians

proper party — see PARTY 1b

prop·er·ty *n, pl* **-ties** [Anglo-French *propreté, proprieté*, from Latin *proprietat-, proprietas*, from *proprius* own,

particular] **1 :** something (as an interest, money, or land) that is owned or possessed — see also ASSET, ESTATE, INTEREST 1, POSSESSION 1e

abandoned property **:** property to which the owner has relinquished all rights ◊ When property is abandoned, the owner gives up the reasonable expectation of privacy concerning it. The finder of abandoned property is entitled to keep it, and a police officer may take possession of abandoned property as evidence without violating the Fourth Amendment to the U.S. Constitution.

after–acquired property **1 :** property (as proceeds) that a debtor acquires after the commencement of a bankruptcy case and that is usu. considered part of the bankruptcy estate **2 :** property acquired after the perfection of a lien or security interest; *esp :* such property acquired after the creation of a lien or security interest that is subject to the lien or becomes collateral for the security interest **3 :** property transferred to the estate of a decedent after execution of the will

common property **:** property owned or used by more than one party; *specif* **:** property owned or leased by tenants in common — compare *tenancy in common* at TENANCY

community property **:** property held jointly by husband and wife; *specif* **:** property esp. from employment and debts acquired by either spouse after marriage that is deemed in states having a community property system to belong to each spouse as an undivided one⁼half interest — compare *ownership in indivision* at OWNERSHIP ◊ The states having community property are Louisiana, Arizona, California, Texas, Washington, Idaho, Nevada, New Mexico, and Wisconsin.

immovable property **:** REAL PROPERTY in this entry; *specif, in the civil law of Louisiana* **:** tracts of land with their component parts

intangible property **:** property (as a

stock certificate or professional license) that derives value not from its intrinsic physical nature but from what it represents

in·tel·lec·tu·al   property \ˌin-tə-'lek-chə-wəl-\ : property that derives from the work of the mind or intellect; *specif* : an idea, invention, trade secret, process, program, data, formula, patent, copyright, or trademark or application, right, or registration relating thereto

lost property : property that has been left in an unknown location involuntarily but through no one's fault ◊ The finder of lost property has title to the property against all the world except the true owner.

marital property : property acquired by either spouse during the course of a marriage that is subject to division upon divorce ◊ In community property states, marital property is the same as community property and is divided equally upon divorce. In nearly all other states, marital property is divided according to what the court determines is equitable.

movable property : property (as personal property or crops) that can be moved

personal property 1 : property (as a vehicle) that is movable but not including crops or other resources still attached to land : property other than real property ⟨a tax on the *personal property* of the corporation⟩ 2 : property belonging to a particular person

qualified terminable interest property : property passing to a surviving spouse that qualifies for the marital deduction if the executor so elects providing that the spouse is entitled to receive income in payments made at least annually for life and that no one has a power to appoint any part of the property to any person other than the surviving spouse — see also *QTIP trust* at TRUST ◊ Under federal tax law the property must be included in the gross estate of the surviving spouse at his or her own death, where it is subject to taxation.

real property : property consisting of land, buildings, crops, or other resources still attached to or within the land or improvements or fixtures permanently attached to the land or a structure on it; *also* : an interest, benefit, right, or privilege in such property — called also *immovable property*

separate property : property of a spouse that is not community property or marital property; *esp* : property acquired by a spouse before marriage or individually during marriage (as by gift or often by inheritance)

tangible property : property that has a tangible and corporeal existence and intrinsic economic value because of it ⟨the insurance policy restricted property damage coverage to *tangible property*⟩ — compare INTANGIBLE PROPERTY in this entry

2 : one or more rights of ownership

property interest — see INTEREST 3b

property right *n* **1** : a right or interest in or involving property (as real property) ⟨a conflict between environmental regulations and *property rights*⟩ **2** : PROPERTY INTEREST at INTEREST 3b

property tax *n* : a tax levied on real or personal property (as by a municipality) — compare EXCISE, INCOME TAX

pro·phy·lac·tic \ˌprō-fə-'lak-tik, ˌprä-\ *adj* : designed or tending to prevent harm or wrong ⟨a ~ rule against profiting from inside information⟩

pro·po·nent \prə-'pō-nənt\ *n* **1** : one who argues in favor of something **2** : one who offers a will for probate

¹pro·pri·e·tary \prə-'prī-ə-ˌter-ē\ *n, pl* **-tar·ies 1** : something that is used, produced, or marketed under exclusive legal right of the inventor or maker; *specif* : a drug (as a patent medicine) that is protected by secrecy, patent, or copyright against free competition as to name, prod-

uct, composition, or process of manufacture **2** : a business secretly owned by and run as a cover for an intelligence operation
²proprietary *adj* **1 a** : held as property of a private owner **b** : of, relating to, or characteristic of a proprietor ⟨~ rights⟩ **2** : used, made, or marketed by one having the exclusive legal right ⟨a ~ process⟩ **3** : privately owned and managed and run as a profit-making organization ⟨a ~ insurer⟩ ⟨a ~ clinic⟩ **4** : of or relating to the acts of a municipality which profit or benefit the municipality and for which it is answerable in negligence
proprietary lease — see LEASE
pro·pri·e·tor \prə-'prī-ə-tər\ *n* : one who has legal right or exclusive title to something : OWNER; *also* : one (as a lessee) having an interest (as control or present use) less than absolute or exclusive right
pro·pri·e·tor·ship *n* **1** : the fact or state of being a proprietor **2** : a business entity consisting of a single owner : SOLE PROPRIETORSHIP — compare CORPORATION, PARTNERSHIP
prop·ter af·fec·tum \'präp-tər-ə-'fektəm\ *adv* [Medieval Latin] : because of partiality ⟨challenge a juror *propter affectum*⟩
propter de·fec·tum \-di-'fek-təm\ *adv* [Medieval Latin] : because of a defect (as residence or relationship) ⟨the disqualification of a juror *propter defectum*⟩
pro ra·ta \,prō-'rā-tə, -'rä-, -'ra-\ *adv* [Latin] : proportionately according to an exactly calculable factor (as share or liability) — **pro rata** *adj*
pro rata clause *n* : a clause in an insurance policy limiting an insurer's liability for a loss to a proportionate share in relation to coverage collectible from other insurers for the same loss — called also *pro rata liability clause, standard other insurance clause*
pro·scribe \prō-'skrīb\ *vt* **pro·scribed; pro·scrib·ing** [Latin *proscribere* to publish, proscribe, from *pro-* before + *scribere* to write] : to condemn or forbid as harmful or unlawful

pro·scrip·tion \prō-'skrip-shən\ *n* **1** : the act of proscribing : the state of being proscribed **2** : an imposed restraint or restriction — **pro·scrip·tive** \-'skrip-tiv\ *adj* — **pro·scrip·tive·ly** *adv*
pro se \'prō-'sā, -'sē\ *adv or adj* [Latin] : on one's own behalf : without an attorney ⟨a defendant's right to proceed *pro se*⟩ ⟨a *pro se* action⟩
pros·e·cute \'prä-si-,kyüt\ *vb* **-cut·ed; -cut·ing** [Latin *prosecutus*, past participle of *prosequi* to pursue] *vt* **1** : to institute and carry forward legal action against for redress or esp. punishment of a crime **2** : to institute and carry on a lawsuit with reference to ⟨every action shall be *prosecuted* in the name of the real party in interest —*Federal Rules of Civil Procedure* Rule 17(a)⟩ ~ *vi* : to institute and carry on a civil or criminal action — **pros·e·cut·able** \,prä-si-'kyü-tə-bəl\ *adj*
prosecuting attorney *n* : an attorney who represents the government in instituting and proceeding with criminal actions : DISTRICT ATTORNEY
prosecuting witness — see WITNESS
pros·e·cu·tion \,prä-si-'kyü-shən\ *n* **1** : the act or process of prosecuting; *esp* : the institution and carrying on of a criminal action involving the process of seeking formal charges against a person and pursuing those charges to final judgment **2** : the party by whom criminal proceedings are instituted or conducted — compare DEFENSE 3, PLAINTIFF
prosecution history estoppel — see ESTOPPEL 1
pros·e·cu·tive \'prä-si-,kyü-tiv\ *adj* : of or relating to prosecution ⟨~ function⟩
pros·e·cu·tor \'prä-si-,kyü-tər\ *n* **1** : a person who institutes a prosecution (as by making an affidavit or complaint charging the defendant) **2** : a government attorney who presents the state's case against the defendant in a criminal prosecution
pros·e·cu·to·ri·al \,prä-si-kyü-'tōr-ē-əl\ *adj* : of, relating to, or being a prosecutor or prosecution
pros·e·cu·to·ry \'prä-si-kyə-,tōr-ē\ *adj* : PROSECUTORIAL

pro·spec·tive \prə-'spek-tiv, 'prä-ˌspek-\ *adj* **1** : relating to or effective in the future ⟨a statute's ~ effect⟩ **2** : likely to come about : expected to happen ⟨~ inability to perform the contract⟩ **3** : likely to be or become ⟨a ~ buyer⟩ — **pro·spec·tive·ly** *adv*

pro·spec·tus \prə-'spek-təs\ *n, pl* **-tus·es** \-tə-səz\ : a preliminary printed statement describing a business or other enterprise and distributed to prospective buyers, investors, or participants; *specif* : a description of a new security issue supplied to prospective purchasers and providing a disclosure of detailed information concerning the company's business and financial standing ◊ Under the Securities Act of 1933, the prospectus is part of the registration statement that must be filed with the Securities and Exchange Commission before a security may be offered or sold to the public. The Securities Act defines *prospectus* broadly as "any prospectus, notice, circular, advertisement, letter, or communication, written or by radio or television, which offers any security for sale or confirms the sale of any security."

¹pros·ti·tute \'präs-tə-ˌtüt, -ˌtyüt\ *n* : a person who engages in sexual activity indiscriminately esp. for money — compare PANDERER, PIMP

²prostitute *vt* **-tut·ed; -tut·ing** [Latin *prostitutus*, past participle of *prostituere*, from *pro-* before + *statuere* to cause to stand, place] : to offer as a prostitute

pros·ti·tu·tion \ˌpräs-tə-'tü-shən, -'tyü-\ *n* : the act or practice of engaging in sexual activity indiscriminately esp. for money; *also* : the crime of engaging in such activity

pro tan·to \prō-'tan-tō, -'tän-\ *adv or adj* [Late Latin] : for so much : to a certain extent ⟨the obligation is *pro tanto* discharged —*Uniform Commercial Code*⟩ ⟨entered into a *pro tanto* release pending the appeal⟩

pro·tect *vt* **1** : to shield from injury or harm ⟨~*ing* public health and safety⟩ **2** : to secure or preserve against encroach-

ment, infringement, restriction, or violation : maintain the status or integrity of esp. through legal or constitutional guarantees ⟨~ a work against copyright infringement⟩ ⟨the First Amendment ~*s* speech⟩ **3** : to restrict competition for (as domestic industries) by means of tariffs or trade controls — **pro·tect·able** *or* **pro·tect·ible** *adj*

pro·tect·ed class *n* : a group of people intended by a legislature to benefit from the protection of a statute; *also* : SUSPECT CLASS

pro·tec·tion *n* **1** : the act of protecting : the state of being protected ⟨entitled to constitutional ~⟩ **2 a** : one that protects **b** : supervision or support of one having less power ⟨~ of endangered species⟩ **3** : the freeing of the producers of goods of a country from foreign competition in their home market by restrictions (as high duties) on foreign competitive goods **4 a** : immunity from prosecution purchased by criminals through bribery **b** : money extorted by racketeers posing as a protective association **5** : coverage for loss provided by insurance

protection order — see ORDER 3b
pro·tec·tive *adj* : of, relating to, or providing protection
protective custody — see CUSTODY c
protective order — see ORDER 3b
protective search — see SEARCH
protective sweep *n* : a quick protective search limited in scope to a cursory visual inspection of places in which a person might hide
protective trust — see TRUST
pro tem *adv or adj* : PRO TEMPORE — often styled with a terminal period in legal contexts ⟨Justice *pro tem.*⟩
pro tem·po·re \prō-'tem-pə-rē, -pō-ˌrā\ *adv or adj* [Latin] : for the time being : chosen or appointed to occupy a position either temporarily or in the absence of a

\ə\abut \ᵊ\kitten \ər\further \a\ash \ā\ace
\ä\cot, cart \au̇\out \ch\chin \e\bet \ē\easy
\g\go \i\hit \ī\ice \j\job \ŋ\sing \ō\go \ȯ\law
\ȯi\boy \th\thin \t̲h̲\the \ü\loot \u̇\foot \y\yet
\zh\vision *see also* Pronunciation Symbols page

regularly elected official ⟨an administrator *pro tempore*⟩
pro•test *n* **1** : a solemn declaration of opinion and usu. of disagreement: as **a** : a solemn written declaration by a notary public or U.S. consul on behalf of the holder of an instrument (as a note) announcing dishonor and declaring the liability of all parties to the instrument for any loss or damage arising from such action; *also* : the action of making or causing to be made such a declaration with due service of notice of dishonor **b** : a declaration made by the master of a ship before a notary, consul, or other authorized officer upon arrival in port after a disaster declaring that any loss was not the fault of the crew but due to the disaster **c** : a declaration made by a party esp. before or while paying a tax or performing a demanded act by which the declarer asserts that the justice or legality of the tax or act is disputed and that compliance is not voluntary **2** : the act of objecting or a gesture of disapproval; *esp* : a usu. organized public demonstration of disapproval — **protest** *vb* — **under protest** : with noted objections (as of insufficient payment) and claims ⟨cashed a check *under protest*⟩
pro•tes•tant \prə-'tes-tənt\ *n* : a person challenging an action of an administrative agency
pro•thon•o•ta•ry \prə-'thä-nə-₁ter-ē, ₁prō-thə-'nä-tə-rē\ *n, pl* **-ries** [Late Latin *protonotarius*, from *proto-* first in time + Latin *notarius* stenographer] : a chief clerk of any of various courts of law — **pro•thon•o•tar•i•al** \prə-₁thä-nə-'ter-ē-əl\ *adj*
pro•to•col \'prō-tə-₁kȯl\ *n* **1** : an original draft, minute, or record of a document or transaction **2 a** : a preliminary memorandum often formulated and signed by diplomatic negotiators as a basis for a final convention or treaty **b** : the records or minutes of a diplomatic conference or congress that show officially the agreements arrived at by the negotiators

prove \'prüv\ *vt* **proved; proved** *or* **proven** \'prü-vən\; **prov•ing** **1** : to test the truth, validity, or genuineness of ⟨~ a will at probate⟩ **2 a** : to establish the existence, truth, or validity of ⟨the charges were never *proved* in court⟩ **b** : to provide sufficient proof of or that ⟨*proved* the defendant guilty beyond a reasonable doubt⟩ — **prov•able** \'prü-və-bəl\ *adj* — **prov•able•ness** *n* — **prov•ably** \'prü-və-blē\ *adv*
pro•vi•sion \prə-'vi-zhən\ *n* : a stipulation (as a clause in a statute or contract) made beforehand
pro•vi•sion•al \prə-'vi-zhə-nəl\ *adj* **1** : provided for a temporary need : suitable or acceptable in the existing situation but subject to change or nullification ⟨a ~government⟩ ⟨~ custody of a minor⟩ **2** : of, relating to, or being temporary judicial acts or proceedings (as of attachment, injunction, or sequestration) allowed before final judgment to protect the interests of one or more parties to an action ⟨a ~remedy⟩ — **pro•vi•sion•al•ly** *adv*
pro•vi•so \prə-'vī-zō\ *n, pl* **-sos** *or* **-soes** [Medieval Latin *proviso quod* provided that] **1** : an article or clause (as in a statute or contract) that introduces a condition **2** : a conditional stipulation
prov•o•ca•tion \₁prä-və-'kā-shən\ *n* **1** : the act of provoking **2** : something that provokes, arouses, or stimulates
pro•voke \prə-'vōk\ *vt* **pro•voked; pro•vok•ing** **1** : to incite to anger **2** : to provide the needed stimulus for — **pro•vok•er** *n*
prox•i•mate \'präk-sə-mət\ *adj* **1** : next immediately preceding or following (as in a chain of causation, events, or effects) : being or leading to a particular esp. foreseeable result without intervention — see also *proximate cause* at CAUSE 1 **2** : very or relatively close or near ⟨would be sufficiently ~ to the commencement of the defendant's trial —*Johnson v. New Jersey*, 384 U.S. 719 (1966)⟩ — **prox•i•mate•ly** *adv*
proximate cause — see CAUSE 1

prox·im·i·ty \präk-'si-mə-tē\ *n* : the quality or state of being proximate

proxy \'präk-sē\ *n, pl* **prox·ies** [Middle English *procucie,* contraction of *procuracie,* from Anglo-French, from Medieval Latin *procuratia,* alteration of Latin *procuratio* appointment of another as one's agent] **1** : the act or practice of a person serving as an authorized agent or substitute for another — used esp. in the phrase *by proxy* **2 a** : authority or power to act for another **b** : a statement or document giving such authorization; *specif* : an oral consent or written document (as a power of attorney) given by a stockholder to a specified person or persons to vote corporate stock **3 a** : a person authorized to act or make decisions for another ⟨appointed a health-care ~⟩ **b** : something serving to replace or substitute for another thing

proxy contest *n* : a shareholder's challenge to an action or the control of corporate management accomplished through the solicitation of proxies from other shareholders — called also *proxy fight*

proxy marriage *n* : a marriage performed in the absence of either the bride or groom who authorizes a proxy to represent him or her at the ceremony

proxy statement *n* : a document containing information about a proposed corporate action that the corporation is required to submit to shareholders for their vote on the action

PRP *abbr* potentially responsible party — used esp. in environmental law

pru·dence \'prüd-ᵊns\ *n* : attentiveness to possible hazard : caution or circumspection as to danger or risk ⟨a person of ordinary ~⟩

pru·dent \'prüd-ᵊnt\ *adj* : characterized by, arising from, or showing prudence — **pru·dent·ly** *adv*

prudent man rule *n* : a rule giving discretion to a fiduciary and esp. a trustee to manage another's affairs and invest another's money with such skill and care as a person of ordinary prudence and intelligence would use in managing his or her own affairs or investments — called also *prudent person rule;* compare LEGAL LIST

pru·ri·ent \'prur-ē-ənt\ *adj* : marked by or arousing an unwholesome sexual interest or desire — **pru·ri·ent·ly** *adv*

¹pub·lic *adj* **1 a** : exposed to general view ⟨~ indecency⟩ **b** : known or recognized by many or most people **2 a** : of, relating to, or affecting all of the people or the whole area of a nation or state ⟨~ statutes⟩ **b** : of or relating to a government : authorized by, administered by, or acting for the people as a political entity ⟨~ expenditures⟩ ⟨the ~ prosecutor⟩ **c** : of, relating to, or being in the service of the community or nation ⟨holding ~ office⟩ **d** : provided for, used by, or containing the records of a government agency ⟨the post office and other ~ buildings⟩ **3** : of or relating to people in general **4** : of or relating to business or community interests as opposed to private affairs ⟨~ policy⟩ ⟨a matter of ~ concern⟩ **5** : devoted to the general or national welfare ⟨actions motivated by ~ spirit⟩ **6** : accessible to or shared by all members of the community ⟨a ~ hearing⟩ ⟨a ~ park⟩ — compare PRIVATE **7** : capitalized in shares that can be freely traded on the open market — often used with *go* — **pub·lic·ly** *adv*

²public *n* **1** : a place accessible or visible to the public — usu. used in the phrase *in public* **2** : the people as a whole

public act *n* : PUBLIC LAW 1

public administrator — see ADMINISTRATOR

pub·li·ca·tion *n* **1** : the act or process of publishing **2** : a published work

public bill — see BILL 1

public corporation — see CORPORATION

public defender *n* : a lawyer usu. holding public office who represents criminal

\ə\abut \ᵊ\kitten \ər\further \a\ash \ā\ace
\ä\cot, cart \au̇\out \ch\chin \e\bet \ē\easy
\g\go \i\hit \ī\ice \j\job \ŋ\sing \ō\go \ȯ\law
\ȯi\boy \th\thin \t̲h̲\the \ü\loot \u̇\foot \y\yet
\zh\vision *see also* Pronunciation Symbols page

defendants unable to pay for legal assistance

public do·main \-dō-'mān\ *n* **1** : land owned directly by the government **2** : the realm or status of property rights that belong to the community at large, are unprotected by copyright or patent, and are subject to appropriation by anyone

public duty doctrine *n* : a doctrine in tort law: a government entity (as a state or municipality) cannot be held liable for the injuries of an individual resulting from a public officer's or employee's breach of a duty owed to the public as a whole as distinguished from a duty owed to the particular individual — called also *public duty rule;* see also SPECIAL DUTY DOCTRINE

public fig·ure *n* : an individual or entity that has acquired fame or notoriety or has participated in a particular public controversy — see also LIMITED PURPOSE PUBLIC FIGURE; compare PUBLIC OFFICIAL ◊ A public figure must prove actual malice in order to prevail in a defamation action.

public forum *n* : a place that has a long-standing tradition of being used for, is historically associated with, or has been dedicated by government act to the free exercise of the right to speech and public debate and assembly — see also LIMITED PUBLIC FORUM

pub·li·ci ju·ris \'pə-blə-,sī-'jùr-is, 'pü-bli-sē-'yùr-ēs\ *adj* [Latin] : belonging to the public : subject to a right of the public to enjoy

public interest — see INTEREST 3a

public invitee *n* : a person invited to enter or remain on property for a purpose for which the property is held open to the public

public land *n* : land owned by a government

public law *n* **1** : an enactment of a legislature that affects the public at large throughout the entire territory (as a state or nation) which is subject to the jurisdiction of the legislature or within a particular subdivision of its jurisdiction : GEN-ERAL LAW — called also *public act, public statute;* compare LOCAL LAW 1a **2 a** : the area of law that deals with the relations of individuals with the state and regulates the organization and conduct of government — compare PRIVATE LAW **b** : international law regulating the relations among sovereign states or nations as distinguished from private international law

publicly held corporation *n* : PUBLIC CORPORATION at CORPORATION

public nuisance — see NUISANCE

public offering *n* : an offering of corporate securities to the general public or to potential purchasers whose level of knowledge or access to information about the securities is dependent upon the disclosures of the corporation — compare PRIVATE OFFERING ◊ Public offerings are subject to the requirements of the Securities Act of 1933 for filing a registration statement before the offering can take place.

public office *n* : an office created by a constitution or legislative act, having a definite tenure, and involving the power to carry out some governmental function

public officer *n* : a person who has been elected or appointed to a public office

public official *n* : PUBLIC OFFICER; *specif* : a person holding a public office the nature of which requires that in order for the person to prevail in a defamation action he or she must show actual malice on the part of the defendant — compare PUBLIC FIGURE

public person *n, in the civil law of Louisiana* : a juridical person (as the state) acting in a sovereign capacity

public record *n* : a record required by law to be made and kept: **a** : a record made by a public officer or a government agency in the course of the performance of a duty **b** : a record filed in a public office ◊ Public records are subject to inspection, examination, and copying by any member of the public.

public records exception *n* : an exception to the hearsay rule allowing admission into evidence of records, reports, statements, or data compilations made by public offices or agencies that set forth activities of the office or agency, matters observed pursuant to a duty under law that are required to be reported, or factual findings resulting from an investigation made pursuant to lawful authority that are to be used in civil actions or proceedings or in criminal actions against the government

public right *n* : a right created by the legislature that may be exercised against the government — often used in pl.

public sale — see SALE

public statute *n* : PUBLIC LAW 1

public trust doctrine *n* : a doctrine asserting that the state holds land lying beneath navigable waters as trustee of a public trust for the benefit of its citizens

public use — see USE 2

public utility *n* : a business organization (as an electric company) performing a public service and subject to special government regulation

pub·lish *vt* **1** : to make known to another or to the public generally ◊ For purposes of defamation, a defamatory communication made to only one third party may be considered published. **2 a** : to proclaim officially ⟨~ an enactment⟩ **b** : to declare (a will) to be a true and valid expression of one's last will **c** : to reproduce (an opinion) in a reporter **3 a** : to disseminate to the public or provide notice of to the public or to an individual (as through a mass medium) ⟨ordered to ~ the citation in the legal notices for three weeks⟩ — see also *notice by publication* at NOTICE **b** : to distribute or offer for distribution to the public copies of (a copyrightable work) by some transfer of ownership, rental, lease, or loan **4** : UTTER — **pub·lish·er** *n*

puff *n* **1** : an act or instance of puffing **2** : a statement that amounts to puffing ⟨whether the seller's statement was a "~" or an express warranty —J. J. White and R. S. Summers⟩

puff·ery \'pə-fə-rē\ *n* : PUFFING

puff·ing \'pə-fiŋ\ *n* : the practice of making exaggerated commendations esp. for promotional purposes; *also* : the exaggerated commendations made ◊ Generally, a seller cannot be held liable for misrepresentation for statements that amount to mere puffing. Nor can puffing be considered to create an express warranty.

Pullman abstention — see ABSTENTION

pun·ish \'pə-nish\ *vt* **1** : to impose a penalty on for a fault, offense, or violation **2** : to inflict a penalty for the commission of (an offense) in retribution or retaliation or as a deterrent ~ *vi* : to inflict punishment — **pun·ish·abil·i·ty** \ˌpə-ni-shə-'bi-lə-tē\ *n* — **pun·ish·able** \'pə-ni-shə-bəl\ *adj* — **pun·ish·er** *n*

pun·ish·ment *n* **1** : the act of punishing **2** : a penalty (as a fine or imprisonment) inflicted on an offender through the judicial and esp. criminal process — see also CRUEL AND UNUSUAL PUNISHMENT

pu·ni·tive \'pyü-nə-tiv\ *adj* : inflicting, involving, or aiming at punishment — **pu·ni·tive·ly** *adv* — **pu·ni·tive·ness** *n*

punitive damages — see DAMAGE 2

pur autre vie \pər-'ō-trə-'vī, pùr-'ō-trə-'vē\ [Anglo-French] : for another's life — see also *estate pur autre vie* at ESTATE 1

¹pur·chase *vb* **pur·chased; pur·chas·ing** *vt* **1** : to acquire (real property) by means other than descent or inheritance **2** : to obtain by paying money or giving other valuable consideration; *specif* : to take (property) by a voluntary transaction (as a sale, mortgage, pledge, lien, or gift) that creates an interest and that is governed by the Uniform Commercial Code — see also BONA FIDE PURCHASER ~ *vi* : to purchase something — **pur·chas·able** *adj* — **pur·chas·er** *n*

²purchase *n* : an act or instance of purchasing: as **a** : the acquiring of real property by any means other than descent or inheritance **b** : the acquiring of an interest in property esp. in exchange for valuable consideration — see also WORD OF PURCHASE

¹purchase money *n* : the consideration paid or to be paid by the purchaser of property

²purchase money *adj* : involving or being a debt secured by the property purchased with the money borrowed — see also *purchase money mortgage* at MORTGAGE

purchase money mortgage — see MORTGAGE

purchase money resulting trust — see TRUST

purchase money security interest — see INTEREST 1

pure *adj* **1 a** : unmixed with any other matter **b** : free from dirt or taint **2** : being thus and nothing other ⟨a ∼ no-fault compensation system⟩ — **pure·ly** *adv* — **pure·ness** *n*

pure accident *n* : UNAVOIDABLE ACCIDENT

pure premium *n* : NET PREMIUM

pure race *adj* : of, relating to, or being a recording act in which the first party to properly record documentation of an interest in property has priority regardless of notice of other claims ⟨a *pure race* statute⟩ — compare ³NOTICE, RACE-NOTICE

pure risk *n* : a risk that can only result in loss — compare SPECULATIVE RISK

pure speech *n* : the communication of ideas through spoken or written words or through conduct limited in form to that necessary to convey the idea — compare COMMERCIAL SPEECH, SYMBOLIC SPEECH ◇ Pure speech is accorded the highest degree of protection under the First Amendment to the U.S. Constitution.

pur·ga·tion \pər-'gā-shən\ *n* : the act or the result of purging

purge \'pərj\ *vt* **purged; purg·ing 1** : to clear (as oneself or another) of guilt ⟨*purged* himself of contempt⟩ **2** : to become no longer guilty of ⟨∼ the contempt⟩

pur·loin \pər-'lȯin, 'pər-ˌlȯin\ *vt* : STEAL

pur·par·ty \'pər-ˌpär-tē\ *n* [Anglo-French *pourpartie*, from Old French *pur*, *pour* for + *partie* division] : a share or portion of an estate allotted by a partition to a coparcener

pur·pose \'pər-pəs\ *n* : an objective, effect, or result aimed at or attained; *specif* : the business activity in which a corporation is chartered to engage — **pur·pose·ful** \-fəl\ *adj* — **pur·pose·ful·ly** *adv* — **pur·pose·ful·ness** *n*

pur·pose·ly *adv* : with a deliberate, conscious, or express purpose : INTENTIONALLY

pur·pres·ture \pər-'pres-chər\ *n* [Anglo-French, alteration of Old French *porpresure*, from *porprendre* to seize, occupy, enclose, from *por-* for + *prendre* to take, from Latin *prehendere*] : wrongful appropriation of land subject to the rights of others : an encroachment upon or enclosure of real property (as highways, sidewalks, or harbors) subject to common or public rights

pur·view \'pər-ˌvyü\ *n* [Anglo-French *purveu est* it is provided (opening phrase of a statute)] **1** : the body of a statute or the part that begins with *Be it enacted* and ends before the repealing clause **2** : the limit or scope of a law

put *n* : PUT OPTION at OPTION 3

pu·ta·tive \'pyü-tə-tiv\ *adj* : thought, assumed, or alleged to be such or to exist ⟨the child's ∼ father⟩ ⟨ignorantly entered into a ∼ marriage before the divorce from a previous spouse was final⟩ — **pu·ta·tive·ly** *adv*

put option — see OPTION 3

¹pyr·a·mid \'pir-ə-ˌmid\ *n* **1** : a group of holding companies superimposed on one another to give those in control of the top holding company control over all of the companies with a small investment **2** : the series of operations involved in pyramiding on an exchange **3** : a pyramid scheme

²pyramid *vi* : to speculate (as on a security or commodity exchange) by using paper profits as a margin for additional transactions — *vt* **1** : to use (as profits) in speculative pyramiding **2** : to increase the impact of (as a tax assessed at the production level) on the ultimate consumer by treating as a cost subject to markup

³**pyramid** *adj* : of, relating to, or being an illegal scheme in which participants give money or other valuables in exchange for the opportunity to receive payment for recruiting others to participate in the scheme

Q

Q.B. *abbr* Queen's Bench

QDRO \'kwä-drō\ *abbr* qualified domestic relations order

QTIP \'kyü-,tip\ *abbr* qualified terminable interest property

QTIP trust — see TRUST

qua \'kwä, 'kwā\ *prep* [Latin, which way, as, from ablative singular feminine of *qui* who] **:** in the capacity or character of ⟨a legitimate interest of the stockholder ~ stockholder⟩

quae·re \'kwir-ē, 'kwer-\ *n* [Latin, imperative of *quaerere* to seek, ask] **:** QUESTION — usu. used to introduce a question ⟨~: whether the legislature intended such a result?⟩

qual·i·fied \'kwä-lə-,fīd\ *adj* **1 :** fitted (as by training or experience) for a given purpose or condition **2 a :** being in compliance or accordance with specific requirements or conditions ⟨a ~ voter⟩ **b :** eligible under applicable requirements for favorable tax treatment (as exemption of funds from taxation until retirement) ⟨a ~ pension plan⟩ **3 :** limited or modified in some way **:** less than absolute — **qual·i·fied·ly** \-,fī-əd-lē, -,fīd-lē\ *adv*

qualified charitable remainder trust — see TRUST

qualified disclaimer *n* **:** an irrevocable and absolute refusal to accept a particular interest in the estate of a decedent (as a spouse) that is made in accordance with federal tax requirements and results in favorable tax consequences (as exemption from a gift tax) ◊ Property disclaimed under a qualified disclaimer is not treated as a gift and is not included in the gross estate of the decedent. Thus property disclaimed by a surviving spouse could pass to his or her children without incurring a gift tax. A disclaiming party can-

not, however, direct the disposition of the disclaimed interest and must not have accepted the interest or its benefits (as dividends).

qualified domestic relations order — see ORDER 3b

qualified endorsement — see ENDORSEMENT

qualified immunity — see IMMUNITY

qualified ownership — see OWNERSHIP

qualified privilege — see PRIVILEGE 1a

qualified residence interest — see INTEREST 5

qualified terminable interest property — see PROPERTY

qualified witness — see WITNESS

qual·i·fy \'kwä-lə-,fī\ *vb* **-fied; -fy·ing** *vt* **1 :** to limit or modify in some way **2 :** to make or consider eligible or fit ⟨his training and experience *qualified* him as an expert witness⟩ **3 :** to issue a certificate or license to ~ *vi* **1 :** to meet certain requirements or criteria ⟨~ for a tax credit⟩ **2 :** to acquire competent power or capacity ⟨has just *qualified* as a lawyer⟩

qualifying event *n* **:** an event or condition (as a terminal illness) that permits an acceleration or continuation of benefits or coverage; *esp* **:** an event involving an employee covered by a group health insurance plan that would result in a termination of coverage for the employee or a qualified beneficiary if not for federal provisions for the continuation of such coverage (as for six months) ◊ Qualifying events for continuation of group health insurance coverage include the death, divorce, or legal separation of the employee, termination from employment for a reason other than gross misconduct, reduction in working hours, and change in status of a child who ceases to be classified as a dependent under the terms of the plan. An employee is entitled to notice of the right to continuation after a qualifying event occurs.

qual·i·ty *n, pl* **-ties 1 :** a special, distinctive, or essential character: as **a :** a character, position, or role assumed ⟨those acts of ownership, which the person called to the succession can only do in ∼ of heir —*Louisiana Civil Code*⟩ **b :** the character of an estate as determined by the manner in which it is to be held or enjoyed **2 :** degree of excellence ⟨made no warranties as to the product's ∼⟩

quan·tum me·ru·it \'kwän-təm-'mer-ü-it, -yü-\ *n* [Latin, as much as he/she deserved] **1 :** a claim or count grounded on an implied contract that the defendant would pay the plaintiff as much as deserved for services or materials provided; *specif* **:** a count in a common-law action for assumpsit claiming payment of the value of labor provided **2 :** a theory or doctrine that permits recovery by a party for services or materials provided despite the absence of an express contract when they were accepted and used by the defendant under circumstances which gave reasonable notice that the plaintiff expected to be paid for them — compare UNJUST ENRICHMENT

quantum va·le·bant \-və-'lē-ˌbant, -vä-'lā-ˌbänt\ *n* [Latin, as much as they were worth] **1 :** a count in a common-law action of assumpsit to recover the value of goods or materials furnished **2 :** a theory or doctrine that permits recovery for materials provided on the basis of an implied contract

quash \'kwäsh, 'kwȯsh\ *vt* [Anglo-French *quasser*, from Middle French *casser*, *quasser*, from Late Latin *cassare*, from Latin *cassus* void] **:** to make void **:** ANNUL 2 ⟨∼ a subpoena⟩

quash·al \'kwä-shəl, 'kwȯ-\ *n* **:** an act of quashing something ⟨opposed the ∼ of the indictment⟩

¹qua·si \'kwā-ˌzī, -ˌsī; 'kwä-zē, -sē\ *adj* [Latin, as if, as it were, from *quam* as + *si*

if] **:** having such a resemblance to another thing as to fall within its general category ⟨a *quasi* corporation⟩

²quasi *adv* **:** in some significant sense or degree — often used in combination ⟨*quasi-fiscal*⟩ — see also QUASI-JUDICIAL, QUASI-LEGISLATIVE

quasi contract — see CONTRACT

quasi–delict *n, in the civil law of Louisiana* **:** QUASI-OFFENSE

quasi easement — see EASEMENT

quasi estoppel — see ESTOPPEL 1

quasi in rem \-in-'rem\ *adv or adj* [Latin, as if against a thing] **:** as if one were proceeding against the thing — used esp. in reference to proceedings (as for attachment of property) in which one seeks satisfaction of a claim against a person by adjudication of rights to a particular property over which jurisdiction can be obtained — see also *quasi in rem jurisdiction* at JURISDICTION; compare IN PERSONAM, IN REM ◊ The plaintiff in a quasi in rem action uses the court's jurisdiction over the defendant's property in hopes of obtaining a remedy for a claim (as for money) against the defendant. A quasi in rem action is often used when jurisdiction over the defendant cannot be obtained due to his or her absence from the state.

quasi in rem jurisdiction — see JURISDICTION

quasi–judicial *adj* **:** of, relating to, or being an administrative act, body, or procedure that is concerned with the adjudication of specific rights and obligations rather than the promulgation of rules, that requires discretion and decision, and that may be subject to notice and hearing requirements and judicial review

quasi–legislative *adj* **:** of, relating to, or being an administrative act, body, or procedure that is concerned with the promulgation of rules and regulations or the

\ə\abut \ᵊ\kitten \ər\further \a\ash \ā\ace
\ä\cot, cart \au̇\out \ch\chin \e\bet \ē\easy
\g\go \i\hit \ī\ice \j\job \ŋ\sing \ō\go \ȯ\law
\ȯi\boy \th\thin \t͟h\the \ü\loot \u̇\foot \y\yet
\zh\vision *see also* Pronunciation Symbols page

adoption of laws, charters, or orders and that is based on authority derived from the legislature by statute ⟨quasi-judicial decisions are more closely scrutinized than ~ decisions —*In re Investigation of Unfair Election Practice Objections*, 451 N.W.2d 49 (1990)⟩

quasi-offense *n*, *in the civil law of Louisiana* : a negligent unlawful act that causes damage to another and for which the law imposes an obligation for damages — compare OFFENSE

Queen's Bench *n* : a division of the High Court of Justice of England and Wales that hears civil cases (as commercial cases) and appeals of criminal cases — used during the reign of a queen; compare KING'S BENCH

ques·tion *n* **1** : a particular query directed to a witness — compare INTERROGATORY

hy·po·thet·i·cal question \ˌhī-pə-'the-ti-kəl\ : a question directed to an expert witness (as a physician) that is based on the existence of facts offered in evidence and the answer to which is an opinion to be considered in light of the evidence ◊ Modern rules of evidence have lessened the need for a hypothetical question setting forth all of the facts to be assumed in answering the question. An expert witness may state an opinion based on data or facts considered reliable in his or her field even if not already disclosed or not admissible as evidence.

leading question : a question so framed or presented as to suggest a particular answer ⟨*leading questions* should not be used on the direct examination of a witness except as may be necessary to develop his testimony —*Federal Rules of Evidence* Rule 611(c)⟩ ◊ Leading questions are permitted in direct examination of an adverse witness or one who is a child or has a communication disorder. They are ordinarily permitted in cross-examination.

2 : a particular matter or issue that is in dispute, uncertain, or to be inquired into

certified question **1** : a question of state

law that may determine the outcome of a case pending in a federal court and that is submitted by the federal court to the state's highest court when there is no controlling state precedent **2** : a question of law submitted to a federal or state court by a lower court or tribunal ⟨appealed the decision on the *certified question*⟩

federal question : a question that falls under the jurisdiction of a federal court because it requires a resolution of the construction or application of federal law — see also *federal question jurisdiction* at JURISDICTION

political question : a question that the court declines to consider because it involves a political matter that is not justiciable without infringing on the powers of the executive or legislative branch or is not accompanied by guiding policy or discoverable and manageable standards for resolving it — see also POLITICAL QUESTION DOCTRINE

question of fact : a question that depends on an examination of factual matters, is usu. decided by a jury, and is usu. not considered on appeal

question of law : a question that depends on an examination of law rather than fact, is decided by a judge rather than by a jury, and may be examined on appeal

3 : a proposition submitted to a vote (as in a referendum)

question of fact — see QUESTION 2

question of law — see QUESTION 2

quick assets — see ASSET 2

quid pro quo \ˌkwid-ˌprō-'kwō\ *n* [New Latin, something for something] : something (as consideration) given or received for something else

quid pro quo sexual harassment *n* : sexual harassment in which the satisfaction of sexual demands is made the condition of job benefits or continued employment or is used as the basis for employment decisions regarding the individual — compare HOSTILE ENVIRONMENT SEXUAL HARASSMENT

¹qui·et *adj* : free from disturbance, interference, or dispute (as from an adverse claim) ⟨~ enjoyment of property⟩
²quiet *vt* : to establish or make (title) secure by means of an action that produces a final determination of the respective rights of parties who are in dispute over property — compare CLOUD ON TITLE

qui tam \ˌkwī-'tam, ˌkwē-'täm\ *adj* [Late Latin, who as much, who as well; from the first words of a clause referring to the plaintiff as one who sues as much for the state as for himself or herself] : of, relating to, or being a qui tam action ⟨a *qui tam* plaintiff⟩

qui tam action *n* : an action that is brought by a person on behalf of a government against a party alleged to have violated a statute esp. against defrauding the government through false claims and that provides for part of a penalty to go to the person bringing the action ⟨the whistleblower brought a *qui tam action* against the contractor for presenting fraudulent claims for payment⟩

quit·claim \'kwit-ˌklām\ *vt* : to release a claim to; *specif* : to release a claim to and convey by quitclaim deed ⟨required under the divorce decree to ~ the property to his wife⟩ — **quitclaim** *n*
quitclaim deed — see DEED

Quo·rum \'kwōr-əm\ *n* [Middle English, a select number of English justices of the peace formerly required to be present at sessions to constitute a lawful bench, from Latin, of whom, genitive plural of *qui* who; from the wording of the commission once issued to justices of the peace in England] : the number (as a majority) of members or officers that must be present to conduct business ⟨lacked a ~ at the meeting of shareholders⟩

quo·ta \'kwō-tə\ *n* [Medieval Latin, from Latin *quota pars* how great a part] **1** : a proportional part or share assigned to each in a body **2** : a specific amount that serves as a minimum or maximum ⟨a law against traffic ticket ~s⟩

quotient verdict — see VERDICT

quo war·ran·to \'kwō-wə-'ran-tō, -'rän-\ *n* [Medieval Latin, by what warrant; from the wording of the writ] **1** : an extraordinary writ requiring a person or corporation to show by what right or authority a public office or franchise is held or exercised **2** : a proceeding in the nature of a writ of quo warranto for determining by what authority or right an office or franchise is held or exercised and seeking as an extraordinary remedy the discontinuance of an unlawful exercise of office or franchise

R

race–no•tice \'rās-,nō-təs\ *adj* [*race* from the notion of two parties rushing to the courthouse in order to be the first to record a claim or interest on the same property] : of, relating to, or being a recording act which stipulates that an unrecorded deed, mortgage, or lien shall not be valid against a recorded one unless the recording party (as a subsequent purchaser from the same seller) had notice of the interest or claim of the other party when recording — compare ³NOTICE, PURE RACE ◊ If one party purchases a property and records the deed, a subsequent purchaser is normally held to know about it — to have "constructive notice" of it — as a matter of law since it is a matter of public record. Under a race-notice statute, however, a subsequent purchaser cannot have constructive notice of an unrecorded deed, and so the recorded deed has priority unless the purchaser actually knew about — had "actual notice" of — the unrecorded deed.

rack•e•teer \,ra-kə-'tir\ *n* : one that engages in racketeering — **racketeer** *vb*

rack•e•teer•ing \,ra-kə-'tir-iŋ\ *n* **1** : the extortion of money or advantage by threat or force **2** : a pattern of illegal activity (as extortion and murder) that is carried out in furtherance of an enterprise (as a criminal syndicate) which is owned or controlled by those engaged in such activity — see also *Racketeer Influenced and Corrupt Organizations Act* in the IMPORTANT LAWS section; compare ORGANIZED CRIME

raid•er *n* : one that attempts a usu. hostile takeover of a business corporation — compare WHITE KNIGHT

rain•mak•er \'rān-,mā-kər\ *n* : a person (as a partner in a law firm) who brings in new business — **rain•mak•ing** *n*

rank and file *n* : the general membership of a union

¹ran•som *n* : a consideration paid or demanded for the release of someone or something from captivity — see also KIDNAPPING

²ransom *vt* : to free from captivity by paying a price

¹rape *vt* **raped; rap•ing** [Latin *rapere* to seize and take away by force] : to commit rape on — **rap•er** *n* — **rap•ist** *n*

²rape *n* : unlawful sexual activity and usu. sexual intercourse carried out forcibly or under threat of injury against the will usu. of a female or with a person who is beneath a certain age or incapable of valid consent because of mental illness, mental deficiency, intoxication, unconsciousness, or deception — see also STATUTORY RAPE ◊ The common-law crime of rape involved a man having carnal knowledge of a woman not his wife through force and against her will, and required at least slight penetration of the penis into the vagina. While some states maintain essentially this definition of rape, most have broadened its scope esp. in terms of the sex of the persons and the nature of the acts involved. Marital status is usu. irrelevant. Moreover, the crime is codified under various names, including *first degree sexual assault, sexual battery, unlawful sexual intercourse,* and *first degree sexual abuse.*

rape shield law *n* : a law that prohibits or limits use of evidence (as testimony) regarding prior sexual conduct of an alleged rape victim

rat•able \'rā-tə-bəl\ *adj* : made or calculated according to a proportionate rate : PRO RATA ⟨a ~ distribution of the bankruptcy estate⟩ — **rat•ably** \-blē\ *adv*

rate *n* **1** : a fixed ratio between two things

2 : a charge, payment, or price fixed according to a ratio, scale, or standard: as **a** : a charge per unit of a commodity provided by a public utility **b** : a charge per unit of freight or passenger service — see also JOINT RATE **c** : a unit charge or ratio used in assessing property taxes **3 a** : a quantity, amount, or degree of something measured per unit of something else **b** : an amount of payment or charge based on another amount; *specif* : the amount of premium per unit of insurance — **rate** *vt*

rate base *n* : the total fair value of public utility property that is used in rendering services and that comprises the investment on which a fair rate of return is based in setting utility rates

rat·i·fy \'ra-tə-ˌfī\ *vt* **-fied; -fy·ing** : to make valid or effective; *esp* : to adopt or affirm (as the prior act or contract of an agent) by express or implied consent with the effect of original authorization ⟨unable to rescind the contract because he *ratified* it by accepting the benefits⟩ — compare REFORM — **rat·i·fi·ca·tion** \ˌra-tə-fə-'kā-shən\ *n* — **rat·i·fi·er** \'ra-tə-ˌfī-ər\ *n*

ra·tio de·ci·den·di \'rā-shē-ˌō-ˌde-sə-'den-ˌdī, 'rā-ˌshō-, -ˌdā-sē-'den-dē\ *n* [Latin, grounds for deciding] : the principle or rule constituting the basis of a court decision

ra·tio·nal \'ra-shə-nəl\ *adj* **1** : having reason or understanding **2** : relating to, based on, or guided by reason, principle, fairness, logic, a legitimate state interest, or a consideration of fact ⟨age distinctions are not subject to strict scrutiny, but they must have a ~ relationship to a legitimate state interest —*In re J. M.,* 642 A.2d 1062 (1994)⟩ — **ra·tio·nal·i·ty** \ˌra-shə-'na-lə-tē\ *n* — **ra·tio·nal·ly** *adv*

rational basis *n* : a reason or ground (as for legislation or an action by a government agency) that is not unreasonable or arbitrary and that bears rational relationship to a legitimate state interest — see also RATIONAL BASIS TEST

rational basis test *n* : a test less inten-

sive than strict scrutiny or an intermediate review that involves a determination of whether a statutory or regulatory classification of persons (as by age or offender status) has a rational basis and does not deny equal protection under the Constitution ⟨if the classification neither affects a fundamental right, nor creates a suspect classification, nor is based on gender, then the *rational basis test* is applied —*Charlton v. Kimata,* 815 P.2d 946 (1991)⟩ — called also *rational relationship test*

rav·ish \'ra-vish\ *vt* [Middle English, to seize and take away by violence, from Middle French *raviss-,* stem of *ravir,* ultimately from Latin *rapere* to seize, rob] : RAPE — **rav·ish·ment** *n*

re \'rā, 'rē\ *prep* [Latin, ablative of *res* thing] : with regard to : IN RE

re- *prefix* **1** : again : anew ⟨reinvest⟩ **2** : back : backward ⟨reconvey⟩

reach *vt* **1** : to extend application to **2** : to obtain an interest in or possession of ⟨unable to ~ all the assets of the debtor⟩ **3 a** : to arrive at and consider ⟨the justices did not ~ that issue⟩ **b** : to amount to ⟨did not ~ a due process violation⟩ — **reach** *n* — **reach·able** *adj*

re·ad·just \ˌrē-ə-'jəst\ *vt* : to adjust again; *esp* : to voluntarily reorganize (a corporation) ~ *vi* : to become readjusted — **re·ad·just·ment** *n*

re·af·firm \ˌrē-ə-'fərm\ *vt* **1** : to affirm again **2** : to agree to the payment of (a dischargeable debt) with a creditor prior to the discharge of debts in bankruptcy ⟨~ed her debt in order to keep her car⟩ — **re·af·fir·ma·tion** \-ˌa-fər-'mā-shən\ *n*

reaffirmation hearing — see HEARING

real *adj* [Anglo-French, concerning land, property, or things (rather than persons), from Middle French, from Medieval Latin and Late Latin; Medieval Latin *realis* relating to things (in law), from

\ə\abut \ᵊ\kitten \ər\further \a\ash \ā\ace \ä\cot, cart \au̇\out \ch\chin \e\bet \ē\easy \g\go \i\hit \ī\ice \j\job \ŋ\sing \ō\go \ȯ\law \ȯi\boy \th\thin \t̲h̲\the \ü\loot \u̇\foot \y\yet \zh\vision *see also* Pronunciation Symbols page

Late Latin, actual, from Latin *res* thing, fact] **1 a :** of or relating to real property ⟨a ~ action⟩ — see also *real property* at PROPERTY **b** *in the civil law of Louisiana* **:** attached to a thing rather than a person ⟨a ~ obligation is transferred along with the thing to which it is attached⟩ — see also REAL RIGHT; compare PERSONAL **2 :** ACTUAL **3 :** adjusted for inflation esp. to reflect actual purchasing power ⟨~ income⟩

real defense — see DEFENSE 2b

real estate *n* **:** REAL PROPERTY at PROPERTY

real estate investment trust — see TRUST

real estate mortgage investment conduit \-'kän-ˌdü-ət, -ˌdyü-\ *n* **:** REMIC

real evidence — see EVIDENCE

re•align \ˌrē-ə-'līn\ *vt* **:** to make new divisions or groupings of; *esp* **:** to regroup (one or more litigants) to reflect the true arrangement of interests in a suit ◊ After examining the ultimate interests of the parties involved in a suit, the court might choose to realign the plaintiffs and defendants so that, for example, one of the defendants becomes a plaintiff. — **re•align•ment** *n*

re•al•ize \'rē-ə-ˌlīz\ *vt* **-ized; -iz•ing 1 :** to convert into money **2 :** to obtain or incur (as a gain or loss) esp. as the result of a sale, exchange, or other disposition of an asset ⟨*realized* a loss when the house was sold⟩ — compare RECOGNIZE — **re•al•i•za•tion** \ˌrē-ə-lə-'zā-shən\ *n*

real party in interest — see PARTY 1b

real property — see PROPERTY

real right *n, in the civil law of Louisiana* **:** a right that is attached to a thing rather than a person ⟨the right of ownership . . . may be burdened with a *real right* in favor of another person as allowed by law —*Louisiana Civil Code*⟩ ◊ A real right is not restricted to real property since it can also be attached to movable property. Real rights include ownership, use, pledge, usufruct, mortgage, and predial servitude.

Re•al•tor \'rē-əl-tər, 'rēl-, -ˌtor\ *collective mark* — used for a real estate agent who

is a member of the National Association of Realtors

re•al•ty \'rē-əl-tē, 'rēl-\ *n* **:** REAL PROPERTY at PROPERTY

re•ap•por•tion \ˌrē-ə-'pōr-shən\ *vt* **:** to apportion anew; *esp* **:** to apportion (seats in a house of representatives) in accordance with new population distribution ~ *vi* **:** to make a new apportionment — **re•ap•por•tion•ment** *n*

re•ar•gu•ment \ˌrē-'är-gyə-mənt\ *n* **:** new or repeated argument; *esp* **:** presentation of new or additional arguments to a court on a matter of law or fact which a petitioner claims was overlooked or misunderstood by the court ◊ Reargument requires the granting of a motion, which must be filed within a specified period after entry of the court's judgment. — **re•ar•gue** \-'är-ˌgyü\ *vt*

rea•son *n* **1 :** an underlying ground, justification, purpose, motive, or inducement ⟨required to provide ~*s* for the termination in writing⟩ **2 a :** the faculty of comprehending, inferring, or distinguishing esp. in a fair and orderly way **b :** the proper and sane exercise of the mind

rea•son•able *adj* **1 a :** being in accordance with reason, fairness, duty, or prudence **b :** of an appropriate degree or kind **c :** supported or justified by fact or circumstance ⟨a ~ belief that force was necessary for self-defense⟩ **d :** COMMERCIALLY REASONABLE **2 :** applying reason or logic; *broadly* **:** RATIONAL 1 ⟨a ~ mind⟩ — **rea•son•able•ness** *n* — **rea•son•ably** *adv*

reasonable accommodation *n* **:** something done to accommodate a disabled person that does not jeopardize safety or pose an undue hardship for the party (as an employer) doing it; *also* **:** something done to accommodate a religious need that does not create undue hardship for an employer

reasonable care *n* **:** DUE CARE

reasonable cause — see CAUSE 2

reasonable diligence *n* **:** DUE DILIGENCE 1

reasonable doubt *n* **:** a doubt esp. about the guilt of a criminal defendant that arises or remains upon fair and thorough consideration of the evidence or lack thereof ⟨all persons are presumed to be innocent and no person may be convicted of an offense unless each element of the offense is proved beyond a *reasonable doubt —Texas Penal Code*⟩ — see also STANDARD OF PROOF; compare CLEAR AND CONVINCING, PREPONDERANCE OF THE EVIDENCE ◊ Proof of guilt beyond a reasonable doubt is required for conviction of a criminal defendant. A reasonable doubt exists when a factfinder cannot say with moral certainty that a person is guilty or a particular fact exists. It must be more than an imaginary doubt, and it is often defined judicially as such doubt as would cause a reasonable person to hesitate before acting in a matter of importance.

reasonable force — see FORCE 3

reasonable person *n* : a fictional person with an ordinary degree of reason, prudence, care, foresight, or intelligence whose conduct, conclusion, or expectation in relation to a particular circumstance or fact is used as an objective standard by which to measure or determine something (as the existence of negligence) ⟨we have generally held that a *reasonable person* would not believe that he or she has been seized when an officer merely approaches that person in a public place and begins to ask questions — *State v. Cripps*, 533 N.W.2d 388 (1995)⟩ — called also *reasonable man*

reasonable prob·a·bil·i·ty *n* : a probability that the result of a proceeding would have been different if not for the unprofessional errors of counsel or nondisclosure of exculpatory material by the prosecution which is sufficient to undermine confidence in the outcome

reasonable suspicion *n* : an objectively justifiable suspicion that is based on specific facts or circumstances and that justifies stopping and sometimes searching (as by frisking) a person thought to be involved in criminal activity at the time — see also *reasonable cause* at CAUSE 2; compare *probable cause* at CAUSE 2,

TERRY STOP ◊ A police officer stopping a person must be able to point to specific facts or circumstances even though the level of suspicion need not rise to that of the belief that is supported by probable cause. A reasonable suspicion is more than a hunch.

reasonable use — see USE 2

reasonably equivalent value *n* : value that is a fair amount for property transferred by a debtor esp. in bankruptcy and that is not therefore evidence of a fraudulent conveyance — see also *fair consideration* at CONSIDERATION

re·bate \'rē-ˌbāt\ *n* : a refund or deduction of part of a payment, price, or charge — **re·bate** \'rē-ˌbāt, ri-'bāt\ *vb*

re·but \ri-'bət\ *vt* **re·but·ted; re·but·ting** [Anglo-French *reboter, rebuter* to answer a charge, bar from an action, literally, to repulse, rebuff, from Old French *reboter,* from *re-* back + *boter* to push, butt] : to refute, counteract, or disprove (as opposing evidence) by evidence or argument ⟨~ damaging testimony⟩ ⟨~ a presumption⟩ — **re·but·ta·ble** *adj* — **re·but·ta·bly** *adv*

rebuttable presumption — see PRESUMPTION

re·but·tal \ri-'bət-ᵊl\ *n* : the act or procedure of rebutting; *also* : evidence or argument that rebuts

rebuttal evidence — see EVIDENCE

rebuttal witness — see WITNESS

¹**re·but·ter** *n* [Anglo-French *reboter,* from *reboter* to rebut] : the answer of a defendant in matter of fact to a plaintiff's surrejoinder

²**rebutter** *n* : one that rebuts

re·call \ri-'kȯl, 'rē-ˌkȯl\ *n* **1** : a call to return ⟨a ~ of workers⟩ **2** : the right or procedure by which an official may be removed by vote of the people ⟨a ~ petition⟩ **3** : the act of revoking **4** : a public call by a manufacturer for the return

\ə\abut \ᵊ\kitten \ər\further \a\ash \ā\ace
\ä\cot, cart \au̇\out \ch\chin \e\bet \ē\easy
\g\go \i\hit \ī\ice \j\job \ŋ\sing \ō\go \ȯ\law
\ȯi\boy \th\thin \t̲h̲\the \ü\loot \u̇\foot \y\yet
\zh\vision *see also* Pronunciation Symbols page

of a defective or esp. unsafe product —
re·call \ri-'kȯl\ *vt*
re·cant \ri-'kant\ *vt* : to renounce or withdraw (prior statements or testimony) ⟨sur-
prised the prosecution by ~*ing* statements made earlier to the police⟩ ~ *vi*
: to renounce or withdraw prior statements or testimony — **re·can·ta·tion**
\ˌrē-ˌkan-'tā-shən\ *n*
re·cap·i·tal·ize \ˌrē-'ka-pət-ᵊl-ˌīz\ *vt* : to
change the capital structure of (a corporation) — **re·cap·i·tal·i·za·tion** \-ˌka-pət-
ᵊl-ə-'zā-shən\ *n*
¹**re·cap·ture** \ˌrē-'kap-chər\ *vt* -**tured**;
-**tur·ing** **1** : to capture again **2** : to recover
or take (as an excess or gain) by law or
agreement; *esp* : to recover (a tax benefit) by higher or additional taxation of
income or property that ceases to qualify
for a credit or deduction or by taxing
gain realized from the sale or exchange
of such property ⟨the government *recaptured* the depreciation by taxing the gain
resulting from the difference between the
sale price and the basis after deprecia-
tion⟩
²**recapture** *n* **1** : the act or process of re-
capturing **2** : an amount recaptured or
subject to recapture
re·ceipt \ri-'sēt\ *n* **1** : the act, process, or
fact of taking possession **2** : something
(as income) received — usu. used in pl. **3**
: a writing acknowledging the receiving
of goods or money
re·ceiv·able \ri-'sē-və-bəl\ *adj* **1** : capable
of being received **2** : subject to call for
payment ⟨notes ~⟩ — see also ACCOUNT
RECEIVABLE — **receivable** *n*
re·ceiv·er \ri-'sē-vər\ *n* **1** : an officer
charged with receiving tax payments or
returns and other related duties (as the
maintenance of tax rolls) **2** : a person
appointed by the court to hold in trust and
administer property in litigation; *esp* : one
appointed to administer, conserve, rehabilitate, or liquidate the assets of an insolvent corporation for the protection or
relief of creditors — compare CONSERVA-
TOR, LIQUIDATOR
receiver's certificate *n* : a debt instrument

that is issued by the receiver of a corporation and that may have priority over other
liens against the company
re·ceiv·er·ship \ri-'sē-vər-ˌship\ *n* **1** : the
office or function of a receiver **2** : a proceeding in which a receiver is appointed
3 : the state of being in the hands of a
receiver — compare BANKRUPTCY
re·cess \'rē-ˌses, ri-'ses\ *n* : a temporary
adjournment of a trial, hearing, or legislative session — **recess** *vb*
re·cid·i·vate \ri-'si-də-ˌvāt\ *vi* -**vat·ed**;
-**vat·ing** [Medieval Latin *recidivatus*,
past participle of *recidivare* to fall back,
relapse, from Latin *recidivus* falling back,
recurring] : to return to criminal activity
re·cid·i·vism \ri-'si-də-ˌvi-zəm\ *n* : relapse into criminal behavior
re·cid·i·vist \ri-'si-də-vist\ *n* : an habitual
criminal — **recidivist** *adj* — **re·cid·i·
vis·tic** \ri-ˌsi-də-'vis-tik\ *adj*
re·cip·ro·cal \ri-'si-prə-kəl\ *adj* **1 a** : MU-
TUAL **2 b** : BILATERAL ⟨a ~ contract⟩
2 : characterized by correspondence or
equivalence esp. in return or response
with another of the same category ⟨was
prevented from obtaining ~ discovery
of the names of the State's alibi rebuttal witnesses —*Mauricio v. State*, 652
N.E.2d 869 (1995)⟩; *also* : marked by
such correspondence or equivalence between its own components ⟨a ~ arrange-
ment⟩ **3** : marked by reciprocity between
states — **re·cip·ro·cal·ly** *adv*
reciprocal dealing *n* : an arrangement violative of antitrust laws in which a party
with greater economic power agrees to
buy a product from a seller if the seller
buys something in return
reciprocal exchange *n* : an unincorporated association in which members (as
individuals, partnerships, trustees, or corporations) exchange contracts and pay
premiums through an attorney-in-fact for
the insurance of each other ⟨liability of
each member of the *reciprocal exchange*
was limited to ten times the annual pre-
mium⟩ — called also *interinsurance exchange, reciprocal insurance exchange,
reciprocal interinsurance exchange*

reciprocal insurance *n* : insurance through a reciprocal exchange — called also *interinsurance*

reciprocal insurance exchange *n* : RECIPROCAL EXCHANGE

reciprocal interinsurance exchange *n* : RECIPROCAL EXCHANGE

reciprocal negative easement — see EASEMENT

reciprocal will — see WILL

rec·i·proc·i·ty \ˌre-sə-ˈprä-sə-tē\ *n*, *pl* **-ties** **1** : the quality or state of being reciprocal **2** : the exchange, recognition, or enforcement of licenses, privileges, or obligations between states of the U.S. or between nations

re·ci·sion \ri-ˈsi-zhən\ *or* **re·cis·sion** \-shən\ *n* : RESCISSION

re·ci·tal \ri-ˈsīt-ᵊl\ *n* : a formal statement or setting forth of some relevant matter of fact in a deed or other document ⟨a ∼ of a factual reason for a transaction⟩ ◊ A recital is often preceded by *whereas.*

reck·less *adj* : characterized by the creation of a substantial and unjustifiable risk to the lives, safety, or rights of others and by a conscious and sometimes wanton and willful disregard for or indifference to that risk that is a gross deviation from the standard of care a reasonable person would exercise in like circumstances ⟨a ∼ state of mind may be inferred from conduct⟩ — see also *involuntary manslaughter* at MANSLAUGHTER, *reckless homicide* at HOMICIDE, RECKLESSNESS; compare CARELESS — **reck·less·ly** *adv*

reckless dis·re·gard of the truth *or* **reckless disregard for the truth** **1** : disregard of the truth or falsity of a defamatory statement by a person who is highly aware of its probable falsity or entertains serious doubts about its truth or when there are obvious reasons to doubt the veracity and accuracy of a source ⟨the knowingly false statement and the false statement made with *reckless disregard of the truth*, do not enjoy constitutional protection —*Garrison v. Louisiana*, 379 U.S. 64 (1964)⟩ **2** : a reckless lack of attention to the truth that misleads or deceives another (as a magistrate) ⟨whether false statements were made intentionally or in *reckless disregard of the truth* in support of the warrant —*State v. O'Neil*, 879 P.2d 950 (1994)⟩

reckless endangerment *n* : the offense of recklessly engaging in conduct that creates a substantial risk of serious physical injury or death to another person ◊ Reckless endangerment is a misdemeanor but sometimes rises to a felony, as when a deadly weapon is involved.

reckless homicide — see HOMICIDE

reck·less·ness *n* : the quality or state of being reckless; *also* : reckless conduct — compare NEGLIGENCE ◊ Recklessness may be the basis for civil and often criminal liability. Unlike negligence it requires conscious disregard of risk to others.

re·claim \ˌrē-ˈklām\ *vt* **1** : to make fit or available for human use ⟨∼*ing* land that had been strip-mined⟩ **2 a** : to demand the return of by right **b** : to regain possession of

rec·la·ma·tion \ˌre-klə-ˈmā-shən\ *n* **1** : the act or process of reclaiming ⟨the ∼ of goods delivered to an insolvent buyer⟩ **2** : a right to reclaim (as under commercial law)

rec·og·ni·tion \ˌre-kəg-ˈni-shən\ *n* **1** : the act, process, or fact of recognizing **2** : the state of being recognized

recognition strike — see STRIKE

re·cog·ni·zance \ri-ˈkäg-nə-zəns\ *n* [Anglo-French *recognisance, reconisance,* literally, recognition, from Old French *reconoisance,* from *reconoistre* to recognize, from Latin *recognoscere*] **1** : an obligation entered into on the record before a court or magistrate requiring the performance of an act (as the paying of a debt) usu. under penalty of a money forfeiture; *also* : the sum liable to forfeiture

\ə\abut \ᵊ\kitten \ər\further \a\ash \ā\ace
\ä\cot, cart \au̇\out \ch\chin \e\bet \ē\easy
\g\go \i\hit \ī\ice \j\job \ŋ\sing \ō\go \ȯ\law
\ȯi\boy \th\thin \t͟h\the \ü\loot \u̇\foot \y\yet
\zh\vision *see also* Pronunciation Symbols page

2 : a simple personal obligation or undertaking (as to appear in court) entered into before a magistrate and having no money penalty attached ⟨released on his own ~⟩

rec·og·nize *vt* **-nized; -niz·ing 1** : to acknowledge formally: as **a** : to admit as being of a particular status ⟨~ a precedent⟩ ⟨~ a union⟩; *specif* : to acknowledge (as a right, cause of action, or defense) as valid **b** : to admit as being one entitled to be heard : give the floor to **c** : to acknowledge the de facto existence or the independence of ⟨refused to ~ the new government⟩ **2** : to account for as real, received, or incurred and treat and record appropriately; *specif* : to account for (a gain, loss, expense, or income) on current accounting or tax records ⟨*recognized* the gain when she included it as income on her tax return⟩ — compare REALIZE

recognized market *n* : a market in which a secured party sells collateral upon a debtor's default, which does not rely on competitive bidding or haggling, and in which prices are stated publicly and presumed to be commercially reasonable ◊ Under the Uniform Commercial Code, a creditor is not required to notify a debtor of the sale of collateral in a recognized market.

re·cog·ni·zor \ri-'käg-nə-ˌzȯr\ *n* : one that is obligated under a recognizance

rec·on·cile \'re-kən-ˌsīl\ *vb* **-ciled; -cil·ing** *vt* **1 a** : to restore to harmony ⟨*reconciled* the parties⟩ ⟨*reconciled* the marriage⟩ **b** : to bring to resolution ⟨~ differences⟩ **2 a** : to check (a financial account) against another for accuracy **b** : to account for ~ *vi* : to become reconciled; *specif* : to voluntarily resume cohabitation as spouses prior to a divorce becoming final with the mutual intention of remaining together and reestablishing a harmonious relationship ⟨denied the complaint for divorce because the parties had *reconciled*⟩ — **rec·on·cil·abil·i·ty** \ˌre-kən-ˌsī-lə-'bi-lə-tē\ *n* — **rec·on·cil·able** \ˌre-kən-'sī-lə-bəl\ *adj* — **rec-**

on·cile·ment *n* — **rec·on·cil·i·a·tion** \ˌre-kən-ˌsi-lē-'ā-shən\ *n*

re·con·duc·tion \ˌrē-kən-'dək-shən\ *n*, [French *reconduction*, from Latin *reconducere* to lead back, lease again, from *re*back + *conducere* to conduct, hire, lease] *in the civil law of Louisiana* : a renewal of a lease

re·con·struc·tion *n* **1** : a rebuilding of a nonfunctional patented article that amounts to creation of a new article and constitutes infringement of the patent ⟨the complete replacement of the mechanism was a ~ and not a repair⟩ **2** : the practice or process of recreating an incident (as an accident) for the purpose of investigating the specific facts and circumstances surrounding it ⟨heard testimony on the speed of the vehicle from an expert in accident ~⟩

re·con·ven·tion \ˌrē-kən-'ven-chən\ *n* [French, from Middle French, from *re*again, back + *convention* agreement between two parties] *in the civil law of Louisiana* : the act or process of making a counterclaim ⟨judicial efficiency is served by requiring the defendant to assert in ~ all causes of action against the plaintiff —*Ballex v. Naccari*, 657 So. 2d 511 (1995)⟩

re·con·ven·tion·al demand \ˌrē-kən-'ven-chə-nəl-\ *n*, *in the civil law of Louisiana* : COUNTERCLAIM ⟨allowed to make a *reconventional demand* arising from a different transaction with the plaintiff⟩

re·con·vey \ˌrē-kən-'vā\ *vt* : to convey back or again ⟨the lender ~*ed* title to the borrower upon satisfaction of the debt⟩

¹re·cord \ri-'kȯrd\ *vt* **1** : to put in a record **2** : to deposit or otherwise cause to be registered in the appropriate office as a record and notice of a title or interest in property ⟨~ a deed⟩ ⟨~ a mortgage⟩ — see also RECORDING ACT **3** : to cause (as sound, images, or data) to be registered on something in reproducible form ⟨~ a telephone conversation⟩ ~ *vi* : to record something

²rec·ord \'re-kərd\ *n* **1** : the documentary account of something ⟨confidential medical ~s⟩: as **a** : an official document that records the acts of a public body or officer **b** : an official copy of a document deposited with a designated officer **c** : the official set of papers used and generated in a proceeding ⟨the appeals court reviewed the trial ~⟩ **d** : documented evidence or history of one or more arrests or convictions — see also BUSINESS RECORDS EXCEPTION, PUBLIC RECORDS EXCEPTION **2** : something (as a disc or tape) on which images, sound, or data has been recorded — **of record 1** : on the record of the court in connection with a particular proceeding ⟨the attorney *of record*⟩ **2** : being documented or attested

re•cor•dal \ri-'kȯr-dəl, 're-kər-dəl\ *n* : RECORDATION

re•cor•da•tion \ˌre-ˌkȯr-'dā-shən, ˌrē-\ *n* : the act or process of recording ⟨~ of a lien⟩

record date *n* : the date on which a corporation determines the identity of its shareholders and their holdings (as for determining who is entitled to notice of a shareholder meeting or who is entitled to vote at such a meeting or to receive dividends) — called also *date of record*

re•cord•er *n* **1** : a judge of a municipal court **2** : a public officer charged with making a record of writings or transactions (as conveyances) ⟨a ~ of deeds⟩

re•cord•ing act *n* : a statute setting forth the requirements for recording a deed or interest (as in real property) and the standards for determining priority among different parties with claims on the same property — see also ³NOTICE, PURE RACE, RACE-NOTICE

record owner — see OWNER

record title — see TITLE

re•coup \ri-'küp\ *vt* : RECOVER 1 ⟨would ~ the overpayment from current claims payments — *City of Cordova v. Medicaid Rate Commn.*, 789 P.2d 346 (1990)⟩

re•coup•ment \ri-'küp-mənt\ *n* **1** : the process or fact of recouping ⟨~ of expenses⟩ **2 a** : a keeping back of all or part of a sum sought by a plaintiff in the interest of equity — see also EQUITABLE

RECOUPMENT **b** : a reduction in damages because of a demand by the defendant arising out of the same occurrence or transaction **c** : the right of a defendant to have the claim of the plaintiff reduced or eliminated by reason of a breach of contract or duty by the plaintiff in the same occurrence or transaction; *also* : an affirmative defense alleging such a breach **d** : a counterclaim that arises out of the same occurrence or transaction as that of the original action — compare SET-OFF ◇ Recoupment involves the type of claim that now must be asserted in a compulsory counterclaim.

re•course \'rē-ˌkȯrs, ri-'kȯrs\ *n* **1 a** : the act of turning to someone or something for assistance esp. in obtaining redress **b** : a means to a desired end esp. in the nature of a remedy or justice; *also* : the end itself **2** : the right or ability to demand payment or compensation; *specif* : the right to demand payment from the endorser or drawer of a negotiable instrument — see also *recourse note* at NOTE; compare NON-RECOURSE ◇ Under Article 3 of the Uniform Commercial Code, the phrase *without recourse* on a negotiable instrument limits the liability of the endorser or drawer. If an endorsement states that it is made without recourse, the endorser is not liable to pay, subject to various conditions, if the instrument is dishonored. Similarly, if a draft states that it is drawn without recourse, the drawer is not liable to pay, subject to various conditions, if the draft is dishonored, provided that it is not a check.

recourse note — see NOTE

re•cov•er \ri-'kə-vər\ *vt* **1** : to get back or get back an equivalent for ⟨~ costs through higher prices⟩ **2 a** : to obtain or get back (as damages, satisfaction for a debt, or property) through a judgment or decree ⟨~ damages in a tort action⟩ **b**

\ə\abut \ᵊ\kitten \ər\further \a\ash \ā\ace
\ä\cot, cart \au̇\out \ch\chin \e\bet \ē\easy
\g\go \i\hit \ī\ice \j\job \ŋ\sing \ō\go \ȯ\law
\ȯi\boy \th\thin \t̲h̲\the \ü\loot \u̇\foot \y\yet
\zh\vision *see also* Pronunciation Symbols page

: to obtain (a judgment) in one's favor ~ *vi* **1** : to get something back **2** : to obtain damages or something else through a judgment ⟨argued that the plaintiff should not be permitted to ~⟩

re·cov·er·able \ri-'kə-və-rə-bəl\ *adj* : capable of being recovered esp. as a matter of law — **re·cov·er·abil·i·ty** \-,kə-və-rə-'bi-lə-tē\ *n*

re·cov·ery \ri-'kə-və-rē\ *n, pl* -er·ies **1** : the act, process, or fact of recovering **2 a** : the obtaining, getting back, or vindication of a right or property by judgment or decree; *esp* : the obtaining of damages **b** : an amount awarded by or collected as a result of a judgment or decree

re·cross–ex·am·i·na·tion \'rē-'krȯs-ig-,za-mə-'nā-shən\ *n* : examination of a witness after redirect examination

re·cus·al \ri-'kyü-zəl\ *n* : an act, procedure, or fact of recusing — compare CHALLENGE

re·cu·sant \'re-kyə-zənt, ri-'kyü-\ *adj* : refusing to submit to authority ⟨the ~ witness failed to appear despite a subpoena⟩ — **recusant** *n*

rec·u·sa·tion \,re-kyə-'zā-shən\ *n* : RECUSAL

re·cuse \ri-'kyüz\ *vt* **re·cused; re·cus·ing** [Anglo-French *recuser* to refuse, from Middle French, from Latin *recusare*, from *re-* back + *causari* to give a reason, from *causa* cause, reason] **1** : to challenge or object to (as a judge) as having prejudice or a conflict of interest **2** : to disqualify (as oneself or another judge or official) for a proceeding by a judicial act because of prejudice or conflict of interest ⟨an order *recusing* the district attorney from any proceeding may be appealed by the district attorney or the Attorney General —*California Penal Code*⟩ — **re·cuse·ment** *n*

re·deem \ri-'dēm\ *vt* **1 a** : REPURCHASE **b** : to repurchase by right and not on the open market ⟨~ preferred shares⟩ **2 a** : to free from a lien or pledge usu. by payment of the amount secured thereby ⟨~ collateral⟩ **b** : to exercise an equity of redemption in (real property) by payment in full

of a mortgage debt after default but prior to a foreclosure becoming effective ⟨a right to ~ property prior to the actual sale under a judgment of foreclosure —*Bowery Sav. Bank v. Harbert Offset Corp.*, 558 N.Y.S.2d 821 (1990)⟩ — see also EQUITY OF REDEMPTION **c** : to exercise a right of redemption in (real property) within the period set by law by a repurchase that voids the effect of foreclosure or sale — see also RIGHT OF REDEMPTION ◊ A mortgagor with a right of redemption might redeem property within the set period following a foreclosure sale by paying the new purchaser the purchase price, interest, taxes, and lawful charges. **d** : to remove the obligation of by payment (as at maturity) ⟨~ a bond⟩ **3 a** : to present and have redeemed **b** : to exchange for something of value ~ *vi* : to redeem something (as real property) ⟨failed to exercise its equity of redemption, and this part of the right to ~ was therefore cut off —*Hausman v. Dayton*, 653 N.E.2d 1190 (1995)⟩

re·deem·able *adj* : capable of being redeemed; *specif* : subject to redemption before maturity or after a specified time and usu. with payment of an added premium ⟨a ~ bond⟩ ⟨~ preferred stock⟩

re·demp·tion \ri-'demp-shən\ *n* : the act, process, or fact of redeeming — see also EQUITY OF REDEMPTION, RIGHT OF REDEMPTION — **re·demp·tive** \-'demp-tiv\ *adj*

re·demp·tion·er \ri-'demp-shə-nər\ *n* : one that redeems; *specif* : one that redeems real property under equity of redemption or right of redemption

red her·ring \,red-'her-iŋ\ *n* [*red herring* something that distracts attention from the main issue, diversion] : a preliminary prospectus (as for the sale of securities) that is not yet approved by the appropriate body (as the Securities and Exchange Commission)

red·hi·bi·tion \,re-də-'bi-shən, ,red-hə-\ *n* [French *rédhibition*, from Latin *redhibitio* return of defective goods to the seller, from *redhibēre* to return (defective goods), from *red-* back + *habēre* to hold, have] *in the civil law of Louisiana* : the rescission of the sale of or a reduction in the purchase price of a thing that has a redhibitory defect; *also* : the action for such a rescission or reduction

red·hib·i·to·ry \red-'hi-bə-ˌtōr-ē\ *adj, in the civil law of Louisiana* : of, relating to, or being redhibition ⟨a ~ action⟩

redhibitory defect *n, in the civil law of Louisiana* : a defect that renders a thing useless or so diminishes its usefulness or value that it must be presumed that the buyer would not have bought it or would have paid a lesser price if aware of the defect ⟨a seller is deemed to know that the thing he sells has a *redhibitory defect* when he is a manufacturer of that thing — *Louisiana Civil Code*⟩ — called also *redhibitory vice* ◊ A seller that knows of a redhibitory defect but omits to declare it, or that declares the thing to have a quality he or she knows it does not, is liable for return of the purchase price with interest and for damages, other expenses, and reasonable attorney's fees. The seller may, however, be allowed credit for value resulting from the use or fruits of the thing.

re·di·rect examination \ˌrē-də-'rekt-, -ˌdī-\ *n* : examination of a witness again after cross-examination

re·dis·trict \ˌrē-'dis-trikt\ *vt* : to divide anew into districts; *specif* : to revise the legislative districts of ~ *vi* : to revise legislative districts

red·lin·ing \'red-ˌlī-niŋ\ *n* **1** : the illegal and discriminatory practice of refusing to lend to or insure people in a particular area (as a slum) **2** : the practice of showing changes to a draft of a document by marking with red lines

re·dress \ri-'dres, 'rē-ˌdres\ *n* **1 a** : relief from distress **b** : a means of obtaining a remedy **2** : compensation (as damages) for wrong or loss — **re·dress** \ri-'dres\ *vt*

re·duce \ri-'düs, -'dyüs\ *vt* **re·duced; re·duc·ing 1** : to make smaller **2 a** : to convert (a chose in action) into a chose in possession ⟨enforcement action sought

to ~ to possession her property interest in the . . . determination of money damages — *Haynes v. Contat*, 643 N.E.2d 941 (1994)⟩ **b** : to convert by enforcement through litigation ⟨may ~ his claim to judgment, foreclose or otherwise enforce the security interest — *Uniform Commercial Code*⟩ — **re·duc·ibil·i·ty** \-ˌdü-sə-'bi-lə-tē, -ˌdyü-\ *n* — **re·duc·ible** \-'dü-sə-bəl, -'dyü-\ *adj* — **re·duc·ibly** *adv* — **re·duc·tion** \ri-'dək-shən\ *n* — **reduce to practice** : to cause to undergo reduction to practice

reduction to practice : the process of demonstrating that an invention works correctly for its desired purpose ◊ Under federal patent law reduction to practice is taken into account in establishing priority of invention.

re·en·try \ˌrē-'en-trē\ *n* : a retaking possession of property by a lessor or grantor in exercise of the right to do so upon the failure of the lessee or grantee to fulfill a covenant or condition — see also *power of termination* at POWER 2b

re·exam·ine \ˌrē-ig-'za-mən\ *vt* : to examine again

re·fer \ri-'fər\ *vt* **re·ferred; re·fer·ring** : to send or direct for treatment, aid, service, information, or decision ⟨*referred* the debtor to an attorney with expertise in bankruptcy⟩; *specif* : COMMIT 1c

ref·er·ee \ˌre-fə-'rē\ *n* : an officer appointed by a court or quasi-judicial body (as a workers' compensation board) to investigate a case, report findings, and often to make orders subject to review ⟨the board may affirm, reverse, modify or supplement the order of the ~ — *Oregon Revised Statutes*⟩

ref·er·ence \'re-frəns, -fə-rəns\ *n* **1** : an act of referring; *specif* : mention or citation of one document (as a statute) in another ⟨a municipality may adopt by ~ all or a part of this title — *Alaska Statutes*⟩ — see

\ə\abut \ᵊ\kitten \ər\further \a\ash \ā\ace \ä\cot, cart \au̇\out \ch\chin \e\bet \ē\easy \g\go \i\hit \ī\ice \j\job \ŋ\sing \ō\go \ȯ\law \ȯi\boy \th\thin \t͟h\the \ü\loot \u̇\foot \y\yet \zh\vision *see also* Pronunciation Symbols page

also INCORPORATE **2 :** a referral esp. to a legislative committee or master; *also* **:** an order referring a matter to a master ⟨evidence upon all matters embraced in the ~ —*Federal Rules of Civil Procedure* Rule 53(c)⟩

ref•er•en•dum \ˌrə-fə-'ren-dəm\ *n, pl* **-da** \-də\ *or* **-dums** [New Latin, from Latin, neuter of *referendus*, gerundive of *referre* to refer] **:** the submission to popular vote of a measure passed on or proposed by a legislative body or by popular initiative; *also* **:** the popular vote on a measure so submitted

re•fer•ral \ri-'fər-əl\ *n* **:** the act or an instance of referring ⟨appealed the ~ of the bill to the Ways and Means committee⟩

re•fi•nance \ˌrē-fə-'nans, -'fī-ˌnans\ *vt* **1 :** to renew or reorganize the financing of **2 :** to revise the terms of (a debt obligation) esp. in regard to interest rate or payment schedule ⟨~ a mortgage⟩ ~ *vi* **:** to finance something anew

re•form \ri-'fòrm\ *vt* **1 :** to put (a writing) into a corrected form that more accurately reflects the agreement of the parties ⟨allows a writing signed by mistake to be ~*ed* —W. M. McGovern, Jr. *et al.*⟩ — compare RATIFY **2 :** to induce or cause to abandon wrongful or harmful ways ⟨a ~*ed* drug dealer⟩ ~ *vi* **:** to become changed for the better

ref•or•ma•tion \ˌre-fər-'mā-shən\ *n* **:** the act or an instance of reforming; *specif* **:** the equitable remedy of reforming a writing (as a deed or contract) and enforcing it as reformed ◊ Reformation is allowed primarily to correct mistakes such as typographical errors or incorrectly chosen words. Occasionally reformation is permitted in cases of fraud or misrepresentation. Clear and convincing evidence of the mistake and of the intended agreement is usu. required; sometimes parol evidence is sufficient to establish the agreement. This remedy is not applicable to wills.

re•for•ma•to•ry \ri-'fòr-mə-ˌtòr-ē\ *n, pl* **-ries :** a penal institution to which esp.

young or first offenders are committed for training and reformation

reform school *n* **:** a reformatory for boys or girls

ref•u•gee \ˌre-fyù-'jē\ *n* **:** an individual seeking refuge or asylum; *esp* **:** an individual who has left his or her native country and is unwilling or unable to return to it because of persecution or fear of persecution (as because of race, religion, membership in a particular social group, or political opinion)

refund annuity — see ANNUITY

Reg. *abbr* **1** regulation **2** register

re•gime \rā-'zhēm, ri-\ *n* **:** a system of principles, rules, or regulations for administration (as of property) ⟨the mandatory consecutive sentencing ~ —*People v. Garcia*, 642 N.E.2d 1077 (1994)⟩ ⟨community property ~⟩ — used esp. in the civil law of Louisiana ◊ Under the Louisiana Civil Code there are various regimes for various types of property, such as community or separate property. These regimes, while usu. established by the law, may also be modified or created by agreement of the parties.

¹reg•is•ter \'re-jə-stər\ *n* [Anglo-French *registre*, from Medieval Latin *registrum*, alteration of Late Latin *regesta*, pl., register, from Latin, neuter plural of *regestus*, past participle of *regerere* to bring back, pile up, collect] **1 :** a written record containing regular entries of items or details; *specif* **:** POLICE REGISTER **2 a :** a book or system of public records (as titles or patents) **b :** a roster of qualified or available individuals **c :** the formal record maintained by a corporation of the names and addresses of holders of its registered securities **3 :** REGISTRY **4** [probably alteration of Middle English *registrer* registrar] **:** REGISTRAR

²register *vb* **-tered; -ter•ing** *vt* **1 :** to make or secure official entry of in a register ⟨~ a car⟩ ⟨~ a title⟩ **2 :** to enroll formally esp. as a voter or student **3 :** to secure special protection for (a piece of mail) by prepayment of a fee ~ *vi* **1 :** to enroll one's name in a register **2 :** to enroll one's name officially as a prerequisite for voting

registered bond — see BOND 2

registered security — see SECURITY

reg·is·tra·ble \'re-jə-strə-bəl\ *also* **reg·is·ter·able** \-stə-rə-bəl\ *adj* : capable of being registered

reg·is·trant \'re-jə-strənt\ *n* : a person who registers or is registered

reg·is·trar \'re-jə-ˌsträr\ *n* : an official recorder or keeper of records

reg·is·tra·tion \ˌre-jə-'strā-shən\ *n* **1** : the act of registering **2** : an entry in a register **3** : a document certifying an act of registering

registration statement *n* : a detailed public disclosure of the terms and conditions of a public offering of a new issue of stock by a corporation ◊ A registration statement is required by the Securities and Exchange Commission before new shares may be offered for sale to the public. It includes, among other things, information about a corporation's capital structure, its financial condition and operations, and the personal relationships of the directors and officers of the company to the issuer. A condensed version of the registration certificate serves as a prospectus.

reg·is·try \'re-jə-strē\ *n, pl* **-tries 1** : REGISTRATION ⟨an instrument filed for ~ in the conveyance records —*Louisiana Civil Code*⟩ **2** : the nationality of a ship according to its entry in a register **3** : a place of registration : a place where official records and documents are kept ⟨the ~ of motor vehicles⟩ ⟨~ of deeds⟩

reg·u·lar income *n* : income (as wages or pension benefits) that is received at fixed or uniform intervals

regular session *n* : a session (as of a court) that is designated to happen at fixed intervals or specified times

reg·u·late *vt* **-lat·ed; -lat·ing 1** : to govern or direct according to rule **2 a** : to bring under the control of law **b** : to make regulations for or concerning

reg·u·la·tion *n* **1** : the act of regulating or state of being regulated **2** : an authori-

tative rule; *specif* : a rule or order issued by a government agency and often having the force of law — see also *Administrative Procedure Act* in the IMPORTANT LAWS section ◊ An agency is often delegated the power to issue regulations by the legislation that created it. Regulations must be made in accordance with prescribed procedures, such as those set out in the federal or a state Administrative Procedure Act. Federal regulations are first published in the *Federal Register* and later codified in the *Code of Federal Regulations*.

Regulation D \-'dē\ *n* : a regulation of the Securities and Exchange Commission governing the limited offer and sale (as by a private offering) of unregistered securities

Regulation J \-'jā\ *n* : a regulation of the Board of Governors of the Federal Reserve System governing the collection of checks and other cash and noncash items and the handling of returned checks by Federal Reserve banks

Regulation Q \-'kyü\ *n* : a regulation of the Board of Governors of the Federal Reserve System prohibiting member banks from paying interest on demand deposits

Regulation T \-'tē\ *n* : a regulation of the Board of Governors of the Federal Reserve System regulating the extension of credit by and to securities brokers and dealers and imposing initial margin requirements and payment rules on securities transactions

Regulation U \-'yü\ *n* : a regulation of the Board of Governors of the Federal Reserve System imposing credit restrictions on banks that extend credit for the purpose of buying or carrying margin stock if the credit is secured directly or indirectly by margin stock

Regulation X \-'eks\ *n* : a regulation of the Department of Housing and Urban

\ə\abut \ᵊ\kitten \ər\further \a\ash \ā\ace
\ä\cot, cart \aú\out \ch\chin \e\bet \ē\easy
\g\go \i\hit \ī\ice \j\job \ŋ\sing \ō\go \ó\law
\ói\boy \th\thin \t̲h̲\the \ü\loot \ú\foot \y\yet
\zh\vision   *see also* Pronunciation Symbols page

Development that implements the Real Estate Settlement Procedures Act

Regulation Z \-'zē\ *n* : a regulation of the Board of Governors of the Federal Reserve System that implements the federal Truth in Lending Act as to member banks

reg·u·la·tor \'re-gyə-ˌlā-tər\ *n* : one (as a government agency) that regulates

reg·u·la·to·ry \'re-gyə-lə-ˌtōr-ē\ *adj* **1** : of or relating to regulation **2** : making or concerned with making regulations

regulatory agency — see AGENCY 4

regulatory offense *n* : a violation of a regulation that is not part of a criminal code and that carries the punishment of a fine or imprisonment : ADMINISTRATIVE CRIME — called also *regulatory crime*

regulatory search — see SEARCH

regulatory taking *n* : an appropriation or diminution of private property rights by a governmental regulation which exceeds the government's legitimate police power (as the power to enact safety regulations) and for which the owner may seek a writ of mandamus, declaratory relief, or just compensation (as by inverse condemnation) — compare PHYSICAL TAKING, ZONING ◊ In order to determine whether a regulatory taking is effected by a regulation, a court will consider the government's interest that is being furthered by the regulation, the breadth or specificity of the regulation, and the extent of the regulation's impact on the owner's property rights and expectations. The U.S. Supreme Court has held that an owner can bring an action for compensation when the taking has deprived the owner of all use of the property even temporarily. Otherwise, the owner may be entitled only to declaratory relief.

reh *abbr* rehearing

re·ha·bil·i·tate \ˌrē-ə-'bi-lə-ˌtāt, ˌrē-hə-\ *vt* **-tat·ed; -tat·ing 1** : to restore to a former capacity; *specif* : to restore credibility to (a witness or testimony) ⟨the State simply brought out all of the prior statements to qualify or explain the inconsistency and to ~ the witness — *People v. Page*, 550 N.E.2d 248 (1990)⟩ —

compare IMPEACH ◊ A witness whose trial testimony is inconsistent with his or her pretrial usu. sworn statements is considered impeached. Such a witness may be rehabilitated usu. on redirect examination. There are various state and federal evidentiary rules governing what evidence (as character evidence) is admissible to rehabilitate a witness. **2 a** : to restore to a former state (as of good repair or solvency) ⟨if the debtor wishes to liquidate rather than reorganize or ~ the farming operation — J. H. Williamson⟩ **b** : to restore (as a convicted criminal defendant) to a useful and constructive place in society through therapy, job training, and other counseling — **re·ha·bil·i·ta·tion** \-ˌbi-lə-'tā-shən\ *n*

re·hear \ˌrē-'hir\ *vt* **-heard** \-'hərd\; **-hear·ing** : to consider again or anew after decision or dismissal in the same or another forum : hold an additional hearing about ⟨would defer to an arbitrator's decision without ~*ing* the matter — M. A. Kelly⟩

re·hear·ing \ˌrē-'hir-iŋ\ *n* : a reconsideration of a cause (as an appeal) after final decision or dismissal usu. by the same tribunal that is usu. granted due to some error in the original hearing and that may encompass new matters (as evidence or issues)

reh'g *abbr* rehearing

re·im·burse \ˌrē-əm-'bərs\ *vt* **-bursed; -burs·ing 1** : to pay back (a sum lost or expended) to someone ⟨will ~ the court costs⟩ **2** : to make restoration or payment of an equivalent to ⟨~ the employee for travel expenses⟩ — **re·im·burse·ment** *n*

re·in·scribe \ˌrē-in-'skrīb\ *vt, in the civil law of Louisiana* : to inscribe (as a mortgage) again esp. after expiration of the period of inscription (as ten years) ◊ A recorded mortgage or document creating a privilege is reinscribed by filing a notice of reinscription with the recorder. — **re·in·scrip·tion** \-'skrip-shən\ *n*

re·in·sur·ance \ˌrē-ən-'shur-əns, -'in-ˌshur-\ *n* : insurance or indemnification by a second insurer of all or part of a risk assumed by another insurer as contracted for by the first insurer — see also CEDE; compare DIRECT INSURANCE, RETROCESSION 3

re·in·sure \ˌrē-ən-'shu̇r\ *vt* : to insure again : transfer or assume (liability) through reinsurance ⟨frequently ~ part of their exposure —R. I. Mehr⟩

re·in·sur·er \ˌrē-ən-'shu̇r-ər\ *n* : an insurance company that insures all or part of the liability of another insurance company

re·in·vest \ˌrē-ən-'vest\ *vt* **1** : to invest again or anew **2 a** : to invest (as income from investments) in additional securities **b** : to invest (as earnings) in a business rather than distribute as dividends or profits

re·is·sue patent \ˌrē-'i-ˌshü-, -'is-ˌyü-\ *n* : a patent that is issued to fix defects (as invalid claims) of an original patent and that replaces and is granted for the remainder of the term of the original patent

REIT *abbr* real estate investment trust

re·ject \ri-'jekt\ *vt* : to refuse to accept, acknowledge, or grant — compare REVOKE

re·jec·tion \ri-'jek-shən\ *n* : the act or an instance of rejecting: as **a** : a refusal to accept an offer **b** : a refusal to accept nonconforming goods as performance of a contract ◊ Rejection and revocation are two remedies available to the buyer under the Uniform Commercial Code after the delivery of defective goods. Goods may be rejected if they do not conform to the contract. The rejection must be made within a reasonable period after delivery, before the goods have been accepted, and notice of the rejection must be given to the seller. Acceptance of the goods can be revoked if a defect substantially impairing their value to the buyer is discovered after acceptance, but such revocation must be made within a reasonable period after the buyer has discovered, or should have discovered, the defect.

re·join·der \ri-'jȯin-dər\ *n* [Anglo⸗ French, from *rejoindre, rejoinder* to make rejoinder, literally, to join again, meet, from Old French, from *re-* again

+ *joindre* to join] : an answer to a reply; *specif* : the defendant's answer to the plaintiff's reply or replication under common-law pleading

re·late back *vi* **re·lat·ed back; re·lat·ing back** : to apply or take effect retroactively esp. based on relation back ⟨the amendment *relates back* to the date of the original pleading —*Federal Rules of Civil Procedure* Rule 15(c)⟩

re·la·tion back *n* : the assigning of a prior date (as the date of execution of a document) to an act (as filing of a document and esp. a pleading) as the time of its effect esp. to avoid a time limit ⟨the *relation back* of amendments to the date of the original pleading⟩; *also* : the legal fiction that an action (as the filing of a document) was taken on a previous date to avoid the expiration of a time limit

rel·a·tive *adj* **1** : not absolute **2** *in the civil law of Louisiana* : having or allowing some legal effect ⟨a ~ impediment⟩ ⟨a ~ simulation⟩ — see also *relative nullity* at NULLITY — **rel·a·tive·ly** *adv*

relative nullity — see NULLITY

re·la·tor \rē-'lā-tər\ *n* : a party other than the plaintiff upon whose information, knowledge, or relation of facts an action is brought when the right to bring the action is vested in another: as **a** : the private person who brings a qui tam action **b** : a party who has standing and on whose behalf a writ (as of mandamus) is petitioned for by the state as plaintiff ⟨~ then filed . . . a petition in prohibition requesting this court to prohibit respondents from transferring the funds —*State ex rel. Tate v. Turner*, 789 S.W.2d 240 (1990)⟩ — see also EX RELATIONE

¹re·lease *vt* **re·leased; re·leas·ing 1 a** : to relieve or free from obligation, liability, or responsibility ⟨the debtor is *released* from all dischargeable debts⟩ **b** : to give up (a claim, title, or right) to the benefit

\ə\abut \ᵊ\kitten \ər\further \a\ash \ā\ace
\ä\cot, cart \au̇\out \ch\chin \e\bet \ē\easy
\g\go \i\hit \ī\ice \j\job \ŋ\sing \ō\go \ȯ\law
\ȯi\boy \th\thin \t̲h̲\the \ü\loot \u̇\foot \y\yet
\zh\vision *see also* Pronunciation Symbols page

of another person : SURRENDER **2** : to set free from confinement ⟨was *released* on personal recognizance⟩

²release *n* **1 a** : discharge from an obligation or responsibility that bars a cause of action ⟨did not effect a ~ of the school for any negligence⟩ **b** : the giving up or renunciation of a right or claim that bars a cause of action ⟨was a ~ of the remainder of the debt⟩ ◊ A release may in some situations require consideration in order to be valid. A release of one joint obligor sometimes is considered to release all the obligors. **2** : an act or instrument that effects a release ⟨signed a ~ issued by the insurer⟩ — called also *release of all claims;* compare HOLD HARMLESS **3** : the act or instance of freeing esp. from custody

rel•e•vance \'re-lə-vəns\ *n* : the quality or state of being relevant : relation to the matter at hand ⟨ruled on the ~ of the testimony⟩ ⟨~ in discovery has been broadly interpreted⟩

rel•e•van•cy \'re-lə-vən-sē\ *n, pl* **-cies** : RELEVANCE

rel•e•vant \'re-lə-vənt\ *adj* **1** : tending logically to prove or disprove a fact of consequence or to make the fact more or less probable and thereby aiding the trier of fact in making a decision ⟨determined that the evidence was ~⟩; *also* : having a bearing on or reasonably calculated to lead to a matter that bears on any issue in a case for purposes of pretrial discovery — see also *relevant evidence* at EVIDENCE **2** : having significant and demonstrable bearing on facts or issues ⟨was not a ~ case⟩

relevant evidence — see EVIDENCE

re•li•ance \ri-'lī-əns\ *n* **1** : the act of relying ⟨~ on a promise⟩ **2** : RELIANCE INTEREST at INTEREST 1

reliance interest — see INTEREST 1

re•lic•tion \ri-'lik-shən\ *n* [Latin *relictio* act of leaving behind, from *relinquere* to leave behind] **1** : the gradual recession of water leaving land permanently uncovered **2** : land uncovered by reliction — compare ACCRETION

re•lief *n* : redress, assistance, or protection given by law esp. from a court ⟨should state what ~ the plaintiff seeks⟩: as **a** : release from obligation or duty ⟨~ from judgment⟩ **b** : an order from a court granting a particular remedy (as return of property) ⟨injunctive ~⟩ ⟨declaratory ~⟩ — see also REMEDY

re•lieve *vt* **re•lieved; re•liev•ing** : to set free from a duty, burden, or liability ⟨cannot be *relieved* of his negligence⟩ ⟨the trust cannot ~ the trustees of those very basic duties that the law imposes — *Hosey v. Burgess,* 890 S.W.2d 262 (1995)⟩

re•lit•i•gate \,rē-'li-tə-,gāt\ *vb* **-gat•ed; -gat•ing** *vt* : to litigate (a case or a matter) again or anew ~ *vi* : to litigate a case or a matter again or anew — **re•lit•i•ga•tion** \-,li-tə-'gā-shən\ *n*

re•ly *vi* **re•lied; re•ly•ing** : to depend with confidence : place faith

re•main•der *n* [Anglo-French, from Old French *remaindre* to remain] **1** : an estate in property in favor of one other than the grantor that follows upon the natural termination of a prior intervening possessory estate (as a life estate) created at the same time and by the same instrument — compare *future interest* at INTEREST 1, REVERSION

charitable remainder : a remainder in favor of a charity

contingent remainder : a remainder that is to take effect in favor of an unidentifiable person (as one not yet born) or upon the occurrence of an uncertain event — called also *executory remainder*

cross remainder : either of two or more remainders in favor of two or more persons so that upon the termination of one remainder that share goes to the other or others

executory remainder : CONTINGENT REMAINDER in this entry

remainder vested subject to open : a vested remainder that is subject to diminution by the shares of other remaindermen (as children born later)

vested remainder : a remainder in the favor of an ascertained person who has a present interest and is entitled to take possession upon the termination of the prior estate **2** : that which remains or is left; *specif* : the property in a decedent's estate that is not otherwise devised or bequeathed ⟨I leave the rest, residue, and ~ of my estate to my son Michael⟩

re·main·der·man \ri-'mān-dər-mən\ *n, pl* **-men** \-₁men, -mən\ : one who has received or is to or may receive a remainder

remainder vested subject to open — see REMAINDER

¹re·mand \ri-'mand\ *vb* [Anglo-French *remander*, from Middle French, to order back, from Late Latin *remandare* to send back word, from Latin *re-* back + *mandare* to order] *vt* **1** : to return (a case or matter) from one court to another esp. lower court or from a court to an administrative agency ⟨the judgment of the trial court is reversed and the cause ~*ed* to the superior court for further proceedings consistent with this opinion —*McCarton v. Estate of Watson*, 693 P.2d 192 (1984)⟩ — compare AFFIRM **2** : to send (an accused) back into custody by court order (as pending trial) : turn (a prisoner) over for continued detention ~ *vi* : to return a case to a lower court or other tribunal ⟨the court ~*ed* for resentencing —K. A. Cohen⟩

²remand *n* **1** : the act of remanding or state of being remanded **2** : an order remanding a case or person

re·me·di·a·ble \ri-'mē-dē-ə-bəl\ *adj* : capable of being remedied — **re·me·di·a·bil·i·ty** \-₁mē-dē-ə-'bi-lə-tē\ *n*

re·me·di·al \ri-'mē-dē-əl\ *adj* **1 a** : intended as or providing a remedy **b** : concerned with the correction, removal, or abatement of an evil, defect, or disease ⟨~ treatment of an inmate to improve behavior⟩ ⟨a workers' compensation claimant who received ~ attention from a doctor⟩ ⟨a ~ statute correcting the previous law⟩ **2** : of, relating to, or being a law ⟨ ⟩ for the purpose of providing a

method of enforcing an already existing substantive right : PROCEDURAL

remedial action *n* : an action taken to effect long-term restoration of environmental quality (as under the Comprehensive Environmental Response, Compensation, and Liability Act) — compare REMOVAL ACTION

re·me·di·ate \ri-'mē-dē-₁āt\ *vt* : to make the target of remedial action ⟨the commissioner of environmental protection . . . shall conduct remedial actions necessary to ~ the pollution at or on the site — *General Statutes of Connecticut*⟩

re·me·di·a·tion \ri-₁mē-dē-'ā-shən\ *n* **1** : the act or process of remedying **2** : the act or process of remediating

¹rem·e·dy *n, pl* **-dies** : the means to enforce a right or to prevent or obtain redress for a wrong : the relief (as damages, restitution, specific performance, or an injunction) that may be given or ordered by a court or other tribunal for a wrong ⟨if the contract is null and void, the ~ is to rescind and to put the parties in the position in which they were prior to the attempted agreement —*First Nat'l Mortgage Corp. v. The Manhattan Life Ins. Co.*, 360 So. 2d 264 (1978)⟩ ⟨specific performance and other equitable *remedies*⟩ — **rem·e·di·less** *adj*

²remedy *vt* **-died; -dy·ing** : to provide or serve as a remedy for

REM·IC \'re-mik\ *n* [real estate mortgage investment conduit] : an entity (as a corporation, partnership, or trust) that functions as a vehicle for investment in mortgage obligations and esp. collateralized mortgage obligations and receives favorable tax treatment by restricting its own investment to the maintenance of cash flow and reserves and to investment in properties acquired from foreclosure on the underlying mortgages — called also *real estate mortgage investment conduit;*

\ə\abut \ᵊ\kitten \ər\further \a\ash \ā\ace
\ä\cot, cart \aů\out \ch\chin \e\bet \ē\easy
\g\go \i\hit \ī\ice \j\job \ŋ\sing \ō\go \ȯ\law
\ȯi\boy \th\thin \th\the \ü\loot \ů\foot \y\yet
\zh\vision *see also* Pronunciation Symbols page

compare *pass-through security* at SECU-
RITY, *real estate investment trust* at
TRUST
re•mise \ri-'mīz\ *vt* re•mised; re•mis•ing
[Middle French *remis*, past participle of
remettre to put back, from Latin *remittere*
to send back] : to give, grant, or release a
claim to
re•mis•sion \ri-'mi-shən\ *n* : the act or
process of remitting
re•mit \ri-'mit\ *vb* re•mit•ted; re•mit•ting
[Latin *remittere* to let go back, send back,
give up, forgive, from *re-* back + *mittere*
to let go, send] *vt* **1 a** : to release from
the guilt or penalty of **b** : to refrain from
exacting ⟨~ a tax⟩ **c** : to cancel or refrain
from inflicting ⟨~ the fine⟩ **2** : to submit or refer for consideration, judgment,
decision, or action; *specif* : REMAND **3**
: to restore or consign to a former status or condition **4** : to send (money) to a
person or place esp. in payment of a demand, account, or draft ~ *vi* : to send
money (as in payment) — re•mit•ment *n*
— re•mit•ta•ble *adj*
re•mit•tance \ri-'mit-ᵊns\ *n* **1 a** : a sum
of money remitted **b** : an instrument by
which money is remitted **2** : transmittal
of money (as to a distant place)
¹re•mit•ter *n* [Anglo-French, from *remitter*
to remit] : REMITTITUR
²remitter *n* : one that remits; *specif* : one
that sends a remittance
re•mit•ti•tur \ri-'mi-tə-tər\ *n* [Latin, it is
sent back, remitted, third person singular
present indicative passive of *remittere* to
send back, remit] **1 a** : a procedure under
which a court may order the reduction of
an excessive verdict; *esp* : a procedure in
which the court requires the plaintiff to
remit the portion of the verdict deemed
excessive in lieu of a grant of a defendant's motion for a new trial or of a reversal if the court is an appellate court **b** : a
remission to a defendant by a plaintiff of
the portion of a verdict considered excessive by the court **c** : the formal agreement
or stipulation of a plaintiff waiving or re-
leasing the right to receive the portion of a
verdict considered excessive — compare

ADDITUR **2** : a sending back of a case and
its record from an appellate or superior
court to a trial or inferior court for further proceedings (as additional findings
of fact) or for entry of a judgment in accordance with instructions or the decision
of the higher court
re•mon•strance \ri-'män-strəns\ *n* : an
earnest presentation of reasons in opposition to something; *specif* : a document
formally stating points of opposition or
grievance
re•mote *adj* re•mot•er; -est **1 a** : far removed in space, time, or relation ⟨ances-
tors of a more ~ degree⟩ **b** : exceeding
the time allowed under the rule against
perpetuities for the vesting of interests
⟨the residuary clause . . . violates the rule
against ~ vesting —*Estate of Grove*, 70
Cal. App. 3d 355 (1977)⟩; *also* : being
in violation of the rule against perpetuities ⟨a ~ contingent estate⟩ **2** : acting,
acted on, or controlled indirectly or from
a distance **3 a** : not proximate or acting
directly **b** : not arising from the effect
of that which is proximate **4** : small in
degree ⟨a ~ possibility of paternity⟩ —
re•mote•ly *adv* — re•mote•ness *n*
remote cause — see CAUSE 1
re•mov•al *n* : the act or process of removing : the fact of being removed
removal action *n* : an action under environmental legislation and esp. under
the Comprehensive Environmental Response, Compensation, and Liability Act
that involves short-term abatement of
pollution (as removal of toxic substances)
— compare REMEDIAL ACTION
re•move \ri-'müv\ *vb* re•moved; re•mov-
ing *vt* : to change the location, position,
station, status, or residence of: as **a** : to
have (an action) transferred from one
court to another and esp. from a state
court to a federal court — see also SEPA-
RABLE CONTROVERSY ◊ Section 1441
et seq. of title 28 of the U.S. Code allows a defendant who is brought into a
state court to remove the action to federal district court when diversity of citizenship exists, when the action involves a

claim or right arising under the U.S. Constitution or under laws or treaties of the U.S., or when the defendant is a foreign country or its agency or instrumentality. Civil actions and criminal prosecutions brought against an officer or agency of the U.S. for any act under color of office may also be removed. **b** : to dismiss from office ⟨an independent counsel . . . may be *removed* from office . . . only by the personal action of the Attorney General —*U.S. Code*⟩ **c** : to take away ⟨should his incapacity be *removed* by a judgment of a court —*Louisiana Civil Code*⟩ — **re·mov·abil·i·ty** \-ˌmü-və-'bi-lə-tē\ *n* — **re·mov·able** *also* **re·move·able** \-'mü-və-bəl\ *adj* — **re·mov·able·ness** *n*

ren·der \'ren-dər\ *vt* **1** : to transmit to another : DELIVER **2** : to furnish for consideration, approval, or information: as **a** : HAND DOWN ⟨~ a judgment⟩ **b** : to agree on and report (a verdict) — compare ENTER **3** : to give in acknowledgment of dependence or obligation : make payment of **4** : to direct the execution of ⟨~ justice⟩ — **ren·der·able** *adj*

ren·di·tion \ren-'di-shən\ *n* **1** : the act or result of rendering ⟨the Court's ~ of judgment⟩ **2** : extradition of a fugitive who has fled to another state

rendition warrant — see WARRANT

re·ne·go·tia·ble \ˌrē-ni-'gō-shə-bəl, -shē-ə-\ *adj* : capable of being renegotiated : subject to renegotiation

re·ne·go·ti·ate \ˌrē-ni-'gō-shē-ˌāt\ *vt* : to negotiate again (as for more money or to adjust interest rates or repayments); *specif* : to determine under statutory procedure the existence and amount of excess profits on (a government contract) in order to eliminate or obtain a refund of such profits ~ *vi* : to negotiate again; *specif* : to adjust a government project price in order to eliminate or recover excessive profits — **re·ne·go·ti·a·tion** \-ni-ˌgō-shē-'ā-shən, -ˌgō-sē-\ *n*

re·new \ri-'nü, -'nyü\ *vt* **1** : to make like new : restore to freshness, vigor, or perfection; *specif* : to prevent the lapse of (a

judgment) due to expiration of a statute of limitations **2** : to do or state again ⟨~*ed* his objection to the evidence⟩ **3** : to grant or obtain again or as an extension ⟨~ a lease⟩ ~ *vi* **1** : to become new or as new **2** : to make a renewal (as of a contract) — **re·new·abil·i·ty** \-ˌnü-ə-'bi-lə-tē, -ˌnyü-\ *n* — **re·new·able** \-'nü-ə-bəl, -'nyü-\ *adj*

re·new·al /ri-'nü-əl, -'nyü-/ *n* **1** : the act or process of renewing ⟨a ~ of the copyright⟩ **2** : the quality or state of being renewed **3** : something renewed **4** : something used for renewing; *specif* : expenditure that betters existing fixed assets **5** : the rebuilding of a large area (as of a city) by a public authority

renewal note — see NOTE

re·nounce \ri-'naúns\ *vb* **re·nounced; re·nounc·ing** *vt* **1** : to announce one's abandonment or giving up of a right to or interest in : DISCLAIM 1 ⟨~ an inheritance⟩ **2** : to refuse to follow, obey, or recognize any further ⟨~ allegiance to one's country⟩ ~ *vi* : to make a renunciation

¹rent *n* **1 a** : a return made by a tenant or occupant of real property to the owner for possession and use thereof; *esp* : a sum of money agreed upon between a landlord and tenant for the use of real property **b** *in the civil law of Louisiana* : a contract by which one party conveys to another to hold as owner a tract of land or other immovable property in perpetuity in exchange for payment of an annual sum or quantity of fruits **c** : the amount paid by a hirer of personal property to the owner for the use thereof **d** : a royalty under a mineral lease **2** : the portion of the income of an economy (as of a nation) attributable to land as a factor of production in addition to capital and labor — **for rent** : available for use or service in return for payment

²rent *vt* **1** : to grant the possession and enjoyment of in exchange for rent **2** : to take and hold under an agreement to pay rent

\ə\abut \ᵊ\kitten \ər\further \a\ash \ā\ace
\ä\cot, cart \aú\out \ch\chin \e\bet \ē\easy
\g\go \i\hit \ī\ice \j\job \ŋ\sing \ō\go \ò\law
\òi\boy \th\thin \t͟h\the \ü\loot \ú\foot \y\yet
\zh\vision *see also* Pronunciation Symbols page

~ *vi* **1** : to be for rent **2 a** : to obtain use and possession of a place or property in exchange for rent **b** : to allow the possession and use of property in exchange for rent — **rent·er** *also* **ren·tor** \'ren-tər\ *n*

¹rent·al *n* **1** : an amount paid or collected as rent **2** : something that is rented **3** : an act of renting **4** : a business that rents something

²rental *adj* **1 a** : of or relating to rent **b** : available for rent ⟨~ property⟩ **2** : dealing in rental property ⟨a ~ agency⟩

rent control *n* : government regulation of the amount charged as rent for housing and often also of eviction — **rent–con·trolled** *adj*

ren·tier \rän-'tyā, 'rän-ˌtyä\ *n* [French, from *rente* income from a property, rent] : a person who lives on income from property or securities

rent strike *n* : a refusal by a group of tenants to pay rent (as in protest against high rates)

re·nun·ci·a·tion \ri-ˌnən-sē-'ā-shən\ *n* : the act or practice of renouncing; *specif* : the act of refusing to continue to acknowledge, recognize, or be bound by a contract or obligation : REPUDIATION

ren·voi \ren-'voi\ *n* [French, act of sending back, reference, from Middle French, from *renvoyer* to send back] : the reference of a matter involving a conflict of laws to the law of the foreign jurisdiction involved including reference to the jurisdiction's rules governing conflicts of laws — compare WHOLE LAW

re·open \ˌrē-'ō-pən\ *vt* **1** : to take up again ⟨~ discussion⟩ **2** : to resume the discussion or consideration of (a closed matter) ⟨~ the contract to negotiate benefits⟩ **3** : to try or hear (an action) anew esp. for the purpose of hearing new evidence

re·open·er \ˌrē-'ō-pə-nər\ *n* : REOPENING CLAUSE

re·open·ing clause \ˌrē-'ō-pə-niŋ-\ *n* : a clause in a collective bargaining agreement providing for reconsideration of an issue (as wages) during the life of the agreement

reorg. *abbr* reorganization

re·or·ga·ni·za·tion \ˌrē-ˌòr-gə-nə-'zā-shən\ *n* **1** : the act of reorganizing : the state of being reorganized **2 a** : the rehabilitation of the finances of a business in accordance with a plan approved by a bankruptcy court under the provisions of chapter 11 of the Bankruptcy Code **b** : any of various procedures (as recapitalization or merger) that affect the tax structure of a corporation under the Internal Revenue Code and often produce favorable tax treatment

A reorganization \'ā-\ : a reorganization that consists of a merger or consolidation which complies with the requirements of applicable state statute

B reorganization \'bē-\ : a reorganization involving the acquisition by one corporation of the stock of another corporation in exchange solely for all or some of the voting stock of the acquiring corporation or its parent either of which has control of the acquired corporation immediately after the acquisition

C reorganization \'sē-\ : a reorganization involving the acquisition by one corporation of substantially all of the property of another corporation in exchange solely for all or part of the voting stock of the acquiring corporation or its parent regardless of any liability assumed by the acquiring corporation as a result of the acquisition

D reorganization \'dē-\ : a reorganization involving a transfer by a corporation of all or part of its assets to another corporation that results in control of the other corporation being immediately placed in the transferor or one or more of its shareholders or both but under which the stock or securities of the other corporation must be distributed in a qualified transaction — see also SPIN-OFF, SPLIT-OFF, SPLIT-UP

E reorganization \'ē-\ : a reorganization that consists of a recapitalization

F reorganization \'ef-\ : a reorganization consisting merely of a change in the identity, form, or place of organization of a corporation

G reorganization \\'jē-\ : a reorganization involving a transfer by a corporation of all or part of its assets to another corporation under a bankruptcy or similar proceeding provided that the stock or securities of the other corporation are distributed in a qualified transaction **3** : alteration of the existing structure of governmental units (as bureaus or legislative committees) and the lines of control and authority between them usu. to promote greater efficiency and responsibility

reorganization plan *n* : a plan submitted for approval to a bankruptcy court by a corporation seeking to reorganize under chapter 11 of the Bankruptcy Code that sets out the proposed restructuring

re•or•ga•nize \ˌrē-'ȯr-gə-ˌnīz\ *vb* **-nized; -niz•ing** *vt* : to rearrange the plan or structure of : organize again or anew; *specif* : to cause (a business) to undergo a reorganization ~ *vi* : to reorganize something

rep. *abbr* **1** report, reporter **2** representative **3** republic

rep•a•ra•tion \ˌre-pə-'rā-shən\ *n* **1 a** : the act of making amends, offering expiation, or giving satisfaction for a wrong or injury **b** : something done or given as amends or satisfaction **2** : the payment of damages; *specif* : compensation in money or materials payable by a defeated nation for damages to or expenditures sustained by another nation as a result of hostilities with the defeated nation — usu. used in pl.

re•peal \ri-'pēl\ *vt* [Anglo-French *repeler*, from Old French, from *re-* back + *apeler* to appeal, call, from Latin *appellare* to address, entreat, call by name] : to rescind or annul by authoritative act; *esp* : to revoke or abrogate by legislative enactment ⟨legislatures ~*ing* statutes in light of a recent Supreme Court decision⟩ — **repeal** *n*

re•peal•er *n* : a legislative act or clause in an act that repeals an earlier act

re•peal•ing clause *n* : a clause in a statute repealing a previous enactment

re•peat offender *n* : a person who has been convicted of a crime on more than one occasion

re•pel•lent \ri-'pe-lənt\ *n* : a method used to avoid or discourage a hostile corporate takeover

re•place•ment *n* **1 a** : the act of replacing : the state of being replaced **b** : an insurer's option under a policy to replace or repair damaged property rather than pay the insured for the loss **2** : something that replaces; *specif* : a new fixed asset or portion of an asset that takes the place of one discarded (as because of deterioration)

replacement cost *n* : the cost of replacing property with property of like kind and equal quality or effectiveness

¹**re•plev•in** \ri-'ple-vən\ *n* [Anglo-French *replevine*, from *replevir* to give security, from Old French, to give security for, from *re-* back + *plevir* to pledge] : an action originating in common law and now largely codified by which a plaintiff having a right in personal property claimed to be wrongfully taken or detained by the defendant seeks to recover possession of the property and sometimes to obtain damages for the wrongful detention; *also* : a procedure allowing the plaintiff as a provisional remedy to take possession of the property prior to judgment on the action ◊ Under section 2-716 of the Uniform Commercial Code, a buyer who is a party to a contract that has been breached by the seller has a right of replevin for goods that are identified to the contract if cover cannot reasonably be effected.

²**replevin** *vt* : REPLEVY

replevin bond — see BOND 1a

re•plev•i•sor \ri-'ple-və-sər, -ˌsȯr\ *n* : the plaintiff in a replevin action

¹**re•plevy** \ri-'ple-vē\ *n, pl* **re•plev•ies** : REPLEVIN

²**replevy** *vt* **re•plev•ied; re•plevy•ing** [probably from Anglo-French *replevi*, past participle of *replevir* to give secu-

rity, from Old French, to give security for, from *re-* back + *plevir* to pledge] : to take or get back by replevin — **re·plev·i·able** \ri-ˈple-vē-ə-bəl\ *adj*

rep·li·ca·tion \ˌre-plə-ˈkā-shən\ *n* [Anglo⸗ French, from Middle French, from Late Latin *replicatio*, from Latin, action of folding back, from *replicare* to fold back] : REPLY

re·ply *n* : a plaintiff's or complainant's response to a plea, allegation, or counterclaim in the defendant's answer

reply brief *n* : a brief that is filed with the plaintiff's reply and that sets forth the arguments in support thereof

re·po \ˈrē-ˌpō\ *n, pl* **repos** **1** : REPURCHASE AGREEMENT **2** : REPOSSESSION

¹re·port *n* : a usu. detailed account or statement: as **a** : an account or statement of the facts of a case heard and of the decision and opinion of the court or of a quasi⸗ judicial tribunal determining the case **b** : a written submission of a question of law (as by a lower court) to an appellate court for review before final decision is entered **c** : a usu. formal and sometimes official statement giving the conclusions and recommendations of a person (as a master) or group (as a legislative committee) authorized or delegated to consider a matter or proposal ⟨the committee made an unfavorable ∼ on the bill⟩ **d** : a usu. formal account of the results of an investigation given by a person or group delegated or authorized to make the investigation **e** : an analysis of operations and progress and a statement of future plans made at stated intervals by an administrator or executive or group of executives to those to whom such a report is owed ⟨the board of directors issued its annual ∼ to the stockholders⟩

²report *vt* **1 a** : to make a written record or summary of ⟨∼ a case⟩ **b** : to make a shorthand record of **2 a** : to give a formal or official account or statement of **b** : to return or present (a matter officially referred for consideration) with conclusions or recommendations; *specif* : REPORT OUT **c** : to announce or relate as

the result of a special search, examination, or investigation **d** : to make known to the proper authorities ⟨∼ed the fire⟩ **e** : to make a charge of misconduct against ⟨∼ed him for harassment⟩ — *vi* **1** : to present oneself ⟨∼ed for jury duty⟩ **2** : to make, issue, submit, or present a report ⟨the committee will ∼ this afternoon⟩

re·port·able *adj* : required by law to be reported ⟨∼ income⟩

re·port·er *n* : one that reports: as **a** : one who makes authorized statements and publications of court decisions or legislative proceedings; *also* : a publication in which such reports are reproduced — see also CITATION; compare ADVANCE SHEET **b** : one who makes a shorthand record of a speech or proceeding; *specif* : COURT REPORTER

reporter's privilege — see PRIVILEGE 1b

re·port·ing pay *n* : payment made to a worker who reports for work without having previously been told that no work is available

report out *vt* : to return after consideration and often with revisions to a legislative body for action ⟨after much debate the committee *reported* the bill *out*⟩

re·pos·sess \ˌrē-pə-ˈzes\ *vt* : to regain possession of; *esp* : to take possession of again by judicial process or self-help upon default of the payment of installments due — compare FORECLOSE, SEIZE 2 — **re·pos·ses·sor** \-ˈze-sər\ *n*

re·pos·ses·sion \ˌrē-pə-ˈze-shən\ *n* : the act or an instance of repossessing

rep·re·sent *vt* **1** : to substitute in some capacity for : act the part of, in place of, or for (as another person) usu. by legal right: as **a** : to serve esp. in a legislative body by delegated authority usu. resulting from an election **b** : to provide legal representation to as a lawyer **c** : to act as the representative of in a class action **2 a** : to describe as having a specified character or quality **b** : to give one's impression and judgment of : state in a manner intended to affect action or judgment

rep·re·sen·ta·tion *n* **1** : one that represents: as **a** : a statement or account made to influence opinion or action — compare WARRANTY 3 **b** : an incidental or collateral statement of fact on the faith of which a contract is entered into ⟨the contract of sale contains a ~ by the purchaser — *U.S. Code*⟩; *specif* : a statement of fact made by an applicant to an insurer for the purpose of obtaining insurance **2** : the act or action of representing: as **a** : the action or fact of one person standing for another so as to have the rights and obligations of the person represented **b** : the substitution of an individual or class in place of a person (as when a child or children take the share of an estate that would have fallen to a deceased parent) — see also PER STIRPES **c** : the action of representing or the fact of being represented esp. in a legislative body **d** : the act or action by a lawyer of providing legal advice to a client and appearing (as in court) to speak and act on the client's behalf **3** : the body of persons representing a constituency

¹rep·re·sen·ta·tive *adj* **1** : serving to represent **2 a** : standing or acting for another esp. through delegated authority ⟨an agent acting in a ~ capacity⟩ **b** : of, based on, or constituting a government in which the people are represented by individuals chosen from among them usu. by election **3** : of or relating to representation

²representative *n* : one that represents another or others in a special capacity: as **a** : one that represents a constituency as a member of a legislative or other governing body; *specif* : a member of the House of Representatives of the U.S. Congress or a state legislature **b** : one that represents another as agent, deputy, substitute, or delegate and that usu. is invested with the authority of the principal **c** : one that represents or stands in the place of a deceased person : PERSONAL REPRESENTATIVE **d** : one that represents another as successor or heir **e** : one named as the plaintiff or defendant in a class action to litigate on behalf of the class

¹re·prieve \ri-'prēv\ *vt* **re·prieved; re·priev·ing** [alteration of earlier *repry* to

send back (to prison), return to custody, perhaps from Anglo-French *repris*, past participle of *reprendre* to take back, from Old French] : to delay the punishment of (as a condemned prisoner)

²reprieve *n* **1 a** : the act of reprieving : the state of being reprieved **b** : a formal temporary suspension of the execution of a sentence esp. of death as an act of clemency **2** : an order or warrant of reprieve

re·pri·sal \ri-'prī-zəl\ *n* [Anglo-French *reprisaile, reprisaille*, from Middle French, from Old Italian *ripresaglia*, from *ripreso*, past participle of *riprendere* to take back, from *ri-* back + *prendere* to take, from Latin *prehendere*] **1 a** : the act or practice in international law of resorting to force short of war in retaliation for damage or loss suffered **b** : an instance of such action **2** : a retaliatory act ⟨may not fire a complaining employee in ~⟩

re·pub·lic *n* **1** : a government having a chief of state who is not a monarch and who in modern times is usu. a president; *also* : a political unit (as a nation) having such a form of government **2** : a government in which supreme power resides in a body of citizens entitled to vote and is exercised by elected officers and representatives responsible to them and governing according to law; *also* : a political unit (as a nation) having such a form of government

re·pub·li·ca·tion \,rē-,pə-blə-'kā-shən\ *n* **1** : the act or an instance of republishing **2** : the state of being republished

re·pub·lish \,rē-'pə-blish\ *vt* **1** : to publish again or anew ⟨~*ing* the defamatory statements⟩ **2** : to execute (a will) anew usu. through the execution of a codicil incorporating the will by reference and with the result of rendering an otherwise invalid will valid

re·pu·di·ate \ri-'pyü-dē-,āt\ *vt* **-at·ed;**

\ə\abut \ᵊ\kitten \ər\further \a\ash \ā\ace
\ä\cot, cart \aú\out \ch\chin \e\bet \ē\easy
\g\go \i\hit \ī\ice \j\job \ŋ\sing \ō\go \ó\law
\ói\boy \th\thin \t̲h̲\the \ü\loot \ú\foot \y\yet
\zh\vision *see also* Pronunciation Symbols page

-at·ing : to disavow or reject an obligation (as a debt) or duty (as performance under a contract); *specif* : to indicate an inability or unwillingness to perform as promised under (a contract) — **re·pu·di·a·tor** \-,ā-tər\ *n*

re·pu·di·a·tee \ri-,pyü-dē-,ā-'tē, -ə-'tē\ *n* : a party to a contract that has been repudiated by another party to the contract

re·pu·di·a·tion \ri-,pyü-dē-'ā-shən\ *n* : the rejection or renunciation of a duty or obligation (as under a contract); *esp* : ANTICIPATORY REPUDIATION ◊ A party aggrieved by a repudiation may consider a repudiated contract to have been breached and bring an action for relief.

re·pug·nan·cy \ri-'pəg-nən-sē\ *n, pl* **-cies** **1** : the quality or fact of being inconsistent, irreconcilable, or in disagreement; *specif* : a contradiction or inconsistency between sections of a legal instrument (as a contract or statute) ⟨if two acts which cover the same subject matter are repugnant . . . , the latter operates to the extent of the ~ as a repeal of the former — *In re Miller*, 107 F. Supp. 1006 (1952)⟩ **2** : an instance of contradiction or inconsistency

re·pug·nant \ri-'pəg-nənt\ *adj* : characterized by contradiction and irreconcilability ⟨the arbitrator's decision was not ~ to the Act — M. A. Kelly⟩

repugnant verdict — see VERDICT

¹re·pur·chase \,rē-'pər-chəs\ *vt* **-chased; -chas·ing** : to buy back ⟨~ shares of stock⟩

²repurchase *n* : the act or an instance of purchasing something again or back; *specif* : a corporation's buying back of some of its stock at market price (as to increase the amount of treasury stock or as a preliminary step to going private)

repurchase agreement *n* : a contract giving the seller of securities (as Treasury bills) the right to repurchase after a stated period and the buyer the right to retain interest earnings

rep·u·ta·tion *n* : overall quality or character as seen or judged by people in general within a community — see also *character evidence* at EVIDENCE, *reputation testimony* at TESTIMONY

rep·u·ta·tion·al \,re-pyə-'tā-shə-nəl\ *adj* : of or relating to reputation ⟨a ~ injury caused by the libel⟩

reputation testimony — see TESTIMONY

re·quest for admission : a written request served upon another party to an action (as under Federal Rule of Civil Procedure 36) asking that the party admit the truth of certain matters relevant to the action — called also *request for admissions, request to admit* ◊ A party upon whom a request for admission has been served must provide an answer for each matter of which an admission is requested by admitting it, denying it, or giving reasons why it can be neither admitted nor denied. A matter admitted does not have to be proven at trial, but it is established for the purpose of the pending action only.

request for instructions : a written request setting forth instructions that the submitting party requests the court use in instructing the jury

request for pro·duc·tion : a discovery request served by one party to an action on another (as under Federal Rule of Civil Procedure 34) for the presentation for inspection of specified documents or tangible things or for permission to enter upon and inspect land or property in the other party's possession

request to admit : REQUEST FOR ADMISSION

re·quired records doctrine *n* : a doctrine holding that the privilege against self-incrimination does not apply to business records that are customarily kept in accordance with government regulation and that have aspects such that the records can be characterized as public

requirements contract — see CONTRACT

req·ui·si·tion \,re-kwə-'zi-shən\ *n* **1** : the taking of property by a public authority for a public use : the exercise of the power of eminent domain **2** : a formal demand made by one international jurisdiction (as a nation) upon another for the surrender or extradition of a fugitive from justice in accordance with an extradition treaty

res \'räs, 'rēz\ *n* [Latin] **1** : a thing (as a

property, interest, or status) as opposed to a person that is the object of rights and esp. that is the subject matter of litigation ⟨a court with jurisdiction over the ~ of the suit⟩ — compare IN PERSONAM, IN REM, QUASI IN REM **2 :** CORPUS ⟨the ~ of the trust was the marital home — *Stopka v. Commercial Embroidery, Inc.*, 428 N.E.2d 1130 (1981)⟩

res ad·ju·di·ca·ta \'rēz-ə-ˌjü-di-'kä-tə, 'räs-äd-ˌyü-\ *n* [Late Latin] **:** RES JUDICATA

re·sale \'rē-ˌsāl, ˌrē-'sāl\ *n* **:** the act or an instance of selling again; *specif* **:** the selling of goods again by the same seller by right and after a breach by the original buyer ⟨a purchaser who buys in good faith at a ~ takes the goods free of any rights of the original buyer — *Uniform Commercial Code*⟩ — **re·sal·able** \ˌrē-'sā-lə-bəl\ *adj*

resale price maintenance *n* **:** a form of illegal price-fixing in which a manufacturer compels different retailers to resell a product at the same price and thereby prevents competition

re·scind \ri-'sind\ *vb* [Latin *rescindere* to cut loose, annul, from *re-* away, back + *scindere* to cut, split] *vt* **1 :** to take back and make void ⟨~*ed* its suspension of his license⟩ **2 :** to abrogate (a contract or transaction) by mutual agreement, judicial decree, or unilateral declaration because of fraud, mistake, duress, misrepresentation, illegality, a breach, or another sufficient ground with both parties restored to their positions before the contract was made ⟨denied that the other party had the right to ~ the contract⟩ — compare CANCEL, TERMINATE **3 :** to make void by the same or by a superior authority ⟨~ a regulation⟩ ~ *vi* **:** to rescind something (as a contract) — **re·scind·able** \-'sin-də-bəl\ *adj*

re·scis·sion \ri-'si-zhən\ *n* **:** the act, process, or fact of rescinding esp. a contract; *specif* **:** the equitable judicial remedy of rescinding a contract in a suit brought by one of the parties — compare REFORMATION — **re·scis·so·ry** \ri-'si-zə-rē, -'si-sə-\ *adj*

res·cue doctrine *n* **:** a common-law doctrine that permits a plaintiff to recover from a party whose negligence was the proximate cause of a peril from which the plaintiff reasonably undertook to rescue a third party ◊ The act of rescue itself is considered foreseeable, and the negligence of the defendant is considered to be the proximate cause of injury to the rescuer as well as to the one rescued.

re·sen·tence \ˌrē-'sent-ᵊns, -ᵊnz\ *vt* **:** to sentence again

res·er·va·tion *n* **1 :** the act or an instance of reserving ⟨~ of rights⟩ **2 :** the creation by and for a grantor of a new right or interest (as an easement) in real property granted to another; *also* **:** the right or interest so created or the clause creating it in a deed — compare EXCEPTION **3 a :** public land reserved for a special purpose (as conservation) **b :** a tract of land reserved for use by an American Indian tribe — see also *Indian Removal Act of 1830* in the IMPORTANT LAWS section; compare *Indian title* at TITLE ◊ The federal government has jurisdiction over certain serious felonies committed on American Indian reservations, and a member of a tribe is vested with the rights of an American citizen even if in a tribal court proceeding. Prior to the Indian Civil Rights Act of 1968, states could obtain civil and criminal jurisdiction over a reservation or other American Indian lands by legislative action, but that Act created the requirement that such jurisdiction be acquired with the consent of the tribe as manifest in an election among tribal adults. This requirement was not retroactive. Federal land claim settlement acts pertaining to particular states have included statutes expressly assigning civil and criminal jurisdiction to the states involved.

¹re·serve *vt* **re·served; re·serv·ing :** to keep back or set apart: as **a :** to keep (a

\ə\abut \ᵊ\kitten \ər\further \a\ash \ā\ace
\ä\cot, cart \au̇\out \ch\chin \e\bet \ē\easy
\g\go \i\hit \ī\ice \j\job \ŋ\sing \ō\go \ȯ\law
\ȯi\boy \th\thin \t̲h̲\the \ü\loot \u̇\foot \y\yet
\zh\vision *see also* Pronunciation Symbols page

right, power, or interest) esp. by express declaration ⟨all rights *reserved*⟩ — compare WAIVE **b :** to defer a determination of (a question of law) ⟨the justices *reserved* the question because it was not an issue in the case⟩

²reserve *n* **1 :** something stored or kept available for future use ⟨an energy company with various unproven oil ~*s*⟩ **2 :** an act of reserving **3 :** money kept in a separate account to meet future liabilities

legal reserve **:** the minimum amount as determined by government standards of the deposits held by a bank or of the assets of a life insurance company required by law to be kept as reserves

loss reserve **1 :** a reserve allocated by a bank for the purpose of absorbing losses ⟨a loan *loss reserve*⟩ **2 :** an insurance company's reserve representing the discounted value of future payments to be made on losses which may have already occurred

policy reserve **:** an insurance company's reserve representing the difference in value between the net premiums and assumed claims for a given year in life insurance

unearned premium reserve **:** a reserve of funds which represents premiums paid to an insurance company but not yet applied to policy coverage and from which a policyholder is paid a refund in the event of cancellation prior to the period for which premiums have been paid **4 :** RESERVE PRICE — **with reserve :** with a reserve price and with a seller reserving the right to reject all bids ◊ A sale at auction is with reserve if there is no explicit indication to the contrary. — **without reserve :** without a reserve price and with the seller bound to accept the highest bid

reserved powers — see POWER 2a

reserve price *n* **:** a price announced at an auction as the lowest that will be considered

res ges•tae \'rās-'ges-ˌtī, 'rēz-'jes-ˌtē\ *n pl* [Latin, things done, deeds] **1 :** the acts, facts, circumstances, statements, or occurrences that form the environment of a

main act or event and esp. of a crime and are so closely connected to it that they constitute part of a continuous transaction and can serve to illustrate its character ⟨the decedent's statement . . . was too far removed in time and place to be admissible as part of the *res gestae* — *Lynch v. State*, 552 N.E.2d 56 (1990)⟩ **2 a :** an exception or set of exceptions to the hearsay rule that permits the admission of hearsay evidence regarding excited utterances or declarations relating to mental, emotional, or bodily states or sense impressions of a witness or participant — compare *dying declaration* and *spontaneous declaration* at DECLARATION 2c, EXCITED UTTERANCE ◊ Res gestae in common law encompassed a variety of different exceptions to the hearsay rule, but most modern rules of evidence (as the Federal Rules of Evidence) have abandoned use of res gestae and specify the different exceptions on their own terms. **b :** an exception to the exclusionary rule against the use of other crimes as evidence that permits such use when another crime is closely enough connected to the one in dispute as to form part of a continuous episode or transaction

res•i•dence \'re-zə-dəns\ *n* **1 :** the act or fact of living in a place **2 a :** the place where one actually lives as distinguished from a domicile or place of temporary sojourn ⟨a person can have more than one ~ but only one domicile⟩ ◊ A distinction is usu. maintained between *domicile* and *residence* based on the relative permanency of a domicile and the intent to make it a principal place of abode. In some contexts, however, such as for determining proper venue *domicile* and *residence* are used as synonyms. Similarly *residence* and *domicile* are sometimes used as synonyms with regard to the place of incorporation of a business. **b :** a place in which a corporation does business or is licensed to do business **3 :** the status of a resident **4 :** DWELLING

res•i•den•cy \'re-zə-dən-sē\ *n, pl* **-cies 1 :** an often official place of residence **2**

: the condition of being a resident of a particular place

res·i·dent \\'re-zə-dənt\ *n* : one who has a residence in a particular place but does not necessarily have the status of a citizen — compare CITIZEN 1, DOMICILIARY — **resident** *adj*

residua *pl of* RESIDUUM

re·sid·u·al \ri-'zi-jə-wəl\ *adj* : of, relating to, or constituting a residue : RESIDUARY

residual estate *n* : RESIDUARY ESTATE at ESTATE 3a

¹**re·sid·u·ary** \ri-'zi-jə-,wer-ē\ *adj* : of, relating to, consisting of, or constituting a residue

²**residuary** *n, pl* **-ar·ies** **1** : RESIDUE **2** : RESIDUARY LEGATEE

residuary clause *n* : a clause in a will disposing of a residue

residuary devise — see DEVISE

residuary estate — see ESTATE 3a

residuary legacy — see LEGACY

residuary legatee *n* : one designated to receive the residue of an estate

res·i·due \'re-zə-,dü, -,dyü\ *n* : something that remains after a part is taken, separated, or designated; *specif* : the part of a testator's estate remaining after the satisfaction of all debts, charges, taxes, and legacies other than residuary legacies

re·sid·u·um \ri-'zi-jə-wəm\ *n, pl* **re·sid·ua** \-jə-wə\ [Latin] : RESIDUE ⟨a lapsed or void legacy of personal property shall fall into the ~ and go to the residuary legatee —*Official Code of Georgia Annotated*⟩

residuum rule *n* : a rule requiring that the decision or order of an administrative agency be supported by at least a small amount of evidence which is not inadmissible hearsay in order to be upheld on review ◊ The residuum rule has been rejected in most jurisdictions.

res in·ter ali·os acta \'rēz-'in-tər-'ā-lē-,ōs-'ak-tə, 'rās-'in-ter-'ä-lē-,ōs-'äk-tä\ *n* [Late Latin, literally, thing done among others] : something transacted between other parties ◊ This term is used in reference to matters not involving the same parties as those in litigation. Evidence of such matters is generally inadmissible.

res ip·sa \-'ip-sə\ *n* : RES IPSA LOQUITUR

res ipsa lo·qui·tur *also* **res ipsa lo·qui·tor** \-'lō-kwə-tər\ *n* [Latin, the thing speaks for itself] : a doctrine or rule of evidence in tort law that permits an inference or presumption that a defendant was negligent in an accident injuring the plaintiff on the basis of circumstantial evidence if the accident was of a kind that does not ordinarily occur in the absence of negligence ⟨a plaintiff who establishes the elements of *res ipsa loquitur* can withstand a motion for summary judgment and reach the jury without direct proof of negligence —*Cox v. May Dept. Store Co.*, 903 P.2d 1119 (1995)⟩ ◊ For res ipsa loquitur to apply, the accident in question must not be due to any voluntary action or contribution by the plaintiff. The doctrine has traditionally required that a defendant have exclusive control over the instrumentality of an injury, but now it is commonly applied when multiple defendants have joint or sometimes successive control (as by the manufacturer and retailer of a defective product). In addition to the control requirement, and sometimes superseding it, is the requirement that a defendant have responsibility for the instrumentality as well as responsibility to the plaintiff. In order for res ipsa loquitur to succeed in a medical malpractice suit, the fact that the accident is one that ordinarily does not occur without a failure to exercise due care must be readily apparent to the layperson as common knowledge. The accident alone should afford reasonable evidence of negligence, as when a foreign object is left inside a surgical patient.

res ju·di·ca·ta \'rēz-,jü-di-'kä-tə, 'rās-,yü-\ *n* [Latin, judged matter] **1** : a thing, matter, or determination that is adjudged or final: as **a** : a claim, issue, or cause of action that is settled by a judgment conclusive as to the rights, questions, and

\ə\abut \ᵊ\kitten \ər\further \a\ash \ā\ace
\ä\cot, cart \aú\out \ch\chin \e\bet \ē\easy
\g\go \i\hit \ī\ice \j\job \ŋ\sing \ō\go \ò\law
\òi\boy \th\thin \t̲h̲\the \ü\loot \ù\foot \y\yet
\zh\vision *see also* Pronunciation Symbols page

facts involved in the dispute **b** : a judgment, decree, award, or other determination that is considered final and bars relitigation of the same matter ⟨the trial court interpreted the earlier order as a dismissal with prejudice and thus *res judicata* as to the subsequent complaint —*Southeast Mortg. Co. v. Sinclair,* 632 So. 2d 677 (1994)⟩; *also* : the barring effect of such a determination **2** : a principle or doctrine that generally bars relitigation or reconsideration of matters determined in adjudication ⟨the doctrine of *res judicata* precludes the presentation of issues in a post-conviction petition which have previously been decided upon direct appeal —*Stowers v. State,* 657 N.E.2d 194 (1995)⟩: as **a** : a broad doctrine in civil litigation that requires and includes the barring of relitigation of settled matters under merger, bar, collateral estoppel, and direct estoppel : FORMER ADJUDICATION — compare BAR 3b, *estoppel by judgment* at ESTOPPEL 2a, MERGER 4 **b** : a specific doctrine that precludes relitigation of claims and issues arising from the same cause of action between the same parties and their privies after a final judgment on the merits by a competent tribunal or after some other final determination having the same effect ⟨*res judicata* precludes only subsequent suits on the same cause of action; collateral estoppel may preclude relitigation of issues in later suits on any cause of action —J. H. Friedenthal *et al.*⟩ — called also *claim preclusion* **3** : an affirmative defense based on res judicata

res no·va \'rēz-'nō-və, 'räs-\ *n* [Latin, new matter] : a case or issue that has never before been decided by a court ⟨plaintiff admits the case is *res nova* in Alabama —*McDermott v. Hambright,* 238 So. 2d 876 (1970)⟩

res·o·lu·tion \ˌre-zə-'lü-shən\ *n* **1** : a formal expression of opinion, will, or intention voted by an official body (as a legislature) or assembled group — see also CONCURRENT RESOLUTION, JOINT RESOLUTION **2** : an expression or document

containing authorization usu. by a corporate board of directors of a particular act, transaction, agent, or representative ⟨a corporate ~ authorizing counsel to bind the corporation to a settlement⟩

re·sol·u·to·ry \ri-'zäl-yə-ˌtōr-ē, 're-zə-lə-ˌtōr-ē, ˌre-zə-'lü-tə-rē\ *adj* [Late Latin *resolutorius* dissolving, from Latin *resolvere* to loosen, dissolve, break up, from *re-* away, back + *solvere* to loosen, release] : operating to annul or terminate

resolutory condition — see CONDITION

¹re·solve \ri-'zälv\ *vb* **re·solved; re·solv·ing** *vt* **1** : to deal with successfully : clear up ⟨~ a dispute⟩ **2 a** : to declare or decide by formal resolution and vote **b** : to change by resolution or formal vote ⟨the house *resolved* itself into a committee⟩ ~ *vi* : to form a resolution

²resolve *n* **1** : something that is resolved **2** : a legal or official determination; *esp* : a legislative declaration

RES·PA \'res-pə\ *abbr* Real Estate Settlement Procedures Act — see also IMPORTANT LAWS section

res·pite \'res-pət, ri-'spīt\ *n, in the civil law of Louisiana* : a judicially approved or enforced agreement that provides a debtor with time or a delay for the payment of creditors

re·spon·de·at superior \ri-'spän-dē-ət-\ *n* [Medieval Latin, let the superior give answer] : a doctrine in tort law that makes a master liable for the wrong of a servant; *specif* : the doctrine making an employer or principal liable for the wrong of an employee or agent if it was committed within the scope of employment or agency ⟨to recover . . . upon a theory of *respondeat superior,* it is incumbent upon plaintiff to prove that the collision occurred while the driver was within the scope of his employment —*Perdue v. Mitchell,* 373 So. 2d 650 (1979)⟩ — compare SCOPE OF EMPLOYMENT, *vicarious liability* at LIABILITY 2b

re·spon·dent \ri-'spän-dənt\ *n* : one who answers or defends in various proceedings: as **a** : an answering party in an equitable proceeding **b** : a party against whom a petition (as for a writ of habeas corpus) seeking relief is brought **c** : an answering party in a proceeding in juvenile court or family court; *specif* : a party against whom a divorce proceeding is brought **d** : a party prevailing at trial who defends the outcome on appeal : APPELLEE

re•spon•den•tia \ˌrē-ˌspän-'den-chē-ə\ *n* [New Latin, from Latin *respondent-, respondens,* present participle of *respondere* to answer, correspond; from the fact that the loan is only a personal obligation on the part of the borrower who must "answer" for the money] : a loan secured by the goods on one's ship — compare BOTTOMRY

re•spon•si•ble *adj* **1 a** : liable to be called on to answer **b** : liable to be called to account as the primary cause, motive, or agent **c** : liable to legal review or in case of fault to penalties **2** : characterized by trustworthiness, integrity, and requisite abilities and resources ⟨awarded the contract to the lowest ~ bidder⟩ **3** : able to choose for oneself between right and wrong **4** : marked by or involving accountability ⟨a ~ office⟩ — **re•spon•si•bil•i•ty** *n* — **re•spon•si•ble•ness** *n* — **re•spon•si•bly** *adv*

responsive pleading — see PLEADING 1
responsive verdict — see VERDICT
rest *vi* : to bring to an end voluntarily the introduction of evidence in a case ⟨the defense ~*s*⟩ ~ *vt* : to cease presenting evidence pertinent to (a case) ⟨I ~ my case⟩

Re•state•ment \ˌrē-'stāt-mənt\ *n* : any of several volumes produced by the American Law Institute and authored by legal scholars and experts that set forth statements of major areas of law (as contracts, torts, trusts, and property) and are widely referred to in jurisprudence but are not binding

res•ti•tu•tion \ˌres-tə-'tü-shən, -'tyü-\ *n* **1 a** : a restoration of something to its rightful owner **b** : a making good of or giving an equivalent for some injury **2 a** : the equitable remedy of restoring to an aggrieved party that which was obtained in unjust enrichment **b** : a remedy for breach of contract that consists of restoring the aggrieved party to the status quo that existed before the contract was made **3** : an amount to be paid for the purpose of restitution ⟨ordered to pay ~ to the victim of his crime⟩ — compare FINE — **res•ti•tu•tion•al** \ˌres-tə-'tü-shə-nəl, -'tyü-\ *adj* — **res•ti•tu•tion•ary** \ˌres-tə-'tü-shə-ˌner-ē, -'tyü-\ *adj* — **res•ti•tu•tive** \'res-tə-ˌtü-tiv, -ˌtyü-\ *adj* — **res•ti•tu•to•ry** \ˌres-tə-'tü-tə-rē, -'tyü-; rə-'sti-tyə-ˌtōr-ē\ *adj*

re•strain \ri-'strān\ *vt* **1 a** : to prevent from doing something — see also *restraining order* at ORDER 3b **b** : to limit, restrict, or keep under control **2** : to moderate or limit the force, effect, development, or full exercise of **3** : to deprive of liberty and esp. of physical movement

restraining order — see ORDER 3b
re•straint \ri-'strānt\ *n* **1 a** : an act or fact of restraining — see also PRIOR RESTRAINT **b** : the state of being restrained **2 a** : a means of restraining **b** : a device that restricts movement (as of prisoners or violent psychiatric patients)

restraint of trade 1 : an act, fact, or means of curbing the free flow of commerce or trade ⟨covenant not to compete with an employer after leaving is in *restraint of trade* and must be reasonable to be enforced⟩ **2** : an attempt or intent to eliminate or stifle competition, to effect a monopoly, to maintain prices artificially, or otherwise to hamper or obstruct the course of trade and commerce as it would be if left to the control of natural and economic forces ⟨the Sherman Antitrust Act declared every contract, combination, and conspiracy in *restraint of trade* to be illegal⟩; *also* : the means (as a contract or combination) employed in such an endeavor — see also HORIZON-TAL RESTRAINT, PER SE RULE 2, RULE OF REASON, VERTICAL RESTRAINT, *Sherman Antitrust Act* in the IMPORTANT LAWS section

restraint on alienation : something that serves to prevent a party from alienating property; *specif* : a provision in an instrument (as a deed or will) that purports to prohibit or penalize the use of the power of alienation ◊ Though not necessarily unlawful, restraints on alienation are disfavored in the law.

re·strict *vt* **1** : to subject to bounds or limits ⟨~ the height of buildings⟩ ⟨~ visitation rights⟩ **2** : to place under restrictions as to use or distribution ⟨~*ed* the land to recreational use⟩

re·strict·ed *adj* : subject or subjected to restriction ⟨a ~ area⟩ ⟨~ use⟩

restricted security — see SECURITY

re·stric·tion *n* **1** : something that restricts: as **a** : a regulation that restricts or restrains **b** : a limitation on the use or enjoyment of property or a facility **2 a** : an act of restricting **b** : the state of being restricted

re·stric·tive \ri-'strik-tiv\ *adj* **1 a** : of or relating to restriction **b** : serving or tending to restrict **2** : prohibiting further negotiation — **re·stric·tive·ly** *adv* — **re·stric·tive·ness** *n*

restrictive covenant *n* **1** : a covenant acknowledged in a deed or lease that restricts the free use or occupancy of property (as by forbidding commercial use or types of structures) ⟨one who purchases for value and without notice takes the land free from the *restrictive covenant* — *American Jurisprudence* 2d⟩ ◊ For a restrictive covenant to run with the land it must be intended to do so by the original parties to it, it must directly concern the land itself and be enforceable, and there must be privity between the original parties and between the original and subsequent grantee. **2** : COVENANT NOT TO COMPETE ⟨*restrictive covenants* unenforceable upon physicians —*Annotated Laws of Massachusetts*⟩ ◊ A restrictive

covenant in a work contract must be reasonable to be enforceable, which means that it must be reasonably necessary to protect the legitimate interests of the employer or partnership, must not impose undue hardship on the individual concerned, and must not harm the public interest (as by causing undue restraint of trade).

restrictive endorsement — see ENDORSE-MENT

re·struc·ture \ˌrē-'strək-chər\ *vb* **-tured; -tur·ing** *vt* : to change the makeup, organization, or pattern of ⟨~ a corporation⟩ ⟨companies trying to ~ their debt — Claudia MacLachlan⟩ ~ *vi* : to restructure something

re·struc·tur·ing \ˌrē-'strək-chə-riŋ\ *n* : the act or process of changing the structure of something (as a corporation or its ownership of securities)

resulting trust — see TRUST

resulting use — see USE 1b

re·tain \ri-'tān\ *vt* **1** : to keep in possession or use **2** : to keep in one's pay or service; *specif* : to employ (as a lawyer) by paying a retainer

re·tain·age \ri-'tā-nij\ *n* : a percentage of a contract price retained from a contractor as assurance that subcontractors will be paid and that the job will be completed

retained earnings *n pl* : EARNED SURPLUS at SURPLUS

re·tain·er \ri-'tā-nər\ *n* [Anglo-French *retener* act of engaging or employing, from *retener, retenir* to engage, retain] **1** : the act of a client by which the services of a lawyer are engaged **2** : a fee paid to a lawyer for advice or services or for a claim on services when needed

retaining lien — see LIEN

re·tal·i·ate \ri-'ta-lē-ˌāt\ *vi* **-at·ed; -at·ing** : to act in revenge — **re·tal·i·a·tion** \-ˌta-lē-'ā-shən\ *n* — **re·tal·i·a·tive** \-'ta-lē-ˌā-tiv\ *adj* — **re·tal·ia·to·ry** \-'tal-yə-ˌtōr-ē\ *adj*

retaliatory discharge — see DISCHARGE

retaliatory eviction — see EVICTION

re·ten·tion \ri-'ten-chən\ *n* **1** : the act of retaining or the state of being retained **2**

: the portion of the insurance on a particular risk not reinsured or ceded by the originating insurer

re•tire *vb* **re•tired; re•tir•ing** *vi* : to withdraw from an action ⟨the jury *retired* for deliberations⟩ — *vt* : to withdraw from circulation or from the market ⟨~ a loan⟩ ⟨~ stock⟩

re•trac•tion \ri-'trak-shən\ *n* : an act of taking back or withdrawing ⟨~ of a confession⟩ ⟨her ~ of the defamatory statement⟩

re•trax•it \ri-'trak-sit\ *n* [Latin, he/she has withdrawn] : the withdrawing of a suit in court by the plaintiff that results in a dismissal with prejudice

re•treat *n* : the act or process of withdrawing from a dangerous situation ◊ Many jurisdictions require that a person must have at least attempted a retreat, if it was possible to do so with safety, in order for a defense of self-defense to prevail. Retreat from an attack in one's own home, however, is usu. not required. — **retreat** *vb*

re•tri•al \ˌrē-'trī-əl, 'rē-ˌtrī-\ *n* : a trial of a matter already tried ◊ A retrial is barred by double jeopardy following a mistrial for which there was no manifest necessity.

ret•ri•bu•tion \ˌre-trə-'byü-shən\ *n* : punishment imposed (as on a convicted criminal) for purposes of repayment or revenge for the wrong committed

re•trib•u•tive \ri-'tri-byə-tiv\ *adj* : of, relating to, or marked by retribution ⟨~ justice⟩ — **re•trib•u•tive•ly** *adv*

ret•ro•ac•tive \ˌre-trō-'ak-tiv\ *adj* : extending in scope or effect to a prior time or to conditions that existed or originated in the past; *esp* : made effective as of a date prior to enactment, promulgation, or imposition ⟨a ~ tax⟩ — see also EX POST FACTO LAW — **ret•ro•ac•tive•ly** *adv* — **ret•ro•ac•tiv•i•ty** \-ak-'ti-və-tē\ *n*

ret•ro•ces•sion \'re-trə-ˌse-shən\ *n* [French *rétrocession*, from Medieval Latin *retrocessio* retreat, from Late Latin, act of going back, from Latin *retrocedere* to go back] **1** : the return of title to property to its former or true owner; *specif, in*

the civil law of Louisiana : the return to a decedent's heirs of property of the decedent that had been sold or assigned by coheirs ◊ An heir's right to retrocession has been repealed. **2** : the act of ceding back something (as jurisdiction) **3 a** : the process by which all or part of the risks assumed in an insurance contract are reassigned or ceded by a reinsurer to another insurance company **b** : the amount reassigned or ceded

ret•ro•spec•tive \ˌre-trə-ˌspek-tiv\ *adj* : affecting things past : RETROACTIVE; *specif* : of, relating to, or being a law that takes away or impairs vested rights, creates new duties or obligations, or attaches new disabilities with respect to acts and transactions completed before its enactment — **ret•ro•spec•tive•ly** *adv*

re•try \ˌrē-'trī\ *vt* **re•tried; re•try•ing** : to try again

¹re•turn *vt* **1 a** : to give (an official account or report) to a superior (as by a list or statement) ⟨~ the names of all residents in the ward⟩ ⟨~ a list of jurors⟩ **b** : to bring back (as a writ, verdict, or indictment) to an office or tribunal ⟨the sheriff must ~ the execution . . . to the proper clerk within sixty days — J. H. Friedenthal *et al.*⟩ ⟨the grand jury ~*ed* six indictments⟩ ⟨~*ed* a verdict of not guilty⟩ **2** : to bring in or produce (as earnings or profit) : YIELD — **re•turn•able** *adj*

²return *n* **1 a** : the delivery of a court order (as a writ) to the proper officer or court **b** : PROOF OF SERVICE **2** : RETURN DAY **3** : an account or formal report (as of an action performed or duty discharged of facts and statistics) ⟨census ~*s*⟩; *esp* : a set of tabulated statistics prepared for general information — usu. used in pl. **4 a** : a report of the results of balloting ⟨election ~*s*⟩ **b** : an official declaration of the election of a candidate ⟨each house shall be the judge

\ə\abut \ᵊ\kitten \ər\further \a\ash \ā\ace
\ä\cot, cart \aú\out \ch\chin \e\bet \ē\easy
\g\go \i\hit \ī\ice \j\job \ŋ\sing \ō\go \ó\law
\ói\boy \th\thin \t͟h\the \ü\loot \ú\foot \y\yet
\zh\vision   *see also* Pronunciation Symbols page

of the elections, ~s, and qualifications of its own members — *U.S. Constitution* art. I⟩ **5** : a formal document executed in accordance with law on a required form showing taxable income, allowable deductions and exemptions, and the computation of the tax due — called also *tax return* **6** : the profit from labor, investment, or business : YIELD **7** : something returned; *specif* : a paper (as a check or draft) calling for payment that is returned by a bank to the clearinghouse because of a defect (as lack of funds or insufficient endorsement)

return day *n* : a day when a return is to be made: as **a** : a day on which the defendant in an action or proceeding is to appear in court (as for arraignment) **b** : a day on which the defendant in an action must file an answer **c** : a day on which a hearing on an action or proceeding (as a motion) is to be held **d** : a day on which proof of service must be returned **e** : a day fixed by law for the canvassing of election returns — called also *return date*

return of service : PROOF OF SERVICE

rev'd *abbr* reversed

re·ven·di·cate \ri-'ven-də-ˌkāt\ *vt* **-cat·ed;** **-cat·ing** [back-formation from *revendication*, from French, from Middle French, probably from *revendiguer* to revendicate, from *re-* back + *vendiguer* to lay claim to something, from Latin *vindicare*] *in the civil law of Louisiana* : to bring an action to enforce rights in (specific property) esp. for the recognition of ownership and the recovery of possession from one wrongfully in possession — **re·ven·di·ca·tion** \-ˌven-də-'kā-shən\ *n* — **re·ven·di·ca·to·ry** \-'ven-də-kə-ˌtōr-ē\ *adj*

rev·e·nue \'re-və-ˌnü, -ˌnyü\ *n, often attrib* **1** : the total income produced by a given source ⟨a property expected to yield a large annual ~⟩ **2** : the gross income returned by an investment **3** : the yield of sources of income (as taxes) that a political unit (as a nation or state) collects and receives into the treasury for public use **4** : a government department

concerned with the collection of national revenue

revenue bill — see BILL 1

revenue bond — see BOND 2

revenue law *n* : a law relating to the imposition or collection of taxes to defray the expenses of government

Revenue Ruling *n* : an official interpretation of a tax law by the Internal Revenue Service that is published to provide guidance esp. to taxpayers and IRS officials

revenue stamp *n* : a stamp for use as evidence of a tax (as on a package of cigarettes, a proprietary article, or a mortgage or deed) : TAX STAMP

re·ver·sal *n* **1** : an act or the process of reversing **2** : an instance of reversing ⟨the ~ of the lower court's decision⟩

re·verse *vb* **re·versed; re·vers·ing** *vt* : to set aside or make void (a judgment or decision) by a contrary decision — compare AFFIRM ~ *vi* : to reverse a decision or judgment ⟨for these reasons, we ~⟩ — **re·ver·si·ble** *adj*

reverse discrimination *n* : discrimination against whites or males (as in employment or education)

reverse mortgage — see MORTGAGE

reverse palm·ing off *n* : the wrongful misappropriation of another's goods or services by removing the correct name or trademark and selling or offering the goods under a different name

reverse stock split *n* : a method of increasing the value of shares of corporate stock by calling in all outstanding shares and reissuing fewer shares having greater value — compare STOCK SPLIT

reversible error — see ERROR

re·ver·sion \ri-'vər-zhən\ *n* [Anglo-French, from Middle French, from Latin *reversio* act of turning back, from *revertere* to turn back] **1** : the returning of an estate upon its termination to the former owner or to his or her successor in interest **2 a** : the present vested interest in the residue of an estate that remains in its owner after the grant therefrom of a lesser estate (as a life estate) and that will commence in possession by operation of law upon termination of the lesser estate **b :** the future interest in property left in a grantor or his or her successor in interest that is not subject to a condition precedent — compare POSSIBILITY OF REVERTER, REMAINDER — **re•ver•sion•ary** \-zhə-ˌner-ē\ *adj*

reversionary interest — see INTEREST 1

re•ver•sion•er \ri-ˈvər-zhə-nər\ *n* : one that has or is entitled to a reversion; *broadly* : someone having a vested right to a future estate

re•vert \ri-ˈvərt\ *vi* **1 :** to come or go back (as to a former status or state) ⟨if the donee of a general power fails to exercise it . . . the appointive assets ~ to the donor's estate —W. M. McGovern, Jr. *et al.*⟩ **2 :** to return to the grantor or his or her heirs as a reversion — **re•vert•ible** \-ˈvər-tə-bəl\ *adj*

re•vert•er \ri-ˈvər-tər\ *n* [Anglo-French, from *reverter* to return, from Old French *revertir* to return, revert, from Latin *revertere* to turn back] **1 :** REVERSION **2** : POSSIBILITY OF REVERTER ◊ Although *reversion* and *possibility of reverter* or *reverter* are sometimes used synonymously, many authorities disapprove such use.

re•vest \ˌrē-ˈvest\ *vt* : to vest again or anew

¹re•view \ri-ˈvyü\ *n* : a judicial reexamination and reconsideration of the legality or constitutionality of something (as the proceedings of a lower tribunal or a legislative enactment or governmental action) — see also JUDICIAL REVIEW

²review *vt* : to reexamine judicially — **re•view•abil•i•ty** \-ˌvyü-ə-ˈbi-lə-tē\ *n* — **re•view•able** \ri-ˈvyü-ə-bəl\ *adj*

re•vi•val \ri-ˈvī-vəl\ *n* : an act or instance of reviving

re•vive \ri-ˈvīv\ *vt* **re•vived; re•viv•ing :** to restore the force, effect, or validity of (as a contract, will, action, or judgment)

rev•o•ca•ble \ˈre-və-kə-bəl, ri-ˈvō-\ *adj* : capable of being revoked

revocable trust — see TRUST

rev•o•ca•tion \ˌre-və-ˈkā-shən\ *n* : an act or instance of revoking

rev•o•ca•to•ry \ˈre-və-kə-ˌtōr-ē, ri-ˈvä-\ *adj* : of, relating to, or effecting a revocation ⟨a ~ instrument⟩

revocatory action *n, in the civil law of Louisiana* : an action brought by a creditor seeking to have set aside a contract made by his or her debtor that increases the debtor's insolvency

re•voke \ri-ˈvōk\ *vt* **re•voked; re•vok•ing** : to annul by recalling or taking back: as **a :** to destroy the effectiveness of (a will) by executing another or by an act of destruction (as tearing or crossing out) **b** : to put an end to (a trust) **c :** to withdraw (an offer) esp. before acceptance **d** : to withdraw (acceptance of goods) by refusing to keep goods because of nonconformity — see also REJECTION **e :** to take back (as a license or a grant of parole or probation) esp. because of misconduct — **re•vok•er** *n*

re•volv•ing credit *n* : a credit which may be used repeatedly up to the limit specified after partial or total repayments have been made

Rev. Rul. *abbr* Revenue Ruling

rev. stat. *abbr* revised statutes

re•zone \rē-ˈzōn\ *vt* **re•zoned; re•zon•ing** : to zone again or anew

Rich•ard Roe \ˈri-chərd-ˈrō\ *n* : a male party to a legal proceeding whose true identity is unknown or whose true name is being withheld; *esp* : the second of two such parties — compare JANE ROE, JOHN DOE

RICO \ˈrē-kō\ *abbr* Racketeer Influenced and Corrupt Organizations (Act) — see also the IMPORTANT LAWS section

rid•er *n* **1 :** an addition to a document (as an insurance policy) often attached on a separate piece of paper **2 :** a clause or provision appended to a legislative bill to obtain a usu. distinct object

right \ˈrīt\ *n* [Old English *riht*, from *riht* righteous] **1 a :** qualities (as adherence

\ə\abut \ᵊ\kitten \ər\further \a\ash \ā\ace
\ä\cot, cart \aú\out \ch\chin \e\bet \ē\easy
\g\go \i\hit \ī\ice \j\job \ŋ\sing \ō\go \ó\law
\ói\boy \th\thin \t͟h\the \ü\loot \ú\foot \y\yet
\zh\vision   *see also* Pronunciation Symbols page

to duty or obedience to lawful authority) that together constitute the ideal of
moral propriety or merit moral approval
b : something that is morally just ⟨able
to distinguish ~ from wrong⟩ **2** : something to which one has a just claim: as **a**
: a power, privilege, or condition of existence to which one has a natural claim
of enjoyment or possession ⟨the ~ of lib-
erty⟩ ⟨that all men . . . are endowed by
their Creator with certain unalienable ~*s*
—*Declaration of Independence*⟩ — see
also NATURAL RIGHT **b** : a power, privilege, immunity, or capacity the enjoyment of which is secured to a person by
law ⟨one's constitutional ~*s*⟩ **c** : a legally enforceable claim against another
that the other will do or will not do a
given act ⟨the defendant may be under a
legal duty . . . to exercise reasonable care
for the plaintiff's safety, so that the plaintiff has a corresponding legal ~ to insist
on that care —W. L. Prosser and W. P.
Keeton⟩ **d** : the interest that one has in
property : a claim or title to property —
often used in pl. ⟨a security interest is not
enforceable . . . and does not attach unless . . . the debtor has ~*s* in the collateral
—*Uniform Commercial Code*⟩ ⟨leasing
mineral ~*s*⟩ — see also REAL RIGHT **e** *pl*
: the interest in property possessed (as under copyright law) in an intangible thing
and esp. an item of intellectual property
⟨obtained publishing ~*s*⟩ **3** : a privilege
given stockholders to subscribe pro rata
to a new issue of securities generally below market price — **right·ful** \-fəl\ *adj*
— **right·ful·ly** \-fə-lē\ *adv* — **of right 1**
: as an absolute right **2** : demandable or
enforceable under the law ⟨appeal *of right*
to the circuit courts of appeal —L. H.
Campbell⟩
right heir — see HEIR
right of action 1 : a right to begin and
prosecute an action in the courts (as for
the purpose of enforcing a right or
redressing a wrong) **2** : CHOSE IN ACTION
at CHOSE
right of common : PROFIT A PRENDRE
right of entry 1 a : the legal right of taking

or resuming possession of real property in
a peaceable manner **b** : POWER OF TER-
MINATION at POWER 2b **c** : the legal right to
enter upon real property of another for a
special purpose (as to show leased property to a prospective purchaser or to make
repairs) without being guilty of trespass
2 : the right of an alien to enter a nation, state, or other political jurisdiction
for some special purpose (as journalism
or academic study)
right of first re·fus·al \-ri-'fyü-zəl\ : the
right to have the first opportunity to purchase property upon the owner's decision
to sell at the same terms offered by a third
party or at predetermined terms — called
also *preemptive right*
right of petition : a right guaranteed by the
First Amendment to the U.S. Constitution
to petition the government for a redress of
grievances
right of privacy : the right of a person to
be free from intrusion into or publicity
concerning matters of a personal nature
— called also *right to privacy;* compare
INVASION OF PRIVACY ◊ Although not
explicitly mentioned in the U.S. Constitution, a penumbral right of privacy has
been held to be encompassed in the Bill of
Rights, providing protection from unwarranted governmental intrusion into areas
such as marriage and contraception. A
person's right of privacy may be overcome by a showing that it is outweighed
by a compelling state interest.
right of pu·blic·i·ty : the right to prevent
unauthorized use of one's name or likeness by a third person for commercial
benefit
right of redemption : the right to regain
ownership of property by freeing it from
a debt, charge, or lien (as by paying to the
creditor what is due to release the secured
property); *specif* : a mortgagor's statutory
right to redeem after a judicial foreclosure
and sale
right of reentry : POWER OF TERMINATION
at POWER 2b
right of survivorship : the right of the survivor of owners of property held jointly

to take the entire property; *esp* : the right of the survivor of joint tenants to sole ownership of the entire property

right of use *in the civil law of Louisiana* : a personal servitude conferring a specified use of an estate that is less than full enjoyment

right of way 1 : an easement or servitude over another's land conferring a right of passage **2 a** : the area over which a right of way exists **b** : the strip of land over which is built a public road **c** : the land occupied by a railroad esp. for its main line **d** : the land used by a public utility (as for a transmission line) **3 a** : a precedence in passing accorded to one vehicle over another by custom, decision, or statute **b** : the right of traffic to take precedence

rights arbitration — see ARBITRATION

right–to–know *adj* : of, relating to, or being a law requiring businesses (as chemical manufacturers) producing or importing hazardous substances to provide information about the substances to the community and inform and train employees who handle it

right to privacy : RIGHT OF PRIVACY

right–to–work *adj* : of, relating to, or being a law prohibiting labor agreements that require all employees to be union members

right–wrong test *n* : M'NAGHTEN TEST

¹ri•ot *n* : a disturbance of the peace created by an assemblage of usu. three or more people acting with a common purpose and in a violent and tumultuous manner to the terror of the public; *also* : the crime of rioting

²riot *vi* : to create or engage in a riot — **ri•ot•er** *n*

riot gun *n* : a small arm used to disperse rioters rather than to inflict serious injury or death; *esp* : a short-barreled shotgun

ri•ot•ous \'rī-ə-təs\ *adj* **1** : of the nature of a riot ⟨~ conduct⟩ **2** : participating in a riot ⟨a ~ assemblage⟩ — **ri•ot•ous•ly** *adv* — **ri•ot•ous•ness** *n*

ri•par•i•an \rə-'per-ē-ən\ *adj* : of or relat-ing to or living or located on the bank of a watercourse (as a river or stream) or sometimes a lake; *broadly* : of or relating to or living or located on the bank of a body of water — compare LITTORAL

riparian right *n* : the right of one owning riparian land to have access to and use of the shore and water

ripe *adj* **1** : of, relating to, or being a claim for relief that is ready for judicial resolution because the injury is certain to occur and is not merely hypothetical or speculative — compare MOOT **2** : ready and appropriate for disclosure because reasonably determined to be valid and not required to be kept secret for business reasons — used of corporate information — **ripe•ness** *n*

ripeness doctrine *n* : a doctrine prohibiting federal courts from exercising jurisdiction over a case until an actual controversy is presented involving a threat of injury that is real and immediate

risk *n* **1 a** : possibility of loss or injury **b** : liability for loss or injury if it occurs ⟨the ~ of loss passes to the buyer when the goods are duly delivered to the carrier *—Uniform Commercial Code*⟩ ⟨the ~ of personal injury and property damage should be placed with the manufacturer rather than the consumer *—Case & Comment*⟩ **2 a** : the chance of loss to the subject matter of an insurance contract : uncertainty with regard to loss; *also* : the degree of probability of such loss — compare PERIL **b** : a person or thing that is a specified hazard to an insurer ⟨a poor ~ for insurance⟩ **c** : an insurance hazard from a specified cause or source ⟨a war ~⟩ — **risk•less** *adj*

risk capital — see CAPITAL

risk–util•i•ty test *n* : a test used in product liability cases to determine whether a manufacturer is liable for injury to a consumer because the risk of danger created

\ə\abut \ə\\kitten \ər\further \a\ash \ā\ace \ä\cot, cart \au̇\out \ch\chin \e\bet \ē\easy \g\go \i\hit \ī\ice \j\job \ŋ\sing \ō\go \ȯ\law \ȯi\boy \th\thin \th̲\the \ü\loot \u̇\foot \y\yet \zh\vision *see also* Pronunciation Symbols page

by the product's design outweighs the benefits of the design

RJI *abbr* request for judicial intervention

road·block *n* : a road barricade set up by law enforcement officers esp. for the purpose of detecting criminal activity

rob·bery *n, pl* **-ber·ies** [Anglo-French *robberie, roberie,* from Old French, from *rober* to take something away from a person by force] : the unlawful taking away of personal property from a person by violence or by threat of violence that causes fear : larceny from the person or immediate presence of another by violence or threat of violence and with intent to steal

   aggravated robbery : robbery committed with aggravating factors (as use of a weapon, infliction of bodily injury, or use of an accomplice)

   armed robbery : robbery committed by a person armed with a dangerous or deadly weapon

   simple robbery : robbery that does not involve any aggravating factors

robe *n* : the legal profession; *esp* : the position of a judge — usu. used with *the* ⟨[his] . . . decision to decline the ~ —H. B. Zobel⟩

roll *n* **1** : a document containing an official record **2** : an official list ⟨the public relief ~*s*⟩: as **a** : a list of members of a legislative body ⟨the clerk called the ~ and recorded the votes⟩ **b** : a list of practitioners in a court or the courts of a state — usu. used in pl. **c** : a record kept by an authorized official of persons or property or both that are subject to taxation

roll call *n* : the act or an instance of calling off a list of names (as for checking attendance); *specif* : an act or instance of calling the roll of a legislative body to determine if there is a quorum or to vote on a matter

roll·over \'rōl-ˌō-vər\ *n* : the act or process of rolling over

roll over *vt* **1 a** : to defer payment of (an obligation) **b** : to renegotiate the terms of (a financial agreement) **2** : to place (invested funds) in a new investment of the same kind ⟨*roll over* IRA funds⟩

roll·up \'rōl-ˌəp\ *n* : LIMITED PARTNERSHIP ROLLUP TRANSACTION

¹Ro·man·ist \'rō-mə-nist\ *n* : a specialist in the law of ancient Rome

²Romanist *adj* : of or relating to the law of ancient Rome ⟨~ tradition⟩

Ro·man law *n* : the legal system of the ancient Romans that includes written and unwritten law, is based on the traditional law and legislation of the assemblies, resolves of the senate, enactments of the emperors, edicts of the praetors, writings of the jurisconsults, and the codes of the later emperors, and that is the basis for much of the modern civil law systems

root \'rüt, 'rut\ *n, in the civil law of Louisiana* : DESCENDANT — **by roots** : PER STIRPES

r.o.r. *abbr* released on recognizance

round lot *n* : the standard unit of trading in a security market usu. amounting to 100 shares of stock — compare ODD LOT

roy·al·ty *n, pl* **-ties** **1** : a right delegated (as to an individual or corporation) by a sovereign **2 a** : a share of the profit or product reserved by the grantor esp. of an oil or mineral lease — compare OVERRIDING ROYALTY **b** : a payment made to an author or composer for each copy of a work sold or to an inventor for each article sold under a patent

R.S. *abbr* revised statutes

ru·bric \'rü-brik\ *n* : an established rule, tradition, or custom

¹rule *n* **1 a** : a prescribed guide for conduct or action **b** : a regulating principle or precept **2 a** : an order or directive issued by a court in a particular proceeding esp. upon petition of a party to the proceeding that commands an officer or party to perform an act or show cause why an act should not be performed ⟨a ~ directing the district court to show cause why its ruling should not be vacated —*People v. District Court,* 797 P.2d 1259 (1990)⟩ **b** : a usu. judicially promulgated regulation having the force of law that governs judicial practice or procedure ⟨~*s* of evidence⟩ ⟨~*s* of appellate procedure⟩ — see also RULE OF

COURT **c** : RULE OF LAW 1 **3** : all or part of a statement (as a regulation) by an administrative agency that has general or particular applicability and future effect and that is designed to implement, interpret, or prescribe law or policy or that describes the organization, procedure, or practice of the agency itself ⟨a ∼ subject to statutory notice and comment requirements for informal rulemaking⟩ **4 a** : a regulation or bylaw governing procedure or conduct in a body, organization, institution, or proceeding **b** : a resolution of a legislative rules committee setting forth the terms for consideration of a particular bill by the entire body **5** : the exercise of authority or control ⟨majority ∼⟩ — see also HOME RULE, RULE OF LAW 2

²rule *vb* **ruled; rul·ing** *vt* **1** : to exercise authority or power over **2** : to determine and declare authoritatively; *esp* : to command or determine judicially ⟨*ruled* the evidence inadmissible⟩ ∼ *vi* **1** : to exercise supreme authority **2** : to lay down a rule or ruling ⟨*ruled* in favor of the plaintiff⟩

rule against perpetuities *often cap R&P* : a common-law rule stating that in order for a future interest to be good it must vest after its creation (as at the death of a testator) within a life in being or lives in being plus 21 years plus the period of gestation of any beneficiary conceived but not yet born — compare LIFE IN BEING, STATUTORY RULE AGAINST PERPETUITIES, WAIT AND SEE

rule in Shel·ley's case \-'she-lēz-\ *often cap R* [from *Wolfe v. Shelley*, a 1581 English case invoking the rule] : a former common-law rule that converted a life estate of an ancestor into an estate in fee and destroyed the remainder to the heirs that was created in the same instrument as that creating the life estate — see also *executory interest* at INTEREST 1

rule·mak·ing *n* : the making of rules; *specif* : the quasi-legislative formulation of rules (as regulations) by an administrative agency that must be carried out in

line with procedure prescribed by statute (as the Administrative Procedure Act) ⟨issued a notice of proposed ∼⟩ — see also FORMAL RULEMAKING, INFORMAL RULEMAKING — **rulemaking** *adj*

rule of com·plete·ness : a rule permitting a party to require introduction of the rest of or more of a document or recorded statement that is being used as evidence by the opposing party ◊ The rule of completeness applies when fairness demands consideration of the part of a document left out at the same time as the part that has been introduced.

rule of con·ve·nience : a common-law rule providing that in the interest of convenience and fairness a class (as of descendants) which is to receive a gift need not be closed until the distribution of the principal occurs

rule of court : a regulation governing practice or procedure in a particular court

rule of decision : something (as a law, rule of law, body of law, or prior decision) that governs a decision or adjudication ⟨a claim or defense as to which State law supplies the *rule of decision* —*Federal Rules of Evidence* Rule 302⟩

rule of four : a rule in the U.S. Supreme Court under which a petition for certiorari will be granted and the case in question reviewed if four of the nine justices so decide

rule of law 1 : an authoritative legal doctrine, principle, or precept applied to the facts of an appropriate case ⟨adopting the *rule of law* that is most persuasive in light of precedent, reason and policy — *Wright v. Wright*, 904 P.2d 403 (1995)⟩ **2** : government by law : adherence to due process of law

rule of len·i·ty \-'le-nə-tē\ : a rule requiring that those ambiguities in a criminal statute relating to prohibitions and penalties be resolved in favor of the defendant

\ə\abut \ə\kitten \ər\further \a\ash \ā\ace \ä\cot, cart \aů\out \ch\chin \e\bet \ē\easy \g\go \i\hit \ī\ice \j\job \ŋ\sing \ō\go \ò\law \òi\boy \th\thin \t͟h\the \ü\loot \ů\foot \y\yet \zh\vision *see also* Pronunciation Symbols page

when to do so would not be contrary to legislative intent

rule of necessity : a rule permitting or requiring a judge or other official to adjudicate a case despite bias or personal interest when disqualification would result in the lack of any competent tribunal

rule of reason : a standard used in restraint of trade actions that requires the plaintiff to show and the factfinder to find that under all the circumstances the practice in question unreasonably restricts competition in the relevant market — compare PER SE RULE 2 ◊ The rule of reason does not apply to per se violations of the Sherman Antitrust Act.

rules committee *n* : a committee of a legislative house that determines the rules and procedure for expediting the business of the house and has the power to control the date and extent of debate of a proposed bill and the degree to which it may be amended

Rule 10b–5 \-,ten-,bē-'fīv\ *n* [*10b–5* from the section of the Securities Exchange Act of 1934 pursuant to which the rule was formulated] : a rule adopted by the Securities and Exchange Commission in furtherance of the Securities Exchange Act that outlaws fraud, deceit, misrepresentation, and manipulation in securities dealing in broad terms

rul·ing *n* : an official or authoritative determination, decree, statement, or interpretation (as by a judge on a question of law) ⟨followed a previous ~ on the same question⟩ — see also REVENUE RULING; compare DECISION, DISPOSITION, FINDING, HOLDING, JUDGMENT, OPINION, VERDICT

ruling letter — see LETTER 1

run *vi* **ran; run; run·ning 1 a** : to be or continue to be in operation or effect **b** : to proceed toward expiration or effectiveness ⟨statute of limitations began to ~ when she received notice of the injury⟩ — compare TOLL **2** : to continue to accrue or become payable in an amount increasing with the passing of time ⟨interest *running* from a particular date⟩ — **run with the land** : to pass as a right or encumbrance upon the transfer of real property ⟨the restrictive covenant *ran with the land*⟩

S

sab•o•tage \'sa-bə-ˌtäzh\ *n* [French, from *saboter* to clatter with wooden shoes, botch, sabotage, from *sabot* wooden shoe] **1 :** the willful destruction of an employer's property or the hindering of normal operations by other means **2 :** the injury, destruction, or knowingly defective production of materials, premises, or utilities used for war or national defense — compare CRIMINAL SYNDICALISM, SEDITION

safe harbor *n* **:** something (as a statutory or regulatory provision) that provides protection (as from a penalty or liability) ⟨had no *safe harbor* from prosecution⟩

sal•able *or* **sale•able** \'sā-lə-bəl\ *adj* **:** MERCHANTABLE

sal•a•ry *n, pl* **-ries :** fixed compensation paid regularly for services — **sal•a•ried** *adj*

sale *n* **1 a :** the transfer of title to property from one party to another for a price; *also* **:** the contract of such a transaction — see also ¹SHORT 2; compare BARTER, DONATION, EXCHANGE, GIFT

  absolute sale **:** a sale that takes place without conditions and with title simply passing to the buyer upon payment of the price — compare CONDITIONAL SALE in this entry

  bulk sale **:** a sale not in the ordinary course of the seller's business of more than half of the seller's inventory — called also *bulk transfer* ◊ Article 6 of the Uniform Commercial Code governs bulk sales. Under section 6-102(c), in order for a sale to be considered a bulk sale, the buyer (or an auctioneer or liquidator if the sale is an auction) must have been given notice or been able upon reasonable inquiry to have had notice that the seller will not afterward continue to operate the same or a similar kind of business.

  cash sale **:** a sale in which payment must be made in cash ◊ Under U.C.C. section 2-310, payment must be made in cash at the time and place that the buyer receives the goods unless there is a prior agreement between the parties for a sale on credit.

  conditional sale **:** a sale that is complete only when one or more conditions are met; *specif* **:** a sale in which the seller extends credit to the buyer to purchase the item and takes a security interest in the item with the buyer receiving title when the debt has been fully paid off — compare ABSOLUTE SALE in this entry

  execution sale **:** a sale carried out to execute a judgment under authority of a judicial officer (as a court clerk) but not by court order

  forced sale **:** a sale of property ordered by a court in order to satisfy a creditor's judgment against a debtor

  foreclosure sale **:** a sale of property upon default of a mortgage to satisfy the debt

  judicial sale **:** a sale of property conducted by an authorized official by order of a court **:** FORCED SALE in this entry

  private sale **:** an often unadvertised sale of property that is not open to the general public and does not take place at a set time or place

  public sale **:** a sale (as an auction) that is publicly advertised and that takes place at a location open to the public

  sale in gross **:** a sale of a tract of land

\ə\abut \ᵊ\kitten \ər\further \a\ash \ā\ace
\ä\cot, cart \aů\out \ch\chin \e\bet \ē\easy
\g\go \i\hit \ī\ice \j\job \ŋ\sing \ō\go \ȯ\law
\ȯi\boy \th\thin \t̲h̲\the \ü\loot \ů\foot \y\yet
\zh\vision *see also* Pronunciation Symbols page

that is not made with a guarantee as to the exact amount of land involved; *also* : the sale of an undivided property (as in execution of a judgment)

sale on ap•prov•al : a conditional sale whose completion depends on acceptance of the goods by a buyer (as a consumer) receiving them primarily for use with the option to return them if they do not meet his or her approval even though they conform to contract

sale or return : a conditional sale whose completion depends on acceptance of the goods by a buyer (as a merchant) receiving them primarily for resale with the option to return them if they are not resold even though they conform to contract

sheriff's sale : a forced sale of property by a sheriff or deputy sheriff

tax sale : a forced sale of property resulting from nonpayment of taxes by the owner — compare *tax lien* at LIEN **b** : a contract for selling or disposing of a security or an interest in a security for value — see also ¹SHORT 2b, WASH SALE **2** : the transfer of a controlled substance to another person for money or other consideration **3** : a selling of goods at lower than usual prices **4** *pl* **a** : operations and activities involved in promoting and selling goods and services ⟨vice-president of ~*s*⟩ **b** : gross receipts **c** : income calculated under the accrual basis of accounting

saleable *var of* SALABLE

sale in gross — see SALE

sale on approval — see SALE

sale or return — see SALE

sales tax *n* : a tax levied on the sale of goods and services that is usu. calculated as a percentage of the purchase price and collected by the seller

sal•vage \'sal-vij\ *n* **1 a** : compensation paid for saving a ship or its cargo from the perils of the sea or for recovering it from an actual loss (as in a shipwreck) **b** : the act of saving or rescuing a ship or its cargo **c** : the act of saving or rescuing property in danger (as from fire) **2 a** : property saved from destruction (as in a

wreck or fire) **b** : damaged property acquired by an insurer after payment for the loss — compare ABANDONMENT 1d

salvage value *n* **1** : the value of damaged property **2** : the actual or estimated value realized on the sale of a fixed asset at the end of its useful life ◊ Salvage value is used in calculating depreciation.

same evidence test *n* : a test for double jeopardy that involves a determination of whether the same facts would support both a prior and second conviction

¹**sanc•tion** \'saŋk-shən\ *n* **1** : a punitive or coercive measure or action that results from failure to comply with a law, rule, or order ⟨a ~ for contempt⟩ **2** : explicit or official approval **3** : an economic or military coercive measure adopted usu. by several nations in concert for forcing a nation violating international law to desist or yield to adjudication

²**sanction** *vt* **1** : to give official approval or consent to : RATIFY **2** : to impose a sanction on ⟨~*ed* the lawyer for professional misconduct⟩

sanc•tion•able \'saŋk-shə-nə-bəl\ *adj* : deserving or liable to be sanctioned ⟨~ conduct⟩

sane *adj* : mentally sound; *specif* : able to understand one's actions and distinguish right from wrong

san•i•ty *n* : the quality or state of being sane — compare INSANITY

sat•is•fac•tion *n* **1 a** : the act or fact of satisfying **b** : execution of an accord by performance of the substituted obligation — often used in the phrase *accord and satisfaction* — compare ACCORD 3, TRANSACTION 3 **c** : a document indicating that an obligation has been satisfied ⟨a ~ of mortgage⟩ **2** : the quality or state of being satisfied

satisfaction piece *n* : a formal written acknowledgment by an obligee (as a mortgagee) that an obligation has been satisfied and that the obligor is discharged

sat•is•fy *vt* **-fied; -fy•ing 1 a** : to carry out the terms or obligation of (as by payment of money) ⟨refused to ~ the judgment against her⟩ ⟨~ a condition precedent⟩; *broadly* : to cause to be discharged, settled, or paid ⟨sought to ~ his claim against the debtor⟩ **b** : to meet an obligation to ⟨~ a creditor⟩ **2** : to convince by argument or evidence **3** : to conform to ⟨~ requirements⟩

sav·ing clause *n* : a clause in a statute exempting something from the statute's operation or providing that the rest of it will stand if part is held invalid; *also* : a contractual clause providing that if part of the contract is invalidated the rest shall remain in effect — called also *savings clause*

sav·ings and loan association *n* : a cooperative association organized to hold savings of members in the form of dividend-bearing shares and to invest chiefly in home mortgage loans

savings bank — see BANK

savings bank trust — see TRUST

savings bond — see BOND 2

savings clause *n* : SAVING CLAUSE

savings statute *n* : a statute explicitly excepting certain proceedings, remedies, penalties, rights, or liabilities from the effect of a repeal, amendment, or law — called also *saving statute*

saving to suitors clause : a clause in federal law found at title 28 section 1333(1) of the U.S. Code that allows a party to pursue a remedy for a maritime claim in a state court when entitled to such remedy and that effectively means that a party may pursue an in personam maritime claim in an ordinary civil action seeking a common-law remedy with the right to a jury trial

S.B. *abbr* senate bill

SBA *abbr* Small Business Administration — see also the IMPORTANT AGENCIES section

scab *n* **1** : a worker who refuses to join a labor union **2** : a union member who refuses to strike or returns to work before a strike has ended **3** : a worker who accepts employment or replaces a union worker during a strike : STRIKE BREAKER **4** : one who works for less than union wages or on nonunion terms

scale *n* : a set of graduated wage rates; *also* : a wage consistent with such rates — compare MINIMUM WAGE

scalp *vt* : to buy and sell so as to make small quick profits ⟨~ stocks⟩; *esp* : to resell at greatly increased prices ~ *vi* : to profit by slight market fluctuations — **scalp·er** *n*

sched·ule \'ske-jül, *esp Brit* 'she-dyül\ *n* **1 a** : a list or statement of supplementary details appended to another document **b** : a formal list, table, catalog, or inventory **2** : a plan that indicates the time and sequence of each element — **schedule** *vt*

sched·uled *adj* : insured or effective in accordance with a schedule listing particular property, injuries, or services covered ⟨~ personal property⟩ ⟨~ coverage⟩

scheme *n* **1** : a combination of elements (as statutes or regulations) that are connected, adjusted, and integrated by design : a systematic plan or program ⟨an administrative inspection ~⟩ **2** : a crafty, unethical, or fraudulent project ⟨a ~ to defraud investors⟩

sci·en·ter \sī-'en-tər\ *n* [Latin, knowingly, from *scient-*, *sciens*, present participle of *scire* to know] **1** : knowledge of the nature of one's act or omission or of the nature of something in one's possession that is often a necessary element of an offense ⟨the ~ element constitutionally required for an obscenity statute — *Wall Dist. v. Newport News*, 323 S.E.2d 75 (1984)⟩; *also* : intent to engage in particular esp. criminal conduct ⟨a few environmental statutes . . . do away altogether with the need to prove ~ . . . requiring no proof of criminal intent whatsoever —R. J. Kafin *et al.*⟩ **2** : a mental state in fraud (as securities fraud) that is characterized by an intent to deceive, manipulate, or defraud

sci. fa. *abbr* scire facias

scin·til·la \sin-'ti-lə\ *n* : a small trace or

\ə\abut \ə\kitten \ər\further \a\ash \ā\ace \ä\cot, cart \au\out \ch\chin \e\bet \ē\easy \g\go \i\hit \ī\ice \j\job \ŋ\sing \ō\go \o\law \oi\boy \th\thin \th\the \ü\loot \u\foot \y\yet \zh\vision *see also* Pronunciation Symbols page

barely perceptible amount of something (as evidence supporting a position)

sci•re fa•ci•as \\'sī-rē-'fā-shē-əs, -shəs, -shē-ˌas; 'skē-rā-'fä-kē-ˌäs\\ *n* [Medieval Latin, you should cause to know] **1 :** a judicial writ founded upon some matter of record and requiring the party proceeded against to show cause why the record should not be enforced (as by revival of the judgment), annulled, or vacated **2 :** a legal proceeding instituted by a scire facias

scope of employment : the range of conduct and activity within which an employee can reasonably be considered to be carrying out the business of his or her employer ⟨workers' compensation for injuries arising out of the course and *scope of employment*⟩ — see also RESPONDEAT SUPERIOR ◊ The liability of an employer for an act committed by an employee depends on whether the act falls within the scope of employment.

S corporation — see CORPORATION

scriv•en•er \\'skri-və-nər\\ *n* [Middle English, alteration of *scriveyn*, from Anglo-French *escrivein*, ultimately from Latin *scriba* public record keeper, from *scribere* to write] **:** a professional or public copyist or writer of official or formal documents (as deeds or contracts)

scru•ti•ny \\'skrüt-ᵊn-ē\\ *n, pl* **-nies :** searching study or inquiry; *specif* **:** judicial investigation of the constitutionality of a statutory classification of persons under the equal protection clause of the U.S. Constitution — see also INTERMEDIATE 2, STRICT SCRUTINY; compare RATIONAL BASIS TEST

¹seal *n* [Old French *seel*, from Latin *sigillum*, from diminutive of *signum* mark, sign] **:** a device (as an emblem, symbol, or word) used to identify or replace a signature and to authenticate (as at common law) written matter — see also *contract under seal* at CONTRACT — **under seal :** with an authenticating seal affixed

²seal *vt* **1 :** to authenticate or approve by or as if by a seal **2 :** to close off (as records) from public access

¹search *n* **1 :** an exploratory investigation (as of an area or person) by a government agent that intrudes on an individual's reasonable expectation of privacy and is conducted usu. for the purpose of finding evidence of unlawful activity or guilt or to locate a person ⟨warrantless *~es* are invalid unless they fall within narrowly drawn exceptions —*State v. Mahone*, 701 P.2d 171 (1985)⟩ — see also EXIGENT CIRCUMSTANCES, PLAIN VIEW 2, *probable cause* at CAUSE 2, REASONABLE SUSPICION, *search warrant* at WARRANT; compare SEIZURE ◊ The Fourth Amendment to the U.S. Constitution prohibits unreasonable searches and requires that a warrant may issue only upon probable cause and that the warrant must particularly describe the place to be searched. Some searches, such as a search incident to an arrest, have been held to be valid without a warrant.

administrative search : an inspection or search carried out under a regulatory or statutory scheme esp. in public or commercial premises and usu. to enforce compliance with regulations or laws pertaining to health, safety, or security ⟨one of the fundamental principles of *administrative searches* is that the government may not use an administrative inspection scheme as a pretext to search for evidence of criminal violations —*People v. Madison*, 520 N.E.2d 374 (1988)⟩ — called also *administrative inspection, inspection, regulatory search;* see also *probable cause 2* at CAUSE 2 ◊ The U.S. Supreme Court held in *Camara v. Municipal Court*, 387 U.S. 523 (1967), that a reasonable administrative search may be conducted upon a showing of probable cause which is less stringent than that required for a search incident to a criminal investigation. The Court stated that the reasonableness of the search can only be determined by "balancing the need to search against the invasion which the search entails." Cases following *Camara* have stated that the probable cause requirement is fulfilled by showing that the search meets reasonable administrative standards established in a nonarbitrary regulatory scheme.

bor·der search : a search made of a person upon crossing into the U.S. at a border or its equivalent (as the airport at which the person arrives in the U.S.) ◇ Probable cause is not required for a border search.

consent search : a warrantless search conducted upon the voluntarily given consent of a person having authority over the place or things to be searched

inventory search : a warrantless search (as of an impounded automobile) conducted for the purpose of placing personal property in safekeeping to prevent loss of the property and claims against police for such loss

protective search : a search (as a frisk) conducted by a law enforcement officer for the purpose of ensuring against threats to safety (as from a concealed weapon) or sometimes to prevent the destruction of evidence

regulatory search : ADMINISTRATIVE SEARCH in this entry

shake·down search \'shāk-ˌdaůn-\ : a search for illicit or contraband material (as weapons or drugs) in prisoners' cells that is usu. random and warrantless ◇ In *Hudson v. Palmer*, 468 U.S. 517 (1984), the U.S. Supreme Court held that Fourth Amendment protections do not extend to searches of prisoners' cells.

strip search : a search for something concealed on a person conducted after removal of the person's clothing **2** : an act of boarding and inspecting a ship on the high seas in exercise of the right to do so under international law (as in time of war) **3** : an examination of a public record or registry — see also TITLE SEARCH

²**search** *vt* : to conduct a search of ⟨~ a premises⟩ ⟨~ a person⟩ ⟨~ a title⟩ — *vi* : to conduct a search ⟨~ for drugs in a school locker⟩ — **search·er** *n*

search and seizure warrant *n* : SEARCH WARRANT at WARRANT

search warrant — see WARRANT

sea·son·able \'sē-zə-nə-bəl\ *adj* : occurring within the time agreed to by parties to a commercial transaction or within a reasonable time ⟨~ notice of the rejection of goods⟩ — **sea·son·ably** \-blē\ *adv*

SEC *abbr* Securities and Exchange Commission — see also the IMPORTANT AGENCIES section

sec·ond·ary \'se-kən-ˌder-ē\ *adj* **1** : of second rank, status, importance, or value **2** : derived from something original or primary **3** : of, relating to, or being the second order or stage in a series — **sec·ond·ar·i·ly** \ˌse-kən-'der-ə-lē\ *adv* — **sec·ond·ar·i·ness** \'se-kən-ˌder-ē-nəs\ *n*

secondary beneficiary — see BENEFICIARY b

secondary boycott *n* : a boycott of an employer with which a union does not have a dispute that is intended to induce the employer to cease doing business with another employer with which the union does have a dispute — compare PRIMARY BOYCOTT ◇ Secondary boycotts are usu. illegal under the National Labor Relations Act.

secondary evidence — see EVIDENCE

secondary liability — see LIABILITY 2b

secondary market *n* **1** : the market in which previously issued securities are sold — compare PRIMARY MARKET **2** : the market in which existing mortgages are bought and sold

secondary mean·ing *n* : a developed association in the public's mind between the mark, name, or trade dress of a product and a specific manufacturer originating it that renders the mark, name, or trade dress protectable under trademark law ⟨the general descriptive name of the product acquired *secondary meaning*⟩

secondary pick·et·ing *n* : the picketing of

\ə\abut \ə\kitten \ər\further \a\ash \ā\ace \ä\cot, cart \aů\out \ch\chin \e\bet \ē\easy \g\go \i\hit \ī\ice \j\job \ŋ\sing \ō\go \ò\law \òi\boy \th\thin \t̲h̲\the \ü\loot \ů\foot \y\yet \zh\vision *see also* Pronunciation Symbols page

an employer who conducts business with an employer with whom a union has a dispute ◊ Secondary picketing that is not for the purpose of informing the public of the dispute violates the Labor Management Relations (Taft-Hartley) Act.

secondary strike — see STRIKE

sec·ond degree *n* : the grade given to the second most serious forms of crimes ⟨assault in the *second degree*⟩ — **second-degree** *adj*

second-degree murder — see MURDER

second mortgage — see MORTGAGE

sec·re·tary *n, pl* **-tar·ies** *often cap* **1** : an officer of a business concern who may keep records of directors' and stockholders' meetings and of stock ownership and transfer and help supervise the company's interests **2** : a government officer who superintends an administrative department

Secretary of the Senate : an officer of the Senate chiefly responsible for administration and operation

se·cret testament *n* : MYSTIC WILL at WILL

sec·tion 1983 \'sek-shən-,nīn-tēn-,ā-tē-'thrē\ *n* : the section of title 42 of the U.S. Code that makes a person liable for depriving another of any rights, privileges, or immunities secured by the U.S. Constitution and laws while acting under color of any statute, ordinance, regulation, custom, or usage of a state

se·cure *vt* **se·cured; se·cur·ing 1** : to put beyond hazard of losing or not receiving ⟨~ the blessings of liberty — *U.S. Constitution* preamble⟩ **2 a** : to protect or make certain (as by lien) ⟨make a just and equitable partition and ~ the parties' respective interests — *Denton v. Lazenby*, 879 P.2d 607 (1994)⟩ **b** : to give security for (as a loan) or otherwise assure the payment, performance, or execution of with security ⟨the court imposed a lien on his property to ~ the judgment⟩ **c** : to give or pledge security to (as a creditor); *broadly* : to cause to have security or a security interest ⟨a creditor *secured* by a lien on real property⟩

secured *adj* **1 a** : guaranteed or protected by security ⟨a ~ claim⟩ **b** : constituting security ⟨~ property⟩ **2** : having a security interest ⟨an interest rendering the primary lender ~⟩ **3** : involving or providing for the creation of a security interest ⟨a ~ sale⟩

secured creditor — see CREDITOR

secured party — see PARTY 1a

secured transaction *n* : a transaction that is intended to create a security interest in personal property (as goods) or fixtures and that is governed by Article 9 of the Uniform Commercial Code — compare SECURITY AGREEMENT

se·cur·i·tize \si-'kyùr-ə-,tīz\ *vt* **-tized; -tiz·ing** : to convert (assets) into securities typically by transferring them (as by sale) to a special trust, partnership, or corporation that issues them as securities with a resulting reallocation or reduction of risk and increase in liquidity for the company (as a bank) acting as the sponsor of the transaction — see also *asset-backed security* at SECURITY — **se·cur·i·ti·za·tion** \si-,kyùr-ə-tə-'zā-shən\ *n*

se·cur·i·ty \si-'kyùr-ə-tē\ *n, pl* **-ties 1 a** : something (as a mortgage or collateral) that is provided to make certain the fulfillment of an obligation ⟨used his property as ~ for a loan⟩ **b** : SURETY — see also SECURITY FOR COSTS **2** : evidence of indebtedness, ownership, or the right to ownership; *specif* : evidence of investment in a common enterprise (as a corporation or partnership) made with the expectation of deriving a profit solely from the efforts of others who acquire control over the funds invested ⟨a ~ involves some form of investment contract⟩ — see also DUE DILIGENCE

asset-backed security : a security (as a bond) that represents ownership in or is secured by a pool of assets (as loans or receivables) that have been securitized

bearer security : a security (as a bearer bond) that is not registered and is payable to anyone in possession of it

cer·tif·i·cat·ed security \sər-'ti-fə-,kā-təd-\ : a security that belongs to or is divisible into a class or series of shares, participations, interests, or obligations, is a commonly recognized medium of investment, and is represented on an instrument payable to the bearer or a specified person or on an instrument registered on books by or on behalf of the issuer

convertible security : a security (as a share of preferred stock) that the owner has the right to convert into a share or obligation of another class or series (as common stock)

debt security : a security (as a bond) serving as evidence of the indebtedness of the issuer (as a government or corporation) to the owner

equity security : a security (as a share of stock) serving as evidence of an ownership interest in the issuer; *also* : one convertible to or serving as evidence of a right to purchase, sell, or subscribe to such a security

ex•empt•ed security : a security (as a government bond) exempt from particular requirements of the Securities and Exchange Commission (as those relating to registration on a security exchange)

fixed–income security : a security (as a bond) that provides a fixed rate of return on an investment (as because of a fixed interest rate or dividend)

government security : a security (as a Treasury bill) that is issued by a government, a government agency, or a corporation in which a government has a direct or indirect interest

hybrid security : a security with characteristics of both an equity security and a debt security

mortgage–backed security : a security that represents ownership in or is secured by a pool of mortgage obligations; *specif* : a pass-through security based on mortgage obligations

pass–through security : a security representing an ownership interest in a pool of debt obligations from which payments of interest and principal pass from the debtor through an intermediary (as a bank) to the investor; *esp* : one based on a pool of mortgage obligations guaranteed by a federal government agency — compare COLLATERALIZED MORTGAGE OBLIGATION, REMIC

registered security **1** : a security (as a registered bond) whose owner is registered on the books of the issuer **2** : a security that is to be offered for sale and for which a registration statement has been submitted

restricted security : a security accompanied by restrictions on its free transfer or registration of transfer

shelf security : a corporate security held for deferred issue in a shelf registration

treasury security : a security issued by a government treasury : TREASURY 3

un•cer•tif•i•cat•ed security \,ən-sər-'ti-fə-,kā-təd-\ : a security that belongs to or is divisible into a class or series of shares, participations, interests, or obligations, that is a commonly recognized medium of investment, that is not represented by an instrument, and the transfer of which is registered on books by or on behalf of the issuer

unregistered security : a security for which a registration statement has not been filed

when–is•sued security : a security traded on a conditional basis prior to its issue

3 a : measures taken to guard against espionage or sabotage, crime, attack, or escape **b** : an organization or department whose task is security

security agreement *n* : an agreement which creates or provides for a security interest ⟨perfect a security interest in collateral described in a *security agreement*⟩ — compare SECURED TRANSACTION

security deposit *n* : money provided by a tenant to a landlord to secure performance of a rental agreement or compensate for possible loss or damage

\ə\abut \ə\kitten \ər\further \a\ash \ā\ace
\ä\cot, cart \aú\out \ch\chin \e\bet \ē\easy
\g\go \i\hit \ī\ice \j\job \ŋ\sing \ō\go \ó\law
\ói\boy \th\thin \th\the \ü\loot \ú\foot \y\yet
\zh\vision *see also* Pronunciation Symbols page

security for costs : security sometimes required of a party to litigation in order to assure payment of expenses

security interest — see INTEREST 1

se·di·tion \si-'di-shən\ *n* [Latin *seditio*, literally, separation, from *sed* apart + *itio* act of going, from *ire* to go] : the crime of creating a revolt, disturbance, or violence against lawful civil authority with the intent to cause its overthrow or destruction — compare CRIMINAL SYNDICALISM, SABOTAGE — **se·di·tious** \-shəs\ *adj* — **se·di·tious·ly** *adv*

seg·re·gate \'se-gri-ˌgāt\ *vb* **-gat·ed; -gat·ing** *vt* : to cause or force the separation of; *specif* : to separate (persons) on the basis of race, religion, or national origin ~ *vi* : to practice or enforce a policy of segregation — **seg·re·ga·tive** \-ˌgā-tiv\ *adj*

seg·re·ga·tion \ˌse-gri-'gā-shən\ *n* **1** : separation of individuals or groups and esp. racial groups — compare DESEGREGATION

de facto segregation : segregation of racial groups that arises as a result of economic, social, or other factors rather than by operation or enforcement of laws or other official state action

de jure segregation : segregation intended or mandated by law or otherwise intentionally arising from state action ◊ De jure segregation is illegal.

2 : separate confinement of prisoners within a penal institution

seise *var of* SEIZE

sei·sin *or* **sei·zin** \'sēz-ᵊn\ *n* [Anglo French *seisine*, from Old French *saisine* act of taking possession, from *saisir* to seize, of Germanic origin] **1** : the possession of land or chattels: as **a** : the possession of land arising from livery of seisin — see also LIVERY OF SEISIN **b** : the possession of a freehold estate in land by one having title thereto **2** : the right to immediate possession of an estate or to immediate succession ⟨~ of an heir upon death of the testator⟩

seize *vt* **seized; seiz·ing 1** *or* **seise** : to put in possession of property or vest with the right of possession or succession ⟨stand

seized of land⟩ **2** : to take possession or custody of (property) esp. by lawful authority ⟨~ drugs as evidence⟩ ⟨the judgment of criminal forfeiture shall authorize the Attorney General to ~ the interest or property subject to forfeiture —*Federal Rules of Criminal Procedure* Rule 32(b)(2)⟩ ⟨can ~ the goods subject to his security interest and . . . keep them in satisfaction of the debt —J. J. White and R. S. Summers⟩ — compare FORECLOSE, REPOSSESS **3** : to detain (a person) in such circumstances as would lead a reasonable person to believe that he or she was not free to leave ⟨determined that the defendant was *seized* when surrounded by police officers⟩ — **seiz·able** *adj*

seizin *var of* SEISIN

sei·zure \'sē-zhər\ *n* : the act, fact, or process of seizing: as **a** : the seizing of property that involves meaningful interference with a person's possessory interest in it ⟨~ of evidence found in plain view⟩ — see also PLAIN VIEW 2 **b** : the seizing of a person (as for arrest or investigation) — see also ARREST, STOP; compare SEARCH ◊ The Fourth Amendment to the U.S. Constitution guarantees the right against unreasonable searches and seizures. It requires that a warrant may issue only upon probable cause, and that the warrant particularly describe the persons or things to be seized. Not all seizures, however, require a warrant. A seizure that constitutes an arrest requires probable cause to be reasonable, and a stop usu. requires reasonable suspicion of the particular person or persons stopped, although stops like those at drunk driving checkpoints may be justified by a plan that places explicit and neutral limitations on the conduct of police officers with no requirement of individualized suspicion.

se·lec·tive incorporation *n* : a theory or doctrine of constitutional law that those rights guaranteed by the first eight amendments to the U.S. Constitution that are fundamental to and implicit in the concept of ordered liberty are incorporated into the Fourteenth Amendment's due process clause — compare TOTAL INCORPORATION

se·lect·man \si-'lekt-mən, -ˌman\ *n* : one of a board of officials elected in towns of all New England states except Rhode Island to serve as the chief administrative authority of the town

self–deal·ing \'self-'dē-liŋ\ *n* : engagement in a transaction that is intended primarily to benefit one's self or the narrow interests of a few (as corporate insiders) rather than those to whom one owes a duty by virtue of one's position ⟨∼ by a trustee⟩ — **self–dealing** *adj*

self–de·fense \'self-di-'fens\ *n* **1** : the use of force to defend oneself **2** : an affirmative defense (as to a murder charge) alleging that the defendant used force necessarily to protect himself or herself because of a reasonable belief that the other party intended to inflict great bodily harm or death — see also JUSTIFICATION 2

self–ex·e·cut·ing \'self-'ek-sə-ˌkü-tiŋ\ *adj* : taking effect immediately without the need for implementing legislation or further judicial action ⟨a ∼ judgment⟩

self–help \'self-'help\ *n* : the act of redressing or preventing a wrong by one's own actions rather than through legal proceedings ◊ The Uniform Commercial Code permits creditors to repossess collateral by self-help if it can be done without a breach of the peace.

self–in·crim·i·nat·ing \'self-in-'kri-mə-ˌnā-tiŋ\ *adj* : tending to incriminate oneself ⟨a ∼ statement⟩

self–in·crim·i·na·tion \ˌself-in-ˌkri-mə-'nā-shən\ *n* : incrimination of and by oneself esp. through testimony — see also *privilege against self-incrimination* at PRIVILEGE

self–in·sur·ance \ˌself-in-'shur-əns, -'in-ˌshur-\ *n* : insurance of oneself, one's interests, or one's components (as of a governmental unit) through the use of a fund that one maintains to cover losses

self–in·sure \ˌself-in-'shur\ *vt* : to insure by self-insurance (as in workers' compensation) ⟨an employer wishing to ∼ its liability —*Pennsylvania Statutes*⟩ ∼ *vi*

: to use self-insurance ⟨a governmental agency that ∼s⟩ — **self–in·sur·er** *n*

self–proved \'self-'prüvd\ *adj* : SELF-PROVING 1

self–prov·ing \'self-'prü-viŋ\ *adj* **1** : containing proof of its own validity ⟨a ∼ will⟩ **2** : providing or being the evidence that renders something self-proving; *esp* : being an affidavit signed by the witnesses to a will attesting to the will's validity

self–serving declaration — see DECLARATION 2c

sell *vb* **sold; sell·ing** *vt* **1** : to transfer ownership of by sale — compare BARTER, CONVEY, GIVE **2** : to offer for sale ∼ *vi* : to dispose of something by sale : make a sale — compare DONATE — **sell·er** *n* —

sell short : to sell something one does not own : make a short sale

sem·ble \'sem-bəl\ [Anglo-French, third person singular present indicative of *sembler* to seem] : it seems ⟨∼ that the two statutes are consistent⟩ — used chiefly to indicate obiter dictum usu. parenthetically following a citation or to introduce a tentative thought

sen·ate \'se-nət\ *n* : the upper chamber in a bicameral legislature; *esp, cap* : the upper house of the U.S. Congress or a state legislature

sen·a·tor \'se-nə-tər\ *n* : a member of a senate — **sen·a·to·ri·al** \ˌse-nə-'tōr-ē-əl\ *adj*

se·nior \'sē-nyər\ *adj* : having higher rank or priority ⟨a ∼ lienholder⟩; *specif* : having a claim on corporate assets and income prior to other securities

se·nior·i·ty \sēn-'yòr-ə-tē\ *n* **1** : the quality or state of being senior **2** : the senior status attained by length of continuous service (as in a company); *also* : the length of such continuous service

senior lien — see LIEN

senior mortgage — see MORTGAGE

\ə\abut \ᵊ\kitten \ər\further \a\ash \ā\ace \ä\cot, cart \aú\out \ch\chin \e\bet \ē\easy \g\go \i\hit \ī\ice \j\job \ŋ\sing \ō\go \ò\law \ói\boy \th\thin \th̲\the \ü\loot \ú\foot \y\yet \zh\vision *see also* Pronunciation Symbols page

¹**sen·tence** \'sent-ᵊns, -ᵊnz\ *n* [Old French, opinion, judicial sentence, from Latin *sententia*, ultimately from *sentire* to feel, think, express an opinion] **1** : a judgment formally pronouncing the punishment to be inflicted on one convicted of a crime **2** : the punishment that one convicted of a crime is ordered to receive

concurrent sentence : a sentence that runs at the same time as another

consecutive sentence : a sentence that runs before or after another

cumulative sentence : CONSECUTIVE SENTENCE in this entry; *also* : the combination of two or more consecutive sentences

death sentence : a sentence condemning the convicted defendant to death

de·ter·mi·nate sentence \di-'tər-mə-nət-\ : a sentence for a fixed rather than indeterminate length of time

general sentence : a sentence that does not allocate the punishment imposed for the individual counts on which the defendant was convicted ◊ General sentences are impermissible.

in·de·ter·mi·nate sentence \ˌin-di-'tər-mə-nət-\ : a sentence of minimum and maximum duration with the exact length to be later determined (as by a parole board)

life sentence : a sentence of imprisonment for the rest of the convicted defendant's life

mandatory sentence : a sentence that is specifically required or falls within a range required by statute as punishment for an offense ⟨imposed the minimum *mandatory sentence* for distributing drugs near a school⟩

presumptive sentence : a sentence that is the presumed punishment for an offense and is subject to the upward or downward adjustment of its severity depending on aggravating and mitigating factors

split sentence : a sentence of which part is served in prison and the other suspended and usu. replaced by probation

suspended sentence : a sentence the imposition or execution of which is suspended by the court

²**sentence** *vt* **sen·tenced; sen·tenc·ing** : to impose a sentence on

sentencing guide·lines \-'gīd-ˌlīnz\ *n pl* : a set of rules for computing sentences that is promulgated by a commission on sentencing and that typically provides classifications (as of offenses or offenders), scales (as of severity of crimes), and suggested punishments

SEP *n* : SIMPLIFIED EMPLOYEE PENSION

sep·a·ra·bil·i·ty clause \ˌse-pə-rə-'bi-lə-tē-\ *n* : SEVERABILITY CLAUSE

sep·a·ra·ble controversy \'se-pə-rə-bəl-\ *n* : a separate and independent claim or cause of action that by itself is removable to the federal courts even though it is joined with others that are not removable ◊ If a case involves a separable controversy, the entire case may be removed and determined as a whole, or the court may remand those matters that were not removable and determine the rest.

sep·a·rate \'se-pə-ˌrāt\ *vb* **-rat·ed; -rat·ing** *vt* : to cause the separation of ～ *vi* : to undergo a separation ⟨the couple *separated* last year⟩ — compare DIVORCE

sep·a·rate but equal \'se-prət-, -pə-rət-\ *n* : the doctrine set forth by the U.S. Supreme Court that sanctioned the segregation of individuals by race in separate but equal facilities but that was invalidated as unconstitutional — see also *Brown v. Board of Education of Topeka* and *Plessy v. Ferguson* in the IMPORTANT CASES section

sep·a·rat·ed \'se-pə-ˌrā-təd\ *adj* : being in a state of estrangement between spouses usu. requiring the maintenance of separate residences and the intent to live apart permanently : being in a state of separation ⟨has been ～ for a year⟩

separate estate — see ESTATE 2

separate maintenance *n* : maintenance paid (as by court order) from one spouse to another during separation ⟨entitlement to *separate maintenance* does not extend to the division of marital assets —

Kennedy v. Kennedy, 662 So. 2d 179 (1995)⟩

separate opinion — see OPINION

separate property — see PROPERTY

sep·a·ra·tion \ˌse-pə-'rā-shən\ *n* **1** : cessation of cohabitation between a married couple by mutual agreement with intent that it be permanent; *also* : LEGAL SEPARATION — compare DIVORCE ◊ In some cases in which the estrangement is extreme, a separation is considered to have occurred even when the couple retain the same residence if they have stopped communicating and engaging in sexual relations and intend to be separated. **2** : termination of a contractual relationship (as employment or military service)

separation agreement *n* : a contractual agreement setting forth terms pertaining to property, child support, or other matters in the separation of a married couple ⟨incorporated the *separation agreement* into the divorce decree⟩

separation from bed and board : LEGAL SEPARATION

separation of church and state : the separation of religion and government mandated under the establishment clause and the free exercise clause of the U.S. Constitution that forbids governmental establishment or preference of a religion and that preserves religious freedom from governmental intrusion

separation of powers **1** : the constitutional allocation of the legislative, executive, and judicial powers among the three branches of government **2** : the doctrine under which the legislative, executive, and judicial branches of government are not to infringe upon each other's constitutionally vested powers — see also NONDELEGATION DOCTRINE

¹se·ques·ter \si-'kwes-tər\ *vt* **-tered; -tering** [Anglo-French *sequestrer*, from Middle French, from Latin *sequestrare* to hand over to a trustee, from *sequester* third party to whom disputed property is entrusted, agent, from *secus* beside, otherwise] **1** : to place (as a jury or witness) on or isolation ◊ Juries are se-

questered in order to preserve their impartiality. Witnesses are sequestered so that their testimony is not influenced by the testimony of prior witnesses. **2 a** : to seize esp. by a writ of sequestration **b** : to deposit (property) in sequestration

²sequester *n* : SEQUESTRATION 3

se·ques·trate \'sē-kwəs-ˌtrāt, 'se-; si-'kwes-ˌtrāt\ *vt* **-trat·ed; -trat·ing** : SEQUESTER

se·ques·tra·tion \ˌsē-kwəs-'trā-shən, ˌse-\ *n* **1** : the act of sequestering : the state of being sequestered **2 a** : a writ authorizing an official (as a sheriff) to take into custody the property of a defendant usu. to enforce a court order, to exercise quasi in rem jurisdiction, or to preserve the property until judgment is rendered **b** *in the civil law of Louisiana* : a deposit in which a neutral person agrees to hold property in dispute and to restore it to the party to whom it is determined to belong **3** : the cancellation of funds for expenditure or obligation in order to enforce federal budget limitations set by law

se·ques·tra·tor \'sē-kwəs-ˌtrā-tər, si-'kwes-\ *n* **1** : an official who executes a writ of sequestration **2** : someone who holds property in sequestration

serial bond — see BOND 2

¹se·ri·a·tim \ˌsir-ē-'ā-təm, -'a-, -'ä-\ *adv* [Medieval Latin, from Latin *series* succession of persons or things, series, from *serere* to join, bind together] : in a series : individually in a sequence ⟨we will consider the complaints ∼⟩

²seriatim *adj* : occurring or following in a series ⟨talked to the various trustees in ∼ telephone calls —*Professional Hockey Corp. v. World Hockey Ass'n*, 191 Cal. Rptr. 773 (1983)⟩

se·ri·ous bodily harm *n* : SERIOUS BODILY INJURY

serious bodily injury *n* : bodily injury which involves substantial risk of death,

\ə\abut \ᵊ\kitten \ər\further \a\ash \ā\ace
\ä\cot, cart \au̇\out \ch\chin \e\bet \ē\easy
\g\go \i\hit \ī\ice \j\job \ŋ\sing \ō\go \ȯ\law
\ȯi\boy \th\thin \th̲\the \ü\loot \u̇\foot \y\yet
\zh\vision *see also* Pronunciation Symbols page

protracted and obvious disfigurement, or protracted loss or impairment of the function of a bodily member or organ or mental faculty — compare BODILY INJURY

ser·vant *n* : a person who serves others: as **a** : an individual who performs duties about the person or home of a master or personal employer **b** : a person in the employ and subject to the direction or control of an individual or company — see also RESPONDEAT SUPERIOR; compare AGENT, MASTER

serve *vt* **served; serv·ing 1** : to deliver, publish, or execute (notice or process) as required by law ⟨no notice of any such request was ever *served* on the husband — *National Law Journal*⟩ **2** : to make legal service upon (the person named in a process) : inform or notify by legal service ⟨unless the city had been *served* with prior notice of a defect —Gene Mustain⟩ **3** : to put in (a term of imprisonment) ⟨has *served* five years of her sentence⟩

¹ser·vice *n* **1** : the act of delivering to or informing someone of a writ, summons, or other notice as prescribed by law ⟨after ∼ of process⟩ — see also *notice by publication* at NOTICE, SUBSTITUTED SERVICE, SUMMONS ◊ Although service of process is primarily the means for a court to exert personal jurisdiction over a person, some form of service (as by publication of notice in a newspaper) is also usu. required for exercise of in rem or quasi in rem jurisdiction. **2 a** : useful labor that does not produce a tangible commodity — usu. used in pl. ⟨payment for ∼s rendered⟩ **b** : the maintenance or repair of tangible property ⟨machinery for the ∼ and improvement of the residence⟩

²service *vt* **ser·viced; ser·vic·ing** : to provide services for: as **a** : to meet interest and sinking fund payments on (debt) ⟨didn't have the cash flow to ∼ a large loan⟩ **b** : to collect payments and maintain a payment schedule for (a loan) esp. after sale of the loan to a secondary mortgage market (as the Federal National Mortgage Association) — compare ORIGINATE

service mark *n* : a mark (as a name) used esp. in advertising to identify and distinguish services (as transportation) of one person from another and to indicate the source of the services — see also *Trademark Act of 1946* in the IMPORTANT LAWS section; compare TRADEMARK

servient estate — see ESTATE 4

ser·vi·tude \'sər-və-ˌtüd, -ˌtyüd\ *n* **1** : a condition in which an individual lacks liberty esp. to determine his or her course of action or way of life; *specif* : the state of being a slave ⟨involuntary ∼⟩ — see also *Amendment XIII* and *Amendment XV* to the CONSTITUTION in the back matter **2** : a right by which property owned by one person is subject to a specified use or enjoyment of another — used chiefly in the civil law of Louisiana; see also *dominant estate* and *servient estate* at ESTATE 4; compare EASEMENT

   apparent servitude : a predial servitude whose existence is perceivable by exterior signs or works (as an aqueduct or road) on the property

   legal servitude : a predial servitude that is created by a limitation under the law on the use of the property

   natural servitude : a predial servitude that arises from the situation of the estates (as from one being situated downhill from another)

   personal servitude : a servitude that burdens property in favor of a specific named person — see also RIGHT OF USE, USUFRUCT

   predial servitude : a servitude that burdens one item of immovable property (as a tract of land) in favor of another ◊ A predial servitude is transferred along with the ownership of the dominant estate, and the servient estate is always taken subject to the servitude. A predial servitude cannot be transferred separately from the dominant estate.

ses·sion *n* : a meeting or series of meetings of a body (as a court or legislature) for the transaction of business; *also* : the period between the first meeting of a legislative or judicial body and the final adjournment

— see also REGULAR SESSION, SPECIAL SESSION

set aside *vt* **1** : to disagree with and overturn (a decision or act of a lower tribunal) upon review : OVERRULE, VACATE ⟨*set aside* the decree⟩ **2** : to deprive of legal effect or force : ANNUL, VOID ⟨may *set aside* the contract⟩

set-off \'set-ˌȯf\ *n* **1** : the reduction or discharge of a debt by setting against it a claim in favor of the debtor; *specif* : the reduction or discharge of a party's debt or claim by an assertion of another claim arising out of another transaction or cause of action against the other party **2 a** : a right to seek reduction or discharge of a debt or claim by countering a party's claim with an independent claim **b** : a counterclaim made by a defendant against a plaintiff for reduction or discharge of a debt by reason of an independent debt owed by the plaintiff to the defendant — compare RECOUPMENT 2

set off *vt* : to reduce or discharge by set-off : OFFSET

set·tle *vb* **set·tled; set·tling** *vt* **1** : to resolve conclusively ⟨~ a question of law⟩ **2** : to establish or secure permanently ⟨a *settled* legal principle⟩ **3** : CLOSE ⟨~ the sale of securities⟩ ⟨~ the estate⟩ **4** : to resolve a disagreement about (a court order) ⟨no hearing to consider these objections and to ~ the order had been conducted — *Saba v. Gray,* 314 N.W.2d 597 (1981)⟩ **5 a** : to fix (a price) by mutual agreement **b** : to conclude (a lawsuit) by entering into an agreement negotiated by the parties usu. out of court **c** : to close (as an account) by payment; *also* : to close by compromise and payment of less than the full amount claimed or due ~ *vi* **1** : to conclude a lawsuit by entering into an agreement ⟨the plaintiff chose to ~ out of court⟩ **2** : to make a settlement of a transfer of funds **3** : to adjust differences or accounts ⟨*settled* with his creditors⟩

set·tle·ment *n* **1** : the act or process of settling **2 a** : an agreement reducing or resolving differences; *esp* : an agreement between litigants that concludes the liti-

gation ⟨the states finally agreed upon a ~ and a consent decree —W. J. Brennan, Jr.⟩ ⟨entered into a property ~ prior to the divorce⟩ **b** : a formal and permanent grant or conveyance **c** : the sum, estate, or income granted or paid under a settlement ⟨if the monetary limits of a defendant's insurance policy can be discovered in order to obtain reasonable ~s —J. H. Friedenthal *et al.*⟩ **3** : CLOSING ⟨~ costs⟩ **4** : the transfer of funds between a payor bank and a collecting bank in order to complete transactions for customers

settlement option — see OPTION 4

set·tlor \'set-ˌlȯr, 'set-ᵊl-ˌȯr\ *n* : a person who creates a trust — compare BENEFICIARY a, TRUSTEE 2a

sev·er \'se-vər\ *vt* **sev·ered; sev·er·ing 1** : to end (a joint tenancy) by ending one or all of the unities of time, title, possession, or interest (as by conveying one tenant's interest to another party) **2** : to separate (as a contract) into different parts (as independent obligations) in order to treat each separately **3 a** : to try (criminal offenses or defendants) separately in order to avoid prejudice **b** : to split (a criminal trial) into multiple trials in order to avoid prejudice **c** : to try (civil claims or issues pleaded in the same case) separately — **sev·er·ance** \'se-vrəns, -və-rens\ *n*

severability clause *n* : a clause (as in a contract) which states that provisions are severable; *esp* : a clause in a statute that makes the statute's parts or provisions severable so that one part can be invalidated without invalidating the whole — called also *separability clause*

sev·er·able \'se-vrə-bəl, 'se-və-rə-\ *adj* : capable of being severed : DIVISIBLE ⟨a ~ contract⟩ ⟨a ~ bequest⟩ — compare ENTIRE — **sev·er·abil·i·ty** \ˌse-vrə-'bi-lə-tē, ˌse-və-rə-\ *n*

sev·er·al *adj* [Anglo-French, from Medieval Latin *separalis,* from Latin *separ*

\ə\abut \ᵊ\kitten \ər\further \a\ash \ā\ace
\ä\cot, cart \au̇\out \ch\chin \e\bet \ē\easy
\g\go \i\hit \ī\ice \j\job \ŋ\sing \ō\go \ȯ\law
\ȯi\boy \th\thin \th̲\the \ü\loot \u̇\foot \y\yet
\zh\vision *see also* Pronunciation Symbols page

separate] **1 a :** of or relating separately to each individual involved; *specif* : enforceable separately against each party ⟨each promisor owed a ∼ duty⟩ — see also *several liability* at LIABILITY 2b, *several obligation* at OBLIGATION **b :** being separately or individually responsible, liable, or obligated ⟨a ∼ obligor⟩ — compare JOINT **2 :** separate or distinct from one another ⟨to regulate commerce with foreign nations and among the ∼ States —*U.S. Constitution* art. I⟩ — **sev·er·al·ly** *adv*

several liability — see LIABILITY 2b
several obligation — see OBLIGATION
sev·er·al·ty \'se-vrəl-tē, 'se-və-rəl-\ *n* [Anglo-French *severalté* separation, individual ownership, from *several* separate, several] **1 :** sole, separate, and exclusive ownership : one's own right without a joint interest in another person ⟨agrees to assign the lease, or some portion of it (in common or in ∼) to another operator —*Pacific Enterprises Oil Co. v. Pacific Petroleum Corp.*, 614 So. 2d 409 (1993)⟩ ⟨held the estate in ∼⟩ **2 :** the quality or state of being individual, particular, or several

sex discrimination *n* : discrimination based on sex and esp. against women
sex·u·al abuse \'sek-shə-wəl-, -shwəl-\ *n* **1 a :** the infliction of sexual contact upon a person by forcible compulsion **b :** the engaging in sexual contact with a person who is below a specified age or who is incapable of giving consent because of age or mental or physical incapacity **2 :** the crime of engaging in or inflicting sexual abuse

sexual assault — see ASSAULT
sexual battery — see BATTERY
sexual harassment *n* : employment discrimination consisting of unwelcome verbal or physical conduct directed at an employee because of his or her sex; *also* : the tort of engaging in such discrimination — see also HOSTILE ENVIRONMENT SEXUAL HARASSMENT, QUID PRO QUO SEXUAL HARASSMENT ◊ Sexual harassment has been found by federal courts to violate the protection in the Civil Rights Act of 1964 against discrimination in employment. There are also state statutes under which sexual harassment actions may be brought. In order to recover against an employer under a sexual harassment suit, the plaintiff has to show that the harassment affected the employment (as by being severe or pervasive) and that the employer is liable under respondeat superior because of actual or constructive knowledge of the harassment. Strict liability is often imposed for harassment of an employee by a supervisor or for quid pro quo sexual harassment.

shakedown search — see SEARCH
¹sham \'sham\ *n* : something that is false, deceptive, misleading, or otherwise not genuine
²sham *adj* : not genuine : intended to mislead or deceive : FALSE, ILLUSORY ⟨the sale for one dollar was a ∼ transfer of property⟩
sham pleading — see PLEADING 1
sham transaction *n* : a transaction that is made to mislead or deceive others : a transaction having no economic effect that is made to create tax benefits ◊ The Internal Revenue Service may deny tax benefits for sham transactions.
share *n* **1 :** a portion belonging to, due to, or due from an individual ⟨a joint tortfeasor is liable for her ∼ of the damages⟩; *specif* : the part allotted or belonging to one of a number owning together any property or interest ⟨the ∼ of a joint tenant⟩ ⟨his ∼ passed to his widow⟩ **2 a :** any of the equal interests into which ownership of something (as a fund) is divided; *specif* : any of the equal interests or rights into which the entire capital stock of a corporation is divided **b :** a certificate representing such a share
shared custody — see CUSTODY b
share·hold·er *n* : one that owns a share in a fund (as a mutual fund) or property; *esp* : STOCKHOLDER — see also DERIVATIVE ACTION, EQUITY 4c, PROXY CONTEST — **share·hold·ing** *adj or n*
shareholder control agreement *n* : a writ-

ten unanimous agreement of shareholders that transfers control of specified areas of corporate governance (as election of directors and officers, issue of dividends, employment of shareholders, or arbitration of disputes) from directors and officers to the shareholders

shareholder resolution *n* : a formal resolution by shareholders ratifying or requesting a specified action by a corporate board

shareholder's derivative suit *n* : DERIVATIVE ACTION

share·hold·ers' meeting \'shar-ˌhōl-dərz-\ *n* : ANNUAL MEETING

share·own·er \'shar-ˌō-nər\ *n* : SHAREHOLDER

shark re·pel·lent \-ri-'pe-lənt\ *n* : any measure taken by a corporation to discourage a hostile takeover attempt

shelf registration *n* : a provision of Securities and Exchange Commission regulations governing public offerings that allows corporations to defer sale of some shares after registration until market conditions are more favorable

shelf security — see SECURITY

shell corporation — see CORPORATION

shelter trust — see TRUST

Shep·ard·ize \'she-pər-ˌdīz\ *vt* **-ized; -iz-ing** : to look up (a case citation) in *Shepard's Citations* esp. in order to check the status of the case, parallel citations, or the use of the case in other jurisdictions ◊ *Shepard's Citations* is a citator and electronic service of Shepard's/McGraw⸗Hill, Inc.

sher·iff *n* [Old English *scīrgerēfa*, from *scīr* shire + *gerēfa* reeve (king's agent)] : an official of a county or parish charged primarily with judicial duties (as executing the processes and orders of courts and judges)

sheriff's deed — see DEED

sheriff's sale — see SALE

shield law *n* : a law that prevents or protects against disclosure or revelation of information: as **a** : RAPE SHIELD LAW **b** : a law that protects journalists from disclosure of confidential news sources

shifting use — see USE 1b

shipment contract — see CONTRACT

shock *adj* : of, relating to, or being a criminal sentence or condition of release involving participation in a program of vigorous physical training, discipline, regimentation, and rehabilitation therapy ⟨~incarceration⟩ ⟨~ probation⟩ ⟨~ parole⟩

shop *n* : a business establishment : a place of employment — see also CLOSED SHOP, OPEN SHOP, UNION SHOP

shop committee *n* : a committee composed of union members appointed or elected to handle employee grievances within a shop

shop·lift \'shäp-ˌlift\ *vi* : to steal displayed goods from a store ~ *vt* : to steal (displayed goods) from a store

shop·lift·er *n* : one who shoplifts

shop right *n* : the right of an employer to use without payment of any royalty an employee's invention developed in the course of employment

shop steward *n* : a union member elected or appointed to serve as the representative of the union in a plant, department, or shop and charged mainly with negotiating the settlement of grievances of employees with employers, maintaining compliance with the collective bargaining agreement, recruiting new union members, and collecting union dues

¹short *adj* **1** : treated or disposed of quickly in court ⟨the calendar for ~ causes⟩ **2 a** : not having goods or property that one has sold in anticipation of a fall in prices ⟨a seller who was ~ at the time of the sale⟩ **b** : consisting of or relating to a sale of securities or commodities that the seller does not possess or has not contracted for at the time of the sale ⟨a ~ sale⟩ ⟨a ~ position⟩ ◊ The purpose of a short sale is to profit from an anticipated drop in the price of a security or com-

\ə\abut \ˈə\kitten \ər\further \a\ash \ā\ace
\ä\cot, cart \au̇\out \ch\chin \e\bet \ē\easy
\g\go \i\hit \ī\ice \j\job \ŋ\sing \ō\go \ȯ\law
\ȯi\boy \th\thin \t̲h̲\the \ü\loot \u̇\foot \y\yet
\zh\vision *see also* Pronunciation Symbols page

modity. Typically, an investor directs a broker to borrow a quantity of stocks and to sell them at the current price. If the price drops, the investor then repurchases an equal quantity at the lower price, returns the borrowed stocks, and retains the difference in price as profit. If the price rises instead of falling, the investor may choose or be compelled to repurchase the stocks at a higher price and to accept a loss.

²short *adv* **:** by or as if by a short sale ⟨sold the stock ∼⟩

short–form merger — see MERGER

short rate *n* **1 :** an insurance premium charge for less than a year of coverage that is more than a pro rata part of the annual premium **2 :** an insurance policy written for less than one year — called also *short term*

short–swing profit *n* **:** a profit made by a corporate insider who purchases stock and sells it or sells stock and purchases it within a prescribed period ◊ Section 16(b) of the Securities Exchange Act of 1934 provides that a corporation may recover short-swing profits realized by an insider within six months.

short term *n* **:** SHORT RATE

short–term capital gain — see GAIN

show *vt* **showed; shown** *or* **showed; show•ing :** to demonstrate or establish by argument, reasoning, or evidence ⟨must ∼ a compelling need for the court action⟩ — **show cause :** to establish by reasoning and evidence a valid reason for something ⟨if a debtor wishes to extend a plan beyond three years, he must *show cause* — J. H. Williamson⟩ ⟨must *show cause* why the petition may not be granted⟩

show cause order — see ORDER 3b

show•ing *n* **:** an act or instance of establishing through evidence and argument ⟨appears to require a more specific ∼ of need by those who seek to perform drug-testing — D. A. Grossbaum⟩ ⟨failed to make a prima facie ∼ of a constitutional violation warranting suppression of the evidence⟩

show•up \'shō-ˌəp\ *n* **:** a presentation of a criminal defendant or arrestee individually to a witness for identification — compare LINEUP ◊ A showup identification may withstand a due process challenge when there is an emergency situation, when the presentation is accidental, or when otherwise the totality of the circumstances render it justifiable.

side•bar \'sīd-ˌbär\ *n* **:** SIDEBAR CONFERENCE ⟨had failed to request a ∼ before injecting the collateral offense into the trial —*Dockery v. State*, 659 So. 2d 219 (1994)⟩; *also* **:** the place near or before the bench where a sidebar conference takes place ⟨the judge informed both attorneys . . . that they . . . could stand at ∼ while questions were posed —*Commonwealth v. Urena*, 632 N.E.2d 1200 (1994)⟩ — compare BENCH, STAND — **sidebar** *adj*

sidebar conference *n* **:** a conference between the judge, the lawyers, and sometimes the parties to a case that the jury does not hear

sight *adj* **:** payable on presentation — see also *sight draft* at DRAFT

sight draft — see DRAFT

sign *vt* **1 :** to affix a signature to **:** ratify or attest by hand or seal ⟨∼ a bill into law⟩; *specif* **:** to write or mark something (as a signature) on (a document) as an acknowledgment of one's intention to be bound by it **2 :** to assign or convey formally ⟨∼*ed* the property over to his brother⟩ — **sign•er** *n*

sig•na•to•ry \'sig-nə-ˌtōr-ē\ *n, pl* **-ries :** a signer with another or others ⟨*signatories* to a petition⟩; *esp* **:** a government bound with others by a signed convention — **signatory** *adj*

sig•na•ture *n* **1 a :** the act of signing one's name or of making a mark in lieu thereof **b :** the name of a person written with his or her own hand to signify that the writing which precedes accords with his or her wishes or intentions **c :** any mark (as initials, stamp, or printed name) made on a document and intended to serve as an indication of the party's execution or authentication of the document and intent to be bound by it — see also PRIVATE

SIGNATURE **2** : a distinguishing or identifying mark, feature, or quality; *esp* : a distinctive method of committing a crime that is characteristic of an offender

signature crime *n* : any of two or more crimes that involve the use of a method, plan, or modus operandi so distinctive that it logically follows that the crimes must have been committed by the same person ◇ Evidence of other criminal acts is usu. not admissible against a defendant. Evidence of other crimes to prove that the crime in question is a signature crime committed by the defendant, however, is usu. allowed.

si·lence *n* **1** : the state of keeping or being silent; *esp* : forbearance from speech or comment **2** : failure to make something known esp. in violation of a duty to do so ⟨acceptance by ~⟩ — see also *estoppel by silence* at ESTOPPEL 1

si·lent *adj* **1** : making no utterance : resolved not to speak esp. about a certain topic ⟨the right to remain ~⟩ **2** : making no mention or account : omitting explanation and leaving questions unanswered ⟨a criminal statute ~ as to the requirement of intent⟩ **3** : taking no active part in the conduct of a business ⟨a ~ member of a firm⟩ — see also *silent partner* at PARTNER

silent partner — see PARTNER

silent record *n* : a record of a criminal proceeding which does not show that the defendant acted with knowledge or understanding of his or her rights (as in entering a plea of guilty or waiving the right to counsel)

silent witness the·o·ry *n* : a theory or rule in the law of evidence: photographic evidence (as photographs or videotapes) produced by a process whose reliability is established may be admitted as substantive evidence of what it depicts without the need for an eyewitness to verify the accuracy of its depiction

sim·ple *adj* **1** : oral or written but not under seal or of record **2** : not extreme, aggravated, or complicated ⟨~ kidnapping⟩ **3** : having no limitations or restric-

tions — see also FEE SIMPLE — **sim·ply** *adv*

simple assault — see ASSAULT

simple battery — see BATTERY

simple contract — see CONTRACT

simple interest — see INTEREST 5

simple mortgage clause *n* : OPEN MORTGAGE CLAUSE

simple negligence — see NEGLIGENCE

simple robbery — see ROBBERY

simple trust — see TRUST

sim·pli·ci·ter \sim-'pli-sə-tər\ *adv* [Latin, from *simplic-*, *simplex* simple] **1** : in a simple degree or manner : SIMPLY ⟨was murder ~⟩ **2** : PER SE

sim·pli·fied employee pension *n* : a pension that is funded by employer contributions or through a salary reduction arrangement and that places fewer administrative burdens on the employer than do other plans and allows employer deduction of contributions and employee withdrawal at any time — called also *SEP*

sim·u·late \'sim-yə-ˌlāt\ *vt* **-lat·ed; -lat·ing** *in the civil law of Louisiana* : to make or carry out in a manner that does not express one's true intent ⟨a *simulated* sale of the debtor's property in which no consideration was paid⟩

sim·u·la·tion \ˌsim-yə-'lā-shən\ *n, in the civil law of Louisiana* **1** : the act of simulating **2** : a contract that by mutual agreement does not express the true intent of the parties — see also COUNTERLETTER; compare *disguised donation* at DONATION ◇ Although a simulation does not have effect as between the parties, its lack of effect may not be asserted against third parties, such as creditors or bona fide purchasers, to avoid liability.

si·mul·ta·ne·ous death act \ˌsī-məl-'tā-nē-əs-\ *n* : an act providing for the disposition of property or insurance benefits when there is no sufficient evidence that persons (as spouses) died other than si-

\ə\abut \ᵊ\kitten \ər\further \a\ash \ā\ace
\ä\cot, cart \au̇\out \ch\chin \e\bet \ē\easy
\g\go \i\hit \ī\ice \j\job \ŋ\sing \ō\go \ȯ\law
\ȯi\boy \th\thin \t͟h\the \ü\loot \u̇\foot \y\yet
\zh\vision *see also* Pronunciation Symbols page

multaneously (as in an accident) ◊ The simultaneous death act is a uniform act that has been adopted by most states. It covers situations where the title to or transfer of property depends on priority of death. In general, for determining the disposal of property, each decedent is considered to have survived the other, and an insured individual is considered to have survived a beneficiary.

single–act statute *n* : LONG-ARM STATUTE

sin•gle publication rule *n* : a rule in the law of libel that treats an edition of a print source (as a magazine) as one publication giving rise to one cause of action for libel regardless of how many copies were printed and where they were distributed

sinking fund — see FUND 1

sit *vi* **sat; sit•ting** **1** : to occupy a place as a member of an official or formal body ⟨~ in Congress⟩ ⟨~ on a board of directors⟩ **2** : to hold a session : conduct official business ⟨the court ~*s* in the state capital⟩

si•tus \'sī-təs, 'sē-, -ˌtüs\ *n* [Latin, position, site, from *sinere* to leave in place, allow] : a location that is or is held to be the site of something (as property or a crime or tort) and that commonly determines jurisdiction over it ⟨the ~ of a conspiracy⟩

S.J.D. *abbr* [New Latin *scientiae juridicae doctor*] doctor of juridical science, doctor of the science of law

skip person *n* : a person to whom property is transferred in a generation-skipping transfer; *also* : a trust whose interests are all held by or may only be distributed to skip persons — see also DIRECT SKIP; compare GENERATION-SKIPPING TRANSFER

¹slan•der \'slan-dər\ *vt* : to utter slander against — **slan•der•er** *n*

²slander *n* [Anglo-French *esclandre*, from Old French *escandle*, *esclandre* scandal, from Late Latin *scandalum* moral stumbling block, disgrace, from Greek *skandalon*, literally, snare, trap] **1** : defamation of a person by unprivileged oral communication made to a third party; *also* : defamatory oral statements **2** : the

tort of oral defamation ⟨sued his former employer for ~⟩ — compare DEFAMATION, FALSE LIGHT, LIBEL ◊ An action for slander may be brought without alleging and proving special damages if the statements in question have a plainly harmful character, as by imputing to the plaintiff criminal guilt, serious sexual misconduct, or conduct or a characteristic affecting his or her business or profession. — **slan•der•ous** \'slan-də-rəs\ *adj* — **slan•der•ous•ly** *adv* — **slan•der•ous•ness** *n*

slander of goods : DISPARAGEMENT 1

slander of title : a false and malicious written or spoken public statement disparaging a person's title to property that causes harm for which special damages may be awarded ⟨damages for the filing of a fraudulent lien and for *slander of title* —M & P Concrete Prods. v. Woods*, 590 So. 2d 429 (1991)⟩ — called also *defamation of title, disparagement of property, disparagement of title;* compare DEFAMATION, DISPARAGEMENT 1

slight negligence — see NEGLIGENCE

slip law *n* [*slip* from the fact that it was printed on a single piece of paper] : an initial separate publication of a new statute made prior to its inclusion in the general laws

slip opinion — see OPINION

slow•down \'slō-ˌdaun\ *n* : a slowing down of business operations by employees ⟨the term "strike" includes any strike . . . and any concerted ~ —*U.S. Code*⟩

small business *n* : an independently owned and operated business that is not dominant in its field of operation and conforms to standards set by the Small Business Administration or by state law regarding number of employees and yearly income — called also *small business concern;* see also *Small Business Administration* in the IMPORTANT AGENCIES section

small business corporation — see CORPORATION

small claim *n* : a claim for the recovery of money or property whose value is below a certain amount

small claims court *n* : a special court intended to simplify and expedite the resolution of minor disputes involving small claims

[1]**smart money** *n* [*smart* pain] : PUNITIVE DAMAGES at DAMAGE 2

[2]**smart money** *n* **1** : money invested by one having inside information or much experience **2** : well-informed investors or speculators

smug•gle \'sma-gəl\ *vb* **smug•gled; smug•gling** *vt* : to import or export secretly and illegally esp. to avoid paying duties or to evade enforcement of laws ⟨~ drugs⟩ ⟨convicted of *smuggling* weapons⟩ ~ *vi* : to export or import something in violation of customs laws

so•cial contract *n* : an actual or hypothetical agreement among individuals forming an organized society or between the community and the ruler that defines and limits the rights and duties of each

social guest *n* : a person who comes onto the property of another on a social basis ◊ A social guest can be either a licensee or an invitee. Some jurisdictions make no distinction, in effect categorizing all social guests as invitees, which means that the property owner is required to exercise due care in guarding or warning any social guest against injury. In other jurisdictions a social guest may be categorized as a licensee, in which case the property owner has a duty only to refrain from willfully or recklessly injuring or endangering the guest.

social host *n* : a person who furnishes another with alcohol in a social setting and not as a licensed vendor ⟨courts . . . reluctant to impose liability on *social hosts* based on . . . negligence principles alone, without the support of express legislative policy —*Ferreira v. Strack*, 652 A.2d 965 (1995)⟩ ◊ Social hosts have sometimes been found criminally liable for serving alcohol to a minor or to an already usu. obviously intoxicated person, and have sometimes been found civilly liable for injury to or by an intoxicated minor. Less often, a person categorized as a so-

cial host has been found civilly liable for subsequent injury to a third party caused by an intoxicated adult guest, esp. in an automobile accident.

social insurance *n* : insurance of the individual against certain hazards (as unemployment, old age, and disability) that is undertaken, facilitated, or enforced by government as a social policy

social security *n* **1** : the principle or practice or a program of public provision (as through social insurance or assistance) for the economic security and social welfare of the individual and his or her family; *esp, often cap both Ss* : a U.S. government program established in 1935 to include old-age and survivors insurance, contributions to state unemployment insurance, and old-age assistance **2** : money paid out through a social security program ⟨collects *social security*⟩ — see also *Social Security Act* in the IMPORTANT LAWS section, *Social Security Administration* in the IMPORTANT AGENCIES section

so•ci•e•ty \sə-'sī-ə-tē\ *n, pl* **-ties 1** : the benefits of love, care, affection, and companionship that family members receive from each other ⟨sought damages for loss of ~ from his wife's wrongful death⟩ — compare CONSORTIUM **2** : a voluntary association of individuals dedicated to common ends ⟨a conservation ~⟩ **3** : a community, nation, or broad grouping of people having common traditions, institutions, and collective activities and interests — **so•ci•e•tal** \-sī-ət-ᵊl\ *adj*

sod•omy \'sä-də-mē\ *n* [Anglo-French *sodomie* sexual intercourse between men, from Old French, from Late Latin *Sodoma* Sodom, from the supposed homosexual practices of the men of the city in Genesis 19:1-11] : the crime of oral or anal sexual contact or penetration between persons or of sexual intercourse be-

\ə\abut \ᵊ\kitten \ər\further \a\ash \ā\ace \ä\cot, cart \au̇\out \ch\chin \e\bet \ē\easy \g\go \i\hit \ī\ice \j\job \ŋ\sing \ō\go \ȯ\law \ȯi\boy \th\thin \t̲h̲\the \ü\loot \u̇\foot \y\yet \zh\vision *see also* Pronunciation Symbols page

tween a person and an animal; *esp* : the crime of forcing another person to perform oral or anal sex — **sod•om•ize** \'sä-də-,mīz\ *vt*

soft goods — see GOOD 2

so•la•ti•um \sō-'lā-shē-əm\ *n, pl* **-tia** \-shē-ə\ [Late Latin *solacium, solatium,* from Latin, solace] : compensation for grief or wounded feelings (as from the wrongful death of a relative)

sole *adj* : belonging exclusively or otherwise limited to one usu. specified individual, unit, or group

sole custody — see CUSTODY b

sole proprietorship *n* : a business owned and controlled by one person who is solely liable for its obligations — compare CORPORATION, PARTNERSHIP

so•lic•it \sə-'li-sət\ *vt* **1** : to make petition to ⟨~ the court⟩ **2** : to ask, induce, advise, or command (a person) to do something and esp. to commit a crime — compare COERCE, IMPORTUNE **3** : to attempt to persuade (a person) to purchase something **4** : to attempt to bring about or obtain by soliciting a person ⟨~ bribes⟩ ~ *vi* **1** : to make solicitation **2** *of a prostitute* : to offer to have sexual relations with someone for money

so•lic•i•ta•tion \sə-,li-sə-'tā-shən\ *n* : an act or practice or an instance of soliciting ⟨~ of a proxy for a shareholder vote⟩; *specif* : the crime of soliciting someone to commit a crime (as murder)

so•lic•i•tee \sə-,li-sə-'tē\ *n* : one that is solicited

so•lic•i•tor \sə-'li-sə-tər\ *n* **1** : one that solicits; *esp* : an agent that solicits customers (as in insurance) or charitable contributions **2** : a British lawyer who advises clients, represents them in the lower courts, and prepares cases for barristers to try in higher courts **3** : the chief law officer of a municipality, county, or government department — see also CITY ATTORNEY

solicitor general *n, pl* **solicitors general** : a law officer appointed primarily to assist an attorney general; *also* : a federal law officer responsible for representing the government in court and esp. the U.S. Supreme Court

sol•i•dar•i•ty \,sä-lə-'dar-ə-tē\ *n, in the civil law of Louisiana* : the quality or state of being solidary : existence of a solidary obligation ⟨will not presume ~⟩

sol•i•dary \'sä-lə-,der-ē\ *adj* [French *solidaire* characterized by community of interests, from Middle French, from Latin *(in) solidum* for the whole, involving all] *in the civil law of Louisiana* **1** : existing jointly and severally **2** : being a party to a solidary obligation ⟨when one obligor owes an indivisible performance to distinct obligees, the obligees are ~ obligees —*Foreman v. Montgomery,* 496 So. 2d 1280 (1986)⟩ — **sol•i•dar•i•ly** \,sä-lə-'der-ə-lē\ *adv*

solidary liability — see LIABILITY 2b

solidary obligation — see OBLIGATION

sol•ven•cy \'säl-vən-sē\ *n* : the quality or state of being solvent

sol•vent \'säl-vənt\ *adj* : able to pay all legal debts as they become due

Son of Sam law \-'sam-\ *n* [after *Son of Sam,* pseudonym of serial killer David Berkowitz, whose profits from the sale of his story a 1977 New York statute attempted to divert to his victims] : a law preventing criminals from profiting from media depictions (as in books or films) of their crimes

¹sound *adj* **1 a** : free from injury or disease : exhibiting normal health **b** : free from flaw, defect, or decay ⟨a ~ design⟩ **2 a** : free from error, fallacy, or misapprehension ⟨based on ~ judicial reasoning⟩ **b** : legally valid ⟨a ~ title⟩ **3** : showing good judgment or sense — **sound•ly** *adv* — **sound•ness** *n* — **of sound mind** : having the mental capacity to make a will esp. as demonstrated by the ability to understand the nature of one's property, identify the natural objects of one's bounty, and understand the nature of the dispositions being made in the will

²sound *vi* : to be based or founded : have a specified basis for an action — used with *in* ⟨those remedies for rent which ~ed in contract —O. W. Holmes, Jr.⟩ ⟨~*ing* in tort⟩

source *n* **1 :** a point of origin ⟨the ~ of the conflict⟩ **2 :** one that supplies information ⟨held the reporter in contempt for refusing to reveal her ~⟩

source of law : something (as a constitution, treaty, custom, or statute) that provides the authority for judicial decisions and for legislation; *specif* **:** a labor contract as the source of authority for an arbitrator's decision

¹sov·er·eign \'sä-vrən, 'sə-, -və-rən\ *also* **sov·ran** \-vrən\ *n* **:** a person or political entity (as a nation or state) possessing or held to possess sovereignty ⟨a controversy between two ~s . . . the United States on the one hand and the State of California on the other —*U.S. Code*⟩ — see also *sovereign immunity* at IMMUNITY

²sovereign *also* **sovran** *adj* **1 :** possessed of supreme power ⟨a ~ ruler⟩ **2 :** enjoying autonomy ⟨~ states⟩ **3 :** relating to, characteristic of, or befitting a sovereign

sovereign acts doctrine *n* **:** a doctrine granting the United States immunity from contractual obligations for acts performed in its sovereign capacity

sovereign immunity — see IMMUNITY

sov·er·eign·ty *also* **sov·ran·ty** \'sä-vrən-tē, 'sə-, -və-rən-\ *n, pl* **-ties** **1 a :** supreme power esp. over a body politic **b :** freedom from external control **:** AUTONOMY **2 :** one that is sovereign; *esp* **:** an autonomous state

sovran, sovranty *var of* SOVEREIGN, SOVEREIGNTY

speak·er *n, often cap* **:** the presiding officer of a deliberative assembly ⟨*Speaker* of the House of Representatives⟩

speak·ing *adj* **:** addressing matters not set forth in the pleadings ⟨a ~ demurrer⟩ ⟨a ~ motion⟩

spec \'spek\ *vt* **specced** *or* **spec'd** \'spekt\; **spec·cing** \'spe-kiŋ\ **:** to write specifications for

spe·cial *adj* **1 :** distinguished by some unusual quality ⟨~ circumstances justifying an award of attorney's fees⟩ **2 :** relating

to a single thing or class of things **:** having an individual character or trait ⟨owed them a ~ duty not owed to the public at large⟩ **3 a :** supplemental to the regular **b :** assigned or provided to meet a need not covered under established procedures **4 :** designed or selected for a particular purpose, occasion, or other end ⟨family courts are courts of limited and ~ jurisdiction —*Cleveland v. Cleveland*, 559 P.2d 744 (1977)⟩ **5 :** containing particulars and details ⟨a ~ pleading⟩ — **spe·cial·ly** *adv*

special act *n* **:** an act of a legislature that is not of general application in all territory subject to the legislative power but affects private persons or only part of a class of persons in the same situation or only part of a more general subject matter or is intended to apply only in a particular subdivision of the entire territory

special administrator — see ADMINISTRATOR

special agency — see AGENCY 2a

special agent — see AGENT

special appearance *n* **:** an appearance by a party in court for the sole purpose of challenging the court's assertion of personal jurisdiction over the party — compare GENERAL APPEARANCE ◊ Under the Federal Rules of Civil Procedure and the rules of states that have adopted it, the use of a special appearance to challenge jurisdiction has been abolished, and jurisdiction may be challenged in the pleadings or in a pretrial motion.

special assessment *n* **:** a specific tax levied on private property to meet the cost of public improvements that provide a special benefit enhancing the value of the property

special benefit — see BENEFIT 1

special contract — see CONTRACT

special counsel *n* **:** counsel appointed to fill a particular need; *specif, cap* **:** a government official charged with protecting employees from illegal practices by employers and esp. from employer reprisal for whistleblowing

special court–martial *n* : a court-martial that consists of at least three officers, a trial judge advocate, and a defense counsel and that has authority to impose a limited sentence and hear only noncapital cases — compare GENERAL COURT-MARTIAL, SUMMARY COURT-MARTIAL

special damages — see DAMAGE 2

special demurrer — see DEMURRER

special deposit — see DEPOSIT 2a

special district *n* : a political subdivision of a state established to provide a single public service (as water supply or sanitation) within a specific geographical area

special duty doctrine *n* : an exception to the public duty doctrine that imposes liability for injury on a government entity when there is a special duty owed to the plaintiff but not to the public at large — called also *special duty exception* ◊ The special duty doctrine applies when the duty owed to the plaintiff arises by statute or when the plaintiff has justifiably come to rely on the government's assumption of that duty.

special employee *n* : an employee under workers' compensation law who is assigned by his or her employer to work for another employer

special employer *n* : an employer under workers' compensation law that borrows an employee from another employer

special endorsement — see ENDORSEMENT

special exception *n* : a use of property that is allowed under a zoning ordinance under specified conditions : CONDITIONAL USE at USE 2

special facts doctrine *n* : a doctrine holding that a corporate officer with superior knowledge gained by virtue of being an insider owes a limited fiduciary duty to a shareholder in transactions involving transfer of stock

special finding — see FINDING

special grand jury *n* : a grand jury

summoned by a court usu. at its discretion in addition to or in place of the regular grand jury (as when the regular grand jury has already been discharged)

special guaranty *n* : a guaranty made to a specific person and enforceable only by that person

special hazard rule *n* : an exception to the going and coming rule that allows an employee to recover from an employer for injuries sustained while going to or coming from work ◊ The special hazard rule applies when the place at which the injury occurred was along the only available route or when the employee would not have been there if not for the employment and usu. the risks associated with the location are distinctive or greater than the risk common to the public.

special interrogatory *n* : an interrogatory addressed to a jury seeking a determination of a specific issue or issues of ultimate fact for the purpose of testing the deliberations and conclusions of the jury for consistency with the general verdict or when the court requires the jury to return a special verdict

special judge *n* : a judge appointed to serve when a sitting judge is unable or unqualified to serve

special jury *n* : a specially selected panel of jurors called upon request of a party from a list of presumably more intelligent or knowledgeable prospective jurors for a case involving complicated issues of fact or serious felonies — called also *blue-ribbon jury, struck jury*

special law *n* **1** : LOCAL LAW 1a **2** : a law that applies to a particular place or esp. to a particular member or members of a class of persons or things in the same situation but not to the entire class and that is unconstitutional if the classification made is arbitrary or without a reasonable or legitimate justification or basis — called also *local law, special legislation;* compare GENERAL LAW

special lien — see LIEN

special master *n* : MASTER 2

special meeting *n* : a meeting held for a special and limited purpose; *specif*: a corporate meeting held occasionally in addition to the annual meeting to conduct only business described in a notice to the shareholders

special mis·sion exception *n* : an exception to the going and coming rule that allows recovery under workers' compensation to an employee who was injured while going to or coming from work on an errand that was part of the employee's regular duties or that was at the request of the employer or otherwise within the scope of the employment

special mortgage — see MORTGAGE

special permit *n* : SPECIAL EXCEPTION

special power — see POWER 2b

special power of appointment — see POWER OF APPOINTMENT

special power of attorney — see POWER OF ATTORNEY

special proceeding — see PROCEEDING

special prosecutor *n* : a prosecutor appointed to prosecute particular cases that the regular prosecutor is unable or unqualified to prosecute or for other reasons does not prosecute — see also INDEPENDENT COUNSEL

special session *n* : an extraordinary session (as of a court or a legislative body)

special tax *n* : a tax levied to fund a particular government project or program

spe·cial·ty *n*, *pl* **-ties** **1** [from the special form of the contract] : FORMAL CONTRACT at CONTRACT **2** : a doctrine providing that a person extradited can be prosecuted only for the charges described in the order for extradition **3** : real property (as a parcel of land or esp. a structure) that is of such specialized character that no market for it exists and for which value upon condemnation is determined by the cost of reproduction less depreciation — used esp. in New York

special use permit *n* : an authorization from an appropriate government body (as a zoning board) for a use of property that is a special exception : lawful approval for a special exception

special use valuation *n* : a method of valuation allowed under the Internal Revenue Code in calculating estate taxes on farm property or on real property used in a closely held business in which the property is valued on the basis of its current use rather than at the market value for its highest and best use

special verdict — see VERDICT

special warranty deed — see DEED

spe·cie \'spē-shē, -sē\ *n* [from *in specie*, from Latin, in kind] : money in coin — **in specie** : in the identical form and without alteration or substitution ⟨an agreement to be carried out *in specie*⟩

spe·cif·ic \spə-'si-fik\ *adj* **1** : relating to a particular thing **2** : intended for or restricted to a particular end or object **3** : being of a particularly identified kind or nature — **spe·cif·i·cal·ly** \-i-klē, -kə-lē\ *adv* — **spec·i·fic·i·ty** \,spe-sə-'fi-sə-tē\ *n*

spec·i·fi·ca·tion \,spe-sə-fə-'kā-shən\ *n* : a detailed precise presentation of something or of a plan or proposal for something: as **a** : a written statement containing a description of particulars (as of charges or contract terms) **b** : a written description of an invention or discovery for which a patent is sought that embodies the manner and process of making and using the invention or discovery and concludes with a claim of that aspect for which the applicant demands credit **c** : a written description of construction work to be done forming part of the contract — usu. used in pl.

specific bequest — see BEQUEST

specific denial — see DENIAL

specific devise — see DEVISE

specific intent — see INTENT

specific jurisdiction — see JURISDICTION

specific legacy — see LEGACY

specific lien — see LIEN

specific performance — see PERFORMANCE

specs *n pl* : SPECIFICATIONS

spec·u·late \'spe-kyə-,lāt\ *vb* **-lat·ed; -lat·ing** *vi* **1** : to theorize on the basis of insufficient evidence ◊ A jury is not

\ə\abut \ə\kitten \ər\further \a\ash \ā\ace \ä\cot, cart \aů\out \ch\chin \e\bet \ē\easy \g\go \i\hit \ī\ice \j\job \ŋ\sing \ō\go \ȯ\law \ȯi\boy \th\thin \th\the \ü\loot \ů\foot \y\yet \zh\vision *see also* Pronunciation Symbols page

permitted to speculate on a matter about which insufficient evidence has been presented in reaching its verdict. **2 :** to assume a business risk in hope of gain; *esp* **:** to buy or sell in expectation of profiting from market fluctuations ~ *vt* **:** to take to be true on the basis of insufficient evidence — **spec•u•la•tor** \-ˌlā-tər\ *n*

spec•u•la•tion \ˌspe-kyə-'lā-shən\ *n* **:** an act or instance of speculating: as **a :** assumption of unusual business risk in hopes of obtaining commensurate gain **b :** a transaction involving such speculation

spec•u•la•tive \'spe-kyə-lə-tiv, -ˌlā-\ *adj* **1 :** involving, based on, or constituting intellectual speculation; *also* **:** theoretical rather than demonstrable ⟨~ medical testimony concerning the cause of death⟩ **2 :** of, relating to, or being a financial speculation ⟨~ securities⟩ ⟨~ home building⟩ — **spec•u•la•tive•ly** *adv*

speculative risk *n* **:** a risk that may result in either a loss or a gain — compare PURE RISK

speech *n* **:** words or conduct used to communicate or express a thought **:** EXPRESSION — see also COMMERCIAL SPEECH, FREEDOM OF SPEECH, FREE SPEECH, OBSCENE, SYMBOLIC SPEECH, *Amendment I* to the CONSTITUTION in the back matter

speech or de•bate clause *n*, *often cap S&D&C* **:** a clause in Article I of the U.S. Constitution granting members of Congress a privilege from arrest and legislative immunity for any speech or debate made in either of the houses — called also *speech and debate clause*

speedy trial \'spē-dē-\ *n* **:** a trial conducted according to prevailing rules and procedures that takes place without unreasonable or undue delay or within a statutory period ◊ The right to a speedy trial is guaranteed to criminal defendants by the Sixth Amendment to the U.S. Constitution. The purposes of the right as explained by the U.S. Supreme Court are to keep a person who has not yet been convicted from serving lengthy jail time, to lessen the time that the accused must endure the anxiety and publicity of

the impending trial, and to minimize the damage that delay might cause to the person's ability to present a defense. Although the Constitution does not set out any specific time within which a trial must commence in order to be deemed speedy, some states have enacted laws establishing a limit whose expiration results in a dismissal of the charges.

spending power — see POWER 2a

¹spend•thrift \'spend-ˌthrift\ *n* **:** a person who spends money foolishly, profusely, or wastefully

²spendthrift *adj* **1 :** of, relating to, or being a spendthrift **2 :** of or relating to a spendthrift trust

spendthrift trust — see TRUST

Spiel•berg Doctrine \'spēl-ˌbərg-\ *n* [after the *Spielberg* Manufacturing Company, subject of an unfair labor practice complaint that prompted the formation of the doctrine] **:** a doctrine in labor law: the National Labor Relations Board will defer to an arbitrator's decision regarding a contract dispute if the arbitrator's decision was not repugnant to the National Labor Relations Act, the arbitration proceedings provided a hearing as fair as would have been provided before the NLRB, and the contract required binding arbitration — compare COLLYER DOCTRINE

spin–off \'spin-ˌof, -ˌäf\ *n* **:** a transfer of corporate assets to a subsidiary in return for a distribution to the shareholders of the corporation of all of the stock or controlling stock of the subsidiary without surrender of any stock by the shareholders of the corporation **:** a D reorganization involving a distribution of the stock of another company to the corporation's shareholders; *also* **:** a new company created by such a distribution — compare SPLIT-OFF, SPLIT-UP

¹split *vb* **split; split•ting :** to divide into parts or portions: as **a :** to divide into factions, parties, or groups **b :** to mark (a ballot) or cast or register (a vote) so as to vote for candidates of different parties **c :** to divide (stock) by issuing a larger number of shares to existing shareholders

usu. without increase in total par value — see also STOCK SPLIT **d :** to divide (a cause of action) into separate parts or claims for the purpose of instituting an action for less than all ◇ Splitting a cause of action is usu. prohibited. ∼ *vi* **:** to become divided or separated ⟨the Supreme Court, *splitting* five to four, sustained the law —R. H. Bork⟩
²split *adj* **1 :** divided into portions, parts, or fragments ⟨a ∼ trial⟩ ⟨a ∼ stock⟩ **2 :** divided by or in opinion ⟨a ∼ court⟩ ⟨a ∼ decision⟩
split–funded plan *n* **:** a retirement plan combining life insurance and an investment fund
split gift — see GIFT
split–off \'split-,ȯf, -,äf\ *n* **:** a transfer of corporate assets to a subsidiary involving the surrender of a part of the stock owned by the corporation's shareholders in exchange for controlling stock of the subsidiary **:** a D reorganization involving a distribution of part but not all of a corporation's stock for a subsidiary's stock; *also* **:** a new company created by such a distribution — compare SPIN-OFF, SPLIT-UP
split sentence — see SENTENCE
split–up \'split-,əp\ *n* **:** a transfer by a corporation of all its assets in complete liquidation to two or more subsidiaries that involves the surrender of all stock by the shareholders in exchange for new stock in the transferee corporations **:** a D reorganization involving a distribution of the stock of two or more subsidiaries to the shareholders who in return surrender all their stock in the distributing corporation — compare SPIN-OFF, SPLIT-OFF
spo•li•a•tion \,spō-lē-'ā-shən\ *n* **1 :** the destruction, alteration, or mutilation of evidence esp. by a party for whom the evidence is damaging **2 :** alteration or mutilation of an instrument (as a will) by one who is not a party to the instrument
spo•li•a•tor \'spō-lē-,ā-tər\ *n* **:** one who spoils or damages the value of something
spon•sor *n* **1 :** a legislator who introduces and supports a legislative proposal (as a

bill or amendment) **2 :** a person who assumes responsibility for some other person (as an immigrant) or thing **3 a :** one that securitizes assets **b :** one that promotes, advocates, or favors a business venture (as investment in a security or limited partnership) — **sponsor** *vb* — **spon•sor•ship** *n*
spontaneous declaration — see DECLARATION 2c
spontaneous exclamation *n* **:** SPONTANEOUS DECLARATION at DECLARATION 2c
spontaneous utterance *n* **:** SPONTANEOUS DECLARATION at DECLARATION 2c
spot zoning *n* **:** the usu. illegal rezoning of a small parcel of land within the limits of another zone that is illegal when not done in accord with a comprehensive zoning plan or when arbitrary or discriminatory — compare VARIANCE
spray *vt* **:** to disperse among a number of recipients ⟨authorized to ∼ trust income —W. M. McGovern, Jr. *et al.*⟩
spread *n* **1 a :** the difference between any two prices for similar articles ⟨the ∼ between the list price and the market price of an article⟩ **b :** the difference between the highest and lowest prices of a product or security for a given period **c :** the difference between bid and asked prices (as of a stock) **2 a :** a simultaneous put option and call option in which the put price and the call price differ so that no profit is made unless the price falls below or rises above the put or call price respectively by more than enough to cover the cost of the option; *also* **:** the difference between the put price and call price **b :** a transaction in which a participant hedges with simultaneous long and short options in different commodities or different delivery dates in the same commodity **3 :** an arbitrage transaction operated by buying and selling simultaneously in two markets when there is an abnormal difference in price

\ə\abut \ᵊ\kitten \ər\further \a\ash \ā\ace
\ä\cot, cart \au̇\out \ch\chin \e\bet \ē\easy
\g\go \i\hit \ī\ice \j\job \ŋ\sing \ō\go \ȯ\law
\ȯi\boy \th\thin \t͟h\the \ü\loot \u̇\foot \y\yet
\zh\vision *see also* Pronunciation Symbols page

between the two markets; *also* : the difference in price **4** : the difference between the yields on investments in fixed-income securities equal in quality but with different maturity dates or with the same maturity dates but unequal quality

springing use — see USE 1b

sprin·kle *vt* **sprin·kled; sprin·kling** : SPRAY

square *adj* : fitting the factual or legal situation at bar ⟨we have been shown no ∼ holding of a Florida court to that effect —*Milhet Caterers, Inc. v. North Western Meat, Inc.*, 185 So. 2d 196 (1966)⟩ — **square·ly** *adv*

squat·ter \'skwä-tər\ *n* : a person who occupies real property without a claim of right or title ◊ In most jurisdictions, a squatter cannot gain title to land through adverse possession because adverse possession requires possession of the property under a claim of right or color of title.

squeeze·out \'skwēz-,aùt\ *n* : a corporate action or series of actions (as a refusal to declare dividends or the restricting of decision-making power in corporate governance) through which majority shareholders deprive minority shareholders of the benefit of stock ownership usu. as part of an attempt to force sale of minority shares — compare FREEZEOUT ◊ *Freezeout* and *squeezeout* are sometimes used as synonyms.

ss *abbr* [Latin *scilicet* that is to say] specifically — used in the statement of venue which follows the caption of a legal document and esp. between the name of the state and the particular subdivision (as county)

SSI *abbr* supplemental security income

stake *n* **1** : the subject matter (as property or an obligation) of an interpleader **2** : an interest or share in an esp. commercial undertaking

stake·hold·er \'stāk-,hōl-dər\ *n* **1** : a person holding property or owing an obligation that is claimed by two or more adverse claimants and who has no claim to or interest in the property or obligation

⟨the ∼ can interplead the claimants⟩ **2** : a person having an interest or share in a commercial undertaking

stale *adj* : impaired in legal effect or force by reason of not being used, acted upon, or demanded in a timely fashion ⟨the search warrant was invalid because it was based on ∼ information⟩ ⟨a ∼ claim⟩

stalk \'stòk\ *vt* : to subject to stalking ∼ *vi* : to engage in stalking — **stalk·er** *n*

stalk·ing *n* : the act or crime of willfully and repeatedly following or harassing another person in circumstances that would cause a reasonable person to fear injury or death esp. because of express or implied threats; *broadly* : a crime of engaging in a course of conduct directed at a person that serves no legitimate purpose and seriously alarms, annoys, or intimidates that person ◊ Stalking is often considered to be aggravated when the conduct involved also violates a restraining order protecting the victim.

stamp *n* : an official mark or seal set on something (as a deed) chargeable with a government or state duty or tax or on papers requiring execution under certain conditions to signify that the duty or tax has been paid or the condition fulfilled; *esp* : REVENUE STAMP

stamp tax *n* : a tax collected by means of a stamp purchased and affixed (as to a deed)

¹stand *vb* **stood; stand·ing** *vi* **1** : to be in a particular state or situation ⟨∼ accused⟩ **2** : to remain valid or effective ⟨let the ruling ∼⟩ ∼ *vt* : to submit to ⟨∼ trial⟩ — **stand in judgment** : to submit to the judgment of the court — **stand in the shoes of** : to assume the rights or obligations of — **stand mute** : to be effectively silent: as **a** : to exercise the privilege against self-incrimination (as in a trial) **b** : to raise no objections ⟨the prosecution agreed to *stand mute* at the sentencing⟩ — **stand on** : to depend on esp. as the basis of an argument or claim ⟨a party who *stands on* the writing as a complete and exclusive embodiment of the contract —J. J. White and R. S. Summers⟩

²stand *n* : the place taken by a witness for testifying in court ⟨take the ~⟩ — compare BAR, BENCH, DOCK, SIDEBAR

stan•dard *n* **1** : something established by authority, custom, or general consent as a model, example, or point of reference ⟨the ~ of the reasonable person⟩ **2** : something established by authority as a rule for the measure of quantity, weight, extent, value, or quality **3** : the basis of value in a monetary system

standard deduction — see DEDUCTION

standard mortgage clause *n* : a mortgage clause that is usu. considered to form a separate contract between the insurer and mortgagee under which the mortgagee can collect payment even if the policy is void or voidable with regard to the insured (as because of fraud or non-payment) — called also *union mortgage clause*

standard of care : the degree of care or competence that one is expected to exercise in a particular circumstance or role

standard of proof : the level of certainty and the degree of evidence necessary to establish proof in a criminal or civil proceeding ⟨the *standard of proof* to convict is proof beyond a reasonable doubt⟩ — see also CLEAR AND CONVINCING, PREPONDERANCE OF THE EVIDENCE; compare BURDEN OF PROOF, *clear and convincing evidence* at EVIDENCE, REASONABLE DOUBT ◊ Preponderance of the evidence is the least demanding standard of proof and is used for most civil actions and some criminal defenses (as insanity). Clear and convincing proof is a more demanding standard of proof and is used in certain civil actions (as a civil fraud suit). Proof beyond a reasonable doubt is the most demanding standard and the one that must be met for a criminal conviction.

standard oth•er insurance clause *n* : PRO RATA CLAUSE

standby letter of credit — see LETTER OF CREDIT

¹stand•ing *adj* : continuing in existence, use, or effect indefinitely ⟨a ~ order⟩

²standing *n* **1** : the status of being qualified to assert or enforce legal rights or duties in a judicial forum because one has a sufficient and protectable interest in the outcome of a justiciable controversy and usu. has suffered or is threatened with actual injury ⟨only one who already has ~ can argue the public interest in support of his claim —*Hawaii's Thousand Friends v. Anderson*, 768 P.2d 1293 (1989)⟩ **2** : a principle requiring that a party have standing in order to justify the exercise of the court's remedial powers

standing committee *n* : a permanent committee; *esp* : one in a house or senate with jurisdiction over legislation in a particular area (as the judiciary or the armed services)

stand•still agreement \'stand-ˌstil-\ *n* : an agreement providing for the preservation of the status quo for a specified or indefinite period: as **a** : an agreement under which litigation is forestalled between two parties **b** : an agreement under which a party agrees to refrain from taking further steps to acquire control of a corporation (as by additional purchases of stock)

star chamber *n* **1** *cap S&C* : an old English court abolished in 1641 that exercised wide civil and criminal jurisdiction under rules of procedure suited to the prerogatives of the king and that was marked by secrecy, the absence of juries, self-incrimination, and an inquisitorial as opposed to accusatorial system of justice **2** : a tribunal or proceeding resembling the Star Chamber esp. in being secretive or arbitrary

sta•re de•ci•sis \'ster-ē-di-'sī-sis, 'stär-ē-; 'stä-rä-dā-'kē-sēs\ *n* [New Latin, to stand by things that have been settled] : the doctrine under which courts adhere to precedent on questions of law in order to insure certainty, consistency, and stability in the administration of justice with departure from precedent permitted for compelling

\ə\abut \ᵊ\kitten \ər\further \a\ash \ā\ace
\ä\cot, cart \aú\out \ch\chin \e\bet \ē\easy
\g\go \i\hit \ī\ice \j\job \ŋ\sing \ō\go \ó\law
\ói\boy \th\thin \t͟h\the \ü\loot \ú\foot \y\yet
\zh\vision *see also* Pronunciation Symbols page

reasons (as to prevent the perpetuation of injustice)

Stat. *abbr* statutes

state *n, often attrib* **1 a :** a politically organized body of people usu. occupying a definite territory; *esp* : one that is sovereign **b :** the political organization that has supreme civil authority and political power and serves as the basis of government — see also *compelling state interest* at INTEREST 3a, SEPARATION OF CHURCH AND STATE **c :** a government or politically organized society having a particular character ⟨a police ∼⟩ **2 :** the operations or concerns of the government of a country : the sphere of administration and supreme political power of a country (as in international relations) ⟨secrets of ∼⟩ ⟨affairs of ∼⟩ **3 a :** one of the constituent units of a nation having a federal government; *specif* : one of the fifty such units comprising the great part of the U.S. — see also STATE LAW **b :** the territory of a state

state action *n* **1 :** an action that is either taken directly by the state or bears a sufficient connection to the state to be attributed to it ◊ State actions are subject to judicial scrutiny for violations of the rights to due process and equal protection guaranteed under the Fourteenth Amendment to the U.S. Constitution. Such an action may be the subject of a claim brought under federal law (as section 1983) by one alleging a violation of constitutional rights, privileges, or immunities. **2 :** state efforts to displace competition with regulation or a state-supervised monopoly ◊ Such efforts are immune from antitrust liability.

state bank — see BANK

state court *n* **:** a court established in accordance with a state constitution and having jurisdiction to adjudicate matters of state law

stated capital — see CAPITAL

stat·ed value *n* **:** the value assigned in a corporation's books to stock and esp. to no-par value stock ◊ Stated value is sometimes based on the actual amount received when stock is issued, but it can also be an arbitrarily low value. It has no relation to the market value of the stock.

state law *n* **:** the law of a state; *specif* : a law or body of laws promulgated by a state legislature

state·ment *n* **1 a :** an official or formal report or declaration ⟨a ∼ of policy⟩ **b :** an oral or written assertion (as by a witness) or conduct intended as an assertion — see also HEARSAY, PRIOR CONSISTENT STATEMENT, PRIOR INCONSISTENT STATEMENT **2 :** a financial record or accounting

Statement of Financial Af·fairs : a written statement filed by a debtor in bankruptcy that contains information regarding esp. financial records, location of any accounts, prior bankruptcy, and recent or current debt — called also *statement of affairs*

Statement of Intention : a written statement filed by a debtor prior to the meeting of creditors in a chapter 7 bankruptcy case that indicates what property the debtor intends to surrender and retain

state of mind exception *n* **:** an exception to the hearsay rule that allows the use of hearsay evidence regarding the state of mind of the declarant (as in a statement of intent or motive)

state prison *n* **:** a prison maintained by a state esp. to incarcerate those convicted of serious crimes (as felonies)

state's attorney *n* **:** a district attorney that represents a state — compare UNITED STATES ATTORNEY

state's evidence *n* **:** a participant or accomplice in a crime who gives evidence to the prosecution esp. in return for a reduced sentence — used chiefly in the phrase *turn state's evidence*

states' rights *n pl* **1 :** rights and powers not forbidden to the states nor vested in the federal government by the U.S. Constitution **2** *sing in constr* **:** a doctrine based on states' rights that has been used to justify state resistance to federal authority in matters seen as the exclusive concern of the states and that is most often associated with the states favoring slavery and secession in the 19th century — compare FEDERALISM

sta·tus \'stā-təs, 'sta-\ *n* [Latin, mode or condition of being, from *stare* to stand] **1 a :** the condition of a person or a thing in the eyes of the law **b :** position or rank in relation to others **2 :** a state of affairs ⟨the ~ of the negotiations⟩

status offender *n* : a juvenile under the jurisdiction of the court because of acts that would not be criminal if committed by an adult but that indicate the child is beyond parental control — compare JUVENILE DELINQUENT, YOUTHFUL OFFENDER

status quo \-'kwō\ *n* [Latin, state in which] : the existing state of affairs; *specif* : the last actual and uncontested state of affairs that preceded a controversy and that is to be preserved by preliminary injunction — compare STATUS QUO ANTE

status quo an·te \-'kwō-'an-tē\ *n* [Latin, state in which previously] : the state of affairs that existed previously ⟨rescind the contract and restore the parties to the *status quo ante*⟩

stat·ute \'sta-chüt\ *n* [Latin *statutum* law, regulation, from neuter of *statutus*, past participle of *statuere* to set up, station, from *status* position, state] **1 :** a law enacted by the legislative branch of a government — see also CODE, STATUTORY LAW **2 :** an act of a corporation or its founder intended as a permanent rule **3 :** an international instrument setting up an agency and regulating its scope or authority ⟨the ~ of the International Court of Justice⟩

statute law *n* : STATUTORY LAW

statute of frauds 1 *often cap S&F* **a :** a state law modeled on the English Statute of Frauds or dealing with the enforcement and requirements of agreements in particular circumstances — see also *Statute of Frauds* in the IMPORTANT LAWS section; compare MAIN PURPOSE RULE, *part performance 2* at PERFORMANCE ◊ There are many statutes of frauds, but use of the

term often implies a single entity. This is at least partially due to the great stature of the original law, which represents the general principle that a contract must be in writing to be enforceable. **b :** a provision in the Uniform Commercial Code under which a contract for the sale of goods for $500 or more is not enforceable unless signed by the party sought to be held to it or by an authorized agent **2 :** a defense employing a statute of frauds (as in the denial of an enforceable agreement)

statute of limitation : STATUTE OF LIMITATIONS

statute of limitations 1 a : a statute establishing a period of time from the accrual of a cause of action (as upon the occurrence or discovery of an injury) within which a right of action must be exercised — compare LACHES, STATUTE OF REPOSE **b :** a criminal statute establishing the period of time within which an offense can be punished after its commission **2 :** a period of time established by statute of limitations for commencing an action or prosecution **3 :** an affirmative defense that the statute of limitations has expired

statute of mortmain : MORTMAIN STATUTE

statute of re·pose \-ri-'pōz\ : a statute that bars a cause of action after a period of time running from a particular act (as the delivery of a product) or event even if the cause of action has not accrued (as upon discovery of a defect) ⟨the *statute of repose* began to run upon completion of the house even though the defect was not discovered for several years⟩

stat·u·to·ry \'sta-chə-ˌtōr-ē\ *adj* **1 :** of or relating to a statute or statutes ⟨a ~ provision⟩ **2 :** enacted, created, regulated, or defined by statute ⟨a ~ presumption⟩ ⟨a ~ insider⟩ — **stat·u·to·ri·ly** \ˌsta-chə-'tōr-ə-lē\ *adv*

\ə\abut \ᵊ\kitten \ər\further \a\ash \ā\ace
\ä\cot, cart \au\out \ch\chin \e\bet \ē\easy
\g\go \i\hit \ī\ice \j\job \ŋ\sing \ō\go \o\law
\oi\boy \th\thin \th\the \ü\loot \u\foot \y\yet
\zh\vision *see also* Pronunciation Symbols page

statutory employee *n* : one (as a contractor or person working under a contractor) who does work for a statutory employer from whom he or she is entitled to the exclusive remedy of workers' compensation benefits

statutory employer *n* : one who employs another (as a contractor) to perform work in the course of a business and who is liable for workers' compensation according to a statute establishing such an employment relationship or liability

statutory foreclosure *n* : a foreclosure in which a mortgagee or trustee executes a power of sale given in a mortgage or deed of trust and does so in accordance with statutory provisions — compare STRICT FORECLOSURE

statutory guardian — see GUARDIAN

statutory law *n* : the law that exists in legislatively enacted statutes esp. as distinguished from common law — compare COMMON LAW

statutory lien — see LIEN

statutory merger — see MERGER

statutory omnibus clause *n* : a statutory provision requiring that coverage of an automobile insurance policy be extended to a person using the vehicle with the express or implied permission of the insured — compare OMNIBUS CLAUSE 2

statutory rape *n* : rape consisting of sexual intercourse with a person beneath an age (as 14 years) specified by statute ◊ Many state statutes also specify a minimum age of the perpetrator or an age differential (as at least four years) between the perpetrator and the victim. Consent of the victim and belief that the victim is of the age of consent are usu. considered immaterial. Statutory rape is now codified under various names, such as *rape in the second degree, rape in the third degree, unlawful sexual intercourse with a minor,* and *criminal sexual conduct in the second degree.*

statutory rule against perpetuities : a statute setting forth the requirements for the vesting of a future interest in property and superseding the common-law rule

against perpetuities; *esp* : a uniform statute invalidating a future interest in property that is not certain to vest or terminate within a life in being plus 21 years or that does not vest or terminate within 90 years after its creation

¹stay *vt* **stayed; stay·ing** : to temporarily suspend or prevent by judicial or executive order ⟨may not grant an injunction to ~ proceedings in a state court — *U.S. Code*⟩

²stay *n* : a temporary suspension or injunction of an action or process by a usu. discretionary judicial or executive order ⟨a ~ of execution of the judgment⟩ ⟨~ of a lower court's judgment pending certiorari — W. J. Brennan, Jr.⟩ — see also AUTOMATIC STAY; compare *cease-and-desist order* at ORDER 3b, MANDAMUS, SUPERSEDEAS

steal *vt* **stole; sto·len; steal·ing** [Old English *stelan*] : to take or appropriate without right or consent and with intent to keep or make use of — see also ROBBERY, THEFT

stepped–up basis — see BASIS 3

step transaction doctrine *n* : a doctrine in tax law: a series of separate but related transactions may be viewed as a single transaction and the tax liability may be based on that transaction rather than the individual transactions in the series

stet \'stet\ *n* [Latin, let it stand, third person singular present subjunctive of *stare* to stand] : an order staying all proceedings in an action — used esp. in Maryland

stew·ard *n* : SHOP STEWARD

sting *n* : an elaborate confidence game; *specif* : such a game worked by undercover police in order to catch criminals

stip·u·late \'sti-pyə-ˌlāt\ *vb* **-lat·ed; -lat·ing** [Latin *stipulatus,* past participle of *stipulari* to exact (as from a prospective debtor) a formal guarantee when making an oral contract] *vi* **1** : to make an agreement or covenant about something (as damages) **2** : to demand a particular promise in an agreement — used with *for* ⟨may . . . assume or ~ for obligations of all kinds — *Louisiana Civil Code*⟩ **3** : to agree respecting an aspect of legal proceedings — used with *to* ⟨*stipulated* to a dismissal of the claim with prejudice — *National Law Journal*⟩ ⟨pleaded guilty to the charge of battery and *stipulated* to the underlying facts —*Luna v. Meinke*, 844 F. Supp. 1284 (1994)⟩ ~ *vt* **1** : to specify esp. as a condition or requirement of an agreement ⟨parties may not ~ the invalidity of statutes or ordinances —*West v. Bank of Commerce & Trusts*, 167 F.2d 664 (1948)⟩ ⟨the contract *stipulated* that the lessor was responsible for maintenance⟩ ⟨within a *stipulated* period of time⟩ **2** : to establish (procedure or evidence) by agreement during a proceeding ⟨defendant *stipulated* that evidence was sufficient to support his conspiracy conviction —*National Law Journal*⟩ ⟨based on *stipulated* facts⟩

stipulated authority — see AUTHORITY

stipulated damages — see DAMAGE 2

stip·u·la·tion \ˌsti-pyə-'lā-shən\ *n* **1** : an act of stipulating **2** : something stipulated: as **a** : an agreement between parties regarding some aspect of a legal proceeding ⟨a ~ of facts⟩ ⟨admitted the charges in a prehearing ~ —*New York Law Journal*⟩ **b** : a condition, requirement, or item specified in a legal instrument; *specif* : STIPULATION POUR AUTRUI

stipulation pour au·trui \-ˌpür-ō-'trē, -'trwʸē\ *n* [French, stipulation for other persons] *in the civil law of Louisiana* : a contract or provision in a contract that confers a benefit on a third-party beneficiary ◊ A stipulation pour autrui gives the third-party beneficiary a cause of action against the promisor for specific performance. In order for a third party to be a third-party beneficiary of a stipulation pour autrui there usu. has to be a legal or factual relationship between the stipulator and the beneficiary.

stip·u·la·tor \'sti-pyə-ˌlā-tər\ *n* **1** : one that stipulates **2** *in the civil law of Louisiana* : the promisee in a stipulation pour autrui who bargains for and receives the promise that benefits the third-party beneficiary

stir·pi·tal \'stir-pə-təl, 'stər-\ *adj* : of or relating to per stirpes distribution

stock *n* **1 a** : the equipment, materials, or supplies of a business **b** : a store or supply accumulated; *esp* : the inventory of the goods of a merchant or manufacturer **2** : the ownership element in a corporation usu. divided into shares and represented by transferable certificates; *also* : the certificate evidencing ownership of one or more shares of stock

capital stock **1** : the stock that a corporation may issue under its charter including both common and preferred stock **2** : the outstanding shares of a joint stock company considered as an aggregate **3** : CAPITALIZATION 4

common stock : a class of stock whose holders share in company profits (as through dividends) on a pro rata basis, may vote for directors and on important matters such as mergers, and may have limited access to information not publicly available

cumulative preferred stock : preferred stock whose holders are entitled to the payment of cumulative dividends as well as current dividends before common stockholders are paid

growth stock : stock issued by a growth company

margin stock : stock that may be purchased in a margin account

no–par value stock : stock issued with no par value which may be carried for corporate accounting purposes as part of the capital stock or as part of the capital surplus to the extent allowed by law — called also *no-par stock*

pen·ny stock : the stock of a small company not listed on a major exchange and traditionally selling at less than a dollar a share

preferred stock : a class of corporate stock whose holders are guaranteed pay-

\ə\abut	\ᵊ\kitten	\ər\further	\a\ash	\ā\ace
\ä\cot, cart	\aú\out	\ch\chin	\e\bet	\ē\easy
\g\go	\i\hit	\ī\ice	\j\job	\ŋ\sing	\ō\go	\ò\law
\òi\boy	\th\thin	\t͟h\the	\ü\loot	\ú\foot	\y\yet
\zh\vision	*see also* Pronunciation Symbols page

ment of dividends and a share of asset distribution before the holders of common stock but are usu. denied voting rights

treasury stock : stock that is reacquired and held by the issuing company (as to increase the market value of traded shares)

voting stock : stock (as common stock) entitling the holder to vote in matters of corporate governance

wa•tered stock : stock issued with a par value greater than the value of the underlying assets

stock appreciation right *n* : a form of deferred compensation that allows an employee to receive as a bonus the cash value of the appreciation of stock over a period of years and that defers taxation until paid

stock bo•nus plan *n* : a form of deferred compensation that is funded by employer contributions of corporate securities with dividends usu. reinvested

stock exchange *n* **1** : a place where security trading is conducted on an organized system **2** : an association or group of people organized to provide an auction market among themselves for the purchase and sale of securities

stock•hold•er *n* : an owner of corporate stock — compare BONDHOLDER — **stock•hold•ing** *n or adj*

stockholder of record : the person who is recorded on the books of a company as the owner of stock and who may be an agent or trustee for the true owner

stock index *n* : an index that tracks the performance of a particular group of stocks

stock in trade : the equipment, merchandise, or materials necessary to or used in a trade or business

stock manipulation *n* : illicit behavior that creates or attempts to give the appearance of active trading in a security (as to induce others to buy or sell)

stock market *n* **1** : STOCK EXCHANGE 1 **2** : a market for particular stocks **3** : the market for stocks throughout a country

stock option — see OPTION 3

stock option plan *n* : a form of deferred compensation that allows an employee to buy corporate stock at a set price (as the prevailing market price at the time of the contract) at any time (as when the market price has risen) during a designated number of years

stock power — see POWER 2b

stock split *n* : the division of the outstanding shares of a corporation into a larger number of shares thereby reducing the value of each share but not the total value of each holding — compare REVERSE STOCK SPLIT ◊ The purpose of a stock split is to make the stock more attractive to potential investors by reducing the price per share.

stole *past of* STEAL

stolen *past part of* STEAL

stood *past and past part of* STAND

¹stop *vb* **stopped; stop•ping** *vt* **1** : to cause to halt ⟨*stopped* payment⟩ **2** : to subject to a legal stop ~ *vi* : to cease activity or motion

²stop *n* : an act or instance of stopping; *specif* : a temporary detention that constitutes a limited seizure of a person for the purpose of inquiry or investigation and that must be based on reasonable suspicion — see also TERRY STOP; compare ARREST

stop and frisk statute *n* : a state law that allows a police officer to stop any person without making an arrest based on a reasonable suspicion that the person has committed or is about to commit a crime

stop order — see ORDER 4b

stop•page in tran•si•tu \'stä-pij-,in-'tran-zə-,tü, -'tran-sə-, -,tyü\ *n* [Latin *in transitu* in passing from one place to another] : the right of a seller of goods to stop them on their way to the buyer and resume possession of them (as on discovery of the buyer's insolvency) — called also *stoppage in transit*

stop payment *n* : a depositor's order to a bank to refuse to honor a specified check drawn by him or her

strad•dle \'strad-°l\ *n* : the purchase of an

equal number of put options and call options on the same underlying securities with the same price and maturity date
straight bill of lading — see BILL OF LADING
straight deductible *n* : a deductible that is a constant value (as a specified amount)
straight life annuity — see ANNUITY
straight life insurance — see LIFE INSURANCE
straight–line *adj* : marked by equal payments over a given term ⟨using the ~ method of depreciation⟩
straight–line depreciation — see DEPRECIATION
straight voting *n* : a system of voting for corporate directors in which each shareholder may cast one vote for each share of stock owned for each seat in contention — compare CUMULATIVE VOTING
strang·er *n* : someone who is not a party or in privity with a party (as to a contract or legal action) ⟨may be enforced against a ~ to the contract⟩
straw man *n* : an intermediary for a transaction (as a conveyance of real property)
street name *n* : a brokerage firm's name in which securities owned by another (as an individual investor) are listed (as to expedite transfer at time of sale by avoiding handling of the actual certificates)
stretch–out *n* : a labor practice in which workers are required to do extra work with slight or no additional pay
strict *adj* **1** : characterized by narrowness : not demonstrating a broad or liberal view ⟨~ interpretation⟩ **2 a** : firm or rigid in requirement or control **b** : severe in discipline **3 a** : inflexibly maintained or adhered to **b** : rigorously conforming to a principle or norm or condition ⟨a ~ bill of interpleader⟩ **4** : not requiring fault — see also *strict liability* at LIABILITY 2b — **strictly** *adv*
strict construction *n* : interpretation (as of a writing or legislation) based on a literal or technical understanding of the words used
strict foreclosure *n* **1** : a proceeding in which the amount due on a mortgage is

determined and a period of time within which it must be paid is fixed with the understanding that in the event of the mortgagor's default title will be vested in the mortgagee free of any right of the mortgagor to redeem — compare STATUTORY FORECLOSURE **2** : the acceptance by a creditor of collateral as discharge of an obligation which under the Uniform Commercial Code denies the creditor the right to a deficiency judgment ◊ Under the U.C.C.'s strict foreclosure provision, notice must be given to other parties having a security interest in the property. If one of these parties objects to the strict foreclosure, there must be a foreclosure sale instead. In some states, deficiency judgments are allowed in strict foreclosure cases as well as foreclosures by sale.
¹stric·ti ju·ris \'strik-ˌtī-'jùr-is, 'strik-tē-'yùr-ēs\ *adj or adv* [Latin] : according to or determined by strict interpretation of the law ⟨the rights of a guarantor are *stricti juris* —*Sitzer v. Lang*, 243 S.E.2d 95 (1978)⟩
²stricti juris *n* : a rule of legal interpretation requiring or dictating close, narrow, or strict interpretation ⟨failure to apply the rule of *stricti juris* to the parol evidence —*Brown v. Capitol Fish Co.*, 282 S.E.2d 694 (1981)⟩
stric·tis·si·mi ju·ris \strik-'ti-sə-ˌmī-'jùr-is, -mē-'yùr-ēs\ *adv* [Latin] : according to the strictest interpretation of the law
strict liability — see LIABILITY 2b
strict scrutiny *n* : the highest level of judicial scrutiny that is applied esp. to a law that allegedly violates equal protection in order to determine if it is narrowly tailored to serve a compelling state interest — see also INTERMEDIATE 2, RATIONAL BASIS TEST
¹strike *vb* **struck; struck** *also* **strick·en; strik·ing** *vi* **1** : to remove or delete something **2** : to stop work in order to force

\ə\abut \ə\kitten \ər\further \a\ash \ā\ace
\ä\cot, cart \aù\out \ch\chin \e\bet \ē\easy
\g\go \i\hit \ī\ice \j\job \ŋ\sing \ō\go \ò\law
\òi\boy \th\thin \th\the \ü\loot \ù\foot \y\yet
\zh\vision *see also* Pronunciation Symbols page

an employer to comply with demands — *vt* **1** : to remove or delete from a legal document and esp. from the record of a trial ⟨it *struck* that part of [the] injunction —*National Law Journal*⟩ **2** : to remove (a prospective juror) from a venire **3** : to engage in a strike against (an employer)
²strike *n* **1** : the removal of a potential juror from a venire — compare CHALLENGE **2** : a concerted work stoppage, interruption, or slowdown by a body of workers to enforce compliance with demands made on an employer — see also RENT STRIKE, *Labor Management Relations Act* in the IMPORTANT LAWS section; compare JOB ACTION

economic strike : a strike that is brought against an employer because of a dispute regarding economic benefits or conditions (as wages) ◊ Workers engaged in an economic strike can legally be replaced permanently. No-strike clauses in collective bargaining agreements have been held to bar only economic strikes and not strikes protesting an unfair labor practice.

general strike : a simultaneous strike by all unionized workers of all trades and industries

jurisdictional strike : a strike that is called against an employer as a result of a dispute with another union as to the right to perform particular work

organizational strike : RECOGNITION STRIKE in this entry

primary strike : a strike by workers against their employer with whom they have a dispute

recognition strike : a strike by workers against their employer seeking to force the employer to recognize the union as their collective bargaining agent — called also *organizational strike*

secondary strike : SYMPATHY STRIKE in this entry

sit–down strike : a strike during which employees remain in and occupy the employer's premises as a protest and means of forcing compliance with demands ◊ This form of strike has been

illegal according to both statute and case law since the early 1940s.

sym•pa•thy strike : a strike by workers not involved in a labor dispute in support of other striking employees or unions — called also *secondary strike*

wild•cat strike : a strike by workers that is not authorized by the union

strike•break•er \'strīk-,brā-kər\ *n* : an individual hired to replace a striking worker

strike down *vt* : ANNUL, NULLIFY ⟨the trustee . . . can *strike down* transfers — J. J. White and R. S. Summers⟩; *esp* : to declare (a law) illegal and unenforceable ⟨the court *struck down* death penalty provisions —L. H. Tribe⟩

strike fund — see FUND 1

strike suit *n* : a derivative action based on no bona fide claim and brought with the intent to force defendants to settle out of court

¹strip *vt* **stripped**; **stripping** : to divide (a debt security) into separately traded securities entitling the owner usu. to either principal or interest alone from the obligation

²strip *n* : a security traded separately from another after stripping; *specif* : a derivative mortgage-backed security created by the segregation of cash flow from the underlying mortgages or other mortgage-backed securities and entitling the investor to a specified percentage (as 100 percent) of the interest or principal paid

STRIP *n, pl* **STRIPs** [*s*eparate *t*rading of *r*egistered *i*nterest and *p*rincipal of securities] : a treasury security that entitles the investor usu. to payment of interest or principal exclusively and that is registered in a Federal Reserve bank under a federal program that provides for such separate trading of the components of U.S. Treasury obligations — compare *zero-coupon bond* at BOND 2

strip–search *vt* : to conduct a strip search of

strip search — see SEARCH

strong mark *n* : a trademark or service mark that is distinctive and is used in a fictitious, arbitrary, or fanciful manner in connection with a product — compare WEAK MARK ◊ A strong mark is afforded greater trademark protection than a weak mark.

¹struck *past and past part of* STRIKE

²struck *adj* : being the object of or subjected to a labor strike ⟨a ~ employer⟩

struck jury *n* **1** : a jury that is selected from a venire of usu. forty people from which potential jurors are struck by attorneys for each side alternately until a specified number (as twelve) of jurors are left **2** : SPECIAL JURY

su·able \'sü-ə-bəl\ *adj* : capable of being or liable to be sued

sua spon·te \'sü-ə-'spän-tē, -'spōn-tā\ *adv or adj* [Latin, of its own accord] : on the court's own motion or initiative ⟨authorize the court to order a new trial *sua sponte* —J. H. Friedenthal *et al.*⟩ ⟨the court's *sua sponte* dismissal⟩

sub- *prefix* **1** : under : beneath : below ⟨*sub*standard⟩ **2 a** : subordinate : secondary : next lower than or inferior to ⟨*sub*agent⟩ **b** : subordinate portion of : subdivision of ⟨*sub*chapter⟩ ⟨*sub*committee⟩ **c** : assigning to another by the same method ⟨*sub*license⟩ ⟨*sub*contract⟩

sub·agent \'səb-ˌā-jənt, ˌsəb-'ā-\ *n* : an agent who is appointed by another agent (as an insurance agent) and for whom the principal agent is responsible or liable

sub·chap·ter \'səb-ˌchap-tər\ *n* : a subdivision of a chapter (as of a statute or code)

subchapter S \-'es\ *n* : a subchapter of chapter 1 of the Internal Revenue Code that allows a small business corporation's taxable income to be computed in a manner similar to that used for a partnership — see also *S corporation* at CORPORATION

subchapter S corporation *n* : S CORPORATION at CORPORATION

sub·com·mit·tee \'səb-kə-ˌmi-tē\ *n* : a subdivision of a committee that is assigned a portion of the committee's jurisdiction, holds hearings, amends legislation, and reports to the committee

sub·con·tract \ˌsəb-'kän-ˌtrakt\ *n* : a contract between a party to an original contract and a third party that assigns part of the performance (as building a house) of the original contract to the third party — **subcontract** \ˌsəb-'kän-ˌtrakt, -kən-'trakt\ *vb*

subcontractor *n* : one (as an individual or business) that contracts to perform part or all of the obligations of another's contract

sub·di·vide \ˌsəb-də-'vīd, 'səb-də-ˌ\ *vt* : to divide into several parts; *specif* : to divide (a tract of land) into two or more lots for sale or building development

sub·di·vi·sion \'səb-də-ˌvi-zhən\ *n* **1** : an act or instance of subdividing ⟨obtain approval of his ~ of the land⟩ **2** : a tract of land subdivided into lots ⟨to provide streets and sewers for the ~⟩ **3** : a part made by subdividing ⟨as prescribed in ~ one of this section⟩

sub·ject \'səb-ˌjekt\ *n* : the person upon whose life a life insurance policy is written and upon whose death the policy is payable : INSURED — compare BENEFICIARY b, POLICYHOLDER

subject matter jurisdiction — see JURISDICTION

sub ju·di·ce \ˌsəb-'jü-də-sē, ˌsùb-'yü-di-ˌkā\ *adv* [Latin] : before the court : at bar ⟨in the case *sub judice*⟩

sub·lease \'səb-ˌlēs\ *n* : a lease that is given by a tenant or lessee to another person of part or all of the leased premises for a shorter term than that of the original lease and under which some interest is retained — compare *assignment of lease* at ASSIGNMENT — **sublease** *vt*

sub·les·see \ˌsəb-le-'sē\ *n* : a lessee under a sublease

sub·les·sor \ˌsəb-'le-ˌsòr, -le-'sòr\ *n* : one that grants a sublease

sub·let \'səb-ˌlet\ *vb* **-let; -let·ting** *vt* : to make or obtain a sublease of ~ *vi* : to lease all or part of a leased property

sub·li·cense \ˌsəb-'līs-ᵊns\ *n* : a license granted by a licensee that grants some or all of the rights (as to a patent) acquired under the original license — **sublicense** *vb*

sub·lim·it \ˌsəb-'li-mət\ *n* : a liability limit in an insurance policy for a particular risk (as loss of jewelry by theft) that is below the aggregate liability limit of the policy

sub·mis·si·ble \səb-'mi-sə-bəl\ *adj* : sufficient for submission to a trier of fact : capable of being submitted for decision ⟨the claimant has the burden of proving a ~ case —*Manor Square, Inc. v. Heartthrob of Kansas City, Inc.*, 854 S.W.2d 38 (1993)⟩

sub·mis·sion \səb-'mi-shən\ *n* **1** : an agreement to submit a dispute to and abide by the decision of an arbitrator ⟨an award falls within the general rule that acts of arbitrators must . . . be coextensive with the ~ —*Albert v. Goor*, 218 P.2d 736 (1950)⟩ **2** : an act of submitting something ⟨upon ~ of a properly completed memorandum —J. H. Friedenthal *et al.*⟩; *also* : something submitted **3** : an act of submitting to the authority or control of another

sub·mit *vb* **sub·mit·ted; sub·mit·ting** *vt* **1** : to yield or subject to control or authority ⟨to ~ himself to the jurisdiction of the tribal court —*Sheppard v. Sheppard*, 655 P.2d 895 (1982)⟩ **2 a** : to present or propose to another for review, consideration, or decision; *specif* : to commit to a trier of fact or law for decision after the close of trial or argument ⟨the trial court could properly ~ both counts to the jury —Rorie Sherman⟩ **b** : to deliver formally **3** : to put forward as an opinion or contention ~ *vi* **1** : to yield oneself ⟨parties to a contract may agree in advance to ~ to the jurisdiction of a given court —*National Equipment Rental, Ltd. v. Szukhent*, 375 U.S. 311 (1964)⟩ **2** : to defer to or consent to abide by the opinion of another

sub nom. *abbr* sub nomine

sub nom·i·ne \ˌsəb-'nä-mə-nē, -ˌnā; 'sùb-'nō-mē-ˌnā\ *prep* [Latin] : under the name of ⟨the testator made him a trustee *sub nomine* "Charlie Smith"⟩ — often

used in full or abbreviated form in legal citations to indicate the name under which the litigation continued ⟨*Castro v. Beecher*, 522 F. Supp. 873, 877 (D. Mass. 1981), aff'd *sub nom.*, *NAACP v. Beecher*, 679 F.2d 965 (1st Cir. 1982)⟩

¹sub·or·di·nate \sə-'bȯrd-ᵊn-ət\ *adj* **1** : placed in or occupying a lower rank, class, or position **2** : submissive to or controlled by authority

²sub·or·di·nate \sə-'bȯrd-ᵊn-ˌāt\ *vt* **-nat·ed; -nat·ing** : to assign lower priority to (as a debt or creditor) : postpone satisfaction of until after satisfaction of another ⟨the equitable assignee will be *subordinated* to the rights of the assignor's trustee in bankruptcy —J. D. Calamari and J. M. Perillo⟩

sub·or·di·na·tion \sə-ˌbȯrd-ᵊn-'ā-shən\ *n* : an act or instance of subordinating; *also* : the remedy of subordinating a claim — see also EQUITABLE SUBORDINATION

subordination agreement *n* : an agreement by which one party subordinates its claim to that of another

sub·orn \sə-'bȯrn\ *vt* [Latin *subornare*, from *sub-* secretly + *ornare* to prepare, equip] **1** : to induce or procure to commit an unlawful act and esp. perjury ⟨an attempt to ~ a witness⟩ **2** : to induce (perjury) or obtain (perjured testimony) from a witness ⟨an attorney and his client were jointly charged with ~*ing* perjury and perjury, respectively —W. R. LaFave and J. H. Israel⟩ — **sub·orn·er** *n*

sub·or·na·tion \ˌsə-ˌbȯr-'nā-shən\ *n* : an act or instance of suborning ⟨~ of perjured statements⟩ ⟨to protect witnesses from intimidation and ~ —*WBZ-TV4 v. DA for the Suffolk Dist.*, 562 N.E.2d 817 (1990)⟩ ◇ Subornation of perjury is a crime.

¹sub·poe·na *also* **sub·pe·na** \sə-'pē-nə\ *n* [Latin *sub poena* under penalty] : a writ commanding a designated person upon whom it has been served to appear (as in court or before a congressional committee) under a penalty (as a charge of contempt) for failure to comply — compare SUMMONS

²**subpoena** *also* **subpena** *vt* **-naed; -na-ing** : to call before a court or hearing by a subpoena ⟨the inspector is given the power to ~ any relevant . . . witnesses — *Harvard Law Review*⟩; *also* : to command the production of (evidence) by a subpoena duces tecum ⟨*subpoenaed* documents⟩

subpoena ad tes·ti·fi·can·dum \-,ad-,tes-tə-fə-'kan-dəm, -,äd-,tes-tē-fē-'kän-,düm\ : a subpoena that commands a witness to appear and give testimony

subpoena du·ces te·cum \-'dü-səs-'tē-kəm, -'dyü-, -sēz-; -'dü-kes-'tā-,küm\ *n* [New Latin, under penalty you shall bring with you] : a subpoena that commands the production of specified evidence in a person's possession ◊ Unlike a search warrant, a subpoena duces tecum can be issued without a showing of probable cause.

sub·ro·gate \'sə-brō-,gāt\ *vt* **-gat·ed; -gat·ing** [Latin *subrogatus*, past participle of *subrogare, surrogare* to elect as a substitute, from *sub-* under + *rogare* to request] : to put in the place of another by the doctrine of subrogation : substitute (as a second creditor) for another with regard to a legal right or claim ⟨~*s* the trustee to the priority and avoidance rights of certain unsecured creditors —J. J. White and R. S. Summers⟩ ⟨the surety who pays the principal obligation is *subrogated* . . . to the rights of the creditor —*Louisiana Civil Code*⟩

sub·ro·ga·tion \,sə-brō-'gā-shən\ *n* **1** : an equitable doctrine holding that when a third party pays a creditor or obligee the third party succeeds to the creditor's rights against the debtor or obligor; *also* : a doctrine holding that when an insurance company pays an insured's claim of loss due to another's tort the insurer succeeds to the insured's rights (as the right to sue for damages) against the tortfeasor — called also *equitable subrogation* **2** : an act or instance of subrogating ⟨where an insurer has acquired by an assignment or by ~ the right to recover for money — J. M. Landers *et al.*⟩ ◊ Subrogation can

take place either by operation of law or by contractual agreement.

sub·ro·gee \,sə-brō-'gē, -'jē\ *n* : the party (as a second creditor) that succeeds to another's rights by subrogation

sub·ro·gor \,sə-brō-'gȯr\ *n* : the party (as an insured) that yields his or her rights to another (as an insurer) by subrogation

sub·scribe \səb-'skrīb\ *vb* **sub·scribed; sub·scrib·ing** [Latin *subscribere*, literally, to write beneath, from *sub-* under + *scribere* to write] *vt* **1** : to write (one's name) underneath or at the end of a document ⟨we now ~ our names as witnesses —W. M. McGovern, Jr. *et al.*⟩ **2 a** : to sign (as a document) with one's own hand in token of consent, obligation, or attestation ⟨such witnesses shall ~ the will in the presence of the testator —*West Virginia Code*⟩ **b** : to pledge (a gift or contribution) by writing one's name with the amount **c** : to sell (stock) by subscription ⟨over two million shares have been *subscribed*⟩ ~ *vi* **1** : to sign one's name to a document; *also* : to give consent or approval by signing one's name **2** : to agree to purchase and pay for securities esp. of a new offering ⟨a right to ~ to a share of stock —D. Q. Posin⟩ — **sub·scrib·er** *n*

sub·scrip·tion \səb-'skrip-shən\ *n* **1** : the act of signing one's name (as in attesting or witnessing a document) **2** : something that is subscribed; *specif* : a sum subscribed or pledged ⟨a charitable ~⟩ **3** : an agreement to purchase securities (as stocks) of a new issue and esp. of a prospective corporation — compare WARRANT 3b

sub·se·quent \'səb-si-kwənt, -,kwent\ *adj* : following in time, order, or space — see also *condition subsequent* at CONDITION; compare PRECEDENT

sub·sid·i·ary \səb-'si-dē-,er-ē, -'si-də-rē\

\ə\abut \ᵊ\kitten \ər\further \a\ash \ā\ace
\ä\cot, cart \aú\out \ch\chin \e\bet \ē\easy
\g\go \i\hit \ī\ice \j\job \ŋ\sing \ō\go \ȯ\law
\ȯi\boy \th\thin \t̲h̲\the \ü\loot \ú\foot \y\yet
\zh\vision *see also* Pronunciation Symbols page

n, pl **-ar·ies** : a company having the majority of its stock owned by another company — compare AFFILIATE ◊ The parent company of a subsidiary generally has the same policy-making powers as any majority owner and can do such things as appoint directors and hire officers. The subsidiary is controlled by the parent through these powers, and the parent may be held liable for the acts of the subsidiary if the subsidiary is found to be an instrumentality of the parent. — **subsidiary** *adj*

sub si·len·tio \ₜsəb-sə-'len-chē-ₜō, -sī-; ₜsùb-sē-'len-tē-ₜō\ *adv* [Latin] : under or in silence : without notice being taken or without making a particular point of the matter in question ⟨overruled *sub silentio* this court's holding in Collora —*State v. Olsen*, 498 N.W.2d 661 (1993)⟩

sub·stance *n* **1** : SUBSTANTIVE LAW ⟨was a question of ~ and not process⟩ — compare PROCEDURE **2** : something (as language) essential esp. to establishing a valid right, claim, or charge ⟨a title defective in form, not ~⟩

sub·stan·dard *adj* : deviating from or falling short of a standard or norm: as **a** : of a quality lower than that prescribed by law **b** : constituting a greater than normal risk to an insurer

sub·stan·tial \səb-'stan-chəl\ *adj* **1 a** : of or relating to substance **b** : not illusory : having merit ⟨failed to raise a ~ constitutional claim⟩ **c** : having importance or significance : MATERIAL ⟨a ~ step had not been taken toward commission of the crime —W. R. LaFave and A. W. Scott, Jr.⟩ **2** : considerable in quantity : significantly great ⟨would be a ~ abuse of the provisions of this chapter —*U.S. Code*⟩ — compare DE MINIMIS — **sub·stan·ti·al·i·ty** \-ₜstan-chē-'a-lə-tē\ *n* — **sub·stan·tial·ly** *adv*

substantial capacity test *n* : a test used in many jurisdictions when considering an insanity defense which relieves a defendant of criminal responsibility if at the time of the crime as a result of mental disease or defect the defendant lacked the capacity to appreciate the wrongfulness of his or her conduct or to conform the conduct to the requirements of the law — called also *ALI test, Model Penal Code test;* compare DIMINISHED CAPACITY, IRRESISTIBLE IMPULSE TEST, M'NAGHTEN TEST ◊ This test was first formulated in the Model Penal Code and has been adopted by many jurisdictions.

substantial compliance *n* : compliance with the substantial or essential requirements of something (as a statute or contract) that satisfies its purpose or objective even though its formal requirements are not complied with

substantial evidence — see EVIDENCE

substantial factor *n* : an important or significant factor that is not necessarily the only factor leading to a plaintiff's injury but is sufficient to have caused the injury by itself — compare BUT-FOR

substantial justice *n* : justice of a sufficient degree esp. to satisfy a standard of fairness; *also* : justice administered according to the substance and not necessarily the form of the law ⟨all pleadings shall be so construed as to do *substantial justice* —*Federal Rules of Civil Procedure* Rule 8(f)⟩ — see also FAIR PLAY AND SUBSTANTIAL JUSTICE

substantial performance — see PERFORMANCE

substantial right *n* : an important or essential right that merits enforcement or protection by the law : a right related to a matter of substance as distinguished from a matter of form

sub·stan·tive \'səb-stən-tiv\ *adj* **1** : of or relating to a matter of substance as opposed to form or procedure ⟨a ~ issue⟩ ⟨the ~ instructions to the jury⟩ ⟨was dismissed on procedural and ~ grounds⟩ — compare PROCEDURAL **2** : affecting rights, duties, or causes of actions ⟨a ~ statutory change⟩ ⟨a ~ rule of law⟩ **3** : existing in its own right; *specif* : of or relating to a substantive crime ⟨the object of a RICO conspiracy is to violate a ~ RICO provision —*United States v. Elliot*, 571 F.2d 880 (1978)⟩

substantive crime *n* : a crime that does not have as an element the performance of some other crime : a crime that is not dependent on another ⟨indicted and convicted of conspiracy to attempt to enter the bank and the *substantive crime* of attempting to enter the bank — *United States v. Clay*, 495 F.2d 700 (1974)⟩ — called also *substantive offense;* compare ACCESSORY, CONSPIRACY

substantive due process *n* : DUE PROCESS 2

substantive evidence — see EVIDENCE

substantive law *n* : law that creates or defines rights, duties, obligations, and causes of action that can be enforced by law — compare ADJECTIVE LAW, PROCEDURAL LAW ◊ There are restrictions on applying new substantive law (as statutory or case law) retroactively.

substantive offense *n* : SUBSTANTIVE CRIME

substantive right *n* : a right arising from substantive law

substantive rule *n* : LEGISLATIVE RULE

substantive unconscionability *n* : unconscionability of a contract that arises from the terms of the contract and esp. from terms that are found to be one-sided, unjust, or overly harsh — compare PROCEDURAL UNCONSCIONABILITY

substituted basis — see BASIS 3

substituted contract — see CONTRACT

substituted judgment — see JUDGMENT 2

sub·sti·tut·ed service *n* : the service of a writ, process, or summons otherwise than by personal service (as by mail or publication or by leaving it at a defendant's place of business or residence or with an agent) — called also *constructive service*

sub·sti·tute gift *n* : SUBSTITUTIONAL GIFT at GIFT

sub·sti·tu·tion \ˌsəb-stə-'tü-shən, -'tyü-\ *n* : the substituting of one person or thing for another: as **a** *in the civil law of Louisiana* : a disposition not in trust by which a donee, heir, or legatee is charged to hold property transferred and return it to a third person — compare FIDEI COMMISSUM, VULGAR SUBSTITUTION ◊ Substitutions

are prohibited. **b** : replacement of a party to an action with a successor or representative upon motion to the court when the party is unable to continue litigating (as because of death, incompetency, transfer of interest, or loss of the office for which the party was suing or being sued in an official capacity) **c** : the replacement of a new agreement or obligation for an old one — see also NOVATION — **sub·sti·tu·tion·al** \-shə-nəl\ *n* — **sub·sti·tu·tion·ary** \-shə-ˌnər-ē\ *adj*

substitutional gift — see GIFT

sub·sure·ty \ˌsəb-'shùr-ə-tē\ *n* : one who is a surety along with another surety who may be liable for the entire loss upon the default of the principal

sub·sure·ty·ship *n* : the relation between two or more sureties who are bound to answer for the same duty where one has the whole duty of performance with respect to the other

sub·ten·an·cy \ˌsəb-'te-nən-sē\ *n* **1** : the quality or state of being a subtenant **2** : the interest in property that one holds as a subtenant

sub·ten·ant \ˌsəb-'te-nənt\ *n* : one who rents property from a tenant of the property

sub·ver·sion \səb-'vər-zhən\ *n* : a systematic attempt to overthrow or undermine a government or political system by persons working from within; *also* : the crime of committing acts in furtherance of such an attempt — **sub·ver·sion·ary** \-zhə-ˌner-ē\ *adj* — **sub·ver·sive** \-'vər-siv\ *adj or n* — **sub·ver·sive·ly** *adv* — **sub·ver·sive·ness** *n*

suc·ceed \sək-'sēd\ *vi* **1** : to come next after another in office or position **2 a** : to take something by succession ⟨*∼ed* to his mother's estate⟩ **b** : to acquire the rights, obligations, and charges of a decedent in property comprising an estate ⟨the heir, who accepts, is considered as having *∼ed*

to the deceased from the moment of his death —*Louisiana Civil Code*⟩ ∼ *vt* **1** : to follow in sequence and esp. immediately **2** : to come after as heir or successor
suc•ces•sion \sək-'se-shən\ *n* **1 a** : the order in which or the conditions under which one person after another succeeds to a property, dignity, position, title, or throne ⟨the sequence of ∼ to the presidency⟩ **b** : the right of a person or line of ancestry to succeed **c** : the line of ancestry having such a right **2 a** : the act or process of following in order **b** : the act or process of one person's taking the place of another in the enjoyment of or liability for rights or duties or both **3** : the act or process by which a person becomes entitled to the property or property interest of a deceased person and esp. an intestate : the transmission of the estate of a decedent to his or her heirs, legatees, or devisees; *also* : the estate of the deceased including assets and liabilities — used chiefly in the civil law of Louisiana

intestate succession **1** : the transmission of property or property interests of a decedent as provided by statute as distinguished from the transfer in accordance with the decedent's will; *also* : the operation of such statutory provisions in transmitting intestate property ⟨would take the property by *intestate succession*⟩ **2** *in the civil law of Louisiana* : property that is not disposed of by will but by operation of statute ⟨who presents himself to claim an *intestate succession* —*Louisiana Civil Code*⟩

testate succession : the transmission of property in accordance with a valid will

vacant succession in the civil law of Louisiana : an estate that has not been claimed, of which the heirs are unknown, or that has been renounced by all of the heirs

4 a : the continuance of a corporation's status as a legal person ⟨perpetual corporate ∼⟩ **b** : the act or process by which one corporation assumes ownership of

another ⟨documents . . . that all aim to prepare your company for its new owner's ∼ —Saul Berkowitz⟩ **5** : the act or process by which one state takes over or follows upon another and becomes entitled to its rights and position in international law
succession tax *n* **1** : ESTATE TAX **2** : INHERITANCE TAX
suc•ces•sive \sək-'se-siv\ *adj* **1 a** : of or relating to succession ⟨∼ rights⟩ **b** : created by succession **2** : following in order : following each other without interruption ⟨∼ bankruptcy filings⟩ **3** : of, relating to, or being a petition for habeas corpus that raises a claim already adjudicated — **suc•ces•sive•ly** *adv* — **suc•ces•sive•ness** *n*
successive tortfeasor *n* : any of two or more tortfeasors whose negligent acts are independent though causing injury to the same third party
suc•ces•sor \sək-'se-sər\ *n* : one that follows : one that succeeds another (as in a position, title, office, or estate)
successor in interest : a successor to another's interest in property; *esp* : a successor in ownership of a business that is carried on and controlled substantially as it was before the transfer
sud•den emergency doctrine *n* : a doctrine of tort law: a person who is confronted with a sudden and unexpected perilous situation not of his or her own making and who acts as would a reasonably prudent person under the circumstances will not be held liable even if later reflection shows that the wisest course was not chosen
sudden heat *n* : HEAT OF PASSION
sudden heat of passion : HEAT OF PASSION
sudden passion *n* : HEAT OF PASSION
sue *vb* **sued; su•ing** *vt* [Anglo-French *suer*, *suire*, literally, to follow, pursue, from Old French *sivre*, ultimately from Latin *sequi* to follow] : to bring an action against : seek justice from by legal process ∼ *vi* : to bring an action in court

sue–and–labor clause *n* : a clause in marine insurance contracts by which the insured agrees to take steps necessary to safeguard the covered property from loss or to minimize losses that occur and the insurer agrees to pay for the reasonable costs of such steps

sue out *vt* : to apply for and obtain in judicial proceedings ⟨*sued out* a summons⟩

suf·fer·ance \'sə-frəns, -fə-rəns\ *n* : consent or sanction implied by a lack of interference or failure to enforce a prohibition — see also *estate at sufferance* at ESTATE 1, *tenancy at sufferance* at TENANCY

suf·fi·cien·cy *n* : the quality or state of being sufficient ⟨the ~ of the evidence to convict⟩

suf·fi·cient *adj* : enough to meet the needs under the law of a situation or a proposed end — **suf·fi·cient·ly** *adv*

sufficient cause — see CAUSE 2

suf·frage \'sə-frij\ *n* [Latin *suffragium* vote, political support, from *suffragari* to support with one's vote] **1** : a vote in deciding a controverted question or the choice of a person for an office or trust ⟨no State . . . shall be deprived of its equal ~ in the Senate —*U.S. Constitution* art. V⟩ **2** : the right of voting : FRANCHISE; *also* : the exercise of such right

sug·gest *vt* **1** : to mention or imply as a possibility **2** : to enter on the record as a suggestion

sug·ges·tion *n* **1 a** : the act or process of suggesting **b** : something suggested **2** : an entry on the record of a fact or circumstance (as the death or insolvency of a party) material to a case and essential for the court in making its determination ⟨reference to a party's death in a pleading was not the equivalent of a formal ~ of death on the record —*Kissic v. Liberty Nat'l Life Ins. Co.*, 641 So. 2d 250 (1994)⟩

sug·ges·tive *adj* : giving a suggestion or making a hint: as **a** : being a trademark, trade dress, trade name, or service mark that requires the consumer to use thought and imagination to perceive the nature

of the product or service ◇ Suggestive marks are entitled to trademark protection without proof of secondary meaning. **b** : relating to or being a lineup that in some way suggests to the witness which member of the lineup is in fact the defendant

sui·cide clause *n* : a provision limiting the liability of an insurer to a return of net premiums paid if an insured commits suicide within a stipulated period

sui ge·ner·is \'sü-ˌī-'je-nə-rəs, 'sü-ē-\ *adj* [Latin, of its own kind] : constituting a class alone : unique or particular to itself ⟨the lawyer's . . . ad that makes no distinction among various legal and factual nuances in each *sui generis* case has the potential to mislead —*National Law Journal*⟩

sui ju·ris \-'jür-is, -'yü-rēs\ *adj* [Latin, of one's own right] **1** : having full legal capacity to act on one's own behalf : not subject to the authority of another **2** : qualified to enjoy full rights of citizenship (as of holding public office or serving on a jury)

suit *n* [Anglo-French *siute, suite, suit* request to initiate legal proceedings, literally, pursuit, from *siute*, feminine past participle of *suire* to follow, from Old French *sivre* — see SUE] : a proceeding to enforce a right or claim; *specif* : an action brought in a court seeking a remedy for injuries suffered or a determination of rights : LAWSUIT

suit·or \'sü-tər\ *n* **1** : a party to a suit **2** : one that seeks to take over a business ⟨approved the merger before the ~ obtained a 10% stake —*Wall Street Journal*⟩

sum cer·tain \'səm-'sərt-ᵊn\ *n* : an amount that can be determined with certainty from the information presented (as on a negotiable instrument) without resort to outside sources

---

\ə\abut \ᵊ\kitten \ər\further \a\ash \ā\ace
\ä\cot, cart \au̇\out \ch\chin \e\bet \ē\easy
\g\go \i\hit \ī\ice \j\job \ŋ\sing \ō\go \ȯ\law
\ȯi\boy \th\thin \t͟h\the \ü\loot \u̇\foot \y\yet
\zh\vision *see also* Pronunciation Symbols page

sum·ma·ry \'sə-mə-rē\ *adj* : done immediately, concisely, and without usual formal procedures; *esp* : used in or done by summary proceeding — compare PLENARY — **sum·mar·i·ly** \sə-'mer-ə-lē\ *adv*

summary court–martial *n* : a court-martial consisting of one commissioned officer and having authority to impose no sentence in excess of one month's confinement or forfeiture of two-thirds of one month's pay — compare GENERAL COURT-MARTIAL, SPECIAL COURT-MARTIAL

summary distribution *n* : an abridged form of administration allowing distribution of an estate after the filing of an inventory showing assets sufficient only to pay superior claims (as to family members claiming statutory shares) — compare COLLECTION BY AFFIDAVIT

summary judgment — see JUDGMENT 1a

summary proceeding — see PROCEEDING

summary process *n* : a procedure allowed to enforce a claim or right in a summary manner; *specif* : a procedure to repossess real property esp. from a tenant upon nonpayment or other default : a summary eviction

sum·ma·tion \sə-'mā-shən\ *n* : CLOSING ARGUMENT

sum·ming–up *n* : CLOSING ARGUMENT

sum·mon *vt* : to command by service of a summons to appear in court

¹sum·mons \'sə-mənz\ *n, pl* **sum·mons·es** \-mən-zəz\ : a written notification that one is required to appear in court: as **a** : a document in a civil suit that is issued by an authorized judicial officer (as a clerk of court) and delivered to a plaintiff or the plaintiff's attorney for service on the defendant and that notifies the defendant that he or she must appear and defend (as by filing an answer) within a specified time or a default judgment will be rendered for the plaintiff **b** : a document that summons a defendant to appear before a court to answer a minor criminal charge and that is issued in lieu of a warrant for arrest by an authorized judicial

officer (as a magistrate) upon request of a prosecuting attorney **c** : a notification to appear for jury service **d** : a notification to appear as a witness — see also JOHN DOE SUMMONS, SERVICE; compare SUBPOENA

²summons *vt* **sum·monsed** \-mənzd\; **sum·mons·ing** \-mən-ziŋ\ : SUMMON; *esp* : to bring into court by a summons ⟨hereby *summonsed* to serve as a trial juror⟩

Sun·day closing law *n* : a law that requires certain commercial establishments to close on Sundays or that restricts the sales that may be made on that day

sun·set *adj* : having or being a provision stipulating the termination or repeal of something (as a law, grant, or insurance coverage) on a specified date ⟨~ laws requiring periodic review of programs to justify their continuance⟩

sun·shine *adj* : forbidding or restricting closed meetings of legislative or executive bodies and sometimes providing for public access to government records ⟨~ laws⟩ — see also *Freedom of Information Act* in the IMPORTANT LAWS section

sup ct *abbr* supreme court

su·per·in·ten·dent *n* : one who has the oversight and charge of a place, institution, department, organization, or operation; *specif* : the executive head of a police department

su·pe·ri·or *adj* : of higher status, rank, or priority

superior court *n, often cap S&C* **1** : a court of general jurisdiction intermediate between the inferior courts and the higher appellate courts **2** : a court having original jurisdiction and conducting jury trials

superior knowledge — see KNOWLEDGE

su·per·ma·jor·i·ty \'sü-pər-mə-ˌjȯr-ə-tē\ *n* : a large majority ⟨a provision requiring a ~ vote — say, 80 % of the common shares instead of the usual bare majority rule —R. C. Clark⟩

su·per·sede \ˌsü-pər-'sēd\ *vt* **-sed·ed; -sed·ing 1** : to subject to postponement or suspension; *esp* : to suspend the operation of (a judgment or order) by means of a supersedeas **2 :** to take the place of in authority **:** PREEMPT, OVERRIDE **3 :** to take the place of and render null or ineffective

su·per·se·de·as \ˌsü-pər-'sē-dē-əs\ *n* [Medieval Latin, you should desist (word used in the writ)] **1 :** a common-law writ commanding a stay of legal proceedings that is issued under various conditions and esp. to stay an officer from proceeding under another writ **2 :** an order suspending the proceedings of an inferior court and esp. the enforcement of a judgment until reviewed on appeal

supersedeas bond — see BOND 1a

superseding cause — see CAUSE 1

su·per·vene \ˌsü-pər-'vēn\ *vi* **-vened; -ven·ing :** to take place after or later in the course of something else as an additional and usu. unforeseeable development with intervening or countering effect

supervening cause — see CAUSE 1

su·per·vi·sor *n* **:** one that directs or oversees a person, group, department, organization, or operation; *specif* **:** the popularly elected chief administrative official of a township or other subdivision in some states of the U.S.

supp. *abbr* supplement

sup·ple·men·tal \ˌsə-plə-'ment-ᵊl\ *adj* **:** serving to complete or make an addition ⟨~ appropriations⟩; *specif* **:** of, relating to, or being a supplemental pleading — **supplemental** *n*

supplemental jurisdiction — see JURISDICTION

supplemental pleading — see PLEADING 1

sup·ple·men·ta·ry \ˌsə-plə-'men-tə-rē, -trē\ *adj* **:** added or serving as a supplement

supplementary proceeding — see PROCEEDING

¹sup·port *vt* **1 a :** to promote the interests or cause of **b :** to uphold or defend as valid or right **c :** to argue or vote for **2 :** to provide with substantiation or corroboration ⟨~ an alibi⟩ **3 :** to provide with the means of livelihood (as housing, f⸱ `lothing) esp. in accordance with

an agreement or court order **4 :** to hold up or in position **:** maintain the physical integrity of ⟨the right to have one's land ~*ed* by the underlying land⟩

²support *n* **1 :** the act or process of supporting **:** the condition of being supported ⟨pledged the candidate their ~⟩ **2 :** a means of obtaining the necessities of life (as food, shelter, and clothing) **:** a source of livelihood esp. in the form of alimony or child support **3 :** something that provides support

sup·press \sə-'pres\ *vt* **1 :** to put down by authority or force **2 a :** to keep secret **b :** to stop or prohibit the publication or revelation of **3 a :** to exclude (illegally obtained evidence) from use at trial ⟨~ narcotics found in violation of the right against unreasonable search and seizure⟩ **b :** to fail to disclose (material evidence favorable to a defendant) in violation of due process ⟨accused the prosecution of ~*ing* evidence⟩ — compare BRADY MATERIAL ⁓ *vi* **:** to suppress evidence — **sup·press·ible** *adj* — **sup·pres·sion** \-'pre-shən\ *n*

suppression hearing — see HEARING

su·pra \'sü-prə\ *adj* [Latin] **:** earlier in this writing **:** ABOVE ⟨in the discussion ~⟩ — used in books, articles, and cases to refer the reader to previous pages, sections, or footnotes of the text or previous citations of other works ⟨see cases cited ~ note 16⟩ — compare IDEM, INFRA

su·prem·a·cy clause \sə-'pre-mə-sē-\ *n*, *often cap S&C* **:** a clause in Article VI of the U.S. Constitution that declares the constitution, laws, and treaties of the federal government to be the supreme law of the land to which judges in every state are bound regardless of state law to the contrary

su·preme court *n* **1 :** the highest court in a nation or state; *specif, cap S&C* **:** the

\ə\abut \ᵊ\kitten \ər\further \a\ash \ā\ace
\ä\cot, cart \au̇\out \ch\chin \e\bet \ē\easy
\g\go \i\hit \ī\ice \j\job \ŋ\sing \ō\go \ȯ\law
\ȯi\boy \th\thin \t̲h̲\the \ü\loot \u̇\foot \y\yet
\zh\vision *see also* Pronunciation Symbols page

highest court in the judicial branch of the U.S. government that has original jurisdiction over controversies involving ambassadors or other ministers or consuls but whose main activity is as the court of last resort exercising appellate jurisdiction over cases involving federal law **2** *cap S&C* : a court of original jurisdiction in New York ◊ The court of last resort in New York is the Court of Appeals.

Supreme Court of Appeals : the court of last resort in West Virginia

Supreme Court of Judicature : the highest judicial body of England and Wales that includes the Court of Appeal and High Court of Justice

Supreme Judicial Court *n* : the court of last resort in Maine and Massachusetts

sur \'sùr, 'sūer\ *prep* [Anglo-French, on, upon, from Latin *super* over] : on the basis of : with regard to ⟨~ petition for rehearing⟩

¹sur·charge \'sər-ˌchärj\ *vt* **1** : to impose a surcharge on ⟨~ a trustee for failing to exercise due care⟩ **2** : to show an omission in (an account) for which credit ought to have been given

²surcharge *n* **1** : an additional or excessive charge **2** : a penalty imposed on a fiduciary for failing to exercise due care in the management of assets

sure·ty \'shùr-ə-tē\ *n, pl* **-ties** [Anglo⸗ French *seurté*, literally, guarantee, security, from Old French, from Latin *securitat-, securitas*, from *securus* secure] **1** : a formal engagement (as a pledge) given for the fulfillment of an undertaking **2** : one (as an accommodation party) who promises to answer for the debt or default of another ◊ At common law a surety is distinguished from a guarantor by being immediately liable as opposed to becoming liable only upon default of the principal. Under the Uniform Commercial Code, however, a surety includes a guarantor, and the two terms are generally interchangeable.

surety bond — see BOND 1a

surety company — see COMPANY

sure·ty·ship *n* : the contractual relationship in which a surety engages to answer for the debt or default of a principal to a third party

sur·plus \'sər-ˌpləs\ *n* **1 a** : an amount that remains when a use or need is satisfied **b** : an excess of receipts over disbursements **c** : the value of assets after subtracting liabilities **2** : an excess of the net worth of a corporation over the par value of its capital stock — compare UNDIVIDED PROFITS

capital surplus : all surplus other than earned surplus

earned surplus : the surplus that remains after deducting losses, distributions to stockholders, and transfers to capital stock accounts

paid–in surplus : surplus resulting from the sale of stock at amounts above par

sur·plus·age \'sər-ˌplə-sij\ *n* : excessive or nonessential matter; *esp* : matter contained in a pleading that is unnecessary or irrelevant

surplus line *adj* : of, relating to, or being insurance provided by a company not authorized to do business in the state except through a specially licensed broker ◊ Surplus line insurance can only be purchased if efforts to acquire suitable insurance from authorized companies are unsuccessful.

sur·prise *n* **1** : a condition or situation in which a party to a proceeding is unexpectedly placed without any fault or neglect of his or her own and that entitles the party to relief (as a new trial) **2** : an aspect of procedural unconscionability that consists of hiding a term of a contract in a mass of text

sur·re·but·tal \ˌsər-ri-'bət-ᵊl\ *n, often attrib* [*sur-* over + *rebuttal*] : the response to the rebuttal of the opposing party in a proceeding ⟨testimony of defense ~ witnesses —*Arizona Rules of Court*⟩

sur·re·join·der \ˌsər-ri-'jöin-dər\ *n* : an answer to a rejoinder

¹sur·ren·der *vt* **1 a** : to yield to the control or possession of another ⟨~ the leased premises⟩ ⟨~ collateral to a creditor⟩ **b** : to give up completely or agree to forgo **c** : to cancel (one's insurance policy) voluntarily **2** : to give over to the custody of the law ⟨~ a defendant⟩ ~ *vi* : to give oneself up

²surrender *n* : an act or instance of surrendering ⟨discharge an obligor by ~ of a promissory note⟩; *esp* : the yielding of an estate by a tenant to the landlord so that the leasehold interest is extinguished by mutual agreement

surrender value *n* : CASH SURRENDER VALUE

sur·ro·ga·cy \'sər-ə-gə-sē\ *n, pl* **-cies** : the office of a surrogate

sur·ro·gate \'sər-ə-gət\ *n* [Latin *surrogatus*, past participle of *surrogare, subrogare* to substitute, from *sub-* in place of, under + *rogare* to ask] **1** : one acting in the place of another; *esp* : one standing in loco parentis to a child **2** *often cap* : the judge or judicial officer of a Surrogate's Court or Surrogate's office — **surrogate** *adj*

Surrogate's Court *n* : a probate court in New York

Surrogate's office *n* : an office in New Jersey which carries out duties in probate, the administration of estates, and the guardianship of minors

sur·tax \'sər-ˌtaks\ *n* : an additional tax over and above a normal tax

sur·vi·val act *n* : SURVIVAL STATUTE

survival action *n* : an action for the recovery of damages for injury to a fatally injured person that is brought by his or her personal representative — compare WRONGFUL DEATH ACTION ◊ A survival action depends on the existence of a cause of action that the decedent would have had if he or she had survived. A wrongful death suit is concerned with injury to beneficiaries, not the decedent.

survival statute *n* : a statute that considers the cause of action for injury to a decedent as surviving his or her death and thereby permits survival actions — called also *survival act*

sur·vi·vor *n* : one (as a joint tenant or a child) who is recognized as outliving another and is commonly entitled to insurance benefits (as under social security) or

property upon the death of the decedent — see also *joint-and-survivor annuity* at ANNUITY

sur·vi·vor·ship *n* **1** : the right of one or more joint tenants who have survived another to take the interest of the person who has died **2** : the state of being a survivor

¹sus·pect \'səs-ˌpekt, sə-'spekt\ *adj* [Latin *suspectus*, from past participle of *suspicere* to look up at, regard with awe, suspect, from *sub-, sus-* up, secretly + *specere* to look at] : regarded or deserving to be regarded with suspicion or heightened scrutiny

²sus·pect \'səs-ˌpekt\ *n* : a person suspected of a crime; *also* : a person apprehended for but not yet charged with an offense

³sus·pect \sə-'spekt\ *vt* **1** : to imagine (one) to be guilty on slight evidence or without proof **2** : to imagine to exist or be probable ⟨they had reasonable cause to ~ abuse⟩

suspect class *n* : a class of individuals marked by immutable characteristics (as of race or national origin) and entitled to equal protection of the law by means of judicial scrutiny of a classification that discriminates against or otherwise burdens or affects them ⟨a classification that does not impact a *suspect class* or impinge upon a fundamental constitutional right will be upheld if it is rationally related to a legitimate government interest —*Doe v. Poritz*, 622 A.2d 367 (1995)⟩ — called also *protected class;* see also SUSPECT CLASSIFICATION ◊ *Suspect class* and *suspect classification* are often used synonymously in regard to a group of persons, but *suspect class* does not refer to the process of classifying itself.

suspect classification *n* : a statutory classification that is subject to strict scrutiny by the judiciary of its consistency with constitutional equal protection guar-

\ə\abut \ᵊ\kitten \ər\further \a\ash \ā\ace
\ä\cot, cart \au̇\out \ch\chin \e\bet \ē\easy
\g\go \i\hit \ī\ice \j\job \ŋ\sing \ō\go \ȯ\law
\ȯi\boy \th\thin \t̲h̲\the \ü\loot \u̇\foot \y\yet
\zh\vision *see also* Pronunciation Symbols page

antees because it affects a suspect class; *also* : SUSPECT CLASS

sus•pend *vt* **1** : to debar temporarily from a privilege, office, or function **2 a** : to stop temporarily ⟨~ trading⟩ **b** : to make temporarily ineffective ⟨~ a license⟩ **c** : STAY ⟨~ a hearing⟩ **d** : to defer until a later time — see also *suspended sentence* at SENTENCE

suspended sentence — see SENTENCE

sus•pen•sion *n* : the act of suspending : the state or period of being suspended ⟨the ~ of an employee⟩

sus•pen•sive \sə-'spen-siv\ *adj, in the civil law of Louisiana* **1** : having the effect of suspending ⟨granted a ~ appeal⟩ — see also *suspensive condition* at CONDITION **2** : characterized by suspension

suspensive condition — see CONDITION

sus•pi•cion *n* : the act or an instance of suspecting something : a mental state usu. short of belief in which one entertains a notion that something is wrong or that a fact exists without proof or on slight evidence — see also REASONABLE SUSPICION — **sus•pi•cion•less** *adj*

sus•tain \sə-'stān\ *vt* **1** : to support as true, legal, or just **2** : to allow or uphold as valid ⟨~ an objection⟩ — compare OVERRULE 1 — **sus•tain•able** *adj*

swap \'swäp\ *n* **1** : an exchange of securities **2** : a derivative contract in which two parties (as corporations) agree to exchange rates esp. relating to debt

swear *vb* **swore; sworn; swear•ing** [Old English *swerian*] *vt* **1** : to utter or take solemnly ⟨~ an oath⟩ **2 a** : to assert as true or promise under oath ⟨a *sworn* affidavit⟩ **b** : to assert or promise emphatically or earnestly ⟨*swore* to uphold the constitution⟩ **3 a** : to put to an oath **b** : to bind by an oath ~ *vi* : to take an oath

swear in *vt* : to induct into office by administration of an oath

swear out *vt* : to procure (a warrant) by making a sworn statement; *also* : to make (a sworn affidavit) to procure a warrant

sym•bol•ic delivery \sim-'bä-lik-\ *n* : CONSTRUCTIVE DELIVERY at DELIVERY

symbolic speech *n* : conduct that is intended to convey a particular message which is likely to be understood by those viewing it ⟨it is well established that wearing certain clothing can be a form of protected *symbolic speech* —*City of Harvard v. Gaut,* 660 N.E.2d 259 (1996)⟩ — compare COMMERCIAL SPEECH, PURE SPEECH ◊ Symbolic speech is entitled to free speech protection under the First Amendment to the U.S. Constitution unless its regulation is within the constitutional power of the government and is justified by an important government interest, and the restriction placed on it by regulation is no greater than is essential to the furtherance of that interest.

sympathy strike — see STRIKE

syn•al•lag•mat•ic \ˌsi-nə-ˌlag-'ma-tik, sə-ˌna-ləg-\ *adj* [Greek *synallagmatikos* of a contract, from *synallagmat-, synallagama* contract, covenant, from *synallassein* to enter into a contract, from *syn-* together with, at the same time as + *allassein* to change, exchange, barter, from *allos* other] *in the civil law of Louisiana* : BILATERAL

synallagmatic contract — see CONTRACT

syn•dic \'sin-dik\ *n* [French, government officer, from Late Latin *syndicus,* from Greek *syndikos* court assistant, advocate, from *syn-* together with + *dikē* right, judgment] *in the civil law of Louisiana* : a trustee of property owned by an insolvent or bankrupt debtor

syn•di•cal•ism \'sin-di-kə-ˌli-zəm\ *n* [French *syndicalisme,* from (*chambre*) *syndicale* trade union, from *chambre* chamber + *syndicale,* feminine of *syndical* of or relating to a syndic or to a committee that assumes the powers of a syndic, from *syndic* government office] : a doctrine or practice promoting the revolutionary seizure of government and industry — see also CRIMINAL SYNDICALISM

¹syn•di•cate \'sin-di-kət\ *n* [French *syndicat* the office or jurisdiction of a syndic] **1** : a group organized to carry out a particular transaction or enterprise **2 :** an association of organized criminals

²**syn·di·cate** \'sin-di-ˌkāt\ *vb* **-cat·ed; -cat·ing** *vt* **:** to form or manage as or through a syndicate ⟨a *syndicated* tax shelter⟩ ~

vi **:** to unite to form a syndicate — **syn·di·ca·tion** \ˌsin-di-'kā-shən\ *n*
syn·di·ca·tor \'sin-di-ˌkā-tər\ *n* **:** one that syndicates; *esp* **:** one that organizes investment in limited partnerships by different parties

---

\ə**abut**   \ᵊ**kitten**   \ər**further**   \a**ash**   \ā**ace**
\ä**cot, cart**   \au̇**out**   \ch**chin**   \e**bet**   \ē**easy**
\g**go**   \i**hit**   \ī**ice**   \j**job**   \ŋ**sing**   \ō**go**   \ȯ**law**
\ȯi**boy**   \th**thin**   \t̲h̲**the**   \ü**loot**   \u̇**foot**   \y**yet**
\zh**vision**   *see also* Pronunciation Symbols page

T

tac·it \'ta-sət\ *adj* **1** : implied (as by an act or by silence) rather than express ⟨a ~ admission⟩ **2** *in the civil law of Louisiana* : arising by operation of law ⟨a ~ mortgage⟩ — **tac·it·ly** *adv*

tack *vt* : to combine (a use, possession, or period of time) with that of another esp. in order to satisfy the statutory time period for acquiring title to or a prescriptive easement in the property of a third party ⟨successive adverse users in privity with prior adverse users can ~ successive adverse possessions of land —*Hall v. Kerlee*, 461 S.E.2d 911 (1995)⟩

Taft–Hartley fund — see FUND 1

¹tail *n* [Anglo-French, literally, cutting, from Old French, from *taillier* to cut, prune] **1** : the condition of being limited or restricted by entailing ⟨a tenant in ~⟩ **2** : ENTAIL 2

²tail *adj* : limited as to tenure — see also *fee tail* at FEE 1

taint \'tānt\ *vt* : to damage or destroy the validity of ⟨evidence ~ed by an illegal search⟩ — **taint** *n*

taint hearing — see HEARING

take *vb* **took; tak·en; tak·ing** *vt* **1 a** : to obtain control, custody, or possession of often by assertive or intentional means **b** : to seize or interfere with the use of (property) by governmental authority; *specif* : to acquire title to for public use by eminent domain **2 a** : to undertake the duties of ⟨~ office⟩ **b** : to bind oneself by ⟨~ an oath⟩ **3** : to get in writing **4 a** : to accept the tender of (as a promise) **b** : to accept (as an oath, affidavit, or deposition) in a legal capacity (as by administering or witnessing) **5 a** : to set in motion ⟨~ an appeal⟩ **b** : to claim or exercise as an option or right ⟨~ depreciation⟩ **6** : to put or set forth ⟨~ an exception⟩ — *vi* : to obtain ownership or possession of property ⟨~ free of a security interest⟩; *specif* : to receive the title to an estate ⟨~ as an heir⟩ — **take the Fifth** : to exercise the privilege against self-incrimination based on the Fifth Amendment to the U.S. Constitution

take·over \'tāk-ˌō-vər\ *n* : the acquisition of control or possession (as of a corporation) ⟨a hostile ~⟩

tak·er *n* : one that takes: as **a** : one that takes property by will or descent ⟨a residuary ~⟩ **b** : one to whom a negotiable instrument is transferred

take up *vt* **1** : to pay the amount of (as a note) : pay in full for **2** : to proceed to deal with ⟨*take up* a motion⟩

tak·ing *n* **1** : a seizure of private property or a substantial deprivation of the right to its free use or enjoyment that is caused by government action and esp. by the exercise of eminent domain and for which just compensation to the owner must be given according to the Fifth Amendment to the U.S. Constitution — see also INVERSE CONDEMNATION, PHYSICAL TAKING, REGULATORY TAKING ◊ A governmental action that results in a mere diminution in property value is less likely to be considered a taking than one that deprives the owner of economically viable use of the property. **2** : the wrongful acquisition of control over property (as in larceny) or a person

ta·les \'tā-ˌlēz\ *n pl* [from the Medieval Latin phrase *tales de circumstantibus* such (persons) of the bystanders; from the use of the phrase in the writ summoning them] *often attrib* : persons added to a jury from among those available in or about the courthouse or in the county to make up a deficiency in the number of jurors regularly summoned ⟨a ~ juror⟩

tales·man \'tālz-mən, 'tā-lēz-\ *n, pl* **tales-**

men \-mən\ : a person summoned as one of the tales added to a jury

tam·per *vi* **1** : to bring improper influence to bear (as by bribery or intimidation) — used with *with* ⟨~*ed* with the jurors⟩ **2** : to alter or interfere in an unauthorized or improper manner — used with *with* ⟨~*ed* with evidence⟩

tan·gi·ble \'tan-jə-bəl\ *adj* : capable of being perceived esp. by the sense of touch

tangible asset — see ASSET 2

tangible property — see PROPERTY

tar·get *n* : the object to be affected or achieved by an action or development; *specif* : a company that is the object of a takeover

target offense *n* : an offense (as murder) that is the object of a conspiracy

tar·iff \'tar-əf\ *n* [Italian *tariffa*, from Arabic *ta'rīf* notification] **1 a** : a schedule of duties imposed by a government on imported or in some countries exported goods **b** : a duty or rate of duty imposed in such a schedule **2** : a document filed with the appropriate government agency that sets forth the rates, charges, and other provisions pertaining to services furnished by a business (as a carrier) or public utility

¹tax *vt* [Medieval Latin *taxare* to assess for taxation, tax, from Latin, to assess, value, fix] **1** : to assess or determine judicially the amount of (costs of an action in court) **2** : to levy a tax on ⟨~ the corporation⟩ ⟨~ capital gains⟩ — **tax·er** *n*

²tax *n, often attrib* **1** : a charge usu. of money imposed by legislative or other public authority upon persons or property for public purposes **2** : a sum levied on members of an organization to defray expenses

tax·able \'tak-sə-bəl\ *adj* **1** : subject to being taxed : making one liable to taxation ⟨a ~ amount⟩⟨a ~ event⟩ **2** : that may be properly charged by the court against the plaintiff or defendant in a suit ⟨~ costs⟩ **3** : used as the basis of a tax computation ⟨a ~ period⟩ — **tax·abil·i·ty** \,tak-sə-'bi-lə-tē\ *n*

taxable distribution *n* : a generation-

skipping transfer of property held in trust that is subject to a generation-skipping transfer tax payable by a skip person when he or she receives a distribution of income or principal — compare DIRECT SKIP, TAXABLE TERMINATION

taxable estate — see ESTATE 3a

taxable income *n* : income that is subject to taxation and is characterized by the accrual of some gain or benefit to the taxpayer; *specif* : the total amount of income remaining as the basis of taxation for a given period after all allowable deductions have been applied to gross income

taxable termination *n* : a generation-skipping transfer of property held in trust that is subject to a generation-skipping transfer tax payable by the trustee when an interest in the property terminates (as at the death of the parent of a skip person), no interest is held by one who is not a skip person, and a distribution to a skip person may be made — compare DIRECT SKIP, TAXABLE DISTRIBUTION

taxable year *n* : a period of time used as the basis of tax computation that is usu. the annual accounting period of a calendar year or fiscal year — called also *tax year*

tax anticipation note — see NOTE

tax·a·tion *n* **1** : the action of taxing: as **a** : the imposition of taxes **b** : the judicial determination of costs **2 a** : revenue obtained from taxes **b** : the amount assessed as a tax **3** : a particular system of taxing ⟨progressive ~⟩

tax base *n* **1** : a sum (as the total assessed valuation of property in a county) used as the basis of taxation **2** : the source of tax revenue for a governmental body ⟨change the *tax base* of a school district to reduce the property tax burden⟩

tax benefit rule *n* : a tax rule requiring that if an amount (as of a loss) used as a deduction in a prior taxable year is recovered

---

\ə\abut \ᵊ\kitten \ər\further \a\ash \ā\ace
\ä\cot, cart \au̇\out \ch\chin \e\bet \ē\easy
\g\go \i\hit \ī\ice \j\job \ŋ\sing \ō\go \ȯ\law
\ȯi\boy \th\thin \t̷h\the \ü\loot \u̇\foot \y\yet
\zh\vision *see also* Pronunciation Symbols page

in a later year it must be included in the gross income for the later year to the extent of the original deduction ◊ If the amount of the loss was not taken as a deduction in the year the loss occurred, the recovered amount is not counted as income.

tax certificate *n* : a certificate issued to the purchaser of property at a tax sale that certifies the sale and entitles the purchaser to a tax deed upon expiration of the period for right of redemption if all taxes and charges have been paid ⟨voided the *tax certificate* when it was determined that the original owner was exempt from paying the delinquent taxes⟩ — called also *tax sale certificate;* compare *tax deed* at DEED

tax court *n, often cap T&C* : a court having jurisdiction over questions of law and fact arising under the tax laws of a government; *specif* : the federal court hearing tax cases

tax credit *n* : an amount that may be subtracted from the sum of tax otherwise due and that is distinguished from a deduction applied to gross income in the calculation of taxable income — compare EXEMPTION

tax deed — see DEED

tax–deferred *adj* : not taxable until a future date or event (as withdrawal or retirement)

tax evasion *n* : a willful and esp. criminal attempt to evade the imposition or payment of a tax ⟨convicted of *tax evasion*⟩

tax–exempt *adj* **1** : exempted from taxation; *also* : based on such exemption ⟨~ status⟩ **2** : providing interest or income that is exempted from taxation ⟨a ~ municipal bond⟩

tax–free *adj* : TAX-EXEMPT

taxing power — see POWER 2a

tax lien — see LIEN

tax·pay·er *n* : a person (as an individual or corporation) that pays or is liable for a tax — **tax·pay·ing** *adj*

tax preference item *n* : an item (as an amount of depreciation) favorable to a taxpayer in the ordinary computation of

tax liability that is taxed in the computation of alternative minimum tax

tax return *n* : RETURN 5

tax roll *n* : a record of the properties in a taxing district that includes the taxes due and paid on each property and is sometimes combined with a record of assessed values

tax sale — see SALE

tax sale certificate *n* : TAX CERTIFICATE

tax shelter *n* : an entity (as a partnership) or investment plan or arrangement whose principal purpose is the avoidance or evasion of income tax; *also* : an interest offered or purchased on the premise that it will provide favorable tax consequences ⟨purchased limited partnership *tax shelters*⟩

tax stamp *n* : a stamp affixed to an item as evidence that a tax on it has been paid; *esp* : one that the dealer of a controlled substance is required to purchase by payment of a tax according to a state law ⟨an additional count of failure to purchase a *tax stamp*⟩

tax title — see TITLE

tax write–off *n* : a tax deduction of an amount of depreciation, expense, or loss ⟨cancelled the debt and took a *tax write-off* on the loss⟩

tax year *n* : TAXABLE YEAR

temporary alimony — see ALIMONY

temporary custody — see CUSTODY b

temporary restraining order — see ORDER 3b

ten·an·cy \'te-nən-sē\ *n, pl* **-cies 1** : the holding of or a mode of holding an estate in property: **a** : a form of ownership of property : TENURE **b** : the temporary possession or occupancy of property that belongs to another

holdover tenancy : a tenancy that arises when one remains in possession of property after the expiration of the previous tenancy (as one under a lease), that may be established as a tenancy at will by the recognition of the landlord (as by accepting rent), and that may sometimes be statutorily converted to a periodic tenancy for the same or a different term than that of the original tenancy ⟨liable for payment of rent in a *holdover tenancy*⟩ — called also *tenancy at sufferance*

joint tenancy : a tenancy in which two or more parties hold equal and simultaneously created interests in the same property and in which title to the entire property is to remain to the survivors upon the death of one of them (as a spouse) and so on to the last survivor ⟨a right to sever the *joint tenancy*⟩ — see also TENANCY BY THE ENTIRETY in this entry; compare TENANCY IN COMMON in this entry

life tenancy : the tenancy of one with a life estate; *also* : LIFE ESTATE at ESTATE 1 ⟨created a *life tenancy* for her husband⟩

pe·ri·od·ic tenancy \ˌpir-ē-ˈä-dik-\ : a tenancy that is carried forward by specified time periods (as months) without a lease and that may be terminated by the landlord or tenant after giving proper notice

tenancy at sufferance : HOLDOVER TENANCY in this entry

tenancy at will : a tenancy that is terminable at the will of the landlord or tenant provided that applicable statutory requirements for notice are met

tenancy by the entirety : a tenancy that is shared by spouses who are considered one person in law and have the rights of survivorship inherent in joint tenancy and that becomes a tenancy in common in the event of divorce ⟨property subject to a *tenancy by the entirety* cannot be encumbered by one tenant acting alone —*Mays v. Brighton Bank*, 832 S.W.2d 347 (1992)⟩ — called also *tenancy by the entireties;* compare *estate by the entirety* at ESTATE 1

tenancy for years : a tenancy that is for a specified period of time — compare TENANCY AT WILL in this entry

tenancy in common : a tenancy in which two or more parties share ownership of property but have no right to each other's interest (as upon the death of

another tenant) — compare JOINT TENANCY in this entry

tenancy in partnership : a tenancy that binds partners to the use of partnership property only for partnership purposes and that does not permit the separate assignment by a partner of his or her right to the property

2 : the period of a tenant's occupancy or possession

tenancy at sufferance — see TENANCY
tenancy at will — see TENANCY
tenancy by the entirety — see TENANCY
tenancy for years — see TENANCY
tenancy in common — see TENANCY
tenancy in partnership — see TENANCY

ten·ant \ˈte-nənt\ *n* [Anglo-French, from Old French, from present participle of *tenir* to hold, from Latin *tenēre*] : one who holds or possesses property by any kind of right : one who holds a tenancy in property; *specif* : one who possesses property in exchange for payment of rent — see also LESSEE; compare TENANCY

tenant by the entirety : any of the parties holding a piece of property as a tenancy by the entirety

tenant in common : any of the parties holding a piece of property as a tenancy in common

¹ten·der *n* **1 a** : an act or instance of tendering **b** : an unconditional offer of payment or performance (as in discharge of an obligation) that is coupled with a manifestation of willingness and ability to follow through (as by producing a check) **c** : TENDER OF DELIVERY ⟨sufficient ∼⟩ **2** : something offered in payment or performance; *specif* : MONEY ⟨the proper amount of ∼ required⟩ — see also LEGAL TENDER

²tender *vb* [Anglo-French *tendre* to offer, propose for acceptance, literally, to stretch, hold out, from Old French, from Latin *tendere*] *vt* **1 a** : to make a ten-

\ə\abut \ᵊ\kitten \ər\further \a\ash \ā\ace
\ä\cot, cart \aù\out \ch\chin \e\bet \ē\easy
\g\go \i\hit \ī\ice \j\job \ŋ\sing \ō\go \ò\law
\òi\boy \th\thin \t̲h̲\the \ü\loot \ù\foot \y\yet
\zh\vision *see also* Pronunciation Symbols page

der of ⟨~ goods⟩ ⟨~ delivery⟩ ⟨~ payment⟩ ⟨~ performance⟩ **b :** to offer as an amount in settlement of a claim by an injured party against an insured ◊ An insurance company might be obligated to tender the limits of a policy to an injured party when a higher amount is likely to be awarded at trial. **2 :** to extend for acceptance or consideration (as in proof of something) esp. in a proceeding ⟨~ a plea to the court⟩ ⟨~ an issue⟩ **3 :** to offer for sale ⟨~ shares⟩ ~ *vi* **:** to offer securities for sale ⟨make an informed decision to ~⟩

tender of delivery : an offer of goods by a seller to a buyer that consists of putting or holding them at the disposition of the buyer and giving the buyer any notification reasonably necessary for taking delivery ⟨a cause of action for breach of warranty usually accrues upon *tender of delivery*⟩ — compare DELIVERY

tender offer *n* **:** a public offer to purchase a specified number or range of shares from shareholders usu. at a premium and in an attempt to gain control of the issuing company

tender years exception *n* **:** an exception to the hearsay rule in some jurisdictions that allows the use of an out-of-court statement by a young child in an abuse or neglect case if the time, content, and circumstances of the statement provide sufficient indications of reliability and the child will testify or else is unavailable as a witness but there is corroborating evidence of the act in question

ten·e·ment \'te-nə-mənt\ *n* [Anglo-French, from Old French, from Medieval Latin *tenementum*, from Latin *tenēre* to hold] **1 a :** any of various forms of property (as land) that is held by one person from another **b :** an estate in property **2 :** DWELLING

ten·ta·tive minimum tax \'ten-tə-tiv-\ *n* **:** a tax that to the extent it exceeds regular tax liability is the alternative minimum tax liability and that is determined by adjusting taxable income by adding tax preference items under Internal Rev-

enue Code section 57 and subtracting an exemption amount under section 55

tentative trust — see TRUST

ten·ure \'ten-yər\ *n* [Anglo-French, feudal holding, from Old French *teneüre*, from Medieval Latin *tenitura*, ultimately from Latin *tenēre* to hold] **1 :** the act, manner, duration, or right of holding something ⟨~ of office⟩; *specif* **:** the manner of holding real property **:** the title and conditions by which property is held ⟨freehold ~⟩ **2 :** a status granted to a teacher usu. after a probationary period that protects him or her from dismissal except for reasons of incompetence, gross misconduct, or financial necessity — **te·nur·ial** \te-'nyür-ē-əl\ *adj* — **te·nur·ial·ly** \-ə-lē\ *adv*

term *n, often attrib* **1 :** a specified period of time ⟨the policy ~⟩ **2 :** the whole period for which an estate is granted; *also* **:** the estate itself **3 a :** the period in which the powers of a court may be validly exercised **b :** SESSION **4 :** a word, phrase, or provision of import esp. in determining the nature and scope of an agreement — usu. used in pl. ⟨the ~s of the contract⟩

ter·mi·na·ble \'tər-mə-nə-bəl\ *adj* **:** capable of being terminated — see also *qualified terminable interest property* at PROPERTY, *terminable interest* at INTEREST 1

terminable interest — see INTEREST 1

ter·mi·nate \'tər-mə-ˌnāt\ *vb* **-nat·ed; -nat·ing** *vi* **:** to come to an end in time or effect ~ *vt* **1 :** to bring to a definite end esp. before a natural conclusion ⟨~ a contract⟩ — compare CANCEL, RESCIND **2 :** to discontinue the employment of — **ter·mi·na·tion** \ˌtər-mə-'nā-shən\ *n*

term insurance *n* **:** insurance in effect for a set term; *specif* **:** TERM LIFE INSURANCE at LIFE INSURANCE

term life insurance — see LIFE INSURANCE

term loan — see LOAN

term of art : a word having a particular meaning in a field (as the law) — called also *word of art*

terre tenant \'ter-, 'tər-\ *n* [Anglo-French *terre tenaunt* freeholder, from Old French *terre* land + *tenant* holding, from present participle of *tenir* to hold] : one in actual possession of land; *specif* : one who purchases land after a lien of mortgage or judgment has attached — used chiefly in the law of Pennsylvania

ter·ri·to·ri·al·i·ty \ˌter-ə-ˌtōr-ē-'a-lə-tē\ *n* **1** : territorial status **2** : the jurisdiction of a sovereign state over matters within the limits of its territory esp. as exercisable apart from the minimum contacts standard for personal jurisdiction over nonresidents

territorial jurisdiction *n* : JURISDICTION 3

territorial wa·ters *n pl* : the waters under the sovereign jurisdiction of a nation or state including both marginal sea and inland waters

ter·ri·to·ry \'ter-ə-ˌtōr-ē\ *n, pl* **-ries** **1** : a geographical area belonging to or under the jurisdiction of a governmental authority **2** : a political subdivision of a country **3** : a part of the U.S. (as Guam or the U.S. Virgin Islands) not included within any state but organized with a separate legislature — compare TRUST TERRITORY — **ter·ri·to·ri·al** \ˌter-ə-'tōr-ē-əl\ *adj* — **ter·ri·to·ri·al·ly** *adv*

ter·ror *n* : an intense fear of physical injury or death ⟨inflict ~ by forced entry or unlawful assembly⟩; *also* : the infliction of such fear ⟨an act of ~⟩

ter·ror·ism \'ter-ər-ˌi-zəm\ *n* **1** : the unlawful use or threat of violence esp. against the state or the public as a politically motivated means of attack or coercion **2** : violent and intimidating gang activity ⟨street ~⟩ — **ter·ror·ist** \-ist\ *adj or n* — **ter·ror·is·tic** \ˌter-ər-'is-tik\ *adj*

ter·ror·ize \'ter-ər-ˌīz\ *vt* **-ized; -iz·ing** : to inflict terror upon — **ter·ror·i·za·tion** \ˌter-ər-ə-'zā-shən\ *n*

Ter·ry stop \'ter-ē-\ *n* [from *Terry v. Ohio*, 392 U.S. 1 (1968), case in which the right of police to stop and question a suspect was first discussed] : a stop and limited search of a person for weapons justified by a police officer's reasonable conclusion that a crime is being or about to be committed by a person who may be armed and whose responses to questioning do not dispel the officer's fear of danger to the officer or to others — compare REASONABLE SUSPICION

test action *n* : TEST CASE at CASE

tes·ta·cy \'tes-tə-sē\ *n, pl* **-cies** : the state of being testate esp. as determined in probate of a will ⟨a rule favoring ~ over intestacy in the interpretation of wills⟩ ⟨partial ~⟩

tes·ta·ment \'tes-tə-mənt\ *n* [Latin *testamentum*, from *testari* to call as a witness, make a will, from *testis* witness] **1** : an act by which a person determines the disposition of his or her property after death ⟨a ~ of property⟩ **2** : WILL ◊ A testament was formerly concerned specifically with personal property, as in the phrase *last will and testament*. Now a will covers both personal and real property and the terms *will* and *testament* are generally synonymous, but the phrase lives on. — **tes·ta·men·ta·ry** \ˌtes-tə-'men-tə-rē\ *adj*

testamentary capacity *n* : the capacity in executing a will to understand the nature and extent of one's property and how one is disposing of it and to recognize the natural objects of one's bounty

testamentary gift — see GIFT

testamentary guardian — see GUARDIAN

testamentary heir — see HEIR

testamentary power of appointment — see POWER OF APPOINTMENT

testamentary trust — see TRUST

¹tes·tate \'te-ˌstāt, -stət\ *adj* [Latin *testatus*, past participle of *testari* to make a will] **1** : having made a valid will ⟨died ~⟩ **2** : disposed of or governed by a will ⟨~ property⟩ ⟨a ~ estate⟩

²testate *n* : TESTATOR

testate succession — see SUCCESSION

tes·ta·tion \te-'stā-shən\ *n* : the act or power of disposing of property by testament or will ⟨freedom of ~⟩

tes·ta·tor \'te-ˌstā-tər\ *n* : a person who dies leaving a will

tes·ta·trix \te-'stā-triks, 'te-ˌstā-\ *n, pl* **-tri·ces** \te-'stā-trə-ˌsēz, ˌtes-tə-'trī-sēz\ : a female testator

test case — see CASE 1a

tes·te \'tes-tē\ *n* [Medieval Latin *teste meipso* (or *seipso*) by my (or his) own witness] **1** : the witnessing or concluding clause of an instrument (as a writ) **2** : WITNESS — used esp. formerly to indicate that what follows is named as authority for what precedes

tes·ti·fy \'tes-tə-ˌfī\ *vb* **-fied; -fy·ing** [Latin *testificari*, from *testis* witness] *vi* : to make a solemn declaration under oath or affirmation for the purpose of establishing a fact : give testimony ~ *vt* : to declare in testimony — **tes·ti·fi·er** *n*

testimonial evidence — see EVIDENCE

tes·ti·mo·ni·um clause \ˌtes-tə-'mō-nē-əm-\ *n* [Latin *testimonium* testimony] : the authenticating clause of an instrument (as a deed) that typically begins "In witness whereof" and furnishes such information as when it was signed and before what witnesses

tes·ti·mo·ny \'tes-tə-ˌmō-nē\ *n, pl* **-nies** [Latin *testimonium*, from *testis* witness] : evidence furnished by a witness under oath or affirmation and either orally or in an affidavit or deposition

former testimony : testimony that a witness gives at a different proceeding (as another hearing or a deposition) ◊ Under Federal Rule of Evidence 804, former testimony is admissible as an exception to the hearsay rule when the declarant is unavailable and if a predecessor in interest in a civil proceeding or the party against whom the testimony is offered had an opportunity and similar motive to develop the testimony.

negative testimony : testimony concerning what did not happen; *esp* : testimony concerning what one did not perceive ⟨*negative testimony* that the witness did not hear a train whistle⟩ ◊ Negative testimony is sometimes accorded the same weight as positive testimony when the witness was in a position to perceive something and was eagerly attentive.

opinion testimony : testimony relaying opinion as opposed to direct knowledge of the facts at issue ◊ Opinion testimony may be allowed in evidence when it helps the factfinder understand or determine the facts at issue. Such testimony by a lay witness must be rationally based on his or her perception. A qualified expert witness may also give opinion testimony. The expert's opinion may be based on facts or data that he or she perceives directly or of which he or she is made aware other than by direct perception at or before trial.

positive testimony : testimony that presents an affirmative declaration of fact and is based on the personal knowledge of the testifier

reputation testimony : testimony concerning a person's reputation among associates or in the community — **tes·ti·mo·ni·al** \ˌtes-tə-'mō-nē-əl\ *adj* — **tes·ti·mo·ni·al·ly** *adv*

theft *n* [Old English *thiefth*] : LARCENY; *broadly* : a criminal taking of the property or services of another without consent ◊ Theft commonly encompasses by statute a variety of forms of stealing formerly treated as distinct crimes.

grand theft : theft of property or services whose value exceeds a specified amount or of a specified kind of property (as an automobile) ◊ Grand theft is a felony.

identity theft : the unauthorized use of another's means of identification (as name or social security number) for the purpose of commiting theft or another crime

petty theft : theft of property or services whose value is below a specified amount — called also *petit theft* ◊ Petty theft is a misdemeanor but may be aggravated by prior convictions.

Thibodeaux abstention — see ABSTENTION

thief *n, pl* **thieves** [Old English *thēof*] : one who commits theft

third degree *n* : the grade given to the third most serious forms of crimes — **third-degree** *adj*

third–degree murder — see MURDER

third party — see PARTY 1a, b

third–party beneficiary — see BENEFICI-ARY d

third–party claim *n* **1** : a claim made against a third party in a third-party complaint — compare COUNTERCLAIM, CROSS-ACTION, CROSS-CLAIM **2** : a claim made by an injured third party (as a third-party beneficiary of workers' compensation insurance) against an insurer or insured for indemnification

third–party complaint *n* : a complaint filed against a third party by a defendant or plaintiff alleging that the third party is liable for all or part of a claim or counterclaim in dispute between the original parties

third–party defendant *n* : a third party who is the object of a third-party complaint

third–party plaintiff *n* : a defendant who files a third-party complaint against a third party

third–party practice *n* : IMPLEADER

third–party rec·ord·keep·er \-'re-kərd-ˌkē-pər\ *n* : a party (as an accountant or bank) summoned to produce records pertaining to a tax investigation of another party ◊ The original party is entitled to receive notice of and to challenge the issuance of a summons to a third-party recordkeeper.

third–party standing *n* : standing sometimes granted to a party claiming to protect the rights or interests of a third party — compare BATSON CHALLENGE ◊ Third-party standing is granted esp. when a statute is challenged as unconstitutionally overbroad or when a party (such as a criminal defendant) challenges the exclusion of a juror who is being denied equal protection by being excluded esp. because of race or gender.

third possessor *n, in the civil law of Louisiana* : one who acquires mortgaged property and is not personally bound for the obligation secured by the mortgage

30–day letter — see LETTER 1

threat *n* : an expression of an intention to injure another : MENACE 1 ⟨criminal laws against making terroristic ~s⟩

¹thresh·old \'thresh-ˌhōld\ *n* : a point of beginning : a minimum requirement for further action; *specif* : a determination (as of fact or the existence of a reasonable doubt) upon which something else (as further consideration or a right of action) hinges ⟨the ~ for inquiry⟩

²threshold *adj* : of, relating to, or being a threshold ⟨the ~ issue in a negligence action is whether the defendant owed a duty of care to the plaintiff —*Noakes v. City of Seattle*, 895 P.2d 842 (1995)⟩ ⟨a ~ showing of the need for psychiatric evaluation⟩

thrift *n* : an institution that promotes saving and provides mortgages; *esp* : SAVINGS AND LOAN ASSOCIATION — called also *thrift institution*

time–barred \'tīm-'bärd\ *adj* : barred by the passage of time under a statute of limitations, statute of repose, or procedural rule ⟨petition for post-conviction relief was ~⟩

time deposit — see DEPOSIT 2a

time draft — see DRAFT

time·ly \'tīm-lē\ *adj* : falling within a prescribed or reasonable time ⟨~ notice⟩ — **time·li·ness** *n* — **timely** *adv*

time note — see NOTE

time, place, or manner restriction *n* : a restriction on the time, place, or manner of expression that is justified when it is neutral as to content and serves a significant government interest and leaves open ample alternative channels of communication ⟨an injunction excluding demonstrators from the front of the building was held to be a reasonable *time, place, or manner restriction*⟩ — called also *time, place, and manner restriction*

time policy *n* : a marine insurance policy covering property for a specified period

\ə\abut \ə\kitten \ər\further \a\ash \ā\ace
\ä\cot, cart \aů\out \ch\chin \e\bet \ē\easy
\g\go \i\hit \ī\ice \j\job \ŋ\sing \ō\go \ȯ\law
\ȯi\boy \th\thin \th̲\the \ü\loot \ů\foot \y\yet
\zh\vision   *see also* Pronunciation Symbols page

time•share \'tīm-,shar\ *n, often attrib* : an agreement or arrangement in which parties share the ownership of or right to use property (as a resort condominium) and that provides for occupation by each party esp. for periods of less than a year — called also *timesharing* — **timeshare** *vt*

¹tip *n* **1** : information provided to the police or authorities regarding crime **2** : a piece of inside information esp. of advantage in securities trading

²tip *vt* **tipped; tip•ping** : to provide a tip to or about — often used with *off* — **tip•per** *n*

tip•pee \,ti-'pē\ *n* : one who receives a tip esp. in insider trading

tip•ster \'tip-stər\ *n* : one who provides a tip to the police

tit. *abbr* title

ti•tle *n* [Anglo-French, inscription, legal right, from Old French, from Latin *titulum* inscription, chapter heading, part of the law that sanctions an action] **1 a** : the means or right by which one owns or possesses property; *broadly* : the quality of ownership as determined by a body of facts and events

after–acquired title : title that vests automatically in a grantee when acquired by a grantor who purported to sell the property before acquiring title; *also* : a doctrine that requires such vesting — compare *estoppel by deed* at ESTOPPEL 1 ◊ The doctrine of after-acquired title generally does not apply when the grantor receives title by quitclaim deed; to vest title in the grantee the deed must include words expressing such an intention.

clear title : title that exists free of claims or encumbrances on the property ⟨had *clear title* to the farm⟩; *broadly* : MARKETABLE TITLE in this entry

equitable title : title vested in one who is considered by the application of equitable principles to be the owner of property even though legal title is vested in another ⟨the purchaser under a contract for sale had *equitable title* to and an insurable interest in the property⟩; *specif*

: the right to receive legal title upon performance of an obligation

good title : title to property (as a negotiable instrument or real property) that is valid in fact or law or beyond a reasonable doubt ⟨a holder in due course acquires *good title* to the item⟩; *esp* : MARKETABLE TITLE in this entry

In•di•an title : title held by American Indians that consists of the right to occupy certain land with the permission of the United States government ⟨appears to be no question that Congress may limit or extinguish *Indian title*, and any rights appurtenant to the title, without obtaining the consent of the Indian peoples —*In re Rights to Use Water in Big Horn River Sys.*, 753 P.2d 76 (1988)⟩ — compare RESERVATION

just title in the civil law of Louisiana : a juridical act (as a sale or donation) sufficient to transfer ownership or a real right; *also* : the title that derives from such an act ⟨have a *just title*⟩ ◊ For the purposes of acquisitive prescription, the requirement of just title is satisfied by an act that would have been sufficient to transfer ownership if it had been executed by the true owner.

legal title : title that is determined or recognized as constituting formal or valid ownership (as by virtue of an instrument) even if not accompanied by possession or use ⟨the trustee held *legal title* to the property⟩ ⟨retained *legal title* to the goods until the debt was paid⟩ — compare *legal interest* at INTEREST 1

lu•cra•tive title \'lü-krə-tiv-\ : title to property acquired by gift, succession, or inheritance ⟨the property acquired by *lucrative title* remained the separate property of the spouse⟩

marketable title : title that is subject to no reasonable doubt as to its validity or freedom from encumbrance and that can be reasonably sold, purchased, or mortgaged ⟨seller warrants that seller has *marketable title* to the property⟩; *specif* : title of such quality that a purchaser under contract should be compelled to accept it — called also *merchantable title* ◊ *Clear title* and *good title* are commonly used to indicate marketable title.

onerous title 1 *in the civil law of Louisiana* : title that depends on the giving of consideration for the property 2 : title to property that is acquired through the labor or skill of a spouse and is included in community property

paper title : title shown on a document ⟨had an equitable interest in the property though *paper title* was held by her husband⟩

par•a•mount title \'par-ə-ˌmaůnt-\ : title that renders inferior any other title to the property ⟨warranted that the purchaser would have quiet enjoyment free from disturbance by one holding *paramount title*⟩

particular title *in the civil law of Louisiana* : title by which one possesses or owns particular property received (as by purchase, gift, or legacy) before or after the death of an ancestor ⟨a successor by *particular title* does not continue the possession of his ancestor —A. N. Yiannopoulos⟩ — see also *particular legacy* at LEGACY; compare UNIVERSAL TITLE in this entry

record title : title shown on the public record

tax title : title obtained by the purchaser of property at a tax sale; *also* : title held by a governmental body to property seized because of tax delinquency

universal title : title acquired by the conveyance causa mortis of a specified proportion (as one-fourth) of all of the conveyor's property interests or all of a specified type of the conveyor's property interests esp. so that upon the conveyor's death the recipient stands as a universal successor ⟨was a legatee under *universal title*⟩

b : an instrument (as a deed) that is evidence of ownership **c** : CERTIFICATE OF TITLE 1a ⟨paid tax and ~ fees⟩ **2 a** : the name or heading of something (as a proceeding, statute, or book) **b** *often cap* : a

division of a statutory or regulatory code or of an act ⟨*Title* IX⟩

title insurance *n* : insurance that compensates for loss from title defects or encumbrances (as liens) that were unknown but should have been discovered at the time the policy was issued

title search *n* : a search of public records to determine the condition of title to real property usu. that is the subject of a transaction (as a purchase or mortgage) ⟨the borrower was required to pay for a *title search*⟩

T–note *n* : TREASURY NOTE at NOTE

¹toll *n* [Old English, tax or fee paid for a liberty or privilege, ultimately from Late Latin *telonium* custom house, from Greek *tolōnion*, from *telōnēs* collector of tolls, from *telos* tax, toll] : a charge for the use of a transportation route or facility; *broadly* : a charge for use ⟨a water ~⟩

²toll *vb* [Anglo-French *tollir*, *toller* to take away, make null, bar, ultimately from Latin *tollere* to lift up, take away] *vt* **1** : to take away (as a right) **2 a** : to remove the effect of ⟨the court did not ~ the statute of repose after the statutory period had expired⟩ **b** : SUSPEND 2a ⟨~ the running of the statute of limitations⟩ — compare RUN ~ *vi* : to be suspended ⟨statute of limitations ~s for a period of seventy-five days following the notice —*Parker v. Yen*, 823 S.W.2d 359 (1991)⟩

³toll *n* : a suspension of effect ⟨the court extended the statute of limitations ~⟩

took *past of* TAKE

Tor•rens system \'tōr-ənz-\ *n* [after Sir Robert *Torrens* (1814–1884), British pioneer in Australia] : a title registration system used esp. in Massachusetts, Hawaii, Illinois, and Minnesota ◊ When a certificate of title is first applied for in the Torrens system, the title is searched or examined, a court hearing is held (as in a land court), and a decree confirming ti-

\ə\abut \ᵊ\kitten \ər\further \a\ash \ā\ace
\ä\cot, cart \aů\out \ch\chin \e\bet \ē\easy
\g\go \i\hit \ī\ice \j\job \ŋ\sing \ō\go \ȯ\law
\ȯi\boy \th\thin \t̲h̲\the \ü\loot \ů\foot \y\yet
\zh\vision   *see also* Pronunciation Symbols page

tle and ordering registration (as with the registrar of deeds) is issued. A certificate of title is then given to the owner, after which the property may be conveyed by executing deeds, delivering the certificate of title to be cancelled, and issuing a new certificate to the new owner. The title registered in a Torrens system is usu. guaranteed and marketable, making title insurance unnecessary and greatly reducing the time spent researching the state of the title during subsequent conveyances.

tort \'tòrt\ *n* [Anglo-French, wrongful or illegal act, from Old French, injury, from Medieval Latin *tortum*, from Latin, neuter of *tortus* twisted, from past participle of *torquēre* to twist] **:** a wrongful act other than a breach of contract that injures another and for which the law imposes civil liability **:** a violation of a duty (as to exercise due care) imposed by law as distinguished from contract for which damages or declaratory relief (as an injunction) may be obtained; *also* **:** a cause of action based on such an act ⟨the court declined to recognize the ~ —*National Law Journal*⟩ ⟨cannot sue in ~⟩ —compare CRIME, DELICT

tort·fea·sor \'tòrt-,fē-zər\ *n* [Anglo-French *tortfesor* wrongdoer, from *tort* wrong + *fesor*, *faisour* doer, maker, from Old French, from *fais-*, stem of *faire* to do, make, from Latin *facere*] **:** a person who commits a tort, delict, or quasi-offense

tor·tious \'tòr-shəs\ *adj* **:** constituting a tort **:** recognized as a tort ⟨a ~ act⟩ ⟨~ interference with contract⟩ — **tor·tious·ly** *adv*

tort reform *n* **:** change or alteration of laws imposing civil liability for torts esp. to limit liability for punitive damages

total breach — see BREACH 1b

to·tal disability *n* **:** a degree of disability considered sufficient (as according to statute or in an insurance policy) to make one unable to engage in gainful work

total incorporation *n* **:** a doctrine in constitutional law: the Fourteenth Amendment's due process clause embraces all the guarantees in the Bill of Rights and applies them to cases under state law — compare SELECTIVE INCORPORATION ◇ The total incorporation doctrine has never been adopted by a majority of the U.S. Supreme Court. The majority opinions of the Supreme Court have instead adhered to a fundamental fairness standard or applied selective incorporation in determining whether a state has violated the Fourteenth Amendment's due process clause.

total loss — see LOSS

Totten trust — see TRUST

town clerk *n* **:** a public officer charged with recording the official proceedings and vital statistics of a town

town counsel *n* **:** CITY ATTORNEY

tox·ic tort \'täk-sik-\ *n* **:** a tort in which there is personal injury or property damage due to exposure to toxic substances

¹trade *n* **1 a :** the business or work in which one engages regularly **b :** an occupation requiring manual or mechanical skill **c :** the persons engaged in an occupation **2 :** the business of buying and selling or bartering commodities **3 :** an act or instance of trading; *also* **:** an exchange of property usu. without use of money

²trade *vb* **trad·ed; trad·ing** *vi* **1 :** to engage in the exchange, purchase, or sale of goods **2 :** to give one thing in exchange for another **3 :** to engage in selling ~ *vt* **1 :** to give in exchange for another commodity; *also* **:** to make an exchange of **2 :** to engage in frequent buying and selling of (as stocks or commodities) usu. in search of quick profits — **trad·able** *also* **trade·able** *adj*

³trade *adj* **1 :** of, relating to, or used in trade or in a particular trade or business **2** *also* **trades :** of, composed of, or representing the trades or labor unions

trade acceptance *n* **:** a time draft or bill of exchange for the amount of a specific purchase drawn by the seller on the buyer, bearing the buyer's acceptance, and often noting the place of payment (as a bank)

trade dress *n* **:** the overall image of a product used in its marketing or sales that is composed of the nonfunctional elements of its design, packaging, or labeling (as colors, package shape, or symbols) ◊ Trade dress is protected by the Trademark (Lanham) Act of 1946 if it is not a functional part of the product, has acquired secondary meaning, and there is likelihood of confusion as to the source of the product on the part of the consumer if a competing product has a similar trade dress.

trade libel *n* : DISPARAGEMENT 1

trade·mark \'trād-ˌmärk\ *n* : a mark that is used by a manufacturer or merchant to identify the origin or ownership of goods and to distinguish them from others and the use of which is protected by law — see also DILUTION, INFRINGEMENT, STRONG MARK, WEAK MARK, *Trademark Act of 1946* in the IMPORTANT LAWS section; compare COPYRIGHT, PATENT, SERVICE MARK ◊ The Patent and Trademark Office registers trademarks and service marks that are used in interstate commerce or in intrastate commerce that affects interstate commerce. There are also state registration statutes for marks used in intrastate commerce. A trademark or service mark need not be registered for an owner to enforce his or her rights in court. The common law recognizes ownership of a trademark, established by actual and first use of the mark, but it extends only to the areas or markets where the mark is used. Federal registration of a trademark gives rise to a federal cause of action for infringement in addition to the common-law claim. Registration also serves as evidence of the owner's exclusive right to the continuous use and validity of the mark, and as constructive notice to the world of the claim to the mark. To be a valid trademark at common law and for federal registration, a mark must be distinctive; a descriptive mark may become distinctive by acquiring secondary meaning.

trade name *n* : a name or mark that is used by a person (as an individual proprietor or a corporation) to identify that person's business or vocation and that may also be used as a trademark or service mark ◊ Like a trademark or service mark, a trade name is protected by law against infringement. A trade name that has been used for at least 6 months can be recorded with the Customs Bureau, and any infringing imports will be barred.

trade secret *n* : a formula, process, device, or item of information used by a business that has economic value because it is not generally known or easily discovered by observation or examination and for which reasonable efforts to maintain secrecy have been made ◊ Trade secrets are a form of intellectual property. Many states have enacted laws which create an action for damages or injunctive relief against misappropriation of trade secrets by improper means. Information contained in a patent is not protected as a trade secret.

trade union *n* : LABOR UNION

trade usage *n* : USAGE OF TRADE

trading partnership — see PARTNERSHIP

tra·di·tion *n* [French, legal transfer] *in the civil law of Louisiana* : transfer or acquisition of property esp. by delivery with intent of both parties to transfer the title ⟨delivery of the act of transfer or use of the right by the owner of the dominant estate constitutes ~ —*Louisiana Civil Code*⟩

¹traf·fic *n, often attrib* **1 a** : import and export trade **b** : the business of bartering or buying and selling **c** : illegal or disreputable usu. commercial activity ⟨the drug ~⟩ **2 a** : the movement (as of vehicles or pedestrians) through an area or along a route **b** : the vehicles, pedestrians, ships, or planes moving along a route **c** : the information or signals transmitted over a communications system **3 a** : the passengers or cargo carried by a transportation system **b** : the business of transporting passengers or freight

---

\ə\abut \ə\kitten \ər\further \a\ash \ā\ace \ä\cot, cart \au̇\out \ch\chin \e\bet \ē\easy \g\go \i\hit \ī\ice \j\job \ŋ\sing \ō\go \ȯ\law \ȯi\boy \th\thin \th̲\the \ü\loot \u̇\foot \y\yet \zh\vision *see also* Pronunciation Symbols page

²traffic *vb* **traf·ficked; traf·fick·ing** *vi* : to carry on traffic ～ *vt* **1** : to travel over **2** : to engage in the trading or bartering of — **traf·fick·er** *n*

traffic court *n* : a local court having limited jurisdiction over violation of statutes, ordinances, and regulations governing the use of roads and motor vehicles

tranche \'trä\nsh\ *n* [French, literally, slice, from Old French, from *trenchier*, *trancher* to cut] : a division or portion of a pool or whole: as **a** : an issue of bonds derived from a pooling of like obligations that is differentiated from other issues esp. by maturity or rate of return **b** : a bond series issued for sale in a foreign country

trans·act \tran-'zakt, -'sact\ *vi* **1** : to carry on business **2** *in the civil law of Louisiana* : to settle a dispute by a transaction ～ *vt* **1** : to carry to completion ⟨～ a sale⟩ **2** : to carry on the operation or management of ⟨～ business⟩

trans·ac·tion \tran-'zak-shən, -'sak-\ *n* **1** : something transacted; *esp* : an exchange or transfer of goods, services, or funds **2 a** : an act, process, or instance of transacting **b** : an action or activity involving two parties or things that reciprocally affect or influence each other **3** *in the civil law of Louisiana* : an onerous contract that is intended by the parties to prevent or end actual or possible litigation and in which they make reciprocal concessions — compare ACCORD, SATISFACTION

transactional immunity — see IMMUNITY

¹trans·fer \trans-'fər, 'trans-ˌfər\ *vt* **transferred; trans·fer·ring** : to cause a transfer of — **trans·fer·abil·i·ty** \transˌfər-ə-'bi-lə-tē, ˌtrans-fər-\ *n* — **trans·fer·able** *also* **trans·fer·ra·ble** \trans-'fər-ə-bəl\ *adj* — **trans·fer·or** \trans-fər-'òr, trans-'fər-ər\ *n* — **trans·fer·ral** \trans-'fər-əl\ *n*

²trans·fer \'trans-ˌfər\ *n* **1** : a conveyance of a right, title, or interest in real or personal property from one person or entity to another **2** : a passing of something

from one another ⟨～ of venue⟩ ⟨the ～ of power⟩

transfer agent — see AGENT

trans·fer·ee \ˌtrans-ˌfər-'ē\ *n* : a person to whom something is transferred or conveyed

trans·fer·ence \trans-'fər-əns, 'transˌfər-\ *n* : an act, process, or instance of transferring

transferred intent — see INTENT

transfer tax *n* : a tax (as a gift tax or estate tax) imposed on the transfer of property

trans·gress \tranz-'gres, trans-\ *vt* **1** : to go beyond limits set or prescribed by : VIOLATE **2** : to pass beyond or go over (a limit or boundary) ～ *vi* **1** : to violate a law **2** : to go beyond a boundary or limit

tran·si·to·ry action \'tran-zə-ˌtòr-ē-, -sə-\ *n* : an action that may be brought in any venue where there is personal jurisdiction over the defendant — compare LOCAL ACTION

trans·la·tive \tranz-'lā-tiv, trans-\ *adj* : constituting a transfer or conveyance ⟨an act ～ of ownership⟩

trans·mis·sion \tranz-'mi-shən, trans-\ *n* : an act, process, or instance of transmitting

trans·mit \tranz-'mit, trans-\ *vt* **transmit·ted; trans·mit·ting 1** : to send or convey from one person or place to another **2** : to transfer esp. by inheritance — **trans·mit·ta·ble** \-'mi-tə-bəl\ *adj* — **trans·mit·tal** \-'mit-ᵊl\ *n*

trans·mu·ta·tion \ˌtranz-myü-'tā-shən, ˌtrans-\ *n* **1** : a doctrine in property law which allows the conversion of a separate property interest into marital or community property by agreement between spouses or by contribution of marital or community assets to the separate property (as for maintenance or improvements); *also* : a doctrine in property law which allows the conversion of a marital or community property interest into separate property **2** : an act or instance of converting a property interest in accordance with the doctrine of transmutation ⟨absent a ～ by deed⟩

trans·mute \tranz-'myüt, trans-\ *vt* **trans-**

muted; **trans·mut·ing** : to convert or transform the type of ownership of (property) by transmutation ⟨did not ~ the properties themselves into marital assets —*In re Siddens*, 588 N.E.2d 321 (1992)⟩

¹tra·verse \'tra-ˌvərs, trə-'vərs\ *n* : a denial of a matter of fact alleged in the opposing party's pleadings; *also* : a pleading in which such a denial is made

²tra·verse \trə-'vərs, 'tra-ˌvərs\ *vt* [Anglo⸗ French *traverser*, literally, to lay across, bar, impede, from Old French, from Late Latin *transversare* to cross, from Latin *transversus* lying across] : to deny (as an allegation of fact or an indictment) in a legal proceeding

trea·son \'trēz-ᵊn\ *n* [Anglo-French *treison* crime of violence against a person to whom allegiance is owed, literally, betrayal, from Old French *traïson*, from *traïr* to betray, from Latin *tradere* to hand over, surrender] : the offense of attempting to overthrow the government of one's country or of assisting its enemies in war; *specif* : the act of levying war against the United States or adhering to or giving aid and comfort to its enemies by one who owes it allegiance — **trea·son·ous** \-əs\ *adj*

trea·sure *n* : personal property that is hidden in something else for an extended period and whose owner cannot be determined

trea·sur·er *n* : an officer entrusted with the receipt, care, and disbursement of funds: as **a** : a governmental officer charged with keeping, receiving, and disbursing public revenues **b** : the executive financial officer of a club, society, or business corporation — **trea·sur·er·ship** *n*

treasure trove \-'trōv\ *n* : treasure that anyone finds; *specif* : gold or silver in the form of money, plate, or bullion that is found hidden and whose ownership is not known ◊ State law determines who is entitled to a treasure trove.

trea·sury /'tre-zhə-rē, 'trā-/ *n, pl* **-sur·ies** **1 a** : a place in which stores of wealth are kept **b** : the place of deposit and disbursement of collected funds; *esp* : one where public revenues are deposited, kept, and disbursed **c** : funds kept in such a depository **2** *cap* **a** : a governmental department in charge of finances and esp. the collection, management, and expenditure of public revenues **b** : the building in which the business of such a governmental department is transacted **3** *cap* : a government security (as a note or bill) issued by the Treasury

Treasury bill — see BILL 7
Treasury bond — see BOND 2
Treasury note — see NOTE
treasury security — see SECURITY
treasury share *n* : a share of treasury stock
treasury stock — see STOCK

trea·ty *n, pl* **treaties** [Anglo-French *treté*, from Middle French *traité*, from Medieval Latin *tractatus*, from Latin, handling, treatment, from *tractare* to treat, handle] **1** : the action of treating and esp. of negotiating **2** : an agreement or arrangement made by negotiation: as **a** : PRIVATE TREATY **b** : a contract in writing between two or more political authorities (as states or sovereigns) formally signed by representatives duly authorized and usu. ratified by the lawmaking authority of the state ⟨the president . . . shall have power, by and with the advice and consent of the Senate, to make *treaties* —*U.S. Constitution* art. II⟩ — compare EXECUTIVE AGREEMENT **3** : a document embodying a negotiated agreement or contract **4** : an agreement or contract (as between companies) providing for treaty reinsurance

treaty reinsurance *n* : reinsurance under a general agreement that automatically reinsures in accordance with its terms all risks of a given class to a predetermined extent as soon as they are insured by the direct underwriter — compare FACULTATIVE REINSURANCE

treble damages — see DAMAGE 2

¹tres·pass \'tres-pəs, -ˌpas\ *n* [Anglo⸗

French *trespas* violation of the law, actionable wrong, from Old French, crossing, passage, from *trespasser* to go across, from *tres* across + *passer* to pass] : wrongful conduct causing harm to another: as **a** : a willful act or active negligence as distinguished from a mere omission of a duty that causes an injury to or invasion of the person, rights, or esp. property of another; *also* : the common‑law form of action for redress of injuries directly caused by such a wrongful act — compare TRESPASS ON THE CASE in this entry **b** : TRESPASS QUARE CLAUSUM FREGIT in this entry

continuing trespass : a trespass that continues until the act (as of depriving another of his or her property without the intent to steal it) or instrumentality (as an object placed wrongfully on another's land) causing it is ended or removed

criminal trespass : trespass to property that is forbidden by statute and punishable as a crime as distinguished from trespass that creates a cause of action for damages

trespass ab initio : a trespass that arises upon a lawful act which because of subsequent unlawful or wrongful conduct is deemed under a legal fiction to have been trespassory from the beginning

trespass de bo•nis as•por•ta•tis \-dē-'bō-nis-,as-pòr-'tā-tis, -dā-'bō-nēs-,äs-pòr-'tä-tēs\ [probably from Medieval Latin (*trangressio*) *de bonis asportatis* (trespass) concerning property carried off] : a common-law form of action to recover for trespass involving the carrying off of one's goods by another

trespass on the case : a common-law form of action to recover for another's wrongful act that indirectly causes one's injury — called also *action on the case*, *case*

trespass qua•re clau•sum fre•git \-'kwer-ē-'klò-zəm-'frē-jət, -'kwä-rā-'klaù-sùm-'frä-gēt\ [probably from Medieval Latin (*transgressio*) *quare clausum fregit* (trespass) whereby he or she broke into a close (tenement protected by law of trespass)] : a trespass that involves wrongful and tortious entry on another's real property

trespass to try title : an action brought as a means of obtaining redress for a trespass to real property and determining the title to the property

trespass vi et ar•mis \-'vī-,et-'är-mis, -'vē-, -,mēs\ [Latin *vi et armis* with force and arms] : a trespass involving intentional infliction of injury on a person

²**trespass** *vi* : to commit a trespass; *esp* : to enter wrongfully or without proper authority or consent upon the real property of another ~ *vt* : to commit a trespass against

trespass ab initio — see TRESPASS

trespass de bonis asportatis — see TRESPASS

tres•pass•er \'tres-,pa-sər, -pə-\ *n* : one who trespasses; *esp* : one who enters or remains on the real property of another wrongfully or without the owner's or possessor's authority or consent — compare INVITEE, LICENSEE ◊ The general rule is that the owner or possessor of real property has the duty merely to refrain from willfully, wantonly, or recklessly injuring a trespasser whose presence is known. This rule is usu. applied to licensees as well, although a licensee is usu. owed a higher degree of care when an entrance fee is charged or when active operations (as of machinery) are taking place on the property.

trespass on the case — see TRESPASS

tres•pas•so•ry \'tres-pə-,sòr-ē\ *adj* : constituting a trespass ⟨a ~ taking of property⟩

trespass quare clausum fregit — see TRESPASS

trespass to try title — see TRESPASS

trespass vi et armis — see TRESPASS

tri•able \'trī-ə-bəl\ *adj* : liable or subject to judicial or quasi-judicial examination or trial

tri•al *n* [Anglo-French, from *trier* to try] : a judicial examination of issues of fact or law disputed by parties for the purpose of determining the rights of the parties — compare HEARING, INQUEST — **at trial** : in or during the course of a trial

trial by jury : JURY TRIAL

trial by or·deal \-ȯr-'dēl, -'ȯr-ˌdēl\ : a formerly used criminal trial in which the guilt or innocence of the accused was determined by subjection to dangerous or painful tests (as submersion in water) believed to be under divine control

trial court *n* : the court before which issues of fact and law are tried and first determined as distinguished from an appellate court

trial de novo *n* : a trial in a higher court in which all the issues of fact or law tried in a lower court or tribunal are reconsidered as if no previous trial had taken place — compare MISTRIAL

trial judge advocate *n* : a judge advocate detailed to act as a prosecutor of an accused before a court-martial

trial jury *n* : a jury impaneled to try a case : PETIT JURY

trial lawyer *n* : a lawyer who engages chiefly in trying esp. plaintiff's cases before courts of original jurisdiction

tri·bal court \'trī-bəl-\ *n* : a court administered through self-government of an American Indian tribe esp. on a reservation and having federally prescribed jurisdiction over custody and adoption cases involving tribal children, criminal jurisdiction over offenses committed on tribal lands by members of the tribe, and broader civil jurisdiction over claims between tribe members and nonmembers ◊ Criminal prosecutions of tribal members in tribal courts must respect constitutional rights specifically listed in the Indian Civil Rights Act, which also provides for a federal habeas corpus remedy in lieu of federal appellate review. Parties to a civil action that arguably falls within the jurisdiction of a tribal court must first exhaust remedies there before seeking adjudication in a federal court, whether they are both tribal members or not. A dispute over such jurisdiction is ultimately a federal question.

tri·bu·nal \trī-'byün-ᵊl, tri-\ *n* [Latin, platform for magistrates, from *tribunus* tribune, from *tribus* tribe] **1** : the seat of a judge or one acting as a judge **2** : a court or forum of justice : a person or body of persons having to hear and decide disputes so as to bind the parties

tri·er \'trī-ər\ *n* : TRIER OF FACT

trier of fact : the judge in a bench trial or jury in a jury trial that carries the responsibility of determining the issues of fact in a case — called also *factfinder, finder of fact, trier*

TRO *abbr* temporary restraining order

tro·ver \'trō-vər\ *n* [short for *action of trover and conversion;* Anglo-French *trover* act of finding (alluding to goods lost by the plaintiff and found by the defendant), from *trover* to find, from Old French] : an action at common law to recover the value of chattels or goods wrongfully converted by another to his or her own use — compare DETINUE

true bill — see BILL 3b

true lease — see LEASE

true threat *n* : a threat that a reasonable person would interpret as a real and serious communication of an intent to inflict harm ◊ True threats are not protected as free speech by the First Amendment to the U.S. Constitution and render the person making the threat liable to criminal prosecution.

true value *n* **1** : FAIR MARKET VALUE — called also *true cash value* **2** : the depreciated book value of personal property for purposes of taxation of such property used in business

trust *n* **1 a** : a fiduciary relationship in which one party holds legal title to another's property for the benefit of a party who holds equitable title to the property **b** : an entity resulting from the establishment of such a relationship — see also BENEFICIARY, CESTUI QUE TRUST,

\ə\abut \ᵊ\kitten \ər\further \a\ash \ā\ace
\ä\cot, cart \au̇\out \ch\chin \e\bet \ē\easy
\g\go \i\hit \ī\ice \j\job \ŋ\sing \ō\go \ȯ\law
\ȯi\boy \th\thin \t͟h\the \ü\loot \u̇\foot \y\yet
\zh\vision *see also* Pronunciation Symbols page

CORPUS, *declaration of trust* at DECLA-
RATION 4, PRINCIPAL, SETTLOR ◇ Trusts
developed out of the old English use. The
traditional requirements of a trust are a
named beneficiary and trustee (who may
be the settlor), an identified res, or property, to be transferred to the trustee and
constitute the principal of the trust, and
delivery of the res to the trustee with the
intent to create a trust. Not all relationships labeled as trusts have all of these
characteristics, however. Trusts are often
created for their advantageous tax treatment.

accumulation trust : a trust in which
principal and income are allowed to accumulate rather than being paid out
◇ Accumulation trusts are disfavored
and often restricted in the law.

active trust : a trust in which legal title
remains in the trustee who has a duty to
act affirmatively (as in exercising control, discretion, and judgment) with regard to the property — compare PASSIVE
TRUST in this entry

alimony trust : a trust created often in
accordance with a separation agreement
in which property is transferred to the
trust as a source of support for a divorced spouse with a remainder to
someone else

bank account trust : TOTTEN TRUST in
this entry

business trust : a trust that is created
for the purpose of making profit and
that is usu. characterized by some kind
of commercial activity, transferable certificates of interest, existence continuing after the death of beneficiaries, limited liability, legal title in the hands of
trustees, and officers having duties of
management — called also *common-
law trust, Massachusetts trust* ◇ A trust
that qualifies as a business trust is eligible for bankruptcy protection under
chapter 13 of the Bankruptcy Code.

bypass trust : a trust in which a spouse
leaves his or her estate upon death to
a trust naming the surviving spouse as
beneficiary usu. with remainders to chil-

dren or other descendants — called also
*bypass shelter trust, credit shelter trust,
shelter trust* ◇ The purpose of a bypass
trust is to reduce the surviving spouse's
taxable estate. Such trusts do not qualify
for the marital deduction.

charitable lead trust \-'lēd-\ : a trust in
which a charity is named as the beneficiary for a period of time after which
named individuals succeed as beneficiaries

charitable remainder annuity trust : a
charitable remainder trust in which the
named beneficiaries receive a fixed payment of not less than five percent of the
fair market value of the original principal over the course of a specified period after which the remaining principal
passes to charity

charitable remainder trust : a trust in
which individuals are named as beneficiaries to receive income for a period of
time (as the lifetimes of the beneficiaries) after which the principal passes to
charity ◇ Charitable remainder trusts
qualify for tax exemptions under section
664 of the Internal Revenue Code.

charitable remainder uni·trust \-'yü-
nə-ˌtrəst\ : a charitable remainder trust
in which the named beneficiaries receive payments of a fixed percentage
and not less than five percent of the
value of the trust assets as determined
annually for a specified period after
which the remainder passes to charity

charitable trust : a trust created for the
purpose of performing charity or providing social benefits ◇ Unlike most
trusts, a charitable trust does not require
definite beneficiaries and may exist in
perpetuity.

Clif·ford trust \'kli-fərd-\ : a grantor
trust lasting at least ten years with income payable to a beneficiary and principal reverting to the settlor upon termination ◇ Prior to the Tax Reform Act of
1986, a Clifford trust could be used as a
tax shelter that diverted income from the
settlor, who was in a higher tax bracket,
to a beneficiary, often a child, who was

in a lower tax bracket. Under the current rules, the settlor is treated as the owner of any portion of a trust in which he or she has a reversionary interest, and therefore taxes are calculated at the settlor's rate.

common–law trust : BUSINESS TRUST in this entry

com•plex trust : a trust under which any or all income does not have to be distributed and principal may be distributed — compare SIMPLE TRUST in this entry

constructive trust **1** : an implied trust imposed by a court to prevent the unjust enrichment of one who has wrongfully obtained (as through fraud or bad faith) title to the property or a property interest of another — called also *trust de son tort, trust ex delicto, trust ex maleficio;* compare RESULTING TRUST in this entry **2** : an equitable remedy to prevent unjust enrichment through the imposition of a constructive trust

credit shel•ter trust : BYPASS TRUST in this entry

discretionary trust : a trust that gives the trustee authority to exercise his or her discretion in distributing principal or income to the beneficiary

dry trust : PASSIVE TRUST in this entry

executed trust : a trust in which nothing is left to be done by the trustee but preserve the property and execute the purpose of the trust to benefit the beneficiaries

executory trust : a trust in which the settlor or trustee has duties to perform (as securing the property, ascertaining the objects of the trust, or making distributions)

express trust : a trust intentionally created by the settlor; *specif* : a trust created by a positive act of the settlor and set down in writing that expresses the intention to create a trust, identifies the property to be placed in trust, and names beneficiaries

generation–skip•ping trust : a trust in which the principal will eventually go to a skip person usu. following payment of income for life to a non-skip person : a trust created by a generation-skipping transfer of property in trust

grantor trust : a trust that is taxed at the settlor's tax rate because the settlor has the power to control the beneficial enjoyment of the trust, retains a reversionary interest in the trust, has administrative powers over the trust, has the power to revoke the trust, or benefits from the income of the trust — see also CLIFFORD TRUST in this entry

hon•or•ary trust \'ä-nə-,rer-ē-\ : a trust that is created for a purpose which is not charitable and that names no specific beneficiary ◊ An honorary trust may be upheld as valid where allowed by statute providing that its purpose (as for the care of an animal or grave) is sufficiently clear. Unlike a charitable trust, however, an honorary trust is subject to the rule against perpetuities.

Illinois land trust : LAND TRUST in this entry

implied trust : a trust arising by operation of law when the circumstances of a transaction imply the creation of a trust that is not expressly created by the parties and esp. when a trust is necessary to avoid an inequitable result or to prevent fraud

individual policy pension trust : an insurance trust created as a retirement plan in which individual life insurance policies are purchased for employees and held in trust by the employer to fund the plan

insurance trust : a trust in which the principal consists of an insurance policy or its proceeds

inter vivos trust : a trust that becomes effective during the lifetime of the settlor — called also *living trust;* compare TESTAMENTARY TRUST in this entry

\ə\abut   \ə\kitten   \ər\further   \a\ash   \ā\ace
\ä\cot, cart   \aü\out   \ch\chin   \e\bet   \ē\easy
\g\go   \i\hit   \ī\ice   \j\job   \ŋ\sing   \ō\go   \ȯ\law
\ȯi\boy   \th\thin   \t̲h̲\the   \ü\loot   \u̇\foot   \y\yet
\zh\vision   *see also* Pronunciation Symbols page

investment trust : a business trust that is a closed-end investment company

involuntary trust : IMPLIED TRUST in this entry; *esp* : CONSTRUCTIVE TRUST in this entry

irrevocable trust : a trust that cannot be revoked by the settlor after its creation except upon the consent of all the beneficiaries

land trust : a trust created to effectuate a real estate ownership arrangement in which the trustee holds legal and equitable title to the property subject to the provisions of a trust agreement setting out the rights of the beneficiaries whose interests in the trust are declared to be personal property — called also *Illinois land trust, naked land trust*

living trust : INTER VIVOS TRUST in this entry

marital deduction trust : a marital trust created in order to qualify for the marital deduction; *esp* : POWER OF APPOINTMENT TRUST in this entry

marital trust : a testamentary trust naming a surviving spouse as the beneficiary — see also MARITAL DEDUCTION TRUST and POWER OF APPOINTMENT TRUST in this entry

Mas·sa·chu·setts trust \ˌma-sə-ˈchü-səts-, -zəts-\ : BUSINESS TRUST in this entry

naked land trust : LAND TRUST in this entry

naked trust : PASSIVE TRUST in this entry

nominee trust : a trust created for the purpose of holding property for beneficiaries whose identities are kept secret

oral trust : a trust created by the settlor's spoken statements esp. for the purpose of transferring real property as part of an agreement between the settlor and the trustee

passive trust : a trust or use under which the trustee has no duties to perform : a trust in which legal and equitable titles are merged in the beneficiaries — called also *dry trust, naked trust;* compare ACTIVE TRUST in this entry

pour–over trust : a trust that receives the assets that make up its principal by operation of a testamentary disposition to it usu. of the residue of an estate or from another trust upon the settlor's death

power of appointment trust : a marital trust that provides a surviving spouse with a life estate in property and a power of appointment allowing appointment of the property to the surviving spouse or to his or her estate ◊ A power of appointment trust made in accordance with Internal Revenue Code section 2056(b)(5) qualifies for the marital deduction.

protective trust : a trust that attempts to shield assets from the beneficiaries' creditors by providing that it is within the trustee's discretion to refuse to pay a beneficiary or that a beneficiary forfeits his or her interest in the trust upon a creditor's attempt to reach it

purchase money re·sult·ing trust : a resulting trust arising where not abolished by statute when property is purchased with title in the name of one person but using the money of another

QTIP trust \ˈkyü-ˌtip-\ : a trust to which qualified terminable interest property is transferred for purposes of taking the marital deduction

qualified charitable remainder trust : a trust that is either a charitable remainder annuity trust or a charitable remainder unitrust

real estate investment trust : a business trust similar to a closed-end investment company except that it invests in real estate either as an owner having equity in the property or as a lender holding mortgages on the property

resulting trust : an implied trust based upon the presumed intentions of the parties as inferred from all the circumstances that the party holding legal title to trust property holds it for the benefit of the other — compare CONSTRUCTIVE TRUST in this entry

revocable trust : a trust over which the settlor has retained the power of revocation *savings bank trust* : TOTTEN TRUST in this entry

shelter trust : BYPASS TRUST in this entry

simple trust : a trust under which all current income must be distributed and no principal may be distributed

spendthrift trust : a trust that is created for the benefit of a spendthrift who is paid income therefrom and that cannot be reached by creditors to satisfy the spendthrift's debts

tentative trust : TOTTEN TRUST in this entry

testamentary trust : a trust created in a will to be effective upon the settlor's death

Tot•ten trust \'tät-ᵊn-\ : a trust created by a deposit in a bank by one person as trustee for another that is revocable until the death of the depositor — called also *bank account trust, savings bank trust, tentative trust*

trust de son tort \-də-ˌsōn-'tȯrt, -ˌsȯⁿ-'tȯr\ [Anglo-French *de son tort* (*desmesne*) from his or her (own) wrongful act] : CONSTRUCTIVE TRUST 1 in this entry

trust ex delicto : CONSTRUCTIVE TRUST 1 in this entry

trust ex maleficio : CONSTRUCTIVE TRUST 1 in this entry

unit trust : a trust operating as a vehicle for investment whose portfolio consists of long-term bonds that are held to maturity

voting trust : a trust created by the transfer of legal title to shares of stock to a trustee or trustees who exercise the corporate voting rights conferred by ownership of the shares as agreed in the trust instrument ◊ The shareholders transferring legal title to their shares retain the equitable title and continue to receive dividends and other distributions. They also receive certificates as evidence of their interest in the trust, which provides the holder with the rights of a shareholder except for voting rights.

2 a : a combination of firms or corporations formed by an agreement establishing a trust whereby shareholders in the separate corporations exchange their shares for shares representing proportionate interest in the principal and income of the combination and surrender to the trustees the management and operation of the combined firms or corporations **b** : a combination or aggregation of business entities formed by any of various means; *esp* : one that reduces competition or is thought to present a threat of reducing competition — compare ANTITRUST **3 a** : a charge or duty imposed in faith or confidence or as a condition of some relationship **b** : something committed or entrusted to one to be used or cared for in the interest of another ⟨no religious test shall ever be required as a qualification to any office or public ~ under the United States — *U.S. Constitution* art. VI⟩ **c** : the condition, obligation, or right of one to whom something is confided : responsible charge or office ⟨acted diligently in carrying out his ~ as chairman of the board⟩ **d** : CUSTODY ⟨a child committed to their ~⟩ **— in trust** : in a trust ⟨property held *in trust* for the children⟩

trust account *n* : an account opened with a trust company (as a bank) under which an inter vivos or testamentary trust is set up (as for the escrow of funds)

trust agreement *n* : an agreement establishing and setting forth the material terms of a trust

trust•bust•er \'trəst-ˌbəs-tər\ *n* : one and esp. a federal officer who seeks to break up trusts by prosecution under the antitrust laws **— trust–bust•ing** \-tiŋ\ *n*

trust company — see COMPANY

trust deed — see DEED

trust de son tort — see TRUST

¹trust•ee \ˌtrəs-'tē\ *n* **1** : one to whom something is entrusted : one trusted to keep or administer something: as **a** : a member of a board entrusted with administering the funds and directing the policy of an institution or organization **b** : a country charged with the supervision of a trust territory **2 a** : a natural or legal person to whom property is committed to be administered for the benefit of a beneficiary (as a person or charitable organization) : the holder of legal title to property placed in a trust — compare CESTUI QUE TRUST, SETTLOR **b** : one (as a corporate director) occupying a position of trust and performing functions comparable to those of a trustee **c** : TRUSTEE IN BANKRUPTCY — **trust·ee·ship** *n*

²**trustee** *vb* **trust·eed; trust·ee·ing** *vt* : to commit to the care of a trustee ~ *vi* : to serve as trustee

trust·eed \ˌtrəs-'tēd\ *adj* : managed or administered by a trustee

trustee in bankruptcy : an officer of the court in whom ownership of a debtor's property is vested for the benefit of the creditors and who administers the property for the purpose of making payments to the creditors according to the priority of their claims: as **a** : the trustee in a chapter 7 or chapter 11 case who is charged with duties that include collecting the property comprising the bankruptcy estate and reducing it to money for payment of claims **b** : the trustee in a chapter 12 or chapter 13 case who is charged with duties that include distributing payments made by the debtor in accordance with a confirmed plan — called also *bankruptcy trustee;* see also DEBTOR IN POSSESSION

trustee process *n* : the process of attachment by garnishment — used esp. in the northeastern U.S.

trust ex delicto — see TRUST

trust ex maleficio — see TRUST

trust fund — see FUND 1

trust fund doctrine *n* : a doctrine holding that shareholders to whom assets of an insolvent corporation have been transferred are liable to creditors upon dissolution

of the corporation; *broadly* : a doctrine holding that corporate assets are held as a trust fund for the benefit of shareholders and creditors and that corporate officers have a fiduciary duty to deal with them properly

trust indenture *n* : a document under which a trust (as one created by the issuer of bonds in accordance with the Trust Indenture Act of 1939) is conducted

trust instrument *n* : a document (as a formal declaration of trust or trust agreement) embodying the creation and provision of a trust

trus·tor \ˌtrəs-'tȯr, 'trəs-tər\ *n* : SETTLOR

trust receipt *n* : a trust agreement between a lender and a borrower by which the lender gives up possession of goods without abandoning title and the borrower agrees to hold the goods in trust for the lender and if the goods are sold to turn the proceeds over to the lender in settlement of the debt ◊ The Article Nine security interest replaces the trust receipt where the Uniform Commercial Code has been adopted.

trust territory *n* : a non-self-governing territory placed under an administrative authority by the United Nations

trust·wor·thy *adj* : worthy of confidence; *specif* : being or deriving from a source worthy of belief or consideration for evidentiary purposes ⟨a ~ informant⟩ — **trust·wor·thi·ness** *n*

trusty \'trəs-tē\ *n, pl* **trust·ies** : a convict considered trustworthy and allowed special privileges

try *vt* **tried; try·ing** [Anglo-French *trier* to choose, sort, ascertain, examine judicially, from Old French, to choose, sort] **1** : to examine or investigate judicially ⟨no fact *tried* by a jury, shall be otherwise reexamined in any court of the United States, than according to the rules of the common law — *U.S. Constitution* amend. VII⟩ ⟨in all actions *tried* upon the facts without a jury — *Federal Rules of Civil Procedure* Rule 52(a)⟩ **2** : to conduct the trial of : put on trial ⟨if . . . the judge before whom the defendant has been *tried* is unable to perform the duties to be performed by the court after a verdict or finding of guilt —*Federal Rules of Criminal Procedure* Rule 25(b)⟩ **3 :** to participate as lawyer or counsel in the trial of **:** bring to trial on behalf of a client ⟨was unqualified to ~ death penalty cases⟩

turn *vi* **:** to have a specified decisive factor — used with *on* ⟨the first of the cases . . . ~*ed* on first amendment issues —K. A. Cohen⟩

turnover order — see ORDER 3b

tur·pis cau·sa \'tər-pis-'kȯ-zə, 'tùr-pēs-'kaù-sä\ *n* [Latin, immoral reason] **:** a cause or consideration that is base or immoral and therefore not sufficient to support a contractual obligation

tur·pi·tude \'tər-pə-ˌtüd, -ˌtyüd\ *n* **:** inherent baseness or depravity; *also* **:** a base act

tu·tor \'tü-tər, 'tyü-tər\ *n, in the civil law of Louisiana* **:** a guardian of a minor or sometimes of a person with mental retardation — compare COMMITTEE, CONSERVATOR, CURATOR — **tu·tor·ship** *n*

tu·trix \'tü-ˌtriks, 'tyü-\ *n, pl* **tu·tri·ces** \tü-'trī-ˌsēz, tyü-; 'tü-trə-ˌsēz, 'tyü-\ *or* **tu·trix·es** \-ˌtrik-səz\ **:** a female tutor

twelve–mile limit *n* **:** a limit of a nation's territorial waters extending twelve miles from shore

twist·ing *n* **:** the making of a misrepresentation by an insurance agent to cause a policyholder to surrender or lapse an insurance policy esp. for the purpose of replacing it with another policy

two issue rule *n* **:** a rule of procedure: a general verdict that is returned in a case having more than one theory of liability and that is supported by at least one issue will stand regardless of error as to other issues

two witness rule *n* **:** a rule requiring the testimony of at least two witnesses in order to convict for perjury

ty·ing *adj* **:** of, relating to, or being an arrangement or agreement in which a seller will sell a product to a buyer only if the buyer will also buy another product; *also* **:** of or being the product that will not be sold without the other ◇ A tying arrangement violates antitrust laws.

U

uber·ri·mae fi·dei \yü-'ber-i-,mē-'fī-dē-,ī, ü-'ber-ē-,mī-'fē-dā-,ē\ *adj* [Latin, of the most abundant good faith] **:** of the utmost or perfect good faith ⟨contracts of insurance are traditionally contracts *uberrimae fidei*⟩

uber·ri·ma fi·des \yü-'ber-i-mə-'fī-,dēz, ü-'ber-ē-,mä-'fē-,dās\ *n* [Latin, most abundant good faith] **:** utmost or perfect good faith ⟨acted in *uberrima fides*⟩ ◊ The terms *uberrima fides* and *uberrimae fidei*, although grammatically distinct in Latin, are often used interchangeably in English.

U.C.C. *abbr* Uniform Commercial Code — see also the IMPORTANT LAWS section

UCCC *abbr* Uniform Consumer Credit Code — see also the IMPORTANT LAWS section

UCMJ *abbr* Uniform Code of Military Justice — see also the IMPORTANT LAWS section

UFCA *abbr* Uniform Fraudulent Conveyance Act — see also the IMPORTANT LAWS section

UFTA *abbr* Uniform Fraudulent Transfer Act — see also the IMPORTANT LAWS section

ultimate fact — see FACT

ul·tra·haz·ard·ous \,əl-trə-'ha-zər-dəs\ *adj* **:** being of such extreme danger or risk of harm that strict liability will be imposed

ultrahazardous activity *n* **:** an uncommon activity involving a risk of injury that cannot be eliminated by the exercise of the utmost care — see also ABNORMALLY DANGEROUS ACTIVITY

ul·tra vi·res \'əl-trə-'vī-,rēz, 'ül-trä-'vē-,rās\ *adv or adj* [Latin, beyond the power or means (of)] **:** beyond the scope or in excess of legal power or authority (as of a corporation) ⟨the agency acted *ultra vi-*

res⟩ ⟨the agreement was *ultra vires*⟩ — compare INTRA VIRES

um·brel·la *adj* **:** being or relating to a supplemental insurance policy that extends the coverage of an underlying policy on the same risk ⟨an ~ policy⟩ ⟨~ liability insurance⟩

um·pire *n* **:** a person having authority to decide finally a controversy or question between parties: as **a :** one appointed to decide between disagreeing arbitrators **b :** an impartial third party chosen to arbitrate disputes arising under the terms of a labor agreement **c :** one appointed to mediate between the appraisers of an insured and insurer in order to determine the amount of a loss

un- *prefix* **1 :** not ⟨*un*counseled⟩ **2 :** contrary to ⟨*un*constitutional⟩

un·alien·able \,ən-'āl-yə-nə-bəl, -'ā-lē-ə-\ *adj* **:** not alienable **:** INALIENABLE

un·avoid·able accident *n* **:** an accident that is not proximately caused by the negligence of any party or that is unforeseeable or not preventable by exercise of reasonable precautions and for which liability based on fault is not imposed — compare ACT OF GOD

unavoidable casualty *n* **:** UNAVOIDABLE ACCIDENT; *also* **:** an unavoidable circumstance that prevents the timely performance of a procedural act (as the filing of an answer) by a party or the party's lawyer — compare EXCUSABLE NEGLECT ◊ As with excusable neglect, showing evidence of unavoidable casualty will relieve a party from a default judgment or a time limit.

uncertificated security — see SECURITY

un·clean hands *n pl* **:** an equitable doctrine: a complainant will be denied relief if he or she has engaged in misconduct (as acting in bad faith) directly relating to the complaint; *also* : the condition of having engaged in such misconduct and being barred from equitable relief ⟨may not be invoked by a plaintiff with *unclean hands* —*Royal Sch. Labs., Inc. v. Town of Watertown*, 358 F.2d 813 (1966)⟩ ◊ Unclean hands on the part of the plaintiff is often pleaded as an affirmative defense by the defendant.

un·con·di·tion·al \ˌən-kən-'di-shə-nəl\ *adj* : not conditional or limited : ABSO-LUTE, UNQUALIFIED — **un·con·di·tion·al·ly** *adv*

un·con·scio·na·bil·i·ty \ˌən-ˌkän-chə-nə-'bi-lə-tē\ *n* **1** : the state or condition of being unconscionable ⟨the issue of ~ is to be decided by the court —J. D. Calamari and J. M. Perillo⟩ — see also PROCE-DURAL UNCONSCIONABILITY, SUBSTAN-TIVE UNCONSCIONABILITY **2** : a doctrine in contract law: a court may grant relief from or deny enforcement of all or part of a contract if it is found to be unconscionable

un·con·scio·na·ble \ˌən-'kän-chə-nə-bəl\ *adj* : unreasonably unfair to one party, marked by oppression, or otherwise unacceptably offensive to public policy ⟨an ~ clause⟩ ⟨finds the contract . . . to have been ~ at the time it was made —*Uniform Commercial Code*⟩ — compare CONSCIONABLE — **un·con·scio·na·bly** *adv*

un·con·sti·tu·tion·al \ˌən-ˌkän-stə-'tü-shə-nəl, -'tyü-\ *adj* : contrary to or failing to comply with a constitution; *esp* : violative of a person's rights guaranteed by the U.S. Constitution ⟨an ~ search and seizure⟩ — **un·con·sti·tu·tion·al·i·ty** *n* \-ˌtü-shə-'na-lə-tē, -ˌtyü-\ — **un·con·sti·tu·tion·al·ly** *adv*

unconstitutional conditions doctrine *n* : a doctrine in constitutional law that bars a government from imposing a condition on the grant of a benefit requiring the waiver of a constitutional right

un·coun·seled \ˌən-'kaun-səld\ *adj* : not provided with counsel : not receiving the advice of counsel ⟨an ~ defendant⟩

un·der·cap·i·tal·ized \ˌən-dər-'ka-pət-ᵊl-ˌīzd\ *adj* : having too little capital for efficient operation ⟨~ companies⟩

un·der·in·clu·sive \ˌən-dər-in-'klü-siv\ *adj* : not sufficiently inclusive : excluding something that should be included; *specif* : not affecting others similarly situated with respect to the purpose of the law and esp. in violation of equal protection ⟨an ~ classification⟩ ⟨all four ordinances are overbroad or ~ in substantial respects — *Church of the Lukumi Babalu Aye v. City of Hialeah*, 508 U.S. 520 (1993)⟩ — compare OVERINCLUSIVE — **un·der·in·clu·sive·ness** *n*

un·der·in·sur·ance \ˌən-dər-in-'shùr-əns\ *n* **1** : insufficient insurance **2** : insurance coverage protecting usu. against uninsured or underinsured motorists by compensating the insured if the tortfeasor's liability policy limits fall short of the insured's losses : insurance providing uninsured motorist coverage

un·der·in·sured \ˌən-dər-in-'shùrd\ *adj* : not sufficiently insured : having insufficient insurance to cover losses or damages ⟨an ~ motorist⟩

un·der·in·sur·er \ˌən-dər-in-'shùr-ər\ *n* : an insurer providing underinsurance coverage

un·der·signed \'ən-dər-ˌsīnd\ *n, pl* **undersigned** : one whose name is signed at the end of a document ⟨the ~ jointly and severally agree⟩

un·der·tak·ing *n* **1** : a promise or pledge esp. required by law **2** : something (as cash or a written promise) deposited or given as security esp. in a court ◊ Undertakings are often required of one party during property actions (as for attachment) in order to compensate the other party should the court's action (as in attaching the property) be found unjustified later.

un·der·ten·ant \'ən-dər-ˌte-nənt\ *n* : a tenant (as a sublessee) who takes some part

\ə\abut   \ᵊ\kitten   \ər\further   \a\ash   \ā\ace
\ä\cot, cart   \au\out   \ch\chin   \e\bet   \ē\easy
\g\go   \i\hit   \ī\ice   \j\job   \ŋ\sing   \ō\go   \o\law
\oi\boy   \th\thin   \th\the   \ü\loot   \ù\foot   \y\yet
\zh\vision   *see also* Pronunciation Symbols page

of the tenancy of another tenant (as a lessee) — used esp. in New York

un·der·write \'ən-dər-ˌrīt, ˌən-dər-'rīt\ *vt* **-wrote** \-ˌrōt, -'rōt\; **-writ·ten** \-ˌrit-ᵊn, -'rit-ᵊn\; **-writ·ing** **1 a :** to assume liability for (a risk) as an insurer ⟨the insurer ~*s* individuals, not the group, in franchise health insurance⟩ **b :** to issue or set the terms of (an insurance policy) **2 :** to agree to purchase (all or part of a security issue) usu. on a fixed date at a fixed price with the purpose or plan to resell by means of a public offering ⟨was a security brokerage firm which as part of its business *under-wrote* speculative new issues — *UFITEC, S.A. v. Carter*, 135 Cal. Rptr. 607 (1977)⟩ **3 a :** to put up funds for or guarantee financial support of **b :** to assess the risk of (as a loan)

un·der·writ·er \'ən-dər-ˌrī-tər\ *n* **1 a :** a person (as an individual or a company) who underwrites an insurance policy **:** INSURER **b :** a person who assesses risks to be covered by an insurance policy **2 :** a person (as an individual or company) who underwrites a security issue — compare ISSUER ◊ The Securities Act of 1933 requires dealers, issuers, and underwriters to file registration statements for the securities that they sell.

un·di·vid·ed *adj* **:** shared with others having an interest in the whole **:** held jointly, in common, or in indivision with other co-owners ⟨each such tenant in common holds an equal ~ share in the title — O. L. Browder *et al.*⟩ ⟨each spouse owns a present ~ one-half interest in the community property — *Louisiana Civil Code*⟩ — compare DIVIDED, ENTIRE

undivided profits *n pl* **:** earnings of a business that have been retained instead of being distributed to stockholders or owners or designated as surplus — compare SURPLUS 2

un·due \ˌən-'dü, -'dyü\ *adj* **1 :** not due **:** not yet payable ⟨an ~ bill⟩ **2 :** exceeding or violating propriety or fitness ⟨would impose ~ hardship on the debtors⟩ ⟨such a requirement would place an ~ burden on employers⟩

undue influence *n* **:** improper influence that deprives a person of freedom of choice or substitutes another's choice or desire for the person's own — compare COERCION, DURESS, NECESSITY ◊ It is a doctrine of equity that a contract, deed, donation, or testamentary disposition can be set aside if the court finds that someone has exercised undue influence over the maker at the time that the contract, conveyance, or will was made. To establish a prima facie case it is usu. necessary to show a susceptibility to undue influence (as from mental impairment), the opportunity and disposition on someone's part to exercise such influence, and that the transaction would not have been made except for the undue influence.

un·du·ly \ˌən-'dü-lē, -'dyü-\ *adv* **:** in an undue manner **:** to an excessive degree ⟨~ influenced the testator⟩

un·earned income *n* **:** income (as interest and dividends) that is not gained by labor, service, or skill — compare EARNED INCOME

unearned premium reserve — see RESERVE

un·eman·ci·pat·ed \ˌən-i-'man-sə-ˌpā-təd\ *adj* **:** not emancipated; *specif* **:** still under parental authority ⟨an ~ minor⟩

un·em·ploy·ment compensation *n* **:** compensation paid at regular intervals (as by a state agency) to an unemployed worker and esp. one who has been laid off — called also *unemployment benefit* ◊ Unemployment compensation is usu. a fixed percentage of the former wages of an unemployed worker.

unemployment insurance *n* **:** a social insurance program that provides unemployment compensation for a limited period to involuntarily unemployed workers

un·en·force·able \ˌən-in-'fȯr-sə-bəl\ *adj* **:** not enforceable in a court — **un·en·force·abil·i·ty** \-ˌfȯr-sə-'bi-lə-tē\ *n*

un·fair com·pe·ti·tion *n* **:** the common-law tort of passing off one's goods as another's; *broadly* **:** any of various torts (as disparagement) that interfere with the business prospects of a competitor or injure consumers

unfair labor practice *n* : any of various acts by an employer or labor organization that violate a right or protection under applicable labor laws ◊ The unfair labor practices that are specified in the National Labor Relations Act are the following: 1) the interference, restraint, or coercion of employees in the exercise of their rights by an employer; 2) domination of a labor organization by an employer; 3) encouragement or discouragement of union membership by discrimination in hiring or conditions of employment by an employer; 4) discrimination against an employee for filing charges of or testifying regarding an unfair labor practice by an employer; 5) refusal of an employer to bargain with the collective bargaining agent; 6) restraint or coercion of employers or employees by a labor organization; 7) coercion of an employer by a labor organization to discriminate against an employee; 8) refusal of a labor organization to bargain collectively with an employer; 9) engaging in illegal strikes or boycotts by a labor organization; 10) excessive or discriminatory initiation fees for a labor organization; 11) coercion of an employer by a labor organization to pay for work not done; 12) picketing by a labor organization to force an employer to recognize or employees to select another collective bargaining agent when there has already been an election.

unfair trade practice *n* : any of various deceptive, fraudulent, or otherwise injurious (as to a consumer) practices or acts that are declared unlawful by statute (as a consumer protection act) or recognized as actionable at common law

un·fore·see·able \ˌən-fōr-'sē-ə-bəl\ *adj* : not capable of being reasonably anticipated or expected : such that a person of ordinary prudence would not expect to occur or exist under the circumstances ⟨an ∼ misuse⟩ ⟨an ∼ injury⟩ — **un·fore·see·abil·i·ty** \-ˌsē-ə-'bi-lə-tē\ *n*

uni·fied bar \'yü-nə-ˌfīd-\ *n* : INTEGRATED BAR

unified credit *n* : a tax credit applied against the unified transfer tax that is a cumulative credit gradually reduced by the amount of credit allowed for gifts made in preceding calendar periods ◊ The total unified credit allowed as of 1987 is $192,800. The amount of the credit to be used in each period cannot exceed that period's tax liability, and so the credit may be gradually used up over a period of years. The unified credit is phased out once the amount of taxable gifts rises above a certain level.

unified transfer tax *n* : a tax imposed under the Internal Revenue Code on the cumulative total of gifts made over a certain amount by a person during his or her lifetime or after death — called also *unified estate and gift tax;* see also UNIFIED CREDIT ◊ The unified transfer tax system creates liability for a single tax rather than separate liability for a gift tax and an estate tax.

uni·form *adj* : of, relating to, or based on a uniform act

uniform act *n* : an act (as the Uniform Commercial Code) sponsored by the National Conference of Commissioners on Uniform State Laws that is intended to be enacted by each individual state with or without changes

uni·lat·er·al \ˌyü-nə-'la-tə-rəl\ *adj* **1** : done or undertaken by one party ⟨a ∼ mistake as to the terms⟩ **2** : of, relating to, or affecting one side of a subject **3** : containing a promise to perform made by only one party esp. because the other has already performed (as by paying an amount) ⟨an option contract is ∼⟩ — **uni·lat·er·al·ly** *adv*

unilateral contract — see CONTRACT
unilateral mistake — see MISTAKE
un·in·sured mo·tor·ist coverage \ˌən-in-

'shərd-'mō-tə-rist-\ *n* : insurance coverage that compensates the insured or another protected person (as a passenger) for damages caused by another motorist without any insurance — called also *uninsured motorist insurance;* see also UNDERINSURANCE

union *n* **1** : an act or instance of uniting or joining two or more things into one; *esp* : the formation of a single political unit from two or more separate and individual units **2** : something that is made one : something formed by a combining or coalition of its members: as **a** : a confederation of independent individuals (as nations or persons) for some common purpose **b** : a political unit constituting an organic whole formed usu. from previously independent units (as England and Scotland in 1707) which have surrendered their principal powers to the government of the whole or to a newly created government (as the U.S. in 1789) **c** : LABOR UNION

union·ize \'yü-nyə-,nīz\ *vb* **-ized; -iz·ing** *vt* : to organize into a labor union ⟨to prevent them from *unionizing* the employees⟩; *also* : to establish a labor union in ⟨a *unionized* shop⟩ ~ *vi* : to form or join a labor union — **union·i·za·tion** \,yü-nyə-nə-'zā-shən\ *n*

union mortgage clause *n* : STANDARD MORTGAGE CLAUSE

union shop *n* : a unionized business in which the employer by agreement is free to hire nonmembers as well as members of the union but union membership within a specified time (as 30 days) is a condition of continued employment — compare AGENCY SHOP, CLOSED SHOP, OPEN SHOP ◊ State law determines whether a collective bargaining agreement can have a clause creating a union shop. Many states having right-to-work laws bar union shop agreements.

uni·tary \'yü-nə-,ter-ē\ *adj* **1** : having the character of a single thing that is a constituent of a whole; *specif* : of, relating to, or being a business with subsidiaries in other states or nations that has its state income tax figured by including the subsidiaries' income, determining the portion of that income attributable to activities within the state, and taxing that percentage ⟨a ~ business operating throughout the U.S.⟩ ⟨imposed a ~ tax on a multinational corporation⟩ **2** : marked by unity : not dual or segregated : INTEGRATED **3** ⟨a ~ school district⟩ — **uni·tar·i·ness** *n*

unit deed — see DEED

Unit·ed States attorney *n* : an attorney in the Department of Justice who is appointed either by the president or the attorney general of the United States and acts as the prosecutor in federal criminal cases and as counsel for the U.S. in civil actions within the federal judicial district to which he or she is assigned

United States Claims Court *n* : a former court succeeded by the United States Court of Federal Claims

United States Court of Appeals for the Armed Forces : the highest military court presided over by civilian judges and reviewing decisions of lower military courts on criminal matters ◊ This court was formerly called the United States Court of Military Appeals.

United States Court of Federal Claims *n* : a federal court having nationwide trial jurisdiction over claims against the United States — see also FEDERAL CIRCUIT ◊ The claims over which this court has jurisdiction include those based on the Constitution, acts of Congress, regulations of an executive agency, contracts with the United States, actions for damages not sounding in tort, claims of American Indian groups against the United States, and certain tax cases (as claims for tax refunds). Private bills are referred to it from Congress for advisory findings as to whether there is a genuine legal or equitable claim for relief. The court does not have jurisdiction over claims for pensions or claims based on treaties with foreign nations.

United States Court of International Trade *n* : a federal court having nationwide exclusive jurisdiction over a variety of cases involving international trade and customs duties including those initiated against the United States — see also FEDERAL CIRCUIT

United States Court of Military Appeals *n* : UNITED STATES COURT OF APPEALS FOR THE ARMED FORCES

United States Court of Veterans Appeals *n* : a federal court having exclusive jurisdiction to review decisions of the Board of Veterans' Appeals — see also FEDERAL CIRCUIT

United States marshal *n* : MARSHAL 1

United States trustee *n* : a person appointed and supervised by the Attorney General who has various administrative responsibilities in bankruptcy cases in the region encompassing one or more federal judicial districts to which he or she has been assigned

unit trust — see TRUST

uni·ty \'yü-nə-tē\ *n, pl* **-ties 1** : the quality or state of not being multiple : the quality or state of being one, single, whole, or the same ⟨only if there is ~ of ownership of the immovable and movables⟩ **2** : an aspect (as time, title, interest, or possession) of a joint tenancy that must be identical as it relates to the cotenants ⟨such a conveyance severs the joint tenancy by removing the *unities* of time and title⟩ ◊ At common law, all four unities were required to be present for a joint tenancy. Conveying the interests of the cotenants at the same time creates the unity of time. Conveying the interests of the cotenants in the same instrument creates the unity of title. Conveying the same interest (as fee simple absolute) to the cotenants creates the unity of interest. Conveying a common right of possession or enjoyment creates the unity of possession.

uni·ver·sal \ˌyü-nə-'vər-səl\ *adj* **1** *in the civil law of Louisiana* **a** : encompassing or burdening all of one's property esp. causa mortis ⟨granted him a ~ usufruct⟩ — see also *universal legacy* at LEGACY; compare *universal title* at TITLE **b** : of or relating to a universal conveyance or ˌ   ance under a universal title ⟨a

~ donee⟩ — see also UNIVERSAL SUCCESSOR **2** : not confined by limitations or exceptions : general in application — **univer·sal·ly** *adv*

universal agency — see AGENCY 2a

universal agent — see AGENT

universal legacy — see LEGACY

universal life insurance — see LIFE INSURANCE

universal successor *n, in the civil law of Louisiana* : a successor (as an heir, universal legatee, or legatee under universal title) who succeeds to the rights and obligations of the ancestor in title, continues possession by the ancestor's title, and is responsible for the debts of the succession — compare PARTICULAR SUCCESSOR ◊ Neither a usufructuary under universal title nor a universal usufructuary is a universal successor.

universal title — see TITLE

universal variable life insurance — see LIFE INSURANCE

un·ju·di·cial \ˌən-jü-'di-shəl\ *adj* : not becoming or suitable to a judge ⟨~ conduct⟩

un·just *adj* : characterized by injustice : deficient in justice and fairness ⟨an ~ sentence⟩ — **un·just·ly** *adv* — **un·just·ness** *n*

unjust en·rich·ment *n* **1** : the retaining of a benefit (as money) conferred by another when principles of equity and justice call for restitution to the other party; *also* : the retaining of property acquired esp. by fraud from another in circumstances that demand the judicial imposition of a constructive trust on behalf of those who in equity ought to receive it — see also *quasi contract 1* at CONTRACT **2** : a doctrine that requires an equitable remedy on behalf of one who has been injured by the unjust enrichment of another

un·jus·ti·fi·able \ˌən-'jəs-tə-ˌfī-ə-bəl, -ˌjəs-tə-'fī-\ *adj* : not justifiable — **un·jus·ti·fi·ably** *adv*

\ə\abut \ᵊ\kitten \ər\further \a\ash \ā\ace
\ä\cot, cart \aů\out \ch\chin \e\bet \ē\easy
\g\go \i\hit \ī\ice \j\job \ŋ\sing \ō\go \ȯ\law
\ȯi\boy \th\thin \th̲\the \ü\loot \ů\foot \y\yet
\zh\vision *see also* Pronunciation Symbols page

un·jus·ti·fied \ˌən-'jəs-tə-ˌfīd\ *adj* : not justified ⟨an ~ intrusion⟩

un·law·ful *adj* **1** : not lawful : not authorized or justified by law **2** : acting contrary to or in defiance of the law ⟨an ~ possessor⟩ — **un·law·ful·ly** *adv* — **un·law·ful·ness** *n*

unlawful arrest — see ARREST

unlawful assembly *n* : the offense of assembling with a certain minimum number of others for the purpose of engaging in a riot or other unlawful conduct that threatens public safety, peace, or order; *also* : a group so assembled

unlawful detainer *n* **1** : the act of wrongfully remaining in possession of property (as after expiration of a lease) **2** : an action intended to remedy unlawful detainer by restoring possession of property to its owner — called also *unlawful detainer action*

unlawful force — see FORCE 3

un·liq·ui·dat·ed \ˌən-'li-kwə-ˌdā-təd\ *adj* : not liquidated; *esp* : not calculated or established as a specific amount ⟨an ~ claim⟩

un·mar·ket·able \ˌən-'mär-kə-tə-bəl\ *adj* : not marketable; *esp* : being or relating to title that a reasonably prudent person would not accept in the ordinary course of business or that is reasonably likely to be the subject of litigation

un·nat·u·ral act *n* : CRIME AGAINST NATURE

un·nec·es·sary hard·ship *n* : a deprivation of an owner's right to the beneficial use of property that is caused when a zoning ordinance makes it impossible to receive a reasonable return from the property ◊ Unnecessary hardship may justify the granting of a variance if the use permitted by the variance will not alter the essential character of the locality. Unnecessary hardship must involve unique characteristics of the property itself, not economic difficulties of the owner.

un·pat·ent·able \ˌən-'pat-ᵊn-tə-bəl\ *adj* : not patentable

un·per·fect·ed \ˌən-pər-'fek-təd\ *adj* : not perfected ⟨an ~ security interest⟩

un·pre·med·i·tat·ed \ˌən-prē-'me-də-ˌtā-təd\ *adj* : not premeditated

un·priv·i·leged \ˌən-'priv-lijd, -'pri-və-\ *adj* : not privileged ⟨~ communication⟩

un·pros·e·cut·ed \ˌən-'prä-sə-ˌkyü-təd\ *adj* : not prosecuted ⟨an ~ charge⟩

un·prov·able \ˌən-'prü-və-bəl\ *adj* : not provable

un·proved \ˌən-'prüvd\ *adj* : UNPROVEN

un·prov·en \ˌən-'prü-vən\ *adj* : not proven ⟨an ~ allegation⟩

un·qual·i·fied \ˌən-'kwä-lə-ˌfīd\ *adj* : not qualified

un·re·al·ized \ˌən-'rē-ə-ˌlīzd\ *adj* : not yet realized ⟨~ appreciation⟩

un·rea·son·able *adj* : not reasonable : beyond what can be accepted: as **a** : clearly inappropriate, excessive, or harmful in degree or kind ⟨an ~ delay⟩ ⟨an ~ restraint of trade⟩ **b** : lacking justification in fact or circumstance ⟨an ~ inference⟩; *esp* : IRRATIONAL b ⟨the agency decision was ~⟩ **c** : not supported by a warrant or by a valid exception to a warrant requirement (as when there is reasonable suspicion) and therefore unconstitutional ⟨the right of the people to be secure in their persons, houses, papers, and effects, against ~ searches and seizures, shall not be violated — *U.S. Constitution* amend. IV⟩ — see also SEARCH, SEIZURE — **un·rea·son·able·ness** *n* — **un·rea·son·ably** *adv*

unreasonably dangerous *adj* : characterized by a hazard due to design, defect, or a failure to warn that would not be contemplated by an ordinary user of the product and that is not outweighed by utility ⟨impose strict liability on the manufacturer or seller of an *unreasonably dangerous* product that injures an ultimate user⟩ — see also *products liability* at LIABILITY 2b

un·re·but·ta·ble \ˌən-ri-'bə-tə-bəl\ *adj* : not rebuttable ⟨an ~ presumption⟩

un·re·cord·ed \ˌən-ri-'kȯr-dəd\ *adj* : not recorded; *esp* : not set down in the appropriate public record ⟨had priority over an ~ security interest in the property⟩

un·reg·is·tered \ˌən-'re-jə-stərd\ *adj* : not registered ⟨charged with operating an ~

motor vehicle⟩ — see also *unregistered security* at SECURITY

unregistered security — see SECURITY

un·re·view·able \ˌən-ri-'vyü-ə-bəl\ *adj* : not reviewable ⟨the failure to raise distinctly at trial the matter being objected to ordinarily renders a claim ~ on appeal — *State v. Person*, 577 A.2d 1036 (1990)⟩

un·se·cured \ˌən-si-'kyu̇rd\ *adj* : not secured: as **a** : not guaranteed or protected as to payment, performance, or satisfaction by a security interest or by property given or pledged as security ⟨~ debt⟩ ⟨an ~ claim⟩ **b** : characterized by a lack of security or of a security interest ⟨~ status⟩

unsecured creditor — see CREDITOR

un·sound \ˌən-'sau̇nd\ *adj* : not sound: as **a** : not healthy or whole **b** : not mentally normal : not wholly sane ⟨of ~ mind⟩ **c** : not firmly made, placed, or fixed **d** : not valid or true ⟨an ~ argument⟩ — **un·sound·ly** *adv* — **un·sound·ness** *n*

un·sworn \ˌən-'swōrn\ *adj* : not sworn ⟨could only provide an ~ statement⟩

un·time·ly \ˌən-'tīm-lē\ *adj* : not timely; *esp* : not made or filed within a period of time specified by procedural rule ⟨an ~ petition⟩ — **un·time·li·ness** *n* — **un·timely** *adv*

un·wor·thy *adj* : not meritorious; *specif*, *in the civil law of Louisiana* : being or relating to an heir who is deprived of the right to inherit from a person because of a failure in a duty towards the person — **un·wor·thi·ness** *n*

un·writ·ten law *n* : law based chiefly on custom rather than legislative enactments

UPA *abbr* Uniform Partnership Act — see also the IMPORTANT LAWS section

UPC *abbr* Uniform Probate Code — see also the IMPORTANT LAWS section

up·hold *vt* **-held; -hold·ing** : to judge valid : let stand ⟨~ an award⟩; *specif* : to hold constitutional ⟨~ the practice of having religious invocations and benedictions at high school graduation ceremonies — *Sands v. Morongo Unified Sch. Dist.*, 809 P.2d 809 (1991)(dissent)⟩ ⟨~ a statute⟩

us·age \'yü-sij, -zij\ *n* : an habitual or uniform practice esp. in an area or trade — compare CUSTOM

usage of trade : a practice or method of dealing that is regularly observed in a place, vocation, or trade and that one justifiably expects to be followed by another party to a commercial transaction — compare COURSE OF DEALING, COURSE OF PERFORMANCE ◊ Evidence of a usage of trade may be admissible as supplementing the express terms of a disputed contract when it does not contradict them.

U.S.C. *abbr* United States Code — see also the IMPORTANT LAWS section

¹use \'yüs\ *n* **1 a** : an arrangement in which property is granted to another with the trust and confidence that the grantor or another is entitled to the beneficial enjoyment of it — see also TRUST, *Statute of Uses* in the IMPORTANT LAWS section ◊ Uses originated in early English law and were the origin of the modern trust. Uses became popular in medieval England, where they were often secretly employed as a method of evading laws (as those prohibiting mortmain) and penalties (as attainder) and to defeat creditors. In response, the Statute of Uses was enacted in 1535. The purpose of the Statute was to execute the use, investing the legal ownership of the property in the cestui que use, or one entitled to the beneficial enjoyment, and abolishing the ownership of the grantee. The Statute did not have blanket application, however. Certain uses, particularly those in which the grantee was not merely a passive holder of the property, were not executed under the Statute. These uses were called trusts, and they were the basis of the modern trust. **b** : the right to the utilization and benefit of property to which legal title is held by another ⟨the secret conveyance of ~s in early English law⟩; *broadly* : the fact or right of having the benefits and profits of property

beneficial use : the use of a cestui que use analogous to a beneficial interest in a trust : USE 1b

re·sult·ing use : a use that equity attributes back to a grantor when there is no person declared to receive it or no transfer of consideration

shift·ing use : a use that is transferred or takes effect in derogation of some estate upon the happening of a future event

spring·ing use : a use that arises upon the happening of a future event and is not in derogation of any other estate

2 : the utilization of property, resources, or services

beneficial use **1** : use of property that allows an owner to derive a benefit or profit in the exercise of a basic property right ⟨the owner was entitled to just compensation when he was forced to sacrifice all *beneficial use* of the property⟩ — see also UNNECESSARY HARDSHIP; compare TAKING **2** : use of water for a reasonable or beneficial purpose consistent with the public interest ⟨authorize the diversion of water for *beneficial use*⟩

conditional use : use of property in a zone for a particular purpose that is allowed under conditions set forth in a zoning ordinance : SPECIAL EXCEPTION

fair use : a use of copyrighted material that does not constitute an infringement of the copyright provided the use is fair and reasonable and does not substantially impair the value of the work or the profits expected from it by its owner; *also* : the privilege of making a fair use of copyrighted work ◊ Among the factors determining if a use of a copyrighted work is a fair use are these: the purpose of the use, the character of the use (as in being commercial or educational in nature), the nature of the copyrighted work, and the amount of the work used.

nonconforming use : use of property in a manner that does not conform to the restrictions of a zoning law (as an ordinance); *specif* : one in lawful existence when a restriction takes effect and so allowed to continue

public use **1** : use by or to the benefit of the public; *broadly* : use that serves a legitimate or conceivable public purpose ⟨nor shall private property be taken for *public use*, without just compensation — *U.S. Constitution* amend. V⟩ — see also EMINENT DOMAIN; compare TAKING ◊ If a taking of property is not for public use then the consent of the owner is required. **2** : use of an invention by one who is under no limitation, restriction, or obligation of secrecy to the inventor ◊ Under federal law one is not entitled to a patent for an invention that was in public use more than a year prior to the date of application for the patent.

reasonable use **1** : a use of one's property or of water that is for a suitable and beneficial purpose and that does not lead to unreasonable interference with another's use of property or with the natural flow of water **2 a** : a rule whereby one may alter the natural flow of a watercourse as part of the reasonable use of property even though some harm results to another landowner **b** : a rule whereby a use of the water under the surface of one's land that causes harm to an adjacent landowner is reasonable if made for a suitable purpose in connection with the overlying land ◊ This rule originated when cities began to use land in the country for wells that caused injury to adjacent farmers; the water was not for use there and so unreasonableness ultimately depended not on waste or harm but on the final destination of the water. **c** : a rule that recognizes a landowner as entitled to make a reasonable use of property if it does not cause unreasonable harm to another and that may be applied to the alteration of a watercourse, the drainage of surface water, and the use of water beneath the surface

3 : utilization of a motor vehicle in a manner that is not completely foreign to its purpose ⟨insurance for accidents arising from the ownership, maintenance, or ~ of the car⟩

²use \'yüz\ *vt* **used; us·ing** : to put into service : have enjoyment of — **us·er** *n*

use and occupation *n* : an action in which the owner of property seeks compensation for use and occupation of the premises by another (as a tenant remaining in possession after expiration of a lease)

use·ful life *n* : an estimated amount of time during which an asset or facility will yield income or be useful — see also DEPRECIATION 1

use immunity — see IMMUNITY

use·less ges·ture exception \-'jes-chər-\ *n* : an exception to the knock and announce rule that excuses police from having to announce their purpose before entering a premises in execution of a warrant if facts known to the officers justify them in being virtually certain that the occupant already knows their purpose

use tax *n* : a tax imposed on the use of personal property and esp. property purchased in another state; *specif* : a one-time tax imposed on the exercise or enjoyment of any right or power over tangible personal property that is incident to the ownership, possession, custody, or leasing of it ⟨a law allowing the payment of a sales tax to be credited against the amount of *use tax* due⟩ ⟨the manufacturer became liable for a *use tax* when items were withdrawn from inventory for internal use⟩

use value *n* : value of property based on its use rather than on the market ⟨*use value* of agricultural land⟩

usu·fruct \'yü-zə-ˌfrəkt, -sə-\ *n* [Latin *ususfructus* from *usus et fructus*, literally, use and enjoyment] : the right to the use and enjoyment of another's property and its profits ⟨a ~ in the crops of the estate⟩; *esp, in the civil law of Louisiana* : a personal servitude of limited duration that confers the right of use and full enjoyment of another's property and its fruits ◊ Under the civil law of Louisiana, one having a usufruct in land must

deliver it to the owner with its basic substance undiminished at the end of the term; one having a usufruct in consumables acquires ownership of them, but must return their value or things of the same quantity or quality at the end of the usufruct.

¹usu·fruc·tu·ary \ˌyü-zə-'frək-chə-ˌwer-ē, -sə-\ *n, pl* **-ar·ies** : one who has a usufruct in property ⟨the right of usufruct expires upon the death of the ~ —*Louisiana Civil Code*⟩ — compare *naked owner* at OWNER

²usufructuary *adj* : of, relating to, or having the character of a usufruct ⟨a ~ right⟩

usu·rer \'yü-zhər-ər\ *n* : one that engages in usury

usu·ri·ous \yu̇-'zhu̇r-ē-əs\ *adj* **1** : practicing usury **2** : involving usury ⟨~ interest⟩ — **usu·ri·ous·ly** *adv* — **usu·ri·ous·ness** *n*

usurp \yu̇-'sərp, -'zərp\ *vb* [Latin *usurpare* to take possession of without a strict legal claim, from *usus* use + *rapere* to seize] *vt* : to seize and hold (as office, place, or powers) in possession by force or without right ⟨the courts may not ~ the powers of the legislature⟩ ~ *vi* : to seize or exercise authority or possession wrongfully — **usur·pa·tion** \ˌyü-sər-'pā-shən, -zər-\ *n* — **usurp·er** \yu̇-'sər-pər, -'zər-\ *n*

usu·ry \'yü-zhə-rē\ *n* [Medieval Latin *usuria* interest, lending at exorbitant interest, alteration of Latin *usura* use, interest (i.e., sum paid for use of money), from *usus* use] **1** : the lending of money at exorbitant interest rates; *specif* : the crime of charging or contracting to charge an unlawfully high rate of interest **2** : a rate or amount of interest charged in usury — compare *legal interest* at INTEREST 5

util·i·ty *n, pl* **-ties 1** : fitness for some purpose or worth to some end **2 a** : PUBLIC UTILITY **b** : a service or commodity provided by a public utility ⟨paid for rent

---

\ə\abut \ᵊ\kitten \ər\further \a\ash \ā\ace
\ä\cot, cart \au̇\out \ch\chin \e\bet \ē\easy
\g\go \i\hit \ī\ice \j\job \ŋ\sing \ō\go \ȯ\law
\ȯi\boy \th\thin \t̲h̲\the \ü\loot \u̇\foot \y\yet
\zh\vision *see also* Pronunciation Symbols page

and *utilities*⟩; *also* : equipment or material used in providing such a service or commodity ⟨an easement limited to purposes of travel which does not include the right to install *utilities* — *Ware v. Public Serv. Co.*, 412 A.2d 84 (1980)⟩ **3** *pl* : stocks or bonds of utility companies ⟨*utilities* performed poorly⟩

uti pos·si·de·tis \ˈyü-tī-ˌpä-sə-ˈdē-təs, ˈü-tē-ˌpȯ-sē-ˈdā-tēs\ *n* [Late Latin, as you (now) possess (it); from the wording of an interdict in Roman law enjoining both parties in a suit to maintain the status quo until the decision] : a principle in international law that recognizes a peace treaty between parties as vesting each with the territory and property under its control unless otherwise stipulated

UTMA *abbr* Uniform Transfer to Minors Act — see also the IMPORTANT LAWS section

ut·ter *vt* : to put (as a counterfeit note) into circulation as if genuine ⟨convicted of ~*ing* a forged check⟩ — **ut·ter·er** *n*

V

v. *abbr* versus

va·cant *adj* **1** : not filled or occupied **2 a** : not put to use ⟨~ land⟩ **b** : having no heir or claimant ⟨a ~ estate⟩

vacant succession — see SUCCESSION

va·cate *vb* **va·cat·ed; va·cat·ing** *vt* **1** : to make void : ANNUL, SET ASIDE ⟨~ a lower court order⟩ **2 a** : to make vacant **b** : to give up the occupancy of ~ *vi* : to vacate an office, post, or tenancy

va·ca·tion *n* **1** : a period in which activity or work is suspended; *specif* : an interval between judicial terms **2** : an act or instance of vacating ⟨~ of a judgment⟩

va·ca·tur \və-'kā-tər\ *n* [Medieval Latin, it is made null and void] : VACATION 2 ⟨sought ~ of the arbitration award⟩

va·gran·cy \'vā-grən-sē\ *n, pl* **-cies** **1** : the act or practice of wandering about from place to place **2** : the crime of wandering about without employment or identifiable means of support ⟨the court struck down the ~ law as unconstitutionally vague⟩ ◊ Most vagrancy laws have been abolished.

va·grant \'vā-grənt\ *n* [Anglo-French *wagerant, vageraunt*, from present participle of *vagrer, walcrer* to wander about, drift, probably from Old Norse *valka* to roll, wallow] : one who has no established residence and wanders about without lawful or identifiable means of support ⟨~s may not be punished for being ~s; only persons who commit culpable acts are liable for criminal sanctions — *State v. Richard*, 836 P.2d 622 (1992)⟩

vague \'vāg\ *adj* : characterized by such a lack of precision that a person of ordinary intelligence would have to guess if particular conduct is being proscribed : characterized by a failure to describe forbidden conduct in terms sufficient to provide fair warning ⟨an unconstitutionally ~ law⟩

— see also VOID-FOR-VAGUENESS DOCTRINE; compare OVERBROAD — **vague·ly** *adv* — **vague·ness** *n*

vagueness doctrine *n* : VOID-FOR-VAGUENESS DOCTRINE

val·id \'va-ləd\ *adj* **1** : having legal efficacy or force ⟨a ~ license⟩; *esp* : executed with proper authority and form ⟨a ~ contract⟩ ⟨a ~ search⟩ **2** : having a legitimate basis : JUSTIFIABLE ⟨a ~ reason for terminating the employee⟩ **3** : appropriate to the end in view — **va·lid·i·ty** \və-'li-də-tē\ *n* — **val·id·ly** *adv*

val·i·date \'va-lə-,dāt\ *vt* **-dat·ed; -dat·ing** **1 a** : to make valid **b** : to grant official sanction to by marking **2** : to confirm the validity of (an election) — **val·i·da·tion** \,va-lə-'dā-shən\ *n*

valuable consideration — see CONSIDERATION

val·u·a·tion \,val-yü-'wā-shən\ *n* **1** : the act or process of valuing ⟨actuarial ~ of the assets and liabilities of a state pension fund⟩; *specif* : appraisal of property ⟨~ of marital property is a factual finding that will not be upset unless clearly erroneous —*Jensen v. Jensen*, 458 N.W.2d 391 (1990)⟩ **2** : the estimated or determined value (as market value) of a thing ⟨the total assessed ~ of property in the district⟩

valuation hearing — see HEARING

¹val·ue \'val-yü\ *n* **1 a** : a fair return or equivalent in goods, services, or money for something exchanged ⟨received good ~ for the price⟩ **b** : VALUABLE CONSIDERATION at CONSIDERATION **2** : monetary worth; *esp* : MARKET VALUE — **val·ue·less** *adj*

\ə\abut \ᵊ\kitten \ər\further \a\ash \ā\ace \ä\cot, cart \aů\out \ch\chin \e\bet \ē\easy \g\go \i\hit \ī\ice \j\job \ŋ\sing \ō\go \ó\law \ói\boy \th\thin \t̲h̲\the \ü\loot \ů\foot \y\yet \zh\vision *see also* Pronunciation Symbols page

²**value** *vt* **val·ued; valu·ing** : to estimate or determine the monetary value of

value–ad·ded tax *n* : a tax levied at each addition of value in the processing of a raw material, the performance of a service, or the production and distribution of a commodity with each payer except the consumer reimbursed from payment at the next stage — called also *VAT*

valued policy *n* : an insurance policy in which the insurer and insured agree on a stated amount that will be paid in the event of a future loss instead of an amount that would have to be proven as the actual loss

valued policy law *n* : a law requiring insurance companies to pay to the insured in case of total loss the full amount of insurance regardless of the actual value of the property at the time of the loss

van·dal \'vand-ᵊl\ *n* [*Vandal*, member of a Germanic tribe who sacked Rome in A.D. 455] : a person who willfully destroys, damages, or defaces property belonging to another or to the public

van·dal·ism \'vand-ᵊl-ˌi-zəm\ *n* : the willful or malicious destruction or defacement of property ⟨insurance covering property damage from ~ and malicious mischief⟩

van·dal·ize \'vand-ᵊl-ˌīz\ *vt* **-ized; -iz·ing** : to subject to vandalism

variable annuity — see ANNUITY

variable life insurance — see LIFE INSURANCE

variable universal life insurance — see LIFE INSURANCE

var·i·ance \'ver-ē-əns\ *n* **1** : a disagreement between two documents or positions; *esp* : a disagreement between allegations (as in an indictment or complaint) and proof offered at trial that warrants an appropriate remedy (as a directed verdict or an acquittal) when prejudicial to the substantial rights of the defendant **2** : an authorization to do something contrary to the usual restriction ⟨a ~ granted by a state agency⟩; *esp* : permission for a use of real property that is prohibited by a zoning ordinance — see also UNNEC-ESSARY HARDSHIP; compare SPOT ZONING

VAT \ˌvē-ˌā-'tē\ *n* : VALUE-ADDED TAX

vehicular homicide — see HOMICIDE

vel non \ˌvel-'nän, -'nōn\ [Latin] : or not ⟨the existence *vel non* of a genuine issue of material fact —*Morris v. Smith*, 837 P.2d 679 (1992)⟩

vend \'vend\ *vi* : to dispose of something by sale; SELL; *also* : to engage in selling ~ *vt* : to sell esp. as a hawker or peddler

vend·ee \ˌven-'dē\ *n* : one to whom a thing is sold

ven·dor \'ven-dər, ven-'dȯr\ *also* **vend·er** \'ven-dər\ *n* : one that sells something

vendor's lien — see LIEN

ve·ni·re \və-'nī-rē\ *n* [probably from *veniremen*] : a panel from which a jury is to be selected — compare ARRAY

venire fa·ci·as \-'fā-shē-əs\ *n* [Medieval Latin *venire facias* (*juratores* or *juratam*) may you cause (the jurors or the jury) to come (words used in the writ)] : a writ ordering a sheriff to summon a jury

ve·ni·re·man \və-'nī-rē-mən, -'nir-ē-\ *n, pl* **-men** [*venire* (*facias*) + *man*] : VENIREPERSON

ve·ni·re·mem·ber \və-'nī-rē-ˌmem-bər, -'nir-ē-\ *n* : VENIREPERSON

ve·ni·re·per·son \və-'nī-rē-ˌpər-sən, -'nir-ē-\ *n* : a member of a venire — called also *venireman, veniremember*

ven·ture \'ven-chər\ *n* : an undertaking involving chance, risk, or danger; *esp* : a speculative business enterprise — see also JOINT VENTURE

venture capital — see CAPITAL

ven·ue \'ven-ˌyü\ *n* [Anglo-French, place where a jury is summoned, alteration (influenced by *venue* arrival, attendance) of *vinné*, *visné*, literally, neighborhood, neighbors, from Old French, ultimately from Latin *vicinus* neighboring] **1** : the place or county in which take place the alleged events from which a legal action arises — used esp. at common law **2** : the place from which a jury is drawn and in which trial is held — see also CHANGE OF VENUE; compare JURISDICTION **3** : a statement showing that a case is brought to the proper court or authority

ver·bal act \'vər-bəl-\ *n* : an utterance that is direct evidence (as of an offense) and not hearsay ⟨the offer of drugs for sale was admissible as a *verbal act*⟩

ver·dict \'vər-dikt\ *n* [alteration (partly conformed to Medieval Latin *veredictum*) of Anglo-French *veirdit* statement, finding, verdict, from Old French *veir* true (from Latin *verus*) + *dit* saying, from Latin *dictum*] **1** : the usu. unanimous finding or decision of a jury on one or more matters (as counts of an indictment or complaint) submitted to it in trial that ordinarily in civil actions is for the plaintiff or for the defendant and in criminal actions is guilty or not guilty — compare JUDGMENT 1a

compromise verdict : a verdict produced not by sincere unanimous agreement on guilt or liability but by an improper surrender of individual convictions; *specif* : an impermissible verdict by a jury that is unable to agree on liability and so compromises on an award of damages that is less than what it should be if the plaintiff has a right of recovery free from any doubts

di·rect·ed verdict **1** : a verdict granted by the court when the party with the burden of proof has failed to present sufficient evidence of a genuine issue of material fact that must be submitted to a jury for its resolution ⟨the order of the court granting a motion for a *directed verdict* is effective without any assent of the jury —*Federal Rules of Civil Procedure* Rule 50(a)⟩ — see also *judgment notwithstanding the verdict* at JUDGMENT 1a ◊ Motions for summary judgment, a directed verdict, or for judgment notwithstanding the verdict are all based on the assertion that there is no material fact at issue. A motion for a directed verdict is made after the opponent has presented the evidence. **2** : a verdict of acquittal ordered by the court on the ground that the evidence is not sufficient to support a conviction when viewed in

the light most favorable to the prosecution : JUDGMENT OF ACQUITTAL at JUDGMENT 1a ⟨motions for *directed verdict* are abolished and motions for judgment of acquittal shall be used in their place —*Federal Rules of Criminal Procedure* Rule 29(a)⟩

directed verdict of acquittal : DIRECTED VERDICT 2 in this entry

excessive verdict : a verdict that awards damages grossly disproportionate to injury and shocks the court's sense of justice and that may be remedied by a lessening of damages or a new trial — see also REMITTITUR

general verdict : a verdict that is either for the plaintiff or for the defendant and is often returned with answers to interrogatories on questions of fact ⟨where there exists a conflict between the *general verdict* and the interrogatories, the trial court may determine that the answers to the interrogatories prevail —*Berk v. Matthews*, 559 N.E.2d 1301 (1990)⟩ — see also INTERROGATORY, SPECIAL INTERROGATORY; compare SPECIAL VERDICT in this entry

in·struct·ed verdict : DIRECTED VERDICT in this entry

partial verdict **1** : a verdict in which a jury does not find all of the defendants in a trial to be guilty **2 a** : a verdict that finds a defendant guilty on some counts and not guilty on others **b** : a verdict in which a jury is unable to reach or has not yet reached agreement on all of the offenses under consideration ◊ The acceptance of partial verdicts before a jury is finished with deliberations may interfere with the deliberative process; having a jury achieve unanimity on a higher charge first discourages compromise verdicts on lesser included offenses. In some jurisdictions it has been considered proper to afford the jury the

\ə\abut \ə'\kitten \ər\further \a\ash \ā\ace
\ä\cot, cart \au̇\out \ch\chin \e\bet \ē\easy
\g\go \i\hit \ī\ice \j\job \ŋ\sing \ō\go \ȯ\law
\ȯi\boy \th\thin \t͟h\the \ü\loot \u̇\foot \y\yet
\zh\vision *see also* Pronunciation Symbols page

opportunity to render a partial verdict of acquittal on a higher charge to avoid declaring a mistrial because of a hopeless deadlock only on a lesser included offense; such a verdict would prevent double jeopardy on the higher charge.

quo•tient verdict \'kwō-shənt-\ : a usu. impermissible verdict that is based on a numerical average of the amounts written down by jurors (as percentages of fault in a comparative negligence case); *specif* : a verdict that awards damages based on the average of the sums written down by the jurors under an agreement that all will be bound by the average figure ⟨*quotient verdicts* are invalid and constitute grounds for a mistrial — *Faverty v. McDonald's Restaurants of Oregon, Inc.*, 892 P.2d 703 (1995)⟩

repugnant verdict : an impermissible verdict that contradicts itself since the defendant is convicted and acquitted of different crimes having identical elements in the same transaction — used chiefly in New York

re•spon•sive verdict \ri-'spän-siv-\ : a verdict that responds to the indictment and accords with statutorily prescribed findings for a particular charge that include guilty, not guilty, and guilty of a prescribed lesser included offense — used in Louisiana ◊ A responsive verdict of guilty on a lesser included offense must be supported by the evidence.

special verdict : a verdict that consists of specific findings of fact (as of liability) in response to interrogatories, that often includes determinations of damages, and that is used by the court in the formation of a judgment — compare GENERAL VERDICT in this entry

2 : an amount awarded in a verdict ⟨reduced the ~⟩

ver•i•fi•ca•tion \ˌver-ə-fə-'kā-shən\ *n* **1** : an act or process of verifying **2** : a sworn statement of truth or correctness ⟨submitted a ~ signed by the defendant with the petition⟩

ver•i•fy \'ver-ə-ˌfī\ *vt* **-fied; -fy•ing**

[Anglo-French *verifier*, from Medieval Latin *verificare*, from Latin *verus* true + *-ficare* to make] **1** : to confirm or substantiate by oath, affidavit, or deposition ⟨~ a motion⟩ **2** : to establish the truth, accuracy, or reality of

ver•ti•cal agreement \'vər-ti-kəl-\ *n* : an agreement among economic competitors on different levels of production or distribution that affects competition — compare HORIZONTAL AGREEMENT ◊ Unlike horizontal agreements, vertical agreements are not considered illegal per se under antitrust laws, but they must withstand judicial scrutiny to be held valid.

vertical price–fixing *n* : an illegal arrangement in which parties at different levels of a system of production and distribution act to fix the market price of goods; *esp* : RESALE PRICE MAINTENANCE — compare HORIZONTAL PRICE-FIXING ◊ Vertical price-fixing is a per se violation of antitrust laws.

vertical privity *n* **1** : privity between one who acquires property burdened with a restrictive covenant and those who executed the covenant ⟨require *vertical privity* for a restrictive covenant to run with the land⟩ **2** : privity between parties (as a manufacturer and retailer) who occupy adjoining levels in a system of product distribution

vertical restraint *n* : a restraint of trade involving parties (as manufacturers and wholesalers) at different levels of a market structure

vest *vb* [Anglo-French *vestir*, literally, to clothe, from Old French, from Latin *vestire*] *vt* **1 a** : to place in the possession, discretion, or province of some person or authority ⟨all legislative powers herein granted shall be ~*ed* in a Congress of the United States — *U.S. Constitution* art. I⟩ ⟨a timely notice of appeal ~*s* jurisdiction in the appeals court⟩; *specif* : to give to a person a fixed and immediate right of present or future enjoyment of (as an estate) ⟨an interest ~*ed* in the beneficiary⟩ **b** : to grant or endow with a particular authority, right, or property ⟨~ a

judge with discretion⟩ ~ *vi* : to become vested; *specif* : to entitle one unconditionally to the payment of pension benefits upon termination or retirement ⟨his pension interest will ~ after ten years with the company⟩ — compare MATURE
vest•ed \'ves-təd\ *adj* **1** : fully and absolutely established as a right, benefit, or privilege : not dependent on any contingency or condition; *specif* : not subject to forfeiture if employment terminates before retirement ⟨~ pension benefits⟩ **2** : having a vested interest ⟨a ~ employee⟩ ⟨a ~ beneficiary⟩
vested estate — see ESTATE 1
vested interest — see INTEREST 1
vested remainder — see REMAINDER
vested right *n* : a right belonging completely and unconditionally to a person as a property interest which cannot be impaired or taken away (as through retroactive legislation) without the consent of the owner
¹ve•to \'vē-tō\ *n, pl* **ve•toes** [Latin, I forbid, refuse assent to] **1** : an authoritative prohibition **2 a** : a power vested in a chief executive to prevent permanently or temporarily the enactment of measures passed by a legislature **b** : the exercise of such authority — see also POCKET VETO; compare LEGISLATIVE VETO
²veto *vt* **ve•toed; ve•to•ing** : to refuse to admit or approve; *specif* : to refuse assent to (a legislative bill) so as to prevent enactment or cause reconsideration — see also OVERRIDE
vex•a•tious \vek-'sā-shəs\ *adj* : lacking a sufficient ground and serving only to annoy or harass when viewed objectively ⟨disciplined the attorney for engaging in ~ litigation⟩
vi•at•i•cal settlement \vī-'a-ti-kəl-\ *n* [probably from Latin *viaticum* provision for a journey] : an agreement by which the owner of a life insurance policy covering a person (as the owner) with a catastrophic or life-threatening illness receives compensation for less than the expected death benefit of the policy in return for an assignment, transfer, sale,

devise, or bequest of the death benefit or ownership of the policy to the other party (as a company specializing in such transactions)
vi•car•i•ous \vī-'kar-ē-əs\ *adj* : imposed on one person in place of another — see also *vicarious liability* at LIABILITY 2b — **vi•car•i•ous•ly** *adv* — **vi•car•i•ous•ness** *n*
vicarious liability — see LIABILITY 2b
¹vice \'vīs\ *n* **1** : a moral fault or failing **2** : DEFECT **3** : immoral activity (as prostitution)
²vice \'vīs, 'vī-sē\ *prep* [Latin, ablative of *vic-* place, turn] : in the place of ⟨I will preside, ~ the absent chairman⟩; *also* : rather than
vice- *prefix* : one that takes the place of ⟨*vice*-chancellor⟩
vice–chan•cel•lor \'vīs-'chan-sə-lər\ *n* **1** : an officer ranking next below a chancellor and serving as deputy **2** : a judge appointed to act for or to assist a chancellor
vice–con•sul \'vīs-'kän-səl\ *n* : a consular officer subordinate to a consul general or to a consul
vice–presidency *n* : the office of vice president
vice president *n* **1** : an officer next in rank to a president and usu. empowered to serve as president in that officer's absence or discharge **2** : any of several officers serving as a president's deputies in charge of particular locations or functions (as sales) — **vice presidential** *adj*
vic•i•nage \'vis-ªn-ij\ *n* [Anglo-French *veisinage* neighborhood, from *veisin* neighboring, from Old French, from Latin *vicinus*] : a particular vicinity or district: as **a** : the district in which a crime takes place and from which the accused is entitled to have an impartial jury selected as required by the Sixth Amendment to the U.S. Constitution **b** *in the civil law of Louisiana* : the neighborhood in which

\ə\abut \ª\kitten \ər\further \a\ash \ā\ace
\ä\cot, cart \au\out \ch\chin \e\bet \ē\easy
\g\go \i\hit \ī\ice \j\job \ŋ\sing \ō\go \o\law
\oi\boy \th\thin \th\the \u\loot \u\foot \y\yet
\zh\vision *see also* Pronunciation Symbols page

one is obligated not to cause material injury to others (as by a nuisance) in the free exercise of rights of ownership in immovable property ⟨these obligations of ∼ are legal servitudes imposed on the owner of property —*Rodrigue v. Copeland*, 475 So. 2d 1071 (1985)⟩

vi•o•late \'vī-ə-ˌlāt\ *vt* **-lat•ed; -lat•ing** : to go against (as a prohibition or principle) : fail to observe or respect ⟨∼ a law⟩ ⟨civil rights were *violated*⟩ ⟨∼ due process⟩ — **vi•o•la•tion** \ˌvī-ə-'lā-shən\ *n* — **vi•o•la•tive** \'vī-ə-ˌlā-tiv\ *adj* — **vi•o•la•tor** \'vī-ə-ˌlā-tər\ *n*

vi•o•lent felony *n* : a crime consisting of conduct that presents a serious risk of potential injury to another or that is punishable by imprisonment for more than one year — used esp. in federal sentencing of career criminals guilty of crimes involving use of a weapon

vir•ile share \'vir-əl-, -ˌīl-\ *n* [partial translation of French *part* (or *portion*) *virile* equally alloted share (as in an intestate inheritance), from Latin *pars virilis*, literally, male's share] *in the civil law of Louisiana* : an amount for which a solidary obligor (as a partner) is liable: as **a** : an amount due from the obligor under a solidary obligation (as a debt) arising from a contract or quasi contract that is equal to that of each other obligor unless there is an agreement or judgment to the contrary **b** : an amount based on the proportionate fault of the obligor when the obligation arises from an offense (as in negligence) or quasi-offense — called also *virile portion*

vi•sa \'vē-zə, -sə\ *n* : an endorsement made on a passport by the proper authorities denoting that it has been examined and that the bearer may proceed

vis•i•ta•tion \ˌvi-zə-'tā-shən\ *n* **1** : an official visit (as for inspection) ⟨∼ of the home of a neglected child⟩ **2** : access to a child granted esp. to a parent who does not have custody ⟨supervised ∼⟩ ⟨∼ rights⟩

vis•i•ta•to•ri•al \ˌvi-zə-tə-'tōr-ē-əl\ *adj* : VISITORIAL

vis•i•to•ri•al \ˌvi-zə-'tōr-ē-əl\ *adj* : of or relating to inspection or supervision ⟨the ∼ powers of the state board of education⟩

vis major \'vis-'mā-jər\ *n* [Latin, literally, greater force] : an overwhelming force; *also* : ACT OF GOD

vi•ti•ate \'vi-shē-ˌāt\ *vt* **-at•ed; -at•ing** : to make ineffective ⟨fraud ∼s a contract⟩

vi•va vo•ce \ˌvī-və-'vō-sē, ˌvē-və-'vō-ˌchä\ *adv or adj* [Medieval Latin, literally, by living voice] : through speech : by word of mouth ⟨testify *viva voce*⟩

¹void \'vȯid\ *adj* **1** : of no force or effect under law ⟨a ∼ marriage⟩ **2** : VOIDABLE — **void•ness** *n*

²void *vt* : to make or declare void ⟨∼ a contract⟩

void•able \'vȯid-ə-bəl\ *adj* : capable of being voided; *specif* : subject to being declared void when one party is wronged by the other ⟨a ∼ contract⟩ — **void•abil•i•ty** \ˌvȯid-ə-'bi-lə-tē\ *n*

voidable preference *n* : PREFERENCE

void–for–vagueness doctrine *n* : a doctrine requiring that a penal statute define a criminal offense with sufficient definiteness that ordinary people can understand what conduct is prohibited and in a manner that does not encourage arbitrary and discriminatory enforcement ◊ Under the void-for-vagueness doctrine, a vague law is a violation of due process because the law does not provide fair warning of a prohibition and fails to set standards for enforcement that would govern the exercise of the police power.

¹voir dire \'vwär-'dir, 'wär-\ *n* [Anglo-French, to speak the truth] : a formal examination esp. to determine qualification (as of a proposed witness) ⟨the judge admitted the witness's expert testimony after a *voir dire* by the attorney⟩; *esp* : the act or process of questioning prospective jurors to determine which are qualified (as by freedom from bias) and suited for service on a jury

²voir dire *vt* **voir dired; voir dir•ing** : to examine in a voir dire proceeding ⟨a motion to *voir dire* the witness outside the presence of the jury⟩ ⟨*voir diring* prospective jurors as to their beliefs concerning the death penalty —*State v. Ortiz*, 540 P.2d 850 (1975) (concur)⟩

vo·len·ti non fit in·ju·ria \vō-'len-ˌtī-ˌnän-ˌfit-in-'jür-ē-ə, wō-'len-tē-ˌnōn-ˌfit-in-'yü-rē-ä\ [New Latin] : to one who is willing no harm is done — used as a common-law maxim expressing the principle that one is not injured when a risk is voluntarily assumed; compare ASSUMPTION OF RISK

vol·un·tary \'vä-lən-ˌter-ē\ *adj* **1 a** : proceeding from one's own free choice or consent rather than as the result of duress, coercion, or deception ⟨a ~ statement⟩ **b** : not compelled by law : done as a matter of choice or agreement ⟨~ arbitration⟩ **c** : made freely and with an understanding of the consequences ⟨a ~ plea of guilty⟩ **2** : done by design or intention **3** : made without valuable consideration or for nominal consideration ⟨a ~ conveyance⟩ — **vol·un·tar·i·ly** \ˌvä-lən-'ter-ə-lē\ *adv* — **vol·un·tar·i·ness** *n*

voluntary bankruptcy *n* : bankruptcy declared upon petition of the debtor — see also BANKRUPTCY

voluntary bar *n* : a bar to which lawyers are not required to belong to practice law in the state — compare INTEGRATED BAR

voluntary deposit — see DEPOSIT 3a

voluntary dismissal — see DISMISSAL

voluntary dissolution — see DISSOLUTION

voluntary lien — see LIEN

voluntary manslaughter — see MANSLAUGHTER

voluntary waste — see WASTE

vol·un·teer \ˌvä-lən-'tir\ *n* **1** : one that voluntarily undertakes something; *esp* : one who without request, obligation, or an interest pays the debt of another and is denied reimbursement from subrogation **2** : one who receives property without giving valuable consideration

¹vote *n* [Latin *votum* vow, hope, wish] **1 a** : a usu. formal expression of opinion or will in response to a proposed decision;

esp : one given as an indication of approval or disapproval of a proposal, motion, or candidate for office **b** : the total number of such votes made known at a single time ⟨got half the ~⟩ **2** : the collective opinion or preference of a body of persons expressed by voting **3** : the right to cast a vote; *specif* : the right of suffrage **4 a** : the act or process of voting ⟨brought the question to a ~⟩ **b** : a method of voting

²vote *vb* **vot·ed; vot·ing** *vi* **1 a** : to cast or conduct a vote ⟨~ for acquittal⟩ **b** : to exercise a political franchise ⟨encourage people to ~⟩ — *vt* **1** : to choose, endorse, decide the disposition of, defeat, or authorize by vote ⟨~ an appropriation⟩ **2** : to cast votes on a corporate matter on the basis of ⟨*voted* their shares against the proposed merger⟩

voting rights *n pl* **1** : rights of participation in esp. public elections — see also *Voting Rights Act* in the IMPORTANT LAWS section **2** : the rights of shareholders or directors to vote on corporate matters — compare *voting stock* at STOCK, *voting trust* at TRUST

voting stock — see STOCK

voting trust — see TRUST

voting trust certificate *n* : a certificate issued as evidence of the holder's beneficial interest in a voting trust

vouch \'vaüch\ *vb* [Anglo-French *voucher* to call, summon, summon to court as guarantor of a title, ultimately from Latin *vocare* to call, summon] *vt* **1** : to summon into court **2** : to verify (a business transaction) by examining documentary evidence ~ *vi* **1** : to become surety **2 a** : to supply supporting evidence or testimony **b** : to give personal assurance

vouch·er \'vaü-chər\ *n* [Anglo-French, summoning of a person to guarantee title, from *voucher* to summon] **1** : a documentary record of a business transaction

2 : a written affidavit or authorization **3 :** a form or check indicating a credit against future purchases or expenditures

vouch·ing *n* **:** an impermissible practice by a prosecutor of placing the prestige of the government behind its witness or otherwise insinuating to the jury that the prosecutor offers personal assurance of the witness's veracity

vouching–in *n* **:** a common-law procedural device in which a defendant named in a lawsuit notifies another that he or she will look to the other for indemnity of an adverse judgment and that the other will be bound by the judgment if he or she refuses to come and defend in court

¹vow *n* **:** a solemn promise or statement; *esp* **:** one by which a person is bound to an act, service, or condition ⟨marriage ∼*s*⟩

²vow *vt* **1 :** to promise solemnly **2 :** to bind or commit by a vow — *vi* **:** to make a vow — **vow·er** *n*

voy·age policy *n* **:** a marine insurance policy covering only a stated voyage

vul·gar substitution \'vəl-gər-\ *n* [French *substitution vulgaire*, from Latin *substitutio vulgaris*, literally, ordinary substitution, as distinguished from *substitutio pupillaris* substitution of an heir in place of a minor who actually receives the testamentary gift but dies before reaching the age of majority] *in the civil law of Louisiana* **:** a testamentary disposition in which the person making the will names another person to take the gift in the event that the instituted heir does not accept it or is already deceased

vulture fund — see FUND 2

W

Wade hearing — see HEARING
wage *n* **1** : a payment usu. of money for labor or services usu. according to a contract and on an hourly, daily, or piece-work basis — often used in pl. **2** *pl* : the share of the national product attributable to labor as a factor in production
wage assignment — see ASSIGNMENT
wait and see *n* : a doctrine in property law that postpones determining the question of validity of a future interest that has not yet vested (as a contingent remainder) until circumstances make clear whether or not the interest will vest within a time limit — compare RULE AGAINST PERPE-TUITIES ◊ A minority of states have adopted the wait and see doctrine.
waive \'wāv\ *vt* **waived; waiv•ing** [Anglo⸗French *waiver, weiver,* literally to abandon, forsake, from *waif, weif* forlorn, stray, probably from Old Norse *veif* something loose or flapping] **1** : to relinquish (as a right or privilege) voluntarily and intentionally ⟨the defendant *waived* a felony hearing on the charge —*National Law Journal*⟩ — compare FORFEIT, RE-SERVE **2** : to refrain from enforcing or requiring ⟨some statutes ~ the age requirement —W. M. McGovern, Jr. *et al.*⟩ — **waiv•able** *adj*
waiv•er \'wā-vər\ *n* [Anglo-French, from *waiver* to waive] : the act of intentionally or knowingly relinquishing or abandoning a known right, claim, or privilege; *also* : the legal instrument evidencing such an act — compare ESTOPPEL, FORFEITURE ◊ Acts or statements made while forming or carrying out a contract may constitute a waiver and prevent a party from enforcing a contractual right (as when an insurer is barred from disclaiming liability because of facts known to it when it issued the insurance policy).

Varying standards are applied by courts to determine if there has been a waiver of various constitutional rights (such as the right to counsel) in criminal cases.
walk•out \'wȯk-ˌau̇t\ *n* **1** : STRIKE **2** : the action of leaving a meeting or organization as an expression of disapproval
wan•ton \'wänt-ᵊn, 'wȯnt-\ *adj* : manifesting extreme indifference to a risk of injury to another that is known or should have been known : characterized by knowledge of and utter disregard for probability of resulting harm ⟨a ~ act⟩ ⟨by such ~ or willful misconduct⟩ — see also RECKLESS ◊ *Wanton, reckless,* and *willful* are often used to refer to an aggravated level of negligence that borders on intent and that is often ground for an award of punitive damages. —**wan•ton•ly** *adv* — **wan•ton•ness** *n*
war crime *n* : an act committed usu. during an international war for which individual criminal liability will be imposed by a domestic or international tribunal; *specif* : a violation of the laws or customs of war as embodied or recognized by international treaty, court decisions, or established practice — usu. used in pl. ◊ Following World War II, the Charter of the International Military Tribunal at Nuremberg first codified war crimes including crimes against humanity. Also encompassed in the legal concept of war crimes is the crime of planning or waging a war of aggression or a war in violation of international treaties.
war criminal *n* : an individual who has committed a war crime

\ə\abut \ᵊ\kitten \ər\further \a\ash \ā\ace
\ä\cot, cart \au̇\out \ch\chin \e\bet \ē\easy
\g\go \i\hit \ī\ice \j\job \ŋ\sing \ō\go \ȯ\law
\ȯi\boy \th\thin \t̲h̲\the \ü\loot \u̇\foot \y\yet
\zh\vision *see also* Pronunciation Symbols page

ward \'word\ *n* **1** : a division of a city for representative, electoral, or administrative purposes **2 a** : a person who by reason of incapacity (as minority or incompetency) is under the control of a guardian **b** : a person who by reason of incapacity is under the protection of a court either directly or through a guardian appointed by the court — called also *ward of the court;* compare INTERDICT — **ward•ship** *n*

war•den *n* [Anglo-French *wardein, gardein* guardian, from *warder, garder* to guard, protect] **1** : an official charged with special supervisory duties or with the enforcement of specified laws or regulations ⟨a game ~⟩ **2** : an official in charge of the operation of a prison

ware•house receipt *n* : a receipt issued by a person engaged in the business of storage for hire that constitutes a document of title

war powers — see POWER 2a

¹**war•rant** \'wȯr-ənt, 'wär-\ *n* [Anglo-French *warant, garant* protector, guarantor, authority, authorization, of Germanic origin] **1** : WARRANTY 2 ⟨an implied ~ of fitness⟩ **2** : a commission or document giving authority to do something: as **a** : an order from one person (as an official) to another to pay public funds to a designated person **b** : a writ issued esp. by a judicial official (as a magistrate) authorizing an officer (as a sheriff) to perform a specified act required for the administration of justice ⟨a ~ of arrest⟩ ⟨by ~ of commitment⟩

administrative warrant : a warrant (as for an administrative search) issued by a judge upon application of an administrative agency

anticipatory search warrant : a search warrant that is issued on the basis of an affidavit showing probable cause that there will be certain evidence at a specific location at a future time — called also *anticipatory warrant*

arrest warrant : a warrant issued to a law enforcement officer ordering the officer to arrest and bring the person named in the warrant before the court or a magistrate ◊ A criminal arrest warrant must be issued based upon probable cause. Not all arrests require an arrest warrant.

bench warrant : a warrant issued by a judge for the arrest of a person who is in contempt of court or indicted

death warrant : a warrant issued to a warden or other prison official to carry out a sentence of death

dis•pos•ses•so•ry warrant \ˌdis-pə-'ze-sə-rē-\ : a warrant issued to evict someone (as a lessee) from real property — used esp. in Georgia

distress warrant : a warrant ordering the distress of property and specifying which items of property are to be distrained

extradition warrant : a warrant for the extradition of a fugitive; *specif* : RENDITION WARRANT in this entry

fugitive warrant : an arrest warrant issued in one jurisdiction for someone who is a fugitive from another jurisdiction — called also *fugitive from justice warrant*

general warrant : a warrant that is unconstitutional because it fails to state with sufficient particularity the place or person to be searched or things to be seized

no–knock search warrant : a search warrant allowing law enforcement officers to enter premises without prior announcement in order to prevent destruction of evidence (as illegal drugs) or harm to the officers — compare EXIGENT CIRCUMSTANCES

rendition warrant : a warrant issued by an official (as a governor) in one jurisdiction (as a state) for the extradition of a fugitive in that jurisdiction to another that is requesting the extradition

search warrant : a warrant authorizing law enforcement officers to conduct a search of a place (as a house or vehicle) or person and usu. also to seize evidence — called also *search and seizure warrant* ◊ The Fourth Amendment to the U.S. Constitution requires that a search warrant for a criminal investigation be issued only upon a showing of probable cause, as established usu. by a sworn affidavit. The search warrant has to specify the premises and persons to be searched as well as what is being searched for. Not all searches require a search warrant. Warrantless searches are permitted when they are of a kind that the courts have found to be reasonable (as by being limited) or when they are prompted by a level of suspicion or belief (as reasonable suspicion or probable cause) that is consistent with the level of intrusion of the search. Some searches have been found to be so intrusive that a court hearing is required before the search is permitted.

3 a : a short-term obligation of a governmental body (as a municipality) issued in anticipation of revenue **b :** an instrument issued by a corporation giving to the holder the right to purchase the capital stock of the corporation at a stated price either prior to a stipulated date or at any future time ⟨stock ~⟩ — compare SUBSCRIPTION — **war·rant·less** *adj*

²**warrant** *vt* [Anglo-French *warentir*, *garantir*, from *garant* protector, guarantor] **1 :** to guarantee esp. by giving assurances that make one liable or responsible: as **a :** to give a warranty (as of title) to **b :** to protect or assure by warranty ⟨the ~*ed* goods⟩ ⟨an assignor is not liable for defaults of the obligor and does not ~ his solvency —*Restatement (Second) of Contracts*⟩ **c :** to state as a warranty : guarantee to be as represented ⟨the seller ~*s* that the car is without defects⟩ ⟨expressly ~*ed* "prior endorsements guaranteed" —J. J. White and R. S. Summers⟩ **2 a :** to authorize by a warrant ⟨a ~*ed* search⟩ **b :** to serve as or give adequate reason or authorization for ⟨~*ed* the awarding of attorney's fees⟩ ⟨was not ~*ed* by the facts⟩ **3 :** to give proof of the authenticity or truth of ⟨a formally ~*ed* statement⟩

war·rant·ee \ˌwȯr-ən-'tē, ˌwär-\ *n* : a person to whom a warranty is given or made
warrant of attorney : a power of attorney authorizing another (as an attorney) to appear in court and confess judgment on the grantor's behalf
war·ran·tor \ˌwȯr-ən-'tȯr, ˌwär-; 'wȯr-ən-tər, 'wär-\ *n* : a person who makes or gives a warranty
war·ran·ty \'wȯr-ən-tē, 'wär-\ *n, pl* **-ties** [modification (influenced by *warrant*) of Anglo-French *garantie*, from *garantir* to protect, warrant] **1 :** a promise in a deed that gives the grantee of an estate recourse (as through an action for damages) against the grantor and the grantor's heirs in case the grantee is evicted by someone holding a paramount title — called also *covenant of warranty;* see also *special warranty deed* and *warranty deed* at DEED **2 a :** a promise in a contract (as for a sale or lease) which states that the subject of the contract is as represented (as in being free from defective workmanship) and which gives the warrantee recourse against the warrantor ⟨a ~ against defects is implied by the sale⟩ — see also *breach of warranty* at BREACH 1a; compare CAVEAT EMPTOR ◊ A warranty was originally considered to extend only to those parties having privity of contract (as the manufacturer and dealer of an automobile), but cases have held that a warranty also extends to the final consumer who does not contract directly with the manufacturer. Both express and implied warranties may be modified, limited, or even waived by agreement of the parties. Breach of a warranty generally does not constitute breach of the entire contract.
express warranty : a warranty that is created in a contract by a statement of fact (as a description) which is made about the object of the contract and which forms a basis of the bargain

\ə\abut \ᵊ\kitten \ər\further \a\ash \ā\ace
\ä\cot, cart \au̇\out \ch\chin \e\bet \ē\easy
\g\go \i\hit \ī\ice \j\job \ŋ\sing \ō\go \ȯ\law
\ȯi\boy \th\thin \t͟h\the \ü\loot \u̇\foot \y\yet
\zh\vision *see also* Pronunciation Symbols page

implied warranty : a warranty that is not expressly stated but that is recognized or imposed by the law based on the nature of the transaction

warranty of fit•ness : a usu. implied warranty that the property being sold is fit for the purpose for which the buyer is purchasing it ◇ Under the Uniform Commercial Code, a seller must know the purpose for which goods are being bought and that the buyer is relying on the seller's skill or judgment in order for a warranty of fitness to be implied.

warranty of habitability : a usu. implied warranty in a residential lease that the leased premises will be habitable ◇ If a landlord breaches a warranty of habitability, a tenant may have such remedies as terminating the tenancy, recovering damages, or withholding rent. The warranty is based in many jurisdictions either on case law or statute.

warranty of merchantability : a usu. implied warranty that the property being sold is merchantable (as by being of a quality that is generally acceptable in that line of trade) ◇ Under the U.C.C., a warranty of merchantability is not implied unless the seller is a merchant with respect to the goods sold.

b : a usu. written guarantee of the integrity of a consumer product and of the maker's responsibility for the repair or replacement of defective parts — see also *Consumer Product Safety Act* in the IMPORTANT LAWS section **3** : a statement made in an insurance policy by the insured that a fact relating to the subject of the insurance or the risk exists or will exist or that some related act has been done or will be done — compare REPRESENTATION ◇ A warranty in an insurance policy must be true or be fulfilled in order for the policy to be valid.

affirmative warranty : a warranty stating that a fact or condition is currently true

promissory warranty : a warranty stating that a fact or condition is and will remain true

warranty deed — see DEED
warranty of fitness — see WARRANTY 2a
warranty of habitability — see WARRANTY 2a
warranty of merchantability — see WARRANTY 2a
war risk insurance *n* : insurance that protects against loss due to acts of war
wash sale *n* [probably from the comparison of such a sale to the act of washing, which does not affect the nature of the thing washed] : a sale and purchase of securities that produces no change of the beneficial owner; *specif* : a sale of securities within 30 days before or after the purchase of substantially identical securities ◇ Any loss from such a sale is not deductible for most taxpayers under the Internal Revenue Code.
waste *n* **1** : destruction of or damage to property that is caused by the act or omission of one (as a lessee, mortgagor, or life tenant) having a lesser estate and is usu. to the injury of another (as an heir, mortgagee, or remainderman) with an interest in the same property ⟨an action for ∼⟩

ame•lio•rat•ing waste \ə-'mēl-yə-ˌrā-tiŋ-\ : waste that leads to improvement of property (as by clearing the way for rebuilding something) — called also *ameliorative waste*

permissive waste : waste caused by the failure of a tenant to take ordinary or proper care of the property

voluntary waste : waste caused by the intentional commission of a destructive act by a tenant

2 : a reduction of the value of assets (as in a trust) caused by a failure to exercise proper care or sound judgment in managing them; *esp* : a transfer of corporate assets (as through excessive executive compensation or a merger) for no legitimate business purpose or for less than what a person of ordinary sound business judgment would consider to be adequate consideration ⟨the essence of a claim of ∼ of corporate assets is the diversion of corporate assets for improper or unnecessary purposes —*Michelson v.*

Duncan, 407 A.2d 211 (1979)⟩ ◊ Waste injures the interests of shareholders.

wasting asset — see ASSET 2

Wa•ter Court *n* : a court in Colorado and Montana with jurisdiction over the determination and administration of rights to water

watered stock — see STOCK

way of necessity : EASEMENT BY IMPLICATION at EASEMENT

ways and means *n pl* **1** : methods and resources for raising the necessary revenues for the expenses of a nation or state **2** *often cap W&M* : a legislative committee with jurisdiction over ways and means

weak mark *n* : a trademark or service mark that is descriptive or suggestive of the product or service and entitled to a lesser degree of protection than a strong mark — compare STRONG MARK

well–plead•ed complaint rule *n* : a rule of procedure that federal question jurisdiction cannot be acquired over a case unless an issue of federal law appears on the face of a properly pleaded complaint ◊ The well-pleaded complaint rule is not satisfied by a defense based on federal law, including a defense of federal preemption, or by anticipation of such a defense in the complaint.

Whar•ton's Rule \'hwȯrt-ᵊnz-\ *n* [after Francis *Wharton* (1820–89), American lawyer and author, who formulated it] : a rule that prohibits the prosecution of two persons for conspiracy to commit a particular offense when the offense in question can only be committed by at least two persons ◊ Wharton's Rule does not apply when legislative intent is to the contrary (as when the legislation imposes a separate punishment for conspiracy to commit a particular crime).

when–issued security — see SECURITY

whis•tle•blow•er \'hwi-səl-,blō-ər\ *n* : an employee who brings wrongdoing by an employer or other employees to the attention of a government or law enforcement agency and who is commonly vested by statute with rights and remedies for retaliation — compare QUI TAM ACTION —

whis•tle•blow•ing \-iŋ\ *n*

white–col•lar crime \'hwīt-'kä-lər-\ *n* : crime that is committed by salaried professional workers or persons in business and that usu. involves a form of financial theft or fraud (as in securities dealing)

white knight *n* : a party (as a corporation) invited to take over a corporation and thereby prevent its acquisition by another — compare RAIDER

whole law *n* : the entire body of laws of a state including its provisions for conflict of laws — compare INTERNAL LAW, RENVOI

whole life insurance — see LIFE INSURANCE

wildcat strike — see STRIKE

wilful *var of* WILLFUL

¹will *n* **1** : the desire, inclination, or choice of a person or group **2** : the faculty of wishing, choosing, desiring, or intending **3** : a legal declaration of a person's wishes regarding the disposal of his or her property after death; *esp* : a formally executed written instrument by which a person makes disposition of his or her estate to take effect after death — see also CODICIL, LIVING WILL, TESTAMENT

antenuptial will : a will that was executed by a person prior to that person's marriage and is usu. revocable by the court if no provision was made for the person's spouse unless an intention not to make such a provision is manifest

conditional will : a will intended to take effect upon a certain contingency and usu. construed as having absolute force when the language pertaining to the condition suggests a general purpose to make a will

counter will : MUTUAL WILL in this entry

holographic will : a will written out in the hand of the testator and accepted as valid in many states provided it meets

\ə\abut \ᵊ\kitten \ər**further** \a\ash \ā\ace
\ä\cot, cart \au̇\out \ch\chin \e\bet \ē**easy**
\g**go** \i\hit \ī\ice \j\job \ŋ\sing \ō\go \ȯ\law
\ȯi\boy \th\thin \t͟h**the** \ü\loot \u̇\foot \y\yet
\zh\vision *see also* Pronunciation Symbols page

statutory requirements (as that no important parts have been altered or replaced in the hand of another and that it has been properly witnessed)

international will : a will written in any language and executed in accordance with procedures established as a result of an international convention so as to be valid as to form regardless of the location of its execution or the assets, nationality, domicile, or residence of the testator ◊ A properly executed international will is still subject to local probate laws; the validity deriving from adherence to statutory requirements for such wills is purely formal, and a will invalid in respect to such requirements may still be valid under other rules.

joint and mutual will : a single will jointly executed by two or more persons and containing reciprocal provisions for the disposition of property owned jointly, severally, or in common upon the death of one of them — called also *joint and reciprocal will*

joint will : a single will jointly executed by two or more persons and containing their respective wills ⟨the execution of a *joint will* or mutual wills does not create a presumption of a contract not to revoke the will or wills —*Maine Revised Statutes*⟩ — compare JOINT AND MUTUAL WILL in this entry ◊ A joint and mutual will is a joint will, but a joint will need not contain reciprocal provisions.

mutual will : one of two separate wills that share reciprocal provisions for the disposition of property in the event of death by one of the parties ⟨a *mutual will* executed in connection with an agreement based on sufficient consideration is both contractual and testamentary in nature —*Pruss v. Pruss*, 514 N.W.2d 335 (1994)⟩ — called also *counter will, reciprocal will;* compare JOINT AND MUTUAL WILL in this entry

mystic will *in the civil law of Louisiana* : a will signed, sealed, witnessed, and notarized according to statutory procedure — called also *mystic testament, se-cret testament* ◊ The Louisiana Civil Code requires that for a mystic will to be valid, the will document itself or the envelope containing it must be closed and sealed and thus presented to the notary public and witnesses, or closed and sealed in their presence, and the testator must declare that it contains his or her signed will. The envelope or closed document must be subscribed by the testator, witnesses, and notary public.

non•in•ter•ven•tion will \ˌnän-ˌin-tər-'ven-chən-\ : a will that provides for an executor to administer the estate without judicial involvement

nuncupative will : a will allowed in some states that is dictated orally before witnesses and set down in writing within a statutorily specified time period (as 30 days) and that is allowed only for one in imminent peril of death from a terminal illness or from military or maritime service

pour–over will : a will that provides for a transfer of assets (as the residue of the estate) to a trust (as an inter vivos trust) upon the death of the testator

reciprocal will : MUTUAL WILL in this entry

— at will : subject to an individual's discretion; *specif* : without a requirement that the employer have just cause for terminating an employee ⟨could be discharged *at will*⟩

²will *vt* **1** : to order or direct by will ⟨~ed that his money be given to charity⟩ **2** : to dispose of by will ⟨~ed the house to their children⟩

will•able \'wi-lə-bəl\ *adj* : capable of being willed

will contest *n* : a dispute or proceeding (as a trial) begun by one who objects to probate of a will on the ground that it is invalid — see also NO CONTEST CLAUSE ◊ The party who contests the will has the burden of proof, and the personal representative of the estate must defend it. Will contests must be brought within a time period prescribed by statute, and in some states are heard by a jury.

will·ful *or* **wil·ful** \'wil-fəl\ *adj* : not accidental : done deliberately or knowingly and often in conscious violation or disregard of the law, duty, or the rights of others ⟨~ injury⟩ ⟨a ~ violation of a court order⟩ — **will·ful·ly** *adv* — **will·ful·ness** *n*

willful blind·ness *n* : deliberate failure to make a reasonable inquiry of wrongdoing (as drug dealing in one's house) despite suspicion or an awareness of the high probability of its existence ◊ Willful blindness involves conscious avoidance of the truth and gives rise to an inference of knowledge of the crime in question.

will substitute *n* : a device (as a trust) used instead of a will to transfer property upon death

wind up *vt* **wound up; wind·ing up** : to bring to an end by taking care of unfinished business ⟨ordered to *wind up* his practice⟩; *specif* : to conclude by removing liabilities and distributing any remaining assets to partners or shareholders ⟨*wind up* the business and affairs of a corporation in dissolution⟩ ⟨*wind up* a receivership⟩

wire fraud — see FRAUD

¹**wire·tap** \'wīr-ˌtap\ *vb* **-tapped; -tap·ping** *vi* : to engage in wiretapping ⟨had probable cause to ~⟩ ~ *vt* : to interpret through wiretapping ⟨a *wiretapped* telephone conversation⟩; *also* : to connect to the telephone line of for the purpose of wiretapping ⟨*wiretapped* her home⟩ — compare BUG, EAVESDROP

²**wiretap** *n* **1** : an act or instance of wiretapping ⟨we have held previously that ~s are a form of a search — *Whack v. State*, 615 A.2d 1226 (1992)⟩ **2** : an electrical connection for wiretapping — compare PEN REGISTER

wire·tap·ping \'wīr-ˌta-piŋ\ *n* : interception of the contents of communication through a secret connection to the telephone line of one whose conversations are to be monitored usu. for purposes of criminal investigation by law enforcement officers ◊ Wiretapping and wiretap evidence are strictly regulated under federal and state laws. An order authorizing wiretapping may be issued only when there is probable cause to believe that a person is committing, has committed, or is about to commit a particular offense, and there must be probable cause to believe that communications relating to such an offense will be obtained. Wiretapping must not be employed when a conversation is privileged, and officers must minimize interception of conversations that are not material to the investigation.

with·draw *vb* **-drew; -drawn; -draw·ing** *vt* **1** : to remove (money) from a place of deposit or investment **2** : to dismiss (a juror) from a jury **3 a** : to eliminate from consideration or set outside a category or group ⟨~ his candidacy⟩ **b** : to cease to proceed with ⟨*withdrew* the question after an objection was sustained⟩ **c** : to take back ⟨~ a plea⟩ **d** : to remove (a motion) from consideration under parliamentary procedure — *vi* **1** : to remove oneself from participation ⟨~ from a case⟩; *specif* : to cease participation in a conspiracy by an affirmative act of renunciation esp. involving confession to the authorities or communication of abandonment to coᵃconspirators **2** : to remove a motion from consideration under parliamentary procedure

with·draw·al *n* **1** : the act or fact of withdrawing ⟨~ from a conspiracy⟩ **2** : removal of money from a place of deposit or investment ⟨a penalty for early ~⟩

with·hold·ing tax *n* : a deduction (as from wages, fees, or dividends) levied at a source of income as advance payment on income tax

¹**wit·ness** *n* [Old English *witnes* knowledge, testimony, witness, from *wit* mind, sense, knowledge] **1 a** : attestation of a fact or event ⟨in ~ whereof the parties have executed this release⟩ **b** : evidence

\ə\abut \ᵊ\kitten \ər\further \a\ash \ā\ace
\ä\cot, cart \au̇\out \ch\chin \e\bet \ē\easy
\g\go \i\hit \ī\ice \j\job \ŋ\sing \ō\go \ȯ\law
\ȯi\boy \th\thin \t͟h\the \ü\loot \u̇\foot \y\yet
\zh\vision *see also* Pronunciation Symbols page

(as of the authenticity of a conveyance by deed) furnished by signature, oath, or seal **2 :** one who gives evidence regarding matters of fact under inquiry; *specif* : one who testifies or is legally qualified to testify in a case or to give evidence before a judicial tribunal or similar inquiry ⟨a ~ before a congressional committee⟩ ⟨no person . . . shall be compelled in any criminal case to be a ~ against himself — *U.S. Constitution* amend. V⟩ — compare AFFIANT, DEPONENT

adverse witness : a witness who is called by or associated with an opposing party or who by statement, conduct, or other evidence (as of relationship) shows bias against or is injurious to the case of the party by whom the witness is called ⟨sought to have his witness declared an *adverse witness* subject to impeachment⟩ — called also *hostile witness;* see also *leading question* at QUESTION 1

alibi witness : a witness upon whom a criminal defendant relies in establishing an alibi

char·ac·ter witness : a witness who testifies as to the character or reputation esp. of a criminal defendant : a witness who gives character evidence

expert witness : a witness (as a medical specialist) who by virtue of special knowledge, skill, training, or experience is qualified to provide testimony to aid the factfinder in matters that exceed the common knowledge of ordinary people

hostile witness : ADVERSE WITNESS in this entry

lay witness : a witness who is not an expert witness

material witness : a witness whose testimony is necessary for trial and whose presence may sometimes be secured by the state by subpoena, custody, or recognizance

prosecuting witness : a witness (as the victim of a crime) whose own allegations initiate the prosecution of the defendant

qualified witness : a witness who has sufficient understanding of a record-

keeping system to provide testimony that forms the proper foundation for admission of evidence under the business records exception to the hearsay rule

rebuttal witness : a witness called upon to rebut evidence already presented

3 : one who is called on to be present at a transaction so as to be able to testify to its occurrence; *specif* : one who sees the execution of an instrument and signs it to confirm its authenticity ⟨a ~ to a will⟩ **4** : EYEWITNESS ⟨a ~ to an assault⟩ — **bear witness** : to furnish or constitute proof or evidence

²witness *vt* **1 :** to furnish evidence or proof of **2 :** to act as witness of: as **a :** to see the execution of (an instrument) and sign for the purpose of establishing authenticity ⟨~ a will⟩ **b :** to be formally present as a witness of (as a transaction or the execution of a convict) **3 a :** to see or experience directly **b :** to take note of ~ *vi* : to bear witness : give evidence

³witness *adj* : being an object or location used to ascertain a precise boundary point esp. on a corner of a tract when marking that point itself is impractical or impossible ⟨a ~ tree⟩ ⟨a ~ corner⟩

witness protection pro·gram *n* : a state or federal program designed to protect prosecution witnesses in serious criminal cases esp. from bodily injury or tampering (as by providing aid in establishing a new identity in a new location)

witness stand *n* : STAND

word of art : TERM OF ART

word of limitation : a word in a deed or will esp. following the name of an intended grantee or devisee that serves to describe the nature or extent of the estate granted or devised — usu. used in pl. ⟨construed "and his heirs" in "to John and his heirs" as *words of limitation* describing an estate in fee simple rather than as words of purchase giving a future interest in the estate to his heirs⟩; compare WORD OF PURCHASE

word of purchase : a word in a deed or will that shows who is to receive the estate — usu. used in pl.; compare WORD OF LIMITATION

work·ers' compensation *n* **1** : compensation for injury to an employee arising out of and in the course of employment that is paid to the worker or dependents by an employer whose strict liability for such compensation is established by statute ◊ Where established by statute, workers' compensation is generally the exclusive remedy for injuries arising from employment, with some exceptions. Workers' compensation statutes commonly include explicit exclusions for injury caused intentionally, by willful misconduct, and by voluntary intoxication from alcohol or illegal drugs. **2** : WORKERS' COMPENSATION INSURANCE

workers' compensation insurance *n* : insurance purchased by an employer or created through self-insurance that provides coverage for workers' compensation claims by injured employees

work·house *n* : a correctional facility for persons guilty of minor criminal violations

working capital — see CAPITAL

working interest — see INTEREST 1

work made for hire *n* : work (as art, music, writing, or a computer program) that is the property of an employer when made by one acting as an employee or is the property of the party for whom it is specially ordered or commissioned when that is expressly stipulated in writing — used in copyright law

work·man's compensation *n* : WORKERS' COMPENSATION

work·men's compensation *n* : WORKERS' COMPENSATION

work·out *n* : an undertaking or plan intended to resolve a problem of indebtedness esp. in lieu of bankruptcy or foreclosure proceedings

work product *n* : the set of materials (as notes), mental impressions, conclusions, opinions, or legal theories developed by or for an attorney in anticipation of litigation or for trial

work product doctrine *n* : a doctrine or

rule that protects an attorney's work product from discovery — called also *work product rule* ◊ This doctrine applies to work product of all kinds, but it may be waived for certain materials (as documents) if the party seeking discovery shows that it has a substantial need of the materials in preparing its own case and that it is unable without undue hardship to obtain the substantial equivalent of the materials by other means.

work release *n* : release of a prisoner from confinement during the day for the purpose of outside employment — **work–release** *adj*

work stoppage *n* : a cessation of work by employees as a job action ◊ *Work stoppage* is often used to refer to a cessation of work that is less serious and more spontaneous than one referred to as a *strike*. As used in the Labor Management Relations Act, *strike* refers to "any ... concerted stoppage of work by employees ... and any concerted slowdown or other concerted interruption of operations by employees."

work–to–rule *n* : the practice of working to the strictest interpretation of the rules as a job action

World Court *n* : INTERNATIONAL COURT OF JUSTICE

wor·thi·er title *n, often cap W&T* : a common-law doctrine providing that an heir receiving a devise of an estate that is the same as the estate he or she would receive by descent if the grantor died without a will receives the property by descent rather than by devise since descent has been thought to convey a better title ◊ The doctrine of worthier title today is usually considered in light of its implication for inter vivos transfers (that is, transfers made between living persons) to an heir. When a grantor makes an inter vivos conveyance of property followed by a fu-

\ə**abut** \ᵊ**kitten** \ər**further** \a**ash** \ā**ace**
\ä**cot, cart** \aù**out** \ch**chin** \e**bet** \ē**easy**
\g**go** \i**hit** \ī**ice** \j**job** \ŋ**sing** \ō**go** \ò**law**
\òi**boy** \th**thin** \t͟h**the** \ü**loot** \ù**foot** \y**yet**
\zh**vision** *see also* Pronunciation Symbols page

ture estate to his or her heirs, the conveyance is deemed to create a reversion in the grantor rather than a remainder, so that the heirs take by descent and receive a superior title than that which would have been received through the remainder.

wrap–around mortgage — see MORT-GAGE

writ \'rit\ *n* [Old English, something written] **1** : a letter that was issued in the name of the English monarch from Anglo-Saxon times to declare his grants, wishes, and commands **2** : an order or mandatory process in writing issued in the name of the sovereign or of a court or judicial officer commanding the person to whom it is directed to perform or refrain from performing a specified act ◊ The writ was a vital official instrument in the old common law of England. A plaintiff commenced a suit at law by choosing the proper form of action and obtaining a writ appropriate to the remedy sought; its issuance forced the defendant to comply or to appear in court and defend. Writs were also in constant use for financial and political purposes of government. While the writ no longer governs civil pleading and has lost many of its applications, the extraordinary writs esp. of habeas corpus, mandamus, prohibition, and certiorari indicate its historical importance as an instrument of judicial authority.

alias writ : a writ issued upon the failure of a previous one

alternative writ : a writ commanding one to perform a mandated act or else to show cause why the act need not be performed — compare PEREMPTORY WRIT in this entry

extraordinary writ : a writ granted as an extraordinary remedy at the discretion of the court in its jurisdiction over officials or inferior tribunals — called also *prerogative writ;* see also CER-TIORARI, HABEAS CORPUS, MANDAMUS, PROCEDENDO, PROHIBITION, QUO WAR-RANTO; compare WRIT OF RIGHT 2 in this entry ◊ Extraordinary writs were

originally writs exercised by royal prerogative.

judicial writ : a writ issued by a court under its own seal for judicial purposes in the course of a proceeding or to enforce a judgment — compare ORIGINAL WRIT in this entry

original writ : a writ formerly used in England that issued out of chancery as the means of bringing a suit and defendant before the court — compare JUDI-CIAL WRIT in this entry ◊ The original writ was superseded by the summons in 1873.

peremptory writ : a writ (as of mandamus) that presents an absolute order without the alternative to show cause ⟨a *peremptory writ* of prohibition⟩ — compare ALTERNATIVE WRIT in this entry

pre•rog•a•tive writ \pri-'rä-gə-tiv-\ : EX-TRAORDINARY WRIT in this entry

writ of assistance **1** : a writ issued to a law officer (as a sheriff or marshal) for the enforcement of a court order or decree; *esp* : one used to enforce an order for the possession of lands **2** : a writ provided for under British rule in colonial America that authorized customs officers to search unspecified places for any smuggled goods ◊ Many colonial courts refused to issue writs of assistance, which were a focus of bitter resentment against arbitrary searches and seizures. Opposition to such writs inspired the provision in the U.S. Constitution requiring that a search warrant describe with particularity the place and items to be searched.

writ of coram nobis : WRIT OF ERROR CORAM NOBIS in this entry

writ of error : a common-law writ directing an inferior court to remit the record of an action to the reviewing court in order that an error of law may be corrected if it exists ◊ The writ of error has been largely abolished and superseded by the appeal.

writ of error coram nobis : a writ calling the attention of the trial court to facts which do not appear on the record despite the exercise of reasonable diligence by the defendant and which if known and established at the time a judgment was rendered would have resulted in a different judgment ⟨petitioned for a *writ of error coram nobis* on the ground that newly discovered evidence exonerated him⟩ — called also *coram nobis, writ of coram nobis*

writ of right 1 : a common-law writ formerly used to restore property held by another to its rightful owner **2 :** a writ granted as a matter of right — compare EXTRAORDINARY WRIT in this entry

write down *vt* **wrote down; writ·ten down; writ·ing down :** to reduce the book value of (an asset) ⟨*write down* accounts receivable⟩ — **write–down** \'rīt-ˌdaün\ *n*

write–off \'rīt-ˌóf\ *n* **1 :** the elimination of an asset or amount due from the books **2 :** TAX WRITE-OFF

write off *vt* **1 :** to eliminate (an asset) from the books **:** enter as a loss or expense ⟨*write off* a bad loan⟩ **2 :** to use as a deduction in calculating taxable income ⟨*write off* the cost as a business expense⟩

write up *vt* **:** to increase the book value of (an asset) — **write–up** \'rīt-ˌəp\ *n*

writ of assistance — see WRIT
writ of certiorari : CERTIORARI
writ of coram nobis — see WRIT
writ of debt : DEBT 2
writ of error — see WRIT
writ of error coram nobis — see WRIT
writ of right — see WRIT
writ·ten premium *n* **:** premium received by an insurer in a particular period and esp. annually

¹wrong *n* **1 :** a violation of the rights of another; *esp* **:** TORT **2 :** something (as conduct, practices, or qualities) contrary to justice, goodness, equity, or law ⟨the difference between right and ~⟩

²wrong *vt* **:** to do a wrong to **:** treat with injustice

wrong·do·er \'róŋ-ˌdü-ər\ *n* **:** one (as a criminal or tortfeasor) who does wrong

wrong·do·ing \'róŋ-ˌdü-iŋ\ *n* **:** injurious,

criminal, or improper behavior ⟨denied any ~⟩

wrong·ful \'róŋ-fəl\ *adj* **1 :** constituting a wrong; *esp* **:** injurious to the rights of another ⟨a ~ act or omission⟩ **2 :** UNLAWFUL ⟨remained in ~ occupation of the property⟩ ⟨a ~ occupant⟩ — **wrong·ful·ly** *adv* — **wrong·ful·ness** *n*

wrongful birth *n* **:** a malpractice claim brought by the parents of a child born with a birth defect against a physician or health-care provider whose alleged negligence (as in prenatal testing or diagnosis) effectively deprived the parents of the opportunity to make an informed decision whether to avoid or terminate the pregnancy; *also* **:** the birth or injury at issue in such a claim ⟨recognize a cause of action for *wrongful birth*⟩ ◊ Two factors behind the general recognition of the wrongful birth claim are scientific advances in prenatal diagnosis of birth defects and the legalization of abortion. Wrongful birth and wrongful life are distinct from malpractice claims alleging actual physical injury to a fetus caused by a negligently performed procedure.

wrongful con·cep·tion \-kən-'sep-shən\ *n* **:** WRONGFUL PREGNANCY

wrongful death *n* **:** a death caused by the negligent, willful, or wrongful act, neglect, omission, or default of another ⟨sought damages for the *wrongful death* of their murdered daughter⟩

wrongful death action *n* **:** an action that is brought by and in the name of the personal representative (as a spouse or parent) of one who dies a wrongful death and that seeks damages for the benefit of the survivors or the estate of the decedent — compare SURVIVAL ACTION ◊ A wrongful death action is intended to compensate for injury to beneficiaries and not the injury to the decedent. The right to bring such an action is defined by statute.

\ə**abut** \ᵊ**kitten** \ər**further** \a**ash** \ā**ace**
\ä**cot, cart** \aü**out** \ch**chin** \e**bet** \ē**easy**
\g**go** \i**hit** \ī**ice** \j**job** \ŋ**sing** \ō**go** \ó**law**
\ói**boy** \th**thin** \th̲**the** \ü**loot** \ù**foot** \y**yet**
\zh**vision** *see also* Pronunciation Symbols page

wrongful discharge — see DISCHARGE

wrongful dishonor *n* : a wrongful refusal by a payor bank to honor an item that is properly payable ⟨a payor bank is liable to its customer for damages proximately caused by the *wrongful dishonor* of an item — *Uniform Commercial Code*⟩

wrongful life *n* : a malpractice claim brought by or on behalf of a child born with a birth defect alleging that he or she would never have been born if not for the negligent advice or treatment provided to the parents by a physician or health-care provider; *also* : the life or injury at issue in such a claim ⟨recovery for *wrongful life*⟩ ◊ Wrongful life claims have usu. been rejected by the courts. The injury is not the birth defect, but the life itself, and courts are reluctant to declare life an injury. A specific calculation of damages for wrongful life would entail affixing a monetary value to the difference between life in an impaired state and nonexistence. There is no legally established right not to be born.

wrongful preg·nan·cy *n* : a malpractice claim brought by the parents of a healthy but unwanted child usu. against a physician or health-care provider for alleged negligence in performing a sterilization or abortion procedure and sometimes against a pharmacist or pharmaceutical manufacturer of contraceptives; *also* : the pregnancy or injury at issue in such a claim ⟨an action for *wrongful pregnancy*⟩ — called also *wrongful conception* ◊ A majority of courts faced with the issue have disallowed damages for child-rearing expenses in wrongful pregnancy cases. It is more common to recover for medical expenses, pain and suffering, lost wages, or loss of consortium from pregnancy and childbirth.

XYZ

¹x \'eks\ *n, often cap* **1 :** a mark used in place of a signature when the maker is incapable of signing his or her name (as because of illiteracy or a physical ailment) **2 :** a mark used in indicating a choice or applicable item (as on an insurance form)
²x *abbr* **1** ex-distribution **2** ex-dividend **3** ex-rights **4** ex-warrants
xd *abbr* ex-dividend
xr *abbr* ex-rights
xw *abbr* ex-warrants
year–and–a–day rule *n* **:** a common-law rule that relieves a defendant of responsibility for homicide if the victim lives for more than one year and one day after being injured ◇ The year-and-a-day rule, which dates from at least 1278, is frequently criticized as anachronistic since modern medicine makes pinpointing cause of death easier than it was formerly. However, the rule still exists or is reflected in the law of some jurisdictions.
yellow–dog contract — see CONTRACT
¹yield \'yēld\ *vt* **:** to produce as return from an expenditure or investment **:** furnish as profit or interest ⟨an account that ∼*s* 6 percent⟩ ∼ *vi* **1 :** to give place or precedence (as to one having a superior right or claim) **2 :** to relinquish the floor of a legislative assembly ⟨∼ to the senator from Maine⟩
²yield *n* **1 :** agricultural production esp. per acre of crop **2 :** the return on a financial investment usu. expressed as a percentage of cost ⟨the bond ∼ was 8 percent⟩
Younger abstention — see ABSTENTION
youth·ful offender *n* **:** a young person (as one within a statutorily specified age range) who commits a crime but is granted special status entitling him or her to a more lenient punishment (as one involving probation or confinement in a special youth correctional facility) than

would otherwise be available — compare JUVENILE DELINQUENT, STATUS OFFENDER ◇ Young individuals who are no longer juveniles may be categorized as youthful offenders. Youthful offender treatment is generally designed to free a young person from the negative consequences of being convicted and punished as an adult, in the hope that he or she will be rehabilitated. Factors in the determination of youthful offender status include the crime and the criminal history of the individual.
ZBA *abbr* zero bracket amount
Z–bond \'zē-ˌbänd\ *n* **:** ACCRUAL BOND at BOND 2
ze·ro brack·et amount *n* **:** a deduction from gross income that was permitted for federal taxpayers and reflected in tax tables until its replacement by the standard deduction in 1986
zero–coupon bond — see BOND 2
zip·per clause *n* [from the comparison of such a clause to the closing action of a zipper] **:** a clause in a labor contract indicating that the agreement is an exclusive and complete expression of consent ◇ A zipper clause may constitute a waiver of the right to bargain over issues negotiated in or outside the terms of a contract until its expiration.
¹zone *n* **:** a specifically designated section of a larger area or territory: as **a :** a section of a municipality controlled by specific restrictions on permitted use (as for residences or agriculture) **b :** a distance within which the same fare is charged by a common carrier **c :** a stretch of roadway

\ə\abut \ᵊ\kitten \ər\further \a\ash \ā\ace
\ä\cot, cart \aù\out \ch\chin \e\bet \ē\easy
\g\go \i\hit \ī\ice \j\job \ŋ\sing \ō\go \ò\law
\òi\boy \th\thin \th̲\the \ü\loot \ù\foot \y\yet
\zh\vision *see also* Pronunciation Symbols page

or a space within which certain traffic regulations are in force

²zone *vt* **zoned; zon·ing 1 a :** to partition (as a city or town) by ordinance into sections reserved for different purposes (as residence or business) **b :** to designate the permitted use of (property) by placement in a municipal zone ⟨land *zoned* for agricultural use⟩ **2 :** to restrict different kinds of (use) to different areas ⟨the power to ∼ land use within its borders⟩

zone of dan·ger : the area within which one is in actual physical peril from the negligent conduct of another person ◊ Some jurisdictions require that a bystander who witnesses a direct injury to another can only recover for negligent infliction of emotional distress if he or she was also in the zone of danger—that is, in actual danger of physical injury.

zone of employment : the area in and around a place of employment that is under the control of the employer ◊ For workers' compensation purposes, an injury to an employee going to or coming from work in the zone of employment is sometimes considered to have occurred in the course of employment.

zone of interest : the range or category of interests that a statute or constitutional guarantee is intended to protect — called also *zone of interests* ◊ The interest of a party seeking to enforce a law or guarantee in a challenge to an action by the government (as by an administrative agency) must fall within the zone of interest protected by the law or guarantee in question, and the party must have suffered an injury in fact to that interest.

zone of privacy : an area or aspect of life that is held to be protected from intrusion by a specific constitutional guarantee (as of the right to be secure in one's person, house, papers, or effects against unreasonable searches or seizures) or is the object of an expectation of privacy ⟨allowed disclosure of medical records, records which were deemed to fall within a *zone of privacy*, upon a showing of proper government interest —*Stenger v. Lehigh Valley Hosp. Ctr.*, 609 A.2d 796 (1992)⟩ — compare EXPECTATION OF PRIVACY, PENUMBRA 2

zoning *n* **:** municipal or county regulation of land use effected through the creation and enforcement of zones under local law

The Judicial System

Classifications of Law   543
The American Court System   548
Court and Law Enforcement Personnel   556
Court Procedures   559

Classifications of Law

Law may be classified in several ways: by system (common and civil law), by source (constitutional, statutory, and case law), by the parties involved (public and private law), by substance (civil and criminal law), and by function (substantive and procedural law). Each of these classifications is discussed in the sections that follow.

Common Law and Civil Law Systems

The two primary systems of American law are the common law system and the civil law system. The common-law system, which developed in England, is the most prevalent system of law in North America. The civil law system in North America is strongest in Louisiana in the United States and in Quebec in Canada; it is also prevalent in Mexico.

The common-law system is based on precedent and the principle of stare decisis. Although the legislative bodies at the federal, state, and local levels enact written statutes, and sometimes collect portions of those statutes into "codes," there is no formal, comprehensive code of common law. Instead, the common law is stated in court decisions, and it is changed or modified by subsequent cases or statutes.

The civil law system may be traced back to the Roman law from which most European law systems originated. It was brought to the Western Hemisphere by the French, Spanish, and Portuguese. The civil law system as it exists in Europe is the result of Napoleon Bonaparte's efforts: he provided for the drafting of the *Code Civil* or *Code Napoleon*, which restated the earlier principles of Roman law in more modern terms. In the civil law system, the Code Civil is a general statement of legal principles that is looked to in the interpretation of statutes and cases, and civilian courts do not follow the principle of stare decisis. The civil law system also does not have a division between law and equity.

Constitutional Law

A constitution is the basic framework for a legal and governmental system. It defines basic principles of law that all other laws must follow and delegates authority to various officials and agencies. Constitutions are created by the people acting in their collective capacity as sovereign in the nation or state in which they live.

The United States Constitution is the supreme law of the United States. No other federal or state law, statute, or case may impose upon its provisions.

The U.S. Constitution is divided into three parts. The first part, Articles I–VII, divides governmental power among the three branches of government (legislative, executive, and judicial) and between the federal and state governments, describes the relationships between the states, and sets out the means for amending the Constitution. Two methods are provided for proposing amendments (two thirds of both houses of Congress, or a Constitutional Convention called for by the legislatures of two thirds of the states), and two methods are provided for ratifying the proposed amendments (three fourths of the legislatures or three fourths of the conventions called in each state). By requiring a supermajority (i.e., at least two thirds), the framers made sure that any constitutional changes would have such general acceptance throughout the nation that the possibility of a legal challenge or outright rebellion would be minimized.

The second part of the Constitution is the Bill of Rights, which consists of the Constitution's first ten amendments. The Tenth Amendment specifies that powers not reserved by the U.S. Constitution for the federal government reside with the states. The first nine amendments provide for and protect individual freedoms. The First Amendment provides for freedom of religion, speech, press, assembly, and petition for redress of grievances. Other amendments protect the ability to keep arms, the freedom from unreasonable searches and seizures, and the right to speedy and public jury trials in criminal cases and jury trials in civil cases. These have been among the most widely debated concepts in constitutional law.

The third part of the Constitution—the additional amendments that have been added over the past 200 years—reflects the efforts to keep it current with respect to changing social and political needs. These amendments cover a wide range of subjects. The Thirteenth Amendment abolished slavery in 1865. The Fourteenth Amendment granted the equal protection of the laws and due process of law to all the citizens and residents of the various states. The Fifteenth, Nineteenth, Twenty-fourth, and Twenty-sixth Amendments extended the right to vote. The Eighteenth Amendment prohibited the manufacture and sale of intoxicating beverages, and the Twenty-first Amendment repealed the Eighteenth Amendment.

States also have constitutions, which are often more detailed than the U.S. Constitution. When a court is interpreting a state constitution, it may find correctly that the state constitution gives people within that state more rights than the same language contained in the U.S. Constitution. Because of the supremacy clause of the U.S. Constitution, however, no state can give its people *fewer* rights than those in the U.S. Constitution.

Statutory Law

Statutes are enacted by the legislative branch of government (whether federal or state) to regulate areas within the legislature's jurisdiction, as granted by the Constitution.

The United States Congress (by authority of Article I, Section 8, of the Constitution) has reserved to itself the power to regulate certain activities and functions, including patents, trademarks, copyrights, federal taxation, customs matters, the postal system, admiralty matters, bankruptcy, and diplomatic matters. It has the exclusive right to pass laws affecting these subjects. Congress also has power to pass legislation in areas not specifically assigned to it by the Constitution—such as labor and pollution control—that fall within its enumerated powers.

A law passed by Congress is not effective until it is signed into law by the president or has been repassed over the president's veto by a two-thirds majority of each house of the Congress, or if the president takes no action within 10 days of receiving it. Laws are published at the end of each session of Congress in the *Statutes at Large (Stat.)*, where the laws are arranged chronologically, and are ultimately compiled in the *United States Code (U.S.C.)*, where the laws are grouped by subject. (Various private publishers also publish annotated editions of the United States Code.) This Code is organized into 50 titles or general subject areas (see Table).

Titles of the United States Code

1. General Provisions	26. Internal Revenue Code
2. The Congress	27. Intoxicating Liquors
3. The President	28. Judiciary and Judicial Procedure
4. Flag and Seal, Seat of Government and the States	29. Labor
	30. Mineral Lands and Mining
5. Government Organization and Employees	31. Money and Finance
6. Surety Bonds [repealed, and most provisions covered under title 31]	32. National Guard
	33. Navigation and Navigable Waters
7. Agriculture	34. Navy [eliminated by the enactment of title 10]
8. Aliens and Nationality	35. Patents
9. Arbitration	36. Patriotic Societies and Observances
10. Armed Forces	37. Pay and Allowances of the Uniformed Services
11. Bankruptcy	
12. Banks and Banking	38. Veterans' Benefits
13. Census	39. Postal Service
14. Coast Guard	40. Public Buildings, Property, and Works
15. Commerce and Trade	41. Public Contracts
16. Conservation	42. The Public Health and Welfare
17. Copyrights	43. Public Lands
18. Crimes and Criminal Procedure	44. Public Printing and Documents
19. Customs Duties	45. Railroads
20. Education	46. Shipping
21. Food and Drugs	47. Telegraphs, Telephones, and Radiotelegraphs
22. Foreign Relations and Intercourse	48. Territories and Insular Possessions
23. Highways	49. Transportation
24. Hospitals and Asylums	50. War and National Defense (with Appendix)
25. Indians	

Each year the state legislatures also pass many laws, which become effective when they either receive gubernatorial approval or are passed over the governor's veto. The exact titles of the state session laws—that is, the collections of statutes passed in each session of the state legislature—vary, as do the titles given to the state law compilations. In Michigan, for example, they are known as *Michigan Compiled Laws*; in Minnesota they are called *Minnesota Statutes Annotated*; in North Dakota they are called the *North Dakota Century Code*. (Like the United States Code, some of these compilations are published in annotated editions by private law-book publishers.)

Relationship of constitutions, statutes, and the courts   Because of the supremacy clause in the Constitution, federal laws must comply only with the federal Constitution, but the laws of any state must comply with provisions of both the state constitution and the federal Constitution. In a conflict between a federal and a state law, the federal law preempts the state law.

Statutory law is superior to case law as a source of law, and courts ordinarily are bound to apply the relevant statutory law to the cases that they decide. However, if a state legislature were to pass a law in violation of the state constitution—for example, a law requiring that all textbooks be submitted to a review board—the appellate court in the state could declare the law unconstitutional. Courts will also interpret statutes and supply legal principles when no rule exists. Once the court issues a decision, the decision becomes part of the case law on the subject.

Case Law

Case law or *common law* is the law made by courts. It is known as case law because it derives from judicial decisions in legal cases rather than from written statutes. This means that as a court decides and reports its decision concerning a particular suit, this case becomes part of the body of law and can be consulted in later cases involving similar problems.

Prior to the development of constitutional and statutory law, controversies were decided on the basis of established customs. If there were no established customs, judges decided a case on the basis of what they considered to be right and wrong. As these decisions began to be recorded, judges were directed to look for guidance to the decision in a prior case that had similar facts. This use of precedents is known as *stare decisis*—literally, "to stand by (previous) decisions." *Stare decisis* is important because it provides for consistency in the application of common law and offers some assurance to a person seeking relief in the courts as to the rules governing the likely outcome of the case.

Cases are published in reporters (such as *United States Reports*) that are produced either by the government or a private publishing firm. Not all cases are published.

Equity law A review of the common law is not complete without examining *equity law*, which has its origins in English common law.

Since legal rules cannot be formulated to deal adequately with every possible contingency, applying them mechanically can sometimes result in injustice. To remedy such injustices, the law of equity was developed. The principle of equity is as old as the English common law, but it was hardly needed until the 14th century, since the law until that time was still relatively fluid and informal. As the common law became firmly established, however, its strict rules of proof began to cause hardship. Power to grant relief in situations involving potential injustices lay with the king and the lord chancellor. Eventually the chancellor's jurisdiction developed into the Court of Chancery, whose function was to administer equity. The chancellor decided each case on its merits and had the right to grant or refuse relief without giving reasons, but common grounds for relief, such as fraud and breach of confidence, came to be recognized. And because the defendant could file an answer, a system of written pleadings developed.

Although a few states in the United States still have separate courts of equity and courts of law, most jurisdictions have merged the procedures of law and equity courts. Although the procedures are merged, the question of whether remedies are legal or equitable is important for determining whether a plaintiff is entitled to a jury trial. Equity law continues to provide unusual and personal remedies for legal disputes of a civil nature. Two of the most familiar equity decrees are the *injunction* and *specific performance*. An injunction restrains a party from doing something that would cause irreparable harm if not enjoined or temporarily halted. For example, an injunction may order a manufacturer to stop dumping certain chemicals into a river. Specific performance requires the performance of a duty agreed on in a contract or other agreement.

Public and Private Law

Another classification of laws is based on the scope of the laws, that is, on the parties to whom they apply. This classification includes public and private law.

Private law governs the relationship between private citizens. Disputes may involve property, contracts, negligence, wills, and any number of other matters. Occasionally, as in marriage and divorce, the state may be involved indirectly, but, as the state is not itself a litigant, the matter remains one of private law.

Public law is a branch of law concerned with regulating the relations of individuals among themselves and with the government as well as the organization and conduct of government itself. Public-law disputes involve the state or its agencies in a direct manner. Usually the state is a litigant; it is often the plaintiff, the party bringing the suit to court. Examples of public law are municipal law, township law, criminal law, admiralty law, securities law, social security law, and aviation law.

When individual laws are referred to, however, there is a different kind of distinction between public and private laws. Specifically, a private law is a law that affects only selected individuals or localities, while a public law affects the welfare of the whole governed unit. A private law provides a kind of exception to the public rule.

Administrative law has become a major part of public law. Administrative law comprises the rules and regulations framed and enforced by a federal or state administrative agency as well as any rulings that the agency makes. Administrative bodies, while primarily executive in nature, may be delegated some legislative or judicial authority. For example, the Federal Aviation Administration not only issues regulations for air transportation but also adjudicates some disputes between airlines and their customers. The rules and regulations created by the federal administrative agencies are first published chronologically in the *Federal Register* (*Fed. Reg.*) and then later organized by subject in the *Code of Federal Regulations* (*C.F.R.*). See Important Agencies for information on some of the federal agencies.

State and local governments also have administrative agencies that issue rules, regulations, and rulings. They may be a part of an executive department of the state government or they may be independent entities. These agencies tend to regulate areas not preempted by federal agencies, but they may also be found in fields subject to both federal and state regulation. State administrative agencies often have jurisdiction over these areas: unemployment and workers' compensation, taxation, education, motor vehicles, zoning, and health and safety. States publish their administrative law in compilations similar to the *Federal Register* and *Code of Federal Regulations*.

Civil and Criminal Law

Cases that come before a court may generally be divided into two categories: *civil* and *criminal*. Civil law deals with acts that injure a person or a person's rights. Civil law provides remedies, such as monetary damages or declaratory relief, that are intended primarily to compensate the injured party. Civil law covers numerous areas, including real estate, domestic relations, partnership, taxes, contracts, and wills and trusts.

Criminal law declares what conduct is criminal and prescribes the punishment to be imposed for it. A criminal action is always prosecuted in the name of the federal government ("The United States of America"), the state ("The People of the State of . . . "; "The State of . . . "), or a political subdivision, because the case is based on the alleged violation of the rights of *all* the people. The remedy sought in a criminal case is intended to punish the offender. The major categories of crimes are crimes against the person (as homicide or assault) or crimes against property (as arson or theft). A single act may be the basis for both civil and criminal penalties.

Substantive and Procedural Law

Substantive law consists of the statutory and case law setting forth rights and obligations upon which a controversy is based, whereas *procedural* or *adjective* law states the rules by which a person can secure his or her substantive rights. Thus, procedural law consists of the rules of procedure or practice according to which the substantive law is administered. Procedural law deals with *pleadings*, which are papers that pass between the parties; *practice*, which refers to the conduct of litigation; and *evidence*, or the admissibility of evidence to achieve fairness while avoiding u   expense or delay.

Although procedural law does not state the law, it outlines the procedures that must be followed in applying the substantive law. Procedural law enables the attorney to decide whether a case should go to federal or state court. It will tell the attorney when a lawsuit must be started, what pleadings are required of all parties, and what kind of evidence can be presented at trial. Procedural law can be as important as the substantive law in determining the outcome of a case because a case may be thrown out if the proper procedures are not followed.

The American Court System

The complexity of a state judicial system is normally in direct proportion to the population of the governmental unit. The judiciaries of many states with small populations are much less complex than the judiciaries of some large cities. Furthermore, some of the municipal judicial systems are nearly as autonomous within the state system as the state system is within the federal system. Article III, Section 1, of the U.S. Constitution creates the federal judicial system. It says: "The judicial power of the United States, shall be vested in one Supreme Court, and in such inferior courts as the Congress may from time to time ordain and establish." Sections 2 and 3 spell out the extent of the judicial power afforded the Supreme Court and the subordinate federal courts. In turn, the constitutions of the various states have created state judicial systems, many of them similar to the federal judicial system. The American judicial system is composed of the federal courts, created by the Constitution or Congress under its constitutional powers, and the state courts, created by state constitutions and legislatures.

The Courts

The term *court* has several meanings. One meaning encompasses all the persons who are assembled for the administration of justice; these include the judge or judges, clerk, marshal, bailiff, court reporter or public stenographer, jurors, and attorneys. *Court* may also refer to the hall, chamber, or place where a judicial proceeding is being held. The courthouse includes the offices occupied by many of the persons associated with the administration of justice. And frequently the judge or judges themselves are referred to as "the Court."

The two principal functions of courts are settling controversies between parties and deciding the rules of law applicable in a particular case. In general, the judicial process as carried out by the courts consists of interpreting the laws and applying them justly to all cases arising in litigation. Most courts do not give advisory opinions. Exceptions exist, however, where the constitutions of some states permit the supreme courts of those states to render advisory opinions to the legislature or governor concerning the constitutionality of a statute.

Jurisdiction

Jurisdiction may be defined as the authority of a court to hear a controversy or dispute. Because there are both federal and state courts, one of the first procedural steps in bringing a suit is to decide the court in which it should be brought. Some courts have exclusive jurisdiction over certain matters, as is the case with tax or bankruptcy courts, but in many cases there may be concurrent jurisdiction between two courts, as a state court and a federal district court. A court must have jurisdiction over either the parties or the property involved in the controversy. There are many federal and state statutes outlining the jurisdiction of the various courts.

Original and appellate jurisdiction Jurisdiction is either original or appellate. A court of *original jurisdiction* has the authority to receive the case when begun, to try the case, and to render a decision based on the law and facts presented. *Appellate jurisdiction*, which is set by statute or constitution, is the authority to review, overrule, or revise the action of a lower court.

The American judicial system, at both the state and federal level, is pyramidal and hierarchical. The courts at the top of the pyramid are supreme courts. Supreme courts are normally appellate courts, although they may have original jurisdiction in some matters. Below the supreme appellate courts are usually intermediate appellate courts. These courts generally hear most initial appeals and have appellate jurisdiction and supervisory control over the trial courts except as laws provide otherwise, but they are also courts of original jurisdiction in certain areas prescribed by constitution or statute. Trial courts are courts of either general or limited jurisdiction whose decisions are subject to review and correction by appellate courts.

Concurrent and exclusive jurisdiction   Jurisdiction is exclusive when only one court is empowered by law to hear the case in question. It is concurrent when the plaintiff has a choice of courts in which to initiate litigation.

Equity   Most courts of general jurisdiction serve as both courts of common law and courts of equity. When these courts maintain separate dockets (agendas) for law and equity cases, they will follow different procedures for each docket. When these courts are allowed to combine law and equity cases, they may award both money damages (financial compensation) and equitable relief (remedial measures). Some states continue to maintain completely separate courts of equity known as *chancery courts*, or courts with chancery divisions that have equity jurisdiction. The judges in these courts of equity are called *chancellors*, and the judgments they render are usually called *decrees*.

Courts of limited jurisdiction   Some trial courts are courts of limited jurisdiction. Courts of limited jurisdiction are ordinarily created by statute, and their jurisdiction is limited to those matters set forth in the statute. Courts of limited jurisdiction include *district courts, county courts, municipal courts, county district courts, juvenile courts*, and *probate courts*. Courts of limited jurisdiction may have exclusive jurisdiction where the amount in controversy does not exceed a fixed amount. They may also have jurisdiction over minor criminal matters, such as misdemeanors or ordinance violations. A record may be kept in courts of limited jurisdiction. However, in small-claims divisions of district courts and in justice of the peace courts, municipal courts, or magistrate courts, it may be that no verbatim record of the proceedings will be kept.

The Federal Court System

The federal courts form a part of the federal judicial system, the jurisdiction of which is prescribed by Article III of the Constitution. The federal court system consists of a Supreme Court of the United States, 13 federal courts of appeals, a large number of district courts that serve as courts of general jurisdiction, and a number of specialized courts created by the Congress under the necessary and proper clause of Article I.

The Supreme Court of the United States   The Supreme Court of the United States was created in accordance with Article III, Section 1, of the U.S. Constitution and was organized on February 2, 1790. The Supreme Court is made up of the Chief Justice of the United States and a number of associate justices; currently there are eight associate justices. The president has the power to nominate the justices, and appointments are made with the advice and consent of the Senate. The Supreme Court's term runs from the first Monday in October of each year until business is completed, usually about the end of June. The nine justices sit *en banc* (in full court). Six justices constitute a quorum (minimum number required to constitute a lawful bench), but certain cases can be acted upon by a single justice acting as a circuit justice.

Article III, Section 2, of the Constitution defines the original and exclusive jurisdiction of the Supreme Court as (1) all controversies between states, and (2) all actions or proceedings against ambassadors or other public ministers of foreign states or their domestic servants, not inconsistent with the law of nations. The Court has original but *not* exclusive jurisdiction over (1) all actions or proceedings brought by ambassadors or other public ministers of foreign states or to which consuls or vice consuls of foreign states are parties, (2) all controversies between the United States and a state, and (3) all actions or proceedings by a state against the citizens of another state or against aliens.

The Court only occasionally hears cases in original jurisdiction, however; its chief function is as an appellate court. The Supreme Court may review cases from the U.S. courts of appeals either by writ of certiorari (a written mandate to call up the records of a subordinate court) granted to petitioners that are party to any civil or criminal case, or by certification of a question of federal law in a civil or criminal case by a court of appeals. Both of these appeals are granted at the court's discretion. There is also a very limited right of direct appeal from a three-judge district court panel. A majority of Supreme Court cases come on petition for certiorari.

The Supreme Court may also review, by writ of certiorari, the final judgment of the highest court of a state in which a decision on a case may be rendered if (1) there is a question as to the validity of a treaty or statute of the United States, (2) the validity of a state statute has been questioned as being unconstitutional or illegal, or (3) a title, right, privilege, or immunity is claimed under the Constitution or treaties or statutes of the United States.

The Supreme Court normally reviews fewer than 200 cases each year. By contrast, it refuses to review about 2,000 cases each year: the majority of its decisions consist of denials of certiorari to review decisions of courts of appeals or state supreme courts.

The Supreme Court also possesses statutory power to prescribe rules of procedure to be followed in the lower federal courts. Studies are carried out and rules recommended by the Judicial Conference of the United States, the main policy-making group for the federal judiciary. The Supreme Court has set rules of procedure governing such matters as bankruptcy proceedings, copyright cases, appellate proceedings, civil law, and criminal law. These rules of procedure for the federal courts are published with the decisions of the Supreme Court in the *United States Reports* (abbreviated *U.S.*) and also as appendices to some of the titles of the *United States Code*.

United States Courts of Appeals   The courts of appeals were created in 1891, to relieve the Supreme Court of the task of considering all appeals for cases originally decided by the federal trial courts. By statute, they are empowered to review all final decisions and certain provisional decisions of federal district courts, except when direct review by the Supreme Court is provided for. The courts of appeals are also empowered to review and enforce orders of many federal administrative agencies, and also to review appeals from the Tax Court of the United States. Decisions of the courts of appeals are final but subject to discretionary review by the Supreme Court. Each of the 50 states is assigned to one of 11 judicial circuits (see Fig. 1). There is an additional circuit for the District of Columbia, and another for the Federal Circuit. Each court of appeals usually hears cases in divisions consisting of a panel of three judges; however, it may sit *en banc* with all judges present. The number of judges assigned to each court of appeals is fixed by statute. Individual judges make decisions for the court only in procedural matters.

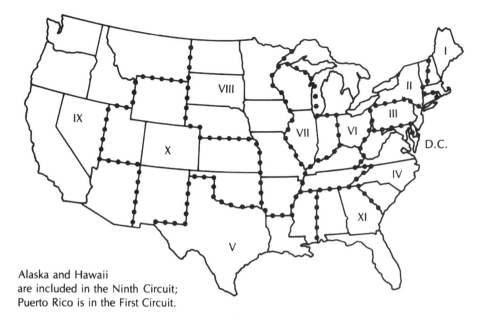

Alaska and Hawaii
are included in the Ninth Circuit;
Puerto Rico is in the First Circuit.

Fig. 1 Circuits of the United States Courts of Appeals

United States District Courts   The district courts are federal trial courts with general federal jurisdiction. There is at least one district court in each state, while some larger states have as many as four. There are in all 92 federal district courts in the 50 states plus one in the District of Columbia and one in Puerto Rico. The number of federal district court judges is fixed by statute. Normally only one judge hears a case, but in certain cases a three-judge panel is required.

Each district court is served by a clerk, a U.S. attorney, a U.S. marshal, and one or more U.S. magistrates, bankruptcy judges, probation officers, and court reporters. Magistrates are federal judicial officers who serve under the general supervision of the federal district, but who also have some responsibilities as defined in the Federal Magistrate Act of 1979. These responsibilities include the power to conduct some trials, to enter sentences for misdemeanors or infractions, to conduct hearings (including evidentiary hearings), and to hear and determine pretrial matters pending before the court.

The jurisdiction of the federal district courts is set forth in the *United States Code*. These courts possess only original jurisdiction. Among the cases tried are those involving crimes against the United States, cases involving diversity of citizenship (cases in which a citizen of one state brings a suit against a citizen of another state), admiralty and maritime cases, cases involving review and enforcement of orders of most federal administrative agencies, and civil cases arising under federal statutes, treaties, or the Constitution. When the federal district court exercises diversity jurisdiction, it is not necessary for a question of federal law to be involved. In the diversity cases, the district court applies the law of the state in which the case arose. Bankruptcy and parole cases form a large part of their work in addition to the regular civil and criminal cases.

In each district court, the bankruptcy judges constitute a unit of the court known as the bankruptcy court for that district. Each bankruptcy court may have its own clerk. The bankruptcy court has exclusive jurisdiction to hear all matters arising under the bankruptcy code and any matters

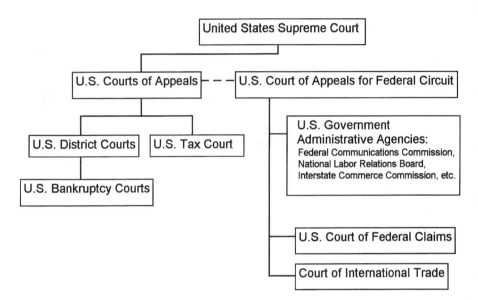

Fig. 2 Federal Court System

concerning the administration of a bankruptcy estate. Decisions of a bankruptcy court may be reviewed first by the district court, then by a federal court of appeals.

Special United States Courts   In addition to the courts discussed above, Congress, often under the necessary and proper clause of Article I, has created special courts from time to time to deal with particular kinds of cases. Appeals from decisions of these courts may ultimately be reviewed by the Supreme Court. Among those courts are the District of Columbia's local courts—the Superior Court and the District of Columbia Court of Appeals—which are not part of the federal court system. Other courts include the U.S. Court of Appeals for the Armed Forces, which is concerned exclusively with military criminal law, and the Territorial Courts, which function as district courts for the territories of Guam, the U.S. Virgin Islands, and the Northern Mariana Islands. The three major special courts—the U.S. Court of Federal Claims, the Court of International Trade, and the U.S. Tax Court—are described below. The former U.S. Court of Customs and Patent Appeals has been superseded by the Court of Appeals for the Federal Circuit (see Fig. 2).

United States Court of Federal Claims   The U.S. Court of Federal Claims was originally established in 1855 as the Court of Claims. It has original jurisdiction to render judgment on claims other than tort claims against the United States. Examples are claims for compensation for the taking of property, claims arising under construction and supply contracts, claims by civilian and military personnel for back pay and retirement pay, and claims for the refund of federal income and excise taxes. The demonstrated purpose for the establishment of the court was to relieve Congress of pressure to pass private bills to resolve claims. If the monetary amount of damages is small, claims may be settled by the federal executive departments involved, but large claims are filed either in the district courts or in the Court of Federal Claims, which have concurrent jurisdiction. Judgments of the court are final and conclusive, subject to review by the Court of Appeals for the Federal Circuit.

Court of International Trade   The Court of International Trade was created in 1926 as the U.S. Customs Court. Through subsequent legislation it was integrated into the federal court system and became a court of record. This court deals with questions of external revenue, while the U.S. Tax Court deals with questions of internal revenue. The Court of International Trade has exclusive jurisdiction of civil actions under the tariff laws, such as controversies over the appraised value of imported merchandise. The court has a chief judge and eight additional judges, not more than five of whom can belong to the same political party. The Chief Justice of the United States may temporarily designate and assign any of its judges to serve as a federal-circuit or district-court judge. Ordinarily cases are tried before a single judge, although a three-judge panel may be used. Appeals are taken to the Court of Appeals for the Federal Circuit. The principal offices of the court are in New York City, but its nine judges are divided among three divisions that can conduct trials in ports other than New York.

United States Tax Court   The U.S. Tax Court is a court of record established in 1942, and it consists of 19 members. The Tax Court tries and decides controversies involving deficiencies or overpayment in income, estate, gift, and personal-holding-company surtaxes in cases where deficiencies have been determined by the Commissioner of Internal Revenue. It hears taxpayers' claims against the Internal Revenue Service after the machinery of administrative adjudication within the Treasury Department has been exhausted. Other than in small tax cases, all decisions are subject to review by the federal courts of appeals (excluding the Court of Appeals for the Federal Circuit) and ultimately by the Supreme Court. The Tax Court, which is located in Washington, D.C., has 19 divisions, one for each of its judges. Trials are public and are conducted by single judges in locations throughout the country.

State Court Systems

The judicial power of the states is limited by the full faith and credit clause of the U.S. Constitution, which states: "full faith and credit shall be given in each state to the public acts, records, and judicial proceedings of every other state." It is further limited by the due process clause of the Fourteenth Amendment, which states: "No state shall make or enforce any law which shall abridge the privileges or immunities of citizens of the United States; nor shall any state deprive any person of life, liberty, or property, without due process of law; nor deny to any person within its jurisdiction the equal protection of the laws."

Federal courts have exclusive jurisdiction in those areas provided for under the Constitution—namely, conflicts between states, conflicts between a state and the United States, petitions for federal regulatory agencies to enforce a decision, and prosecution of national criminal laws—and under federal statutes; state courts cannot share this jurisdiction. State courts, in turn, usually have exclusive jurisdiction over matters not held by the federal courts. Two areas that have remained exclusive to the states are probate and domestic relations. State courts may hold concurrent jurisdiction with federal courts in many other areas; there are many situations where claims may be litigated in either a federal or state court, as when the requirements for federal diversity jurisdiction are met but there is no federal law involved in the case. It is in the state courts, however, that most of the litigation problems that arise in the lives of most U.S. citizens are resolved. Conflicts resolved by state courts include those involving domestic relations, common crimes and misdemeanors, business relationships, morals offenses, personal injury and property damage, real estate, and aspects of business practice such as sales and secured transactions.

The states frequently experiment with restructuring their court systems, although the basic structure of a supreme court, an intermediate appellate court, and a trial court of general jurisdiction is usually maintained (see Fig. 3).

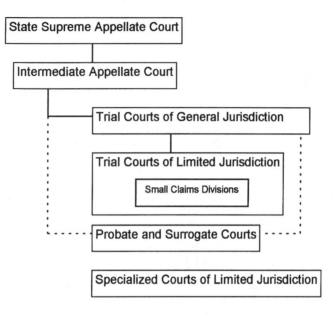

Fig. 3 State Court System

State supreme courts   The highest court in a state is usually called the Supreme Court, although in some states it is called the Court of Appeals (New York and Maryland), the Supreme Court of Appeals (West Virginia), or the Supreme Judicial Court (Maine and Massachusetts).

The supreme court in most states is given supervisory control over and appellate jurisdiction from all other courts in the state judicial system, limited only by the constitution and statutes. The supreme appellate court draws its authority from the state constitution. Appeals to the supreme court from lower state courts may be either mandatory (required by law) or discretionary (granted by the court). The court rules and/or statutes will set forth the grounds on which either may be accomplished. In a few states that do not have an intermediate appellate court, appeals are made directly to the supreme appellate court. States with an intermediate appellate court usually require that an appeal from a court of original jurisdiction go to the intermediate court, but in a very few cases direct appeal to the supreme appellate court may be allowed. For example, in Illinois direct appeal to the state supreme court is possible in cases in which a circuit court imposes the death penalty. In states with an intermediate appellate court, the supreme court may have complete control over those cases that it is willing to hear. Ordinarily the state supreme court has very few areas of original jurisdiction.

Intermediate appellate courts   Most states have intermediate courts of appeal. In most cases the intermediate appellate court was created to lessen the caseload of the supreme appellate court. Intermediate appellate courts ordinarily have initial appellate jurisdiction over the final judgments of a state's trial court of general jurisdiction. The jurisdiction of the intermediate court of appeal may be established by statute, by rule of the supreme appellate court, or both. Intermediate courts of appeal may exercise original jurisdiction when it is required for the complete determination of a case on review and may issue certain writs when permitted by statute or court rule.

Trial courts of general jurisdiction   Below the supreme and intermediate appellate courts in the state judicial hierarchy is the trial court of general jurisdiction. It may be called the *circuit court*, the *superior court*, the *district court*, the *court of common pleas*, or, in New York, the *supreme court*.

This court ordinarily has the authority to try both civil and criminal cases except where the constitution or a statute has limited that jurisdiction; it is also normally empowered to try cases arising under both equity and common law. The circuit court usually has appellate jurisdiction and supervisory control over subordinate courts except as provided by law, and it ordinarily possesses the power to issue extraordinary writs. A basic rule to remember is that the circuit court has original jurisdiction in any matter unless that jurisdiction has been specifically placed in some other court by the state constitution or by statute.

Circuit courts are geographically organized, with each circuit serving one or more counties. Each circuit may have one or more judges assigned to it, although each case is usually heard by a single judge.

State courts of general jurisdiction are courts of record. This means that their acts, decisions, and proceedings are documented in a written record that is maintained by the clerk of the court. Records of court decisions and the processes that led to those decisions are important. Without such records it is difficult to challenge a decision successfully in a higher court.

Trial courts of limited jurisdiction   Whether called *municipal courts* or *district courts* or by some other name, most states have trial courts of limited jurisdiction. The jurisdiction of these courts may vary from matters of the type usually handled by the circuit court to lesser matters such as traffic offenses, minor criminal matters, ordinance violations, and probable-cause hearings. These courts may also be given exclusive jurisdiction over common-law claims up to a determined monetary limit, such as $10,000 or $25,000. The jurisdiction of the court will ordinarily determine whether it is a court of record, and that in turn determines whether and to what court an appeal may be taken. The territorial authority of these courts is ordinarily confined to the city or county in which the court is located.

These courts may also have a *small-claims division*. Cases heard in the small-claims division are limited as to the amount that the court may award as damages. Lawyers are usually prohibited from representing litigants in small-claims cases, and no juries and no appeals are permitted.

Specialized courts of limited jurisdiction   Specialized courts of limited jurisdiction include *probate* or *surrogate courts, family courts, traffic courts*, and in some instances subordinate courts variously designated as *justice of the peace courts*, *magistrate courts*, and *police courts*.

Many states have separate *probate* or *surrogate courts*. The jurisdiction of such courts is limited in subject matter but not by geographical or monetary restrictions. In some states probate courts may be organized into districts, with a single court serving more than one county. The jurisdiction of the probate court is ordinarily limited to the settlement of estates, wills, and guardianship of minors and legally incompetent persons. In some states the probate courts also have jurisdiction over juvenile delinquents, neglected children, dependents, the adoption of children, and other matters such as name changes. Appeals from probate court may be taken to the intermediate appellate court or to the trial court of general jurisdiction.

Several states have either *juvenile* or *family-law courts*. Juvenile courts standing alone will ordinarily have exclusive original jurisdiction over all neglected, dependent, or delinquent children under a certain age. Family-law courts will have exclusive jurisdiction over divorce, separation, annulment, support actions, suits involving temporary custody of children, and adoption. In some cases, the functions of the juvenile and family-law courts are combined, and the court has original jurisdiction over all of these matters.

Traffic courts are courts of limited jurisdiction geographically, monetarily, and with respect to the punishment that may be meted out. Jurisdiction is ordinarily limited to misdemeanors and traffic violations. While the traffic court is not a court of record, it is sometimes possible to appeal a traffic court's decision, depending on the statute that created the court.

A few states have retained the *police court*. Jurisdiction is limited to misdemeanor offenses and to the conduct of preliminary examinations determining whether there is sufficient evidence to bind the case over to the court with jurisdiction for further proceeding. In some states the police court has jurisdiction to try civil cases within geographical and monetary limits.

American Indian Tribal Courts

Outside the structure of the federal and state courts are the Native American—officially *American Indian*—*tribal courts*. These courts function under their own structures, enabling statutes, and court rules, and are limited only by the most fundamental concepts of U.S. Constitutional law.

In any divorce case in a state court, if any of the children of the marriage are American Indian, the state court must surrender jurisdiction regarding issues of custody and visitation to a tribal court for decision. Similarly, a state court cannot exercise jurisdiction over an American Indian child with regard to adoption or other issues determinative of the child's familial status.

Tribal courts also adjudicate matters arising on or concerning tribal lands, such as hunting and fishing rights, oil and gas rights, development rights, and rights of ownership and rental. Some of these rights may be granted by treaties with the federal government. Contracts with American Indian tribes may require that disputes or enforcement be brought before tribal courts. In recent years American Indian tribes have become increasingly engaged in gambling enterprises as a way of generating needed revenues for their communities, and cases involving gambling debts owed by non-Native Americans may be adjudicated in tribal courts. Similarly, criminal cases arising from violation of tribal laws may be adjudicated in tribal courts.

Court and Law Enforcement Personnel

Officers of the Court

The officers of the court are persons assembled at the court to administer justice. They include the judge, who is the principal officer of the court, the lawyers, the clerk of the court, the sheriff, the marshal, the bailiff, and possibly a constable or court officer.

Judges   A judge may be elected or appointed. Judges in the federal judiciary, with the exception of the judges for the Article I courts, are appointed for life by the president with the advice and consent of the Senate. Candidates for the federal judiciary are cleared through the office of the Deputy U.S. Attorney General, who receives reports of each candidate from the FBI and the American Bar Association. The Senate Judiciary Committee then conducts hearings on the nomination and makes a recommendation to the full Senate.

There are five methods of selecting judges in the states. The leading method is selection by partisan election, often following nomination at party primaries or conventions. Slightly less common is the nonpartisan election. The remaining states use either elections by the legislature, gubernatorial appointments, or the Missouri Plan. The Missouri Plan, so called because of its place of origin, was designed to overcome the weaknesses of the elective system. It permits the governor to select a judge from a list of nominees recommended by a special commission but also requires the judge to be voted on in a public referendum after serving a period of time.

At trials and hearings the judge presides and rules on issues occurring during the trial. In jury cases, the judge presides over the selection of the jury and instructs the jury concerning the law of the case. The judge may also be called upon to rule on motions made before the start of the trial.

From the time the oath of office is taken, judges at all levels are bound to conduct themselves in an ethical manner and to adhere to a code of judicial conduct. A Model Code of Judicial Conduct was adopted by the American Bar Association in 1972 and was most recently amended in 1990. Its seven basic canons are as follows:

Canon 1   A judge should uphold the integrity and independence of the judiciary.

Canon 2   A judge should avoid impropriety and the appearance of impropriety in all activities.

Canon 3   A judge should perform the duties of office impartially and diligently.

Canon 4   A judge may engage in activities to improve the law, the legal system, and the administration of justice.

Canon 5   A judge should regulate extra-judicial activities to minimize the risk of conflict with judicial duties.

Canon 6   A judge should regularly file reports of compensation received for quasi-judicial and extra-judicial activities and of monetary contributions.

Canon 7   A judge or a candidate for judicial office should refrain from political activity inappropriate to judicial office.

Some states, such as New York and California, have adopted the Model Code with some modifications as state law. Violation of the canons of the Model Code and the state codes subjects a judge to disciplinary action.

State laws determine whether the court officers are referred to as judges or justices. In most states, as in the federal judiciary, the term *justice* is reserved for the members of the supreme appellate court.

Administration of the courts   The Chief Justice of the United States is the chief administrative officer of the federal judiciary. As the title implies, he or she is not merely the Chief Justice of the Supreme Court, but the Chief Justice of the entire United States. Each federal court of appeals and district court has a chief judge. With the assistance of a circuit executive, the chief judge of a circuit administers most of the work of the court of appeals. The chief judge of a federal district court usually takes responsibility for most of the administration of that court. However, chief judges do not have authority over their fellow judges in rendering case decisions. In deciding cases, the authority of chief judges is the same as that of any other judge.

Chief justices of the state supreme appellate courts, depending upon the language of the state constitution, may or may not be the chief judicial officers in the state. As chief justices, however, they do have influence over the administration of the entire court system through the supreme appellate court's superintending or rulemaking power. They are also responsible for the administration of the appellate courts.

Chief judges of intermediate appellate courts are responsible for the administration of those courts according to the constitution, statute, or court rule describing their responsibilities. Within the power given it, each court establishes rules to assist in the administration of the court.

Attorneys   Attorneys are also officers of the court. They are responsible for the preparation, management, and trial of their clients' cases. Like judges, they are held to a code of professional conduct. The Model Rules of Professional Conduct, adopted by the American Bar Association in 1983 and regularly amended, seek to guide the attorney in the conduct of his or her various roles in relation to clients, the court, the public, and society in general. If a lawyer is found guilty of violating these ethical standards, he or she is subject to discipline, including reprimands, fines, suspension, and even disbarment. Most states have adopted the Model Rules with some modifications as state law.

Other court personnel   Other officers assigned to the court include the clerk and the sheriff. The *clerk* schedules trials and officially records all court business. The clerk is responsible for maintaining the completeness, accuracy, and integrity of the court files, and in that capacity receives and files all court papers, including copies of summonses, complaints, answers, amendments, motions, and appearances, and also issues some papers, as summonses and writs, upon the order of a judge. In addition, the court clerk is responsible for the care of the jury. The *sheriff*, in addition to keeping the peace in the jurisdiction, serves summonses, complaints, and other court documents and carries out court orders. Some of the civil functions of the sheriff may be performed by a designated court officer.

There is a *marshal* for each federal judicial district and for the Superior Court of the District of Columbia. Marshals are appointed by the president, with the advice and consent of the Senate, to serve four-year terms. They and their deputies are primarily responsible for providing security within and outside the courtroom for federal judges, court officials, witnesses, and jurors. They are also responsible for (1) serving as marshals of the federal district court and of the federal court of appeals when those courts are sitting in the district; (2) executing all writs, processes, and orders issued under the authority of the United States, including those of the courts; and (3) paying the salaries and expenses of the U.S. attorneys and their staffs, and the marshals' own staffs. Marshals and their deputies may also exercise the same powers as sheriffs of the state in which they are located.

The *bailiff* is responsible for the protection of everyone in the courtroom and for maintaining the dignity and decorum of court proceedings.

Courts of record also employ a *court reporter*, who is responsible for making a complete and accurate verbatim record of every word spoken during a trial or hearing before the court. This record may be taken down by sound recording or stenography, or by using a stenotype machine.

Additional court personnel may include law clerks and secretaries assigned to judges, a vast number of office workers in the office of the clerk of court, probation officers with their clerical staffs, and law clerks to the court reporters. In the federal district courts there are bankruptcy trustees with their staffs. The larger courts may also employ a number of messengers and librarians.

Law Enforcement Agencies

The United States Department of Justice   The U.S. Department of Justice, created in 1870, is headed by the U.S. Attorney General, who directs all the affairs and activities of the department. The Department of Justice conducts the United States' case in appeals before the Supreme Court whenever the United States in involved. The Solicitor General usually argues special cases for the government in the Supreme Court, while members of his or her staff represent the government in other cases. The Justice Department also represents the government in legal matters generally, giving legal advice and opinions to the president and the heads of executive departments when requested.

The Attorney General supervises these activities and also directs the U.S. attorneys and U.S. marshals in the judicial districts around the country. (There is one U.S. district attorney and one

U.S. marshal for every federal judicial district.) The Deputy Attorney General is primarily concerned with criminal law or investigative matters; he or she also directs the Executive Office of United States Attorneys. The Associate Attorney General generally supervises criminal matters. An Assistant Attorney General for Administration is responsible for matters relating to the internal administration of the department. The assistant attorney general in charge of the Office of Legal Counsel serves as legal adviser to the president and the heads of executive branch agencies.

Divisions within the Department of Justice include the Antitrust Division, the Civil Rights Division, the Civil Division, the Criminal Division, the Environment and Natural Resources Division, and the Tax Division. The divisions may institute investigations or supervise or direct litigation in federal courts. Other bureaus and administrative units within the Department of Justice are the Federal Bureau of Investigation, the Bureau of Prisons, the U.S. Marshals Service, the Immigration and Naturalization Service, the Drug Enforcement Administration, the Foreign Claims Settlement Commission, and the U.S. Sentencing Commission.

State law enforcement offices   The *state attorney general* is the principal law enforcement officer in a state. The office brings actions in the name of the state when appropriate, serves as legal counsel to the legislative and executive branches, and issues opinions clarifying or interpreting statutes. The attorney general may also intervene in suits where it is felt the state's interest should be represented. The office, however, is much weaker than that of the U.S. Attorney General.

The chief local law enforcement officer may be called the *prosecuting attorney, state attorney*, or *district attorney.*

The office of the *public defender* is now active in many states. Public defenders provide legal counsel for people of limited means in both trial and appellate courts.

Court Procedures

Legal procedures vary from state to state and from court to court. This lack of uniformity has led legislatures and bar associations to try to reduce the number of disparities among various jurisdictions by standardizing court procedures, legal terminology, and legal documents. Standardizing legal procedures is of great value to the courts and the legal profession in the efficient administration of justice and the handling of cases in court.

In an effort to simplify common-law pleading, Congress in 1938 adopted a set of rules known as the *Federal Rules of Civil Procedure*. These rules set out each step in a civil proceeding, including the method of preparing required documents in all federal courts. Since then, the majority of the states have adopted similar rules. Consequently, the rules of procedure in the state courts are to a certain extent now uniform.

Types of Court Action

The courts have responsibility in three general areas—criminal, civil, and equity law. In most jurisdictions, the same courts try cases in all three areas. In a few jurisdictions, special courts known as chancery courts hear equity cases, and some states have separate courts for civil and criminal cases. Under the Federal Rules of Civil Procedure, there is no longer a distinction between law and equity in the preparation of pleadings in federal civil law cases.

Criminal actions   An individual or a group breaking a law designed to protect society from harm is considered to have committed a crime. Because the public has suffered as a result of the crime, the people of the state or of the United States bring the action; they are represented in court by a public official who may be known as a *district attorney*, a *public prosecutor*, or a *United States* *attorney.* The jurisdiction of each court determines the types of crimes that are to be prosecuted there. Courts of limited jurisdiction generally hear lesser crimes, or misdemeanors, while courts of general jurisdiction try the more serious crimes, or felonies.

Civil actions   A civil case may arise when the actions of an individual or a group cause harm to another, who then goes to court seeking compensation for that harm. The injured party, called the *plaintiff* or *complainant*, asks the court to grant damages in the form of a payment of money. In some jurisdictions, if either party in the case requests it, a jury may hear the trial. If neither party requests a jury, the judge renders judgment after hearing both sides. In most civil actions the party who brings the action must present a *preponderance of the evidence* or the action will fail.

Equity actions   In most jurisdictions equity actions are encompassed within civil actions, although a few states provide separate courts of equity. In equity cases the party who brings suit is called the *petitioner* or *complainant*. The petitioner asks the court to order the opposing party, usually known as the *respondent*, to perform or to cease from performing a specific act. Equity will be sought when relief is not available to the petitioner through money damages. There is no right to jury trial at equity; the judge alone makes the decision. The decision of the judge in a case in equity is, technically, a *decree* rather than a judgment; in practice, however, the words are commonly interchanged.

Steps in Criminal Procedure

Arrest   An individual may file an informal complaint with a law enforcement officer, after which a judge signs a warrant, which is written authority for a law-enforcement officer to make an arrest. The officer may also make an arrest without a warrant if there is probable cause to do so. In some cases a grand jury must be convened to determine whether there is cause to indict an alleged criminal perpetrator. An accused taken into custody must be informed of his or her rights of representation and against self-incrimination.

Bail   Bail is a deposit of money that helps to guarantee that an accused person will appear for trial at the time and date specified. After the accused has been taken into custody, the court may set bail and temporarily release the accused person. If he or she does not appear, bail is forfeited, and the accused is considered a fugitive. If the accused can reasonably be expected to appear when ordered, the court may release the accused on his or her own recognizance (that is, without bail), depending on local rules and the seriousness of the crime.

Preliminary hearing   A preliminary hearing is held to determine whether there is probable cause for holding the accused for trial. A preliminary hearing may also be held to fix bail. In the case of certain less serious crimes the preliminary hearing may follow the arraignment (see below).

Arraignment   The next step in a criminal procedure is an arraignment. Arraigning an accused person has three purposes: (1) to establish the identity of the accused; (2) to inform the accused of the charges; and (3) to allow the court to hear the plea of the accused—that is, the answer to the charge, or a declaration of guilt or innocence.

After being formally charged, and usually before the start of a trial, a defendant may arrange with the prosecution to enter a guilty plea to a lesser charge, if the prosecution is willing to charge the defendant with a lesser crime.

Trial   The U.S. Constitution guarantees a right to a jury trial in a criminal trial; this right, however, may be waived by the defendant. If the trial is to be held before a jury, it is selected and sworn in. A trial jury typically consists of 12 citizens who listen to the facts and present their decision, the verdict. In criminal actions a unanimous vote of the jurors is usually necessary. In a jury trial, the judge rules on points of law and the jury decides questions of fact.

After the jury has been sworn in, the trial usually follows this sequence: (1) opening statement by the prosecutor; (2) opening statement by the defendant's lawyer (this may be delayed, however, until the beginning of step 4); (3) presentation of evidence by the prosecutor; (4) presentation of evidence by the defendant's lawyer; (5) closing argument by the prosecutor; (6) closing argument by the defendant's lawyer; and (7) the judge's charge or instructions to the jury.

The judge charges the jury, instructing them regarding the law that relates to the case, and provides guidance in reaching a verdict. The judge prepares the instructions, but prior to the trial each attorney prepares and submits to the judge a set of requested *jury instructions*. In this way, each attorney can make sure that the judge does not overlook any point that the attorney considers important.

Verdict   The jury retires to a private room and considers the case. A vote of the jury is taken to arrive at a decision. The defendant may be acquitted, found guilty, or a mistrial may be declared by the judge if the jury cannot reach a decision. If the defendant is found guilty, the judge has the authority to impose sentence, although in some jurisdictions the jury will determine the sentence. In serious cases, another hearing might be held to determine the sentence. The sentence is based on specific findings of fact, as the presence of aggravating or mitigating circumstances, and conclusions of law. The verdict is signed by the judge and recorded so that it may be included in the transcript of the case. If the accused is found guilty, the case may be appealed. After acquittal, a criminal defendant cannot be tried again for the same crime. If a mistrial is declared, there must be a new trial with a new jury.

Steps in Civil Procedure

Civil procedure consists of four fairly well-defined phases: (1) pleadings, (2) discovery, (3) trial and judgment, and (4) conclusion of litigation.

Phase 1: Pleadings   The general term *pleadings* refers to the series of written claims and defenses that establish what is in controversy or at issue, on what grounds the action is being based, and who is involved.

Complaint   As the first step in a civil lawsuit, the plaintiff's attorney files a *complaint*, which may also be known as a *petition* or a *declaration*, against the defendant. Where courts of equity exist, the first pleading in an equity action is called a *bill of complaint* or a *bill in equity*. The complaint states the specific injury suffered by the plaintiff, the acts of the defendant alleged to have caused that injury, and the remedy, as damages, being sought.

Summons   The defendant must be given positive notice that a complaint has been filed and that a response to the complaint must be made. This notice is called a *summons*, and in most states it must be served with a copy of the complaint. Once the action has been initiated by filing and serving the complaint and summons, it cannot be terminated unless specified legal steps are taken. Also, once notice is received, the defendant must make some response to the summons and complaint within a specified time in order to avoid a default judgment.

Objections   Rules of court procedure require that a complaint be clear, definite, and complete and that it be prepared in accordance with the law and the rules of the court. When the defense believes that the complaint is not in accordance with court rules or the law, the attorney may object to it by means of various documents such as a *demurrer*, a *motion to strike*, a *motion to quash*, or a *motion for more definite statement*. These documents, and others, attempt to invalidate the complaint on the ground that it is not supported by a cause of action recognized by law. As these documents are based on points of law, most courts require a supporting document to be prepared and attached. This document may be a brief, a legal memorandum, or a memorandum of points and authorities.

Answer   The next step in a civil action is the preparation of an answer, in which the defendant responds to the factual allegations in the complaint. The answer must state any affirmative defenses, as estoppel, that the defendant intends to use against the plaintiff's claims or the defendant will not usually be allowed to assert them during the trial. Court rules in many jurisdictions permit the answer to contain a *counterclaim* against the plaintiff. The counterclaim does not reply to an allegation but states a cause of action that the defendant has against the plaintiff. The defendant may also make a *cross-claim* or *cross-complaint* against another defendant. The cross-claim may be filed and served as a document separate from the answer, or it may be combined with the answer into one document. Additional parties other than the original plaintiff and defendant may be joined and made subject to the counterclaims, cross-claims, and third-party claims during the exchange of pleadings.

Phase 2: Discovery   When the initial pleading stage of litigation is concluded, the attorneys will attempt to locate all witnesses and uncover all evidence while learning as much as possible about the issues. This process is known as discovery. Numerous discovery devices are available, and the attorney must decide which devices to use and when. Some of these devices are discussed below.

Interrogatories   Information may be obtained by means of a written set of questions in a court document, usually entitled *interrogatories*, that require written answers. Testimony may also be taken by asking witnesses oral questions. This discovery activity is known as taking a *deposition* or using *oral interrogatories*. The manner in which the questioning can be conducted is precisely determined by the rules of civil procedure.

Subpoena   When witnesses are required to give testimony in court, they must receive official notice that they are to appear. This notice is called a *subpoena*. Some states require that witnesses who are to give depositions be subpoenaed. If an attorney knows that a witness may refer to certain documents or other evidence in the testimony—either in court or in a deposition—or if the attorney wants certain items admitted as evidence, a document called a *subpoena duces tecum* ("under penalty you shall bring with you") is required. This document tells a person to appear at a specified time and place with those particular exhibits (documents, photographs, or other items) related to the suit.

Other discovery devices   The attorney may petition the court for the right to inspect evidence or documents and also for the right to order a physical or mental examination of a party.

Pretrial conference   After all preliminary work has been completed and the case has been set for trial, the attorneys of record may meet informally with the judge to discuss the issues involved in the lawsuit. These conferences are not required in all states. At a pretrial conference the attorneys discuss the issues, the allegations, and the facts involved in the case. As the issues are discussed, information is exchanged; and sometimes evidence is produced that results in a request to dismiss the litigation without trial. Sometimes certain aspects of the case can be settled by *stipulation*, or agreement, between the attorneys with the approval of the judge. Because trials are expensive in terms of time, emotion, and money, both parties may reevaluate the situation and decide to settle out of court.

Conclusion of litigation without trial   Many lawsuits never go to court. Sometimes the reason is personal, having to do with the attitude of the parties. On the other hand, a high percentage of lawsuits are terminated before trial for legal reasons. Sometimes the pleadings and evidence gathered during discovery show that there is no factual issue to be tried, and so the judge enters a summary judgment upon motion by one of the parties. Sometimes one of the parties or the attorney deliberately does not respond within the time specified and a default judgment is entered. At other times the parties mutually agree to terminate the suit. There may also be a discontinuance or dismissal for a variety of reasons. The plaintiff may voluntarily discontinue the case, or the case may be involuntarily dismissed upon motion by the defendant because the statute of limitations has run out or the plaintiff has failed to prosecute—that is, has not taken steps to bring the case finally to trial. A dismissal without prejudice allows the plaintiff to act on the cause of action again later on; a dismissal with prejudice bars later action. Whatever the reason for concluding a case without trial, the attorneys of record must prepare, file, and serve certain documents, as motions and supporting briefs, in order to bring the case to a conclusion.

Release   When a case is dismissed as the result of a settlement out of court, the party who is to make restitution usually will not do so unless given a properly executed agreement most often called *release* or *release of all claims*. In this document, the person who receives the settlement agrees never again to bring suit for additional costs on the matter in dispute.

Phase 3: Trial and judgment   If a case cannot be settled by mutual agreement and if there are no grounds for dismissal or default, the case must go to trial for a decision on the merits. Rules have been developed which carefully prescribe the procedures to be followed for setting the matter for trial, conducting the trial, and entering the judgment of the court.

Trial   When either attorney feels that the case is ready for trial, the clerk of the court is notified through the filing of a *memorandum setting for trial* or a *notice of trial*. The calendar clerk places the trial on the calendar, meaning that it is added to the list of cases that are going to be tried. The clerk notifies the parties to the action when and where the trial will be held. For the customary sequence of a trial, refer to the preceding section on steps in a criminal proceeding. In civil cases the plaintiff's attorney rather than a prosecutor argues the case, and in most jurisdictions the plaintiff's attorney is permitted a rebuttal immediately following the defense lawyer's final argument. After the plaintiff has presented evidence, and before presentation of the defense, the defendant may move for a dismissal for failure to state a claim for which relief may be granted.

Judgment   Not all civil actions are entitled to be adjudicated by jury trial. The U.S. Constitution preserves the right to jury trial for common-law actions, but actions originally brought in equity courts do not enjoy this right. Where there is a right to a jury trial, the plaintiff may waive this right. When there is no jury, the judge hears the case, applies the law, and issues a judgment in favor of one party or the other based on the facts and the merits of the case. When a case is heard before a jury, the jury decides in favor of one of the parties on the basis of the facts presented and sets the amount of damages. In civil cases the judgment or decree is issued in favor of the party judged to have met its burden of proof. The party in whose favor judgment is made is the *prevailing party*.

Phase 4: Conclusion of litigation   After the court hands down a judgment, the losing party has several options: (1) to satisfy the judgment (as by paying the damages); (2) to fail to perform satisfaction, in which case the prevailing party may have to take measures to enforce the judgment (as by attaching the losing party's property); or (3) to appeal the case to a higher court. If the losing party chooses to appeal, no payment is made to the prevailing party. The attorney for the losing party must make the appeal within the time limit prescribed by law or lose the right to appeal.

Satisfaction   The judgment is a court order requiring the losing party to provide satisfaction in some manner to the prevailing party. Satisfaction may take several forms: the losing party may be required to pay court costs and monetary damages to the prevailing party, to perform a specified action requested by the other party, or to stop a certain action to which the other party objects. Once satisfaction has been made, the court must be given a document indicating that the judgment has been satisfactorily carried out.

In settling court costs the prevailing party must submit for the court's approval a statement of all recoverable expenses incurred in the course of litigation. The appropriate motion is filed and served on opposing counsel. The opposing party may object to the costs indicated and file a motion to that effect. The court will rule on both motions. If the court allows all costs, the order signed by the judge is filed, and official copies are served on opposing counsel. Normally each side pays its own attorneys' fees. However, in some limited circumstances the losing party may have to pay the prevailing party's attorneys' fees in addition to the court costs.

When the prevailing party has been paid all money owed, both damages and costs, the prevailing attorney files a document stating the amount of money received and declaring that full satisfaction of claims has been made. It also shows that judgment was entered into the official records. The document must be signed by the prevailing party, filed, and served on opposing counsel.

If the losing party fails to provide satisfaction as adjudged, various special proceedings may take place that could result in the seizure of person or property by the court.

Important Cases

Adkins v. Children's Hospital, 261 U.S. 525 (1923), invalidated a board established by Congress to set minimum wages for women workers in the District of Columbia. The court ruled in a 5–3 vote that the law authorizing the Wage Board infringed upon Fifth Amendment guarantees of life, liberty, and property, including employers' and employees' right to contract in whatever manner they pleased. The effects of *Adkins* were reversed in *West Coast Hotel Co. v. Parrish.*

Baker v. Carr, 369 U.S. 186 (1962), forced the Tennessee legislature to reapportion itself on the basis of population, thus ending the excessively high representation of rural areas in the state legislature and establishing that the Supreme Court may intervene in apportionment cases. Traditionally, rural areas dominated Tennessee's and other states' legislative politics. In the *Baker* case, the Court held that every vote should carry equal weight regardless of a voter's place of residence. A subsequent ruling, *Reynolds v. Sims*, 377 U.S. 533 (1964), built on *Baker* by requiring virtually every state legislature to be reapportioned, ultimately causing the political power in most state legislatures to shift from rural to urban areas.

Board of Education, Island Trees School District v. Pico, 457 U.S. 853 (1982), restricted the ability of school boards to censor school libraries. The Court, in reversing a New York state decision that allowed a local school board to remove books it found offensive, ruled that while a board may exercise a certain amount of discretion in creating a library to reflect community values, it cannot arbitrarily impose its own will on the effort and trample citizens' First Amendment rights. Books that can be shown to be vulgar or irrelevant may be removed, but books that simply contain unpopular ideas may not be.

Bowers v. Hardwick, 478 U.S. 186 (1986), held that the fundamental right to privacy as guaranteed by the Constitution does not extend to sex acts regarded as sodomy under state law, even if such acts take place between consenting adults in the confines of the home. The case originated when a gay Georgia man was arrested in his home for engaging in oral sex there with another man in violation of a state sodomy law. The Supreme Court, in a sharply divided opinion (5–4), upheld the constitutionality of the Georgia statute on the grounds that it reflected a legitimate belief by society that certain sex acts are immoral and unacceptable. In a notable dissent, Justice Harry Blackmun argued that the ruling violated one of the most fundamental rights of all, "the right to be let alone."

Bradwell v. Illinois, 83 U.S. 130 (1873), upheld an Illinois Supreme Court decision that denied a woman (Bradwell) the right to practice law because of her gender. The case was appealed to the U.S. Supreme Court on the ground that the state court's decision was at odds with the privileges and immunities clause of the Fourteenth Amendment, but the high court took the same narrow view of the clause that it had established (only the day before) in the Slaughterhouse Cases (see also *Butchers' Benevolent Assoc. of New Orleans v. Crescent City Livestock Landing and Slaughterhouse Co.*). As a result, sex-discriminatory statutes did not begin being struck down on Fourteenth Amendment grounds until well into the 20th century.

Brown v. Board of Education of Topeka, 347 U.S. 483 (1954); 349 U.S. 294 (1955), ruled unanimously that racial segregation in public schools violated the Fourteenth Amendment to the

Constitution, which says that no state may deny equal protection of the laws to any person within its jurisdiction. The 1954 decision declared that separate educational facilities were inherently unequal. *Brown* reversed the Court's earlier ruling in *Plessy v. Ferguson* that permitted "separate but equal" public facilities. The 1954 decision was limited to the public schools, but it was believed to imply that segregation was not permissible in other public facilities. The 1955 decision laid out guidelines for ending segregation and advised that school boards must proceed "with all deliberate speed" to satisfy the guidelines.

Butchers' Benevolent Association of New Orleans v. the Crescent City Livestock Landing and Slaughter-house Co., *popularly* The Slaughterhouse Cases, 83 U.S. 36 (1873), limited the protections provided by the Fourteenth Amendment (which prohibits states from denying any person "the equal protection of the law"). Specifically the Supreme Court ruled that a state-sanctioned slaughtering monopoly did not abridge other slaughterhouse owners' privileges and immunities as U.S. citizens and deprive them of property rights, as they had claimed. The Court thereby refused to extend federal protection of civil rights to the property rights of businesspersons, but in so doing it unwittingly weakened the power of the Fourteenth Amendment to protect the civil rights of blacks and other minorities.

Civil Rights Cases — see UNITED STATES V. STANLEY

Cruzan v. Missouri Department of Health, 497 U.S. 261 (1990), upheld the constitutionality of a person's right to refuse life-sustaining medical treatment as long as clear and convincing evidence is presented that such refusal is desired by the person. In this particular case, the Court ruled that a comatose patient had not sufficiently conveyed her wishes and therefore that life-sustaining treatment must continue; but the Court allowed that when demonstrable evidence of a patient's wishes is given, life-sustaining treatment may be removed in the interest of preserving individual liberty and the quality of life.

Danbury Hatters Case — see LOEWE V. LAWLOR

Dred Scott Case — see SCOTT V. SANDFORD

Engel v. Vitale, 370 U.S. 421 (1962), held that state-sanctioned prayer in public schools is unconstitutional. The Court found that even when a prayer is essentially nondenominational and pupils who so desire may be excused from reciting it, if the action is state sponsored the state is in violation of the constitutional separation of church and state. Later rulings would similarly affirm that devotional exercises in public schools went against the establishment of religion clause.

Erie Railroad Co. v. Tompkins, 304 U.S. 64 (1938), required federal courts to apply state law in diversity cases (i.e., cases in which the litigants are from different jurisdictions). Prior to *Erie* diversity cases were decided on the basis of what was held to be a kind of federal common law, which consisted of the "laws of the several states" plus federal courts'—not states'—interpretations of those laws (*Swift v. Tyson,* 41 U.S. 1 (1842)). Supporters of this earlier position believed that a federal common law was conducive to national development, while opponents claimed that it rode roughshod over states' rights. In an unprecedented ruling, Justice Louis D. Brandeis declared the earlier Supreme Court decision (*Swift*) unconstitutional, thus changing the course of diversity proceedings. Henceforth there would be no federal "common law" in diversity cases but only federal application of state laws.

Ex Parte McCardle, 74 U.S. 506 (1869), recognized that the Supreme Court's appellate jurisdiction can be limited by Congressional act, thus establishing Congress's legislative supremacy over both the executive and judicial branches of the federal government. William H. McCardle, a Mississippi editor who was jailed for sedition after criticizing federal Reconstruction efforts, appealed to the Supreme Court for a writ of habeas corpus. Since Congress had passed a law stripping the Court of its power of judicial review with regard to Reconstruction measures, the Court dismissed McCardle's appeal on the ground that it lacked jurisdiction over such matters. The case marked the peak of the Radical Republican power to determine national policy.

Ex Parte Milligan, 71 U.S. 2 (1866), prohibited the federal government from establishing military courts to try civilians (except where regular courts were no longer functioning in an actual theater of war). Lambdin P. Milligan had been arrested in his Indiana home in 1864 and tried in a military court on charges of aiding the Confederacy. The Supreme Court declared that neither the president nor Congress had the authority to set up such a court; Milligan, as a consequence, had been deprived of his constitutional right to trial by jury (and so was freed).

Ex Parte Young, 209 U.S. 123 (1908), determined that a federal court may enjoin a state from enforcing a law the constitutionality of which has been challenged. The particular law in this case was a railroad rate reduction statute in Minnesota that had been challenged by railroad company shareholders on the ground that it deprived them of their property without due process of law. The shareholders applied in a federal district court for an injunction, which was granted but subsequently ignored by state authorities. The Supreme Court found for the shareholders and the district court, holding that the right to enjoin did not violate Eleventh Amendment restrictions on the power of federal courts to hear suits against states.

Furman v. Georgia, 408 U.S. 238 (1972), ruled that capital punishment laws, as then enforced, were unconstitutional. The Court stated that the death penalty itself did not violate the Constitution but the manner of its application in many states did. It was shown that capital punishment was likely to be imposed in a discriminatory way and that blacks in particular were far more likely to be executed than whites. The decision required a system for applying the death penalty that would not be discriminatory against any racial or other minority. Many states have since passed laws that meet the Court's requirements of specifying the crimes or circumstances for which the death penalty is to be considered.

Gibbons v. Ogden, 22 U.S. 1 (1824), established that states cannot, by legislative enactment, interfere with the power of Congress to regulate commerce. The state of New York had authorized a monopoly on steamboat operation in state waters, and this action was upheld by a state chancery court. The Supreme Court, however, ruled that competing steamboat operators were protected by terms of a federal license to engage in trade along a coast. The decision was an important development in the interpretation of the commerce clause of the Constitution, and it freed all navigation of monopoly control.

Gideon v. Wainwright, 372 U.S. 335 (1963), held that the Sixth Amendment guarantees a defendant's right to counsel and that an indigent defendant must be provided with a court-appointed lawyer in all felony cases. The case is important for overruling an earlier decision, *Betts v. Brady*, 316 U.S. 455 (1942), that prevented the extension of the due process clause of the Fourteenth Amendment to state as well as federal criminal proceedings. *Gideon* was frequently cited in later cases, as the Court continued to expand due process guarantees and other fundamental rights in trial procedures.

Gitlow v. New York, 268 U.S. 652 (1925), extended First Amendment freedom-of-speech and Fourteenth Amendment equal-protection provisions to the states as well as the federal government.

Although Socialist Benjamin Gitlow's conviction in a New York court on criminal anarchy charges was upheld by the Supreme Court ("a state may punish utterances endangering the foundations of organized government and threatening its overthrow by unlawful means"), the Court used the case to note that freedoms of speech and the press are among the fundamental rights and liberties constitutionally protected from impairment by the states. The ruling was the first of a number of decisions holding that the Fourteenth Amendment extended the provisions of the Bill of Rights to state action.

Gregg v. Georgia, 428 U.S. 153 (1976), upheld the constitutionality of the death penalty for first-degree murder as long as the individual character of the offender and the circumstances of the crime are taken into account. A two-part proceeding was thus required, one to determine guilt or innocence, and another to determine the sentence. Opponents of a Georgia death penalty statute had claimed that it violated Eighth Amendment guarantees against cruel and unusual punishment. However, the Supreme Court found that the statute contained sufficient guidelines regarding jury deliberation and discretion to enable the law to be imposed without constituting arbitrary or discriminatory application. In two related cases decided the same day, the Court cautioned against states requiring *mandatory* death sentences for certain crimes, since such a requirement precluded the possibility of considering mitigating circumstances.

Griswold v. Connecticut, 381 U.S. 479 (1965), invalidated a law prohibiting the use of contraceptives, even by married persons. An executive of the Planned Parenthood League of Connecticut had been convicted of counseling clients to use contraceptives. In overturning the conviction, Justice William O. Douglas (writing for the Court) stated that there was a "zone of privacy" within a "penumbra" created by fundamental constitutional guarantees that includes the right to personal privacy. The state of Connecticut was found to have unconstitutionally interfered with that privacy in enacting and enforcing the ban on contraception.

Hammer v. Dagenhart, 247 U.S. 251 (1918), struck down the Keating-Owen Act, 39 Stat. 675 (1916), which had regulated child labor. The Supreme Court ruled that the Keating-Owen Act exceeded federal authority and represented an unwarranted encroachment on state powers to determine local labor conditions. In a notable dissent, Justice Oliver Wendell Holmes, Jr., pointed to the evils of excessive child labor, to the inability of states to regulate child labor, and to the unqualified right of Congress to regulate interstate commerce—including the "power to prohibit." The Court's ruling would not be overturned until 1941 (see also *United States v. Darby Lumber Co.*).

Heart of Atlanta Motel v. United States, 379 U.S. 241 (1964), upheld the constitutionality of the Civil Rights Act of 1964, thus giving federal law enforcement officials the power to prevent racial discrimination in the use of public facilities. An Atlanta motel had refused to rent rooms to blacks, claiming that the establishment was privately owned and operated only within state, thus making it immune from federal statute. The government sued on the ground that the motel received out-of-state patrons (it was located near two interstate highways) and thus came under both the public accommodations section of the Civil Rights Act and the interstate commerce clause of the Constitution. In a unanimous vote, the Court sustained the government's position and enjoined the motel from discriminating on the basis of race.

In re Debs, 158 U.S. 564 (1895), upheld the government's use of the injunction against unlawful strikes. At issue was labor leader Eugene V. Debs's violation of a federal court injunction against the 1894 Pullman [Train] Car Company plant strike. The Supreme Court upheld the injunction on the grounds of national sovereignty and the government's authority to remove obstructions to interstate commerce and the mails. The Pullman injunction was used as a model for strike stoppages until decisions during the New Deal era began to weaken its hold.

International Shoe Co. v. Washington, 326 U.S. 310 (1945), expanded states' powers to claim jurisdiction over out-of-state parties. Prior to the ruling, states often could not establish jurisdiction (in personam jurisdiction) over outside parties, even when such parties could be shown to have contracted with or tortiously injured a state or its citizens. The Supreme Court held that when such "minimum contacts" are maintained with a state, notions of fair play and substantial justice require that the contacting party be made subject to that state's laws. Following the decision many states enacted "long-arm" statutes that extended their power to apply in personam jurisdiction. In *Shaffer v. Heitner*, 433 U.S. 186 (1977), the Court applied the same "minimum contacts" standard to cases involving questions of in rem (property) and quasi in rem (intangible property) jurisdiction.

Korematsu v. United States, 323 U.S. 214 (1944), sanctioned the government's wartime internment of Japanese-American residents of the West Coast. The petitioner, Fred Korematsu, was charged with violating a restricted zone and failing to report to an assembly area as required under the presidential order that created the relocation camps. The Court did not ultimately examine the constitutionality of the government forcing people into detention but simply debated the action of Korematsu, finding against him in a 6–3 vote. In dissent, Justice Frank Murphy denounced the decision as the "legalization of racism."

Lochner v. New York, 198 U.S. 45 (1905), struck down a New York law setting 10 hours' labor a day as the legal maximum. In a case in which a baker had contracted with his employees for longer than the 10-hour working day, Justice Rufus W. Peckham declared that the Fourteenth Amendment prohibited the states from curtailing a person's liberty to make his or her own economic arrangements with his or her employees. This decision drew a stinging rebuke from Justice Oliver Wendell Holmes, Jr., whose opinion became the prevailing interpretation of the Fourteenth Amendment by the 1930s, when legislation such as maximum-hours laws were held to be constitutional.

Loewe v. Lawlor, *popularly* The Danbury Hatters Case, 208 U.S. 274 (1908), held labor unions to be subject to the antitrust laws. In 1902 the United Hatters of North America, having failed to organize the firm of D. E. Loewe in Danbury, Connecticut, called for a nationwide boycott of the firm's products. The firm brought suit under the Sherman Antitrust Act, and in 1908 the union was assessed triple damages. The case was a severe setback to the use of the secondary boycott by unions.

Malloy v. Hogan, 378 U.S. 1 (1964), extended the Fifth Amendment protection against self-incrimination to criminal defendants in state courts. Previously "pleading the Fifth," i.e., choosing to remain silent in the course of a criminal investigation or trial, was reserved only for federal defendants. In this case, involving a Connecticut gambler who was charged with contempt for refusing to identify the owner of a pool hall, the Court used the due process clause of the Fourteenth Amendment to extend the provisions of the Fifth Amendment to the states, thus expanding the rights of all criminal defendants. Five years later in *Benton v. Maryland*, 395 U.S. 784 (1969), the Court used the same process to extend the guarantee against double jeopardy to state defendants.

Mapp v. Ohio, 367 U.S. 643 (1961), established that illegally obtained evidence cannot be produced at trial in a state court to substantiate criminal charges against the defendant. The Court relied on the earlier decision in *Weeks v. United States*, 222 U.S. 383 (1914). *Weeks* established the exclusionary rule, which states that a person whose Fourth Amendment protections against unreasonable search and seizure have been violated has a right to exclude any evidence so obtained from use in a court of law. In *Mapp* the Court held that the exclusionary rule had to be applied universally to all criminal proceedings, overturning the ruling in *Wolf v. Colorado*, 338 U.S. 25 (1949), insofar as it failed to hold the exclusionary rule applicable to state court proceedings, and thus greatly broadening the constitutional protections available to defendants. In *United States v. Leon*, 468 U.S. 897 (1984), the court validated an exception to the exclusionary rule, holding that evidence which is obtained "in good faith" with a search warrant that is later ruled invalid remains admissible, a central point made in support of the decision being the unacceptable social cost of excluding such evidence.

Marbury v. Madison, 5 U.S. 137 (1803), declared, for the first time, an act of Congress unconstitutional, thus establishing the doctrine of judicial review. The Supreme Court held that a section of the Judiciary Act of 1789 (specifically, Section 13, which authorized the Court to issue a writ of mandamus) was unconstitutional and thus invalid. Chief Justice John Marshall declared that in any conflict between the Constitution and a law passed by Congress, the Constitution must always take precedence.

Martin v. Hunter's Lessee, 14 U.S. 304 (1816), affirmed the Supreme Court's right to appellate jurisdiction—that is, the right to review all state court judgments in cases arising under the federal Constitution or a law of the U.S. At issue was a Virginia superior court's refusal to obey an earlier Supreme Court judgment concerning title ownership in a property dispute. Justice Joseph Story's landmark opinion rejected the Virginia court's position and firmly established the Supreme Court as the ultimate authority in interpreting the Constitution.

Martin v. Mott, 25 U.S. 19 (1827), affirmed the president's right as commander in chief to call out the state militia. Complying with an order from President James Madison during the War of 1812, the New York governor called out some militia companies. Mott, a private in one of those companies, refused to obey the order; he was court-martialed and fined for this refusal. Martin, a U.S. Marshal, seized Mott's property to enforce the judgment when Mott did not pay the fine. Mott brought a civil suit to recover his property. The Court held that the president had validly used his Article I power to call out the militia, that he had sole authority to decide whether or not a situation permitting use of the statutory power existed, and that this decision was "conclusive upon all other parties" (as the states). The case set a major precedent in support of President Abraham Lincoln's decision to assemble troops in the cause of defending the national union.

McCulloch v. Maryland, 17 U.S. 316 (1819), affirmed the constitutional doctrine of Congress's "implied powers." The decision established that Congress had not only the powers expressly conferred upon it by the Constitution but also all authority "appropriate" to its carrying out such powers—including, in this case, the authority to establish a national bank. The doctrine of implied powers became a powerful force in the steady growth of federal power.

Minor v. Happersett, 88 U.S. 162 (1875), denied the constitutional basis for the right of women to vote, thus sustaining the disenfranchisement of women until passage of the Nineteenth Amendment in 1920. In a unanimous decision, the justices upheld a state's right to bar women from voting, finding that nothing in the Constitution "confer[s] the right of suffrage on anyone" and that citizenship alone is not sufficient cause. A year after the decision suffragist Susan B. Anthony succeeded in getting a proposed constitutional amendment introduced in Congress, but it was defeated that year and every subsequent year until 1920.

Miranda v. Arizona, 384 U.S. 436 (1966), specified a code of conduct for police interrogations of criminal suspects held in custody. Known as the Miranda warnings, these guidelines include informing arrested persons prior to questioning that they have the right to remain silent, that anything they say may be used against them, and that they have the right to the counsel of an attorney. Ernesto Miranda had been convicted on serious charges after having signed a confession without first being told his rights. The Court held that the prosecution could not use his statements unless the police had complied with several procedural safeguards to guarantee his Fifth Amendment privilege against self-incrimination. The 5–4 Miranda decision shocked the law enforcement community and was hotly debated. Several later decisions by a more conservative court served to limit the scope of the Miranda safeguards.

Missouri v. Holland, 252 U.S. 416 (1920), held that Congress may enact legislation to fulfill the terms of a treaty, even if such legislation otherwise constitutes an invasion of individual state sovereignty. The state of Missouri had sought to preserve exclusive authority over its game laws by enjoining U.S. game wardens from enforcing the Migratory Bird Treaty Act of 1918, which obligated Canada and the United States to protect certain migratory species. The Supreme Court disallowed the injunction, arguing that Congress must be able to act in the national interest, even if by means of unpopular legislation pursuant to an international treaty.

Muller v. Oregon, 208 U.S. 412 (1908), sustained a state law that limited to 10 the daily working hours of women factory employees on the ground that their "maternal functions" might be impaired. Aside from the contrast it provides to *Lochner v. New York*, the case is important for being the first to see extensive sociological and economic data—gathered, in this case, by (then attorney) Louis D. Brandeis, who argued the case—marshaled in support of an argument. After *Muller*, the so-called "Brandeis brief" would be the model for social reformers arguing their cases in courts of law.

Munn v. Illinois, 94 U.S. 113 (1877), upheld the power of government to regulate private industries. A Chicago grain warehouse firm (Munn) had been found guilty of violating state law concerning maximum rates that customers could be charged for storage and transportation of grain. The firm appealed to the Supreme Court, which nevertheless ruled that state power to regulate extends to private industries (such as grain storage facilities) that affect the public interest. Although the case marked a turning point in the struggle for public regulation of private enterprise, later court decisions sharply curtailed the government's power to regulate business.

National Labor Relations Board v. Jones & Laughlin Steel Corp., 301 U.S. 1 (1937), sustained the constitutionality of the National Labor Relations Act (1935) and expanded the federal government's power to regulate commerce. The justices held in a 5–4 decision that a labor-management dispute in a Pennsylvania steel factory, though local in nature, had disrupted interstate commerce and was therefore subject to government oversight.

Near v. Minnesota, 382 U.S. 679 (1931), ruled that a state law prohibiting publication of a newspaper that prints malicious or defamatory articles constitutes prior restraint of the press in violation of First Amendment guarantees. This was the first, and one of the most important, prior restraint cases to be heard by the Court. In a sharply divided opinion (5–4), the justices invalidated a Minnesota gag rule that was applied against a local practitioner of yellow journalism. Two weeks before, in *Stromberg v. California*, 283 U.S. 359 (1931), the Court had struck down as an unconstitutional ban on free speech a California law prohibiting the display of a red flag that symbolized Communist opposition to government.

Nebbia v. New York, 291 U.S. 502 (1934), upheld the price-setting activities of a New York dairy control board and provided a legal foundation for government regulation of business "affected with a public interest." The case thus set aside the narrower interpretation made famous by Justice James C. McReynolds in *Munn v. Illinois.*

New York Times Co. v. Sullivan, 376 U.S. 254 (1964), held that even false statements about public officials were entitled to protection under the First and Fourteenth Amendments (freedom of speech; equal protection of the laws) unless "actual malice" could be demonstrated. Sullivan was a Montgomery, Alabama, police commissioner who was implicated (although not named directly) in an ad by a civil rights group published in the *New York Times.* The ad was highly critical of the Montgomery police department, causing Sullivan to sue for libel and defamation of character. The Court, however, held that any public official who sues for damages because of an alleged falsehood must prove that the falsehood had been issued with the knowledge that it was false or with reckless disregard of whether it was false or not. The Court found no such malice on the part of the *Times.* Ten years later, in *Gertz v. Robert Welch, Inc.*, 418 U.S. 323 (1974), the Court affirmed the right of private individuals as opposed to public persons to recover libel damages when only fault rather than "actual malice" is proven.

New York Times Co. v. United States, *popularly* The Pentagon Papers Case, 407 U.S. 713 (1971), removed an injunction against the *New York Times* designed to stop publication of classified government documents known as the Pentagon Papers. In what is regarded as one of the most significant prior restraint cases in history, the Supreme Court, in a 6–3 decision, held that the government had failed to demonstrate the "heavy burden of proof" needed to justify prior restraint of the press, thus freeing the newspaper to resume publishing the politically controversial material.

Northern Securities Co. v. United States, 193 U.S. 197 (1904), revived the all-but-forgotten Sherman Antitrust Act by "trust-busting" a holding company (Northern Securities) and two railroads as a combination in restraint of trade. This was the first of 43 similar cases brought during the following seven years that steadily nibbled away at the *United States v. E. C. Knight Co.* decision and culminated in *Standard Oil Co. of New Jersey v. United States.*

Palsgraf v. Long Island Railroad Co., 248 N.Y. 339, 162 N.E. 99 (1928), developed the legal concept of proximate cause. A man had been running to catch a departing train at the station and was helped onto it by two L. I. Railroad Co. guards. As the guards pulled the man onto the train, the package that he was carrying, which contained fireworks, dropped onto the rails and exploded. The explosion knocked over a scale that hit and injured a woman (Palsgraf) waiting for another train. Chief Justice Benjamin Cardozo (writing for the majority) analyzed the case in terms of negligence: whether the train attendants had breached a duty of due care to the plaintiff. The majority found no negligence on the guards' part and denied recovery to the plaintiff. In the dissent Justice William S. Andrews maintained that the case should have properly been analyzed in terms of causation (whether without the attendants' actions the plaintiff would not have been injured), and that liability should be imposed for injury to anyone within the zone or radius of danger that was a result of those actions. It was this dissent that was often cited in subsequent cases involving proximate cause.

Pentagon Papers Case — see NEW YORK TIMES CO. V. UNITED STATES

Pierce v. Society of Sisters, 285 U.S. 510 (1925), declared unconstitutional state statutes forbidding private and parochial elementary and secondary schools. An order of Catholic nuns filed suit against Oregon officials who were requiring all children of school age to attend public rather than private schools. The Supreme Court found for the sisters, holding that the Fourteenth Amendment guarantees "personal liberty," including the right of parents to choose schooling for their children.

Plessy v. Ferguson, 163 U.S. 537 (1896), established the legality of racial segregation so long as facilities were kept "separate but equal." An organized challenge to Louisiana laws concerning separate rail cars for blacks and whites was brought before the state supreme court but rejected and then taken on appeal to the Supreme Court. The latter court, too, held that separate accommodations did not infringe on black or white passengers' political equality but only made a legitimate social distinction. The case is ultimately as well known for the famous dissent by Justice John Marshall Harlan (the "Constitution is color-blind, and neither knows nor tolerates classes among citizens") as for its place in civil rights history. It would be overturned by *Brown v. Board of Education of Topeka* (1954).

Powell v. Alabama, 287 U.S. 45 (1932), extended the Fourteenth Amendment guarantee of due process of law to state courts. The first and most important of the so-called Scottsboro Cases (after the Alabama town in which they originated), the decision helped to clarify the rights of the accused in state criminal trials involving indigent defendants. Several black youths who were charged with raping two white women were convicted in a state court after receiving only a cursory defense by two poorly prepared state-appointed attorneys. The Supreme Court ruled that the Fourteenth Amendment required state trial judges to assign an individual attorney to each indigent defendant in a capital case and to otherwise ensure that a fair trial, including assistance of counsel, is provided in noncapital cases. This mandate was expanded in *Gideon v. Wainwright* (1963), which provided that all indigent defendants charged with serious crimes (capital or noncapital) must be assigned counsel.

Reed v. Reed, 404 U.S. 71 (1971), declared a state law unconstitutional on the ground that it discriminated against women, the first such decision in the Court's history. The law in question was one that preferred the father over the mother as executor of a son's estate. Despite nearly two centuries of upholding the constitutionality of such gender-discriminatory laws, the Court said in this case that the father-preference represented "the very kind of arbitrary legislative choice forbidden by the [Fourteenth Amendment's] equal protection clause."

Richmond Newspapers, Inc. v. Virginia, 448 U.S. 555 (1980), affirmed the public's and the press's constitutional right to attend criminal trials. The decision overturned a state court ruling that the publicity surrounding a murder case then entering a fourth trial (because of a series of mistrials and reversals) justified the exclusion from the court of members of the press and the public. The Supreme Court ruled that only when a defendant's right to a fair trial is demonstrably threatened, and there is no alternative to closure, can a trial take place beyond the view of the public. One year later, in *Chandler v. Florida*, 449 U.S. 560 (1981), the Court allowed that press access to trials may include television coverage, but cautioned in a subsequent case, *Globe Newspaper Co. v. Superior Court*, 457 U.S. 596 (1982), that tighter restrictions may apply in the case of minors.

Roe v. Wade, 410 U.S. 113 (1973), established a woman's right to have an abortion without undue restrictive interference from the government. The Court held that a woman's right to decide for herself to bring or not bring a pregnancy to term is guaranteed under the Fourteenth Amendment. A Texas law prohibiting abortions had been challenged by an unmarried pregnant woman (Roe) and the court ruled in her favor, finding that the state had violated her right to privacy. In attempting to balance the state's rights against the rights of the individual, Justice Harry A. Blackmun held that the state's legitimate interest in protecting potential life increased as the pregnancy advanced.

While allowing that the state may forbid abortions during the third trimester, Blackmun wrote that a woman is entitled to obtain an abortion freely, after consultation with a doctor, in the first trimester and in an authorized clinic in the second trimester.

Roth v. United States, 354 U.S. 426 (1957), held that obscene material is not protected speech and tendered a basic definition of obscenity: "Whether, to the average person, applying contemporary community standards, the dominant theme of the material taken as a whole appeals to prurient interests." The case involved a publisher (Roth) who had been convicted for mailing obscene materials and who then appealed to the Supreme Court on the ground that his First Amendment rights to freedom of speech had been violated. Although the Court found against him, its ruling was based on an attempt to balance individual freedoms with the interests of the community. Subsequent decisions would place greater emphasis on local standards in the definition of obscenity and broaden the protections accorded to publishers. In *Miller v. California*, 413 U.S. 15 (1973), the Court held that when a state regulates obscene materials the state law must specifically define the sexual conduct depicted or described by the material, and the law must be limited to material which portrays the conduct in a patently offensive way and does not have serious literary, artistic, political, or scientific value.

San Antonio Independent School District v. Rodriguez, 411 U.S. 1 (1973), ruled that the Constitution is silent on the matter of a person's right to an education and therefore a state which finances its schools through local property taxes violates no constitutional principle in so doing, even if marked economic disparities among school districts exist. This case originated as a class-action suit brought by parents in a property-poor Texas district. A federal district court found for the parents, holding that the state had abridged their right to equal protection by allowing property-rich districts to receive and spend more tax dollars per pupil than were spent in the parents' district. The Supreme Court, however, reversed the decision on the grounds that education is not taken up in the Constitution and that Texas, at any rate, was providing a free basic education to every child and therefore was not discriminating against any class of persons. The case had broad nationwide implications for the way schools could be financed.

Santa Clara County v. Southern Pacific Railroad Co., 118 U.S. 394 (1886), defined corporations as "persons" who are entitled to the same equal protection rights as individuals. While falling short of conferring citizen status on corporate entities, the Court nevertheless declared that such entities are constitutionally guaranteed the right to liberty, property, and due process of the law and for legal purposes may be regarded as persons. The case is viewed historically as marking a Court shift away from issues predominantly involving civil rights and toward those predominantly involving property rights and the doctrines of laissez-faire economics.

Schechter Poultry Corp. v. United States, 295 U.S. 495 (1935), did away with the National Industrial Recovery Act (NIRA; 1933). By unanimous vote, the Court held that Congress had exceeded its authority to delegate legislative powers and regulate interstate commerce in enacting NIRA. It also found that the Act gave too much discretionary power to the president. Only with NIRA's successor, the National Labor Relations Act (1935), would the Roosevelt administration be successful in demonstrating to the court that it had devised a workable solution to the national economic emergency created by the Depression.

Schenck v. United States, 249 U.S. 47 (1919), subverted the apparent absolute nature of First Amendment protections of freedom of speech by establishing a "clear and present danger" test by which certain forms of incendiary speech become prosecutable. The case involved two New York Socialists who were convicted under the Espionage Act of 1917 for distributing handbills urging resistance to military conscription during World War I. The two appealed on First Amendment grounds to the Supreme Court, but Justice Oliver Wendell Holmes, Jr., writing for the Court, rejected their arguments and declared that "the character of every act depends upon the circumstances in which it is done. The most stringent protection of free speech would not protect a man in falsely shouting fire in a theater and causing panic. [The] question in every case is whether the words used are used in such circumstances and are of such a nature as to create a clear and present danger that they will bring about the substantive evils that Congress has a right to prevent." (see also *Gitlow v. New York* and *Yates v. United States*)

Scott v. Sandford, *popularly* The Dred Scott Case, 60 U.S. 393 (1857), made slavery legal in all territories, thereby adding fuel to the great controversies that eventually led to civil war. Chief Justice Roger B. Taney declared that a Negro (in this case, Scott) was not entitled to rights as a U.S. citizen. Taney and the other justices in the majority went on to declare that the Missouri Compromise of 1820 (which had forbidden slavery in that part of the Louisiana Purchase north of latitude 36°30', except for Missouri) was unconstitutional because Congress had no power to prohibit slavery in the territories. The decision increased antislavery sentiment in the North and fed the sectional antagonism that burst into war in 1861.

Scottsboro Cases — see POWELL V. ALABAMA

Slaughterhouse Cases — see BUTCHERS' BENEVOLENT ASSOCIATION OF NEW ORLEANS V. THE CRESCENT CITY LIVESTOCK LANDING AND SLAUGHTER-HOUSE CO.

Standard Oil Co. of New Jersey v. United States, 221 U.S. 1 (1911), dissolved 34 companies controlled by John D. Rockefeller's Standard Oil Trust as constituting a monopoly in violation of the Sherman Antitrust Act. While in one sense the case was the high point of the "trust-busting" efforts of two presidents (see also *Northern Securities Co. v. United States*), in another sense it marked a turn toward a more conservative interpretation of the Sherman Act. Chief Justice Edward Douglass White promulgated the idea that a restraint of trade by a monopolistic business must be "unreasonable" to be illegal under the Sherman Act. White's failure, however, to define a "reasonable" restraint, coupled with the imprecise brevity of the Sherman Act, made subsequent antitrust decisions exceedingly difficult to predict.

Swann v. Charlotte–Mecklenburg County Board of Education, 402 U.S. 1 (1971), authorized the use of busing, racial quotas, and gerrymandered school districts to wipe out the lingering effects of segregation in Southern schools. More than 15 years after *Brown v. Board of Education of Topeka* (1954), many Southern schools remained segregated. Having written guidelines for districts in the wake of *Brown*, and having already done away with *Brown's* "all deliberate speed" formula in favor of one mandating desegregation "now" (*Green v. County School Board of New Kent County, Virginia*, 391 U.S. 430 (1968)), the Court delivered in *Swann v. Charlotte-Mecklenburg County* its longest desegregation opinion to date: 30 pages, complete with "mathematical ratios" for school composition and an endorsement of busing and redistricting as means to achieve the desired end.

Tennessee v. Garner, 471 U.S. 1 (1985), declared that police may not use deadly force against a fleeing suspect unless they have probable cause to believe that the suspect might kill or seriously injure persons nearby. The particulars in this case included police knowledge that a suspect was in all likelihood an unarmed minor; nevertheless, the youth was fatally shot upon fleeing the crime scene. In its opinion, the Court stated that "[a] police officer may not seize an unarmed, nondangerous suspect by shooting him dead."

Trustees of Dartmouth College v. Woodward, 17 U.S. 518 (1819), held that the Charter of Dartmouth College granted in 1769 by King George VII of England was a contract and, as such, could not be impaired by the New Hampshire State Legislature. State legislators had tried to alter the contract's terms regarding the continuance of the board of trustees, an effort rejected by the Court. The decision had far-reaching impact in its application to business charters, protecting businesses and corporations from a great deal of government regulation.

United States v. Darby Lumber Co., 312 U.S. 100 (1941), held that the Fair Labor Standards Act (1938) mandating federal wage and hours standards applies to the local manufacture of goods even if those goods are only indirectly part of interstate commerce. The decision overturned *Hammer v. Dagenhart*, which prohibited Congress from encroaching on state powers to determine local labor conditions. In *Darby* the Court ruled that, although only some of the goods manufactured by Darby Lumber Co. were to be shipped through interstate commerce, the production of all Darby goods was subject to federal regulation because such production was part of the mainstream of the company's activities that affected interstate commerce. One year later, in *Wickard v. Filburn*, 317 U.S. 111 (1942), the Court ruled that Congress may regulate certain activities (such as local agriculture) that are neither commercial nor interstate if they exert "a substantial economic effect on interstate commerce."

United States v. E. C. Knight Co., 156 U.S. 1 (1895), permitted combinations of local manufacturers and put most monopolies beyond the reach of the Sherman Antitrust Act of 1890. The E. C. Knight Company, which enjoyed a virtual monopoly of sugar refining in the U.S., was sued by the government under the provisions of the Sherman Act. The Supreme Court ruled (8–1) against the government, declaring that manufacturing (e.g., refining) was a local activity not subject to congressional regulation of interstate commerce. Not until serious trust-busting began under presidents Theodore Roosevelt and William Howard Taft were effective means of enforcement added to the antitrust laws and the power of monopolies somewhat curtailed. (see, e.g., *Northern Securities Co. v. United States*)

United States v. Nixon, 418 U.S. 683 (1974), held that presidential materials (such as documents and tape-recorded communications) can be subpoenaed as evidence to be used in a criminal trial. President Richard M. Nixon had refused to turn over a portion of his private materials to the congressional committee investigating the Watergate incident, claiming that it was his prerogative as president to keep confidential statements secret. The Court, however, ruled that such a prerogative must yield to the need of the judiciary to enforce criminal justice, as long as the confidential statements do not relate strictly to military or diplomatic matters.

United States v. Stanley, *popularly* The Civil Rights Cases, 109 U.S. 3 (1883), declared private acts of racial discrimination beyond the reach of federal jurisdiction, thus invalidating the Civil Rights Act of 1875. Various attempts had been made by private parties to test the provisions of the 1875 law under circumstances involving privately owned but publicly operated facilities (e.g., inns, public conveyances, places of amusement). In finding against supporters of the law, the Court ruled that the Constitution prohibited only state-sponsored, not private, discrimination. Despite a strong dissent by Justice John Marshall Harlan, the decision would not be overturned until the landmark *Heart of Atlanta Motel v. United States* ruling in 1964.

United Steelworkers of America v. Weber, 443 U.S. 193 (1979), held that employees and unions could conduct voluntary training programs designed to improve skills of minority employees even if qualified white employees were excluded provided that the programs were "temporary," did not "trammel" white interests, and were intended to overcome "manifest racial imbalance." The case grew out of a class-action suit filed in district court by a white production worker who alleged that black employees were being promoted in preference to white employees. The Court stressed the voluntary nature of the company's programs and the need to redress past racial imbalances.

University of California Regents v. Bakke, 438 U.S. 265 (1978), held that fixed quotas may not be set for places for minority applicants at professional schools if white applicants are denied a chance to compete for those places. The Court qualified the ruling, however, by saying that race may be considered as a factor in making decisions on admission. At issue was a state medical school admissions program that, because it required a certain number of minority applicants, twice denied admission to a qualified white candidate (Bakke). The Court concluded: "Government may take race into account when it acts not to demean or insult any racial group, but to remedy disadvantages cast on racial minorities by past racial prejudice."

Wallace v. Jaffree, 472 U.S. 38 (1985), struck down a mandatory moment-of-silence statute that was intended as an alternative to requiring school prayer. The Court found that an Alabama statute authorizing schools to take time out for "meditation or prayer" violated the Constitution's ban against using state institutions to establish religion. Two years later, in *Edwards v. Aguillard*, 482 U.S. 578 (1987), the Court found that a Louisiana law requiring public schools that teach evolution to teach creationism too violated the same establishment of religion clause.

Ware v. Hylton, 3 U.S. 199 (1796), upheld the primacy of U.S. treaties over state statutes. It invalidated a Virginia law allowing Virginia residents' Revolutionary War debts to British creditors to be paid off in depreciated currency or confiscated property and affirmed the terms of the federally negotiated Treaty of Paris (1783). The ruling thus established that federal treaties always take precedence over conflicting state laws.

Wayman v. Southard, 23 U.S. 1 (1825), affirmed the constitutional right of Congress to delegate legislative authority, thus laying the basis for the creation of the administrative state. In a unanimous opinion, the Court stated that once policy has been set by Congress according to the procedures set forth in the Constitution, the administration of that policy—the detailed making and application of rules—may be delegated to an authorized agent of the government. Thus was born the role of the federal administrator and government regulatory agencies.

Webster v. Reproductive Health Services, 491 U.S. 397 (1989), upheld a state law barring the use of public facilities or public employees to effect abortions, and required physicians to perform tests to determine the viability of any fetus believed to be at least 20 weeks old. The ruling upheld these restrictions as constitutional without overturning *Roe v. Wade*. In subsequent years the Court ruled that a state may require one parent to be notified when an unmarried minor seeks an abortion (*Ohio v. Akron Center for Reproductive Health*, 497 U.S. 502 (1990)) but that the constitutional right to obtain an abortion remains the law of the land (*Planned Parenthood of Southeastern Pennsylvania v. Casey*, 505 U.S. 833 (1992)).

West Coast Hotel Co. v. Parrish, 300 U.S. 379 (1937), upheld a state law setting minimum wages for women and children, thus overturning two earlier rulings (*Adkins v. Children's Hospital* and *Morehead v. New York ex. rel Tipaldo*, 298 U.S. 587 (1936)) and placing limits on the freedom to contract. Justice George Sutherland wrote in dissent that setting a minimum wage for women constituted arbitrary discrimination based on gender, a position many feminists of the era supported.

West Virginia State Board of Education v. Barnette, 319 U.S. 624 (1943), struck down an earlier ruling (*Minersville School District v. Gobitis* (1940)) that children who are members of the religious group known as Jehovah's Witnesses must join in saluting the American flag in public schools. The Court ruled that First Amendment guarantees regarding freedom of religion protected the right to remain silent if a person's religious beliefs recommend it, and that the government cannot compel a person to do otherwise.

Wong Sun v. United States, 371 U.S. 471 (1962), applied the exclusionary rule to verbal statements obtained in connection with an illegal arrest. Wong Sun and James Wah Toy were arrested for narcotics possession without probable cause and convicted; an informant led agents to Toy who, at the time of his arrest, implicated Wong Sun. Both were questioned after their arraignments but refused to sign statements prepared after their interrogations. Wong Sun voluntarily returned for questioning a few days after his arrest. The Court clarified the fruit of the poisonous tree concept, which excludes evidence gathered as a result of an illegal arrest or search, and refused to allow evidence of statements made by Toy during the illegal search of his premises. Wong Sun's unsigned statement made upon his return was properly admitted as evidence against him, however, because its connection to his illegal arrest was attenuated.

Worcester v. Georgia, 31 U.S. 515 (1832), affirmed the federal government's exclusive right to treat "the Indian nations . . . as distinct, independent, political communities" outside the reach of the states. The case involved a missionary (Worcester) to the Cherokees who failed to obtain a license as required by a Georgia statute. The Supreme Court ruled that, since the Cherokees must be regarded as an independent nation, the Georgia law violated the commerce clauses of the Constitution. The state, however, with President Andrew Jackson's endorsement, ultimately refused to acknowledge the ruling and proceeded forcibly to remove Cherokees from their territory under the umbrella of the Indian Removal Act of 1830.

Wygant v. Jackson Board of Education, 476 U.S. 267 (1986), declared affirmative action an appropriate means to remedy past racial discrimination in hiring and employment. Ironically, the Court ordered in this case that a Jackson, Mississippi, school board reinstate several senior white teachers who had been dismissed to make room for newly hired black teachers, arguing that the board had failed to show a significant history of bias; had it done so, affirmative action would have been appropriate. In two similar cases the following year, the Court upheld the constitutionality of a one black–one white promotion quota (*United States v. Paradise*, 480 U.S. 149 (1987)) and the promotion of a woman over a man who scored higher on a job-qualification test (*Johnson v. Transportation Agency, Santa Clara County*, 480 U.S. 616 (1987)).

Yates v. United States, 354 U.S. 298 (1957), ruled that speech advocating the forcible overthrow of the government is not prosecutable unless it is tied to overt acts. The opinion modified that of *Dennis v. United States*, 341 U.S. 494 (1951), which was largely a restatement of the famous opinion of Justice Oliver Wendell Holmes, Jr., regarding the "clear and present" danger test in *Schenck v. United States*. In the 1940s and 1950s, these two earlier decisions were often cited in conjunction with the Smith Act (1940) and the Internal Security (McCarran) Act (1950) in cases involving so-called un-American activities on the part of presumed Communist organizations. In *Yates*, however, the clear-and-present-danger doctrine underwent revision such that no seditious or subversive speech could be punished unless it constituted an incitement to immediate unlawful action and the incitement was likely to produce, in the circumstances, such action.

Yick Wo v. Hopkins, 118 U.S. 356 (1886), declared that the equal protection clause of the Fourteenth Amendment applies to all persons, not just citizens. The case is notable for having addressed both the rights of noncitizens and the issue of police power directed against them. Yick Wo was a Chinese immigrant who ran a small San Francisco laundry that was shut down by police for being in violation of a city ordinance against operating commercial enterprises out of wooden buildings. It was widely understood that the ordinance targeted Chinese businesses, since such businesses made predominant use of wooden construction (which was not itself prohibited). In its ruling, the Court sanctioned local authorities for arbitrary application of the law and upheld the right of citizens and noncitizens alike to appeal to the Fourteenth Amendment for protection against discrimination.

Youngstown Sheet & Tube Co. v. Sawyer, 343 U.S. 579 (1952), held unconstitutional the president's seizure of the strike-threatened steel industry during the Korean War. President Truman had based the executive order on his constitutional power as commander in chief, but the Court ruled that the president exceeded his authority in seizing private property. Even in a time of war, it ruled, only Congress is able to authorize a lawful seizure (and then must pay proper compensation).

Important Laws

ABA Model Code of Professional Responsibility, guidelines adopted by the American Bar Association in 1969. The Model Code is organized around nine canons, or standards of professional conduct for lawyers, with sections called ethical considerations and disciplinary rules following each one. The Code was updated until the adoption of the Model Rules of Professional Conduct in 1983, and served as a model for state legislation. By 1980 almost every state had a code regulating lawyers based on the Model Code. After 1983, many states repealed their codes and enacted legislation based on the Model Rules instead.

ABA Model Rules of Professional Conduct, guidelines adopted by the American Bar Association in 1983 and periodically amended. These rules serve as models for state legislation governing lawyers, their relationships with their clients, and related matters (as advertising). About 30 states have enacted statutes based on the Model Rules. The Model Rules supersede the ABA Model Code of Professional Responsibility.

Administrative Procedure Act (APA), 5 U.S.C. § 500 et seq. (1946), established practices and procedures for all government agencies to follow in adjudication and rulemaking. The act granted citizens the right to receive ample previous notice of proceedings, the right to submit evidence, the right to have independent hearing officers (to the exclusion of investigating or prosecuting officers), and the right to a decision based solely on testimony and papers actually entered in the proceedings. It also required agencies to publish notices of proposed rulemaking in the Federal Register and to give interested persons an opportunity to participate in the rulemaking by submitting written data or arguments.

Age Discrimination in Employment Act (ADEA), 29 U.S.C. § 621 et seq. (1967), prohibited job discrimination based on age. The law was specifically designed to protect job applicants over 40 years of age. It applies to federal, state, and city governments and to private businesses that have more than 20 employees and engage in interstate commerce. Some exceptions are allowed in the case of law enforcement and fire-fighting personnel, and in those instances in which the employer can offer convincing evidence that age is a bona fide job criterion.

Agricultural Adjustment Act (AAA), 7 U.S.C. § 601 et seq. (1933), gave "parity payments" to farmers who agreed to limit production. The act was designed to correct the imbalance between farm and nonfarm products and return purchasing power to pre-World War I levels. It met with only limited success. Production fell as intended (aided by the severe drought of 1933–36) and prices rose in consequence; but the AAA was of more value to big farmers than to small family farmers, who often could not meet their expenses if they restricted their output. Thus, even before the Supreme Court invalidated the AAA in 1936, on the ground that Congress had exceeded its power to regulate commerce, support for it had diminished. A second, more limited Agricultural Adjustment Act, 7 U.S.C. § 1281 et seq. (1938), similarly produced mixed results, tending to boost commercial farming at the expense of small farmers.

Alien and Sedition Acts, 1 Stat. 570, 577, 596 (1798), internal security laws passed by the U.S. Congress, restricting aliens and curtailing the excesses of an unrestrained press, in anticipation of an expected war with France. The alien laws were aimed at French and Irish immigrants, who were mostly pro-French. These laws raised the waiting period for naturalization from 5 to 14 years, permitted the detention of subjects of an enemy nation, and authorized the chief executive to expel any alien he considered dangerous. The Sedition Act banned the publishing of false or malicious writings against the government and the inciting of opposition to any act of Congress or the president—practices already forbidden by state statutes and the common law but not by federal law. All the Alien and Sedition Acts subsequently expired or were repealed, although the current law found at 50 U.S.C. § 21 is based on the second alien act.

Americans with Disabilities Act (ADA), 42 U.S.C. § 1201 et seq. (1990), provided civil rights protections to individuals with disabilities and guaranteed them equal opportunity in public accommodations, employment, transportation, state and local government services, and telecommunications. Some 43 million disabled people were affected by the law. The employment provisions applied beginning in 1992 to employers with 25 or more employees; those with 15–24 employees would have to be in compliance by 1994. The public accommodations provisions were generally effective beginning January 1992. They required that necessary changes be made to afford access by persons with disabilities to all public facilities, including restaurants, theaters, day-care centers, parks, institutional buildings, and hotels.

Atomic Energy Act, 42 U.S.C. § 2011 et seq. (1946), established the Atomic Energy Commission (AEC) and gave it authority over all aspects of atomic energy, including nuclear warhead research, development, testing, and production. The legislation grew out of the need many outside of government and the military, including scientists who had worked on the Manhattan Project, felt for establishing independent controls over nuclear technology. The act also established a joint congressional committee on atomic energy. In 1954, amendments were added to allow greater participation by private nuclear-industry interests, and in 1974 the AEC and the joint committee were dissolved and their functions transferred to the Nuclear Regulatory Commission, the Energy Research and Development Administration (disbanded in 1977 when the Department of Energy was created), and various congressional subcommittees.

Banking Act of 1933, *popularly* Glass-Steagall Act of 1933, 12 U.S.C. §§ 24, 335, 371, 377, 378 (1933), one of three Depression-era bank reform measures that established federal deposit insurance and helped curb bank speculation. The Glass-Steagall Act created the Federal Deposit Insurance Corporation, which backs deposits using federal dollars, and required the separation of investment banking and commercial banking, thus allowing different interest rates for long-term and short-term financing. A later act, known as the Emergency Banking Relief Act, 12 U.S.C. 51a–51c (1933), created a "bank holiday" (business moratorium) to stop a depositor panic and to allow for the reorganization of solvent banks under federal review-and-licensing guidelines. It also authorized the president to take the United States off the gold standard, ending a foreign drain on gold and reassuring depositors. Finally, the Banking Act of 1935 gave the Federal Reserve Board the power to determine the cash reserves of commercial banks, a move that came to be recognized as an appropriate technique for controlling the money supply.

Bankruptcy Code, 11 U.S.C. § 101 et seq. (1978), title of the U.S. Code governing insolvency and debt adjustment. Individuals, whether merchants or not, as well as private corporations, with the exception of certain financial institutions, are subject to the Bankruptcy Code. A number of federal and state legislative acts during the 19th century laid the basis for the code, but it was not until the development (beginning in the 1960s) of the Bankruptcy Reform Act of 1978, 92 Stat.

2549 (1978), which enacted title 11, that the laws were systematically reviewed and codified. The Code defined bankruptcy procedure and strengthened the hand of bankruptcy judges. Chapter 7 of the code governs liquidation, in which assets are sold and the proceeds are given to creditors. Chapter 9 governs the adjustment of debts of a municipality. Chapter 11 governs corporate reorganization, in which debts are temporarily frozen and business is consolidated as part of a court-approved plan to pay off creditors. Chapter 12 governs the adjustment of debts of a family farmer with regular annual income, and functions much like Chapter 13. Chapter 13 governs wage earners' bankruptcy, in which debts are paid off from disposable income while the court controls other assets. Certain state exemptions to the federal code also exist and vary widely.

Civil Rights Act of 1964, 42 U.S.C. § 2000a et seq. (1964), comprehensive legislation intended to end discrimination based on race, color, religion or national origin. It is often called the most important U.S. law on civil rights since Reconstruction (1865–77). Title I of the act guarantees equal voting rights by removing registration requirements and procedures biased against minorities and the underprivileged. Title II prohibits segregation or discrimination in places of public accommodation involved in interstate commerce. Title VII bans discrimination, including sex-based discrimination, by trade unions, schools, or employers involved in interstate commerce or doing business with the federal government; it also established a government agency, the Equal Employment Opportunity Commission (EEOC), to enforce these provisions. The act also calls for the desegregation of public schools (Title IV), broadens the duties of the Civil Rights Commission (Title V), and assures nondiscrimination in the distribution of funds under federally assisted programs (Title VI). A 1972 amendment, the Equal Employment Opportunity Act, 42 U.S.C. § 2000e et seq., extended Title VII coverage to employees of state and local governments and increased the enforcement authority of the EEOC.

Civil Rights Acts, 14 Stat. 27 (1866), 16 Stat. 140 (1870), 16 Stat., 433 (1871), 17 Stat. 13 (1871), 18 Stat. 336, 337 (1875), a series of acts passed between 1866 and 1875, the provisions of some of which are codified in several sections of title 42 of the U.S. Code. The earlier legislation granted blacks the rights to sue and be sued, to give evidence, and to own property. Federal authorities were authorized to enforce penalties upon anyone interfering with registration, voting, holding of office, or jury service of blacks. The Civil Rights Act of 1875 prohibited racial discrimination by innkeepers, public transportation, and owners of public establishments, but it was struck down by the Supreme Court in *United States v. Stanley*, 109 U.S. 3 (1883). Because of that decision, which held that the Fourteenth Amendment protected against discrimination by a government but not by an individual, Congress did not enact civil rights legislation until the Civil Rights Acts of 1957 and 1964.

Civil Service Act, 5 U.S.C. § 1101 et seq., formerly 5 U.S.C. § 632 et seq. (1883), established the tradition and mechanism of permanent federal employment based on merit rather than on political party affiliation (the spoils system). Civil service reform became a leading issue in the midterm elections of 1882. In January 1883, Congress passed a comprehensive civil service bill sponsored by Senator George H. Pendleton of Ohio, providing for the open selection of government employees—to be administered by a Civil Service Commission—and guaranteeing the right of citizens to compete for federal appointment without regard to politics, religion, race, or national origin. Only about 10 percent of the positions in the federal government were covered by the new law, but nearly every president after Chester A. Arthur, who signed the bill into law, broadened its scope. By 1990 more than 90 percent of federal employees were protected by the act.

Clayton Antitrust Act, 15 U.S.C. §§ 12 et seq. (1914), law enacted to clarify and strengthen the Sherman Antitrust Act (1890). The vague language of the latter had provided large corporations with numerous loopholes, enabling them to engage in certain restrictive business arrangements which, though not illegal per se, resulted in concentrations that had an adverse effect on competition. Whereas the Sherman Act declared monopoly illegal, the Clayton Act defined in some detail varied types of illegal business practices that are conducive to the formation of monopolies or that result from them. Certain forms of holding companies and interlocking directorates are forbidden, as are discriminating freight agreements and the distribution of sales territories among so-called natural competitors. Two sections of the Clayton Act were later amended by the Robinson-Patman Act, 15 U.S.C. § 13c (1936), and the Celler-Kefauver Act, 15 U.S.C. § 18 (1950), to fortify its provisions. The Robinson-Patman Act, 15 U.S.C. §§ 13–13b, 21a (1988), made more enforceable section 2, which relates to price and other forms of discrimination among customers. The Celler-Kefauver Act strengthened section 7, prohibiting one firm from securing either the stocks or physical assets (i.e., plant and equipment) of another firm when the acquisition would reduce competition.

Clean Air Act, 42 U.S.C. §§ 7401 et seq. (1970), established air pollution control standards and gave citizens' groups the right to sue alleged violators. Most notably, it set auto emission standards and required manufacturers to drastically reduce the amount of pollutants discharged from new cars. Enforcement authority was assigned to the Environmental Protection Agency (EPA). A 1977 amendment extended certain deadlines for reaching specified auto emission levels while applying tighter restrictions on coal burning and other pollution sources; and a 1990 amendment imposed more stringent requirements on urban areas and mandated the increased use of cleaner-burning fuels.

Code Civil, *popularly* Code Napoleon *or* Napoleonic Code, codification of the principles of the civil law enacted in France under Napoleon in 1804. It clarified and made uniform the private law of France and followed Roman law in organizing the code into three books dealing with the law of persons, things, and modes of acquiring ownership of things. It also borrowed many principles and concepts from Roman civil law. Under the civil law system, judges are to apply these principles and decide cases in accordance with legislation rather than precedent.

Code Napoleon — see CODE CIVIL

Code of Federal Regulations (CFR), compilation of administrative laws governing federal regulatory agency practice and procedures. Revised annually, it contains the whole of the daily *Federal Register* together with previously issued regulations that are still current. Like the U.S. Code, it is divided into 50 titles, each representing a general subject area (e.g., commerce, military) and containing the applicable rules and regulations for agency activities in that area. The purpose of the CFR is to make available the large body of laws that govern federal practice. It can usually be found in university law libraries, large public libraries, and most federal depository libraries.

Code of Justinian, the collections of laws and legal interpretations developed under the sponsorship of the Byzantine emperor Justinian I from A.D. 529 to 565. Strictly speaking, the works did not constitute a new legal code. Rather, Justinian's committees of jurists provided basically two reference works containing collections of past laws and extracts of the opinions of the great Roman jurists. Also included were an elementary outline of the law and a collection of Justinian's own new laws.

Communications Act of 1934, 47 U.S.C. § 151 et seq. (1934), legislation enacted in scattered sections of the U.S. Code governing the growing communications field. It created the Federal

Communications Commission and established regulations for wire and radio common carriers (as for licensing and setting charges).

Comprehensive Environmental Response, Compensation, and Liability Act (CERCLA) (*popularly* Superfund), 42 U.S.C. §§ 9601 et seq. (1980), created a trust fund ($1.6 billion) to be used by the Environmental Protection Agency (EPA) in the cleanup of toxic waste sites. Any party responsible for creating or contributing to a dangerous toxic dump site was made subject to government suit and liable for damages, the compensation to be used to replenish the fund. Within two years the EPA was itself the target of congressional investigation, as various "sweetheart" deals (financially beneficial arrangements) between the EPA and polluters were discovered and many hazardous waste sites remained untouched. In 1986 the Superfund Amendments and Reauthorization Act (SARA) (codified throughout 42 U.S.C § 9601 et seq.) was signed, substantially increasing the size of the fund ($8.5 billion), establishing a new tax on corporations (particularly those in the chemical industry), and adding more controls to the EPA's management of the fund and the government's cleanup efforts.

Compromise of 1850, 9 Stat. 446, 452, 453, 462, 467 (1850), series of compromise measures passed by the U.S. Congress in an effort to settle several outstanding slavery issues and to avert the threat of dissolution of the Union. The measures were offered by the "great compromiser," Senator Henry Clay of Kentucky. In an attempt to give satisfaction both to those favoring and those opposing slavery, the important sections of the omnibus bill called for the admission of California as a free state, the organization of the territories of New Mexico and Utah with the slavery question left open, settlement of the Texas-New Mexico boundary dispute, a more rigorous provision for the return of runaway slaves, and the prohibition of the slave trade in the District of Columbia. These measures were accepted by moderates in all sections of the country, and the secession of the South was postponed for a decade. The Compromise, however, contained the seeds of future discord.

Consumer Product Safety Act (CPSA), 15 U.S.C. § 2051 et seq. (1972), created the Consumer Product Safety Commission, empowered to promulgate safety standards for consumer products as well as to do research and maintain information on consumer products. Also created penalties for violations of safety standards.

Copyright Act of 1976, 17 U.S.C. § 101 et seq. (1976), replaced prior Copyright Act of 1909, revising extensively U.S. copyright law. This act preempted state common-law copyright, thus completing the coverage of the national copyright system. In addition to other changes, it eliminated the requirement that works to be copyrighted be deposited with the Library of Congress, and it changed the term of copyright from 28 years with a single renewal to the life of the author plus 50 years (with certain exceptions). It also broadened categories of materials that may be copyrighted, stating that copyright subsists in original works of authorship fixed in any tangible medium of expression. Such works include literary, musical, and dramatic works; pantomimes and choreographic works; pictorial, graphic, and sculptural works; motion pictures and other audio-visual works; sound recordings and computer software. The act clarified the conventions of fair use; specified proper copyright notification (usually the symbol © or the word "Copyright"); established the Copyright Royalty Tribunal to oversee cable television and jukebox licensing of copyrighted works, in accordance with royalty rates set by the tribunal; placed limitations on the use of copyrighted works by libraries and educational institutions; and established a mechanism for review of issues pertaining to computer software.

De Donis Conditionalibus, legislation in late 13th-century England that allowed a conveyor of land to limit its inheritance to the direct descendants of the conveyee and to claim it back if the conveyee's direct line died out (fee tail). The statute consolidated the power to convey in the present possessor of land, effectively strengthening the authority of the feudal lords.

Depository Institutions Deregulation and Monetary Control Act (DIDMCA), 12 U.S.C. 248-1, 1735f-7a (1980), changed some of the rules—many of them obsolete—under which U.S. financial institutions had operated for nearly half a century. The principal objectives were to improve monetary control and equalize more nearly its cost among depository institutions; to remove impediments to competition for funds by depository institutions, while allowing the small saver a market rate of return; and to expand the availability of financial services to the public and reduce competitive inequalities among financial institutions offering them. The major changes were: (1) Uniform Federal Reserve requirements were phased in on transaction accounts (such as demand deposits, NOW accounts, telephone transfers, and automatic transfers) at all depository institutions—commercial banks (whether Federal Reserve members or not), savings and loan associations, mutual savings banks, and credit unions. (2) The Federal Reserve Board was authorized to collect all data necessary for the monitoring and control of money and credit aggregates. (3) Access to loans at the discount rate from Federal Reserve banks was widened to include any depository institution issuing transaction accounts or nonpersonal time deposits. (4) The Federal Reserve was to price its services, to which all depository institutions would now have access. (5) Regulation Q, which had long set interest-rate ceilings on deposits, was to be phased out over a six-year period. (6) An attempt was made to deal effectively with the state usury laws. (7) NOW accounts were authorized on a nationwide basis and could be offered by all depository institutions. Other services were extended. (8) The permissible activities of thrift institutions were broadened considerably. (9) Deposit insurance at commercial banks, savings banks, savings and loan associations, and credit unions was raised from $40,000 to $100,000. (10) The "truth in lending" disclosure and financial regulations were simplified to make it easier for creditors to comply.

Economic Opportunity Act, 42 U.S.C. §2701 et seq. (1964), provided funds for vocational training, created a Job Corps to train youths in conservation camps and urban centers, encouraged community action programs, extended loans to small businessmen and farmers, established a domestic peace corps (the counterpart of a popular foreign program), and created the Head Start program, a program that was designed to prepare children for success in public schools and that included medical, dental, social service, nutritional, and psychological care.

Economic Recovery Tax Act (ERTA), 26 U.S.C. §§ 15, 21, 22, 29, 30, 32, 40, 422, 424; 42 U.S.C. § 9836a et seq. (1981), reduced individual income tax rates by 25 percent and expanded depreciation allowances and credits for investments. It also allowed the appreciated value of charitable gifts to be counted as part of an alternative tax base.

Electronic Communications Privacy Act (ECPA), 18 U.S.C. §§ 2510–2520 (1986), made it a crime to intentionally intercept a wire or oral or electronic communication or to use or disclose the contents of an intercepted communication, with some exceptions. The privacy of messages sent and received on a computer network is protected under this act. It also criminalized intentional unauthorized access to stored wire or electronic communications, and set out the authorization procedure that government agents must follow before placing a wiretap.

Elementary and Secondary Education Act, 20 U.S.C. § 6301 et seq. (1965), provided federal funding for public and private education below the college level. Developed as part of President

Lyndon B. Johnson's Great Society program, the act was aimed particularly at high-poverty areas. Title I provided for basic-skills instruction in disadvantaged urban neighborhoods; Title II provided funds for library books and textbooks, including aid to parochial schools; Title III offered grants for local-level program innovations; Title IV created federal research and development programs; and Title V served to bolster state departments of education. Perhaps the most enduring legacy of the act are the Title I provisions, which continue to be debated in school districts and educational think tanks across the nation.

Employee Retirement Income Security Act (ERISA), 29 U.S.C. § 1001 et seq. (1974), provided for the regulation of private pension plans. The law stipulated capitalization, membership, and operating requirements and altered vestment formulas to include, for example, mandatory employee vestment after a certain period of time. The law also required pension-fund operators to make periodic reports on the conditions and activities of the fund. Oversight of the act's provisions was assigned to the newly created Pension Benefit Guaranty Corporation. The law also provided for regulation of employee welfare benefit plans, such as group health plans, disability insurance plans, or other plans, funds, or programs benefiting employees. Provisions of the Consolidated Omnibus Budget Reconciliation Act of 1986 (COBRA), codified at 29 U.S.C. § 1161 et seq., provide for continuation of ERISA benefits under such a plan to eligible employees upon termination of employment.

Employment Act, 15 U.S.C. § 1021 et seq. (1946), stated the government's responsibility for maintaining high employment levels and established the Council of Economic Advisers to advise the president and help assure a healthy national economy. The act has its roots in the Great Depression of the 1930s and in the economic policy associated with English economist John Maynard Keynes, which largely became federal policy. Central to the policy was the government's role in managing long-term economic demand (through price competition and regulation of interstate trade), which would ensure full employment. Although ultimately the economic policy was dismantled, the Employment Act was important for establishing the role of professional economists in the government and tasking the government with the creation of a systematic economic plan.

Endangered Species Act (ESA), 16 U.S.C. § 1531 et seq. (1973), obligated the government to protect all animal and plant life threatened with extinction, including in this category "endangered" species, defined as any species "which is in danger of extinction throughout all or a significant portion of its range," and "threatened" species, defined as any species "which is likely to become endangered in the foreseeable future throughout all or a significant portion of its range." It also provided for the drawing up of lists of such species and promoted the protection of critical habitats (areas designated as critical to the conservation of a species).

Espionage Act, 18 U.S.C. § 792 et seq. (1917), served to suppress opposition to the United States entry into World War I by making criticism of U.S. policy a "treasonable" offense. In combination with the Sedition Act of 1918, which amended it, the act was used as the basis for launching an unprecedented campaign against political radicals, suspected dissidents, left-wing organizations, and aliens. The disregard of basic civil liberties during these "Palmer raids," as they came to be known (because of the prominence of Attorney General A. Mitchell Palmer), drew widespread protest and ultimately discredited some high government officials. Once war opposition waned and the so-called Red Scare (i.e., fear of a perceived Bolshevik conspiracy to overthrow the U.S. government) passed, the law was allowed to expire (1921).

Ethics in Government Act, 2 U.S.C. § 288 et seq. (1978), established a comprehensive code of ethics for federal officials. It took account of both the House and Senate ethics codes but applied to the entire government, including the executive branch. It required government officers to file financial disclosure statements in order to make it possible to identify conflicts of interest; and it placed tighter restrictions on executive-branch employees' ability to register as lobbyists after leaving government service. The act also created the office of special prosecutor (known as *independent counsel* after 1983) to investigate and prosecute top executive officials independent of the attorney general's office, and it established the Office of Government Ethics to administer the code's provisions.

Fair Credit Reporting Act (FCRA), 15 U.S.C. § 1601 et seq. (1970), required credit agencies to make their records available to the consumer and report credit information only to authorized third parties. It also provided procedures by which consumers could challenge and correct faulty information and have the corrected version disseminated to the appropriate parties. Related consumer credit legislation includes the Fair Credit Billing Act, 15 U.S.C. § 1666 et seq. (1974), which gave consumers a means to challenge billing errors and required creditors to make all necessary adjustments; the Equal Credit Opportunity Act, 15 U.S.C. § 1691 et seq. (1974; amended 1976), which prohibited the denial of credit based on sex, marital status, age, race, religion, or national origin; and the Fair Debt Collection Practices Act, 15 U.S.C. § 1692 et seq. (1977), which curbed potential abuses by debt collection agencies.

Fair Labor Standards Act of 1938 (FLSA), *popularly* Wages and Hours Act, 29 U.S.C. § 201 et seq. (1938), the first act in the United States prescribing nationwide compulsory federal regulation of wages and hours, sponsored by Senator Robert F. Wagner of New York. The law, applying to all industries engaged in interstate commerce, established a minimum wage of 25 cents per hour for the first year, to be increased to 40 cents within seven years. No worker was obliged to work, without compensation at overtime rates, more than 44 hours a week during the first year, 42 the second year, and 40 thereafter. A 1963 amendment, the Equal Pay Act, 29 U.S.C. § 206 (d), barred gender discrimination in pay rates for the same work done under similar conditions.

Federal Election Campaign Act (FECA), 2 U.S.C. § 431 et seq. (1971), set strict limits on the amount of money a particular corporation, union, or private individual could give to a candidate in a federal election. It also required candidates and political action committees (PACs) to disclose their receipts and identify their contributors. A 1974 amendment specified additional contribution limits and imposed spending limits for candidates in primary and general elections; however, the Supreme Court struck down the latter provision as unconstitutional in *Buckley v. Valeo*, 424 U.S. 1 (1976). The 1974 amendment also set up the Federal Election Commission and established public funding of presidential elections. Two additional amendments (1976, 1979) were aimed at regulating PACs and boosting the level of party participation.

Federal Reserve Act, 12 U.S.C. § 221 et seq. (1913), created a federal reserve system to mobilize banking reserves and issue a flexible currency—federal reserve notes—based on gold and commercial paper. It created a system consisting of a governing board of presidential appointees, the 12 Federal Reserve banks, a committee to oversee the sale of securities on the open market, a general advisory council, and (since 1976) a consumer advisory council. All national banks were required to be members of the Federal Reserve System, and state banks could become members if they met membership qualifications.

Federal Rules of Appellate Procedure, body of procedural rules governing the appeals process in the bringing of cases to a U.S. court of appeals from a U.S. district court or the Tax Court of the

United States. The work of each of the 12 regional courts of appeals is mainly to review decisions of federal administrative agencies and to review judgments of the lower district courts. The appellate rules state the practices and procedures by which such judicial reviews are to be undertaken. Many state appellate procedures are roughly similar to those of the federal government.

Federal Rules of Civil Procedure, body of procedural rules governing civil actions in federal courts. As stated in Rule 1, the rules' purpose is "to secure the just, speedy, and inexpensive determination of every action." Two central elements of civil process covered by the rules are discovery and pretrial conference, the former being a review of the facts by both parties and the latter being a meeting before a judge or magistrate to determine whether a trial is necessary or whether an out-of-court settlement might be reached. The federal rules have served as a model for many state court rules of civil procedure.

Federal Rules of Criminal Procedure, body of procedural rules governing criminal proceedings in federal courts. Two central aims of the rules are to ensure that due process of the law is served and that efficient use is made of judicial resources. The rules cover such elements as pretrial discovery, plea bargaining, introducing evidence, and making objections. Although, as in the case of rules of civil procedure, some states have patterned their rules of criminal procedure after the federal rules, there is greater diversity in criminal procedure than in civil procedure across U.S. jurisdictions.

Federal Rules of Evidence, body of procedural rules governing the use of evidence in both civil and criminal cases in federal courts. The rules establish the methods by which evidentiary information may be presented, covering such elements as relevance, admissibility, competency of witnesses, privileges, confessions and admissions, expert testimony, physical evidence, and authentication. The rules of evidence have been founded on both case law and state statutes and are shaped by understandings of what constitutes admissible and sufficient proof. Many states have patterned their rules of evidence after those of the federal courts.

Federal Tort Claims Act (FTCA), 28 U.S.C. § 1346 et seq. (1946), did away with discretionary immunity (based on sovereignty) for the United States in civil tort actions in federal court. Prior to the enactment (which is Title VI of the Legislative Reorganization Act, 2 U.S.C. § 31), persons who were tortiously injured by agents of the government had no legal recourse (other than having a congressperson introduce a private relief bill) because the U.S. government could not be sued. The act established the conditions for making claims and bringing suit against the federal government. Several exceptions to government liability are included, however, such as acts involving the "discretionary function" of federal agents and injuries incurred while carrying out military duties.

Food, Drug, and Cosmetic Act (FDCA), 21 U.S.C. § 301 et seq. (1938), prohibited interstate commerce in adulterated food products and hazardous or mislabeled household substances and strengthened the enforcement power of the Food and Drug Administration (FDA). The act established new consumer product identification and quality standards and expanded the FDA's role in inspecting food and cosmetics and in testing and licensing drugs. It has been amended several times to broaden its coverage, which now includes medical devices, sanitation certification, labeling and anti-tampering requirements, and FDA oversight in drug marketing. These amendments often came in the wake of heavy lobbying, pro and con, by both consumer advocates and industry representatives.

Freedom of Information Act (FOIA), 5 U.S.C. § 552 (1966), established public access to government information. The vast bulk of information controlled by the federal government was made available under the act, but certain exceptions still apply. These include classified national defense and foreign policy information, privileged or confidential trade and financial information, internal personnel records and documents, information concerning certain law enforcement matters, and geological and geophysical research information concerning wells. Information not exempt from public disclosure was deemed available to virtually anyone regardless of nationality or need to know. Most federal agencies issue bulletins that describe how to obtain the information they hold. In some cases a fee is charged to persons requesting documents to offset records search and duplication costs.

Fugitive Slave Acts, 1 Stat. 302 (1793) and 9 Stat. 462 (1850), repealed by 13 Stat. 200 (1864), statutes passed by Congress in 1793 and 1850 (and repealed in 1864) that provided for the seizure and return of runaway slaves who escaped from one state into another or into a federal territory. The 1793 law enforced Article IV, Section 2, of the U.S. Constitution in authorizing any federal district judge or circuit court judge, or any state magistrate, to decide finally and without a jury trial the status of an alleged fugitive slave. For some time after the beginning of the American Civil War, the Fugitive Slave Acts were considered to still hold in the case of blacks fleeing from masters in border states that were loyal to the Union government. It was not until June 28, 1864, that the acts were repealed.

Fulbright Act, formerly 50 U.S.C. § 1641 (1946), provided for educational grants under an international exchange scholarship program created to increase mutual understanding between the people of the United States and the people of other countries through the medium of educational and cultural exchange. The program was conceived by Senator J. William Fulbright of Arkansas and carried forward by the Fulbright Act of 1946 and subsequent legislation, consolidated and expanded in the Mutual Educational and Cultural Exchange Act of 1961, also known as the Fulbright-Hays Act, 22 U.S.C. § 2458a.

General Agreement on Tariffs and Trade (GATT), integrated set of bilateral trade agreements aimed at the abolition of quotas and the reduction of tariff duties among the contracting nations. By the late 20th century, more than 90 nations were signatories to GATT. GATT includes a long schedule of specific tariff concessions for each contracting nation, representing tariff rates that each country has agreed to extend to others. It also sets forth general rules that are, in effect, a code of commercial policy. They provide for unconditional most-favored-nation clauses, the elimination of quotas and other quantitative trade restrictions, uniform customs regulations, and the obligation of each contracting nation to negotiate for tariff cuts upon the request of another. An escape clause allows contracting countries to alter agreements if their domestic producers suffer excessive losses as a result of trade concessions. Countries that are members of a customs union or free-trade area are permitted to grant preferential tariff rates to each other.

G.I. Bill of Rights — see Servicemen's Readjustment Act

Glass–Steagall Act of 1933 — see Banking Act of 1933

Gulf of Tonkin Resolution, 78 Stat. 384 (1964), terminated by 84 Stat. 2055 (1971), resolution put before the United States Congress by President Lyndon Johnson on Aug. 5, 1964, following allegedly unprovoked attacks by North Vietnamese torpedo boats on two U.S. destroyers in the Gulf of Tonkin between August 2 and August 4. Its stated purpose was to approve and support the determination of the president, as commander in chief, in taking all necessary measures to repel any armed attack against the forces of the United States and to prevent further aggression, and it declared the maintenance of international peace and security in Southeast Asia to be vital to American interests and to world peace. Both houses of Congress passed the resolution on August 7. In later years, especially in view of subsequent revelations concerning U.S. policy and operations in Vietnam, many members of Congress came to see the resolution as giving the president a blanket power to wage war, and it was repealed in 1970.

Hatch Act, 5 U.S.C. § 1501 et seq. (1939), aimed at eliminating corrupt practices in national elections. It was sponsored by Senator Carl Hatch of New Mexico following disclosures that Works Progress Administration officials were using their positions to win votes for the Democratic Party. The Hatch Act forbade intimidation or bribery of voters and restricted political-campaign activities by federal employees. As amended in 1940, it also severely limited contributions by individuals to political campaigns and spending by campaign committees.

Hepburn Act, formerly 49 U.S.C. § 1 et seq. (1906), created the first of the government's regulatory commissions. The Interstate Commerce Commission (ICC) was established in 1887 to oversee trade on the interstate railways but weakened by an 1897 Supreme Court decision. By the early 1900s, public demand for effective national regulation of interstate railroad rates had grown enough to allow President Theodore Roosevelt to undertake a personal campaign to have new legislation passed. The resulting Hepburn Act greatly enlarged the ICC's jurisdiction and forbade railroads to increase rates without its approval. This and similar acts laid the basis for the modern concept of consumer protection through government regulation.

Higher Education Act, 20 U.S.C. § 1001 et seq. (1965), provided needs-based scholarships and loans for undergraduates and authorized a National Teachers Corps. Citing "the appalling frequency with which a student is presently forced to forgo the opportunity of [higher] education because of inability to meet the costs," a Democratic Congress passed the bill as part of President Lyndon B. Johnson's Great Society Program. The act signaled a transition from institutional assistance to individual student aid.

Homestead Act, 43 U.S.C. § 161 et seq. (1862), provided 160 acres of public land free of charge (except for a small filing fee) to anyone either 21 years of age or head of a family, a citizen or person who had filed for citizenship, who had lived on and cultivated the land for at least five years. By the turn of the century, more than 80 million acres had been claimed by homesteaders.

Housing and Urban Development Act, 42 U.S.C. § 3101 et seq. (1965), established a Cabinet-level department to coordinate federal housing programs. Intended as a measure to improve living conditions in urban areas, it provided comprehensive housing assistance to low- and moderate-income families and gave urban interests an active voice in federal housing policy. Previous legislation had authorized low-cost mortgage loans administered by the Federal Housing Administration (FHA), suburban development programs (e.g. the G.I. Bill), and various neighborhood rehabilitation programs, including some urban renewal efforts; but only with the creation of the Department of Housing and Urban Development (HUD) in 1965 did federal assistance become available on a large scale to blighted urban areas. A 1968 amendment set as a target the construction of millions of new housing units and gave HUD more direct administrative authority, but the program was halted by executive order under President Richard M. Nixon and subsequently revised to provide primarily rent assistance. By the 1990s federal housing policy had shifted toward an emphasis on local block grants, various savings and loan programs, and private home ownership.

Immigration Acts, series of acts that regulated the flow of immigrants into the United States. Beginning in the 19th century, Congress enacted a series of restrictive immigration laws that sought to limit or bar those immigrants who were thought to be undesirable (e.g., Chinese and Japanese persons, the illiterate, the sick or handicapped, criminals, political radicals). In the early part of the 20th century a commission set up to study the issue recommended a quota system, which was adopted in the Immigration Act of 1924, formerly 8 U.S.C. § 145 et seq. This act established an annual quota, fixed in 1929 at 150,000. It also established the national-origin system, under which quotas were established for each country based on the number of persons of that national origin who were living in the United States in 1920. It thus discriminated in favor of the countries of northwestern Europe and against immigrants from southern and eastern Europe; it barred Asians completely. Although minor changes were subsequently made, this law was to characterize national immigration policy until 1965, when it was abolished in favor of a first-come, first-serve policy. The new law set an annual ceiling of 170,000 immigrant visas for nations outside the Western Hemisphere, with 20,000 the maximum allowed to any one nation. A ceiling of 120,000 was set for persons from the Western Hemisphere. A law in 1986 granted amnesty to many illegal aliens already in the United States and imposed sanctions on employers who knowingly hire illegal aliens. Additional revisions were made in 1990.

Indian Removal Act of 1830, 4 Stat. 411 (1830), one of the first legislative steps in creating the reservation system from which 25 U.S.C. § 174 is derived. Despite a 1789 act of Congress, 1 Stat. 137, declaring that the land rights of American Indians must be respected and that their title could only be extinguished by treaty, the 1830 act authorized the president to purchase land from tribes east of the Mississippi and grant them perpetual title to land west of the river. In carrying out the law, resistance was met with military force. The discovery of gold in California (1848) started a new sequence of broken treaties and war. An act of March 3, 1871, 15 Stat. 566, terminated native tribes' status as independent powers with which the United States could contract by treaty and brought native peoples under tighter legislative control, ultimately assigning them to reservations. The infamous Dawes General Allotment Act of 1887, 25 U.S.C. § 331 et seq. (1887), divided the reservations into individual parcels and gave every inhabitant a particular piece of the land. The result was disastrous: through the alienation of surplus lands and the patenting of individual holdings, Native American peoples collectively lost 62 percent (86,000,000 acres) of their tribal lands. In 1934, Congress adopted the Indian Reorganization Act, 25 U.S.C. § 461 et seq. (1934), which contemplated an orderly decrease in federal control and a concomitant increase of American Indian self-government. About 160 tribes adopted written constitutions, and a revolving credit fund helped Native Americans improve their economic position. The Snyder Act, 25 U.S.C. § 13 (1921), extended citizenship to all Native Americans, but few took advantage of the law. In the 1950s many petitions for land claims against the United States were granted, with awards totaling nearly $1 billion. In 1968, Congress passed the Indian Civil Rights Act, 25 U.S.C. § 1301 et seq., prohibiting tribes exercising the powers of self-government from infringing on rights (as to freedom of speech and trial by jury) guaranteed under the U.S. Constitution. In subsequent decades Native Americans continued to strengthen their tribal governments and increase their use of the courts to obtain rights to economic resources connected with tribal lands.

Internal Revenue Code, 26 U.S.C. § 1 et seq. (1986), legislation governing federal tax law. The Internal Revenue Code was first enacted into law in 1939 as a compilation of U.S. statutes relating to internal revenue from 1862 to 1938 that were still in force in 1939. A revised Internal Revenue Code was enacted in 1954, and the 1954 Code was revised and redesignated the Internal Revenue Code of 1986 by the Tax Reform Act of 1986. The Code defines the scope and operation of the entire U.S. tax system. It is recognized as one of the longest (6,000 pages, with several volumes of accompanying explanations) and most complex laws in the world. Among its numerous provisions, it sets limits on taxes collected on the manufacture of alcohol, tobacco, and firearms; describes the funding requirements for private pension plans; states the tax requirements for maintaining social insurance; determines government revenues from corporate, excise, estate, and gift taxes; and lays the basis for the collection of personal income taxes. The code is administered by the Internal Revenue Service.

Internal Security Act of 1950, *popularly* McCarran Act, 50 U.S.C. § 781 (1950), repealed by 107 Stat. 2329 (1993), required the registration of communist organizations in the United States and established the Subversive Activities Control Board to investigate persons thought to be engaged in "un-American" activities. It was a key institution in the era of the Cold War, tightening alien exclusion and deportation laws and allowing for the detention of dangerous, disloyal, or subversive persons in times of war or "internal security emergency." Most of its provisions were later declared unconstitutional.

Judiciary Act, 1 Stat. 73 (1789), divided the country into judicial districts and set up courts in each one, along with judges and attorneys with responsibility for civil and criminal actions in their districts. It also created the office of Attorney General of the United States, and provided for Supreme Court review of the final judgments of the highest court of any state in cases involving federal treaties and statutes or state statutes that may be invalid under the Constitution. The constitutionality of the act was twice challenged in the Supreme Court in *Martin v. Hunter's Lessee*, 14 U.S. 304 (1816), and *Cohens v. Virginia*, 19 U.S. 264 (1821), but was upheld each time.

Kansas–Nebraska Act, 10 Stat. 277 (1854), critical national policy change concerning the expansion of slavery into the territories, affirming the concept of popular sovereignty over congressional edict. In 1820 the Missouri Compromise had excluded slavery from that part of the Louisiana Purchase (except Missouri) north of the 36°30′ parallel. The Kansas-Nebraska Act, sponsored by Democratic Senator Stephen A. Douglas, provided for the territorial organization of Kansas and Nebraska under the principle of popular sovereignty, which had been applied to New Mexico and Utah in the Compromise of 1850. Passage of the act was followed by the establishment of the Republican Party as a viable political organization opposed to the expansion of slavery into the territories.

Labor Disputes Act, *popularly* Norris–LaGuardia Act, 29 U.S.C. §§ 101–115 (1932), limited the power of federal courts to issue injunctions in labor disputes, especially against striking unions. It also outlawed yellow dog contracts.

Labor Management Relations Act, *popularly* Taft–Hartley Act, 29 U.S.C. § 141 et seq. (1947), law—enacted over the veto of President Harry S. Truman—amending much of the pro-union National Labor Relations (Wagner) Act of 1935. While preserving the rights of labor to organize and to bargain collectively, the Labor Management Relations Act of 1947 additionally guaranteed employees the right not to join unions (outlawing the closed shop); permitted union shops only where state law allowed and where a majority of workers voted for them; required unions to give 60 days' advance notification of a strike; authorized 80-day federal injunctions when a strike threatened to imperil national health or safety; narrowed the definition of unfair labor practices; specified unfair union practices; restricted union political contributions; and required union officers to deny under oath any Communist affiliations. The Labor Management Reporting and Disclosure (Landrum-Griffin) Act of 1959 set further union restrictions, barring secondary boycotts and limiting the right to picket.

Labor Management Reporting and Disclosure Act (LMRDA), *popularly* Landrum–Griffin Act, 29 U.S.C. § 401 et seq. (1959), instituted federal penalties for labor officials who misused union funds, who had been found guilty of specific crimes, or who had violently prevented union members from exercising their legal rights. The act contained other provisions that strengthened parts of the Labor Management Relations (Taft-Hartley) Act, which was detested by nearly all elements of organized labor. These provisions included a strict ban on secondary boycotts (union efforts to stop one employer from dealing with another employer who is being struck or boycotted) and greater freedom for individual states to set the terms of labor relations within their borders. The latter provision hampered labor organizing in the South, the least unionized region in the United States.

Landrum–Griffin Act — see LABOR MANAGEMENT REPORTING AND DISCLOSURE ACT

Lanham Act — see TRADEMARK ACT OF 1946

Lend–Lease Act, formerly 22 U.S.C. § 411 et seq. (1941), gave the president the authority to aid any nation whose defense he believed vital to the United States and to accept repayment "in kind or property, or any other direct or indirect benefit which the President deems satisfactory." The principal recipients of aid during World War II were the British Commonwealth countries (about 63 percent) and the Soviet Union (about 22 percent), though by the end of the war more than 40 nations had received lend-lease help. Much of the aid, valued at $49.1 billion, amounted to outright gifts. Some of the cost of the lend-lease program was offset by so-called reverse lend-lease, under which Allied nations gave U.S. troops stationed abroad about $8 billion worth of aid. The Lend-Lease Act expired by its own terms following the end of World War II.

Louisiana Civil Code, codification of the civil law enacted by the Louisiana state legislature in 1825. Modeled on the Code Napoleon, the Civil Code codified the French and Spanish laws considered still in force in Louisiana at that time. The Civil Code has undergone revision by legislative act numerous times since 1825, with the most recent comprehensive revision being in 1986. The Civil Code contains the basic law of persons, property, obligations, donations, and successions that Louisiana statutes must accord with and Louisiana judges must apply in deciding cases.

McCarran Act — see INTERNAL SECURITY ACT OF 1950

Missouri Compromise, 3 Stat. 545, measure worked out between the North and the South and passed by the U.S. Congress that allowed for admission of Missouri as a slave state, Maine as a free state, and made free soil all western territories north of Missouri's southern border. It marked the beginning of the prolonged sectional conflict over the extension of slavery that led to the Civil War. It was repealed by the Kansas-Nebraska Act (1854) and declared unconstitutional in the Dred Scott decision of 1857.

Model Penal Code, set of criminal law principles and guidelines issued in 1962 by the American Law Institute, following more than a decade of effort. The code is an attempt to rationalize criminal law in relation to modern society and to establish a logical framework for defining offenses and a consistent body of general principles on such matters as criminal intent and the liability of accomplices. The Model Penal Code had a profound influence on the revision of many individual state codes over the following 20 years; the code itself was never enacted completely, but it inspired and influenced a long period of criminal code reform.

Morrill Land–Grant College Act, 7 U.S.C. § 301 et seq. (1862), provided grants of land to state colleges, whose "leading object" would be to teach subjects "related to agriculture and the mechanic arts," without excluding the general sciences and classical studies. It granted every state establishing such a college 30,000 acres of public land for each of its lawmakers in Congress. Since 1862 some 12 million acres have been distributed, on which some 70 of the so-called land-grant colleges currently flourish.

Napoleonic Code — see CODE CIVIL

National Aeronautics and Space Act, 42 U.S.C. § 2458 (1958), boosted space research and provided funds to increase the study of science. Enacted largely in response to the Soviet Union's launching of Sputnik I, the first man-made satellite to orbit the earth (1957), the act created the National Aeronautics and Space Administration (NASA) to research and develop vehicles and activities for the exploration of space. The related National Defense Education Act, formerly 20 U.S.C. § 401 et seq., provided extensive aid to schools and students in order to bring American education—particularly in the sciences—up to what were regarded as Soviet levels of achievement.

National Bank Act, 12 Stat. 665 (1863), provided for the federal charter and supervision of national banks; they were to circulate a stable, uniform national currency secured by federal bonds deposited by each bank with the comptroller of the currency (often called the national banking administrator). The act regulated the minimum capital requirements of national banks, the kinds of loans they could make, and the reserves that were to be held against notes and deposits; it also provided for the supervision and examination of banks and for the protection of note holders. While the act did not prohibit state banks from issuing their own currency, Congress did impose a 10 percent tax on state bank notes that effectively eliminated such a rival currency. The act was repealed in 1864 by the enactment of the National Bank Act of 1864, 12 U.S.C. § 38 et seq., which reserved the rights of the associations organized under the 1863 act. The inflexibility of national bank-note supplies and a lack of reserves led to the formation of the Federal Reserve System in 1913.

National Environmental Policy Act (NEPA), 42 U.S.C. § 4321 et seq. (1969), established a national Council on Environmental Quality to oversee government activities that could affect the environment and required federal agencies to file environmental impact statements before taking any major action. The law was intended to help "maintain conditions under which man and nature can exist in productive harmony" and, as such, has been labeled by the courts an "environmental full disclosure law." It has often been left to the courts to rule on the accuracy of impact statements that have been contested by environmental or neighborhood groups.

National Industrial Recovery Act (NIRA), formerly 40 U.S.C. § 401 et seq. (1933), Depression-era legislation that created the Public Works Administration (PWA) and National Recovery Administration (NRA) to oversee a series of recovery measures. The PWA was allotted $3.3 billion to create public works operations, but because of time spent planning, the PWA did not become an important factor until late in the New Deal. The NRA was charged with administering codes of fair labor practice within certain industries. The codes were designed to stabilize production, raise prices, and protect labor and consumers. By February 1934, however, many critics felt that far too many codes had come into existence, containing innumerable provisions that were difficult to enforce. In May 1935 the Supreme Court invalidated the code system (*Schechter Poultry Corp. v. United States*, 295 U.S.C. § 495 (1935)). Despite shortcomings, however, the NRA had aided several highly competitive industries, such as textiles, and brought reforms that were reenacted in other legislation: federal wages-and-hours regulation, collective bargaining guarantees, and abolition of child labor in interstate commerce.

National Labor Relations Act (NLRA), *popularly* Wagner Act, 29 U.S.C. § 151 et seq. (1935), the single most important piece of labor legislation enacted in the United States in the 20th century. It was enacted to eliminate employers' interference with the autonomous organization of workers into unions. Sponsored by Senator Robert F. Wagner, a Democrat from New York, the act established the federal government as the regulator and ultimate arbiter of labor relations. It set up a permanent, three-member National Labor Relations Board (NLRB) with the power to protect the right of most workers (with the notable exception of agricultural and domestic laborers) to organize unions of their own choosing and to encourage collective bargaining. The act prohibited employers from engaging in such unfair labor practices as setting up a company union and firing or otherwise discriminating against workers who organized or joined unions. Under the act, the NLRB was given the power to order elections whereby workers could choose which union they wanted to represent them. The act prohibited employers from refusing to bargain with any such union that had been certified by the NLRB as being the choice of a majority of employees.

National Security Act, 50 U.S.C. § 403 (1947), created several major defense and intelligence institutions, including the National Security Council (NSC), the Central Intelligence Agency (CIA), the Secretary of Defense, the Joint Chiefs of Staff, and the U.S. Air Force. The legislation grew out of the nation's wartime experience and a postwar concern over the capabilities and intentions of the Soviet Union. The basic function of the institutions created by the act is to advise the president on domestic, foreign, and military policies related to national security.

Norris–LaGuardia Act — see LABOR DISPUTES ACT

Occupational Safety and Health Act (OSHA), 29 U.S.C. 651 et seq. (1970), sought to make work safer and protect the physical well-being of the worker. It created the Occupational Safety and Health Administration (OSHA) within the Department of Labor to oversee its provisions. The law required employers to maintain certain health and safety standards and submit to periodic government inspection of workplaces. OSHA's efforts to enforce regulations have often been the subject of legal battles.

Omnibus Budget Reconciliation Act (OBRA), 42 U.S.C. § 9801 et seq. (1981), implemented massive government spending reductions and significantly altered the congressional budget process. As the centerpiece of President Ronald Reagan's "supply-side" revolution, the law called for $135 billion to be cut from federal programs while defense spending was greatly increased. The act also shifted responsibility for the budget reconciliation process from congressional committees to the House and Senate floors. Later budget reconciliation acts (1990, 1993) were aimed at extending and adjusting five-year deficit reduction targets as part of the overall federal budget process.

Public Utility Holding Company Act (PUHCA), 15 U.S.C. § 79 et seq. (1935), regulated the control holding companies had over operating public utility companies. The act was designed to break up a system that allowed much financial leverage to be wielded by a relatively small number of private holding companies, and instead create a system based on independent, regional operating units. Oversight for this transformation was assigned to the Securities and Exchange Commission, which was given broad enforcement powers. The change is generally viewed to have been crucial to the development of the nation's electric utilities and is also notable for marking the emergence of a congressional coalition of Republicans and conservative Democrats who opposed this and other legislation perceived as being directed against business interests.

Racketeer Influenced and Corrupt Organizations Act (RICO), 18 U.S.C. §§1961–1968 (1970), made criminal "enterprise," or illicit activity that is run like a business, illegal and applied harsh penalties to those engaged in it. RICO included provisions against fraud, corruption, and violence and allowed federal prosecutors broad powers to attack organized crime elements or other groups involved in certain "patterns" of illicit conduct. It has been used successfully against a wide variety of offenders, and many states have modeled laws on its provisions.

Railway Labor Act (RLA), 45 U.S.C. § 151 (1926), established arbitration and mediation guidelines for labor-management disputes in interstate transportation industries. Because it gave a statutory basis to employees' right to organize and prohibited company interference or coercion, it has been regarded as a precursor to such important labor legislation of the 1930s as the Labor Disputes (Norris-LaGuardia) Act, the National Industrial Recovery Act, and the National Labor Relations (Wagner) Act. But the Railway Labor Act is important in its own right for having established noncompulsory bargaining as the basic framework for achieving labor settlements. A 1934 amendment extended its provisions to airlines and created the National Mediation Board, an independent federal agency empowered to handle disputes.

Real Estate Settlement Procedures Act (RESPA), 12 U.S.C. §2601 et seq. (1974), protected consumers buying real estate by requiring disclosure of all closing costs. The Act required lenders to give mortgage applicants a standard form estimating the settlement costs, and it prohibited kickbacks for referrals among settlement service providers (as title insurers).

Resource Conservation and Recovery Act (RCRA), 42 U.S.C. 6901 et seq. (1976), authorized the Environmental Protection Agency (EPA) to develop a hazardous waste management system, including plans for the handling and storage of wastes and the licensing of treatment and disposal facilities. The states were required to implement the plans under authorized grants from the EPA. The act generally encouraged "cradle to grave" management of certain products and emphasized the need for recycling and conservation.

Revised Uniform Partnership Act — see Uniform Partnership Act

Rural Electrification Act, 7 U.S.C. § 901 et seq. (1936), established a program, overseen by the Rural Electrification Administration (REA), aimed at raising the standard of rural living and slowing the extensive migration of rural Americans to urban centers. More than 98 percent of U.S. farms were equipped with electric power under the program. The REA provided low-interest loans to farm cooperatives for the construction and operation of power plants and power lines in rural areas. Rural electrification brought city conveniences, such as electric lighting and radio, to areas of low population density and allowed for the automation of many farm operations.

Securities Acts, two laws concerning the issuance and exchange of financial securities. The first act, known simply as the Securities Act, 15 U.S.C. § 77a et seq. (1933), stipulated that a company offering securities must register them with the Federal Trade Commission (or, after 1933, the Securities and Exchange Commission [SEC]) and make full public disclosure of all relevant information. Certain private, in-state, governmental, and small-business offerings were exempt. The second act, the Securities Exchange Act, 15 U.S.C. § 78a et seq. (1934), prohibited the buying of stock without adequate funds to pay for it, provided for the registration and supervision of securities markets and stockbrokers, established rules for solicitation of proxies, and prevented unfair use of private information in stock trading. The administration of both acts was assigned to the SEC, which also served as adviser to the court in corporate bankruptcy cases.

Securities Exchange Act — see Securities Acts

Sedition Act of 1918, 40 Stat. 553 (1918), an amendment to the Espionage Act of 1917. The act made it criminal to use speech to incite resistance to the war effort, as well as to criticize the United States or to support a country at war with the United States. The act was repealed in 1921.

Semiconductor Chip Protection Act of 1984 (SCPA), 17 U.S.C. §§ 901–904 (1984), reserved exclusive rights to an original design for a semiconductor chip to the owner of that design for a period of 10 years.

Servicemen's Readjustment Act, *popularly* G.I. Bill of Rights, 38 U.S.C. § 4101 et seq. (1944), provided veterans with loans, educational subsidies, and other benefits. Designed to ease military personnel back into civilian life and at the same time to bolster the postwar economy, the legislation was broadly supported. Through the Veterans Administration (VA), veterans received low-interest mortgage and small-business loans, job training, hiring privileges, and tuition and other incentives to continue their education in school or college. Subsequent amendments also provided for full disability coverage and the building of additional VA hospitals. The act had profound effects on the housing industry and higher education in particular, creating millions of new homes (and jobs) and hundreds of thousands of new college graduates.

Sherman Antitrust Act, 15 U.S.C. § 1 et seq. (1890), curbed concentrations of power that interfere with trade and reduce competition. One of its main provisions outlawed all combinations that restrained trade between states or with foreign nations. This prohibition applied not only to formal cartels but also to any agreement to fix prices, limit industrial output, share markets, or exclude competition. A second key provision made illegal all attempts to monopolize any part of trade or commerce in the United States. These two provisions, which comprise the heart of the Sherman Act, are enforceable by the Department of Justice through litigation in the federal courts. Firms found in violation of the act can be ordered dissolved by the courts, and injunctions to prohibit illegal practices can be issued. Violations are punishable by fines and imprisonment. Moreover, private parties injured by violations are permitted to sue for triple the amount of damages done them. In 1914 Congress passed two legislative measures that provided support for the Sherman Act. One of these was the Clayton Antitrust Act, which elaborated on the general provisions of the Sherman Act and specified many illegal practices that either contributed to or resulted from monopolization. The other measure created the Federal Trade Commission, providing the government with an agency that had the power to investigate possible violations of antitrust legislation and issue orders forbidding unfair competition practices.

Smoot–Hawley Tariff Act, 19 U.S.C § 1001 (1930), deleted by 76 Stat. 72 (1962), raised import duties by as much as 50 percent, greatly adding to the downward spiral of the world economy in the 1930s. Conceived and passed by the House of Representatives in 1929 as a protective measure for domestic industries, including so-called aged industries, the act contributed to the early loss of confidence on Wall Street and signaled American unwillingness to play the role of leader in the world economy. Combined with the drain of gold and foreign currency, it produced results that were catastrophic. Other countries retaliated with similarly high protective tariffs, and respected overseas banks began to collapse. Even today the Smoot-Hawley tariff is occasionally invoked as a symbol of the negative effects of protectionism.

Social Security Act, 42 U.S.C. § 401 et seq. (1935), established a permanent national old-age pension system through employer and employee contributions; later it was extended to include dependents, the disabled, and other groups. Responding to the economic impact of the Great Depression, 5,000,000 elderly people in the early 1930s joined nationwide Townsend clubs, promoted by Francis E. Townsend to support his program demanding a $200 monthly pension for everyone over the age of 60. In 1934 President Franklin D. Roosevelt set up a committee on economic security to consider the matter; after studying its recommendations, Congress in 1935 enacted the Social Security Act, providing old-age benefits to be financed by a payroll tax on employers and employees. Railroad employees were covered separately under the Railroad Retirement Act of 1934. The Social Security Act has been periodically amended, expanding the types of coverage, bringing progressively more workers into the system, and adjusting both taxes and benefits in an attempt to keep pace with inflation.

Statute of Frauds, law enacted in England in 1677 to prevent fraud and perjuries by parties seeking to hold another to an alleged obligation. The original law is the basis of statutes that have been enacted in all U.S. states. It required various contracts and causes of action to be evidenced by a writing signed by the party to be charged or by a lawfully authorized agent. Under the original Statute of Frauds, all leases, estates, and interests in land had the effect of estates at will unless evidenced by writing, with the exception of leases for three years or less; such leases, estates, or interests were not to be assigned, granted, or surrendered unless by means of a writing except when occurring by operation of law. Trusts in land were held to the same basic terms. Causes of action based on a promise to marry or to answer for damages or for the debt, default, or improper or negligent conduct of another were to be evidenced in writing. Contracts for the sale of land were to be in writing; and contracts for the sale of goods above a certain amount were to be evidenced by the receipt of goods or giving of value by the buyer or by writing. Contracts that could possibly be performed in a year did not need to be in writing.

Superfund — see COMPREHENSIVE ENVIRONMENTAL RESPONSE, COMPENSATION, AND LIABILITY ACT

Taft–Hartley Act — see LABOR MANAGEMENT RELATIONS ACT

Tax Reform Act of 1986, 100 Stat. 2085 (1986), revised federal tax laws and created the Internal Revenue Code of 1986. The act eliminated various tax loopholes for high-income earners and reduced the highest rates for both businesses and individuals. The intent of the act was to achieve a "level playing field." The rate reductions were to be made up by increased restrictions on deductions for corporate capital expenditures and a repeal of the investment tax credit. Corporate taxes were thus expected to increase $120 billion in five years, which generally they have done. The act also removed over four million low-income individuals from the tax rolls and made unemployment compensation taxable. Tax reform took place previously in 1976, 1981, and 1984. The Tax Reform Act of 1976 included, among other changes, new provisions relating to childcare and child support, and instituted new laws relating to capital gains and losses, including the one-time exclusion from capital gains tax on the sale of a residence. In 1981, the Economic Recovery Tax Act (*q.v.*) was enacted. The Tax Reform Act of 1984 was aimed at reducing the federal deficit. Among its provisions were tax exemptions for certain fringe benefits, stricter rules regarding deductions for charitable donations, and the creation of tax advantages to corporations to encourage exports. These efforts to amend federal tax laws were followed by the sweeping changes brought by the Tax Reform Act of 1986.

Tax Reform Act of 1984 — see TAX REFORM ACT OF 1986

Tax Reform Act of 1976 — see TAX REFORM ACT OF 1986

Trademark Act of 1946, *popularly* Lanham Act, 15 U.S.C. § 1051 et seq. (1946), created federal protection of trademarks and service marks through registration with the Patent and Trademark Office. The act defined what may be used as a mark, outlined the registration procedure, and created a cause of action for infringement.

Truth in Lending Act (TILA), 15 U.S.C. § 1601 et seq. (1968), required consumer credit institutions to provide customers with accurate written information about the cost of credit, including the annual percentage rate charged and the finance charges added to the loan. Sufficient information must be provided to allow the consumer to make a valid comparison of different lending institutions' loan schedules. In cases where the borrower's home is used to secure the loan, three days must be allowed for the cancellation of a signed credit agreement. The act also prohibited the unsolicited distribution of credit cards and limited the card owner's liability in the case of lost or stolen cards.

Uniform Code of Military Justice (UCMJ), 10 U.S.C. § 801 et seq. (1950), body of laws containing the substantive and procedural law that governs members of the armed services and the military courts.

Uniform Commercial Code (U.C.C.), body of laws developed by a national commission and the American Law Institute to help regularize the law of sales. It has been adopted in part by every state. The code governs sales and leasing, bank deposits and collections, commercial paper and letters of credit, bulk transfers and warehouse receipts, investment securities and secured transactions, and various other commercial transactions.

Uniform Consumer Credit Code (UCCC), body of laws designed to systematize and clairify the law governing retail installment sales, consumer credit, and small loans. The code was promulgated by a national commission on uniform state laws in 1968 and revised in 1974. Four states have adopted the 1974 code.

Uniform Fraudulent Conveyance Act (UFCA), set of laws adopted in 1918 by a national commission on uniform state laws seeking to address the issue of conveyances made by an insolvent or bankrupt debtor who attempts to defraud a creditor. Some conveyances were presumed fraudulent while others required that there be actual intent to commit fraud. The act has been replaced in most states by the Uniform Fraudulent Transfer Act.

Uniform Fraudulent Transfer Act (UFTA), set of laws adopted in 1984 by a national commission on uniform state laws and intended to replace the Uniform Fraudulent Conveyance Act. Changes to the earlier act were necessary in order to bring it in line with changes in bankruptcy law, with the Uniform Commercial Code, and with the Model Rules of Professional Conduct. While, like the UFCA, rendering transfers voidable because of constructive or actual fraudulent intent, the UFTA created a different definition of insolvency, treated the preferential transfer as avoidable in the case of fraud, and changed the remedies available to creditors. Thirty-three states have adopted the UFTA.

Uniform Partnership Act (UPA), set of laws governing business partnerships that was adopted in 1914 by a national commission on uniform state laws but later superseded by a Revised Uniform Partnership Act in 1994. Forty-seven states have adopted the 1914 act, with three of those states repealing their enactments in favor of the 1994 act. Another three states have adopted only the 1994 act. The 1914 act embodied aspects of both the entity and aggregate theories of partnership and governed general and limited partnerships. The Revised Act retained the aggregate theory for some purposes and was intended as a set of default rules to apply when the partnership agreement did not address a situation. The Revised Act also no longer governed limited partnerships.

Uniform Probate Code (UPC), body of laws on wills and estates that was developed by a national commission on uniform state laws and subsequently adopted in whole or in part by about one third of the states. The code provides that some of the formalities of court supervision can be eliminated by selecting one of several procedures suited for inheritance cases of varying degrees of complexity: simple and inexpensive procedures for simple cases, and administration supervised by the court and containing elaborate safeguards for estates that are insolvent or under dispute or that present other difficulties. The code covers elements such as the determination of a will, the functions of an executor, and the process of administering a decedent's estate.

Uniform Transfers to Minors Act (UTMA), body of laws governing gifts of property to minors. It was developed as the Uniform Gifts to Minors Act by a national commission on uniform state laws and subsequently adopted, with minor variations, by every state. It was later revised and given its present name. The state laws based on the act typically permit the selection of a property custodian in lieu of a court-supervised guardianship. The custodian is charged with managing the property wisely on the child's behalf, including making secure investments, keeping accurate records, applying income toward the child's support, and not mixing the property with the custodian's own. The custodian's responsibilities end when the child reaches majority age.

United States Code (U.S.C.), comprehensive body of laws, both general and permanent, passed by Congress and organized topically under 50 titles. The first edition of the code was issued in 1926, and a second, cumulative edition was released in 1932. This pattern of providing cumulative updates every six years continues to the present day, although various interim supplements are also published. A typical citation to the code (e.g., 15 U.S.C. § 290) gives the title number (a number from 1 to 50), the abbreviated title of the code itself (U.S.C.), and the section number under which the statute may be found.

Voting Rights Act, 42 U.S.C. § 1971 (1965), eradicated the tactics previously used in the South to disenfranchise black voters. Despite the Civil Rights Act of 1964, most Southern blacks found it difficult to exercise their voting rights. In 1965, mass demonstrations were held to protest the violence and other means used to prevent black voter registration. After a peaceful protest march at Selma, Alabama, was violently broken up by white authorities, President Johnson responded with the Voting Rights Act, which abolished literacy tests and other voter restrictions and authorized federal intervention against voter discrimination. The subsequent rise in black voter registration transformed politics in the South.

Wages and Hours Act — see FAIR LABOR STANDARDS ACT OF 1938

Wagner Act — see NATIONAL LABOR RELATIONS ACT

War Powers Act, 50 U.S.C. § 1541 et seq. (1973), restrained the president's ability to commit U.S. forces overseas. Whereas previously, both by constitutional right and by custom, the executive branch had exercised full authority to send troops abroad, under the provisions of this act Congress was to play a more prominent role in making such decisions. The law required the president to consult with and report to Congress before involving U.S. forces in foreign hostilities. Generally considered a measure to help prevent "future Vietnams," the act has nevertheless met with some resistance among presidents and has not always been strictly interpreted by Congress.

Wire Fraud Act, 18 U.S.C. § 1343 (1952), prohibited interstate wire, radio, or television transmissions whose contents included "any scheme or artifice to defraud." Adopted as an amendment to the Communications Act of 1934, which established the Federal Communications Commission as the regulatory agency of the communications industry, the provisions of the Wire Fraud Act were modeled after those of the Mail Fraud Act of 1872, which extended federal jurisdiction to crimes within the states' jurisdiction that were injurious to private individuals. Unlike common-law definitions of fraud, which rely on specific intent, the Mail and Wire Fraud acts make it a crime to use the mails or electronic communications media to defraud, regardless of whether the scheme succeeds in deceiving a victim. Both acts have also been interpreted broadly by the courts as devices to use in prosecuting corrupt state and local officials who have abused their offices and deprived citizens of their right to honest government.

Workers' Compensation Acts, series of federal and state laws providing for the compensation of workers for losses suffered as a result of work-related injuries. The original federal law, the Federal Employees' Compensation Act, 5 U.S.C. § 8101 et seq. (1916), required that federal employees receive certain medical benefits and other compensation. This act was followed by the Longshore and Harbor Workers' Compensation Act, 33 U.S.C. § 901 et seq. (1927), which provided similar benefits to maritime workers, and the Black Lung Benefits Reform Act, 30 U.S.C. § 902 (1977), which provided benefits to coal miners. Many states have enacted similar legislation to serve state employees; other disabled workers are entitled to benefits provided under Title II of the Social Security Act. Workers' compensation plans usually provide payments for medical treatment, temporary and permanent incapacity, and, in a few cases, retraining and rehabilitation. Such payments are made regardless of negligence.

Workmen's Compensation Act — see WORKERS' COMPENSATION ACT

Important Agencies

Administrative Conference of the United States (ACUS), independent agency established in 1964 to advise the government on ways to improve federal administrative procedures. Most of the members, who are government officials, private lawyers, and university professors, are experts in administrative law. The chairperson is appointed by the president and approved by the Senate for a five-year term. An 11-person executive board or council sets the agenda for six standing committees that study issues involving adjudication, general administration, government procedures, judicial review, regulation, and rulemaking. By statute, membership in the conference must number no fewer than 75 and no more than 101, the majority of whom must be government officials. The ACUS issues reports and recommends changes regarding legal procedures used by government agencies.

Administrative Office of the United States Courts, agency of the judicial branch responsible for carrying out the nonjudicial, administrative business of the federal courts, exclusive of the U.S. Supreme Court. Its functions include the supervision of court administrative personnel, the maintenance of court-related statistical data, and the disbursement of payroll and other funds. Working in consultation with the Judicial Conference of the United States, an important advisory and general-oversight body, the Administrative Office also exercises general supervision of federal probation officers, bankruptcy judges, magistrates, and public defender organizations. The Office was established in 1939.

Board of Immigration Appeals, nine-person tribunal administered by the Department of Justice (under the Deputy Attorney General's office) and given nationwide jurisdiction to hear appeals from decisions of immigration judges or those of the Immigration and Naturalization Service (INS). The Board's decisions are binding on all INS officers and immigration judges unless modified or overruled by the Attorney General, and are subject to judicial review in federal courts. Most of the cases that come before the Board involve deportation orders and the exclusion of aliens applying for admission to the United States. The Board's rulings are one of the most important sources of immigration case law in the country.

Bureau of Alcohol, Tobacco and Firearms (ATF), Treasury Department agency charged with enforcing and administering laws covering the production, taxation, and distribution of alcohol and tobacco products as well as laws relating to the use of firearms and explosives. The ATF's Compliance Operations section makes plant inspections, issues licenses and permits, oversees tax collection on alcohol and tobacco, monitors advertising and labeling practices, and investigates violations, including, in some cases, those involving environmental protection laws. Its Law Enforcement section investigates the illegal use of firearms and explosive devices and illicit trafficking in firearms, distilled spirits, and contraband cigarettes, and it also assists federal, state, and local law enforcement agencies in the suppression of arson-for-profit schemes and narcotics operations involving the use of firearms and explosives.

Bureau of Export Administration (BXA), Commerce Department agency charged with overseeing the nation's export control policy, including enforcement of U.S. export laws. The BXA's administrative section monitors control of regulated export commodities, issues licenses, and conducts policy and technology analysis. Central to the agency's objectives are the control of technology and data that can affect national security or fuel the proliferation of weapons abroad. The bureau's enforcement section investigates breaches of U.S. export control laws and analyzes export intelligence to assess reexport risks and the potential for military application of nonmilitary technology.

Bureau of Indian Affairs (BIA), Interior Department agency that serves as the principal link between federally recognized Native American populations (officially, *American Indian tribes*) and the U.S. government. The BIA, which has its headquarters in Washington, D.C., but is organized into various area and local field offices, is responsible for administering approximately 56 million acres of land held in trust for groups holding a statutory relationship with the United States. It also provides various economic development, educational, and natural-resource management services to help promote self-determination and well-being among Native Americans, though some of its efforts have been protested by local communities.

Bureau of Land Management (BLM), Interior Department agency charged with the management of more than 220 million acres of public land, located primarily in the western United States and Alaska. Resources managed by the BLM include timber, minerals, oil and gas, geothermal energy, wildlife habitats, endangered plant and animal species, recreation areas, lands with cultural importance, wild and scenic rivers, designated conservation and wilderness areas, and open-space lands. The BLM regulates certain multiple-use lands such as grazing lands, issues rights of way for crossing federal lands, manages watersheds, and makes certain land available for sale or lease to encourage the use and development of natural resources. An additional 300 million acres, the mineral rights to which are owned by the federal government, are also managed by the BLM. Land use plans are generally developed with public involvement and frequently include debates between business interests and conservation groups.

Bureau of Prisons, Justice Department agency charged with managing federal correctional facilities and planning for future prison needs. It oversees the detention of federal offenders and provides health, religious, employment, training, and educational services to inmates. It also conducts research and evaluation activities and provides technical assistance and training for state and local corrections authorities.

Central Intelligence Agency (CIA), independent government agency in the executive branch charged with carrying out intelligence and counterintelligence operations in support of national security. The CIA is under the direction of the president and the National Security Council (NSC), the president's principal policy-making body on national security issues. The CIA advises the president and the NSC on intelligence and counterintelligence needs; collects, evaluates, and disseminates intelligence and foreign counterintelligence data; conducts counterintelligence operations outside the United States; and conducts special activities approved by the president. Clandestine activities are carried on under various guises—including the diplomatic cover used by virtually every intelligence service, as well as such fronts as corporations that the CIA creates or acquires.

Commodity Futures Trading Commission (CFTC), independent government agency established in 1975 to regulate trading in futures. The CFTC, made up of five commissioners appointed by the president and approved by the Senate, works to ensure that trading on the 11 U.S. futures exchanges is fair and that the integrity of the marketplace is preserved. To that end it monitors trading, registers brokers, reviews contracts, audits records and bank accounts, investigates fraud, adjudicates customer complaints, engages in market analysis, and exercises enforcement authority. No more than three of its five members may belong to the same political party.

Consumer Product Safety Commission (CPSC), independent federal regulatory agency charged with protecting the public from unreasonable risks of injury associated with consumer products. The CPSC, composed of five commissioners appointed by the president and approved by the Senate, works with industry to develop voluntary safety standards—and certain mandatory ones when voluntary efforts fail. It also works with state and local authorities to develop uniform standards; collects and disseminates data on the cause and prevention of consumer product injuries; requires manufacturers to certify that certain products conform to applicable safety standards; bans or requires the recall of products that violate certain hazard control standards; and enforces standards through administrative action or litigation. Established in 1973, the commission has operated since 1986, when Congress restricted funds, with only two of its five seats filled.

Council of Economic Advisers (CEA), executive-branch body responsible for advising the president on policy matters relating to the national economy. The council analyzes the national economy and its various segments; appraises the federal government's economic programs and policies; recommends to the president policies for economic growth and stability; and prepares various reports. The administration of the federal budget, as approved by Congress, is controlled by the Office of Management and Budget (OMB), which also advises the president on budget matters and assists in the development of efficient management procedures for the executive branch.

Department of Agriculture (USDA), federal executive division responsible for programs and policies relating to the farming industry and the use of national forests and grasslands. The USDA works to stabilize or improve domestic farm income, develop or increase foreign markets, curb poverty and hunger, protect soil and water resources, make credit available for rural development, and ensure the quality of food supplies. Among its numerous agencies and services are the Food Safety and Inspection Service (FSIS), which inspects and monitors meat and poultry products; the Grain Inspection Packers and Stockyards Administration (GIPSA), which enforces grain standards and ensures fair-trade practices in the marketing of livestock and related products; the Agricultural Marketing Service (AMS), which oversees food grading and classification standards in the marketing of farm produce and establishes minimum prices for certain commodities such as milk; the Commodity Credit Corporation (CCC), which provides loans, purchases, and payments to commodity producers in the interest of stabilizing prices and farm income; the Federal Crop Insurance Corporation (FCIC), which offers producers financial protection in the case of crop loss; and the National Forest Service, which regulates the use of the nation's 191.6-million-acre National Forest System. Other units under the USDA are involved in rural community development, consumer information, overseas marketing, agricultural research, and various staff activities.

Department of Commerce (DOC), federal executive division responsible for programs and policies relating to international trade, national economic growth, and technological advancement. Among the agencies under its control are the Bureau of the Census, which monitors the population of the United States; the Bureau of Economic Analysis (BEA), which monitors the U.S. economy; the Bureau of Export Administration (*q.v.*); the Economic Development Administration (EDA), which provides financial assistance to economically distressed communities; the International Trade Administration (*q.v.*); the Minority Business Development Agency (MBDA), which provides assistance to minority firms; the National Oceanic and Atmospheric Administration (NOAA), which provides maritime and marine-resources information and reports the weather of the United States; the National Telecommunications and Information Administration (NTIA), which serves as the government's source of information regarding telecommunications and related technology; the Patent and Trademark Office (*q.v.*); the Technology Administration, which works with business to develop technology, policies, and standards in order to strengthen U.S. industrial competitiveness; and the U.S. Travel and Tourism Administration (USTTA), which provides information and services relating to the U.S. tourism industry.

Department of Defense (DOD), federal executive division responsible for ensuring U.S. national security and supervising U.S. military forces. It includes the Joint Chiefs of Staff, the departments of the Army, Navy, and Air Force, and numerous defense agencies and allied services. The department is based in the Pentagon. All military personnel are subject to the Uniform Code of Military Justice, the armed forces' principal body of criminal law. Each military branch maintains its own legal-services division headed by a judge advocate general as well as its own criminal investigative service.

Department of Education, federal executive division responsible for carrying out government education programs and policies. It seeks to ensure access to education and to improve the quality of education nationwide. In addition to administering programs in elementary and secondary education, higher education, vocational and adult education, special education, bilingual education, civil rights, and educational research, the department provides funds and services to the American Printing House for the Blind, Gallaudet University, Howard University, the National Institute for Literacy, and the National Technical Institute for the Deaf.

Department of Energy (DOE), federal executive division responsible for coordinating and administering national energy policy. The department promotes energy efficiency and the use of renewable energy through various research and financial assistance programs. Its national security and environmental management programs serve to develop nuclear energy resources, including nuclear power plants and weapons, while its Office of Environmental Management oversees waste management and cleanup activities at inactive facilities, including sites with chemical and nuclear waste. Its Fossil Energy Office develops policies and regulations concerning the use of natural gas, coal, and electric energy, and its regional power administrations transmit electric power produced at federal hydroelectric projects. The DOE also conducts investigations in cases involving whistleblower reprisal complaints, and it holds hearings and listens to appeals in cases involving complaints about its regulations. Included in the DOE is the Federal Energy Regulatory Commission (*q.v.*).

Department of Health and Human Services (HHS), federal executive division responsible for carrying out government programs and policies relating to human health, welfare, and income security. The department consists of five major components—the Administration for Children and Families (ACF), the Administration on Aging, the Health Care Financing Administration (*q.v.*), the Public Health Service (PHS), the Substance Abuse and Mental Health Services Administration (SAMHSA)—and various ancillary agencies. The ACF administers programs in child welfare, youth services, family assistance (including Aid to Families with Dependent Children [AFDC]), community services (including block grants), and minority development and refugee services. The Administration on Aging administers programs designed to serve older persons. The PHS, which includes the Centers for Disease Control and Prevention (CDC), the Food and Drug Administration (*q.v.*), and the National Institutes of Health (NIH), has broad responsibility for protecting the health of the nation's population. SAMHSA focuses its efforts on the prevention and treatment of addictive and mental disorders. HHS also maintains an inspector general's office to investigate reports of fraud or abuse, and a civil rights office to ensure that programs are administered free from discrimination.

Department of Housing and Urban Development (HUD), federal executive division responsible for carrying out government housing and community development programs. HUD works to ensure equal access to housing and community-based employment opportunities; finances new housing, public housing, and housing rehabilitation projects; insures mortgages for single-family homes and multifamily units; and carries out programs that serve the housing needs of low-income and minority families, the elderly, disabled, and mentally ill. HUD housing offices also work to protect consumers against fraudulent practices by land developers, ensure the safety of manufactured (mobile) homes, and defend home buyers against abusive mortgage-loan practices. Its community planning and development offices administer block grant programs designed to rehabilitate blighted urban neighborhoods. The department also maintains various oversight units to monitor programs, hear complaints, and adjudicate claims.

Department of Justice, federal executive division responsible for law enforcement and allied programs and services. Headed by the Attorney General of the United States, the department is the largest employer of lawyers, criminal investigators, and law enforcement agents in the nation. It maintains separate divisions for investigating and prosecuting cases under federal antitrust laws, civil rights laws, criminal laws (including those covering organized crime), environmental laws, tax laws, and others. In addition, several major agencies are under its control, including the Federal Bureau of Investigation (*q.v.*), the Bureau of Prisons (*q.v.*), the Drug Enforcement Administration (*q.v.*), the Immigration and Naturalization Service (*q.v.*), the Office of Justice Programs (*q.v.*), the U.S. Marshals Service (*q.v.*), and the U.S. National Central Bureau (USNCB), which represents the United States in INTERPOL, the International Criminal Police Organization. The department also maintains a civil division to represent the U.S. government in cases involving tort claims or commercial litigation, and an Office of Community Oriented Policing Services (COPS) to assist in the development of community policing programs. For additional information see the entries for Board of Immigration Appeals and Foreign Claims Settlement Commission.

Department of Labor (DOL), federal executive division responsible for enforcing labor statutes and promoting the general welfare of U.S. wage earners. In addition to the Employment Standards Administration (*q.v.*), Occupational Safety and Health Administration (*q.v.*), and Pension and Welfare Benefits Administration (*q.v.*), DOL controls numerous agencies involved in the administration of employment and training programs, unemployment insurance programs, trade adjustment (i.e., worker dislocation) assistance programs, veterans and senior citizens programs, and mine safety programs. Its Bureau of Labor Statistics (BLS) provides data on labor economics, and its Office of the American Workplace (OAW) researches and develops programs in cooperative labor-management relations and high-performance work practices. The department also maintains several review and appeals boards for settling disputes involving employee compensation, unemployment insurance, benefits, health and safety regulations, and service contracts.

Department of State, federal executive division responsible for carrying out U.S. foreign policy. It is the president's principal means of conducting treaty negotiations and effecting agreements with foreign nations. Under its control are the U.S. Mission to the United Nations, six regional bureaus of political affairs, the U.S. Foreign Service (including 164 embassies and numerous subagencies), and various offices of diplomatic security, foreign intelligence, policy analysis, international narcotics control, protocol, and passport and medical services. The department's legal adviser advises the secretary of state on all matters of international law arising in the conduct of foreign relations.

Department of the Interior, federal executive division responsible for most of the nation's federally owned lands and natural resources as well as reservation communities for American Indians. In addition to the Bureau of Land Management (*q.v.*) and the Bureau of Indian Affairs (*q.v.*), the department administers the Minerals Management Service (MMS), which leases offshore and certain other lands for the development of energy and mineral resources; the Office of Surface Mining (OSM), which oversees regulation regarding coal mining; the Bureau of Reclamation, which manages federal water and power resources; the U.S. Fish and Wildlife Service (*q.v.*); the National Park Service (NPS), which manages the nation's 365 federal recreational areas, including historic sites; the U.S. Geological Survey (USGS), which is involved in the examination, mapping, and classification of public lands; and other research services. The department also maintains an Office of Hearings and Appeals to adjudicate cases involving contracts and other disputes.

Department of the Treasury, federal executive division responsible for fiscal policy. It advises the president on fiscal matters, serves as fiscal agent for the government, performs certain law enforcement activities, and manufactures currency. Among its constituent agencies are the Bureau of Alcohol, Tobacco and Firearms (*q.v.*); the Bureau of Public Debt, which borrows money for the government and raises new money by selling government securities; the Bureau of Engraving and Printing, which issues bank notes, treasury securities, and postage stamps; the Internal Revenue Service (*q.v.*); the Office of the Comptroller of the Currency (OCC), which regulates national banks; the Office of Thrift Supervision (*q.v.*); the U.S. Customs Service (*q.v.*); the U.S. Mint, which issues coinage and serves as the depository for the nation's gold bullion; and the U.S. Secret Service, which protects the president and other White House personnel. The Treasury Department also operates the Federal Law Enforcement Training Center (FLETC) at Glynco, Georgia, a facility that serves more than 70 federal law enforcement organizations.

Department of Transportation (DOT), federal executive division responsible for programs and policies relating to transportation. Besides the Federal Aviation Administration (*q.v.*), the National Highway Traffic Safety Administration (*q.v.*), and the U.S. Coast Guard (*q.v.*), it controls the Federal Highway Administration (FHWA), which plans, develops, and oversees construction of interstate highways; the Federal Railroad Administration (FRA), which issues and enforces rail safety regulations and administers railroad financial assistance programs; the Federal Transit Administration (FTA), which manages mass transit development and improvement programs; the Maritime Administration (MA *or* MARAD), which supervises the U.S. merchant marine; and various specialized regulatory, research, and development agencies, including offices for hazardous materials transportation and pipeline safety.

Department of Veterans Affairs (VA), federal executive division responsible for programs and policies relating to veterans and their families. The VA administers benefits that include compensation payments for disability or death related to military service, pensions and life insurance, educational assistance and vocational rehabilitation, home loan guaranty, burial, and medical care. Through its numerous regional offices and facilities, the VA serves some 27 million veterans and manages benefits that amount to some $30 billion annually. It maintains separate appeals boards to settle disputes involving entitlement claims and vendor contracts.

Drug Enforcement Administration (DEA), Justice Department agency charged with enforcing laws that cover trafficking in controlled substances. The DEA works with other agencies, such as the Federal Bureau of Investigation (*q.v.*), the Internal Revenue Service (*q.v.*), the U.S. Coast Guard (*q.v.*), and the U.S. Customs Service (*q.v.*), to control the cultivation, production, smuggling, and distribution of illicit drugs. Most of its efforts are directed against international narcotics smuggling organizations, but it also coordinates domestic efforts aimed at closing down interstate operations. It maintains 70 overseas offices and over 100 domestic offices as well as an intelligence center, forensic laboratories, and an air wing.

Employment Standards Administration (ESA), Labor Department agency charged with administering certain programs concerning fair labor practices. Among the programs it directs are those dealing with minimum wage and overtime standards, nondiscrimination and affirmative action, migrant and child labor, and workers' compensation for federal and certain private employers and employees. It is one of the chief regulatory authorities in the area of employment practices, offering technical assistance to government contractors and other employers to ensure compliance with federal employment laws and investigating complaints on behalf of workers.

Environmental Protection Agency (EPA), independent agency in the executive branch charged with controlling and abating environmental pollution. The EPA maintains separate programs dealing with air and radiation, water, solid waste, and pesticides and toxic substances. Among the agency's principal tasks are establishing pollution control standards, regulating the discharge of certain materials, issuing permits for the treatment or disposal of hazardous waste, monitoring air and water quality, administering the so-called "Superfund" for the cleanup of toxic waste sites, tracking the transport of hazardous compounds, registering insecticides and similar chemical treatments, and generally providing regulatory guidance to industry and other federal agencies. Although the EPA encourages voluntary compliance with federal environmental laws, it has authority to enforce regulations where violations occur. It maintains regional offices in 10 major U.S. cities in an effort to cooperate with state and local authorities in carrying out its mission.

Equal Employment Opportunity Commission (EEOC), independent agency charged with enforcing and administering laws that cover discrimination in employment. The EEOC works to prevent discrimination based on race, color, national origin, religion, sex, disability, or age in hiring, promoting, firing, setting wages, testing, training, and other terms and conditions of employment. It issues rules, regulations, and guidelines and has the authority to conduct investigations, attempt conciliation in cases involving discrimination, and litigate matters in federal courts. The EEOC also coordinates all federal equal employment opportunity programs, including affirmative action plans, and has jurisdiction over federal employees' and applicants' complaints concerning employment discrimination. Its five commissioners, only three of whom may belong to the same political party, are appointed by the president and approved by the Senate for five-year terms. The EEOC has long suffered from a chronic backlog of cases.

Farm Credit Administration (FCA), independent financial regulatory agency charged with overseeing the operation of farm credit institutions. Dealing with the banks, associations, affiliated service organizations, and other entities that collectively comprise what is known as the Farm Credit System, the FCA works to protect the interests of those who borrow from or invest in system institutions. Although it is normally prohibited from participating in the management or operations of farm credit institutions, the FCA may so participate when violations of its regulations occur. It has the power to issue cease-and-desist orders, to levy civil monetary penalties, to remove officers of farm credit institutions, to establish financial and operating reporting requirements, and to assume conservatorship over failing institutions. The FCA also has oversight responsibility for the Federal Agricultural Mortgage Corporation (Farmer Mac), a federally chartered secondary mortgage loan and guaranty institution.

Federal Aviation Administration (FAA), Transportation Department agency charged with the administration and enforcement of civil aviation standards and regulations. Among other tasks, the FAA issues aircraft manufacturing, maintenance, and flight safety standards, and performs inspections; develops air traffic rules and regulations, and operates a network of airport traffic control towers; trains and certifies flight engineering, traffic control, and other personnel; engineers and tests air navigation equipment; administers airport development, safety, and security programs; maintains relations with foreign aviation authorities; and conducts research and issues technical publications, including aeronautical charts. It also works with U.S. military organizations to control navigable airspace and ensure an effective air defense system.

Federal Bureau of Investigation (FBI), Justice Department agency charged with conducting investigations in cases involving federal jurisdiction. The FBI gathers and reports facts, locates witnesses, makes arrests, and compiles evidence for the U.S. Attorney General's office in Washington, D.C., and for U.S. Attorneys' offices in the federal judicial districts of the nation. Its jurisdiction includes a wide range of responsibilities in the criminal, civil, and security fields, with priority assigned to organized crime/drugs, counterterrorism, white-collar crime, foreign counterintelligence, and violent crime.

Federal Communications Commission (FCC), independent agency charged with regulating all interstate and foreign communications by radio, television, wire, satellite, and cable. The FCC controls about 3 million corporate and individual communications licenses. FCC standards and regulations apply only to the technical aspects of communication systems (such as frequency and equipment), not broadcast content (although it does have rules covering obscenity and slander). It allocates frequencies; licenses stations and operators; regulates common carrier telephone, cable, and satellite systems; oversees wireless systems, including cellular phones, pagers, and mobile radios; promotes the use of communications technology for ensuring the safety of life and property; and participates in the national defense. The five-person commission is supplemented by a decision review board and a corps of administrative law judges.

Federal Deposit Insurance Corporation (FDIC), independent government corporation created in 1933 (after the disastrous collapse of the banking system) with the duty to insure bank deposits in eligible banks against loss in the event of a bank failure and to regulate certain banking practices. The FDIC's income is derived from assessments on insured banks and from interest on the required investment of its surplus funds in government securities. It also has authority to borrow up to $30 billion from the U.S. Treasury. The corporation insures bank deposits in eligible banks, and some savings and loan institutions, up to the statutory limit ($100,000). It also acts as receiver for all national banks placed in receivership and for designated state banks; performs periodic audits of banks for insurance purposes; approves or disapproves mergers, consolidations, and acquisitions in certain cases; issues cease-and-desist orders when it detects violations of approved practices; and performs other duties related to ensuring public confidence in banks and protecting the money supply.

Federal Election Commission (FEC), independent agency responsible for administering and enforcing laws that cover federal election campaigns. The FEC oversees the public financing of presidential elections, ensures public disclosure of campaign finance activities, monitors campaign contributions and expenditures, regulates the campaign activities of political action committees (PACs), and investigates reports of violations. It is composed of six commissioners appointed by the president with the advice and consent of the Senate.

Federal Energy Regulatory Commission (FERC), independent agency within the Department of Energy (DOE) responsible for regulating the transmission and sale of energy resources (such as natural gas and electricity). The five-member commission has the authority to set rates and charges for the transportation and sale of natural gas, the transmission and sale of electricity, the licensing of hydroelectric power, and the transportation of oil by pipeline. In addition, FERC issues licenses and permits for the construction of hydroelectric projects, for the maintenance of facilities at international borders, and for the construction of gas pipelines and facilities. Besides issuing its own rules and regulations and reviewing those of the DOE (which is bound by the decision of FERC), FERC holds public hearings presided over by an administrative law judge in certain cases involving proposed rule or rate changes.

Federal Housing Administration (FHA), agency within the Department of Housing and Urban Development charged with assisting lower-income and nontraditional home buyers in financing home purchases. The FHA was created in 1934 to help out home buyers and the housing industry, which was devastated by the onset of the Great Depression. Today, the FHA fulfills its mission primarily through programs that provide, guarantee, or insure loans to first-time, lower-income, or nontraditional home buyers.

Federal Housing Finance Board (FHFB), independent regulatory agency in the executive branch charged with overseeing the Federal Home Loan Bank system, a nationwide system of banks, savings associations, credit unions, and insurance companies that make long-term home mortgage loans. The FHFB was created in 1989, together with the Office of Thrift Supervision (*q.v.*) and the Resolution Trust Corporation (which ceased operating in 1995, with some functions transferred to the FDIC), under the Financial Institutions Reform, Recovery, and Enforcement Act of 1989 (FIRREA), which was enacted to address widespread problems in the savings and loan industry. The FHFB's mission is to ensure that federal home loan banks remain adequately capitalized and operate in a safe and sound manner. It prescribes rules and conditions under which the banks may provide loans, regulates the banks' financial management and investment activities, supervises federally mandated community investment and affordable housing programs, conducts performance reviews and financial audits, appoints bank directors, approves payment of dividends, and generally ensures that the banks carry out their housing finance mission. In the secondary mortgage market the FHFB deals with the Government National Mortgage Association (Ginnie Mae), the Federal National Mortgage Association (Fannie Mae), and the Federal Home Loan Mortgage Corporation (Freddie Mac), all of which are government or government-sponsored agencies specializing in mortgage-backed securities (MBSs).

Federal Labor Relations Authority (FLRA), independent government agency charged with administering laws that protect the right of federal employees to bargain collectively. The FLRA establishes policies and guidelines concerning federal service labor-management relations, ensures compliance with statutory collective bargaining rights and obligations, determines the appropriateness of bargaining units, supervises and conducts federal service representation elections, ensures conformance with government rules and regulations, investigates complaints about unfair labor practices, and adjudicates disputes. It also maintains a panel devoted to resolving impasses in negotiations between agencies and unions.

Federal Maritime Commission (FMC), independent agency in the executive branch charged with regulating the marine commerce of the United States. The FMC ensures that ocean carriers, shipping terminals, and marine operators are in compliance with federal shipping statutes; accepts or rejects tariff filings; issues freight licenses; administers passenger indemnity programs; monitors steamship conferences (commercial associations among shipping companies) to detect any unauthorized, concerted activity; conducts financial audits; investigates and adjudicates complaints; and generally ensures that waterborne foreign and domestic trade in the United States is conducted in a fair and equitable manner. No more than three of its five appointed commissioners may belong to the same political party.

Federal Mediation and Conciliation Service (FMCS), independent government agency charged with representing the public interest in labor-management disputes that affect interstate commerce. The FMCS seeks to prevent or minimize work stoppages by assisting labor and management to settle their disputes through mediation. It has no law-enforcement authority but rather offers its expertise, facilities, and services to help ensure effective collective bargaining, mediation, and voluntary arbitration.

Federal Reserve System, central banking authority of the United States. It acts as a fiscal agent for the U.S. government, is custodian of the reserve accounts of commercial banks, makes loans to commercial banks, and is authorized to issue Federal Reserve notes that constitute the entire supply of paper currency of the country. Created by the Federal Reserve Act of 1913, the system consists of the Board of Governors of the Federal Reserve System, the 12 Federal Reserve banks, the Federal Open Market Committee, the Federal Advisory Council, and, since 1976, a Consumer Advisory Council; there are several thousand member banks. The Board of Governors of the Federal Reserve System determines the reserve requirements of the member banks within statutory limits, reviews and determines the discount rates established by the 12 Federal Reserve banks, and reviews the budgets of the reserve banks. The Federal Open Market Committee (FOMC) is responsible for the determination of Federal Reserve bank policy in the purchase and sale of securities on the open market. The Federal Advisory Council's role is purely advisory. All national banks are required to be members of the Federal Reserve System, and state banks may become members if they meet membership qualifications. The Federal Reserve System may exercise its regulatory powers by adjusting the legal reserve ratio—*i.e.*, the proportion of its deposits that a member bank must hold in its reserve account—thus increasing or reducing the amount of new loans that the commercial banks can make. The money supply may also be influenced through manipulation of the discount (also called rediscount) rate, which is the rate of interest charged by Federal Reserve banks on short-term secured loans to member banks. A third method of regulation is through open-market operations, now employed daily to make small adjustments in the market. (Federal Reserve bank sales or purchases of securities on the open market tend to reduce or increase the size of commercial-bank reserves.)

Federal Trade Commission (FTC), independent agency charged with preventing unfair or deceptive trade practices. Although the FTC has no authority to punish violators, it may monitor compliance with trade laws, conduct legal investigations, issue cease-and-desist orders, convene public hearings presided over by an administrative law judge, request formal injunctions from or file civil suits in U.S. district courts, and ensure that court orders are followed. The FTC seeks to protect consumers by regulating advertising, marketing, and consumer credit practices; and works to protect businesses by preventing antitrust agreements and other unfair practices. In addition to performing those quasi-judicial and quasi-legislative functions, the FTC promotes voluntary compliance through a variety of cooperative procedures, such as issuing industry guides and writing advisory opinions, and advocates in the courts and among legislatures and government agencies for the support of free and fair trade.

Food and Drug Administration (FDA), agency of the Department of Health and Human Services authorized by Congress to inspect, test, approve, and set safety standards for foods and food additives, drugs, chemicals, cosmetics, and household and medical devices. The FDA is empowered to prevent untested products from being sold and to take legal action to halt sale of undoubtedly harmful products or of products which involve a health or safety risk. Through court procedure, the FDA can seize products and prosecute the persons or firms responsible for legal violation. FDA authority is limited to interstate commerce. The agency cannot control prices nor directly regulate advertising except of prescription drugs and medical devices.

Foreign Claims Settlement Commission of the United States, independent agency within the Department of Justice charged with adjudicating claims of U.S. nationals against foreign governments. Working either under specific jurisdiction conferred by Congress or pursuant to international claims settlement agreements, the commission processes claims by U.S. servicemen and civilians, such as those held as foreign prisoners of war, or by the survivors of such servicemen and civilians. The commission also furnishes technical assistance and advice to other federal agencies in planning new foreign claims adjudication programs and negotiating international claims settlement agreements.

General Accounting Office (GAO), agency within the legislative branch charged with auditing and evaluating government programs and activities to ensure effective and efficient disbursement of public funds. The GAO, headed by the Comptroller General of the United States, is the investigative arm of Congress, performing reviews requested by committee chairpersons and ranking minority members as well as those required by law or initiated independently by the GAO itself. The GAO also advises Congress on legal issues involving government programs and activities, assists in drafting legislation and reviewing legislative proposals, and assists government agencies in interpreting the laws governing the expenditure of public funds.

General Services Administration (GSA), independent agency charged with the management of government property and records. The GSA, often in conjunction with private contractors and subcontractors, constructs and operates government buildings, procures and distributes supplies, operates transportation and communications equipment and services, manages automatic data processing systems, and oversees government document and information security programs. The GSA's Board of Contract Appeals is responsible for resolving disputes arising out of contracts with the GSA, the Department of the Treasury, the Department of Education, the Department of Commerce, and other independent government agencies.

Health Care Financing Administration (HCFA), agency of the Department of Health and Human Services charged with administering the Medicare and Medicaid programs. Medicare provides health insurance coverage for people age 65 and over, younger people who are receiving social security disability benefits, and people who are undergoing certain treatments for kidney disease. Medicaid, which is jointly financed by state and federal governments, covers health-care expenses for all recipients of Aid to Families with Dependent Children (AFDC), and most states also cover the needy elderly, blind, and disabled who are enrolled in the Supplemental Security Income (SSI) program as well as certain infants and low-income pregnant women.

Immigration and Naturalization Service (INS), Justice Department agency charged with administering and enforcing federal immigration laws. The INS facilitates entry into the United States of persons legally admissible as immigrants or visitors; grants certain benefits to those seeking asylum, temporary or permanent resident status, or naturalization; works to prevent unlawful entry, employment, or receipt of benefits by persons not entitled to them; and seeks to apprehend or remove aliens who enter or remain illegally in the United States. One of its principal law enforcement units is the U.S. Border Patrol.

Internal Revenue Service (IRS), Treasury Department agency charged with administering and enforcing federal tax laws, except those relating to alcohol, tobacco, firearms, and explosives. The IRS issues rulings and regulations to supplement the provisions of the Internal Revenue Code; determines, assesses, and collects internal revenue taxes; determines pension plan qualifications and exempt organization status; and provides certain taxpayer services such as publishing educational literature and adjudicating complaints. It maintains seven major regional offices in addition to its headquarters in Washington, D.C.

International Trade Administration (ITA), Commerce Department agency charged with overseeing all issues concerning import administration, international economic policy and programs, and trade development. The ITA's International Economic Policy office assists in the development of world and regional trade development strategies, and its Trade Development office focuses on strengthening the export competitiveness of U.S. industrial sectors in international markets. Its Import Administration office works to protect American industry from injurious and unfair foreign trade practices, such as commercial dumping or nonpayment of duties, and ensures the proper administration of foreign trade zones. Its U.S. and Foreign Commercial Service provides informational and marketing services to the U.S. exporting and international business community.

Interstate Commerce Commission (ICC), independent government agency charged with regulating interstate surface transportation. The ICC's jurisdiction includes railroads, trucking companies, bus lines, household-goods transporters, freight forwarders, water carriers, transportation brokers, and pipelines not regulated by the Federal Energy Regulatory Commission. Its activities include certification of carriers, regulation of rates and charges, overseeing mergers and consolidations, approval of railroad construction and railroad bankruptcy procedures, and general consumer protection. Although preliminary public hearings on matters before the commission may be held at designated locations throughout the United States, final decisions are made in formal proceedings held at the Washington, D.C., headquarters.

Legal Services Corporation, quasi-official federal organization that provides financial assistance to certain public legal-services programs. The corporation seeks to ensure that persons involved in noncriminal proceedings who would otherwise be unable to afford legal assistance have access to such assistance. To that end it makes grants to and contracts with individuals, firms, corporations, and organizations for the purpose of providing for the legal needs of these clients.

Merit Systems Protection Board (MSPB), independent government agency charged with overseeing the personnel practices of the federal government. As successor to the U.S. Civil Service Commission, the MSPB is charged with preserving the integrity of federal merit systems (that is, systems in which appointments and promotions are based on competence rather than political favoritism) and the rights of federal employees working in the systems. The MSPB hears and adjudicates appeals by federal employees of adverse personnel actions (such as removals, suspensions, and demotions), orders corrective and disciplinary action when appropriate, reviews regulations issued by the Office of Personnel Management, and conducts special studies of the merit systems. Decisions involving allegations of discrimination may also be reviewed by the Equal Employment Opportunity Commission, and all MSPB decisions may be appealed to the U.S. Court of Appeals for the Federal Circuit.

National Credit Union Administration (NCUA), independent agency in the executive branch responsible for chartering, insuring, supervising, and examining federal credit unions. The NCUA grants federal credit union charters to groups sharing a common bond of occupation or association, or to groups within a well-defined neighborhood, community, or rural district. It issues policies and regulations, conducts annual examinations, and maintains a warning system designed to identify problems. It also manages separate national insurance and emergency loan funds.

National Highway Traffic Safety Administration (NHTSA), Department of Transportation agency charged with reducing deaths, injuries, and economic losses resulting from motor vehicle crashes by setting and enforcing safety standards and by providing grants enabling state and local governments to conduct effective local highway safety programs. The responsibilities of the NHTSA include investigating safety defects in motor vehicles; establishing and enforcing fuel economy standards; assisting states and local communities in reducing the threat of drunk drivers; promoting the use of safety belts, child safety seats, and air bags; investigating odometer fraud; establishing and enforcing regulations concerning vehicular theft; and providing information on motor vehicle safety topics to consumers.

National Labor Relations Board (NLRB), independent government agency charged with preventing or remedying unfair labor practices by private sector employers and unions. As official administrator of the nation's principal labor law, the National Labor Relations (Wagner) Act, the NLRB has authority to investigate charges of unfair labor practices, issue complaints, prosecute cases before board members and an administrative law judge, pursue injunction proceedings, obtain compliance with board orders and court judgments, and conduct secret-ballot elections among employees to determine whether or not they desire to be represented by a labor union in bargaining with employers about their wages, hours, and working conditions. The NLRB can act only when it is formally requested to do so. Individuals, employers, or unions may initiate cases by filing charges of unfair labor practices or petitions for employee representation elections with the board field offices serving the area in which the case arises.

National Mediation Board, independent government agency charged with mediating labor-management disputes in the railroad and airline industries. The board's major responsibilities include the mediation of disputes over wages, hours, and working conditions that arise between rail or air carriers and organizations representing their employees, and the investigation of disputes over representation that arise between classes of carrier employees and labor organizations. Disputing parties who fail to reach an accord in direct bargaining may request the board's services or the board may, in the interest of preventing disruptions to commerce, invoke its own services. If mediation fails the board may also seek to induce the parties to submit the dispute to arbitration.

National Security Agency (NSA), Defense Department agency charged with carrying out certain U.S. communications-security and intelligence-gathering activities. Besides prescribing and overseeing certain security principles and procedures for the U.S. government, and conducting certain foreign intelligence operations, the NSA regulates certain communications channels and operates a national computer security center in support of its defense mission.

National Transportation Safety Board (NTSB), independent government agency charged with investigating certain types of accidents (such as those involving aircraft or trains) and conducting safety studies to identify areas needing improvement in the transportation industry. The NTSB investigates air, rail, pipeline, marine, highway, and other transportation accidents to determine their cause and make recommendations to prevent such accidents from recurring. It also conducts transportation safety studies, publishes reports, establishes regulatory guidelines for reporting accidents, reviews the adequacy of safeguards concerning the transport of hazardous materials, and hears on appeal the suspension or revocation of certificates and licenses issued by the Department of Transportation.

Nuclear Regulatory Commission (NRC), independent government agency charged with overseeing civilian use of nuclear energy. The NRC licenses persons and companies to build and operate nuclear reactors and other facilities and to own and use nuclear materials. It issues standards, rules, and regulations for the maintenance of such licenses and regularly inspects nuclear facilities to ensure compliance with public health and safety, environmental quality, national security, and antitrust laws. The NRC also investigates nuclear incidents and reports of violations, conducts public hearings on nuclear safety and other issues, and reviews power plant operational data to detect trends concerning safety issues.

Occupational Safety and Health Administration (OSHA), Labor Department agency charged with ensuring that employers furnish their employees with a working environment that is free from recognized health and safety hazards. OSHA develops and promulgates occupational safety and health standards; develops and issues regulations; conducts investigations and worksite inspections; and issues citations and proposes penalties for noncompliance with OSHA standards and regulations. The independent Occupational Safety and Health Review Commission (OSHRC), one member of which is an administrative law judge, is charged with ruling on cases forwarded to it by the Department of Labor when disagreements arise over the results of safety and health inspections performed by OSHA.

Office of Government Ethics (OGE), independent agency charged with preventing conflicts of interest among executive branch officers and agencies and with overseeing standards of ethical conduct that apply to all executive agencies. The OGE issues rules and regulations pertaining to ethics standards for executive agencies; ensures compliance with executive branch financial disclosure requirements; orders corrective action when necessary; provides ethics training and program assistance; and recommends new legislation or amendments as appropriate.

Office of Justice Programs (OJP), Justice Department agency charged with assisting state and local governments with developing more efficient and effective crime prevention and control measures. OJP works with federal, state, and local government officials to control drug abuse and trafficking, rehabilitate crime-ridden neighborhoods, improve the administration of justice, meet the needs of crime victims, and find new ways to address problems such as gang violence, prison crowding, juvenile crime, and white-collar crime. Most of the work is accomplished through grants, though some research and technical assistance is also provided.

Office of Special Counsel (OSC), independent investigative and prosecutorial agency within the executive branch charged with protecting federal employees from prohibited personnel practices, especially reprisal for whistleblowing. OSC investigates allegations of activities prohibited by civil service laws, rules, and regulations; provides a secure channel through which information regarding possible violations, mismanagement, waste of funds, abuse of authority, or dangers to public health may be reported without fear of retaliation and without disclosure of identity; and litigates matters before the Merit Systems Protection Board (*q.v.*) and/or takes corrective or disciplinary measures as appropriate.

Office of Thrift Supervision (OTS), Treasury Department agency charged with regulating the nation's approximately 1,700 savings associations to maintain the safety, soundness, and viability of the industry. Created in 1989 as successor to the Federal Home Loan Bank Board, OTS develops regulations governing thrift institutions; examines and supervises companies that own thrifts; controls the acquisition of thrifts by holding companies; takes enforcement actions against savings institutions that violate laws or regulations; promotes housing and other financial services in areas with the greatest need; and interacts with members of Congress and the public to disseminate information and advance its objectives.

Patent and Trademark Office (PTO), Commerce Department agency charged with granting patents and registering trademarks. The PTO examines patent applications and, in granting a patent, provides inventors with exclusive rights to the results of their creative work. Trademarks, registered for ten years, with renewal rights of equal term, are examined by the PTO for compliance with various statutory requirements to prevent unfair competition and consumer deception. In addition, the PTO maintains public-access files containing over 30 million documents, including U.S. and foreign patents and U.S. trademarks; hears and decides appeals from prospective inventors and trademark applicants; participates in legal proceedings involving patents and trademarks; maintains a roster of patent agents and attorneys; and advocates strengthening intellectual property protection worldwide.

Pension and Welfare Benefits Administration (PWBA), Labor Department agency charged with overseeing management of the nation's nearly 1 million pension plans and 4.5 million health and welfare plans. Under the Employment Retirement Income Security Act (*q.v.*), administrators of private pension and welfare plans must provide plan participants with easily understandable summaries of plans; must file those summaries with the PWBA; must report annually on the financial operation of the plans; and must meet other fiduciary standards—all of which are overseen and enforced by PWBA. Vesting, participation, and funding standards are primarily enforced by the Internal Revenue Service. The independent Pension Benefit Guaranty Corporation (PBGC), a wholly owned government corporation, guarantees payment of pension benefits in approximately 66,000 covered plans.

Securities and Exchange Commission (SEC), independent government agency charged with regulating securities markets. The SEC's principal functions are to register securities and issuers in order to ensure full and fair disclosure of pertinent financial information; to register and oversee the activities of securities brokers and dealers; to issue rules and regulations regarding securities transactions; to register and regulate the activities of mutual funds and other investment companies; to oversee the operation of public utility holding companies in order to ensure compliance with the laws governing them; to register investment advisers; to participate in corporate reorganization proceedings administered in federal courts in order to protect the interests of public investors; and to safeguard the interests of purchasers of publicly offered debt securities. The SEC may conduct investigations into complaints or other indications of securities violations; obtain court orders enjoining certain acts; revoke registrations; and prosecute violators in federal courts.

Small Business Administration (SBA), independent government agency charged with protecting and advancing the interests of small business concerns. The SBA offers a variety of financial assistance programs to small businesses, ensures that small businesses receive a fair portion of government contracts, licenses and regulates small business investment companies, operates minority enterprise development and women's business ownership programs, studies the impact on small businesses of legislative proposals and other public policy issues, and performs other functions in support of small business development.

Social Security Administration (SSA), agency of the Department of Health and Human Services charged with administering the national program of contributory social insurance. Under the program, employees, employers, and the self-employed pay contributions that are pooled in special trust funds. When earnings stop or are reduced because the worker retires, dies, or becomes disabled, monthly cash benefits are paid to replace part of the earnings the family has lost. Principal benefits programs include hospital insurance programs, retirement and disability insurance programs, and Supplemental Security Income insurance programs for the aged, blind, and disabled.

State Justice Institute, quasi-official agency established to further the development and improvement of judicial administration in the state courts of the United States. To achieve its objectives the Institute provides funds through grants, cooperative agreements, and contracts to state courts and organizations and serves as a national information clearinghouse.

U.S. Coast Guard (USCG), branch of the U.S. Armed Forces and agency within the Department of the Treasury charged with enforcing U.S. maritime laws and ensuring the safety of the nation's ports and waterways. In addition to enforcing federal maritime laws and applicable international agreements, and assisting other federal law enforcement agencies in their work, the Coast Guard performs marine safety-inspection and licensing activities, enforces rules and regulations governing the safe use of U.S. ports and waterways, maintains various aids to navigation (such as lights and buoys), administers statutes governing the construction of certain bridges, and performs various other activities (such as search and rescue operations and marine environmental response) in support of its mission.

U.S. Customs Service, Treasury Department agency charged with collecting import revenues and enforcing customs and related laws. Among its major tasks are assessing and collecting customs duties, excise taxes, fees, and penalties due on imported merchandise; interdicting and seizing contraband, including narcotics and illegal drugs; processing persons, carriers, cargo, and mail into and out of the United States; administering certain navigation laws; detecting and apprehending persons engaged in fraudulent practices designed to circumvent customs and related laws; and assisting other government agencies in enforcing various export-control, trade, and criminal statutes and regulations.

U.S. Fish and Wildlife Service (FWS), Interior Department agency charged with protecting the nation's fish and wildlife resources. In addition to operating 500 national wildlife refuges, 166 waterfowl production areas, and 78 national fish hatcheries, FWS maintains a nationwide network of wildlife law enforcement agents. It is also responsible for developing the list of federally recognized endangered and threatened species and enforcing the laws governing the protection of those species.

U.S. International Trade Commission (USITC), independent agency charged with conducting specialized studies of international trade and tariffs, including examinations of U.S. and foreign customs laws, and making recommendations to the president, Congress, and other government agencies. The USITC conducts investigations, holds public hearings, and carries out research projects pertaining to the issue of foreign importation vis-à-vis U.S. domestic production and consumption, seeking to identify, among other things, unfair or injurious practices in import trade. As part of its broad powers, the USITC advises the president regarding proposed trade agreements, reviews rates of duty on specific articles, investigates market disruptions, monitors the effects of subsidized goods entering the United States, studies import interference with domestic agricultural programs, and issues tariff schedules, trade summaries, and other publications.

U.S. Marshals Service, Justice Department agency charged with carrying out all law enforcement activities relating to the federal justice system. The Marshals Service provides security for the federal courts, apprehends federal fugitives, operates the federal witness protection program, maintains custody of and transports federal prisoners, executes court orders and arrest warrants, receives and manages property forfeited to the government by drug traffickers and other federal offenders, and participates in emergency response and other crisis situations. It is the nation's oldest federal law enforcement agency, having been established in 1789.

U.S. Postal Service (USPS), independent agency charged with processing and delivering mail and with protecting the mails from loss, theft, or abuse in accordance with U.S. postal laws. Besides providing mail processing and delivery services, the USPS oversees the application of postal rates and fees as determined by its Board of Governors and the independent Postal Rate Commission; develops and applies mail classification standards; and serves, through its Postal Inspection Service, as the federal law enforcement agency holding jurisdiction in criminal matters affecting the integrity and security of the mail.

U.S. Sentencing Commission, independent body in the judicial branch responsible for developing sentencing policies and practices for the federal courts. The commission, created in 1984, issues guidelines prescribing the appropriate form and severity of punishment for offenders convicted of federal crimes. It also evaluates the effect of the sentencing guidelines on the criminal justice system, advises Congress regarding the modification or enactment of statutes relating to criminal law and sentencing matters, and conducts research into sentencing, protection, and related issues.

Constitution of the United States[1]

We the People of the United States, in order to form a more perfect Union, establish justice, insure domestic tranquility, provide for the common defense, promote the general welfare, and secure the blessings of liberty to ourselves and our posterity, do ordain and establish this Constitution for the United States of America.

Article I.

Section 1. All legislative powers herein granted shall be vested in a Congress of the United States, which shall consist of a Senate and House of Representatives.

Section 2. The House of Representatives shall be composed of members chosen every second year by the people of the several states, and the electors in each state shall have the qualifications requisite for electors of the most numerous branch of the state legislature.

No Person shall be a Representative who shall not have attained to the age of twenty-five years, and been seven years a citizen of the United States, and who shall not, when elected, be an inhabitant of that state in which he shall be chosen.

Representatives and direct taxes shall be apportioned among the several states which may be included within this union, according to their respective numbers, which shall be determined by adding to the whole number of free persons, including those bound to service for a term of years, and excluding Indians not taxed, three-fifths of all other persons[2]. The actual enumeration shall be made within three years after the first meeting of the Congress of the United States, and within every subsequent term of ten years, in such manner as they shall by law direct. The number of representatives shall not exceed one for every thirty thousand, but each state shall have at least one Representative; and until such enumeration shall be made, the state of New Hampshire shall be entitled to choose three, Massachusetts eight, Rhode Island and Providence Plantations one, Connecticut five, New York six, New Jersey four, Pennsylvania eight, Delaware one, Maryland six, Virginia ten, North Carolina five, South Carolina five, and Georgia three.

When vacancies happen in the representation from any state, the executive authority thereof shall issue writs of election to fill such vacancies.

The House of Representatives shall choose their Speaker and other officers; and shall have the sole power of impeachment.

---

[1]This version of the Constitution follows the engrossed copy signed by General George Washington and the deputies from twelve states at the Constitutional Convention on September 17, 1787. It has been edited to some extent for this book to reflect modern spelling, capitalization, and punctuation. [A version reflecting the original language and spelling can be found on the Internet at: http://www.house.gov/Constitution/Constitution.html.]

[2]The part of this paragraph relating to the mode of apportionment of representatives among the several states has been modified by the first sentence in Amendment XIV, which eliminates reference to "free persons" and "other persons." The reference to direct taxes in proportion to population of the state has been changed by Amendment XVI, which permits the institution of an income tax.

Section 3. The Senate of the United States shall be composed of two Senators from each state, *chosen by the legislature thereof*[3], for six years; and each Senator shall have one vote.

Immediately after they shall be assembled in consequence of the first election, they shall be divided as equally as may be into three classes. The seats of the Senators of the first class shall be vacated at the expiration of the second year, of the second class at the expiration of the fourth year, and of the third class at the expiration of the sixth year, so that one-third may be chosen every second year; *and if vacancies happen by resignation, or otherwise, during the recess of the legislature of any state, the executive thereof may make temporary appointments until the next meeting of the legislature, which shall then fill such vacancies*[4].

No person shall be a Senator who shall not have attained to the age of thirty years, and been nine years a citizen of the United States, and who shall not, when elected, be an inhabitant of that state for which he shall be chosen.

The Vice President of the United States shall be President of the Senate, but shall have no vote, unless they be equally divided.

The Senate shall choose their other officers, and also a President pro tempore, in the absence of the Vice President, or when he shall exercise the office of President of the United States.

The Senate shall have the sole power to try all impeachments. When sitting for that purpose, they shall be on oath or affirmation. When the President of the United States is tried, the Chief Justice shall preside: and no person shall be convicted without the concurrence of two-thirds of the members present.

Judgment in cases of impeachment shall not extend further than to removal from office, and disqualification to hold and enjoy any office of honor, trust or profit under the United States: but the party convicted shall nevertheless be liable and subject to indictment, trial, judgment, and punishment, according to law.

Section 4. The times, places and manner of holding elections for Senators and Representatives, shall be prescribed in each state by the legislature thereof; but the Congress may at any time by law make or alter such regulations, except as to the places of choosing Senators.

The Congress shall assemble at least once in every year, and such meeting shall be *on the first Monday in December, unless they shall by law appoint a different day.*[5]

Section 5. Each house shall be the judge of the elections, returns, and qualifications of its own members, and a majority of each shall constitute a quorum to do business; but a smaller number may adjourn from day to day, and may be authorized to compel the attendance of absent members, in such manner, and under such penalties as each house may provide.

Each house may determine the rules of its proceedings, punish its members for disorderly behavior, and, with the concurrence of two-thirds, expel a member.

Each house shall keep a journal of its proceedings, and from time to time publish the same, excepting such parts as may in their judgment require secrecy; and the yeas and nays of the members of either house on any question shall, at the desire of one-fifth of those present, be entered on the journal.

Neither house, during the session of Congress, shall, without the consent of the other, adjourn for more than three days, nor to any other place than that in which the two houses shall be sitting.

---

[3]This statement has been modified by the first paragraph of Amendment XVII, which places the election of Senators with the people rather than with the state legislatures.
[4]This statement has been modified by the second paragraph of Amendment XVII.
[5]This starting date has been changed to January 3 by Amendment XX.

Section 6. The Senators and Representatives shall receive a compensation for their services, to be ascertained by law, and paid out of the treasury of the United States. They shall in all cases, except treason, felony and breach of the peace, be privileged from arrest during their attendance at the session of their respective houses, and in going to and returning from the same; and for any speech or debate in either house, they shall not be questioned in any other place.

No Senator or Representative shall, during the time for which he was elected, be appointed to any civil office under the authority of the United States, which shall have been created, or the emoluments whereof shall have been increased during such time; and no person holding any office under the United States, shall be a member of either house during his continuance in office.

Section 7. All bills for raising revenue shall originate in the House of Representatives; but the Senate may propose or concur with amendments as on other bills.

Every bill which shall have passed the House of Representatives and the Senate, shall, before it become a law, be presented to the President of the United States; if he approve he shall sign it, but if not he shall return it, with his objections to that house in which it shall have originated, who shall enter the objections at large on their journal, and proceed to reconsider it. If after such reconsideration two-thirds of that house shall agree to pass the bill, it shall be sent, together with the objections, to the other house, by which it shall likewise be reconsidered, and if approved by two-thirds of that house, it shall become a law. But in all such cases the votes of both houses shall be determined by yeas and nays, and the names of the persons voting for and against the bill shall be entered on the journal of each house respectively. If any bill shall not be returned by the president within ten days (Sundays excepted) after it shall have been presented to him, the same shall be a law, in like manner as if he had signed it, unless the Congress by their adjournment prevent its return, in which case it shall not be a law.

Every order, resolution, or vote to which the concurrence of the Senate and House of Representatives may be necessary (except on a question of adjournment) shall be presented to the President of the United States; and before the same shall take effect, shall be approved by him, or being disapproved by him, shall be repassed by two-thirds of the Senate and House of Representatives, according to the rules and limitations prescribed in the case of a bill.

Section 8. The Congress shall have power to lay and collect taxes, duties, imposts and excises, to pay the debts and provide for the common defense and general welfare of the United States; but all duties, imposts and excises shall be uniform throughout the United States;

To borrow money on the credit of the United States;

To regulate commerce with foreign nations, and among the several states, and with the Indian tribes;

To establish an uniform rule of naturalization, and uniform laws on the subject of bankruptcies throughout the United States;

To coin money, regulate the value thereof, and of foreign coin, and fix the standard of weights and measures;

To provide for the punishment of counterfeiting the securities and current coin of the United States;

To establish post offices and post roads;

To promote the progress of science and useful arts, by securing for limited times to authors and inventors the exclusive right to their respective writings and discoveries;

To constitute tribunals inferior to the Supreme Court;

To define and punish piracies and felonies committed on the high seas, and offenses against the law of nations;

To declare war, grant letters of marque and reprisal, and make rules concerning captures on land and water;

To raise and support armies, but no appropriation of money to that use shall be for a longer term than two years;

To provide and maintain a navy;

To make rules for the government and regulation of the land and naval forces;

To provide for calling forth the militia to execute the laws of the Union, suppress insurrections and repel invasions;

To provide for organizing, arming, and disciplining, the militia, and for governing such part of them as may be employed in the service of the United States, reserving to the states respectively, the appointment of the officers, and the authority of training the militia according to the discipline prescribed by Congress;

To exercise exclusive legislation in all cases whatsoever, over such district (not exceeding ten miles square) as may, by cession of particular states, and the acceptance of Congress, become the seat of the government of the United States, and to exercise like authority over all places purchased by the consent of the legislature of the state in which the same shall be, for the erection of forts, magazines, arsenals, dock-yards, and other needful buildings;—and

To make all laws which shall be necessary and proper for carrying into execution the foregoing powers, and all other powers vested by this Constitution in the government of the United States, or in any department or officer thereof.

Section 9. The migration or importation of such persons as any of the states now existing shall think proper to admit, shall not be prohibited by the Congress prior to the year one thousand eight hundred and eight, but a tax or duty may be imposed on such importation, not exceeding ten dollars for each person.

The privilege of the writ of habeas corpus shall not be suspended, unless when in cases of rebellion or invasion the public safety may require it.

No bill of attainder or ex post facto law shall be passed.

No capitation, or other direct, tax shall be laid, unless in proportion to the census or enumeration herein before directed to be taken.[6]

No tax or duty shall be laid on articles exported from any state.

No preference shall be given by any regulation of commerce or revenue to the ports of one state over those of another: nor shall vessels bound to, or from, one state, be obliged to enter, clear, or pay duties in another.

No money shall be drawn from the treasury, but in consequence of appropriations made by law; and a regular statement and account of the receipts and expenditures of all public money shall be published from time to time.

No title of nobility shall be granted by the United States: and no person holding any office of profit or trust under them, shall, without the consent of the Congress, accept of any present, emolument, office, or title, of any kind whatever, from any king, prince, or foreign state.

Section 10. No state shall enter into any treaty, alliance, or confederation; grant letters of marque and reprisal; coin money; emit bills of credit; make any thing but gold and silver coin a tender in payment of debts; pass any bill of attainder, ex post facto law, or law impairing the obligation of contracts, or grant any title of nobility.

No state shall, without the consent of the Congress, lay any imposts or duties on imports or exports, except what may be absolutely necessary for executing its inspection laws: and the net produce of all duties and imposts, laid by any state on imports or exports, shall be for the use of the treasury of the United States; and all such laws shall be subject to the revision and control of the Congress.

---

[6]This paragraph has been replaced by Amendment XVI, permitting the institution of an income tax.

No state shall, without the consent of Congress, lay any duty of tonnage, keep troops, or ships of war in time of peace, enter into any agreement or compact with another state, or with a foreign power, or engage in war, unless actually invaded, or in such imminent danger as will not admit of delay.

Article II.

Section 1.   The executive power shall be vested in a President of the United States of America. He shall hold his office during the term of four years, and, together with the Vice President, chosen for the same term, be elected, as follows:

Each state shall appoint, in such manner as the legislature thereof may direct, a number of electors, equal to the whole number of Senators and Representatives to which the state may be entitled in the Congress: but no Senator or Representative, or person holding an office of trust or profit under the United States, shall be appointed an elector.

The electors shall meet in their respective states, and vote by ballot for two persons, of whom one at least shall not be an inhabitant of the same state with themselves. And they shall make a list of all the persons voted for, and of the number of votes for each; which list they shall sign and certify, and transmit sealed to the seat of the government of the United States, directed to the President of the Senate. The President of the Senate shall, in the presence of the Senate and House of Representatives, open all the certificates, and the votes shall then be counted. The person having the greatest number of votes shall be the President, if such number be a majority of the whole number of electors appointed; and if there be more than one who have such majority, and have an equal number of votes, then the House of Representatives shall immediately choose by ballot one of them for President; and if no person have a majority, then from the five highest on the list the said house shall in like manner choose the President. But in choosing the President, the votes shall be taken by states, the representation from each state having one vote; a quorum for this purpose shall consist of a member or members from two-thirds of the states, and a majority of all the states shall be necessary to a choice. In every case, after the choice of the President, the person having the greatest number of votes of the electors shall be the Vice President. But if there should remain two or more who have equal votes, the Senate shall choose from them by ballot the Vice President.[7]

The Congress may determine the time of choosing the electors, and the day on which they shall give their votes; which day shall be the same throughout the United States.

No person except a natural-born citizen, or a citizen of the United States at the time of the adoption of this Constitution, shall be eligible to the office of President; neither shall any person be eligible to that office who shall not have attained to the age of thirty-five years, and been fourteen years a resident within the United States.

In case of the removal of the President from office, or of his death, resignation, or inability to discharge the powers and duties of the said office[8], the same shall devolve on the Vice President, and the Congress may by law provide for the case of removal, death, resignation or inability, both of the President and Vice President, declaring what officer shall then act as President, and such officer shall act accordingly, until the disability be removed, or a President shall be elected.

The President shall, at stated times, receive for his services, a compensation which shall neither be increased nor diminished during the period for which he shall have been elected, and he shall not receive within that period any other emolument from the United States, or any of them.

---

[7]This paragraph has been replaced by Amendment XII, authorizing separate votes for President and Vice President, and that Amendment by section 3 of Amendment XX.

[8]This statement has been affected by Amendment XXV.

Before he enter on the execution of his office, he shall take the following oath or affirmation:—"I do solemnly swear (or affirm) that I will faithfully execute the office of President of the United States, and will to the best of my ability, preserve, protect and defend the Constitution of the United States."

Section 2.   The President shall be commander-in-chief of the Army and Navy of the United States, and of the militia of the several states, when called into the actual service of the United States; he may require the opinion, in writing, of the principal officer in each of the executive departments, upon any subject relating to the duties of their respective offices, and he shall have power to grant reprieves and pardons for offenses against the United States, except in cases of impeachment.

He shall have power, by and with the advice and consent of the Senate, to make treaties, provided two-thirds of the Senators present concur; and he shall nominate, and by and with the advice and consent of the Senate, shall appoint ambassadors, other public ministers and consuls, judges of the Supreme Court, and all other officers of the United States, whose appointments are not herein otherwise provided for, and which shall be established by law: but the Congress may by law vest the appointment of such inferior officers, as they think proper, in the President alone, in the courts of law, or in the heads of departments.

The President shall have power to fill up all vacancies that may happen during the recess of the Senate, by granting commissions which shall expire at the end of their next session.

Section 3.   He shall from time to time give to the Congress information of the state of the Union, and recommend to their consideration such measures as he shall judge necessary and expedient; he may, on extraordinary occasions, convene both houses, or either of them, and in case of disagreement between them, with respect to the time of adjournment, he may adjourn them to such time as he shall think proper; he shall receive ambassadors and other public ministers; he shall take care that the laws be faithfully executed, and shall commission all the officers of the United States.

Section 4.   The President, Vice President and all civil officers of the United States, shall be removed from office on impeachment for, and conviction of, treason, bribery, or other high crimes and misdemeanors.

Article III.

Section 1. The judicial power of the United States, shall be vested in one Supreme Court, and in such inferior courts as the Congress may from time to time ordain and establish. The judges, both of the supreme and inferior courts, shall hold their offices during good behavior, and shall, at stated times, receive for their services, a compensation, which shall not be diminished during their continuance in office.

Section 2.   The judicial power shall extend to all cases, in law and equity, arising under this Constitution, the laws of the United States, and treaties made, or which shall be made, under their authority;—to all cases affecting ambassadors, other public ministers and consuls;—to all cases of admiralty and maritime jurisdiction;—*to controversies to which the United States shall be a party;—to controversies between two or more states;—between a state and citizens of another state;—between citizens of different states*[9],—between citizens of the same state claiming lands

---

[9]This portion of this paragraph has been affected by Amendment XI.

under grants of different states, and between a state, or the citizens thereof, and foreign states, citizens or subjects.

In all cases affecting ambassadors, other public ministers and consuls, and those in which a state shall be party, the Supreme Court shall have original jurisdiction. In all the other cases before mentioned, the Supreme Court shall have appellate jurisdiction, both as to law and fact, with such exceptions, and under such regulations as the Congress shall make.

The trial of all crimes, except in cases of impeachment, shall be by jury; and such trial shall be held in the state where the said crimes shall have been committed; but when not committed within any state, the trial shall be at such place or places as the Congress may by law have directed.

Section 3.   Treason against the United States, shall consist only in levying war against them, or in adhering to their enemies, giving them aid and comfort. No person shall be convicted of treason unless on the testimony of two witnesses to the same overt act, or on confession in open court.

The Congress shall have power to declare the punishment of treason, but no attainder of treason shall work corruption of blood, or forfeiture except during the life of the person attainted.

Article IV.

Section 1.   Full faith and credit shall be given in each state to the public acts, records, and judicial proceedings of every other state. And the Congress may by general laws prescribe the manner in which such acts, records and proceedings shall be proved, and the effect thereof.

Section 2.   The citizens of each state shall be entitled to all privileges and immunities of citizens in the several states.

A person charged in any state with treason, felony, or other crime, who shall flee from justice, and be found in another state, shall on demand of the executive authority of the state from which he fled, be delivered up, to be removed to the state having jurisdiction of the crime.

No person held to service or labor in one state, under the laws thereof, escaping into another, shall, in consequence of any law or regulation therein, be discharged from such service or labor, but shall be delivered up on claim of the party to whom such service or labor may be due.[10]

Section 3.   New states may be admitted by the Congress into this Union; but no new state shall be formed or erected within the jurisdiction of any other state; nor any state be formed by the junction of two or more states, or parts of states, without the consent of the legislatures of the states concerned as well as of the Congress.

The Congress shall have power to dispose of and make all needful rules and regulations respecting the territory or other property belonging to the United States; and nothing in this Constitution shall be so construed as to prejudice any claims of the United States, or of any particular state.

Section 4.   The United States shall guarantee to every state in this Union a republican form of government, and shall protect each of them against invasion; and on application of the legislature, or of the executive (when the legislature cannot be convened) against domestic violence.

---

[10]This paragraph, insomuch as it concerns slavery, has been affected by Amendment XIII, which abolishes slavery.

Article V.

The Congress, whenever two-thirds of both houses shall deem it necessary, shall propose amendments to this Constitution, or, on the application of the legislatures of two-thirds of the several states, shall call a convention for proposing amendments, which, in either case, shall be valid to all intents and purposes, as part of this Constitution, when ratified by the legislatures of three-fourths of the several states, or by conventions in three-fourths thereof, as the one or the other mode of ratification may be proposed by the Congress; provided that no amendment which may be made prior to the year one thousand eight hundred and eight shall in any manner affect the first and fourth clauses in the ninth section of the first article; and that no state, without its consent, shall be deprived of its equal suffrage in the Senate.

Article VI.

All debts contracted and engagements entered into, before the adoption of this Constitution, shall be as valid against the United States under this Constitution, as under the Confederation.

This Constitution, and the laws of the United States which shall be made in pursuance thereof; and all treaties made, or which shall be made, under the authority of the United States, shall be the supreme law of the land; and the judges in every state shall be bound thereby, anything in the Constitution or laws of any state to the contrary notwithstanding.

The Senators and Representatives before mentioned, and the members of the several state legislatures, and all executive and judicial officers, both of the United States and of the several states, shall be bound by oath or affirmation, to support this Constitution; but no religious test shall ever be required as a qualification to any office or public trust under the United States.

Article VII.

The ratification of the conventions of nine states, shall be sufficient for the establishment of this Constitution between the states so ratifying the same.

Done in convention by the unanimous consent of the states present the seventeenth day of September in the year of our Lord one thousand seven hundred and eighty seven and of the Independence of the United States of America the twelfth, In witness whereof we have hereunto subscribed our names,

Go. Washington—Presidt. and deputy from Virginia
[signed also by the deputies of twelve states: Connecticut, Delaware, Georgia, Maryland, Massachusetts, New Hampshire, New Jersey, New York, North Carolina, Pennsylvania, South Carolina, and Virginia.]

Amendments to the Constitution

ARTICLES IN ADDITION TO, AND AMENDMENTS OF, THE CONSTITUTION OF THE UNITED STATES OF AMERICA, PROPOSED BY CONGRESS, AND RATIFIED BY THE LEGISLATURES OF THE SEVERAL STATES, PURSUANT TO THE FIFTH ARTICLE OF THE ORIGINAL CONSTITUTION[11]

Amendment [I]

Congress shall make no law respecting an establishment of religion, or prohibiting the free exercise thereof; or abridging the freedom of speech, or of the press; or the right of the people peaceably to assemble, and to petition the Government for a redress of grievances.

Amendment [II]

A well regulated militia, being necessary to the security of a free state, the right of the people to keep and bear arms, shall not be infringed.

Amendment [III]

No soldier shall, in time of peace be quartered in any house, without the consent of the owner, nor in time of war, but in a manner to be prescribed by law.

Amendment [IV]

The right of the people to be secure in their persons, houses, papers, and effects, against unreasonable searches and seizures, shall not be violated, and no warrants shall issue, but upon probable cause, supported by oath or affirmation, and particularly describing the place to be searched, and the persons or things to be seized.

---

[11]The amendments themselves are formally titled articles, following the pattern of the first 10 to be ratified. Only the 13th, 14th, 15th, and 16th had numbers assigned to them when ratified. The first ten amendments are known as the Bill of Rights, and they were part of 12 articles proposed to the legislatures of the states by the First Congress in 1789. The first article concerned the apportionment of Representatives and was never ratified. The second article effectively forced a two-year wait for voted pay increases for Senators and Representatives to take effect until there was an intervening election for Representatives. This article, having no time limit for it, became the 27th Amendment in 1992, after ratification by three-fourths of the 50 states.

Amendment [V]

No person shall be held to answer for a capital, or otherwise infamous crime, unless on a presentment or indictment of a grand jury, except in cases arising in the land or naval forces, or in the militia, when in actual service in time of war or public danger; nor shall any person be subject for the same offence to be twice put in jeopardy of life or limb; nor shall be compelled in any criminal case to be a witness against himself, nor be deprived of life, liberty, or property, without due process of law; nor shall private property be taken for public use, without just compensation.

Amendment [VI]

In all criminal prosecutions, the accused shall enjoy the right to a speedy and public trial, by an impartial jury of the state and district wherein the crime shall have been committed, which district shall have been previously ascertained by law, and to be informed of the nature and cause of the accusation; to be confronted with the witnesses against him; to have compulsory process for obtaining witnesses in his favor, and to have the assistance of counsel for his defense.

Amendment [VII]

In suits at common law, where the value in controversy shall exceed twenty dollars, the right of trial by jury shall be preserved, and no fact tried by a jury, shall be otherwise reexamined in any court of the United States, than according to the rules of the common law.

Amendment [VIII]

Excessive bail shall not be required, nor excessive fines imposed, nor cruel and unusual punishments inflicted.

Amendment [IX]

The enumeration in the Constitution, of certain rights, shall not be construed to deny or disparage others retained by the people.

Amendment [X]

The powers not delegated to the United States by the Constitution, nor prohibited by it to the States, are reserved to the States respectively, or to the people.